Your Study Guides Map Perfectly to the Wiley CPAexcel Review Course

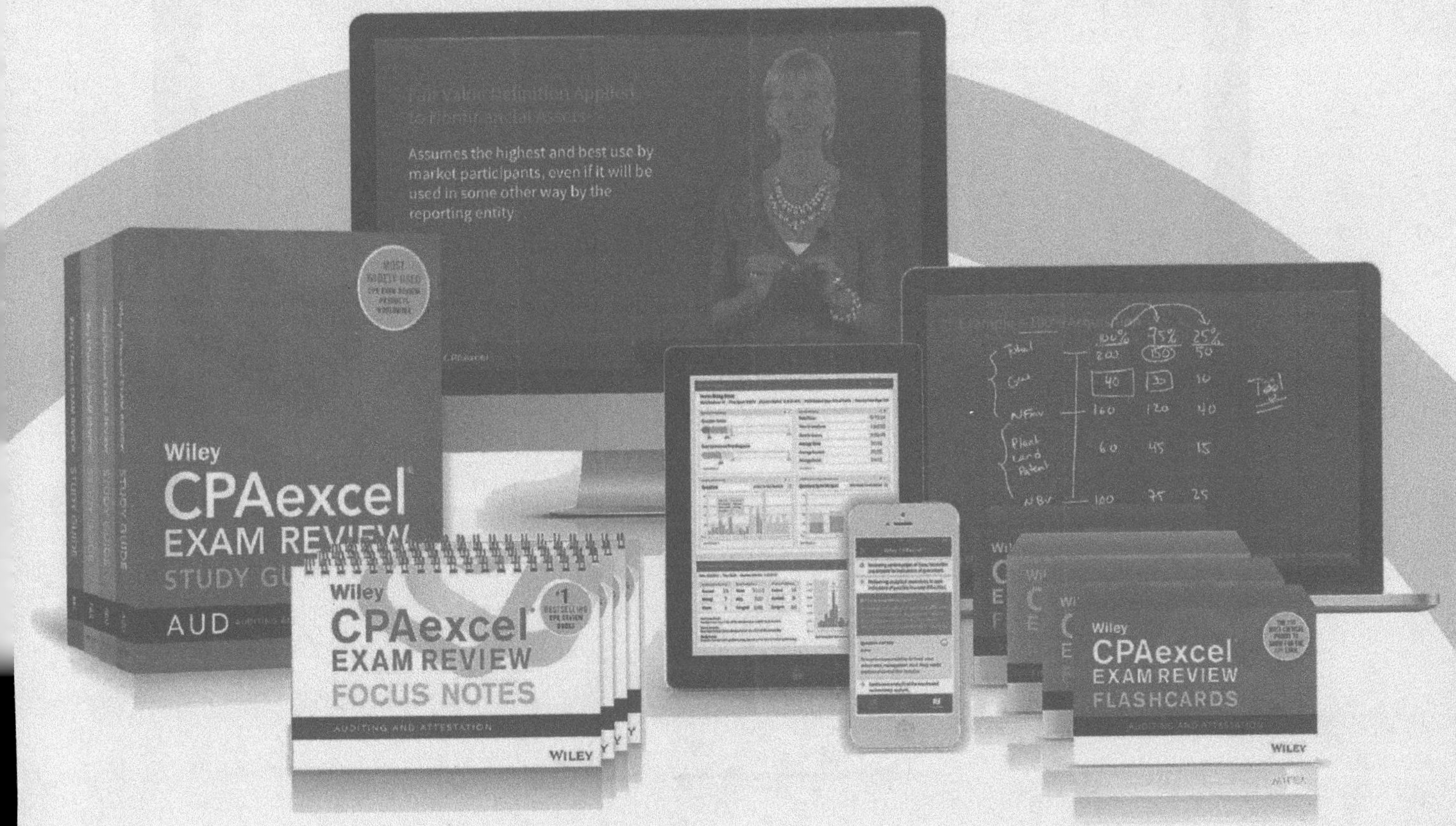

Why Study with the Full CPA Review Course?

- ✔ Everything You Need to Pass
- ✔ Unlimited Access Until You Pass
- ✔ 9 Out of 10 Students Pass

Get Your 14-Day Free Trial at **efficientlearning.com/cpatrial**

Bite-Sized Lessons Make It Easy

- ✔ **Manageable lessons that can be completed in 30 to 45 minutes**
- ✔ **Video, text, and assessments in each lesson**
- ✔ **Unlimited practice exams emulate the exam day experience**
- ✔ **Mobile app syncs automatically with the online course and may be used offline**
- ✔ **Lesson progress and mastery metrics show how you're progressing**

Your Plan to Pass Is Waiting

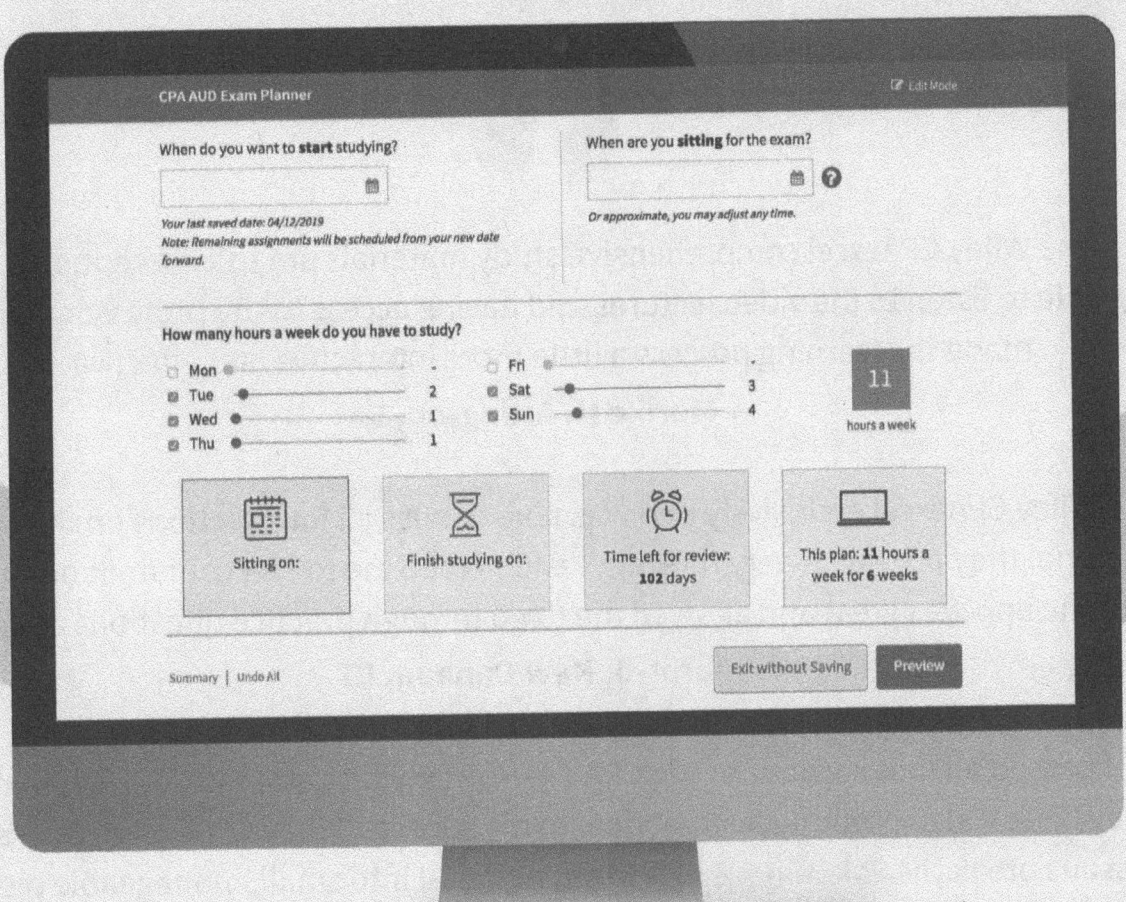

Wiley CPAexcel's Exam Planner is at the heart of why 9 out of 10 pass using our system.

✓ **Enter your exam date**

✓ **Enter your weekly study hours**

✓ **See 700 lessons scheduled to the day**

You Can Do This!

Wiley CPAexcel® Exam Review

STUDY GUIDE

2022

FINANCIAL ACCOUNTING AND REPORTING

Wiley CPAexcel® Exam Review

STUDY GUIDE

2022

FINANCIAL ACCOUNTING AND REPORTING

Meghann Cefaratti, Ph.D.
Donald R. Deis Jr., Ph.D., CPA, CFE
Pam Smith, Ph.D., CPA, MBA

Wiley Efficient Learning™

Contents

Contents

Contents

About the Authors

Wiley CPA content is authored by a team of accounting professors and CPA Exam experts from top accounting colleges such as the University of Texas at Austin (frequently ranked the #1 accounting school in the country), Northern Illinois University (frequently ranked in the top 10 in its peer group and top 20 overall), and the University of North Alabama.

Professor Allen H. Bizzell
CPAexcel® Author and Video Lecturer
Ph.D., CPA (inactive)
Former Associate Dean and Accounting Faculty, University of Texas (Retired)
Associate Professor, Department of Accounting, Texas State University (Retired)

Professor Gregory Carnes
CPAexcel® Author, Mentor, and Video Lecturer
Ph.D., CPA
Dean, College of Business, Raburn Eminent Scholar of Accounting, University of North Alabama
Former Dean, College of Business, Lipscomb University
Former Chair, Department of Accountancy, Northern Illinois University

Professor Meghann Cefaratti
CPAexcel® Author and Video Lecturer
Ph.D., CIA
Grant Thornton Professor of Accountancy, Department of Accountancy, Northern Illinois University

Professor Donald R. Deis Jr.
CPAexcel® Author and Video Lecturer
Ph.D., CPA, CFE
TAMUS Regents Professor and Ennis & Virginia Joslin Endowed Chair in Accounting, College of Business, Texas A&M University—Corpus Christi
Former Director, School of Accountancy, University of Missouri—Columbia
Former Professor and Director, Accounting Ph.D. Program, Louisiana State University—Baton Rouge

Instructor Elizabeth Grant
CPAexcel® Author and Video Lecturer
MAS, CPA
Instructor, Department of Accountancy, Northern Illinois University

Professor Marianne M. Jennings
CPAexcel® Author and Video Lecturer
J.D.
Professor Emeritus of Legal and Ethical Studies, W.P. Carey School of Business, Arizona State University

Instructor Tamara Phelan
CPAexcel® Author and Video Lecturer
MBA, CPA, CMA
Instructor, Department of Accountancy, Northern Illinois University

Professor Robert A. Prentice
CPAexcel® Author and Video Lecturer
J.D.
Ed and Molly Smith Centennial Professor In Business Law and Distinguished Teaching Professor, J.D. McCombs School of Business, University of Texas

Professor Pam Smith
CPAexcel® Author and Video Lecturer
Ph.D., MBA, CPA
KPMG Endowed Professor of Accountancy, Department of Accountancy, Northern Illinois University

Professor Dan N. Stone
CPAexcel® Author and Video Lecturer
Ph.D., MPA, CPA (inactive)
Rosenthal Endowed Chair, Von Allmen School of Accountancy, University of Kentucky

Professor Donald E. Tidrick
CPAexcel® Author and Video Lecturer
Ph.D., CPA, CMA, CIA
Deloitte Professor of Accountancy, Northern Illinois University
Former Associate Chair, Department of Accounting, Director of Professional Program in Accounting and
  Director of the CPA Review Course, University of Texas at Austin

About the Financial Accounting Professors

Dr. Meghann Cefaratti is the Grant Thornton Professor in the Department of Accountancy at Northern Illinois University, where she teaches financial reporting and auditing. She earned her Ph.D. in Accounting from Virginia Tech, and her dissertation received the 2011 Best Dissertation Award from the Forensic Accounting Section of the American Accounting Association. Her research interests include internal auditing, fraud risk, internal control, information systems and cybersecurity, and judgment and decision-making in auditing contexts. Before becoming a professor, Meghann was an auditor with the Air Force Audit Agency.

Dr. Donald R. Deis Jr. is Texas A&M University Regents Professor and the Ennis & Virginia Joslin Endowed Chair in Accounting within the College of Business at Texas A&M University—Corpus Christi. Prior to joining TAMUCC, Dr. Deis was the Joseph A. Silvoso Distinguished Director of the School of Accountancy at the University of Missouri-Columbia and was the Ernst & Young Endowed Research Professor and Director of the Accounting Ph.D. Program at Louisiana State University—Baton Rouge. His primary research focus is on the quality of audits provided by public accounting firms, fraud, corporate governance, and the privatization of government services.

Dr. Pam Smith is KPMG Endowed Professor of Accountancy at Northern Illinois University. She has won more than a dozen teaching awards at all levels: department, college, university, state, and international. Dr. Smith is a leader in the creation and operation of NIU's nationally ranked ethics program, BELIEF (Building Ethical Leaders using an Integrated Ethics Framework). She is co-author of NIU's *Building Ethical Leaders* handbook. Her primary teaching and research interests are in financial reporting, mergers and acquisitions, risk management, and ethical business practices

Welcome to Financial Accounting and Reporting

Overview

Welcome to Financial Accounting and Reporting (FAR)! This lesson introduces you to the professors of the FAR lessons and provides you an overview of the test.

Study Guide

The content presented throughout FAR is based on the AICPA Blueprint specifications. The CPA Examination Blueprint for FAR is presented in the following area headings, together with exam allocation for each content area:

AREA	Allocation
I. Conceptual Framework and Financial Reporting	25–35%
II. Select Financial Statement Accounts	30–40%
III. Select Transactions	20–30%
IV. State and Local Governments	5–15%

The exam consists of multiple-choice questions and task-based simulations. Specifically, the four-hour FAR exam is structured as follows:

Testlet 1: 33 multiple-choice questions
Testlet 2: 33 multiple-choice questions
Testlet 3: 2 task-based simulations
Testlet 4: 3 task-based simulations
Testlet 5: 3 task-based simulations

Here we present a broad overview from which to begin your journey toward successful completion of the CPA exam. Generally, the topics are presented in the study text in the same sequence as they are presented in the Blueprint. However, in a few cases, the order of the topics is different from in the Blueprint to present topics in a logical sequence for learning purposes. CPAexcel will continually provide you with the "map" and the resources needed to be a CPA!

Area I. Conceptual Framework and Financial Reporting

Completion of the lessons in this area will ensure that you have the conceptual foundation for success in subsequent sections. This area covers the FASB's standard-setting process and Accounting Standards Codification. A must-know in this section is the fundamentals of the conceptual framework and accrual accounting. A strong understanding of these concepts will provide you with the base needed to figure out specific questions. Trust your training and your gut instinct when answering the questions. Area I also reviews the reporting and presentation of a basic set of financial statements: the statement of financial position, the income statement, the statement of comprehensive income, the statement of shareowners' equity, and the statement of cash flows. There are a series of lessons on how to consolidate financial statements. Public companies that are U.S. registrants must also comply with the reporting and disclosure requirements of the Securities and Exchange Commission, which includes earnings per share and segment and interim reporting. A solid understanding of the content in this area is important as you travel into the next section, which provides details on the financial statement accounts.

Area II. Select Financial Statement Accounts

This area covers the accounting and reporting of balance sheet accounts starting with cash all the way through equity. For each topic, think about what is recognized and when, and for how much. Also make note if there are important disclosure requirements. Concentrate on the tools you need to solve problems (diagrams, T-accounts, journal entries, etc.). If you know what tools to use to answer questions and understand how to record a transaction and how the financial statements are affected, you are 85% there. Keep in mind that even though this section lists balance sheet accounts, every balance sheet account impacts the income statement. Accounts receivable impacts revenue, inventory impacts cost of goods sold, fixed assets impact depreciation and gains or losses on disposal, accrued liabilities impact operating expenses, and debt impacts interest expense.

Area III. Select Transactions

This area addresses the accounting and reporting of select transactions that are not covered in Area II. Many of these transactions are complex, and you may find the content very challenging. If you have covered these topics in classes, you will "relearn" them quickly. If the topics are new to you (or you never understood them the first time), be patient with yourself and take the time you need to gain a basic understanding of the accounting. The select transactions presented in this area are related to revenue recognition, compensation arrangements such as pensions and stock awards, income taxes, and leases. Area III also includes the accounting and reporting associated with business combinations, derivative financial instruments and hedging, and foreign currency denominated transactions. This area also includes the accounting for accounting changes and error corrections.

Don't just ignore the topics you find really challenging. You are smart and capable of learning the basics related to the topics. You don't have to be an expert, but you do need to know the basics! I am confident that you will succeed in your goals if you spend quality time studying the material and practicing with all question formats.

~ Professor Pam Smith

We wrap up this section with financial reporting and accounting for not-for-profit entities. FASB made a major change in this area so you should expect questions about donor restrictions, contributions, categories of net assets, and financial statements. Healthcare organizations and colleges and universities are also covered. The concepts are very straightforward and you will do well in this area after completing your study.

~ Professor Don Deis

Area IV. State and Local Governments

Financial reporting and accounting for state and local governments is the final section of your FAR study. If you have experience working with governments or you took a governmental accounting course, you probably just need to brush up on the area and learn about some of the recent changes made by GASB. If you are new to governmental accounting, you will need to focus on the types of funds used, budgetary and encumbrance accounting, modified accrual accounting, government-wide financial statements, fund-level financial statements, accounting for infrastructure, types of fund balance, categories of net position, interfund transfers, nonexchange transactions, and deferred inflows and deferred outflows of resources. It may sound pretty dry, but the exam questions for governmental accounting are fairly predictable and easy! You should do very well in this area.

~ Professor Don Deis

Conceptual Framework, Standard-Setting and Financial Reporting

Overview of US GAAP

FASB and Standard Setting

This lesson presents an overview of the standard-setting process in the United States.

After studying this lesson, you should be able to:

1. Describe the role of the Financial Accounting Standards Board.

2. Describe the primary purpose of financial reporting.

3. List the three aspects of financial reporting addressed by GAAP.

4. Identify the major organizations in U.S. accounting standards.

I. **Introduction**

   A. Financial accounting and reporting is concerned with providing relevant information to all users of the financial statements: investors, creditors, competitors, employees, and regulatory bodies. Financial statement information is used to make informed decisions regarding allocation of resources. A common use is whether to invest in a firm or to lend money to it.

   B. Financial information is disseminated in many forms including news releases, prospectuses for future securities offerings, filings with the Securities and Exchange Commission (SEC), and annual reports to shareholders. Financial statements are the culmination of the accounting process and represent the most comprehensive financial information disclosures made by firms. The footnotes and other textual and tabular information provide supplementary information and help to explain the amounts disclosed in those statements.

II. **Generally Accepted Accounting Principles (GAAP)**

Definition
Generally Accepted Accounting Principles (GAAP): The rules of financial reporting for business enterprises. GAAP are also called *accounting standards*.

   A. **What GAAP Addresses**—GAAP is a set of reporting rules to address three aspects of financial reporting:

      1. **Recognition**—A recognized item is recorded in an account and ultimately affects the financial statements.

Note
Recognition is an accounting concept that indicates that the item is recorded on the financial statements. In contrast, *realization* is an economic concept that indicates that cash is paid or received. GAAP focuses on accrual accounting and therefore is concerned with recognition more than with realization.

      2. **Measurement**—Concerns the dollar amount assigned to an item.

      3. **Disclosure**—Many unrecognized amounts are reported in the footnotes to complete the portrayal of the firm's financial position and performance.

   B. GAAP affects what is disclosed in financial statements and in what amount. For example, GAAP requires that many assets be reported at their historical cost, rather than at current market value. Without a relatively uniform set of GAAP, business entities would be free to report whatever amounts they desired.

III. Organizations Involved in Developing Accounting Standards

A. **Financial Accounting Standards Board (FASB)**—The FASB is currently the standard-setting body in the United States.

B. The **Securities and Exchange Commission (SEC)** is the federal government agency that administers the securities laws of the United States. These laws affect firms that issue debt and equity securities to the public. Such firms register with the SEC and are called *registrants*. The financial statements of these firms must be filed with the SEC and must be audited by independent third parties (CPA firms).

C. Congress granted the SEC the authority to establish GAAP for the firms within its jurisdiction (publicly traded firms) but generally has ceded this authority to a private sector body (currently, the FASB). In a few instances, the SEC has exercised its right to reverse or modify an accounting standard adopted by the private sector body. The SEC also has pressured the FASB to establish certain principles more quickly.

D. The FASB considers the potential reaction of the SEC to its proposed standards. The SEC frequently responds to the FASB's initial "exposure" draft providing useful commentary for the final pronouncement.

E. The **American Institute of Certified Public Accountants (AICPA)** is the national professional organization for practicing CPAs and has had a great impact on accounting principles over the years. The mission of the AICPA is to provide its members with resources, information, and leadership so that they may in turn provide valuable services for the benefit of their clients, employers, and the general public.

F. In 1939, the AICPA appointed its Committee on Accounting Procedure (CAP), the first private sector body charged with the responsibility of promulgating GAAP. CAP issued 51 Accounting Research Bulletins (ARBs). To the extent that an ARB has not been rescinded or superseded, it constitutes GAAP.

G. In 1959, the AICPA created the Accounting Principles Board (APB), another committee, to take over the work of CAP. The APB is the second private sector group designated to formulate GAAP. Members were required to be CPAs. The APB issued 31 opinions, many of which remain as GAAP, in whole or in part.

H. In 1971, the AICPA appointed the Wheat Committee, which recommended the formation of yet another private sector body—the FASB—to take over the reins from the APB. In 1973, the FASB assumed the role of standard setter for the accounting profession. The FASB is not affiliated with the AICPA.

> **Note**
> *The FASB operated with seven Board members from its inception in 1973 until 2008 when the Board was reduced to five members. The Board membership increased back to seven in early 2011. The FAF Chairman, Jack Brennan, gave this rationale for the change: "Returning the Board to the seven-member structure will enhance the FASB's investment in the convergence agenda with the International Accounting Standards Board (IASB), while addressing the unprecedented challenges facing the American capital markets in the months and years ahead."*

I. The **FASB** is one of three parts of the current accounting standard-setting mechanism in the United States. The other two are the Financial Accounting Foundation (FAF)—the parent body, and the Financial Accounting Standards Advisory Council (FASAC):

   1. FAF—Appoints the members of the FASB and its advisory councils, ensures adequate funding for the FASB, and exercises oversight over the FASB. Funding sources include fees levied on publicly traded firms under the Sarbanes-Oxley Act, contributions, and publication sales. The trustees of the FAF are appointed from organizations with an interest in accounting standards.

   2. FASB—Establishes financial accounting standards for business entities. The FASB is an independent body, subject only to the FAF.

   3. FASAC—Provides guidance on major policy issues, project priorities, and the formation of task forces.

J. The FASB is the current private-sector body that establishes GAAP for business entities.**The mission of the FASB** (in brief) is to:

1. Improve the usefulness of financial reporting

2. Maintain current accounting standards

3. Promptly address deficiencies in accounting standards

4. Promote international convergence of accounting standards

5. Improve the common understanding of the nature and purposes of information in financial reports.

K. Facts in Brief about the FASB

1. Seven full-time members with renewable (for one additional term) and staggered 5-year terms.

2. Subject to FAF policies and oversight.

3. Members cannot have employment or investment ties with other entities.

4. Members need not be CPAs although typically the public accounting profession is represented; also the preparer (reporting firm) and investor communities are represented.

L. In promulgating GAAP, the FASB applies the following principles:

1. Accounting standards should be unbiased and not favor any particular industry; standards are for the benefit of financial statement users;

2. The needs and views of the economic community should be considered; the views of the accounting profession should not take precedence;

3. The process of developing standards should be open to the public and allow due process to provide opportunity for interested parties to make their views known;

4. The benefits of accounting standards should exceed their cost.

M. The FASB Uses the Following Process when Issuing an Accounting Standard—The FASB:

1. Considers whether to add a project to its agenda, in consultation with the FAF—the FASB receives many requests from its constituencies including the SEC, auditing firms, investors, and reporting firms to address new financial reporting issues and clarify existing standards

2. Conducts research on the topic and issues a Discussion Memorandum detailing the issues surrounding the topic; the FASB's conceptual framework plays a role in this process by providing a theoretical structure for guiding the development of a specific standard

3. Holds public hearings on the topic

4. Evaluates the research and comments from interested parties and issues an Exposure Draft—the initial accounting standard

5. Solicits additional comments, modifies the Exposure Draft if needed

6. Finalizes the new accounting guidance and approves with a majority vote (four of seven affirmative votes) and issues an Accounting Standards Update (ASU)

N. FASB's Emerging Issues Task Force (EITF)—This group was formed to consider emerging reporting issues and to accelerate the process of establishing rulings on such issues. In this sense, the EITF acts as a "filter" for the FASB, enabling the FASB to focus on more pervasive issues. When a consensus of the 15 members is reached on an issue, no further action by the FASB is required. EITF pronouncements are included in GAAP. If the EITF is unable to reach a consensus, the FASB may become involved, ultimately revising an existing standard or adopting a new one.

IV. The Political Nature of the Accounting Standard-Setting Process

A. Parties, Preferences, and Outcomes—The parties interested in the outcome of the standard-setting process may have opposing preferences and interests. Firm managers (referred to as "preparers" or "preparer firms") often prefer standards with lower compliance costs and that tend to portray their firms in a more positive light (higher earnings and assets, lower liabilities).

B. Financial statement users, on the other hand, prefer unbiased, transparent reporting. They want the facts. Investors also want conservative reporting-disclosure of less positive results under conditions of uncertainty or where the firm has a choice of reporting alternatives under GAAP. The FASB has pledged to adopt unbiased accounting standards, and thus has the interests of financial statement users in mind when developing accounting standards.

C. The FASB considers its conceptual framework, the collection of Statements of Financial Accounting Concepts (SFACs), a "constitution" or underlying set of theoretical concepts in its deliberations. However, the FASB does not create GAAP in a vacuum. Historically, the Board has been very responsive to the views of affected parties through its due diligence process and actively solicits public comment before adopting a final accounting standard.

D. User groups (e.g., industry associations, financial institutions) influence the outcome of FASB standards by:

1. Making their views public through the financial press

2. Providing input during the due process procedure

3. Putting pressure on the SEC directly to change a proposed standard, or through the U.S. Congress

E. The Board is careful to pay attention to this type of input, particularly when it helps clarify the issues. However, although the FASB has pledged to be unbiased rather than promulgate standards favoring a particular reporting position or industry, it has admitted to responding to pressure from interested parties.

F. For example, negative *economic consequences* is often the argument of an interested party. Economic consequences refers to the effect of a proposed standard on a firm's financial statements. A common argument against a proposed standard is that it will cause earnings to decline, thus reducing the firm's ability to raise capital. Although some observers believe that the FASB should not be sensitive to the views of reporting firms, there have been some spectacular cases in which the FASB has delayed an accounting standard or even reversed itself in light of the concerns reporting firms have had about the "economic consequences" of a proposed standard.

V. Enforcement of GAAP

A. Methods of Enforcement

1. Accounting standards are not laws; they are not determined by legislatures but rather by private sector bodies. They are *generally accepted*. GAAP are a type of regulation, imposed on the economic system by its constituents. Without GAAP, the economy and capital markets as we know them would not work. Investors need to have confidence in the numbers they receive. Without some kind of common language, the system could not function. Corruption would become much more prevalent than it is today.

2. However, the private-sector bodies that contribute to the formulation of GAAP have no enforcement authority. Rather, there are economic sanctions for firms not complying with GAAP. These sanctions include increased difficulty in raising debt and equity capital.

3. The SEC, however, does have the authority to penalize firms and managers subject to its jurisdiction when financial statements do not comply with GAAP. Public companies are violating the securities laws if they publish financial statements that materially depart from GAAP.

4. The SEC sends a *deficiency* letter to a registrant when an accounting irregularity is found. If the firm disagrees, the SEC may issue a "stop order" preventing trading in the firm's securities until the disagreement is resolved. Outright violations of the securities laws may result in criminal sanctions against managers, or fines against the company.

5. The enactment of the Sarbanes-Oxley Act of 2002 significantly affects the enforcement procedures relating to audits of public companies, and penalties for noncompliance with GAAP. The Auditing section of CPAexcel covers the implications of this Act in depth.

Accrual Accounting

This lesson presents an overview of GAAP and the basic theory of accrual accounting.

After studying this lesson, you should be able to:

1. List the components of an external financial report.

2. Define accruals and deferrals and give examples of each.

3. Reconcile cash basis income to accrual basis income.

4. Reconcile accrual basis income to cash basis income.

5. Evaluate the components of accrual and deferral accounts using T-accounts.

I. Introduction

A. **External Financial Report**—The general-purpose external financial report (also called the annual report) is prepared by applying Generally Accepted Accounting Principles (GAAP). The general-purpose external financial report has the following key components.

1. Income Statement

2. Statement of Comprehensive Income

3. Balance Sheet (Statement of Financial Position)

4. Statement of Changes in Owners' Equity

5. Statement of Cash Flows

6. Footnote Disclosures and supplementary schedules

7. Auditor's Opinion

B. **GAAP**—The composition of GAAP includes principles, methods, and procedures that are generally accepted by the accounting profession. The majority of GAAP includes the pronouncements issued by the Financial Accounting Standards Board (FASB) and its predecessors.

C. **Authoritative GAAP**

1. **Codification**

a. The Accounting Standards Codification (ASC) is the compilation and organization of all GAAP sources. For publicly traded entities, the SEC has additional reporting guidelines.

b. Accounting and financial reporting practices not included in the Codification are nonauthoritative.

c. The Codification does not include guidance for non-GAAP matters including:

i. Other Comprehensive Basis of Accounting

ii. Cash Basis

iii. Income Tax Basis

iv. Regulatory Accounting Principles

2. **No specified GAAP**

a. If guidance for a transaction or event is not specified in the Codification, authoritative GAAP for similar transactions or events should be considered before considering nonauthoritative GAAP. Sources of nonauthoritative guidance include widely recognized and prevalent practices, FASB Concepts Statements, AICPA Issues Papers, and others. There is no implied hierarchy for these sources.

      i. The guidance for similar transactions or events is not followed if that guidance either prohibits the application of the guidance to the particular transaction or event, or indicates that the accounting treatment not be applied by analogy.

3. SEC guidance

    a. Authoritative GAAP include relevant SEC rules and interpretative releases (applicable only to publicly traded firms). The Codification includes relevant portions of SEC content but does not contain the entire text of relevant SEC rules, regulations, interpretive releases and staff guidance. For example, the Codification does not include SEC content related to Management's Discussion and Analysis and other items appearing outside the financial statements. The Codification does not replace or affect guidance issued by the SEC and is provided on a convenience basis.

II. Accrual Basis of Accounting

  A. GAAP, and therefore the financial statements, reflects the accrual basis of accounting rather than the cash basis of accounting. Both U.S. and international GAAP reflect the accrual basis of accounting. GAAP addresses the recognition, measurement, and disclosures associated with financial reporting.

Example

A firm sells $40,000 worth of goods during the year, and collects $30,000 on the resulting accounts receivable. There is no uncertainty regarding the collection of the remaining $10,000. Under the accrual basis, $40,000 of revenues would be recognized for the year; under the cash basis, only $30,000 would be recognized. The next year, when the remaining $10,000 of cash is collected, the cash basis would recognize $10,000 of revenue. The accrual basis would recognize no additional revenue. The accrual basis provides a more comprehensive measurement of the change in value of the firm resulting from income producing activities for a period because it does not limit the recognition of resource changes to the cash flows for that period. Accrual accounting much more fully reflects the economic substance of transactions.

  B. Accrual basis accounting recognizes and reports the **economic activities** of the firm in the period the activity was **incurred**, regardless of when the cash activity takes place. The table below depicts the possible scenarios and the terminology related to timing differences. In essence, cash can precede or follow an economic transaction. The economic transaction is one that generates revenue or expense.

  C. As with any job, you have to have the right tool for that task. The questions and problems associated with this lesson test your knowledge of:

    1. Accruals and deferrals,

    2. Construction and evaluation of T-accounts, and

    3. Reconciliation of cash to accrual and accrual to cash.

  D. You may need to refresh your understanding of these concepts before you go any further in your study in FAR because accrual basis concepts are critical in all FAR lessons.

The table displays a common theme for **accruals** and **deferrals**:

- When the economic event occurs, first you create an accrual account. (You are accruing the cash owed or to be paid as an asset or liability.)

- When the cash activity occurs, first you create a **deferral** account. (You are deferring the recognition of an expense or revenue as an asset or liability.)

Transaction	Event	Account created	Examples
Revenue	Cash received before revenue earned	Deferred revenue—liability	Rent, subscriptions, gift certificates
	Revenue earned before cash received	Accrued asset—asset	Sales on account, interest, rent
Expense	Cash paid before expense incurred	Deferred expense—asset	Prepaid insurance, supplies, rent, PPE
	Expense incurred before cash paid	Accrued expense—liability	Salaries, wages, interest, taxes

Using the payment and receipt of $100 for rent, the entries made by the renter and rentee are shown below.

	Landlord (Rentee)	Tenant (Renter)
CASH RECEIVED THEN RENT EARNED		

Dec. entries: Rent paid December 31	Cash 100
	   Unearned Rent (liability) 100
	(Rent revenue is deferred)
		Prepaid Rent (asset) 100
		   Cash 100
		(Rent expense is deferred)

Jan. entries: January rent earned	Unearned Rent 100
	   Rent revenue 100
		Rent expense 100
		   Prepaid Rent 100

	Landlord (Rentee)	Tenant (Renter)
RENT EARNED THEN CASH RECEIVED		

Dec. entries: December rent paid on January 1	Accrued Rent Revenue (asset) 100
	   Rent Revenue 100
	(Rent revenue is accrued)
		Rent expenses 100
		   Accrued Rent Expenses
		   (liability) 100
		(Rent expense is accrued)

Jan. entries: December rent collected	Cash 100
	   Accrued Rent Revenue 100
		Accrued Rent Expense 100
		   Cash 100

Important points to note. The revenue and expense are recorded in the period the economic event occurred (e.g., using the space). The accrual and deferral accounts are simply holding the revenue or expense amounts on the balance sheet until they can be recognized on the income statement.

Example

Assume Mayer Corporation had $28,000 of revenue in the first year of operations, $6,000 was on account and $22,000 was paid in cash. Mayer Corporation incurred operation expenses of $15,800, $12,000 was paid in cash and $3,800 was owed on account at year-end. In addition, Mayer Corporation prepaid $2,400 for insurance that will not be used until the next year.

Below are an Income Statement, Balance Sheet and Statement of Cash Flows under the cash basis and accrual basis of accounting. Note that the ending cash balance is exactly the same under both cash and accrual basis. The difference is the *timing* of the receipt and payment of cash.

Cash Basis

Income Statement		Balance Sheet	
Sales	$22,000	Cash	**$7,600**
Op Exp	(12,000)		
Ins Exp	(2,400)		
Total	$7,600		

Statement of Cash Flows—Direct Method

Operating Activities		
Sales		$22,000
Operating expense	(12,000)	
Insurance expense	(2,400)	
		(14,400)
Total Cash Flow from Operating Activities		**$7,600**

Note: Δ = change in the account balance.

Example
Continuation:

Below are an Income Statement, Balance Sheet and Statement of Cash Flows under the accrual basis of accounting.

Accrual Basis

Income Statement		Balance Sheet	
Sales	$28,000	Cash	$7,600
Op Exps	(15,800)	Acct Rec	6,000
		Prepaid	2,400
			$16,000
		Acct Pay	3,800
		Equity	12,200
Total	$12,200		$16,000

Statement of Cash Flows—Indirect Method

Operating Activities

Net Income	$12,200
ΔAccounts Receivable	(6,000)
ΔPrepaid Expenses	(2,400)
ΔAccounts Payable	3,800
Total Cash Flow from Operating Activities	**$7,600**

Example
J&L Pecans maintain accounting records on an accrual basis. In 20X6 J&L decided to convert to cash basis accounting. During 20X5 J&L reported $95,178 of net income. On January 1, 20X5 and December 31, 20X5 J&L had the following amounts.

	January	December
Accounts receivable	9,250	15,927
Unearned revenue	2,840	4,111
Accrued expenses	3,435	2,108
Prepaid expense	1,917	3,232

Conversion of J&L's income from accrual basis to cash basis can be viewed various ways. One way is to use the accounting equation. Starting with the accounting equation, we follow simple algebra to isolate the change in cash. (Note: Δ = change in account value.)

1) $A = L + E$

2) $\Delta A = \Delta L + \Delta E$

3) $\Delta cash + \Delta other\ assets = \Delta L + \Delta E$

4) $\Delta cash = \Delta L + \Delta E - \Delta other\ assets$

1) is the accounting equation; 2) is the change in all of the variables in the accounting equation (still an equality); 3) is separating the changes in cash from the changes in all other assets; and 4) is isolating cash on the left side of the equation. Using equation 4) we can convert J&L Pecans from accrual to cash:

Conversion of Accrual Basis to Cash Basis
For the Year 20X5

Net income on an accrual basis	$95,178
Subtract increase in accounts receivable ($9,250 – $15,927)	(6,677)
Add increase in unearned service revenue ($2,840 – $4,111)	1,271
Subtract decrease in accrued expense ($3,435 – $2,108)	(1,327)
Subtract increase in prepaid expenses ($1,917 – $3,232)	(1,315)
Net income on an cash basis	$87,130

If you are asked to change from cash to accrual, you can still use the accounting equation formula, **but the signs would be opposite** those used in the conversion from accrual to cash.

Conversion of Cash Basis to Accrual Basis
For the Year 20X5

Net income on a cash basis	$87,130
Add increase in accounts receivable ($9,250 – $15,927)	6,677
Subtract increase in unearned service revenue ($2,840 – $4,111)	(1,271)
Add decrease in accrued expense ($3,435 – $2,108)	1,327
Add increase in prepaid expenses ($1,917 – $3,232)	1,315
Net income on an accrual basis	$95,178

Note

Converting cash to accrual (and vice versa) is challenging. In addition, the wording of the questions can be tricky. The key is to be clear on what the question is asking.

If the question is asking you to convert a revenue or expense account from cash to accrual (or vice versa), it is easiest to use a T-account.

If you are asked to convert net income from cash to accrual (or vice versa), the formula based on the accounting equation can help you remember whether to add or subtract changes in assets and liabilities when adjusting net income. However, T-accounts can also be used.

Take a deep breath and slowly work through the questions in this lesson. Everyone struggles with this area.

Try both approaches and use what works best for you. There are many ways to think through cash/accrual reconciliations; we have no doubt that you will figure out a way that works for you and you will master the topic. Keep up the great work!

Financial Accounting Standards Codification

This lesson presents the Financial Accounting Standards Codification.

After studying this lesson, you should be able to:

1. Describe the goals and purpose of the Codification.

2. Identify the main areas of the Codification.

3. Illustrate how you would research using the Codification.

I. Financial Accounting Standards Codification

> **Caution**
> It is important that you practice using the Codification before the CPA Exam so that you do not waste valuable time struggling with the interface during the exam. The Codification website has several useful tutorials for first-time users.

A. **Goals of the Codification**—The FASB Codification Research System is the online, real-time database by which users access the Codification. The Codification system became effective on July 1, 2009. The online nature of the Codification and its internal structure were designed to achieve the following goals:

   1. Simplify the structure and accessibility of authoritative GAAP.

   2. Provide all authoritative literature in a single location.

   3. Reduce the time and effort required to research an accounting issue.

   4. Reduce the risk of noncompliance with GAAP.

   5. Facilitate updating of accounting standards.

   6. Assist the FASB with research and convergence (IFRS) efforts.

B. **Updating the Codification**

   1. Changes to authoritative GAAP are accomplished through FASB Accounting Standards Updates (ASU), including amendments to SEC content. No longer will separate FASB Statements or other documents be separately published. ASUs are designated chronologically by year. For example, ASU 2014-12 refers to the twelfth ASU issued by the FASB in 2014.

   2. An ASU is a separate document posted on the FASB website and incorporated in the Codification. The ASU will (1) summarize the key aspects of the update, (2) detail how the Codification will change, and (3) explain the basis for the update. ASUs are not authoritative— ASUs are a vehicle to update the codification and are not permanent in their own right, but a way to amend the codification. When changes to the codification happen, the FASB updates the Codification and issues the ASU simultaneously.

   3. During the transition period for an ASU to become effective, the Codification shows the new guidance as "Pending Text." When the new guidance is effective, the previous guidance (if any) is deleted and the new guidance takes its place.

   4. Although updates no longer use the old FASB numbering system, the Codification provides access to the original standards used in creating the Codification.

   5. The Codification provides links enabling users to provide feedback, which then is directly transmitted to the FASB.

C. **Codification Structure**

   1. **Overall structure**—Accounting guidance within the Codification has the following structure:

Areas—Topics—Subtopics—Sections—Subsections—Paragraphs

   a. Each area has at least one topic. Within a topic, there are subtopics. Within subtopics, there are sections, and so forth. The topic, subtopic, and section levels reflect the structure used by international accounting standards.

2. **Areas**—The highest level in the Codification is the area, of which there are nine, each with a specific numeric identifier:

   a. General principles (100)

   b. Presentation (200) (does not address recognition or measurement)

   c. Assets (300)

   d. Liabilities (400)

   e. Equity (500)

   f. Revenue (600)

   g. Expenses (700)

   h. Broad transactions (800) (transactions involving more than one area such as interest, and subsequent events)

   i. Industry (900) (special industry accounting)

3. **Topics**—There are approximately 90 topics across the nine areas. For example, all asset topics are within 300–399. The number of topics varies by area, depending on the content within each area. For example, 310 is the receivables topic, within the Asset area.

4. **Subtopics**—There is at least one subtopic within each topic. The "overall" subtopic appears within each topic. The number of subtopics within a topic varies by area, again depending on content. Each carries a numeric identifier. The "overall" subtopic contains the "big picture" level guidance for a topic. The other subtopics provide additional specific guidance and exceptions. For example, 310-40 is the Troubled-Debt Restructurings by Creditors subtopic within the Receivables topic, which is within the Asset area.

5. **Sections**—Each subtopic has the following 16 sections with the associated numeric identifier:

00	Status
05	Overview and Background
10	Objectives
15	Scope and Scope Exceptions
20	Glossary
25	Recognition
30	Initial Measurement
35	Subsequent Measurement
40	Derecognition
45	Other Presentation Matters
50	Disclosure
55	Implementation Guidance and Illustrations
60	Relationships
65	Transition and Open Effective Date Information
70	Grandfathered Guidance
75	XBRL Definitions

    a. The listing of sections is uniform across all subtopics, unless no material exists for a section within a particular subtopic. For example, 310-40-35 is the Subsequent Measurement section within the Troubled-Debt Restructurings by Creditors subtopic within the Receivables topic, which is within the Asset area.

    b. The section level is the primary research level because the accounting guidance in the form of paragraphs resides within the sections.

    c. For SEC guidance, the same section numbering system is used with the addition of the letter *S* preceding the section number.

6. **Subsections**—In some cases, a section is divided into subsections to facilitate the exposition. These are not numbered.

7. **Paragraphs**

    a. The actual accounting standard material is provided in paragraphs within sections or subsections. For example, 310-40-35-2 is paragraph 2, Troubled-Debt Restructuring, within the General subsection within the Subsequent Measurement section within the Troubled-Debt Restructurings by Creditors subtopic within the Receivables topic, which is within the Asset area.

    b. Paragraphs follow a hierarchical structure allowing lower level paragraphs to be associated with higher-level paragraphs within a group, similar to threads in an online discussion group. Greater-than symbols (>, >>, >>>) are used for nesting paragraphs.

    c. Paragraph numbers do not change over time. New paragraphs will use a letter extension.

    d. Entities are encouraged to use purely verbal references to Topic levels within the Codification for the footnotes to their financial statements because FASB standard numbers are no longer used. For example, to refer to requirements concerning interest capitalization, the footnote would refer to "as required by the Interest Topic of the FASB Accounting Standards Codification."

    e. The Codification standardized certain terms. For example, the Codification uses the term "entity" rather than "firm" or "company" and thus uses the term "intra-entity" rather than "intercompany." Moreover, the word "shall" is used for required treatments, rather than "should," "must," or other terms.

8. **Industry**

    a. Area 900 holds industry topics and contains only the guidance that is not otherwise applicable in the other eight areas. For consistency, the topics within the industry area are structured the same way as in the other areas. Agriculture is industry topic 905 for example. Within that topic, the receivables subtopic is listed and numbered as Agriculture—Receivables: 905-310.

    b. The general area topics include relevant guidance referenced to specific industries. Thus, the Codification is cross-referenced.

D. Researching the Codification

1. The Codification provides four different ways for researching an issue:

    a. Browse the structure (illustrated above) in the menu provided.

    b. Search by key word(s); this mode allows narrowing of a search both by related term and by major area within the Codification structure.

    c. Enter the specific Codification location (using the numerical system within the Codification); this is designed for users who know their topic and section of interest.

    d. Search by previous GAAP standard number (e.g., by FAS 13).

2. In addition, the Codification allows users to aggregate findings by similar content. For example, all Status sections for a topic can be accessed and joined without separately accessing the Status section for each subtopic.

3. Moreover, information can be combined. For example, all content in a subsection may be viewed in one document without having to separately access each individual section.

E. What is Excluded from the Codification?

    1. The Codification does not include accounting guidance related to:

        a. Other Comprehensive basis of accounting

        b. Cash basis accounting

        c. Income tax basis accounting

        d. Regulatory accounting principles (e.g., insurance)

        e. Governmental accounting standards

Conceptual Framework of Financial Reporting by Business Enterprises

Objectives and Qualitative Characteristics

This lesson presents an overview of the conceptual framework related to the objectives of financial reporting and the qualitative characteristics of accounting information.

After studying this lesson, you should be able to:

1. Describe the objective of financial reporting.

2. Describe the qualitative characteristics of accounting information.

3. List the primary qualitative characteristics of accounting information.

4. List the enhancing qualitative characteristics of accounting information.

I. Conceptual Framework Outline

A. The FASB's Statements of Financial Accounting Concepts, as amended, comprise the conceptual framework for financial accounting. The framework does not constitute GAAP but rather provides consistent direction for the development of specific GAAP. The conceptual framework is a "constitution" for developing specific GAAP.

B. A listing of the parts of the conceptual framework follows. This outline lists the major subsections of the framework in a progression leading from definitions and general concepts to specific accounting principles, the ultimate purpose of the framework.

   1. Objective of financial reporting

   2. Qualitative characteristics of accounting information

   3. Accounting assumptions

   4. Basic accounting principles

   5. Cost constraint

   6. Elements of financial statements

II. Objective of Financial Reporting

A. The objective of general-purpose financial reporting is to provide information about the entity useful to current and future investors and creditors in making decisions as capital providers.

B. Useful information includes information about:

   1. The amount, timing, and uncertainty of an entity's cash flows;

   2. Ability of the entity to generate future net cash inflows;

   3. An entity's economic resources (assets) and claims to those resources (liabilities) that provides insight into the entity's financial strengths and weaknesses, and its liquidity and solvency;

   4. The effectiveness with which management has met its stewardship responsibilities;

   5. The effect of transactions and other events that change an entity's economic resources and the claims to those resources.

17

III. Qualitative Characteristics of Accounting Information

A. For financial statement information to be useful, it should have several qualitative characteristics. There are two primary characteristics and four enhancing characteristics, each of which has subcomponents. The following diagram shows the primary and enhancing characteristics and their components, as contributing to the objective of financial reporting.

Objective of Financial Reporting: Decision Usefulness
Primary Qualitative Characteristics

1. Relevance	**2.** Faithful representation
a. Predictive value	a. Completeness
b. Confirmatory value	b. Neutrality
c. Materiality	c. Free from error

Enhancing Qualitative Characteristics

1. Comparability

2. Verifiability

3. Timeliness

4. Understandability

B. Primary Characteristics (Relevance, Faithful Representation)—For information to be useful for decision-making, it must be both relevant and a faithful representation of the economic phenomena that it represents.

1. Relevance (primary characteristic)—Information is relevant if it makes a difference to decision makers in their role as capital providers. Information is relevant when it has predictive value, confirmatory value, or both.

a. Predictive value—Information has predictive value if it assists capital providers in forming expectations about future events.

b. Confirmatory value—Information has confirmatory value if it confirms or changes past (or present) expectations based on previous evaluations. For example, if reported earnings for a period bear out market expectations, then it has confirmatory value.

c. Materiality—Information that is material will impact a user's decision. Materiality is somewhat pervasive throughout the objectives of financial reporting in the sense that the financial statements should present material information because it is decision useful. The FASB believes that materiality is an entity specific attribute and that material information is relevant to the decision maker. Therefore, materiality is an attribute of relevance.

2. Faithful representation (primary characteristic)—Information faithfully represents an economic condition or situation when the reported measure and the condition or situation are in agreement. Financial information that faithfully represents an economic phenomenon portrays the economic substance of the phenomenon. Information is representationally faithful when it is complete, neutral, and free from material error. Faithful representation replaces reliability as a primary qualitative characteristic.

Example
If a firm reports gross plant assets of $100,000, the firm must actually have purchased that much in plant assets and be currently using them in operations.

---

a. **Completeness:** Information is complete if it includes all data necessary to be faithfully representative.

b. **Neutral:** Information is neutral when it is free from any bias intended to attain a prespecified result, or to encourage or discourage certain behavior.

Example
Firms may be reluctant to report losses. Neutrality requires that losses, if they are probable and estimable, be reported regardless of any possible effect on the firm.

c. **Free from error:** Information is free from error if there are no omissions or errors.

C. **Enhancing Characteristics**—These are complementary to the primary characteristics and enhance the decision usefulness of financial reporting information that is relevant and faithfully represented.

1. **Comparability**—The quality of information that enables users to identify similarities and differences between sets of information. Consistency in application of recognition and measurement methods over time enhances comparability.

2. **Verifiability**—Information is verifiable if different knowledgeable and independent observers could reach similar conclusions based on the information.

3. **Timeliness**—Information is timely if it is received in time to make a difference to the decision maker. Timeliness can also enhance the faithful representation of information.

4. **Understandability**—Information is understandable if the user comprehends it within the decision context at hand. Users are assumed to have a reasonable understanding of business and accounting and are willing to study the information with reasonable diligence.

D. **Relevance and Faithful Representation May Conflict**—In such cases, a trade-off is made favoring one or the other.

Examples
1. *Relevance over faithful representation.* The pervasive use of accounting estimates (depreciation, bad debt expense, pension estimates) is an example of emphasizing relevance over faithful representation. Firms are providing estimates, rather than certain amounts. Reasonable approximations, although they cannot be perfectly reliable, are preferred by financial statement users to either (1) perfect information issued too late to make a difference, or (2) no information at all.

2. *Faithful representation over relevance.* In the opinion of many, the use of historical cost as a valuation base is an example of emphasizing faithful representation over relevance. Historical cost is very reliable because it is based on objectively verifiable past information. However, historical cost is considered to be less current and, therefore, less relevant than market value.

Note
Candidates should be able to identify the components of relevance and faithful representation. It helps to remember that there are three components to both qualities.

Assumptions and Accounting Principles

This lesson presents an overview of accounting assumptions and principles in the related conceptual framework.

After studying this lesson, you should be able to:

1. List and describe the assumptions in the conceptual framework.

2. List and describe the principles in the conceptual framework.

I. Accounting Assumptions

A. Entity Assumption—We assume there is a separate accounting entity for each business organization.

Example

The owners and the corporation are separate. The owners own shares in the corporation; they do not own the assets of the firm. The corporation owns the assets. The financial statements represent the corporation, not the owners. A firm cannot own itself. Treasury shares are not assets to the firm—no one owns treasury shares. A firm can sue and be sued. If a firm is sued, the owners are not liable.

B. Going-Concern Assumption

1. In the absence of information to the contrary, a business is assumed to have an indefinite life, that is, it will continue to be a going concern. Therefore, we do not show items at their liquidation or exit values.

2. This assumption, also called the continuity assumption, supports the historical cost principle for many assets. Income measurement is based on historical cost of assets because assets provide value through use, rather than disposal. Thus, net income is the difference between revenue and the historical cost of assets used in generating that revenue. Without the going-concern principle, historical cost would not be an appropriate valuation basis.

Example

Prepaid assets, such as prepaid rent, would not be assets without the assumption of continuity.

C. Unit-of-Measure Assumption—Assets, liabilities, equities, revenues, expenses, gains, losses, and cash flows are measured in terms of the monetary unit of the country in which the business is operated. Price level changes cause the application of this assumption to weaken the relevance of certain disclosures.

Example

The amounts of all assets are added together even though amounts recorded at different times represent different purchasing power levels.

1. **Capital maintenance and departures from the unit of measure assumption**

    a. The concept of capital maintenance is related to the unit of measure assumption. Capital is said to be maintained when the firm has positive earnings for the year, assuming no changes in price levels. When a firm has income, it has recognized revenue sufficient to replace all the resources used in generating that revenue (return *of* capital), and has resources left over in addition (income, which is return *on* capital). That income could be distributed as dividends without eroding the net assets (capital) existing at the beginning of the year. GAAP is based on the concept of "financial" capital maintenance. As long as dividends do not exceed earnings, and earnings is not negative, financial capital has been maintained.

    b. An alternative concept of capital maintenance is *physical* capital maintenance. This concept holds that earnings cannot be recognized until the firm has provided for the physical capital used up during the period. To measure the capital used up, changes in price level must be considered.

> **Example**
>
> A firm uses up $5,000 worth of supplies in providing its service during the year, but to replace those supplies for use next year, $5,500 will have to be paid (10% increase in specific price of supplies). The *financial* capital maintenance model uses the $5,000 cost of supplies as the measure of revenue needed to maintain capital. If revenue for the current period is $5,000 and the firm had no other expenses, earnings would be zero and capital would just be maintained. The *physical* capital model would require revenue of $5,500 for capital to be maintained.
>
> GAAP does not require adjustments for price level changes and thus applies the *financial* capital maintenance concept in financial reports.

  D. Time Period Assumption—The indefinite life of a business is broken into smaller time frames, typically a year, for evaluation purposes and reporting purposes. For accounting information to be relevant, it must be timely. The reliability of the information often must be sacrificed to provide relevant disclosures. The use of estimates is required for timely reporting but also implies a possible loss of reliability.

II. Accounting Principles

  A. Measurement—At the time of origination, assets and liabilities are recorded at the market value of the item on the date of acquisition, usually the cash equivalent. This origination value is referred to as historical cost. For many assets and liabilities, this value is not changed even though market value changes. Other assets, such as plant assets and intangibles, are disclosed at historical cost less accumulated depreciation or amortization. Given the going-concern assumption, revaluation to market value is inappropriate for plant assets, because the value of these assets is derived through use, rather than from disposal.

  B. There are measurement attributes other than historical costs that are used to represent items reported on the financial statements. Below is a brief summary and example of each measurement attribute.

    1. Net realizable value—This value is used to approximate liquidation value or selling price. It is the net value to be received after the costs of sale are deducted from the current market value

      a. Example: Lower cost or market for inventory valuation uses NRV.

    2. Current replacement cost—This value represents how much you would have to pay to replace an asset. Current replacement cost would represent current market value from the buyer's perspective.

      a. Example: Replacement cost is also used in inventory valuation.

    3. Fair value—This value is also referred to as current market value. It is the price that would be received to sell an asset (or the price to settle a liability) in an orderly transaction from the perspective of a market participant at the measurement date (see the fair value lessons for further discussion of fair value).

      a. Example: Current market value (or fair value) is used to value trading and available-for-sale securities.

4. **Amortized cost**—This value is historical cost less the accumulated amortization or depreciation of the asset.

    a. Example: Buildings and equipment are reported at historical cost less accumulated depreciation.

5. **Net present value**—This is the value determined from discounting the expected future cash flows.

    a. Example: The discounted future cash flows are used in many capital budgeting decisions.

C. **Revenue Recognition Principle**—This principle addresses three important issues related to revenues. Below is a general view of revenue—see the Revenue Recognition lessons for more details.

1. **Revenue Defined**—*What* revenue is: Revenue refers to increases in assets or the extinguishment of liabilities stemming from the delivery of goods or the provision of services—that is, the main activities of the firm.

2. **When to Recognize Revenue**—Revenues are recognized when the entity completes its performance obligation to a customer and the revenue is earned and realized (or realizable) . The performance obligation is completed when the goods or services are delivered (revenue is earned) and cash or promise of cash is received (realized). In general, there are five steps to allocate the components of revenue.

    1. Identify the contract with the customer (promise to deliver a good or service)

    2. Identify if there is more than one performance obligation

    3. Determine the transaction price

    4. Allocate the transaction price to the separate performance obligations (if there is more than one performance obligation)

    5. Recognize revenue when each performance obligation is satisfied.

3. **Measure Revenue**—*How* to measure revenue: Revenues are measured at the cash equivalent amount of the good or service provided.

Example

A contract is entered into with the customer to deliver an automobile and provide a warranty on the parts associated with the automobile.

There are two separate performance obligations: Deliver the automobile and provide parts if needed.

Determine the price of the automobile without the warranty or the price that the warranty is sold for separate from the automobile.

Allocate the transaction price to the separate performance obligations.

Recognize revenue when each performance obligation is satisfied. With respect to the automobile, revenue would be recognized upon delivery; with respect to the warranty, the revenue would be recognized over the warranty period.

D. **Expense Recognition Principle**—This principle addresses when to recognize expenses and is sometimes referred to as the matching principle.

1. The matching principle says: *Recognize expenses only when expenditures help to produce revenues.* Revenues are recognized when earned and realized or realizable; the related expenses are recognized, and the revenues and expenses are "matched" to determine net income or loss.

2. Expenses that are directly related to revenues can be readily matched with revenues they help produce.

3. Cost of goods sold and sales commissions are expenses that are directly associated and, therefore, matched with revenue. Other expenses are allocated based on the time period of benefit provided. Depreciation and amortization are examples. Such expenses are not directly matched with revenues. Still other expenses are recognized in the period incurred when there is no determinable relationship between expenditures and revenues. Advertising costs are an example.

E. **Full Disclosure Principle**—Financial statements should present all information needed by an informed reader to make an economic decision. This principle is sometimes referred to as the adequate disclosure principle.

> **Example**
> An aircraft manufacturer enters into a contract to build 200 airplanes for an airline company. As of the balance sheet date, production has not begun. Thus, there is no recognition of this contract in the accounts. However, a footnote should explain the financial aspects of the contract. This information is potentially of greater interest than many items recognized in the accounts.

Constraints and Present Value

This lesson presents an overview of accounting assumptions and principles in the related conceptual framework.

After studying this lesson, you should be able to:

1. List and describe the constraints in the conceptual framework.

2. Describe how cash flow and present value are used in accounting measurements.

I. Cost Constraint

A. The cost constraint on GAAP limits recognition and disclosure if the cost of providing the information exceeds its benefit. Firms may not omit disclosures if they are material and mandated by GAAP.

Example

A firm would not report its entire inventory subsidiary ledger in the footnotes or financial statements. The reporting of total inventory cost is sufficient. Reporting more detailed information is not worth the cost of doing so.

B. **Conservatism**—Conservatism (also called prudence) is the reporting of less optimistic amounts (lower income, net assets) under conditions of uncertainty or when GAAP provides a choice from among recognition or measurement methods.

1. Conservatism is a guideline that is used to limit the reporting of aggressive accounting information. Conservatism is used to avoid misleading internal and external users of the financial statements.

2. If estimates of an outcome are not equally likely, the preferred approach is to report the most likely estimate, rather than the more conservative estimate, if the latter is less likely.

3. It should be noted that overly conservative estimates can be misleading and cause over reporting in subsequent periods.

Examples

1. Conservatism usually arises when there is uncertainty and management must make estimates. The allowance for uncollectible accounts receivable is an estimate, but an overly conservative accrual of the allowance in the current year will lead to lower net income and assets in the current period, but would over report income in subsequent years.

2. When estimating a contingent liability that arises from a lawsuit, often legal counsel provides a range of outcomes, for example $500,000—$1,000,000 loss. Accruing the most conservative loss in the current period, $1,000,000, will result in a gain in the subsequent period when the loss is settled for an amount less than $1,000,000, for example $800,000.

DR: Contingent Liability	$1,000,000	
CR: Cash		$800,000
CR: Gain on settlement of contingent liability		200,000

II. Financial Statements, Recognition Criteria, Elements

A. A full set of financial statements should include the following:

1. Financial Position at year-end (balance sheet)

2. Earnings for the year (income statement)

3. **Comprehensive Income for the year**—total nonowner changes (statement of comprehensive income)

4. **Cash Flows during the year** (statement of cash flows)

5. **Investments by and Distributions to Owners during the year** (statement of owner's equity)

B. **Recognition and Measurement Criteria**—In relation to measurement and recognition of items in a financial report, the following criteria must be met:

1. **Definition**—The definition of a financial statement element is met.

2. **Measurability**—There is an attribute to be measured, such as historical cost.

3. **Relevance**—The information to be presented in the financial report is capable of influencing decisions. The information is timely, has predictive ability, provides feedback value, and is material.

4. **Faithful Representation**—The information is complete, neutral and free from material error.

C. **Elements of Financial Statements**—Ten elements that appear in a financial report.

1. **Assets**—Resources that have probable future benefits to the firm, controlled by management, resulting from past transactions. Note the three aspects of this definition.

2. **Liabilities**—Probable future sacrifices of economic benefits arising from present obligations of an entity to transfer assets or provide services to other entities as a result of past transactions or events.

3. **Equity**—Residual interest in the firm's assets, also known as net assets. Equity is primarily comprised of past investor contributions and retained earnings.

4. **Investments by Owners**—Increases in net assets of an entity from transfers to it by existing owners or parties seeking ownership interest

5. **Distributions to Owners**—Decreases in net assets of an entity from the transfer of assets, provision of services, or incurrence of liabilities by the enterprise to owners

6. **Comprehensive Income**—Accounting income (transaction based) plus certain holding gains and losses and other items. It includes all changes in equity other than investments by owners and distributions to owners.

7. **Revenues**—Increases in assets or settlements of liabilities of an entity by providing goods or services

8. **Expenses**—Decreases in assets or incurrences of liabilities of an entity by providing goods or services. Expenses provide a benefit to the firm

9. **Gains**—Increases in equity or net assets from peripheral or incidental transactions

10. **Losses**—Decreases in equity or net assets from peripheral or incidental transactions. Losses provide no benefit to the firm.

III. **Using Cash Flow Information and Present Value in Accounting Measurements**—The concepts statement addresses the use of present-value measurements. Like all concepts statements, it does not constitute GAAP but is used in the development of GAAP.

A. **Measurement Issues**

1. This Statement addresses only measurement issues, not recognition. The statement applies to initial recognition, fresh-start measurements, and amortization techniques based on future cash flows. A fresh-start measurement establishes a new carrying value after an initial recognition and is unrelated to previous amounts (e.g., mark-to-market accounting and recognition of asset impairments).

2. If the fair value of an asset or liability is available, there is no need to use present-value measurement. If not, present value is often the best available technique to estimate what fair value would be if it existed in the situation.

B. **Present Value Measure**—When a present-value measure is used:

1. The result should be as close as possible to fair value if such a value could be obtained.

2. The expected cash flow approach is preferred, because present-value measurements should reflect the uncertainties inherent in the estimated cash flows.

C. **Capture Economic Differences**—A present value measurement that fully captures the economic differences between various estimates of future cash flows would include the following:

1. An estimate of future cash flows

2. Expectations about variations in amount or timing of those cash flows

3. Time value of money as measured by the risk-free rate of interest

4. The price for bearing the uncertainty inherent in the asset or liability

5. Any other relevant factors

D. **Two Approaches**—The statement contrasts two approaches to computing present value:

> **Note**
> *The risk and uncertainty is incorporated into either the discount rate or the cash flows—not both!*

1. **The traditional approach** (referred to as discounted cash flows) incorporates factors 2–5 above in the discount rate and uses a single most-likely cash flow in the computation. The traditional approach uses the interest rate to capture all the uncertainties and risks inherent in a cash flow measure. This is the approach that continues to be applied in some present value applications in financial accounting.

2. **The expected cash flow approach** uses a risk-free rate as the discount rate. That is, factors 2–5 are incorporated into the risk-adjusted expected cash flow and the discount factor is the risk-free rate.

E. **Expected Cash Flow Approach**—The expected cash flow approach uses expectations about all possible cash flows instead of a single most-likely cash flow. Both uncertainty as to timing and amount can be incorporated into the calculation. The Board believes that the expected cash flow approach is likely to provide a better estimate of fair value than a single value because it directly incorporates the uncertainty in estimated future cash flows.

Examples

1. *Example of Uncertain Amount*—The amount of a cash flow may vary as follows: $200, $400, or $600 with probabilities of 10%, 60%, and 30%, respectively. The expected cash flow is $440 = $200(.10) + $400(.60) + $600(.30). The expected cash flow approach uses a range of cash flows with probabilities attached. Thus, the uncertainties of the cash flows themselves are reflected in the distribution of cash flows. Calculation of the present value is determined by using the probability weight cash flows discounted using the risk-free rate.

2. *Example of Uncertain Timing*—A $100 cash flow might be received in 1, 2, or 3 years with probabilities of 10%, 60%, and 30%, respectively. Assuming an interest rate of 5%, the expected present value = $100(pv1, .05, 1)(.10) + $100(pv1, .05, 2)(.60) + $100(pv1, .05, 3)(.30). [(pv 1, .05, 1) is the symbol for the present-value of a single payment of $1, due in 1 year discounted at 5%.] Calculation of the present value is determined by using the probability weight cash flows discounted using the risk free rate.

---

1. Different rates of interest may also be used in each of the single present value terms to reflect different risk for the different timing of cash flow.

F. The expected cash flow approach has been incorporated into Accounting for Asset Retirement Obligations.

Fair Value Framework

Fair Value Framework—Introduction and Definitions

This lesson provides the definition of fair value and the components of that definition. The definition includes the concepts related to market participant and principal or most advantageous market. The lesson describes how the definition would be applied to assets, liabilities, and equity. In addition, the use of practical expedient is described as well as the concept of net asset value (NAV) as a practical expedient.

After studying this lesson, you should be able to:

1. Define "fair value" for accounting purposes.

2. Describe the individual components of the fair value definition and how each component impacts the application of the definition.

3. Demonstrate the application of the fair value definition to assets, liabilities, and shareholders' equity and to a net portfolio of assets and liabilities.

4. Explain when a practical expedient can be used to determine fair value.

I. **Introduction**—Fair value is used to measure and report financial statement items as required or permitted by a number of GAAP pronouncements (ASCs). Some pronouncements provide different definitions of "fair value" and provide only limited guidance in the determination of fair value for GAAP purposes. As a consequence, inconsistencies have occurred in how fair value is measured in practice. ASC 820 provides a framework for how to measure fair value to achieve increased consistency and comparability in fair value measurements and expanded disclosure when fair value measurements are used.

   A. **Objectives**—In order to accomplish the objectives of ASC 820, the following are provided:

      1. A definition of fair value for GAAP purposes;

      2. A framework for measuring (determining) fair value for accounting purposes;

      3. A set of required disclosures about fair value measurement when it is used.

II. **Fair Value Defined**

> **Definition**
> *Fair Value*: The price that would be received to sell an asset or paid to transfer a liability in an orderly transaction between market participants at the measurement date.

In order to fully understand and apply this definition, several components of the definition need to be described further:

1. Fair value is a market-based measurement, not an entity-specific measurement.

2. The determination of fair value for a particular asset or liability (or equity item) may be either a stand-alone asset or liability (e.g., a financial instrument or a nonfinancial operating asset) or a group of assets/liabilities (e.g., a reporting unit or business). Fair value determination should consider the attributes (e.g., condition, location, restriction on asset use or sale, etc.) of the specific asset or liability being measured.

> **Note**
> *The fair value definition focuses on **how** to measure fair value not **when** to measure fair value.*

3. The transaction to sell the asset or transfer the liability is a hypothetical transaction at the measurement date that would occur under current market conditions; it is not a transaction that would occur in a forced liquidation or distress sale.

4. Even when there is no observable market to provide pricing information about the sale of an asset or the transfer of a liability at the measurement date, a fair value measurement assumes that a transaction takes place at that date.

5. The assumed transaction establishes a basis for estimating the price to sell the asset or transfer the liability.

6. The hypothetical transaction to sell the asset or transfer the liability is assumed to occur in the principal market or, alternatively, in the absence of a principal market, the most advantageous market for the asset or liability, to which the entity has access, after taking into account transaction costs and transportation costs.

   a. The **principal market** is the one with the greatest volume and level of activity for the asset or liability within which the reporting entity could sell the asset or transfer the liability.

   b. The **most advantageous market** is the one in which the reporting entity could sell the asset at a price that maximizes the amount that would be received for the asset or that minimizes the amount that would be paid to transfer the liability.

7. The price determined in the principal or most advantageous market should not be adjusted for transaction costs—incremental direct cost to sell the asset or transfer the liability—which do not measure a characteristic of the asset or liability. However, cost incurred to transport the asset or liability to its principal or most advantageous market (the location characteristic of an asset) would be used to adjust fair value for measurement purposes.

> **Note**
> Notice that although transaction and transportation costs are taken into account in determining the most advantageous market, transaction costs are not used (i.e., not deducted from the asset market price or added to the liability transfer cost) in determining the fair value of an asset or liability in the most advantageous market.

8. Market participants, as used in the definition, are buyers and sellers of the asset or liability that are:

   a. Independent of the reporting entity

   b. Acting in their economic best interest

   c. Knowledgeable of the asset or liability and the transaction involved

   d. Able and willing, but not compelled, to transact for the asset or liability

III. Application of Definition to Assets, Liabilities, and Shareholders' Equity

A. Application to Assets

1. The determination of fair value of a nonfinancial asset assumes the highest and best use of the asset by market participants, even if the intended use of the asset by the reporting entity is different; the concept of *highest and best use* does not apply to measuring the fair value of financial assets (or liabilities).

2. The highest and best use must take into account what is physically possible, legally permissible and financially feasible at the measurement date.

3. The highest and best use of an asset may be:

   a. **In use**—Maximum value to market participants would occur through its use in combination with other assets as a group; *or*

   b. **In exchange**—Maximum value to market participants would occur principally on a stand-alone basis (i.e., the price that would be received in a current transaction to sell the [single] asset).

B. Application to Liabilities

1. The determination of fair value of a liability assumes that the liability is transferred to a market participant at the measurement date; it is not settled or canceled.

   a. The liability to the counterparty (i.e., the party to whom the obligation is due) is assumed to continue after the hypothetical transaction.

   b. Nonperformance risk relating to the liability is assumed to be the same after the hypothetical transaction as before the transaction.

2. The determination of fair value of a liability should consider the effects of the reporting entity's credit risk (or credit standing) on the fair value of the liability in each period for which the liability is measured at fair value; a third-party credit enhancement should not be considered.

3. A separate input or an adjustment to other inputs to account for a restriction that prevents the transfer of liabilities should not be made in measuring fair value.

4. When a quoted price for the transfer of an identical or similar liability is not available, and the identical liability is held by another party as an asset, the liability should be measured from the perspective of the party that holds the item as an asset.

C. Application to Shareholders' Equity

1. The requirements for the determination of fair value apply to instruments classified in shareholders' equity that are measured at fair value (e.g., equity interest issued as consideration in a business combination).

2. The measurement assumes the instrument is transferred to a market participant at the measurement date and is measured from the perspective of a market participant that holds the instrument as an asset.

3. A separate input or an adjustment to other inputs to account for a restriction that prevents the transfer of a shareholder equity instrument should not be made in measuring the fair value.

4. When a quoted price for the transfer of an identical or similar shareholders' equity instrument is not available and the identical instrument is held by another party as an asset, the instrument should be measured from the perspective of the party that holds the item as an asset.

D. Application to Net Financial Assets and Financial Liabilities

1. An exception to the requirement that fair value of qualified financial assets and financial liabilities be measured separately is permitted when a reporting entity manages risk associated with a portfolio of financial instruments on a net exposure basis, rather than on a gross exposure basis.

2. An entity that holds financial assets and financial liabilities and manages those instruments on the basis of their net risk exposure may measure the fair value of those financial assets and financial liabilities at:

   a. The price that would be received to sell a NET asset position for a particular risk, or

   b. The price that would be paid to transfer a NET liability position for a particular risk.

IV. Applicability—ASC 820 applies to items that use fair value measurement either as required or as permitted by GAAP, except in very limited situations. Specifically, the guidance of ASC 820 does **not** apply to:

A. Accounting principles that address share-based payment transactions

B. ASCs that require or permit measurements that are similar to fair value but that are not intended to measure fair value, including:

1. Accounting principles that permit measurements that are determined using vendor-specific objective evidence of fair value; *or*

2. Accounting principles that address fair value measurement for purposes of inventory pricing

C. Accounting principles that address fair value measurements for purposes of lease classification or measurement

D. ASCs that permit practicability exceptions to fair value measurement (see below)

E. **Pervasive Applicability**—Other than the exceptions noted above, the content of ASC 820 must be followed when fair value measurement is used, either as required or permitted by other pronouncements.

V. **Practical Expedient Exception**—ASC 820 allows a company to use a "practical expedient" to measure the fair value of an investment that does not have a quoted market price but reports a net asset value per share (NAV). These investment vehicles are often referred to as alternative investments. Examples are hedge funds, private equity funds, real estate funds, venture capital funds, common/collective funds, and offshore funds.

For example, a private equity fund (PE) may invest in start-up companies, rare archeological artifacts, artwork, and real estate. The PE fund most likely reports the investment in these items at fair value or investment value. The PE fund may report NAV to the investors; if the PE fund meets the criteria as an alternative investment, the investor can use NAV as a practical expedient to measure fair value. The following diagram shows the structure of an alternative investment.

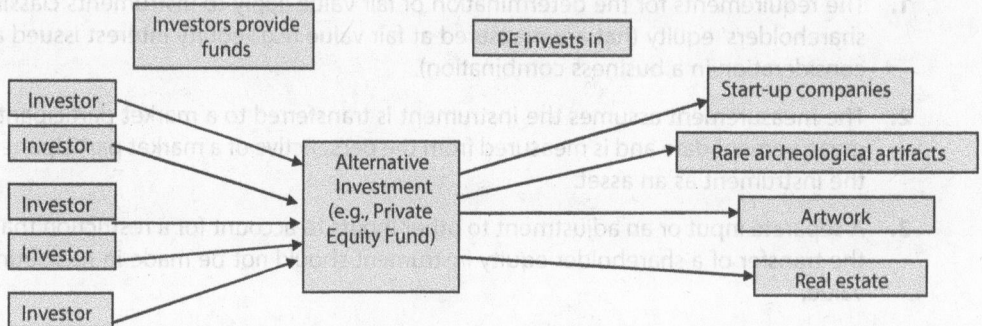

A. Alternative investments must meet the criteria in order to use NAV as the practical expedient:

1. Does not have a "readily determinable fair value."

2. The investment meets the criteria for an investment company as stipulated in ASC 940-10-15-2 or does not meet the criteria to be an investment company but follows industry practice and issues financial statements consistent with the measurement principles for an investment company.

B. **Classification in the Fair Value Hierarchy**—The investor is not allowed to "look through" the alternative investment fund and classify the investment in the fair value hierarchy according to the investments made by the PE fund. The investor owns a share of the PE fund, not a share of the start-up company or the real estate.

1. Alternative investments that are reported at NAV as a practical expedient are NOT categorized in the fair value hierarchy (Level 1, 2, or 3) but are separately reported in the footnotes with disclosures that indicate that NAV is being used and these disclosures must reconcile to the amounts reported on the balance sheet.

2. Companies that use NAV as a practical expedient for measuring fair value must disclose sufficient information so that financial statement users understand the nature and the risks of the investment. The disclosure must include information about the terms and conditions in which the company can redeem its investments.

C. There are other instances where practical expedient is allowed. An entity is allowed to use a practical expedient in other circumstances, such as in the valuation of benefit plans or for a private company's measurement of share-based payments.

Recognition and Measurement

The measurement of fair value is based on an exit price — the amount that would be received to sell an asset or paid to transfer a liability. In some cases, that amount will be the same amount as an entry price, but not in all cases. A number of methods may be used to determine a hypothetical exit price that establishes fair value. This lesson discusses the relationship between an exit price and an entry price, and identifies those situations where the prices may be different amounts. This lesson also identifies those methods and describes their use in determining fair value.

After studying this lesson, you should be able to:

1. Identify reasons why an entry price and an exit price may not be the same on the recognition date.

2. Identify and apply the techniques or approaches used to determine fair value.

3. Identify when a change in techniques may be appropriate and the consequence of such a change.

4. Describe the nature of an entry price and an exit price and distinguish between the two.

5. Identify when the fair value option can be applied.

6. Apply the definition of fair value to specific accounts or transactions.

I. **Fair Value Determination**—When an asset is acquired or a liability is assumed in a transaction, the price paid to acquire the asset or the price received to assume the liability is an entry price. The price paid when an asset is initially recognized may or may not equal fair value. Fair value of an asset or a liability is the price that would be received to sell an asset or paid to transfer a liability which is an exit price.

   A. Conceptually, an entry price and an exit price are different.

   B. In many cases, the entry price (transaction price) and the exit price (fair value) will be the same at the date of initial recognition of an asset or liability and, therefore, constitute the fair value of the asset or liability at that date.

   C. In some cases, however, the entry (transaction) price may not be the exit price and therefore not be fair value at the date of initial recognition of an asset or liability. For example, the transaction price might not be fair value (exit price) if:

   1. The transaction is between related parties;

   2. The transaction takes place when the seller is under duress (e.g., in a liquidation sale);

   3. The unit of account for the transaction price is different from the unit of account that would be used to measure the asset or liability at fair value. For example, if the asset or liability measured at fair value is part of a business in a business combination, there are unstated rights associated with an asset that are measured separately, or the quoted price includes transaction costs, such as with oil; *or*

   4. The market in which the transaction price takes place is different from the principal market (or most advantageous market).

   D. If an entity is required or permitted to measure an asset or liability initially at fair value and the transaction price at initial recognition differs from fair value, a gain or loss is recognized in earnings at initial recognition of the asset or liability (unless otherwise required by GAAP for that item).

   1. The asset or liability would be recorded at fair value.

   2. The difference between the transaction (entry) price and the recorded fair value (exit price) would be recognized as a loss or gain in the period of initial recognition.

II. Measurement Techniques

A. **Valuation Techniques/Approaches**—In the determination of fair value for GAAP purposes, three valuation techniques or approaches could be used:

1. **Market approach**—This approach uses prices and other relevant information generated by market transactions involving assets or liabilities that are identical or comparable to those being valued.

2. **Income approach**—This approach converts future amounts to a single present amount. Discounting future cash flows would be an income approach to determining fair value.

3. **Cost approach**—This approach uses the amount that currently would be required to replace the service capacity of an asset (i.e., current replacement cost), adjusting for obsolescence.

B. **Valuation Technique/Approach Selection**—Which approach (or approaches) is appropriate to measure fair value will depend on the circumstances, including the availability of sufficient data for the respective approaches, and will maximize the use of relevant observable inputs and minimize the use of unobservable inputs.

1. In some cases, a single valuation technique will be appropriate (e.g., using quoted prices in an active market for identical assets or liabilities).

2. In some cases, multiple valuation techniques will be appropriate (e.g., when valuing an entire business).

   a. When multiple valuation techniques are used, the different results should be evaluated and weighted.

   b. When multiple valuation techniques are used, professional judgment will be required to select the fair value from within the range of alternative values that is most representative in the circumstances.

3. Under all valuation techniques, the valuation must take into account appropriate risk adjustments, including a risk premium for uncertainty.

C. **Consistent Application of Approach/Technique**

1. Valuation techniques used to measure fair value should be consistently applied.

2. A change in valuation technique or its application is appropriate if the change will result in a more representative fair value.

   a. A change in valuation technique or application may be appropriate, for example, if new markets develop, new information becomes available, previous information is no longer available, or valuation techniques improve.

   b. Changes in fair value resulting from changes in valuation techniques or applications are treated as changes in accounting estimates.

III. Fair Value Option

A. An entity can apply the fair value option to an eligible item only on the date when one of the following events occurs (an election date):

1. When the item is first recognized;

2. When an eligible firm commitment is established;

3. Specialized accounting for an item ceases to exist;

4. An investment becomes subject to equity method accounting (but is not consolidated) or to a VIE that is no longer consolidated; *or*

5. An event that requires the item to be measured at fair value, such as a business combination or significant modifications to debt instruments.

B. Entities that elect to use the fair value measurement (referred to as the fair value option) for eligible financial assets and financial liabilities must adhere to certain requirements. Those requirements include:

    1. The fair value option may be applied on an instrument-by-instrument basis, with limited exceptions.

        a. The fair value option may be elected for a single eligible item without electing it for other identical items with the following exceptions:

            i. If multiple advances are made to one borrower as part of a single contract and the individual advances lose their identity, the fair value option must be applied to all advances under the contract;

            ii. If the fair value option is applied to an investment that would otherwise be accounted for under the equity method of accounting, it must be applied to all of the investor's financial interests, both equity and debt, in that entity; *or*

            iii. If the fair value option is applied to an eligible insurance/reinsurance contract, it must be applied to all claims/obligations and features/coverages under the contract.

        b. The fair value option does not have to be applied to all instruments issued or acquired in a single transaction (except as noted in 1, above). The fair value option may be applied to some of the individual instruments issued or acquired (e.g., shares of stock or bonds) in a single transaction, but not to other individual instruments issued or acquired in that transaction.

    2. The fair value option is irrevocable unless and until a new election date for the specific item occurs.

    3. The fair value option is applied only to an entire instrument and not to only specific risks, specific cash flows, or portions of an instrument.

    4. If the fair value option is elected for held-to-maturity securities, those securities will be treated and reported as trading securities.

        a. Gains and losses resulting from change in fair value will not be reported in other comprehensive income.

        b. Gains and losses resulting from changes in fair value will be reported in current income.

IV. Instruments Not Eligible for Fair Value Option—Entities may NOT use fair value to measure and report the following financial assets and financial liabilities:

    A. An investment in a subsidiary that is to be consolidated

    B. An interest in a variable interest entity that is to be consolidated

    C. Employers' and plans' obligations (or assets) for pension benefits, other postretirement benefits, postemployment benefits, and other employee-oriented plans

    D. Financial assets and liabilities recognized under lease accounting

    E. Demand deposit liabilities of financial institutions

    F. Financial instruments that are classified by the issuer as a component of shareholders' equity

Inputs and Hierarchy

Many inputs may be used when determining fair value. In some cases, the inputs are based on limited assumptions and observable points; for example, when quoted prices in an active market are appropriate and available. In other cases, a number of assumptions and a variety of inputs may be needed to develop a fair value measure. This lesson identifies the kinds of inputs that may be used and the relative importance of each.

After studying this lesson, you should be able to:

1. Distinguish between observable and unobservable inputs in determining fair value.

2. Describe the three levels of the fair value hierarchy and give examples of each.

3. Categorize valuation inputs and/or results into the three levels of the fair value hierarchy.

I. **Inputs**—Inputs refer to the various assumptions that market participants would use in determining fair value, including assumptions about the risk inherent in using a particular valuation technique, as well as the risk inherent in using various inputs (data, assumptions, etc.) with each valuation technique.

   A. Inputs used may be

      1. **Observable**—Inputs used in pricing an asset, liability, or equity item that are developed based on market data obtained from sources independent of the reporting entity; *or*

      2. **Unobservable**—Inputs that reflect the reporting entity's own assumptions used in pricing the asset, liability, or equity item that are developed based on the best information available in the circumstances.

   B. Valuation techniques used to measure fair value should maximize the use of observable inputs and minimize the use of unobservable inputs.

II. **Fair Value Hierarchy**—The fair value hierarchy (provided in ASC 820) prioritizes or ranks the inputs to valuation techniques used to measure fair value into three levels:

   A. **Level 1**—Inputs in this, the highest level, are unadjusted quoted prices in active markets for assets or liabilities (or equity items) identical to those being valued that the entity can obtain at the measurement date.

      1. Quoted prices in an active market provide the most reliable evidence of fair value and, except in unusual circumstances, should be used to measure fair value when available.

      2. Quoted prices should not be adjusted because the entity holds a sizable position in the asset or liability relative to the trading volume in the market (often referred to as the "blockage factor").

      3. Adjustments to quoted prices generally result in a fair value measurement categorized in a lower level of the fair value hierarchy (i.e., Level 2 or 3).

   B. **Level 2**—Inputs in this level are observable for assets or liabilities (or equity items), either directly or indirectly, other than quoted prices described in Level 1, above.

      1. This level includes:

         a. Quoted prices for similar assets or liabilities in active markets;

         b. Quoted prices for identical or similar assets or liabilities in markets that are not active markets in which there are few relevant transactions, prices are not current or vary substantially, or for which little information is publicly available;

         c. Inputs, other than quoted prices, that are observable for the assets or liabilities being valued, including, for example, interest rates, yield curves, implied volatilities and credit spreads; *and*

    d. Inputs that are derived principally from, or corroborated by, observable market data by correlation or other means (referred to as "market-corroborated inputs").

  2. Depending on factors specific to the asset or liability being valued, these inputs may need to be adjusted when applied to the asset or liability for factors such as: condition, location, and the level of activity in the relevant market.

  3. When market participants would apply a premium or discount related to a characteristic of an asset or liability being valued (e.g., a control premium), an entity should apply the premium or discount in measuring fair value.

  4. If significant unobservable inputs are used to adjust observable inputs, the resulting measurement may be categorized in Level 3.

C. Level 3—Inputs in this, the lowest level, are unobservable for the assets or liabilities (or equity items) being valued and should be used to determine fair value only to the extent observable inputs are not available.

  1. Unobservable inputs should reflect the entity's assumptions about what market participants would assume and should be developed based on the best information available in the circumstances, which might include the entity's own data.

  2. The reporting entity should not ignore information available about market participants' assumptions and should adjust its own data if information indicated that market participants would use different assumptions.

  3. When market participants would apply a premium or discount related to a characteristic of the asset or liability being valued (e.g., a control premium), an entity should apply the premium or discount in measuring fair value.

  4. When a valuation technique uses unobservable inputs to determine fair value subsequent to initial recognition and fair value at initial recognition is the transaction price, the valuation technique should be calibrated (adjusted) at initial recognition so that the results of the valuation technique equals the transaction price.

Note

If net asset value (NAV) is used as a practical expedient to determine fair value, NAV is not reported within the fair value hierarchy but rather is separately disclosed in the footnotes of the financial statements. See the "Fair Value Framework—Introduction and Definitions" lesson for more discussion on use of practical expedients.

Disclosure Requirements

Any time fair value measurement is used GAAP requires specific disclosures when financial statements are issued. This lesson identifies the most important of those disclosures.

After studying this lesson, you should be able to:

1. Describe significant disclosures required for assets, liabilities, and equity items measured at fair value on a **recurring** basis.

2. Describe significant disclosures required for assets, liabilities, and equity items measured at fair value on a **nonrecurring** basis.

3. Describe the significant disclosure requirements for the election of the fair value option applied to assets, liabilities, and equity items.

I. U.S. GAAP requires disclosures about the assets and liabilities measured at fair value so that the financial statement user can understand the risks and uncertainties associated with those measurements.

    A. The entity must disclose information about the valuation techniques and inputs used to derive the fair value measurement. This includes the judgments and assumptions needed to complete the valuation. The entity must also disclose how the changes in fair value affect the entities results of operations and cash flows.

    B. The disclosures are categorized as those fair value measurements that are done on a recurring basis and those fair value measurements done on a nonrecurring basis.

II. **For Assets and Liabilities That Are Measured at Fair Value on a Recurring Basis**—In periods subsequent to initial recognition, the reporting entity must disclose the following information about the major assets and liabilities carried at fair value in the statement of financial position (balance sheet). These disclosures are required for each interim and annual period:

    A. For each class of assets and liabilities, the fair value measurements either on the balance sheet or in the footnotes at the reporting date

    B. Segregated into each of the three levels within the fair value hierarchy

    C. For measurements classified in Levels 2 and 3, a description of the valuation techniques and inputs used to measure fair value and a discussion of changes in valuation techniques during the period, if any

    D. For fair value measurements in Level 3, the entity must disclose the unobservable inputs, a reconciliation of the beginning and ending balances, separately presenting changes during the period attributable to the following:

        1. Total gains or losses recognized, showing separately those included in earnings and those included in other comprehensive income, and the line item(s) in which they are recognized in the respective statements

        2. Purchases, sales, issuances, and settlements, disclosed separately

        3. Transfer in and/or out of Level 3 disclosed separately, the reasons for such transfers

    E. For fair value measurements in Level 3:

        1. A narrative description of the uncertainty of the fair value measurement to changes in unobservable inputs

    F. The amount of total gains or losses for the period that are attributable to the change in unrealized gains or losses relating to assets and liabilities still held at the reporting date and a description of where those unrealized amounts are reported in the income statement or statement of comprehensive income.

G. For nonfinancial assets, disclose if highest and best use differs from current use and why.

III. For Assets and Liabilities That Are Measured at Fair Value on a Nonrecurring Basis—An asset or liability is measured at fair value on a nonrecurring basis because that asset or liability is impaired or there is other evidence that fair value measurement must be used. The disclosures for items reported at fair value on a nonrecurring basis are the same as the disclosures on a recurring basis, but, in addition, the following also must be disclosed:

A. The reasons for the measurement and if the measurement estimate is at a date that is not at the end of the reporting period, the entity must disclose the date for the measurement

B. For fair value measurements in Level 3, unobservable inputs, a description of the valuation process used and quantitative information about the unobservable inputs used

IV. Other Disclosure Issues

A. The quantitative disclosures required above must be presented using a tabular format.

B. Reporting entities are encouraged, but not required, to combine the fair value information disclosures under this ASC with fair value information disclosures required by other accounting pronouncements.

C. If net asset value (NAV) is used as a practical expedient to determine fair value, NAV is not reported within the fair value hierarchy but rather is separately disclosed in the footnotes of the financial statements. See the "Fair Value Framework—Introduction and Definitions" lesson for more discussion on use of practical expedients.

1. Alternative investments that are reported at NAV as a practical expedient are NOT categorized in the fair value hierarchy (Level 1, 2, or 3) but are separately reported in the footnotes with disclosures that indicate that NAV is being used and these disclosures must reconcile to the amounts reported on the balance sheet.

2. Companies that use NAV as a practical expedient for measuring fair value must disclose sufficient information so that financial statement users understand the nature and the risks of the investment. The disclosure must include information about the terms and conditions in which the company can redeem its investments.

V. Disclosure Related to the Fair Value Options

A. Fair Value Option Disclosures Objectives—**When the fair value option is elected, the disclosures should be sufficient** to enable users of financial statements to understand management's reasons for electing or partially electing the fair value option.

B. Required Disclosures for Interim and Annual Statements of Financial Position (Balance Sheet)—As of each date for which a Statement of Financial Position (Balance Sheet) is presented, the following must be disclosed:

1. Management's reasons for electing a fair value option for each eligible item or group of similar eligible items

2. If the fair value option is elected for some, but not all, eligible items within a group of similar eligible items:

a. A description of those similar items and the reasons for partial election

b. Information to enable users to understand how the group of similar items relates to individual line items on the Statement of Financial Position

3. For each line item in the Statement of Financial Position that includes an item or items for which the fair value option has been elected:

a. Information to enable users to understand how each line item in the statement relates to major categories of assets and liabilities

b. The aggregate carrying amount of items included in each line item in the statement that are not eligible for the fair value option, if any

4. The difference between the aggregate fair value and the aggregate unpaid principal balance of:

    a. Loans and long-term receivables that have contractual principal amounts and for which the fair value option is used

    b. Long-term-debt instruments that have contractual principal amounts and for which the fair value option has been elected

5. For loans held as assets for which the fair value option has been elected:

    a. The aggregate fair value of loans that are 90 days or more past due

    b. If the entity's policy is to recognize interest income separately from other changes in fair value, the aggregate fair value of loans in nonaccrual status (i.e., loans for which interest income is not accrued)

    c. The difference between the aggregate fair value and the aggregate unpaid principal balance for loans that are 90 days or more past due, are in nonaccrual status, or both

6. For investments that would have been accounted for under the equity method if the entity had not chosen to apply the fair value option, the information required by ASC 323, *The Equity Method of Accounting for Investments*, including:

    a. The name of each investee and the percentage ownership of its common stock

    b. The accounting policies of the investor with respect to investments in common stock

C. Required Disclosures for Interim and Annual Income Statements—For each period for which an Income Statement is presented, the following must be disclosed about items for which the fair value option has been elected:

1. For each line item in the Statement of Financial Position (Balance Sheet), the amount of gains and losses from fair value changes included in earnings for the period and in which line in the Income Statement those gains/losses are reported

2. A description of how interest and dividends are measured and where they are reported in the Income Statement

3. For loans and other receivables held as assets:

    a. The estimated amount of gains and losses included in earnings for the period attributable to changes in instrument-specific credit risk, and

    b. How those gains and losses were determined.

4. For liabilities with fair values that have been significantly affected during the reporting period by changes in the instrument-specific credit risk:

    a. The estimated amount of gains and losses from fair value changes included in earnings that are attributable to changes in the instrument-specific credit risk

    b. How the gains and losses were determined

    c. Qualitative information about the reasons for those changes

D. Other Disclosure Requirements

1. In annual reports only, the methods and significant assumptions used to estimate fair value (of items for which the fair value option has been elected) must be disclosed.

2. If an entity elects the fair value option at the time an investment becomes subject to the equity method of accounting or when it ceases to consolidate a subsidiary, it must disclose:

    a. Information about the nature of the event, and

    b. Where the effect on earnings shows in the Income Statement.

General-Purpose Financial Statements

Financial Statements

After studying this lesson, you should be able to:

1. Describe the form and content of the Income Statement.
2. Describe the form and content of the Balance Sheet.
3. Describe the form and content of the Statement of Cash Flows.

I. **Summary of the Primary Financial Statements**—Here we present an overall summary of the basic financial statements. Later lessons will cover each statement in more depth.

A. **Income Statement—Statement of Profit or Loss**

1. The income statement measures the performance of the firm for the period. It is dated for the entire period (e.g., for the year ended December 31, 20xX).

2. The income statement is prepared by applying the all-inclusive approach. That is, almost all revenues, expenses, gains, and losses are shown on the income statement and are included in the calculation of net income. A major exception here is prior period adjustments, which are the effects of corrections of errors affecting prior year net income. Prior period adjustments are shown on the Statement of Retained Earnings as adjustments to the beginning balance of retained earnings in the year the error is discovered.

3. There are other items that would appear to be income items but are not reflected in net income. These include unrealized gains and losses on investments in securities available-for-sale, certain pension cost adjustments, and foreign currency translation adjustments. These items are included in *comprehensive income*, which now is a required disclosure. However, except for items included in *comprehensive income* but not also in net income, prior period adjustments, and a few other items, the reporting of net income in the income statement reflects an all-inclusive approach.

B. **Statement of Comprehensive Income**

1. The statement of comprehensive income reports all non-owner changes in equity over a period of time—the same time period as the income statement. This statement is also dated for the year ended December 31, 20xX.

2. The statement of comprehensive income includes net income (or loss) and the items included in comprehensive income that are not part of net income. Those items include:

   a. Unrealized gains and losses on available-for-sale securities

   b. Adjustments in the calculation of the pension liability

   c. Foreign currency translation adjustments

   d. Deferrals of certain gains or losses on hedge accounting.

C. **Balance Sheet—Statement of Financial Position**

1. The balance sheet discloses the resources of the firm at a point in time. It is dated as of a specific date (e.g., December 31, 20xX).

2. The balance sheet is formally referred to as the Statement of Financial Position, but balance sheet is the more commonly used term. A business enterprise discloses its economic resources (assets) and the manner of financing the acquisition of those resources (creditors, owners' contributions, and prior year's earnings) in the balance sheet.

3. Formats for presentation

a. The presentation format for a balance sheet is typically one of two formats: the account format or the report format.

b. In the account format, the assets are shown on the left side of the page, and the liabilities and owners' equity are shown on the right side. This format emphasizes the balance sheet equation: A = L + OE.

Account Format

Debits	**Credits**
Assets	Liabilities
	Stockholders' Equity

c. In the report format, which is the most popular form, the three categories of accounts are listed from top to bottom, as in a report, with assets always shown first.

Report Format

Assets
Liabilities
Stockholders' Equity

4. Classification of accounts

a. Regardless of balance sheet format, assets, liabilities, and equities are presented on the balance sheet in a prescribed order, which is summarized below.

i. Assets are presented in order of decreasing liquidity. The most liquid assets (such as cash) are shown first, and less liquid assets are shown last (such as property, plant, and equipment).

ii. Liabilities are shown in order of maturity. Current liabilities are presented first and then long-term liabilities are presented.

iii. Owners' Equity (also referred to as Shareholders', Stockholders', or Shareowners' Equity) items are shown in order of permanence.

Example
For a corporation, the contributed capital accounts are shown first and retained earnings are typically shown as the final item in Stockholders' Equity. Retained earnings are thought to be less permanent due to the fact that dividends are a distribution of earnings.

5. Balance sheet presentation

a. Balance sheet presentation reflects the classification of assets and liabilities. The classification criteria used for each is indicated below and is affected by the firm's operating cycle. The operating cycle of a firm is the period of time required to purchase or produce inventory, sell the inventory, and collect cash from the resulting receivables. For most firms, the operating cycle is significantly less than one year. For firms in some industries, such as construction, the operating cycle is longer than one year.

b. Current assets—Assets that are in the form of cash, or will be converted into cash, or consumed within one year or the operating cycle of the business, whichever is longer.

Example
Cash, accounts receivable, short-term investments, inventory, and prepaid assets are current assets.

    c. **Current liabilities**—Liabilities that are due in the upcoming year or in the operating cycle of the business, whichever is longer, and that will be met through the transfer of a current asset or the creation of another current liability. Both criteria must be met in order for a liability to be classified as current.

Example
Accounts payable, wages payable, income tax payable, unearned revenues, and warranty liability are current liabilities. (For the last two items, only the portion to be extinguished within one year of the balance sheet would be classified as current.) Also, the current portion of long-term debt is classified as current; it is the amount of debt previously classified as long-term that is now due within one year of the balance sheet date.

    d. **Long-term assets and long-term liabilities**—These are defined by exclusion. All assets that do not meet the criteria necessary to be classified as current are classified as long-term assets. Likewise, all liabilities that do not meet the criteria necessary to be classified as current are classified as long-term liabilities.

Example
Long-term investments, plant assets, certain deferred charges, and intangible assets are non-current assets. Notes and bonds payable and mortgages payable are long-term liabilities.

  6. Valuation and measurement

Note
CPA Exam questions tend to emphasize sections of the balance sheet. For example, a question might focus on the property, plant, and equipment section of the balance sheet or on the long-term liability section of the balance sheet. As we cover the individual items presented on the balance sheet, these problems will be a primary focus.

    a. Balance Sheet Valuation is summarized below but will be emphasized more in the coverage of individual balance sheet items. The point here is that the meaning of the dollar amount of an item listed in the balance sheet depends on the account being measured.

    b. Several different measurement bases are currently used in the balance sheet. For example, an account receivable listed at $10,000 does not necessarily mean the same thing as $10,000 listed for an intangible asset.

Account Type	Measurement Basis
Property, Plant and Equipment, Intangibles	Historical Cost and Depreciated/Amortized Historical Cost
Receivables	Net Realizable Value
Inventory	Lower of Cost or Market
Investments in Marketable Securities	Market Value
Liabilities	Present Value
Owners' Equity	Historical Value of Cash Inflows and Residual Valuation

D. **Statement of Stockholders' Equity**—The statement of stockholders' equity (sometimes referred to as shareholders' equity) presents the changes in the owners' equity over a period of time—the same time period as the income statement. Like the income statement, this statement is dated for the year ended (e.g., December 31, 20xX). This statement presents the changes in contributed capital, additional paid-in capital, and retained earnings. These changes arise from the purchase and sale of shares of the entities stock, the changes in comprehensive income, and the payment of dividends.

E. **Statement of Cash Flows**

1. The statement of cash flows is the third of the three major financial statements required to be reported. It describes the major changes in cash by meaningful category. Like the income statement, it is dated for the entire period (e.g., for the year ended December 31, 20xX).

2. The purpose of the Statement of Cash Flows is to explain the change in cash and cash equivalents that has occurred during the past accounting year. Cash equivalents are short-term investments that:

   a. Are convertible into a known and fixed amount of cash; *and*

   b. Have an original maturity to the purchaser of three months or less.

Example
A US treasury obligation purchased when there are three months or less remaining to maturity is a cash equivalent. Investments in stocks are not cash equivalents because they have no maturity value and are not convertible into a specific unchanging amount of cash.

3. In reviewing the statement of cash flows, it is important to remember the articulation between the balance sheet and the statement of cash flows. If the statement of cash flows employs a pure cash definition of funds, the first asset listed on the balance sheet will be cash. If the statement of cash flows employs a broader definition of funds (cash and cash equivalents), the first asset listed on the balance sheet will be Cash and Cash Equivalents.

4. The presentation of cash flows in the statement of cash flows follows a classification system established by the FASB. Cash flows are classified into three categories: operating, investing, and financing.

   a. **Operating**—Those cash flows related to transactions that flow through the income statement.

Example
Operating cash inflows include receipts from customers and interest. Cash outflows include payments to suppliers, to employees, and to taxing authorities.

b. **Investing**—Cash flows related to the acquisition and disposal of long-term assets and investments (other than cash equivalents and trading securities; these are operating).

Example
Investing cash outflows include purchases of plant assets and investments. Cash inflows include proceeds from the sale of these items.

c. **Financing**—Cash flows related to the liabilities and owners' equity sections of the balance sheet.

Example
Financing cash inflows include issuing debt and equity securities. Cash outflows include retirement of debt and equity securities, and dividend payments.

Income Statement

This lesson presents an overview of the Income Statement.

After studying this lesson, you should be able to:

1. List and define the components of the Income Statement.

2. Identify the difference between economic income and accounting income.

3. Prepare an Income Statement.

I. **Background**

A. **Definitions of Revenues, Expenses, Gains, and Losses**

Definitions

Revenues: Revenues represent increases in net assets or settlements of liabilities by providing goods and services. Revenues are related to the company's primary business operations.

Expenses: Expenses represent decreases in net assets or incurred liabilities through the provision of goods or services. Expenses are related to the company's primary business operations. Expenses provide benefit to the firm. Losses do not.

Gains: Gains represent increases in equity or net assets from peripheral or incidental transactions.

Losses: Losses represent decreases in equity or net assets from peripheral or incidental transactions. Losses do not provide value or benefit to the firm.

B. **All-Inclusive versus Current Operating Performance Views of the Income Statement**

1. **All-inclusive income statement**—The current income statement under GAAP is mostly an all-inclusive one in which essentially all revenues, expenses, gains, and losses are shown on the income statement and included in the net income calculation.

    a. **Exceptions**—There are exceptions to all-inclusive income statements.

        i. **Prior-period adjustments**—Prior-period adjustments are shown on the Statement of Retained Earnings and are the correction of accounting errors affecting income of prior years.

        ii. **Other comprehensive income items (OCI)**

            1. Foreign currency translation adjustments

            2. Unrealized holding gains and losses on securities available for sale

            3. Pension and other postretirement benefit plan cost adjustments

            4. Certain deferred derivative gains and losses

        iii. The OCI items above are disclosed in the statement of comprehensive income discussed in a later lesson. The different income amounts for a period are related as follows:

Net Income + Other Comprehensive Income = Comprehensive Income

        iv. Retrospective changes in accounting principle affecting income. These are treated as direct adjustments to retained earnings.

2. **Current operating performance income statement**

    a. At the other end of the spectrum is the current operating performance approach to income statement preparation, which would limit the income statement to normal, recurring items.

    b. Many other items would be run through owners' equity and thus escape the attention of financial statement users who rely more heavily on the income statement.

    c. Due to enhanced opportunities to manipulate net income, the all-inclusive approach was selected over the current operating approach for income statement presentation purposes.

  C. Concepts of Income—The accountant and economist have different ways to measure income. There are many different ways to approach the problem. GAAP takes an objective, arm's-length transaction approach to measurement and recognition.

    1. Definition

Definition

Accounting Income: Revenues less expenses plus gains less losses.

---

    a. That is, accounting income reflects recorded transactions, events, and adjustments.

    b. For many assets and liabilities, changes in market value are not recognized until substantiated by a transaction between willing parties.

    c. Investments with readily determinable market values are an exception. These investments (trading securities, securities available for sale) are reported at market value. Moreover, inventories are written down to lower of cost or market.

    2. Definition

Definition

Economic Income: The change in the net worth of a business enterprise during an accounting period.

---

    a. The net worth of a business enterprise is described as the fair value (FV) of net assets (rather than total owners' equity per GAAP).

    b. Thus, the FV of a business on December 31 of a given year is compared with the FV of the business on January 1 of that year to determine economic income.

    c. Net income for the period would include all changes in FV of assets and liabilities during the period.

    d. Any investments by owners would be added and any dividends paid or treasury stock purchased would be subtracted, when making this calculation.

Fair Value of Net Assets at Jan. 1	+	Net Income for the Period (including increases in FV)	+	Owner Investments	−	Dividends and Stock Repurchases	=	Fair Value at Dec. 31

    e. The use of fair values and other price level changes takes into account the changes in the value of the firm's assets and liabilities and goes beyond the recording of transactions. However, because GAAP is concerned with reliability of information, transaction-based reporting is the current model used.

II. Structure of the Statement

  A. Continuing Operations and Other Items of Income—The income statement is divided roughly into two portions.

1. **Top portion**—The top portion includes routinely occurring items and other items that are appropriately included in income from continuing operations.

   a. The subtotal income from continuing operations is used by investors as a broad measure of operating income.

   b. GAAP does not prescribe the specific format in which information should be presented in the top portion of the Income Statement.

   c. Income from continuing operations includes all income items other than those in the bottom portion of the income statement.

2. **Bottom portion**—The bottom portion includes items that are specifically defined by GAAP as being unrelated to continuing operations.

   a. These items are not representative of the firm's ability to generate income and are unique items that will not be repeated. They are, however, components of total income.

   b. GAAP is very specific about the measurement and presentation of items in the bottom portion. For example, there is very specific guidance on the presentation and measurement of discontinued operations.

   c. Discontinued operations are required to be presented at the bottom portion of the income statement. Discontinued operations are major components of an entity that are either sold or planned to be sold and thus are no longer part of continuing operations.

B. **Sample Income Statement**—A generalized income statement appears next.

ABX Company

Income Statement

For the Year Ended December 31, 20X0

Net sales

− Cost of goods sold

= Gross margin

− Operating expenses

+ Miscellaneous revenues and gains

− Miscellaneous expenses and losses

± Unusual or infrequent items

= Income from continuing operations before tax

− Less income tax expense

= Income from Continuing Operations

± Income from Discontinued Operations (net of tax)

= Net income

C. **Presentation Requirements**—There is no prescribed way of displaying the items above income from continuing operations. For example, some firms provide a subtotal called "operating income," which appears before miscellaneous items, but such disclosure is not mandated by GAAP.

D. **Presentation Order**—Below income from continuing operations, the prescribed presentation is the order as shown above.

E. **Income Tax Expense**—Income tax expense is attributable only to income from continuing operations. The tax effects of items below continuing operations are shown along with the item itself in a process called "intraperiod tax allocation."

F. **Multiple Disclosures**

1. The total income tax effect for a given year is accomplished through multiple disclosures. The items for which intraperiod tax allocation is applied include:

   a. Discontinued operations

   b. Other comprehensive income items

   c. Adjustment for retroactive accounting principle changes

   d. Prior-period adjustments

2. The first item is reported in the income statement; the second is reported in a special OE account called accumulated other comprehensive income, and the last two are reported in the retained earnings statement.

Example

Intraperiod tax allocation and discontinued operations disclosure. A loss on discontinued operations before tax is $12,000, and the associated tax rate is 30%. The disclosure in the income statement below continuing operations would appear as:

Less discontinued operations, net of $3,600 tax savings........$8,400

G. **Intraperiod Tax Allocation**—Pertains to the tax effects for only one year. It is the allocation of the total tax consequence for that year among income from continuing operations, and the four items listed above. This process contrasts with *interperiod* tax allocation, which records a period's total tax consequence in current taxes payable and deferred tax accounts. Interperiod tax allocation is a much more extensive process and is covered in another lesson.

III. **Unusual or Infrequent Income Items**

A. GAAP requires that unusual or infrequent items be separately reported if material, as a component of income from continuing operations or alternatively, disclosed in notes to financial statements. Note that there is no longer a category for "extraordinary items" at the bottom of the income statement. Any unusual or infrequent items (such as an impairment loss) is shown as a component of income from continuing operations.

IV. **Formats Leading to Income from Continuing Operations**—Income from continuing operations includes the revenues, expenses, gains, and losses that are normal and recurring. In addition to including those items that are specifically related to primary business operations, income from continuing operations also includes those revenues, expenses, gains, and losses that are the result of incidental or peripheral activities. The presentation of income from continuing operations follows one of two formats, the single-step format or the multiple-step format. Note the required per share disclosures shown at the bottom of the income statements. Earnings per share are discussed in detail in later lessons.

A. **Formats in Practice**

1. Two formats have become accepted in practice: single-step and multiple step statements. There are many variants of each.

   a. Both formats provide the same information although the multiple-step format provides more subtotals and organization.

   b. Income from continuing operations and net income are the same amounts regardless of the format used.

   c. The format differences affect only the ordering in calculating income from continuing operations.

2. The presentation below income from continuing operations is mandated by U.S. GAAP and is the same regardless of how the top portion is presented.

B. Single-Step Format—The single-step format involves a presentation of income from continuing operations that is largely based on a single comparison. Total revenues and gains are compared with total expenses and losses in the single-step format. A single-step illustration for the Wolf Company follows.

Wolf Company		
Income Statement		
For the Year Ended December 31, 20xX		
Revenues and Gains:		
Net Sales	$1,000,000	
Rent Revenue	10,000	
Investment Revenue	20,000	
Gain on Sale of Operational Assets	30,000	1,060,000
Expenses and Losses:		
Cost of Goods Sold	400,000	
Distribution Expenses	10,000	
General and Administrative Expenses	20,000	
Depreciation Expense	30,000	
Interest Expense	10,000	
Loss on Sale of Investments	20,000	(490,000)
Unusual or Infrequent Gains and Losses:		
Casualty Loss	(100,000)	
Gain on Sale of Real Estate	200,000	100,000
Pretax Income from Continuing Operations		670,000
Income Tax Expense		(201,000)
Income from Continuing Operations		469,000
Income from Discontinued Operations		
Results of Operations (less income tax expense of $30,000)	70,000	
Loss on Disposal of Business Segment (less income tax savings of 60,000)	(140,000)	(70,000)
Net Income		$399,000
Earnings per Share:		
Income from Continuing Operations		4.69
Income from Discontinued Operations		(.70)
Net Income		$3.99

C. Multiple-Step Format—The multiple-step format involves a presentation of income from continuing operations that includes multiple comparisons of revenues, expenses, gains, and losses. In doing so, the reader is provided with the operating margin of the company, which is the excess of operating revenues over operating expenses. In other words, these revenues and expenses are directly tied to the company's primary business operations. Operating expenses can be divided into various subcategories of items that relate to the company's operations. Common categories of operating expenses are general and administrative expenses and selling expenses. General and administrative expenses are expenses are incurred in the day-to-day operations of a business that are not directly tied to a specific function or department within the company. Selling expenses usually consist of costs associated to sales activities of the business. Beyond the operating margin, the incidental or peripheral gains and losses are shown in the presentation of income from continuing operations. Next is a multiple-step illustration for the Wolf Company.

Wolf Company
Income Statement
For the Year Ended December 31, 20xX

Sales Revenue	$1,100,000	
Less Sales Returns and Allowances	(100,000)	
Net Sales		1,000,000
Cost of Goods Sold		(400,000)
Gross Margin		600,000
Operating Expenses:		
Distribution Expenses	10,000	
General and Administrative Expenses	20,000	
Depreciation Expense	30,000	(60,000)
Operating Margin		540,000
Other Revenues and Gains:		
Rent Revenue	10,000	
Investment Revenue	20,000	
Gain on Sale of Operational Assets	30,000	60,000
Other Expenses and Losses:		
Interest Expense	10,000	
Loss on Sale of Investments	20,000	(30,000)
Unusual or Infrequent Gains and Losses:		
Casualty Loss	(100,000)	
Gain on Sale of Real Estate	200,000	100,000
Pretax Income from Continuing Operations		670,000
Income Tax Expense		(201,000)
Income from Continuing Operations		469,000
Income from Discontinued Operations:		
Results of Operations (less income tax expense of $30,000)	70,000	
Loss on Disposal of Business Segment (less income tax savings of $60,000)	(140,000)	(70,000)
Net Income		$399,000
Earnings Per Share:		
Income from Continuing Operations		4.69
Income from Discontinued Operations		(.70)
Net Income		$3.99

Balance Sheet/Statement of Financial Position

This lesson presents an overview of the balance sheet.

After studying this lesson, you should be able to:

1. Identify the measurement bases used to measure the items on the Balance Sheet.

2. Distinguish between a current and noncurrent asset or liability.

3. Prepare a Balance Sheet.

I. The Balance Sheet

A. Background on the Balance Sheet

1. The statement of financial position is another name for the balance sheet.

2. It is the only statement dated as of a point in time. The title consists of three lines:

> ABC Company
>
> Balance Sheet
>
> As of December 31, 20X4

3. Only asset, liability, and owners' equity accounts are represented (and related contra (–) and adjunct (+) accounts) and as such the balance sheet reports the entity's financial position at a point in time.

4. Total assets = Total liabilities + Owners' equity.

5. Many different measurement (valuation) bases are represented—total assets of $10 million is not really $10 million of the types of same dollars. Most reported account balances do not represent current market value.

6. The balance sheet provides information useful in assessing the entity's financial strengths and weaknesses, especially risk (relative proportion of debt to equity, for example), and the allocation of assets.

7. A classified balance sheet distinguishes current and noncurrent assets and liabilities which helps users assess liquidity.

8. Account balances reflect only the transaction-based U.S. GAAP recognition and measurement system. A transaction or event is required for recognition of all items. The balance sheet does not report all assets of the firm, only the assets acquired through a transaction. For example, internally generated goodwill is not recorded (recognized), and the recorded value of other intangibles such as trademarks may be significantly less than their current value.

B. Factors Limiting the Interpretation of Balance Sheet Information

1. Assets and liabilities are acquired at different times and are not affected in the same way by inflation and specific price-level changes. This causes the recorded value of these accounts to be different from their current or real value and makes comparisons difficult.

2. Several different measurement bases are used (historical cost, depreciated historical cost, market (fair) value, realizable value, present value) which compromises the comparability characteristic of accounting information.

3. Consolidation of subsidiaries compounds the difficulties with interpretation of account balances when the parent and subsidiaries use different accounting methods.

4. The value of many assets is derived primarily through use (exceptions are investments, receivables); this value may differ considerably from book value and market value. How does the user really interpret book value when book value and market value are different?

C. **Measurement Bases for Balance Sheet Valuation**—Because so many different measurement bases are represented in the balance sheet, the totals for assets and liabilities are difficult to interpret and compare across firms.

> **Definition**
> *Measurement Base*: The attribute of an account being measured and reported

1. **Historical cost or other historical value**—Some accounts are measured and reported at a fixed, unchanging historical amount. Examples include land, some investments, cash, prepaids, many current liabilities, contributed capital accounts, and treasury stock.

2. **Depreciated, amortized, or depleted historical cost**—Other accounts reflect the remaining portion of a fixed unchanging historical amount. In some cases, the original cost or other relevant amount is maintained in one account, with a contra or adjunct account being subtracted from or added to that account for the purpose of reporting net book value (carrying value). Examples include property, plant and equipment; intangibles; natural resources.

3. **Market value, a type of current value**—Examples include investments in marketable securities (stocks and bonds) for which the holding firm does not have significant influence and does not intend to hold to maturity (in the case of bonds). *Fair value*, often used synonymously with *market value*, is the selling price for assets and amount currently required to retire a liability. These are *exit* values rather than *entry* values.

4. **Net realizable value**—This is another type of current value but one that is less in amount than the historical value. Net realizable value is the amount the firm expects to receive from the sale or collection of the item. Examples include accounts receivable and inventories.

5. **Present value**—The present value of a future cash flow is its discounted value. This is the primary measurement basis for noncurrent debt (mainly bonds and long-term notes). The present value is the measure of current sacrifice when extinguishing the debt at the balance sheet date.

6. **Aggregate of more than one valuation basis**—Retained earnings-net income reflects all measurement bases through revenue and expense recognition.

D. **Classification of Assets and Liabilities**—Assets and liabilities are classified as current or noncurrent. U.S. GAAP defines only current items; the noncurrent classification represents items that are not classified as current. The purpose of this classification is to distinguish items that will affect the firm's liquidity in the near term (one year) from those that will not. Classification helps financial statement users assess the ability of a firm to pay its debts in the near future. Owners' equity accounts are not classified because they do not represent resources or obligations.

1. **Current asset (CA)**

   a. An asset expected to be realized in cash or to be consumed or sold during the normal operating cycle, or within one year of the balance sheet date, whichever is longer.

   b. The operating cycle is the period of time from purchasing inventory to paying for the payable incurred on inventory purchase to the sale of goods to the collection of receivable and then to purchasing inventory all over again.

   c. For most firms the operating cycle is less than one year, but some firms, such as construction and engineering companies, have operating cycles exceeding one year. Construction in process, an inventory account found in construction firms' balance sheets, is a current asset even though the constructed asset may require several years to complete.

2. **Current liability (CL)**

   a. A liability expected to be extinguished through the use of current assets or by the incurrence of other current liabilities.

   b. The *incurrence of other CL* part of the definition means that CL that are continuously refinanced (rolled over) by replacing them with other CL due later (but within one year of the balance sheet date) must still be classified as CL, even though no CA will be used to extinguish them in the year after the balance sheet date.

Example

A note payable due 3/1/x2 is expected to be refinanced continuously on a 4-month basis, each time substituting a new 4-month note for the old. This note should be classified as a CL in the 12/31/x1 balance sheet because there is no certainty that the firm will not use CA in the next year to pay off the debt. The debtor firm cannot control the creditor who may decide not to refinance. Interest rates may increase substantially changing the strategy of the debtor firm. However, if the new note is due later than 12/31/x2 then the original note is classified as NCL.

Only if the firm refinances an otherwise current liability with a noncurrent liability before the balance sheet is issued (or is available to be issued) can the original liability be reclassified as noncurrent. *Refinance* here includes:

- Replacing the liability with a new liability that is due one year from the balance sheet date

- Entering into an irrevocable agreement to do so with a capable creditor

- Issuing stock to extinguish the debt

---

3. **Noncurrent assets (NCA) and noncurrent liabilities (NCL)**—Defined by default as assets and liabilities that are not current. The current/noncurrent distinction is important because firms would rather report more CA and less CL to appear more liquid and less risky in the short run. There is great incentive to move CLs into the NCL category, for example.

4. **Ratios for liquidity**

   a. Current ratio = CA/CL. This ratio is frequently used as a measure of liquidity. Many analysts use a minimum value of 2 when evaluating firms because the extra CA provides a buffer for uncertainty, and CA includes inventories and prepaids that are not considered very liquid.

   b. Quick or acid-test ratio = (Cash + Short-term investments + AR)/CL. This ratio provides a more rigorous test of liquidity.

   c. Effect of transactions on ratios.

> **Exam Tip**
> The CPA Exam may ask the effect of certain transactions on ratios. Analyze the effect by determining whether the numerator or denominator has experienced the greater percentage change.

Example

Assume the current ratio exceeds 1. What is the effect on the current ratio of paying an account payable? Answer: Both CA (cash) and CL (accts pay) decrease by the same amount. The ratio increases because the denominator falls by a greater percentage.

E. **Balance Sheet Account Types by Category**

1. For balance sheet reporting, assets and liabilities are typically reported in order from most liquid to least liquid. For example, current assets begin with cash and cash equivalents, then short-term investments, receivables, inventories and finally prepaids.

2. Current assets

    a. Cash, cash equivalents, short-term investments, accounts receivable, other receivables, inventories, prepaids

    b. Cash is the only account for which the following are the same:

        i. Nominal value

        ii. Market value

        iii. Realizable value

        iv. Present value

        v. Future value

3. Noncurrent assets

    a. Long-term investments, property, plant and equipment, intangibles, "other" assets (including long-term prepaids)

    b. Goodwill is by far the largest intangible in terms of dollar amount for many firms and equals the excess of the purchase price paid for another business over the market value of its net assets. Only when a firm is purchased by another is goodwill recognized in the balance sheet of the purchaser. Internally, generated goodwill is expensed.

4. Current liabilities—Accounts payable, accrued liabilities, unearned revenue, income tax payable, notes payable, current portion of long-term debt (the portion due within one year of the balance sheet date).

5. Noncurrent liabilities—Notes payable, bonds payable, lease liabilities, pension liabilities, postretirement healthcare liabilities, deferred taxes. (Although this item can appear in all four possible classifications (i.e., CA, NCA, CL, and NCL), the NCL category is by far the largest.)

6. Owners' equity—two main types

    a. Contributed capital (common stock, preferred stock, contributed capital in excess of par), treasury stock (a contra account)

    b. Retained earnings (total net income to date less total dividends to date)

F. Reporting Within the Balance Sheet—The use of contra accounts (−) and "adjunct" accounts (+); valuation accounts.

1. Contra and adjunct accounts

    a. Accounts can be accompanied by contra and adjunct accounts

    b. A contra account has a balance opposite that of the associated account in terms of debit and credit. Contras can be debit or credit balances, and can be considered valuation accounts or merely accumulations of items such as depreciation and amortization over time

    c. An adjunct account has a balance that is the same as that of the associated account in terms of debit and credit. An adjunct can have either a debit or a credit balance. An adjunct account is added whereas a contra is subtracted

2. Valuation accounts

    a. A valuation account is one used to increase or decrease the book value of an item to a measure of current value.

    b. Not all contra or adjunct accounts are valuation accounts, but all valuation accounts are contras or adjuncts.

    c. Examples

Examples
1. Accumulated depreciation is a contra account to property, plant, and equipment but is not a valuation account because net book value in this case is not equal to market value.

Property, plant, and equipment	$40,000 (cost)
Accumulated depreciation	(5,000)
Net book value	$35,000 (undepreciated cost)

2. Allowance for uncollectible accounts is a contra account to accounts receivable and is a valuation account because net accounts receivable is an approximation to net realizable value, a measure of current value.

Accounts receivable	$60,000 (sales value)
Allowance for doubtful accounts	(8,000)
Net book value	$52,000 (net realizable value)

3. Valuation allowance for investments in marketable securities can be a contra or adjunct account and is a valuation account because it decreases or increases the net book value of the investment to current market value. The account is a contra if the market value is less than original cost, and is an adjunct if the market value exceeds original cost.

Investments in marketable securities	$30,000 (cost)
Valuation allowance	4,000
Market value	$34,000 (market value)

4. Bond premium and discount are adjunct and contra accounts respectively but are not valuation accounts because the net bond liability is generally not equal to market value.

Bonds payable	$100,000 (face value)
Bond premium	3,000
Net bond liability	$103,000 (net carrying value)

G. The Balance Sheet and Firm Valuation

1. The total owners' equity of most publicly traded firms (also known as net assets or A – L) is significantly less than the market value of the firm because investors place a higher value on firms that include the investors' expectation of future earnings. Firms are usually worth much more than the sum of their individual net assets, even at market value.

2. There are three important valuations for a firm:

    a. **Total OE or net assets**—This is the amount determined by current U.S. GAAP and is found in the balance sheet;

    b. **Market value of net identifiable assets**—The amount of cash that would remain after selling all identifiable assets (including identifiable intangibles) and paying off all liabilities. This amount is also called the firm's "split up" or liquidation value. To determine this amount, the firm must have its assets appraised;

    c. **Total value of the firm**—Its *market capitalization*—that is, the total value of the firm's outstanding stock. For publicly traded firms, this value can be found on Internet financial sites.

3. Identifiable assets and liabilities with market values different from their book values cause the difference between total OE and the market value of net identifiable assets. Examples include investments and natural resources.

4. The difference between a firm's market capitalization and the market value of net identifiable assets is goodwill—an amount that cannot be identified with any individual recorded asset. However, goodwill is recorded for accounting purposes only when one firm purchases all or a controlling interest of another firm.

H. Market Capitalization—The market capitalization is generally many times recorded OE in amount. The purpose of the balance sheet is not to provide a firm's market value, but rather to provide information that is a starting point for valuing a firm and assessing its riskiness. The relative investment in plant assets, natural resources, investments, and in affiliated companies, along with the ratio of debt to equity provides investors with valuable information about the financial structure and direction of the firm. The trend in balance sheet values over time also provides useful information.

1. In addition, the balance sheet is largely historical, and is limited to transactions that have already taken place. It is not the responsibility of financial statements to provide current value. Rather, current value is a constantly changing amount based on investors' perceptions in the market at the time. In sum, the information in the balance sheet and other financial statement information is an input to market valuation, not the other way around. Stock prices react to changes in financial statement information and other information.

I. Debt Disclosures—These are perhaps the most important items found in the balance sheet, dollar for dollar. They indicate a quantifiable financial risk faced by the firm in the future.

J. Control and Subsidiary Accounts

1. The accounts reside in the ledger. The general ledger contains all accounts to be used in preparing the balance sheet. Some of these accounts are called **control** accounts because they report the aggregate balance of several subsidiary accounts.

Example
The accounts receivable (AR) control account balance (in the general ledger) is the sum of the subsidiary AR account balances. For example, a firm has 100 subsidiary AR accounts, each one for a different customer. The sum of the 100 subsidiary AR balances equals the balance in the control AR account balance, which is reported on the balance sheet.

---

2. Control and subsidiary accounts are used for any account that consists of many individual accounts. Inventory, plant assets (property, plant, and equipment) and accounts payable are examples.

3. A chart of accounts typically assigns account numbers to accounts for use in computerized information systems. For example, assets may be assigned numbers 100–199, liabilities 200–250, etc. Cash might be assigned the number 100, with AR control assigned number 104. Each account in the AR subsidiary ledger then could be numbered 104-1, 104-2, etc.

K. Accounting Cycle Review

1. The periodic accounting process leading to the preparation of financial statements is called the accounting cycle. The cycle steps used by a firm are specific to the information technology applied. The following is a representative list, in chronological order.

    a. Analyze relevant source documents (e.g., sales invoices) and record journal entries in a journal, a temporary listing of accounts affected and the amount by which they are to be changed by transaction, event, or adjustment.

    b. Post (distribute) the information from the journal to the accounts in the ledger, on a periodic basis. Only after posting, the account balances are updated.

    c. Record adjusting journal entries at the end of the accounting period. These journal entries record changes in resources and obligations not signaled by a new transaction or event. Examples include accrual of wages expense from the last payday to the end of the fiscal period, expiration of prepaids, and recognition of estimated expenses such as depreciation and warranty expense. These journal entries are also posted to the accounts.

d. Prepare trial balances. Some firms prepare a trial balance, which is a test of the equality of the sum of debit account balances and credit account balances, before and after adjusting journal entries. A trial balance is a quick test for the presence of an error in recording or posting.

e. Prepare the income statement, balance sheet, and statement of cash flows (often in that order). The first two are prepared directly from the ledger accounts or trial balance; the cash flow statement requires additional analysis.

f. Close the temporary account balances (revenues, expenses, gains, losses) setting them to zero, and transfer the net income amount to retained earnings.

2. Throughout the accounting cycle, U.S. GAAP is applied primarily at the two journal entry steps (1 and 3), and in preparing the financial statements and note disclosures. Otherwise, the cycle is largely mechanical and usually not performed manually.

L. Special Journals

1. Similar to the control-subsidiary account distinction for ledger accounts, firms may use special journals, and a general journal. High volume similar transactions are recorded in special journals (e.g., the sales journal) with very infrequent transactions being recorded in the general journal. Special journals facilitate the review and control of similar transactions (all sales, all cash receipts etc.).

2. Advantages of special journals

a. Special journals simplify the recording of journal entries because each recording affects the same accounts each time. Your check register is an example; it is a cash receipts/payments journal. Each entry you make always affects cash, and you need only write into the register the other item affected (e.g., utility bill).

b. The number of postings also is reduced because only the sum of the changes in the special journal accounts for the period need to be posted to the respective accounts.

c. Separation of duties for improved internal control is fostered with the use of special journals. Only particular individuals may be authorized to access the sales journal for example, but not the cash receipts journal, or the general journal.

3. Sales journal as an example of a special journal—A sales journal for a firm might record all cash and credit sales and have the following six columns:

Date	Customer	Invoice #	DR Cash	DR AR	CR Sales

Each line entered into the journal is a complete journal entry. Cash sales use all columns except for the DR AR column, and credit sales use all columns except for the DR Cash column. Special journals dispense with the *flush left* formatting for debits and *indenting right* for credits.

4. Periodic posting is as follows:

a. Sum of the DR Cash column for a period is posted to the cash account;

b. Sum of the DR AR column for a period is posted to the AR control account while each individual amount in that column is posted to the appropriate AR subsidiary account;

c. Sum of the CR Sales account is posted to the sales account.

5. Posting is usually performed within the computerized system and is mechanical from the user's point of view. Posting references enables cross-referencing between journal and ledger. For example, the posting to the AR control account from the special journal might indicate the location of the total from the sales journal within the information system.

Statement of Comprehensive Income

This lesson presents the Statement of Comprehensive Income, how it is prepared and presented by the reporting entity.

After studying this lesson, you should be able to:

1. Define "comprehensive income."
2. List the components of other comprehensive income.
3. Prepare a Statement of Comprehensive Income.
4. Illustrate the reporting alternatives for comprehensive income.

I. **Presentation of Comprehensive Income** is presented either in a separate statement or in the statement of income.

   A. U.S. GAAP requires the disclosure of comprehensive income in a financial report in one of two ways:

      1. **Single statement of comprehensive income**—This alternative presents the components of profit or loss (net income) within this single statement leading to net income as a subtotal. Displaying the other comprehensive income items leads to total comprehensive income.

      2. **Two statements**—A separate income statement is presented (and as such it becomes part of a complete set of financial statements) immediately before the statement of comprehensive income. The net income amount resulting from the first statement is used as the beginning amount for the second statement, which then reports the other comprehensive income items leading to comprehensive income.

   B. Net income is not replaced by comprehensive income. The purpose of requiring the reporting of comprehensive income is to report the net change in equity (other than from transactions with owners) in a single amount and to provide a more complete picture of the total earnings of the firm for a period. This reporting contributes to the objective of reporting an "all-inclusive" income amount.

II. **Comprehensive Income Defined**

   A. Comprehensive income was designed to report the change in net assets during the period from all sources other than from transactions with owners acting as owners. There are two components of comprehensive income:

      1. Net income *and*

      2. "Other" comprehensive income.

      3. It is the second category that causes comprehensive income to differ from net income. "Other" comprehensive income items are not currently recognized in net income. They are recorded directly as increases or decreases in owners' equity.

Definition
Comprehensive income: The sum of (1) net income and (2) other comprehensive income.
CI = NI + OCI

III. **"Other" Comprehensive Income Items (OCI)**

   A. The following items are items included in the second category above; that is, they are included in comprehensive income but not in income:

1. Unrealized gains and losses on debt securities classified as available-for-sale (AFS).

2. Unrecognized pension and postretirement benefit cost and gains. Currently, GAAP does not recognize all changes in these liabilities and assets immediately in income. Rather, some are recognized in other comprehensive income.

3. Foreign currency translation adjustments are changes in the value of foreign currency and accounts measured in foreign currency

4. Certain deferred gains and losses from derivatives.

B. OCI items are typically reported net of tax. Alternatively, firms may report each item on a pretax basis with the net aggregate income tax effect reported as a separate item.

C. Comprehensive income does not include the following:

1. Retrospective effects of changes in accounting principle

2. Prior-period adjustments

> **Note**
> *Effective for testing on or after January 1, 2018, only debt securities are classified as available-for-sale with unrealized gains and losses in OCI.*

D. The above two items are both reported as adjustments to retained earnings. Therefore, comprehensive income accounts for most but not all nonowner changes in owners' equity.

IV. Reporting Comprehensive Income—The following two examples of formats for reporting comprehensive income use assumed values.

Example
Separate Statement of Comprehensive Income:

ABX Inc.
Statement of Comprehensive Income
For the Year Ended December 31, 20X7

Net income		$24,000
Other comprehensive income, net of tax		
Net unrealized holding loss on AFS debt securities	($7,000)	
Unrealized pension cost adjustment	(2,000)	
Other comprehensive income		(9,000)
Comprehensive income		$15,000

Comprehensive income is the sum of net income and other comprehensive income.

Example
Combined statement of income and comprehensive income:

For this illustration, only the lower half of the income statement is shown.

ABX Inc.
Statement of Income and Comprehensive Income
For the Year Ended December 31, 20X7

Income from continuing operations		$14,000
Discontinued Operations, net of tax		10,000
Net income		$24,000
Other comprehensive income, net of tax		
Net unrealized holding loss on AFS debt securities	($7,000)	
Unrealized pension cost adjustment	(2,000)	
Other comprehensive income		(9,000)
Comprehensive income		$15,000

Comprehensive income is the sum of net income and other comprehensive income.

V. Accumulated Other Comprehensive Income (AOCI)

A. Accumulated other comprehensive income (AOCI) is the amount carried over from the previous period and then either increased or decreased during the current period. This total is the running total of other comprehensive income items through the Balance Sheet date. Irrespective of the reporting option chosen for comprehensive income, U.S. GAAP requires that the total of other comprehensive income be separately displayed in the owners' equity section of the Balance Sheet in an account with a title such as AOCI. AOCI is an owners' equity (OE) account.

B. In addition, the accumulated balances of each individual component of OCI must be reported. This information can appear in the Balance Sheet, Statement of Owners' Equity, or footnotes. This disclosure allows the user to understand the changes in individual components of other comprehensive income.

C. Both net income and OCI items occur each year and together yield comprehensive income. Net income is closed to retained earnings and OCI is closed to AOCI each year. Both retained earnings and AOCI are OE accounts.

D. Think of OCI as a separate but parallel "income" track, along with net income. "Net income is to retained earnings as OCI is to AOCI."

E. An item recognized in OCI one year may be recognized in net income in a later year. To avoid double counting in OE, the OCI item from the previous year is removed from AOCI. This is called a reclassification adjustment. The entity must disclose the reclassification adjustments and the effect of the reclassification adjustment on NI and OCI.

Example
A firm recognizes a $5,000 unrealized gain on an AFS debt investment in Year 1 OCI. In Year 2, the AFS debt investment is sold for a $5,000 gain (recognized in net income causing retained earnings to increase by $5,000). At the end of Year 2, the $5,000 unrealized gain from Year 1 in AOCI is removed by reducing AOCI by $5,000 (the reclassification adjustment). The gain in OCI is "reclassified" as a gain recognized in net income. Without the reclassification adjustment, total OE would count the $5,000 twice. Reclassification adjustments are reported in the footnotes.

F. The tax cuts and jobs act of 2017 significantly reduced tax rates for corporations. Typically, when there is a change in tax laws or rates, an entity must remeasure deferred tax assets and liabilities and present the changes in net income. If the item that originated the deferred tax difference was in AOCI at the old rate, that amount will remain in AOCI even though the related deferred tax asset or liability will be adjusted through net income. These are referred to as **stranded tax effects**.

ASU 2018-02 provides the entity with the option to reclassify the income tax effects in AOCI resulting from the the 2017 Act directly to retained earnings and not through net income. The entity is required to make disclosures about its policy on reclassifying stranded tax effect regardless of whether they elected the new standard or not. The disclosure must state whether or not the entity elected to reclassify the stranded amounts and the policy used to release the tax effects from AOCI. That is, are the stranded tax effects released from AOCI on an individual account basis or on a portfolio basis? The entity can apply the new standard retrospectively or in the period of adoption.

Statement of Changes in Equity

This lesson presents an overview of the Statement of Changes in Equity.

After studying this lesson, you should be able to:

1. Identify the components included in the Statement of Owners' Equity.

2. Construct a Statement of Owners' Equity.

I. Background

    A. Firms are required to report the changes in their owners'-equity (OE) accounts for the period. Supplementary schedules or footnotes may be used, but often large firms report the Statement of Changes in Equity to meet this requirement.

        1. Other titles for this statement include Statement of Changes in Owners' Equity, Owners' Equity Statement, Statement of Shareholders' Equity, and Statement of Owners' Equity. Some firms prefer to only report a separate statement of retained earnings and report the other changes in the notes.

        2. In addition to the changes in OE accounts for the period, firms must also report the changes in the number of shares of equity securities. This information is the counterpart to some of the account changes in the statement of changes in equity, but measured in shares. Some firms report the share information in a column adjacent to the changes in the relevant accounts measured in dollars.

    B. The Statement of Changes in Equity effectively expands the OE section of the balance sheet by listing all the changes in those accounts, explaining how the beginning balance increased or decreased in deriving the ending balance. Reporting investments by owners and distributions to owners are important aspects of this disclosure. The statement is dated like the Income Statement and Statement of Cash Flows—for a period.

    C. The format of the statement varies.

II. Format of the Statement—The most common formats encountered are the vertical and horizontal formats.

III. Vertical Format—In this format, each OE account is reported in a separate column of a spreadsheet-type document. The following is an example of this format for a single period.

Business Enterprises, Inc.
Statement of Changes in Equity
For the Year Ended December 31, 20X2

	Common Stock	Contributed Capital in Excess of Par	Accumulated Other Comprehensive Income	Retained Earnings	Treasury Stock	Total OE
Balance, 1/1/x2	$40,000	$180,000	$20,000	$230,000	($30,000)	$440,000
Issued stock	5,000	30,000				35,000
Issued stock dividend	2,000	11,000		(13,000)		
Purchased treasury stock					(20,000)	(20,000)
Declared cash dividend				(25,000)		(25,000)
Net income				90,000		90,000
Other comprehensive income			(6,000)			(6,000)
Balance, 12/31/x2	$47,000	$221,000	$14,000	$282,000	($50,000)	$514,000

A. Each column reconciles the beginning and ending account balance for one account by disclosing all the changes in the account during the period. Total OE is also shown as a column. This format allows a check of accuracy by comparing total OE computed as (1) the sum of each transaction affecting OE, and (2) the sum of individual OE account balances.

B. In most cases, each event causing a change in OE requires at least two entries per row (more than one column affected). The total OE column is usually but not always affected. The stock dividend, for example, has no effect on total OE. Later lessons review the underlying accounting leading to the line items in this statement. Both net income (from the income statement) and cash dividends declared are entered into the retained-earnings column and total-OE column and have opposite effects. Treasury stock is a contra-OE account, a direct reduction to owners' equity.

C. The statement of comprehensive income is presented either in a separate statement or in a combined statement with net income. The firm is not required to report the components of other comprehensive income in this statement. However, accumulated other comprehensive income totals are reported.

D. Nonetheless, accumulated other comprehensive income (AOCI) has its own column. Recall that AOCI is the running total of all other comprehensive income (OCI) items. Any firm with AOCI will report it in the statement of changes in equity, regardless of its policy concerning reporting the statement of comprehensive income.

IV. Horizontal Format—Alternatively, the statement can be presented in horizontal format. Each account is explained from beginning balance to ending balance in one set of rows, one account schedule on top of another. The first two accounts for this format are shown as follows:

Common stock, 1/1/x2	$40,000	
Issued stock	5,000	
Issued stock dividend	2,000	
Common stock, 12/31/x2		47,000
Contributed capital in excess of par, 12/31/x2	180,000	
Issued stock	30,000	
Issued stock dividend	11,000	
Contributed capital in excess of par, 1/1/x2		$221,000

    A. After all the remaining accounts are entered, the totals of each account (to the left of each account schedule) add to total OE.

V. Comparative Statements—SEC registrants report three years of OE statements, as is the case with the income statement and statement of cash flows. The current year statement is shown comparatively with the statement for the previous two years. Again, either the vertical or the horizontal format is used for presentation.

    A. The comparative multiyear display for the vertical format for single year statements results in the statements of three years stacked one on top of the other. This type of display, thus, is vertical within each year and horizontal across years.

    B. The comparative multiyear display for the horizontal format for single year statements adds two more sets of columns, one for each year shown comparatively. This type of display, thus, is horizontal within each year and vertical across years.

VI. Other Columns—Other columns found in the statement of changes in equity include:

Preferred stock

Contributed capital in excess of par, preferred

Contributed capital from treasury stock

Equity attributable to noncontrolling interests (minority interest)

Equity attributable to the shareholders of the parent (the reporting company). The sum of this total and for minority interest yields the total OE of the reporting company.

VII. Other events—Other events reported in the statement of changes in equity (and columns affected) include:

Retrospective change in accounting principle affecting prior earnings (retained earnings and total OE)

Restatement of income statement for an error affecting prior earnings—prior period adjustment (retained earnings and total OE)

Contributed capital from conversion of bonds (contributed capital and total OE)

Contributed capital from stock options and stock award plans (contributed capital and total OE)

    A. The first two items above explain how the beginning retained earnings balance is affected by retroactive application of an accounting policy or error correction.

Statement of Cash Flows

Sources and Uses of Cash

This lesson provides an overview of the purpose, content, and format of the Statement of Cash Flows. Cash may include other highly liquid items called *cash equivalents*. This lesson also presents the definition of "cash equivalents" and provides examples.

After studying this lesson, you should be able to:

1. Describe the purpose of a Statement of Cash Flows.

2. Define and identify cash equivalents and restricted cash.

3. List the categories included in a Statement of Cash Flows.

I. **Statement of Cash Flows—Requirements and Purpose**

   A. **Statement Requirement**—A Statement of Cash Flows (SCF) is required for all business enterprises that report both financial position (Balance Sheet) and results of operations (income statement) for a period.

      1. The SCF is one of the basic financial statements, like the income statement and statement of financial position (Balance Sheet).

      2. An SCF is not required for certain investment-type entities (e.g., employee benefit plan entities).

   B. **Statement Purposes**

      1. The basic purpose of the SCF is to provide information about the cash receipts and cash payments for an entity to help investors, creditors, and others assess:

         a. Past ability to generate and control cash inflows and cash outflows related to operating, investing, and financing activities;

         b. Probable future ability to generate cash inflows sufficient to meet future obligations and pay dividends; *and*

         c. The likely need for external borrowing.

      2. The SCF also provides information about investing and financing activities that do not involve cash inflows (receipts) or outflows (payment) (e.g., acquiring a major long-term asset by incurring a liability).

   C. The SCF must explain all of the changes in cash, cash equivalents, and restricted cash between the beginning and end of the reporting period on the Balance Sheet.

Definition

Cash equivalents: Short-term, highly liquid investments that are readily convertible to known amounts of cash. Cash equivalents are sufficiently close to maturity so that the risk of changes in value due to changes in interest rate is insignificant.

---

      1. Investments usually are considered cash equivalents only when the original maturity is three months or less (e.g., treasury bills, money market funds). Investments in equity securities cannot be cash equivalents because they are not convertible to a known amount of cash.

      Example
A T-bill purchased with a three-month term is a cash equivalent. But a T-bill with a four-month term does not become a cash equivalent after holding it one month.

2. Restricted cash is identified by the entity as the cash that is held for a specific purpose and is not available for the company to freely use. Often the restriction of the cash is part of a collateral or other type of agreement with a third party. For all restricted cash, the entity must disclose the nature of the restriction. Frequently, restricted cash is reported on a separate line item on the statement of financial position.

3. The entity should disclose its policy for designating items as cash equivalents and restricted cash. A change in policy for designating cash equivalents or restricted cash is a change in accounting principle.

4. Since the components of cash, cash equivalents, and restricted cash may be reported on separate lines on the statement of financial position, the entity must disclose how the change in cash presented on the SCF reconciles to the components of cash presented on the statement of financial position. This reconciliation can be on the face of the SCF or in the notes to the financial statements.

D. Information Reported

1. The SCF must report information in the following categories (subsequent lessons discuss each of these in more detail):

   a. Cash inflows and outflows from operating activities

   b. Cash inflows and outflows from investing activities

   c. Cash inflows and outflows from financing activities

   d. Effects of foreign currency translation on cash flows

   e. Reconciliation of net cash inflows/outflows (sum of the items listed above) with the reported change in cash, cash equivalents, and restricted on the Statement of Financial Position (Balance Sheet).

2. Noncash investing and financing activities are those that do not use cash to complete the transaction (e.g., the purchase of land with a note payable). The transaction involves investing (in the land) and financing (the note payable) but no cash. Noncash transactions can be significant. To provide complete information to the financial statement user, noncash investing and financing activities must be disclosed on the face of the statement of cash, in a supplemental schedule or in the footnotes.

E. SCF Graphic Presentation—See the following illustration.

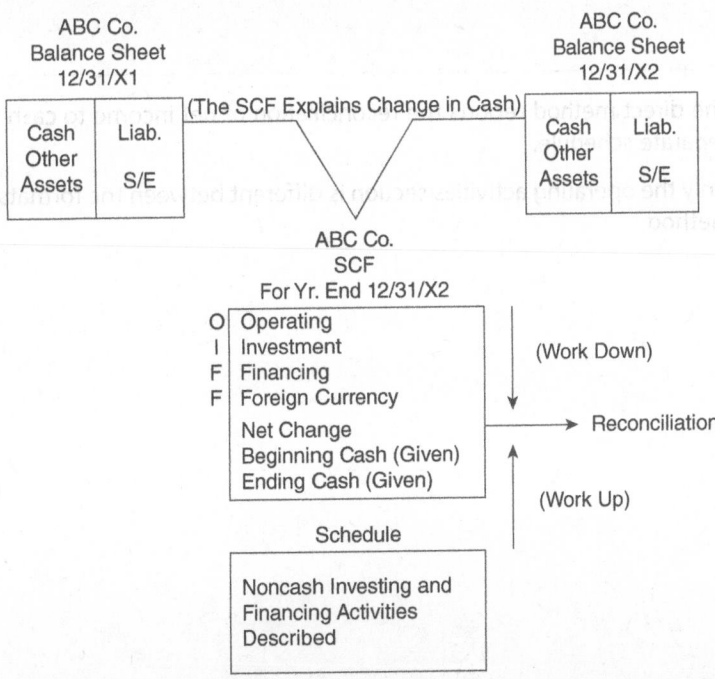

F. Summary of SCF Presentation

1. The categories used to explain the net change in cash and equivalents (operating, investing, financing, and foreign currency) should be presented in the order shown and can be remembered as OIFF ("Oh, If—I could only remember").

2. The categories are used to explain the net change in cash, cash equivalents, and restricted cash, and include items of both inflow (receipts) and outflow (payments).

3. The beginning and ending cash, cash equivalents, and restricted cash are given on the Balance Sheets for the ends of the prior and current periods.

4. The change in cash, cash equivalents, and restricted cash is a known amount. The difference between the beginning and ending balances is the overall net change presented on the Statement of Cash Flows.

5. The OIFF elements must exactly explain the known amount of change in cash (and equivalents).

6. The new cash flow derived from the OIFF elements (working down) equals the derived change in cash, cash equivalents, and restricted cash (working up).

7. The disclosure of noncash investing and financing activities can be on a separate schedule or in the footnotes, or at the bottom of the SCF. The noncash activities are not presented in the body of the SCF.

II. Two Formats Allowed by GAAP

A. The operating section of the SCF can be presented using either the direct or the indirect format.

B. The direct method reports the actual operating cash inflows and outflows in the operating section. The indirect method reports the reconciliation of net income and net operating cash flow in the operating section. Both lead to the same subtotal: net operating cash flow. The following table shows the differences and similarities between the approaches.

	Direct method	Indirect method
Operating activities:	Operating Cash Flows	Reconciliation
Investing activities:	Investing Cash Flows	Investing Cash Flows
Financing activities:	Financing Cash Flows	Financing Cash Flows

C. The direct method reports the reconciliation of net income to cash flows from operations in a separate schedule.

D. Only the operating activities section is different between the formats. Most firms use the indirect method.

Operating, Investing, and Financing Activities

This lesson presents the elements that make up the major sections of the Statement of Cash Flows and the requirements for disclosure of noncash investing and financing activities. This lesson presents the direct method for determining the Cash Flows from Operating Activities. In addition, this lesson presents how the conversion of foreign currency to the U.S. dollar impacts the change in cash.

After studying this lesson, you should be able to:

1. Distinguish what items are included in cash flows from operations using the direct method.
2. Distinguish what items are included in cash flows from investing activities.
3. Distinguish what items are included in cash flows from financing activities.
4. Construct a Statement of Cash Flows and reconcile beginning cash to ending cash balance.

I. Cash Flows from Operating Activities—Direct Method

This category reports cash inflows and cash outflows that relate to items that are included in the determination of net income. The items that make up Cash Flow from Operating Activities may be presented in the Statement of Cash Flow (SCF) using either the direct method or the indirect method. This lesson covers the direct method.

A. The major cash flow items in this category are:

Inflows (Cash Received)	Outflows (Cash Paid)
From customers	To suppliers (goods/services and operating expenses)
Dividends (from investments)	To employees (payroll)
Interest received	Interest paid
	Income taxes

B. One of the hallmarks of classifying an item as operating cash flows is that it is associated with net income. Notice that interest paid and received and dividends received are all operating cash flows, but dividends paid is a financing cash flow. The first three flows are associated with income statement items (interest expense and revenue, dividend revenue), but dividends paid is not an income item; rather, it is a direct reduction in retained earnings. Dividends paid are a distribution of income to owners and are not on the income statement, so they are not in cash flows from operations. Any cash inflow or cash outflow not properly classified as an investing or financing activity would be included as cash flow from operating activities (e.g., collection of a lawsuit settlement). The Net Cash Flow from Operating Activities can be positive or negative.

C. To derive net cash provided by operating activities using the direct method, each item in the income statement is adjusted from an accrual basis to cash basis. This means that individual items of gross receipts of cash (from revenue activities) and gross payments of cash (from expenses incurred) must be converted from accrual to cash basis.

Under GAAP, the income statement is prepared on the accrual basis, which recognizes accruals and deferrals. Therefore, the items of revenue and expense do not necessarily reflect cash received and cash paid. Income Statement items affected by accrual accounting must be adjusted to reflect the actual cash generated or used.

D. In order to convert revenue and expense items on the accrual-based income statement to the amount of cash they generated or used, the effects of accruals and deferrals must be removed. The following subsections describe and illustrate the conversion process for the major types of items including cash collected from customers, cash payments to suppliers, and cash payments for (any) operating expense:

1. **Collection from customers**—Revenues on an income statement may include accruals (revenue earned but not collected) and exclude deferrals (cash collected but revenue not earned). To derive the cash collected from customers, these accruals/deferrals must be reversed.

Example

Assume the following information is from the Income Statement (20X2) and Balance Sheets (20X1 and 20X2) of ABC Co.:

Revenue (sales—20X2)	$900,000
Accounts Receivable 12/31/X1	$60,000
Accounts Receivable 12/31/X2	75,000
Net Increase in Accounts Receivable—20X2	$5,000
Unearned Revenue 12/31/X1	–0–
Unearned Revenue 12/31/X2	25,000
Net Increase in Unearned Revenue—20X2	$25,000

Schedule Calculation of Cash Collected from Customers—20X2:

Revenues	$900,000
Deduct: Increase in Receivables	(15,000)*
Add: Increase in Unearned Revenue	25,000**
Cash Collected from Customers	$910,000

*Since Receivables increased by $15,000, that amount was recognized as revenue (Debit A/R; Credit Revenue) but was not collected in cash. (A decrease in Receivables would increase cash collected.)

**Since Unearned Revenues increased by $25,000, that amount was collected in cash (Debit Cash; Credit Unearned Revenue) but was not reported in revenues (a decrease in Unearned Revenue would decrease cash collected).

Entry Calculation of Cash Collected from Customer—20X2:

DR: Increase in Receivables (given)	$15,000	
DR: Cash (Amount to Balance)	910,000	
CR: Increase in Unearned Revenue (given)		$25,000
CR: Revenues (given)		900,000

2. **Cash payments to suppliers**—Cost of Goods Sold on an income statement may include changes in inventory and/or changes in accounts payable. To determine cash paid to suppliers for purchases, these changes must be considered.

Example

The following information is from the Income Statement (20X2) and the Balance Sheets (20X1 and 20X2) of ABC Co.:

Cost of Goods Sold	$400,000
Inventory (12/31/X1)	100,000
Inventory (12/31/X2)	120,000
Net Increase in CGS—20X2	20,000
Accounts Payable 12/31/X1	80,000
Accounts Payable 12/31/X2	90,000
Net Increase Accounts Payable—20X2	$10,000

Schedule Calculation of Cash Paid to Suppliers—20X2:

Cost of Goods Sold—20X2	$400,000
Add: Increase in Inventory	20,000[a]
Total Purchases	420,000
Deduct: Increase in Accts. Payable	10,000[b]
Cash Payments to Suppliers	$410,000

[a]Since Inventory increased, more goods were purchased than were in Cost of Goods Sold. (A decrease in Inventory would reduce purchases.)

[b]Since Accounts Payable increased by $10,000, that amount of purchases (DR Purchases; CR Accounts Payable) was not paid. (A decrease in Accounts Payable would increase cash paid.)

Entry Calculation of Cash Paid to Suppliers:

DR: Cost of Goods Sold (given)	$400,000	
DR: Increase in Inventory (given)	20,000	
CR: Increase in Accts. Payable (given)		$10,000
CR: Cash paid to Suppliers (amt to bal.)		410,000

3. **Cash payments for operating expenses**—Expenses on an income statement may include accruals (expenses incurred but not paid) and/or deferrals (cash paid but expense not incurred). To derive cash paid for operating expenses these accruals/deferrals must be reversed.

   a. The required adjustments, as described above, and the example that follows apply to all types of expenses, even though the example uses General Operating Expense (I/S) and Prepaid Expense (B/S) items. The same analysis would apply to Selling, General and Administrative Expenses, Interest Expense, or Income Tax Expense.

Example

Assume the following information is from the Income Statement (20X2) and Balance Sheets (20X1 and 20X2) of ABC Co.

Operating Expenses—20X2	$150,000
Prepaid Expenses 12/31/X1	10,000
Prepaid Expenses 12/31/X2	5,000
Net Decrease Prepaid Expenses—20X2	5,000
Operating Expense Payable 12/31/X1	20,000
Operating Expense Payable 12/31/X2	35,000
Net Increase Operating Expense Payable—20X2	$15,000

Schedule Calculation of Cash Paid for Operating Expenses—20X2:

Operating Expense—20X2	$150,000
Deduct: Decrease in Prepaid Expense	5,000[a]
Subtotal	145,000
Deduct: Increase in Expenses Payable	15,000[b]
Cash Payments for Operating Expenses	$130,000

[a]Since Prepaid Expense decreased, Operating Expenses included $5,000 paid for (prepaid) in a prior period, not paid for in the current period. (An increase in Prepaid Expense would increase cash paid).

[b]Since Operating Expenses Payable increased by $15,000, that amount of expenses (Debit Operating Expenses; Credit Expense Payable) was not paid. (A decrease in Expense Payable would increase cash paid).

Entry Calculation of Cash Paid for Operating Expenses—20X2:

DR: Operating Expenses (given)	$150,000	
CR: Decrease in Prepaid Expense (given)		$5,000
CR: Increase in Expense Payable (given)		15,000
CR: Cash Paid for Operating Expenses (amount to balance)		130,000

4. **Cash payments for other types of expenses**—The calculation methodology used to derive cash flow from operating expenses (in the examples above) can be used for other types of expenses (e.g., interest, income taxes, etc.)

E. **Presentation of Cash Flow from Operating Activities—Direct Method** would appear as shown below. Using the cash flow values developed in the prior examples, in addition we have provided cash outflows for payments to employees, interest expense, and income tax expense.

Cash flow from operating activities		
Cash Collected from Customers (per above)		$910,000
Cash Payments:		
To Suppliers (per above)	$410,000	
To Employees (assumed)	50,000	
For Operating Expense (per above)	130,000	
For Interest (assumed)	20,000	
For Income Taxes (assumed)	40,000	
Total Cash Payments		650,000
Net Cash Provided by Operating Activities		$260,000

F. **Reconciliation of Net Cash Flow from Operating Activities with Net Income**—If the Direct Method is used to present Net Cash Flow from Operating Activities, a separate schedule must be provided that reconciles Cash Flows from Operating Activities to Net Income.

1. The reconciliation shows the adjustments to Net Income necessary to arrive at Cash Flow from Operating Activities.

2. The schedule that presents the reconciliation is identical to the Cash Flow from Operating Activities section in the Statement of Cash Flows presented using the Indirect Method.

3. Using values developed above and assuming other adjustments that will be covered in the Indirect Method, the reconciliation would be presented as follows:

Net Income		$110,000
Adjustment to Reconcile Net Income to Net Cash provided by Operating Activities:		
Depreciation Expense (assumed)*	$150,000	
Loss on Equipment Sale (assumed)*	5,000	
Undistributed Equity Revenue (assumed)*	(28,000)	
Amortization of Premium on Bond Investment (assumed)*	3,000	
Increase in Accounts Receivable (above)	(15,000)	
Increase in Inventory (above)	(20,000)	
Decrease in Prepaid Expense (above)	5,000	
Increase in Accounts Payable (above)	10,000	
Increase in Expense Payable (above)	15,000	
Increase in Unearned Revenues (above)*	25,000	
Total Adjustments		150,000
Net Cash Provided by Operating Activities		$260,000

(Note: Items marked with an asterisk (*) are assumed at this point to illustrate a complete reconciliation of net income and cash flow from operating activities. The analysis of each of these items and the calculation of each amount is shown in the following section covering the Indirect Method of deriving Net Cash Provided by Operating Activities).

II. Cash Flows from Investing Activities

This category reports cash inflows and cash outflows that relate to "investment" in and disposal of noncash assets.

A. The major cash flow items in this category are the following:

Inflows (Cash received)	Outflows (Cash paid)
Sale of long-term assets	Purchase of long-term assets
Collection of loan principal	Lending (to others)
Disposal of debt and equity securities (of others, e.g., held-to-maturity or available-for-sale classifications)	Investment in debt and equity securities (of others, e.g., held-to-maturity or available-for-sale classifications)
Sale of other productive assets (e.g., patent or equipment; but not Inventory)	Purchase of other productive assets (e.g., patent or equipment; but not Inventory)

B. Investment in and disposal of debt and equity securities of other entities. This includes investments in debt securities classified as held-to-maturity or available-for-sale.

C. Firms classify cash flows from purchases, sales, and maturities of debt investments in trading securities based on the intended purpose of the investment. If the firm plans to hold the securities only for a short time, then the related cash flows are classified as operating. If the intent of holding is other than for short-term speculation, then the related cash flows are classified as investing.

D. The net of these items constitutes Net Cash Flow from Investing Activities and can be positive or negative.

E. The items that make up Cash Flow from Investing Activities are presented in the same manner, regardless of whether the direct or indirect approach is used to present Cash Flow from Operating Activities.

III. Cash Flows from Financing Activities

This category reports cash inflows and cash outflows that relate to how the entity is financed.

A. The major cash flow items in this category are the following:

Inflows (Cash received)	Outflows (Cash paid)
Sale of (own) stock	Repurchase own (Treasury) stock
Proceeds from borrowing (bonds, notes, etc.)	Paying back lenders (principal only)
	Payment of dividends

B. The net of these items constitutes Net Cash Flow from Financing Activities, and can be positive or negative.

C. The items that make up Cash Flow from Financing Activities are presented in the same manner, regardless of whether the direct or indirect approach is used to present Cash Flow from Operating Activities.

IV. Effects on Cash of Foreign Currency Translation

The SCF also shows the effect on the change in cash (between the beginning and the end of the period) that results from changes in currency exchange rates between the U.S. dollar and foreign currencies.

Note
See the lessons "Import Transactions" and "Export Transactions" for a complete description of foreign currency transactions and translation.

A. Companies that have transactions in foreign currencies or convert financial statements expressed in a foreign currency to statements expressed in dollars may incur a change in the dollar value of cash simply because of exchange rate changes.

Example
A foreign subsidiary has a (nondollar) cash balance that does not change during 20X2 of 100,000 euro. Assume the (spot) exchange rates were:

12/31/X1: 1 euro = $ .10

12/31/X2: 1 euro = $ .11

The dollar value of cash for U.S. reporting would be:

12/31/X1 (100,000 euro × .10) $10,000
12/31/X2 (100,000 euro × .11)   <u>11,000</u>
Net Increase in Cash $1,000

B. Changes in cash caused by changes in exchange rates must be shown "as part of the reconciliation of the change in cash and cash equivalents during the period."

1. Foreign currency transactions that occur during the period and affect cash flow should be converted to their dollar equivalent using (1) the exchange rate in effect at the date of each transaction or (2) an average exchange rate for the period, if not materially different from the specific rates in effect on the dates of the transactions.

2. Cash balances held in foreign currency at period-end should be converted to dollars using the spot (current) exchange rate at the date of the Balance Sheet.

C. The net of the above items constitutes Net Effect (on Cash) of Foreign Currency Translation.

D. The items that make up Net Effect of Foreign Currency Translation are presented in the same manner, regardless of whether the direct or indirect approach is used to present Cash Flow from Operating Activities.

V. Reconciliation of Change in Cash

The net effect of operating, investing, financing cash flows and the net effect of foreign currency translation will be the difference between cash (including cash equivalents and restricted cash) at the beginning and end of the period.

A. The items in this category are:

> Net Increase (or Decrease) in Cash (during X2)
>
> ± Beginning Cash (1/1/X2)
>
> = Ending Cash (12/31/X2)

B. The beginning and ending Cash would include cash, cash equivalents, and restricted cash reported on the respective (1/1/X2 and 12/31/X2) Balance Sheets.

C. The difference between beginning and ending Cash is the net change (increase or decrease) in Cash.

D. The net change in Cash is the amount that must be exactly explained by the cash flows associated with Operating, Investing, and Financing Activities plus or minus the impact of foreign currency translation.

VI. Noncash Investing and Financing Activities

Significant noncash investing and financing activities must be reported.

A. Noncash activities must be presented at the bottom of the SCF or in a disclosure (e.g., schedule or footnote).

B. If an Investing or Financing Activity involves part cash and part noncash, the cash portion should be a part of (on the face of) the SCF; the noncash portion should be disclosed in Noncash Investing and Financing Activities.

Example

A $100,000 note payable is settled by a cash payment of $60,000 and issuing stock with a fair value of $40,000.

The cash portion ($60,000) would be a Financing Cash Outflow.

The noncash portion ($40,000) would be disclosed as a noncash financing activity in the Schedule of Noncash Investing and Financing Activities.

Operating Cash Flows—Indirect Method

This lesson presents the components of, and calculations to determine, cash flows from operating activities using the indirect method. This lesson also includes a summary comparison of the determination of cash flows from operating activities using the direct and the indirect method.

After studying this lesson, you should be able to:

1. Construct the operating section on the Statement of Cash Flows using the indirect method.

2. Evaluate the similarities and differences in the Statement of Cash Flows under the direct and indirect methods.

I. **Cash Flow from Operating Activities—Accrual Reconciliation**

The indirect method of presenting cash flow from operating activities is a reconciliation of net income (accrual basis) to cash generated by operations (cash basis).

A. **Accruals and Deferrals**—Under GAAP, net income is based on accrual accounting, which recognizes economic events through accruals and deferrals which means many items used in determining net income do not reflect cash flows (e.g., losses and gains). Therefore, net income does not reflect net cash flow from operations. Using the indirect method, net income is adjusted to derive net cash flow from operating activities by:

1. Adding back noncash charges (reductions) included in deriving net income; and

2. Subtracting out noncash credits (increases) included in deriving net income.

B. Under the indirect method, net income must be adjusted for the following items to get cash flow from operating activities. Below is a list of items that are typically used to reconcile accrual-based net income to cash flows from operations.

1. Items that are underlined added back to net income underlined are those that were deducted to derive net income, but cash was not used in the transaction. Examples of the items that are added back in the reconciliation are:

   a. Depreciation expense

   b. Amortization expense

   c. Depletion expense

   d. Losses (from sale of assets, etc.)

   e. Loss under equity method of accounting for Investments

   f. Amortization of premium on bond investment

   g. Amortization of discount on bonds payable

   h. Decreases in current assets (accounts receivable, inventory, prepaid assets, etc.)

   i. Increases in current liabilities (accounts payable, deferred taxes, etc.)

   j. Increase in unearned revenue

2. Items that are subtracted from net income are those that were added to derive net income, but cash was not received in the transaction. Examples of items that are deducted in the reconciliation are:

   a. Gains (from sale of assets, etc.)

   b. Amortization of discount on bond investment

   c. Amortization of premium on bond payable

   d. Undistributed income under equity method of accounting for investments

    e. Increases in current assets (accounts receivable, inventory, prepaid assets, etc.)

    f. Decreases in current liabilities (accounts payable, deferred taxes, etc.)

    g. Decrease in unearned revenue

II. Cash Flows from Operating Activities—Noncash Items

To convert net income to cash generated or used by operations, there are noncash items that must be included in the reconciliation.

A. Depreciation/Amortization/Depletion Expenses

These are noncash expenses that must be added back to net income. Often the amount of depreciation/amortization/depletion expense is not given and you need to solve for the expense:

1. A T-account is the best way to derive depreciation/amortization/depletion expense (collectively referred to as depreciation expense going forward). Use the information provided in the problem and fill in the known amounts for the accumulated depreciation, asset value, and any gain or loss. Solve for the unknown values to back into the unknown depreciation expense.

Example

Assume the following information is from the balance sheets (20X1 and 20X2) and additional disclosures of ABC Co.:

Accumulated Depreciation (A/D) 12/31/X1	$400,000
Accumulated Depreciation (A/D) 12/31/X2	500,000
Net Increase—20X2	$100,000

Additional information:

Equipment with a book value of $25,000 (cost = $75,000 and accumulated depreciation = $50,000) was sold for $30,000.

T-account calculation of depreciation expense:

Accumulated Depreciation

	400,000 Beg Balance
Sale of assets 50,000	150,000 (plugged) Depreciation expense
	500,000 Ending Balance

In the determination of cash flows from operations, $150,000 of depreciation expense should be added back to net income because depreciation expense is not a cash outflow.

B. Losses/Gains

1. These are noncash deductions or additions in computing net income that must be added back to or subtracted from net income (by the amount recognized as a loss or gain).

2. If the amount of a loss or gain is not provided, it must be derived from information that is given.

Example

Continuing with the example of ABC Co., assume the additional information:

During 20X2, equipment with a cost of $75,000 and accumulated depreciation of $50,000 was sold for $20,000.

Calculation of loss:

Price		$20,000
Less: Cost	$75,000	
A/D	50,000	
Book Value		25,000
Loss on Sale		$ 5,000

In the determination of cash flows from operations, the $5,000 loss should be added back to net income because the loss is not a cash outflow.

C. Equity Method Adjustments

1. An investor that uses the equity method to account for an investment must recognize its share of the investee's net income or net loss in the period it is reported by the investee, regardless of whether any dividends are paid by the investee. Therefore, the investor would make the following entries:

   a. Investee reports Net Income, Investor entry:

   DR: Investment in Investee (asset)
   CR: Equity Investment Income

   b. Investee reports Net Loss, Investor entry:

   DR: Equity Investment Loss
   CR: Investment in Investee (asset)

2. In either case, the investor has increased or decreased its net income without any related cash flow.

3. If the investee paid a cash dividend during the period, the Investor entry would be:

   DR: Cash
   CR: Investment in Investee (asset)

4. Therefore, under the equity method, only cash dividends received from the investee cause a cash flow. The adjustments to net income to get cash flow would be:

   a. If an equity investment loss, add back the amount of the loss.

   b. If an equity investment income, subtract out the amount recognized as income that was not received as cash dividends.

Example

Assume ABC Company owns 40% of XYZ Company and appropriately accounts for its investment using the equity method. During 20X2, XYZ had net income of $100,000 and paid cash dividends of $30,000.

Calculation:

XYZ Co.	ABC Co.
Net Income $100,000 × .40 =	$40,000
Less: Cash Dividend 30,000 × .40 =	12,000
ABC Revenue **not** Received as Cash	$28,000

In the determination of cash flows from operations, $28,000 should be subtracted from net income.

D. Amortization of Bond Premiums/Discounts

Bond premiums and discounts arise from both an investment in bonds or the issuing of bonds, at the time the bonds are bought or sold. The subsequent amortization of a premium or discount will enter into net income (through interest income or interest expense) but will not generate or use cash. Therefore, the effects of premium or discount amortization must be added back to or subtracted from net income. Two illustrations are given:

1. **Amortization of premium on bond investment**—When bonds are purchased for more than maturity value, a premium results.

   a. The related entry would be:

   DR: Investment in Bonds (at face value)
   DR: Premium on Bond Investment
       CR: Cash

   b. The cash outflow would be recognized in the period the investment is made as a component of cash flow from investing activities.

   c. The subsequent amortization of the premium would be recorded by a periodic entry:

   DR: Interest Income
       CR: Premium on Bond Investment

   The debit to Interest Income reduces the amount of net income but does not use cash. Therefore, the amortization should be added back to net income. If the bonds had been acquired at less than maturity value, the resulting amortization of the discount would have to be subtracted from net income.

2. **Amortization of discount on bonds payable**—When bonds are issued for less than maturity value, a discount results.

   a. The related entry would be:

   DR: Cash
   DR: Discount on Bonds Payable
       CR: Bonds Payable

The cash inflow would be recognized in the period the bonds were sold as a component of cash flow from financing activities. The subsequent amortization of the discount would be recorded by a periodic entry:

The debit to Interest Expense reduces the amount of net income, but does not use cash. The amount of amortization should be added back to net income. If the bonds had been issued (sold) at more than maturity value, the resulting amortization of the premium would have to be subtracted from net income.

> DR: Interest Expense
> CR: Discount on Bonds Payable

E. **Increases and Decreases in Current Assets and Current Liabilities**—Increases and decreases in current assets and current liabilities reflect differences between the amount of revenue or expense recognized for net income and the amount of cash received or paid. Two examples illustrate the relevant points:

   1. Increase in accounts receivable

     a. When sales are made on account, the related entry would be:

> DR: Assets Receivable
> CR: Sales

The sales amount (credit) is included in net income, but unless the account receivable is collected within the same period there is no increase in cash. Therefore, net income would have to be decreased by the amount of the uncollected account receivable. The aggregate change in accounts receivable will have the same effect on net income as shown above. Therefore, the amount of the aggregate change in receivables (and other current assets) must be used to adjust net income to get the related cash flows.

Example
Assume ABC Company's accounts receivable balances for 20X1 and 20X2 were:

Accounts Receivable 12/31/X1	$60,000
Accounts Receivable 12/31/X2	75,000
Net Increase—20X2	$15,000

Because accounts receivable increased by $15,000, sales of that amount are included in net income, but the cash has not been collected. Therefore, in the determination of cash flows from operations, $15,000 should be subtracted from net income.

If accounts receivable had decreased, more cash would have been collected than sales recognized for the period. The decrease in accounts receivable would be added to net income to derive the cash flow from operations.

Increases and decreases in other current assets would be treated in the same manner.

   2. Increase in accounts payable

     When purchases are made on account, the related entry would be:

DR: Purchases (or other expense)
CR: Account Payable

The purchase account (debit) is included in net income, but unless the accounts payable is paid within the same period, there is no decrease in cash. Therefore, net income would have to be increased by the amount of the unpaid account payable. The aggregate change in accounts payable will have the same effect on net income as shown above. Therefore, the amount of the aggregate change in payables (and other current liabilities) must be used to adjust net income to get the related cash flows.

Example
Assume ABC Company's accounts payable balances for 20X1 and 20X2 were:

Accounts Payable 12/31/X1	$80,000
Accounts Payable 12/31/X2	90,000
Increase—20X2	$10,000

Because accounts payable increased by $10,000, an expense (COGS) is included in net income, but the cash has not been paid. Therefore, in the determination of cash flows from operations, $10,000 would be added to net income.

If accounts payable had decreased, more cash would have been paid than expenses recognized for the period. Then the amount of decrease would have to be deducted from net income to determine the related cash flow.

Increases and decreases in other current liabilities would be treated in the same manner.

3. **Increases and decreases in unearned revenues**—Increases and decreases in unearned revenue reflect differences between the amount of revenue recognized in net income and the amount of cash received. Therefore, the amount of these increases or decreases must be added back to or subtracted from net income to get the related cash flow. The following example illustrates the required adjustment.

Example
Assume the following information is from the balance sheets for 20X1 and 20X2 of ABC Co.:

Unearned Revenue 12/31/X1	$ -0-
Unearned Revenue 12/31/X2	25,000
Increase—20X2	$25,000

The increase occurred as the result of ABC making an entry such as:

DR: Cash
CR: Unearned Revenues

The debit to cash increased cash flow, but the credit to unearned revenue did not enter into the determination of net income. Therefore, net income understates cash flow for the period. The amount of increases in unearned revenues must be added back to net income to determine cash flow.

If unearned revenue had decreased, it would have caused an increase in net income (DR: Unearned Revenue; CR: Revenue) without generating a related cash flow. Therefore, the amount of a decrease in unearned revenue must be subtracted from net income to determine the related cash flow.

III. Presentation of Cash Flow from Operating Activities—Indirect Method

Using the cash flow values developed in prior illustrations, the cash flow from operating activities under the indirect method would be presented as follows:

Cash Flow From Operating Activities

Net Income (assumed)		$110,000
Adjustments to Reconcile Net Income to Net Cash provided by Operating Activities:		
Depreciation Expense (above)	$150,000	
Loss on Equipment Sale (above)	5,000	
Undistributed Equity Revenue (above)	(28,000)	
Amortization of Premium on Bond Investment (assumed)	3,000	
Increase in Accounts Receivable (above)	(15,000)	
Increase in Inventory (assumed)*	(20,000)	
Decrease in Prepaid Expenses (assumed)*	5,000	
Increase in Accounts Payable (above)	10,000	
Increase in Expenses Payable (assumed)*	15,000	
Increase in Unearned Revenues (above)	<u>25,000</u>	
Total Adjustments		$150,000
Net Cash Provided by Operating Activities		$260,000

*Note: Items marked with an asterisk (*) were developed in the illustration of the direct method in the previous lesson and are included here as assumed. Under the indirect method, the adjustment for Inventory and prepaid expenses would have been developed the same way the change in accounts receivable was developed. The adjustment for expenses payable would have been developed the same way the change in accounts payable was developed.

IV. Comparison of the Direct/Indirect Method of Determining Cash Flows from Operating Activities

The direct method and the indirect method are alternative ways of developing and presenting cash flow from operating activities. The most significant aspects of the two methods are:

A. The direct method presents cash flows in terms of the specific sources from which cash was received (inflows) and to which cash was paid (outflows).

B. The indirect method develops cash flows by adjusting net income and does not (necessarily) identify the specific sources of cash inflows or outflows.

C. Under either method, the cash flow from operating activities will be the same amount.

D. Under either method, the other major sections of the statement of cash flows—investing, financing, foreign currency effects, and the reconciliation of the change in cash—**will be the same.**

E. The direct method is preferred (by the FASB).

F. Both methods require disclosure of Noncash Investing and Financing activities.

G. The direct method requires an additional schedule to reconcile net income to cash flow from operating activities.

H. The indirect method requires an additional disclosure of the amount (of cash) paid for interest and income taxes.

Direct Method		**Indirect Method**
Statement		
Components of Cash Flows from Operating Activities (subtotal is same)	<—Different—>	Components of Cash Flows from Operating Activities (subtotal is same)
Cash Flows from Investing Activities	<—Same—>	Cash Flows from Investing Activities
Cash Flows from Financing Activities	<—Same—>	Cash Flows from Financing Activities
Effect of Foreign Currency Translation	<—Same—>	Effect of Foreign Currency Translation
Reconciliation with Cash Change	<—Same—>	Reconciliation with Cash Change
Additional Disclosures		
Noncash Investing and Financing	<—Same—>	Noncash Investing and Financing
Reconcile Cash Flows from Operating Activities with Net Income—in supporting schedule	<—(N/A)—>	(In Body of Statement)
(N/A—In Body of Statement)	<—(N/A)—>	Payments for Interest
(N/A—In Body of Statement)	<—(N/A)—>	Payments for Income Tax

Notes to Financial Statements

Notes to Financial Statements

This lesson presents a discussion of the notes to the financial statements.

After studying this lesson, you should be able to:

1. Describe the reason for footnote disclosures.

2. List the disclosures required in the footnotes.

I. **Notes to the Financial Statements**

   A. **Financial Report Disclosures**—To achieve the objectives of the full disclosure principle, the three primary financial statements are supplemented by footnote disclosures and disclosures that appear in related schedules. Summaries of the major required financial report disclosures follow.

   1. **Summary of significant accounting policies**—The first footnote is typically a summary of significant accounting policies—the principles and methods chosen by management where GAAP allows a choice. Such disclosure is required. Users' understanding of financial statement amounts is greatly facilitated by knowing the methods used in preparing the statements. This footnote usually includes information about the following:

      a. The chosen depreciation method

      b. The chosen method of valuing inventory

      c. The securities classified as cash and cash equivalents

      d. The basis for consolidation:

         i. Amortization policies

         ii. Revenue recognition policies

   2. This summary must include information about all significant accounting policies but is not required in interim statements if the policies have not changed.

   3. **Related party transactions**—Companies must disclose the following information:

      a. The nature of the relationship between the related entities (Related parties include a parent and its subsidiaries, a firm and its principal owners and management and members of their immediate families, a firm and its equity-method investees, and others.)

      b. A description of all related-party transactions for the accounting years in which an income statement is presented in the financial report

      c. The dollar amounts of the related-party transactions for the accounting years in which an income statement is presented in the financial report

      d. In relation to related parties, any receivables or payables from or to related parties as of the date of each balance sheet presented in the financial report

   B. **Noncurrent Liability Disclosures**—Companies are required to disclose the following information about liabilities:

   1. Combined aggregate amount of maturities on borrowings for each of the five years following the balance sheet

   2. Sinking fund requirements

3. The aggregate amount of payments for unconditional obligations to purchase fixed or minimum amounts of goods or services

4. The fair value of each financial debt instrument in the financial statements or in the notes

5. The nature of the firm's liabilities, interest rates, maturity dates, conversion options, assets pledged as collateral, and restrictions

C. **Capital Structure Disclosures**—Companies are required to provide the following information related to capital structure:

1. **Rights and privileges** of outstanding securities

2. The **number of shares issued** during the annual fiscal period and any subsequent interim period presented

3. **Liquidation preference** of preferred stock

4. If the liquidation value of preferred stock is considerably in excess of par value or stated value of preferred stock, this information should be disclosed in the equity section of the balance sheet.

5. **Other preferred stock disclosures**—The following information can be disclosed in the footnotes or in the equity section of the balance sheet:

   a. Aggregate or per-share amounts at which preferred stock can be called or is subject to redemption through sinking fund operations

   b. Aggregate or per-share amounts of arrearages for cumulative preferred stock

6. **Redeemable preferred stock**—For each of the five years following the balance sheet date, the amount of redemption requirements for all types of redeemable capital stock must be disclosed in the notes to the financial statements.

D. **Errors and irregularities**—A later lesson discusses the accounting for these items.

1. Errors are unintentional.

2. Irregularities are intentional.

3. Both require footnote disclosure. If prior-year income is affected, a prior-period adjustment is recorded that corrects the beginning balance of retained earnings and any other accounts affected in the year of discovery.

E. **Illegal Acts**—Examples include illegal contributions and bribes. The Foreign Corrupt Practices Act was passed by the US Congress to discourage such acts. The nature and impact of illegal acts on the financial statements should be disclosed fully in the notes.

II. **Management's Discussion and Analysis (MD&A)**—This is a narrative written by management and, although not considered part of the footnotes, is nonetheless an important disclosure supplementing the financial statements.

A. Publicly held firms are required to include the MD&A in the annual report. It provides management's discussion about the operations of the firm, its liquidity, and capital resources.

B. Additional discussion involves management's view of the firm's financial condition, changes in financial condition, and results of operations through analysis of the financial statements. Explanations of the reasons for major changes in financial performance and financial position are examples. Discussion of the effects of significant and unusual events provides further insight.

C. Forward-looking information is provided that is not reflected in the financial statements. This includes management's general prognosis about future sales, effects of competition, and expected effects of general macroeconomic conditions. An example is a discussion of the effect of inflation or specific price-level changes on future sales and earnings. Another is a discussion of the possible effects of uncertainties on the firm's financial statements.

III. Disclosures for the Effects of Changing Prices

A. Background

1. During times of price instability, financial reporting can be distorted, especially for items measured using historical cost. Both the balance sheet and income statement items (e.g., depreciation expense) are affected. Both inflation (general price-levels) and specific price changes affect the interpretation of reported amounts.

2. In the past, large firms were required to provide extensive footnote disclosure about the effects of price changes on the financial statements. Because inflation has subsided, there currently is no such requirement although disclosure of information on the effects of changing prices continues to be encouraged.

3. The remaining material in this subtopic provides a summary of price level changes.

B. General Price-Level Changes

Definitions

Inflation: The increase in general prices for a period of time; deflation is the decrease in general prices. When inflation is 4%, there has been a 4% increase in the general price level index.

General Prices: A market basket of items that the typical consumer purchases.

1. The Bureau of Labor Statistics publishes the CPI-U (Consumer Price Index for All Urban Consumers), which is an index reflecting the aggregate increase in the price of many goods and services used by individuals. It is one measure of inflation commonly quoted in the financial press. If inflation is 2% for an annual period, then the CPI-U has increased 2% for the year.

Definition

Nominal Dollars: Measurements in the price level in effect at a transaction date. These measurements are not adjusted for inflation.

2. Financial statement amounts are measured in nominal dollars. If a firm purchased equipment and paid $10,000, that transaction is measured and reported in nominal dollars at $10,000. Price level changes are ignored.

Definition

Constant Dollars: Measurements in the general price level as of a specific date. Constant dollar measurements reflect an adjustment for inflation and allow comparisons using dollars with the same purchasing power.

3. If equipment is purchased for $10,000 when the general price level index is 100, the constant dollar measurement for that equipment when the general price level index is 120 at a later date is $12,000 ($10,000 × 120/100). If the price of equipment had kept pace with inflation, the firm would have to spend $12,000 now to obtain the equipment it purchased for $10,000 on a previous date.

Note

In the adjustment ratio above (120/100), the numerator is the price level for the date on which the constant dollar measurement is desired. The denominator is the price level in effect on the date the transaction occurred.

a. Constant dollar adjustments allow comparisons of dollar amounts for transactions occurring on different dates. The effect of inflation is stripped away leaving "real" dollar measurements.

C. Specific Price Changes

Definition
Specific Price Change: The change in the price of a specific good or service over a period of time.

1. If the price of crude oil increased from $17 to $18 per barrel, then the specific price level of oil increased 5.9% ($18 – $17)/$17.

2. **Restrictions**—Specific price changes refer only to specific goods and services and are not necessarily correlated with inflation (general price level increase) although frequently they are.

Examples
1. The price of potato chips increased 3% during a period in which inflation was 2%. The specific price of potato chips moved in the same direction as inflation but the rate of increase was higher.

2. The price of computer chips has steadily declined over the last several years even though there has been moderate inflation. The specific price of computer chips has moved in a direction opposite that of inflation.

D. Effects of General Changes

Definition
Purchasing Power: The purchasing power of an asset is the amount of goods and services that can be obtained by transferring the asset to another party.

1. During inflation, the purchasing power of an asset having a fixed unchangeable value decreases.

Example
The purchasing power of a $10 bill decreases during periods of inflation because the amount of goods and services that the bill can purchase declines. (There was a time that going to a movie cost $1.00. Now it costs as much as $8.00 for a movie. A dollar does not go as far as it used to.)

E. Monetary and Nonmonetary Items—Assets and liabilities are categorized as (1) monetary or (2) nonmonetary, depending on whether the item has a fixed unchangeable value.

1. **Monetary items**—The specific price of monetary items cannot change. A $50 bill is always "worth" $50. An account receivable recorded at $3,000 is a monetary item because the claim the creditor has on the debtor is fixed at $3,000.

   a. Examples of monetary items—Cash, most receivables, accounts payable, all liabilities payable in fixed dollar amounts, and certain investments in debt securities.

2. **Nonmonetary items**—The specific price of nonmonetary items can change. The value of an item of inventory purchased for $300 can change before it is sold. The item of inventory does not command a fixed value.

   a. Examples of nonmonetary items—Inventory, plant assets, investments in equity securities, unearned rent, and other liabilities payable in goods and services

F. Purchasing Power Gains and Losses—The change in the purchasing power of an item due to a change in the general price level is measured only for monetary items because the specific price of nonmonetary items can change. During inflation, the amount of goods a $10 bill can purchase definitely decreases but the same cannot necessarily be said for an item of inventory originally costing $10. The value of the inventory item may increase with inflation but the value of the $10 bill cannot increase.

1. **Purchasing power gain**—A purchasing power gain results from holding monetary assets during deflationary times or having monetary liabilities during inflationary times.

Example

A firm owes $4,000 on a note due in one year. If inflation is 10% during that year (beginning price level of 100, ending price level of 110), the purchasing power of the dollars paid at the end of the year is 10% less than the dollars borrowed. Thus, the firm has a purchasing power gain because the firm is paying 10% less in purchasing power to extinguish the debt than it received from the creditor. (This is why interest rates increase with inflation, to compensate the creditor for the loss in purchasing power during the term of the borrowing.)

Amount of debt required at 12/31, for the firm to be in the same purchasing power position it was in at 1/1:

$4,000(110/100) =	$4,400
Amount of debt actually owed at 12/31:	$(4,000)
Purchasing power gain	$400

If the debt increased to $4,400 by year-end, the firm would be in the same purchasing power situation as it was at the beginning of the year.

But it actually owes only $4,000. Therefore, the firm is $400 ahead in purchasing power at 12/31.

2. **Purchasing power loss**—A purchasing power loss results from holding monetary assets during inflationary times or having monetary liabilities during deflationary times.

Example

A firm has a cash balance of $4,000 at the beginning of the year. If inflation is 10% during the year (beginning price level of 100, ending price level of 110), and the firm has had no change in its cash balance, the value of the dollars held at year's end is 10% less in terms of purchasing power. Thus, the firm has a purchasing power loss because the firm has 10% less in purchasing power than it had at the beginning of the year.

Amount of cash required at 12/31 to be in the same purchasing power position it was in at 1/1:

$4,000(110/100) =	$4,400
Amount of cash actually held at 12/31:	$(4,000)
Purchasing power loss	$400

The firm's $4,000 cash will buy $400 less in goods and services at year-end compared with the amount it could buy at the beginning of the year.

3. Computation of purchasing power gain or loss with both monetary assets and liabilities.

 **Example**

	1/1/x8	12/31/x8
General price level indices	120	140
Monetary assets held	$2,000	$3,800
Monetary liabilities owed	1,500	2,500
Net monetary assets	$ 500	$1,300

Assume the price level index rose evenly throughout the year; therefore, the average price level in 20x8 was 130.

	Nominal dollars	Adjustment ratio	Constant dollars
Net monetary assets, 1/1/x8	$500	140/120	$583
Increase in net monetary assets	800	140/130	862
Net monetary assets at 12/31 needed to keep pace with inflation			$1,445
Net monetary assets actually held at 12/31			1,300
Purchasing power loss, 20x8			$145

Summary
Purchasing Power Gain or Loss

	Period of	
Holding net monetary	Inflation	Deflation
Assets	Loss	Gain
Liabilities	Gain	Loss

Risks and Uncertainties

This lesson addresses the required disclosures by firms of the risks and uncertainties they face.

After studying this lesson, you should be able to:

1. Explain the scope of the required disclosures and the kinds of risks and uncertainties that are required to be disclosed.

2. Identify the five areas of required disclosure.

3. Describe the main disclosure requirements within the five areas.

4. Define and describe the four concentrations within the significant concentration areas of disclosure.

I. Background

A. Information about the risks and uncertainties faced by the firm enhances the ability of financial statement users to predict the future cash flows and operations of the firm. GAAP requires certain information about risks and uncertainties to be disclosed. The applicable accounting standard provides for selectivity whereby specified criteria are used to screen all the possible risks so that the required disclosures are limited to matters that materially affect a particular entity.

B. The disclosures are primarily concerned with risks and uncertainties that could materially affect financial statement amounts within one year of the date the financial statements are issued (the near term).

C. The required disclosures involve the following sources of risk and uncertainty. Each is discussed in more detail later in this lesson.

1. Nature of the entity's operations
2. Use of estimates in financial statements
3. Certain significant estimates
4. Current vulnerability due to significant concentrations in certain aspects of operations
5. The entity's ability to exist as a going concern

D. The five areas are not mutually exclusive; rather, there may be some overlap.

E. The requirements of the standard apply to annual and complete interim statements but not to condensed or summarized interim statements. The disclosure requirements only apply to the current year's statements in comparative financial statements.

F. The requirements apply only to those included in the standard and not to risks and uncertainties related to:

1. Management or key personnel
2. Proposed changes in government regulations
3. Proposed changes in accounting principles
4. Deficiencies in internal control
5. Possible effects of acts of God, war, sudden catastrophe

II. Nature of Operations

A. Different types of businesses have different risks. Knowledge of the firm's (1) products and services, (2) geographical locations and (3) principal markets will assist users in assessing risks concerning the firm's operations. For example, identification of competition and vulnerability to technological change are aided with this knowledge.

B. Financial statements and notes are required to include a description of the major products or services of the firm, and its principal markets and their locations. If the firm operates in more than one type of business, the relative importance of the operations in each business is disclosed, along with the basis of this determination (based on assets, revenues, or earnings for example).

C. These disclosures are not required to be on a quantified basis; relative importance can be described in such terms as major, intermediate, minor, and other similar ways.

III. Use of Estimates

A. The firm must communicate that: (1) use of estimates is inescapable in preparing financial statements that conform with GAAP, (2) the use of estimates results in approximate amounts, not certainty, and (3) estimates involve assumptions about future events.

B. The degree to which estimates can be relied upon is affected by many factors including whether the business and economic environment is stable or unstable at the time. This area of disclosure reminds users that they should not place an unwarranted degree of reliability on the reported amounts in financial statements.

IV. Certain Significant Estimates

A. When estimates used to value assets, liabilities, or contingencies are subject to a reasonable possibility of material change, disclosures may be required. Disclosure about an estimate is required when information available before the financial statements are issued or are available to be issued indicates that the following two criteria are met:

1. It is at least reasonably possible that an estimate will change in the near term;

2. The effect of the change would be material.

   a. Materiality is based on the effect of using the new estimate on the financial statements.

B. The disclosures must include:

1. The nature of the uncertainty that may cause an estimate to change and a statement that it is at least reasonably possible that a change in an estimate will occur in the near term. If the estimate concerns a loss contingency, the disclosure must also include an estimate of the possible loss or range of loss, or state that such an estimate cannot be made.

2. The estimated effect of the change as of the date of the financial statements must be disclosed.

C. If the criteria above are not met because the firm uses a risk-reduction technique, the disclosures are encouraged but not required.

D. The following are examples of assets and liabilities, related revenues and expenses, and disclosures of gain or loss contingencies that may be particularly sensitive to change in the near term:

1. Inventory subject to obsolescence

2. Equipment subject to technological obsolescence

3. Deferred tax asset valuation allowances

4. Capitalized software costs

5. Environmental remediation obligations

6. Litigation obligations

7. Obligations for defined benefit pension plans and other postemployment benefits

V. Significant Concentrations

A. Susceptibility to risk and uncertainty increases when diversification is lacking –when the firm has concentrations in various aspects of its business. Examples of concentrations include excessive reliance on one customer, having one product or service account for most of the firm's revenues, and reliance on one or a small number of suppliers.

B. The standard is concerned with "severe impacts" caused by concentrations. A severe impact is a significant financially disruptive effect on the normal functioning of the firm, where "severe" is greater than material but less than catastrophic. Bankruptcy is considered catastrophic for example.

C. The standard applies only to the following defined set of four concentrations, rather than all possible concentrations.

   1. Concentrations in the volume of business with a particular customer, supplier, lender, grantor, or contributor. The loss of the relationship is an example of an event that could cause a severe impact. The standard states that it is always at least reasonably possible to lose such a customer, grantor or contributor although the impact may not be severe.

   2. Concentrations in revenue from specific products, services, or fund-raising sources. A price or demand change could cause a severe impact.

   3. Concentrations in specific sources (suppliers) of services, materials, labor, licenses or other rights used in operations. Losses of a key supplier or a patent are examples of events that could cause a severe impact.

   4. Concentrations in the market or geographic area of operations. The standard states that it is always at least reasonably possible that operations located outside the firm's home country will be disrupted in the near term.

D. Disclosure of a concentration is required if all the following criteria are met. These concentrations are called *disclosable concentrations*.

   1. The concentration exists at the balance sheet date;

   2. The entity is vulnerable to the risk of a near-term severe impact because of a concentration *and*

   3. It is at least reasonably possible that events capable of causing a severe impact will occur in the near term. (Note: Reasonably possible is less than probable.)

E. For disclosable concentrations (those meeting the above criteria), the following is to be disclosed:

   1. Information adequate to inform users about the nature of the risk associated with the concentration

   2. For concentrations of labor (one of the four listed concentrations, see above) subject to collective bargaining agreements, the firm must disclose (a) the percentage of the labor force covered by the agreement, and (b) the percentage of the labor force covered by the agreement that will expire within one year.

   3. For concentrations of operations located outside of the entity's home country (one of the four listed concentrations, see above), the firm also must disclose the carrying amounts of net assets and the geographic areas in which they are located.

VI. Management's Going-Concern Assessment

A. Management must assess the entity's ability to continue as a going concern. Management's assessment should be based on facts and circumstances that are "known or reasonably knowable" as of the date the financial statements are issued. Note this assessment is not as of the balance sheet date, but rather should include information up to the date that the financial statements are issued.

B. There is uncertainty regarding the entity's ability to meet maturing obligations if there is "substantial doubt" that the entity can meet its obligations as they become due. Substantial doubt means that it is probable that the entity will be unable to meet its obligations. Probable is the threshold associated with contingencies and is broadly interpreted to mean greater than 70% or 80% probably that the event will occur.

C. Both quantitative and qualitative information should be considered when assessing the entity's ability to meet its obligations. The *look-forward* period for this assessment is one year from the issuance of the financial statements. Per ASU 2014-15, the following information should be taken into consideration:

1. **The company's current financial condition**—Including its current liquid resources (e.g., available cash or available access to credit).

2. **Conditional and unconditional obligations** —Due or anticipated in the next year (whether or not they are recognized in the financial statements).

3. **Funds necessary to maintain operations**—Considering the company's current financial condition, obligations, and other expected cash flows in the next year.

4. **Other conditions**—That could adversely affect the company's ability to meet its obligations in the next year (when considered in conjunction with the above). For example: Negative financial trends (e.g., recurring operating losses, working capital deficiencies, or negative operating cash flows).

    a. Other indications of financial difficulties (e.g., default on loans, denial of supplier credit, a need to restructure debt or seek new debt, noncompliance with statutory capital requirements, or a need to dispose of substantial assets)

    b. Internal matters (e.g., labor difficulties, substantial dependence on the success of a project, uneconomic long-term commitments, or a need to significantly revise operations)

    c. External matters (e.g., significant litigation, loss of a key customer, franchise, license, patent or supplier, or an uninsured natural disaster)

D. Disclosures are required only when conditions give rise to substantial doubt about the entity's going concern. No disclosures are required if there is no going concern uncertainties. If the substantial doubt is alleviated because management developed a plan to mitigate the effects of the uncertainties, the disclosures are still needed and the disclosures would include a description of management's plans to alleviate the substantial doubt. Disclosures include:

1. The principal conditions that give rise to the uncertainties

2. Management's evaluation of these conditions (essentially management's response to the factors found in C. above

3. Management's plans to alleviate the substantial doubt

Subsequent Events

This lesson presents the accounting and reporting for subsequent events.

After studying this lesson, you should be able to:

1. Define a subsequent event.

2. Distinguish between subsequent events that require recognition or disclosure on the financial statements.

3. Provide the key disclosure requirements for subsequent events.

I. **Subsequent Events**

    A. **Definition and Examples**

> **Definition**
>
> *Subsequent Events*: Events or transactions that have a material effect on the financial statements. Subsequent events occur *after* the date of the financial statements but *before* the statements are issued or are available to be issued.

        1. **Examples**

            a. Examples include lawsuits, changes in corporate structure, issuances of debt and equity securities, major acquisitions, and significant gains and losses.

            b. Although the financial statement date is the "closing date" for reporting, users of financial statements typically read the disclosures as if they are current as of the date of issue. Furthermore, the full disclosure principle mandates that all relevant information be disclosed.

        2. **Two categories**—There are two categories of subsequent events, each requiring different accounting treatment:

            a. The condition leading to the subsequent event **existed** at the balance sheet date;

            b. The condition leading to the subsequent event **did not exist** at the balance sheet date —the condition arose after the balance sheet date.

    B. **Subsequent Events—Conditions Existed at the Balance Sheet Date**—The financial statements should reflect all information regarding these events up to the balance sheet date. This category of subsequent events requires recognition in the financial statements and includes all events that provide evidence about conditions existing at the balance sheet date including estimates used in the process of preparing the statements. Footnotes may be included to supplement and explain the recognition.

>
>
> **Examples**
>
> 1. A major customer's financial situation has been deteriorating during the reporting year (year 4), with bankruptcy being declared early in year 5. As a result, a receivable from that customer is deemed worthless after the year 4 balance sheet date but before the issuance of the financial statements. The loss from the write-off of the receivable should be recognized in year 4 income, and the year 4 balance sheet should reflect the write-off because the condition leading to the bankruptcy existed at the balance sheet date.
>
> 2. Information is discovered early in year 5 indicating that the total useful life of certain plant assets will be significantly less than originally estimated due to obsolescence. This condition developed gradually during year 4. The useful lives of the affected assets should be re-estimated and depreciation expense for year 4 should reflect those revised estimates.

II. **Subsequent Events—Conditions Did Not Exist at the Balance Sheet Date**—This category of subsequent event requires only footnote disclosure of events that have material effects on the financial statements. The footnote disclosures include a description of the nature of the event and an estimate of the financial effect, or a statement that an estimate cannot be made. Recognition is inappropriate because the condition existed after the balance sheet date

---

Examples

1. A major customer declared bankruptcy as a result of a casualty in early 20X5. As a result, a receivable from that customer is deemed worthless after the 20X4 balance sheet date but before the issuance of the financial statements. The loss from the worthless receivable is disclosed in the footnotes, but recognition is postponed until the 20X5 statements, because the casualty occurred after 20X4.

2. A firm completes a large issuance of bonds early in 20X5, before the issuance of the 20X4 statements. The footnotes to the 20X4 statements should disclose the relevant information about the issuance, but recognition is postponed until the 20X5 statements.

III. **Period of evaluation for subsequent events**

1. The period during which to evaluate subsequent events is the period between the balance sheet date, and either:

    a. The date the financial statements are **issued**—when they are widely distributed (e.g., filed with the SEC) for general use, *or*

    b. The date the financial statements are **available to be issued**—when they are complete, comply with GAAP, and have all the approvals necessary for issuance.

2. Public entities or any entities that widely distribute their financial statements use the *issued* date.

3. All other entities use the **available to be issued date**. These entities are not required to evaluate subsequent events after the point of availability. However, a non-SEC filer must also disclose the date through which the subsequent events were evaluated and whether that date is the date the financial statements are issued or available to be issued.

IV. **Related Situations**—The recognition and disclosure requirements for subsequent events apply to both annual and interim financial statements but do not apply to subsequent events or transactions that are governed by other applicable GAAP.

1. **Contingent liabilities**

    a. The examples presented here are addressed in detail in other lessons. Here we present an overview as it relates to subsequent events.

    b. The reporting principles for contingent liabilities are similar to those of subsequent events and in some cases overlap. However, for recognized contingencies (those that are probable and estimable as of the balance sheet date), the event confirming the loss, reduction in asset, or recognition of liability need not take place before the issuance of the financial statements.

    c. For example, a firm recognizes warranty expense and a warranty liability at the end of 20X4 on sales recognized in 20X4 because warranty claims are probable and the amount to service the claims is estimable. The condition giving rise to the expense and liability existed at the balance sheet date (the obligation to service the claims and the probable nature of the claims), but the warranty claims need not occur before the issuance of the balance sheet in order for the liability to be recognized at the end of 20X4.

    d. In addition, for contingent liabilities, the quality that distinguishes recognition from footnote disclosure only is the likelihood of the future event and whether the economic sacrifice is estimable. Thus, although the situation appears to be similar to subsequent events accounting, a specific accounting principle governs this accounting.

    e. Gain contingencies are not recognized, although it could be argued that the conditions giving rise to the gain existed before the balance sheet date.

f. Refinancing current debt

    a. The examples present here are addressed in detail in other lessons; here we present an overview as it relates to subsequent events.

    b. A firm can reclassify a current liability as noncurrent if it accomplishes one of the following after the balance sheet date but before the financial statements are issued:

        i. Issue stock to extinguish the debt;

        ii. Refinance the current liability with a non-current liability; *or*

        iii. Enter into an irrevocable agreement to refinance the current liability with a noncurrent liability.

    c. The recognition (change in classification to noncurrent) takes place during the subsequent event period, but it can be argued that the decision was made to effect the reclassification after the balance sheet date. Thus, although the situation appears to be similar to subsequent events accounting, a specific accounting principle governs this accounting.

    d. Stock dividends and splits after the balance sheet date are treated as if they occurred as of the balance sheet date. Although it could be argued that because the dividend or split should not be recognized because it took place after the balance sheet date, a specific accounting principle requires recognition.

Exit or Disposal Activities and Discontinued Operations

This lesson presents the accounting and reporting for exit or disposal activities and discontinued operations.

After studying this lesson, you should be able to:

1. Calculate the gain or loss on the disposal or involuntary conversion of a plant asset.

2. Complete the journal entry to record the disposal or involuntary conversion of a plant asset.

3. Define what is meant by a "component of an entity."

4. Calculate the gain or loss on a discontinued operation.

5. Complete the financial statement presentation of a discontinued operation.

I. The following categories capture the types of exit or disposal activities: 1) those disposals that occur in the normal course of business that are disposals of individually insignificant assets, 2) disposals that meet the criteria of a discontinued operation, and 3) individually significant disposals that do not meet the criteria of a discontinued operation. Each category is discussed further below.

II. **Exit or Disposal Activity in the Ordinary Course of Business**

A. A company may voluntarily sell, dispose, or abandon plant assets that are individually insignificant to the operations of the business. These disposals occur and are not the primary source of revenue for the entity, but are incidental to operations. In the case of fire, flood, or other event, the plant asset may be destroyed involuntarily. In either case, the asset must be depreciated up to the date of the disposal. The first thing that must be done before recording an exit or disposal activity is to record depreciation.

B. Sale of a plant asset requires removing the asset and accumulated depreciation, recording the receipt of cash, and recognition of the gain or loss on the sale. When the cash received from the sale exceeds the assets net book value (asset cost – accumulated depreciation), then a gain is recognized. When the cash received is less than the assets net book value, then a loss is recognized. The gain or loss on the disposal of an asset is reported on the income statement with other items from customary business activities.

Example
Assume Shelby Company purchased a plant asset for $20,000 with a 10-year life on January 1, 20X0. On July 1, 20X8, Shelby Company sold the plant asset for $5,000. The entries for the sale of the plant asset are as follows:

Depreciation expense	$1,000	
Accumulated depreciation		$1,000

(to record 6 months of depreciation in the year of sale — (20,000/10 years) × 6/12)

Cash	$5,000	
Accumulated depreciation	$17,000[1]	
Plant Asset		$20,000
Gain on sale of plant asset		$ 2,000

(to record the gain on the sale of the plant asset)

*((20,000/10 years) × 8.5 years held) = 17,000)

C. If the asset is abandoned or there is an involuntary conversion because the asset is destroyed, then no cash is received and the gain or loss equals the net book value of the asset on the date of the abandonment or conversion. The loss on abandonment or conversion is an ordinary loss and part of continuing operations on the income statement. The next section presents the accounting and reporting for discontinued operations.

III. Discontinued Operations

A. A discontinued operation is when a component or group of components of an entity are 1) disposed for by sale or other than sale, or classified as held-for-sale, and 2) the disposal "represents a strategic shift that has (or will have) a major effect on an entity's operation and financial results." (ASU 2014-08) A strategic shift includes the disposal of a major geographical area, a major line of business, a major equity method investment, or other major parts of the entity.

B. **Comparative Financial Statements**—The income of a discontinued operation, and any gain or loss from its disposal, are separated from income from continuing operations, for **all periods presented**, even though in previous periods the income from the segment was part of continuing operations. This requirement enhances the consistency of comparative financial statements. Discontinued operations are shown below income from continuing operations in the income statement. Earnings per share is presented for discontinued operations on the face of the income statement.

1. **Income statement**: The gain or loss from the discontinued operation is presented on the face of the income statement as income (loss) from discontinued operation (net of tax). In contrast, gains or losses from the disposal that does not qualify as a discontinued operation is included in income from continuing operations.

Example

The income of Old, a reporting unit of Car, Inc., is $20 and $5 for years 6 and 7. Total Car income is $100 each year. In year 7 Old is discontinued and put up for sale. Year 7's comparative income statement shows the change in reporting for year 6.

	Year 6	Year 7
Income from continuing operations	$80	$95
Discontinued operation	$20	$5
Net income	$100	$100

The year 6 income statement published in year 6 included Old's income of $20 in income from continuing operations because in that year Old was part of the continuing operations of Car, Inc. However, in year 7, that is no longer the case and Old's results are separated from income from continuing operations for both years presented.

2. **Balance sheet**: All assets and liabilities of the discontinued operation for all comparative periods are presented separately on the balance sheet. These assets and liabilities cannot be presented as a net single amount; rather the gross amount of assets and liabilities must be shown.

IV. Two Values to Report

—The following are separately disclosed and computed in the income statement below income from continuing operations:

A. **Income**—Income from the discontinued operation (DOP) for the portion of the year to disposal (or if disposal occurs in a later year, income for the entire year).

B. Gain or Loss—On disposal of the operation.

1. The gain or loss is the net proceeds from sale of the component less book value of the component's net assets. Net proceeds are equal to the gross amount received on sale less the cost to dispose of the assets. Thus, the cost to dispose increases a loss and decreases a gain.

Example
Disposal loss or gain calculation:

Component data:

Assets net of applicable depreciation	$400
Liabilities	$150
Amount received on sale	$220
Cost to sell	$20

Book value of net assets = $400 − $150 = $250. Proceeds = $220 − $20 = $200. Loss on disposal = $250 − $200 = $50.

C. All items reported for discontinued operations are net of tax (after tax).

D. The measurements for the DOP disposal loss is the same as for individual impaired assets held for disposal (impairment is covered in a different lesson). The only difference is the location on the income statement the gain or loss is reported. The gain or loss recognized for individual assets is included in income from continuing operations whereas the gain or loss from DOP is reported as *discontinued operations* below income from continuing operations.

E. Gain on Disposal—Actual gains on disposal (when the decision to discontinue the operation and the disposal occur in the same period) are recognized but estimated gains are not. A gain occurs when the net proceeds from the sale of the component exceed the BV (book value) of the net assets of the component.

F. Loss on Disposal—When the BV of the net assets of the component exceeds the component's fair value less cost of disposal at year-end, then the component assets are written down to fair value less cost of disposal. The latter amount (fair value less cost of disposal) is estimated at the end of the year, and the loss is recognized even though disposal or sale has not taken place.

G. If the disposal takes place in the year the decision is made, then the disposal loss reported is the actual amount.

H. If the actual disposal loss is different from the estimated loss recognized previously, then in the period of disposal the difference is recognized as a gain or loss.

Example
If the previously recognized estimated loss was $40,000 and the actual loss in the year of disposal was $30,000, then in the year of disposal a $10,000 gain is recognized and reported in the DOP section of the income statement.

I. The disposal loss or gain is a separate line item in the DOP section of the income statement in addition to the separate operating income of the component during the period. Alternatively, the two amounts can be netted with footnote disclosure showing them both. The assets are separated from the others in the BS when disposal takes place after the decision to eliminate the component.

Example

In year 3, a firm decided to discontinue an operation (DOP) that qualifies for separate DOP reporting. The operation's operating income was $60 in year 2 and negative $20 in year 3 (operating loss). For simplicity, assume the firm shows only two years comparatively. At the end of year 3 the BV of the component's net assets is $400. The fair value of the component is $250, and the firm expects to incur $20 of direct incremental cost to dispose of the component in year 4. Income from continuing operations for year 2 reported in year 2 was $300. Income from continuing operations in year 3 is $320. All amounts are after-tax.

The latter portion of the comparative income statement:

	Year 3		Year 2
Income from continuing operations		$320	$240
Income from DOP	(20)		60
Loss on disposal of DOP	(170)*	(190)	
Net income		$130	$300

*$170 = $400 BV − ($250 fair value − $20 cost to sell)

All amounts shown above are after tax.

Note that income from continuing operations for year 2 reported in the year 2 income statement was $300. For comparative purposes, the components year 2 income is separated from income from continuing operations. The assets of this component are also reported on a separate line on the balance sheet.

J. After the disposal of an operation is completed, there may be adjustments to amounts previously reported in the DOP section of the income statement. These adjustments might stem from resolution of contingencies, settlement of pension obligations, and others that occur after disposal. Such adjustments are reported in the DOP section of the income statement in the year they occur.

V. **Disclosures**—There are several disclosure requirements for both (1) disposals that meet the criteria for a discontinued operation and (2) individually significant disposals that do not meet these criteria.

A. For disposal of an individually significant component that does not meet the definition of a discontinued operation, the entity must disclose pretax profit or loss reported in the income statement for the period in which the disposal group is sold or is classified as held for sale.

B. For a disposal that meets the criteria of a discontinued operation the entity must disclose the following (ASU 2014-08):

1. Fact and circumstances leading to the disposal and reasons for the strategic shift and the effect of the strategic shift on operations

2. For the initial period in which the disposal group is classified as held for sale and for all prior periods presented in the statement of financial position, a reconciliation of (1) total assets and total liabilities of the discontinued operation that are classified as held for sale in the notes to the financial statements to (2) total assets and total liabilities of the disposal group classified as held for sale that are presented separately on the balance sheet

3. Operating and investing cash flows for the periods for which the discontinued operation's results of operations are reported in the income statement

4. Depreciation and amortization, capital expenditures, and significant operating and investing noncash items for the periods for which the discontinued operation's results of operations are reported in the income statement

5. Entities that have significant continuing involvement with a discontinued operation after the disposal date must provide additional disclosures regarding the nature of activities, including cash flows from or to the discontinued operation.

Evaluating Financial Statements

Ratios—Liquidity/Solvency and Operational

This lesson presents financial statement ratios for liquidity/solvency and operational analysis.

After studying this lesson, you should be able to:

1. Calculate and interpret liquidity and solvency ratios.

2. Calculate and interpret operational ratios.

I. Background

Definition
Financial Statement Ratio Analysis: The development of quantitative relationships between various elements of a firm's financial statements.

A. Ratio analysis enables comparisons across firms, especially within the same industry, and facilitates identifying operating and financial strengths and weaknesses of a firm.

B. The names given to ratios frequently indicate the nature of the quantitative analysis needed to develop the ratios.

Example
Debt to Equity Ratio = Total **Debt** (Liabilities) / Owner's **Equity**

C. Ratios can be grouped according to the major purpose or type of measure being analyzed. The major purposes or types of measures being analyzed are:

1. Liquidity/Solvency

2. Operational Activity

3. Profitability

4. Equity/Investment Leverage

D. Below is a diagram of the "big picture" of all ratios. This overview helps put the dozens of individual ratios into perspective and helps "see" how the balance sheet / income statement relationships tie together. This diagram also makes it easy to see the difference between ROA and ROE. **Return on Assets** (ROA)—measures operating performance *independent* of financing. **Return on Equity** (ROE)—explicitly *includes* the amount and cost of financing.

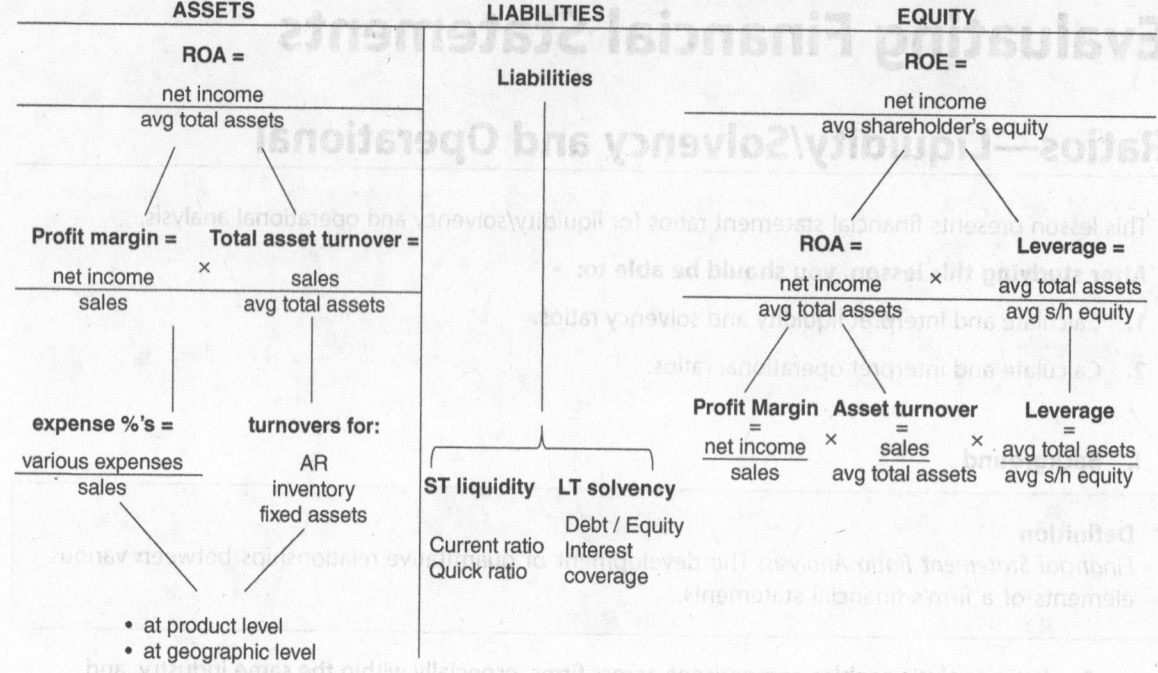

II. Liquidity/Solvency Ratios

A. Major liquidity measures

Definition

Liquidity Ratios (also known as *Solvency Ratios*): Measure the ability of the firm to pay its obligations as they become due.

1. **Working capital**: Measures the extent to which current assets exceed current liabilities and, thus, are uncommitted in the short term. It is expressed as:

Working Capital = Current Assets – Current Liability

Working Capital Ratio = Current Assets / Current Liabilities

The more common name of this ratio is "current ratio."

2. Measures the quantitative relationship between current assets and current liabilities in terms of the "number of times" current assets can cover current liabilities.

   a. Is a widely used measure of the firm's ability to pay its current liabilities

   b. Changes in Current Assets and/or Current Liabilities have determinable effects on the Working Capital Ratio (WCR):

WCR = Current Assets / Current Liabilities

An increase in current assets (alone) increases the WCR.

A decrease in current assets (alone) decreases the WCR.

An increase in current liabilities (alone) decreases the WCR.

A decrease in current liabilities (alone) increases the WCR.

If the WCR equals 1.00, equal increases or equal decreases in current assets and liabilities will not change the WCR; it will remain 1.00.

c. If the WCR **exceeds** 1.00:

    i. Equal increases in current assets and liabilities decrease the WCR.

$$WCR = CA\ 20,000\ /\ CL\ 10,000 = 2$$
$$WCR = (CA\ 20,000 + 10,000)\ /\ (CL\ 10,000 + 10,000) = 30,000\ /\ 20,000 = 1.5$$

    ii. Equal decreases in current assets and liabilities increase the WCR.

$$WCR = CA\ 30,000\ /\ CL\ 20,000 = 1.5$$
$$WCR = CA\ 20,000\ /\ CL\ 10,000 = 2$$

d. If the WCR is **less than** 1.00:

    i. equal increases in current assets and liabilities increase the WCR.

$$WCR = CA\ 10,000\ /\ CL\ 20,000 = .50$$
$$WCR = (CA\ 10,000 + 10,000)\ /\ (CL\ 20,000 + 10,000) = 20,000\ /\ 30,000 = .66$$

    ii. Equal decreases in current assets and liabilities decreases the WCR.

$$WCR = 20,000\ /\ 30,000 = .66$$
$$WCR = 10,000\ /\ 20,000 = .50$$

3. The **acid-test ratio** measures the quantitative relationship between highly liquid assets and current liabilities in terms of the "number of times" that cash and assets that can be converted quickly to cash cover current liabilities:

Acid-Test Ratio (also known as Quick Ratio) = (Cash + (Net) Receivables + Marketable Securities) / Current Liabilities

4. The **securities defensive-interval ratio** measures the quantitative relationship between highly liquid assets and the average daily use of cash in terms of the number of days that cash and assets can be quickly converted to support operating costs

Securities Defensive-Interval Ratio = (Cash + (Net) Receivables + Marketable Securities) / Average Daily Cash Expenditures

5. The **times interest earned ratio** measures the ability of current earnings to cover interest payments for a period.

Times Interest Earned Ratios = (Net Income + Interest Expense + Income Tax) / Interest Expense

6. The **times preferred dividend earned ratio** measures the ability of current earnings to cover preferred dividends for a period.

Times Preferred Dividend Earned Ratio = Net Income / Annual Preferred Dividend Obligation

III. Operational Activity Ratios—These measure the efficiency with which a firm carries out its operating activities.

    A. Accounts receivable turnover measures the number of times that accounts receivable turnover (are incurred and collected) during a period. Indicates the quality of credit policies (and the resulting receivables) and the efficiency of collection procedures.

> Accounts Receivable Turnover = (Net) Credit Sales / Average (Net) Accounts Receivable (e.g., Beginning + Ending/2)

    B. Number of days' sales in average receivables measures the average number of days required to collect receivables; it is a measure of the average age or receivables.

> Number of Days' Sales in Average Receivables = (300 or 360 or 365 (or other measure of business days in a year)) / Accounts Receivable Turnover (computed above)

    C. Inventory turnover measures the number of times that inventory turnover (is acquired and sold or used) during a period. Indicates over or under stocking of inventory or obsolete inventory.

> Inventory Turnover = Cost of Goods Sold / Average Inventory (e.g., Beginning + Ending/2)

    D. Number of days' supply in inventory measures the number of days inventory is held before it is sold or used. Indicates the efficiency of general inventory management.

> Number of Days' Supply in Inventory = (300 or 360 or 365 (or other measure of business days in a year)) / Inventory Turnover (computed above)

    E. Operating number of cycle measures the average length of time to invest cash in inventory, convert the inventory to receivables, and collect the receivables; it measures the time to go from cash back to cash.

> Operating Number of Cycle = Days in Operating = Number of Days' Sale in A/R + Length Cycle Number of Days' Supply in Inventory

Ratios—Profitability and Equity

This lesson presents financial statement ratios for profitability and equity analysis.

After studying this lesson, you should be able to:

1. Calculate and interpret profitability ratios.

2. Calculate and interpret equity ratios.

I. Background

Definition
Financial Statement Ratio Analysis: The development of quantitative relationships between various elements of a firm's financial statements.

A. Ratio analysis enables comparisons across firms, especially within the same industry, and facilitates identifying operating and financial strengths and weaknesses of a firm.

B. The names given to ratios frequently indicate the nature of the quantitative analysis needed to develop the ratios.

Example
Debt to Equity ratio = Total **Debt** (Liabilities) / Owner's **Equity**

C. Ratios can be grouped according to the major purpose or type of measure being analyzed. The major purposes or types of measures being analyzed are:

1. Liquidity/solvency

2. Operational activity

3. Profitability

4. Equity/investment leverage

II. Profitability Ratios—These measure aspects of a firm's operating (income/loss) results on a relative basis.

A. **Profit margin (on sales)** measures the net profitability on sales (revenue).

Profit Margin (on Sales) = Net Income / (Net) Sales

B. **Return on total assets** measures the rate of return on total assets and indicates the efficiency with which invested resources (assets) are used.

Return on Total Assets = (Net Income + (add back) Interest Expense (net of tax effect)) / Average Total Assets

C. **Return on common stockholders' equity** measures the rate of return (earnings) on common stockholders' investment.

Return on Common Stockholders' Equity = (Net Income—Preferred Dividend (obligation for the period only)) / Average Common Stockholders' Equity (e.g., (Beginning + Ending)/2)

D. **Return on owners' (all stockholders') equity** measures the rate of return (earnings) on all stockholders' investment.

Return on Owners' (all Stockholders') Equity = Net Income / Average Stockholders' Equity (e.g., (Beginning + Ending)/2)

E. **Earnings per share (EPS—basic formula)** measures the income earned per (average) share of common stock. Indicates ability to pay dividends to common shareholders.

Earnings Per Share (EPS—Basic Formula) = (Net Income—Preferred Dividends (obligation for the period only)) / Weighted Average Number of Shares Outstanding

F. **The price-earnings (P/E) ratio** measures the price of a share of common stock relative to its latest earnings per share. Indicates a measure of how the market values the stock, especially when compared with other stocks.

Price-Earnings Ratio (P/E Ratio) = Market Price for a Common Share / Earnings per (Common) Share (EPS)

G. **Common Stock Dividends Pay Out Ratio**

Total Basis = Cash Dividends to Common Shareholders / Net Income to Common Shareholder

H. **Per share basis** measures the extent (percentage) of earnings distributed to common shareholders.

Per Share Basis = Cash Dividends per Common Share / Earnings per Common Share

I. **Common stock yield** measures the rate of return (yield) per share of common stock.

Common Stock Yield = Dividend per Common Share / Market Price per Common Share

III. **Equity/Investment Leverage Ratios**—These provide measures of relative sources of equity and equity value.

A. The **debt to equity ratio** measures relative amounts of assets provided by creditors and shareholders.

Debt to Equity Ratio = Total Liabilities / Total Shareholders' Equity

B. The **owners' equity ratio** measures the proportion of assets provided by shareholders.

Owners' Equity Ratio = Shareholders' Equity / Total Assets

   C. The **debt ratio** measures the proportion of assets provided by creditors. Indicates the extent of leverage in funding the entity.

> Debt Ratio = Total Liabilities / Total Assets

   D. **Book value per common stock** measures the per share amount of common shareholders' claim to assets. (See the section on this ratio in the "Book Value per Share" lesson for more details.)

> Book Value per Common Stock = Common Shareholders' Equity / Number of Outstanding Common Shares

   E. **Book value per preferred share** measures the per share amount of preferred shareholders' claim to assets.

> Book Value per Preferred Share = Preferred Shareholders' Equity (including dividends in arrears) / Number of Outstanding Preferred Stocks

Consolidated Financial Statements

Introduction to Consolidated Financial Statements

This lesson presents the criteria for consolidated financial statements, the exceptions to those criteria, and an overview to the consolidating process.

After studying this lesson, you should be able to:

1. Identify the alternative accounting methods that a parent may use to carry an investment in a subsidiary on its books.

2. Describe the effects of the alternative accounting methods on the consolidating process and on the consolidated statements.

3. Describe when consolidated financial statements are required under U.S. GAAP (and when they are not appropriate).

4. Describe the information needed in order to prepare consolidated financial statements.

5. Describe where the consolidating process is carried out.

6. List the basic sequence of steps used in carrying out the consolidating process.

7. Identify the specific circumstances that affect how the consolidating process is carried out.

I. **Background**

    A. Consolidated financial statements are required when one entity has effective control over another entity.

        1. Controlling interest is usually present when an entity (investor/parent) has a greater than 50% ownership (directly or indirectly) of another entity (investee/subsidiary) and, therefore, can direct the activities of the investee/subsidiary; or

        2. Control is also evident when an entity (variable-interest holder) is the principal beneficiary of a variable-interest entity.

    B. In either of the foregoing cases, the entities are separate legal entities, but are under common economic control.

        1. The shareholders of the parent entity control that entity, which, in turn, has control of the subsidiary entity.

        2. The shareholders of the variable-interest holder entity control that entity, which, in turn, has control of the variable-interest entity.

    C. Because the entities are under common economic control, GAAP requires consolidated financial statements.

        1. **Consolidated financial statements** present the financial information of two or more separate legal entities, usually a parent company and one or more of its subsidiaries, as though they were a single economic entity (remember the economic entity concept from the conceptual framework).

        2. The **consolidating process** is the sequence of steps or activities carried out in order to combine the financial information of two or more entities. The consolidating process results in consolidated financial statements.

D. The process of presenting consolidated financial statements can be represented graphically in the following way:

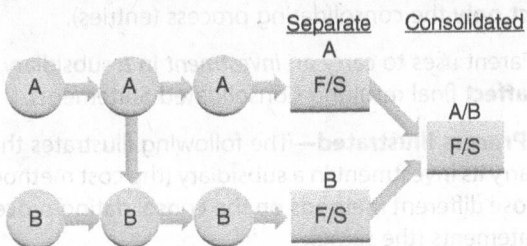

II. Justification—The preparation and presentation of consolidated financial statements is justified based on:

A. The presumption that consolidated statements are more meaningful than separate financial statements.

    1. "There is a presumption that consolidated statements are more meaningful than separate statements and that they are usually necessary for a fair presentation when one of the entities in the group directly or indirectly has a controlling financial interest in the other entities" (ASC 810-10-1).

B. The supposition that economic substance (common controlling interest) take precedence over legal form (separate legal entities).

III. Exceptions—There are certain limited exceptions to when an entity must consolidate another entity. Those exceptions include:

A. If an investor/parent has majority ownership of an investee/subsidiary (> 50% of the voting stock of the investee), but is prevented from exercising that majority ownership to control the financial and operating policies or activities of the subsidiary, it will not consolidate the subsidiary. Effective control may be lacking (even for a majority owned subsidiary) when it is:

    1. A foreign subsidiary largely controlled by the foreign government through prohibition on paying dividends, control of day-to-day operations, or other impediments to control.

    2. A domestic subsidiary in bankruptcy and under the control of the courts.

B. Certain entities are precluded from consolidating controlled entities by industry-specific guidelines, including:

    1. Registered investment companies.

    2. Brokers/dealers in securities.

C. A variable-interest (investment) or subsidiary (unconsolidated subsidiary) that is not included in consolidated statements would be reported as an "Investment" by the interest-holder/investor.

    1. The variable-interest investment would be measured as the entity's claim to the net asset value of the variable-interest entity.

    2. The unconsolidated subsidiary investment would be measured using either fair value or the equity method of accounting, depending on the extent of influence that can be exercised over the subsidiary by the parent.

IV. Parent's Accounting for a Subsidiary to be Consolidated

A. A Parent records a subsidiary **on its books** as an *investment* (in Subsidiary).

B. Subsequently, a Parent may carry an *investment* in a subsidiary that will be consolidated **on its books** using:

    1. Cost method;

    2. Equity method;

    3. Any other method it chooses.

V. A Parent Must Report Entities Under Its Control in Consolidated Statements

   A. The method a parent uses to carry an *investment* in a subsidiary on its books (cost, equity, or other) **will affect only** the consolidating process (entries).

   B. The method a Parent uses to carry an *investment* in a subsidiary on its books (cost, equity, or other) **will not affect** final resulting Consolidated Statements.

   C. Consolidating Process Illustrated—The following illustrates the use of alternative methods by a parent to carry its investment in a subsidiary (the cost method and the equity method) and the effects of those different methods on the consolidating process (different) and on the final consolidated statements (the same).

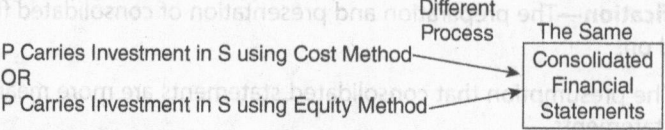

VI. Information Requirements—In order to consolidate the financial statements of two or more entities, certain specific information is needed, including:

   A. Financial statements (or adjusted trial balances) of the separate affiliated entities to be consolidated

   B. Data as of the date of a business combination (i.e., acquisition date):

      1. Book values of assets acquired and liabilities assumed as of the acquisition date

      2. Fair values of assets acquired and liabilities assumed as of the acquisition date

      3. Fair value of any noncontrolling interest in the acquired entity as of the acquisition date

      4. Fair value of any equity interest in the acquired entity owned by the parent prior to the acquisition date

   C. Intercompany (i.e., between the companies being consolidated) transaction data (for the operating period) and intercompany balances (as of period end)

VII. Consolidating Process

   A. The consolidating process is carried out on a consolidating worksheet, not on the books of any entity.

      1. The basic information for the worksheet comes from the account balances of the separate entities.

      2. The consolidating process is primarily concerned with adjusting and eliminating those balances to develop information that would report the separate entities as though they were a single entity.

      3. The consolidating process and the results of that process are not recorded on the books of any of the affiliated entities.

      4. The result of the consolidating process is the full set of consolidated financial statements.

   B. The basic sequence of steps in carrying out the consolidating process are (each of these requirements is covered in detail in the following lessons):

      1. Record trial balances—Record account titles and balances of the separate entities on the consolidating worksheet from the adjusted trial balances, separate statements, or other sources.

      2. Record adjusting entries—Develop and post to the worksheet consolidating adjusting entries, if any.

3. **Record eliminating entries**—Develop and post to the worksheet consolidating eliminating entries; these entries are likely to include:

   a. Investment eliminating entry (always required)

   b. Intercompany receivables/payables elimination(s)

   c. Intercompany revenue/expense elimination(s)

   d. Intercompany profit elimination(s)

4. Complete consolidating worksheet.

5. Prepare formal consolidated financial statements from worksheet.

VIII. **Factors Affecting the Consolidation Process**—Although the general process is the same for carrying out all consolidating processes, the specific adjustments, eliminations and related amounts depend on the specific circumstances. The following alternatives will affect the specific adjustments and eliminations made during the consolidating process:

A. Whether the consolidating process is being carried out at the date of the business combination or at a subsequent date

B. Whether the parent owns 100% (all) of the voting stock of a subsidiary or less than 100% of the voting stock

C. Whether on its books the parent carries its investment in a subsidiary using the cost or equity method of accounting

D. Whether transactions between the affiliated entities (parent and its subsidiaries) originate with the parent or with a subsidiary

Consolidating Process

Consolidation at Acquisition

This lesson discusses the preparation of consolidated financial statements immediately following a business combination or following an operating period that occurs after the combination. This lesson describes and illustrates the specific requirements of the consolidating process carried out **immediately following the acquisition** of a subsidiary by a parent.

After studying this lesson, you should be able to:

1. Describe the characteristics of consolidated financial statements immediately following a business combination.

   Prepare consolidated financial statements immediately following a business combination, including:

   - calculate consolidated balances on the consolidated balance sheet,

   - understand consolidating investment eliminating entries, and

   - understand intercompany receivable/payable eliminating entries.

2. Describe the effects that the method a parent uses to carry an investment (on its books) in a subsidiary has on the investment balance that must be eliminated in the consolidating process.

I. **Business Combinations**—A business combination must be accounted for using the acquisition method of accounting. Immediately following an acquisition the consolidated balance sheet will be different from the parent's (acquiring entity's) financial statements. If an income statement, statement of cash flows, or statement of retained earnings were prepared at the date of acquisition, it would represent information of the parent company only because there will not yet have been any activity including the subsidiary.

II. **Consolidated Balance Sheet**—At the date of the combination, a consolidated balance sheet will "combine" the assets, liabilities, and shareholder claims (majority and noncontrolling, if any) of the parent and its newly acquired subsidiary(ies).

III. **Consolidated Income Statement/Retained Earnings Statement/Cash Flow Statement**—At the date of combination, a consolidated income statement, statement of retained earnings, or statement of cash flow would be the same as the statements of the parent entity.

   A. Under the acquisition method of accounting for the combination, the operating results of the acquired entity up to the date of the combination is part of what the parent paid for in the cost of the investment in the subsidiary.

   B. There has not yet been an operating period (and operating results) during which the Subsidiary was controlled by the parent. Therefore, the consolidated income statement, retained earnings statement, and cash flow statement will be the same as the parent's at the date of the combination.

IV. **Carrying Investment in Subsidiary**—At the date of combination, the method the parent will use to account for the investment in the subsidiary (cost, equity or other) is not a consideration—that is, there is no "carrying" period yet.

V. **Overview**—The following example will depict the information needed to answer questions regarding the date of acquisition.

Example

P (Passing) purchased 100% of S (Score) for $200,000 on January 1, year 1. The book value of S ($150,000) equals the fair value of all of S's assets and liabilities except for equipment, which had an FMV of $100,000 (the carrying value was $80,000). Any excess purchase price is attributed to goodwill. P owes S $10,000 and S has a receivable from P of $10,000.

The decomposition of the purchase price is:

Decompose the purchase price

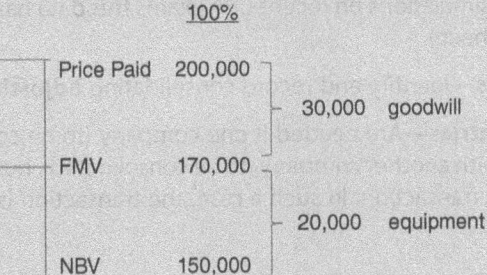

Below are the balance sheets of P and S immediately after the acquisition. The far right-hand columns represent the *consolidated entity* as of **January 1, year 1** (the date of the acquisition).

	Passing		Score		ELIM	CONSOLIDATED	
	Debit	Credit	Debit	Credit		Debit	Credit
Current Assets	80,000		30,000			100,000[1]	
Inventory	150,000		350,000			500,000	
Equipment (Net)	430,000		80,000			530,000[2]	
Investment in Score	200,000					0	
Goodwill						30,000	
Current Liabilities		150,000		110,000			250,000[3]
Long-Term Debt		460,000		200,000			660,000
Common Stock		200,000		140,000			200,000[4]
Retained Earnings		50,000		10,000			50,000[4]
Totals	860,000	860,000	460,000	460,000		1,160,000	1,160,000

[1] **P's current assets**   80,000
S's current assets   30,000
Less interco AR   (10,000)
Consolidated current assets   100,000

[2] **P's equipment**   430,000
S's equipment   80,000
Plus FMV adjust   20,000
Consolidated equipment   530,000

[3] **P's current liabilities**   150,000
S's current liabilities   110,000
Less interco AP   (10,000)
Consolidated current liabilities   250,000

[4] **Only P's**

VI. Focus on the end result (the consolidated balances) for most of the CPA Exam questions. If you need to complete an entire consolidating worksheet, knowing how to derive the ending balances will help you get to consolidated totals. If you want a refresher on the process of consolidation (or have never studied consolidation in your course work) then you will want to review the following description of the steps to consolidation.

VII. Process Steps to Follow—The steps to be followed in deriving consolidated financial statements from the separate trial balances or statements of the separate companies are:

A. Record Trial Balances—Record account titles and balances on worksheet from trial balance, separate financial statements, or other sources of the separate companies that are to be consolidated. (In simulations on recent CPA Exams this data has been provided in the form of a preprinted worksheet.)

B. Adjusting Entries—Identify and record consolidating **adjusting** entries required, if any:

1. **Adjusting entries**—Are needed if one company (to be consolidated) has recorded a transaction with another company (to be consolidated), but the receiving company has not recorded the transaction. In such a case, the transaction is "in-transit" to the receiving company.

2. **Examples are**

   a. Payment of accounts payable by one company at year-end, but not yet received/ recognized by the other company

   b. Dividend declared by one company (e.g., subsidiary) at year-end, but not yet recognized by the receiving company (e.g., parent)

3. **Rule**—The rule for handling *in-transit* intercompany transactions is to make an adjusting entry on the consolidating worksheet to complete the transaction as though it had been received by the receiving company (i.e., as though the transaction were completed on both sets of books).

   a. **Example**—At the time P acquired S, S had recorded a payment of $5,000 to P on an Accounts Payable; the payment was still in transit (i.e., P had not yet received the payment). What entry would be made **on the consolidating worksheet immediately after the combination** as an adjusting entry?

DR: Cash	$5,000
CR: Accounts Receivable	$5,000

4. **Posting of adjusting entries**—The effects of adjusting entries are eventually posted to the appropriate separate company books as a result of actual completion of the in-transit transaction.

C. Eliminating Entries—Identify and record balance sheet eliminating entries: The common balance sheet eliminating entries at the date of combination are:

1. **Investment elimination entry**—All consolidations **require** an investment elimination entry to eliminate investment in the subsidiary account (brought on to the consolidating worksheet (W/S) by the parent) against the subsidiary's shareholders' equity (brought on to the W/S by the subsidiary).

   a. **Avoids double counting**—This elimination avoids *double counting* that would otherwise result on the consolidated B/S—that is, counting the asset *investment* (from the parent) and the assets and liabilities (from the subsidiary) to which the Investment gives the parent a claim.

b. **Entry when parent owns 100% of subsidiary**—Sample investment elimination (on the consolidating worksheet) when there is no noncontrolling interest (formerly *minority interest*) in the subsidiary:

DR: Common Stock (of subsidiary)

Additional Paid-in Cap (of subsidiary)

Retained Earnings (of subsidiary)

Identifiable Assets (of subsidiary to FV, as needed)

Goodwill (if Investment cost > FV of subsidiary's NA)

CR: Identifiable Liabilities (of subsidiary to FV, as needed)

Investment in subsidiary (from parent's books)

---

   i. In the sample entry, identifiable assets (liabilities) would be debited (credited) if the fair value of identifiable assets (liabilities) is greater than the book value of identifiable assets (liabilities) at the acquisition date.

     1. This debit or credit would be to specific assets or liabilities (for example: inventory, equipment, land, or accounts payable, etc.) to adjust them to fair value (on the worksheet) at the date of the business combination.

     2. If depreciable assets are increased (debited), at the date of acquisition no assessment of impairment is required. (But, at the end of every subsequent period, additional depreciation expense must be taken on the consolidating worksheet).

     3. If the identifiable assets or liabilities had a fair value less than book value, the specific assets or liabilities would be written down to fair value (on the worksheet).

   ii. In the sample entry, goodwill would be debited if the Investment value is greater than the FV of net identifiable assets.

     1. Recall from a prior lesson that *investment value* is the fair value of consideration paid by the acquirer (parent) to acquire the subsidiary plus the fair value of the noncontrolling interest at the acquisition date.

     2. If goodwill is recognized (debited), at the date of acquisition no assessment of impairment is required. (But, at the end of every subsequent period, goodwill must be assessed for impairment; it is not amortized.)

   iii. Allocation assuming fair value exceeds book value of the net identifiable assets at the date of acquisition and that the investment value exceed the fair value of the net (identifiable) assets.

c. **Entry when parent owns less than 100% of subsidiary**—Sample investment elimination entry (on the consolidating worksheet) when there is a noncontrolling interest in the subsidiary.

   i. Subsidiary's shareholder equity not owned by the parent (either directly or indirectly) belongs to the noncontrolling interest.

   ii. It is the **noncontrolling interest (minority) claim** to consolidate net assets attributable to the subsidiary, which includes the subsidiary's net assets at fair value and the full fair value of any goodwill recognized on the acquisition.

iii. Sample entry

DR: Common Stock (of subsidiary)

Add'l Paid-in Cap (of subsidiary)

Retained Earnings (of subsidiary)

Identifiable Assets (of subsidiary to FV, as needed)

Goodwill (if Investment value > FV of subsidiary's NA)

CR: Identifiable Liabilities (of subsidiary to FV, as needed)

Investment in subsidiary (from parent's books)

Noncontrolling Interest (% claim to consolidated net assets attributable to the subsidiary)

iv. **The noncontrolling interest account**—Will show on the consolidated balance sheet as a separate item within shareholders' equity.

2. **Intercompany receivables/payables eliminations**—Receivables and payables between companies being consolidated must be eliminated to the extent the amounts are intercompany (between the companies).

a. **Examples** and the amount to eliminate are:

i. **Accounts receivable/account payable (100%)**—All intercompany receivables and payables between the affiliated firms that exist at the date of the combination must be eliminated.

1. **Illustration facts**—Assume that at the date Company P acquired controlling interest of Company S in a legal acquisition, Company S owed Company P $10,000 for services it had received from Company P. Therefore, the separate companies would bring onto the consolidating worksheet the following balances:

Company P / Receivable from S = $ 10,000

Company S / Payable to Company P = $ 10,000

2. **Eliminating entry**—On the consolidating worksheet, the following eliminating entry would be made:

DR: Payable to P $10,000

CR: Receivable from S $10,000

3. **Consequence**—As a consequence of the eliminating entry, on the consolidating worksheet (and the consolidated financial statements) there will be no receivable/payable between Companies P and S shown; it is as though they are a single entry.

ii. **Interest**—Interest receivable/interest payable (100%): If an intercompany receivable/payable was for interest, an entry similar to the one above would be made for 100% of the intercompany balance.

iii. **Dividends**—Dividends receivable/dividends payable (intercompany %): dividends receivable and dividends payable between the affiliated firms that exist at the date of the combination must be eliminated.

    1. **Illustration facts**—Assume that at the date Company P acquired controlling interest of Company S in a legal acquisition, Company S had a $100,000 dividends payable balance on its books and that Company P owned 5% of Company S just prior to acquiring controlling interest. As a consequence, 5% of Company S's dividends payable is a dividends receivable to Company P. The separate companies would bring onto the consolidating worksheet the following balances:

Company P / Dividends Receivable (from Co. S) = $5,000

Company S / Dividends Payable = $100,000

---

    2. **Eliminating entry**—On the consolidating worksheet the following eliminating entry would be made:

DR: Dividends Payable $5,000

    CR: Dividends Receivable $5,000

---

    3. **Consequence**—As a consequence of the eliminating entry, on the consolidating worksheet (and the consolidated financial statements) Company P's dividends receivable will have been eliminated and Company S's dividends payable will have been reduced to $95,000, the amount due to nonaffiliates. Note that only the intercompany (between P and S) portion of the dividend is eliminated.

iv. **Bonds**—Investment in bonds/bonds payable (intercompany %): Bonds issued by one affiliate (bonds payable) and held by another affiliate (investment in bonds) at the date of the combination must be eliminated against each other.

    1. **Illustration facts**—Assume that at the date Company P acquired controlling interest of Company S in a legal acquisition, Company P already held $100,000 of Company S's bonds, which it had acquired at par ($100,000). Company S had total bonds payable of $1,000,000. Therefore, the separate companies would bring onto the consolidating worksheet the following balances:

Company P / Investment in S Bonds = $100,000

Company S / Bonds Payable (at par) = $1,000,000

---

    2. **Eliminating entry**—On the consolidating worksheet the following eliminating entry would be made:

DR: Bonds Payable $100,000

    CR: Investment in Bonds $100,000

---

    3. **Consequence**—As a consequence of the eliminating entry, on the consolidating worksheet (and the consolidated financial statements) Company P's investment in Company S's bonds will have been eliminated and Company S's bonds payable will have been reduced to $900,000, the amount due to nonaffiliates. Note that only the intercompany (between P and S) portion of the bonds is eliminated.

4. Other eliminations—If either the investment in bonds or the bonds payable accounts had a related premium or discount, these amounts would have been eliminated as well and would have resulted in a gain or loss depending on the nature of the premium or discount (debit or credit). (Eliminating intercompany bonds with premiums or discounts is covered in the following section dealing with the consolidating process following the date of acquisition.)

VIII. **Complete Worksheet**—After the separate company account balances and the adjusting and eliminating entries have been posted to the worksheet, it can be complete, mostly by "adding" across and down.

IX. **Formal Consolidated Statements**—Prepare formal consolidated statements: Once the worksheet is completed, it is the basis for preparing the formal consolidated financial statements.

Consolidation Subsequent to Acquisition

On its books, a parent may carry an investment in a subsidiary to be consolidated using any accounting method it desires because the investment will be eliminated in the consolidating process. The method a parent uses will affect the entries for the investment eliminating entry made on the worksheet in the consolidating process, but will not affect the final consolidated statements— they will be the same regardless of the method used by the parent to carry the investment on its books. While the parent can use any method it chooses to carry the investment, the two traditional methods are the cost method and the equity method. (Those are the only methods assumed on the CPA Exam.) This lesson covers the consolidating process when the parent uses the cost method.

After studying this lesson, you should be able to:

1. Describe the characteristics of the cost method of accounting for an investment.

2. Describe the necessary treatment of the consolidating worksheet when a parent uses the cost method to account for an investment in a subsidiary.

3. Record the adjusting (reciprocity) entry and the investment-eliminating entry on the consolidating worksheet when a parent uses the cost method to account for an investment in a subsidiary.

4. Record other eliminating entries that may be necessary on the consolidating worksheet as a direct result of the investment-eliminating entry.

I. **Consolidation After Acquisition**—After the date of acquisition, the parent company (P) will account for its Investment in S using either the equity method or cost method. Remember that P's stand-alone financial statements are not GAAP compliant because P must consolidate all subsidiaries under its control. In order to consolidate P and S, you must first understand how P accounted for the Investment in S, because upon consolidation the Investment in S is eliminated.

II. **If P uses the Equity Method**—If the equity method is used to carry the investment in the subsidiary, the parent:

   A. *Does* adjust on its books the carrying value of its investment in the subsidiary to reflect:

      1. The parent's share of the subsidiary's income or loss.

> DR: Investment in Subsidiary
>
>   CR: Income from Equity Investment

      2. The parent's share of dividends declared by the subsidiary.

> DR: Dividends Receivable/Cash
>
>   CR: Investment in Subsidiary

      3. The amortization (e.g., "depreciation") of any difference between the FV of identifiable assets (but not goodwill) and the book value of those assets. Example entry (assuming FV > BV):

> DR: Dividends Receivable/Cash
>
>   CR: Investment in Subsidiary

      4. This entry reduces the income recognized from the subsidiary (and the related investment increase) by the amount of "depreciation" the parent must recognize on its fair value greater than book value. Below are the T-accounts on P's books with respect to the equity method accounting for S.

Equity Method Accounting

Investment in S		Income from Equity Investment in S	
Initial investment	P's share of S's dividends	Depreciation/ amortization of purchase price differential	P's % share of S's NI
P's % share of S's NI	Depreciation/ amortization of purchase price differential		
Ending Balance			Ending Balance

Example

P (Passing) purchased 100% of S (Score) for $200,000 on January 1, 20X2. On that date the book value equaled the fair value of all of S's assets and liabilities except for equipment, which had an FMV of $100,000. Any additional excess purchase price is attributed to goodwill. The equipment has a remaining life of four years.

Below, we show the decomposition of the price paid for S and reconstruct the T-accounts for the equity method accounting recorded by P. Understanding the components of the purchase price and the equity method accounting aids understanding of the consolidation.

The decomposition of the purchase price is as follows:

Decompose the Purchase Price

100%

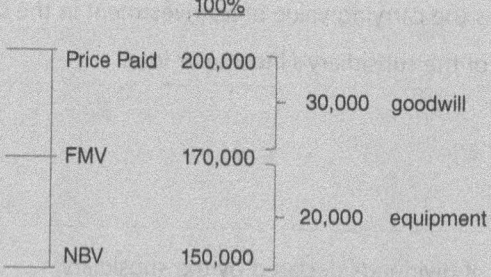

Price Paid 200,000	
	30,000 goodwill
FMV 170,000	
	20,000 equipment
NBV 150,000	

T-Account
Equity Method Accounting

Investment in S		Income from Equity Investment in S	
Cost 200,000	0 dividends		50,000—P's share of S's NI
		Depreciation of equipment 5,000	
P's % S's NI 50,000	5,000 depreciation of equipment		
Ending Balance 245,000			45,000

The consolidating worksheet presents the trial balance of P and S and the Consolidated balances as follows. The consolidating worksheet does not reflect the eliminating entries in the consolidation process. Rather our focus is on the end result after consolidation. The footnotes below show how certain balances were derived.

	Passing		Score		ELIM	CONSOLIDATED	
	Debit	Credit	Debit	Credit		Debit	Credit
Current Assets	80,000		30,000			**110,000**	
Inventory	150,000		350,000			**500,000**	
Equipment (net)	430,000		80,000			**525,000**[1]	
Investment in Score	245,000					**0**	
Goodwill	0		0			**30,000**[2]	
Current Liabilities		150,000		110,000			**260,000**[3]
Long-Term Debt		255,000		150,000			**405,000**
Common Stock		200,000		140,000			**200,000**[4]
Retained Earnings		50,000		10,000			**50,000**
Sales		500,000		75,000			**575,000**
Income from S		45,000					**0**
Expenses	295,000		25,000			**325,000**[3]	
Totals	1,200,000	1,200,000	485,000	485,000		**1,490,000**	**1,490,000**

[1]**P's Equipment**	430,000
S's Equipment	80,000
FMV adjustment	20,000
Depreciation of FMV adj	(5,000)
Total	525,000

[2]**Goodwill**	30,000
Impairment	0
Total	30,000

[3]**P's Expenses**	295,000
S's Expenses	25,000
Depreciation of FMV adj	5,000
Total	325,000
[4]**Only P's**	

NOTE: Push-down accounting would require that S record the fair market revaluations on the general ledger on the date of acquisition. Push down accounting is required for SEC Registrants with 100% owned subsidiaries. Push-down accounting essentially "pushes down" the revaluations on to the general ledger of S so that the revaluations are not allocated during the consolidation process. In the example above, the push-down accounting entry made by S would be:

Equipment 20,000

Goodwill 30,000

Revaluation Capital (an equity account) 50,000

Upon consolidation the revaluation capital account would be eliminated.

III. If P Uses the Cost Method to Account for the Investment in S—In this case the parent:

   A. DOES NOT adjust on its books **the carrying value of its investment in the subsidiary** to reflect:

      1. The parent's share of the subsidiary's income or loss;

      2. The parent's share of dividends **declared by** the subsidiary;

      3. The "depreciation"/amortization of any difference between the fair value of the subsidiary's identifiable net assets and the book value of the subsidiary's identifiable net assets.

   B. DOES recognize its share of dividends declared by the subsidiary **as dividend income** (not as an adjustment to the investment account).

      1. Example entry

> DR: Dividends Receivable/Cash
>   CR: Dividend Income

IV. Investment Elimination—The investment elimination entry is made to eliminate the adjusted Investment account (as of the beginning of year) against the subsidiary Shareholders' Equity (as of the beginning of year).

   A. Sample entry assuming the parent owns 100% of the subsidiary:

> DR: C/S (of subsidiary)
>   Additional Paid-in Capital (of subsidiary)
>   R/E (of subsidiary including change since acquisition)
>   Identifiable Assets (of subsidiary to FV at acquisition, as needed)
>   Goodwill (If Investment > FV of subsidiary's NA at acquisition)
>   CR: Identifiable Liabilities (of subsidiary to FV at acquisition, as needed)
>   Investment in subsidiary

   B. The effects of this entry on the worksheet are to:

      1. Eliminate the investment account of the parent (as of the beginning of the year) against the shareholder equity accounts of the subsidiary (as of the beginning of the year);

      2. Adjust identifiable assets and liabilities of the subsidiary to fair value as of the date of the business combination;

      3. Recognize goodwill, if any, as of the date of the business combination. Goodwill would be recognized at the original amount by which the investment value > FV of identifiable net assets acquired.

V. Fair Value of Subsidiary's Identifiable Assets/Liabilities Different than Book Value—When the fair value of the subsidiary's identifiable assets and/or liabilities are different than the book value at the date of acquisition, depreciation/amortization must be recognized on the worksheet for any amount of Identifiable Assets recognized by the Investment elimination (above).

   A. Recall that the extent to which the parent's investment (and the fair value of noncontrolling interest, if any) as of the acquisition date is greater than the book value of subsidiary's identifiable net assets at the acquisition date is not identified on the separate books.

1. Any difference is implicit in the acquisition date difference between the Investment on the parent's books (plus the noncontrolling interest, if any) and the Shareholders' Equity on the subsidiary's books (which is also the book value of the subsidiary's net assets).

2. It is only when the two values (P's Investment + any noncontrolling interest and S's Shareholders' Equity) are brought together in the Investment elimination entry on the worksheet that the difference becomes explicit. The subsidiary's identifiable assets and liabilities are adjusted to fair value on the worksheet and, if the investment value is different than the resulting net asset value, goodwill (or a bargain purchase gain) is recognized. Any adjustment (increase or decrease) to depreciable or amortizable assets on the worksheet will result in the need for an adjustment (increase or decrease) to depreciation or amortization expense on the worksheet.

B. When the subsidiary's assets are written up to fair value (in the investment elimination entry, for example) it is as though the parent and noncontrolling interest, if any, paid more for the assets than the subsidiary paid for them. Therefore, additional depreciation or amortization must be taken.

C. **Sample Entry on Worksheet (at End of 1st Period)**—Assuming depreciable and amortizable assets were written up as part of the investment eliminating entry:

> DR: Depreciation Expense
>
>   Amortization Expense
>
>   CR: Accumulated Depreciation
>
>   Intangible Assets (Not Goodwill!)

D. **Sample Entry on Worksheet (at End of Subsequent Periods)**—assuming depreciable and amortizable assets were written up as part of the investment eliminating entry:

> DR: Retained Earnings P – Beginning*
>
>   Depreciation Expense**
>
>   Amortization Expense**
>
>   CR: Accumulated Depreciation***
>
> *For expense recognized in prior year(s) on consolidating worksheet(s)
> **For current year expense
> ***For cumulative prior and current amounts

E. If at acquisition the fair value of the subsidiary's identifiable net assets was greater than the parent's investment (plus the fair value of the noncontrolling interest, if any), a bargain purchase would have resulted.

1. In this case, the bargain purchase amount would have been recognized by the parent as a gain in the period of the business combination.

2. At the end of the period of the business combination, the bargain purchase gain would have been closed to the parent's Retained Earnings, and would be included in that Retained Earnings in all subsequent periods.

Consolidation Less than 100% Ownership

In many instances the Parent company purchases less than 100% of the Subsidiary. When P owns more than 50% of S, P will consolidate S to create consolidated statements. The percentage of S not owned by P is reflected in the consolidated financial statements as Noncontrolling Interest (NCI). On the balance sheet NCI is presented in the equity section of the consolidated balance sheet. On the income statement NCI is presented as Income to NCI—a reduction of consolidated net income.

After studying this lesson, you should be able to:

1. Allocate the purchase price for a less than 100% acquisition.

2. Calculate the components of the balance sheet and income statement that would be represented on the consolidated statements with a less than 100% acquisition.

3. Calculate the amount of income to the noncontrolling interest that would be represented on the consolidated income statement.

4. Calculate the amount of equity attributed to the noncontrolling interest on the consolidated balance sheet.

I. **Noncontrolling Interest (NCI)**—If the parent does not own 100% of the subsidiary, the Noncontrolling Interest must be determined and recognized in the consolidated statements.

   A. **Consolidated Income Statement**

   1. For each operating period, the noncontrolling interest percentage claim to consolidated net income will be shown as a separate line item on the consolidated income statement. This account is usually shown as Income to Noncontrolling Interest.

   2. The noncontrolling interest claim to consolidated net income is the noncontrolling interest percentage share of the subsidiary's reported net income, plus (minus) its percentage share of depreciation/amortization expense on fair value in excess of (less than) book value and its percentage share of any other revenues/expenses or gains/losses attributable to the subsidiary recognized on the consolidating worksheet.

   B. **Consolidated Balance Sheet**

   1. On each consolidated balance sheet, the noncontrolling interest will be recognized as a separate line item (e.g., Noncontrolling Interest Equity) in the Shareholders' Equity section.

   2. The amount of the noncontrolling equity interest is the noncontrolling percentage claim to the subsidiary's book value at the acquisition date, plus (minus) its claim to the unamortized difference between fair values and book values at acquisition, plus its claim to goodwill recognized at acquisition, minus its share of any goodwill/impairment /losses.

II. **Determining NCI Equity**

   A. Determining the value of the NCI Equity reported by the consolidated entity can be done via calculation. NCI Equity is represented on the consolidated financial statements and is created during the consolidation process. This account does not exist on the individual financial statements of P or S. The CPA Exam frequently will ask you to provide the value of the NCI Equity or the Income that should be allocated to the NCI. Here we show you how to calculate these values. It is also important because the calculation shows the conceptual relationship between S's NBV and the amount of S's NBV that is allocated to the noncontrolling interest. NCI Equity is the NBV of S that is allocated to the noncontrolling interest and is represented on the consolidated balance sheet.

   B. First determine the NBV of S as of the date of consolidation. Add to S's NBV the 100% purchase price differential less 100% of any depreciation/amortization or goodwill impairment. Multiply the S's adjusted NBV by the NCI % to arrive at NCI Equity. NCI Equity represents the amount of S's NBV allocated to the non-controlling shareholders of S including any FMV adjustments from the date of acquisition.

122

Calculation of Income to NCI	End of Year
S's Net Income	$
Less: Depreciation/amortization of differential	$
Less: Goodwill impairment loss	$
S's adjusted Net Income	$
NCI % ownership of S	%
Income to Noncontrolling Interest	$

C. Often CPA Exam questions will not provide enough information to complete the above calculation. In these cases you can also calculate ending NCI Equity by "rolling forward" the beginning NCI Equity using the following calculation.

Calculation of NCI Equity	End of Year
NCI Equity at the beginning of the year*	$
Plus: NCI % of S's Net Income	
Less: NCI % of S's dividends	
Less: NCI % of Goodwill impairment loss	$
Less: NCI % Depreciation/amortization of differential	$
NCI Equity at the end of the year	$

*Make sure you use the full fair value of the beginning NCI equity. That is, make sure this number includes the NCI share of any fair market revaluations and goodwill from the date of the acquisition.

III. Determining Income to NCI

A. The portion of S's net income that is allocated to the NCI is created during the consolidation process and can be calculated. 100% of S's revenues and expenses are represented on the consolidated income statement. The NCI portion of S's net income that is not available for distribution to the shareholders of P must be subtracted out of total net income.

B. To calculate income to the NCI, start with S's net income and adjust it for the depreciation and/or amortization of the purchase price differential from the date of acquisition. You will also subtract any goodwill impairment loss that occurred during the current year. Once you have S's net income adjusted for the amounts related to the purchase price differential, multiply by the NCI percentage ownership and this will give you the amount of income to the NCI.

Calculation of Income to NCI	End of Year
S's Net Income	$
Less: Depreciation/amortization of differential	$
Less: Goodwill impairment loss	$
S's adjusted Net Income	$
NCI % ownership of S	%
Income to Noncontrolling Interest	$

Example

P (Passing) purchased 80% of S (Score) for $200,000 on January 1, 20X2. On that date the full value of the Noncontrolling interest is $50,000. The book value equaled the fair value of all of S's assets and liabilities except for equipment, which had an FMV of $100,000 (the carrying value of the equipment is $80,000). Any additional excess purchase price is attributed to goodwill. The equipment has a remaining life of four years. During 20X2 S reported net income of $50,000 and did not pay dividends.

Below is the decomposition of the value of S allocated between the controlling and noncontrolling interest. In addition we have reconstructed the T-accounts for the equity method accounting that would have been recorded by P during the year. Understanding the components of the equity method accounting, and tying the ending balances of these T-accounts to the consolidation worksheet, is useful in understanding the consolidations process.

The decomposition of the purchase price is:

	100%	80%	20%
Total	250	200	50
Goodwill	80	64	16
FMV	170	136	34
Equip	20	16	4 (4 yr life)
BV	150	120	30

The decomposition of the purchase price is:

Below are the equity-method accounts:

Equity-Method Accounting

Investment in S		Income from Equity Investment	
Cost 200,000	0 dividends		40,000 P's share of S's NI
	Depreciation of equip 4,000		
P's % of S's NI 40,000	4,000 depreciation equip		
Ending Balance 236,000			36,000

Below is the consolidation worksheet with the trial balance of P and S on December 31, 20X2. The *consolidated entity* as of **December 31, 20X2,** is presented in the final two columns. The focus here is **not** the consolidation process. That is, the focus is not on completion of eliminating entries. The focus is on the ending balances reported by the consolidated entity. The footnotes below the worksheet show the computations to derive the ending balances.

	Passing		Score		Elimination	CONSOLIDATED	
	Debit	Credit	Debit	Credit		Debit	Credit
Current Assets	80,000		30,000			**110,000**	
Inventory	150,000		350,000			**500,000**	
Equipment (net)	430,000		80,000			**525,000**[1]	
Investment in S	236,000					**0**	
Goodwill	0	0				**80,000**[2]	
Current Liabilities		150,000		110,000			**260,000**
Long-Term Debt		260,000		150,000			**410,000**
NCI Equity	0	0					**59,000**[3]
Common Stock		200,000		140,000			**200,000**[4]
Retained Earnings		50,000		10,000			**50,000**
Sales		500,000		75,000			**575,000**
Income from S		36,000					**0**
Expenses	300,000		25,000			**330,000**[5]	
Income to NCI	0	0				**9,000**[4]	
Totals	1,196,000	1,196,000	485,000	485,000		**1,554,000**	**1,554,000**

[1]**Equipment**

P's equipment	430,000
S's equipment	80,000
FMV adjustment	20,000
Depreciation	(5,000)
Total	525,000

[2]**Goodwill**

Beg. balance	80,000
Impairment	(0)
Total	80,000

[3]**NCI Equity**

Book Value of SNaN	200,000
FMV adjustment	100,000
Depreciation	(5,000)
Total	295,000
NCI %	x .20
NCI Equity	59,000

*Note: S's ending Net Book Value (NBV) is beginning NBV plus Net Income less Dividends. In this example beginning NBV $150,000 (140,000 CS + 10,000 RE) plus NI (75,000 Sales − 25,000 Expenses) = Ending NBV $200,000.

[4]Income to NCI

S's NI	50,000
FMV Depreciation	(5,000)
	45,000
NCI %	x .20
Income to NCI	9,000

[5]Expenses

P's expenses	300,000
S's expenses	25,000
Depreciation	5,000
Total	330,000

Intercompany (I/C) Transactions and Balances

Intercompany I/C Transactions and Balances— Introduction

Transactions between entities that are to be consolidated are referred to as "intercompany transactions," or "transactions between affiliated companies." To the extent the entities being consolidated have intercompany transactions, or account balances that resulted from intercompany transactions, those transactions or balances have to be eliminated in the consolidating process. This lesson provides an overview of the elimination of intercompany transactions in the consolidating process.

After studying this lesson, you should be able to:

1. Describe the conceptual basis for the elimination of intercompany transactions.

2. Identify the primary types of intercompany transactions and balances that will need to be eliminated in preparing consolidated financial statements.

3. Describe how intercompany receivables/payables and intercompany revenues/expenses come about.

4. Record the entries required on the consolidating worksheet to eliminate intercompany receivables/payables and revenues/expenses.

I. **Conceptual Basis**

   A. From the perspective of the **separate legal entities**, transactions between them, and the related gains/losses and changes in account balances, should be recognized on their separate books. Even if the parent owns less than 100% of the subsidiary (but more than 50% as required for consolidation)—the entire amount of the intercompany transaction must be eliminated.

   B. For **consolidated financial statements** purposes the separate entities are treated as a single economic entity. As a consequence, only transactions with nonaffiliates should be recognized in consolidating financial statements.

   C. The results of transactions with other entities to be included in the consolidated financial statements must be eliminated, including the results of:

      1. Transactions between a parent and its subsidiaries

      2. Transactions between affiliated subsidiaries

   D. The kinds of transactions (and their related consequences) that must be eliminated, and those not to be eliminated, can be illustrated as follows:

PS Consolidation

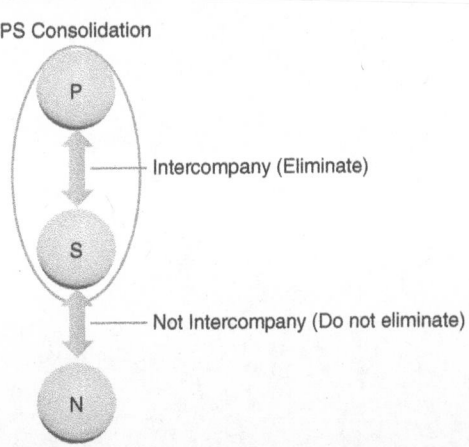

Intercompany (Eliminate)

Not Intercompany (Do not eliminate)

II. **Intercompany Items**

   A. The primary types of intercompany transactions and related intercompany balances are:

      1. Receivable/payables

      2. Revenues/expenses

      3. Inventory

      4. Fixed assets

      5. Bonds

III. **I/C Receivables and Payables**

   A. Recall that intercompany receivables and payables result from one affiliated company providing goods or services to another affiliated company and permitting the buying affiliated to "charge" the amount owed.

Example

Assume that, during the period, Company P, the parent company, provided services to its subsidiary, Company S, and that Company S owed Company P $10,000 for those services at the end of the period. Each company would bring the following account balances onto the consolidating worksheet:

Company P / Receivable from S = $10,000 (DR)

Company S / Payable to P = $10,000 (CR)

On the consolidating worksheet the following eliminating entry would be required so that no intercompany receivable or payable will show on the consolidated financial statements:

DR:	Payable to P	$10,000
	CR: Receivable from S	$10,000

   B. Typical intercompany accounts receivable/accounts payable and the amount of each to eliminate are:

      1. (Trade) Accounts Receivable/Accounts Payable (100%): The full amount of the intercompany receivable and intercompany payable must be eliminated.

      2. Loan Receivable/Loan Payable

      3. Interest Receivable/Interest Payable (100%)

      4. Dividends Receivable (100%)/Dividends Payable (Intercompany %): Note that only the intercompany amount of the dividends payable must be eliminated. Any dividend payable to noncontrolling shareholders will not be eliminated.

IV. I/C Revenues and Expenses

A. Recall that intercompany revenues and expenses result from one affiliated company providing services for a fee to another affiliated company.

Example

Assume that, during the period, Company P, the parent company, provided services to its subsidiary, Company S for $10,000. Each company would bring the following account balances onto the consolidating worksheet:

Company P / I/C Revenue (from S) = $10,000 (CR)

Company S / I/C Expense (to P) = $10,000 (DR)

On the consolidating worksheet the following eliminating entry would be required so that no intercompany revenue or expense will show on the consolidated financial statements:

DR: I/C Revenue (from S) $10,000

CR: I/C Expense (to P) $10,000

B. The full amount (100%) of intercompany revenues and expenses must be eliminated, even if the original transaction occurred at no profit to the "selling" affiliate.

C. Typical intercompany revenues and expenses and the amount of each to eliminate are:

1. Management Services Expense/Management Services Revenue (100%)

2. Interest Expense/Interest Revenue (100%)

Intercompany (I/C) Inventory Transactions

When one affiliated entity sells inventory (finished goods, raw materials, etc.) to another affiliated entity, an intercompany inventory transaction has occurred. Intercompany transactions need to be eliminated and the account balances adjusted to the values as if the transaction did not occur. This lesson identifies the accounts that will be affected, and describes and illustrates the eliminations that are needed on the consolidating worksheet.

After studying this lesson, you should be able to:

1. Identify the accounts affected by intercompany inventory transactions.

2. Analyze facts and calculate the amounts needed to be eliminated for intercompany inventory transactions under various circumstances, including:

   - when intercompany inventory transactions occur at cost,

   - when intercompany inventory transactions occur at more (or less) than cost,

   - when intercompany balances are in ending inventory and/or in beginning inventory,

   - when intercompany sales are made by a parent (to a subsidiary) or by a subsidiary (to a parent), and

   - when intercompany sales by a subsidiary are from a 100% owned subsidiary or less than 100% owned subsidiary.

3. Record intercompany inventory eliminations on a consolidating worksheet under the various circumstances identified above.

I. Objective

   A. ALL intercompany transactions *must be removed (eliminated)* as if the transaction never occurred. You cannot have a transaction with YOURSELF! Transactions of the consolidated entity are ONLY those with outside third parties.

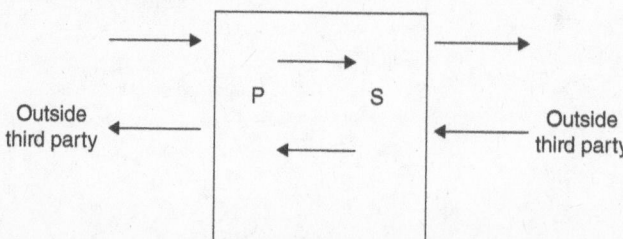

II. Terms and Concepts

   A. Intercompany Transactions—Include buying, selling, and transfers. They also include the profits or losses and the outstanding balances that result from these transactions.

   1. A **downstream** transaction is when the parent sells to the subsidiary. Any intercompany profit that results from the sale will be on the books of the parent.

   2. An **upstream** transaction is when the subsidiary sells to the parent. Any intercompany profit that results from the sale will be on the books of the subsidiary.

   3. A transaction may also be between two subsidiaries with a common parent, or any other combination of tiering the transaction.

III. **Accounts Affected**—Intercompany inventory transactions affect the following accounts:

    A. **Sales/Cost of Goods Sold**—The level of sales and cost of goods sold (COGS) (of the selling affiliate) are overstated because for consolidated purposes it is as though no sale occurred and, therefore, the effects of the sale should be eliminated.

    B. **Inventory**—Any intercompany profit (or loss) in the ending inventory of the buying affiliate overstates(or understates) the carrying value of that inventory for consolidated purposes and should be eliminated.

IV. Tool to use to help you organize information and answer questions:

Diagram:

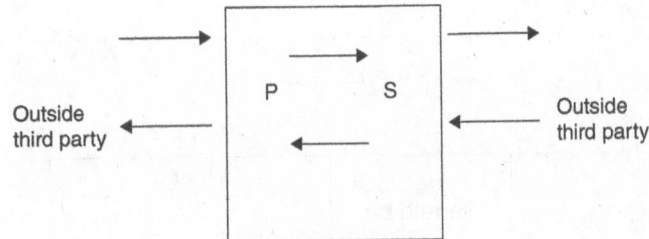

Tables to organize data:

What is				
		What is		
	Should be	P	S	Difference
Sales				
COGS				
Inventory				

V. Example Application Using Tools

Example

P purchased inventory for $16,000, and sold it to S for $20,000 (Gross profit = 20% = 4,000 / 20,000).

S purchased inventory for $20,000 and sold it to P for $38,000 (Gross profit = 47.4% = 18,000 / 38,000)

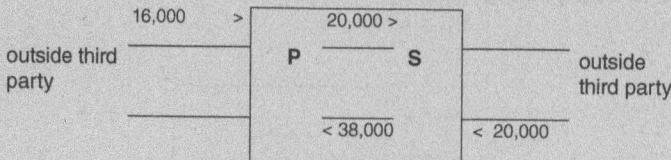

Downstream:

		What is		
	Should be	P	S	Difference
Sales	0	20,000	0	20,000 DR
COGS	0	16,000	0	16,000 CR
Inventory	16,000	0	20,000	4,000 CR

Upstream:

		What is		
	Should be	P	S	Difference
Sales	0	0	38,000	38,000 DR
COGS	0	0	20,000	20,000 CR
Inventory	20,000	38,000	0	18,000 CR

A. The following sections of this lesson present a step-by-step walk-through of the elimination of intercompany inventory transactions. Use the method/technique that works best for you!

VI. Elimination of Intercompany Sales/COGS

A. For **consolidated purposes**, sales by one affiliate to another affiliate will overstate sales and cost of goods sold brought onto the worksheet by the selling affiliate and, if the inventory was sold between the affiliates at a profit, overstate inventory (or purchases) brought onto the worksheet by the buying affiliate.

1. Sales and cost of goods sold (or purchases) for consolidated purposes should consist only of the effects of sales to and purchases from nonaffiliates.

2. Even though they may have no effect on consolidated net income (because the sale was at cost to the selling affiliate), intercompany sales and cost of goods sold (or purchases) overstate the absolute amount of sales and cost of goods sold (or purchases) for consolidated purposes and, therefore, must be eliminated against each other to prevent incorrect values for ratios and other analytical purposes.

B. Illustration—I/C Sale with NO Profit—Assume Company P sold inventory that cost it $8,000 to its 100% owned subsidiary, Company S, for $8,000 cash (P to S = a downstream sale). Entries made by the respective companies on their books would be:

Company P		
DR: Cash	$8,000	
CR: Sale		$8,000
DR: COGS	$8,000	
CR: Inventory		$8,000
Company S		
DR: Inventory	$8,000	
CR: Cash		$8,000

1. Because Company P sold the goods at its cost, there is no intercompany profit in the sales, cost of goods sold or in the inventory held by Company S.

2. All the resulting balances are brought on to the consolidating worksheet by the separate companies at year's end.

C. Eliminating Entry—Even though the intercompany sale resulted in no net profit or loss, on the consolidating worksheet, the following eliminating entry would be made to eliminate (only) the intercompany sale/COGS. (The eliminating entry for intercompany profit and profit in ending inventory will be illustrated in the following subsection.)

	Should be	What is		Difference
		P	S	
Sales	0	8,000	0	8,000 DR
COGS	0	8,000	0	8,000 CR
Inventory	8,000	0	8,000	0

DR: Sales	$8,000	
CR: COGS		$8,000

1. This elimination is a reversal of the original intercompany sale and COGS.

2. As a consequence of this eliminating entry, on the consolidating worksheet (and consolidated financial statements) no sales or COGS results from transactions between the affiliated companies; it is as though they never occurred.

3. The same kind of eliminating entry (i.e., same DR and CR at the amount of intercompany sale) would be made if all the intercompany inventory had been resold by the buying affiliate to nonaffiliates during the period of intercompany sale.

VII. IC Sales with Profit/Loss—Elimination of intercompany inventory profit (or loss) in ending inventory:

   A. Ending Inventory Value—Profit (or loss) recognized on an intercompany sale that is related to inventory **that has not been resold** (to a non-affiliate) by the buying affiliate, will also overstate (or understate) the carrying value of the remaining intercompany ending inventory (as brought onto the worksheet by the buying affiliate).

   B. Illustration Facts—Assume Company P sold inventory that cost it $8,000 to its 100% owned subsidiary, Company S, for $12,000 cash (P to S = a downstream sale). Entries made by the respective companies on their books would be:

Company P		
DR: Cash	$12,000	
CR: Sale		$12,000
DR: COGS	$8,000	
CR: Inventory		$8,000
Company S		
DR: Inventory	$12,000	
CR: Cash		$12,000

1. Because Company P sold the goods to Company S at more than its (P's) cost, the inventory carrying value to Company S includes an intercompany profit that must be eliminated for consolidated purposes.

2. All the resulting balances are brought on to the consolidating worksheet by the separate companies at year's end.

   C. Eliminating Entry—On the consolidating worksheet, the following eliminating entries (or combined entry) would be made to simultaneously eliminate the intercompany sales, intercompany cost of goods sold, and intercompany profit in ending inventory (i.e., intercompany inventory not resold.)

     1. **Illustration #1**—Assume from the example that 100% (all) of the intercompany inventory is still in the buying affiliate's inventory (on hand) at year end:

Company P Sales Price (to Co. S)	$12,000
Company P COGS (from nonaffiliate)	8,000
Intercompany Profit (all on hand)	$ 4,000

2. Entries to eliminate intercompany sales/COGS and profit in ending inventory:

DR: Sales (I/S)	$12,000
CR: COGS (I/S)	$12,000
DR: COGS (I/S)	$4,000
CR: Inventory (B/S)	$4,000

a. In the first entry, the debit to sales and credit to COGS have the effect of eliminating (reversing) the intercompany amounts brought onto the worksheet by the selling affiliate.

b. In the second entry, the debit to COGS (an I/S account) reduces consolidated net income by $4,000 (the unrealized profit in intercompany inventory) and the credit to Inventory eliminates the intercompany profit of $4,000 from ending inventory brought onto the worksheet by the buying affiliate.

c. The two eliminating entries shown above could be (and often are) combined into a single entry, as follows:

		What is		
	Should be	P	S	Difference
Sales	0	12,000	0	12,000 DR
COGS	0	8,000	0	8,000 CR
Inventory	8,000	0	12,000	4,000 CR

DR: Sales (I/S)	$12,000
CR: COGS (Inventory—I/S)	$8,000
CR: Inventory (B/S)	$4,000

d. As a consequence of the eliminating entries (or entry), no intercompany sales or COGS are recognized from the intercompany transaction and the inventory would be reported at its cost from a nonaffiliate, $8,000.

3. Illustration #2—Assume from the example above that 50% (half) of the intercompany inventory has been resold and, therefore, only 50% is still in the buying affiliates inventory (on-hand) at year-end. S sold the inventory for $10,000:

Company P Sales Price (to Co. S)	$12,000
Company P COGS (from nonaffiliate)	8,000
Total Intercompany Profit	$ 4,000
% of Intercompany Inventory on hand	× .50
Intercompany Profit to eliminate	$ 2,000

4. Entries to eliminate intercompany sale/COGS and profit in ending inventory:

DR: Sales (I/S)	$12,000	
CR: COGS (Inventory—I/S)		$12,000
DR: COGS (I/S)	$2,000	
CR: Inventory (B/S)		$2,000

a. In the first entry, the debit to sales and credit to COGS have the effects of eliminating (reversing) the intercompany amounts brought onto the worksheet by the selling affiliate.

b. In the second entry, the debit to COGS (an I/S account) reduces consolidated net income by $2,000 (the unrealized profit in ending inventory) and the credit to Inventory eliminates from the remaining ending inventory the intercompany profit of $2,000 brought onto the worksheet by the buying affiliate.

c. No intercompany profit-eliminating entry is required for the goods that have already been resold and therefore, are not in ending inventory.

d. The two eliminating entries present above could be (and often are) combined into a single entry:

		What is		
			What is	
	Should be	P	S	Difference
Sales	10,000	12,000	10,000	12,000 DR
COGS	4,000	8,000	6,000	10,000 CR
Inventory	4,000	0	6,000	2,000 CR

DR: Sales (I/S)	$12,000	
CR: COGS (I/S)(+$2,000 − $12,000)		$10,000
CR: Inventory (B/S)		$2,000

e. The correctness of the above entries can be confirmed by looking at the resulting balances on the consolidating worksheet after the eliminating entries are recorded:

i. Intercompany sales are $0 (zero).

ii. Cost of goods sold is : DR. $8,000 (P) + $6,000 (S) + $2,000 (E) – CR. $12,000 (E) =$4,000, the cost from a nonaffiliated of 1/2 the inventory now sold (1/2 × $8,000 = $4,000).

> **Note**
> S's selling price to an outside third party will always be the amount reported on the consolidated statements. So if you are not given the selling price to the third party, it doesn't matter, because the selling price you want to eliminate is just the price from P to S.

1. The $8,000 in COGS is the cost to P from a nonaffiliated recognized when it sold the inventory to S.

2. The $6,000 in COGS is 1/2 the $12,000 cost to S of the inventory acquired from P and recognized as COGS when it sold half the goods to nonaffiliates.

3. The $2,000 and $12,000 are the eliminating entries (E) posted to COGS.

VIII. **Sale by Subsidiary to Parent**—Intercompany Inventory Sale by subsidiary to parent: The prior illustrations assumed that the sale was made by the parent company to a subsidiary—a downstream sale. If a subsidiary sells to its parent, the transaction is an upstream sale. The intercompany elimination for upstream sales depends, in part, on the parent's percentage ownership of the subsidiary.

    A. **Parent owns 100% of the subsidiary**

        1. **Eliminate sales/COGS**—All the intercompany sale/COGS would be eliminated as above. It is a mere reversal of the original intercompany sale and cost of goods sold.

        2. **Profit elimination**—All the intercompany profit and profit in ending inventory carrying value would be eliminated as above and would reduce the parent's claim to net income and asset (inventory) carrying value, since there are no noncontrolling claims to the subsidiary.

    B. **Parent Owns Less than 100% of the Subsidiary—If You Have a Worksheet Without Income Statement**—If the elimination occurs on a consolidating worksheet that does not include an income statement (i.e., only a balance sheet is provided), the elimination would be allocated on the worksheet between the parent and the noncontrolling shareholders' interest in proportion to their respective ownership percentages.

        1. **Eliminate sale/COGS**—All the intercompany sale/COGS would be eliminated as above. It is a mere reversal of the original intercompany sale and cost of goods sold.

        2. **Profit elimination**—All the intercompany profit and the profit in ending inventory would be eliminated, but the profit elimination would be allocated between the parent and the noncontrolling shareholders' interest in proportion to their respective ownership percentages as part of the allocation of net income.

            a. **Worksheet with income statement**—If the elimination occurs on a consolidating worksheet that includes an income statement, the elimination would be the same as presented above to eliminate intercompany profit in ending inventory:

> DR: COGS (I/S)
>
>   CR: Inventory (B/S)

                i. Eliminating entry on worksheet with balance sheet only. Assume that P owns 80% and noncontrolling interest owns 20% of the subsidiary.

> DR: Retained Earnings—P $3,200
>
> DR: Noncontrolling Interest   800
>
>   CR: Inventory (B/S) $4,000

                ii. The debits reduce Company P's consolidated retained earnings ($3,200) and noncontrolling interest ($800); the credit eliminates the profit in ending inventory ($4,000), all on the consolidated balance sheet.

C. Illustration facts—Assume Company P owns 80% of its subsidiary, Company S. Company S sold inventory that cost it $8,000 to Company P for $12,000 cash (an upstream sale). All the inventory is still held by Company P at year's end. The elimination of intercompany profit in ending inventory would be allocated as follows:

Parent	.80 × $4,000 =	$3,200
Noncontrolling Interest	.20 × $4,000 =	800
Total Profit Eliminated		$ 4,000

D. Eliminating entry on worksheet with balance sheet only:

DR: Retained Earnings—P	$3,200
DR: Noncontrolling Interest	800
CR: Inventory (B/S)	$4,000

E. The debits reduce Company P's consolidated retained earnings ($3,200) and noncontrolling interest ($800); the credit eliminates the profit in ending inventory ($4,000), all on the consolidated balance sheet.

IX. Eliminate Profit/Loss in Beginning Inventory—Elimination of intercompany inventory profit (or loss) in beginning inventory:

A. Profit/Loss Remain—Because the intercompany inventory profit (or loss) eliminated from ending inventory (illustrated above) occurs ONLY on the consolidating worksheet, the intercompany profit (or loss) will remain:

1. On the books of the selling affiliate as an element of profit (or loss) closed to its retained earnings;

2. On the books of the buying affiliate as an overstatement (or understatement) of its beginning inventory for the subsequent period.

B. Eliminate on Worksheet—The intercompany profit (or loss) in retained earnings and beginning inventory will be brought onto the consolidating worksheet of the subsequent period by the selling and buying affiliate, respectively, and must be eliminated on the worksheet.

C. Eliminating Entry—On the subsequent consolidating worksheet, the following eliminating entry would be made to simultaneously eliminate the intercompany profit in (beginning) retained earnings (of the selling affiliate) and the overstatement of the beginning inventory (of the buying affiliate):

DR: Retained Earnings
    CR: Inventory—Beginning (I/S)

1. If a loss in intercompany inventory had been eliminated in the prior period, the debit and credit would be reversed.

2. The amount of intercompany profit (or loss) in retained earnings and beginning inventory to be eliminated is the same amount as eliminated in the ending inventory of the prior period.

3. The debit to retained earnings eliminates the intercompany profit recognized in the prior period on the books of the selling affiliate and brought on to the worksheet of the current period in its (selling affiliates) retained earnings; the credit to beginning inventory as reported on the worksheet income statement eliminates the intercompany profit in the beginning inventory shown on the books of the buying affiliate and brought on to the worksheet of the current period.

4. The credit to beginning inventory on the consolidating worksheet causes a reduction in beginning inventory in the income statement section of the worksheet that reduces cost of goods sold as follows (using assumed amounts, including intercompany profit in beginning inventory of $20,000):

	Without Elimination		With Elimination
Begin Inventory	$120,000	<———>	$100,000
+ Purchases	100,000		100,000
= Available for Sale	$220,000		$200,000
− Ending Inventory	50,000		50,000
= Cost of Goods Sold	$170,000		$150,000

a. The credit to beginning inventory in the income statement section (and the resulting reduction in cost of goods sold) causes the intercompany profit eliminated (deferred) in the prior period to be treated as though it is confirmed (recognized) in the subsequent period.

b. If the intercompany inventory on hand at the beginning of the period is not sold to a nonaffiliate as of the end of the period, the related intercompany profit will be eliminated (deferred) again as part of the elimination of intercompany profit in ending inventory of that period.

Intercompany (I/C) Fixed Asset Transactions

When one affiliated entity sells fixed assets to another affiliated entity, an intercompany fixed asset transaction has occurred. This transaction needs to be eliminated and the account balances brought to the balances as if the transaction had not occurred. This lesson identifies the accounts that will be affected and illustrates the adjustments or eliminations that will be needed on the consolidating worksheet.

After studying this lesson, you should be able to:

1. Identify the accounts affected by intercompany fixed-asset transactions.

2. Analyze facts and calculate the amounts needed to be eliminated for intercompany fixed asset transactions under various circumstances, including:

   - for the effects of intercompany fixed asset transactions in the period of the transfer and on post-transfer depreciation expense and accumulated depreciation,

   - when intercompany fixed asset sales are made by a parent (to a subsidiary) or by a subsidiary (to a parent), and

   - when intercompany fixed asset sales by a subsidiary are from a 100% owned subsidiary or less than 100% owned subsidiary.

3. Record intercompany fixed-asset eliminations on a consolidating worksheet under the various circumstances identified above.

I. Objective

A. **ALL** intercompany transactions **must be removed (eliminated)** as if the transaction never occurred. You cannot have a transaction with YOURSELF! Transactions of the consolidated entity are ONLY those with outside third parties.

B. Transfer of a depreciable or nondepreciable asset between parent and subsidiary for anything other than original cost must be stated on the consolidated trial balance as if the transfer had not occurred.

II. Accounts Affected—Intercompany fixed asset transactions affect the following accounts:

A. **Fixed Asset**—Any gain (or loss) recognized by the selling affiliate will cause the cost to the buying affiliate to overstate (or understate) the carrying value of the asset for consolidated purposes and must be corrected so that the asset is reported at original cost from a nonaffiliate.

B. **Accumulated Depreciation**—The sale of the fixed asset will cause the selling affiliate to write off its accumulated depreciation (on the asset sold), which will understate accumulated depreciation for consolidated purposes; the accumulated depreciation should be reinstated.

C. **Depreciation Expense/Accumulated Depreciation**—Any gain (or loss) included in the cost to the buying affiliate will cause subsequent depreciation taken by the buying affiliate and brought onto the consolidating worksheet to overstate (or understate) depreciation expense and accumulated depreciation for consolidated purposes in each subsequent period; these elements must be adjusted.

D. Tools to use to help you organize information and answer questions:

   1. Diagrams:

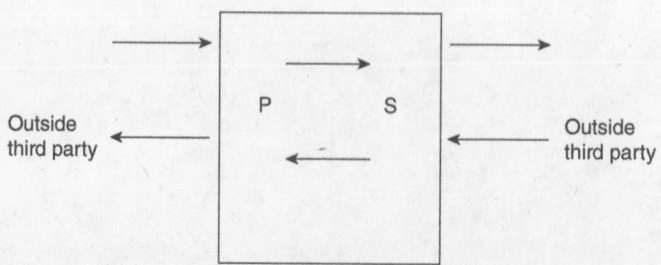

2. Tables to organize data:

	Should be	What is	Difference
Equipment			
Accum Depr			
Depr Expense			
Gain on Sale			

E. Nondepreciable Assets

1. Suppose on December 31, P sold land to S for $150,000. The land originally cost P $130,000. S still holds the land.

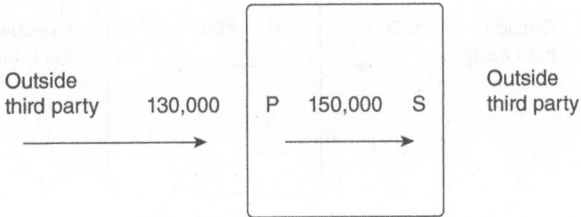

2. To understand the transaction, it helps to first evaluate the journal entries each company made at the date of the sale. Here are the entries that P and S would have made on December 31.

On P's Books
DR: Cash   150,000
     CR: Land   130,000
     Gain on Sale   20,000

On S's Books
DR: Land   150,000
     CR: Cash   150,000

3. To help keep straight what the consolidated amount should be, prepare a table that compares the original asset basis to the intercompany asset basis.

	Should be	What is	Difference
Land	130,000	150,000	20,000 CR
Gain on Sale	0	20,000	20,000 DR

4. If this transaction had never occurred, Land "Should be" $130,000 on the consolidated financial; therefore, $130,000 is in the "Should be" column. Because of the intercompany transaction, the Land "Is" recorded on S's books at $150,000. P recorded a gain as a result of this transaction, and there should be no gain because from the consolidated perspective you cannot have a transaction with yourself! To adjust the asset to $130,000 the eliminating entry is a credit land for $20,000 and a debit to Gain on sale.

5. In the years subsequent to the intercompany sale, the Land will be adjusted each year on the consolidating worksheet. The offset to the adjustment of the Land will be to Retained Earnings. The gain in the year of sale would have been closed to the seller's Retained Earnings (in this case P's Retained Earnings). During the consolidation process, the following eliminating entry would be made each year that the land is still held by the buyer (in this case S).

DR: Retained Earnings	20,000	
CR: Land		20,000

III. Depreciable Assets

A. Now suppose on December 31, P sold equipment to S for $7,000, and the equipment originally cost $9,000. The equipment had an original life of 10 years and P held the equipment for 3 years before the sale to S.

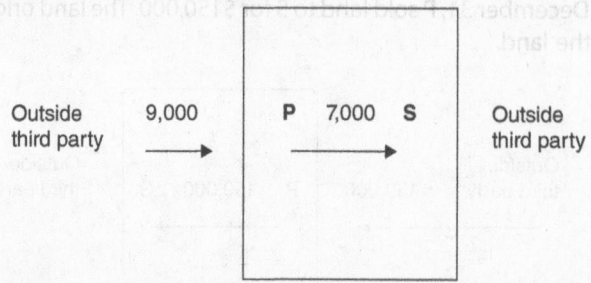

B. To understand the transaction, it helps to first evaluate the journal entries each company made at the date of the sale. Here are the entries that P and S would have made on December 31..

Original cost to P	9,000	NBV	6,300
Less AD (900 × 3 yrs)	(2,700)	Selling Price	7,000
NBV	6,300	Gain on Sale	700

On P's Books

DR: Depreciation Expense	900	
CR: Accumulated Depreciation		900
DR: Cash	7,000	
Accumulated Depreciation	2,700	
CR: Equipment		9,000
Gain on Sale		700

On S's Books

DR: Equipment	7,000	
CR: Cash		7,000

	Should be	What is	Difference
Equipment	9,000	7,000	2,000 DR
Accum Depr	2,700	0	2,700 CR
Depr Expense	900	900	0
Gain on Sale	0	700	700 DR

142

1. The eliminating entry in year 1 is the "difference" column:

Equipment	2,000	
Gain on Sale	700	
Accumulated Depreciation		2,700

2. The table for year 2 would appear as follows:

	Should be	What is	Difference
Equipment	9,000	7,000	2,000 DR
Accum Depr	3,600	1,000	2,600 CR
Depr Expense	900	1,000	100 CR
Retained Earnings	–	–	700 DR

Note

The intercompany gain on the date of sale, divided by the remaining useful live of the asset, will always equal the difference in depreciation taken by the buyer and seller (this holds true only if the useful life of the asset remains unchanged). This calculation will serve as a check figure for the Should Be/What Is/Difference table.

IV. Summary of Intercompany Sales of Depreciable Assets

The table below summarizes the impact of an upstream or downstream sale on various calculations and on the consolidating entries in both the year of the intercompany sale and the years after the intercompany sale. The first column shows the impact on the calculation of Consolidated Net Income (CNI), Income to the Controlling Interest (CI), and Income to the Noncontrolling Interest (NCI). The second column shows the impact on the calculation of the Noncontrolling Interest Equity (NCI Equity). The third column shows the impact on the consolidating entries.

CY = Current year: PY= Prior Year: NI = Net Income: EOY = End of year:

A. Downstream (P sells to S):

	Calculation of CNI, CI, NCI	Calculation of NCI Equity	Consolidating Entries
Year of sale	1. Adjust P's independent NI for CY gain or loss 2. Adjust P's independent NI for CY depreciation adjustment (if sale is not at EOY)	N/A	Eliminate intercompany gain or loss, adjust asset basis, accumulated depreciation, and depreciation expense
Years after sale	Adjust P's independent NI for CY depreciation adjustment	N/A	Eliminate prior year intercompany gain or loss through retained earnings, adjust asset basis, accumulated depreciation, and depreciation expense

B. Upstream (S sells to P)

	Calculation of CNI, CI, NCI	Calculation of NCI Equity	Consolidating Entries
Year of sale	1. Adjust S's independent NI for CY gain or loss 2. Adjust S's independent NI for CY depreciation adjustment (if sale is not at EOY)	1. Adjust S's NBV for CY gain or loss 2. Adjust S's NBV for CY depreciation adjustment (if sale is not at EOY)	Eliminate intercompany gain or loss, adjust asset basis, accumulated depreciation, and depreciation expense
Years after sale	Adjust S's independent NI for CY depreciation adjustment	1. Adjust S's NBV for PY gain or loss 2. Adjust S's NBV for PY PLUS CY depreciation adjustment	Eliminate prior year intercompany gain or loss through retained earnings and NCI equity, adjust asset basis, accumulated depreciation, and depreciation expense

C. The following sections of this lesson present a step-by-step walk through of the elimination of intercompany fixed asset transactions. Use the method/technique that works best for you.

V. **Elimination of Intercompany Gain (or Loss) and Reinstatement of Accumulated Depreciation— In Year of Intercompany Transactions**

A. **Illustration Facts**—Assume that on January 2, 20X1 Company P sold a depreciable fixed asset to its 100% owned subsidiary, Company S, for $30,000 cash (P to S = a downstream sale). At the time of the sale, the asset had the following values on Company P's books:

Original Cost	$40,000
Accumulated Depreciation	15,000
Net Book Value	$25,000

1. The asset net book value had an original expected life of 8 years, no expected residual value, and is being depreciated using the straight-line method. Entries made by the respective companies on their books to record the intercompany sale would be:

Company P		
DR: Cash	$30,000	
DR: Accumulated Depreciation	15,000	
CR: Fixed Asset		$40,000
CR: Gain on Sale		5,000
Company S		
DR: Fixed Asset	$30,000	
CR: Cash		$30,000

2. All the resulting balances are brought onto the consolidating worksheet by the separate companies at year's end.

B. Eliminating Entry—On the consolidating worksheet, the following eliminating entry would be made to simultaneously eliminate the intercompany gain, reinstate the carrying value of the asset to its cost to the parent from a nonaffiliate, and reinstate the accumulated depreciation: (The eliminating entry for overstated depreciation expense and accumulated depreciation taken by the purchasing subsidiary will be illustrated in the following section.)

DR: Fixed Asset	$10,000	
DR: Gain on Sale	5,000	
CR: Accumulated Depreciation		$15,000

1. This eliminating entry on the consolidating worksheet will:

    a. Reestablish the fixed asset to its original cost from a nonaffiliate—$40,000

    b. Eliminate the gain of $5,000 brought onto the consolidating worksheet by the selling affiliate—Company P

    c. Reestablish the accumulated depreciation as of the date of the intercompany sale to the amount based on original cost—$15,000

2. As a consequence of this eliminating entry, on the consolidating worksheet (and consolidated financial statements) the intercompany gain will have been eliminated and the fixed asset and related accumulated depreciation will be reported at amounts based on original cost from a non-affiliate.

VI. Elimination of Overstated (or Understated) Depreciation Expense and Accumulated Depreciation

A. Illustration Facts (continued from above): Company S would record on its books the depreciable fixed asset purchased from its Parent at $30,000. It elects to continue to use straight-line depreciation with no expected residual value over the remaining 5 years of the asset life. Therefore, each year Company S would record depreciation expense of $6,000 ($30,000/5 yrs.) as follows:

DR: Depreciation Expense	$6,000	
CR: Accumulated Depreciation		$6,000

1. These amounts would be brought onto the consolidating worksheet by Company S.

B. Analysis of Facts—On the books of the selling affiliate (prior to the intercompany sale) the asset had a book value of $25,000 (cost $40,000—accumulated depreciation $15,000 = $25,000), which would have been depreciated at the rate of $5,000 per year ($25,000/5 yrs.).

1. Because the purchase price to the buying affiliate included a $5,000 intercompany profit (Cost $30,000 – BV $25,000 = $5,000) the buying affiliate will recognize depreciation expense on its books (and brought onto the worksheet) of $6,000 per year ($30,000/5 yrs.).

2. The extra $1,000 per year is attributable to the intercompany profit ($5,000) depreciated over 5 years. In summary, an analysis for each year shows:

Depreciation after the intercompany transaction	=	$6,000
Depreciation based on original cost	=	5,000
Excess depreciation expenses (per year)	=	$1,000

3. The excess depreciation expense (and related accumulated depreciation) must be eliminated on the consolidating worksheet.

C. Eliminating Entry—On the consolidating worksheet the following eliminating entry would be made to reduce the depreciation expense and the related accumulated depreciation:

> DR: Accumulated Depreciation $1,000
> CR: Depreciation Expense $1,000

1. This eliminating entry on the consolidating worksheet will:

    a. Reduce the depreciation expense recognized to the amount ($5,000) based on the original cost from a nonaffiliate;

    b. Reduce the accumulated depreciation to the amount ($5,000, for the first year) based on the original cost from a nonaffiliate.

2. As a consequence of the eliminating entry, (net) depreciation expense for consolidated purposes will be $5,000 ($6,000 – $1,000) and accumulated depreciation will be $20,000 ($15,000 reinstated as part of the gain elimination above + $5,000 net depreciation recognized for the current period). The correctness of the accumulated depreciation is confirmed by:

> Original Cost $40,000/8 years Life = $5,000 per Year × 4 Years since Acquisition of the Asset = $20,000.

VII. Elimination in Years Subsequent to Intercompany Transaction—Elimination of Intercompany Gain (or loss) and Adjustment of Asset and Accumulated Depreciation—In Years Subsequent to Intercompany Transaction:

    A. Effects/Eliminations—Because the elimination made at the end of one period is recorded only on the consolidating worksheet (and not on the entity books), in years subsequent to the intercompany sale the following affects and eliminations apply:

        1. The gain (or loss) on the sale of fixed assets recognized by the selling affiliate will have been closed through net income to retained earnings. Therefore, the unconfirmed portion of the gain (or loss) will have to be eliminated from retained earnings brought onto the worksheet by the selling affiliate.

        2. The cost of the asset as recorded by the buying affiliate will continue to misstate the cost from a nonaffiliate. Therefore, the asset value brought onto the worksheet by the buying affiliate will have to be adjusted to its cost from a nonaffiliate; the amount of the adjustment will remain the same and will have to be made for as long as the asset remains on the books of the buying affiliate.

        3. The accumulated depreciation on the buying affiliate's books will continue to be misstated (by a decreasing amount) until the asset is fully depreciated because it does not include the accumulated depreciation written off by the selling affiliate. Therefore, accumulated depreciation related to the intercompany fixed asset will have to be adjusted each period until the asset is fully depreciated.

    B. Correct Depreciation Expense—Because the buying affiliate has the asset on its books at its cost from the selling affiliate, the annual depreciation expense (and related accumulated depreciation) recognized will be misstated for consolidated purposes because it will include depreciation on the intercompany gain (or loss). Therefore, the depreciation expense for the period brought onto the consolidating worksheet by the buying affiliate will have to be corrected to eliminate the depreciation related to the intercompany gain or loss.

C. Illustration Facts (continued from above): As a result of entries made on the books of the affiliated companies P and S during the prior period in which the intercompany fixed-asset transaction occurred and the depreciation expense taken for the current period, the following account balances will be brought onto the worksheet at the end of the second period:

Company P (Selling Affiliate)	
Retained Earnings (Original Intercompany Gain)	$ 5,000
Company S (Buying Affiliate)	
Fixed Assets	$30,000
Accumulated Depreciation ($30,000/5 yrs. = $6,000 × 2 yrs)	$12,000
Depreciation Expense (current year only)	$ 6,000

1. Each of these account balances is analyzed below.

D. Analysis of Facts—The following should be noted about the account balances (above) brought onto the consolidated worksheet:

1. Retained earnings of the selling affiliate contain the $5,000 intercompany gain recognized on the sale of the asset to the buying affiliate. At the end of the second period, $1,000 of the intercompany gain will have been confirmed as a result of the depreciation on the intercompany gain taken during the first period. Therefore, the unconfirmed intercompany gain in retained earnings to be eliminated on the consolidating worksheet at the end of the second year is $4,000.

2. Fixed assets of the buying affiliate are reported at its cost, $30,000. The original cost from a nonaffiliate was $40,000. Therefore, the fixed assets will have to be written up $10,000 on the consolidating worksheet. This write up of $10,000 will increase the assets' reported value for consolidated purposes to $40,000, its original cost from a nonaffiliate.

3. Accumulated depreciation of the buying affiliate, $12,000, consists of two years depreciation on the intercompany asset at $6,000 per year ($30,000 cost/5 year remaining life = $6,000). The $12,000 includes $2,000 of depreciation expense related to the intercompany gain, $1,000 each for the prior year and the current year end which have the following affects:

   a. The depreciation of the gain related to the prior period ($1,000) reduces the amount of accumulated depreciation written off by the selling affiliate. Recall that Company P, the selling affiliate, wrote off $15,000 in accumulated depreciation when it sold the fixed asset to the buying affiliate.

   b. The $1,000 in excess depreciation taken by the buying affiliate (on the $5,000 gain) during the prior period reinstates $1,000 of the $15,000 written off by the selling affiliate. Thus, at the end of the second year only $14,000 needs to be reinstated.

   c. The depreciation of the gain related to the current period ($1,000) must be reversed in order to report depreciation expense for the current period at $5,000. (See next item.)

4. Depreciation expense for the current period of $6,000 ($30,000/5 years) will have been recognized by the buying affiliate on its books and brought onto the consolidating worksheet. That $6,000 includes $1,000 depreciation ($5,000 gain/5 years) on the gain recognized by the selling affiliate and must be eliminated for consolidated purposes. Therefore, depreciation expense (and

related accumulated depreciation) brought to the worksheet by the buying affiliate must be reversed by $1,000.

E. Eliminating Entries—On the consolidating worksheet at the end of the second period the following entries would be made:

1. To simultaneously eliminate the unconfirmed gain in retained earnings, reinstate the carrying value of the asset to its original cost to the parent and reinstate the accumulated depreciation:

DR: Retained Earnings	$4,000	
DR: Fixed Asset	10,000	
CR: Accumulated Depreciation		$14,000

2. To reduce the depreciation expense and related accumulated depreciation for the current period:

DR: Accumulated Depreciation	$1,000	
CR: Depreciation Expense		$1,000

3. The two entries could be made as a single entry:

DR: Retained Earnings	$4,000	
DR: Fixed Asset	10,000	
CR: Accumulated Depreciation		$13,000
CR: Depreciation Expense		1,000

4. The effects of the eliminated entries (or entry) for consolidating purposes will be to:

a. Reestablish the fixed asset to its original cost from a non-affiliate—$40,000.

b. Eliminate the unconfirmed intercompany gain in retained earnings—$4,000.

c. Reduce depreciation expense recognized for the period to the amount based on original cost from a non-affiliate—$5,000.

d. Reestablish accumulated depreciation to the amount based on depreciation of original cost—$25,000—as follows:

Brought onto worksheet	$12,000
Reinstatement on worksheet	13,000
Total Accumulated Depreciation	$25,000

e. Proof:

Written off by selling affiliate	$15,000	
Two years additional depreciation	10,000	
(Cost $40,000/8 years) × 5 years =	$25,000	

5. **Remaining Three-Year Period**—The eliminating entries made above will continue to be made as part of the consolidating process for the remaining three year estimated life of the fixed asset:

   a. The following elements of the eliminations will not change during the three-year period:

      i. The amount of addition to fixed asset remains $10,000.

      ii. The amount of depreciation expense eliminated remains $1,000.

   b. The following elements of the elimination will change:

      i. The amount of unconfirmed intercompany profit in retained earnings to be eliminated will decrease by $1,000 each year.

      ii. The amount of accumulated depreciation to be reinstated will decrease by $1,000 each year.

   c. The eliminating entries for each of the remaining three years would be:

	Year 6	Year 7	Year 8
DR: Retained Earnings	$ 3,000	$ 2,000	$ 1,000
DR: Fixed Asset	10,000	10,000	10,000
CR: Accumulated Depre.	$12,000	$11,000	$10,000
CR: Depreciation Exp.	1,000	1,000	1,000

   d. If the asset is retained beyond the 8th year, the following eliminating entry will be required until the asset is disposed:

DR: Fixed Asset	$10,000	
CR: Accumulated Depreciation		$10,000

VIII. **Sale By Subsidiary to Parent**—Intercompany fixed asset by subsidiary to parent: The prior illustration assumed that the sale was made by the parent company to a subsidiary —a downstream sale. If a subsidiary sells to its parent the transaction is an upstream sale. The intercompany elimination for upstream sales depends, in part, on the parent's percentage ownership of the subsidiary.

   A. **Parent Owns 100% of the Subsidiary**

      1. The worksheet eliminating entries made when the parent **owns 100%** of a subsidiary, which sells fixed assets to the parent are the same as those made when the parent sells fixed assets to the subsidiary; there is no noncontrolling interest in the subsidiary.

      2. All of the intercompany gain (or loss), net asset adjustment and subsequent depreciation expense adjustment would affect the parent's claim to net income and net asset carrying value.

B. Parent Owns Less than 100% of the Subsidiary

1. The worksheet eliminating entries made when the parent **owns less than 100%** of a subsidiary that sells fixed assets to the parent are the same as those made when the parent sells fixed assets to the subsidiary, but the gain (or loss) eliminated, the net asset adjustment and the subsequent depreciation expense adjustment would be allocated between the parent and the noncontrolling shareholders' interest in proportion to their respective ownership percentages. Those entries are repeated below as a means of review and to show the allocations necessary when a less than 100% owned subsidiary sells fixed assets to its parent.

2. **Worksheet with Income Statement**—If the elimination occurs on a consolidating worksheet that includes an income statement, the eliminations assuming an intercompany gain would be:

   a. **For Period of Intercompany Sale**

   DR: Fixed Asset
   DR: Gain on Sale
      CR: Accumulated Depreciation

   b. To reestablish the fixed asset to its original cost, eliminate the intercompany gain, and reestablish accumulated depreciation written off by the selling affiliate. The debit to the gain will reduce the amount of income that will be allocated between the parent and the noncontrolling shareholders (interest) in proportion to their respective ownership percentages.

   DR: Accumulated Depreciation
      CR: Depreciation Expense

   c. To eliminate the depreciation expense (and related accumulated depreciation) taken by the buying affiliate on the intercompany gain. The credit to depreciation expense will increase the amount of income that will be allocated between the parent and the noncontrolling shareholders' interest in proportion to their respective ownership percentages.

   d. **For periods subsequent to intercompany sale**

   DR: Fixed Assets
   DR: Retained Earnings
      CR: Accumulated Depreciation

   e. To reestablish the fixed asset to its original cost, eliminate the *un*confirmed portion of the intercompany gain in retained earnings and reestablish accumulated depreciation to the amount based on depreciation of original cost. The debit to fixed asset will remain constant; the debit to retained earnings and the credit to accumulated depreciation will decrease each year as a portion of the intercompany gain is confirmed.

   f. The debit to retained earnings of S, the selling affiliate, will reduce the sub's retained earnings by the amount of the **un**confirmed profit.

> DR: Accumulated Depreciation
>   CR: Depreciation Expense

    g. To eliminate the depreciation expense (and related accumulated depreciation) taken by the buying affiliate on the intercompany gain. The credit to depreciation expense will increase income that will be allocated between the parent and noncontrolling interest.

3. **Worksheet without income statement**—If the elimination occurs on a consolidating worksheet that does not include an income statement (i.e., only a balance sheet is provided), the eliminations would be allocated on the worksheet between the parent and the noncontrolling shareholders' interest in proportion to their respective ownership percentages. The eliminating entries each year, assuming a gain, would be:

> DR: Fixed Asset
> DR: Retained Earnings
>   CR: Accumulated Depriciation

    a. There would be no separate entry to adjust depreciation expense as in 2. f. above because there is no income statement. The debit to retained earnings includes both the adjustment for the gain and depreciation expense. A simpler way to think of this is to adjust the fixed asset and accumulated depreciation to the balance needed (as if the intercompany sale had not occurred), and plug the difference to retained earnings!

Intercompany (I/C) Bond Transactions

When one affiliated entity owns the bonds issued by another affiliated entity an intercompany bond transaction has occurred and those bonds are intercompany bonds. Such transactions will result in the need to adjust and/or eliminate a number of account balances brought on to the consolidating worksheet by the separate entities. This lesson identifies the accounts that will be affected, and illustrates the adjustments or eliminations that will be needed on the consolidating worksheet.

After studying this lesson, you should be able to:

1. Identify the accounts affected by intercompany bond transactions.

2. Analyze facts and calculate the amounts needed to be eliminated for intercompany bond transactions under various circumstances, including:

   - when intercompany bonds have premiums or discounts associated with either the intercompany bond investment or bond liability,

   - when intercompany bonds are issued by a parent (and held by a subsidiary) or issued by a subsidiary (and held by a parent), and

   - when intercompany bonds are issued by a subsidiary that is a 100% owned subsidiary or less than 100% owned subsidiary.

3. Record intercompany bond eliminations on a consolidating worksheet under the various circumstances identified above.

Exam Tip

Intercompany bond transactions are sometimes tested on the CPA Exam; however, these transactions are tested less frequently. You should review and be familiar with how I/C Bond transactions are eliminated and the impact of the consolidated balance sheet only AFTER you are comfortable with I/C Inventory and I/C Fixed Asset transactions.

I. **Intercompany Bonds**—Occur when one affiliate owns the bonds issued by another affiliate.

II. **Intercompany Bonds May Result from**

   A. Bonds issued by one company are held by another company at the time the two companies become affiliated as a result of a business combination.

   B. One affiliate acquires the bonds issued by another affiliate (after the two companies are already affiliated as a result of a business combination).

III. **Intercompany Bond Consequences**

   A. When one affiliate acquires the bonds of another affiliate, for consolidated purposes it is as though the bonds have been retired; they have been constructively retired for consolidated purposes.

   B. Therefore, on the consolidating worksheet the bonds payable (and related accounts) brought on by the issuing company must be eliminated against the investment in bonds (and related accounts) brought on by the buying affiliate.

IV. **Accounts Affected**—Intercompany bonds affect the following accounts brought onto the consolidating worksheet by the separate companies:

   A. **Bonds Payable**—To the extent the bonds are held by an affiliate, the bonds have been constructively retired and the liability must be eliminated against the investment in the bonds held by an affiliate (in IV C, below)

B. **Premium or Discount on Bonds Payable**—Any premium (issue price > face value of bonds) or discount (issue price < face value) related to bonds payable that are constructively retired must also be eliminated.

   1. Since the face value of the bonds payable will be exactly eliminated against the face value of the bond investment, any premium or discount on bonds payable that is eliminated will result in a gain or loss on constructive retirement.

      a. Elimination of a Premium on Bonds Payable = Gain (on constructive retirement)

      b. Elimination of a Discount on Bonds Payable = Loss (on constructive retirement)

C. **Investment in Bonds**—Any investment in the bonds of an affiliate has been constructively retired and the asset must be eliminated against the owned portion of the bonds payable of the affiliate (in IVS A, above).

D. **Premium or Discount on Investment in Bonds**—Any premium (cost > face value of bonds) or discount (cost < face value) on the bond investment being eliminated also must be eliminated. Since the face value of the bond investment will be exactly eliminated against the face value of the bonds liability, any premium or discount on the bond investment that is eliminated will result in a loss or gain on constructive retirement:

   1. Elimination of a Premium on Investment in Bonds = Loss (on constructive retirement)

   2. Elimination of a Discount on Investment in Bonds = Gain (on constructive retirement)

E. **Interest Income/Interest Expense**—Any interest income recognized by the affiliate with the investment in intercompany bonds and the interest expense related to the intercompany bonds recognized by the issuing affiliate must be eliminated. Since for consolidated purposes the bonds are considered retired at the time they became intercompany, no subsequent interest income or interest expense can be recognized for consolidated purposes;

F. **Interest Receivable/Interest Payable**—Any intercompany interest receivables and interest payable resulting from intercompany bonds must be eliminated against each other.

V. **Elimination of Intercompany Bonds and Related Premiums/Discounts—At Date Bonds Become Intercompany**

A. **Illustration Facts**—Assume that on January 1, 20X1 Company P had the following account balances related to its 10% bonds.

Bonds Payable (face amount)	$100,000
Premium on Bonds Payable	3,000

B. The bonds have a three-year remaining life and pay interest annually on December 31.

C. On January 1, 20X1 P's subsidiary, Company S, acquired all of P's bonds in the market for $106,000 ($100,000 face amount plus a $6,000 premium). Entries and related account balances on the books of the respective companies would be:

Company P (account balances)	
Bonds Payable	$100,000
Premium on Bonds Payable	3,000
Carrying Value	$103,000

Company S (entry)

Investment in P Bonds (face)	$100,000*	
Premium on Investment in P Bonds	6,000*	
Cash		$106,000

* These two debits likely would be combined in practice.

D. Analysis of Intercompany Bond Facts—At the time Company S acquired its parent's bonds, the bonds became intercompany and for consolidated purposes will be treated as if they are retired.

 1. The constructive retirement of the bond investment ($100,000) against the bond liability ($100,000) will necessitate the elimination of the related premiums on the investment and on the liability.

 2. The elimination of the related premiums will result in recognition of a $3,000 loss on constructive retirement for consolidated purposes, calculated as:

Premium on Bonds Payable (Credit)	= $3,000	Gain
Premium on Investment Bonds (Debit)	= $6,000	Loss
Net Loss on Constructive Retirement	= $3,000	Loss

E. Eliminating Entry—If an eliminating entry was made on a consolidating worksheet immediately following the intercompany bond transaction, the entry would be:

DR: Bonds Payable	$100,000	
Premium on Bonds Payable	3,000	
Loss (on Constructive Retirement)	3,000	
CR: Investment in Bonds Payable		$100,000
Premium on Investment in Bonds		6,000

 1. The loss (or gain) is attributable to the company that issued the bonds, Company P in this illustration.

VI. Book Transactions Subsequent to Intercompany Bonds Relationship—Although the intercompany bonds are constructively retired and eliminated for consolidated purposes, the bond liability and the bond investment will continue to exist on the books of the separate companies.

A. As a consequence, the companies will make the following entries on their separate books for each of the three years' remaining life of the bonds:

Company P

Interest Expense	$10,000	
Interest Payable/Cash		$10,000
(Annual interest @ $100,000 × .10)		
Premium on Bonds Payable	$ 1,000	
Interest Expense		$ 1,000
(Annual amortization @ $3,000/3 years)		

Company S

Interest Receivable/Cash	$10,000	
Interest Income		$10,000
(Annual interest @ $100,000 × .10)		
Interest Income	$ 2,000	
Premium on Investment in Bonds		$ 2,000
(Annual amortization @ $6,000/3 years)		

  B. Although the above bond-related entries will be recorded on the books of the separate companies, for consolidated purposes the bonds were constructively retired at the date the bonds became intercompany owned.

  C. Therefore, the effects of the bond-related entries that apply after the bonds become intercompany must be eliminated for consolidated purposes.

VII. Elimination—Year End—Elimination of Intercompany Bonds and Related Accounts—At End of Year of Intercompany Bond Transaction.

  A. Illustration Facts (continued from above): As a result of the transactions described above, at the end of 20X1, (the year in which the bonds became intercompany), the following account balances would exist on the books of the separate companies and be brought onto the consolidating worksheet:

Company P

Bonds Payable (face amount)	$100,000 (CR)
Premium on Bonds Payable ($3,000 − $1,000)	2,000 (CR)
Interest Expense ($10,000 − $1,000)	9,000 (DR)

Company S

Investment in P Bonds (face amount)	$100,000 (DR)
Premium on Bonds Investment ($6,000 − $2,000)	4,000 (DR)
Interest Income ($10,000 − $2,000)	8,000 (CR)

B. Eliminating Entry—The following eliminating entry would be made on the consolidating worksheet at the end of the period in which the bonds become intercompany bonds:

DR: Bonds Payable	$100,000	
Premium on Bonds Payable	2,000	
Interest Income	8,000	
Loss on Constructive Retirement	3,000	
CR: Investment in P Bonds		$100,000
Premium on Bond Investment		4,000
Interest Expense		9,000

C. Recall, this eliminating entry is required because for consolidated purposes the bonds must be treated as though they were retired at the time they became intercompany. Therefore, all subsequent balances and effects must be eliminated. The eliminating entry accomplishes the following:

   1. Eliminates the intercompany liability and investment ($100,000)

   2. Eliminates the non-amortized premiums on the liability ($2,000) and on the investment ($4,000)

   3. Eliminates the net interest income recognized by Company S, the owner of the bonds (interest received $10,000 minus $2,000 premium amortization = $8,000)

   4. Eliminates the net interest expense recognized by Company P, the issuing affiliate (interest paid $10,000 minus $1,000 premium amortization = $9,000)

   5. Recognizes for consolidated purposes the $3,000 loss on the constructive retirement of the bonds

VIII. Elimination—Subsequent Years

Elimination of intercompany bonds and related accounts—in years subsequent to intercompany transaction.

A. Gain/Loss

   1. The gain or loss on constructive retirement of intercompany bonds is determined as the net amount of premium(s) and/or discount(s) related to the bonds when they become intercompany and is recognized at the date (in the period) in which the bonds become intercompany.

   2. However, as shown above, the separate companies will continue to carry on their books and amortize the premium and/or discount. At the end of each period, the effects of such amortization will be to recognize on the separate company books a portion (by the amount being amortized for the period) of the gain or loss already recognized for consolidated purposes (at the time the bonds became intercompany).

   3. Therefore, in subsequent periods the amount needed to be recognized in eliminating entries for consolidated purposes that has not been recognized on the separate books will decrease each period. When the premium and/or discount related to intercompany bonds is fully amortized on the separate books (i.e., at maturity), the separate books will have recognized the total gain or loss recognized for consolidated purposes when the bonds became intercompany.

B. **Illustration Facts** (continued from above): The following illustration shows the effects on the separate company books of amortizing the premiums from the facts in the above illustration:

	I/C Date 1/1/X1	X1 Amortize Net Income Affect +/–	Balance 12/31/X1	X2 Amortize Net Income Affect +/–	Balance 12/31/X2
Co. P Prem. on B/P (CR)	$3,000	(+1,000)	2,000	(+1,000)	1,000
Co. S Prem. on B/I (DR)	$6,000	(–2,000)	4,000	(–2,000)	2,000
Net (DR)	$3,000	(–1,000)	2,000	(–1,000)	1,000
Consolidated Loss	$3,000				

1. **Net value**—Note that the net value of the premiums at the date the bonds became intercompany, $3,000, is the amount of loss recognized at that time for consolidated purposes.

2. **Subsequent year**—Each subsequent year the amortization taken on the books of the separate companies causes $1,000 (net) of the $3,000 to be recognized on the books of the companies. The books are "catching up" a portion of the $3,000 already recognized for consolidated purposes.

3. Therefore, in subsequent periods the amount of gain or loss needed to be recognized for consolidated purposes will decrease.

4. **Account balances**—As a result of transactions by the separate companies during 20X1 and 20X2 (including the closing of accounts at the end of 20X1), at the end of 20X2 the following account balances would exist on the books of the separate companies and be brought onto the consolidating worksheet:

Company P

Bonds Payable (face amount)	$100,000 (CR)
Premium on Bonds Payable	1,000 (CR)
Interest Expense ($10,000 – $1,000)	9,000 (DR)

Company S

Investment in P Bonds (face amount)	$100,000 (DR)
Premium on Bonds Investment ($6,000 – $2,000 – $2,000)	2,000 (DR)
Interest Income ($10,000 – $2,000)	8,000 (CR)

C. Eliminating Entry—The following eliminating entry would be made on the consolidating worksheet at the end of 20X2, the period after the one in which the bonds became intercompany bonds:

DR: Bonds Payable	$100,000	
Premium on Bonds Payable	1,000	
Interest Income	8,000	
Retained Earnings—P	2,000	
CR: Investment in P Bonds		$100,000
Premium on Bond Investment		2,000
Interest Expense		9,000

D. This entry is the same as for the prior year except:

1. The amount of the premiums has decreased by the amounts of amortization taken in the second year;

2. The debit to Retained Earnings replaces the debit to Loss because the loss occurred in the prior period for consolidated purposes. The amount of the debit to Retained Earnings ($2,000) is $1,000 less than the debit to the loss in the prior period ($3,000) because $1,000 of the loss—the net amortization for the first period—has now been closed to retained earnings on the separate books;

3. A similar entry would be made on the consolidating worksheet at the end of 20X3, except the premiums will have been fully eliminated on the separate books (thus, no eliminating entry will be required for them) and the debit to retained earnings will be $1,000, the amount not yet recognized in the retained earnings of the separate companies through amortization of the premiums.

IX. **Bonds Issued by Subsidiary**—Intercompany bond Issued by a subsidiary: The prior illustration assumed that the bonds were issued by the parent and acquired by a subsidiary. If a subsidiary issues bonds, which are subsequently acquired by the parent, the consolidating eliminations will depend, in part, on the parent's percentage ownership of the subsidiary.

A. **Parent Owns 100% of the Subsidiary**

1. The worksheet eliminating entries made when the parent owns 100% of a subsidiary, which has its bonds reacquired by its parent, are the same as those made when the parent was the issuer.

2. The gain or loss on constructive retirement will be attributable to the issuing subsidiary, but the full amount will effect the parent's claim to net income since there is no noncontrolling interest in the subsidiary.

3. The eliminating entry in years subsequent to the bonds becoming intercompany will debit (loss) or credit (gain) the retained earnings of the subsidiary, rather than the parent, but the consolidated income and retained earnings effects will be the same.

B. **Parent Owns < 100% of the Subsidiary**

1. The worksheet eliminating entries made when the parent owns < 100% of a subsidiary, which has its bonds reacquired by its parent, are essentially the same as those made when the parent was the issuer, but the gain or loss on constructive retirement would be allocated between the parent and the noncontrolling shareholders' interest in proportion to their respective ownership on the consolidated income statement and balance sheet. Those entries are repeated below as a means of review and to show the allocations necessary when the subsidiary issues the bonds.

2. **Worksheet with Income Statement**—If the elimination occurs on a consolidating worksheet that includes an income statement, the elimination assuming a discount on the bond issue, a premium on the bond investment, and a net loss on the constructive retirement would be:

   a. **For period of intercompany bond transaction**

   DR: Bonds Payable
       Loss on Constructive Retirement
       CR: Investment in Intercompany Bonds
           Discount on Bonds Payable
           Premium on Investment in Bonds

   b. To eliminate the intercompany bond liability and bond investment, related premium and discount, and recognize the resulting loss on constructive retirement. Since the loss is attributable to the issuer, the subsidiary's net income will be reduced which will reduce its contribution to consolidated net income. The amount of the loss attributable to noncontrolling shareholders will be allocated to that interest when the share of consolidated net income attributable to noncontrolling interest is allocated to those shareholders on the consolidated income statement.

   c. **For periods subsequent to the intercompany bond transaction**

   DR: Bonds Payable
       Retained Earnings—S
       CR: Investment in Intercompany Bonds
           Discount on Bonds Payable
           Premium on Investment in Bonds

   d. This entry is the same as that made in the period following the intercompany bond transaction, except that retained earnings of the subsidiary is debited rather than loss because the loss occurred in a prior period. The debit will reduce retained earnings of the subsidiary, which will be allocated between the parent and the noncontrolling shareholders' interest in proportion to their respective ownership percentages.

3. **Worksheet without income statement**—If the elimination occurs on a consolidating worksheet that does not include an income statement (i.e., only a balance sheet is provided) the eliminations would be allocated on the worksheet between the parent and the noncontrolling shareholders' interest in proportion to their respective ownership percentages. The eliminating entry each year, assuming a discount on the bond issue, a premium on the bonds investment, and a net loss on constructive retirement, would be:

   DR: Bonds Payable
       Retained Earnings—S
       CR: Investment in Intercompany Bonds
           Discount on Bonds Payable
           Premium on Investment in Bonds

4. This debit to retained earnings of S replaces a debit to loss because there is only a balance sheet. Otherwise, the purpose and effect of each debit and credit is the same as previously described.

Combined Financial Statements

Sometimes there is a need to aggregate the financial information of two or more affiliated entities, but the preparation of consolidated financial statements is not appropriate because none of the affiliated entities controls (is the parent) of the other firms. In such circumstances, the preparation of combined financial statements may be appropriate. This lesson is concerned with the concept and preparation of combined financial statements.

After studying this lesson, you should be able to:

1. Identify when combined financial statements are appropriate.

2. Describe how combined financial statements are prepared.

I.   **Basis for Combined Financial Statements**—Like consolidated financial statements, combined financial statements are the product of bringing together the financial statements of two or more related firms. However, the circumstances when combined financial statements (as opposed to consolidated financial statements) would be appropriate, as well as the process of combining financial statements (as opposed to consolidating financial statements), are somewhat different.

   A. Consolidated financial statements are justified only when the controlling financial interest of the firms being consolidated rests directly or indirectly with one of the firms (a "parent") to be included in the consolidation.

   B. There are circumstances when there is not a parent company, or when a parent does not have effective control of subsidiaries, but bringing together (combining) the financial statements of two or more related firms would be more meaningful than their separate financial statements.

   C. Combined financial statements (as distinguished from consolidated statements) would be appropriate when:

      1. **Common control**: One individual (not a corporation) owns a controlling interest in two or more businesses that have related operations;

      2. **Common management**: Two or more businesses are under common management;

      3. **Unconsolidated subsidiaries**: A parent lacks effective control over two or more subsidiaries (unconsolidated subsidiaries) for which it wishes to show summary results.

II. **Process for Combining Financial Statements**—The process of preparing combined financial statements is similar to the process of consolidating financial statements.

   A. **Intercompany Items**—Intercompany transactions and balances (i.e., between the companies being combined) are eliminated, including:

      1. Intercompany receivables and payables

      2. Intercompany revenues and expenses

      3. Intercompany gains and losses

      4. Intercompany ownership and related equity—The carrying value of an investment in a company to be combined is eliminated against an equal amount of equity of that company; thus, there are no differences (between the debit and credit) to be allocated.

   B. Any other "unusual" matters would be treated in the same manner as in consolidated financial statements, including:

      1. Minority ownership in any combined company

      2. Foreign operations

      3. Income taxes

      4. Different fiscal periods

C. Unlike consolidated financial statements, the resulting combined financial statements do not represent the financial position, results of operations, or cash flows of a single controlling entity but, rather, the aggregate results of the combined companies after eliminating intercompany account activity and balances.

Variable Interest Entities (VIEs)

Consolidated financial statements may be required in certain other circumstances where one entity has control over another entity through means other than equity ownership. This control usually occurs through a variable interest in another entity. This lesson identifies a variable interest entity (VIE) and when the VIE should be consolidated with the primary beneficiary.

After studying this lesson, you should be able to:

1. Understand the concept of variable-interest entities (VIEs) and when VIEs must be consolidated.

2. Identify a primary beneficiary and when the VIE should be consolidated.

I. **Eligibility for Consolidated Financial Statements**—Whether an entity (e.g., an investee), in which another entity (e.g., an investor) has an interest, must be consolidated depends on the nature of the relationship between entities. GAAP establishes a two-step (or two-tier) process for determining whether the relationship requires an entity to be consolidated with another entity. The entity being considered for consolidation must be assessed to determine (1) if it is a variable-interest entity (VIE) and, if so, the primary beneficiary of the VIE, and (2) if the entity is not a VIE, whether an investor has equity ownership that enables it to exercise control of the investee.

II. **Variable-Interest Entity Assessment**—Each entity that is considered for consolidation must first be evaluated to determine if it is a variable-interest entity (VIE) and, if it is, which other entity is its primary beneficiary.

    A. A VIE is a legal entity, which by design either:

        1. Cannot finance its activities without additional subordinated financial support (i.e., its expected losses exceed its total equity investment at risk), or

        2. Its equity holders, as a group, do not have the direct or indirect ability to make decisions about the VIE's activities.

    B. Structurally, a VIE may be a legal trust, partnership, joint venture, limited company or corporation.

        1. Typically, a VIE is established by another entity or entities (the sponsors) to carry out a well-defined, limited business purpose, with the sponsor(s)—also the variable-interest holders—providing most resources to the VIE, often in the form of loans or loan guarantees.

        2. The activities of and decision-making in a VIE are governed largely by the agreement that establishes the entity and generally resides with the variable-interest holders; nonsponsor equity owners may play little role in the operation of the entity.

        3. The risks and rewards associated with the VIE are largely attributable to the variable-interest holders, not the equity owners who may bear little risk and receive only a small rate of return.

        4. The value of the VIE to the variable-interest holders depends on (varies with) the success of the VIE; the variable-interest holders' interest increases if the net asset value of the VIE increases or decreases if the net asset value of the VIE decreases.

    C. In summary, even though the equity investors in a VIE are its legal owners, because of contractual or other arrangements, they play little role in the operation of the entity and carry little risk or receive little benefit from ownership; those risks and benefits accrue to the variable-interest holders (usually also the sponsors). Thus, a VIE is an entity in which another entity has a controlling interest achieved by a means other than holding a majority of the voting rights.

    D. An entity with a variable interest in a VIE must qualitatively assess whether it is the primary beneficiary of the VIE; if so, it is deemed to have a controlling financial interest in the VIE.

    E. An entity will be considered the primary beneficiary of a VIE if it meets both of the following conditions:

1. It has the power to direct activities of the VIE that most significantly impact the VIEs economic performance (called the power criterion), and

2. It has the obligation to absorb losses from or right to receive benefits of the VIE that potentially could be significant to the VIE (called the losses/benefits or risks/rewards criterion).

F. Only one entity (e.g., sponsor), if any, will be the primary beneficiary of a VIE.

G. An entity that is determined to be the primary beneficiary of a VIE (and, therefore, has a controlling financial interest) will consolidate the financial statements of the VIE.

H. An entity that is determined to be the primary beneficiary of a VIE and, therefore, consolidates its financial statements, must assess whether it continues to be the primary beneficiary on an ongoing basis.

III. **Voting Interest Assessment**—If an entity being considered for consolidation (e.g., an investee) is not a variable-interest entity, it would be assessed to determine whether an investor has majority ownership of its voting securities and, if so, that nothing prevents the investor from exercising his or her control of the operating and financial activities of the investee.

A. Controlling ownership of an investee by an investor results from a business combination carried out in the form of a legal acquisition.

1. A business combination carried out as a legal merger or legal consolidation results in only one remaining firm. Financial statements are prepared for that single firm; there are no sets of financial statements to consolidate.

2. A business combination carried out as a legal acquisition results in one legal entity (the parent) having majority ownership, either directly or indirectly, of the other legal entity (the subsidiary). Each firm is a separate legal (and accounting) entity, but under the common control of the parent shareholder.

3. In form, the parent and subsidiary are separate legal entities; in substance, they are a single "economic entity." If the parent can exercise its majority ownership to control the operating and financial activities of the subsidiary, consolidated parent-subsidiary financial statements must be the primary form of financial reporting for the entities.

B. A majority owned (> 50% of voting stock, controlled either directly or indirectly) subsidiary must be consolidated with its parent unless the parent lacks the ability to exercise its majority ownership to control the operating and financial activities of the subsidiary (i.e., the parent lacks effective control of the subsidiary).

1. Effective control may be lacking due to:

   a. Foreign subsidiary being largely controlled by the foreign government through:

      i. Prohibition on paying dividends

      ii. Control of day-to-day operations

   b. Domestic subsidiary in bankruptcy and under the control of the courts.

C. Unless a parent lacks effective control of a subsidiary, the subsidiary's financial statements must be consolidated with parent's financial statements for public reporting.

D. If a majority-owned subsidiary is not consolidated because the investor lacks effective control (for one of the reasons given above), the subsidiary is an "unconsolidated subsidiary."

1. An unconsolidated subsidiary would be reported as an "Investment" asset by the parent.

2. The parent would account for its investment in an unconsolidated subsidiary using either fair value or the equity method, depending on the extent of influence that it can exercise over the investee.

Public Company Reporting Topics (SEC, EPS, Interim, and Segment)

U.S. Securities and Exchange Commission (SEC)

SEC—Role and Standard-Setting Process

After studying this lesson, you should be able to:

1. Describe the components of SEC's organizational structure.
2. Describe the SEC's role in the standard-setting process.
3. List the main pronouncements issued by the SEC.
4. Recognize that there are mandatory exemptions from first time adoption as well as voluntary exceptions.

I. Introduction

A. The SEC is a federal agency created by Congress after the 1929 stock market crash. It administers the U.S. securities laws, most notably the Securities Act of 1933 and the Securities Exchange Act of 1934. The SEC requires registrants (those publicly held companies under its purview) to adhere to U.S. GAAP when reporting financial statements, except those non-U.S.-domiciled companies who may report using IFRS without a reconciliation to U.S. GAAP (see discussion below).

B. Although the SEC has the legal authority to prescribe accounting standards for publicly traded corporations, it continues to believe that standard setting should remain in the private sector, subject to its oversight. The SEC often agrees with the FASB's accounting standards, while communicating its preferences in comments on FASB Exposure Drafts and other documents. In a few cases, the SEC has rejected a FASB standard and in others has applied pressure to have a standard or proposed standard modified, or to come to a decision more quickly.

II. The SEC's Main Purposes

A. "The mission of the U.S. Securities and Exchange Commission is to protect investors, maintain fair, orderly, and efficient markets, and facilitate capital information" (http://www.sec.gov/about/whatwedo.shtml). An important component of the mission is ease and access to information that is relevant to the decision maker. (Remember that relevance is a primary characteristic in the FASB's conceptual framework!)

B. The SEC regulates the issuance of securities by publicly traded companies and regulation of the trading of those securities on secondary markets. The SEC's intent is to ensure that there is adequate information in the public domain before firms issue securities and before those securities are subsequently traded. Some of the most critical information used by the participants in the marketplace is the financial information provided by the registrant. This is why the SEC is so involved with financial reporting and accounting standards.

C. The SEC's EDGAR (Electronic Data Gathering, Analysis and Retrieval System) database facilitates the collections, validations, and indexing of financial statement information. The purpose of EDGAR is to increase the efficiency of the securities markets by providing timely and accessible data.

D. The global economy has called for the need for one high-level, comprehensive set of accounting standards. The SEC has been the champion and driver in the United States to converge GAAP and IFRS. In 2005, SEC and top European Union officials agreed to a roadmap toward convergence between U.S. GAAP and IFRS.

E. In 2008, the SEC began accepting the financial statements of foreign private issuers prepared in compliance with IFRS without reconciliation to U.S. GAAP. This is a significant step toward acknowledging the IFRSs as issued by IASB. The reconciliation (complete on Form 20-F) was considered to be an unnecessary requirement if the goal was one set of high-quality standards. In addition, the cost of completing the reconciliation was viewed as a deterrent for foreign issuers to access the U.S. capital markets. Eliminating the requirement will hopefully encourage more foreign businesses to list their securities in the United States.

   1. A foreign private issuer is any foreign issuer other than a foreign government, *except* an issuer that meets the following conditions (Rule 205, Securities Act 1933):

   a. More than 50% of the outstanding voting securities are directly or indirectly owned by residents of the United States and

   b. Any of the following:

   i. The majority of its executive officers or directors are U.S. citizens or residents.

   ii. More than 50% of the assets of the issuer are located in the United States.

   iii. The business of the issuer is administered principally in the United States.

F. When the SEC determines that a firm has reported in such a way that GAAP has been violated, it sends a deficiency letter to the firm. If not resolved, the SEC can then stop the trading of the firm's securities. If warranted the Department of Justice becomes involved and criminal charges for violations of the securities laws are filed.

III. SEC Organizational Structure

A. The SEC is a member of the International Organization of Securities Commissions (IOSCO), which consists of more than 100 securities regulatory agencies or exchanges across the globe.

> **Note**
> *Although the SEC can prescribe accounting standards, it has delegated that task to the private sector (currently the FASB). However, the SEC maintains the enforcement power for all publicly traded companies to assure compliance with U.S. GAAP.*

B. The SEC has five commissioners appointed by the president of the United States and five divisions (collectively referred to as "the commission").

   1. The Division of Corporation Finance—This division oversees the compliance with the securities acts and examines all filings made by publicly held companies. All filings go to this division.

   2. The Division of Enforcement—When there is a violation of a securities law (except the Public Utility Holding Company Act), this division completes the investigation and takes appropriate actions. This division makes recommendations to the Justice Department concerning any punishments or potential criminal prosecution.

   3. The Division of Trading and Markets—This division oversees the secondary markets, exchanges, brokers, and dealers.

   4. The Division of Investment Management—This division oversees the investment advisers and investment companies under the Investment Company Act of 1940 and the Investment Advisers Act of 1940.

   5. Division of Economic and Risk Analysis—This division was created in 2009 in response to the credit market crisis. The purpose of the division is to integrate financial economics and data analytics into the core mission of the SEC (www.sec.gov).

C. The Office of the Chief Accountant of the SEC is the most important office for standard setting. This office houses the technical expertise on accounting principles, auditing standards and financial disclosure requirements. This office also issues position papers for the SEC to consider and is the link between the SEC and the accounting profession. The Office of the Chief Accountant has oversight of the FASB and AICPA and is the voice of the SEC regarding standard-setting issues.

D. Laws Administered by the SEC

    1. The Securities Acts of 1933 and 1934

    2. The Public Utility Holding Company Act of 1935

    3. Trust Indenture Act of 1939

    4. Investment Company Act of 1940

    5. Investment Advisors' Act of 1940

    6. Securities Investor Protection Act of 1970

    7. Sarbanes-Oxley Act of 2002

IV. Participation in Standard Setting

A. Even though the SEC delegates the creation of accounting standards to the private sector, the SEC frequently comments on accounting and auditing issues. The SEC communicates through an array of venues. SEC pronouncements, along with the FASB Accounting Standards Codification, comprise authoritative U.S. GAAP. Public companies must adhere to SEC pronouncements as well as U.S. GAAP; private companies do not have to adhere to SEC pronouncements. The main pronouncements published by the SEC are listed next.

    1. Financial Reporting Releases (FRR)—These are formal pronouncements and are the highest-ranking authoritative source of accounting for public companies.

    2. Staff Accounting Bulletins (SAB)—These provide the SEC's current position on technical issues. Although SABs are not formal pronouncements (in the sense that they have not gone through any due process), they still are of importance to financial statement preparers, because they reflect the staff's current thinking on various technical issues.

B. Accounting and Auditing Enforcement Releases (AAER)—These report the enforcement actions that have been taken against accountants, brokers, or others.

Example
AAER No. 1585 against WorldCom on its massive accounting fraud was the mechanism to publicly report that the SEC was taking action against WorldCom.

SEC Reporting Requirements

After studying this lesson, you should be able to:

1. Identify the main reporting requirements for the 1933 and 1934 Securities Acts.

2. Identify the forms used for the registration of securities and subsequent reporting.

3. Identify the content that should be contained in these forms.

I. Introduction

A. The 1933 Securities Act requires publicly traded firms offering securities for sale to the public in primary and secondary markets to file a registration statement, and to provide each investor with a proxy statement before each shareholders' meeting.

B. The 1934 Securities Act regulates the trading of securities after they are issued and provides the requirements for periodic reporting and disclosures.

C. The formal SEC rules are found in the Code of Federal Regulations. All publicly traded companies (either public equity or public debt) must comply with the securities regulations. The governing regulations are Regulation S-X and Regulation S-K.

1. Regulation **S-X** governs the form and content of financial statements and **financial** statement disclosures. These include:

   a. Income statement

   b. Balance sheet

   c. Changes in shareholders equity

   d. Cash flow statement

   e. Footnotes to financial statements

   f. Qualification of accountants (independence rules)

2. Regulation **S-K** governs the form and content of **nonfinancial** statement disclosures. These disclosures are the content of the 10-K outside of the financial statements (remember that "S-K" governs the "10-K" nonfinancial statement content). The nonfinancial statement disclosures are

   a. Description of the business

   b. Description of stockholder matters

   c. Management's discussion and analysis (MD&A)

   d. Changes in and disagreements with accountants

   e. Information on directors and management

Definition of a Security
Section 2.1 of the 1933 Act defines a security as: "Any note, stock, treasury stock, bond, debenture, evidence of indebtedness, certificate of interest, or participation in any profit-sharing agreement,

collateral trust certificate, reorganization certificate or subscription, transferable share, investment contract, voting trust certificate, certificate of deposit for a security, fractional undivided interest in oil, gas, or other mineral rights, or in general, any interest or instrument commonly known as a *security*, or any certificate of interest or participation in, temporary or interim certificate for, receipt of, guarantee of, or warrant or right to subscribe to or to purchase any of the foregoing."

D. The SEC allows reduced disclosures for "smaller reporting companies" (SRC). An SRC is one that has:

1. Less than $250 million in public float as of the last business day of the most recent second fiscal quarter, or

2. No public float or public float less than $700 million AND annual revenues less than $100 million in the most recent fiscal year.

II. Initial Registration of Securities—The Securities Act of 1933

A. A company that wants to sell debt or stock in interstate offerings to the general public is required to register those securities with the SEC. Registration requires extensive disclosures about the company, management, and the intended use of the proceeds from the issue. The intent of the securities laws is, in part, to regulate the disclosure of financial information by firms issuing publicly traded securities.

> **Note**
> *The definition of an SRC applies only to reduced disclosures for SEC filings (such as forms 10-K, 10-Q, S-1, MD&A). An SRC does not change the qualification for delayed filing (i.e., nonaccelerated filer).*

B. Form S-1 is the basic registration form for new securities and it includes a list of required disclosures. The financial information includes a balance sheet dated within 90 days of the filing. Part 1 on Form S-1 is the prospectus that is supplied to each potential purchaser of the security.

1. A prospectus describes the issuing company, the business operations and risks, the financial statements, and the expected use of the proceeds. The basic financial statements requirements are:

   a. Two years of balance sheets

   b. Three years of income statements, statements of cash flow, and statements of shareholders' equity

   c. The financial statements must be audited.

   d. Prior statements are presented on a comparative basis.

   e. The SEC requires five years of selected financial information.

2. Part 2 of Form S-1 includes information about the cost of issuing and distributing the security, more detailed information about the directors and officers and additional financial statement schedules.

C. Small registrations, under a certain monetary threshold or number of purchasers are considered to be private placements and are exempt from certain disclosures.

D. The offering process is diagrammed below:

Issuer → Underwriter → Dealer → Public

1. The underwriter provides marking and distribution of the securities. The underwriter is often contractually obligated to sell the securities under one of the following arrangements:

   a. **Firm commitment**—The underwriter purchases the entire issue at a fixed price.

   b. **Best efforts**—The underwriter sells as many shares as possible.

   c. **All or none**—If the underwriter is unable to sell all (or a significant portion) then the issue may be canceled.

2. Once the stock is issued, it may be traded over the counter by dealers or on an organized exchange.

III. Subsequent Reporting of Securities—The Securities Exchange Act of 1934

    A. The 1934 Securities Exchange Act enacted reporting requirements for the purpose of fully disclosing relevant information about publicly traded firms. The SEC's reporting principles for information in the reports are found in Regulation S-X, Financial Reporting Releases (FRRs), and Staff Accounting Bulletins (SAB). Regulation S-X helps reduce redundancy in reporting by allowing for integrated disclosures whereby a company may satisfy certain Form 10-K disclosure requirements by referencing its shareholder annual report as long as that report includes the required disclosures. The following is a list of the most common required forms:

        1. Annual filing—Form 10-K

        2. Quarterly filing—Form 10-Q

        3. Report significant events affecting the company—Form 8-K

        4. Proxy Statement—The report by which management requests the right to vote through proxy for shareholders at meetings

    B. Filing Deadlines. Filing deadlines depend on the size of the company. Company size is as follows:

        1. Large accelerated filer—A company with worldwide market value of outstanding voting and nonvoting common equity held by nonaffiliates of $700 million or more;

        2. Accelerated filer—A company with worldwide market value of outstanding voting and nonvoting common equity held by nonaffiliates that is $75 million or more but less than $700 million;

        3. Nonaccelerated filer—A company with worldwide market value of outstanding voting and nonvoting common equity held by nonaffiliates less than $75 million.

Filer	10-K	10-Q
Large accelerated filer	60 days after fiscal year end	40 days after quarter end
Accelerated filer	75 days after fiscal year end	40 days after quarter end
Nonaccelerated filer	90 days after fiscal year end	45 days after quarter end

        4. The distinction as an accelerated filer is important because companies that are accelerated filers are required to have an auditor attestation over internal control over financial reporting (ICFR). In 2020 the SEC has made modifications to include revenue tests so that smaller reporting companies (SRC) with less than $100 million in annual revenue are excluded from the accelerated filer definitions.

Filing status	Public float	Annual revenues	Required to obtain auditor attestation over ICFR?
Large accelerated filer	$700 million and greater	No requirement	Yes
Accelerated filer	$75 million to less than $700 million	$100 million or more	Yes
Nonaccelerated filer	$75 million to less than $700 million	Less than $100 million	No
	Less than $75 million	No requirement	No

    C. Form 10-K is the required vehicle for reporting annual financial information to the SEC. The 10-K is separated into four parts. The content of each part is outlined in the following chart:

Part I

1. Description of the business
   A. Risk factors
   B. Unresolved staff comments
2. Description of properties
3. Legal proceedings involving the company
4. Submission of matters to a vote of stockholders

Part II

5. Market price of common stock, dividends & stockholder matters
6. Selected financial data
7. Management's Discussion and Analysis (MD&A) offi nancial condition and results of operations
   A. Quantitative and qualitative disclosures about market risk
8. Financial statements and supplementary financial information
9. Change in disagreements with accountants on accounting and financial disclosure
   A. Controls and procedures

Part III

10. Directors and officers
11. Executive compensation and transactions with executives
12. Security ownership by certain beneficial owners and by management
13. Certain relationships and related-party transactions
14. Principal accountant fees and services

Part IV

15. Exhibits; signatures; certification

1. The SEC requires the Management's Discussion and Analysis (MD&A) to be included in its reporting and, as such, provides a discussion of important aspects of the firm from the viewpoint of management. This report covers the firm's financial condition, changes in financial condition, results of operations, liquidity, capital resources and operations, identifies trends and significant events and uncertainties. The discussion also includes information about the effects of inflation and changing prices in nonquantitative form, and explanation of significant or unusual events and uncertainties and their effect or expected effect on the firm's financial performance. Also, the firm's important accounting policies are discussed in the MD&A.

   a. Forward-looking or prospective information is included for the purpose of assessing future cash flows. Prospective information is useful to the financial statement user because it promotes understanding of events, circumstances, trends, and uncertainties when there are material trends and uncertainties. When material, prospective information is required to aid the analysis of long and short-term liquidity, capital resources, material changes in a line item on the financial statements, and any preliminary merger negotiations.

   b. Prospective information should be prepared in accordance with GAAP, using information that is consistent with the plans of the entity, and with due professional care so as not to mislead the user of the financial statements. Prospective financial statements should disclose information as to the purpose of the statements, assumptions, and significant accounting policies.

2. In general, SEC registrants must disclose more information to the SEC than in the annual reports to shareholders. For off-balance-sheet financing relationships, the SEC requires firms to disclose all contractual liabilities and contingent liabilities, whether they are recognized in the accounts.

D. Form 10-Q reports the quarterly information to the SEC within 45 days (nonaccelerated filer) of the end of the quarter. (Only the first three quarters are reported because the 10-K reports the annual information.) Large companies designated as accelerated filers must file within 40 days. Disclosures are less extensive than in the 10-K and include information for the specific quarter and year-to-date information.

1. The quarterly report is intended to provide investors with an update since the last annual report. The 10-Q is not required to be audited, but must be reviewed by the independent auditor.

2. The financial statements presented are:

a. Balance sheet for the quarter and prior fiscal year end

b. Quarterly and year-to-date income statements for this quarter and the same period in the previous year

c. Cumulative year-to-date statements of cash flow for the current and prior fiscal years

E. Form 8-K reports significant events affecting the company such as material impairment, bankruptcy, entry or termination of a definitive agreement, changes in the registrant's CPA, changes in control etc. These are all events that the public shareholder should be aware of, as the events are significant enough to influence decisions.

F. Proxy statements are materials sent to the shareholders for vote. Proxy materials can address things such as election of directors, changes in the corporate charter, issuance of new securities, plans for a major business combination etc. Frequently these items are voted on during the shareholders annual meeting, but sometimes these matters need to be addressed during interim periods, in which case the proxy materials regarding the issue must be circulated.

IV. Corporate Governance

A. The Foreign Corrupt Practices Act of 1977 prohibits bribes of foreign governmental or political officials for the purpose of securing contracts or business. It requires publicly held companies to maintain an adequate system of internal control.

B. The Sarbanes-Oxley Act of 2002 (SOX) contains provisions to enhance corporate governance and to mitigate financial accounting abuses. A few of the significant provisions related to financial reporting are presented below.

1. The SEC requires registrants to have annual audits of their financial statements. The auditing firm must be registered with the Public Company Accounting Oversight Board (PCAOB), a private-sector organization created by the 2002 Sarbanes-Oxley Act (the SEC has oversight authority for the PCAOB). The PCAOB provides oversight of registered auditing firms.

2. Auditors are prohibited from providing nonaudit services to audit clients.

3. Audit committees are required to be composed of nonmanagement members of the board of directors, and the chair has to have financial experience.

4. Annual filing must include a management's report on the internal controls. This report must attest to the existence and effectiveness of the company's internal controls over corporate reporting.

5. There are Increased penalties for fraud and white-collar crime. Willfully failing to maintain audit records for five years is a felony. Criminal charges can be brought against corporate officers who fail to certify financial reports or who willfully certify statements they know do not comply with SOX.

Earnings Per Share

Introduction to Earnings per Share

This is the first of three lessons on earnings per share (EPS). This lesson provides the basic and diluted EPS calculations as well as the disclosure requirements.

After studying this lesson, you should be able to:

1. Complete a calculation of basic EPS.

2. Complete a calculation of diluted EPS.

3. Identify the disclosure requirements for EPS.

I. Earnings per Share—Only public entities are required to present earnings per share (EPS). Nonpublic entities often choose to present EPS, but are not required to do so. There are two EPS figures that firms disclose: basic and diluted. Basic EPS is the EPS based only on actual transactions for the year. Diluted EPS is a "worst-case" figure reflecting the potential dilution of stock options and convertible securities. EPS allows comparisons of performance for firms of any size.

II. EPS Background

A. EPS is computed only for common stock. It represents the amount of earnings on a per-share basis. If EPS were $4, this means that $4 of dividends could have been paid, on average, to each share of common stock outstanding during the year, from earnings in that year. It does not mean the firm is obligated to pay that much, or that it will pay that much. Also, actual common stock dividends paid do not reduce EPS.

B. There are **two different EPS figures**, each of which is reported for several intermediate subtotals in addition to net income.

Definitions

Basic EPS (BEPS): Includes only actual common shares outstanding.

Diluted EPS (DEPS): Includes securities that may become common stock in the future, such as convertible stock and stock options, in addition to actual shares of common outstanding.

1. The securities that may become common stock in the future are called potential common stock (PCS) or potentially dilutive securities. If a firm has no PCS then only BEPS is reported.

C. Disclosure of EPS—ASC 260 provides guidance on the disclosure of earnings per share information on the face of the income statement. This guidance is provided for companies with a simple capital structure and for those companies with a complex capital structure.

1. Simple capital structure—A simple capital structure is one in which the corporation only has common stock outstanding or one in which the corporation has common stock and nonconvertible preferred stock outstanding.

a. Formula—If the corporation only has common stock outstanding, the Basic Earnings per Share (BEPS) is calculated by the formula shown below.

$$BEPS = (Net\ Income)/(Weighted\ Average\ Common\ Shares\ Outstanding)$$

b. Formula—If the company has common stock and nonconvertible preferred stock outstanding, the Basic Earnings per Share is calculated by the formulas shown below.

BEPS = (Net Income Available to Common)/(Weighted Average Common Shares Outstanding)

BEPS = (Net Income– Preferred Stock Dividend)/(Weighted Average Common Shares Outstanding)

2. **Complex capital structure**

   a. A complex capital structure typically includes common stock, along with equity contracts and convertible securities. These securities may become common stock in the future and thus must be included in an EPS figure so that users can assess the impact of these potential changes on EPS.

   b. A company with a complex capital structure is required to disclose the Basic Earnings per Share and the Diluted Earnings per Share. This is called dual EPS reporting.

      i. **Formula**—The Diluted Earnings per Share is calculated by the formula shown below, which includes the effects of potential common stock (PCS)

Note
The potential common stock may affect both the numerator and denominator.

DEPS = (Net Income Available to Common Adjusted for Effects of PCS)/(Weighted Average Common Shares Plus Shares Issuable from PCS)

Example
A convertible bond is a PCS. Under certain conditions, discussed below, they are assumed converted into common stock. If they were actually converted, no interest would be paid and net income (numerator of DEPS) would increase. Likewise, the common shares from conversion would have been outstanding, thus increasing the denominator of DEPS.

III. **Disclosure Requirements**

   A. EPS amounts (all after tax) must be disclosed for the following line items in the income statement:

	Simple Capital Structure (No PCS)	Complex Capital Structure (PCS Present)
On the face of the Income Statement		
1. Income from Continuing Operations	BEPS	BEPS and DEPS
2. Net Income	BEPS	BEPS and DEPS
Either on the face of the Income Statement or in Footnotes		
3. Discontinued Operations	BEPS	BEPS and DEPS

   B. BEPS and DEPS for the first two amounts must be shown with equal prominence. The terms basic EPS and diluted EPS are not required terms. Earnings per share, and earnings per share-assuming dilution, are also acceptable.

   C. **Elaboration**

      1. As the previous table shows, the maximum EPS disclosures in a simple capital structure is three BEPS amounts and in a complex capital structure the maximum disclosure is three BEPS and three DEPS (or six total EPS amounts).

      2. Financial statement users wishing to compute EPS for intermediate subtotals such as income before discontinued operations may do so with the required disclosures.

3. If BEPS and DEPS are equal, both are reported so that users know there are PCS but there was no material dilutive effect.

IV. Basic EPS—A Closer Look

A. Effect of Preferred Stock (numerator of BEPS)

BEPS = (Net Income Available to Common)/Weighted Average Shares Outstanding

BEPS = (Net Income − Preferred Stock Dividends)/Weighted Average Shares Outstanding

B. Preferred Stock Cumulative/Not

1. The amount of preferred stock dividends subtracted in the numerator of BEPS depends on whether the preferred stock is cumulative or not, and if not, on the amount declared in the period.

> **Study Tip**
> Most preferred stock is cumulative.

2. Amount Subtracted Table—Amount of Preferred Dividend Subtracted in EPS Numerator:

	Cumulative Preferred	Noncumulative Preferred
Current-period dividends declared	1 full year's dividends	Amount declared
Current-period dividends not declared	1 full year's dividends	None

3. *Cumulative* means that if a year's preferred dividend is not paid (skipped), no other dividends may be paid before the skipped dividends (dividends in arrears) are paid. Regardless of whether dividends are declared on cumulative preferred stock, one full year's dividends is subtracted from the numerator of BEPS because no common dividends can be paid on these earnings before the preferred dividends are declared. This also means that in a year in which dividends in arrears from a previous year are paid in addition to the current year dividend, still only one year is subtracted from the current-year BEPS numerator because BEPS in the previous year has already been reduced by the skipped dividends.

4. Noncumulative preferred stock—Receives dividends only if declared. Skipped dividends are never paid.

5. Tax Effect—There is no tax effect to consider for preferred stock dividends because dividends paid are not deductible for tax purposes.

6. Examples—A firm has had 1,000 shares of 7%, $100 preferred stock outstanding for several years. The annual dividend on the preferred is $7,000 = .07($100)(1,000). Year 4 is the current year.

a. The preferred stock is cumulative and there are no dividends in arrears. $7,000 is subtracted from income in computing BEPS whether or not the dividend is declared in Year 4. Even if only a partial dividend (say $4,000) is paid, the full $7,000 is subtracted.

b. The preferred stock is cumulative and there are two years' dividends in arrears. $7,000 is subtracted from income in computing BEPS whether or not the dividend is declared, and regardless of the amount declared.

c. The preferred stock is noncumulative. No dividends are declared in Year 4. There is no subtraction in computing Year 4 BEPS.

> **Note**
> In all these cases, it is the amount of dividends declared that matters, not the amount paid.

d. The preferred stock is noncumulative and $2,000 of dividends is declared in Year 4. Subtract $2,000 only.

e. The preferred stock is noncumulative, three years' dividends have been skipped, and $2,000 of dividends is declared in Year 4. Subtract $2,000 only.

Basic Earnings per Share

This is the second of three lessons on earnings per share (EPS). This lesson explains the calculation of weighted average shares outstanding.

After studying this lesson, you should be able to:

1. Complete a calculation of weighted average shares outstanding with stock issuance, repurchase, dividends, and splits.

I. **Weighted Average (WA) Computation (Denominator of BEPS)**

    A. The denominator of BEPS is the weighted average (WA) shares outstanding during the period (not the number outstanding at the end of the period unless there has been no change in the number of shares outstanding all year). Treasury shares purchased during the period reduce the WA. The reason for weighting the shares is that shares outstanding a longer portion of the year represent capital investment that has been working longer for the firm than shares outstanding a shorter portion of the year. The numerator of EPS is income, an amount representing the entire year. The income earned on the capital investment must be related to the period for which the investment was used by the firm.

    B. The calculation weights each change in shares for the portion of the period the new shares are outstanding (add), or for the period the shares were not outstanding as in the case of a purchase of treasury shares (subtract).

	# Shares
Shares outstanding January 1	2,000
Issue shares April 1	1,200
Purchase shares for treasury October 1	400
Issue shares December 1	120
Issue shares December 31	200

The WA shares outstanding (denominator of BEPS) =
$2,000(12/12) + 1,200(9/12) - 400(3/12) + 120(1/12) = 2,810$

The WA shares outstanding (denominator of BEPS) = $2,000(12/12) + 1,200(9/12) - 400(3/12) + 120(1/12) = 2,810$

        1. Explanation—The April 1 issuance caused 1,200 shares to be issued. These shares were outstanding 9 months. This is equivalent to 900 shares being outstanding the entire year. The shares issued December 31 were not outstanding for any period of time during the year and are not included in the WA. If the firm had no preferred stock and net income was $5,620 for the period, BEPS would be $2.00 ($5,620/2,810).

II. **Share Adjustments**—Stock dividends and splits are adjustments to the number of shares outstanding for all investors holding stocks.

    A. Two for One Stock Split—A 10% stock dividend gives an investor holding 1,000 shares an additional 100 shares. Each investor maintains the percentage of the firm previously owned. There are 10% more shares outstanding but each share is worth proportionately less. A two-for-one stock split doubles the number of shares outstanding but the value of each share is halved. These are not substantive changes in shares outstanding the way a new stock issuance is. They bring no resources into the firm.

B. General Rule WA Calculation—All stock dividends and splits are assumed to have been outstanding since the inception of the firm. Apply the percentage of the stock dividend or the factor in a split (factor = 3 in a three-for-one split) to all changes in outstanding stock occurring before the stock dividend or split.

Example

Assume the data from the previous example, with the addition of a stock split and dividend:

Shares outstanding January 1	2,000
Issue shares April 1	1,200
Two-for-one stock split May 1	
Purchase shares for treasury October 1	400
30% stock dividend November 1	
Issue shares December 1	120
Issue shares December 31	200

The WA shares outstanding (denominator of BEPS) = {[2,000(12/12) + 1,200(9/12)]2 − 400(3/12)}1.30 + 120(1/12) = 7,420

The factor of 2 for the two-for-one split is applied to the shares outstanding at the beginning of the year and the April 1 issuance. The 30% stock dividend is likewise applied to all changes before it. The factor used is 1.30 because the 30% stock dividend increases the shares already outstanding on that date by 30%.

C. Adjust for EPS—If a stock dividend or split occurs between the balance sheet date and issuance of the balance sheet, all share amounts are adjusted for EPS purposes.

III. Contingent Shares

A. Shares that are issuable for little or no cash consideration upon satisfaction of certain conditions are contingent shares. They are considered outstanding as of the date the conditions have been met.

B. Weighting Fraction Period—The weighting is for the fraction of the period the conditions were met.

Example

If 2,400 shares are issuable contingent on a particular performance measure that is met by the firm on August 1, then even though the shares may not be issued until the next period, 1,000 shares are included in the WA for BEPS for the current period (2,400 × 5/12).

C. Contingency—If the contingency is a future earnings level, no contingent shares are included in the WA of BEPS because the contingency cannot be met until a future period. The same holds for a current-period earnings level because the contingency cannot be met until the last day of the year.

IV. Illustration of BEPS Reporting

Example

All amounts after-tax:		Common stock:
Income from continuing operations	$40,000	Shares outstanding Jan.1: 10,000
Discontinued operations (net)	(10,000)	Issued 2,000 shares May 1
		Issued 20% stock dividend June 14
		Purchased 1,000 treasury shares July 1
Net income	$30,000	

The firm has 1,000 shares of 4%, $100 par cumulative preferred stock. No dividends were declared on the preferred stock in this year.

WA shares = [10,000 + 2,000(8/12)]1.2 − 1,000(6/12) = 13,100. This value is used for all EPS figures.

Annual preferred dividend requirement: 1,000($100)(.04) = $4,000

Presentation of EPS:

Income from continuing operations: ($40,000 − $4,000)/13,100	$2.75
Discontinued operations: ($10,000/13,100)	(.76)
Net income ($30,000 − $4,000)/13,100 (rounded)	$1.99

Note

Only income from continuing operations and net income subtract the preferred dividends from the numerator. The discontinued operations are not income amounts but rather individual components on a per-share basis.

V. Additional Example

Additional Example—The following example is provided for additional practice. You should verify the calculations for practice.

Example

This example shows an alternative way to compute the weighted average shares. The Simple Company is located in Knoxville, Tennessee and has an accounting year that ends on December 31 of each year. A modified income statement for the 20X7 accounting year is presented below.

Income from Continuing Operations	$1,500,000
Discontinued Operations (less Income Tax Expense of $90,000)	210,000
Net Income	$1,710,000

The tax rate for 20X7 was 30%.

The capital structure of the Simple Company includes common stock and nonconvertible, cumulative, preferred stock. Relevant information related to these securities is shown below.

Common Stock, Par Value of $1

Common Shares Outstanding on January 1, 20X7	270,000	Shares
Sold Common Shares on September 1, 20X7	18,000	Shares
Common Shares Outstanding on December 31, 20X7	288,000	Shares

Requirement: Determine the earnings per-share disclosure for the 20X7 accounting year.

Preferred Stock Dividend: 7,500 × $20 × 6% = $9,000 Weighted Average of Common Shares Outstanding:

Shares		Months	
270,000	×	8	2,160,000
288,000	×	4	1,152,000
		12	3,312,000

3,312,000/12 = 276,000 Shares*

Basic Earnings Per Share Calculation:

Income from Continuing Operations	($1,500,000 − $9,000)/276,000	=	$5.40
Discontinued Operations	$210,000/276,000	=	0.76
Net Income	($1,710,000 − $9,000)/276,000	=	$6.16

*This agrees with the calculation method shown in the previous discussion:
270,000 + 18,000(4/12) = 276,000

Diluted Earnings per Share

This is the third of three lessons on Earnings Per Share (EPS). This lesson presents how to incorporate potentially dilutive securities into the diluted EPS calculation.

After studying this lesson, you should be able to:

1. Calculate the potentially dilutive effect of convertible preferred stock on basic EPS.

2. Calculate the potentially dilutive effect of stock options and warrants using the "treasury stock method" on basic EPS.

3. Calculate the potentially dilutive effect of multiple dilutive securities on basic EPS.

I. Diluted EPS

Diluted EPS is conceptually different from BEPS. It is an imaginary calculation based on events that have not happened as of the balance sheet date. The FASB believes that requiring a second EPS number reflecting the effects of securities that may become common stock in the future enhances the value of per-share disclosures.

II. Background

Definition
Diluted EPS (DEPS): Reflects the maximum dilution or **lowest value of EPS** that is possible given the firm's outstanding securities at the balance sheet date.

A. Effect PCS into BEPS

DEPS incorporates the effect of potential common stock (PCS)-securities that can become common stock in the future, into BEPS. There may be both numerator and denominator effects. BEPS is used as the benchmark value into which the numerator and denominator changes stemming from PCS are incorporated. Thus, DEPS equals BEPS adjusted by the effects of PCS.

III. How Potential Common Stock Affects EPS

Note
An important thing to remember is that PCS is not common stock at the balance sheet date. They are assumed to be exercised (stock options and warrants) or converted (convertible preferred stock and bonds) as of the beginning of the year (or date of issuance if later). Upon assumed exercise or conversion, the numerator and denominator effects are computed, and are considered for incorporation into EPS.

Example
A firm has 10, 8%, $1,000 convertible bonds outstanding the entire period. Each bond is convertible into 20 shares of common stock. The tax rate is 30%. At the beginning of the period, the bonds are assumed converted. The result is that interest of $560 after tax would not have been paid (10)($1,000)(.08)(1 − .30). That is the numerator effect. The denominator effect is the 200 shares of common stock that would be issued on conversion (10)(20).

IV. Dilution and Antidilution

A. Diluted PCS

Only dilutive PCS are incorporated into DEPS.

1. Explanation

This means when we add the numerator effect of a PCS to the numerator of BEPS, and the denominator effect to the denominator of BEPS, the result is a lower EPS number. A dilutive PCS means that DEPS is lower than BEPS as a result of assumed conversion or exercise of the PCS.

B. An antidilutive PCS (one that increases EPS when it is added into BEPS) is ignored for purposes of computing DEPS.

C. Control Number

For purposes of testing for dilution and antidilution, the control number is income from continuing operations.

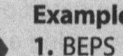

Examples

1. BEPS = $1,000/2,000 = $.50. A potential common stock is assumed converted and the numerator and denominator effects are $200 and 500, respectively. DEPS = ($1,000 + $200)/(2,000 + 500) = $.48. The numerator and denominator effects are added to the numerator and denominator of BEPS. In this case, the PCS is dilutive because DEPS is lower than BEPS. BEPS would be reported at $.50 and DEPS would be reported at $.48.

2. BEPS = $1,000/2,000 = $.50. A potential common stock is assumed converted and the numerator and denominator effects are $200 and 300, respectively. DEPS = ($1,000 + $200)/(2,000 + 300) = $.52. In this case, the PCS is antidilutive because DEPS is higher than BEPS. The PCS is not entered into BEPS. BEPS = DEPS in this case.

3. Income from continuing operations is $1,200 and the WA shares outstanding is 2,400. A loss from discontinued operations of $200 is also reported, resulting in net income of $1,000. The firm has a PCS with no numerator effect but a denominator effect of 200 (200 shares issuable on exercise).

Income from continuing operations	BEPS	DEPS
$1,200/2,400 =	$.50	
$1,200/2,600 =		$.462
Discontinued operations loss		
$200/2,400 =	(.083)	
$200/2,600 =		(.077)
Net income		
$1,000/2,400 =	$.417	
$1,000/2,600 =		$.385

The EPS amounts above would be reported as shown. However, the result for the discontinued operations is antidilutive because the DEPS result (negative .077) is larger (less negative) than for BEPS (negative .083). Because the result is dilutive for income from continuing operations (the control number), all EPS amounts use the same denominator.

Conversely, if income from continuing operations is negative and including the denominator effect of a PCS in the calculation of DEPS for that income figure causes it to be less negative (larger), then no PCS is assumed converted for any income amount. BEPS = DEPS in this case, for all amounts to be shown on a per-share basis.

V. Treasury Stock Method

Incorporating stock options and warrants into DEPS

A. To enter stock options and warrants (which are PCS) into DEPS, a three-step process is used called the treasury stock method.

Example

Assume a firm's BEPS = $1,200/700 = $1.71. The firm has 2,000 stock options outstanding the entire year. The exercise price is $30. The average market price of common stock for the period is $40.

1. Assume exercise of the options. Shares issued on exercise = 2,000

2. Purchase treasury shares with the proceeds from exercise: 2,000($30)/$40 = number of treasury shares purchased = (1,500)

3. Incremental shares = denominator effect = 500

Divide the total proceeds from exercise [$60,000 = 2,000($30)] by the average price per stock the firm would be required to pay for its own shares ($40). The result is that the firm would buy back 1,500 of its own shares. The net number of new shares outstanding as a result of the treasury stock method is 500. DEPS = $1,200/(700 + 500) = $1.00. DEPS is less than BEPS. Therefore the options are dilutive and are entered into DEPS.

The purpose of assuming the purchase of treasury stock is to reduce the total dilution from exercise. Otherwise, the denominator effect would be 2,000, not 500. There is no numerator effect.

B. Antidilutive Options

Options are antidilutive when the option price exceeds the market price. In the above example, if the average market price were $25, the three steps would produce a negative number, causing DEPS to increase. The easy way to remember this is that no one would exercise such a stock option and pay more than market price.

VI. If-Converted Method

Incorporating convertible securities into DEPS.

A. To enter convertible securities (which are PCS) into DEPS, the if-converted method is used.

B. Convertible Assumed Converted

The convertible is assumed converted as of the beginning of the period or date of issuance, whichever is later. The numerator and denominator effects are computed and entered into DEPS. If DEPS decreases, the PCS is dilutive and the security is included in the computation of DEPS.

Example

(Convertible bonds) BEPS for a firm is $3,000/1,000 = $3.00. The firm also has 10, 8%, $1,000 convertible bonds outstanding the entire period. Each bond is convertible into 20 shares of common stock. The tax rate is 30%. At the beginning of the period, the bonds are assumed converted under the if-converted method. The numerator effect is the interest of $560 after tax that would not have been paid (10)($1,000)(.08)(1 – .30). The denominator effect is the 200 shares of common stock that would be issued on conversion (10)(20). DEPS = ($3,000 + $560)/(1,000 + 200) = $2.97. DEPS is less than BEPS. Therefore, the bonds are dilutive and are entered into DEPS.

C. Interest Expense

If the bonds were sold at a discount or premium, interest expense will reflect periodic amortization. The interest expense recognized should be added back (after tax), not the cash interest paid, because earnings was reduced by the expense.

D. Issued Midyear

If the bonds were issued at midyear, the numerator and denominator effects each would be multiplied by 1/2, resulting in smaller increases to the BEPS numerator and denominator.

E. No Tax Effect

Convertible preferred stock is handled the same way as convertible bonds except there is no tax effect.

Example

Net income is $3,400 and WA shares are 700. The annual preferred dividend claim on convertible preferred stock is $400 and if converted, 100 common shares would be issued. In computing BEPS, convertible preferred stock is treated just like nonconvertible preferred stock.

BEPS = ($3,400 − $400)/700 = $4.29

The numerator effect is the dividends that would not be paid if the convertible preferred stock were converted. The denominator effect is the common shares issued on conversion.

DEPS = ($3,400 − $400 + $400)/(700 + 100) = $4.25

The $400 of dividends is added back (after being subtracted in calculating BEPS) in calculating DEPS. DEPS is less than BEPS. Therefore, the convertible preferred stock is dilutive and is entered into DEPS.

VII. The Dilution/Antidilution Method

when there is more than one PCS

A. Two or More PCS

The previous examples have used only one PCS. What happens if there are two or more? Which one is entered into BEPS first? The solution is to incorporate the PCS into DEPS in order of most dilutive first, then the next dilutive PCS and so forth. The PCS with the most dilutive potential is the one with the lowest ratio of numerator effect/denominator effect (N/D).

B. Process

The process is to enter the PCS with the lowest N/D into DEPS first. Then compare the next lowest N/D with the resulting DEPS. Continue to add PCS into DEPS until a PCS is encountered with a higher N/D than the previous DEPS figure, or until all PCS are entered. Use income from continuing operations as the control number.

Example
Data for Year 5:

Income from Continuing Operations	$26,000
Discontinued Operations after tax	12,000
Net Income	$38,000

Common stock shares outstanding all period: 10,000

BEPS for income from continuing operations = $26,000/10,000= $2.60

Potential Common Stock Outstanding All Period:	Numerator Effect	Denominator Effect	Numerator/ Denominator (N/D)
Warrants	$ 0	2,000	$ 0
Convertible bonds issue A	3,000	1,000	3.00
Convertible bonds issue B	2,000	1,500	1.33

The warrants are considered first because the ratio of its numerator effect to denominator effect (N/D) is the lowest of the three.

Income from continuing operations is used as the control number. The warrants are entered into DEPS for income from continuing operations because its N/D of $0 is less than BEPS. The tentative DEPS = ($26,000 + $0)/(10,000 + 2,000) = $2.17.

The convertible bonds issue B is the next to consider because it has the second lowest N/D. Its ratio is $1.33 which is less than the tentative DEPS of $2.17 and thus is entered into DEPS. The new tentative DEPS = ($26,000 + $0 + $2,000)/(10,000 + 2,000 + 1,500) = $2.07.

The convertible bonds issue A is not entered into DEPS because its N/D exceeds the previous tentative DEPS of $2.07. Thus, the final DEPS for income from continuing operations is $2.07. This process thus determines the denominator for all DEPS numbers.

The complete EPS presentation for this firm:

	BEPS	DEPS
Income from Continuing Operations	$2.60	$2.07
Discontinued Operations		
$12,000/10,000	1.20	
$12,000/(10,000 + 2,000 + 1,500)		.89
Net Income		
$38,000/10,000	$3.80	
($38,000 + $0 + $2,000)/(10,000 + 2,000 + 1,500)		$2.96

VIII. Additional Examples

This section provides an example Income Statement and analysis of the stock options. You should verify the calculations for practice.

Example

The Complex Company is located in Knoxville, Tennessee and has an accounting year that ends on December 31. A modified income statement for the 20x7 accounting year is presented below.

Income from Continuing Operations	$1,500,000
Discontinued Operations (less Income Tax Expense of $90,000)	$210,000
Net Income	$1,710,000

The tax rate for 20x7 was 30%.

The capital structure of the Complex Company includes common stock, nonconvertible, cumulative, preferred stock, and stock options. Relevant information related to these securities is shown below.

Common Stock, Par Value of $1

Common Shares Outstanding on January 1, 20x7	270,000 Shares
Sold Common Shares on September 1, 20x7	18,000 Shares
Common Shares Outstanding on December 31, 20x7	288,000 Shares

Non-Convertible, Cumulative, 6% Preferred Stock, Par Value of $20

Preferred Shares Outstanding throughout the year	7,500 Shares

Stock Options - The options represent 6,000 shares. The option price is $20. The average market price for the 20x7 accounting year is $25. The stock options were outstanding for the entire 20x7 accounting year.

Requirement: Determine the earnings per share disclosure for the 20x7 accounting year.

Solution:

Preferred Stock Dividend:

$7,500 \times \$20 \times 6\% = \$9,000$

Weighted Average of Common Shares Outstanding:

Shares		Months	
270,000	$\times$	8	2,160,000
288,000	$\times$	4	1,152,000
		12	3,312,000
			3,312,000/12 = 276,000 Shares*

*This agrees with the calculation method shown in the previous discussion: $270,000 + 18,000(4/12) = 276,000$

Analysis of Stock Options–Treasury Stock Method:

1. Since the average market price is greater than the option price, the stock options are dilutive.

2. To determine the impact of the stock options on the Diluted Earnings per Share Calculation, the treasury stock method is applied.

Step 1: The Stock Options are assumed exercised and 6,000 new shares are issued at $20 per share.

Step 2: The cash from the exercise of the stock options, $120,000, is used to purchase treasury stock at the average market price for the period ($6,000 \times \$20 = \$120,000$). The number of treasury shares would be 4,800 shares ($120,000/25 = 4,800$).

Under step 1, 6,000 new shares would be issued, and under step 2, 4,800 shares would be acquired. The net increase in shares outstanding would be 1,200 shares, the denominator effect.

Effect of the Stock Options:

Adjustment to the Numerator:	$0.00	
Adjustment to the Denominator	1,200	shares
N/D Ratio $0/1,200:	$0.00	

Basic Earnings Per Share Calculation:

Income from Continuing Operations
($1,500,000 − $9,000)/276,000 = $5.40
Discontinued Operations
$210,000/276,000 = $0.76
Net Income
($1,710,000 − $9,000)/276,000 = $6.16

Diluted Earnings Per Share Calculation:

Income from Continuing Operations
($1,500,000 − $9,000)/(276,000 + 1,200) = $5.38
Discontinued Operations
($210,000/276,000 + 1,200) =   0.76
Net Income
($1,710,000 − $9,000)/(276,000 + 1,200) = $6.14

Example

This example has both nonconvertible preferred and convertible preferred.

Background/Requirement

The Complex Company is located in Knoxville, Tennessee and has an accounting year that ends on December 31. A modified income statement for the 20x7 accounting year is presented below.

Income from Continuing Operations	$1,500,000
Discontinued Operations (less Income Tax Expense of $90,000)	$210,000
Net Income	$1,710,000

The tax rate for 20x7 was 30%.

The capital structure of the Complex Company includes common stock, nonconvertible and convertible, cumulative, preferred stock. Relevant information related to these securities is shown below.

Common Stock, Par Value of $1

Common Shares Outstanding on January 1, 20x7	270,000 Shares
Sold Common Shares on September 1, 20x7	18,000 Shares
Common Shares Outstanding on December 31, 20x7	288,000 Shares

Nonconvertible, Cumulative, 6% Preferred Stock, Par Value of $20

Preferred Shares Outstanding throughout the year	7,500 Shares

Cumulative, Convertible 4% Preferred Stock, Par Value of $10

Preferred Shares Outstanding throughout the year	5,000 Shares

The preferred stock is convertible at the rate of 5 common shares for one preferred share.

Requirement: Determine the earnings per share disclosure for the 20x7 accounting year.

Solution:

Preferred Stock Dividend on Nonconvertible Preferred Stock:

$7,500 \times \$20 \times 6\% = \$9,000$

Weighted Average of Common Shares Outstanding:

Shares		Months	
270,000	×	8	2,160,000
288,000	×	4	1,152,000
		12	3,312,000
			3,312,000/12 = 276,000 Shares*

*This agrees with the calculation method shown in the previous discussion: 270,000 + 18,000(4/12) = 276,000

Analysis of the Convertible Preferred Shares -- If-Converted Method:

To analyze the impact of the convertible preferred shares on the Diluted Earnings per Share Calculation, the If-Converted Method is applied.

Convertible Preferred Stock Dividend:	$5,000 \times \$10 \times 4\% =$	$2,000	
Common Shares That Would be Issued Upon Conversion:			
	$5,000 \times 5 =$	25,000	Shares
Adjustment to the Numerator		$2,000	
Adjustment to the Denominator		25,000	Shares
N/D Ratio	$\$2,000/25,000$ Shares $=$	$0.08	

Basic Earnings Per Share Calculation:

Income from Continuing Operations	$(\$1,500,000 - \$9,000 - \$2,000)/276,000 =$	$5.39
Discontinued Operations	$\$210,000/276,000 =$	.76
Net Income	$(\$1,710,000 - \$9,000 - \$2,000)/276,000 =$	$6.16

Diluted Earnings Per Share Calculation:

Note: Since the N/D ratio of the convertible preferred shares is less than the basic earnings per share for income from continuing operations, the convertible preferred shares will have a dilutive effect.

Income from Continuing Operations	$(\$1,500,000 - \$9,000)/(276,000 + 25,000) =$	$4.95
Discontinued Operations	$(\$210,000)/301,000 =$	.70
Net Income	$(\$1,710,000 - \$9,000)/(276,000 + 25,000) =$	$5.65

Example

This example shows the EPS disclosure for an accounting year. Example: The Complex Company is located in Knoxville, Tennessee and has an accounting year that ends on December 31. A modified income statement for the 20x7 accounting year is presented below.

Income from Continuing Operations	$1,500,000
Discontinued Operations (less Income Tax Expense of $90,000)	210,000
Net Income	$1,710,000

The tax rate for 20x7 was 30%.

The capital structure of the Complex Company includes common stock, nonconvertible, cumulative, preferred stock, and convertible bonds. Relevant information related to these securities is shown below.

Common Stock, Par Value of $1

Common Shares Outstanding on January 1, 20x7	270,000	Shares
Sold Common Shares on September 1, 20x7	18,000	Shares
Common Shares Outstanding on December 31, 20x7	288,000	Shares

Non-Convertible, Cumulative, 6% Preferred Stock, Par Value of $20

Preferred Shares Outstanding throughout the year	7,500	Shares

6% Convertible Bonds Payable

Total Face Value of Outstanding Bonds	$1,000,000

The bonds were outstanding throughout the year

The bonds are convertible to common shares at the rate of 50 shares for each $1,000 bond.

Requirement: Determine the earnings per share disclosure for the 20x7 accounting year.

Solution:

Preferred Stock Dividend on Non-Convertible Preferred Stock: 7,500 × $20 × 6% = $9,000

Weighted Average of Common Shares Outstanding:

Shares		Months	
270,000	x	8	2,160,000
288,000	x	4	1,152,000
		12	3,312,000
			3,312,000 /12 = 276,000 Shares*

*This agrees with the calculation method shown in the previous discussion: 270,000 + 18,000(4/12) = 276,000

Analysis of the Convertible Bonds - If-Converted Method:

To analyze the impact of the convertible bonds on the Diluted Earnings per Share Calculation, the If-Converted Method is applied.

Bond Interest Expense

$1,000,000 × 6% = $60,000

Bond Interest Expense, Net of Tax

$60,000 (1 − .30) = $42,000

Common Shares That Would be Issued Upon Conversion:

(1,000,000/$1,000) × 50 Shares = 50,000

Adjustment to the Numerator	$42,000		
Adjustment to the Denominator	50,000	Shares	
N/D	$42,000/50,000	Shares	= $0.84

Basic Earnings Per Share Calculation:

Income from Continuing Operations	($1,500,000 − $9,000)/276,000 =	5.40
Discontinued Operations	$210,000/276,000 =	.76
Net Income	($1,710,000 − $9,000)/276,000 =	$6.16

Diluted Earnings Per Share Calculation:

Note: Since the N/D ratio of the convertible bonds is less than the basic earnings per share for income from continuing operations, the convertible bonds will have a dilutive effect.

Income from Continuing Operations		
	($1,500,000 − $9,000 + $42,000)/(276,000 + 50,000) =	$4.70
Discontinued Operations	$210,000/326,000 =	.64
Net Income	$1,710,000 − 9,000 + 42,000)/326,000 =	$5.35

Example

Note: In the last three examples (Complex Company), if the firm had all three potential common stock securities at the same time (stock options, convertible preferred shares, and convertible bonds payable), the equity contracts and convertible securities would be ranked in order of N/D ratio, from lowest to highest. Based on the data from the previous examples this rank ordering is shown below.

Security	N/D
Stock Options	$0.00 = $0/1,200
Convertible Preferred Shares	$0.08 = $2,000/25,000
Convertible Bonds	$0.84 = $42,000/50,000

The calculation of DEPS for income from continuing operations is as follows (all EPS figures are for income from continuing operations):

BEPS = ($1,500,000 − $9,000 − $2,000)/276,000 = $5.39

First, enter the stock options into DEPS because the N/D ratio of $0.00 is less than $5.39. The tentative DEPS figure = ($1,500,000 − $9,000 − $2,000)/(276,000 + 1,200) = $5.37.

Second, enter the convertible preferred into DEPS because the N/D ratio of $.08 is less than $5.37. The tentative DEPS figure = ($1,500,000 − $9,000 − $2,000 + $2,000)/(276,000 + 1,200 + 25,000) = $4.93.

Lastly, enter the convertible bonds into DEPS because the N/D ratio of $.84 is less than $4.93. The tentative DEPS figure = ($1,500,000 − $9,000 − $2,000 + $2,000 + $42,000)/(276,000 + 1,200 + 25,000 + 50,000) = $4.35.

This is the reported amount for DEPS for income from continuing operations.

Segment Reporting

The disclosure requirements for firms with different business segments are considered here.

After studying this lesson, you should be able to:

1. Define an operating segment.

2. Explain how a reportable segment is identified using three quantitative tests.

3. Articulate the 75% rule for reporting.

4. List the major items to be disclosed for a reportable segment.

5. Apply the quantitative tests in an actual situation.

I. Operating Segments

   A. Financial statements provide highly aggregated information. For a firm that conducts activities in several different lines of business, users would benefit from disclosures that provide more disaggregated information. To that end, GAAP requires, under certain circumstances, that information be provided by major business segment.

   > **Note**
   > *The purpose of segment reporting is to assist the financial statement users' understanding of the entity's performance. Because segment reporting provides disaggregated information, it contains predictive value and confirmatory value to the financial statement user.*

   B. Under GAAP, business segments are identified by employing a management approach. That is, segments are identified in the same manner that management segments the company for purposes of making operating decisions. These segments are referred to as operating segments.

   C. Operating segments must have three characteristics.

   1. The segment is involved in revenue producing and expense incurring activities.

   2. The operating results of the segment are reviewed by the company's chief operating decision maker on a regular basis.

   3. There is discrete financial information available for the segment.

   D. Not all subunits of a corporation are operating segments. The corporate headquarters would not be an operating segment for many firms for example.

II. Identification of Reportable Segments—Quantitative Tests—A reportable segment is one that meets one or more of the following three quantitative tests. Not all operating segments are reportable segments. Disclosure is required only for reportable segments.

   > **Note**
   > *In the past, the quantitative tests have been the most frequently tested aspect of segment reporting.*

   A. The operating segment's revenue from all sources (internal and external) is 10% or more of the combined (internal and external) revenues of all of the company's reported operating segments.

   B. The operating segment's operating profit or loss (absolute value) is 10% or more of the greater of the following two amounts (absolute value). Operating profit is pretax.

   1. The combined operating profit of all operating segments that did not report an operating loss

   2. The combined loss of all operating segments that did report an operating loss

   C. The operating segment's identifiable assets are 10% or more of the combined assets of all operating segments.

III. Aggregation of Two or More Segments

A. For the quantitative tests, two or more segments can be aggregated provided this aggregation is consistent with the objective of segment reporting, and the segments are similar in each of the following areas:

1. The nature of products and services

2. The nature of the production processes

3. Customer type or class

4. Distribution methods for products and services

5. The nature of the regulatory environment

> **Note**
> *Each of the three criteria uses 10% or more as the cutoff percentage. The 10% cutoff is an example of a GAAP-imposed materiality threshold.*

 **Example**
If a firm has three major department stores in various parts of the country, each of which meets the operating segment definition, the stores can be aggregated into a single reportable segment to avoid excessive reporting.

IV. Reportable Segments—the 75% Rule—The total external revenue reported by reportable segments must be at least 75% of the company's total consolidated revenues. This is an overall materiality threshold for reporting.

A. If this test is not met initially, more reportable operating segments must be identified, even if the additional segments do not meet one of the three quantitative tests.

B. There is no stated limit on the number of reportable segments, but as a practical matter, if the number reaches ten, then the firm should assess whether adding more segments is worth the cost.

V. Reportable Segments—"All Other" Category—All nonreportable segments are grouped into an *all other* category and their results are combined for reconciliation purposes.

VI. Reportable Segments—Required Disclosures—The required disclosures for reportable segments include the following (note that operating segments that are not reportable segments are not subject to these reporting requirements). Note also that the information reported reflects the way the firm reports information internally, which may not always be in conformity with GAAP. However, this approach was considered to be more useful than a pure GAAP-based reporting model.

A. Factors used to identify operating segments

B. General information about the products and services of the operating segments

C. Internal and external sales revenue

D. A measure of profit or loss, and total assets

E. The nature of differences between the measurement of segment quantitative information such as income and assets, and the measurement of the firm's reported quantitative information

F. Interest revenue

G. Interest expense

H. Depreciation, depletion, and amortization expense

I. Other significant noncash items

J. Unusual or infrequent items

K. Equity in net income of investees, in which the investment is accounted for under the equity method

L. Income tax expense or benefit

M. Reconciliation of the totals of segment revenues, reported profit or loss, assets, and other significant items to the total for the firm as a whole

N. Capital expenditures

VII. Other Required Disclosures—If the following information is not already provided through the required segment information, firms must separately disclose the following:

A. Revenues from external customers from each product and service or groups of similar products or services

B. Revenues from the home country of the firm and from all foreign countries in total. If the revenues from one foreign country are material, then those revenues are to be disclosed separately.

C. The same disclosure as B above is required for long-lived assets other than financial instruments, long-term customer relationships with a financial institution, mortgage and other servicing rights, and deferred tax assets.

D. Major customers: If the revenue from a single customer amounts to 10% or more of the firm's revenues, this fact must be disclosed, including the amount of revenues from each such customer, and the operating segment or segments that earn that revenue. The identity of the customer need not be disclosed.

VIII. Comprehensive Example

Example

The Smith Company has four operating segments that are identified below. Information related to the current accounting year is also shown below. The revenue column constitutes the firm's entire revenues.

Segment	Total Revenues	Operating Profit (Loss)	Identifiable Assets
Clothing	$200	$50	$100
Sports Equipment	$150	($60)	$90
Beverage	$50	($10)	$25
Furniture	$300	$150	$200
Totals	**$700**	**$130**	**$415**

Additional information: Revenues related to internal transactions totaled $20. Of this amount, $10 of revenues was recorded by the clothing segment and $10 was reported by the furniture segment.

Revenue test: 10% of $700 = $70

Reportable Segments: Clothing, Sports Equipment, and Furniture

Operating profit test: 10% of $200 = $20

Note: The combined operating profit for those segments with positive profit ($200) exceeded the absolute value of the combined operating loss for those segments with losses ($70). Therefore, $200 is used for the test.

Reportable Segments: Clothing, Sports Equipment, and Furniture.

Note that sports equipment has an operating loss but the absolute value of that loss exceeds the $20 test amount.

Identifiable asset test: 10% of $415 = $41.5

Reportable Segments: Clothing, Sports Equipment, and Furniture.

Clothing, sports equipment, and furniture all meet at least one of the tests described above and are reportable segments. Only beverages is not a reportable segment (but it is an operating segment).

The results for each of the three quantitative tests are shown above for completeness but an operating segment need meet only one of the tests in order to qualify as a reporting segment.

75% Test:

75% of $680 = $510. ($680 = $700 –$20 internal revenue). Consolidated revenues are computed by removing intersegment revenues.

(The $680 amount is the firm's external revenue.)

External Revenue of Clothing Segment	$190
External Revenue of Sports Equipment Segment	$150
External Revenue of Furniture Segment	$290
Total External Revenue	**$630**

The 75% Test is met collectively by the three reportable segments because $630 equals or exceeds $510. No additional reportable segments need be identified.

Interim Financial Reporting

Interim Reporting Principles

This is the first of two lessons about interim reporting.

After studying this lesson, you should be able to:

1. Explain the underlying principles for interim reporting.

2. Explain and apply the basic principles of interim reporting to revenues and expenses.

3. Compute income tax expense for interim periods.

4. Describe the application of the lower-of-cost-or-market procedure for interim periods.

I. **Background and General Approach to Interim Reporting**—Why interim reporting? *Timeliness* is one of our enhancing characteristics of accounting information.

    A. Interim reports are not audited although for SEC registrants the reports are reviewed—a more limited procedure relative to an audit. As such, interim reports must be analyzed with more caution, compared with annual reports. Interim reports tend to be less accurate, subject to greater estimation error due to the shorter period involved, and are less complete. However, they improve the timeliness (time period assumption) of financial reporting.

    B. The general reporting philosophy for interim reports is that interim periods are to be viewed as an integral part of the annual period, rather than as a separate or discrete period. This principle guides many of the specific accounting principles. For example, materiality is determined with reference to annual reports, not to amounts in interim reports.

    C. In general, firms must use the same accounting methods (e.g., LIFO, straight-line depreciation) for interim reporting as they do for annual reporting.

    D. **Interim Relates to Annual**—When investors read an interim report, they are interested in evaluating the interim period as it relates to the annual period.

        1. Thus, when more than one interim period is affected by an expenditure for example, the related expense is recognized in the periods benefited, rather than recognized in the period cash was paid.

        2. There are exceptions to this principle, however. Although the integral view is required by GAAP, the *discrete* view—considering each interim reporting period as a separate period—is applied in several situations. The following material first highlights items that reflect the discrete view. The later items exemplify the integral view.

    E. **Interim Period Length**—Interim periods can be of any length less than a year; they are not limited to three-month periods (quarterly periods) although for SEC registrants, the quarterly report (10-Q) is the focus of interim reporting. Revenues earned and realizable in an interim period are recognized in that interim period.

    F. The following table summarizes the general rule for recognition during interim periods.

Item	General Rule	Exceptions
Revenues	Same basis as annual reports	None
Cost of Goods Sold	Same basis as annual reports	1. Gross profit method may be used to estimate CGS and ending inventory for each interim period. 2. Liquidation of LIFO base-period inventory, if expected to be replaced by year end, should be charged to CGS at expected replacement cost. 3. Temporary declines in inventory market value not recognized but must recognize other than temporary declines in interim period of decline 4. Planned manufacturing variances should be deferred if expected to be absorbed by year-end.
All Other Costs and Expenses	Same basis as annual reports	Expenditures which clearly benefit more than one interim period may be allocated among periods benefited, e.g., annual repairs, property taxes
Income Taxes	Estimate annual effective tax rate	None
Discontinued Operations	Recognized in interim period as incurred	None

II. **Revenue Recognition**—Revenues are recognized in each interim period, as they would be in an annual period. Revenues earned and realizable in an interim period are recognized in that interim period.

    A. If a firm uses the percentage of completion method on long-term contracts, the profit recognized each quarter is based on the percentage of completion at the end of each quarter. If a loss is anticipated in quarter 3, the entire contract loss is recognized in quarter 3.

    B. Earnings Per Share (EPS) is reported under the discrete view. Each quarterly EPS amount reflects only the events of that quarter. The assumptions and computations leading to the quarterly EPS amount reflect the circumstances within each interim period separately, rather than estimations of year-end circumstances. For example, shares issued in the third quarter affect reported EPS for the third and fourth quarter only, not the first two quarters.

III. **Expense Recognition**

    A. The general rule for expense recognition is:

        1. If the cost or expense has no relationship to other quarters, recognize the entire expense in the quarter in which the cost was incurred (the discrete view).

        a. Examples

            i. Discontinued operations net of applicable tax (if a component qualifying for discontinued operations reporting is considered held for sale in a particular quarter, the usual discontinued operations reporting is required for that quarter with later adjustments to any gain or loss recognized in those later quarters)

            ii. Gains and losses on disposals of plant assets

        b. These items have no relationship to interim periods other than the one in which they occurred.

        c. Arbitrary allocation of these items to other quarters is not permitted.

2. If the cost or expense benefits other quarters or interim periods, allocate the cost to those other quarters and recognize the appropriate amount of expense in those quarters (the integral view).

    a. **Examples**

        i. Depreciation

        ii. Property tax expense

        iii. Rent expense if prepaid for longer than one interim period

        iv. Advertising expense if expenditures benefit more than one interim period

        v. Bad debt expense if the firm uses an annual estimation procedure

    b. These expenses are allocated to the interim periods benefited even though some may be paid in full in one interim period, because they benefit more than one interim period.

    c. Repairs and maintenance expenditures may be cyclical with significant expenditures in one quarter benefiting the entire year. If the expenditures are planned to cover an annual period (or longer), then each interim period should recognize only its portion of the total expenditure as expense.

B. **Expenses Directly Related to Revenue**—Expenses directly related to revenue (cost of goods sold, sales commissions) are recognized in the same period as the related revenue.

C. **Income Tax Expense**—The interim tax accrual includes state, local, and foreign tax expense/liability. So although the federal tax rate may not change, it is very likely that the estimated annual effective tax rate would change as income increases, because most states have graduated rates. Therefore, the final rate(s) applicable to annual income is not known until the end of the year.

1. The income tax expense (which is computed only for income from continuing operations) for each interim period is computed as follows:

    a. The annual rate to be applied to income from continuing operations is re-estimated each quarter (the rate does not consider the tax on discontinued operations, which would be reported in the quarter these items were incurred, at the incremental rate at the time).

    b. That rate is applied to total interim income through the end of the current quarter, yielding total estimated tax to date.

    c. The income tax reported in previous quarters is subtracted from the results in the second step to yield the income tax expense for the current quarter.

    d. This procedure is a good example of the integral view of interim reporting—the interim period is an integral part of an annual period.

Example
Income tax recognized for quarter 1 is $20,000, based on the annual rate that is expected to apply to the firm. At the end of quarter 2, the expected annual income tax rate is 30% and pretax income for the first two quarters is $130,000.

Income tax expense to be recognized for quarter 2 only is $19,000 (.30 × $130,000 – $20,000).

IV. **Declines in Inventory Application to Interim Reports**—The decline in the value of the inventory is determined by applying either the lower of cost or net realizable value (LC –NRV) or the lower of cost or market (LC-M) approach. See the Inventory lesson "Subsequent Measurement of Inventory" for further discussion on the application of these methods.

A. **Temporary declines** in inventory are those expected to reverse by year's end.

1. These are not recognized as losses in the interim periods in which they occur. This treatment is consistent with the integral view of interim reporting.

2. No loss is expected for the year; therefore, a temporary loss should not be recognized in a specific quarter.

3. Later recoveries are not recorded because the previous loss was not recorded.

B. **Permanent declines** in inventory are those not expected to reverse in the current year are recognized as losses in the interim periods in which they occur.

C. Later recoveries are recognized as gains to the extent of previous losses only.

D. The inventory may not be marked up above cost.

V. Related Questions

Question

An inventory loss (decline in inventory value below cost) is incurred in quarter 2 but is expected to be recovered by year-end. However, it was not actually recovered by the end of the year. In what interim periods is the loss recognized?

Answer

The loss is recognized in quarter 4 because it was expected to be temporary as of the end of quarter 2 and no loss was recognized then.

Question

An inventory loss occurred in the first quarter and was not expected to reverse in the current year. But the loss was recovered in the second quarter with the market price increase exceeding the decline from the first quarter. How should this be treated in the interim reports for quarters 1 and 2?

Answer

Write the inventory down in quarter 1, recognize the loss, and then write it back up in quarter 2 but only to cost, recognizing a gain.

Interim Reporting—Details

After studying this lesson, you should be able to:

1. Describe the reporting of LIFO liquidations and cost accounting variances in interim reports.

2. Explain the application of interim reporting principles to accounting changes.

3. List the minimum reporting requirements for interim reports.

I. **LIFO Liquidation**—If a firm uses LIFO for annual reporting, it must also use LIFO for interim reporting. When a LIFO layer is liquidated in a particular interim period (number of units purchased is less than number of units sold in the interim period), the accounting depends on whether the liquidation is expected to be restored by the end of the annual period.

   A. **Restoration Expected**—If the liquidation is expected to be restored, then the interim period cost of goods sold should reflect the estimated cost of the replacement (this preserves the effect of LIFO for the interim period during which the liquidation took place). The firm recognizes an increase in cost of goods sold and recognizes a provision (liability) for the future purchase. This liability is extinguished in a later interim period when the inventory is replenished. As a result, overestimated earnings are avoided. Also, the ending inventory for the interim period reflects the restoration. This is another example of the integral view of interim reporting.

   B. **Restoration Not Expected**—If the liquidation is not expected to be restored, then the interim period cost of goods sold should reflect the actual cost of the layer liquidated.

II. **Cost Accounting Variances**—Purchase price variances, and volume variances expected to be absorbed by the end of the current year are deferred (not recognized in earnings) for the interim period.

   A. This is consistent with the integral view of interim reporting because there is no variance expected for the year.

   B. The reason for the deferral is that, from the point of view of the entire reporting year, there will be no volume variance.

   C. If the variances will not be absorbed (reversed) by other purchases of material or by increased production later in the year, they are recognized in the quarter of incurrence.

III. **Gross Margin Method for Inventory**—The gross margin method (also called the gross profit method) is not allowed for annual reporting purposes, but can be used for interim reporting. This method uses the gross margin percentage to estimate cost of goods sold from purchase information. The estimated cost of goods sold then is used to estimate ending inventory for the quarter without having to count inventory. Footnote disclosure of the use of this method is required.

IV. **Principle Changes**

   A. A change in accounting principle made in an interim period is reported in the same way as for annual statements. The retained earnings balance at the beginning of that interim period is adjusted to reflect the new principle, and the balances of previous interim periods reported comparatively with the interim period of change are retrospectively adjusted.

Example
A new accounting principle is adopted in quarter 3. The beginning retained earnings balance for quarter 3 is adjusted to reflect the new method up to that point, and quarter 1 and 2 statements are retrospectively adjusted to reflect the new principle.

B. Impracticability Exception—However, the impracticability exception for annual periods does not apply to prechange interim periods in the year the change was made. When it is impracticable to apply the retrospective method to prechange interim periods of the same fiscal year, then the change is made as of the beginning of the subsequent fiscal year.

C. For interim periods after an accounting principle change, the effect of the principle change on income from continuing operations and net income, and related per share amounts are shown.

Example

If an accounting principle change is adopted in the second quarter, these disclosures are required for the last three quarters of the fiscal year.

V. Estimate Changes

A. A change in estimate is accounted for in the interim period in which the change in estimate is made. Earlier interim periods are not affected. If material, the effect of the change on net income for the interim period and subsequent periods is reported.

Example

A change in property, plant, and equipment useful lives is made in quarter 3. The new estimate is applied as of the beginning of quarter 3. The effect of the change on earnings for quarter 3 is reported in quarter 3 results. The new estimate is also applied to quarter 4 and the effect of the change on quarter 4 earnings is reported.

VI. Interim Reports and Segment Reporting—When a firm subject to the segmental disclosure requirements issues interim reports, the following interim information is required to be reported for each segment:

A. External revenues (other than from intersegment sales)

    1. Intersegment revenues.

    2. Segment profit or loss.

VII. Reporting Requirements

A. GAAP does not require interim reports. However, the SEC requires that registrants file the 10-Q report for each quarter. Also, quarterly reports are provided as supplemental information within the annual report.

B. If non-SEC registrants choose to report interim financial statements, there is no requirement that the statements be as complete as annual statements. As a result, there is considerable variation in the detail reported. The FASB encourages the reporting of an interim balance sheet and statement of cash flows. Larger firms tend to provide more complete information. When the fourth quarter interim report is not provided, the annual report should disclose significant events for that quarter, along with material adjustments at year's end including unusual or infrequent items or discontinued operations.

C. If an interim report is provided, the minimum required disclosures include information about:

    1. Sales and other revenue, unusual or infrequent items, discontinued operations, net income

    2. Seasonal revenues and expenses allowing users to assess the impact on both the interim period and annual period

    3. Changes in estimated income tax expense

    4. Contingencies

    5. Fair value

    6. Earnings per share

7. Changes in accounting principle and estimates

8. Significant cash flow changes

D. Cumulatives and Comparatives—At any interim period, the financial statements would present the cumulative results as well as the comparative for the prior year.

    1. For example: reporting as of June/30 (Quarter 2):

        a. Income Statements (4):

            i. Income Statement for Quarter 2 (and prior year Q 2)

            ii. Cumulative Income Statement for 1/1—6/30 (and Comparatives for prior year)

        b. Balance Sheets (3):

            i. Balance Sheet as of 6/30 (and Comparatives for prior year)

            ii. Balance Sheet as of 12/31/prior year's end

        c. Statement of Cash Flows: (4)

            i. Statement of Cash Flows for Quarter II (and Comparatives for prior year)

            ii. Cumulative Statement of Cash Flows for 1/1—6/30 (and Comparatives for prior year

Financial Statements of Employee Benefit Plans

Pension Plan Reporting

After studying this lesson, you should be able to:

1. Distinguish defined contribution and defined benefit plans.

2. Identify the two required financial statements for defined contribution pension plans and defined benefit pension plans.

3. Recognize the components of the statement net assets available for benefits.

4. Recognize the components of the statement of changes in net assets available for benefits.

This lesson on pensions reviews the two required financial statements for pension plans.

I. The **two required financial statements** of pension plans are a **Statement of Net Assets Available for Benefits** of the plan and a **Statement of Changes in Net assets Available for Benefits**.

   a. The statement of net assets available provides the balances for the assets that are available for plan distribution. At least two years of balances are presented.

   b. The statement of changes in net assets shows the change in the balances of the assets. In other words, the numbers on the statement represent the annual change figures not the balance.

Test Tip
You are likely to see a multiple-choice question about the two required financial statements for pension plans because this is specifically identified in the AICPA blueprint as a "remembering and understanding" level topic.

II. **Two Types of Pension Plans**—(1) Defined contribution plans and (2) defined benefit plans.

   A. **Defined Contribution Plans**

Definition
Defined Contribution Plans: The amount of the employer contribution is defined by contract. For example, the employer contributes 5% of gross salary to the plan each month.

   1. In a defined contribution plan, the benefits paid during retirement are dependent on the return on the pension fund assets, and, therefore, they are not defined. The employee bears the risk of fund performance in this type of plan. The sponsoring firm has no obligation to the employee beyond the total annual contribution. A 401(k) plan is an example of a defined contribution plan.

   B. **Defined Benefit Plans**

Definition
Defined Benefit Plans: The benefits paid during retirement are based on a formula and therefore are defined. For example, the employer promises (or defines) the amount the employee will receive each month in retirement.

1. In a defined benefit plan, the contribution to the pension fund is not defined. The employer bears the risk in this type of plan because the benefit is defined. The employer is responsible for ensuring that the retired employee's benefits are paid.

2. Additional required disclosures—Actuarial present value of accumulated plan benefits, disclosure of factors impacting a change in actuarial present value of accumulated plan benefits.

3. **Trustee**—Many firms sponsoring defined benefit plans use a trustee to disburse retirement checks and perform other administrative tasks concerning the pension plan. The sponsoring firm makes periodic funding contributions to the trust company. Those contributions and the earnings on them comprise the pension plan assets available for payment of retirement benefits. The periodic trustee report provides detailed information about the funding of the pension plan and benefit payments made by the plan.

III. Example: Statement of Net Assets Available for Benefits

Relevant, Inc. 401(0k) Plan Statement of Net Assets Available for Benefits	December 31, 20X6	December 31, 20X5
Assets	(in thousands)	
Investments, at fair value	$8,721	$7,894
Receivables:		
Employer contributions	249	286
Employee contributions	125	147
Interest, dividends, other	5	12
Total receivables	379	445
Total assets	9,100	8,339
Liabilities		
Administrative expenses and other payables	9	3
Total liabilities	9	3
Net assets available for benefits	$9,091	$8,336

IV. Example: Statement of Changes in Net Assets Available for Benefits

Relevant, Inc. 401(k) Plan Statement of Changes in Net Assets Available for Benefits	Year Ended December 31, 20X6
Additions	(in thousands)
Investment income:	
Net realized and unrealized appreciation in fair value of investments	$742
Interest and dividends	13
Total investment income	755
Contributions	
Employer	180
Participants	441
Rollovers	110
Total contributions	731
Interest income on notes receivable from participants	7
Total additions	1,493
Deductions	
Benefits paid directly to participants	678
Administrative expenses	5

Relevant, Inc. 401(k) Plan Statement of Changes in Net Assets Available for Benefits	Year Ended December 31, 20X6
Total deductions	683
Net increase in net assets before plan transfer out*	810
Net assets available for benefits:	
Beginning of year	8,090
End of year	$8,900

*Note: This is total additions minus total deductions.

Special-Purpose Frameworks

Cash, Modified Cash, Income Tax

In addition to the GAAP-based general-purpose financial statements described in prior lessons, there are other comprehensive bases of accounting that may be used by nonpublic business entities, specialized entities, and individuals to prepare financial statements. This lesson covers the major non-GAAP comprehensive basis of accounting used by nonpublic business entities. These bases of accounting are referred to as Other Comprehensive Basis of Accounting (OCBOA) or Special Purpose Frameworks.

This lesson covers accounting for the major non-GAAP comprehensive basis of accounting used by nonpublic business entities. A separate lesson covers the auditing of financial statements prepared using a "comprehensive basis other than GAAP" as set forth in SAS 800, Special Considerations—Audits of Financial Statements Prepared in Accordance with Special Purpose Frameworks. It should be noted that the cash, tax, and regulatory bases of accounting are commonly referred to as other comprehensive bases of accounting (OCBOA). The term OCBOA was replaced with the term Special Purpose Framework for auditors under SAS 800. OCBOA is no longer used in Generally Accepted Auditing Standards (GAAS). However, OCBOA is still commonly used in practice. A separate lesson is presented by Professor Don Tidrick, author of the Auditing and Attestation section of CPAexcel®.

After studying this lesson, you should be able to:

1. Identify each separate basis of accounting:
   - Cash Basis
   - Modified Cash Basis
   - Income Tax Basis
   - Other

2. Describe the characteristics of each separate accounting basis.

3. Know how each separate accounting basis differs from GAAP.

I. **Special Purpose Framework or Other Comprehensive Bases of Accounting**—General-purpose financial statements, as described in prior lessons, are based on generally accepted accounting principles (GAAP) for public business enterprises. There are circumstances, however, when financial statements not based on GAAP are used by nonpublic business entities to avoid the time-consuming and costly application of GAAP. For example, another comprehensive basis of accounting (other than GAAP) may be used by sole proprietorships, partnerships or small, closely held corporations when the entity does not have loan covenants or other requirements that mandate the preparation of GAAP-based financial statements. There are over 2.8 million partnerships and over 20 million sole proprietorships in the United States. Many of these nonpublic businesses use another comprehensive basis of accounting. The primary acceptable other comprehensive bases of accounting widely used by nonpublic businesses entities, including cash basis, modified cash basis, and income tax basis, are covered in the following subsections. There are several categories of Special Purpose Framework or OCBOA financial statements:

Cash Basis
Modified Cash Basis
Income Tax Basis
Regulatory Basis
Other Basis with Substantial Support

A. Cash Basis Financial Statements

1. Cash basis financial statements are based solely on cash receipts and cash disbursements. In a pure cash basis of accounting, revenues are recognized only when cash is received and expenses are recognized only when cash is disbursed. The principles of accrual accounting are ignored. In cash basis accounting, there is no attempt to recognize revenues when they are earned and no attempt to recognize expenses when they are incurred, nor is there a matching of related expenses to revenues or to the time period in which they would be recognized in accrual basis accounting.

2. Because, in a pure cash basis of accounting, cash received is recognized as revenue (DR. Cash/CR. Revenue) and cash paid is recognized as expense (DR. Expense/CR. Cash), a balance-sheet-like statement would show only the asset Cash and Equity; there would be no other assets or liabilities shown. For example, a payment for capital assets (e.g., property, plant, or equipment) would be recognized as an expense, not as a long-term asset. Similarly, a collection of cash would be recognized as revenue, whether or not the good or service had been provided.

3. Example Journal Entries for Equipment Purchase of $10,000:

Cash Basis		Accrual Basis	
Equipment Expense	10,000	Equipment (asset)	10,000
Cash	10,000	Cash	10,000

4. A pure cash basis accounting and resulting financial statements may be appropriate for small, very closely held businesses (e.g., sole proprietorships, small partnerships, etc.) where the owners/managers whose primary interest and even survival depends on cash flows.

B. Modified Cash Basis Financial Statements

1. Modified cash basis financial statements result from using a combination of elements of cash basis accounting and accrual basis accounting. Conceptually, modified cash basis accounting would be any point on a continuum between pure cash basis at one end and full accrual basis at the other; the greater the number of accrual basis elements adopted, the greater the modification of the cash basis.

2. A modified cash basis of accounting is acceptable as another comprehensive basis of accounting if the modification(s) has substantial support in practice. Substantial support likely would be established if:

   a. The modification is equivalent to an element of accrual basis accounting, and

   b. The modification is logical and consistent with GAAP.

3. The most common and acceptable modifications to cash basis accounting include:

   a. Recognizing the acquisition of property, plant, equipment and inventory as assets (rather than as expenses), and depreciating, amortizing, or otherwise writing-off the assets in a regular manner, or

   b. Recognizing accounts receivable when revenues are earned and accounts payable when obligations are incurred, rather than deferring recognition until collections are received or payments are made, or

   c. Recognizing income taxes (and, perhaps, other significant taxes) when they become payable, rather than when paid.

4. When modifications to cash basis accounting are made, all related accounts must be reported using the same basis of accounting. For example, if long-term assets are recognized, then the related depreciation expense and accumulated depreciation must be recognized. Similarly, if debt is recognized, then the related interest expense (accrued and paid) must be recognized.

C. Income Tax Basis Financial Statements

1. Income tax basis financial statements result from using the federal income tax rules and regulations that a firm uses, or expects to use, in filing its income tax return. In income-tax basis accounting, the effects of events on a business are recognized when taxable income or deductible expense would be recognized on the tax return. Income is recognized on the financial statements in the period it is taxable and expenses are recognized on the financial statements in the period they are deductible. The specific requirements of federal income tax accounting specify different income and expense recognition rules depending on the nature of the item and the type of taxpayer. Therefore, financial statements based on the income tax basis of accounting will include items based on various recognition principles, from pure cash to full accrual accounting, depending on that tax codes treatment of these items.

2. Some items of economic and accounting consequence to an entity are never recognized for tax purposes. These are commonly called permanent differences. For example, proceeds from life insurance on officers or portions of intercompany dividends are not taxable income to an entity but provide cash to the entity. Similarly, the premium on life insurance on officers and certain fines are not deductible for income tax purposes but require the payment of cash. Under the income tax basis of accounting, nontaxable receipts (revenue) and nondeductible payments (expenses) related to these permanent differences generally would be recognized in a statement of revenues and expenses. That recognition may be made in one of three ways:

   a. As separate line items in the revenue and/or expense sections of the statement of revenues and expenses (the most common treatment)

   b. As separate line items shown as additions to or deductions from the net revenues and expenses

   c. The nature and amounts disclosed in the notes to the financial statements

3. Because items and amounts reported for tax purposes are subject to adjustment by the Internal Revenue Service (IRS), the corresponding amounts reported in tax-based financial statements are subject to change as the tax code is changed by U.S. Congress. Therefore, the notes to the financial statements should clearly indicate not only the basis on which the statements were prepared, but also that they are subject to change as a result of IRS determinations. When such adjustments do occur, the treatment in the financial statements will depend on the nature of the item adjusted.

   a. If the adjustment relates to an error in the tax return of a prior year, then a prior period adjustment is appropriate.

   b. If the adjustment relates to an item that is not an error and is not balance sheet related, then the adjustment would be treated as a current-period expense (or income).

   c. If the adjustment relates to an item that is not an error and is balance-sheet related, then the adjustment would be treated as a prior period adjustment.

4. **Other acceptable non-GAAP basis of accounting**—In addition to the cash basis, the modified cash basis, and the income tax basis of accounting, two additional categories of other comprehensive basis of accounting exist. These additional categories of OCBOA are:

   1. A basis of accounting used to comply with a regulatory agency that has jurisdiction over the reporting entity. Regulatory financial statements do fall under the category of a Special Purpose Framework for audit purposes.

      a. Examples would include financial statements filed with state insurance or public utility regulatory agencies.

      b. Regulatory-based financial statements should be restricted to use by the entity and the regulatory agency.

   2. There also may be financial statements that we have not covered. These financial statements are prepared using a basis with a definite set of accounting and reporting criteria that has substantial support and which is applied to all material financial statement items. One example of these might be financial statements that had price level or inflation adjusted financial statements.

Private Company Council

The purpose of this lesson is to provide a description of the Private Company Council (PCC), its purpose, and the process for setting standards applicable to private companies. This lesson presents the definition of a public business entity and the significant accounting alternatives that relate to private companies.

After studying this lesson, you should be able to:

1. Describe the purpose of the PCC and its role in the standard setting process.

2. Describe the definition of a public business entity.

3. Identify the significant accounting differences for private companies.

I. **PCC Purpose**—In May 2012, the Financial Accounting Foundation (FAF) approved the establishment of the Private Company Council (PCC), an organization that will assist in setting accounting standards for private companies. The PCC has two principal responsibilities:

   A. To work with the Financial Accounting Standards Board (FASB) to identify places within existing Generally Accepted Accounting Principles (GAAP) where there are opportunities for alternative accounting for private companies.

   B. To serve in an advisory capacity to the FASB on the appropriate treatment of items under consideration for new GAAP and how those items may impact private companies.

II. **What Is a Public Business Entity?**

   A. The PCC provides a definition for a public business entity because any entity that is not public is a private entity. It may seem kind of backward to not give a definition of a private entity but to give a definition of a public entity, but it is easier to define the characteristics of a public entity and therefore identify what entities cannot apply the standards set by the PCC.

   B. The definition excludes not-for-profit companies and employee benefit plans. A public entity is one that (ASC 2013-12, para. 2):

      1. Is required by the SEC to file or furnish financial statements;

      2. Is required by the Securities Act of 1934 to file or furnish financial statements with a regulatory agency other than the SEC (for example debt securities);

      3. Is required to file or furnish financial statements with foreign or domestic regulatory agencies in order to sell or issue securities;

      4. Has issued securities that are traded, listed, or quoted on an exchange or over-the-counter market; or

      5. Has securities that are not subject to contractual restrictions and is required by law, contract, or regulation to prepare U.S. GAAP financial statements and make them publicly available on a periodic basis.

   C. The stand-alone financial statements of a subsidiary consolidated with a public company are not considered public business entities for purposes of its stand-alone financial statements. However, the subsidiary is considered a public business for purposes of the financial statements that are included in an SEC filing.

III. **PCC Process**

   A. PCC reviews existing U.S. GAAP and identifies standards that require reconsideration. Any proposed alternative GAAP requires a two-thirds vote of all PCC members.

   B. Proposed modifications to U.S. GAAP approved by the PCC are submitted to the FASB for endorsement. If endorsed by a simple majority of FASB members, the proposed modifications are exposed for public comment. Following receipt of public comment, the PCC determines if any changes are warranted and take a final vote. If approved, the final decision is submitted to the FASB for final approval.

C. If the FASB does not endorse the initial proposal or final modification, the FASB provides to the PCC documentation describing the reason(s) for the non-endorsement and possible changes for the PCC to consider.

IV. The PCC Framework

A. The PCC Framework is used to determine whether, and in what circumstances, private companies should have guidance for alternative recognition, measurement, disclosure, display, effective date, and transition reporting under U.S. GAAP. The differences between private companies and public companies are a driving force in determining whether alternative GAAP is warranted.

B. The Framework provides direction to evaluate the trade-off between user-relevance and cost-benefit for private companies. To help identify information needs of users of public company financial statements versus users of private company financial statements, the Framework outlines five factors that differentiate the needs of the financial statement users. These factors can help identify opportunities to reduce the complexity and costs of preparing financial statements for private companies.

1. Number of primary users and their access to management

2. Investment strategies of the primary users

3. Ownership and capital structure

4. Accounting resources available to generate reporting and disclosure information

5. Resources available for learning about new financial reporting guidance on a timely basis

C. The Framework discusses the areas in which financial accounting and reporting guidance might differ for private companies and public companies:

1. The main areas of guidance for private company accounting are with respect to (a) recognition and measurement, (b) disclosures, and (c) presentation.

V. Adoption and Transition to PCC Standards

A. A company can elect to adopt any of the PCC alternatives at the beginning of any annual period with no retrospective application. There is no retroactive application upon adoption, which significantly simplifies the adoption of a PCC accounting alternative and makes the PCC accounting much more accessible to private companies.

1. In addition, the adoption of the PCC alternative can be done without assessing the preferability of the PCC alternative. Eliminating the need to assess preferability provides private companies with greater flexibility when deciding whether or not to adopt PCC accounting.

VI. Accounting for Goodwill

A. A private entity may elect to amortize goodwill on a straight-line basis over 10 years, or less than 10 years if it is more appropriate. At the time of adoption of this standard, the entity must make an election to test goodwill impairment at the entity level or the reporting unit level.

B. A private entity may elect to perform goodwill impairment triggering event evaluation only at the end of a reporting period (annual or interim). That is, the private entity does not have to evaluate for triggering events related to goodwill impairment continuously throughout the year, only at the end of a reporting period.

C. When the private entity completes the impairment testing, it must apply the impairment test following the guidance for a public entity as required under ASC 350. This means that the private entity has the option to apply the pre-step qualitative assessment prior to the quantitative assessment.

VII. Simplified Accounting for Interest Rate Swaps

   A. This simplified hedge accounting applies only to interest rate swaps for variable rate debt to fixed rate debt (cash flow hedge). Many private companies have difficulty obtaining fixed rate debt at a competitive interest rate. Therefore these companies frequently enter into an interest rate swap to convert the variable rate debt to fixed rates.

   B. When certain criteria are met, the private entity can assume the swap is 100% effective. This assumption significantly reduces the testing needed for assessing and measuring ineffectiveness. The criteria are (815-20-25-131D):

   1. Both the variable rate on the swap and the borrowing are based on the same index and reset period.

   2. The terms of the swap are typical (a "plain-vanilla" swap), and there is no floor or cap on the variable interest rate of the swap unless the borrowing has a comparable floor or cap.

   3. The repricing and settlement dates for the swap and the borrowing match or differ by no more than a few days.

   4. The swap's fair value at inception (i.e., at the time the derivative was executed to hedge the interest rate risk of the borrowing) is at or near zero.

   5. The notional amount of the swap matches the principal amount of the borrowing. In complying with this condition, the amount of the borrowing being hedged may be less than the total principal amount of the borrowing.

   6. All interest payments occurring on the borrowing during the term of the swap are designated as hedged whether in total or in proportion to the principal amount of the borrowing being hedged.

   C. When these criteria are met, the private entity can use the practical expedient of settlement value to measure the value of the swap versus measuring the swap at fair value. Settlement value excludes the adjustment for performance risk and is generally viewed to be a simpler valuation.

   D. The private entity must complete documentation requirements related to cash flow hedge accounting and must comply with the disclosure requirements for hedge accounting (Topic 815) and fair value (Topic 820).

   E. This standard can be applied to existing swaps if the swap had a fair value at or near zero at the time the swap was initiated. The swap does not need to have a fair value at or near zero at the date the standard is elected. After the initial election, the entity cannot apply this standard to other swaps that existed at the date of election. In other words, once this standard is adopted, the entity must identify those existing swaps to which it wants to apply the standard. After application, the entity cannot go back and apply to other existing swaps—the application should happen all at once rather than piecemeal.

VIII. Applying Variable Interest Entity (VIE) Criteria to Common Control Arrangements

   A. Private companies may elect to not apply the VIE guidance to legal entities under common control. The VIE guidance is a process for determining whether an entity is a primary beneficiary and therefore required to consolidate another entity. The election to not apply the VIE guidance is allowed only if both the "parent" and the entity being evaluated for consolidation are private entities.

   B. If this exemption is elected it should be applied to all current and future entities under common control. In other words, the private entity cannot pick and choose which common control arrangements are or are not consolidated if the PCC election is adopted. If the PCC election is made, it must apply to all common control arrangement.

   C. The private company does not need to provide the disclosures associated with a VIE, but rather would disclose the information related to the common control arrangement. The disclosure should include a description of the lease arrangements that exposes the private company to provide financial support.

D. The private entity must still apply the consolidation guidance for those entities in which it has voting control.

IX. Simplified Accounting for Intangible Assets Acquired in a Business Combination

A. Private companies have the option to not recognize certain intangible assets associated with a business combination. Specifically, private companies can elect to not recognize customer-related intangibles that cannot be sold or licensed independent of the business (customer contracts and relationships) and noncompete agreements separately from goodwill. These intangible assets are costly and complex to value.

B. In general, the acquirer in a business combination must recognize all intangible assets that are (1) separable or (2) arise from contractual or other legal rights.

C. Private companies will be excluded from this requirement with respect to customer contracts, customer relationships, and noncompete agreements. Customer contracts that are nontransferable would not need to be separately valued and recognized. Customer relationships are often nontransferable because the relationship is unique with the private company. Noncompete agreements are also often nontransferable because the agreement is with an employee (or former employee) and the private entity. A noncompete agreement is a legal arrangement to prohibit another party from competing with the entity in a certain market for a certain period of time.

D. Private companies must recognize other identifiable intangibles such as copyrights, trademarks, and patents, separately from goodwill. In addition, customer-related intangibles that can be sold or licensed independent of other assets of the businesses must be recognized. For example, customer lists and other customer information that can be sold or licensed independently of the business would meet the separability criterion and would be valued and recognized as part of the business combination.

E. If the private company elects the PCC guidance on intangibles, it must also adopt the goodwill accounting alternative described above (ASU 2014-02), which requires goodwill to be amortized over a period of up to 10 years. The tandem requirement ensures that the customer-related and noncompete-related intangible assets embedded in goodwill are essentially amortized. The opposite is not required—if the private company elects to amortize goodwill, it does not have to elect this guidance on the intangible assets.

Select Financial Statement Accounts

Cash and Cash Equivalents

Cash

This lesson presents a summary of the accounting for cash, cash equivalents, and restricted cash.

After studying this lesson, you should be able to:

1. Define cash, cash equivalents, and restricted cash.

2. Choose which cash balances should be classified as cash equivalents or restricted cash.

3. Define compensating balances.

4. List two main internal controls over cash.

I. Articulation

    A. The balance sheet and the statement of cash flows:

        1. If a business enterprise uses the term **cash** on the statement of cash flows, the term used on the balance sheet will likewise be **cash**.

        2. If a business enterprise uses the term **cash and cash equivalents** on the statement of cash Flows, the term on the balance sheet will be **cash and cash equivalents**.

    B. A cash equivalent is a security with a fixed maturity amount and an original maturity to the purchaser of three months or less.

II. Accounting for Cash—The main reporting issue for cash is what to include in this category of assets. Several items are included in the cash account for balance sheet reporting purposes, and there are others that at first appear to be cash but are excluded.

    A. Cash—The current asset, represents unrestricted cash. This is cash that is available to meet current operating expenses and obligations as they arise.

        1. Included in cash—The components of cash include coin and currency, petty cash, cash in bank, and negotiable instruments such as ordinary checks, cashier's checks, certified checks, and money orders.

        2. Current liability—An overdraft of a bank account occurs when checks honored by the bank exceed the balance in the account. An overdraft may be offset against other cash accounts with the same bank, but not against cash accounts with other banks. In the latter case, the overdraft is listed as a current liability.

        3. Excluded from cash—Cash does not include certificates of deposit, legally restricted compensating balances, or restricted cash funds (such as a bond sinking fund). These amounts are either:

            a. Not available for the immediate payment of debts; or

            b. Management's intent is to use these resources for specific purposes. In addition, cash excludes postdated checks received from customers (include these in accounts receivable), advances to employees (a receivable), and postage stamps (a prepaid expense).

    B. Cash Equivalents—Although not cash, cash equivalents are so near cash that they are often combined with cash for financial statement reporting.

Example
Cash equivalents include: U.S. Treasury obligations (bills, notes, and bonds), commercial paper (very short-term corporate notes), and money market funds.

   C. **Compensating Balance**—This is a minimum balance that must be maintained by the firm in relation to a borrowing. Such a balance increases the effective rate of interest on the borrowing and reduces the risk to the lender.

      1. With respect to compensating balances, if the balance is related to a short-term liability, the compensating balance is shown as a current asset (as in the example below), but is not considered a part of the unrestricted cash balance. If the compensating balance is related to a long-term liability, the compensating balance is a non-current asset.

Example
A firm borrows $10,000 for one year at 6% but must maintain a $700 compensating balance in an account with the lender financial institution. The $700 is not included in the cash account but is rather reported in restricted cash, a current asset. The annual effective interest rate is 6.45% [($10,000 x (.06)/$9,300]. The net loan is only $9,300 ($10,000 – $700).

   D. **Cash is a Monetary Asset** —A monetary asset is an asset with fixed nominal (stated) value. The nominal value of a monetary asset does not change with inflation. Cash is the most "monetary" of all assets. There is no uncertainty as to the stated or nominal value of cash at present or in the future. A $100 bill is always worth exactly $100. However, the purchasing power of cash declines with inflation. The amount of real goods and services a fixed amount of cash can buy decreases as the general price level increases. The effect is the opposite during times of deflation.

III. Cash—The Importance of Internal Control Measures

   A. Because cash is easily concealed and has universal value, companies go to great lengths to safeguard their cash. A variety of internal control measures are used to safeguard cash.

   B. The auditing section of this course considers these measures in detail. For cash, the most popular ones are:

      1. Separation of duties

      2. Bank reconciliations

   C. **Separation of Duties**—Separation of duties makes it more difficult for employees to perpetrate fraud and gain access to the firm's cash.

      1. Separation of Duties, in effect, forces employees to collude if they attempt to fraudulently remove any of the company's cash resources. At a minimum, the duties related to cash that should be separated are:

         a. Custody of cash

         b. Recording of cash

         c. Reconciliation of bank accounts

      2. The reason for this minimum separation is to prevent an employee from pilfering cash and concealing the action by altering the records.

   D. **Bank Reconciliations**—Bank reconciliations provide a check mechanism for both the company and the financial institution. In most cases, any errors detected in a bank reconciliation are the result of **honest** mistakes on the part of the company's employees or on the part of the bank's employees.

1. Bank reconciliations are necessary because cash transactions that occur near the end of a month or an accounting year may be recorded by the company but have not been recorded by the financial institution. Likewise, there may be some cash transactions that have been recorded by the financial institution but have not been recorded by the company.

Bank Reconciliations

The purpose of this lesson is to present the forms and components of a bank reconciliation.

After studying this lesson, you should be able to:

1. Complete a bank reconciliation of the book balance and the bank balance to the true cash balance.

I. **Benefits**—Bank reconciliations provide the following benefits:

   A. Enable a periodic comparison of the bank account balance and cash balance

   B. Help identify errors in the firm's records or bank records

   C. Establish the correct ending cash balance

   D. Provide information for adjusting entries

   E. Help reduce cash theft by employees if the reconciler does not have access to cash records or does not have access to cash (authorization to make disbursements, or cash custody)

II. **Simple Bank Reconciliation**—This type of reconciliation explains the difference between the balance per books and the balance per bank at the end of the month. For example, the November 20X7 bank reconciliation would reconcile the balance per books on November 30, 20X7, with the balance per bank on November 30, 20X7.

   A. There are three formats for the simple bank reconciliation:

      1. **Bank to book**—The starting point is the balance per bank. All adjustments are made to this balance to arrive at the balance per book.

      2. **Book to bank**—The starting point is the balance per book. All adjustments are made to this balance to arrive at the balance per bank.

      3. **Bank and book to true balance**—In this format, the bank balance and the book balance are separately reconciled to the **true** cash balance, which is reported in the balance sheet. The adjustments to the two starting points (bank balance and book balance) are those changes in cash that have not been recorded in the bank or the books at the end of the period.

> **Note**
> The third format is the format that is typically emphasized on the CPA Exam and will be the focus of our coverage.

Example

Balance Per Bank, November 30, 20X7 XX

+ Deposits in Transit	+ X
+ Cash on Hand	+ X
− Outstanding Checks	− X
± Errors made by Bank	± X
True Cash	XX
Balance Per Book, November 30, 20X7 XX	
+ Interest Earned	+ X
+ Note Collected	+ X
− Service Charges	− X
− NSF Check	− X
± Errors in **Firm's** Records	± X
True Cash	XX

4. **Explanations of adjustments to the bank balance**

   a. **Deposit in transit**—These deposits have been made by the company but have not cleared the bank as of November 30, 20X7. This situation is typically related to a bank policy. For example, some banks have a policy that all deposits made after 2 p.m. of a given day will be reflected by the bank on the next business day.

   b. **Cash on hand**—This amount reflects petty cash and undeposited cash receipts. You might think of cash on hand as being one step removed from being a deposit in transit. For example purposes, let's say a company makes a deposit at 3 p.m. on November 30, 20X7. Per bank policy, this deposit will be reflected by the bank on the next business day. This 3 p.m. deposit will be a deposit in transit. During the last two business hours of November 30, 20X7, the company collected additional cash of $200. This $200 of undeposited cash receipts will be considered cash on hand. This amount could not have been known by the bank as of November 30, 20X7.

   c. **Outstanding checks**—This amount represents checks written and mailed by the company that have not cleared the bank by November 30, 20X7.

   d. **Errors made by the bank**—This amount represents errors made by the bank. For CPA Exam purposes, it might be presented as a situation in which checks written by the ABC Company are subtracted from the balance of the ABZ Company. Alternatively, a deposit made by the ABZ Company may be added to the balance of the ABC Company. There are many types of errors that can be tested. The key is to determine which balance (book or bank) is in error, and by how much. The amount of the error is the adjustment to appear in the reconciliation.

5. **Adjustments to the book balance**

   a. **Interest earned**—This amount represents interest earned on the checking account. This amount was added to the company's checking balance by the bank on November 30, 20X7. The company will record this amount upon receipt of the November bank statement.

   b. **Note collected**—This amount represents principal and interest added to the company's checking balance by the bank upon collection of a note receivable. To fully understand the transaction, it must be remembered that the company secured the services of the bank to collect a note receivable. When the bank collected the note, the amount was added to the company's checking balance by the bank. The company will record the transaction when it receives the November bank statement or receives separate correspondence related to the note collection.

   c. **Service charges**—This amount represents service charges that the bank deducted from the company's checking balance on November 30, 20X7. The company will record the transaction upon receipt of the November 30, 20X7 bank statement.

   d. **NSF checks**—This represents *nonsufficient funds* checks received from customers. For example, a customer wrote a $500 check to the company, but the customer's checking balance was not large enough to cover the check payment. Upon determining the NSF check, the bank will reduce the company's checking balance. The company will record the NSF check upon receipt of the November 30, 20X7, bank statement or upon receipt of separate correspondence related to the NSF check.

   e. **Errors in firm's records**—This represents errors made in the company's records. For CPA Exam purposes, this situation might include some discussion of incorrect recording of cash receipts and disbursements. For example, a payment of $96 might have been recorded as a payment of $69. Alternatively, a cash receipt of $11,000 might have been recorded as a cash receipt of $1,100.

Example
The firm received a $320 check on account (correctly written by the customer) in November but recorded the amount as $230. The check cleared the bank in November. The firm's cash account is understated. The adjustment in the reconciliation would increase the cash account by $90 ($320 – $230).

Adjusting journal entries: Upon completion of the bank reconciliation, the company will prepare adjusting entries for each of the adjustments to the balance per books. Entries are required only for the adjustments to the book balance. These entries are illustrated below.

Interest earned on checking account:

DR: Cash   XX

  CR: Interest Revenue   XX

Note receivable collected by the bank:

DR: Cash   XX

  CR: Note Receivable   XX

  CR: Interest Revenue   XX

Service charges:

  DR: Service Charge Expense   XX

  CR: Cash   XX

NSF check received from customer:

  DR: Accounts Receivable   XX

  CR: Cash   XX

Note: The entry for the example any above, which understated the cash account by $90 Is:

DR: Cash   90

  CR: Accounts Receivable   90

Receivables

Accounts Receivable—Accounting and Reporting

The purpose of this lesson is to understand the recording and valuation of accounts receivable.

After studying this lesson, you should be able to:

1. Complete the journal entries for recording AR using the gross method and the net method for discounts and allowances.

I. **Receivables**—This subsection provides an explanation of four different types of receivables.

   A. **Accounts Receivable**—Typically related to customer transactions. That is, an account receivable is usually related to the sale of goods to customers or the provision of services to customers. The length of time related to this claim is very short, 30 to 90 days for most business enterprises. Due to this short time frame, an account receivable typically does not have an interest element.

   B. **Notes Receivable**—Often related to noncustomer transactions although many larger consumer items and transactions between businesses require a promissory note. Examples of transactions that relate to a note receivable include the sale of noncash assets, lending transactions, and the conversion of other receivables. A note receivable is usually related to a longer time frame than an account receivable, and due to that fact, all notes have an interest element. Notes provide increased security for the seller firm, are often negotiable, and usually can be converted to cash with a third party more easily than accounts receivable.

   C. **Trade Receivable**—Another name for customer accounts receivable.

   D. **Nontrade Receivables**—Those receivables created in noncustomer transactions.

II. **Balance Sheet Valuation of Receivable**

   A. Receivables are valued on the balance sheet at net realizable value, the amount of cash that the entity expects to collect at due date or at maturity. Depending on the type of receivable, there are several factors that cause the valuation of a receivable to be less than its face or nominal value.

   B. **Factors Affecting Receivable Valuation**— Several items affect the net valuation of receivables (and net sales). Accounts receivable typically reflects more adjustments than notes receivable. Accounts receivable is shown at its net collectible amount. The adjustments to accounts receivable include:

      1. Trade (quantity) discounts

      2. Cash (sales) discounts

      3. Sales returns and allowances

      4. Noncollectible accounts

   C. Recording Methods

      1. In addition, two different methods of accounting for receivables may be used:

        a. The *gross method,* which records receivables at gross invoice price (before cash discount)

        b. The *net method,* which records receivables at net invoice price (after cash discount)

      2. **Using gross and net**—The following example illustrates the journal entries for the first three mentioned previously above using both the gross and net methods. Noncollectible accounts are described in the next section.

Example
Trade discount and initial recording
Assume we sell $2,000 (list price) of goods, terms 3/10, n30. The sale is subject to a 5% trade discount.

	Gross	Net
Accounts Receivable	1,900	1,843
Sales	1,900*	1,843#

*{.95($2,000)}
#{$1,900(.97)}

The 3/10, n30 terminology indicates that a cash discount of 3% is available to the buyer if payment is remitted within 10 days after the sale. Otherwise, the gross price net of any returns and allowances is due 30 days after the sale. The **gross** invoice price is $1,900, the amount after the trade discount but before the cash discount. The net method records the sale at the gross amount less the 3% cash discount, or 97% of the gross invoice price.

3. Cash discount

Example
Payment is received within the 10-day discount period.

	Gross	Net
Cash	1,843	1,843
Sales Discounts	57	
Accounts Receivable	1,900	1,843

The Sales Discount account is a contra account to sales. It reduces gross sales to sales at its net amount. The net method records sales net of cash discount and does not require an adjustment for cash discounts taken by customers. The gross method separately records cash discounts taken by customers.

Payment is received after the 10-day discount period.

	Gross	Net
Cash	1,900	1,900
Sales Discounts Forfeited		57
Accounts Receivable	1,900	1,843

The Sales Discounts Forfeited account is a miscellaneous revenue account. The net method separately records cash discounts not taken by customers.

4. Returns and allowances

Example

A $200 allowance is made for a defect in the merchandise on the fifth day after sale

	Gross		Net
Sales Returns and Allowances	200		194*
Accounts Receivable		200	194

*{($200).97}

Sales Returns and Allowances is a contra account to sales. "Returns" are for merchandise returned from the customer and the "allowance" is for price reductions of the merchandise. A $200 return would be accounted for in the same manner.

D. Adjusting Entries—At the end of the year, material probable and estimable cash discounts (under the gross method) and sales returns and allowances must be recorded in the year of sale for correct reporting of net sales and accounts receivable.

Example

At the end of 20X8, a firm estimates that $30,000 of cash discounts will be taken by customers in 20X9, on 20X8 sales. The following adjusting entry is made at the end of 20X8:

Sales Discounts	30,000	
Allowance for Sales Discounts		30,000

Allowance for Sales Discounts is contra to accounts receivable. The entry thus reduces both net sales and net accounts receivable. In 20X9, assuming $25,000 of discounts are actually taken on 20X8 sales, the allowance for sales discounts account is debited rather than sales discounts (which were recognized in the previous entry). The remaining $5,000 is treated as an estimate change, reducing the amount of estimated sales discounts to be recognized in the 20X9 year-end adjusting entry.

A similar journal entry is required for estimated sales returns and allowances.

Uncollectible—Direct Write-Off and Allowance

This lesson presents the accounting and reporting of uncollectible accounts receivable.

After studying this lesson, you should be able to:

1. Complete the entries for the direct write-off and allowance method for uncollectibles.

I. Introduction

   A. The fourth factor affecting accounts receivable valuation is uncollectible accounts (the first three were trade discounts, cash discounts, and sales returns and allowances). This is the major issue affecting receivable valuation of receivables. Bad debt expense (also called uncollectible accounts expense on the CPA Exam) is the account that records the effect of uncollectible accounts. Bad debt expense is on the income statement. The allowance for uncollectible accounts is a balance sheet account contra to accounts receivable. Bad debt expense traditionally has been considered a cost of doing business rather than a sales adjustment.

   B. Most companies will use one of two methods to account for bad debt expense. The direct write-off method is the first method presented, followed by the allowance method.

II. Direct Write-Off Method

—This method records bad debt expense only when a specific account receivable is considered uncollectible and is written off. It can be used only when the firm is unable to estimate uncollectible accounts receivable reliably. Most large firms do not use this method.

   A. **Negative Aspects of the Direct Write-Off Method**—Aspects of the direct write-off method: First, if the direct write-off method is employed, accounts receivable are overvalued on the balance sheet. Second, for companies employing the direct write-off method, the company usually recognizes the revenue from a credit sale in one year and typically recognizes the bad debt expense in a subsequent year. So, due to poor balance-sheet valuation and poor matching of revenues and expenses, the direct write-off method is **not** considered in accordance with GAAP unless there is no basis for estimating bad debts.

   B. **Positive Aspects of the Direct Write-Off Method**—Aspects of the direct write-off method: Companies that use the direct write-off method justify its use for two reasons. First, the use of the direct write-off method may not be materially different in its effect on the company's financial statements relative to the allowance method. Second, the direct write-off method is simple and practical to use.

   C. **Typical Entries**—Bad Debt Expense and Bad Debts Recovered are both income statement accounts. The first is an expense account, while the second account is a miscellaneous revenue account.

An account is deemed uncollectible:		
Bad Debt Expense	XX	
Accounts Receivable		XX
An account previously written off is collected:		
Cash	XX	
Bad Debts Recovered		XX

III. The Allowance Method—The allowance method is the method of choice and is required under GAAP. This method records an estimate of the allowance and bad debt expense in an adjusting entry. The allowance is a contra account and reduces accounts receivable. Thus, both income and net accounts receivable are reduced in the year of sale by the estimate of uncollectible accounts on the year's sales.

A. Benefits of this Method—The positive aspects of the Allowance Method are twofold. First, the allowance method allows companies to value accounts receivables at net realizable value on the balance sheet. Second, the use of the allowance method allows companies to recognize the revenues and expenses from credit sales in the same accounting year.

B. Typical Entries

1. End-of-period adjusting entry—This is the important entry. The allowance for doubtful accounts is recorded at the end of the period even though the identity of the specific accounts that will be uncollectible and written off in a later period is unknown. The account is contra to accounts receivable.

Bad Debt Expense	XX	
Allowance for Doubtful Accounts		XX

C. Write-Off of Uncollectible Accounts—This entry has no effect on income or net assets or even net accounts receivable because the income effect of uncollectibles has already been recognized in the previous adjusting entry. The debit to the allowance decreases the allowance and thus increases net accounts receivable. The credit to accounts receivable decreases net accounts receivable

Allowance for Doubtful Accounts	XX	
Accounts Receivable		XX

D. Recovery of Accounts Previously Written Off—These two entries reinstate the allowance account and record cash received.

Accounts Receivable	XX	
Allowance for Doubtful Accounts		XX
Cash	XX	
Accounts Receivable		XX

Allowance for Uncollectible

This lesson presents the determination the allowance for uncollectible (doubtful) accounts receivable.

After studying this lesson, you should be able to:

1. Calculate the allowance, bad debt expense, and complete any adjusting entries associated with the estimated uncollectible accounts receivable.

I. **Allowance for uncollectible accounts**

1. An entity will evaluate past history of the collection of accounts receivable to determine a rate from which to estimate future uncollectible accounts. This analysis may result in the application of a percentage to the ending accounts receivable. Alternatively, the company may analyze the ending accounts receivable by **aging** the ending accounts receivable. This aging process involves grouping receivables by the amount of time they have been outstanding. Once the aging schedule is completed, the company then applies the rate of uncollectibility to each group of receivables.

2. The analysis of ending accounts receivable has one simple objective: the determination of the **needed** or desired balance in the allowance account. By **needed** balance, we mean the balance needed to properly value accounts receivable on the balance sheet. The desired allowance balance equals the expected write-offs to occur in the future based on the receivables at the balance sheet date.

3. Once the balance in the allowance account has been determined, the balance that is needed as an allowance is compared to the existing balance in the allowance account. The difference in these two balances is the amount of bad debt expense to be recorded for the accounting period.

 **Example: End-of-Period Adjustment**
Assume the following facts:

Accounts receivable on December is $200,000.

Based on past experience, the company estimates that 6% of ending receivables will be uncollectible.

Prior to the end-of-period adjustment, the allowance for doubtful accounts had an existing $3,000 debit balance due to greater than expected write-offs.

Desired balance in the allowance account:

$200,000 × 6% = $12,000

Because the existing balance in the allowance account is a $3,000 debit balance, the end-of-period adjusting entry is $15,000 (15,000 credit adjustment + 3,000 beginning debit balance = 12,000 ending credit balance).

Example: Allowance activity

The beginning balances of the current year accounts receivable are as follows:

January 1 Balances:

Accounts Receivable	$250,000
Less Allowance for Doubtful Accounts	(6,000)
Net Accounts Receivable	$244,000

The $6,000 remaining in the allowance account at the beginning of the year represents previous years' expected uncollectible accounts that have yet to be written off.

Assume the following events for the current year:

Write off a $4,000 account:

Allowance for Doubtful Accounts	4,000	
Accounts Receivable		4,000

Collect a $1,000 account written off last year:

Accounts Receivable	1,000	
Allowance for Doubtful Accounts		1,000
Cash	1,000	
Accounts Receivable		1,000

Credit sales for the year amount to $400,000; cash of $290,000 is collected on account:

Accounts Receivable	400,000	
Sales		400,000
Cash	290,000	
Accounts Receivable		290,000

Ending balances before adjustment:

Accounts Receivable	$356,000*
Allowance for Doubtful Accounts	3,000**

*$250,000 − $4,000 + $400,000 − $290,000

**$6,000 − $4,000 + $1,000

Assume the firm uses the aging approach to estimating bad debt expense. Total accounts receivable is partitioned into age categories. The older the category, the greater the probability of uncollectible accounts. The uncollectible percentage is based on past experience.

Age Category	Amount of Receivables	Uncollectible Percentage	Expected Uncollectibles
Current	$200,000	.01	$2,000
31–60 days	100,000	.05	5,000
Over 60 days	56,000	.10	5,600
	$356,000		$12,600

Total expected uncollectible accounts—the desired ending allowance balance of $12,600—is the sum of uncollectible accounts across the age categories.

The sum of the total amounts in the age categories equals total gross accounts receivable.

December 31 adjusting entry:

Bad Debt Expense ($12,600 – $3,000)   9,600

      Allowance for Doubtful Accounts   9,600

The desired or needed ending allowance balance is $12,600. With $3,000 already in the allowance account, only $9,600 is required to be reported as bad debt expense. This approach automatically updates for changes in estimates.

December 31 balances:

Accounts Receivable	$356,000
Less Allowance for Doubtful Accounts	(12,600)
Net Accounts Receivable	$343,400

Note

If given a problem similar to this example, the candidate may be required to compute the right-most column above. These amounts are the product of the amount of receivables in the age category times the uncollectible percentage.

II. Current Expected Credit Loss Associated with Uncollectable Accounts Receivable

A. ASU 326-20-55 provides guidance on the measurement of expected credit losses on trade accounts receivable. This guidance is referred to as the current expected credit loss (CECL) model. CECL requires the entity to measure expected credit losses for the accounts receivable as of each balance sheet date and is based on current conditions and reasonable (and supportable) forecasts. This means that in addition to estimating the allowance as shown previously, the entity will adjust the historical uncollectible percentage for forecasted losses. The entity must estimate the CECL over the entire life of the receivable (accounts receivable and notes receivable), even if the likelihood of credit loss is remote.

B. Using the historical uncollectible percentages presented in the table below, the entity would adjust the historical uncollectible rate for the current and expected credit loss. Assume that the entity expects there to be an increase in unemployment over the next year. Based on reasonable and supportable forecasts, the entity determines that the credit loss adjustment is 10%. Note that the historical rate for uncollectibles can be either increased or decreased by the credit loss adjustment. The new rates shown in the table (5.5%, 11%, and 22%) would be used to determine the allowance for uncollectible accounts receivable.

Age Category	Historical Uncollectible Percentage	Credit Loss Adjustment	Uncollectible and Credit Loss Rate
Current	5.0%	10.0%	5.50%
31–60 days	10.0%	10.0%	11.0%
Over 60 days	20.0%	10.0%	22.0%

C. Entities are required to pool receivables with similar risk characteristics (e.g., geographic region or customer type) when estimating the expected credit loss.

D. At each reporting date, the entity reestimates the amount expected to be collected and adjusts the allowance.

E. The entity must disclose enough information about the allowance for credit loss so that the financial statement user can understand the estimation method used, significant inputs, and circumstances that caused a change in the allowance.

Note

An entity must estimate CECL for all financial assets, which includes: accounts receivable, loans (or notes) receivable, investments in debt securities, and lease receivables.

Notes Receivable

This lesson presents the accounting for notes receivable.

After studying this lesson, you should be able to:

1. Calculate the interest component of an interest-bearing note receivable.

2. Complete the journal entries for an interest bearing note receivable.

3. Calculate the implicit interest on a noninterest bearing note receivable.

4. Complete the journal entries for a noninterest bearing note receivable.

I. Introduction

A. A note is a more formal financial instrument than an accounts receivable. The key reporting issues are valuation of the note (at present value).

B. The maker of a note is the buyer or borrower (the debtor firm or individual). This party is making an unconditional promise to pay principal and interest over the note term. The holder of the note (seller or lender) is the creditor and is the firm recording the note receivable on its books.

C. All notes have an interest element. In an interest-bearing note, the interest element is explicitly stated, while in a non-interest-bearing note, the interest element is not explicitly stated but rather is included in the face value of the note.

D. Notes typically result from the sale of property, conversion of accounts receivable, and lending transactions.

II. Types of Notes

A. **Interest-Bearing Notes Receivable**—The interest element is explicitly stated. For example, the note might be identified as a three-year, 9% note receivable. The amount of cash to be collected from an interest-bearing note is the face amount of the note (principal) plus interest.

B. **Non-Interest Bearing Note Receivable**—The interest element is not explicitly stated. For example, the note might be identified as a two-year, $13,000 non-interest-bearing note. The amount of cash to be collected from a non-interest-bearing note is the face amount of the note. That is, the face amount of the note includes principal and interest that will be collected at maturity date.

III. Recording a Note Receivable

A. **Present Value**—In accordance with U.S. GAAP, all notes are recorded at the present value of future cash flows (notes of less than one-year term need not be recorded at present value). The discount rate used in this calculation is the market rate of interest on the date of note creation (this rate may be different from the note's stated rate—the rate that appears on the note). Furthermore, any discounts related to notes will be amortized by applying the effective interest method.

B. **Market Value**—If the stated interest rate is equal to the market rate of interest, the present value of future cash flows will be equal to the face amount of the note. In this situation, no discounts will exist.

C. **Interest/Market Rate**—If the stated interest rate is not equal to the market rate of interest, the present value of future cash flows will not be equal to the face amount of the note. In this situation, a discount related to the note will exist.

D. For a **non-interest-bearing note**, the present value of future cash flows will not be equal to the face amount of the note. In this situation, a discount related to the note will exist.

IV. Determination of Present Value of Future Cash Flows

A. Cash Transaction—If the transaction is a cash transaction, such as a lending transaction, the present value of future cash flows will equal the amount of cash that exchanged hands on the date of note creation.

B. Noncash Transaction—If the transaction is a noncash transaction, such as the sale of a noncash asset and the receipt of a note receivable, the transaction will be recorded at the fair value of the noncash asset or the fair value of the note receivable (present value of future cash flows), whichever one can be more clearly determined.

Example
Simple Interest Note, Stated Rate Equals Market Rate

A calendar-year fiscal-year firm receives a three-year, 6%, $10,000 note on March 1 of the current year from a sale. The note pays interest each September 1 and March 1. The first four entries are shown:

March 1		
Note Receivable	10,000	
Sales		10,000
September 1		
Cash (.06(1/2)$10,000)	300	
Interest Revenue		300
December 31		
Interest Receivable (.06(4/12)$10,000)	200	
Interest Revenue		200
March 1 (following year)		
Cash	300	
Interest Receivable		200
Interest Revenue (.06(2/12)$10,000)		100

Example
Simple Interest Note, Principal and Interest are Due in Annual Installments

A calendar-year fiscal-year firm receives a 12%, $300,000 note on May 1, 20X7. Beginning in 20X8, the note calls for $100,000 of principal, along with interest on the outstanding note balance at the beginning of the period, to be paid each April 30.

Interest revenue recognized:

In 20X7: $300,000(.12)(8/12) =		$24,000
In 20X8: $300,000(.12)(4/12) +	$200,000(.12)(8/12) =	28,000
In 20X9: $200,000(.12)(4/12) +	$100,000(.12)(8/12) =	16,000
In 20X0: $100,000(.12)(4/12) =		4,000

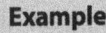

Example
Each Note Payment Includes Principal and Interest
A firm receives a 7%, two-year, $20,000 note from a sale, on January 1, 20X7. The note calls for two equal annual payments to be made beginning December 31, 20X7. The present value of an annuity of $1 for two periods at 7% is 1.80802. Let P = annual payment.

$20,000 = P(1.80802)$

$P = \$11,062$

January 1, 20X7	Note Receivable	20,000	
	Sales		20,000
December 31, 20X7	Cash	11,062	
	Interest Revenue		1,400*
	Note Receivable		9,662

*$20,000(.07) = \$1,400$

This is the interest portion of the first payment.

The $9,662 is return of principal.

December 31, 20X8	Cash	11,062	
	Interest Revenue		724**
	Note Receivable		10,338

**$(\$20,000 - \$9,662)(.07) = \$724$

This entry closes the note receivable account ($20,000 - $9,662 - $10,338 = $0).

Example
Simple Interest Note, Stated Rate, and Market Rates are Unequal
A firm, which is not an equipment dealer, sells used equipment (cost, $40,000; accumulated depreciation, $16,000) and receives a two-year, 4%, $25,000 note on January 1, 20X8. The note calls for annual interest to be paid each December 31 beginning 20X8 with the principal due December 31, 20X9. The equipment has no known market value but the prevailing (market) interest rate at the date of sale is 8%.

Relevant present values of $1 at 8% for two years: single payment, .85734; annuity, 1.78326.

The note is recorded at present value: $25,000(.85734) + .04($25,000)(1.78326) = $23,217. Thus, the note is recorded at a discount of $1,783 ($25,000 – $23,217). The true value of the note on receipt is $23,217 because this amount reflects the current market interest rate. This amount is also used as the fair value of the equipment in computing the gain or loss on disposal.

January 1, 20X8	Note Receivable	23,217	
	Accumulated Depreciation	16,000	
	Loss on Disposal	783	
	Equipment		40,000

(This entry records the note using the net method. The gross method would record the note at $25,000 and credit Discount on Notes for $1,783. Either approach is acceptable and both report the net notes receivable balance at present value.)

December 31, 20X8	Cash .04($25,000)	1,000	
	Note Receivable	857	
	Interest Revenue		1,857*

* .08($23,217)

The $857 amount is the increase in the value of the note for 20X8 because the cash interest was less than the growth in the note's present value over time. Had the gross method been used, the discount account would have been debited for $857 rather than the note receivable account. Under either reporting approach, the net note balance is now $24,074 ($23,217 + $857). This amount is the present value of the remaining payments at December 31, 20X8, which can also be computed as ($25,000 + $1,000)/1.08.

December 31, 20X9	Cash .04($25,000)	1,000	
	Note Receivable	926	
	Interest Revenue		1,926*
	Cash	25,000	
	Note Receivable		25,000

* .08($23,217 + $857)

Example
Non-Interest-Bearing Note

A non-interest-bearing note has a zero stated rate. The term non-interest-bearing is a misnomer, however, because the interest is included in the note's face value. Assume the same information as in the previous example except that there is no stated rate. Now the present value of the note is $21,434 [$25,000(.85734)]. The note is recorded at this amount. The entries are similar except that no cash interest is received. The first interest entry is shown:

December 31, 20X8	Note Receivable	1,715	
	Interest Revenue		1,715*

* .08($21,434)

Criteria for Sale of Receivables

This lesson presents the criteria for when the transfer of receivables is a sale versus security for a loan.

After studying this lesson, you should be able to:

1. List the three criteria for the transfer of AR to qualify as a sale.

2. Complete the journal entries when the transfer of AR is a sale.

3. Define what is meant by selling AR with recourse and without recourse.

I. **Using Accounts Receivable and Notes Receivable as Sources of Cash**—Frequently, business entities use receivables as immediate sources of cash. The firm uses the receivables as collateral for a loan or sells the receivables to a third party rather than wait for the maker of the note to make all the required payments on the note. The reasons for the transactions that will be described are varied. In some cases, a company may elect to forgo the establishment of a collection department. That is, the company could decide that the establishment of a collection department is not economically feasible. In other cases, companies may need the cash related to a note receivable or accounts receivable to meet current operating expenses or to take advantage of a unique opportunity.

II. **The Parties Involved in a Transfer of Receivables are**

   A. The **maker**, which is the debtor that has borrowed funds or purchased an asset and provided a note to the original creditor.

   B. The **original creditor** (transferor), which is the firm that has loaned funds or sold an asset to the maker.

   C. The **third-party financial institution** (transferee), which provides the funds to the original creditor.

III. **Type of Transaction**—When a company transfers receivables to a third party or uses the receivables as collateral for a loan, a determination must be made as to the substance of the transaction: Is it a sale or is it a loan? Codification 860-40 identifies the key characteristics of a sales transaction.

IV. **Criteria for Sale**—Criteria for determining if the transfer of receivables is a sale:

   A. The transaction is a sale of the receivable if three conditions are met. If the three conditions are met, then control has effectively passed to the third party (transferee) and a sale is implied. The three conditions are:

   1. The transferred assets have been isolated from the transferor, even in bankruptcy.

   2. The transferee is free to pledge or exchange the assets.

   3. The transferor does not maintain effective control over the transferred assets either through an agreement that allows and requires the transferor to repurchase the assets or one that requires the transferor to return specific assets.

   B. **Conditions Are Met**—If the above-listed conditions are met, the transaction is accounted for as a sale. The receivable is removed from the books of the transferor and a gain or loss on the sale of the receivable will be recorded.

   C. **Conditions Are not Met**—If the listed conditions are **not** met, the transaction is actually a situation in which the transferor is borrowing funds and using the receivables as collateral for a loan. In this case, the receivable remains on the books of the transferor, and the transferor records a liability related to the borrowing transaction. In this case, the transferor will not record any gain or loss on sale of the receivable. Rather, the transferor will record interest expense related to the borrowing transaction.

V. Terms of Transaction

A. With Recourse or Without Recourse

1. The transaction can be completed with recourse or without recourse. If the transaction is completed with recourse, the transferor is responsible for nonpayment on the part of the original maker of the receivable. This means that if the maker (original debtor) defaults, the original creditor must assume all the payments on the receivable.

Example

Grotex Inc. sells merchandise to Swemby on account. Grotex is the original creditor. Grotex then transfers the receivable to a financial institution and receives 94% of the value of the receivable. Grotex is the transferor and the financial institution is the transferee. If the transfer is with recourse and Swemby fails to pay the receivable, then Grotex must pay the financial institution the full amount of the receivable. During the term of the receivable, Grotex has a contingent liability that can be noted in a footnote, or a contra asset account can be recorded, such as note receivable discounted, or the liability may need to be accrued in the accounts, depending on the probability that Grotex will be required to pay.

2. If the transaction is completed **without recourse**, the transferor is not responsible for nonpayment on the part of the maker of the receivable. Typically, nonrecourse transfers are accounted for as sales because control has passed to the transferee (financial institution).

3. **Notification or Non-Notification Basis**—The transaction can be completed on a notification basis or on a non-notification basis. If the transaction is completed on a notification basis, the maker of the receivable is informed of the transaction and typically is instructed to make payments to the third party. If the transaction is completed on a non-notification basis, the maker of the receivable is not informed of the transaction and continues to make payments to the original creditor.

Example

The discounting of a note receivable is a common transaction involving the transfer of a receivable. The original creditor (transferor) discounts the note to a financial institution that charges a fee on the maturity value of the note. The maturity value is the face value plus interest, at the note's original rate, over the entire term of the note. The transferor receives proceeds equal to the maturity value less the fee. The Tiger Company has a $4,000, 90-day, 8% note receivable, which was received from a customer in settlement of an account receivable. The Tiger Company held the note for 30 days and decided to discount the note at Auburn National Bank. Auburn National Bank charges a 10% discount fee on the maturity value of the note (which includes the interest for the complete term of the note) for the two months it will hold the note. The proceeds to Tiger equal the maturity value less the fee.

Accrued interest for the 30 days the note was held by Tiger: $4,000(.08)(1/12) = $26.67

Cash Proceeds from the Discounting Transaction: Maturity Value of the Note:

$4,000 + ($4,000)(.08)(3/12) =	$4,080
Less Discount Fee: $4,080(.10)(2/12) =	(68)
Equals Cash Proceeds	$4,012

Interest expense (if transaction is a borrowing) or loss (if transaction is a sale):

Carrying Value of Note at Date of Discounting: $4,000 + $26.67	$4,026.67
Less Cash Proceeds	($4,012.00)
Equals Interest Expense or Loss	$14.67

If the transaction is a sale (i.e., if all three criteria of ASC 860 are met), a loss of $14.67 will be recorded. If the transaction is a borrowing transaction, interest expense of $14.67 will be recorded.

Entries assuming a borrowing (all three criteria are not met):

Interest Receivable	26.67	
Interest Revenue		26.67
Cash	4,012.00	
Interest Expense	14.67	
Liability on Note		4,000.00
Interest Receivable		26.67

Entries assuming a sale (all three criteria are met)

Interest Receivable	26.67	
Interest Revenue		26.67
Cash	4,012.00	
Loss on Sale	14.67	
Note Receivable		4,000.00
Interest Receivable		26.67

For the sale transaction, if the note is discounted with recourse, Tiger has a contingent liability for the remaining two months of the note term. If the maker does not pay the note, then Tiger must. Tiger may report the liability in its footnotes or credit Notes Receivable Discounted rather than Notes Receivable in the journal entry immediately above, for $4,000. The Notes Receivable Discounted account is contra to Notes Receivable. This approach more prominently discloses the contingent liability.

Factoring, Assignment, and Pledging

This lesson presents the accounting for factoring receivables and describes the assignment and pledging of AR.

After studying this lesson, you should be able to:

1. Describe the difference between factoring with and without recourse.

2. Describe the difference between assigning and pledging AR.

3. Complete the journal entries when AR is factored with and without recourse.

I. **Other Types of Transactions Involving Transfers of Receivables—Factoring**

   A. **Transferor to factor**—In a factoring, the transferor (original creditor) transfers the receivables to a factor (transferee, a financial institution) immediately as a normal part of business. The transferor prefers to pay the factor a fee in return for the factor's administration of the receivables. The factor often performs credit checks and collects the payments.

   B. **Factoring without recourse**—This type of factoring is usually accounted for as a sale because the factor has no recourse against the transferor if there is a default on the receivables. The factor (transferee) bears the cost of uncollectible accounts, but the seller (transferor) bears the cost of sales adjustments such as sales discounts and returns and allowances because they are considered preconditions.

Example

A firm factors $20,000 of accounts receivable without recourse. The factor charges 5% and holds back an additional 3% for sales returns. Assume that actual sales returns equal the estimated amount. The transferor records the following entries:

Cash $20,000(1.00 – .05 – .03)	18,400	
Receivable from Factor $20,000(.03)	600	
Loss on Sale of Receivables $20,000(.05)	1,000	
Accounts Receivable		20,000
Sales Returns and Allowances	600	
Receivable from Factor		600

If the actual and estimated returns are not equal, the factoring agreement will specify which party receives the savings or bears the cost.

Note

In the example above, the transfer qualified as a sale; therefore, the cost of the factoring is a loss on the sale of receivables.

   C. **Factoring with recourse**—When receivables are factored with recourse, the three criteria of Codification 860-10-40 must be used to determine if the transaction is accounted for as a sale or a loan. The seller (transferor) bears the cost of bad debts as well as the cost of sales adjustments.

1. If accounted for as a sale, the entries are similar to factoring without recourse except that the transferor must estimate and record a recourse liability.

Example

A firm factors $20,000 of accounts receivable with recourse. The factor charges 2%. The firm estimates that its liability for bad debts (the recourse liability) is $1,000. The three criteria of Codification 860-10-40 are met. The holdback for sales adjustments is not illustrated in this example but is handled the same way as for factoring without recourse. The transferor records the following entries:

Cash $20,000(1.00 − .02)	19,600	
Loss on Sale of Receivables $20,000(.02) + $1,000	1,400	
Accounts Receivable		20,000
Recourse Liability		1,000

When accounts are deemed uncollectible, the transferor remits the necessary cash to the factor:

Recourse Liability	1,000	
Cash		1,000

Note

In the example above, the transfer qualified as a sale; therefore ,the cost of the factoring is a loss on the sale of receivables.

2. If accounted for as a loan, the transferor maintains the receivables on its books, and records a loan and interest expense over the term of the agreement.

Example

A firm factors $20,000 of accounts receivable with recourse. The factor charges 2%. The firm estimates that its liability for bad debts (the recourse liability) is $1,000. The three criteria of Codification 860-10-40 are not met. The transferor records the following entries:

Cash $20,000(1.00 − .02)	19,600	
Discount on Factor Liability $20,000(.02)	400	
Factor Liability		20,000
Allowance for Doubtful Accounts	1,000	
Accounts Receivable		1,000

As payments on the receivables are made to the factor, the factor liability is extinguished and interest expense is recognized. The summary entry is:

Factor Liability	20,000	
Accounts Receivable		19,000
Cash (to pay for uncollectible accounts)		1,000
Interest Expense	400	
Discount on Factor Liability		400

Interest expense is recognized in proportion to collections on the receivables. If 75% of the receivables were collected by year-end, then $300 of interest would be recognized as of the balance sheet date.

> **Note**
>
> In the example above, the transfer DID NOT qualify as a sale; therefore, the cost of the factoring is INTEREST EXPENSE, and the accounts receivable are not removed from the books of the transferor until the receivables are collected.

II. **Assignment of Accounts Receivable**—When accounts receivable are assigned, the borrower assigns rights to specific accounts receivable as collateral for a loan. The lender has the right to seek payment from these receivables should the borrower (original creditor for the accounts receivable) default on the loan. The borrower reclassifies the receivables as accounts receivable assigned, a subcategory of total accounts receivable. The borrower maintains the receivable records, and as cash is received, it is remitted to the lender in payment of the loan. The loan and the receivables are not offset on the borrower's balance sheet. When the loan is repaid, any remaining accounts receivable assigned are returned to ordinary accounts receivable status.

III. **Pledging of Accounts Receivable**—Pledging of accounts receivable is less formal than assignment. Rights to specific receivables are not noted as collateral, and accounts receivable are not reclassified. Neither the accounting for the receivables nor the loan is affected by the pledge. Receivables in bulk are transferred to a trustee and can be used for payment of the loan in the event of default by the borrower (original creditor for the accounts receivable). The cash flows from the receivables are used to pay the loan. Footnote disclosure of the pledge is required.

Inventory

Notes Receivable—Impairment

This lesson presents the definition of when a loan is impaired and presents the entries for impairment.

After studying this lesson, you should be able to:

1. Define when a note receivable is impaired.

2. Complete the journal entries for the note impairment.

I. **Impaired loans receivables are written down to**

    A. The present value of the future cash flows expected to be collected using the original effective interest rate for the loan, or

    B. Market value if this value is more determinable.

        A. **The Write-Down (Loss)**—This is accomplished with a debit to bad debt expense and a credit to a contra-receivable account. After the write-down, interest revenue is recognized under any of several methods found in practice, including the interest method and cost-recovery methods (Codifications 310-10-35).

Example

A firm holds a 7%, $10,000 note due December 31, 20X6. Annual interest is due each December 31. The note originated on January 1 several years ago. The 20X5 interest payment was not received and the firm believes, as of December 31, 20X5, that no more interest will be received. In addition, only $7,000 of the principal is expected to be received, and that amount will be delayed one year, to December 31, 20X7.

The carrying value of the note on December 31, 20X5, is $10,700, which includes the $700 annual interest that was not paid by the debtor firm. The interest receivable is closed to note receivable. The resulting $10,700 note receivable balance remains on the books. A valuation account is used to write the note down to present value and the loss (bad debt expense) is recognized on this date. The present value of a single payment of $1 at 7% for two years is .87344. Two years is the remaining term of the note.

December 31, 20X5

Bad Debt Expense	4,586*	
Allowance for Decline in Note Value		4,586
*Carrying Value:		$10,700.00
Less Present Value: $7,000(.87344)		(6,114)
Equals Impairment Loss		$ 4,586

The allowance for decline in note value account is contra to notes receivable. The above entry reduces the net carrying value of the note to $6,114, the present value of remaining cash flows. For the remaining two years of the note term, the firm may choose from a variety of methods to recognize interest revenue. Two are illustrated here:

	Interest Method	Cost-Recovery Method
December 31, 20X6		
Allowance for Decline in Note Value	428	No entry as the new carrying
Interest Revenue .07($6,114)	428	value has not been recovered
December 31, 20X7		
Allowance for Decline in Note Value	458	No entry as the new carrying
Interest Revenue .07($6,114 + $428)	458	value has not been recovered
Cash	7,000	7,000
Allowance for Decline in Note Value	3,700	4,586
Note Receivable	10,700	10,700
Interest Revenue		886

The interest method is applied as it is in any other note or bond situation. Interest revenue for a period is based on the net note balance at the beginning of the period. The cost-recovery method delays recognition of interest revenue until the entire new carrying value ($6,114) is received. The only cash inflow in this situation occurred at the end of 20X7. Thus all the interest revenue is recognized in that year. The total interest revenue over the two years is the same for both methods.

Inventory

Introduction to Inventory

This lesson presents the basics for accounting for inventory including: components of inventory, FOB shipping point, FOB destination, consigned goods, and costs capitalized to inventory.

After studying this lesson, you should be able to:

1. List the three basic components of manufacturing inventory.

2. Define FOB shipping point and FOB destination.

3. Identify what is included in year-end inventory costs (goods in transit, consigned goods, and capitalized costs).

I. Inventory Definition and Description

    A. This section address (1) the items, and (2) costs that should be included in the inventory account.

Definition

Inventory: For a typical business entity inventory includes property held for resale, property in the process of production, and property consumed in the process of production.

    B. A manufacturing company has all three types of inventory items. That is, a manufacturing company has:

        1. Finished goods inventory

        2. Work-in-process inventory

        3. Raw materials inventory

    C. A merchandising company typically holds the inventory item that is best described as property held for resale. That is, a merchandising company has a single type of inventory item, usually referred to as merchandise inventory.

    D. Inventories also include land (if the firm is a real-estate development company), and partially completed buildings and bridges (if the firm is a construction company). Inventories are always current assets to the seller even though they may be noncurrent assets to the buyer.

II. Ending Inventory

    A. What Items are Included in Ending Inventory?

        1. To address this question, you simply apply the ownership criteria. If the merchandise is owned by a business enterprise on the last day of the accounting year, regardless of location, the merchandise should be included in ending inventory.

        2. Most of the merchandise owned by a business enterprise on the last day of the accounting year is typically located on the premises/property of that business enterprise. However, goods awaiting shipment to customers are not included in the firm's inventory if the customer has paid for the goods.

        3. Merchandise owned and located off-site

            a. Goods in transit

                i. Ownership of goods in transit is determined by the test of title: FOB (free-on-board). FOB destination means that title to the goods transfers to the buyer when the goods reach the destination. Therefore, shipping terms of FOB destination Chicago means that the buyer owns the goods when they reach Chicago. FOB shipping point means title passes at the shipping point (the selling company's warehouse), therefore the goods belong to the purchaser as soon as it is loaded on a common carrier. In general, FOB shipping point means title passes at the shipping point and FOB destination means title passes at the destination. The test of title is important for the year-end cut-off because goods in transit can be included in only one firm's inventory: the buyer or seller.

Examples

1. A business entity is located in Auburn, Alabama and has a major supplier located in Seattle, Washington. On December 31, 20X7, some merchandise was placed on a train or a truck and was en route to Auburn, Alabama on that date.

If the goods were shipped FOB shipping point, the purchased goods in transit should be included in the Auburn company's ending inventory.

If the goods were shipped FOB destination, the purchased goods in transit should not be included in the Auburn company's ending inventory.

2. Goods in transit to a customer—A business entity is located in Auburn, Alabama and has a major customer located in Chicago, Illinois. On December 31, 20X7, some merchandise was placed on a train or truck and was en route to Chicago on that date.

If the goods were shipped FOB destination, the sold goods in transit should be included in the Auburn company's ending inventory.

If the goods were shipped FOB shipping point, the sold goods in transit should not be included in the Auburn company's ending inventory.

    b. **Goods on consignment**

        i. A business entity is located in Austin, Texas, and has signed an agreement with a manufacturer to be the sole retailer of the manufacturer's merchandise in the state of Texas. The Austin-based entity sells the merchandise in its Austin-area stores and reaches a consignment agreement with retail establishments in Houston, Dallas, San Antonio, Lubbock, and El Paso. The agreement is the typical consignment agreement. The retail stores outside of Austin will receive the merchandise and attempt to market the merchandise in their selected markets. If the merchandise is sold, the retailer will retain a sales commission and remit the remainder to the Austin-based business entity. If the merchandise is not sold, the retailer will return the merchandise to the Austin-based business entity. In this example, the Austin-based entity is the consignor, and the business establishments located in Houston, Dallas, San Antonio, Lubbock, and El Paso are all consignees.

       ii. In consignment arrangements, the merchandise is owned by the consignor. The merchandise is always included in the consignor's ending inventory even though the inventory typically is never on the consignor's premises.

Example
Trend Inc. has $40,000 worth of its inventory held by a consignee at year-end. Trend also serves as a consignee and holds $30,000 of inventory on consignment for another firm. Only the $40,000 of inventory is included in Trend's ending inventory.

III. **Valuation of Inventory**—The acquisition cost of inventory includes all costs incurred in getting the merchandise to the seller's premises and ready for sale. A good general rule is:

    A. **Capitalize in Inventory All Costs Necessary to Bring the Item of Inventory to Salable Condition.**

1. These costs include freight and insurance in transit paid to the seller firm, any taxes paid on acquisition of inventory, material handling costs, and packaging costs. Interest on the purchase or construction of inventory is never included in inventory. Purchases discounts, and returns and allowances reduce the total cost allocated to inventory. Promotional costs such as advertising are not included in inventory because these costs do not help prepare the inventory for sale.

2. Also not included are interest costs.

Example

A firm incurred the following costs related to the acquisition and sale of inventory:

Direct Purchase Cost	$50,000
Purchases Returns	4,000
Freight-In	9,000
Freight-Out	2,000
Interest on Purchase	1,000
Sales and Other Taxes on Acquisition	3,000
Packaging Costs (for sale)	4,000
Insurance in Transit from Supplier	500
Promotional Expenses	2,500

The inventory should be recorded at the following amount:

Direct Purchase Cost	$50,000
Purchases Returns	(4,000)
Freight-In	9,000
Sales and Other Taxes on Acquisition	3,000
Packaging Costs (for sale)	4,000
Insurance in Transit from Supplier	<u>500</u>
Total Inventory Cost	$62,500

The excluded costs are period expenses.

B. **Inventory Costs**

1. Intermediate accounting considers the general issue of costing inventory but limits its consideration to merchandise inventory—that is, inventory purchased for resale. The Management Accounting section of CPAexcel® addresses a related issue: how to determine the cost of manufactured inventories. Manufactured inventory ultimately should reflect the actual cost of manufacturing.

2. **Fixed overhead is one of the four manufacturing input costs**—The others are direct material, direct labor, and variable overhead. Fixed overhead does not vary with small changes in production volume and, therefore, is often allocated to production based on a predetermined overhead rate. For example, if direct labor hours is used for allocation purposes, and the fixed overhead allocation rate is $4 per direct labor hour, then a production run using 1,000 direct labor hours would receive an allocation of $4,000 of fixed overhead cost. The $4 rate is the ratio: (budgeted fixed overhead)/(budgeted direct labor hours).

3. **Fixed overhead rates**—These are subject to estimation errors and are affected by the choice of denominator measure and the budgeting horizon reflected in the denominator. Assuming no numerator (fixed overhead cost) variation, if actual production is less than the

production budgeted for the denominator, less fixed overhead will be applied to product than is actually incurred. Underapplied fixed overhead resulting from low production volume must be expensed rather than allocated back to product. Low production volume does not imply that the inventory produced should carry a higher cost or is in any way more valuable.

4. To ensure that unallocated fixed overheads are expensed, Codification 330-10-30 requires for external financial reporting purposes, that **normal** activity be used for the denominator level. Normal activity is a measure of the average production volume (as measured in units, direct labor cost or hours, machine hours, or other predicted amount) expected for a budget horizon typically extending beyond one year and takes into account lost production due to planned maintenance. The range in production volume over more than one period establishes the normal capacity amount. Shorter-range budgeted volumes should not be used as the denominator. During periods of abnormally low production, the use of actual production volume would result in higher overhead rates, causing more overhead to be allocated to product. By requiring normal capacity, higher amounts of fixed overhead will not be allocated to the product during low production periods. Fixed overhead that has not benefited production is not an asset and should be expensed as incurred.

5. The standard also requires that costs **including idle facility expense**, excessive spoilage, double freight, wasted materials, and rehandling costs be treated as current-period costs rather than allocated to inventory and carried over to future periods. This is an example of invoking the conceptual framework definition of an asset rather than the matching principle.

6. The FASB also reaffirmed the concept that selling, general, and administrative expenditures not be treated as manufacturing costs but rather as period costs. Selling costs are not production costs.

Periodic Inventory System and Cost-Flow Assumption

This lesson presents the accounting for inventory under a periodic inventory system.

After studying this lesson, you should be able to:

1. Describe the determination and presentation of the net worth element of such a statement.

2. Calculate cost of goods sold.

3. Calculate ending inventory under a periodic system using specific identification, weighted average, FIFO, and LIFO cost flow assumptions.

I. Introduction

   A. In accounting for inventories, business entities may elect to employ a periodic inventory system. If so, the beginning inventory balance is reflected in the merchandise inventory account throughout the year. That is, the merchandise inventory account will have an unchanging balance throughout the accounting year. The firm uses other means to obtain current inventory information for internal purposes. The periodic system is much less expensive to administer than is the perpetual system.

   B. **Recording Acquisitions**—For companies employing the periodic inventory system, acquisitions of merchandise during the year will be recorded in the *purchases and related accounts*. The purchases account is used rather than the inventory account because a continuous record of the cost of inventory on hand at any time is not maintained under the periodic system.

   C. **Typical Entries**

      1. **Beginning inventory**

Merchandise inventory: January 1, 20X7

Purchase of merchandise on account:

Purchases	XX	
Accounts Payable		XX

---

      a. Purchases is a holding account for inventory charges and credits and is closed to ending inventory and cost of goods sold at the end of the period. The inventory account is not used to record purchases in a periodic system.

Paid delivery charges on purchased merchandise

Transportation In	XX	
Cash		XX

Returned damaged or defective merchandise

Accounts Payable	XX	
Purchase Returns and Allowances		XX

Paid for merchandise and received cash discount

Accounts Payable	XX	
Purchase Discounts		XX
Cash		XX

Sold merchandise on account

Accounts Receivable	XX	
Sales		XX

2. **Ending inventory**

    a. **End of the period**—Under the periodic inventory system, a physical count of ending inventory is required. Once the number of units in ending inventory has been counted, a value is assigned to the ending inventory, and the following year-end adjusting entry is prepared.

Merchandise Inventory (Ending)	XX	
Purchase Returns and Allowances	XX	
Purchase Discounts	XX	
Cost of Goods Sold	XX	
Merchandise Inventory (Beginning)		XX
Purchases		XX
Transportation In		XX

Note

The entry shown above allows a business entity to achieve multiple objectives. First, the ending balance of inventory is formally entered into the accounting system. Second, the beginning balance of inventory is closed. Also, the purchases and related accounts are closed. Finally, the cost of goods sold for the year is formally entered into the accounting system. Before this entry, cost of goods sold did not exist in the accounting records. Cost of goods sold is not directly observable in a periodic system. Rather, the value recorded for cost of goods sold is derived from the other amounts in the above entry. Another common way of computing cost of goods sold is by the basic inventory equations:

Net purchases = Gross Purchases + Transportation In (Freight In)

                      − Purchases Returns and Allowances

                      − Purchases Discounts

Beginning Inventory + Net Purchases = Ending Inventory + Cost of Goods Sold

3. Cost of goods sold is the last amount computed. In other words, it is a derived amount based on the other three values in the above equation. Also, Cost of Goods Available for Sale equals the value of either side of the above equation, although in published reports, cost of goods available for sale is shown as the subtotal of beginning inventory and net purchases.

4. The challenge is to determine the allocation of the left side total to the two components of the right side of the equation. Cost of goods sold, a major expense, is not recognized until goods are sold. Costs remain in inventory until sale.

Note

Transportation out (also called delivery expense and freight-out) is not included in inventory. Transportation out is a distribution or selling expense and is not an inventoriable cost.

Example

Data for a firm's inventory and related transactions follows:

Beginning Inventory	$20,000	Ending Inventory	$32,000
Purchases	100,000	Purchases Returns	4,000
Purchases Discounts	8,000	Transportation In	9,000
Transportation Out	6,000		

The firm's cost of goods sold is determined as follows:

Net Purchases   = $100,000 + $9,000 − $8,000 − $4,000

                  = $97,000

Cost of Goods Sold = Beginning Inventory + Net Purchases − Ending Inventory

                  = $20,000 + $97,000 − $32,000

                  = $85,000

II. Cost-Flow Assumption

A. Beginning Inventory + Net Purchases = Ending Inventory + Cost of Goods Sold

B. To assign a value to ending inventory and cost of goods sold, we apply one of four cost-flow assumptions. These cost-flow assumptions are identified below. Although the merits of each flow assumption are discussed below, remember that firms are free to decide which assumption to choose.

C. Specific identification

1. If the business entity has somewhat large, distinguishable products, it might be appropriate to use specific identification. For example, an automobile dealer might find this cost flow assumption appropriate. To continue the example, the dealer counted a total of 49 automobiles in inventory at year-end. The dealer can identify each automobile by vehicle number and match the invoice cost by vehicle number as well. To value its ending inventory, the dealership is able to *specifically identify* the cost of each of the inventory items and then total the individual cost of all the inventory items. Likewise, the dealership can specifically identify the cost of each item sold and total these amounts to determine cost of goods sold for the period.

2. The specific identification assumption is not cost effective for most firms and allows firms to manipulate earnings.

Example

If a firm has many identical items in inventory and desires to maximize net income, it can sell the least expensive items rather than the more expensive items. This example assumes a gradual increase in the specific price level of the inventory. The resulting lower cost of goods sold may erroneously imply to users of the financial statements that the firm can continue the reported level of gross margin (sales less cost of goods sold). However, the firm must eventually begin selling the more expensive items.

D. Weighted Average Cost-Flow Assumption

1. The term *weighted average* always implies the periodic inventory system. If the business entity selects this cost flow assumption, the weighted average cost per unit must be calculated. This calculation is shown below.

Weighted Average Cost per Unit = Cost of Goods Available for Sale / Number of Units Available for Sale

2. The ending inventory valuation is equal to the number of units in ending inventory multiplied by the weighted average cost per unit. Likewise, the cost of goods sold for the period is equal to the number of units sold multiplied by the weighted average cost per unit.

3. The weighted average method treats each unit available for sale (beginning inventory and purchases) as if it were costed at the average cost during the period. It produces cost of goods sold and ending inventory results between those of FIFO and LIFO when prices change during the period.

E. FIFO

1. This cost-flow assumption is based on a *first-in, first-out* philosophy. At the end of the accounting period, it is assumed the ending inventory is composed of units of inventory most recently acquired. Conversely, the cost of goods sold is made up of the *oldest* merchandise. The FIFO cost-flow assumption reflects the way most firms actually move their inventory. *However, GAAP does not require that firms choose the inventory cost-flow assumption that reflects the actual movement of goods.*

2. During periods of rising specific inventory prices, FIFO produces the highest net income because cost of goods sold is costed with the lowest-cost (earliest) purchases in the period. Ending inventory reflects the highest (latest) costs. Sometimes FIFO ending inventory is used as an approximation to the current cost of ending inventory.

F. LIFO

1. This cost-flow assumption is based on a *last-in, first-out* philosophy. At the end of the accounting period, it is assumed the ending inventory is composed of the *oldest* inventory layers, while the cost of goods sold is composed of the units of inventory most recently acquired.

2. During periods of rising specific inventory prices, LIFO produces the lowest net income because cost of goods sold is costed with the highest-cost (latest) purchases in the period. This feature of LIFO is considered an advantage because reported gross margin reflects the latest purchase costs and therefore is more indicative of future gross margin.

3. However, the ending inventory reflects the lowest (earliest) costs. Whenever the firm purchases (or produces) more units than it sells, a layer is added. This layer is costed with the earliest costs of the period in which the layer is added, under the periodic system. After several years of adding layers, ending inventory may reflect very old costs. Ending inventory under LIFO is a less reliable amount compared with FIFO ending inventory.

III. Calculating Cost of Goods Sold in a Periodic System

A. Counting the items in inventory at the end of the year and applying the appropriate costs, depending on the cost-flow assumption, to the items on hand, typically find the ending inventory cost. Cost of goods sold is computed last.

B. To calculate cost of goods sold for a company employing the periodic inventory system, the calculation shown below is used. This approach is the equation approach illustrated previously, placed into a schedule format.

Cost-of-Goods-Sold Calculation:

       Beginning Inventory

 + Net Cost of Purchases

 = Goods Available for Sale

 − <u>Ending Inventory</u>

 = Cost of Goods Sold

Example

The four cost-flow assumptions in a periodic system are illustrated in this example. The purchases and sales of the firm's one product are given in chronological order for the period. Assume the firm always actually sells the oldest units on hand first.

Beginning Inventory:	400 Units @ $10 per Unit
Purchase 1:	100 Units @ $11 per Unit
Sale 1:	200 Units
(Note: No unit cost is given. The cost assigned to each sale depends on the cost-flow assumption chosen.)	
Purchase 2:	200 Units @ $12 per Unit
Sale 2:	400 Units
Purchase 3:	200 Units @ $13 per Unit

The basic equation in units helps to identify the right hand side of the equation for costing purposes:

Beginning Inventory	+ Purchases	= Ending Inventory	+ Sales
400 Units	+ 500 Units	= 300 Units	+ 600 Units

Cost of Goods Available for Sale

   = Cost in Beginning Inventory + Total Purchases Cost

   = 400($10) + 100($11) + 200($12) + 200($13) = $10,100

The sum of ending inventory and cost of goods sold for all four methods must sum to $10,100. This amount is the cost of goods available for sale. During the period, there were 900 units available for sale.

C. Specific Identification and FIFO

1. These two assumptions yield the same results in this case (although they need not in a given situation), because the firm always sells its oldest goods first.

Cost of Goods Sold	= the Cost of the 600 Oldest Units Available During the Period	
	= 400($10) + 100($11) + 100($12)	= $ 6,300
Ending Inventory	= the Cost of the 300 Most Recently Added Units	
	= 100($12) + 200($13)	= 3,800
Sum of Ending Inventory and Cost of Goods Sold		$10,100

D. Weighted Average

1. The average cost per unit for the period = $10,100/900 = $11.22

2. Both cost of goods sold and ending inventory reflect the average cost during the period.

Cost of Goods Sold	= $11.22(600)	= $6,732
Ending Inventory	= $11.22(300)	= 3,366
Sum of Ending Inventory and Cost of Goods Sold		$10,098*

(*off by $2 due to rounding of the average cost per unit)

E. LIFO

Cost of Goods Sold	= the Cost of the 600 Most Recently Acquired Units Available During the Period	
	= 200($13) + 200($12) + 100($11) + 100($10)	= $7,100
Ending Inventory	= the Cost of the 300 Oldest Available Units	
	= 300($10)	= 3,000
Sum of Ending Inventory and Cost of Goods Sold		$10,100

F. Comparison

1. The cost of the inventory item sold by this firm steadily increased during the period. The ranking, highest to lowest in terms of dollar amount, of cost of goods sold and ending inventory:

Cost of Goods Sold		Ending Inventory	
LIFO	$7,100	FIFO	$3,800
W. Ave.	6,732	W. Ave.	3,366
FIFO	6,300	LIFO	3,000

NOTE: *Calculation of cost of goods sold*: This example calculated cost of goods sold directly. Although this may be possible for firms with low unit volume, for most firms using a periodic system, the ending inventory cost is measured first through an inventory count and application of unit costs, and then cost of goods sold is computed by subtracting the ending inventory cost from cost of goods available for sale.

NOTE: *Goods to be considered in the calculation of cost of goods sold*: A periodic system assumes all goods purchased anytime during the year are available for sale. The time period assumption of accounting supports this view. In this example, the last purchase occurred *after* the last sale. Thus, the last purchase could not possibly have been sold. However, LIFO included the last purchase as the very first purchase assumed sold, and the weighted average method also included the purchase in the computation of cost per unit. Given the time period assumption of accounting, the inclusion of the last purchase in the computations is appropriate.

Perpetual Inventory System and Cost-Flow Assumption

This lesson presents the accounting for inventory under a perpetual inventory system.

After studying this lesson, you should be able to:

1. Complete the entries to record inventory under the perpetual system.

2. Calculate ending inventory under the perpetual inventory system using specific identification, weighted average, FIFO and LIFO cost flow assumptions.

I. Typical Entries

A. In illustrating the typical entries for the perpetual inventory system, assume the merchandise inventory account balance on January 1, 20X7 is $100,000.

Purchases of inventory on account

Merchandise Inventory	XX	
Accounts Payable		XX

Paid delivery charges on purchased merchandise

Merchandise Inventory	XX	
Cash		XX

Returned damaged or defective merchandise

Accounts Payable	XX	
Merchandise Inventory		XX

Paid for merchandise and received a cash discount

Accounts Payable	XX	
Merchandise Inventory		XX
Cash		XX

Sold merchandise on account

Accounts Receivable	XX	
Sales		XX
Cost of Goods Sold	XX	
Merchandise Inventory		XX

B. The main differences between these entries and those for the periodic system are:

   A. the use of the inventory account rather than purchases for the acquisition of inventory and adjustments such as returns and discounts; and

   B. the recording of cost of goods sold at sale, rather than at the end of the period.

   C. **End of the Period**—A physical count of ending inventory should be completed to confirm inventory records. If inventory shrinkage has occurred (loss, theft, breakage), or if recording errors have been made, an appropriate adjusting entry would be prepared to reduce inventory to the amount per the physical count. The entry would reduce the inventory account and record a shrinkage loss.

D. **Cost-Flow Assumption**—A perpetual system considers only goods on hand when computing cost of goods sold for a specific sale. As opposed to the periodic system, which considers all goods on hand during the period when computing cost of goods sold, a perpetual system computes cost of goods sold only for the goods that have actually been purchased through the date of sale.

E. **Specific Identification**—The results (values placed on cost of goods sold and ending inventory) for this cost-flow assumption are the same for both the periodic and perpetual systems. The specific cost of each item sold is used to compute the cost of goods sold.

F. **Moving Average**—The term *moving average* always implies the perpetual inventory system. Rather than having a single weighted average cost per unit for the accounting period, the company computes a new weighted average cost per unit after each purchase of inventory. That moving average is used for costing all subsequent sales until another purchase takes place, at which time the moving average is modified by the new purchase. When merchandise is sold, the current weighted average cost per unit is multiplied by the number of units sold to determine the amount of the cost-of-goods-sold entry.

  1. In a period of steadily rising prices, the moving average method (perpetual) results in lower cost of goods sold than the weighted average method (periodic). The moving average method applies earlier (and, therefore, lower) costs to sales during the year relative to the overall higher weighted average cost for the entire period.

G. **FIFO**—The results (values placed on cost of goods sold and ending inventory) for this cost flow assumption are the same for both the periodic and perpetual systems. The cost of the beginning inventory and earliest units purchased are assigned to cost of goods sold leaving the most recent purchase costs to be assigned to ending inventory.

H. **LIFO**—The results for LIFO-perpetual differ from those of LIFO-periodic. In the perpetual system, each sale is costed with the most recent purchase available preceding that sale. The periodic system uses the latest purchases for the entire period. Thus in a year of steadily rising prices, perpetual LIFO yields a lower cost-of-goods-sold figure because it uses earlier purchases. Periodic LIFO would assume the sale of the very latest purchases in the period irrespective of the sequencing of sales and purchases.

Example
The data for the previous example of the four cost-flow assumptions is now applied in a perpetual system in this example. The purchases and sales of the firm's one product are given in chronological order for the period. The firm sells the oldest units on hand first.

Beginning inventory:	400 Units @ $10 per Unit
Purchase 1:	100 Units @ $11 per Unit
Sale 1:	200 Units
Purchase 2:	200 Units @ $12 per Unit
Sale 2:	400 Units
Purchase 3:	200 Units @ $13 per Unit

Beginning Inventory   + Purchases = Ending Inventory + Sales

400 Units   + 500 Units =   300 Units   + 600 Units

Cost of Goods Available for Sale =   Cost in Beginning Inventory + Purchases
                                                            Cost

= 400($10) + 100($11) + 200($12) + 200($13) = $10,100

The sum of ending inventory and cost of goods sold for all four methods must sum to $10,100. This amount is the cost of goods available for sale. During the period, there were 900 units available for sale.

I. Specific Identification and FIFO —The results for both of these assumptions are the same for both the periodic and perpetual systems and are not repeated here.

A **moving average** is not needed until there is a sale to cost. The first sale occurs after the first purchase. The average unit cost of beginning inventory and the first purchase = ($4,000 + $1,100)/500 = $10.20. The following table illustrates the application of the moving averages.

Event	Units	Cost	Moving Average	Computation
Beginning inventory	400	$4,000		
+ Purchase 1	100	1,100		
=	500	5,100	$10.20	= $5,100/500
− Sale 1	(200)	(2,040)		= $10.20(200)
=	300	3,060		
+ Purchase 2	200	2,400		
=	500	5,460	$10.92	= $5,460/500
− Sale 2	(400)	(4,368)		= $10.92(400)
=	100	1,092		
+ Purchase 3	200	2,600		
=	300	3,692	$12.31	= $3,692/300

For example, Sale 1 is costed at $10.20, the moving average of goods on hand just before the sale. Removing those units leaves 300 units in inventory and $3,060 in cost. Purchase 2, at $12 per unit, is added into both the units and cost columns. $12 exceeds the previous moving average; therefore the moving average after Purchase 2 increases. That average is applied to Sale 2 and so forth. The final moving average of $12.31 reflects the higher purchase cost of Purchase 3 and will be used to cost sales the next period until the first purchase in that period is made.

Ending Inventory =	$3,692
Cost of Goods Sold = $2,040 + $4,368	6,408
Total = Cost of Goods Available for Sale	$10,100

J. LIFO—To cost sales, the latest purchases available at time of sale are used.

Cost of Goods Sold:

Sale 1 (200 units):100($11) (Purchase 1) + 100($10)(Beg. Inv.) =	$2,100
Sale 2 (400 units):200($12) (Purchase 2) + 200($10)(Beg. Inv.) =	4,400
Total Cost of Goods Sold	$6,500

Ending Inventory:

From Purchase 3 (all remaining): 200($13) =	$2,600
From Beginning Inventory (100 Units Remaining): 100($10) =	1,000
Total Ending Inventory	$3,600

Check:

Cost of Goods Sold	$6,500
+ Ending Inventory	3,600
= Cost of Goods Available	$10,100

Evaluation of FIFO and LIFO

This lesson emphasizes the differences in FIFO and LIFO cost-flow assumptions.

After studying this lesson, you should be able to:

1. Describe the Income Statement and Balance Sheet effect of using FIFO or LIFO valuation.

2. Describe what is meant by "LIFO liquidation," and what is its effect on the Income Statement.

I. **Evaluation of FIFO and LIFO**

   A. Regardless of price changes, the following effects hold and form the basis for comparing the two methods:

	Ending Inventory	Cost of Goods Sold
FIFO	Reflects latest costs	Reflects earliest costs
LIFO	Reflects earliest costs	Reflects latest costs

   B. Thus, if inventory costs have been rising, LIFO shows lower ending inventory, higher cost of goods sold, and lower income. The opposite is true if costs have been declining.

   C. **FIFO**

      1. In assessing the relative attributes of FIFO, it is important to remember three important points of emphasis.

         a. If FIFO is employed by a business entity, the flow of costs is the same as the physical flow of goods for most firms.

         b. If FIFO is employed by a business entity, the balance sheet valuation of inventory is an approximation to current cost, which is considered more relevant than historical cost.

         c. If FIFO is employed by a business entity, however, the matching of revenues and expenses on the income statement is not considered ideal. Frequently, a company will be matching the revenues of the current year with the cost of merchandise acquired in a prior accounting period.

      2. Thus, if FIFO is chosen, the inventory value in the balance sheet is a current and relevant amount, but cost of goods sold (and, therefore, gross margin and income) are considered to be less current or relevant. FIFO favors the balance sheet. These effects hold regardless of the direction of price level changes (increase or decrease) during the period.

   D. **LIFO**

      1. In assessing the relative attributes of LIFO, it is important to remember three important points of emphasis.

         a. If LIFO is employed by a business entity, the matching of revenues and expenses on the income statement is significantly improved over FIFO. That is, the income statement involves the matching of revenues of the current year with the cost of merchandise acquired in the current year.

         b. If LIFO is employed by a business entity, there are usually income tax advantages associated with that choice. In periods of rising prices, LIFO will result in a higher cost of goods sold and a lower tax burden for the business enterprise. However, due to the LIFO conformity rule, if LIFO is chosen for tax purposes, the firm must also use it for the books. Thus, the firm cannot reduce its taxes with LIFO and at the same time use FIFO for financial reporting purposes in the quest to maximize reported income.

    c. If LIFO is employed by a business entity, the balance sheet presentation of inventory is less than ideal. For the company employing LIFO, inventory on the balance sheet typically reflects the cost of the "oldest" merchandise included in the company's inventory records. This means the balance sheet does not reflect the current cost of inventory and often times, means the inventory is undervalued on the balance sheet.

  2. Thus, if LIFO is chosen, the inventory value in the balance sheet can be a very noncurrent and irrelevant amount, but cost of goods sold (and, therefore, gross margin and income) are considered to be much more current or relevant. LIFO favors the income statement. These effects hold regardless of the direction of price level changes (increase or decrease) during the period.

  3. In addition, LIFO tends to minimize *inventory* profits (also called *phantom* or *illusory* profits).

> **Example**
>
> Inventory costs have been rising. Sales for the year are $100,000 and cost of goods sold is $70,000 under LIFO and $60,000 under FIFO. The $70,000 of cost of goods sold under LIFO is an approximation to the cost of replacing the inventory sold during the period because it represents later purchases in the year. If the firm chooses FIFO, it reports $10,000 more in pretax earnings but that amount really is not disposable income because it must be used to replace higher cost inventory in the next accounting period. The $10,000 is thus illusory income.

E. Cost-Flow Assumptions

  1. In choosing the appropriate cost-flow assumption, a business entity should select the cost-flow assumption that allows the company to do the best job of determining periodic net income.

  2. However, firms often choose FIFO to maximize their reported income. This in turn improves certain financial ratios and may be helpful in meeting requirements placed on the firm by its creditors. In addition, management compensation, if tied to income, will be maximized.

  3. On the other hand, the main reason for choosing LIFO is to minimize income tax. The main advantage of choosing LIFO is tax minimization. The reporting benefit of providing the most current cost of goods sold figure is an unintended consequence for most LIFO firms. A negative consequence to LIFO that sometimes occurs is the tax effect of a LIFO liquidation.

II. LIFO Liquidation

A.
What happens when the number of units purchased or produced is less than the number of units sold? Under LIFO, the computation of cost of goods sold for the current period first uses all the purchases for the period. Then it works backward in time and liquidates layers that were added in previous periods (latest layer added first), until the total number of units sold for the period is costed. A LIFO liquidation is that part of current-period cost of goods sold represented by the cost of goods acquired in prior years.

B. LIFO liquidations occur either from (1) poor planning, or (2) lack of supply.

Example

Assume the following for the current year for a LIFO firm. The beginning inventory is composed of a single layer added in a previous year.

	Units	Unit Cost
Beginning Inventory	100,000	$35.00
Purchases	500,000	$55.00

Merchandise sold during the year: 505,000 Units

Cost of goods sold for the year under LIFO = $27,675,000 = 500,000($55) + 5,000($35). Under LIFO, the current year purchases are used first, and only then are the earlier layers used. (Note: the older inventory items are not actually present; rather, only the cost of those items is included in inventory. Remember that LIFO is a cost-flow assumption, not a description of the actual movement of goods.)

The amount of the LIFO liquidation, thus, is $175,000 ($35 × 5,000). 5,000 more goods were sold than acquired in the year. The $175,000 amount is that part of cost of goods sold represented by the cost of goods acquired in earlier years.

C. LIFO Liquidations are to be Avoided for Two Reasons

1. The main purpose for using LIFO is tax minimization. In the above example, assuming the firm will replenish the 5,000 units liquidated anyway, the firm increases its taxable income by $20 per unit unnecessarily. The $20 amount is the difference between the current-period cost of $55 and the $35 cost in the older layer. Thus, taxable income will increase by $100,000 ($20 x 5,000). If the firm had been able to purchase 505,000 units in the period, this extra tax liability would have been avoided because the entire cost of goods sold would be based on the $55 unit cost.

2. For financial statement reporting, the main advantage of LIFO is in matching current-period costs with current revenues. The liquidation distorts the relationship between current sales and current cost of goods sold. The larger the liquidation, the worse the distortion.

Dollar-Value LIFO

> This lesson presents the calculation to determine ending inventory value using dollar-value LIFO.
>
> **After studying this lesson, you should be able to:**
>
> 1. Explain why a company would want to use dollar value LIFO.
>
> 2. Calculate ending inventory using dollar value LIFO. This calculation includes:
>
>   - converting ending inventory to base year costs;
>
>   - determining the increase in inventory at base year cost;
>
>   - converting the current year layer to current year costs; and
>
>   - adding current layer to beginning of year dollar value LIFO to derive end of year dollar value LIFO.

I. Introduction

A. Remember that in this entire discussion, for external purposes the firm is using LIFO, applied through the DV LIFO method. The firm may use another cost flow assumption (typically FIFO) internally.

B. **Reduces the Effect of the Liquidation Problem**—The dollar-value LIFO conversion technique takes a company's ending inventory in FIFO dollars (usually) and converts them to LIFO dollars. In doing so, the impact of the liquidation problem is reduced.

C. **Allows Companies to Use FIFO Internally**—Most companies prefer to use FIFO for internal management reports and internal operating decisions. dollar-value LIFO allows companies an opportunity to do so.

D. **Reduces Clerical Costs**—As mentioned earlier, most LIFO companies prefer LIFO for external reporting purposes and prefer FIFO for internal purposes. Through the use of Dollar-Value LIFO, a company can maintain a FIFO system for internal purposes, and then convert those results to LIFO for external purposes. Please note that through the use of dollar-value LIFO, a company must maintain only a single inventory system (FIFO) during the accounting period, thus reducing clerical costs.

> **Exam Tip**
> For CPA Exam candidates, a discussion question is frequently included in dollar-value LIFO problems. That discussion question involves a discussion of the advantages of dollar-value LIFO over the quantity of goods LIFO approach (shown previously). These advantages are listed below.

II. Steps in Implementing Dollar-Value LIFO

A. The establishment of inventory pools simply means the company needs to group similar products into inventory groups. For example, a department store might have one inventory pool that includes appliances.

B. The conversion index can be calculated internally or obtained from an external source. Regardless of the method of acquisition, the conversion index represents the calculation shown below.

> Conversion Index = Ending Inventory in Current-Year Dollars / Ending Inventory in Base-Year Dollars

C. *Base-year* dollars refers to the specific price level for the pool in effect at the beginning of the year in which the firm adopted LIFO. When this index is multiplied by the increase in inventory for the year as measured in base-year dollars, the result is the increase in inventory in current costs—the layer added to DV LIFO ending inventory.

Examples

1. A firm using FIFO for many years decides to change to LIFO and use DV LIFO as the specific method of applying LIFO. The beginning inventory in that year is $40,000.

    That value, if not reduced to market via the LC-M valuation process, is the beginning inventory in base year dollars for DV LIFO. If it represents market, then the value must be increased back to cost before applying LIFO.

2. If an external index is unavailable, the conversion index at the end of a year for a pool equals:

    (Current Cost of Ending Inventory) / (Base-Year Cost of Ending Inventory)

    When FIFO is used internally, the ending inventory under FIFO is used as the current cost.

D. Conversion of the FIFO Ending Inventory to LIFO Ending Inventory for Financial Statement Reporting Purposes—This is the objective of the DV LIFO method.

Example

A numerical example illustrates the steps. A firm adopts LIFO (DV LIFO) at the beginning of the current year (Year 1). The beginning inventory under FIFO is $2,000 at cost. That amount is the beginning inventory in base-year dollars (base-year cost). The base-year price index is defined as 1.00. All price changes are measured in relation to the base-year index of 1.00 for simplicity.

The FIFO ending inventory for the current year (Year 1) is $3,200. The ending inventory in base-year dollars is determined to be $2,909. Prices of this type of inventory have increased 10% for the year. An external price index at year-end is 1.10 for this type of inventory. (Note: this agrees with the internal price index, computed as $3,200/$2,909, which also equals 1.10).

1. Convert FIFO ending inventory to ending inventory at base-year cost

    Ending inventory = FIFO ending inventory(1.00/1.10)

    In base-year dollars : $2,909 = $3,200(1.00/1.10)

2. Compute the change in inventory in base-year cost.

Change in inventory in base-year cost	=	Ending inventory in base-year dollars	−	Beginning inventory in base-year dollars
$909	=	$2,909	−	$2,000

This result is important because it shows that there has been a *physical* increase in inventory for the year. With the measurement of the dollar fixed at the base year, the increase could not have been caused by increases in the price level. The $909 amount is the layer added in the current year at base-year cost. But LIFO must measure layers at current cost. The next step accomplishes this objective.

3. Compute the current-year layer at current-year costs.

Current-year layer at current-year cost	=	Current-year layer at base-year cost	×	Conversion index
$1,000	=	$909		(1.10/1.00)

4. Compute ending inventory under DV LIFO (reported in the balance sheet).

Ending DV LIFO inventory	=	Beginning DV LIFO inventory	+	Current-year layer at current-year cost
$3,000	=	$2,000	+	$1,000

1. This process illustrates that DV LIFO uses price-level indices to measure the inventory increase first in base-year cost, and then expresses each year's layer at current cost through the conversion index. The result is a DV LIFO ending inventory that is the sum of layers measured in current dollars for the period the layers were added. This method is called the *double-extension* method because the ending inventory is extended at both base-year cost and ending current-year cost.

2. The balance sheet for Year 1 reports $3,000 of inventory. This amount consists of two layers: beginning inventory of $2,000 and the Year 1 layer of $1,000. The two layers reflect different price-level indices (1.00 and 1.10 respectively).

3. Cost of goods sold is computed as in any periodic inventory context. Ending inventory as computed for DV LIFO is subtracted from cost of goods available for sale. The result is cost of goods sold.

Example

This example extends the previous DV LIFO example two more years to show how layers are accumulated, and how to handle a LIFO liquidation in DV LIFO.

Current (FIFO)	FIFO Cost of Ending Inventory	Ending Price Level Index
Year 2	$4,025	1.15
Year 3	4,100	1.20

Beginning DV LIFO inventory (from Year 1)	$3,000
Ending inventory at base-year cost = $4,025(1.00/1.15) = $3,500	
Increase in inventory at base-year cost = $3,500 − $2,909[*] = $591	
Increase in inventory at Year 2 prices = $591(1.15/1.00)	680
Ending inventory, DV LIFO	$3,680

[*]This amount is from step 1 of Year 1, the ending inventory at base-year cost for Year 1.

The $3,680 amount is really the sum of three layers reflecting different prices. This schedule helps to understand the result of DV LIFO:

Layer	In Base-Year Cost	Conversion Index	DV LIFO
Base	$2,000	1.00	$2,000
Year 1	909	1.10	1,000
Year 2	591	1.15	680
Ending Year 2 DV LIFO inventory			$3,680

Beginning DV LIFO inventory (from Year 2)	$3,680
Ending inventory at base-year cost = $4,100(1.00/1.20) =$3,417	
Decrease in inventory at base-year cost = $3,500[*] − $3,417 = $83	
Decrease Year 2 layer by $83 at base-year cost	
Decrease in Year 2 layer at DV LIFO cost = $83(1.15/1.00) =	(95)
Ending DV LIFO	$3,585

[*]From Year 2 base-year cost.

At current cost, inventory for Year 3 appeared to increase. However, after converting to base-year dollars (removing the effect of the price level increase), the inventory decrease, in physical quantity, was apparent. No layer was added in Year 3. The most recent layer added is reduced under LIFO.

Again, the breakdown of layers at the end of Year 3:

Layer	In Base-Year Cost	Conversion Index	DV LIFO
Base	$2,000	1.00	$2,000
Year 1	909	1.10	1,000
Year 2	508[*]	1.15	584
Ending Year 3 DV LIFO inventory			$3,584[#]

[*]$591 — $83 decrease in base-year dollars
[#]$1 difference due to rounding

Gross Margin and Relative Sales Value Method

This lesson presents the gross margin method for estimating ending inventory and allocation of inventory cost based on relative sales values.

After studying this lesson, you should be able to:

1. Explain margin on sales versus margin on cost and be able to determine cost to sales.

2. Apply the Gross Margin Method to value ending inventory.

3. Apply the Relative Sales Value Method to value ending inventory.

I. Estimating Ending Inventory

    A. For a variety of reasons, companies may need to estimate ending inventory using the gross margin method. A company may use an estimate of ending inventory for internal purposes during interim periods when a physical count is prohibitively expensive or when inventory is destroyed as the result of a casualty. The gross margin method can be used **only** for estimation purposes. It may not be used for financial reporting of inventory.

II. Gross Margin Method

    A. The gross margin method estimates cost of goods sold from sales using a percentage based on historical data. Then, ending inventory can be inferred from beginning inventory, purchases, and cost of goods sold.

    B. To use the gross margin method, a company must have a consistent gross margin percentage (margin as a percentage of sales or margin based on cost). If inventory is heterogeneous, the method should be applied to pools of inventory with relatively homogeneous gross margin percentages.

III. Margin on Sales, Margin on Cost

    A. Formulas:

        1. The margin on sales is gross margin divided by sales, or sales less cost of goods sold divided by sales.

Gross Margin Percentage = Margin on Sales = (Sales – Cost of Goods Sold)/Sales

        2. The margin on cost is sales less cost of goods sold divided by cost of goods sold.

Margin on Cost = (Sales – Cost of Goods Sold) / Cost of Goods Sold

    B. The use of the gross margin method depends on how the margin on sales is expressed.

    C. Margin on cost is always greater than margin on sales because sales exceed cost. The two ways of expressing the margin are related. The following two examples show how each may be converted to the other.

    D. The goal is to use one of the two formulas to determine cost/sales. It is the cost/sales ratio that is used to determine cost of goods sold.

Examples

1. Assume gross margin (also referred to as margin on sales) is 40%. Set sales to 1.00, and margin to .40. This implies that cost is .60 times sales:

Sales	1.00
− Cost	.60
= Margin	.40

Therefore, margin / cost = .40 / .60 = .67. Thus, a gross margin percentage of 40% is equivalent to a margin on cost of 67%.

2. Assume margin on cost is 45%. Set cost to 1.00, and margin to .45. This implies that sales are 1.45 times cost.

Sales	1.45
− Cost	1.00
= Margin	.45

Therefore, margin on sales = .45 / 1.45 = .31. Thus, a gross margin percentage of 31% is equivalent to a margin on cost of 45%.

Formulas can also be used to convert one margin expression to the other:

(Margin on sales) / (1 − Margin on sales) = Margin on cost

(Margin on cost) / (1 + Margin on cost) = Margin on sales

IV. Using the Gross Margin Method

A. The purpose of the previous short section was to describe how each of the two different expressions of margin can be converted into the other. If you are comfortable with this method, the use of the gross margin method is straightforward.

Beg. Inventory + Net Purchases = End. Inventory + Cost of Goods Sold

Beg. Inventory + Net Purchases = End. Inventory + Sales (Cost/Sales)

B. The second equation shows that cost of goods sold is estimated by sales multiplied by the cost-to-sales ratio. This ratio equals 1 − gross margin %, which can easily be computed using the conversion methods shown above. The unknown in the equation is ending inventory. The gross margin method allows an estimate of ending inventory.

Example
A firm's inventory is destroyed by fire on April 4. Beginning inventory is $20,000, net purchases through April 4 are $250,000, and sales through April 4 amount to $320,000.

First, assume the gross margin is 40%. Then the cost/sales ratio is 60%.

Beg. inventory	+	Net purchases	=	End. inventory	+	Sales (cost/sales)
$20,000	+	$250,000	=	?	+	$320,000(.60)
			Ending inventory	=		$78,000

This is an estimate of the cost of inventory destroyed (i.e., the ending inventory at April 4).

Now assume the margin on cost is 45%. From the above examples of converting margins, the gross margin percentage is 31%, and therefore the cost/sales ratio is 69%.

Beg. inventory	+	Net purchases	=	End. inventory	+	Sales (cost/sales)
$20,000	+	$250,000	=	?	+	$320,000(.69)
			Ending inventory	=		$49,200

In this example, the firm could not have counted the inventory destroyed but is able to estimate its cost for insurance purposes by applying the gross margin method. The method is also useful for budgetary and other internal reporting purposes when an exact calculation is not needed.

V. Relative Sales Value Method

A. Firms may be able to obtain significant discounts by purchasing different types of inventory from the same supplier. This may occur, for example, in a liquidation or distress sale. U.S. GAAP requires that the total price be allocated based on the market values or selling prices of the individual inventory items.

Example
Three items of inventory were purchased for $45. The unit selling prices (for the buyer upon resale) are given below.

Inventory item	Unit sales price
A	$20
B	25
C	40
Total	$85

The cost of the inventory ($45) would be allocated to each item based on the relative sales value as demonstrated in the following calculation.

Item A is recorded at $10.59 = (($20 / $85) $45).

Item B is recorded at $13.23 = (($25 / $85) $45).

Item C is recorded at $21.18 = (($40 / $85) $45).

Retail Inventory Method

This lesson presents the retail inventory method for estimating ending inventory.

After studying this lesson, you should be able to:

1. Calculate the cost to retail percentage for the retail inventory method.

2. Calculate ending inventory using the retail inventory method.

I. **The Retail Inventory Method**—This method is used by retailers to estimate ending inventory at cost. Most retailers know the markup on the inventory items and are able to count ending inventory at retail prices (ever see the store employees counting items on a shelf?). This method is used both for internal decision purposes and for financial reporting of cost of goods sold and ending inventory.

II. **The Basic Method**

A. The retail inventory method, which is really a family of related methods, is based on three basic calculations.

B. *First*, ending inventory at retail is calculated or counted at year-end. *Second*, the cost-to-retail ratio is calculated. *Third*, the ending inventory at retail is multiplied by the cost-to-retail ratio to arrive at estimated inventory at cost.

C. Cost of goods sold is an implied amount, rather than a directly calculated amount under this method.

D. The method can be shown in equation form: EI(cost) = EI(retail) × C/R, where EI is ending inventory and C/R is the cost-to-retail ratio for the period. The retail inventory method can be used with FIFO, LIFO, and average cost-flow assumptions. Cost of goods sold is found by subtracting ending inventory at cost from cost of goods available for sale.

> **Note**
> When the retail inventory method is used, the entity must apply LC-M (not LC-NRV) when determining if there had been a decline in the value of the inventory that would warrant an inventory write-down.

E. **Basic Structure of the Retail Inventory Method:**

	Cost	Retail
Beginning Inventory	$200	$300
Purchases	2,000	3,000
Goods Available for Sale	2,200	3,300
Sales		(2,600)
Ending Inventory at Retail		700

Cost to Retail Ratio:

2,200/3,300 = 66 2/3%

Ending Inventory at Retail × Cost Ratio = Ending Inventory at Cost

$700 × 66 2/3% = $467

Cost of goods sold, then, is reported at the implied amount of $1,733 = $200 beginning inventory at cost + $2,000 purchases less $467 ending inventory.

F. This illustrates the "average" retail inventory method. It is one of five variations of the retail inventory method.

III. Terminology and Guidance in Applying the Retail Inventory Method

A. Original Selling Price—Cost plus initial markup.

B. Net Additional Markups—This is the net increase in the original selling price. This amount is the net sum of additional markups above the original selling price less additional markup cancellations. A markup cancellation is a reduction of the additional markup, not a reduction below the original selling price. This amount is added only in the retail column and before computing the cost-to-retail ratio.

C. Net Markdowns—This is the net decrease in the original selling price. This amount is the net difference between markdowns, which are reductions in the original selling price, and markdown cancellations. A markdown cancellation is a reduction of the original markdown, not an increase above the original selling price. Depending on the variation being used, this amount is subtracted only from the retail column when computing the cost-to-retail ratio.

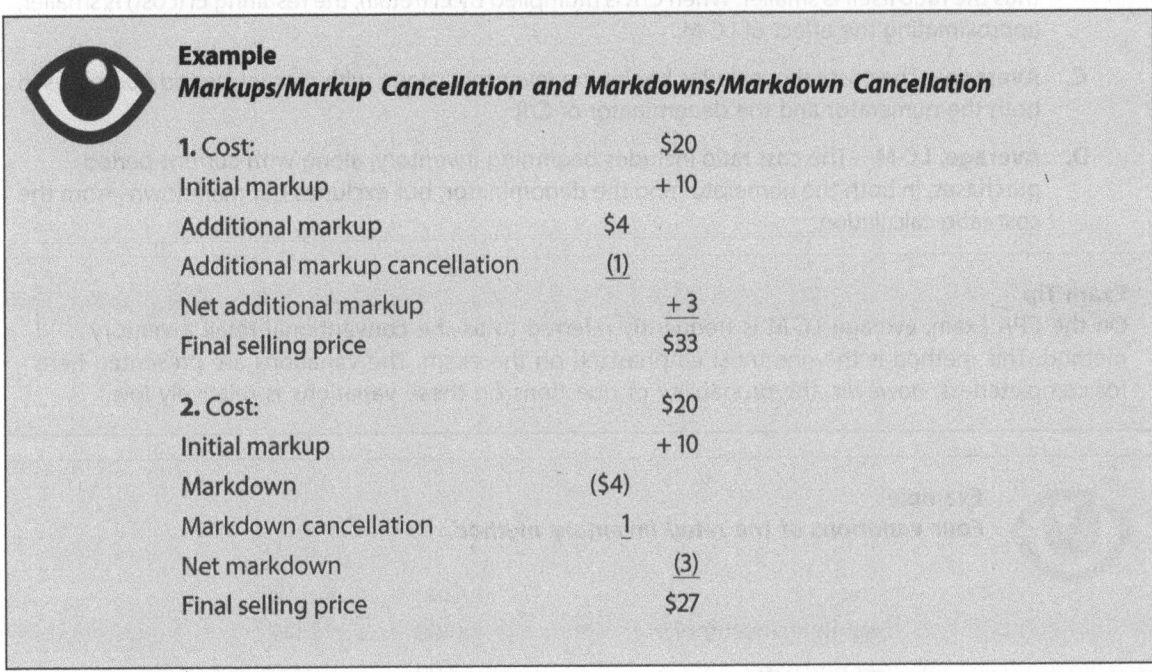

Example
Markups/Markup Cancellation and Markdowns/Markdown Cancellation

1. Cost: $20
Initial markup + 10
Additional markup $4
Additional markup cancellation (1)
Net additional markup +3
Final selling price $33

2. Cost: $20
Initial markup + 10
Markdown ($4)
Markdown cancellation 1
Net markdown (3)
Final selling price $27

D. Net Purchases—Net purchases (purchases less purchase returns plus transportation in) is included in both cost and retail values. Add net purchases to both cost and retail before calculating the cost-to-retail ratio.

E. Employee Discounts—The difference between the normal retail value of merchandise sold to employees and the amount actually paid by employees. This amount is subtracted along with sales from Goods Available for Sale at Retail to arrive at Ending Inventory at Retail, after computing the cost-to-retail ratio.

F. Normal Shortage (spoilage)—Shown at retail value, subtracted along with sales from Goods Available for Sale at Retail to arrive at Ending Inventory at Retail, after computing the cost-to-retail ratio.

G. Abnormal Shortage (losses)—Shown at both cost and retail, the amount of merchandise available for sale has declined. Reduce the cost and retail value of goods available for sale before computing the cost-to-retail ratio. This loss is usually recoverable through insurance.

IV. Variations—The variations of the retail inventory method are directly related to the calculation of the cost ratio. There are five variations, four of which are summarized below. The fifth is covered in the "Dollar-Value LIFO Retail" lesson.

    A. FIFO—The C/R excludes the cost of beginning inventory from the numerator and the retail value of beginning inventory from the denominator. Thus, C/R measures the cost-to-retail ratio only for the current-period purchases on the assumption that all beginning inventory will be sold (first-in, first-out). If ending inventory consists entirely of current-period purchases, the C/R should not include beginning inventory.

    B. FIFO, LC-M—The cost ratio excludes the cost of beginning inventory from the numerator and the retail value of beginning inventory from the denominator. Then, in an effort to arrive at a more conservative cost ratio, the calculation also excludes net markdowns from the cost ratio. This causes the denominator of C/R to be larger, because net markdowns are not subtracted, and thus the ratio itself is smaller. When C/R is multiplied by EI (retail), the resulting EI (cost) is smaller, approximating the effect of LC-M.

    C. Average—The cost ratio includes beginning inventory, along with current-period purchases in both the numerator and the denominator of C/R.

    D. Average, LC-M—The cost ratio includes beginning inventory, along with current-period purchases, in both the numerator and the denominator, but excludes net markdowns from the cost ratio calculation.

Exam Tip

On the CPA Exam, average LC-M is frequently referred to as the conventional retail inventory method. This method is the one most emphasized on the exam. The variations are presented here for completeness; however, the probability of questions on these variations is relatively low.

Example
Four variations of the retail inventory method.

	Cost	Retail
Beginning inventory	$ 100	$ 145
Net purchases	600	900
Net additional markups		70
Net markdowns		− 30
Goods available for sale	$ 700	$ 1,085
Less sales		− 800
Equals ending inventory at retail		$ 285

EI(cost) is not computed above because computing that amount is the objective of the retail method and the amount depends on the variation chosen by the firm. Also, if the *count* of ending inventory at retail is less than $285, a shrinkage loss is indicated. The actual count of ending inventory is the value to use for computing EI(cost) in that case. The $285 amount is the ending inventory *that should be present*, at retail.

FIFO:	C/R	= $600/($900 + $70 − $30)	= .6383
	EI(cost)	= .6383($285)	= $181.92

(Beginning inventory is excluded from the ratio.)

FIFO, LC-M:	C/R	= $600/($900 + $70)	= .6186
	EI(cost)	= .6186($285)	= $176.30

(Beginning inventory is excluded from the ratio and net markdowns are not subtracted in the denominator.)

Average:	C/R	= $700/$1,085	= .6452
	EI(cost)	= .6452($285)	= $183.88

(Beginning inventory is included in the ratio.)

Average, LC-M:	C/R	= $700/($1,085 + $30)	= .6278
	EI(cost)	= .6278($285)	= $178.92

(Beginning inventory is included in the ratio and net markdowns are not subtracted in the denominator.)

Below is a table that summarizes how components are treated when computing cost of sales using the most common method, the average (conventional) retail method.

	Cost	Retail
Beginning inventory	X	X
Purchases	X	X
Freight-in	X	
Purchase returns	(X)	(X)
Net markups		X
Abnormal shortage	(X)	(X)
Goods available (cost/retail ratio)	**XX**	**XX**
Markdowns		(X)
Sales		(X)
Sales returns		X
Employee discounts		(X)
Normal shortage		(X)
Ending inventory retail		**XX**

	Cost	Retail
Beginning inventory	$ 100	$ 145
Purchases (net)	600	900
Net markups		70
Goods available (cost/retail ratio)	**$700**	**1,115**
Markdowns		(30)
Sales (net)		(800)
Ending inventory retail		**$ 285**

Cost to retail ratio is 700 ÷ 1,115 = .6278.

Ending inventory at cost is $285 × .6278 = $178.92

Dollar-Value LIFO Retail

This lesson presents the Dollar-Value LIFO Retail method for estimating ending inventory.

After studying this lesson, you should be able to:

1. Recognize that retail companies that use the LIFO cost flow assumption must use DV LIFO.

2. Identify the order of the DV LIFO Retail calculation.

I. Introduction

A. The **dollar-value LIFO retail method (DV LIFO)** is used by companies that use the LIFO cost-flow assumption when they apply the retail inventory method. The companies must use the dollar-value approach in order to determine the LIFO layers. There are two independent steps:

1. DV LIFO is first applied to inventory at retail only—and in the same way it was illustrated before. This results in the measurement of the current-period layer measured in current retail dollars. So, DV LIFO is restricted to retail dollar application.

2. Then, the FIFO retail method (not LC-M; i.e., subtracting markdowns when computing C/R) cost-to-retail ratio is applied to this retail layer yielding the increase in cost at current prices. Finally, this cost layer is added to beginning inventory at DV LIFO cost to yield ending inventory at DV LIFO cost.

> **Note**
> Since DV LIFO is a form of LIFO, the subsequent measurement and testing for declines in inventory value would be LC-M as described in the lesson on "Subsequent Measurement of Inventory".

II. How to Remember which Step Comes First

A. Because inventory is counted at retail and the method is called DV LIFO retail, apply DV LIFO first, then apply the retail method that deflates the amounts back to cost.

Example
Assume the same information that was presented for the current year as in the previous example in the "Retail Inventory Method" lesson :

	Cost	Retail
Beginning inventory	$ 100	$ 145
Net purchases	600	900
Net additional markups		70
Net markdowns		− 30
Goods available for sale	$ 700	$ 1,085
Less sales		− 800
Equals ending inventory at retail		**$ 285**

Assume the firm adopted DV LIFO at the beginning of the current year. Therefore, the beginning inventory at retail in terms of base year dollars is $145. The price index is set at 1.00 at the beginning of the year and has climbed to 1.08 by the end of the year. The DV LIFO retail method is applied to the current year:

BI DV LIFO	$100.00
EI(retail, FIFO) =	$285.00
EI(retail, base-year dollars) = $285(1.00/1.08) =	$263.89
Increase in EI(retail, base-year dollars) = $263.89 − $145 =	$118.89
Increase in EI(retail, FIFO) = $118.89(1.08/1.00) =	$128.40
Increase in EI(cost, FIFO) = $128.40(.6383)*	81.96
EI DV LIFO	**$181.96**

*Cost ratio for FIFO (not LC-M) from previous example.

Later years are treated the same way. The DV LIFO method is applied as before, to subsequent year's retail dollars. Then, the FIFO cost-to-retail ratio for that year is applied to the retail layer measured in current retail dollars.

Subsequent Measurement of Inventory

This material presents the calculation for lower of cost or market (LC-M or net realizable value (LC-NRV) for subsequent inventory valuation.

After studying this lesson, you should be able to:

1. Identify and apply the appropriate method for subsequent measurement of inventory: lower of cost or market (LC-M) or net realizable value (LC-NRV).

   a. Inventory measured using FIFO or average cost utilizes subsequent measurement that is LC-NRV.

   b. Inventory measured using LIFO or retail method utilizes subsequent measurement that is LC-M.

2. Define cost, market, the floor, and the ceiling used in the LC-M calculations.

3. Complete a calculation for subsequent measurement of inventory, and determine what value should be shown on the balance sheet.

I. Loss on Inventory

A. In addition to the normal valuation of inventory at cost and choice of inventory cost-flow assumption (FIFO, LIFO), GAAP requires that firms recognize an end-of-period loss on inventory if its utility has declined. If market is below cost, then inventory must be written down to market. The loss cannot be postponed until the period of sale.

   1. If cost < market, there is no loss recognition and the inventory is reported at cost.

   2. If cost > market, a loss is recognized and the inventory is written down to market.

II. Subsequent Measurement of Inventory

A. Effective January 1, 2017, if the entity uses FIFO or weighted average inventory valuation method, then the subsequent measurement is cost (as determined by FIFO or weighted average) or net realizable value (LC-NRV).

> **Note**
> LC-NRV applies to all inventory valuation methods that are **not** LIFO or Retail Inventory Method. In essence, this means that LC-NRV is applied to inventories carried at FIFO or weighted average.

B. If the inventory is measured using LIFO or the Retail Inventory Method (RIM), then the subsequent measurement is cost (as determined by LIFO or RIM) or market (L-CM) with market defined below and limited to a ceiling and a floor.

C. The general concept is that an entity must recognize a loss on inventory if the utility of the inventory has declined. If subsequent value of the inventory is below cost, then inventory must be written down and a loss recognized. The loss resulting from a decline in value cannot be postponed until the period of sale.

   1. If cost < market or NRV, there is no loss recognition and the inventory is reported at cost.

   2. If cost > market or NRV, a loss is recognized and the inventory is written down as described below.

D. The result is that inventory is reported at the lower of cost or market (LC-M) or lower of cost or net realizable value (LC-NRV). The total expense or loss is limited to the historical cost of the inventory. But the subsequent valuation requirement shifts a portion of the cost as a loss or expense to the period in which the inventory has declined in value.

III. Inventories NOT Carried at LIFO or RIM (i.e., Carried at FIFO or Weighted Average) use LC-NRV

  A. Subsequent valuation of inventories carried at FIFO or weighted average are measured at the lower of the cost basis or net realizable value. Net realizable value is defined in the Master Glossary in the FASB's Accounting Standards Codification as the "estimated selling prices in the ordinary course of business, less reasonably predictable cost of completion, disposal, and transportation."

Example

An item of inventory had cost using FIFO of $100.

Selling price = $99

Replacement cost = $88

Cost of completion, disposal, and transportation = $9

The entity compares the FIFO cost ($100) to NRV (selling price less cost to sell $99 – $9 = $90). Since the NRV is less than cost, the inventory is written down to its NRV of $90.

IV. Inventories Carried at LIFO or RIM Use LC-M.

  A. Lower of cost or market is applied when the cost is assigned using LIFO or retail inventory method.

  B. Determine Market Value

    1. Market is generally *replacement cost*, subject to a range of values defined by an established *ceiling value* and an established *floor value*.

    2. The ceiling value is net realizable value. That is, the ceiling value is calculated by reducing the sales price by the estimated cost to complete and sell the inventory.

    3. The floor value is net realizable value reduced by the normal profit margin.

  C. Calculate Market Value

    1. If the replacement cost value is within the range established by the ceiling value and the floor value, market is equal to replacement cost.

    2. If the replacement cost value is greater than the ceiling value, market is equal to the ceiling value.

    3. If the replacement cost value is less than the floor value, market is equal to the floor value.

    4. Market is also simply the middle amount (in dollar terms) of the three amounts: replacement cost, net realizable value, and net realizable value less normal profit margin. Market cannot exceed the ceiling or be less than the floor.

Example

At year-end, the following values pertain to an item of inventory:

Cost—determined using LIFO	$100
Replacement cost	80
Selling price	120
Estimated cost of completion and selling	30
Normal profit margin	20

The three values to determine market value:

Replacement cost	80
Net realizable value = $120 − $30	= 90 (ceiling)
Net realizable value less normal profit margin =	$90 − $20
	= 70 (floor)

Market value = $80, which is replacement cost because it is between the ceiling and floor amounts. It is also the middle of the three figures in dollar terms. The final LC-M valuation thus is $80 because market is lower than original cost ($100). The inventory would be reported at $80 and a holding loss of $20 would be recorded (cost of $100 less market of $80). If market had exceeded cost, then the inventory would be reported at cost.

1. If replacement cost were instead $95, then market value would be $90, the middle of the three figures determining market value.

2. If replacement cost were instead $65, then market value would be $70, the middle of the three figures determining market value.

Note
Market value cannot exceed the ceiling or be less than the floor.

D. **Summary**—The LC-M valuation process has two steps:

1. Compute market value (the middle of the three amounts).

2. Value inventory at the lower of original cost or market value (LC-M).

V. **Lower of Cost or Market Comparison**

A. GAAP allows flexibility in application of LC-M, but the lower of cost or market comparison must be completed on a consistent basis from year to year. In making the comparison, a company can employ one of three approaches.

Note
Candidates often become so involved with the first step that they forget to apply the second. Once you have found market, don't forget to compare it to cost (Step 2) for the final valuation under LC-M.

1. **Individual item basis**—If a company has 1,000 inventory items and chooses the individual item approach, a total of 1,000 comparisons will be made to determine the lower of cost or market for ending inventory.

2. **Category basis**—If a company has 1,000 inventory items grouped into 10 categories, a total of 10 comparisons will be made to determine the lower of cost or market for ending inventory.

3. **Total basis**—If a company wishes, it can make a single comparison to determine the lower of cost or market for ending inventory.

B. The individual item basis yields the most conservative (lowest) inventory value (and largest holding loss) because for each item the lower of cost or market is chosen. There is no chance for items with market exceeding cost to cancel against items with cost exceeding market, as there is with the other two approaches.

Example

Inventory	Cost	Market	LC-M Application Level		
			Item	Type	Total
Category A					
Item 1	$10	$7	$7		
Item 2	5	9	5		
Total	$15	$16		$15	
Category B					
Item 3	$19	$24	$19		
Item 4	27	20	20		
Total	$46	$44		44	
Total	**$61**	**$60**	**$51**	**$59**	**$60**

The firm may choose from among $51, $59, and $60 as its LC-M valuation for inventory. All three are lower than cost of $61. The higher the level of applying the LC-M valuation procedure, the higher the resulting valuation.

VI. Lower of Cost or Market—Journal Entry—Once the lower of cost or market comparison is completed and the ending valuation is found (using either LC-M or LC-NRV), the formal entry of this information can be achieved by employing the *direct method* or the *allowance method*. Under the direct method, any holding loss (difference between a higher cost and a lower market value) related to inventory is simply included in cost of goods sold. It is *directly* included in cost of goods sold. Under the allowance method, any holding loss related to inventory is separately identified in a contra inventory account with separate disclosure of the holding loss. Cost of goods sold does not include the holding loss under this method.

Example

A firm uses the category level comparison to determine market value. Total cost of inventory is $30,000, and the total market value is $27,000 at the end of the year. To record the holding loss of $3,000, either of the two approaches can be used. The adjusting entry to record the loss under these approaches is:

Direct method:

Cost of goods sold	3,000	
Inventory		3,000

Allowance method:

Holding loss	3,000	
Allowance to reduce inventory to LC-M		3,000

The allowance method reports $3,000 less of cost of goods sold in the income statement but compensates by reporting a separate holding loss of $3,000. The allowance account, a contra inventory account, reduces net inventory in the balance sheet to $27,000. Both methods yield the same net inventory valuation and income. However, the components of income are different under the two methods.

Inventory Errors

This lesson addresses how to correct for inventory errors.

After studying this lesson, you should be able to:

1. Determine the impact of an inventory error on any component of the Balance Sheet or Income Statement.

2. Complete the journal entry necessary to correct an inventory error.

I. Introduction

A. Inventory effects are analyzed with the basic inventory equation:

> Beginning Inventory + Net Purchases = Ending Inventory + Cost of Goods Sold

B. If beginning inventory is understated, then cost of goods sold is also understated, everything else being the same, because the equation must balance. If ending inventory is understated, cost of goods sold must be overstated, again because the equation must balance.

C. The journal entry and reporting for error corrections depend on both the error and the period of discovery.

Example

The ending inventory for Year 1 is understated $4,000 because the items in one wing of the warehouse were not counted. The effects of this error, ignoring tax effects, are:

	Year 1	Year 2
Beginning inventory:	not affected	understated $4,000
Ending inventory:	understated $4,000	not affected
Cost of goods sold:	overstated $4,000	understated $4,000
Net income:	understated $4,000	overstated $4,000
Retained earnings:	understated $4,000	is now correct*

*This is what is meant by a counterbalancing error. If it is never discovered, retained earnings automatically corrects itself, and with the new count of inventory at the end of the second year, the error disappears. However, the errors in the two years' financial statements do not automatically correct and would be present in the comparative statements.

If the error is discovered in Year 2, the following entry is made to correct the beginning balance of retained earnings:

Inventory	4,000	
Prior period adjustment (to retained earnings)		4,000

A prior–period adjustment is to the account in which the correction of an error in prior year earnings is recorded. The income statement impact of the prior–period error is closed to retained earnings. The prior–period adjustment increases the year 2 beginning balance of retained earnings to its correct amount as if year 1 income were correct. In the comparative statements for years 1 and 2, income for year 1 would be increased to its correct amount. All other affected accounts for year 1 also would be corrected.

If discovery occurs in Year 3, no entry is needed because counterbalancing has taken place. All year 2 ending account balances are correct. However, both year 1 and year 2 statements should be corrected if shown comparatively with year 3. All accounts for those years affected by the error would be restated to their correct amounts.

II. Error in Recording Purchases—What if a purchase at year–end was not recorded in the year of purchase (Year 1), but rather was recorded in the next year (Year 2), the year of payment? Assume the goods were counted in EI in year of purchase.

A. If the Error is Never Discovered

1. 1st year: purchases are understated, CGS understated, net income overstated, ending retained earnings overstated

2. 2nd year: purchases are overstated, CGS overstated, net income understated, ending retained earnings is correct (error has counterbalanced)

3. But the errors remain in both years' statements shown comparatively with later statements.

B. If the Error is Discovered in Year 2

Prior period adjustment (to retained earnings)	XX	
Purchases		XX

1. Retained earnings at the beginning of Year 2 are corrected by this entry, and year 1's income (and any other accounts affected) would be corrected in the Year 1 statement reported comparatively with Year 2.

C. If the Error is Discovered in Year 3

1. No entry is needed because retained earnings are correct—the error has counterbalanced. The statements for Years 1 and 2 would be corrected if shown comparatively with Year 3.

Losses on Purchase Commitments

This lesson addresses what to do with losses on purchase commitments.

After studying this lesson, you should be able to:

1. Explain what to do with losses when the commitment contract can be modified.

2. Explain what to do with losses when the commitment contract cannot be modified.

I. **Introduction**—Companies often commit (in a contract) to the purchase of materials to lock in the unit price of an item needed for production or resale in order to aid in cash flow budgeting and to protect against price increases. Sometime the market price of the item declines below the contract price. The accounting for this price decline depends on whether the contract can be revised in light of the changing market conditions.

II. **The Contract Can be Modified**—In this case, the loss is required to be footnoted as a contingent liability, but is not accrued in the accounts because the loss is not probable given that the contract can be revised.

III. **The Contract Cannot be Modified**—In this case, the loss must be accrued because the loss is probable and estimable. The inventory, when acquired, is recorded at market value and a loss is recognized for the difference between the market value and the contract price. If the contract has not been executed as of the balance sheet date, the following adjusting entry is made:

> Loss on purchase commitment   xx
>
>   Liability on purchase commitment   xx

The amount equals the difference between the unit contract price and market price at year-end, multiplied by the number of units required to be purchased.

A. If the market price drops further in the second year, an additional loss is recognized when the contract is executed. Recoveries result in a gain but only to the extent of the previously recognized loss.

Example
In December, a firm contracted to purchase 200 units of prefabricated housing walls at $4,000 per wall. The contract is neither cancelable nor subject to revision. By December 31, the market price per wall had dropped to $3,900.

The adjusting entry at December 31 is:

Loss on purchase commitment	20,000	
Liability on purchase commitment		20,000[1]

[1]200($4,000 – $3,900)

In January, at payment date, if the market price had decreased to $3,850, the following entry would be made:

Liability on purchase commitment	20,000	
Loss on purchase commitment	10,000[2]	
Inventory $3,850(200)	770,000	
Cash $4,000(200)		$800,000

[2]($3,900 – $3,850)200

If the market price had been $3,950 at payment date, a gain of $10,000 would be recorded and the inventory would be recorded at $3,950 per unit. If the market price exceeded $4,000 at payment date, a gain of $20,000 would be recorded and the inventory would be recorded at $800,000, the original contract price. The contract price is the ceiling for recording the inventory. There is no floor.

Property, Plant and Equipment

Categories and Presentation

This lesson presents the categories and presentation of plant asset account.

After studying this lesson, you should be able to:

1. Distinguish what is included in each category of plant assets.

2. Demonstrate ability to complete the presentation and disclosures for plant assets.

I. **Requirements for Inclusion in Plant Assets**

    A. To be included in plant assets, an asset must:

        1. Be currently used in operations;

        2. Have a useful life extending more than one year beyond the balance sheet date; *and*

        3. Have physical substance. Intangible assets are different from plant assets in that they have no physical substance.

    B. If land is held for investment purposes or for future development, it is excluded from plant assets because it currently is not a productive asset.

II. **Categories Within Plant Assets**

    A. **Plant and Equipment**—This category of fixed assets is composed of buildings, machinery, and equipment. These assets have a finite useful life and can also be referred to as depreciable assets.

    B. **Land Improvements**—This asset differs from land in that it has a finite useful life and is depreciated. Examples of land improvements include parking lots, fencing, external lighting, and some landscaping.

    C. **Land**—This category includes the site of a manufacturing facility, the site of administrative offices, and the site of any storage warehouses. Any plot of land in which a company has constructed facilities specifically related to primary business operations is included in this category. This category does not include real estate held for investment purposes. Land has an indefinite life and is, therefore, not depreciated. *It is the only asset in the plant asset category that is not depreciated or amortized.*

    D. **Natural Resources**—Include such items as a gravel pit, a coal mine, a tract of timber land, and an oil well. This category of assets will produce income until all the natural resources are extracted and sold. These assets are frequently referred to as depletable assets.

    E. **Leasehold Improvements**—This category includes improvements to leased property, such as retail stores or office space. The lessee can depreciate the leasehold improvement over the useful life of the improvement or the life of the lease (whichever is shorter).

Capitalized Costs

This lesson presents what is included in the plant-asset account.

After studying this lesson, you should be able to:

1. Distinguish what costs should be capitalized (versus expensed) upon acquisition of a plant assets.

2. Distinguish what costs should be capitalized (versus expensed) during the life of a plant asset.

Definition

Capitalization: The costs are added to an asset account (balance sheet) rather than to an expense account (income statement). Capitalized amounts are subsequently allocated to expense (depreciated) over time (more on this later).

I. Costs that Are Capitalized Upon Acquisition of Plant Assets

A. The acquisition cost of property, plant, and equipment includes two components, the cash equivalent price or negotiated acquisition cost and the so-called **get-ready costs**.

B. The **get-ready costs** include all costs incurred to get the asset on the company's premises and ready for use. For example, the setting up and testing of new machinery is a **get-ready cost**.

C. The general rule for capitalizing expenditures related to the acquisition of plant assets is similar to the rule for capitalizing costs to inventory.

D. Capitalize all expenditures necessary to bring the plant asset to its intended condition and location.

II. Cost Capitalized During the Life of the Plant Asset

A. If the estimated time of benefit is related to the current accounting period only, the expenditure is recorded as an expense. Such expenditures are called "revenue expenditures" or "period costs."

B. If the estimated time of benefit is related to the current and future accounting periods, the expenditure is capitalized. The term "capitalized" means included in an asset account.

C. If the expenditure is immaterial, the company will account for the expenditure in the most expedient way possible. This usually means the expenditure is recorded as an expense in the period of acquisition.

D. If the expenditure is material in amount, the accounting treatment of the expenditure will be determined by examining the estimated time of benefit related to the expenditure. To be capitalized and then depreciated, an expenditure must make the asset "bigger, better, or last longer." In other words, the asset must have increased or improved functionality, make better products, or have a longer life. Three examples of this concept follow:

1. The estimated useful life of the asset is extended beyond the original estimation (i.e., expenditures for a major overhaul of a bread oven in a commercial bread bakery that might extend the life of the oven beyond the original estimate).

2. The asset becomes more efficient or productive, meaning it can produce higher quantities or operate at a lower cost (i.e., a new laser product sorter might be added to a machine, replacing human efforts to sort out defective products and speeding up the process).

3. Quality of the asset's output is improved (i.e., upgrades to equipment for a textile entity, which enable it to produce a sheet with a higher thread count).

E. If an expenditure merely maintains the asset at its anticipated level of productivity and length of life, the following occurs:

    1. The cost is *not* capitalized on the balance sheet.

    2. Instead, it is recorded as a maintenance expense on the current year income statement.

F. Be familiar with the following terms for capitalizable expenditures:

    1. An *addition* is a new major component of an asset, such as an additional room in or on a building, that did not exist before.

    2. An *improvement* is the replacement of a major component of an asset, such as an air conditioning system for a building.

    3. A *rearrangement* is a restructuring of an asset that does **not** extend its life but creates a new type of benefit. Relocation of an entity to another city is an example.

Example

The following list of expenditures shows a variety of costs related to plant assets and how to account for them.

Expenditure	Accounting treatment
Sales tax on equipment purchase	Capitalize to equipment
Cost of delivery, to set up and test equipment	Capitalize to equipment
Cost to train employees to use equipment	Expense
Title fee on land purchase	Capitalize to land
Attorney fee for land purchase	Capitalize to land
Cost to raze an old building on land purchased	Capitalize to land
Proceeds on salvage material from razing	Reduce recorded land cost
Cost of landscaping	Capitalize to land improvements
Cost to excavate foundation for a building	Capitalize to building
Interest on purchase of plant assets	Expense
Interest during construction of building	Capitalize to building
Back property taxes on land just purchased	Capitalize to land
Annual property taxes on land	Expense
Cost of permits for construction	Capitalize to building

Note

Applying the general rule helps in classifying expenditures. For example, the cost to train employees to use equipment benefits the employees, not the equipment. Razing an old building on land just purchased is part of the process of preparing the land for use. However, the cost to raze a building already owned by the firm increases the loss on disposal of the building.

Valuation

This lesson presents the valuation of plant assets when the exchange involves something other than cash.

After studying this lesson, you should be able to:

1. Calculate the value of plant assets in situations where the exchange involved something other than cash (i.e., credit purchase, securities, donation, group purchase, or self-constructed asset).

Note

In general, plant assets should be valued at the fair value of consideration given in exchange, or at the fair value (cash equivalent price) of the asset acquired, whichever is more readily determinable and reliable.

I. **Cash Equivalent Price or Negotiated Acquisition Cost**

A. **Methods of Acquiring Plant Assets**

1. **Cash purchase**—The cash equivalent price is simply the amount of cash paid for the asset on acquisition date.

2. **Deferred payment plan (credit purchase)**—The cash equivalent price for an asset acquired through a deferred payment plan is the present value of future cash payments using the market rate of interest for similar debt instruments.

Example

The list price of a plant asset is $30,000. The purchaser makes a $10,000 down payment and issues a 2-year non-interest-bearing note for the remainder. The note calls for a single lump-sum payment of $20,000 to be made at the maturity of the note. The market rate of interest on such notes is 10%. The present value of a single payment of $1 received two years in the future at 10% is .82645. The entry to record the plant asset is:

DR: Plant asset	26,529	
CR: Cash		10,000
CR: Note payable $20,000(.82645)		16,529

The note is recorded at present value. The list price of plant assets should not be used for valuation of assets. The list price is mainly a starting point for negotiations between the buyer and seller. Subsequent to acquisition, interest expense is recognized as the note approaches maturity. The interest is expensed. It is not added to the building account.

---

3. **Issuance of securities**—The acquisition cost of an asset acquired through the issuance of stocks or bonds is the fair value of the security or the fair value of the asset acquired, whichever can be most clearly determined. When a significant number of shares is issued, care must be taken to ensure that the issuance did not affect the share price.

4. **Donated assets**—Assets received in donation are recorded at their fair value. A revenue or gain is also recorded.

5. **Group purchases**—If a group of fixed assets is acquired in a single transaction, the total negotiated price is allocated to the individual assets acquired. This allocation is based on the respective fair values of the individual assets acquired.

Example

For a lump-sum price, a firm acquired three plant assets at a bargain price of $50,000. The individual fair values of each asset are:

	Fair or appraised value
Building	$10,000
Land	30,000
Equipment	15,000
Total	$55,000

The recorded cost of each asset is based on its relative fair value. The entry to record the purchase:

DR: Building	($10,000/$55,000)$50,000	9,091	
DR: Land	($30,000/$55,000)$50,000	27,273	
DR: Equipment	($15,000/$55,000)$50,000	13,636	
CR: Cash			50,000

II. Self-Constructed Assets

A. **Components of Capitalized Cost**—The capitalized cost of a self-constructed asset includes four components:

1. **Labor**—The direct labor charges related to the construction of the asset will be capitalized. Usually, labor charges are expensed in the period incurred, but in this instance, the labor charges are capitalized. This component of the cost of the asset includes any fringe benefits related to the basic labor cost.

2. **Material**—The direct materials related to the construction of the asset will be capitalized.

3. **Overhead**—The overhead charges related to the construction of the asset will be capitalized. Usually, the capitalization of overhead charges is accomplished by one of two approaches.

    a. **Incremental overhead approach**—One approach is to capitalize *only* the incremental overhead. For example, if a company typically has $5,000,000 of overhead, but during the period of construction, overhead increased to $5,500,000, the incremental overhead related to the project is $500,000.

    b. **Pro rata overhead allocation approach**—Another approach is to capitalize the overhead on a pro rata basis. For example, if the project represents 15% of the total direct labor hours for the period, 15% of the total overhead will be allocated to the project.

4. **Interest cost incurred during the construction period**—(This topic is separately discussed in detail in a later lesson.) Capitalization of interest is allowed only when assets are constructed. When assets are purchased outright, any interest on debt incurred to purchase the asset cannot be capitalized.

B. **Limitation on Recorded Value**—Fair value at completion

1. In general, GAAP prohibits the recording of assets in excess of their fair values. Recording a constructed asset at an amount exceeding its fair value carries forward losses due to inefficient construction to later.

2. If the total cost of construction exceeds fair value, a loss is recognized for the difference and the asset is recorded at fair value.

Example
The costs incurred to self-construct equipment are:

Labor	$20,000
Material	30,000
Incremental overhead	10,000
Applied overhead	5,000
Capitalized interest	8,000
Total	$73,000

During the construction phase, costs are accumulated in Equipment under Construction. The $73,000 amount is the final recorded amount if the fair value equals or exceeds $73,000. If the fair value were $80,000, the recorded value remains at $73,000 because gains cannot be recognized until realized through lower production costs. The Equipment under Construction account would be closed to Equipment.

Assume, however, that the market value is only $60,000:

Equipment	60,000	
Loss on Construction	13,000	
Equipment under Construction		73,000

Interest Capitalization Basics

This lesson is the first on interest capitalization during construction. This lesson presents when it is appropriate to capitalize interest, calculation of average accumulated expenditures and calculation of interest eligible for capitalization.

After studying this lesson, you should be able to:

1. Identify when interest capitalization is allowed.

2. Calculate the average accumulated expenditures during construction.

3. Calculate the weighted average or specific interest rate.

4. Calculate the amount of interest to be capitalized during the period.

5. Complete the journal entry for interest capitalization.

I. Introduction—Capitalization of Interest

A. Interest cost is typically expensed in the period incurred. However, when a company constructs a fixed asset, the interest cost incurred during the construction period is considered a **get-ready cost** and is, therefore, capitalized. Interest capitalization increases both plant assets and income. Assuming that all interest is first recorded in interest expense, the following adjusting entry capitalizes some or all of that interest:

```
DR: Plant Asset Under Construction  xx
    CR: Interest Expense                    xx
```

B. Interest cost is capitalized only during the construction period. Prior to the construction period, interest cost was expensed. Any interest cost incurred subsequent to the construction period will likewise be expensed.

C. The *justification* for interest capitalization is that had the construction not taken place, the funds used in construction could have been used to reduce interest-bearing debt. This **avoidable** interest is the amount of interest that would have been avoided had the construction not taken place. In a sense, the construction then **caused** that amount of interest, which, therefore, should be included in the cost of the asset constructed.

Note
The definition of an asset is not the underlying justification for interest capitalization. Interest does not increase the probable future value of an asset. Capitalization of interest exemplifies the matching principle as the benefit of the constructed asset will be over its useful life.

D. **Matching Principle**—Interest capitalization exemplifies the matching principle. Until the asset is in service, it cannot produce revenue. The asset is also not yet in its intended condition and location. Thus, expensing of the interest is deferred until the asset can provide revenues against which to match the interest expense.

E. Capitalization of interest applies only to the construction of qualifying assets, such as assets constructed for an enterprise's own use or assets intended for sale or lease that are constructed as discrete projects (ships, real estate developments, etc.).

F. Qualifying assets require a significant time period for construction and are not routinely produced. Rather, the assets must be discrete projects individually constructed. Interest is not capitalized on the construction or manufacture of inventory items, even if the inventory requires significant time for completion (e.g., interest on the production of wine and tobacco products is not capitalized).

II. Interest Is Capitalized During Periods in Which All Three of the Following Conditions Are Met

A. Qualifying expenditures have been made. Cash payments, transfers of other assets, or the incurrence of interest-bearing debt all qualify. The incurrence of short-term non-interest-bearing debt (e.g., accounts payable) does not qualify because the firm has no opportunity cost on such debt.

B. Activities that are necessary to get the asset ready for its intended use are in progress. (Construction is proceeding.)

C. Interest cost is being incurred. Only actual interest cost is capitalized. Imputed interest is not capitalized. The total amount of interest to be capitalized for a period is limited to actual interest incurred in the period.

> **Note**
> *If any of the three conditions is not met, interest capitalization ceases. The capitalization period concludes when the asset is substantially complete and ready for its intended use.*

III. A Two-Step Process Is Involved in Computing Capitalized Interest—The two steps are: (1) compute average accumulated expenditures, and (2) apply the appropriate interest rate(s).

A. Compute Average Accumulated Expenditures—A key concept in determining the amount of interest to be capitalized is avoidable interest. This is the interest on debt that could have been retired had the construction not taken place. To quantify that amount of debt, average accumulated expenditures (AAE) must be computed. AAE is the measure of the amount of debt, on an annual basis, that could have been avoided.

1. AAE = average cash (or other qualifying expenditures) investment in the project during the period. This is the amount of debt that could have been retired during the period.

Examples

1. A firm begins construction on January 1 by making a $40,000 construction payment to a contractor. On July 1, another $40,000 payment is made. AAE = $40,000 + $40,000(6/12) = $60,000. The July 1 payment was invested in the project only half of a year. The $60,000 represents the amount of debt, outstanding the entire year, which could have been retired.

2. The previous example involved a small number of discrete cash payments. This example assumes that cash payments are made continuously throughout the period. The firm starts construction on January 1. By December 31 it has spent $120,000 in qualifying expenditures on the projects. Payments were made evenly throughout the year. AAE = $120,000/2 = ($0 + $120,000)/2 = $60,000. Although $120,000 was expended during the year, on average the firm had $60,000 invested in the project during the year. (This is the same logic as with a bank account; if you deposited equal amounts into your account each day for a year and ended with a $120,000 balance, your average balance would be $60,000 for the year, assuming interest is paid at year's end.)

B. Apply the Appropriate Interest Rate—If AAE is the amount of debt that could have been retired for the year, then an interest rate multiplied by AAE is the amount of interest that could have been avoided. This is the amount of interest to be capitalized, subject to the limitation that capitalized interest cannot exceed actual interest cost for the period.

Example
Using the previous examples of AAE ($60,000), if the interest rate were 10%, then $6,000 of interest would be capitalized ($60,000 × .10) assuming at least that much interest cost was actually incurred. If total interest expense for the period before capitalizing interest amounted to $11,000, then $6,000 of interest would be debited to the asset under construction, and only $5,000 of interest expense would be reported in the income statement.

IV. But What Interest Rate Should Be Used? U.S. GAAP does not limit capitalized interest to specific construction loan interest. Rather, the more general concept of **avoidable** interest is used. Two ways of computing total interest to be capitalized are allowed:

A. Weighted Average Method—Capitalizes interest using the weighted average rate on all interest bearing debt.

B. Specific Method—Capitalizes the interest on specific construction loans first. Then, if needed, capitalize interest on all other debt based on the average interest rate for that debt.

Example

A firm began construction in January and spent $100,000 in qualifying expenditures by year's end. Expenditures were made evenly throughout the period. Debt outstanding the entire year:

	Principal	Annual interest
10% construction loan	$30,000	$3,000
Other debt (average interest rate, 8%)	60,000	4,800
Total	$90,000	$7,800

AAE = $100,000/2 = $50,000

V. Computation of Capitalized Interest

A. Weighted Average Method

Weighted average interest rate = ($7,800)/$90,000 = 8.67%

Capitalized interest = 8.67%($50,000) = $4,335. This amount is less than total interest of $7,800 for the period. Therefore the capitalized interest is $4,335 and the interest expense is $3,465 ($7,800 − $4,335).

B. Specific Method

Capitalized Interest = .10($30,000) + .08($50,000 − $30,000) = $4,600

1. This amount is less than total interest of $7,800 for the period. Therefore the capitalized interest is $4,600 and the interest expense is $3,200 ($7,800 − $4,600).

2. The specific method first uses the construction loan. The principal amount of that loan is only $30,000. But $50,000 (AAE) of debt could have been retired. The additional $20,000 of debt (to sum to the $50,000 AAE) is the portion of the nonspecific debt that could have been retired.

Note
Interest capitalized compounds over several periods. The interest capitalized in Year 1 is included in AAE for Year 2, thus increasing the amount of interest capitalized in Year 2. Interest is, therefore, compounded and included in the asset account.

Note
AAE is used only to compute capitalized interest. The ending balance in construction in progress is typically much larger than AAE for the period. Using the specific method in the above example, the ending balance in construction in progress after capitalizing interest is $104,600 ($100,000 construction payments + $4,600 interest capitalized).

Interest Capitalization Limits

This is the second lesson on interest capitalization. This lesson presents a more detailed discussion of the limits on how much interest can be capitalized. It also offers more detailed examples of the interest eligible for capitalization.

After studying this lesson, you should be able to:

1. Determine the limit on interest that is eligible for capitalization.

2. Calculate the weighted average or specific interest rate.

3. Calculate the amount of interest to be capitalized during the period.

4. Complete the journal entry for interest capitalization.

I. Limit on Interest Capitalization

A. Capitalized interest is limited to actual interest incurred because avoidable debt is the lower of (1) AAE (average accumulated expenditures) and (2) total interest-bearing debt. The actual amount of interest incurred sets the ceiling on interest to be capitalized.

1. When AAE < total interest-bearing debt, reported interest expense for the period is the difference between total interest cost and the amount of interest capitalized. In this case, because AAE is less than total debt, not all debt could have been avoided.

2. When AAE > total interest-bearing debt, all interest cost is capitalized and there is no reported interest expense for the period. In this case, all debt could have been avoided had construction activities not taken place.

B. These points are illustrated in the next example.

1. **Example with more than one nonspecific construction loan**—This example shows how to compute two different weighted averages. Construction on a project began January 1, 20X6 with a construction payment of $100,000 to the contractor. One additional payment of $120,000 was made July 1, 20X6.

2. Debt outstanding during 20X6 (entire year):

5%, $120,000 construction loan

6%, 20,000 note payable unrelated to construction

4%, 30,000 note payable unrelated to construction

AAE = $100,000(12/12) + $120,000(6/12) = $160,000

---

3. **Specific method**

Average interest rate on nonconstruction loans =

((.06)$20,000 + (.04)$30,000) / ($20,000 + $30,000) = .048

Interest capitalized = .05($120,000) + .048($160,000 − $120,000) = $7,920

---

a. **Interest on the specific loan** for the construction is used first, and then interest at the average rate for all other debt is applied to the excess of AAE over the construction loan. Interest is capitalized only up to avoidable debt on the AAE.

b. **If AAE had been less** than the amount of the construction loan (e.g., $100,000), then only the construction loan interest would be capitalized (interest capitalized in that case would be .05 × $100,000 = $5,000).

c. If AAE had been $200,000 (**more than total debt**), then all the interest for the period would be capitalized because total debt is less than $200,000. All the debt could have been avoided. Interest capitalized = .05($120,000) + .048($50,000) = $8,400

4. **Average method**

Average interest rate on all loans =

(.05($120,000) + (.06)$20,000 + (.04)$30,000) / ($120,000 + $20,000 + $30,000) = .0494

Interest capitalized = .0494($160,000) = $7,904

Again, if AAE had been $200,000, then all the interest for the period would be capitalized because total debt is less than $200,000. Interest capitalized = .05($120,000) + (.06)$20,000 + (.04)$30,000 = $8,400

5. **Compounding of Capitalized Interest and Construction Balance**

a. Interest capitalized in one period becomes part of AAE for the next period. Using the example above (average method), the balance in the construction-in-process account at the end of the first period is $227,904 ($100,000 construction payment + $120,000 construction payment + $7,904 capitalized interest).

b. The next year, the calculation of AAE will begin with $227,904(12/12), with the payments during the second year receiving the appropriate rate for the period of time in the project. Thus, the $7,904 of interest capitalized the previous period will be part of the base on which interest is capitalized the next period—interest is compounded.

Note
Interest may be capitalized on a quarterly or annual basis.

CAPITALIZATION OF INTEREST DURING CONSTRUCTION

Qualifying Assets:

Capitalize means to include an expenditure in an asset's cost.

Interest costs, when material, incurred in acquiring the following types of assets, shall be capitalized

1. Assets constructed or produced for a firm's own use

   a. Including construction by outside contractors requiring progress payments

2. Assets intended for lease or sale that are produced as discrete projects

   a. For example, ships and real estate developments

3. But **not** on

   a. Routinely produced inventories (e.g., widgets)
   b. Assets ready for their intended use when acquired
   c. Assets not being used nor being readied for use (e.g., idle equipment)
   d. Land, unless it is being developed (e.g., as a plant site, real estate development, etc.). Then capitalized interest resulting from land expenditure (cash outlay) is added to building.

When to Capitalize Interest (all three must be met):

1. Expenditures for asset have been made
2. Activities intended to get asset ready are in process
3. Interest cost is being incurred

Applicable Interest (net of discounts, premiums, and issue costs):

1. Interest obligations having explicit rates
2. Imputed interest on certain payables/receivables
3. Interest related to capital leases

How Much Interest Cost Is Capitalized?

$$\left(\begin{array}{l} \text{Accumulated expenditures beg. of period (C-I-P* bal.) +} \\ \text{Accumulated expenditures end of period (C-I-P bal.)} \end{array} \right) \div 2 \times \text{Portion of year} = \text{Weighted-average accumulated expenditures}$$

Weighted-average accumulated expenditures + (Interest rate**) = Amount capitalized (cannot exceed total interest incurred)

*C-I-P—Construction-in-Progress

**AICPA questions have given the specific borrowing rate on debt incurred to finance a project and indicated that expenditures were incurred evenly throughout the year. ASC: Topic 835 (SFAS 34) requires that the firm's weighted-average borrowing rate be used after the amount of a specific borrowing is exhausted. Alternatively, only the firm's weighted-average borrowing rate may be used on all expenditures.

Qualifications

1. Amount of interest to be capitalized cannot exceed total interest costs incurred during the entire reporting period

2. Interest earned on temporarily invested borrowings may not be offset against interest to be capitalized

II. Construction Payables—Unpaid construction input costs are not included in AAE until paid in cash. Until cash is paid, debt can be considered avoidable. Payables include wages payable, accounts payable for material, and utilities payable.

> **Example**
>
> If the firm incorporated $20,000 of materials into a project as of the end of the period, but paid only $15,000 for them ($5,000 in accounts payable), qualifying expenditures include only $15,000 for purposes of computing AAE.

III. Land and Capitalized Interest —The effect on interest capitalization of expenditures made for land depends on the purpose for acquiring the land.

    A. For land used as a building site, the cost of the land is included in AAE for the building, and interest is capitalized to the building; (the land is not being constructed.)

    B. For land developed for sale, interest is capitalized to the land;

    C. For land held for speculation, no interest is capitalized because the land is in its condition of intended use, and there is no asset under construction.

IV. Interest on Borrowed Funds—In some cases, the proceeds from a specific construction loan are not fully used for financing the construction until well into the construction phase. Part of the proceeds may be invested in a bank account or a debt security may be purchased. Interest revenue on unused proceeds temporarily invested is not offset against interest to be capitalized. The interest revenue is reported separately and has no effect on interest capitalized.

    A. Exception—If the funds are externally restricted tax-exempt borrowings, then a right of offset exists because the funds are restricted to use in construction.

V. Partial Year Computations—Construction projects may begin or end during a reporting period. Also, new debt may be incurred and other liabilities may be retired during a reporting period.

    A. Guidelines

        1. Interest rate—Adjust the interest rate for the fraction of the year the debt is outstanding. If new interest-bearing debt is incurred during an interest capitalization period, the interest rate reflects the period the debt was outstanding. Assume a firm capitalizes interest quarterly. If $100,000 of 12% debt is incurred May 1, then for quarter 2, $2,000 of interest is included in the numerator of the rate (2 months' interest), and $100,000 is included in the denominator.

        2. Expenditures—Weight by the percentage of the period invested in the project. An expenditure occurring at the beginning of the second month of a quarter receives a weight of 2/3.

> **Example**
>
> **Interest Capitalization**
>
> Assume the company is constructing an asset which qualifies for interest capitalization. By the beginning of July $3,000,000 had been spent on the asset, and an additional $800,000 was spent during July. The following debt was outstanding for the entire month.
>
>   **1.** A loan of $2,000,000, interest of 1% per month, specifically related to the asset.
>
>   **2.** A note payable of $1,500,000, interest of 1.5% per month.
>
>   **3.** Bonds payable of $1,000,000, interest of 1% per month.
>
> The amount of interest to be capitalized is computed below.

Average accumulated expenditures (for the month of July) = ($3,000,000 + $3,800,000) ÷ 2 = $3,400,000

Avoidable interest			**Actual interest**		
$2,000,000 × 1%	=	$20,000	$2,000,000 × 1%	=	$20,000
1,400,000 × 1.3%*	=	18,200	1,500,000 × 1.5%	=	22,500
			1,000,000 × 1%		10,000
$3,400,000		$38,200	$4,500,000		$52,500

$38,200 < $52,500\$38,200 is capitalized

The amount of interest to be capitalized is $38,200. Assuming that all interest was initially recorded as an expense below is the entry that would be made

> DR: Construction-in-progress (asset)   38,200
>
> CR: Interest expense   38,200

*The average rate on other borrowings is ($22,500 + $10,000) ÷ ($1,500,000 + $1,000,000) = 1.3%. Notice that a specific rate is used to the extent possible and the average rate is used only on any excess. Alternatively, the rate on all debt may be used.

VI. Disclosure—The amount of interest capitalized and expensed must be disclosed during a period in which interest is capitalized. Note that the amount of interest paid for the period to be disclosed as part of the Statement of Cash Flows—either as part of the statement, as a supplemental schedule, or in a footnote.

Post-Acquisition Expenditures

This lesson presents a discussion on how to treat post-acquisition expenditures.

After studying this lesson, you should be able to:

1. Distinguish when an expenditure should be capitalized or expensed.

2. Complete the entries for the capitalization of a post-acquisition expenditure.

I. **Introduction**

    A. A post-acquisition cost is capitalized if, as a result of the expenditure, the asset is:

        1. More productive (provides more benefits); *or*

        2. Has a longer useful life.

    B. Otherwise, the expenditure is expensed. Although an argument can be made that ordinary maintenance and repairs prolongs the useful life of an asset, the estimated useful life of an asset assumes a minimum level of periodic service.

    C. Repairs keep the asset in an ordinarily efficient operating condition. Repairs do not typically extend the life of the asset or increase its value. Repairs are typically expensed in the period incurred.

II. **Accounting Treatment for Capitalized Expenditures**

    A. **Additions**—Extensions or enlargements of existing assets.

        1. If an integral part of the larger asset, depreciate the addition over the shorter of its useful life or the remaining useful life of the larger asset.

        2. If not, depreciate the addition over its useful life.

    B. **Modifications**—Improvements (betterments), replacements, and extraordinary repairs all involve a modification of an existing component or part of the larger asset.

    C. **Accounting Approaches**

        1. **Substitution**—Remove the accumulated depreciation and original cost of the old component, recognize the loss, and capitalize the post-acquisition expenditure to the larger asset. This alternative is available only if the accounting system maintained records of the old component cost and accumulated depreciation.

        2. Increase the larger asset account by the post-acquisition cost. This approach is used when the productivity rather than the useful life of the larger asset is enhanced, and when the accounting system does not maintain records of the old component cost and accumulated depreciation.

        3. Debit accumulated depreciation. This approach is used when the expenditure increases the useful life of the larger asset. The debit to accumulated depreciation turns back the clock on the life of the larger asset. This approach is suited especially to extraordinary repairs.

    D. For each of these three approaches, the post-acquisition cost is depreciated over the shorter of its useful life or remaining useful life of the larger asset.

Example
The boiler of a large office building is replaced with a more efficient boiler at a cost of $65,000. The useful life of the building is unaffected but the new boiler will reduce energy costs significantly. The cost of the old boiler was $40,000, and its accumulated depreciation subsidiary ledger account reflects a balance of $35,000. To record the replacement:

DR: Accumulated Depreciation	35,000	
DR: Loss on Replacement	5,000	
CR: Boiler		40,000
DR: Boiler	65,000	
CR: Cash		65,000

Non-Accelerated Depreciation Methods

This is the first of two lessons on depreciation. This lesson presents the concepts for depreciation and certain depreciation methods.

After studying this lesson, you should be able to:

1. Explain the concepts of depreciation.

2. Calculate depreciation under the following methods: straight-line, service hours, and units of production.

I. Nature of Depreciation

A. **Depreciation** is a *systematic and rational* allocation of capitalized plant asset cost to time periods. The term *systematic* implies that the allocation is not random but rather is made on an orderly basis. The term *rational* means that by appealing to how the asset is used, the process can be supported. The process of depreciation matches the cost of the plant asset to periods in which the asset is used to generate revenue.

B. Depreciation is *not* a process of valuation. The amount of depreciation recognized in a period is not necessarily the decline in the market value of the asset, nor is it a measure of the amount of the asset **used up**. If depreciation expense is $10,000, this does not mean that $10,000 of the cost of the asset was used in generating revenue. The $10,000 amount is simply the amount allocated to the period based on the method chosen by the firm. The book value of a depreciable plant asset (original cost less accumulated depreciation to date), is the amount of original cost yet to be depreciated. Only coincidentally does book value equal market value.

C. **Justifications**—There are two *justifications* for depreciation:

1. Assets wear out over time.

2. Assets become obsolete.

Example
Land is not depreciated because it does not wear out and does not become obsolete.

D. The acquisition cost of plant assets is a cost of doing business. Because plant assets have a useful life exceeding one year, their cost is allocated to the periods they benefit. Although the amount of asset decline is not observable, depreciation expense provides at least some measure of the cost of the asset to be included in total expenses on an annual basis.

E. Depreciation is not a source of funds. Although it provides a tax deduction, the same can be said for any deductible expense. Note that most firms use straightline (SL) depreciation for financial reporting, and MACRS (modified accelerated cost recovery system) for income tax reporting. MACRS is the same as the double-declining balance (DDB) method with a half-year convention applied.

F. **Definitions**

Definitions
Book Value: Original cost less accumulated depreciation to date.

Depreciable Cost: Total depreciation to be recognized over the life of the asset. This amount equals original cost less salvage value.

Minimum Book Value: Salvage value. In no case is salvage value depreciated. Thus, book value always includes salvage value. An asset cannot be depreciated such that its book value is less than salvage value.

1. There are three kinds of **noncurrent assets** subject to depreciation or similar process. Different terms are used for each, but all involve a systematic and rational allocation of historical cost to time periods of use:

   a. Plant assets are *depreciated;*

   b. Natural resources are *depleted;*

   c. Intangible assets are *amortized*.

Definitions

Adjusting Journal Entry: The adjusting journal entry for depreciation on nonmanufacturing assets is: DR: Depreciation expense; CR: Accumulated depreciation

Contra Account: Many firms include depreciation expense in Selling, General, and Administrative Expense and report the components in a footnote. Accumulated depreciation is a contra-plant asset account. The use of a contra account preserves the original cost information in the plant asset account.

Manufacturing Assets: For manufacturing assets, depreciation is included in overhead and allocated to production based on machine hours or direct labors. The result is that Work in Process is debited for depreciation cost. When the products are sold, Cost of Goods Sold includes depreciation. A separate expense for depreciation is not recorded for manufacturing assets.

II. Factors in Calculating

A. The amount of depreciation recognized each period is affected by the following four factors. Only the first factor, capitalized cost, is a definite amount. Two estimates are used, and the firm has a free choice among the available methods.

   1. Capitalized cost

   2. Estimated useful life

   3. Estimated salvage value (the cost of the asset not subject to depreciation—that is,the portion of initial cost expected to be returned at the end of the useful life)

   4. Method chosen

B. Several methods of depreciation are acceptable under GAAP. They can be categorized into two basic types: (1) straight-line methods and (2) accelerated methods.

   1. Straight-line methods (a constant rate of depreciation)

   a. **Straight-line method**—Annual depreciation is calculated by the formula shown below

Cost – Salvage Value / Useful Life = Annual Depreciation

   i. Annual depreciation is the same each year.

   ii. **Justification**—The asset will provide essentially the same benefits per year. Buildings are appropriately depreciated on an SL basis.

Example
An asset costing $22,000 with a salvage value of $2,000 and a useful life of 5 years is depreciated $4,000 each year using the SL method ($22,000 – $2,000)/5.

b. **Service hours method**

  i. The life of the asset is defined in terms of service hours, and the depreciation rate per service hour is calculated by using the formula shown below. The number of total service hours the asset will provide must be estimated and used as the denominator.

Depreciation Rate = (Cost – Salvage Value) / (Useful Life in Service Hours)

  ii. Depreciation for any given year is calculated by multiplying the service hours for the year by this constant depreciation rate per service hour. Annual depreciation varies with the number of service hours provided in the year. There is no expectation that depreciation will be the same amount each year.

  iii. **Justification**—The asset will provide essentially the same benefits per service hour. A delivery vehicle is an example of an asset appropriately depreciated on the service-hours method.

Example
An asset costing $22,000 with a salvage value of $2,000 and a useful life of 5 years is depreciated on the service-hours method. The asset is expected to provide 10,000 hours of service. In a given year, 2,500 hours of service are provided. The constant rate is $2 per service hour ($22,000 – $2,000)/10,000. Depreciation for the given year is $5,000 (2,500 × $2).

c. **Units of output method**

  i. The life of the asset is defined in terms of units of output, and the depreciation rate per unit of output is calculated using the formula shown below. The number of total units the asset will produce must be estimated and used as the denominator.

Depreciation Rate = (Cost – Salvage Value) / (Useful Life in Units of Production)

  ii. Depreciation for any given year is calculated by multiplying the units of output for the year by this constant depreciation rate per unit of output. Annual depreciation varies depending on the number of units produced in the year. There is no expectation that depreciation will be the same amount each year.

  iii. **Justification**—The asset will provide essentially the same benefits per unit produced. Oil drilling equipment is an example of an asset appropriately depreciated on the units of production method.

Example
An asset costing $22,000 with a salvage value of $2,000 and a useful life of 5 years is depreciated on the units of production method. The asset is expected to produce 1,000 units. In a given year, 300 units are produced. The constant rate is $20 per unit ($22,000 – $2,000)/1,000. Depreciation for the given year is $6,000 (300 × $20).

Accelerated Depreciation Methods

This is the second of two lessons on depreciation. This lesson presents accelerated depreciation methods.

After studying this lesson, you should be able to:

1. Calculate depreciation under the following methods: sum-of-years digits and double-declining balance.

I. Accelerated Methods—Accelerated methods of depreciation recognize depreciation at a faster rate early in the life of the asset. Later in the life of the asset, the amount of depreciation per period declines. This pattern of depreciation holds regardless of how the asset is used in any given period.

A. Justification

1. The theoretical justification for using an accelerated method is related to the matching principle. It is assumed the asset will be more productive in the earlier years. Therefore, more depreciation expense is recorded during those earlier, more productive years. More expense is matched against revenue in the periods of greater benefit; less expense is matched when the asset provides less benefit.

2. Another justification is obsolescence. Assets subject to obsolescence (high-tech equipment for example) will provide most of their benefits early in their life. Therefore, more depreciation is recognized in those years.

B. Effect—One effect of using accelerated methods is a stable annual total amount of expense related to plant assets. Early in the asset's life, more depreciation is recognized and less maintenance is required. Later in the asset's life just the opposite occurs. But the total annual expense is fairly stable.

C. Methods

1. Sum-of-the-years' digits method

a. First, the sum of the years' digits must be calculated by using the formula shown below.

N = useful life in years.

SYD =(N(N+1))/2 = 1 + 2 + ... + N

SYD is the denominator of the fraction used each year to compute depreciation. The numerator is the number of years remaining at the beginning of the year.

Year 1 Depreciation: (N/SYD)(Cost – Salvage Value)

Year 2 Depreciation: ((N-1)/SYD)(Cost – Salvage Value))

Year N Depreciation: (1/(SYD))(Cost – Salvage Value))

---

b. This method is accelerated because the highest annual amount of depreciation is recognized in year 1, the next highest in year 2, and so forth.

Example

An asset costing $22,000 with a salvage value of $2,000 and a useful life of 5 years is depreciated on the sum-of-the-years' digits method.

SYD = 1 + 2 + 3 + 4 + 5 = 15 = 5(5 + 1)/2

Depreciation, year 1 = (5/15)($22,000 − $2,000) = $6,667

Depreciation, year 2 = (4/15)($22,000 − $2,000) = $5,333

.

.

Depreciation, year 5 = (1/15)($22,000 − $2,000) = $1,333

2. **Declining-balance method**

    a. This method differs from those discussed previously in three ways:

        i. Salvage value is not used in the computation of depreciation.

        ii. Annual depreciation is based on the beginning book value of the asset. This book value declines over time, hence the name of this group of methods. This also is why salvage value is not subtracted. Book value always includes salvage value because salvage value is never depreciated.

        iii. Each year, accumulated depreciation must be checked to ensure that book value does not fall below salvage value.

    b. The method allows rates between 100% and 200% of the straight-line rate.

Double declining balance method

Depreciation in year 1   = Cost(2/N)

Depreciation in year 2   = (Cost − depreciation in year 1)(2/N)

                      = (book value at beginning of year 2)(2/N)

Depreciation in year 3   = (Cost − depreciation in years 1 and 2)(2/N)

The rate (2/N) is twice the straight-line rate. N = useful life in years.

150% of declining-balance method

The calculations are the same as for double-declining balance except that (1.5/N) is the rate used.

Example

An asset costing $22,000 with a salvage value of $2,000 and a useful life of 5 years is depreciated on the double-declining-balance method.

Depreciation, year 1   = $22,000(2/5) = $8,800 Depreciation,

year 2   = ($22,000 − $8,800)(2/5) = $5,280

In some cases, strict use of the declining-balance method results in recognizing more depreciation than depreciable cost. In the year that total depreciation exceeds depreciable cost, firms will change to the straight-line method and depreciate the remaining depreciable cost over the remaining useful life beginning in that year.

3. **Partial or fractional year depreciation**

   a. Assets not purchased at the beginning of a fiscal year must be depreciated on a fractional year basis. Firms often use a simplifying convention such as: depreciate all assets a full year in the year of acquisition, and recognize no depreciation in the year of disposal. Over large groups of assets, these conventions are acceptable if applied consistently.

   b. However, a more exact approach is required on the CPA Exam.

Example

A calendar or fiscal year firm purchased an asset costing $22,000 with a salvage value of $2,000 and a useful life of 5 years on April 1, 20X7. Let:

W1 = the first whole year of depreciation (April 1, 20X7 to March 31, 20X8),

W2 = the second whole year of depreciation (April 1, 20X8 to March 31, 20X9),

and so forth.

Regardless of the depreciation method used, depreciation for reporting years is found as:

20X7 depreciation = (9/12)W1   (asset held 9 months in 20X7)

20X8 depreciation = (3/12)W1 + (9/12)W2   (20X8 contains the last 3 months of the asset's first year, and the first 9 months of the asset's second year)

The remaining years are treated the same way.

If the method chosen is double-declining balance (DDB) , then from the previous example:

W1 = $22,000(2/5) = $8,800

W2 = ($22,000 − $8,800)(2/5) = $5,280

20X7 depreciation = (9/12)W1 = (9/12)($8,800)   = $6,600

20X8 depreciation = (3/12)W1 + (9/12)W2

                   = (3/12)($8,800) + (9/12)($5,280) = $6,160

For DDB, a shortcut approach is available:

20X8 depreciation = (2/5)($22,000 − $6,600) = $6,160

4. **Appraisal methods**—These methods are used when it is impractical to depreciate assets on an individual basis. Accumulated depreciation records are not maintained on individual assets, and no gain or loss is recorded on disposal.

   a. **Inventory (appraisal) method**—This method is applied to groups of smaller homogenous assets. At the end of each year, the assets are appraised and recorded at market value. The appraisal is for the entire group, which saves accounting costs. The decline in market value from the previous year is depreciation expense for the year. If assets were sold during the year, the proceeds from sale reduce depreciation expense.

Example

January 1 appraisal value of group:	$20,000
Proceeds from disposal of some assets in the group:	$3,000
December 31 appraisal value of group:	$12,000

Depreciation expense for the year
= ($20,000 − $12,000) − $3,000 = $5,000

b. Group/composite methods

i. This system applies the straight-line method to groups of assets rather than to assets individually. Accumulated depreciation records are not maintained by asset; rather, only a control account is used to accumulate depreciation. Gains and losses are not recorded. The entry to dispose of an asset plugs the accumulated depreciation account.

The composite depreciation rate = (Annual group SL depreciation) / (Total original cost of group)

ii. Depreciation for a year is the product of the rate and the original cost of assets remaining at the beginning of the year. Asset additions increase the total original cost on which depreciation is computed; asset disposals reduce the total original cost.

Example
A firm purchased the following group of assets:

Asset	Number	Original unit cost	Salvage value	Useful life
A	10	$500	$100	4 years
B	5	600	300	3 years

The composite rate of depreciation =(10($500 − $100)/4 + 5($600 − $300)/3) / (10($500) + 5($600)) = .1875

The .1875 rate means that $.1875 of depreciation is recognized each year for each $1 of acquisition cost in the group. After a few years in which assets have been added and removed, if the original cost of the group of assets remaining on January 1 is $5,000, depreciation for that year is $937.50 ($5,000 × .1875).

Natural Resources

This lesson provides information on the accounting for natural resources.

After studying this lesson, you should be able to:

1. Identify acquisition, exploration, and development costs.

2. Determine the costs that are capitalized as part of the natural resource asset.

3. Calculate the depletion of the natural resource asset.

I. Natural Resources

Definition

Natural Resource: A noncurrent asset that contains the cost of acquiring, exploring, and developing a natural resource deposit (e.g., timber, oil and minerals). It does not include the cost of extracting the resource.

A. The amount capitalized as natural resources is the sum of three different types of costs:

1. **Acquisition costs**—The amount paid to acquire the rights to explore for undiscovered natural resources or to extract proven natural resources.

2. **Exploration costs**—The amount paid to drill or excavate or any other costs of searching for natural resources.

3. **Development costs**—The amount paid after the resource has been discovered but before production begins.

B. **Methods of Accounting for Exploration Costs**

1. **Successful-efforts method**—Only the cost of successful exploration efforts is capitalized to the natural resources account; unsuccessful efforts are expensed.

2. **Full-costing method**—All costs of exploring for the resource are capitalized to the natural resources account. (The total amount capitalized cannot exceed the expected value of resources to be removed.)

3. The choice between the successful-efforts and full-costing methods is among the most important a firm has to make. The choice can have a large effect on net income and total assets. The successful-efforts method best reflects the definition of an asset because only those efforts that located the resource are capitalized to the natural resource account. The full-costing method reflects the matching principle—and capitalizes all costs until the natural resource deposit produces revenue through sale of the inventory. Another justification for full costing is that all exploration efforts contributed to finding the resource.

C. After resources are discovered on the property, the cost to develop the property to enable extraction of the resource is capitalized to the natural resources account. Development costs pertain to facilities that will not be removed when the project is finished.

D. Removable assets such as drilling equipment, vehicles, and the like are recorded in their own separate accounts as plant assets.

II. Depletion

A. After all costs are capitalized to the natural resources account, the resource begins to be removed and depletion is recorded. Depletion is the term used to refer to the allocation of the cost of the natural resource to inventory. Depletion is taken on the natural resource asset (sum of the three costs above less the residual value).

B. Depletion is not an expense but an allocation of the natural resource from noncurrent assets to inventory. When units of the natural resource are depleted, inventory is debited and the natural resource account is credited. Because the useful life is directly associated with the amount of resources extracted, the activity or units of production base method is widely used.

Depletion for a Period = (Depletion Rate) × (Number of Units Removed in Period)

Depletion Rate = (Natural Resources Account Balance – Residual Value) / (Total Estimated Units)

C. The successful-efforts method results in a lower depletion rate but a higher exploration expense in periods of significant exploration.

III. Other Costs Involved in Natural Resource Extraction

Definitions

Extraction Costs: Depreciation on removable assets, wages, and material costs pertaining to the extraction effort; these costs are debited to the inventory of resource, not to the natural resources account.

Production Costs: Additional processing costs after extraction; this cost also is debited to the inventory of resource, not to the natural resources account.

A. When the inventory of resource is sold, the costs that have been debited to it (depletion, extraction, production) are recognized as expense through cost of goods sold.

1. **Depreciation on Assets Used in Extraction**—Depreciation on equipment used in the extraction effort is a component of total extraction costs. It does not contribute to depletion. The entry for extraction costs generally includes a debit to extraction costs and a credit to accumulated depreciation for depreciation on the cost of assets used in extraction. How the equipment is depreciated depends on whether it can be moved from one site to another.

   a. Equipment that can be used at more than one natural resource site—depreciate as usual over its useful life.

   b. Equipment dedicated to one site (often not movable or removable)—depreciate over the shorter of useful life or life of natural resource site. The most efficient method in this case is to use the units-of-production method with the same denominator as the depletion base.

IV. Financial Statement Presentation of Natural Resources

A. The natural resource account is presented as a noncurrent asset. The property associated with the natural resource is not classified as land because the land is not held as a building site, but, rather, to utilize the natural resource on the land.

B. Some firms classify the natural resource as an intangible asset because they have purchased the rights to utilize the land and do not own the land itself. These mineral rights are an intangible asset.

C. Once extracted, the natural resource noncurrent asset is transferred to resource inventory, a current asset.

Example

This example illustrates the flow of the various cost types, the calculation of depletion, and recognition of cost of goods sold.

Acquisition cost of mine	$400,000
Exploration costs, year 1	
Successful	$50,000
Unsuccessful	$150,000
Development costs	$500,000
Extraction and production costs	$200,000
Total estimated tons of ore	100,000
Estimated residual value	$ 20,000
Tons removed in year 1	40,000
Tons sold in year 1	30,000

Entries:

	Successful Efforts	Full costing
DR: Natural resources	950,000*	1,100,000**
DR: Exploration expense	150,000	
CR: Cash	1,100,000	1,100,000

* $400,000 + $50,000 + $500,000
** $400,000 + $50,000 + $500,000 + $150,000

Note:Full costing capitalizes all exploration costs whereas the successful-efforts method capitalizes only the successful efforts and expenses the rest.

	Successful Efforts	Full costing
DR: Inventory of ore	372,000*	432,000**
CR: Accumulated depletion	372,000	432,000

* (($950,000 − $20,000)/100,000 total tons)(40,000 tons removed)
** (($1,100,000 − $20,000)/100,000 total tons)(40,000 tons removed)

Accumulated depletion is contra to the natural resources account. The amounts in this entry for the two methods are the reductions in the book value of the natural resources account allocated to the inventory account. The depletion base is depleted, with the resources flowing to the inventory account. There is no change in net assets or income at this point.

	Successful Efforts	Full costing
DR: Inventory of ore	200,000	200,000
CR: Cash, materials, wages payable	200,000	200,000

The extraction and production costs also increase the inventory account. There is no income effect at this point because no inventory has been sold. Inventory cost has three components: depletion, extraction, and production.

| DR: Cost of goods sold | 429,000[*] | | 474,000[**] | |
| CR: Inventory of ore | | 429,000 | | 474,000 |

[*] ($372,000 + $200,000)(30,000/40,000)

[**] ($432,000 + $200,000)(30,000/40,000)

Of the 40,000 tons removed in the period, 30,000 were sold. Therefore, three-fourths of the inventory cost is expensed. One-fourth of the inventory cost will appear in the ending balance sheet of the firm. The entry to record the sale is not shown. It would be the same for both methods: DR Accounts receivable, CR Sales.

Impairment—Assets for Use and Assets Held-for-Sale

This lesson presents the accounting and reporting for impairment of long-lived assets.

After studying this lesson, you should be able to:

1. Calculate the two steps in the test for impairment of assets held in use.

2. Complete the impairment test for assets held for disposal.

I. **Introduction—Asset Categories**—ASC 360 governs the subsequent measurement and accounting for impaired assets or assets held for disposal.

A. Assets subject to impairment fall into one of three categories:

1. Assets in use

2. Assets held for disposal (sale)

3. Assets to be disposed of other than by sale (by spin-off to shareholders, by exchange for other assets, or by abandonment)

B. **Indicators of Impairment**—Impairment testing must be completed when any of the following conditions occur.

1. Significant decrease in the fair value of the asset

2. Significant change in the way asset is used or physical change in asset

3. An unfavorable change in laws, regulations, or the business climate that would adversely affect the use of the asset

4. Significantly higher than expected costs involved with the construction or acquisition of an asset

5. There have been or projected to be negative operating or cash flow (losses) from the asset.

6. The entity decides to sell the asset before the end of its expected life.

C. Next is a diagram that presents an overview of the decisions that need to be made with respect to asset impairment.

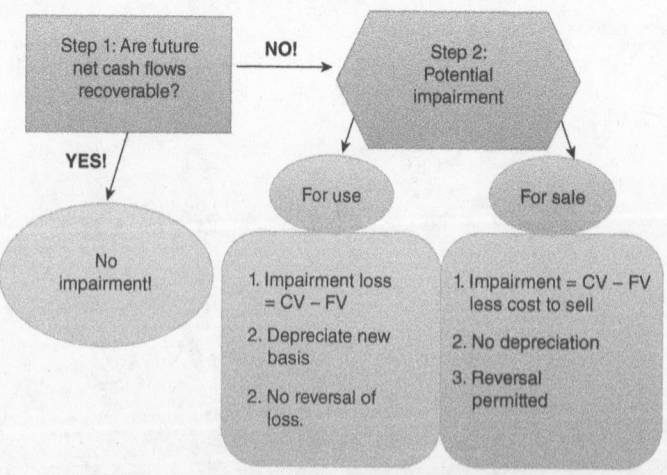

CV = carrying value; the same as net book value (BV or NBV)
FV = fair value

II. **Assets in Use**

A. **Assets in Use**—Assets in use are written down to fair value if their recoverable cost is less than book value. The amount of the impairment loss recognized is the difference between book value and fair value. Note that the determination of impairment is a step separate from the measurement of the loss; both use different values.

1. **Fair value (FV)**—The price that would be acceptable to the firm and another party for the transfer of the asset. **Present value** is used when no active market exists for the asset.

2. **Recoverable cost (RC)**—RC is the sum of expected future net cash inflows from use and ultimate disposal. Costs of maintaining the asset are included in the computation of RC, reducing it. RC is a nominal sum, not a present value. RC is based on how the firm currently uses the asset; the expected remaining useful life is used in computing RC. RC is the net increase in cash expected from using and disposing of the asset over its remaining life. RC always exceeds FV because RC is not a discounted amount.

B. **Test for Impairment**

1. If book value (BV) > RC, then the asset is impaired because book value will not be recovered. If BV is $100 and RC is $70, then there is no accounting justification for reporting the asset at $100.

2. If BV ≤ RC, then the asset is not impaired and no impairment loss is recognized. In this case, the book value is recoverable.

3. Assets should be evaluated for impairment when certain indications are present, rather than on a regular basis. Significant declines in FV, changes in legal climate or physical nature of the asset are examples of signals that suggest an impairment may have occurred.

C. **Measurement of Impairment Loss**

1. An impaired asset is written down to FV. The loss equals BV less FV

2. Note that the *test* for impairment uses BV and RC while the *measurement* of the loss uses BV and FV.

D. **Examples**

Examples

1. An asset with a book value of $100 has a recoverable cost of $120 and a fair value of $75.

Test for Impairment: BV of $100 < RC of $120. The asset is not impaired because the book value is recoverable. There is no loss computation; there is no impairment loss.

2. An asset with a book value of $100 has a recoverable cost of $90 and a fair value of $75.

Test for Impairment: BV of $100 > RC of $90. The asset is impaired because the book value is not fully recoverable.

Loss Measurement: Loss = BV of $100 – FV of $75 = $25. The asset is written down to $75. The loss is a component of income from continuing operations.

The entry to record the loss of $25:

DR: Impairment loss 25
    CR: Asset or Accumulated depreciation 25

Accounting after recognizing the $25 loss

a. The new BV of the asset is the FV of 75 and is used as the cost for future depreciation. The new depreciable cost is $75 less any residual value.

b. An impairment loss on an asset in use cannot be recovered; there is no upward revaluation or gains recognized if FV increases.

c. Additional impairments are possible.

E. Asset Groups—Many, if not most, assets do not function independently but are rather part of a working group. For purposes of the **test for impairment**, assets are grouped at the *lowest* possible organizational level at which cash flows can be identified. The three amounts (BV, FV, RC) are measured at this level. One intended effect of this rule on grouping at the LOWEST level rather than a higher one is to decrease the incidence of merging assets with impairment losses with those for which FV > BV in which case there would be fewer or no impairment losses recognized.

III. Assets Held-for-Sale (Disposal)—Recoverable cost is not used for assets held for disposal. Rather, the test for impairment and the loss computation both use the same values (BV and FV less cost to sell).

A. Decision to Dispose

1. If the decision to dispose of an asset and the ultimate disposal occur in the **same period**, the actual gain or loss on disposal is recognized in income from continuing operations. The disposal loss or gain equals the difference between FV and BV (if BV > FV, then a loss occurs; if BV < FV, then a gain occurs). Depreciation should be recognized to the date of the disposal unless the firm uses a convention for fractional year depreciation. The accumulated depreciation account is removed along with the asset's original cost.

2. If the decision to dispose **precedes** the period of disposal, an estimated loss is recorded if it is probable and estimable. Estimated gains are not recognized.

B. Held for Sale Criteria

1. There are six criteria for determining when an asset is considered held for sale. All six must be met for the accounting provisions to apply. Otherwise, the asset is considered in use.

   a. Management commits to a plan to sell the asset or group of assets.

   b. The asset must be available for immediate sale in its present condition subject only to terms that are usual and customary for such sales. This criterion does not preclude a firm from using the asset while it is held for sale nor does it require a binding agreement for future sale.

   c. An active program to locate a buyer has been initiated.

   d. The sale is expected to take place within one year. In limited cases, the one-year rule is waived for circumstances beyond the firm's control (e.g., due to a new regulation or law, environmental remediation, or deteriorating market).

   e. The asset is being actively marketed for sale at a price that is reasonable in relation to its current value.

   f. Sale of the asset must be probable.

2. If the six criteria are not met at the balance sheet date but are met before issuance, treat the asset as held for use in those statements. If an asset held for sale fails to meet all six criteria at a later date, it is reclassified as held for use.

3. An asset held for sale is impaired if its BV exceeds its fair value less cost to sell at the end of the reporting period.

C. Held for Sale Accounting

1. The asset is written down to (FV less cost to sell)—here the test for impairment and the measurement of the loss are the same. The term "recoverable cost" is not used for assets for sale. If sale is expected beyond one year, the cost to sell is discounted.

2. Only direct incremental costs are used in the computation of cost to sell.

3. The impairment loss recorded equals the difference between the asset's BV and its (FV less cost to sell). The estimated cost to sell increases the loss.

4. The asset is removed from plant assets because it is no longer in use.

5. Depreciation is no longer recognized on the asset.

6. The results of operating the asset during the holding period are recognized in period of occurrence—that is, estimated future operating losses or gains are not recognized until they actually occur. Note that although these assets are held for disposal, they may require maintenance and other cash expenditures. These are expensed as incurred.

7. The asset can be written up or down if held for another period; gains are limited to the amount of the initial impairment loss. (BV cannot exceed the amount immediately before recording the initial impairment loss.)

Example

Assume that a plant asset (cost $100,000; accumulated depreciation $40,000) has a current fair value of $30,000 at the end of Year 4. Management has decided to sell the asset as soon as possible during the next reporting period. The estimated direct cost to sell is $5,000. The six criteria for determining the asset is held for sale are met.

End of Year 4

Plant asset	$100,000	Fair Value	$30,000
Accumulated depreciation	40,000	Cost to sell	(5,000)
Net Book Value	$ 60,000	Asset held for disposal (Year 4 new net book value)	$25,000

$60,000 (old net book value) – $25,000 (Year 4 new net book value) = Year 4 loss on asset held for disposal 35,000

Assume at the end of Year 5, the asset remains unsold. The fair value is now $20,000 and the estimated cost to sell is $12,000.

End of Year 5

Fair Value	$ 20,000
Cost to sell	(12,000)
Asset held for disposal	$ 8,000

$25,000 (Year 4 net book value) – $8,000 (Year 5 net book value) = Year 5 loss on asset held for disposal 17,000

Limit on gains: Assume instead that at the end of Year 5, the fair value had risen to $70,000 and estimated cost to sell remained at $5,000. The difference between fair value and estimated cost to sell has increased from $25,000 to $65,000, an increase of $40,000. This amount exceeds the previous loss of $35,000. The maximum gain allowed is $35,000, the amount of the previous loss. Therefore, the asset would be written back up to $60,000 (the book value immediately before the initial impairment), and a gain of $35,000 would be recognized.

IV. Assets to Be Disposed of Other Than by Sale

A. This category includes disposal by abandonment, by exchange for a similar asset, and by distribution to shareholders as a spin-off. Note that dissimilar asset exchange is not included in this category because that transaction is considered a sale—the culmination of an earnings process.

B. **Accounting**—Continue to classify the asset as held for use until disposal occurs, and continue to depreciate the asset. Apply the impairment standards for assets in use. Compute recoverable cost as for assets in use. These assets are treated as such because even though the plan is to dispose of the asset, the firm will derive the remaining utility of the asset (if any) from operations rather than via disposal. For exchanges and spin-offs, an additional impairment is recorded at disposal if BV > FV.

Nonmonetary Exchange

Commercial Substance

This lesson presents the accounting for nonmonetary exchanges that have commercial substance.

After studying this lesson, you should be able to:

1. Define a nonmonetary asset.

2. Define commercial substance.

3. Calculate the fair value of the asset received and the gain or loss in a nonmonetary exchange.

I. Nonmonetary Assets

Definition

Nonmonetary Asset: Such an asset does not have a fixed nominal or stated value, as is the case with cash, accounts receivable, and other monetary assets.

A. Plant assets, inventories, and many investments are nonmonetary because their value changes with the market. The determination of the fair value   and recorded value of nonmonetary assets presents a challenge when they are acquired in an exchange for other nonmonetary assets.

> **Exam Tip**
> This topic is frequently tested on the exam.

   1. What value should be used when recording the acquired asset?

   2. Should gains or losses be recorded?

   3. ASC 845 governs the accounting for this area.

B. When fair value is the appropriate valuation of the acquired asset, the preferred amount is the fair value of the assets given in exchange. However, if the fair value of the asset acquired is more objectively determinable, then that amount should be used for its valuation.

C. Cash is frequently paid or received on exchange. When recording the journal entry for the exchange, the following common-sense relationships may help:

   1. If cash is paid on the exchange (more common):

Fair Value of Acquired Asset = Fair Value of Asset Exchanged + Cash Paid

   2. If cash is received on the exchange (less common):

Fair Value of Acquired Asset = Fair Value of Asset Exchanged −Cash Received

Example
The fair value of a plant asset exchanged for another plant asset is $40,000. Cash of $6,000 is received on the exchange. The implied fair value of the asset acquired is $34,000 ($40,000 fair value of asset exchanged – $6,000 cash received).

D. However, fair value is not always the appropriate valuation for the acquired nonmonetary asset.

E. **Gain or Loss**—The amount of the gain or loss on exchange is based solely on values pertaining to the asset exchanged. The book value of a plant asset is, for example, the difference between its cost and accumulated depreciation to date. The amount of gain or loss recorded, if any, is:

Gain = Fair Value of Asset Exchanged – Book Value of Asset Exchanged

Loss = Book Value of Asset Exchanged – Fair Value of Asset Exchanged

F. The asset exchanged should be tested for impairment before recording the exchange.

II. Caution on List Price—

The list price of the acquired asset should not be used for fair value-list prices are notoriously inflated. Any associated trade-in allowance is used only to determine the amount of cash to be paid: List price – Trade-in allowance = Cash paid on exchange. The trade-in allowance is not equal to the fair value of the asset exchanged.

Example
The list price of a new machine is $32,000. An old machine is traded in for the new machine, and the seller gives the buyer a trade-in allowance of $18,000 for the old machine. The fair value of the old machine is $12,000.

Cash to be Paid on the Exchange = List Price – Trade-in Allowance

= $32,000 – $18,000   = $14,000

The fair value of the acquired asset equals:

Fair Value of Asset Exchanged + Cash Paid
$12,000.00   + $14,000.00 = $26,000.00

III. ASC 845

A. ASC 845 requires that fair value be used to record a nonmonetary asset acquired in an exchange with another nonmonetary asset, with full recognition of gains and losses, unless any of the following apply:

1. The fair value of neither asset can be determined.

2. The exchange is made solely to facilitate sales to customers (e.g., inventory is exchanged for other inventory in the same line of business to enable one of the firms to make a sale to an outside party).

3. The exchange **lacks commercial substance**—the cash flows of the firm are not expected to change significantly as a result of the exchange, which means:

    a. The cash flows from the acquired asset will not be significantly different from those of the asset exchanged in terms of amount, timing, or risk; *or*

    b. The use value of the acquired asset is not significantly different from that of the asset exchanged, in relation to the fair value of the assets exchanged.

B. Receipt or payment of cash to even the exchange does not necessarily imply that gains and losses should be recognized. For example, in situation 2 above, one firm may pay the other a certain amount of cash to even the exchange of inventory made to facilitate sales to customers. The cash flow does not cause the inventory to be valued at fair value.

C. If any of the above three criteria apply, then the accounting is simpler and based on book value, not fair value. No gain or loss is recorded (there are exceptions—see below), and the acquired asset is recorded at the book value of the asset exchanged plus cash paid on the exchange (or minus cash received on the exchange).

Examples

1. *Commercial Substance*

A plant asset (cost $40,000; accumulated depreciation $13,000) is exchanged for another plant asset with a fair value of $30,000. Cash of $2,000 is also paid to even the exchange. The exchange is determined to have commercial substance.

The implied fair value of the asset exchanged is $28,000 ($30,000 fair value of acquired asset less $2,000 cash paid).

Journal entry for the exchange:

Plant asset	30,000	
Accumulated depreciation	13,000	
Plant asset		40,000
Cash		2,000
Gain on exchange		1,000

The acquired plant asset is valued at the sum of the $28,000 fair value of the asset exchanged and $2,000 cash paid. The $1,000 gain equals the difference between the exchanged asset's fair value of $28,000 and its book value of $27,000 ($40,000 – $13,000). A loss would have occurred if the book value had exceeded its fair value. Both losses and gains are recognized when there is commercial substance to the exchange.

2. *Lack of Commercial Substance*

A plant asset (cost $40,000; accumulated depreciation $13,000) is exchanged for another plant asset with a fair value of $30,000. Cash of $2,000 is also paid to even the exchange. The exchange is determined to lack commercial substance. (Same data as previous example.)

Journal entry for the exchange:

Plant asset	29,000	
Accumulated depreciation	13,000	
Plant asset		40,000
Cash		2,000

The acquired asset is recorded at the sum of the $27,000 book value of the asset exchanged and $2,000 cash paid. No gain or loss is recognized. Another way to determine the debit to the new asset is to subtract the unrecognized gain of $1,000 from the $30,000 fair value of the acquired asset.

IV. Rationale for the Exception to Fair Value Recording

A. If fair value is not available, the firm is forced into using book to record the acquired asset. If the exchange is made simply to facilitate the sale of goods to a customer, or if the exchange lacks commercial substance, then the firm is in essentially the same economic position after the exchange as before. Only the "identity" of the asset has changed. For example, exchanging an office building for a slightly different one leaves the firm in the same position. There is enough uncertainty inherent in fair values that it is considered more prudent to continue the accounting with the historically more reliable amounts (book value). Computationally, the exception also leaves future depreciation calculations unchanged.

B. Judgment is required for determining whether an exchange has commercial substance. The following characteristics of an exchange may indicate commercial substance:

1. The amount of cash paid or received on exchange is significant in relation to the fair value of the assets exchanged;

2. The functions of the assets exchanged are different. For example, exchanging land for equipment would imply at the very least a different timing and duration of cash flows.

No Commercial Substance

This lesson presents the accounting for nonmonetary exchanges that do not have commercial substance.

After studying this lesson, you should be able to:

1. Calculate the fair value of the asset received and the gain or loss in a nonmonetary exchange with no commercial substance and cash is paid or received.

I. Accounting for an Exchange When There Is No Commercial Substance

    A. An exchange lacks commercial substance whenever the cash flows to the firm are not expected to change significantly as a result of the exchange:

        1. The cash flows from the acquired asset will not be significantly different from those of the asset exchanged in terms of amount, timing, or risk; or

        2. The use value of the acquired asset is not significantly different from that of the asset exchanged, in relation to the fair value of the assets exchanged.

        3. When there is no commercial substance, the value of the asset acquired is the book value of the asset given.

    B. There are two exceptions to book value reporting when there is no commercial substance:

        1. When a loss is evident, it is recognized in full, and the acquired asset is recorded at market value. Cash can be paid or received on the exchange for this exception. Thus, losses are always recognized in full—an example of conservatism.

        2. When a gain is evident and cash is received (only), the gain is recognized in proportion to the amount of cash received, and the acquired asset is recorded at market value less the portion of the gain unrecognized. If the proportion represented by cash is 25% or more, then the entire gain is recognized, and the acquired asset is recorded at market value.

Examples

1. No Commercial Substance, Loss, Cash paid

Cost of old asset, $40,000

Accumulated depreciation, $12,000

Fair value of new asset $30,000

Cash of $6,000 is paid to even the exchange

The implied fair value of the old asset is $24,000 ($30,000 fair value of new asset −$6,000 cash paid). A $4,000 loss is evident: $28,000 book value of old asset—$24,000 fair value of old asset. Losses are recognized in full and the new asset is recorded at fair value.

Plant asset	30,000	
Accumulated depreciation	12,000	
Loss	4,000	
Plant asset		40,000
Cash		6,000

2. No Commercial Substance, Loss, Cash Received

Cost of old asset, $40,000

Accumulated depreciation, $12,000

Fair value of new asset $20,000

Cash of $3,000 is received to even the exchange

The implied fair value of the old asset is $23,000 ($20,000 fair value of new asset + $3,000 cash received). A $5,000 loss is evident: $28,000 book value of old asset −$23,000 fair value of old asset. Losses are recognized in full and the new asset is recorded at fair value.

Plant asset	20,000	
Accumulated depreciation	12,000	
Cash	3,000	
Loss	5,000	
Plant asset		40,000

3. No Commercial Substance, Gain, Cash Received

Cost of old asset, $40,000

Accumulated depreciation, $30,000

Fair value of new asset $20,000

Cash of $3,000 is received to even the exchange

The implied fair value of the old asset is $23,000 ($20,000 fair value of new asset + $3,000 cash received). A $13,000 gain is evident: $23,000 fair value of old asset − $10,000 book value of old asset. Cash represents ($3,000/($3,000 + $20,000)) or 13% of the value of the transaction. 13% of the old asset has been "sold" for cash allowing 13% of the gain to be recognized: 13%(13,000) = $1,690. The unrecognized gain is $13,000 − $1,690 = $11,310. The new asset is recorded at fair value less the unrecorded gain = $20,000 − $11,310 = $8,690.

Plant asset	8,690	
Accumulated depreciation	30,000	
Cash	3,000	
Plant asset		40,000
Gain		1,690

4. No Commercial Substance, Gain, Cash Received, Proportion Represented by Cash > 25%

Cost of old asset, $40,000

Accumulated depreciation, $30,000

Fair value of new asset $20,000

Cash of $10,000 is received to even the exchange

The implied fair value of the old asset is $30,000 ($20,000 fair value of new asset + $10,000 cash received). A $20,000 gain is evident: $30,000 fair value of old asset − $10,000 book value of old asset = $20,000. Cash represents ($10,000/($10,000 + $20,000)) of the value of the transaction or 33%, which is more than 25%. This firm has "sold" so much of its asset that the entire transaction is considered a monetary transaction. The entire gain is recognized and the new asset is recorded at fair value.

Plant asset	20,000	
Accumulated depreciation	30,000	
Cash	10,000	
Plant asset		40,000
Gain		20,000

II. Summary of All Cases for Nonmonetary Asset Exchanges

A. Fair value not determinable: recognize no loss or gain, and record the acquired asset at book value of old asset + cash paid or – cash received.

B. Losses (loss = book value of asset exchanged – fair value):

   1. Recognize loss in full, and record the acquired asset at fair value regardless of whether there is commercial substance. (Losses are always recognized in full.)

C. Gains (gain = fair value of asset exchanged – book value):

   1. If there is commercial substance, recognize gain in full, and record the acquired asset at fair value.

   2. If there is no commercial substance and cash is not received on the exchange, recognize no gain, and record the acquired asset at book value of asset exchanged + cash paid.

   3. If there is no commercial substance and cash is received on the exchange, recognize the gain in proportion to the cash received and record the asset acquired at fair value less the unrecognized portion of the gain.

      a. **Exception**—if the proportion of cash received is 25% or more, account for the exchange as if there were commercial substance (recognize gain in full and record acquired asset at fair value).

315

Investments

Introduction—Investments in Equity and Debt Securities

Often an entity will acquire the equity or debt securities of another as an investment. The accounting for that investment by the acquiring entity depends on various factors, including whether the investment is an equity or debt security, the intent of the investor, the amount held, and whether the investment has a readily determinable fair value. This lesson provides an overview of accounting for investments in equity and debt securities and the basis for valuation. The next lessons cover the accounting and reporting for each type of investment in more detail.

After studying this lesson, you should be able to:

1. Define and distinguish between an equity and debt security.

2. Identify the classifications of investments in debt and equity securities for accounting purposes.

I. Accounting for Investments in Equity and Debt Securities

ASU 2016-01, *Financial Instruments—Overall: Recognition and Measurement of Financial Assets and Financial Liabilities*, significantly changed the accounting for investments in the equity of another entity. This standard is effective for fiscal years beginning after December 15, 2017, and eligible for testing on the CPA Exam beginning January 1, 2018. The accounting for an investment by the acquiring entity depends on various factors, including whether the investment is an equity or debt security, the intent of the investor, the amount held, and whether the investment has a readily determinable fair value.

A. Terminology

> **Definition**
>
> *Equity securities*—Securities that represent ownership interest or the right to acquire or dispose of ownership interest.
>
> - Includes common stock, preferred stock (except redeemable preferred stock), stock warrants, call options/rights, put options.
>
> - Excludes debt securities (including convertible debt), redeemable preferred stock, written equity options, cash settled options, and treasury stock.

> **Definition**
>
> *Debt securities*—Securities that represent the right of buyer/holder (creditor) to receive from the issuer (debtor) a principal amount at a specified future date and (generally) to receive interest as payment for providing use of funds.
>
> - Includes bonds, notes, convertible bonds/notes, redeemable preferred stock.
>
> - Excludes common/preferred stock, stock warrants/options/rights, futures/forward contracts.

Exam Tip

Questions on the CPA Exam may provide information regarding the characteristics of a security and ask that you determine whether the security is an equity or debt security. Questions also may ask that you identify the characteristics of a security that gives ownership or rights to ownership. In your studies, make sure you pay attention to the distinguishing characteristics, as those characteristics dictate how the security is accounted for.

An example is redeemable preferred stock. This security may seem like an equity security, but since it is redeemable (usually by the issuing entity for a set value), it is classified as debt because it has a set principal payment as well as a contractually determined stream of cash flows (dividends), similar to the interest on debt.

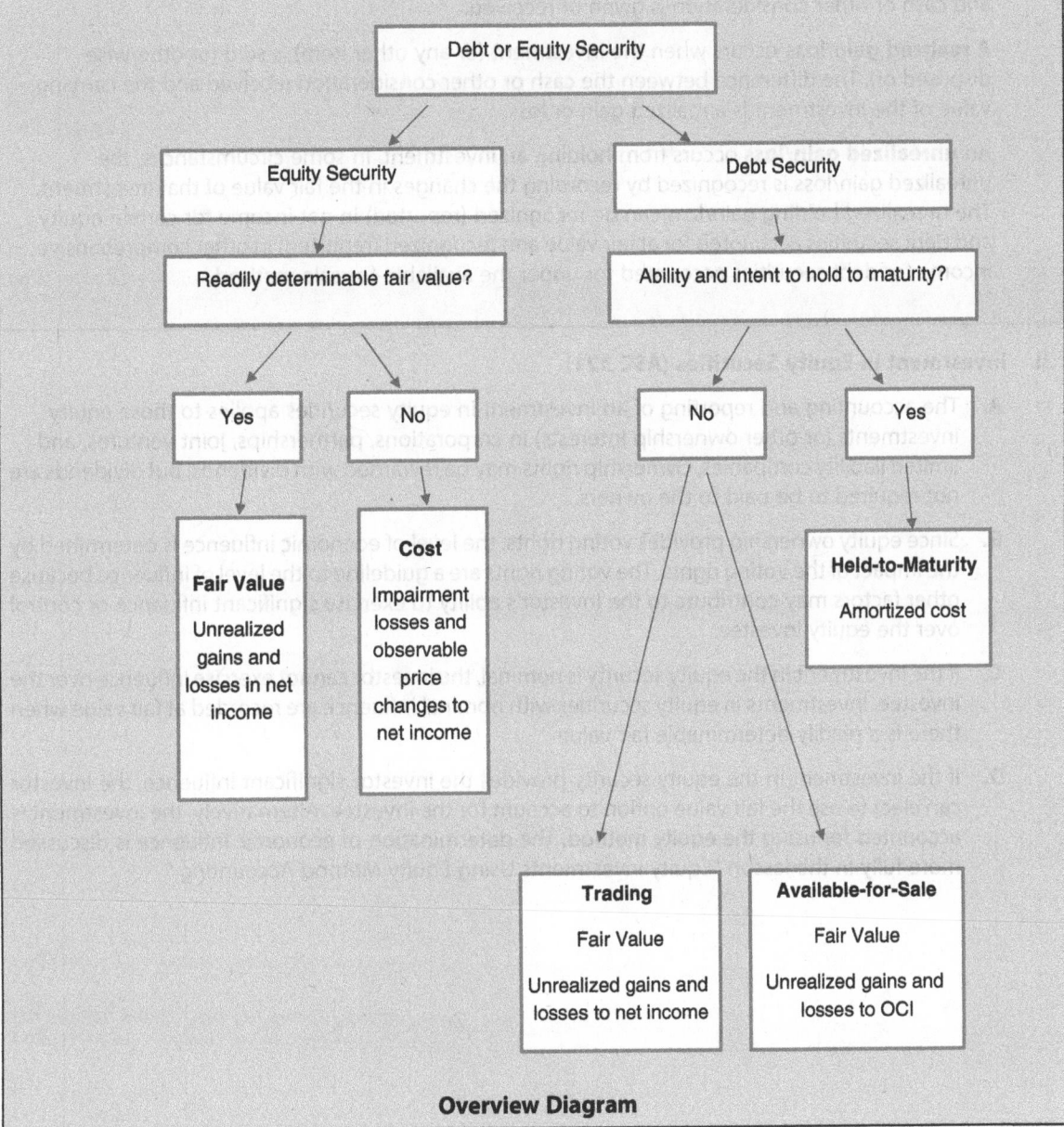

Overview Diagram

Note

It is easy to confuse the terminology related to *recognized* and *realized*, so here we explain the concepts for you to keep in mind as you study the series of lessons on investments.

Recognition is an accounting concept—it means that we have reported the item on the financial statements.

A **recognized gain/loss** occurs when a gain or loss related to an investment (or other item) is recorded (recognized) in the financial statements, regardless of whether the investment has been sold. For example, a gain or loss from the change in fair value of an equity or debt security is reported in the financial statements before the securities are sold.

Realization is an economic concept; it means that there is a culmination of the earnings process, and cash or other consideration is given or received.

A **realized gain/loss** occurs when the investment (or any other item) is sold (or otherwise disposed of). The difference between the cash or other consideration received and the carrying value of the investment is a realized gain or loss.

An **unrealized gain/loss** occurs from holding an investment. In some circumstances, the unrealized gain/loss is recognized by recording the changes in the fair value of that investment. The unrealized holding gain/loss can be recognized (reported) in net income for certain equity and debt securities accounted for at fair value and recognized (reported) in other comprehensive income for debt securities accounted for under the available-for-sale method.

II. Investment in Equity Securities (ASC 321)

A. The accounting and reporting of an investment in equity securities applies to those equity investments (or other ownership interests) in corporations, partnerships, joint ventures, and limited liability companies. Ownership rights may be rewarded with dividends, but dividends are not required to be paid to the owners.

B. Since equity ownership provides voting rights, the level of economic influence is determined by the impact of the voting rights. The voting rights are a guideline to the level of influence because other factors may contribute to the investor's ability to exercise significant influence or control over the equity investee.

C. If the investment in the equity security is nominal, the investor cannot exercise influence over the investee. Investments in equity securities with nominal influence are recorded at fair value when there is a readily determinable fair value.

D. If the investment in the equity security provides the investor significant influence, the investor can elect to use the fair value option to account for the investee. Alternatively, the investment is accounted for using the equity method. The determination of economic influence is discussed more fully in the lesson "Equity Investments Using Equity Method Accounting."

The next table presents an overview of the relationship between the level of economic influence, the valuation basis for the equity investment, and the presentation on the balance sheet.

Percentage equity ownership	< 20%	≥ 20%–50%	> 50%
Level of Economic Influence (influence over operating and financing activities)	Nominal	Significant	Control
Valuation Basis	If readily determinable fair value, use fair value. If no readily determinable fair value, use cost (less any impairment).	Equity method unless the fair value option is elected.	Equity method or cost method
Balance Sheet Presentation	As an investment: current or noncurrent, depending on intent to hold	As an investment: typically, noncurrent	Consolidated financial statements

E. If the investor has **< 20% ownership**, it is presumed that there is **nominal influence or no significant influence** over the operating and financing activities of the investee.

1. If there is a readily determinable fair value for the investee, then the investment must be carried at **fair value** with changes in fair value recorded in net income. See the lesson "Equity Investments at Fair Value."

2. If the investee does not have a readily determinable fair value, then the investment can be carried at **cost less any impairment**. The accounting for this type of investment is included in the lesson "Equity Investments at Cost."

3. The balance sheet presentation of the investment is a **current or noncurrent asset**, depending on management's intent for holding the security for the short term or long term.

F. If the investor has between **20% and 50% ownership**, it is presumed that the investor has **significant influence** over the operating and financing activities of the investee.

1. When there is significant influence over the investee, the investor can use the **equity method of accounting**. See the lesson "Equity Investments Using Equity Method Accounting."

2. If there is a readily determinable fair value for the investment, then the investor has the option to value the investment at **fair value**. If this option is chosen, then the investment is recorded at fair value with the unrealized gains and losses recorded in earnings. Once the investor chooses the fair value option, it is irrevocable and the investment continues to be recorded at fair value.

3. Investments with significant influence are usually reported as a **noncurrent** asset because buying and selling equity shares of this magnitude is relatively difficult to do. For example, if you owned 40% of a company, it would be very difficult for you to sell all of your shares in one block without diluting the selling price.

G. If the investor has >50% ownership of an investment, it is presumed that the investor **controls** the investee. An investment of this magnitude creates a parent/subsidiary relationship.

1. The default accounting for an investment with >50% ownership is the **equity method** of accounting. The parent company will record its equity investment in the subsidiary on the parent's books. Equity method accounting is discussed more fully in the lesson "Equity Investments Using Equity Method Accounting."

2. In some instances, the parent company can choose to use the **cost method** to account for its subsidiary. Cost method accounting is discussed more fully in the lesson "Equity Investments at Cost." The cost method can be used by the parent company because the parent's stand-alone financial statements are not issued on a stand-alone basis. The parent must **consolidate** the subsidiary investment. Upon consolidation, the parent eliminates the investment in the subsidiary, so the parent's investment in the subsidiary is not reported on the consolidated statements.

3. Whether the parent uses the equity method or the cost method to account for its subsidiary, the consolidated financial statements will be the same. The only difference is what is reported on the parent's stand-alone statements. Note that the parent's stand-alone statements are not in compliance with GAAP. GAAP requires that the parent present consolidated statements. Consolidation is discussed more fully in the "Consolidating Process" subsection.

III. Investment in Debt Securities (ASC 320)

A. The accounting and reporting of an investment in debt securities depends on management's intent for holding the debt security. In addition, an important factor in the valuation of the debt security is if there is a readily determinable fair value.

The following table depicts the classifications for the accounting and reporting of investments in debt securities.

Classification	Valuation	Unrealized gain/Loss	Dividend/Interest income (including amortization of premium or discount)
Trading	Fair value	Earnings	Earnings
Available-for-sale	Fair value	Other comprehensive income	Earnings
Held-to-maturity (must have ability and intent to hold until maturity)	Amortized cost	N/A	Earnings

B. Investments in debt securities that are recorded at **fair value** are classified as either trading or available-for-sale, depending on how long management intends to hold the security. Note that **only** investments in debt securities have classification of trading or available-for-sale **(Investments in equity securities no longer have these classifications.)**

   1. If the investment in debt securities is classified as **trading**, the changes in the fair value are recorded in earnings. Most likely this investment would be classified as current because the intent of a trading security is to sell in the near term.

   2. If the investment in debt securities is classified as **available-for-sale**, the changes in the fair value are recorded in other comprehensive income. This investment could be classified as current or noncurrent, depending on how long management intends to hold the security.

C. The critical criteria for accounting for debt investments as **held-to-maturity** (HTM) is whether the company has the positive **ability and intent** to hold the debt security to maturity. HTM securities are carried at **amortized cost**.

D. For all classifications of the investments in debt securities, any **dividend or interest income is reported in current-period earnings**. The amortization of any premium or discount is also included in current-period earnings.

E. In the topic of investments, there are two lessons that provide further detail on the accounting for investment in debt securities. The first lesson discusses the accounting for investments in debt securities at fair value, and the second lesson discusses accounting for investments in debt securities at amortized cost.

Investments in Equity Securities

Equity Investments at Fair Value

This lesson covers the accounting and reporting of investments in equity securities when the investor accounts for the investment at fair value with changes in fair value recognized in net income. Entities are required to report the equity investment at fair value when there is a readily determinable fair value. Alternate accounting methods are used if there is no readily determinable fair value or if the equity ownership gives the investor significant influence over the investee.

After studying this lesson, you should be able to:

1. Distinguish when an equity investment must be accounted for at fair value.

2. Define "readily determinable fair value."

3. Demonstrate the accounting and reporting for equity investments at fair value.

I. Equity Securities

A. ASU 2016-01, *Financial Instruments—Overall: Recognition and Measurement of Financial Assets and Financial Liabilities,* significantly changed the accounting for investments in the equity of another entity. Investments in equity securities with readily determinable fair value are required to be reported at fair value with changes in fair value recognized in net income. **The categories of trading or available-for-sale for investments in equity securities no longer exist.**

ASU 2016-01 resulted in the creation of Accounting Standards Codification (ASC) Topic 321, *Investments—Equity Securities.* The ASC Master Glossary defines equity securities as follows:

> **Definition**
> *Equity securities:* Any security that represents ownership interest or the right to acquire or dispose of ownership interest.
>
> - Includes common stock, preferred stock (except redeemable preferred stock), stock warrants, call options/rights, put options.
>
> - Excludes debt securities (including convertible debt), redeemable preferred stock, and treasury stock.

II. Readily Determinable Fair Value

A. Investments in equity securities should be recorded at fair value when there is a readily determinable fair value. Readily determinable fair value is defined in the (ASC) Master Glossary as follows:

> **Definition**
> An equity security has *readily determinable fair value* if it meets any of the following conditions:
>
> 1. Sales prices or bid-and-ask quotations are currently available on a securities exchange registered with the U.S. Securities and Exchange Commission (SEC) or in the over-the-counter (OTC) market if the OTC prices are publicly reported.
>
> 2. Prices or quotations are in a foreign market that has the breadth and scope of the U.S. markets.
>
> 3. Prices or quotations for investments in mutual funds (or structures similar to mutual funds, such as a limited partnership or venture capital entity) when the fair value per share is published based on current transactions.

B. Equity investments are **not** required to be reported at fair value in the following circumstances:

    1. The equity investment is accounted for under the equity method (i.e., there is significant influence and the fair value option is not elected), *or*

    2. The equity investment is controlled and will be consolidated with the investee, *or*

    3. The equity investment does not have readily determinable fair value; the investor can elect to measure the investment at cost.

        a. Cost is adjusted for any impairment.

        b. Cost also must be adjusted for changes in observable prices of orderly transactions for identical or similar equity investments.

III. Accounting for Equity Investments at Fair Value

Equity investments must be carried at fair value with changes in fair value recorded in net income (unless the exceptions stated above are met).

A. The fair value of an equity security is the price that would be received to sell the security in an orderly transaction between market participants.

B. Initial recognition of the equity investment is at the price paid.

    1. Cost includes purchase price (e.g., per security cost) and includes any costs directly related to the purchase such as brokerage fees, transfer fees, etc. Note that the initial recognition includes transaction costs, but the subsequent measurement of the equity investment is at fair value excluding the transaction costs.

Example

Assume Dean Co. purchases 1,000 shares of Kemnitz Corp for $49,000 plus $1,000 of brokerage fees. Dean's entry to record the purchase would be:

DR: Equity investment in Kemnitz Corp. $50,000

    CR: Cash $50,000

C. Dividends received are recognized as income in the period earned.

Example

Assume Kemnitz declares and pays a dividend of $.50 per share. Dean's share of dividends is 1,000 shares × $.50 = $500. Dean would record dividend income as follows:

DR: Cash $500

    CR: Dividend Income $500

D. A change in fair value of the equity security is the holding gain or loss. Holding gains or losses do not include dividend or interest income. Holding gains or losses also are referred to as unrealized gains or losses as long as the equity security has not been sold. Unrealized gains or losses, for equity investments at fair value, are recognized and reported in earnings (i.e., recognized in the income statement).

Example

Assume the fair value of Kemnitz's shares are $51 per share at the end of the reporting period. Therefore, total fair value of the investment should be reported at $51,000 and the current carrying value is $50,000. The following entry would be made as the fair value adjustment:

DR: Equity investment in Kemnitz Corp.	$1,000	
CR: Unrealized gain on investment		$1,000

1. Realized gains and losses result when the security is sold. In the case where an equity security is reported at fair value with changes in fair value reported in earnings, there will be no realized gain or loss recognized from the sale if the equity security is adjusted to fair value at the date of sale.

Definition

Fair value: The price that would be received to sell an asset or paid to transfer a liability in an orderly transaction between market participants at the measurement date

Examples

Example A

Assume that on January 1, 20X1 Dean Co. purchased 1,000 shares of Kemnitz Corp. for $50,000. Kemnitz shares are sold in two different active markets, and neither is the principal market in which Dean Co. transacts. Below is the price that would be received for Kemnitz Corp. securities on December 31, 20X1.

Investment	Eastern market	Western market
Kemnitz Corp.—1,000 shares	$56,000	$55,000
Transaction costs	3,000	1,000
Net	$53,000	$54,000

Which market is the most advantageous market?

Answer: Western Market is the most advantageous because the net amount that would be received upon the sale is $54,000. Transaction costs are used to help determine the most advantageous market.

What is the Fair Value of the Equity investment in Kemnitz Corp.?

Answer: Dean Co. must price the equity securities in the most advantageous market at $55,000. The fair value of the securities does not include the transaction costs. Transaction costs help determine the most advantageous market, not the fair value.

What is the adjustment to earnings to reflect the change in the fair value of the investment in Kemnitz Corp. at December 31, 20X1?

Answer:

DR: Equity investment in Kemnitz Corp.	$5,000	
CR: Unrealized gain on equity securities (an income statement account)		$5,000

Example B

Now assume that the principal market used by Dean Co. is the Eastern Market.

What is the adjustment to earnings to reflect the change in the fair value of the investment in Kemnitz Corp. at December 31, 20X1?

Answer:

DR: Equity investment in Kemnitz Corp.	$6,000
CR: Unrealized gain on equity securities (an income statement account)	$6,000

Example

Assume that the principal market used by Dean Co. is the Eastern Market and that on December 31, 20X1, the investment in Kemnitz Corp. was adjusted to the fair value of $56,000. Dean decided to sell the Kemnitz Corp. investment on January 20, 20X2, and received $58,000 on the sale.

What is the adjustment to earnings to reflect the sale of the investment in Kemnitz Corp. at January 20, 20X2?

Answer:

DR: Cash	$58,000
CR: Gain on the sale of Kemnitz Corp.	$2,000
CR: Equity investment in Kemnitz Corp.	56,000

Note that the realized gain is calculated based on the most recent carrying value of the equity investment since the last fair value adjustment ($56,000) and the selling price ($58,000). The total gain from the equity investment in Kemnitz Corp. is the sum of the unrealized holding gains ($6,000) and the realized gain on the sale ($2,000), or $8,000.

E. There is no impairment loss related to the sale of an equity security recorded at fair value through earnings because the security is already reported at its fair value.

IV. Presentation of Equity Investments at Fair Value

A. The balance sheet presentation of the equity investment is **current or noncurrent**, depending on management's intent for holding the equity security for the short term or long term.

B. The presentation of the cash flows associated with the purchases and sales of equity securities should be classified on the basis of the nature and purpose for which it acquired the securities. In general, the classification of cash flows would be investing activities unless the purpose of the entities equity transactions is part of its normal operations (i.e., a financial institution), where the classification would be operating activities.

V. Look Through Is Not Permitted

A. "Look through" means that the investor would "look through" the form of the investment to the nature of the securities held by the investee. That is, if Kemnitz Corp. invested in U.S. debt securities, Dean Co.'s investment in Kemnitz is an equity investment even though Kemnitz is totally made up of debt securities.

B. Another illustration is an investment in a limited partnership where the limited partnership invests only in artwork. The investor is an equity owner of the limited partnership, not an owner of the artwork owned by the partnership.

Equity Investments at Cost

This lesson presents the accounting for an equity investment when the investment does not have a readily determinable fair value. When there is no readily determinable fair value, the investor may elect the practicability exception to carry the investment at cost. The cost must be reduced for any impairment, plus or minus price changes from any observable transactions for an identical or similar investment. This lesson presents the impairment testing for equity securities not at fair value and describes when adjustments should be made for observable price changes.

After studying this lesson, you should be able to:

1. Describe when an investor in an equity security may use the practicability exception.

2. Describe the factors that must be considered when determining if the equity investment may be impaired.

3. Complete an impairment calculation and adjustment for an investment in an equity security carried at cost.

4. Identify when an adjustment to an investment in an equity security may occur based on observable factors.

I. Practicability Exception

A. An entity can elect a practicability exception to fair value measurement for investments in an equity security when there is no readily determinable fair value. As the term implies, this exception can be used when it is impracticable to obtain a fair value measurement of the investment. In most cases, the investor uses the practicability exception because the investee is a privately held company. The practicability exception means that the entity can carry the equity investment at cost because determination of a readily determinable fair value cannot be practically obtained.

B. An equity security does **not** have a *readily determinable fair value* in any of the following situations:

1. There are no sales prices or bid-and-ask quotations available on a securities exchange registered with the U.S. Securities and Exchange Commission (SEC) or in the over-the-counter (OTC) market if the OTC prices are publicly reported.

2. There are no prices or quotations in a foreign market that has the breadth and scope of the U.S. markets.

3. There are no prices or quotations for investments in mutual funds (or a limited partnership or venture capital entity) if the fair value per share is published based on current transactions.

C. Election of the practicability exception applies only to equity investments that do not qualify for using net asset value (NAV) as the practical expedient for fair value.

1. NAV is used as a practical expedient for those investees that report their net assets at fair value, and that fair value of the investees is used to determine the per share value of the investors' ownership.

Example
Assume an investor holds 10% equity investment in Probert Co. If there is **no readily determinable fair value** for Probert Co. shares, but Probert's **net assets are reported at fair value** in the amount of $100,000. The investor with a 10% ownership in Probert Co. could qualify for using the **net asset value as a practical expedient** and report the investment at $10,000 ($100,000 ×10%).

However, if Probert Co., **does not report its net assets at fair value** and there is **no readily determinable fair value** for Probert's shares, then the investor may elect the **practicability exception** and report the investment in Probert Co. at cost.

D. The practicability exception can be made on an investment-by-investment basis, but once elected, it must be applied consistently to that investment as long as the investment meets the criteria. The investor must reassess each year whether the equity investment continues to qualify for the practicability exception.

    1. For example, if the investee becomes a public company and fair value is determinable, the equity security will need to be accounted for at fair value with changes in fair value recognized in net income.

II. Initial Investment in an Equity Security Not at Fair Value

A. The initial purchase of the equity security would be recorded at the investor's cost. The initial purchase is an arm's-length transaction and would be the initial fair value of the investment.

B. Dividends received by the investor from the investee are recorded like normal dividends. Cash would be collected, and dividend income is recognized in net income.

III. Impairment of an Investment in an Equity Security Not at Fair Value

A. The impairment model for equity securities that are not reported at fair value has been simplified. Each reporting period the investor must consider qualitative factors in assessing whether the investment is impaired. The qualitative assessment is similar to what is completed for long-lived assets, goodwill, and indefinite-lived intangible assets. ASC 321-10-35-3 lists the following factors to consider in the evaluation of a potential impairment:

> **Exam Tip**
> Questions on the CPA Exam may ask about or use terminology presented in the Wiley CPAexcel lessons. Make sure you are familiar with the terminology as it will aid you in answering questions. The CPA Exam typically will not present acronyms without describing what they stand for. Therefore, no need to worry about memorizing acronyms!

    1. A significant deterioration in the earnings performance, credit rating, asset quality, or business outlook of the investee

    2. A significant adverse change in the regulatory, economic, or technological environment of the investee

    3. A significant adverse change in the general market condition of either the geographical area or the industry in which the investee operates

    4. A bona fide offer to purchase, an offer by the investee to sell, or a completed auction process for the same or similar investment for an amount less than the carrying amount of that investment

    5. Factors that raise significant concerns about the investee's ability to continue as a going concern, such as negative cash flows from operations, working capital deficiencies, or noncompliance with statutory capital requirements or debt covenants

B. If the factors indicate that the equity security is impaired, the impairment loss is recorded. The impairment loss is measured as the amount that the carrying value exceeds the fair value of the equity security.

    1. Since this equity security does not have a readily determinable fair value, the fair value will need to be estimated based on valuation models.

    2. The impairment loss is recorded in net income, and the fair value becomes the new basis of the equity investment.

C. The impairment loss for the equity investment carried at cost using the practicability exception would be recorded as follows:

Assume an equity investment was purchased for $150,000 and is carried at cost using the practicability exception. (The investment does not qualify to use NAV as a practical expedient.) Subsequent factors indicate that there may be an impairment. A valuation model was employed, and it was determined that the fair value of the equity investment is $128,000. The impairment loss would be recorded as $22,000 ($150,000 less $128,000):

| DR: Impairment loss | 22,000 | |
| CR: Investment in equity securities carried at cost | | 22,000 |

IV. Adjustments Based on Observable Transactions

A. When the investor elects the practicability exception and carries the investment in the equity security at cost, the investor must also make a "reasonable effort" to determine if there are known (or can be reasonably known) price changes that should be made to the equity security.

> **Note**
> An impairment loss cannot be reversed unless there are observable price changes in a similar or identical security, as described in the next section.

    1. The investor is not expected to make an exhaustive effort to search for observable transactions. But if the investor is aware that the issuer has similar (or identical) securities with observable transactions, the investor is expected to use information from those transactions to adjust the carrying value of the investment in the equity security.

B. The investor should make an effort to monitor observable price changes in transactions of the same issuer for any security that is similar or identical to the equity security being held. To determine if the security is similar or identical to the one being held, the investor should look at the rights and obligations of the security. Rights and obligations are things like voting rights, distribution rights, preferences, and conversion features.

C. Changes in the observable prices in similar or identical securities may indicate that the investor should make an adjustment to the equity security being held as an investment.

D. Continuing with the previous example, assume an observable transaction is identified regarding the equity investment that was purchased for $150,000 and was impaired by recording an impairment loss of $22,000, as described above. Assume that an observable transaction indicates that the fair value of the equity investment should be $137,000. The adjustment for the unrealized holding gain would be recorded as $9,000 ($137,000 less $128,000):

| DR: Investment in equity securities carried at cost | 9,000 | |
| CR: Unrealized gain on equity securities (reported on the income statement) | | 9,000 |

> **Note**
> If the equity investment was impaired and subsequently there was an observable transaction for a similar or identical equity security indicating there is an increase in the security, then the investor may adjust the investment to equal the change in value indicated by the observable transaction. The adjustment would be a fair value adjustment with an unrealized gain reported on the income statement.
>
> Recognizing an impairment loss and subsequently increasing to fair value is consistent with the desire to reflect the equity investment as close as possible to its fair value.

V. Sale of Securities

A. A realized gain or loss is recognized upon the sale of the equity investment carried at cost. The realized gain or loss is the difference between the equity investment carrying value and the selling price.

Continuing with the previous example, where the equity investment is carried at $137,000, assume that the equity investment is sold for $140,000. The realized gain would be recorded as $3,000 ($140,000 selling price less $137,000 carrying value):

DR: Cash	140,000	
CR: Realized gain on equity securities (reported on the income statement)		3,000
CR: Investment in equity securities carried at cost		137,000

Equity Investments Using Equity Method Accounting

All investments in equity securities are accounted for at fair value unless there is no readily determinable fair value or if the equity ownership gives the investor significant influence over the investee. When the investor has significant influence over the investee, the equity method of accounting can be used or the investor can elect to use fair value and report the investment at fair value. This lesson describes the application of the equity method of accounting.

After studying this lesson, you should be able to:

1. Describe the criteria for significant influence in an equity investment.

2. Illustrate equity method accounting using T-accounts and journal entries.

3. Describe the required disclosures for the equity method of accounting.

4. Describe the accounting when all or part of an equity method investment is disposed of.

I. Significant Influence

A. When the investor has significant influence over the operating and financing activities of the investee, the investor uses either equity method accounting or fair value.

> **Exam Tip**
> This is a very popular topic on the CPA Exam. Study time dedicated to this area will pay off.

1. **Significant influence is presumed if there is 20%–50% ownership of voting stock.** Twenty percent is a guideline. There are circumstances when the investor can exert significant influence with less than 20% ownership and there are circumstances when the investor cannot exert significant influence even with 20% stock ownership.

   a. The following are indicators that the investor **has significant influence** even though ownership is less than 20%.

      i. The investor has representation on the investee's board of directors;

      ii. The investor participates in investee's policy making;

      iii. There are material transactions between the investor and the investee;

      iv. There is technological dependence on the investor; *or*

      v. No other single investor has a material voting ownership in the investee.

   b. The following are indicators that the investor will **not have significant influence**, even though there is more than 20% ownership:

      i. The investee opposes investment;

      ii. There is a standstill agreement between the investor and the investee; this means that the investor cannot acquire more stock or other attempts to exert significant influence;

      iii. Significant influence or control is exercised by shareholders other than the investor. For example:

         a. Investor A owns 35% of the voting stock, but Investor B owns the other 65% (has control) and does not cooperate with Investor A.

         b. Investee is in bankruptcy or legal reorganization and under the control of the courts.

         c. Investee is a foreign entity that operates under foreign government restrictions that preclude exercise of significant influence.

    iv. The investor lacks information for use of equity method (very rare); *or*

    v. The investor cannot obtain representation on the investee board of directors.

> **Tip**
> *Significant influence is not just a bright line rule. You must look at other factors to determine if the investor can exert significant influence over the investee.*

II. Types of Accounting for Equity Investee

A. Typically, on the CPA Exam, when it is stated that the investor has significant influence over the investee, the investor will use **equity method accounting unless the question says that the fair value method is elected**. Equity method accounting is designed so that the investor records changes in the equity investment that reflect the changes in the net assets of the investee.

B. The investor can elect to use **fair value** to measure the equity investment. Once the election is made, the investor must apply fair value consistently.

    1. Under the fair value option, the investment is carried at fair value with changes in fair value recorded in net income.

C. **Control** is presumed when there is greater than 50% ownership of voting stock. In this situation, the investor is the parent of the investee, and the parent will **consolidate** the investee for financial reporting purposes.

> **Note**
> *The investor can elect to record an equity ownership in an investee at fair value. This lesson focuses on equity method accounting.*

    1. The parent company may use a variety of methods (including the equity method) to account for the investment in its subsidiary. However, since the parent will consolidate the subsidiary for financial reporting purposes, the method used by the parent company is irrelevant as the equity investment is eliminated upon consolidation.

III. Equity Method Accounting—at Acquisition

A. The initial investment in securities is recorded at the price of the equity security (e.g., price per share). The price per share assumes the acquisition is an arm's-length transaction negotiated by two independent parties.

    1. All other **costs** related to the purchase of the equity security are expensed because they are not considered an attribute of the investee. Other costs (sometimes referred to as direct costs) are finder's fees, audit fees, and legal fees related to the acquisition.

    The entry at acquisition would be:

> DR: Equity Method Investment
>   CR: Cash (or other consideration)

B. At the time of the initial investment, the investor must also:

    1. Determine book value of assets/liabilities of investee at date of investment;

    2. Determine fair value of assets and liabilities of investee at date of investment. **Assets and liabilities** of the investee are valued at **fair value**.

    3. The fair value of the consideration transferred less the net fair value of the identifiable assets acquired and liabilities assumed is **goodwill**.

    This diagram presents a tool that can be used to organize the components of the purchase of a significant equity investment.

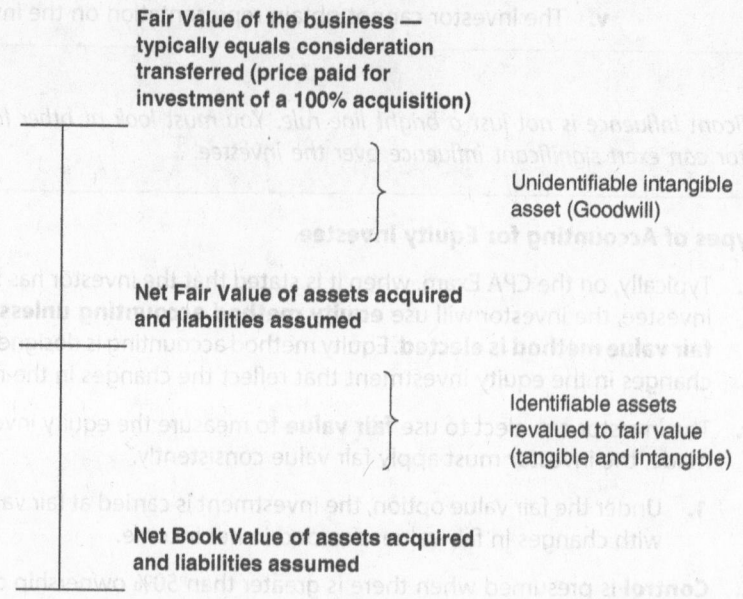

Fair Value of the business —
typically equals consideration
transferred (price paid for
investment of a 100% acquisition)

Unidentifiable intangible
asset (Goodwill)

**Net Fair Value of assets acquired
and liabilities assumed**

Identifiable assets
revalued to fair value
(tangible and intangible)

**Net Book Value of assets acquired
and liabilities assumed**

Example

Assume P Company (P) acquired 20% of S Corp. (S) on July 1 for $500,000. The following diagram shows how to use the tool to organize the data to answer questions. Assume S's net book value (Assets – Liabilities) = $2,000,000. The fair value of S's plant assets is $300,000 more than the book values, and the assets have a remaining useful life of 5 years. **What is the amount of goodwill? What is the entry to record the equity investment?**

	100%	20%
4. Price paid		$ 500,000
5. Goodwill		40,000
3. Identifiable Fair Value	2,300,000	460,000
2. Plant assets	300,000	60,000
1. Book Value	$ 2,000,000	$ 400,000

Steps to Organize the Data

1. The book value of S Corp. is $2,000,000. P's share is $400,000.

2. Plant assets are revalued to fair value for $300,000. P's share is $60,000.

3. The total fair value of the identifiable net assets of S is $2,300,000. P's share is $460,000.

4. The price paid for 20% of S Corp. is $500,000.

5. The difference between the price paid ($500,000) and the fair value of the identifiable net assets ($460,000) is goodwill of $40,000.

Answer: Goodwill = $40,000

Entry:

DR: Equity Method Investment $500,000

    CR: Cash $500,000

IV. Equity Method Accounting—after Acquisition

A. After the date of acquisition, the investor (1) recognizes its share of investee's net income or loss, (2) recognizes its share of investee's dividends, and (3) accounts for any difference between the cost of its investment in the investee and the book value of the investee's net assets it acquired. Equity method accounting affects both the investor's investment account (on the balance sheet) and the income recognized from the investee by the investor (on the income statement). First, we show the **equity method T-accounts**, then the equity method entries.

Equity method investment (on balance sheet)

Original cost of investment	
1. Pro rata share of investee's income since acquisition	**1.** Pro rata share of investee's losses since acquisition
	2. Pro rata share of investee's dividends declared
	3. Amortization of cost in excess of book value (i.e., on amounts allocated to identifiable assets)
	4. Impairment losses

Equity method income (on income statement)

1. Pro rata share of investee's losses since acquisition	**1.** Pro rata share of investee's income since acquisition
2. Amortization of cost in excess of book value (i.e., on amounts to identifiable assets)	
3. Impairment losses	

Note: The entry numbers in the T-accounts represent the entry descriptions presented in the next section.

B. In this section, we show the **equity method entries** depicted in the T-accounts above. Recall the purpose of equity method accounting is to reflect the changes in the investee's net book value. These changes include:

1. Investee's results of operation (income/loss)

The investor's share of the investee's results of operations are recognized by the investor when reported by the investee. The

> **Note**
> When using equity method accounting, dividends are **not** income.

investor recognizes its proportionate share of the investee's reported income/loss, excluding its share of any intercompany profits/losses in assets (e.g., in inventory, etc.).

a. Entry made by the investor if the investee has net income:

> DR: Equity Method Investment
> CR: Equity Method Income

b. Entry made by the investor if the investee has net loss:

> DR: Equity Method Loss
> CR: Equity Method Investment

i. If investee losses reduce the investment to zero, the investor should discontinue applying the equity method unless the investee's imminent return to profitability is assured.

Note on Fair Value Option
If the investor elects to use the fair value option to report an investment that otherwise would be accounted for using the equity method, the investor does **not** recognize its share of the investee's results of operation. The investee's results of operation are assumed to be reflected in the change in fair value of the investment (which is recognized in net income).

c. **Investee's other comprehensive income (OCI)**

If the investee reports changes to equity resulting from items of other comprehensive income, the investor recognizes its proportionate share of those items when reported by the investee.

i. Items of other comprehensive income that might change equity would include:

a. Unrealized gains/losses on available-for-sale debt securities;

b. Foreign currency items; *and*

c. Pension and postretirement benefit items not recognized in period cost.

ii. Entry (assuming OCI items increased equity):

> DR: Equity Method Investment
> CR: Other Comprehensive Income

2. **Investee's dividends**

a. The investor recognizes its proportionate share of investee dividends as a reduction in its investment in the investee. The entry made by the investor when the investee declares/pays a cash dividend would be:

> DR: Dividends Receivable/Cash
> CR: Equity Method Investment

Note on Fair Value Option

If the investor elects to use the fair value option to report an investment that otherwise would be accounted for using the equity method, the investor recognizes the investee's cash dividends as dividend income in earnings.

3. Investee's book value does not equal investment cost or fair value—If the cost of investment to the investor and the fair value of the investee's net assets is different from the investee's book value at the date of investment, the investor will recognize periodic adjustment(s) to its equity investment account and to the equity investment income account.

    a. Differences between the cost of the investment and the book value of the net assets to which the investment gives the investor a claim may be due to:

        i. The identifiable assets/liabilities carrying values on the books of the investee are different from the fair value of those assets/liabilities at the date of the investment.

        ii. Goodwill was paid for by the investor.

    b. When the fair value of the depreciable assets is greater than the book value of those assets, the investor makes an entry for *depreciation* or *amortization* on its share of fair value in excess of book value as it relates to the identifiable depreciable or amortizable assets. There is **no** amortization of goodwill.

        i. Entry:

> DR: Equity Method Income
>   CR: Equity Method Investment

        ii. The investor does not debit expense but reduces the amount of income picked up from the investee and reduces the carrying amount of the investment.

    c. When the fair value of the depreciable assets is less than the book value of those assets, the investor will recognize a bargain purchase gain.

4. If the goodwill associated with the acquisition of the equity investee is impaired, the investor should record that impairment in its equity method accounting.

    a. Entry:

> DR: Equity Method Income
>   CR: Equity Method Investment

Note on Fair Value Option

If the investor elects to use the fair value option to report an equity investment that otherwise would be accounted for using the equity method, the investor does **not** record the entries that are part of the normal equity method accounting. The investment is reported at fair value with the changes in fair value recognized in net income.

Example

Continuing our example of P Company's (P) acquisition of 20% of S Corp. (S) on July 1 for $500,000. Assume that S had a profit of $400,000 for the year, and it was earned evenly throughout the year. In addition, S paid dividends of $300,000 on December 31.

	January 1 to July 1	December 31
Income	$200,000	$200,000
Dividends		$300,000

What would be the equity method entries and T-accounts recorded by P during the year of acquisition?

To record P's share of S's earnings ($200,000 income for July – December) × 20% = $40,000:

DR: Equity Method Investment	$40,000	
CR: Equity Method Income		$40,000

To record P's share of S's dividends: ($300,000 dividends paid on December 31) × 20% = $60,000:

DR: Cash	$60,000	
CR: Equity Method Investment		$60,000

To record P's share of the depreciation of the excess fair value: ($60,000 / 5 years) × ½ year = $6,000:

DR: Equity Method Income	$6,000	
CR: Equity Method Investment		$6,000

The entries above are also presented in the next T-accounts. T-accounts are a great tool to solve CPA Exam questions quickly.

Equity method investment (on balance sheet)

Original cost of investment **$500,000**	Depreciation of cost in excess of book value **$6,000**
Pro rata share of investee's income since acquisition **$40,000**	Pro rata share of investee's dividends declared **$60,000**
Ending balance **$474,000**	

Equity Method Income (on Income Statement)

Depreciation of cost in excess of book value **$6,000**	Pro rata share of investee's income since acquisition **$40,000**
	Ending balance **$34,000**

V. Purchase or Sale of Equity Method Investment

A. If prior ownership with no significant influence is followed by additional purchase of equity shares resulting in significant influence, then a change to equity method accounting will occur when the entity switches from fair value to equity method accounting. A change to the equity method accounting is accounted for **prospectively**.

B. In a sale of all or part of an investment accounted for using the equity method, first update the equity method accounts to date of sale by recording:

1. Investor's share of the investee's income or loss to date of sale.

2. Investor's share of the investee's dividends declared or paid to the date of sale.

3. Investor's depreciation or amortization on of the excess cost over book value to date of sale.

C. The gain or loss on the sale is the difference between selling price (SP) and book (carrying) value (BV) of the equity investment sold.

1. If SP > BV = Realize gain.

2. If SP < BV = Realize loss.

D. If the sale is not for entire investment and results in the investor losing significant influence over the investee (e.g., < 20% ownership), the remaining investment should be accounted for at fair value with any difference between the carrying amount of the remaining investment and its fair value recognized as a gain or loss in current income.

VI. Equity Method Disclosures

When the equity method is used to report investments in common stock, the following disclosures are appropriate:

A. The name of each equity method investee and the percentage of ownership.

B. The name of any investee in which the investor owns 20% or more (but not more than 50%) of the voting stock that is not accounted for using the equity method and the reason for that treatment.

C. The name of any investee in which the investor owns less than 20% of the voting stock that is accounted for using the equity method and the reason for that treatment.

D. Any difference between the carrying amount of the investment and the investor's share of the underlying claim to net assets and how that difference is treated.

E. When a bargain purchase gain is recognized, the amount of the gain recognized, the line item where the gain is recognized and a description of the transaction that resulted in the gain.

F. When there is a quoted market price for the common stock, the market value of each investment.

G. When the equity method is used for investments in corporate joint ventures that are material to the investor, summary information about the assets, liabilities, and results of operation of those joint venture investees.

H. Possible effects of conversion or exercise of outstanding securities (e.g., options, convertible securities, etc.) on the investor's ownership claim.

Investments in Debt Securities

Debt Investments at Fair Value

This lesson covers investments in debt securities when the investor accounts for the investment at fair value. Investments in debt securities reported at fair value are classified as either (1) trading with changes in fair value recorded in earnings or (2) available-for-sale with changes in fair value recorded in other comprehensive income.

After studying this lesson, you should be able to:

1. Determine whether a security meets the definition of a debt security.

2. Evaluate when an investment in a debt security should be classified as a trading or available-for-sale investment.

3. Demonstrate the accounting for a debt security classified as a trading investment.

4. Demonstrate the accounting for a debt security classified as an available-for-sale investment

I. Investments in Debt Securities

A. ASU 2016-01, *Financial Instruments—Overall: Recognition and Measurement of Financial Assets and Financial Liabilities,* significantly changed the accounting for investments. ASU 2016-01 established separate guidance on the accounting for investments in equity and debt securities. Accounting Standards Codification (ASU) 320 is the codified guidance on the accounting and reporting of a debt security.

Definition

Debt securities: Securities that represent the right of buyer/holder (the creditor) to receive from the issuer (the debtor) a principal amount at a specified future date and (generally) to receive interest as payment for providing use of funds.

- Includes bonds, notes, convertible bonds/notes, redeemable preferred stock, and investments in debt securities that result from the securitization of other financial instruments.

- Excludes common/preferred stock, stock warrants, and any derivative financial instruments such as options/rights, futures/forward contracts.

B. **Classifications of Investments in Debt Securities**

1. Upon acquisition of the investment in debt securities, the investor must document the classification of the investment into one of three categories: trading, available-for-sale, or held-to-maturity. This lesson presents the accounting and reporting for trading and available-for-sale.

   a. Investments in debt securities that are reported at fair value are classified as either trading or available-for-sale investments.

2. The entity must review the classification of the investment in debt securities on an annual basis to determine if the classification is appropriate or if a change in classification is warranted.

> **Note**
> The categories of trading or available-for-sale apply only to debt securities and not to equity securities.

II. Trading Classification

A debt security must be classified as trading when it is acquired with the intent to sell in the near term (hours or days). That is, the investor buys and holds the security for the purpose of selling in the near term with the objective of generating profits from short-term price changes. However, the investor can classify securities in this category even though the investor does not intend to sell in the near term.

A. **Measurement**—Investments in debt securities that are classified as trading are measured and reported at **fair value** with the changes in the fair value recorded in **earnings**.

   1. Initially record the investment in the debt security at the price paid. Usually this is the present value of its future cash flows as of the date of the investment.

   2. A valuation account (contra or adjunct) typically is not used when the debt security is classified as trading. A debt security classified as trading is one that will be sold in the near term and is highly liquid. There is no need to keep track of changes in fair value using a valuation account.

B. **Interest income**, including the amortization of any premium or discount on the investment, is recorded in net income.

   1. Record the periodic interest income along with any amortization of the premium or discount first, then calculate the unrealized gain or loss as the difference between the carrying value of the debt and its fair value. The unrealized gain or loss is recorded in net income, and the investment is adjusted to fair value.

C. **Impairment**—There are no impairment losses on investments in debt securities classified as trading. Trading securities are recorded at fair value with the unrealized gains or losses already included in net income.

D. **Financial Statement Presentation**

   1. Trading investments in debt securities usually are presented in the **balance sheet** as a current asset. However, in some instances, management can make a case to report them as noncurrent. Classification as noncurrent should be rare since noncurrent is not consistent with the definition of a trading security held for sale in the near term.

   2. The unrealized holding gains and losses and the interest income (net of any amortization of a premium or discount) is reported in **net income**.

   3. **Cash flows** associated with trading investments in debt securities typically are presented in the statement of cash flows as operating activities. The very nature of trading securities, indicates that part of the entity's operations is to regularly buy and sell securities. If the trading investments are not part of the entity's core operations, then those cash flows are classified as investing activities.

Example
Investment in Debt Securities, Classified as Trading

   1. *Investment in Bond Purchased at Par*
      Assume on January 1, 20X1 the entity purchases a 2-year, $100,000 bond, with a 10% semiannual stated rate, at 10%.

PV of principal ($100,000, 4 periods, 5%)	
Factor = .82270	$ 82,270
PV of interest ($5,000, 4 periods, 5%)	
Factor = 3.546	17,730
Purchase price:	$100,000

Entry on January 1, 20X1, the purchase date:

DR: Investment in debt security—Trading	100,000	
CR: Cash		100,000

Entry on July 1, 20X1, to record interest income ($100,000 × 10% × ½):

CR: Cash	5,000	
CR: Interest income		5,000

Assume on July 1, 20X1, the fair value of the bond is $96,000. The following entry would be made to adjust the investment in the bond to fair value.

DR: Unrealized loss (income statement)   4,000
    CR: Investment in debt security—Trading   4,000
[The carrying value (100,000) is more than fair value (96,000), resulting in a 4,000 unrealized loss.]

The investment in debt securities—Trading would be presented as a current asset on the balance sheet at fair value as follows:

Investment in debt security—Trading $ 96,000

Assume on December 31, 20X1 the fair value of the bond is $97,000. The following entry would be made to adjust the investment in the bond to fair value.

DR: Investment in debt security—Trading   1,000
    CR: Unrealized gain (income statement)   1,000
[The carrying value (96,000) is less than fair value (97,000).
A 1,000 unrealized gain will adjust the investment to fair value.]

On December 31, 20X1, the investment in debt securities—Trading would be presented as a current asset on the balance sheet at fair value as follows:

Investment in debt security—Trading $ 97,000

Assume on January 1, 20X2 the investment in the debt security was sold for $97,500. The entry to record the sale would recognize a realized gain of $500 because the carrying value of the security at the last balance sheet date is $97,000.

DR: Cash   97,500
    CR: Realized gain on the sale of trading investment   500
    CR: Investment in debt security—Trading   97,000

Note

The unrealized gain or loss on a trading security are recognized in the income statement over the period of ownership. The gains or losses during the holding period are unrealized because the security is not yet sold, but those gains and losses parallel the movement in the fair value of the security during each reporting period.

The realized gains or losses is the difference between the carrying value reflecting the most recent fair value adjustment and the fair value on the date sold. In our example, the $500 gain is considered realized in the period the sale occurred. The overall loss was $2,500 (from purchase of $100,000 to sale for $97,500). The change in fair value is spread over the two reporting years with $3,000 unrealized loss in 20X1 and $500 realized gain in 20X2.

The accounting recognition of the realized/unrealized gains or losses is consistent with the classification of the security as "trading," which implies a sale is anticipated in the near term. Until the point that the owner sells the security, the changes in the fair value of the security are not realized (but are recognized!).

Example
Investment in Debt Securities, Classified as Trading

2. *Investment in Bond Purchased at a Discount*

Assume on January 1, 20X1 an entity purchased a 2-year, $100,000 bond, with a 10% semiannual rate, at 12%.

PV of principal ($100,000, 4 periods, 6%)	$79,209
Factor = .79209	
PV of interest ($5,000, 4 periods, 6%)	17,326
Factor = 3.46511	
Purchase price:	$96,535

Below is the amortization schedule for the bond investment.

	Beginning carrying value	Discount	Interest income	Cash received	Amort.	Ending carrying value	Fair value
7/1/X1	96,535	3,465	5,792	5,000	792	97,327	98,500
12/31/X1	97,327	2,673	5,840	5,000	840	98,167	99,000
7/1/X2	98,167	1,833	5,890	5,000	890	99,057	97,000
12/31/X2	99,057	943	5,943	5,000	943	100,000	99,500
Totals			23,465	20,000	3,465		

Entry on January 1, 20X1, the purchase date:

DR: Investment in debt security—Trading	100,000	
CR: Discount on debt security—Trading		3,465
CR: Cash		96,535

Interest income and amortization on July 1, 20X1, the first 6-month period:

DR: Cash	5,000	
DR: Discount on debt security—Trading	792	
CR: Interest income		5,792

Entry to record the fair value adjustment as of July 1, 20X1:

DR: Investment in debt security—Trading	1,173	
CR: Unrealized gain (income statement)		1,173

[The fair value (98,500) is greater than the carrying value of 97,327 (96,535 + 792), resulting in a 1,173 unrealized gain.]

The investment in debt securities—Trading would be presented as a current asset on the balance sheet at fair value as follows:

Investment in debt security—Trading	$101,173
Unamortized discount	(2,673)
Investment in debt security—Trading	$ 98,500

Interest income on December 31, 20X1, the second 6-month period:

DR: Cash	5,000	
DR: Discount on debt security—Trading	840	
CR: Interest income		5,840

Entry to record the fair value adjustment as of December 31, 20X1:

DR: Unrealized loss (income statement)	340	
CR: Investment in debt security—Trading		340

[The fair value (99,000) is less than the carrying value of 99,340 (98,500 plus 840). Therefore, on December 31, 20X1, an unrealized loss of 340 must be recorded.]

The investment in debt securities—Trading would be presented as a current asset on the December 31, 20X1, balance sheet at fair value as follows:

Investment in debt security—Trading	$100,833
Unamortized discount	(1,833)
Investment in debt security—Trading	$ 99,000

III. Available-for-Sale (AFS) Classification

If there is no evidence of positive ability and intent to hold the bond investment to maturity and the entity does not intend to trade the security in the near term, the bond investment is classified as available-for-sale (AFS).

A. A bond investment classified as AFS is reported at **fair value** with the unrealized gains and losses associated with the changes in fair value recorded as an **unrealized holding gain or loss in comprehensive income**.

Note

A valuation account will be used to constantly adjust the carrying amount of the investment in debt securities to fair value. Therefore, you will need to keep track of the carrying value of the debt securities (face amount plus or minus any premium or discount) and the balance in the valuation account. Adjust the valuation account so that debt security is presented at fair value. (See the next example.)

B. The **interest income** on the bond investment (including any amortization of the bond discount or premium) is reported in net income. The interest income entry is the same as when the investment is accounted for as a trading security. After the interest income and bond amortization are recorded, the investment in the bond would be adjusted to fair value.

C. The adjustment to fair value will be shown using the same fact pattern presented above where the bond was purchased at a discount for $96,535, and at the end of the first 6-month period the fair value of the bond is $98,500.

Note

If the fair value option was elected, the debt security still would be reported at fair value, but the unrealized gains and losses would be recognized in earnings rather than in OCI

1. The unrealized gain on the change in the fair value of the bond investment is recorded in other comprehensive income as shown below. Note that the fair value adjustment to the investment account on the balance sheet is achieved by using a contra or adjunct account to adjust the unamortized value of the bond to fair value.

Example
Investment in Debt Securities, Classified as AFS

1. **Investment in Bond Purchased at a Discount**
   Assume on January 1, 20X1 an entity purchased a 2-year, $100,000 bond, with a 10% semiannual rate, at 12%.

PV of principal ($100,000, 4 periods, 6%)	$79,209
Factor = .79209	
PV of interest ($5,000, 4 periods, 6%)	17,326
Factor = 3.46511	
Purchase price	$96,535

Below is the amortization schedule for the bond investment.

	Beginning carrying value	Discount	Interest income	Cash received	Amort.	Ending carrying value	Fair value
7/1/X1	96,535	3,465	5,792	5,000	792	97,327	98,500
12/31/X1	97,327	2,673	5,840	5,000	840	98,167	99,000
7/1/X2	98,167	1,833	5,890	5,000	890	99,057	97,000
12/31/X2	99,057	943	5,943	5,000	943	100,000	99,500
Totals			23,465	20,000	3,465		

Entry on January 1, 20X1, the purchase date:

DR: Investment in debt security—AFS	100,000	
CR: Discount on debt security—AFS		3,465
CR: Cash		96,535

Interest income and amortization on July 1, 20X1, the first 6-month period:

DR: Cash	5,000	
DR: Discount on debt security—AFS	792	
CR: Interest income		5,792

Entry to record the fair value adjustment as of July 1, 20X1:

DR: Fair value adjustment – AFS debt security	1,173	
(balance sheet valuation account)		
CR: Unrealized gain (other comprehensive income)		1,173

[The fair value (98,500) is greater than the carrying value (97,327), resulting in a 1,173 unrealized gain.]

The investment in debt securities—AFS would be presented on the balance sheet at fair value as follows:

Investment in debt security–AFS	$100,000
Unamortized discount	(2,673)
Fair value adjustment	1,173
Investment in debt security–AFS	$ 98,500

Interest income on December 31, 20X1, the second 6-month period:

DR: Cash	5,000	
DR: Discount on debt security—AFS	840	
CR: Interest income		5,840

Entry to record the fair value adjustment as of December 31, 20X1:

DR: Unrealized loss (OCI)	340	
CR: Fair value adjustment—AFS debt security		340
(balance sheet valuation account)		

[The fair value (99,000) is less than the carrying value (99,340)
(98,167 plus the fair value adjustment 1,173). Therefore, on
December 31, 20X1, an unrealized loss of 340 must be recorded.]

The investment in debt securities—AFS would be presented on the December 31, 20X1, balance sheet at fair value as follows:

Investment in debt security—AFS	$100,000
Unamortized discount	(1,833)
Fair value adjustment (1,173 – 340)	833
Investment in debt security–AFS	$ 99,000

D. General guidance on adjustments to investments in debt securities classified as AFS follows.

1. Determine fair value of the AFS debt investments.

2. Determine carrying value of the AFS debt investments.

3. Adjusting the AFS debt investments to fair value.

   a. If the fair value is greater than the carrying value:

      i. Recognize an unrealized holding gain.

      ii. The gain is recorded in other comprehensive income.

   b. If the fair value is less than the carrying value:

      i. Recognize an unrealized holding loss.

      ii. The loss is recognized in other comprehensive income, **and the investment security is assessed for impairment**.

E. If the decline in the fair value of the AFS debt security is below the amortized cost, the security is impaired. The entity must determine how much of the impairment is due to credit loss and how much of the impairment is due to other factors.

F. Credit Loss of an Investment in a Debt Security Classified as AFS,

1. When the fair value of the debt security is less than its amortized cost basis, the entity (investor) must determine if the decline in fair value below amortized cost will be realized and if the decline is the result of credit loss (entity specific credit decline) or other factors (general market conditions).

   a. If the entity intends to sell (or is more likely than not required to sell) the debt security before recovery of the amortized cost, the entity will essentially realize the loss and must determine if any of the loss is due to the deterioration of the credit of the issuer (credit loss).

b. The portion of the decline in fair value that is associated with credit loss is reported in a valuation allowance (a contra account) to the AFS debt investment, and a credit loss expense is recognized in earnings, *not* in other comprehensive income (OCI). The amount of the impairment loss that is not associated with.credit loss is reported in OCI. The entry to establish the allowance associated with the credit loss is:

DR: Credit loss expense

CR: Allowance for credit loss

2. The amount of the allowance for credit loss is limited to the excess of the amortized cost of the debt investment over its fair value. Fair value is the floor to write down the AFS security because it is presumed that the AFS security could be sold at fair value rather than collect the future cash flows. The credit loss can be measured at the individual security level or based on an aggregation of debt securities that share similar risk characteristics.

3. The entity determines whether a credit loss exists by comparing the present value of the cash flows expected to be collected from the security to the security's amortized cost. The estimated cash flows should include factors based on past events, current conditions, and reasonable (and supportable) forecasts. The credit loss is the excess of amortized cost over the present value of the expected cash flows.

Example

Assume that Westin Company holds an investment in a debt security classified as AFS that has a $100,000 principal and unamortized discount of $943, or a net unamortized cost of $99,057. Also assume that the fair value of the security is $97,000. Assume that it is more likely than not that Westin will be required to sell the debt security before the amortized cost can be recovered. Westin must determine if any of the decline in fair value is attributed to a deterioration in the credit of the issuer of the debt security or general market factors. Assume that Westin determines that 60% of the decline is attributed to general market conditions and 40% is attributed to credit factors associated with the issuer.

Investment in debt security—AFS	$100,000
Unamortized discount	(943)
	99,057
Fair value of the security	97,000
Adjustment needed	$ (2,057)

Fair value decline attributed to general conditions $2,057 × .6 = $1,234 (rounded)

Fair value decline attributed to credit $2,057 × .4 = $ 823 (rounded)

The portion of the decline in fair value associated with the decline in credit ($823) is recorded in the allowance for credit loss and recognized in earnings as credit loss expense.

DR: Credit loss expense   823

  CR: Allowance for credit loss   823

The remaining portion of the decline in fair value associated with other factors ($1,234) is recorded as a fair value adjustment and is recognized in other comprehensive income.

DR: Unrealized loss—OCI   1,234

  CR: Fair value adjustment—AFS debt security   1,234

The investment in the AFS debt security would be presented as follows:

Investment in debt security—AFS	$100,000
Unamortized discount	(943)
	99,057
Allowance for credit loss	(823)
Fair value adjustment	(1,234)
Reported value	$ 97,000

4. At each reporting date, the entity must reassess if there is any additional decline in fair value attributed to credit loss and, if so, adjust the allowance for credit loss. The adjustment will result in additional credit loss expense or a reversal of credit loss expense.

   a. The reversal of a credit loss is limited to the balance in the allowance for credit loss account. That is, the allowance for credit losses is a contra account (credit balance) intended to reflect deteriorated credit value associated with the debt investment. The balance cannot go below zero. The allowance for credit loss can never be an adjunct account (debt balance) that would increase the value of the debt investment.

   b. The entity must use consistent valuation estimation methodology applied to the same pool of investments. Any changes in methodology or aggregation of investments must be disclosed.

5. If the entity determines that it will not recover the loss associated with credit loss, the entity must write off any credit losses in the allowance and reduce the basis of the security. The write-off will result in a new amortized cost basis for the security and cannot be adjusted for subsequent recoveries.

   DR: Allowance for credit loss

   CR: Investment in debt security—AFS

6. The entity must present the investment in debt securities classified as AFS at fair value on the balance sheet and disclose the amortized cost basis and the allowance for credit losses. The entity must also disclose information about the allowance for credit loss so that financial statement users can understand the estimation method used, significant inputs, and circumstances that caused a change in the allowance.

G. Financial Statement Presentation

1. AFS investments in debt securities are presented in the balance sheet as a current and/or noncurrent asset, depending on management's intent.

2. AFS investments in debt securities are presented in the statement of cash flows as investing activities.

H. Disposition (sale) of an AFS Investment in Debt Securities

1. First recognize interest income and amortization of premium or discount to date of sale.

2. Determine carrying value of investment to be sold.

3. Recognize any gain or loss at date of sale, if any, as difference between sales price and carrying value of investments sold.

4. Any related unrealized holding gain or loss on securities sold that is in accumulated other comprehensive income at the date of sale is recognized in income.

Example
Sale of Debt Security Classified as AFS

Investment in Bond Purchased at a Discount

Continuing with the fact pattern presented in the earlier example, assume on January 2, 20X2, the **investment in the debt security classified as AFS was sold for $97,500**. The entry to record the sale would recognize a realized loss of $667 comprised of the $1,500 difference between the carrying value ($99,000) and the selling price ($97,500) plus the unrealized gain of $833 in OCI.

Record the sale on January 2, 20X2:

DR: Cash	97,500
DR: Discount on debt security—AFS	1,833
DR: Unrealized gain (other comprehensive income)	833
DR: Realized loss (income statement)	667
CR: Investment in debt security—AFS	100,000
CR: Fair value adjustment—	833
AFS security	
(balance sheet valuation account)	

Debt Investments at Amortized Cost

This lesson presents the criteria necessary for an investment in debt securities to be classified as held-to-maturity and the accounting and financial statement reporting for this investment. Coverage includes recognition of a premium or discount at the time of investment, the amortization of a premium or discount, financial statement presentation, and disposition of held-to-maturity investments.

After studying this lesson, you should be able to:

1. Describe the criteria for classifying investments in debt securities as held-to-maturity.

2. Demonstrate the accounting and reporting for investments in debt securities classified as held-to-maturity.

I. **Classification of Held-to-Maturity Investments**

This classification includes investments in debt securities that the investor intends to hold until the investment matures and has the ability to do so.

A. **Criteria for This Classification**

1. Applies only to investments in **debt** securities because only debt has a maturity.

2. Applies when investor has:

a. *Positive* intent to hold the securities to maturity; and

b. *Ability* to hold the securities to maturity.

3. Held-to-maturity classification is not appropriate if investor may sell due to need for cash or better investment opportunities, or if the debt can be settled (e.g., prepaid) and the investor would not recover all of the recorded investment.

4. Sale of debt securities before maturity that meet the following conditions can be considered held-to-maturity (HTM).

a. Sale is near enough to maturity date so that interest rate risk is substantially eliminated as a factor in pricing.

b. Sale occurs after investor has collected (through periodic payments or prepayment) a substantial portion (at least 85%) of the principal outstanding at acquisition date.

II. **Accounting and Reporting for an HTM Investment**

A. Record investment at cost:

1. Cost includes the purchase price (e.g., per security cost).

2. Carry and report held-to-maturity investments at amortized cost:

a. Recognize periodic interest income.

B. If the bond investment was purchased at a premium and the bond is callable by the issuer, then the bond premium must be amortized to the earliest call date.

1. Because the bond investment can be called (redeemed) by the issuer, ASC 320-20 requires the investor to amortize the premium on the bond investment to the earliest call date, not over the life of the bond.

2. Amortizing a premium to the earliest call date more closely aligns the amortization period with that of the market. Market measures of the bond issued at a premium factor in the impact of the call feature, and amortization to the earliest call date approximates the market's valuation.

C. The next example is the amortization schedule and accounting for a bond investment purchased at a premium where there is no call feature.

1. Note that the fact pattern for this bond is the same fact pattern as the example in the "Bond Accounting Principles" lesson when the entity is the issuer/lender. We recommend that you compare and contrast the accounting for a bond when the entity is the investor (as in this lesson) to when the entity is the issuer/lender (in the "Bond Accounting Principles" lesson).

Example

Investment in Debt Security Classified as HTM Bond Purchased at a Premium

Assume on January 1, 20X1, Haun Company purchased a 2-year, $100,000 bond, with a 10% semiannual stated rate, at 8%.

PV of principal ($100,000 4 periods, 4%) $ 85,480
Factor = .8548

PV of interest ($5,000, 4 periods, 4%)   18,150
Factor = 3.6299

Purchase price $103,630

Below is the amortization schedule for the bond investment:

	Beginning carrying value	Premium	Interest income	Cash received	Amort.	Ending carrying value
7/1/X1	103,630	3,630	4,145	5,000	855	102,775
12/31/X1	102,775	2,775	4,111	5,000	889	101,886
7/1/X2	101,886	1,886	4,075	5,000	925	100,961
12/31/X2	100,961	961	4,039	5,000	961	100,000
Totals			16,370	20,000	3,630	

Entry on January 1, 20X1, the purchase date:

DR: Investment in debt security—HTM   100,000
DR: Premium on debt security—HTM   3,630
　　CR: Cash   103,630

Interest income and amortization of premium on July 1, 20X1, for first 6-month period:

DR: Cash   5,000
　　CR: Premium on debt security—HTM   855
　　CR: Interest Income   4,145

The investment in debt securities—HTM would be presented on the balance sheet at amortized cost as follows:

Investment in debt security—HTM $100,000
Unamortized premium   2,775
Investment in debt security—HTM $102,775

III. Current Expected Credit Loss of an Investment in a Debt Security Classified as HTM

A. ASU 326-20 provides guidance on the measurement of credit losses on financial instruments classified as HTM. This guidance is referred to as the current expected credit loss (CECL) model. CECL replaces the impairment model that was based on actual or incurred losses. The CECL model measures all expected credit losses for the financial asset as of each balance sheet date and is based on historical experience, current conditions, and reasonable (and supportable) forecasts.

B. At each balance sheet date, a valuation allowance for credit loss is estimated and deducted from the amortized cost basis of the HTM debt security. The allowance will result in a reported value that represents the net amount the entity expects to collect. The valuation allowance is a contra account to the HTM debt investment, and a credit loss expense is recognized in earnings. The entry to establish the allowance is:

DR: Credit loss expense

CR: Allowance for credit loss

C. The amount reported on the balance sheet for the HTM debt investment includes the debt principal, the unamortized premium or discount, and the credit loss valuation account. For example, using the information from the example above, assume a $100,000 HTM debt investment, an unamortized premium of $2,775, and a credit valuation allowance of $1,500; the net amount reported on the balance sheet would be $101,275. The $101,275 represents the net amount expected to be collected from the investment.

Investment in debt security—HTM	$100,000
Unamortized premium	2,775
Allowance for credit loss	(1,500)
Net investment in debt security—HTM	$101,275

D. To measure the expected credit loss, an entity can aggregate the HTM debt investments that share similar risk characteristics or estimate the expected credit loss on an individual investment basis. Various methodologies can be used to estimate the credit loss, including discounted cash flows over the contractual term of the investment.

E. At each reporting date, the entity reestimates the amount expected to be collected and adjusts the allowance for credit loss. The adjustment will result in additional credit loss expense or a reversal of credit loss expense.

1. A reversal of a credit loss is limited to the balance in the allowance for credit loss account. That is, the allowance for credit losses is a contra account (credit balance) intended to reflect deteriorated credit value associated with the debt investment. The allowance for credit losses is not an adjunct account (debt balance), which would increase the value of the debt investment.

2. Each reporting period, the entity must use consistent valuation estimation methodology applied to the same pool of investments. Any changes in methodology or aggregation of investments must be disclosed.

F. An HTM debt investment is written off when it is deemed uncollectible. To the extent that the write-off is associated with the credit allowance, the write-off of a debt investment is deducted from the allowance for credit loss account.

DR: Allowance for credit loss

CR: Investment in debt security—HTM

G. The entity must disclose enough information about the allowance for credit loss so that financial statement users can understand the estimation method used, significant inputs, and circumstances that caused a change in the allowance.

IV. **Financial Statement Reporting of Investment in Debt Securities—HTM**

A. Interest income or revenue (including increase/decrease from amortization of discount or premium) is recorded in **net income**.

B. The HTM investment (net of premium or discount) will be reported in the **balance sheet** as

1. **Current**—if maturity is within one year (or operating cycle) of the balance sheet date;

2. **Noncurrent**—if maturity is **not** within one year (or operating cycle) of the balance sheet date.

C. HTM investments in debt securities are presented in the **statement of cash flows** as investing activities.

Investor Stock Dividends, Splits, and Rights

An investor who holds an equity investment in another entity may receive a stock dividend, have the stock split, or receive a right to acquire additional shares. This lesson describes each of these possibilities and summarizes the accounting treatment from the perspective of the investor—the recipient of the stock dividend, split, or right.

After studying this lesson, you should be able to:

1. Complete the calculation and accounting entries for a stock dividend received by an investor.

2. Complete the calculation and accounting entries for a stock split received by an investor.

3. Complete the calculation and accounting entries for a stock right received by an investor.

I. Stock Dividends Received by Investor

A. A stock dividend is when an investor receives additional shares of an investee stock. Unlike a cash dividend, a stock dividend is not income but additional ownership of the entity.

B. When the stock dividend is received, the investor adjusts the **per share** (not total) carrying value of the equity investment. The investor will own additional shares, and therefore the stock dividend will reduce the per share cost basis of the stock.

C. Upon sale of the shares (in part or total), the shares will be removed at new per share carrying value, and any gain or loss will be the difference between the selling price and the new per share value.

Example
Assume Duke Company held the following equity investment in HIKE Corp.

Investment in HIKE Corp	$100,000
Original number of shares	1,000
Per share value ($100,000/1,000)	$100

Now assume that HIKE Corp declared a 10% stock dividend. That means that Duke Company would receive 100 additional shares (1,000 shares × 10%).

The new per share value = $100,000/1,100 shares	$90.90

Now assume that Duke sold 500 shares of HIKE for $110 per share. The gain on the sale would be $9,550 (($110 – $90.90) × 500 shares). The entry would be:

DR: Cash ($110 × 500)	$55,000	
CR: Investment in HIKE Corp		45,450
CR: Gain on sale of investment		9,550

II. Stock Split Received by Investor

A. In a stock split, an investor receives additional shares of the equity investee's stock. An example would be a 2-for-1 split (double the number of shares are owned but at the same value.) When received, a stock split is not income but is additional ownership of the entity. When the stock subsequently is sold, the investor would recognize gain or loss.

    B. Just as in the stock dividend, when the stock split is received, the investor adjusts the **per share** (not total) carrying value of the equity investment. The investor will own additional shares, and therefore the stock split will reduce the per share cost basis of the stock. No journal entry is recorded for a stock dividend or a stock split.

        1. The difference from the stock dividend to the stock split is from the issuer's perspective. The split increases the shares outstanding and reduced the per share par value. A stock dividend increases the shares outstanding but does not reduce the per share par value.

    C. In a reverse stock split, the investor exchanges shares held for fewer shares of the investee. This is rarer, and the reverse split would state-for-3, where the investor would have one third the shares previously held. From the issuer's perspective, par or stated value per share would increase.

> **Note**
> In both a stock split or a reverse stock split, the investor adjusts only per share (not total) cost (carrying value) of investment.

III. Stock Rights Received by Investor

    A. A stock right gives the investor the privilege (right) to purchase additional shares of investee at specific price (strike price) within a specific time. Like stock dividends and splits, stock rights are not income when received.

        1. If the strike price is less than the fair value of the stock, the stock right has a value (in-the-money).

        2. The value of the right is determined by allocating the carrying value of the investment between the shares of stock owned and stock rights received based on their relative fair value.

    B. **Allocation of Value to Rights**

    When the per share fair value of the stock right is known, calculate the value allocated to the stock rights and stock using the formula below:

$$\frac{\text{MV of 1 right}}{\text{MV of stock without right plus MV of 1 right}} \times \frac{\text{Carrying value of}}{\text{investment}} = \frac{\text{Total value}}{\text{of rights}}$$

$$\frac{\text{Total value of rights}}{\text{Number of rights received}} = \text{Per share value of rights}$$

    C. Once the value of the stock rights is calculated, transfer the value of the rights from the equity investment to the investment in stock rights

> DR: Equity Investment in Stock Rights
>   CR: Equity Investment

    D. **Disposition of Stock Rights**

        1. **If sold**, write off the stock rights and recognize a gain/loss.

> DR: Cash
>   CR: Equity Investment in Stock Rights
>   CR: Gain on Sale of Stock Rights

2. **If exercised**, remove the stock rights and record the additional shares purchased with the rights.

DR: Equity Investment
    CR: Equity Investment in Stock Rights
    CR: Cash

3. **If allowed to lapse**, write off the stock rights and recognize a loss.

DR: Loss on Expiration of Stock Rights
    CR: Equity Investment in Stock Rights

Comparison and Transfers of Investments

This lesson presents a side-by-side comparison of the accounting models for investments in equity and debt securities. Investments in equity securities are reported at (1) fair value with changes in fair value reported in net income, (2) at cost, or (3) using the equity method of accounting. Investments in debt securities are reported either at (1) fair value and classified as (a) trading with changes in fair value recorded in earnings or (b) available-for-sale with changes in fair value recorded in other comprehensive income or at (2) amortized cost and classified as held-to-maturity.

After studying this lesson, you should be able to:

1. Demonstrate the accounting for an investment in equity securities at fair value, at cost, and using the equity method of accounting.

2. Compare and contrast the accounting and reporting for equity investment at fair value, at cost, and using the equity method of accounting.

3. Demonstrate the accounting for investments in debt securities reported at fair value classified as a trading or available-for-sale security and debt investments reported at amortized cost.

4. Compare and contrast the accounting and reporting for debt investments at fair value trading, fair value available-for-sale, and at amortized cost.

5. Understand the general rule for transfer of an investment security from one classification to another.

I. Overview of Accounting for Equity Securities: Fair Value, Cost, and Equity Method of Accounting

The diagram below presents an overview of the accounting for equity securities.

Equity Investments

Investments in equity securities are measured at fair value with changes in fair value recognized in net income, except for those with no readily determinable fair value, or result in consolidation, or are accounted for under the equity method of accounting.

< 20% ownership (passive)

Cost method is used when there is no readily determinable fair value and the **practicability exception is elected.**

Applies only to equity investments that do not qualify for using net asset value (NAV) as the practical expedient for fair value.

NAV as a practical expedient: Investees that report its net assets at fair value and that fair value of investee is used to determine the per share value of the investors' ownership.

Initial measurement: Investor's cost.

Subsequent measurement: Cost is reduced for any impairment, (+/-) price changes from any observable transactions for an identical or similar investment. Dividends received are income: Dr: Cash; CR: Dividend income

Presentation: Balance sheet: Current or noncurrent depending on management's intent for holding.

Fair value through net income is used when there is a readily determinable fair value.

Initial measurement: Investor's cost.

Subsequent measurement: Change in fair value is reported as an unrealized holding gain or loss in net income until sold.

Dividends received are income: Dr: Cash; CR: Dividend income

Sale of security: Realized gain or loss is difference between last fair value measurement and selling price.

≥ 20–50% ownership (significant influence)

Equity method of accounting is used when there is significant influence and fair value election is not made.

Initial measurement: Investor's cost.

Subsequent measurement: Equity method accounting which reflects investor's share of investee's earnings and dividends. Adjust for fair value increment at the date of acquisition.

Presentation:
Balance sheet: Noncurrent (generally)

Income statement: Equity method income.

Dividends are NOT income but a reduction of the equity investment.

> 50% ownership (control)

Investor uses equity or cost method to account for investee. For reporting, consolidated financial statements must be prepared.

Separate financial statements of the investor and investee are maintained.

The investor's stand-alone financial statements are not in compliance with GAAP until consolidated.

Presentation: Consolidated financial statements.

II. Numerical Comparison of Accounting Models for Equity Securities

The comparison of the accounting models for equity securities will be based on the same fact pattern to ease comparison. Assume P Corp. purchased 20% of S Inc. for $70,000 on January 1, 20X1. S's results for 20X1, 20X2, and 20X3 are as follows:

	20X1	20X2	20X3
Net Income	$40,000	$35,000	$60,000
Dividends paid	15,000	30,000	20,000
Fair Value:			
January 1	70,000	89,000	86,000
December 31	89,000	86,000	97,000

Fair value: Equity securities with a readily determinable fair value are reported at fair value with unrealized holding gains or losses reported in net income. Using the fair value method requires a fair value adjustment (FVA) entry to adjust the value of the investment to fair value.

Balance Sheet		Income Statement			
Investment in S Debit (Credit)		Unrealized (Gain)/Loss Debit (Credit)		Dividend Income Debit (Credit)	
Purchase	70,000				
FVA 20X1	19,000	FVA 20X1	(19,000)	Dividends 20X1	(3,000)
Balance 20X1	**89,000**	**Balance 20X1**	**(19,000)**	**Balance 20X1**	**(3,000)**
FVA 20X2	(3,000)	FVA 20X2	3,000	Dividends 20X2	(6,000)
Balance 20X2	**86,000**	**Balance 20X2**	**3,000**	**Balance 20X2**	**(6,000)**
FVA 20X3	11,000	FVA 20X3	(11,000)	Dividends 20X3	(4,000)
Balance 20X3	**97,000**	**Balance 20X3**	**(11,000)**	**Balance 20X3**	**(4,000)**

20X1 fair value adjustment (FVA): (89,000 − 70,000) = 19,000 unrealized holding gain

20X2 fair value adjustment (FVA): (89,000 − 86,000) = 3,000 unrealized holding loss

20X3 fair value adjustment (FVA): (86,000 − 97,000) = 11,000 unrealized holding gain

20X1 Dividends: (15,000 × .20) = 3,000

20X2 Dividends: (30,000 × .20) = 6,000

20X3 Dividends: (20,000 × .20) = 4,000

Cost: This method is used when there is < 20% ownership or no significant influence, or there is no readily determinable fair value, or there is no NAV as a practical expedient. Assume there are no indicators of impairment and there are no observable transactions of similar or identical securities.

Balance Sheet		Income Statement	
Investment in S Debit (Credit)		**Dividend Income** Debit (Credit)	
Purchase	70,000	Dividends 20X1	(3,000)
Balance 20X1	**70,000**	**Balance 20X1**	**(3,000)**
		Dividends 20X2	(6,000)
Balance 20X2	**70,000**	**Balance 20X2**	**(6,000)**
		Dividends 20X3	(4,000)
Balance 20X3	**70,000**	**Balance 20X3**	**(4,000)**

20X1 Dividends: (15,000 × .20) = 3,000

20X2 Dividends: (30,000 × .20) = 6,000

20X3 Dividends: (20,000 × .20) = 4,000

Equity method: This method is used when there is ≥ 20% ownership or significant influence and there is no readily determinable fair value.

Balance Sheet		Income Statement	
Investment in S Debit (Credit)		**Equity Method Income** Debit (Credit)	
Purchase	70,000		
20X1 Net Income	8,000	20X1 Net Income	(8,000)
20X1 Dividends	(3,000)		
Balance 20X1	**75,000**	**Balance 20X1**	**(8,000)**
20X2 Net Income	7,000	20X2 Net Income	(7,000)
20X2 Dividends	(6,000)		
Balance 20X2	**76,000**	**Balance 20X2**	**(7,000)**
20X3 Net Income	12,000	20X3 Net Income	(12,000)
20X3 Dividends	(4,000)		
Balance 20X3	**84,000**	**Balance 20X3**	**(12,000)**

20X1 Net Income: (40,000 × .20) = 8,000

20X2 Net Income: (35,000 × .20) = 7,000

20X3 Net Income: (60,000 × .20) = 12,000

20X1 Dividends: (15,000 × .20) = 3,000

20X2 Dividends: (30,000 × .20) = 6,000

20X3 Dividends: (20,000 × .20) = 4,000

III. Overview of Accounting for Debt Securities: Fair Value (Trading and Available-for-Sale) and Amortized Cost (Held-to-Maturity)

The diagram below presents an overview of the accounting for debt securities.

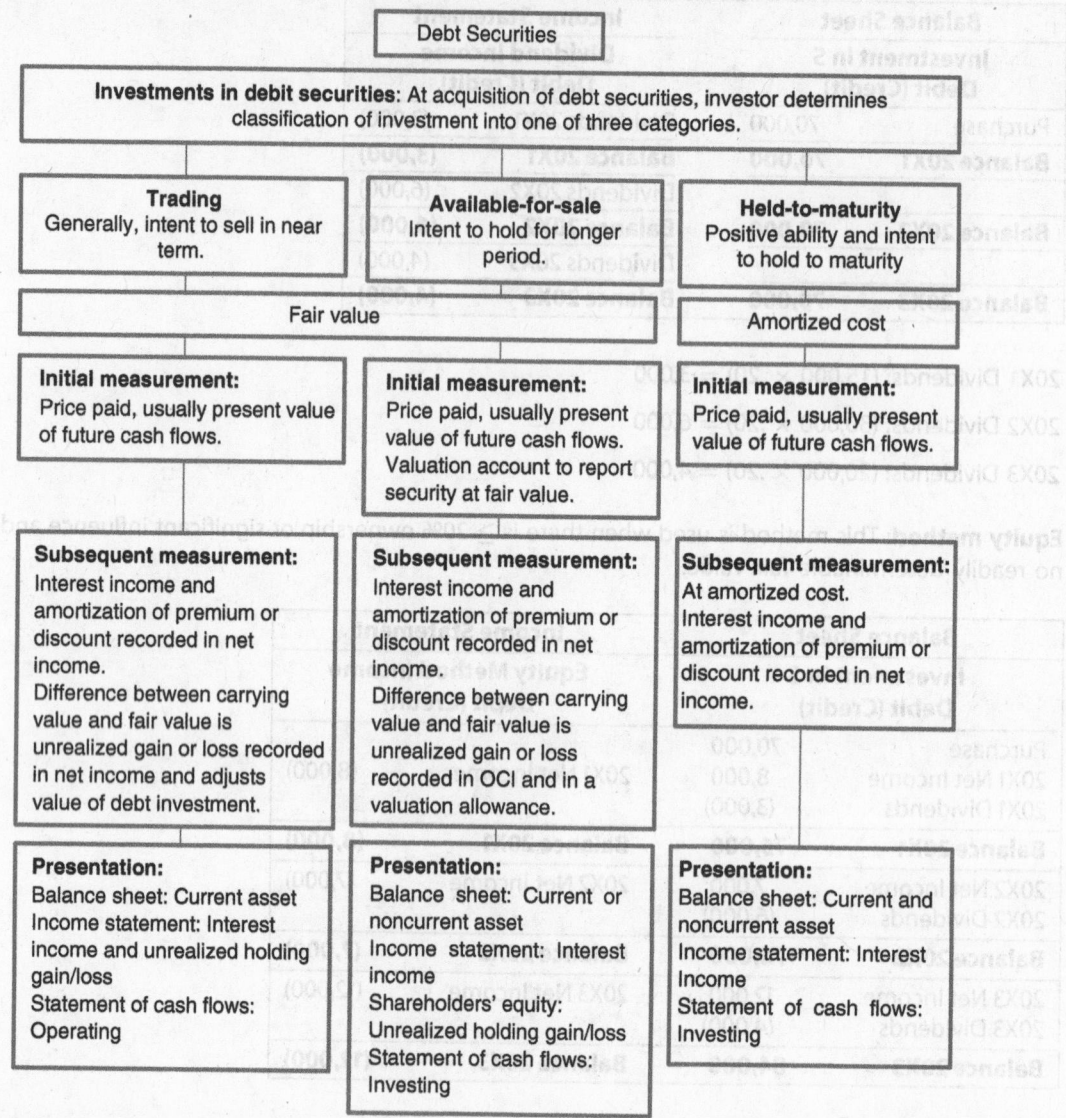

IV. Numerical Comparison of Accounting Models for Debt Securities: Fair Value (Trading and Available-for-Sale) and Amortized Cost (Held-to-Maturity)

Assume on January 1, 20X1 Haun Company purchased a 2-year, $100,000 bond, with a 10% semiannual stated rate, at 8%. Interest is paid on June 30 and December 31 of each year.

PV of principal ($100,000 4 periods, 4%)	$ 85,480
Factor = .8548	
PV of interest ($5,000, 4 periods, 4%)	18,150
Factor = 3.6299	
Purchase price	$103,630

Below is the amortization schedule for the bond investment:

Date	Beginning Carrying Value	Premium	Interest Income	Cash Received	Amort	Ending Carrying Value	Ending Fair Value
June 30, 20X1	103,630	3,630	4,145	5,000	855	102,775	103,000
Dec 31, 20X1	102,775	2,775	4,111	5,000	889	101,886	102,700
June 30, 20X2	101,886	1,886	4,075	5,000	925	100,961	100,500
Dec 31, 20X2	100,961	961	4,039	5,000	961	100,000	100,000

Below is the calculation of the fair value adjustment (FVA):

	Carrying Value (100,000 + Unamortized Premium +/- FVA)	Fair Value	Fair Value Adjustment (FVA)
June 30, 20X1	100,000 + 2,775 + 0 = 102,775	103,000	225
Dec 31, 20X1	100,000 + 1,886 + 225 = 102,111	102,700	589
June 30, 20X2	100,000 + 961 + 814 = 101,775	100,500	(1,275)
Dec 31, 20X2	100,000 + 0 - 461 = 99,539	100,000	461

Assume the investment in the debt security is classified as trading: Debt securities classified as trading are reported at fair value with unrealized holding gains or losses reported in net income. A fair value adjustment (FVA) is made to report the bond at fair value.

Balance Sheet					
Investment in Debt Security Debit (Credit)		Premium on Debt Security Debit (Credit)			Net Fair Value
Purchase	100,000	Purchase		3,630	103,630
June 30, 20X1 FVA	225	June 30, 20X1 Interest		(855)	
Balance June 30, 20X1	**100,225**	**Balance June 30, 20X1**		**2,775**	**103,000**
Dec 31, 20X1 FVA	589	Dec 31, 20X1 Interest		(889)	
Balance December 31, 20X1	**100,814**	**Balance Dec 31, 20X1**		**1,886**	**102,700**
June 30, 20X2 FVA	(1,275)	June 30, 20X2 Interest		(925)	
Balance June 30, 20X2	**99,539**	**Balance June 30, 20X2**		**961**	**100,500**
Dec 31, 20X2 FVA	461	Dec 31, 20X2 Interest		(961)	
Balance Dec 31, 20X2	**100,000**	**Balance Dec 31, 20X2**		**0**	**100,000**

Income Statement			
Unrealized (Gain)/Loss Debit (Credit)		Interest Income Debit (Credit)	
June 30, 20X1 FVA	(225)	June 30, 20X1 Interest	4,145
Dec 31, 20X1 FVA	(589)	Dec 31, 20X1 Interest	4,111
Balance 20X1	**(814)**	**Balance 20X1**	**8,256**
June 30, 20X2 FVA	1,275	June 30, 20X2 Interest	4,075
Dec 31, 20X2 FVA	(461)	Dec 31, 20X2 Interest	4,039
Balance 20X2	**814**	**Balance 20X2**	**8,114**

Assume the investment in the debt security is classified as available-for-sale (AFS): Debt securities classified as AFS are reported at fair value with unrealized holding gains or losses reported in other comprehensive income. In addition, a contra/adjunct account is used on the balance sheet to value the investment at fair value.

Investment in Debt Security Debit (Credit)		Premium on Debt Security Debit (Credit)		FV adjustment— Debt Security Debit (Credit)		Net Fair Value
Purchase	100,000	Purchase	3,630			103,630
		Jun 30, 20X1 Interest	(855)	Jun 30, 20X1 FVA	225	
		Dec 31, 20X1 Interest	(889)	Dec 31, 20X1 FVA	589	
Bal Dec 31, 20X1	100,000	Bal Dec 31, 20X1	1,886	Bal Dec 31, 20X1	814	102,700
		Jun 30, 20X2 Interest	(925)	June 30, 20X2 FVA	(1,275)	
		Dec 31, 20X2 Interest	(961)	Dec 31, 20X2 FVA	461	
Bal Dec 31, 20X2	100,000	Bal Dec 31, 20X2	0	Bal Dec 31, 20X2	0	100,000

Assume the investment in the debt security is classified as held-to-maturity (HTM): Debt securities classified as HTM are reported at amortized cost. There is no adjustment to fair value.

Investment in Debt Security Debit (Credit)		Premium on Debt Security Debit (Credit)		Net Amortized Cost
Purchase	100,000	Purchase	3,630	103,630
		Jun 30, 20X1 Interest	(855)	
		Dec 31, 20X1 Interest	(889)	
Bal Dec 31, 20X1	100,000	Bal Dec 31, 20X1	1,886	101,886
		Jun 30, 20X2 Interest	(925)	
		Dec 31, 20X2 Interest	(961)	
Bal Dec 31, 20X2	100,000	Bal Dec 31, 20X2	0	100,000

V. Transfers Between Classifications

A. Investments in Equity Securities

Changes in the classification of investments in equity securities are accounted for prospectively. The general rule is that transfers between classifications are accounted for at fair value (FV) at the date of transfer. That is, the value of the investment transferred into the new category will be at fair value (if determinable) on the date of the transfer. The treatment of any unrealized gains or losses (G/L) is accounted for in accordance with the new classification.

1. **Possible reason for changes from fair value to cost**—An investment that was initially valued at fair value may change because there is no longer a readily determinable fair value.

2. **Possible reason for changes from fair value to equity method**—An investment that was initially value at fair value may change when the investor gains significant influence over the investee and now accounts for the equity investee using the equity method of accounting.

B. Investments in Debt Securities

Changes in the investments in debt securities are also accounted for prospectively. The general rule is that transfers between classifications are accounted for at fair value (FV) at the date of transfer. That is, the value of the investment in the new category will be at fair value (if determinable) on the date of the transfer. The treatment of any unrealized gains or losses (G/L) is accounted for in accordance with the new classification.

1. **Possible reason for a change from held-to-maturity to fair value**—The investor's ability to hold to maturity has changed because the investor now needs to sell the security to raise needed cash.

The table below depicts the changes in the classification of debt securities.

Transfer from / Transfer to	Held-to-Maturity	Available-for-Sale	Trading
Held-to-Maturity	NA	Establish HTM account at FV. Unrealized G/L in AOCI is amortized over remaining life of the debt.	Establish HTM account at FV. Unrealized G/L in net income. Very Rare
Available-for-Sale	Establish AFS account at FV. Unrealized G/L is recorded in AOCI.	NA	Establish AFS account at FV. Unrealized G/L in net income.
Trading	Establish Trading account at FV. Unrealized G/L is recorded in net income.	Establish Trading account at FV. Unrealized G/L in AOCI is recorded in income.	NA

Intangible Assets—Goodwill and Other

Introduction to Intangible Assets

> This lesson provides information on the accounting for intangible assets.
>
> **After studying this lesson, you should be able to:**
>
> 1. Define an intangible asset.
> 2. Identify the difference between a definite-life and indefinite-life intangible asset.
> 3. Describe how to test for the impairment of definite-life and indefinite-life intangible assets.

I. Introduction

> **Definition**
> Intangible assets are long-term operational assets that lack physical substance or presence, but are currently used in the operation of a business and have a useful life extending more than one year from the balance sheet date.

A. Intangibles are similar to plant assets except that they lack physical substance. Many intangibles are legal rights. ASC 350 governs the accounting for intangibles by (1) dividing intangibles into definite- or indefinite-life intangibles, and (2) requiring that all intangibles be evaluated for impairment.

B. **Sources of Intangibles**—Intangibles are either acquired from other parties or **internally developed**.

   1. An acquired intangible is separately recognized in the accounts if either (1) the benefit of the asset is obtained through contractual or other legal rights (as in a patent), or (2) if the intangible is otherwise separable, i.e., can be sold, transferred, licensed, rented, or exchanged regardless of the acquirer's intent to do so (e.g., customer lists).

   2. Internally developed intangibles are expensed immediately if they are not specifically identifiable, have indeterminate values, or are inherent in a continuing business. Firms must expense the amount of internal expenditures devoted to the development of intangibles. The only costs related to internally developed intangibles that are capitalized are registration fees and legal costs paid to outsiders.

C. **Classification**

   1. **Intangibles are classified as:**

      a. Definite-life intangibles; or

      b. Indefinite-life intangibles.

   2. An intangible has a **definite** life either if the asset has a finite legal life or if the firm believes the useful life is finite. The useful life for amortization is set by economic factors (market and obsolescence) as well as by its legal life.

   3. An intangible has an **indefinite** life if no legal, regulatory, contractual, competitive, or other factor limits the life. Indefinite means there is no foreseeable limit on the period of time over which the intangible is expected to provide cash flows. A renewable and very recognizable trademark is an example.

   4. Only definite-life intangibles are amortized. For example, some licenses and franchises that are renewable or even perpetual are not amortized because their benefits are indefinite in duration and no means exists to determine the useful life.

Example
The intangible asset would have an indefinite life if a city provides a perpetual license to run a ferry across a body of water.

5. However, if an intangible has an indefinite legal life (e.g., trademark) but management believes that the asset has a finite life, then the asset is treated as a definite-life intangible.

6. All intangibles are subject to impairment.

D. **Summary Table**

1. **FV** = fair value;

2. **BV** = book value;

3. **R** = recoverable cost (sum of expected future net cash inflows from use and ultimate disposal; it is a nominal sum, not a present value).

Definite-Life Intangibles

Capitalize | *Amortize* | *Impairment*
External costs[1] | Over useful life | Same as assets in use two steps (no pretest)
 | Usually no residual value |
 | Usually SL method | 1. Impairment if BV > R
 | | 2. Impairment Loss = BV – FV

Indefinite-Life Intangibles Other than Goodwill

Capitalize | *Amortize* | *Impairment*
External costs[2] | Do not amortize | Same as assets held for sale
 | | Qualitative pretest (optional)
 | | Quantitative test:
 | | • Impairment if BV > FV
 | | • Impairment loss = BV – FV

[1]External costs include amounts paid for registration, legal and accounting fees, outside design costs, consulting fees, successful legal defense costs, and the cost of direct purchases of intangibles from others.
[2]Costs of internally developed intangibles including salaries of employees working on patents, materials used, and overhead are expensed as incurred.

E. **Amortization**

1. The amortization of definite-life intangibles is recorded just like depreciation expense. The debit is to an expense account such as amortization expense or selling, general and administrative expense (SG&A) for intangibles devoted to nonmanufacturing activities, and the debit is to work in process (and ultimately cost of goods sold) for manufacturing intangibles. The credit is usually made directly to the intangible rather than to a contra account.

Example

DR: Amortization of copyright (SG&A)   xx
  CR: Accumulated Amortization   xx

2. The straight-line method is typically used to compute amortization.

F. Residual Value—For amortized intangibles, residual value is assumed to be zero unless:

   1. The useful life to the firm is less than legal or economic life;

   2. Another entity could obtain some benefit from the asset after the first firm was finished with it; *and*

   3. There is reliable evidence as to its amount (which would consist of a market for the asset at that time or a commitment from another firm to purchase the asset at end of its useful life).

G. Useful Life—For amortized intangibles, if an asset is valuable only when it is used with other assets, the useful life of the other assets in the group can be a factor in setting useful life. For example, if a number of patents are used for one combined purpose, and the patents do not have any usefulness apart from the group, then the shortest useful life of the assets in the group sets the useful life for them all.

H. Changes in Classification—If an amortized (definite-life) intangible is later deemed to have an indefinite life, then amortization ceases. An impairment might result because fair value would now be used to test for impairment rather than recoverable cost.

I. Separate Recognition—Many intangibles must be separately identified: trademarks and trade names, noncompetition agreements, customer lists, order or production backlogs, copyrights and patents, secret formulas and processes, licensing agreements, and supply contracts. A major reason for identifying these is that intangibles with definite life are amortized. To include them in goodwill would mean they would not be amortized.

J. Types of Intangibles

   1. Marketing-related—Trademarks, Internet domain names, noncompetition agreements.

     a. Some of these items are indefinite-life intangibles. Indefinite-life intangibles include trademarks because they are renewable every 10 years indefinitely.

   2. Customer-related—Customer lists, contractual relationships with customers.

     a. These are definite-life intangibles because they could not have benefit periods of indefinite or unlimited life.

   3. Artistic-related—Copyrights (these are not renewable).

     a. Definite life

   4. Contract-related—Franchises, licensing agreements, broadcast rights, service/supply contracts

     a. Some of these are definite-life intangibles, and some are indefinite-life intangibles (as in the case of a perpetual franchise or one that is renewable indefinitely).

   5. Technology-related—Patents (both product and process type) that have a 20-year life and give the holder the exclusive right to use, manufacture, or sell a product or process. Capitalize successful legal defense costs.

     a. These are definite-life intangibles and, although small modifications can lead to a new patent that effectively extends the life of the old (the BV of the old is added to the new), the new patent is still considered to have a definite life.

   6. Goodwill—Arises only from a business combination in which the fair value of the entity purchased exceeds the fair value of the entity's identifiable net assets (assets—liabilities). (More on goodwill in the next lesson!)

     a. Indefinite life and tested for impairment annually

   7. Defensive intangible asset-is an intangible asset that the entity purchases, but does not intend to use. Rather, the entity intends to hold the asset so it cannot be used by competitors. An entity may "lock up" an intangible asset to reduce competition. Since the entity will receive the benefit from holding this asset through reduced competition, defensive intangible assets have definite life and should be amortized over the period the entity will reap these benefits.

K. Revaluation of Book Value —From time to time, the rights associated with an intangible asset must be legally defended. For example, a company might have a patent on a unique product. If a competitor infringes on the rights represented by the patent and manufactures a similar product, the company holding the patent might elect to defend those rights through legal action. Accounting for the legal costs of this action is dependent on the outcome of the legal action.

L. Successful Legal Defense—If the rights associated with the intangible asset are successfully defended, the economic benefits associated with the intangible asset have been enhanced. Therefore, the related legal costs are recorded as an increase in the capitalized value of the intangible asset.

Example

A firm owns a patent with a total capitalized cost of $45,000. At the beginning of the current year, the patent has been amortized four years of a total estimated nine-year useful life. During the current year, the firm won a patent infringement suit concerning its patent. Legal costs amounted to $15,000. The legal costs are added to the book value of the patent. The book value at the beginning of the current year plus the $15,000 legal costs are amortized over the remaining five years of the patent's life.

Book value of patent at beginning of current year = $45,000 − $45,000(4/9) = $25,000

M. Unsuccessful Legal Defense—If the rights associated with the intangible asset are unsuccessfully defended, the economic benefits associated with the intangible asset have likely been decreased to zero. Therefore, the related legal costs are recorded as legal expenses of the period incurred. In addition, the intangible is written off as a loss.

N. Impairment Test of Definite-Life Intangibles—The test for impairment is a two-step process and it is the same as for plant assets in use.

1. The book value (BV) of the definite-life intangible is compared to the recoverable cost (R) of the intangible asset. Recoverable cost is the sum of net cash inflows attributable to using the asset and from the ultimate disposal. If the BV is greater than the recoverable costs, then the asset is potentially impaired, and the second step must be completed.

2. The second step is to compare the BV to the fair value (FV). If the BV is greater than the FV, the asset is written down to FV. The impairment loss equals BV − FV. Subsequent amortization proceeds based on the new BV.

O. Impairment Test of Indefinite-Life Intangibles other than Goodwill—

1. If the intangible asset is an indefinite life and not subject to amortization, then it must be tested for impairment at least on an annual basis, or when circumstances indicate there may be impairment.

2. The entity may elect to perform a qualitative assessment prior to completing the quantitative impairment test. The qualitative assessment takes into consideration all relevant factors that may impact the fair value of the indefinite-life intangible. Using these factors, the entity must determine whether it is more likely than not (more than 50%) that the indefinite life asset is impaired.

   a. If the entity determines that it is not more likely than not that the indefinite-life intangible is impaired, then the entity does not need to calculate the quantitative impairment test.

   b. If the entity determines that it is more likely than not that the indefinite-life intangible is impaired, then the entity must complete the quantitative impairment test.

3. The quantitative test for impairment is the same as for plant assets held for sale. The FV is used to test for impairment AND measure the loss. An asset is impaired if BV exceeds FV. The impairment loss is the amount that the BV exceeds the FV of the indefinite-life intangible asset.

> **Note**
> Recoverable cost is not used to test for impairment for indefinite-life intangibles because it could be argued that an indefinite-life intangible could have unlimited recoverable costs given the potential for indefinite life. That is, how do you determine the future cash flow streams for a life that is indefinite? You can't!

4. Impairment losses cannot be reversed for either definite-life or indefinite-life intangibles. This is the same as for impairment of assets in use—impairment losses are not recoverable.

> **Note**
> Recall that for plant assets held for sale previous impairment losses can be recovered.

II. Deferred Charges

A. Deferred charges are accounts that are difficult to classify. A variety of practice exists for these accounts. Deferred charges are not included in intangibles but are often listed close to intangibles in the balance sheet and are sometimes confused with intangibles.

B. Examples of deferred charges are listed below.

1. Long-term prepaid insurance

2. Long-term prepaid rent

3. Machinery rearrangement costs—Related to an assembly line for a manufacturing concern, the costs of an efficiency study. These costs are typically amortized over five to ten years.

4. Deferred income taxes—When transactions in the current or past periods give rise to future deductible temporary differences (which reduce future taxable income relative to future pretax accounting income), a deferred tax asset is created. Coverage of this topic is significantly expanded in a subsequent lesson.

5. Deferred bond issue costs—The costs of issuing bonds is recorded in a deferred charge and amortized over the term of the bonds.

III. Cash Surrender Value of Life Insurance

A. Firms that carry whole life insurance policies on key employees enjoy an annual increase in the investment portion of the policy. Cash surrender value is appropriately classified as an investment account but may be reported by some firms in Other Assets in the balance sheet.

Example
The annual premium on a life insurance policy for a corporate executive is $800. In the third year, cash surrender value begins accumulation, at $200.

Entry for third-year premium:

DR:	Insurance Expense	600
DR:	Cash Surrender Value of Life Insurance	200
	CR: Cash	800

In subsequent years, the cash surrender value portion of the premium increases. The fourth year might be $300, for example. At the end of the fourth year, the balance in cash surrender value then would be $500.

IV. Startup Costs

A. Startup costs are those expenditures incurred as a new business is being formed. These costs occur before any business activities commence. Startup costs may also be referred to as preopening costs, preoperating costs, or organization costs. All startup costs are expensed as incurred (ASC 720–15–25–1).

B. Startup activities include:

1. Opening a new facility

2. Introducing a new product or service

3. Conducting business in a new territory

4. Conducting business with an entirely new class of customers

5. Initiating a new process in an existing facility

6. Commencing new operations

C. For example, if New Corporation incurred $60,000 of startup costs, the startup costs would be recorded as:

```
DR: Startup expense   $60,000
                CR: Cash   $60,000
```

Goodwill

This lesson provides information on the accounting for and reporting of goodwill.

After studying this lesson, you should be able to:

1. Describe how goodwill is created and initially measured.

2. Complete the steps to test for and measure goodwill impairment.

I. Introduction

Definition

Goodwill is the result of a business combination and is measured as the excess of the fair value of the acquired company as a whole and the fair value of the identifiable net assets (assets–liabilities) of the acquired company.

A. Goodwill is the only intangible asset that is not identifiable. Goodwill is attributable to many different factors, such as reputation, management skills, location, customer loyalty, etc. Goodwill is the value of the acquiree that cannot be attributable to specific identifiable tangible or intangible assets, or to a favorable liability. Because of the going-concern assumption, goodwill has an indefinite life. The life is assumed to be indefinite because in the absence of evidence to the contrary, the combined entity (acquirer and acquiree) will continue indefinitely.

B. Goodwill is recognized only when the acquirer obtains control of another enterprise. If a firm has never acquired another enterprise, then that firm would not have goodwill in its balance sheet.

Examples
1. 100% Acquisition of Acquiree

Assume ABC Company acquired 100% of XYZ Company for $200,000, which is the FV of XYZ as a whole. At the time of the acquisition, XYZ's net assets had a book value of $100,000.

The fair value of the net identifiable assets of XYZ is $160,000, which means that XYZ has net assets with a fair value in excess of book value.

In the acquisition of XYZ Company, ABC Company paid $40,000 for goodwill ($200,000 – $160,000), as illustrated in the model below.

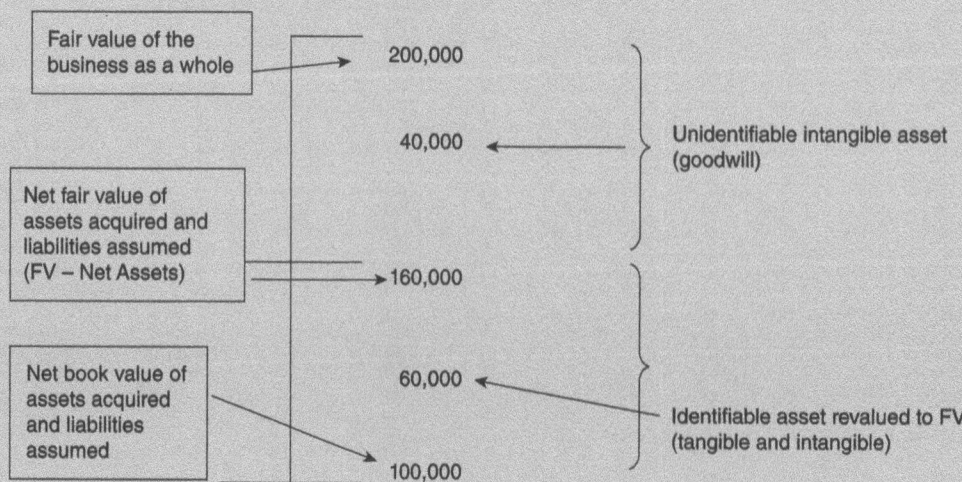

2. Now assume that ABC Company acquired 75% of XYZ Company for $150,000 and that the total value of the remaining 25% is $50,000. The diagram below depicts that the total goodwill is still $40,000, but goodwill is allocated between the controlling interest (acquirer ABC) and the noncontrolling interest (NCI). ABC Company, the controlling interest, is allocated $30,000 and the NCI is allocated the remaining 25%, or $10,000.

	Total value of XYZ 100%	ABC's share 75%	NCI's share 25%	
FV of business	200,000	150,000	50,000	
Goodwill	40,000	30,000	10,000	Calculated difference
FV of identifiable net assets	160,000	120,000	40,000	
FV increment of identifiable net assets	60,000	45,000	15,000	Based on appraisal valuations
BV of identifiable net assets	100,000	75,000	25,000	

C. With respect to determining the **fair value of identifiable net assets**, there are two notable points:

1. The use of the term **net** implies that all liabilities assumed in the acquisition have been subtracted from all assets acquired in the acquisition.

2. The use of the term **identifiable assets** implies that all identifiable assets are included, both tangible (such as property, plant, and equipment) and intangible (such as patents), including those that have a definite life and those that have an indefinite life.

3. The **FV increment of identifiable net assets** is the revaluation of the book value of those assets to their fair value as of the date of the acquisition. These revaluations are recorded by the acquiring company and ultimately reported on the consolidated balance sheet.

D. Recorded goodwill remains on the books of the acquirer unless the acquiree is sold or the goodwill becomes impaired (as described in IV. below).

E. Goodwill represents an expectation on the part of the acquiring business enterprise that, because of synergies, there will be above normal earnings in the years immediately following the acquisition. If the acquiring company had created a new business, it would have had to develop a client base, reputation, and other favorable intangible characteristics. In acquiring an existing business enterprise, the acquiring company pays for the established workforce and customer base, the established business reputation, and other intangible characteristics.

F. Subsequent to the acquisition, the costs to maintain, enhance, or repair purchased goodwill are expensed. The acquirer understandably wishes to maximize the return on its investment and often spends considerable sums to integrate the acquiree operations into its (acquirer's) operations. All such expenditures are expensed. They are not added to the initial goodwill.

II. Internally Developed Goodwill—Internally developed goodwill exists for most business entities. However, internally developed goodwill is not recognized as an asset in the accounting records of a business entity. Internally developed goodwill cannot easily be measured or verified. This is a major reason that only purchased goodwill, resulting from an arm's length transaction, is recognized for accounting purposes.

III. **Bargain Purchases**—Occasionally a firm acquires another enterprise for a price less than the fair value of the acquiree's net assets. This situation is referred to as a bargain purchase. The amount by which the fair value of the acquiree's net assets exceeds the price paid is recognized by the acquirer in the period of the acquisition as a gain.

> **Note**
> A full description of the determination of goodwill and a bargain purchase amount resulting from a business combination is covered in the lesson on business combinations, "Recognizing/Measuring Goodwill or Bargain Purchase Amount," as part of the "Select Transactions" section.

IV. **Goodwill Impairment**

    A. Goodwill, like all indefinite-life intangibles, **must be tested for impairment at least annually** or when certain circumstances indicate that its book value (carrying value) is greater than its fair value (**called an impairment**).

        1. When goodwill is recognized, it must be allocated to a reporting unit. A reporting unit is a component of an operating segment for which discrete financial information is available and regularly used by management for decision-making purposes.

> **Exam Tip**
> The CPA Exam typically does not ask the candidate to identify reporting units, but to know that goodwill is tested at the reporting unit level.

        2. Goodwill impairment testing must be done at the reporting unit level or one level below the reporting unit.

    B. **Qualitative Assessment (Prestep)**

        1. An entity is permitted, and may elect, to begin its determination of whether goodwill is impaired by performing a qualitative assessment.

        2. The purpose of the qualitative assessment is to determine if it is more likely than not (i.e., a likelihood of more than 50%) that the fair value of the reporting unit with which the goodwill is associated has declined below the carrying value of that reporting unit, including its goodwill.

        3. In evaluating whether it is more likely than not that the fair value of a reporting unit is less than its carrying value, an entity should consider all relevant events and circumstances, including:

            a. Microeconomic conditions such as deterioration in general economic conditions, limited access to capital, fluctuation in exchange rates, or other adverse events in equity and credit markets

            b. Industry and market conditions such as deterioration in the industry environment, increased competition, decline in market-dependent multiples, change in the market for the entity's products or services, or a regulatory or political development

            c. Cost factors such as increases in raw materials, labor, or other costs that have a negative effect on earnings and cash flows

            d. Overall financial performance such as negative cash flows or actual or projected declines in revenues, earnings, or cash flows

            e. Entity-specific events such as changes in management, key personnel, strategy, or customers; contemplation of bankruptcy or litigation

            f. Factors affecting a reporting unit such as changes in composition or carrying amount of its net assets, anticipation of selling or disposing all or a portion of a reporting unit, or recognition of goodwill impairment loss by a subsidiary that is a component of a reporting unit

g. If the reporting unit is publicly traded, a sustained decrease in share price (considered both in absolute terms and relative to the peer group)

4. **Qualitative Assessment Outcomes**

    a. After assessing the totality of the above kinds of events and circumstances, an entity determines that it **is not** more likely than not that the fair value of the reporting unit is less than its carrying value, then the quantitative goodwill impairment test **is not required**.

    b. After assessing the totality of the above kinds of events and circumstances, an entity determines that it **is** more likely than not that the fair value of the reporting unit is less than its carrying value, then the quantitative assessment **must be performed**.

C. Quantitative Assessment To Measure Impairment

1. If the qualitative assessment is not completed or if the assessment determines that it is more likely than not that the fair value of the reporting unit is less than its carrying value, then a quantitative calculation must be performed.

2. The fair value of a reporting unit is compared to its carrying amount, including any deferred income taxes and previously recognized goodwill.

3. If the carrying amount of the reporting unit is greater than zero and its fair value exceeds that carrying amount, goodwill of the reporting unit is not impaired and no impairment is recognized.

4. If the carrying amount of the reporting units is greater than its fair value, there is an impairment. The impairment loss is measured as the excess of the carrying value over the fair value. The impairment charge cannot exceed the carrying amount of the goodwill. That is, goodwill is only written down to zero.

Example

Assume that Firm A acquires firm B for $400 million when B's net identifiable assets have a fair value of $300 million. Subsequent to the acquisition, Firm B is considered a reporting unit. As a consequence of the acquisition, Firm A will recognize $100 million in goodwill, determined as cost of investment (fair value of B) $400 million – fair value of identifiable assets $300 million = $100 million goodwill.

One year later, as a result of its qualitative assessment, Firm A cannot rule out the possibility that the goodwill recognized when it acquired Firm B is impaired. Therefore, it carries out the quantitative calculation.

Firm A determines that the fair value of Firm B as a unit is $340 million and that the carrying value of its investment in Firm B is $380 million. Since the fair value ($340 million) is less than the carrying value ($380), goodwill is impaired and an impairment loss of $40 million must be recognized.

Impairment Entry:

DR: Impairment loss—Goodwill $40 million

    CR: Goodwill $40 million

Research and Development Costs

This lesson presents the accounting and reporting for research and development costs (R&D).

After studying this lesson, you should be able to:

1. Identify what costs are considered research and what costs are considered development.

I. Details

A. Definitions

Definitions

Research: The attempt to discover new knowledge aimed at the development of new products, services, processes, or techniques, or the significant improvement in an existing product.

Development: The translation of research findings or knowledge into a plan or design of a new product or significant improvement in an existing product or process whether intended for sale or use. Development includes formulation, design and testing of product alternatives, construction of prototypes, and operations of pilot plants.

1. Development does not include routine or periodic alterations to existing products, processes, or other ongoing operations. It also does not include market research.

Exam Tip
The CPA Exam frequently tests detailed knowledge of the definition and items included in R&D, and also what is not included in R&D.

B. Included in R&D Are Costs Associated With:

1. Laboratory research
2. Conceptual formulation and design of possible products or process alternatives
3. Modification of the formulation or design of a product or process
4. Design, construction, and testing of preproduction prototypes and models
5. Design of tools, jigs, molds, and dies involving new technology
6. Design of a pilot plant

C. Excluded from R&D Are Costs Associated With:

1. Engineering follow-through
2. Quality control and routine testing
3. Troubleshooting
4. Adaptation of an existing capability to a particular customer's needs
5. Routine design of tools, jigs, molds, and dies
6. Legal work in connection with patent applications
7. Software development costs

II. Accounting for R&D

A. General Rule—ASC 730 requires that research and development costs are expensed in the period incurred. Research and development costs include labor costs, materials costs, and overhead costs.

B. Fixed Assets—In relation to the use of fixed assets in research and development activities, three specific situations need to be addressed.

> **Exam Tip**
> ASC 730 views the purchase of an asset that will be used in only one R&D effort as an expense and since it has no future value these costs are immediately expensed.

1. **Fixed Assets Used in Several R&D Projects**—These assets are capitalized and annual depreciation is included in the annual R&D costs. The debit is to R&D expense rather than to depreciation expense; the credit is to accumulated depreciation.

2. **Fixed Assets Used Temporarily in a R&D Project**—The depreciation related to the time frame of the project is included in the annual R&D costs.

3. **Fixed Assets Used in a Single R&D Project and the Asset has no Alternative Uses**—Even though the fixed asset has a useful life exceeding one year and the single R&D project will be in process for more than one year, the entire cost of the fixed asset is expensed as R&D immediately.

C. Patent Costs—The internal costs of developing a patent are considered R&D and therefore are expensed. The result is that the only costs capitalized for internally developed patents are registration and legal costs. This contrasts with the cost of purchasing a patent from an outside party. The entire cost of such a patent is capitalized.

D. Purchased Services—R&D services purchased from other firms are included in R&D. But if a firm performs R&D services for another firm, the costs are accumulated in an inventory account and expensed as cost of goods sold or cost of services provided at the conclusion of the contract.

E. R&D Examples

Examples

1. Maple Inc. does not have the expertise in a specific research area and contracted with Oak Co. to perform research on a new product design to be used by Maple. Maple will expense all of the payments made to Oak as R&D expense. However, Oak Co. will debit inventory for the cost of its research performed for Maple until the contract is completed, at which time contract revenue and expense is recognized. This is not R&D expense to Oak.

2. The following costs were incurred by a firm in the current year:

Materials, labor, and overhead cost incurred for:

Laboratory research	$40,000
Modification of the design of a product or process	10,000
Adaptation of an existing capability to a particular customer's needs	20,000

Purchase cost of fixed assets at beginning of year:

Equipment used the full year for lab research, annual depreciation $30,000; equipment has alternative non-R&D uses $300,000 cost

Equipment used the full year for lab research, annual depreciation $15,000; equipment has alternative R&D uses $150,000 cost

Equipment used the full year for lab research, annual depreciation $25,000; equipment has no alternative use other than in one specific R&D effort $250,000 cost

Total R&D expense for the year equals:

$345,000 = $40,000 + $10,000 + $30,000 + $15,000 + $250,000.

The $20,000 (adaptation of existing capability) is not R&D. The full cost of the third item of equipment is included in R&D for the current year because it has no alternative use (in other R&D or non-R&D uses).

Software Costs

This lesson presents the accounting and reporting for software costs, cloud computing, and the fees associated with cloud computing.

After studying this lesson, you should be able to:

1. Describe the accounting for software costs that are purchased or developed for internal use.

2. Identify the criteria for technological feasibility.

3. Describe the accounting for software costs to be marketed or sold.

4. Determine when a cloud computing (hosting) arrangement contains a license.

5. Describe the accounting for implementation costs associated with a cloud computing (hosting) arrangement.

I. Software Costs for Internal Use

A. An entity may purchase software for internal use and implement the software with no customization (i.e., buy and use off the shelf). These costs are capitalized and amortized over the expected useful life of the software.

B. Alternatively, an entity may purchase software and customize it so that the software fits the entity's unique needs. An entity may also internally develop software for its specific needs. The accounting for modified or internally developed software that is for the entity's own use follows the criteria for research and development (R&D) costs under ASC 985. That is, the stage of the modification or development of the software dictates whether the costs are expensed or capitalized and when amortization commences.

   1. The costs incurred to develop (or modify) the software to the point of technological feasibility is expensed as incurred. The costs incurred after technological feasibility but before the software is put to use is capitalized as an intangible asset.

   2. The capitalized costs of internally developed (or modified) software intended for internal use are amortized over the expected useful life of the software.

C. The critical point for capitalization is technological feasibility. Technological feasibility typically occurs when the model or working model of the software is complete. When there is a working model and evidence that a commitment is made to continue with the development, the software is deemed to be technologically feasible. The costs incurred after the establishment of technological feasibility are capitalized.

D. Some examples provided in ASC 350-40-55 of software that are development (or customized) for internal use are listed next.

   1. A manufacturing entity purchases robots and customizes the software that the robots use to function. The robots are used in a manufacturing process that results in finished goods.

   2. An entity develops software that helps it improve its cash management, which may allow the entity to earn more revenue.

   3. An entity purchases or develops software to process payroll, accounts payable, and accounts receivable.

   4. An entity purchases software related to the installation of an online system used to keep membership data.

   5. A travel agency purchases a software system to price vacation packages and obtain airfares.

   6. A bank develops software that allows customers to withdraw cash, inquire about balances, make loan payments, and execute wire transfers.

E. Costs associated with the maintenance of the software (often referred to as a servicing agreement) are expensed as incurred.

II. Internally Developed Software to Be Marketed or Sold

A. An entity may develop software products to sell, lease, or otherwise market to customers. For example, Microsoft or QuickBooks internally develop software is to sell to customers.

B. Costs incurred to establish technological feasibility are research and development (R&D) costs and are expensed as incurred.

   1. The activities associated with planning, designing, coding, and testing of programs are performed in order to obtain technological feasibility.

C. Once the software product has reached technological feasibility and there is a plan to continue the project, the costs are capitalized as intangible assets.

   1. ASC 985-25 defines technological feasibility of a computer software product as "when the entity has completed all planning, designing, coding, and testing activities that are necessary to establish that the product can be produced to meet its design specifications including functions, features, and technical performance requirements."

   2. After technological feasibility is reached, the entity may capitalize direct costs associated with software product development and indirect costs that are related to the programmers and the facilities. The entity cannot allocate and capitalize general and administrative costs that are not directly related to the product development.

   3. Capitalized costs include costs of coding, testing, debugging, and preparation of final product master and final documentation manual. Capitalized costs do not include duplication of product masters and manuals. Capitalization of the software product as an intangible ends when a product master is ready for duplication.

D. Capitalization of software development stops when the product is available for release to customers. Any costs associated with the maintenance of the software product (fixes or patches issued to users) and costs associated with customer support are expensed as incurred.

E. Once the software is marketed to customers, the intangible asset associated with the software must be amortized. Entities must calculate potential amortization of the capitalized software costs under both the revenue method and the straight-line method. The amortization recorded is whichever calculation results in a larger amortization amount. The computation for both methods must be made each year to ensure the larger amount is recognized. The same method need not produce the larger amount each year. The amortization is an operating expense.

   1. Revenue Method

Amortization for the current year = B × R

where:

B = Book value of capitalized software costs at the beginning of the year

R = (Current-year revenue) ÷ (Current-year revenue + Estimated future revenue)

   2. Straight-Line Method

Amortization for the current year = B ÷ N

where:

B = Book value of capitalized software costs at the beginning of the year

N = Number of years remaining in product sales life at the beginning of the year

3. Remember to calculate both methods and choose the higher of the two amounts each period. Also, remember that the inputs to both methods change each year. The beginning book value changes, as does the estimate of future revenue and remaining years in the product life.

Example:

Assume the software costs incurred in year 1 for a software product developed for sale are:

Costs incurred to establish technological feasibility	$100,000
Costs incurred after establishment of technological feasibility and through the completion of product masters	200,000

Entries in year 1:

DR: R&D expense   100,000

   CR: Cash   100,000

DR: Software costs (intangible asset)   200,000

   CR: Cash   200,000

Now assume the product is marketed at the beginning of year 2 and is expected to have a 3-year sales life.

Revenue from software sales in year 2	$1,000,000
Estimate of revenue for years 3 and 4 (total)	3,000,000
Total current-year and future estimated revenue	4,000,000

Calculation of amortization of software costs for year 2:

Revenue method amortization = 200,000 × (1,000,000 ÷ 4,000,000) = 50,000

Straight-line method amortization = 200,000 ÷ 3 = 66,667

(Use the higher of the two amounts)

Amortization entry for year 2:

DR: Amortization of software costs   66,667

   CR: Software costs (intangible asset)   66,667

The book value of the software costs at beginning of year 3 is 200,000 − 66,667 = 133,333.

Revenue from software sales in year 3	1,750,000
Estimate of revenue for year 4	500,000
Total current-year and future estimated revenue	2,250,000

Calculation of amortization of software costs for year 3:

Revenue method amortization = 133,333 x (1,750,000 ÷ 2,250,000) = 103,703

Straight-line method amortization = 133,333 ÷ 2 = 66,667

(Use the higher of the two amounts)

Amortization entry for year 3:

DR: Amortization of software costs   103,703

    CR: Software costs (intangible asset)   103,703

At the end of year 3, the book value of software cost that is reported in the balance sheet is $29,630 (133,333 – 103,703). This example shows that the same amortization method need not be used each year.

4. After amortizing the capitalized costs for a particular year, the ending book value is compared with the net realizable value of the software (future estimated gross revenues less operating costs). This is essentially an impairment test that is done **each** year. If the ending book value exceeds the net realizable value, the book value is written down to net realizable value, with a loss recognized. The net realizable value becomes the beginning book value for the next period for purposes of amortization. Write-ups are not allowed.

III. Cloud Computing

A. Often an entity utilizes software in a cloud computing arrangement (also known as a hosting arrangement). This means that the entity does not have physical possession of the software but has use of the software on the cloud.

B. First the entity must determine if the cloud computing arrangement includes a software license. The arrangement contains a software license if **both** one and two are true:

1. The customer has the contractual right to take possession of the software at any time during the hosting period without significant penalty.

    a. "Significant penalty" means that the customer can take delivery without incurring significant costs and can use the software separately without a significant reduction in utility or value.

2. It is feasible for the customer either to run the software on its own hardware or to contract with another party unrelated to the vendor to host the software.

C. If the cloud computing arrangement contains a software license, then the license is accounted for like other acquired intangible license agreements. This means that the license is capitalized as an intangible asset and amortized over the life of the license (if definite lived) or tested annually for impairment (if indefinite life).

D. If the cloud computing arrangement does not have a licensing arrangement, it is deemed to be a service contract. The service contract is expensed as incurred. A service contract does not give rise to a recognizable intangible asset.

IV. Cloud Computing Implementation Costs

A. Both licensing arrangements and service contracts that are provided via a cloud computing arrangement will have implementation costs.

1. Implementation costs are those incurred to implement the hosting arrangement. To determine which implementation costs may be capitalized and which costs are expensed, the entity follows the same guidance as capitalizing other intangibles.

    a. Internal and external costs to research, develop, or obtain the software cannot be capitalized and are expensed as incurred. These costs are at the preliminary stage and the software has not yet been implemented. The costs include those for coding, testing, and conversion of old data into new systems.

    b. Internal and external costs associated with implementation of the software for use can be capitalized. Implementation activities are those associated with fees to customize or configure the service and payroll costs to employees who are directly associated with implementation during the development phase.

    c. Once the software is in use, costs can no longer be capitalized and must be expensed in the period incurred.

2. When the cloud computing arrangement is a license, the implementation costs are capitalized to the software intangible asset and amortized as part of the software asset.

3. When the cloud computing arrangement is a service agreement, the implementation costs are capitalized as a prepaid asset. The costs are not capitalized as an intangible asset (because there is no intangible asset) but are prepaid as part of the service agreement. The implementation costs, including the terms in which the entity would exercise the option to extend the agreement, are expensed over the life of the service agreement.

Payables and Accrued Liabilities

Current Liabilities

This lesson is the first of several concerning recognition and reporting of current liabilities. The general nature and definition of liability are discussed, along with classification and valuation of liabilities.

After studying this lesson, you should be able to:

1. Define liability, current liability, and noncurrent liability.

2. Categorize liabilities two different ways.

3. Determine the valuation of current and noncurrent liabilities.

4. Distinguish current from noncurrent liabilities.

Definition
Liabilities: Represent outsider claims to a firm's assets or are enforceable claims for services to be rendered by the firm.

I. **Liabilities in General**

   A. **Definition of Liabilities**

   1. Liabilities have three key elements, which are shown below. This definition is taken from the FASB's conceptual framework. A liability is:

      a. a present obligation to transfer assets or provide services,

      b. that is unavoidable, and

      c. is the result of a past transaction or event.

   2. It is important to note that, for a liability to be recognized in the accounts, it is not necessary to know the identity of the creditor, the exact amount that will be paid, or even the due date. Contingent liabilities, discussed later, are a category of liability for which one or more of these information items are not known as of the balance sheet date. However, the three elements from the conceptual framework above must be met by all liabilities if one is to be recognized in the accounts.

Examples
1. A firm signed a contract to perform services the following year. At the current balance sheet date, the firm has no liability because no resources have been exchanged.

Only a contract has been signed. There is no past transaction that substantiates the liability as of the balance sheet date. There is no future obligation to provide services because neither party has executed the contract. None of the elements of the liability is met.

2. Do airline frequent flyer programs create liabilities for airline companies?

The answer is yes, because all three parts of the definition of a liability are met. The airline has (1) an obligation to provide service (2) that is unavoidable (3) as a result of a past transaction (customers achieving the requisite miles or credit card purchases for a free flight). Airline companies accrue this liability.

B. Classification of Liabilities—Liabilities are classified in two ways: (1) current liabilities (CL) or noncurrent liabilities (NCL), and (2) definite or contingent.

1. Most current liabilities (CL) are due within one year of the balance sheet. All other debt is noncurrent. Liabilities are presented on the balance sheet in increasing order of maturity. That is, current liabilities are presented first, and then, noncurrent liabilities are presented. CL include accounts payable, wages payable, income taxes payable, utilities payable, accrued payables, some notes payable, and many others. Noncurrent liabilities (NCL) include bonds payable, some notes payable, lease liabilities and pension liabilities.

2. Definite liabilities actually exist at the balance sheet. Contingent liabilities have some uncertainty at the balance sheet date. Their existence is contingent on an event that may or may not occur after the balance sheet. A contingent liability may be accrued as a definite liability, is disclosed as a contingency, or is not considered a liability at all. Most liabilities are definite. Examples of contingent liabilities include lawsuits, warranties, and guarantees. Contingent liabilities are covered in a subsequent lesson.

C. Distinction between Current and Noncurrent Liabilities

1. **Current liabilities**—Are those that meet two criteria:

   a. Due in the coming year or the operating cycle of the business, whichever is longer;

   b. An obligation to be met by the transfer of a current asset or the *creation of another current liability*.

      i. The operating cycle is the period from acquiring inventory and other resources, to sale, to receipt of cash from the receivable. Most firms have operating cycles much shorter than a year. One measure of the operating cycle is 365/inventory turnover + 365/AR turnover = number of days required to sell the inventory on hand + number of days required to collect receivables.

2. **Noncurrent liabilities**—Are defined by exclusion. That is, noncurrent liabilities are those that do not meet the criteria necessary for classification as a current liability.

Examples

1. A bond payable liability is due four years from the balance sheet. This liability is classified as noncurrent.

2. If the bond liability matures serially, and a portion of the principal balance is due at the end of each year, then the amount due the following year is classified as a current liability in the balance sheet for the current year and is labeled: current maturities of long-term debt.

---

3. **Valuation of Liabilities**

   a. CLs are reported valued at the amount due, or nominal amount. Liabilities for services are measured at the amount received. For example, the unearned revenue (liability) for an amount received by an airline before a flight is provided is measured at the amount received for the ticket.

   b. NCLs are reported at the present value of all future payments (principal and interest), discounted at the prevailing rate of interest for similar debt on the date of issuance. Present value is the current sacrifice to retire the debt. Interest is the difference between the total future payments and present value. Interest is not recognized until time passes.

Caution

A CL and NCL reported in the balance sheet at equal values (e.g., both $100,000) may require greatly different cash payment totals over their terms due to interest on the NCL principal.

    c. Although in theory all debt should be reported at present value, for practical reasons CL are not discounted because the difference between present and nominal (future) value is typically not material.

II. A Closer Look at Current Liabilities (CL)

    A. The essence of a CL is that it is expected to reduce the firm's liquidity within one year of the balance sheet date or operating cycle whichever is longer. A CL payable with a current asset clearly will reduce the firm's liquidity. But what about the second part of the definition *creation of another CL*?

    B. CLs that are continuously refinanced (rolled over) by replacing them with other CLs due later (but within one year of the balance sheet date) must still be classified as CL, even though no current asset will be used to extinguish them in the year after the balance sheet date.

Examples

1. A note payable due 3/1/X2 is expected to be refinanced continuously on a four-month basis, each time substituting a new four-month note for the old. That is the intent of the debtor firm. The note due 3/1/X2 is classified as a CL in the 12/31/X1 balance sheet because it meets the second part of the CL definition.

Although the expectation is that no current asset will be used to retire the debt, there is no certainty that the debtor firm will be able to continue this practice. For example, the debtor firm cannot control the creditor who may decide not to refinance. Interest rates may increase substantially changing the strategy of the debtor firm.

> **Caution**
> Most liabilities due within one year of the balance sheet are CLs. But there are exceptions—some are classified as NCL.

2. A note is due five months from the balance sheet date but payable in the common stock of the debtor. The debtor does not reduce current assets in payment of this debt. A later lesson discusses another example—the refinancing of short-term debt on a long-term basis.

3. A bond liability due next year for which the firm has created a sinking fund investment (noncurrent asset) for bond retirement is classified as an NCL because payment will reduce noncurrent assets not current assets.

> **Caution**
> Most liabilities due later than one year after the balance sheet date are NCLs but there are exceptions; some are classified as CLs.

4. Long-term obligations callable on demand by the creditor are classified as current. Because the creditor can call in the debt, the debtor must report it as current. A creditor may require this provision in the debt contract to reduce the risk of losing principal. Such provisions also may be added in case the debtor violates a debt restriction. For example, a debt contract requires the debtor to maintain a current ratio (CA/CL) of 3.0 or more. If the ratio falls below 3.0, the debt is due on demand by the creditor, unless the debtor "cures" the violation within the next reporting period.

Specific Current Liabilities

This lesson considers several specific definite current liabilities. Recall that definite liabilities exist at the balance sheet. Additional examples appear in the context of other lessons.

After studying this lesson, you should be able to:

1. Determine when a liability should be accrued.

2. Record sales taxes payable from data about sales and the applicable tax rate.

3. Prepare the journal entries to accrue estimated property taxes and payment of assessed taxes.

I. Definite Liabilities—Definite liabilities are not dependent on any future event. The existence of these liabilities is determined by a current event or a past transaction or event. Definite liabilities include liabilities payable in definite amounts (e.g., accounts payable), those that can only be estimated (e.g., estimated income tax payable), and accrued liabilities that are recorded for expenses recognized before payment is made (e.g., utilities payable). Not all definite liabilities can be measured with certainty. Some are estimated and reported at an approximate amount.

    A. Accounts Payable

        1. These payables are also called trade payables. They represent the amount a business enterprise owes to suppliers and other entities that provide goods or services to the company.

        2. These payables are typically for a short duration, usually 30 days. In some instances, the time period can be 45 or 60 days.

        3. Accounts payable are recognized at the time of purchase or at the time that services are received by the business entity. In relation to purchased merchandise, the payable should be recognized at the point in which the merchandise is included in the company's inventory. The module on inventory discusses this issue in further detail (F.O.B. title test and goods on consignment). Several additional accounts such as purchases, returns and allowances and others are created to accommodate the specifics of inventory purchasing.

    B. Other examples of definite liabilities are accrued rent, interest, utilities, payroll and income taxes. The typical adjusting entry to accrue a liability is as follows:

> DR: Expense   xxx
>   CR: Accrued liability   xxx

II. Property Taxes

    A. Property taxes are levied by state and local governments based on the assessed valuation of property as of a given date. The tax becomes a lien against the property on the date specified by law and thus legally the liability comes into existence on that date. From the perspective of the taxing authority, property taxes do not "accrue" over time. The fiscal periods of the taxing authority and the firm paying the tax (the property owner) often do not coincide.

    B. The issues then are (1) what is the period over which to recognize the tax, and (2) what is the amount of any liability or prepayment for balance sheet reporting.

    C. Accounting Principles

        1. The tax-paying firm accrues the property tax monthly as expense over the fiscal year of the taxing authority because the expense should be recognized in the same period the firm benefits from the services provided by the governmental unit (taxing authority).

2. Until the amount of the tax bill for the year is known, the firm estimates the annual amount for purposes of recording the monthly property tax expense.

3. When the amount of the tax bill for the year becomes known, the difference between the estimated annual amount and the actual annual amount is treated as an increase or decrease to the monthly property tax expense amount based on the annual estimate.

4. Until the tax is paid, the firm records a liability for the recognized expense to date. When the tax is paid, the liability is extinguished and any difference between the estimated taxes and actual is adjusted in the current and future periods.

III. Sales Taxes—Firms collect sales taxes from their customers and periodically submit them to the state or local government. Between collection and submission of the tax, the firm has a liability to the government.

Example

The sales tax rate is 10% and the total amount collected from customers for the month is $77,000. The summary entry to record sales and the sales tax is:

Cash	77,000	
Sales		70,000*
Sales Taxes Payable		7,000

*$77,000/1.10 = $70,000 The cash collected includes the sales tax.

The sales taxes payable account is debited when paid to the state, county, or city. Note that the firm reports only $70,000 of sales.

Payroll and Compensated Absences

Accounting by the employer for vacation and holiday pay programs is the focus of this lesson.

After studying this lesson, you should be able to:

1. Explain the relevance of the four criteria for recognizing compensated absence expense and obligation.

2. Record payroll, including employer payroll tax expenses and payroll liabilities from both employer and employee sources.

3. Distinguish which payroll costs are an expense to the employer.

4. Compute bonus liabilities with income tax effects.

I. Payroll Liabilities

A. In their role as employers, firms incur definite current payroll-related liabilities from two different sources:

1. Employer costs, including gross salary, employer share of fringe benefits, employer share of FICA and Medicare, and federal and state unemployment tax (FUTA and SUTA). The employer recognizes an expense for these costs.

2. Employee costs withheld from paychecks, including income tax withholding, employee share of FICA, Medicare and fringe benefits, and also personal expenses such as parking, union dues and others. The employer does not recognize an expense for these costs but acts as a collection point, resulting in an employer liability.

   a. Payroll tax liabilities are paid by the employer at specific dates set by law.

   b. Social Security legislation levies the OASDI Federal Old Age, Survivor, and Disability Insurance tax, also called FICA (Federal Insurance Contribution Act) tax, on annual salaries and wages up to a certain annual salary limit per employee. In addition, the Medicare tax is levied on all salaries and wages without limit. Both employer and employee pay the same amount for both taxes.

   c. Employers pay federal and state unemployment taxes. Both (1) Federal Unemployment Tax Act (FUTA) and (2) State Unemployment Taxes (SUTA) are levied on each employee's salary up to a certain limit per year. Only employers pay this tax.

Note
Because payroll tax rates and salary limits change, the CPA Exam will provide approximate values. However, we recommend that you be aware of the general magnitude of such costs. Approximate rates and limits:

FICA, 6.5% on the first $110,000 of salary per year

Medicare, 1.5% with no limit

FUTA, 6% on the first $7,000 reduced by up to 5.5% for contributions to SUTA

SUTA, 5.5% on first $7,000

Caution
FICA, FUTA, and SUTA all have salary limits beyond which no more tax is levied either for the employer or the employee (there is no limit for Medicare) for a particular year. Look for these limits in payroll problems and take care not to exceed them when computing these expenses for the employer and for FICA withholdings for the employee.

Example

Gross payroll is $60,000 for a month late in the year (gross pay limits for some employees have been exceeded). Use the approximate tax rates provided.

Net pay=$60,000–Employee with holdings (excludes employer share of fringes)= $60,000–$20,000 income tax – $2,800 FICA – $900 Medicare – $1,000 health– $1,000 retirement – $1,000 union = $33,300

The $65,000 expense includes only the employer's costs. The employees' net pay is reduced by their costs. Rather than increasing the expense debit, the net pay credit is reduced.

Remaining is to record the employer share of FICA and Medicare and the employer's taxes for FUTA and SUTA. The next journal entry records these expenses. The two journal entries could be combined.

FICA tax, 7%, only $40,000 of gross pay subject to tax

Medicare tax, 1.5% of gross pay

State income tax withholding, $2,000 (based on withholding tables)

Federal income tax withholding, $18,000 (based on withholding tables)

State unemployment tax, 5%, only $20,000 of gross pay subject to tax

Federal unemployment tax, 1%, only $20,000 of gross pay subject to tax

Union dues withheld, $1,000

Health insurance premiums, $3,000 (1/3 paid by employees)

Retirement, $4,000 (1/4 paid by employees)

Salary or wage expense	65,000*	
State income tax withholding payable		2,000
Federal income tax withholding payable		18,000
FICA tax payable (.07 × $40,000)		2,800
Medicare tax payable (.015 × $60,000)		900
Health insurance payable		3,000
Retirement payable		4,000
Union dues payable		1,000
Cash (net pay)		33,300

*$65,000 = $60,000 gross + 2/3($3,000 health) + 3/4($4,000 retirement).

Payroll tax expense	4,900	
FICA tax payable (.07 × $40,000)		2,800
Medicare tax payable (.015 × $60,000)		900
FUTA tax payable (.01 × $20,000)		200
SUTA tax payable (.05 × $20,000)		1,000

II. **Bonus Compensation Liabilities**—A bonus is an additional amount of compensation in excess of a base salary. Frequently, liabilities related to bonus compensation are dependent on operating results for the accounting period. The bonus may be based on income before or after the bonus and before or after income tax effects. We recommend converting the problem statement directly into an equation. These types of problems require solving for up to two unknowns.

Examples

1. An employee's bonus is based on operating income after income taxes but before deducting the bonus. Operating Income before bonus and taxes is $90,000, the bonus rate is 10%, and the tax rate is 40%. Let B = bonus, T = tax.

$$B = .10(\$90,000 - T)$$
$$T = .40(\$90,000 - B)$$
$$B = .10(\$90,000 - .40(\$90,000 - B))$$
$$B = \$5,625$$

2. An employee's bonus is based on operating income after income taxes and bonus. Operating income before bonus and tax is $90,000, the bonus rate is 10%, and the tax rate is 40%. Let B = bonus, T = tax.

$$B = .10(90,000 - T - B)$$
$$T = .40(90,000 - B)$$
$$B = .10(90,000 - .40(90,000 - B) - B)$$
$$B = \$5,094$$

III. **Compensated Absences**

A. Compensated absences include vacation, holiday, and sick-leave periods for which the employee is compensated. GAAP requires that accrual accounting be applied if certain criteria are met. The expense of these benefits is accrued during the period employees earn these benefits if all of the following four criteria are met:

1. The obligation is attributable to services rendered as of the balance sheet date.

2. The rights vest (benefits are no longer contingent on continued employment) or accumulate (carry over to future periods).

3. Payment of the obligation is probable.

4. The amount of the obligation is estimable.

B. Some benefits do not require accrual. For example, some holiday-pay benefits, military leave, and maternity leave benefits do not accumulate if the employee does not use these benefits. Therefore, no accrual is required. In general, if the probable and estimable criteria are not met, there is no accrual. Such expenses are recognized when paid (pay-as-you-go).

C. Vesting is more valuable to the employee than accumulation because the employee can leave the firm and be paid the benefits if they are vested. However, if benefits accumulate, the employee does not lose the benefits if the holiday or vacation is not taken by the balance sheet date. Limits on accumulation (e.g., at most 10 weeks of vacation pay can be accumulated for some firms) place a cap on the amount of liability accrued.

IV. **Measurement of the Accrual**—The measurement of the accrual can be based on current or future wage rates although typically current rates are used. Current rates result in a lower expense accrual and do not telegraph future pay raises.

A. If current rates are used for the accrual, and a pay raise is enacted between the accrual of the expense and its payment, the effect of the raise is treated as a change in estimate and is recognized currently and prospectively, retroactive application does not apply.

B. The liability is not discounted but rather is reported at nominal (future) value.

Example
At year's end, employees had earned a total of $35,000 worth of vacation and holiday pay. Of that amount, $12,000 of vacation and holiday pay was paid during the year.

Adjusting entry at year's end:

Salary Expense	23,000	
Liability for Compensated Absences		23,000

Next year, there is an across the board 4% pay rate increase. The remaining holiday and vacation pay is paid.

Liability for Compensated Absences	23,000	
Salary Expense .04($23,000)	920	
Cash		23,920

V. Sick Pay Benefits—Accumulated sick pay benefits need not be accrued (but may be) because the event causing payment (illness) cannot be predicted. However, if unused sick pay benefits are routinely paid to employees (e.g., upon leaving the firm), then accrual is required because in this case the benefits vest.

VI. Benefits not Accrued—In practice, not all earned compensated absence benefits are accrued because not all earned benefits are taken by employees. For example, not all vacation pay benefits are taken because some employees let a portion of their benefits lapse.

Example
The beginning balance of the liability for compensated absences for the year is $50,000. During the current year, $25,000 of additional benefits are earned. The firm estimates that 15% of benefits earned each year will not be paid. Benefits paid for the year totaled $35,000.

Journal entries:

Liability for compensated absences	35,000	
Cash		35,000
Salary expense	21,250	
Liability for compensated absences		21,250

$21,250 = .85($25,000). The expense recognized reflects the amount earned in the period that will probably be paid.

The ending liability balance is $36,250 (= $50,000 − $35,000 + $21,250) and represents the expected future payment for compensated absence benefits earned through the end of the current year.

Asset Retirement Obligations and Environmental Liabilities

This lesson provides information on the accounting for asset retirement and environmental obligations.

After studying this lesson, you should be able to:

1. Identify how asset retirement obligations are measured.

2. Explain how asset retirement obligations are accreted over time.

3. Identify when to accrue an environmental obligation.

I. ASC 410-20 Asset Retirement Obligations

ASC 410-20 addresses the accounting and reporting for asset retirement obligations (AROs) and requires firms to capitalize future asset retirement costs in the underlying asset account and also in an ARO liability. Such future costs include the cost of dismantling an asset, removal, site reclamation, nuclear decommissioning, and closing mines. The costs are incurred at the end of the asset's life but are capitalized when they become estimable, often at the beginning of the asset's useful life. The rationale for capitalizing such costs to the asset is that the retirement activities are integral to the operation of the asset.

II. Scope and Initial Measurement

A. Fair value is used to measure the ARO, and the amount is recognized at the time the cost becomes reasonably estimable. The fair value is the amount the firm would be reasonably expected to pay today to cover the future costs and is the present value of all future payments expected to retire the asset. This amount is debited to the asset and credited to the ARO. The obligation must stem from a legal obligation—one that the firm is required to settle because of a law or contract.

B. If a present value technique is used to measure fair value, then the probability-weighted estimates of future cash flows are discounted using credit-adjusted risk-free rate. The probability-weighted cash flows incorporate risks and uncertainties regarding the future obligation.

C. The amount capitalized does not qualify as an expenditure for purpose of capitalizing interest.

D. ASC 410-20 applies to all *legal* obligations associated with the retirement of a tangible noncurrent asset but does not apply to environmental remediation liabilities arising from improper use of an asset because such costs are not an integral part of the cost basis of the asset. (See next section on environmental obligations.)

III. Subsequent Recognition and Measurement

A. After the asset and ARO are increased by the initial fair value (present value) of future payments to retire the asset, (1) total depreciation or depletion expense over the asset's life is automatically increased by the amount capitalized initially, and (2) the ARO is increased each year due to the passage of time, causing the firm to also record "accretion expense." The annual accretion expense and corresponding increase in ARO is found by multiplying the interest rate used in capitalizing the initial amount by the beginning balance in the ARO. The annual expense is considered an operating expense, not interest expense.

B. Thus, the ARO gradually increases over time (to the final amount expected to be paid) while the net book value of the asset declines through the depreciation or depletion process. Only the initial fair value (present value) is capitalized to the asset and is subject to depreciation or depletion.

Example
Example of ARO

A firm opened a mine on January 1, 20X3, with a total capitalized cost of $4,000,000 (acquisition, exploration, and development). In addition, the firm is legally required to close the mine for the safety of the surrounding community and to reclaim the land for environmental purposes. Operations are expected to cease at the end of 20X7, at which time the closing and reclamation costs will be incurred.

Based on current bids by independent contractors, the following range of closing and reclamation costs is generated:

Closing and reclamation costs	Probability assessment	Expected cash flow
$200,000	.20	$40,000
300,000	.50	150,000
400,000	.30	120,000
		310,000

The risk-free rate of interest on 1/1/X3 is 3%. The firm adds 4% to reflect the effect of its credit standing. Therefore, the credit-adjusted risk-free rate of return is 7%. In addition, the firm assumes annual inflation of 2% over the five-year period of operating the mine. Assume straight-line depletion (although the units of production method would normally be used). Also assume the firm immediately sells ore as it is removed from the site.

Amount capitalized to mine and ARO:

Expected cost to close mine and reclaim land, 1/1/X3	$310,000
Effect of inflation (future value of single payment, 2%, 5 years)	× 1.10408
Expected future cost to close mine and reclaim land, 12/31/X7	$342,265
Present value factor (present value of single payment, 7%, 5 years)	× .71299
Present value (fair value) of cost to close mine and reclaim land	$244,032

1/1/X3			
Developed mine (noncurrent asset, depletable resource)		244,032	
Asset retirement obligation (ARO—a liability)			244,032
(The total capitalized cost of the developed mine is now $4,244,032, the sum of the initial capitalized cost and the amount capitalized for closing the mine and reclaiming the land.)			
12/31/X3			
Depletion expense (to cost of goods sold)		848,806	
Accumulated depletion (contra to Developed mine)			848,806
$4,244,032 ÷ 5 = $848,806			
(Note that annual depletion expense includes $244,032 ÷ 5 = $48,806 of depletion on the capitalized closing and reclamation cost.)			
Accretion expense $244,032 (.07)		17,082	
ARO			17,082
(The $17,082 amount is the increase in the ARO liability due to the passage of time. The initial amount recorded in the ARO grows to its future value; the increase each year is the cost associated with that increase.)			

12/31/X4		
Depletion expense (to cost of goods sold)	848,806	
Accumulated depletion (contra to Developed Mine)		848,806
Accretion expense ($244,032 + $17,082)(.07)	18,278	
ARO		18,278
After the 12/31/X7 entries (the last year), the accumulated depletion balance equals the balance in the Developed mine account. The resulting zero net book value is removed from the accounts. Also, the balance in the ARO account is $342,265. Assume that the actual cost to close the mine and reclaim the land is $360,000:		
ARO	342,265	
Loss on settlement of ARO	17,735	
Cash	360,000	

IV. ASC 410-30 Environmental Obligations

A. ASC 410-30 addresses the accounting and reporting for environmental obligations.

B. Unlike the AROs, an environmental obligation is not associated directly with an asset. An environmental obligation stems from a legal action in violation of one of various Environmental Protection Acts (i.e., Clean Air Act). An environmental liability must be accrued when the liability is both probable and reasonably estimable. Frequently the company would accrue an environmental liability when it has been named the potentially responsible party (PRP) for the environmental remediation.

Contingencies, Commitments, and Guarantees

Contingent Liability Principles

This lesson introduces an important type of liability and the underlying principles for recognition.

After studying this lesson, you should be able to:

1. Define "contingent" liability.

2. Explain when they are recognized in the accounts and when they are footnoted only.

3. Record the journal entries for a regular warranty, a common type of contingent liability.

4. Determine the amount to recognize for a contingent liability when only a range of values can be estimated.

I. Introduction

> **Definition**
> *Contingency*: An existing condition (at the balance sheet date) involving uncertainty as to a possible loss that will be resolved when a future event occurs or fails to occur.

A. Remember that all liabilities are the result of a past event. A contingent liability must exist as of the balance sheet date, which means there must have been a transaction or event implying that a liability may have been incurred. However, a future event also plays an important role in the recognition of a contingent liability.

   1. For example, a firm is a defendant in a lawsuit. The suit is not resolved as of the balance sheet date. The firm does have a definite liability at year-end, but is contingently liable. The outcome of the suit in the following year will result in either a definite liability or no liability at all. Contingent liabilities are generally disclosed and possibly recognized, as discussed below.

   2. General risks and contingencies such as the possibility of a strike or casualty are not recognized or disclosed because no event or transaction has occurred as of the balance sheet date to substantiate that a liability has been incurred. A firm cannot accrue future casualty losses for example.

B. The accounting for contingencies is dependent on the probability of the future event occurring, and whether the amount of the gain or loss is estimable. This lesson considers only contingent liabilities. Other contingencies such as uncollectible accounts receivable and asset impairments are discussed elsewhere.

II. Probability of Future Event

A. In accounting for contingencies, a determination must be made related to the probability of occurrence of the future event (which will resolve the contingency) and the possibility of estimation.

B. In assessing the probability of occurrence, professional judgment is employed to classify the probability into one of three categories. Attorneys or legal counsel assess the likelihood of the event occurring and will classify the event into one of the following categories:

   1. **Probable**—Based on professional judgment, the probability of occurrence is considered very high or a near certainty.

2. **Reasonably possible**—Based on professional judgment, the probability of occurrence is neither very high nor remote. In other words, when probability of occurrence is considered along a spectrum of possibilities, the probability of occurrence is not at either end of the spectrum, but is in the large middle section of the spectrum.

3. **Remote**—Based on professional judgment, the probability of occurrence is considered to be very low, or as the title implies, remote.

C. **Reasonable Estimate of Amount**—Based on professional judgment and experience, a determination is made about the possibility of estimating the amount of the contingency. Either the amount of resulting gain or loss is reasonably estimable or it is not. In addition, firms may be able to estimate a possible range of amounts for the gain or loss, but be unable to assign any amount in the range a higher probability of occurring than any other amount.

D. **The Loss Contingency is Probable and Can be Reasonably Estimated at the Balance Sheet Date**—GAAP requires that if a contingent loss is both *probable* and *estimable*, then an estimated loss and estimated liability is recognized—actually recorded in the accounts in the amount estimated. The guiding theoretical considerations here are conservatism and the definition of a liability. Because the loss (asset decrease or liability increase) will most likely occur in the future and because the firm can estimate the amount, there is no reason to postpone the loss and liability recognition until it actually occurs. The general definition of a liability is met when the contingent liability is probable and estimable.

1. Gain contingencies are not accrued but rather are recorded when the actual gain takes place. For example, if the entity is the plaintiff in a lawsuit where it is probable that the entity will prevail, the entity does not accrue the gain until the actual payment is received (no matter the level of probability or precision of the estimate).

2. Loss contingencies can occur when the entity:

   a. is the defendant in a lawsuit, or

   b. provides product warranty, or

   c. provides rebates or premiums on the product.

Example
Recognized Contingent Liability

A large retailer offers warranties on its products. The firm estimates that total warranty costs will amount to 2% of sales for the year. Warranty claims are expected to occur on an even basis over the two years following sale. Sales were $1,000,000 for the year. There is no beginning warranty liability account balance for the year and there have been warranty claims totaling $6,000 during the year. This is a probable and estimable contingent liability. The actual loss or expense is contingent on a future event: customers making warranty claims. But a past transaction has occurred indicating it is probable that services will have to be provided in the future and the amount is estimable. Therefore, the loss or expense, and liability are recognized in the year of sale with the following adjusting entry.

Warranty Expense	20,000	
Warranty Liability		20,000

The fact that the warranty liability is a contingent liability does not change the fact that it must be recorded in the accounts. Note the entire estimated amount is recorded in the year of sale. The pattern of claims is not a factor in the recognition of the expense. When claims are actually made, the warranty liability is reduced and cash, inventory, and other assets are reduced:

Warranty Liability	6,000	
Cash, Parts Inventory, etc.		6,000

Firms must disclose the accounting policy with respect to warranty accounting, and disclose a schedule of the changes in the warranty liability for the period (increases due to expense, decreases due to claim service).

If the estimate of claims significantly overstates the actual claims cost, then the adjusting entry at the end of the year uses a smaller percentage to compensate. The opposite is true as well. There is no retroactive adjustment; rather the estimate is changed for the current and future periods to reflect the actual level of claims.

If the firm is able to estimate a range of possible losses, with no amount in the range having a higher probability of occurring than any other amount, the amount recognized in the accounts is the **lowest** amount in the range. Use of the lowest amount is the least conservative alternative. The footnotes should describe the entire range, however. In all other cases (other than probable and estimable), no accrual of the loss is required. Footnote disclosure is required unless the probability of occurrence is remote.

Exam Tip

Often in a lawsuit there is a range of probable loss. When there is no amount within the range that is most likely, the lowest amount in that range is accrued as a contingent liability. If a range of values is given but one value in the range has a higher probability assigned to it than any other, the value with the higher probability is used to accrue the contingent liability.

E. **The Loss Contingency is Probable and Cannot be Reasonably Estimated**—In this situation, the loss contingency should be disclosed in the footnotes to the financial statements.

F. **The Loss Contingency is Reasonably Possible**—In this situation, regardless of whether the loss can be reasonably estimated, the loss contingency is disclosed in the footnotes to the financial statements.

G. **The Loss Contingency is Remote**—In this situation, whether the loss can be reasonably estimated or not, the loss contingency can be disclosed in the footnotes to the financial statements. Please note that footnote disclosure is permitted but not required.

Examples of Contingent Liabilities and Additional Aspects

This lesson provides additional examples of recognized contingent liabilities, and addresses unasserted claims, gain contingencies and guarantees.

After studying this lesson, you should be able to:

1. Record a variety of recognized contingent liabilities.

2. Determine when an unasserted claim is recognized in the accounts.

3. State the appropriate reporting of gain contingencies.

4. Explain the reporting of guarantees.

I. Examples of Contingent Liabilities

Examples

1. Recognized Contingent Litigation Liability

The Lion Company was sued during the last quarter of 20X7 because of an accident involving a vehicle owned and operated by the company. After discussing the case with the company's legal representatives, it was decided that the company would probably lose the case, and the amount of damages could be reasonably estimated at $50,000.

Entry:

Estimated Loss from Pending Lawsuit	$50,000	
Estimated Liability from Pending Lawsuit		$50,000

Had the firm believed that the loss was only reasonably possible, the above entry would not be made. The lawsuit and possible loss would be discussed in the footnotes. Only a small percentage of contingent lawsuit losses are recognized.

2. Recognized Contingent Premium Liability

The Wolf Company offered to its customers a premium—a special coffee cup free of charge (cost per cup: $ .75) with the return of 20 coupons. One coupon is placed in each can of coffee when packed. The company estimated, on the basis of past experience that only 70% of the coupons will be redeemed. The following additional data is available for two years.

	Year 1	Year 2
Number of Coffee Cups Purchased	6,000	4,000
Number of Cans of Coffee Sold	100,000	200,000
Number of Coupons Redeemed	40,000	120,000

Entries:

Record the Purchase of Cups:

Year 1:	Premium Inventory	$4,500	
	Cash ($.75 × 6,000)		$4,500
Year 2:	Premium Inventory	$3,000	
	Cash		$3,000

Record the Estimated Premium Expense and Liability:

Year 1:	Estimated Premium Expense	$2,625	
	Estimated Premium Liability		$2,625

$2,625 = (100,000/20) \times \$.75 \times .70$

Year 2:	Estimated Premium Expense	$5,250	
	Estimated Premium Liability		$5,250

$5,250 = (200,000/20) \times \$.75 \times .70$

This is another example of a recognized contingent liability. Because it is probable and estimable, it is recorded like any other recognized liability.

Record the Redemption of the Coupons:

Year 1:	Estimated Premium Liability	$1,500	
	Premium Inventory		$1,500

$1,500 = (40,000/20) \times \$.75 = 1,500$

Year 2:	Estimated Premium Liability	$4,500	
	Premium Inventory		$4,500

$4,500 = (120,000/20) \times \$.75 = 4,500$

II. Unasserted Claims and Assessments

A. Entities may be subject to future claims and assessments not yet filed as of the balance sheet date. Examples include possible IRS actions against the entity for violations of the tax law, EPA claims against the entity for environmental violations, and other events that have occurred as of the balance sheet date.

B. If, at the balance sheet date, it is not probable that a claim or assessment will occur or if the outcome is not expected to be unfavorable to the entity, then no recognition or disclosure is required.

C. If it is probable that a claim or assessment will occur, and there is at least a reasonable probability that the outcome will be unfavorable to the entity, then the claim or assessment is treated as a contingency, even though no claim or assessment has been filed. The event before the balance sheet that would trigger the claim or assessment (such as a previous year's tax return filing or environmental violation) must have occurred, before the entity recognizes or discloses the contingency.

1. If the amount is estimable, the contingent liability is recognized.

2. Otherwise, it is footnoted only.

III. Contingencies Acquired in Business Combinations

A. In mergers and acquisitions, the acquiring firm may acquire contingencies of the acquired firm. The amounts ascribed to contingencies, as is the case for any other identifiable asset or liability, affect the valuation of recorded goodwill on the acquisition. The amount recognized for this type of contingent liability is somewhat different than that discussed above.

B. If the contingency is contractual (e.g., a regular warranty) at acquisition, then contingent liability is recognized by the acquirer at fair value.

C. At acquisition, if the contingency is not contractual and has more than a 50% probability of becoming a definite liability when a future event occurs or does not occur, then the liability is recognized at fair value. Otherwise, there is no recognition.

D. After acquisition, as new information is obtained, the contingency is reported at the greater of acquisition date fair value, and the amount that would be recognized under normal contingency rules. Any changes in the reported liability are recognized as gains or losses.

IV. Gain Contingencies

A. **The Gain Contingency is Probable**—In this situation, whether the gain can be reasonably estimated or not, the gain contingency is disclosed in the footnotes to the financial statements. Probable and estimable gain contingencies, in contrast with loss contingencies, are not recognized in the accounts. Conservatism dictates that the future event must first occur before recognizing the gain and asset increase (or liability decrease).

B. **The Gain Contingency is Reasonably Possible**—In this situation, regardless of whether the gain can be reasonably estimated, the gain contingency is disclosed in the footnotes to the financial statements.

C. **The Gain Contingency is Remote**—In this situation, regardless of whether the gain can be reasonably estimated, footnote disclosure of the gain contingency is not recommended.

V. Guarantees

A. There are many types of guarantees that an entity can provide. The more complex guarantees are beyond the scope of the CPA exam. However, the accounting and disclosure of the guarantee of another entity's indebtedness is something that the CPA candidate should understand. Entities may guarantee the debt of an affiliate to help the affiliate obtain a loan or a line of credit. The guarantor must be ready to comply with the guarantee if the triggering event occurs (e.g., default by the debtor whose debt is guaranteed by the guarantor).

B. The guarantor is required to disclose the following:

1. The nature of the guarantee, the term of the guarantee, how the guarantee came into existence, and the triggering event

2. The maximum future amount payable under the guarantee

3. The carrying amount of the liability

4. A description of recourse provisions or available collateral enabling the guarantor to recover the amounts paid under the guarantee, if any

C. If it is probable that the triggering event will occur and the guarantor will be required to pay under the terms of the guarantee, then the guarantor must accrue a liability associated with the guarantee.

VI. In summary there are three main categories of contingent liabilities:

A. Lawsuits (or other legal action):

1. Accrue and disclose when loss is probable and estimable

2. Disclose when loss is possible (no accrual)

3. No disclosure or accrual when loss is remote

B. Product warranties, rebates, and premiums

1. Accrue an estimated liability based on historical payments and disclose information regarding the liability

C. Financial guarantees of another entity's indebtedness

1. Disclose information regarding the guarantee

2. Accrue a liability associated with the guarantee only when the payment associated with the guarantee is probable

Financial Liabilities and Long-Term Debt

Notes Payable

The general principles applying to all notes payable are covered in this lesson. Accounting for several different types of notes is illustrated with journal entries.

After studying this lesson, you should be able to:

1. Distinguish simple interest notes and installment notes.

2. Choose the correct interest rate for the appropriate computation.

3. Determine whether a note is issued at a premium or discount.

4. Compute the total interest expense over the term of the note.

5. Compute interest expense for a period on a noncurrent note.

6. Apply the gross method and the net method.

7. Apply the effective interest and straight-line methods.

8. Record the initial issuance of notes payable at present value.

9. Compute and record interest expense on notes payable for multiple periods.

10. Record the relevant journal entries for notes issued in exchange for rights or other privileges.

I. Notes Payable Features and Reporting

A. Notes payable are more formal than accounts payable and involve interest. A formal document called a "promissory note" details the rights and duties of both parties to the note. Notes can be classified as current or noncurrent.

B. Current notes payable are reported at the amount due when they mature. Noncurrent notes are reported at the present value of future payments, discounted at the prevailing interest rate at time of issuance.

C. Simple interest notes have a face value that is also the maturity amount, the amount due at the end of the note term. The stated interest rate and face value determine the annual interest to be paid. A 5%, $10,000 (face value) note pays $500 interest per year, with the $10,000 maturity amount due at the end of the note term.

D. **Installment Notes**— Each payment includes principal and interest—have no maturity value because the last payment reduces the note payable balance to zero. These notes are often used to purchase plant assets and may be secured by those assets. A mortgage note is an example.

E. There are two rates of interest relevant to notes payable:

1. Stated rate is the contractual rate listed in the note; this rate determines the cash interest payments.

2. Yield or market rate is the rate on notes of similar risk and term (the prevailing rate).

   If the two rates are equal, the note is issued at face value.

F. When the yield rate is greater than the stated rate, the note is issued at a discount (less than face). When the yield rate is less than the stated rate, the note is issued at a premium (more than face). The issue price or proceeds is the present value, also called principal.

G. The total interest expense over the note term equals the difference between the total payments required under the note and the principal amount. Total interest expense also equals total cash interest over the term plus the discount or minus the premium at issuance.

H. Notes issued for nonmonetary consideration (goods and services) are measured at the more reliable of (a) fair value of the consideration, or (b) present value of future cash payments discounted at the prevailing rate.

I. Periodic interest expense is computed as the product of the yield rate at the date of issuance, and the beginning net note liability (present value). This approach is called the effective interest method and is required by GAAP. The difference between cash interest paid and interest expense recognized at each payment date is the amortization of discount or premium.

J. At subsequent balance sheet dates, notes are reported at the present value of remaining payments, using the yield rate at the date of issuance. Present value also equals face value plus unamortized premium or less unamortized discount.

K. An alternative to the effective interest method is the straight-line method, which is allowed only if it results in interest expense amounts not materially different from the effective interest method. An equal amount of discount or premium amortization is recognized each period.

L. The gross or net method of recording the note and interest expense are both acceptable. The gross method separates the face value (note payable) and discount or premium in different accounts. The net method uses one combined net account (note payable), which is the present value and net note liability under the effective interest method.

M. The fair value of notes must be disclosed—that is, the estimate of the amount required to pay off the note at the balance sheet date. Also disclosed are the details of noncurrent notes such as interest rates, assets pledged, call and conversion provisions and restrictions, and the aggregate maturity amounts for each of the five years following the balance sheet date.

N. Direct loan origination fees and points are recognized over the loan term.

II. Examples

A. Noncurrent Interest-Bearing Note Payable—An interest-bearing note payable is one in which the interest element is explicitly stated. These notes are recorded at the present value of future cash flows, using the market rate of interest as the discount rate. If the stated interest rate and the market rate of interest are not equal, the present value of the future cash flows is not equal to the face amount of the note, and a discount or premium is recorded.

Example
Interest-Bearing Long-Term Notes Payable where Stated and Market Rates Unequal
The Montana Company paid for legal services received by giving the law firm a $10,000 three-year, 6% note payable (interest payable at the end of the year) on January 1 of Year 1. The market rate of interest for a note of this type is 10%. The value of the legal services is not specified. Therefore, the present value of the note is used as the amount to record both sides of the transaction. In some cases, the stated rate is intentionally lowered to ease the cash flow requirements of the debtor firm during the note term.

Present Value of Future Cash Flows

$10,000 × .75131 (PV of $1, N = 3, I = 10%)	=	$7,513
$600 × 2.48685 (PV of an Annuity, N = 3, I = 10%)	=	1,492
Total Present Value of Future Cash Flows		$9,005

Debt Amortization Schedule

Date	Cash Interest	Interest Expense	Discount Amortized	Unamortized Discount	Carrying Value
1/1/Y1				$995	$9,005
12/31/Y1	$600	$900	$300	$695	$9,305
12/31/Y2	$600	$931	$331	$364	$9,636
12/31/Y3	$600	$964	$364	$0	$10,000
Totals	$1,800	$2,795	$995		

Entries:

Year 1:	Legal Expenses	$9,005	
1/1/1	Discount on Note Payable	$995	
	Note Payable		$10,000

This discount account is contra to Note Payable.

The net note payable balance is $9,005.

12/31/1	Interest Expense	$900	
	Discount on Note Payable		$300
	Cash		$600
Year 2:	Interest Expense	$931	
12/31/2	Discount on Note Payable		$331
	Cash		$600
Year 3:	Interest Expense	$964	
12/31/3	Discount on Note Payable		$364
	Cash		$600
	Note Payable	$10,000	
	Cash		$10,000

In this example, we illustrate the gross method. The note payable is listed at face value, with separate recording of the discount. The net method is also acceptable and would record the note payable initially at $9,005 with no discount recorded. Interest expense for Year 1 is .10 × $9,005 (the net note balance at beginning of Year 1).

The legal expenses are recorded at the present value of the future payments at the market or prevailing interest rate. The stated rate of 6% is used only to compute the interest payments. Interest expense is based on the market rate of 10%.

The total interest expense over the note term ($2,795) is the difference between the principal of $9,005 and the sum of the future payments of $11,800 (3 x $600 + $10,000). It also equals the sum of the $1,800 cash interest over the term (3 × $600) and the $995 discount. The discount represents additional interest because the firm received only $9,005 worth of services but must pay $10,000 at the note's maturity.

If the straight-line (SL) method of amortization had been chosen, the journal entry for the three interest payments would be the same, as follows:

Interest expense	932	
Discount on note payable	332	(995/3)
Cash	600	

B. Non-Interest-Bearing Notes Payable—A non-interest-bearing note payable is one in which the interest element is not explicitly stated but rather is included in the face amount of the note. These notes are recorded at the present value of future cash flows, using the market rate of interest as the discount rate.

Example

A firm purchases a used plant asset by issuing a one-year, $10,165 face value note. The note pays no cash interest. The purchase occurred on July 1, Year 1 for this calendar-year firm. The plant asset has a market value of $9,500. The implied market rate of interest is 7% as shown below. A non-interest-bearing note is another example for which the stated rate (0% here) is less than the yield rate.

$10,165(PV of $1, I = ?, N = 1)   = $9,500

(PV of $1, I = ?, N = 1) = $9,500/$10,165 = .93458

This present value factor corresponds to I = 7%.

The purchaser included the 7% interest in the face value of the note. (Net method is shown.)

July 1, Year 1	Equipment	9,500	
	Note Payable		9,500
December 31, Year 1	Interest Expense $9,500(.07/2)	332.50	
	Note Payable		332.50

Interest expense is based on the beginning net liability balance

June 30, Year 2	Interest Expense	332.50	
	Note Payable		332.50
	Note Payable	10,165	
	Cash		10,165

Total interest on the note = $665 = $332.50(2) = $10,165 – $9,500. This solution illustrates the net method. There is no separate accounting for the discount. The gross method could also have been used. The straight-line method is inappropriate in this example, given the magnitude of the difference between the stated and yield rates.

C. Installment Note

Example

On 1/1/X5, a firm purchased a building by paying $100,000 down and signing a $400,000, 6%, 10-year secured mortgage note. The note calls for annual payments beginning 12/31/X5. The prevailing interest rate for a note of this type is 10%. Each payment includes principal and interest, and the note is fully paid with the last payment. The gross or net method can be used as always but the straight-line method is not appropriate because each payment reduces principal.

The annual payment (pmt) is computed using the stated rate and total note amount as indicated in the note:

400,000 = pmt(PV annuity, i =.06, n =10) = pmt(7.36009)

400,000/7.36009 = pmt = $54,347

The amount borrowed is the present value of all payments required on the note using the prevailing or yield rate of 10%. The situation is silent on the fair value of the building. Therefore, the present value of the note (at the yield rate) is used for recording both the note and building.

Amount borrowed = $54,347(PV annuity, i =.10, n =10) = $54,347(6.14457) =$333,939

Journal entries (net method):

1/1/X5	Building	433,939		
	Cash		100,000	
	Mortgage note payable		333,939	
12/31/X5	Interest expense	33,394		333,939(.10)
	Mortgage note payable	20,953		
	Cash		54,347	
12/31/X6	Interest expense	31,299		(333,939 − 20,953)(.10)
	Mortgage note payable	23,048		
	Cash		54,347	

The ending 20X5 balance of the note payable is $312,986 = $333,939 − $20,953, the principal portion of the first payment. The total balance is reported as follows: (1) $23,048 current liability (CL), and $289,938 noncurrent (NCL) = $312,986 − $23,048. The portion of the liability to be paid in 20X6 is the amount classified as current for 20X5 ($23,048).

The ending 20X6 balance of the note payable is $289,938 = $333,939 − $20,953 − $23,048. This balance also can be computed as $54,347(PV annuity, i =.10, n =8) because there are eight payments remaining at this point.

Total interest over the 10 year note term equals the difference between the total payments on the note less the amount borrowed = (10 × $54,347) − $333,939 = $209,531.

Note that each payment affects both interest expense (income statement) and the balance in the net mortgage note payable (balance sheet). In analyzing the effect of the payment on the firm's financial statements, it is important to distinguish the expense from the reduction in principal. Interest is always computed first.

Erroneous reporting of the entire amount of the payment as a reduction in principal overstates the debtor's net income and understates liabilities.

D. Note in Exchange for Rights or Other Privileges—A firm may borrow from a customer and ask for an interest rate less than the prevailing rate in exchange for a reduced price on goods or services to be sold to the customer. Part of the consideration received on the borrowing is a prepayment by the customer for the reduced price. The note is recorded as always using the prevailing rate. The difference between the amount borrowed and the present value of the note is unearned revenue.

Example

At the beginning of 20X4, Duke Inc. borrowed $40,000 by issuing a three-year non-interest-bearing note with face value of $40,000. The prevailing rate on similar notes is 10%. In exchange, Duke agrees to provide the creditor (customer of Duke) with goods at a reduced price over four years.

The present value of the note is $40,000(PV1, i =.10, n =3) = $40,000(.75131) = $30,052.

Journal entries (gross method):

1/1/X4	Cash	40,000		
	Discount on note	9,948		40,000 − 30,052
	Note payable		40,000	
	Unearned revenue		9,948	

Duke receives an interest-free loan in exchange for reducing the prices on its goods to the creditor firm, (Duke's customer). The loan is in substance only for $30,052 and is the basis for interest expense recognition. The remaining $9,948 received by Duke is a prepayment by the customer for reduced prices on the goods it will buy from Duke.

12/31/X4	Interest expense	3,005		.10(30,052)
	Unearned revenue	2,487		9,948/4
	Discount on note		3,005	
	Sales revenue		2,487	

The remaining journal entries for interest proceed as illustrated in other examples. The ending net balance of the note immediately before payment will be $40,000 because the discount will be fully amortized. The recognition of sales revenue proceeds as above over four years assuming the customer purchases equivalent amounts of goods each year.

III. **Joint and Several Liability Arrangements**—Joint and several obligations arise when more than one entity agrees to be liable for the entire amount of an obligation. If one of the entities is unable to make payment when the liability is due, each of the other entities is fully liable for the debt. Such arrangements may arise through a borrowing that involves a note payable.

   A. A firm in such an arrangement for which the total amount of the debt is fixed at the reporting date, reports the obligation at the sum of:

   1. The amount the firm agreed to pay (the required amount according to the arrangement); plus

   2. Any additional amount the firm expects to pay on behalf of the others in the arrangement.

   B. If there is an amount within the range for the second part (2.) that is a better estimate than any other in the range, then that amount is used for (2.). If not, the minimum amount in the range is used.

Bonds Payable

Bond Accounting Principles

Exam Tip
This is a major topic on the CPA Exam. A bond is a long-term debt instrument issued to many different creditor/investors. A bond contrasts with a note that represents the debt for a borrowing from a single creditor.

I. Bond Basics

Definition
Bond: A financial debt instrument that typically calls for the payment of periodic interest with the face value being due at some time in the future. The bondholder (creditor or investor) pays the issuing firm an amount based on the stated and market rates of interest and receives interest and the face amount in return, over the bond term. Bonds and notes are the major sources of general debt funding for corporations.

A. There are seven items of information that must be known to account for a bond:

1. **Face (maturity) value**—The amount paid to the bondholder at maturity. This amount is often $1,000.

2. **Stated (coupon) interest rate**—The rate at which the bond pays cash interest. The rate is stated on the bond. If the rate is 6% and the bond's face value is $1,000, then one bond pays $60 interest each year.

3. **Interest payment dates**—The dates the bond pays the cash interest. Semi-annual interest payments are the norm.

4. **Market (yield, effective) interest rate**—The rate equating the sum of the present values of the cash interest annuity and the face value single payment, with the bond price. If a 6%, $1,000 bond was issued for $900, the market rate of interest equates the $900 amount with the present value of the annuity of $60 (or $30 twice a year), and the $1,000 face value to be paid in the future. The market rate is the true compounded rate of return on the bond. This rate is determined by the market and does not appear on the bond.

5. **Bond date**—The planned issuance date. This date is listed on the bond.

6. **Issuance date**—The date the bonds are actually issued. This date cannot be earlier than the bond date but may be later. This information is not on the bond.

7. **Maturity date**—The date the maturity value is paid, the end of the bond term.

B. Other Terminology

1. **Bond term**—The period from issuance date to maturity date

2. **Bond issue costs**—The cost of printing, registering, and marketing the bonds

3. **Accrued interest on bond sale**—The amount of interest, based on the coupon interest rate for the period, between the issuance date and the immediately preceding interest payment date

4. **Bond price**—The current market price of a bond exclusive of accrued interest

5. **Bond proceeds**—The sum of the bond price and any accrued interest

C. Types of bonds—There are several classifications of bond issues. The most important for the exam are:

1. **Secured versus unsecured (debentures)**—A secured bond issue has a claim to specific assets. Otherwise, the bondholders are unsecured creditors and are grouped with other unsecured creditors. An unsecured bond is backed only by the credit of the issuing firm and is called a debenture.

2. **Serial versus single maturity term**—A serial bond matures serially, that is at regular or staggered intervals. The total face value of this issue is paid gradually rather than all at once, as is the case with a single maturity or term bond.

3. **Callable versus redeemable**—An issuer can retire callable bonds before maturity at a specified price. The bondholder can require a redeemable bond to be retired early.

4. **Convertible versus nonconvertible**—A convertible bond can be converted into capital stock by the bondholder; a nonconvertible bond cannot.

D. Determination of Selling Price of the Bond (Initial Book Value)—The selling price of a bond is equal to the present value of future cash flows face value and cash interest. The discount rate used for this calculation is the market rate of interest on the date the bonds are issued.

1. **Stated rate > market rate**—If the stated interest rate is greater than the market rate of interest, the bonds will sell at a premium.

   a. **The premium**—The amount received above face value and is recorded in Premium on Bonds Payable, an adjunct account to Bonds Payable. If a $1,000 bond sells for $1,100, then the premium is $100. The bond price increases (and yield rate decreases) to the point at which the yield rate equals the market rate for similar bonds.

2. **Stated rate < market rate**—If the stated interest rate is less than the market rate of interest, the bonds will sell at a discount.

   a. **The discount**—The amount below face value and is recorded in Discount on Bonds Payable, a contra account to Bonds Payable. If a $1,000 bond sells for $950, then the discount is $50. The price decreases (and yield rate increases) to the point at which the yield rate equals the market rate for similar bonds.

3. **Stated rate equals market rate**—If the stated rate and market rate are equal, the bond sells at face value and no premium or discount is recorded. (Sell at face value: stated rate = market rate)

Example

A bond issued at a discount:

A 6%, $1,000 bond dated 1/1/x7 is issued on that date to yield 8%. The bond pays interest each June 30 and December 31 and matures four years from issuance. The bond price equals:

$1,000(PV of $1, i = 4%, n = 8)

+ .03($1,000)(PV of $1 annuity, i = 4%, n = 8)

= $1,000(.73069) + $30(6.73274)

= $933

The price (present value) is computed using the market rate of interest. 4% is used rather than 8% because the bonds pay interest semiannually. The 3% interest rate is used only to compute the semiannual interest payment. The bond sells at a discount because investors can earn 8% on competing bonds.

Bond prices are expressed in percentage of face value. This bond was issued at 93.3, or 93.3% of face value. Bond prices are always quoted exclusive of any accrued interest. This example uses only one bond for simplicity. A bond issue of 1,000 bonds would provide $933,000 of debt capital. The amounts in the journal entries and financial statement sections below would be multiplied by 1,000.

The entry to record the issuance of the bond is:

Cash	933	
Discount on Bonds Payable	67	
Bonds Payable		1,000

The noncurrent liability section of the balance sheet immediately after issuance would disclose:

Bonds Payable	$1,000
Less Discount on Bonds Payable	(67)
Net Bonds Payable	$933

The $933 amount is the net bond liability or book value of the bond issue. The bonds payable account is always measured at face value. The discount and premium are contra or adjunct accounts that reduce or increase the net liability to present value. With interest rate changes after issuance, the fair value of the bond most likely is not $933. In the last year of the bond term, the net liability is reported as a current liability, often called *current maturities of long-term debt*.

E. Amortization of Premium/Discounts

1. The discount or premium on a bond issue is amortized over the bond term. The book value of the bond issue must equal face value on the maturity date because that is the amount paid to retire the bonds.

2. The amortization of premiums and discounts is accomplished through the use of the *effective interest method*. Due to materiality, many companies employ the *straight-line amortization method*. The straight-line method is acceptable only if the results do not depart materially from the effective interest method.

Exam Tip

Both methods of amortization are tested on the exam. Questions with more involved requirements often use the straight-line method because the amounts are easier to compute.

3. **Effective interest method**—This method first computes interest expense based on the beginning book value of the bond and the market rate at issuance. The difference between interest expense and the cash interest paid is the amortization of the discount or the premium. The market rate at issuance is always used to compute interest expense. The rate is not changed after issuance because it represents the true interest rate over the bond term. The amortization of discount or premium is a "plug" figure.

Example

Using the previous example of computing the bond price, the June 30 entry in year of issuance under the effective interest method is:

Interest Expense $933(.04)	37	
Discount on Bonds Payable		7
Cash $1,000(.03)		30

The net book value of the bonds is now $940 ($933 + $7). That is the amount on which interest expense at December 31 is computed. The book value changes with each interest entry and will equal $1,000 at maturity. Therefore, each entry recognizes a different amount of interest expense. But the ratio of interest expense to beginning book value is constant and equals the effective interest rate. The resulting book value is the present value of remaining cash payments using the yield rate at issuance.

The initial discount of $67 represents additional interest because only $933 was received from the bondholders, but $1,000 must be paid at maturity. Therefore, total interest expense over the bond issue equals cash interest plus the discount = 8($30) + $67 = $307.

The $67 of additional interest expense (initial discount) is gradually recognized over the term of the bonds; that is why in the entry above, interest expense is $7 more than cash interest paid.

The effect of a premium is opposite that of a discount. It represents a reduction in total interest expense over the bond term because the premium is not paid at maturity. Semiannual interest expense is less than cash interest paid, by the amount of the premium amortization. The book value of the bond issue gradually decreases to face value over the bond term.

4. **Straight-line (SL) method**—This method recognizes a constant amount of amortization each month of the bond term. The straight-line method should not be used when (a) the term to maturity is quite long and there is more than a minor difference between the market and stated rates, or (b) when there is a very significant difference between the market and stated rates regardless of the length of the term. An example of (b) is a zero coupon bond. Such bonds pay no interest (stated rate = 0). However, they yield competitive rates. The effective interest method must be used for these bonds.

Example

Using the previous example of computing the bond price, the June 30 entry in year of issuance under the straight-line method is:

(Note: The interest expense amount is a "plug" figure.)

Interest Expense	38	
Discount on Bonds Payable		8 ($67/48 months)(6 months)
Cash $1,000(.03)		30

The bond term is four years long or 48 months. Six months have elapsed since the issuance of the bonds. The entry at each interest date is the same as the one above for the straight-line method. The interest expense is the same amount for each entry.

Bond Complications

This lesson incorporates additional aspects into accounting for bonds.

After studying this lesson, you should be able to:

1. Record the issuance of a zero coupon bond and subsequent interest expense.

2. Compute and record accrued interest for bonds issued between interest dates.

3. Account for bond issue costs at the issuance of the bonds and throughout the bond term.

4. Analyze the effect of accrued interest and debt issue costs on the firm's financial statements.

I. Zero Coupon Bonds—These bonds pay no interest (coupon rate is zero), but the accounting procedure remains the same except that no cash interest is paid during the term. The entire amount of interest is included in the face value, just like a non-interest-bearing note. Zero coupon bonds, and also "deep-discount" bonds with very low coupon rates, are issued at a large discount.

Example

$400,000 (face value) of zero coupon bonds are issued to yield 5% on January 1, Year 1. The bonds mature in 20 years.

Issue price = $400,000(PV $1, i = 5%, n = 20) = $400,000(0.37689) = $150,756

Journal entries:

1/1/year 1	Cash	150,756	
	Discount on bonds	249,244	
	Bonds payable		400,000
12/31/year 1	Interest Expense	7,538	$150,756(.05)
	Discount on bonds		7,538

The SL method is not appropriate for this type of bond.

II. Bonds Issued between Interest Dates—When bonds are issued between interest dates, the total cash received by the company issuing the bonds equals to the selling price of the bonds plus interest (at the stated rate) accrued since the last interest date. This sum is called the "proceeds." By requiring the investor to pay the interest accrued since the last interest date, the issuing company can pay the usual amount of interest at the next interest date.

Example

A bond issue dated January 1 and paying interest each June 30 and December 31 is issued on April 30. The issuing firm collects 4 months of interest from January 1—April 30. Then, on June 30, the firm pays 6 months of interest. If the original bondholder holds the bonds on June 30, the bondholder receives 6 months of interest because the bond automatically pays 6 months of interest on that date. The bondholder nets 2 months of interest for the period the bonds were held:

     6 months of interest received on June 30

  − 4 months paid at purchase

  = 2 months earned interest

In the entry for bond issuance, accrued interest payable is credited for the interest collected from the bondholders and cash is increased by this amount. There is no interest expense recognized at this point because the bond term has just begun. Accrued interest has no effect on the amount of premium or discount.

Example
Bender Inc. issued $8,000 of 8% bonds at 105 on March 1. The bonds pay interest each December 31 and June 30 and are dated January 1, Year 1. The bonds mature five years after the bond date. The first three entries under the straight-line method (SL) are:

March 1, Year 1

Cash $8,000(1.05) + .08(2/12)($8,000)	8,507	
Premium on Bonds Payable ($8,000).05		400
Accrued Interest Payable .08(2/12)($8,000)		107
Bonds Payable		8,000

June 30, Year 1

Interest Expense	185	
Premium on Bonds Payable ($400/58 months)(4 months)	28	
Accrued Interest Payable	107	
Cash .08(6/12)($8,000)		320

(There are 58 months in the bond term, or four years and ten months, and four months have elapsed since the bond issuance, requiring four months of amortization.) The accrued interest is a separate resource. It is not included in the price and has no effect on the discount or premium.

December 31, Year 1

Interest Expense	279	
Premium on Bonds Payable ($400/58 months)(6 months)	41	
Cash .08(6/12)($8,000)		320

The remaining entries in the bond term are identical to the December 31 entry.

III. Debt Issue Costs

These costs include legal fees, printing costs, and promotion costs related to the issuance of a debt instrument such as a bond or note. Debt issuance costs are the incremental costs of issuing debt (third-party costs), excluding those paid to the lender.

A. Accounting and Reporting:

1. Debt issue costs are reported in the balance sheet as a direct deduction from the liability's carrying amount. This is the same treatment afforded stock issue costs. Debt issue costs are not capitalized as an asset.

2. Debt issue costs are amortized to interest expense over the term of the related debt instrument.

Example
On January 1, Year 1, 20, 5%, $1,000 bonds are issued at 100. The bonds mature in 10 years and pay interest each June 30 and December 31. $1,200 of debt issue costs incurred.

Calculation of the effective interest rate m:

$20,000 − $1,200 = $20,000(PV $1, m, n = 20) + (.05/2)($20,000)(PV $1 annuity, m, n = 20)

$18,800 = $20,000(PV $1, m, n = 20) + $500(PV $1 annuity, m, n = 20)

Using a spreadsheet program or business calculator, m is computed to be 5.8%.

Journal entry for bond issue:

1/1/Year 1	Cash	18,800	
	Bonds payable		18,800

Debt issue costs reduce the proceeds of borrowing and increase the effective interest rate on the bond issue. They also reduce the carrying value of the debt.

Balance sheet presentation:

Noncurrent debt:

Bonds payable	$20,000
Unamortized bond issue costs	(1,200)
Net bond liability	$18,800

The above recording implies the *net* approach. Alternatively, the issue costs may be recorded in a valuation account (*bond issue costs* similar to bond discount) with the bonds payable account recorded at face value.

Journal entry for interest and amortization of bond issue costs:

6/30/Year 1	Interest expense	545		18,800(.058/2)
	Bonds payable		45	
	Cash		500	20,000(.05/2)

Interest expense includes amortization of debt issue costs. Had there been a discount on the bond issue, the amortization of the discount would be included in interest expense as well.

The straight-line (SL) method is an acceptable alternative to the effective interest approach shown above, if its results are not materially different.

If the SL approach is used, the amortization of bond issue costs would be $60 each 6-month period ($1,200/20 periods).

Analysis

The effect of bond issue costs on the issuing firm's financial statements is to (1) reduce the initial net bond liability and (2) increase interest expense in the future.

If instead, the bond issue costs were erroneously recognized as expense, the firm's net income is understated and liabilities are overstated in the year of issuance.

Bond Fair Value Option, International

This lesson addresses the use of the fair value option for bond accounting.

After studying this lesson, you should be able to:

1. Prepare a bond amortization schedule.

2. Apply the fair value option to determine the periodic unrealized gain or loss.

3. Report the unrealized gain or loss in the correct financial statement.

I. Amortization Tables—A bond amortization table shows the amounts for all journal entries and ending net bond liability for the entire bond term. The following is an example of an amortization table showing the use of the effective interest method. One line of an amortization conveys the same information as the journal entry for that year.

Example
On January 1, year 1, the Idaho Company issued bonds with a face value of $100,000 and a stated interest rate of 7%. The bonds will mature on December 31, year 5. Interest on the bonds is paid each December 31. The market rate of interest on January 1, year 1, was 8%.

Selling Price of the Bonds

$100,000 × .68058 (Present Value of $1, n = 5, i = 8%)	$68,058
$7,000 × 3.99271 (Present Value of Annuity, n = 5, i = 8%)	27,949
Total Price	$96,007

Partial Amortization Schedule

Date	Cash Interest	Effective Interest	Discount Amortized	Unamortized Discount	Carrying Value of Bonds
1/1/year 1				$3,993	$96,007
12/31/year 1	$7,000	$7,681	$681	$3,312	$96,688
12/31/year 2	$7,000	$7,735	$735	$2,577	$97,423
12/31/year 3	$7,000	$7,794	$794	$1,784	$98,216
12/31/year 4	$7,000	$7,857	$857	$926	$99,074
12/31/year 5	$7,000	$7,926	$926	$0	$100,000

Under the effective interest method, the carrying value of the bonds at the beginning of the year is used to compute interest expense. The year 1 interest expense of $7,681 equals ($96,007 × .08). The year 2 interest expense of $7,735 equals ($96,688 × .08).

A. When interest payment dates and fiscal year-end do not coincide, the portion of the interest period that falls within a reporting period is used to compute interest expense. The effective interest method "straight lines" the interest calculation during an interest period.

Example

If the Idaho bonds above were dated and issued on March 1, year 1, the amount of interest recognized and discount amortized would be 10/12 of the amounts in the 12/31/year 1 row of the amortization table above. Also, interest payable is credited at 12/31/year 1 for 10/12 of $7,000, rather than cash.

II. Fair Value Option (FVO)

A. The FVO allows certain financial assets and liabilities to be reported at fair value, with unrealized gains and losses reported in earnings in the year they occur. This option reduces the accounting mismatch inherent in using fair value for assets and a different measurement basis for liabilities and reduces earnings volatility because the effect of interest rate changes on investments in debt securities is opposite that on liabilities such as bonds payable.

B. The firm makes an irrevocable decision to choose the FVO on the date of issuance. The choice is by debt instrument. The option can be applied to all or a subset of debt instruments, even within the same type.

  1. If the option is not chosen, then the accounting proceeds as discussed previously.

  2. If the option is chosen, then the accounting also proceeds as discussed above but in addition, the firm increases or decreases the resulting book liability to fair value using a fair value adjustment account (FVA: adjunct or contra account).

    a. Fair value is the quoted market price of the security. If that is not available, the current market rate of interest on similar debt instruments is used to estimate fair value.

    b. The required change in the FVA for the period is recognized as an unrealized gain or loss.

      i. If the required fair value adjustment has increased, the firm recognizes an unrealized loss. The amount required to pay off the liability relative to the book value under the effective interest method at the balance sheet date has increased.

      ii. If the required fair value adjustment has decreased, the firm recognizes an unrealized gain.

      iii. Classification of the unrealized gain or loss:

        a. The portion of the total unrealized gain or loss attributable to credit risk (risk of default or delay in payment of interest or principal) is recognized in other comprehensive income.

        b. The portion attributable to the change in interest rates is recognized in net income.

Example
Fair value option applied. Assume the entire unrealized gain or loss is attributable to interest rate changes.

Amortization Schedule

Date	Cash Interest	Interest Expense	Premium Amortization	Unamortized Premium	Net Liability
1/1/X1				4213	104,213
12/31/X1	7000	6253	747	3466	103,466
12/31/X2	7000	6208	792	2674	102,674
12/31/X3	7000	6160	840	1834	101,834
12/31/X4	7000	6110	890	944	100,944
12/31/X5	7000	6056	944	0	100,000

12/31/X1	Interest expense	6,253	
	Premium	747	
	Cash		7,000

The resulting 12/31/X1 book value before applying FVO is $103,466 (see amortization schedule).

Now assume that the fair value of the bond issue at 12/31/X1 is $102,200. (Interest rates have increased.)

Required fair value adjustment (FVA) = $103,466 − $102,200 = $1,266 DR

12/31/X1	FVA	1,266	
	Unrealized gain		1,266

Financial Statement Effects

Income Statement		Balance Sheet	
Interest expense	$6,253	Bonds payable	$100,000
Unrealized gain	1,266	Premium	3,466
		FVA	(1,266)
		Net liability (fair value)	$102,200

12/31/X2

The fair value of the bond issue at 12/31/X2 is $103,136. (Interest rates have decreased.) From the amortization schedule, the book value, had the FVO not been chosen is $102,674 (see amortization schedule).

Required FVA = $103,136 − $102,674 =	$462 CR
FVA before adjustment	1,266 DR
Adjustment to FVA	$ 1,728 CR

Unrealized loss	1,728	
FVA		1,728

The loss of $1,728 also equals the sum of (1) increase in fair value for the period ($103,136 − $102,200), plus (2) $792 amortization of the premium for the period. Both factors cause the difference between fair value and the net liability per the amortization schedule) to increase.

Modification and Debt Retirement

Refinancing Short-Term Obligations

Current liabilities can be reclassified as noncurrent under the accounting principles covered in this lesson.

After studying this lesson, you should be able to:

1. Understand the three ways a firm can reclassify current liabilities to noncurrent status under GAAP.

I. Introduction

A. Definition—Recall that the definition of a current liability includes *the incurrence of other current liabilities*. This means that if a firm refinances a current liability with another current liability, the liability remains classified as current. Even though no current asset may be required for extinguishment in the coming year, the debtor firm cannot guarantee it will be able to continue to refinance on a short-term basis indefinitely.

If the debtor firm enters into a revolving credit agreement whereby one current liability is continually replaced with another current liability, even though no current assets may actually be used for a significant time period, the agreement does not allow reclassification of the liabilities to noncurrent status. This arrangement falls within the definition of a current liability.

B. Refinancing Short-Term Obligations—Many firms have a preference for classifying liabilities as noncurrent rather than current to improve their reported liquidity position and reduce the perceived immediate riskiness of the firm. Refinancing on a current basis is of no help here, but if a current liability is refinanced on a long-term basis, the classification of a current liability can be successfully changed to noncurrent without extinguishing the original liability.

II. Criteria for Reclassifying Current Liabilities as Noncurrent Liabilities—Reclassification of a current liability to noncurrent status is possible provided two conditions are met.

A. Intent—The intent to refinance the short-term obligation as a long-term obligation must be proven. This proof might be in the form of board of directors' meeting minutes or through written correspondence with the financial institution.

B. Ability

1. The firm must also be able to refinance the obligation and demonstrate that ability before the issuance of the financial statements. There are three ways to meet this requirement. Each must occur in the period between the balance sheet date and the date the financial statements are issued or are available to be issued.

   a. Actually refinance the liability on a long-term basis. In this case, the firm replaces the current liability with a noncurrent liability.

   b. Enter into a noncancellable refinancing agreement supported by a viable lender. The agreement must extend more than one year beyond the balance sheet date. The purpose of the agreement is to refinance the liability on a noncurrent basis.

   c. Issue equity securities replacing the debt.

2. The details of the refinancing arrangement must be disclosed in the footnotes.

Example

On December 31, year 7, the Bulldog Company reports a current note payable that matures on April 1, year 8. The note is payable to an equipment dealer. The year 7 financial statements are issued March 4, year 8. If any of the following three transactions or events occur, then the original note is classified as noncurrent in the year 7 balance sheet:

1. On February 22, year 8, Bulldog issues another note payable maturing in year 9 to replace the existing note.

2. On March 1, year 8, Bulldog signs a noncancellable refinancing agreement with a lender capable of honoring the agreement. The agreement requires the lender to pay the original note in return for a note from Bulldog due after December 31, year 8. The refinancing need not occur before the issuance of the financial statements. Only the agreement must be set in place by that time.

3. In February, Bulldog issues shares of its common stock to the equipment dealer in full payment of the note. (If this occurs before the balance sheet date, then Bulldog has no liability to reclassify.)

However, if the firm extinguishes the original note in February by paying cash, and then replenishes the cash with the issuance of a long-term note, the original note remains a current liability in the year 7 balance sheet because current assets were used for extinguishment.

Also, if a refinancing agreement is cancelable by either party, then there is no reclassification of the note because then there is no guarantee that current assets will not be used in year 8 to pay the note.

Note
The amount of current debt that can be classified as noncurrent cannot exceed the amount available under the agreement (or the amount refinanced or extinguished through issuing stock). The maximum amount may also be limited to the value of collateral put up by the debtor. For example, the amount of a $60,000 note to be refinanced with another lender might be limited to $40,000, the amount of collateral put up by the debtor. In this case, only $40,000 could be classified as noncurrent.

Debt Retirement

The debt retirement topic is usually tested in the context of bond retirements. The general accounting principles are discussed in this lesson. It also reinforces the basic principles by illustrating a comprehensive example.

After studying this lesson, you should be able to:

1. Record the amortization of discount or premium and bond issue costs to the date of retirement on the portion of a bond issue retired.

2. Apply both the effective interest and straight-line methods when recording a bond retirement.

I. Accounting Principles

A. When debt is retired at maturity, any discount or premium, and debt issue costs, are fully amortized. The final payment extinguishes the liability at its maturity value, which is also the net liability amount at maturity. No gain or loss is recognized.

Exam Tip
This topic, in the context of bonds payable, is frequently tested on the CPA Exam.

B. Firms may retire their debt at any time (before maturity) unless the debt agreement prohibits it. The amount paid to retire bonds early reflects the current yield rate and may be different from the book value of the bonds on the retirement date. The result is that a gain or loss is recorded. The gain or loss is included in income from continuing operations.

C. Debt is considered extinguished when one of two conditions is met.

1. The debtor pays the creditor and is relieved of any obligation related to the debt.

2. The debtor is legally released from being the primary obligor of the liability, and it is probable that the debtor will make no further payments. This legal release may be done by the creditor or by the courts. (An example is the release from a mortgage note upon sale of the related property.)

D. If the debtor firm places assets into an irrevocable trust for the purpose of retiring debt (in-substance defeasance), the liability nonetheless remains on the balance sheet, along with the assets, separately reported. The liability is not extinguished, nor is a gain or loss recorded.

II. Accounting for Debt Extinguishment

A. Extinguishment of debt can be accomplished in a variety of ways. The company can simply pay off the debt. Also, debt may be replaced by a new debt issue (a refinancing, also called a "refunding"). For a refunding, the present value of the new debt issue is used as the price of retiring the old issue. Alternatively, the company may purchase a bond issue on the open market and retire the bonds payable. Finally, the company may retire callable bonds by exercising the *call* feature of the bonds if the bonds are callable, and pay the call price.

B. Regardless of the method, however, the accounting is the same:

1. Record interest and amortization of discount or premium, and amortization of debt issue costs, to the date of extinguishment. Accrued interest from the most recent interest payment date will be included in the amount paid to retire the bonds.

2. Remove the related debt accounts at their remaining amounts (face value, unamortized discount or premium, and any unamortized debt issue costs)

3. Record the gain or loss, which is the difference between the current bond price and the net bond liability. The net bond liability is the face value of the bond plus or minus unamortized premium or discount, and less unamortized bond issue costs. If the current bond price exceeds the net bond liability, a loss is recognized, and vice versa.

Example
The Washington Company exercised its **call** privilege related to an outstanding bond payable. The book value of the bond payable was $105,000, including unamortized premium on bond payable of $5,000. The call price was $104,000. The entry to record the transaction is shown below.

Bonds Payable	$100,000	
Premium on B/P	$ 5,000	
Cash		$104,000
Gain		$ 1,000

III. More Involved Example of Bond Retirement

Example
$10,000 of bonds were issued 5/1/Year 1 at 91. The bonds mature 12/31/Year 6. Bond issue costs of $680 were incurred on issue and the straight-line method is used to amortize both the discount and bond issue costs. The bonds pay interest each December 31. On 1/1/Year 4, 60% of the issue was retired at 97.

The bond term is 5 years and 8 months, or 68 months. The bonds are retired when 3 years or 36 months remain in the bond term. The original discount was $900 (.09 x $10,000).

Entry for retirement:

Bonds Payable .60($10,000)	6,000	
Loss	322	
Bond Discount .60($900)(36/68)		286
Bond Issue Costs .60($680)(36/68)		216
Cash .97(.60)($10,000)		5,820

Exam Tip
The CPA Exam has asked the following type of question in relation to an early retirement of bonds: "In computing the gain or loss on the above bond retirement, the price paid for the bonds is compared to which of the following values?" The question refers to the net bond liability of the bonds retired.

Troubled Debt

This lesson discusses troubled debt restructure and modification.

After studying this lesson, you should be able to:

1. Identify when a debt restructure is troubled.

2. Categorize a troubled-debt restructure into one of three types.

3. Record a settlement troubled debt restructure for both debtor and creditor.

4. Account for a modification of terms troubled-debt restructure when the restructured cash flows are less than the book value of the liability being restructured.

5. Determine the new interest rate to be applied by the debtor firm in a troubled-debt restructure for which the sum of restructured cash flows exceeds the original debt amount.

6. Record interest expense during the restructured debt term.

I. Introduction

    A. Restructuring of debt is commonplace. Extension of terms, changes in interest rates, and other aspects of the debt agreement are examples. In a troubled debt restructure (TDR), however, the creditor grants a concession by agreeing to terms less favorable than under the original debt agreement. For a restructuring to be considered a TDR, the *both* of the following must hold:

        1. The creditor granted a concession in the expectation that more ultimately will be received from the debtor compared with other strategies, such as forcing the debtor into bankruptcy.

        2. The debtor is in financial difficulty, which means that without the concession, it is likely that the debtor will default.

    B. The accounting for the restructure depends on whether the debt is settled (a settlement) or whether it continues (a modification of terms).

    C. In all TDR cases, the present value of the consideration paid under the restructured agreement is less than the carrying value of the debt (including any unpaid interest) at date of restructure.

        1. If the debt is settled, the fair value of consideration transferred is less than the carrying value of the debt at date of restructure (creditor grants a concession).

        2. If the debt is modified, the present value of the restructured cash flows (computed using the original interest rate) is less than the carrying value of the debt at date of restructure (creditor grants a concession).

II. Debtor and Creditor Recording and Reporting of Settlement Troubled-Debt Restructures

    A. **Debtor**—In settlement restructures, the debtor:

        1. Records a gain for the difference between the book value of the debt, including any unpaid accrued interest, and the fair value of consideration transferred in full settlement of the debt (debtor always records a gain of this type and never a loss)

        2. Records a gain or loss, if any, on the disposal of nonmonetary assets transferred in full settlement of the debt (if the debtor pays cash only to settle the debt, there is no gain or loss of this type recorded)

3. Removes the debt accounts from the books

4. Records any stock issued in settlement at the fair value

B. **Creditor**—In settlement restructures, the creditor:

1. Records a loss for the difference between the book value of the receivable and the fair value of assets or stock of the debtor received

2. Removes the receivable accounts from the books

3. Records assets received at fair value

Example

On January 1, a debtor owed a creditor a $10,000 note due on this date. In addition, $1,000 of unpaid interest from the previous year was also due. (A 10% original interest rate is implied.) The debtor could not pay the entire amount and the two parties agreed on a restructure in which the debtor would transfer land (cost, $4,000; fair value, $2,000) and issue stock (fair value and total par value, $5,000) in full settlement of the debt.

Debtor			Creditor		
Note Payable	10,000		Investment in Stock	5,000	
Interest Payable	1,000		Loss on Debt Restructure	4,000	
Loss on Land Disposal	2,000		Land	2,000	
Gain on Debt Restructure		4,000	Note Receivable		10,000
Capital Stock		5,000	Interest Receivable		1,000
Land		4,000			

The debtor's gain is the difference between the book value of the debt settled ($11,000, which includes interest) less the market value of items transferred ($2,000 land + $5,000 stock). This equals the creditor's loss on restructure (and equals the concession) because the two parties reported the same book value for the debt and receivable plus interest. The debtor's loss on disposal is the loss that would be recorded had the land been sold for cash.

III. **Debtor Reporting of Modification of Terms for Troubled-Debt Restructure**

A. For debtor accounting purposes, there are two very different cases for modification of terms for TDRs. The cases are distinguished by the relationship between the prerestructure book value of the debt, and the nominal sum of restructured future cash flows. The book value of the original debt always includes unpaid accrued interest. The creditor's accounting for modification terms TDRs is not parallel to the debtor's accounting and is covered in the lesson on loan impairment.

Note

Sometimes a restructuring is a combination settlement and modification of terms, In these cases, the settlement portion is recorded first with the liability reduced by the fair value of consideration paid (no gain is recorded). The remainder of the debt restructure is treated as a modification of terms, detailed below.

1. **Modification type 1**—In modification of terms, restructures in which the nominal sum of the restructured flows is *less than or equal* to the book value of the debt plus accrued interest, the debtor:

   a. Reduces the carrying value of the debt to the nominal sum of restructured cash flows

   b. Records a gain for the difference between the book value and the nominal sum of restructured cash flows

   c. Records no further interest; all future cash payments are returns of principal

2. **Modification type 2**—In modification of terms restructures in which the nominal sum of the restructured flows is *greater* than the book value of the debt plus accrued interest, the debtor:

   a. Records no gain or loss and does not change the carrying value of the debt

   b. Computes the new rate of interest equating the present value of restructured cash flows and the book value of the debt

   c. Records interest expense based on the new rate for the remainder of the loan term

IV. Examples of Modification of Terms for TDRs

Example
Modification Type 1
On January 1, Year 1, a debtor owed a creditor a $10,000 note due on this date. In addition, $1,000 of unpaid interest from the previous year was also due. The debtor could not pay the entire amount and the two parties agreed on a restructure in which the debtor would make the following payments:

	Restructured cash flows	
December 31, Year 1	Interest	400
	Principal	3,000
December 31, Year 2	Interest	400
	Principal	3,000
Total restructured cash flows		6,800

The *interest* cash flows are not really interest because all flows are returns of principal in this case. However, restructuring agreements may refer to such smaller flows as interest. The nominal sum of $6,800 is less than the $11,000 book value of debt.

Entries for Debtor:

January 1, Year 1	Interest Payable	1,000	
	Note Payable	10,000	
	Gain		4,200
	Note Payable		6,800

This entry reduces the carrying value of the debt to $6,800. The gain is the difference between the book value of the old debt plus interest ($11,000) and the nominal sum of restructured flows. The old debt accounts are closed and a new note payable is recorded. An alternative is to simply reduce the old note account $3,200 and close the interest payable account.

December 31, Year 1	Note Payable	3,400	
	Cash		3,400
December 31, Year 2	Note Payable	3,400	
	Cash		3,400

Analysis

The accounting for this case (sum of new flows < book value) is a significant departure from the normal procedure for noncurrent debt accounting, which would report the new note payable at present value, rather than nominal value as in this situation.

Compared with the normal procedure (recording at present value), there are three effects of the above accounting for modification type 1 TDRs on the debtor's financial statements:

1. Liabilities are larger (nominal sum is larger than the present value).

2. Income is smaller in year of restructure (the gain is smaller than if the note payable were recorded at present value).

3. Future interest expense is smaller (there is no interest recognized).

A. **Example of Modification Type 2**

Example
On January 1, Year 1, a debtor owed a creditor a $10,000 note due on this date. In addition, $1,000 of unpaid interest from the previous year was also due. The debtor was unable to pay the total amount and the parties agreed to a restructure in which the debtor would make a single lump sum payment of $11,440 on December 31, Year 1. In this case, the nominal sum of restructured cash flows ($11,440) exceeds the book value of $11,000. Thus, there will be interest paid at the end of Year 1. The new interest rate is found as:

(PV of $1, i = ?, n = 1)($11,440) = $11,000

(PV of $1, i = ?, n = 1)($11,440) = $11,000/($11,440) = .96154

This present value factor corresponds to 4%, indicating the concession made by the creditor. Rather than earning 10%, the creditor will earn only 4%. Another way to consider the concession is to compute the present value of the restructured flows using the original interest rate:

$11,440(PV of $1, i = .10, n = 1) = $11,440(.90909) = $10,400

This amount is less than the $11,000 book value of the debt, again reflecting the debtor's concession.

Entries for Debtor:

January 1, Year 1	No entry needed (or the old debt accounts can be closed and a new note payable of $11,000 can be created)		
December 31, Year 1	Interest Expense .04($11,000)	440	
	Note Payable	10,000	
	Interest Payable	1,000	
	Cash		11,440

B. This illustrates a restructure agreement requiring only a single payment. Other examples might require only an annuity of payments. Either way, only one present value factor is used, and the calculation of the new interest rate is straightforward.

C. However, many restructurings include both single payments and annuities as restructured flows. In these cases, there are two unknowns in terms of present value factors. The candidate may be called upon to set up the solution for such a situation, and explain how to solve for the new effective rate. It is even possible that a simulation may enable the actual calculation. The following example is an illustration.

D. Example of Modification Type 2

Example
On 1/1/X1 a debtor owed a creditor a $6,573 (face) non-interest-bearing note due on this date. The interest rate implied on this note is 8%. The debtor was unable to pay the total amount and the parties agreed to a restructure in which the debtor would make the following restructured payments: (1) restructured face value of $5,000 due 12/31/X6, (2) annual interest payments at 10% of the new face value, beginning 12/31/X1.

In this example, the sum of restructured cash flows is $8,000 [$5,000 + (6 x $500)], which exceeds the debt book value ($6,573). It is important to be sure that the restructure is a TDR before proceeding.

There are two ways to find out.

(1) Use the original interest rate of 8% to determine the present value of new flows. If that present value is less than $6,573, then the creditor is making a concession.

PV of new flows = $5,000(pv of $1, i =.08, n =6) + $500(pv $1 annuity, i =.08, n =6)

PV = $5,000(.63017) + $500(4.62288) = $5,462 < $6,573 therefore, the restructuring is a troubled-debt restructure.

(2) Compute the new effective rate (m) implied by the new flows. If that rate is less than 8%, then the creditor is making a concession.

$5,000(pv of $1, m, n =6) + $500(pv $1 annuity, m, 6) = $6,573

The solution for m can be computed using the internal rate of return (IRR) function within standard spreadsheet programs. See below. m = 4%, which is less than 8%. Therefore, the restructuring is a troubled-debt restructure.

Spreadsheet solution for m. The original liability balance is placed into cell A1 as a negative amount (the investment). Each succeeding cell is a separate cash flow in which each new cell indicates a new period. The next five cells are the annual interest payments of $500. The cash flow for 20X6 (cell A7) includes both principal ($5,000) and interest because they occur simultaneously. In cell B7 the IRR function is inserted and the spreadsheet formula returns 4% for m in that cell.

	A	B
1	−6,573	
2	500	
3	500	
4	500	
5	500	
6	500	
7	5,500	= IRR(A1:A7)

The first two required journal entries are:

12/31/X1	Interest expense	263		(6,573)(.04)
	Note payable	237		
	Cash		500	
12/31/X2	Interest expense	253		($6,573 − $237).04
	Note payable	247		
	Cash		500	

At 12/31/X6, the note balance is $5,000 and is retired with the final payment of that amount.

Debt Covenant Compliance

Several aspects of debt covenants are discussed in this lesson.

After studying this lesson, you should be able to:

1. Describe the basic content of a debt covenant.

2. Articulate the reasons for debt covenants.

3. List several attributes that serve as the restriction included in debt covenants.

4. Note the different ways in which compliance with a debt covenant can be demonstrated.

5. Be aware of the possible responses by the creditor in the event of noncompliance.

I. Background—Debt Covenants

A. A debt covenant is a part of the larger contract underlying the debt instrument. A bond indenture (contract) details the rights and duties of the issuing firm (debtor, borrower) and the bondholder (creditor, lender), for example. A covenant, also called a "restriction," is a section of the contract that describes the responses available to the creditor if certain events or conditions occur, such as the debtor's current ratio declining below a certain level. The covenant may allow the creditor to call the debt (demand immediate payment). Covenants also protect the debtor from such actions should the conditions not occur (debtor maintains compliance with the covenant).

B. Covenants can be established either unilaterally by the creditor, or through negotiation between creditor and debtor. Firms emerging from corporate reorganization or bankruptcy may be subject to more stringent covenants. A description of the covenant is disclosed in the notes to the debtor's financial statements.

C. Covenants are one form of protection for the creditor. Others include requiring the issuing firm to redeem bonds according to a prespecified schedule (sinking fund debentures), requiring the issuing firm to accumulate a sinking fund for the eventual retirement of bonds, and structuring the bonds as serial bonds.

D. The debtor must periodically demonstrate compliance with the covenants. The frequency may be quarterly, semiannually, or annually and is set at the time of borrowing. Information in the audited annual financial statements reflects a higher degree of verifiability compared with quarterly statements. The frequency may reflect the perceived riskiness of the borrower. For example, for a troubled line of credit, demonstration of compliance might be required monthly.

E. Covenants are periodically revisited and modified as debtor financial health and macroeconomic conditions change. At a minimum, adjustments should be considered annually. In a line of credit, a review also occurs upon renewal of the credit line.

II. Specific Attributes Used in Covenants

A. A wide variety of measures is used in debt covenants. Typically, a minimum or maximum value for the measure is the condition beyond which the debtor is in violation. The following list provides examples.

1. **Current ratio** (Current Assets/Current Liabilities)—A measure of liquidity. If the debtor's current ratio falls below 2.0 for example (a minimum level), the debtor has violated the covenant. The creditor then has the right to respond in specific ways defined in the contract. This aspect is discussed below.

2. **Working capital** (Current Assets – Current Liabilities)—A minimum level is specified in the covenant.

3. **Income measures,** such as net income before tax, net income, income from continuing operations, and EBITDA (earnings before interest, taxes, depreciation, and amortization). The covenant specifies a minimum absolute level, or possibly one based on a percentage of the previous year's amount.

4. **Interest coverage ratio**(EBITDA/Interest Expense)—A minimum level is specified.

5. **Retained earnings balance, or total owners' equity balance**—A minimum level is specified.

6. **Debt to equity ratio**—A maximum level is specified.

7. **Total debt**—A maximum level is specified.

8. **Interest expense**—A maximum level is specified.

9. **Total assets or net assets**—A minimum level is specified.

B. Covenants also may describe a restriction on the debtor's transactions during the debt term for the protection of the creditor. Otherwise, the debtor is in violation of the covenant.

   1. Limit dividends or treasury share purchases to a specific amount, or prohibit them.

   2. Limit additional borrowings. A "leverage" covenant may limit total debt to some multiple of an earnings variable, such as EBITDA. Alternatively, the firm may be required to maintain a minimum specified interest coverage ratio if additional debt capital is acquired.

   3. Require that the borrower not voluntarily cause a reduction in net assets (weakening of the balance sheet) or not take any action that might impede the ability to service the debt.

   4. Prohibit risky investments or expansion projects.

C. A covenant also may require that the firm's debt rating not fall below a minimum level. Two rating agencies are Standard & Poor's Corporation and Moody's Investor Services. S&P ratings are: Highest, AAA; High, AA; Medium, A; Minimum investment grade, BBB. Moody's corresponding ratings are: Aaa, Aa, A, Baa. A debtor, for example, may be required to maintain at least an A S&P rating for compliance with the covenant.

D. "Covenant-lite" loans are drawn with fewer or less stringent covenants. Such loans provide less protection for the creditor. One reason for less onerous covenants is that loans can be sold on a secondary market, effectively passing the risk on to investors. The ability to refinance the loans is another factor.

III. The Compliance Process

A. Ensuring compliance with covenants is an ongoing task for many debtor firms. Both management and audit committees continuously monitor the financial condition of the firm so that adjustments can be made in time to avoid situations that would cause the firm to be out of compliance. A forward-looking process facilitates risk assessment and risk management.

B. The debtor develops a system that signals conditions which may lead to a violation well before it actually happens. All relevant personnel within the organization must participate, to avoid the potentially devastating effects of a violation.

C. Periodic internal self-evaluation precedes the formal compliance review that involves the creditor. All administrative requirements pertaining to the covenant within the debt agreement including progress reports are fulfilled on a timely basis.

D. Capital budgeting and other planning processes within the firm consider the potential effect on debt covenant compliance.

E. A periodic sensitivity analysis determines the leeway available on key factors used in the covenant, within current operations. How much room does the firm have to alter its tactics and strategies and continue to comply with its covenants?

IV. Specific Compliance Strategies

A. **Operating Strategies**—Relevant strategies available to the debtor are implied by the covenant. If the covenant requires a limitation or elimination of dividends, for example, then that strategy must be followed to avoid a violation. In this example, shareholders should be informed about the reduction and the reason for it.

1. Improving products and services, enhancing marketing, encouraging innovation, seeking the best management talent, and avoiding risk are ways to improve operating results and help maintain compliance. Leverage should be used sparingly, and only if the expectations for increased profitability are sufficiently strong to warrant increased debt, if allowed under the covenant.

2. Increasing liquidity is another aspect that helps compliance for several types of covenants. Covenants involving the current ratio and working capital are examples. Refinancing short-term debt to noncurrent classification is a specific strategy that would assist the debtor in complying with this type of covenant. In general, specific transactions may enable compliance with covenant ratios.

Example

Beta Co. has a loan covenant requiring it to maintain a current ratio of 1.5 or better as of year-end. As Beta approaches year-end, current assets are $20 million ($1 million in cash, $9 million in accounts receivable, and $10 million in inventory), and current liabilities are $13.5 million. Therefore, its current ratio is 1.48 (20/13.5), which is below the minimum.

Several actions below are being considered to maintain compliance with the debt covenant by year-end:

A. Sell $1 million in inventory and deposit the proceeds in the entity's checking account.

B. Borrow $1 million short term and deposit the funds in the entity's checking account.

C. Sell $1 million in inventory and pay off some of its short-term creditors.

D. Do nothing at all.

Which choice will allow Beta to meet its loan covenant?

Only Action C will increase the current ratio to 1.5 or more. Current assets decrease by $1 million from paying current liabilities, which also decrease $1 million. The current ratio after Action C would be 1.52: (20 − 1)/(13.5 − 1) = 19/12.5 = 1.52.

Action A leaves current assets and current liabilities unchanged, along with the current ratio, leaving Beta in noncompliance.

Action B increases both current assets and current liabilities by $1 million, resulting in a 1.45 current ratio: (20 + 1)/(13.5 + 1) = 21/14.5 = 1.45. The noncompliance is worse after Action B.

Action D is the status quo, leaving the current ratio below the minimum.

---

3. Refinancing debt when interest rates decline can improve both earnings and liquidity.

B. **Accounting Choices**—Where GAAP allows a choice or allows leeway in estimation of certain variables, the debtor firm may consider choosing the methods which contribute to maintaining compliance with the debt covenant.

1. Although net income is not a formal variable in all covenants, higher earnings will contribute to a greater probability of compliance with many covenants. Choices such as FIFO, straight-line depreciation, longer useful lives for plant assets, higher recoverable costs for plant assets, the specific method of capitalizing interest, full-costing method of accounting for natural resource exploration costs, and others can help in this regard.

    a. However, the effect of choices on the quality of earnings must also be considered. Firms with low quality of earnings may suffer in the equity capital markets.

    b. Also, some covenants require consistent application of accounting policies and compute compliance based on the policies in effect at the time of the borrowing. An improvement in an accounting-related measure used in a debt covenant caused by a change in accounting policy therefore may not be "counted" toward improved debt covenant compliance.

  2. Off-balance sheet activities, such as structuring leases as operating leases, will reduce reported debt, a variable used in several measures incorporated into covenants.

V. Creditor Response to a Covenant Violation

A. The debt contract describes the actions that may be taken by the creditor in the event of a covenant violation by the debtor. Typically these are options rather than requirements.

  1. The financial position of the creditor, and the general relationship between the firms, may affect how the creditor responds to a violation.

B. If the covenant states that the debt can be called in the event of noncompliance (e.g., if the debtor's working capital falls below the minimum $20 million as specified in the covenant), then the creditor has the option to demand immediate payment.

C. Other actions include increasing the interest rate, requiring the borrower to specify assets as collateral, accelerating the payment terms (other than immediate payment), reducing the amount available in a line of credit, and repossessing collateral.

D. Additional restrictions may be placed on the debtor. If a covenant is violated because of reduced earnings, for example, then the debtor may be prohibited from paying dividends or taking on more debt until the violation is cured.

E. The creditor may agree to renegotiate or restructure the debt.

F. Legal action may be taken against the debtor, including the initiation of a breach of contract lawsuit.

VI. Debtor Strategies after a Covenant Violation

A. The debtor may have few options after a covenant violation, depending on the response by the creditor. Therefore, the debtor firm seeks to avoid a violation and the potential negative impact on its operations.

  1. If a violation leads to a debt default, operations can be disrupted, access to the capital markets is hindered, higher borrowing costs and penalties may be incurred, employee morale may decline, administrative time is wasted, suppliers and customers may end their relationship with the debtor, and the debtor's going concern may be placed in doubt.

  2. Likewise, creditors do not want debtors to default. Covenant violations place the creditor in an uncertain position and at a minimum cause additional work for its managers. Defaults also may attract scrutiny from bank examiners, which in turn may require an increase in a reserve against the possible loan loss. A default also raises the possibility that a loss is imminent.

B. Many debtors are not in a position to pay the debt immediately and often request a renegotiation of the debt terms enabling lower or deferred payments.

C. A debtor may also ask for a waiver granting time to cure the violation or to void the violation. These requests are more likely when the reasons for the violation are beyond the immediate control of the debtor. General economic downturns and inflation with their respective effects on the debtor's earnings and liquidity are factors. For example, goodwill impairments due to declining stock prices can cause parent firm earnings to decline with no change in the parent's core operations.

D. The debtor may request relief from the covenant. This involves a request to either eliminate or weaken the covenant by amending the debt contract. For example, if the violated leverage covenant is 5 times EBITDA, the debtor may request to increase the multiple to 6.5. Such a change to the covenant may occur when the compliance review or general review of the contract occurs or earlier, depending on the severity of the violation.

VII. Classification of Debt When a Covenant Is Violated

A. If a liability is callable on demand without qualification, then the liability is classified as a current liability, even if not due within one year from the balance sheet date. This category includes liabilities that are not callable as of the balance sheet date but will become due on demand within one year of the balance sheet date.

B. If a liability is callable on demand if a debt covenant is violated, and there is violation, the liability is classified as a current liability if there are no other relevant circumstances.

C. If a liability is callable on demand if a debt covenant is violated, and there is violation, but that violation is waived by the creditor, then the liability is classified as a noncurrent liability.

D. If a liability callable on demand if a debt covenant is violated, and there is a violation, if the creditor grants a grace period and it is probable that the debtor will rectify that violation within the grace period, then the liability is classified as a noncurrent liability. Otherwise, the liability is classified as a current liability.

E. The violations assumed above are called "objective acceleration clauses" because the potential covenant violations are listed as specific events, such as failure to make an interest payment or the current ratio has decreased below the minimum specified in the covenant.

   1. Other clauses are less objective and are called "subjective acceleration clauses." They enable the creditor to call the debt for reasons not objectively specified, such as a decline in the earnings of the debtor or deterioration of the debtor's balance sheet. If circumstances suggest the possible calling of the debt, then the liability is classified as current. However, if the likelihood of acceleration of the due date is considered remote (including similar past situations in which the creditor did not call the debt), then the classification remains noncurrent.

Distinguishing Liabilities from Equity

This lesson considers the theoretical question of whether a transaction yields a liability, equity, or both.

After studying this lesson, you should be able to:

1. Explain how mandatorily redeemable shares are classified.

2. Account for obligations to issue shares of a fixed dollar amount.

3. Record the journal entries for an obligation to issue a fixed number of shares.

4. Account for written put options.

I. **Background**—Although the definitions of *liability* and *equity* have been established for a long time, new transactions have developed that put these definitions to the test. The expectation is that new definitions will be forthcoming, along with affected specific accounting principles. Until then, the determination of whether an item is a liability or equity proceeds on a somewhat piecemeal basis. This lesson considers (1) transactions involving the firm's stock, and (2) compound financial instruments. Additional discussion of financial instruments as they affect liabilities and equity is found in the lessons on derivatives.

II. **Adopted Standards**—The FASB has adopted accounting standards that require certain items related to equity are to be reported as liabilities. These items obligate the firm to deliver assets of a fixed monetary value, either cash or equity shares, in the future, and they include:

   A. Mandatorily redeemable shares

   B. Certain stock appreciation rights (discussed in a previous lesson)

   C. Financial instruments obligating the issuing firm to issue stock worth a fixed value

   D. Written put options and other financial instruments obligating the issuing firm to repurchase its own shares

III. **Mandatorily Redeemable Shares**—Mandatorily redeemable financial instruments are classified as liabilities if both of the following criteria are met. (1) They are obligations to repurchase the firm's equity shares or are indexed to such an obligation, and (2) They require or may require the issuer to settle the obligation by transferring assets. However, if the redemption is required only upon liquidation of the entity, then the classification is equity. An example of an instrument that is classified as debt is a written put option on the issuer's shares that is to be settled in cash. Mandatorily redeemable financial instruments are initially measured at fair value.

IV. **Obligations to Issue Shares of a Fixed Dollar Value**

   A. Firms may pay for services or goods by issuing stock after the goods or services are received. Recall that when shares are issued immediately upon receipt of goods or services, the expense or asset, and the stock issued, are measured at the more reliable of the fair values (good/service, or stock). When there is a period of time between receipt of consideration and the issuance of stock, the stock price can change. The issue then arises at the receipt of consideration: Does the firm have a liability, or equity? The answer depends on whether the agreement specifies shares worth a fixed dollar amount, or a fixed number of shares.

   B. **Shares Worth a Fixed Dollar Amount (Variable Number of Shares)**—When a firm agrees to issue shares in the future worth a fixed dollar amount, a liability rather than equity is recognized. The vendor is not at risk for fluctuations in the price of the stock to be received because shares worth the fixed amount will be received, regardless of the stock price.

Example
A firm and a vendor agree that the firm will pay for service provided April 1, 20X2 with shares of the firm's $1 par common stock two months after that date. The value of shares to be issued is $10,000; the parties agree that this is the fair valuation of the services.

4/1/X2	Service expense	10,000	
	Liability for stock issuance (liability account)		10,000

On May 31, 20X2, the share price of the firm's stock is $40. The number of shares to be issued therefore is 250 ($10,000/$40).

5/31/X2	Liability for stock issuance	10,000		
	Common stock		250	250($1)
	Contributed capital in excess of par-common		9,750	250($40 − $1)

C. Fixed Number of Shares—By comparison, when the number of shares is fixed rather than the dollar amount, the issuing firm records an owner's equity account upon receipt of consideration. During the period between providing the goods or service, and receipt of stock, the vendor is at risk in the same way any other shareholder is at risk. If the stock price declines during this time, the value received by the vendor will also decline.

Example
Using the information in the previous example, assume the two parties agree that the firm will issue 200 shares of $1 common stock two months after the service is provided. The market price of the stock on April 1, 20X2 is $50.

4/1/X2	Service expense	10,000		
	Stock issuance obligation (OE account)		10,000	
5/31/X2	Stock issuance obligation	10,000		
	Common stock		200	200($1)
	Contributed capital in excess of par-common		9,800	200($50 − $1)

The fair value of the services was $10,000 on April 1. That amount determines the increase in contributed capital. The share price at the time of issuance is not relevant.

V. Written Put Options

A. As part of a share repurchase plan, firms may write an option allowing other entities to sell the firm's stock to the firm at a fixed price (option price) on a specific date or during a specified period. The purchaser (option holder) pays a fee for the option. The fee typically approximates the fair value of the option using an option-pricing model (the same type of model used to value employee stock options discussed in a previous lesson).

B. The purchaser of the option is betting that the firm's stock will decline in price. The firm is betting the price will stay above the option price.

C. The fair value of the option is reported as a liability. Changes in the option's fair value are recognized at each year-end before the exercise. An increase in the fair value represents a potential decrease in the share price because the option is more valuable. The option will be exercised if the share price during the exercise period is less than fixed option price. At exercise, the firm extinguishes the liability and pays the option price. If the option is not exercised (because the share price exceeds the option price during the exercise period), the liability is extinguished and a gain is recorded.

Example

On January 1, 20X1, a firm wrote put options for 100 shares of its common stock. Holders of the option will be able to sell the firm's stock back to the firm for $50 per share on December 31, 20X2. The estimated fair value of one option is $10. Journal entries for the firm follow:

1/1/X1	Cash	1,000	100($10)
	Put option liability		1,000

On December 31, 20X1, the fair value of an option is re-estimated to be $12.50. The increase in fair value reflects an increased likelihood that the price of the firm's stock will be less than $50 on the exercise date.

12/31/X1	Loss on put option	250	100($12.50 − $10)
	Put option liability		250

On December 31, 20X2, the price of the firm's stock is $45 per share. The option is exercised because the purchaser (option holder) will receive $50 per option when the shares are worth only $45. The purchaser can purchase a share of the stock for $45 on the market and sell it back to the firm for $50—a gain of $5 per share. However, the purchaser has incurred a net loss of $500: $1,000 fee less the $500 gain on exercise [100($50 − $45)].

12/31/X2	Put option liability	1,250	
	Treasury stock	4,500	100($45) (fair value)
	Cash		5,000 100($50)
	Gain on put option		750

The treasury stock is recorded at fair value. The $500 net gain to the firm over the two years is computed two ways:

1. $500 = $750 gain for 20X2 −$250 loss for 20X1 = $500

2. $500 = $1,000 fee − $500 (excess of $5,000 paid for stock − $4,500 fair value)

D. When the option is not exercised (stock price did not fall below the option price), the put option liability is closed and a gain is recognized. The overall gain to the firm is the fee. In this example, if the stock price were $55 on December 31, 20X2, the option would not be exercised and the firm would record the following journal entry:

12/31/X2	Put option liability	1,250	
	Gain on put option		1,250

The firm's overall gain is $1,000 ($1,250 gain for 20X2 −$250 loss for 20X1).

VI. Compound Financial Instruments

A. At present, GAAP addresses this issue on an individual standard basis. The expectation is that this area will be revised based on a more general standard. Previous lessons addressed the following two items, for example.

1. Convertible bonds are treated the same as nonconvertible bonds at issuance and throughout the term—as debt. There is no separation of the debt and equity components. Only at conversion does the equity component surface. There is an exception—when convertible bonds can be settled in cash. This exception is consistent with the notion of a liability—that is, the obligation to transfer assets in the future as a result of a past transaction.

2. Bonds with detachable warrants separate the debt and equity components at issuance. This treatment is just the opposite as that for most convertible bonds.

Equity

Owners' Equity Basics

This lesson begins several addressing the accounting for owners' equity (OE) by a corporation. The overview of this large area is provided here. This lesson continues with the basics by addressing the rights of stockholders, and the categories of capital stock found in the owners' equity section of the balance sheet.

After studying this lesson, you should be able to:

1. Distinguish the two major types of OE.

2. Identify OE accounts from a list that includes other types of accounts.

3. List several different accounts that fall under "additional paid-in capital."

4. Compare the corporate form of business organization to other forms of business organization.

5. List and distinguish the rights of common and preferred shareholders.

6. Compute the number of shares in the authorized, issued, outstanding, and treasury states or categories.

7. Apply stock dividends and splits to the computation of the number of shares in each category.

Definition

Owners' Equity: The owners' equity (OE) accounts represent the residual interest in the net assets of an entity that remain after deducting its liabilities.

I. **Two Main OE Categories**

   A. The two main categories of OE are listed below.

      1. Earned

      2. Contributed

   B. **Earned Capital**—There is no one measurement basis for earned capital (retained earnings) because all of the measurement bases that are reflected in net income are also reflected in retained earnings.

   C. **Contributed Capital**—The primary measurement basis for contributed capital is the historical value of direct investments made in the firm by investors, in return for shares of capital stock.

   D. **Equation**

Total Owners' Equity = Total Assets − Total Liabilities

---

   1. This balance sheet equation can be used to show the equality of changes in the three types of balance sheet accounts during a period.

Example
The following changes in a firm's aggregate account balances occurred during the year:

	Increase
Assets	$8,900
Liabilities	2,700
Capital stock	6,000
Additional paid-in capital	600

Assume a $1,300 dividend payment and that the year's earnings were the only changes in retained earnings for the year. Net income for the year can be found as follows:

Increase in Assets   =   Increase in Liabilities + Increase in OE

$8,900   = $2,700 + $6,000 + $600 + net income − $1,300

Net income   = $900

II. Presentation of Equity Accounts

A. **Major Account Types**—For a corporation, the major account types in OE are:

1. **Preferred stock,** the total par value of issued preferred stock;

2. **Common stock,** the total par value of issued common stock unless the stock is no-par stock and a stated value is not used;

3. **Additional paid-in capital, preferred**—This account reports the amount received for preferred stock issuances in excess of the par value;

    a. *Additional paid-in capital* is also referred to as *contributed capital in excess of par* and *paid-in capital in excess of par.*

4. **Additional paid-in capital, common**—This account reports the amount received for common stock issuances in excess of the par value;

    a. In general, additional paid-in capital is a category of OE used for several different sources such as paid-in capital from treasury stock transactions, stock award plans, and others.

5. **Retained earnings,** the net of the firm's earnings to date less dividends to date, plus or minus other items including prior period adjustments and certain accounting changes.

6. **Accumulated other comprehensive income,** the running total of all other comprehensive income items through the balance sheet date. See the lesson on the "Statement of Comprehensive Income." This category can be considered part of the "earned" component of OE, although the transactions causing changes in this category are not run through earnings and therefore are not included in retained earnings.

7. **Treasury stock,** which is the cost or par value of the common stock of a firm purchased by that firm, depending on the method used by the firm. Treasury stock of Coca-Cola Company, for example, is stock of Coca-Cola purchased by Coca-Cola. This account is a negative or contra OE account.

B. Types of Ownership

1. The types of ownership, and, therefore, the types of accounts recorded in OE, include

   a. A sole proprietorship

   b. The partnership form of business

   c. The corporate form of business

2. **Sole proprietorship**

   a. With a proprietorship, the ownership of the business enterprise consists of a single individual or party.

3. **Partnership**

   a. With a partnership, the ownership of the business enterprise consists of two or more participants.

4. **Corporation**

   a. With the corporate form of business, the stock may be closely held by a small number of investors or, in the case of a publicly traded company, the stock may be held by a large number of investors with the stock traded on an organized exchange.

   b. The stockholders' section of the corporate balance sheet includes the contributed capital accounts, such as common stock and contributed capital in excess of par, the retained earnings account and others referred to above.

   c. Capital stock (preferred or common) is the means by which ownership is conveyed. If there is only one class of stock, it is common stock.

5. **Advantages and disadvantages of the corporate form of business**

   a. Shareholders have limited liability; the corporation is a separate legal entity. Shareholders are not liable for the actions of the corporation and can lose only their investment. Partners and sole proprietors have unlimited liability. If the business cannot satisfy its debts, the creditors can seek relief from the owners of those types of businesses.

   b. A firm "goes public"—i.e., becomes a corporation—because it is easier to raise significant amounts of capital. Any investor in the world can purchase shares of a publicly traded corporation. Current shareholders can likewise sell their shares easily. In contrast, each time the ownership composition of a partnership changes, the partnership agreement is redrawn.

   c. Lack of mutual agency for a corporation. The actions of one shareholder (unless that shareholder is an officer of the corporation) do not bind the corporation or other shareholders. In contrast, each partner's actions bind the partnership.

   d. Double taxation of corporate profits. A corporation must pay income taxes and file an annual tax return. Dividends to shareholders are taxed on their personal returns. This double taxation is mitigated to some extent through the dividends received deduction if a shareholder of one corporation is another corporation (discussed in the taxation section of this review course). In contrast, partnerships and sole proprietorships file only an information return. The owners pay income tax on their portion of the income from the business.

   e. Corporations are subject to a great deal more regulation, including SEC reporting requirements for publicly held corporations.

6. **Hybrid organizations**—These organizations have some of the characteristics of both corporations and partnerships or sole proprietorships.

    a. S corporation. This is a classification for tax purposes. If the relevant tax rules are followed, limited liability is retained but the income is taxed only once, at the owner level.

    b. Limited liability companies allow all owners to be involved in the management of the business with each being liable only to the extent of their investment. Double taxation is avoided.

    c. Limited liability partnerships are less generous with respect to the limited liability feature.

III. **Legal Capital**— Par value is the minimum legal issue price for capital stock in most states and appears on the stock certificate.

  A. **No Par Value Alternatives**—If the stock has no par value, two alternatives exist:

    1. The firm may designate a stated value, which serves the same function as par value except that it does not appear on the certificate.

    2. The firm may not use a par value or stated value at all, in which case the stock is referred to as no par stock.

  B. **Measured at Par or Stated**

    1. The preferred stock and common stock accounts are always measured at par or stated value.

    2. Any excess of issuance price over the par value is credited to additional paid-in capital (preferred or common).

  C. **No Par Stock Credited**—If the stock is no-par stock, then the entire issuance proceeds is credited to the capital stock account and there is no additional paid-in capital account (contributed capital in excess of par).

  D. **Legal Capital**—The legal capital or minimum capital of a corporation is usually the par value of the stock or the stated value of the stock issued.

    1. **Establishes minimum investment**—This legal requirement establishes the minimum investment necessary to become a part of the ownership group of a corporation.

    2. **Protection for creditors**—Legal capital provides a measure of protection for the creditors of the corporation.

      a. Dividends may not be paid from legal capital.

      b. If there were no such protection, management could liquidate the corporation by paying back the shareholders their investment, leaving the creditors with assets that might not be worth their book value.

      c. In many states, firms may not pay dividends to common stock in an amount that would cause total assets to be less than total liabilities plus the liquidation preference of preferred stock. The liquidation preference of preferred stock is the amount payable on liquidation of the company.

  E. **Stock Not Discounted**—In most states, stock cannot be sold at a discount.

    1. If stock is sold at a discount, a contingent liability equal to the difference between the par or stated value and the acquisition cost of the stock is borne by the original shareholder.

    2. This requirement is an attempt to provide some legal protection for creditors.

  F. **Treasury Stock Transactions**—Another attempt to provide some protection for creditors is a limit on the amount of treasury stock transactions.

    1. In many states, treasury stock may not be purchased in excess of the amount of unrestricted or unappropriated retained earnings.

    2. The corollary of this constraint is that the cost of treasury stock is a restriction on retained earnings.

Example

A firm has $100,000 of assets, but only $30,000 is liquid current assets.

Total debt equals $70,000.

The firm has no retained earnings.

The legal capital of the firm is $30,000.

Although the firm has sufficient recorded assets to cover the creditor and shareholder interests, if the $30,000 of liquid assets was paid to the shareholders, buying out their interests, the $70,000 book value of remaining assets may not be sufficient to cover the creditors' claims because the assets may have a market value significantly less than $70,000.

The creditors would incur a loss.

This would be in direct violation of the order of rights upon liquidation of a corporation: Stockholders receive assets after all the creditors are satisfied.

IV. **Rights of Shareholders, States of Stock**

    A. **Common Stock Rights**—In return for purchasing a share of common stock, the common shareholder receives the following rights:

        1. **Voting rights**

            a. Common shareholders have the right to participate in the decision-making process of a corporation by voting for the board of directors, the external auditors, and other major issues.

            b. That is, the shareholders have a right to participate in major operating and financing decisions through the exercise of voting rights.

            c. They do not, however, have the right to participate in day-to-day management functions.

        2. **Dividend rights**

            a. Common shareholders have rights related to the receipt of dividends.

            b. The dividend rights of common shareholders are subordinate rights in that preferred shareholders receive their dividend allocation prior to any allocation to the common shareholders.

            c. Dividends are not mandatory.

            d. The Board of Directors must declare dividends before the firm is liable to the shareholders for dividends.

        3. **Preemptive rights**

            a. The preemptive rights of common shareholders allow current shareholders to maintain their existing percentage of the firm in the event of a new stock issuance by the firm.

            b. Preemptive rights are not always present, depending on state law and the corporate charter.

            c. The preemptive right is important to shareholders owning an appreciable percentage of the firm.

            d. Without the preemptive right, management could issue shares in an effort to reduce the percentage ownership (and influence) of a shareholder who disagrees with the current management over major issues affecting the direction of the firm.

Example

A firm plans to issue 100,000 shares of common stock.

A shareholder currently owns 2% of the outstanding common stock.

The shareholder must be allowed to purchase 2,000 of the new shares if the preemptive right is present.

The shareholder cannot be compelled to make the purchase, however.

4. **Rights related to liquidation**—In the event of liquidation, common shareholders are again in a subordinate role.

   a. The creditors are satisfied first.

   b. Then, the preferred shareholders are eligible to receive the liquidation values for the preferred shares.

   c. Finally, the remaining assets are distributed to the common shareholders. The common shareholders are the very last to receive assets on liquidation. They have the residual interest in the firm.

   d. Positive total owners' equity does not necessarily imply that any shareholders will receive assets upon liquidation. If the fair value of assets is less than total liabilities at liquidation, no shareholder would receive any assets.

B. **Preferred Stock Rights**—Preferred stock is called *preferred* because these shares typically are paid dividends before common stock. Preferred shareholders, however, usually give up their right to vote in return for the dividend preference.

   1. **The rights of preferred shareholders are**

      a. **Nonvoting**—Typically, preferred shareholders do not have voting rights. That is, preferred shareholders are not participants in the major operating and financing decisions made by the company.

      b. **Dividend preferences**—In relation to dividends, preferred shareholders receive their dividend allocation first. Then, the remainder of the dividend is allocated to common shareholders.

      c. **Additional features**—Additional features, such as withcumulativepreferred stock and participating preferred stock, can enhance this dividend preference for preferred shareholders. The process of allocating dividends to the two types of stock is illustrated in a later lesson.

      d. **Dividends in arrears**

         i. If preferred stock is cumulative and dividends for a year are not paid, then the dividends are said to be in arrears.

         ii. No dividends may be paid to any other class of stock, including the current preferred stock dividend requirement, until the dividends in arrears are paid.

         iii. This is how the dividend preference for preferred stock is preserved. However, there is no liability for dividends in arrears until the dividends are declared.

         iv. Undeclared dividends in arrears are disclosed in the footnotes until the dividends are paid.

e. **Liquidation preferences**

    i. In the event of liquidation, the creditors are paid first.

    ii. Second, the preferred shareholders receive their specified liquidation values per share. This amount may be different from par value, or the value paid for the shares. The liquidation preference per share of preferred stock must be disclosed in the equity section of the balance sheet when the preference exceeds par value. There is no preemptive right for preferred shareholders because preferred stock does not vote in the affairs of the corporation.

    iii. Finally, any remainder is allocated to the common shareholders.

C. **Number of Common Shares Issued, Outstanding, and in the Treasury**

    1. **Common Stock**—When a corporation is formed, the total number of shares that may be issued is called the *authorized shares*. This amount can be increased only by vote of the shareholders. For common stock, this total can be broken down into:

        a. Number issued: The number of shares ever issued by the firm but not retired

        b. Number outstanding: The number of shares currently held by stockholders

        c. Number in the treasury: The number of shares purchased by the issuing firm and not yet reissued. Treasury shares are included in the number of issued shares:

Issued Shares = # Outstanding Shares + # Treasury Shares

Note

The number of issued shares is always greater than or equal to the number of outstanding shares.

    2. **Treasury not outstanding**—Cash and property dividends are not paid on treasury stock because treasury shares are not outstanding.

    3. **Shares outstanding**—Earnings per share and most other per-share calculations are made on shares outstanding because these shares represent the *active* shares—those in the hands of the investors. These are the shares that vote and receive dividends.

    4. **Dividends and splits**—Stock dividends and splits not substantive transactions. They do not cause a change in the firm's assets or relative ownership in the firm. For calculation purposes, they are retroactively applied to all issuances of stock preceding the stock dividend or split.

Examples

1. *Shares Outstanding Computation*

A corporation had 70,000 shares of common stock authorized and 30,000 shares outstanding at the beginning of the year. During the year, the following events occurred:

January	Declared 10% stock dividend
June	Purchased 10,000 shares for the treasury
August	Reissued 5,000 shares
November	Declared 2-for-I stock split

At the end of the year, the number of outstanding shares of common stock are:

$(30,000(1.10) - 10,000 + 5,000)2 = 56,000$

Stock dividends and splits are applied retroactively to all shares outstanding and are applied to all substantive changes in shares outstanding that occur before the stock dividend or split.

2. *Number of Shares Issued and Outstanding Calculation*

Of the 12,500 shares of common stock issued by a firm, 2,500 shares were in the treasury at the beginning of the year. During the year, the following transactions occurred in chronological order:

   a. 1,300 treasury shares were reissued under a stock compensation plan.

   b. A 3-for-1 stock split took effect.

   c. 500 shares of treasury stock were purchased.

Issued shares include outstanding shares and treasury shares. Treasury shares are issued but not outstanding. Stock splits are applied to all outstanding shares because a split reduces the par value of each share of issued stock. Treasury shares must be adjusted for splits because treasury shares typically are reissued.

Number of shares issued at year end: $12,500(3) = 37,500$

Number of shares outstanding at year end: $(10,000 + 1,300)3 - 500 = 33,400$

3. *Number of Shares Issued and Outstanding Computation*

A firm issued 10,000 shares of common stock. Of these, 500 were held as treasury stock at December 31, 20X3. During 20X4, transactions involving the firm's common stock were as follows:

May—100 shares of treasury stock were sold.

August—1,000 shares of previously unissued stock were sold.

November—A 2-for-1 stock split took effect.

Laws in the firm's state of incorporation protect treasury stock from dilution. At December 31, 20X4, the number of common stock issued and outstanding:

Issued $= (10,000 + 1,000)2 = 22,000$

Outstanding $= (9,500 + 100 + 1,000)2 = 21,200$

The treasury shares are already issued. Therefore, in the calculation of issued shares, no separate adjustment for treasury shares is needed.

D. Disclosures

   1. Footnote disclosures for equity can be extensive if the entity has several classes of stock. The following are required disclosures.

   a. Rights and preferences of each class of stock including liquidation preferences and voting rights

   b. Number of shares authorized, issued, and outstanding for each class of stock

   c. Par value for each class of stock

   d. Treasury shares

   e. Restrictions regarding dividends and dividends in arrears

   f. Call and conversion information

Stock Issuance

The different ways that stock is issued are addressed in this lesson.

After studying this lesson, you should be able to:

1. Prepare the journal entry for the issuance of par stock, no-par stock with stated value, and true no-par stock for cash.

2. Record a stock subscription and defaults by subscribers.

3. Classify the stock subscriptions receivable account.

4. Record the journal entry for stock issued in exchange for a nonmonetary asset or service.

5. Allocate the total issuance proceeds to several securities in a basket sale.

6. Account for stock issuance costs.

I. There Are Several Types of Stock Issuance Transactions

A. Cash Transaction—In recording a cash sale of common stock, the corporation will credit the stock account for the par or stated value of the stock sold. Any remainder is recorded in an account such as contributed capital in excess of par value or in excess of stated value.

Example

A firm issues 2,000 shares of $4 par common stock for $10 each.

Cash	20,000	
Common Stock		8,000 OE account, only par value
Paid-in capital in excess of par		12,000 OE account, all the rest

B. Preferred Stock—Is handled the same way; the issuance of preferred stock credits the preferred stock account and contributed capital in excess of par (preferred).

C. True No Par Stock—When the stock is true no-par stock (without stated value),

1. The entire proceeds from issuance of stock are credited to the common stock account.

2. No contributed capital account is recorded.

D. Stock Sold on a Subscription Basis

1. Sale of stock on a subscription basis requires a contract specifying

   a. Share price

   b. Number of shares

   c. And the payment dates

2. **When stock is sold** on a subscription basis, the implication is that the selling price of the stock will be received in a series of payments from the shareholder. Once the full amount is received, the stock will be issued.

3. **At the signing of the contract**—Subscribers may make their first payment.

> **Note**
> If the stock has no par value but a stated value is specified, the contributed capital account is titled: Paid-in capital in excess of stated value (common).

438

4. Initial payment

Cash	amount of payment
Stock subscriptions receivable	sum of remaining payments
Common stock subscribed	(par) × (# of shares subscribed)
Contributed capital in excess of par	(contract price − par) × (# shares)

5. Subsequent payments

Cash	amount of payment
Stock subscriptions receivable	amount of payment

6. Issuance of shares after final payment

Common stock subscribed	(par) × (# of shares subscribed)
Common stock	(par) × (# of shares subscribed)

7. **Account classifications**—Stock subscriptions receivable: contra-common stock subscribed (contra OE)

8. **Common stock subscribed**—Owners' equity

9. **Recorded at signing**—Note that the contributed capital in excess of par is recorded when the contract is signed indicating that, in all probability, the shares will be issued.

10. **Credited upon final payment**—Common stock is not credited until the final payment is made because the shares are not issued at that time.

11. **Default by subscriber**—If the subscriber fails to make all the payments and defaults, the journal entry to record the default depends on the contract and applicable state law.

12. Possibilities include:

   a. Return all payments to subscriber.

   b. Issue shares in proportion to payments made.

   c. The subscriber receives no refund or shares.

Example
An individual subscribes to 200 shares of $10 par common stock at a subscription price of $15. After making payments totaling $1,200, the subscriber defaults.

Summary entry before default:

Cash	1,200	
Stock subscriptions receivable	1,800	
Common stock subscribed		2,000
Contributed capital in excess of par		1,000

Analysis

It is important to remember that the receivable (a confusing account name) is not an asset but rather a contra-equity account. There is no increase in OE for the unpaid portion. The increase in the firm's assets and OE from the above transaction is $1,200, not $3,000.

Default assumption (1), return all payments to subscriber:

The above entry is reversed.

Default assumption (2), issue shares in proportion to payments made:

$1,200/$15 = 80 shares fully paid. Required ending balances:

Common stock: 80($10)	= $800
Contributed capital in excess of par: 80($15-$10)	= $400

Common stock subscribed	2,000	
Contributed capital in excess of par	600	
Subscriptions receivable		1,800
Common stock		800

OE increases $1,200 as a result of this entry.

Default assumption (3), no refund or shares to subscriber:

Common stock subscribed	2,000	
Contributed capital in excess of par	1,000	
Subscriptions receivable		1,800
Contributed capital from default		1,200*

*Equals amount paid in by subscriber

d. Stock issued in exchange for nonmonetary consideration

   i. Value most clearly determined—When stock is sold and a nonmonetary asset is received, the recording of the transaction will be based on the fair value of the stock sold or the fair value of the asset received (or services received), whichever can be most clearly determined.

   ii. Small number of shares—When the stock is actively traded, and the number of shares issued is small in relation to the number of shares already outstanding, generally the market price of the issued shares is the more reliable of the two measures.

   iii. Significant number of shares—If the number of shares issued is significant, then the market value of the consideration received may be a better measure because the issuance of a large number of shares could affect the market price of the stock.

Example
1. A firm issued 300 shares of $5 par common stock for used equipment.
2. The market value of the equipment is not easily determinable.
3. The firm's stock was quoted at $30 a share on a national stock exchange.
4. The firm has hundreds of thousands of shares outstanding.

Equipment 300($30)	9,000	
Common stock 300($5)		1,500
Contributed capital in excess of par - common		7,500

If services are received in exchange for stock issuance, the debit is to an expense.

II. Basket Sale

A. A basket sale occurs when two or more securities are bundled together and sold in a single transaction.

B. The total amount received must be allocated to the individual securities sold.

C. Allocating Methods—For example, common stock and preferred stock might be bundled together and sold in a single transaction. In allocating the proceeds to the common stock sold and the preferred stock sold, the company will use the proportional method or the incremental method.

    1. Proportional method—When both securities have established market values, the allocation will be based on their respective fair values.

    2. Incremental method—When only one security has an established fair value, that security is assigned proceeds equal to the known fair value. Any incremental proceeds are allocated to the remaining security sold.

Examples

100 shares of a firm's $10 par common stock, along with 50 shares of the firm's $12 par preferred stock are issued as a unit for a total consideration of $4,200.

    1. The market prices of the shares are: common, $35; preferred, $20.

	Total market values		Allocation of proceeds	
Common	$35(100)	$3,500	($3,500/$4,500)$4,200	$3,267
Preferred	$20(50)	1,000	($1,000/$4,500)$4,200	933
Total		$4,500		$4,200

Entry to record issuance:

Cash	4,200	
Preferred stock 50× $12		600
Contributed capital in excess of par-preferred ($933– $600)		333
Common stock 100× $10		1,000
Contributed capital in excess of par-common ($3,267– $1,000)		2,267

2. The market price for the common stock is $35. The preferred stock does not sell actively and no current quote is available.

Total allocation to common = $35(100) = $3,500

Remaining amount of proceeds to preferred: $4,200 – $3,500= $700

Entry to record issuance:

Cash	4,200	
Preferred stock 50 × $12		600
Contributed capital in excess of par-preferred ($700 – $600)		100
Common stock 100 × $10		1,000
Contributed capital in excess of par-common ($3,500 – 1,000)		2,500

III. Stock Issue Costs Are Treated as a Reduction in the Proceeds of the Stock Issuance—This reduces the contributed capital in excess of par account.

A. **Rationale**—There is no future benefit of the issue costs—that is, the costs have served their purpose as soon as the stock is issued. No future periods benefit. This view emphasizes the balance sheet. The accounting is the same as for debt issue costs.

> **Note**
> The annual costs of maintaining the stockholder records and processing dividends are expensed as incurred.

Example
A firm issued 100 shares of $5 par common stock for $26 per share and incurred $75 of stock issue costs.

Cash (100 × $26)− $75	2,525
Common stock	500
Contributed capital in excess of par, common	2,025

There is no further accounting for the issue costs.

Preferred Stock

The accounting treatment for the issuance, redemption, retirement and conversion of preferred stock is addressed by this lesson.

After studying this lesson, you should be able to:

1. Prepare the journal entries for the issuance and retirement of preferred stock.

2. Record the conversion of convertible preferred stock.

3. Identify the type of preferred stock that is classified as debt.

I. Issuance

A. Preferred stock often has a larger par value than common stock, and has a dividend stated in dollar terms or as a percentage of face value. An issue of 6%, $100 par preferred stock is equivalent to an issue of $6, $100 par preferred stock for example. Upon issuance, any excess of proceeds over total par value of shares issued is credited to contributed capital in excess of par. The credit to the preferred stock account is relatively much larger than the credit to contributed capital excess compared with common stock, which usually carries a small par value.

B. Convertible preferred stock allows the preferred shareholder to convert the preferred shares to common shares. The journal entry for issuance of convertible preferred stock does not allocate any of the proceeds to the conversion feature. As with convertible bonds, the securities are recorded at issuance in the same way nonconvertible securities would be.

C. Preferred Stock with Warrants—Preferred stock, like bonds, may be issued with warrants for the purchase of common stock entitling the holder to purchase common stock at a fixed price. The issue price of the preferred stock is allocated to (1) the preferred stock accounts, and (2) another OE account for the common stock warrants. The allocation is based on fair value. When the warrants are exercised, cash is debited, the warrant account is closed, common shares are issued, and the common stock accounts are established.

II. Calling and Redeeming Preferred Stock

—When preferred stock is called (by the issuer) or redeemed (by the stockholder) or is acquired and retired, all related OE accounts are removed. The issuer can call in callable preferred stock at a specified price during a specified period. No gain or loss is recognized for any of these events because the transactions are between the firm and its owners.

A. Any **debit difference** is recorded in retained earnings.

B. Any **credit difference** is recorded in a contributed capital account.

C. Any **dividends in arrears** must be paid when the shares are acquired (retained earnings is debited).

D. The General Journal Entry:

Preferred stock	Par value of stock called or redeemed
Contributed capital in excess of par	Amount recorded on original issuance*
Retained earnings	If difference is a debit
Cash	Amount paid to the shareholders
Contributed capital from retirement of Preferred stock	If difference is a credit

*This amount is limited to the original recorded amount on the shares now acquired back by the issuing firm.

Example
100 shares of 6%, $50 par callable cumulative preferred stock with two years of dividends in arrears are called at $53. The shares were issued for $51 a share.

Journal entries:

Retained earnings 2(.06)($50)(100)	600	
Cash (for dividends in arrears)		600
Preferred stock ($50)(100)	5,000	
Contributed capital in excess of par, preferred ($51 − $50)100	100	
Retained earnings ($53 − $51)100	200	
Cash $53(100)		5,300

III. Conversion of Preferred Stock—When convertible preferred stock is converted into common stock, the preferred stock accounts are transferred to the common stock accounts. Again, there is no gain or loss.

    A. Retained Earnings Debited—If the total recorded value of the preferred stock is less than the par value of the common stock issued on conversion, retained earnings is debited for the difference.

    B. The General Journal Entry:

Preferred stock	Par value of stock converted
Contributed capital in excess of par	Amount recorded on original issuance*
Retained earnings	If needed
Common stock	Par value of common stock issued
Contributed capital in excess of par, common	If difference is a credit

*This amount is limited to the original recorded amount on the shares now being converted to common.

Example
100 shares of 6%, $50 par convertible preferred stock are converted into $10 par common stock at a rate of two shares of common per share of preferred. The preferred stock was for $51 a share.

Journal entry:

Preferred stock ($50)(100)	5,000	
Contributed capital in excess of par, preferred ($51 − $50)100	100	
Common stock 100(2)($10)		2,000
Contributed capital in excess of par, common		3,100

If each share of preferred stock was convertible into six shares of common stock, the conversion entry would be:

Preferred stock ($50)(100)	5,000	
Contributed capital in excess of par, preferred ($51 − $50)100	100	
Retained earnings	900	
Common stock 100(6)($10)		6,000

IV. Redeemable Preferred Stock

A. Redeemable preferred stock may require the issuing firm to (1) redeem the stock (purchase the stock from the shareholder) at a specified future date at a specified price, or (2) redeem the stock at the option of the shareholder.

1. A preferred stock or other financial instrument issued in the form of shares is mandatorily redeemable if the issuer is unconditionally required to redeem the instrument by transferring its assets at a specified or determinable date(s) or when an event certain to occur takes place. If the obligation to redeem is dependent on a future uncertain event, the instrument is considered to be **mandatorily redeemable** when that event occurs, or when the event becomes certain to occur.

B. Balance Sheet Classification—Mandatorily redeemable financial instruments (such as redeemable preferred stock) must be classified as debt (rather than owners' equity) unless the redemption is required to occur only if the issuing firm goes out of business.

1. At the end of each year the liability is reported at the present value of the amount to be paid at maturity. The implicit rate at date of issuance is used for the discounting. Interest expense is recorded for the amount of cash dividends paid, as adjusted for the change in present value for the maturity amount.

2. If either the maturity date or maturity value (redemption price) is not known, the fair value is used for balance sheet reporting and the change in fair value is used for interest expense measurement.

Treasury Stock

Accounting generalizations and the specifics of the cost method are covered in this lesson. It also addresses the specifics of the par method and compares it to the cost method. Share retirement and donated stock also are covered.

After studying this lesson, you should be able to:

1. Identify the main accounting aspects of all treasury stock transactions.

2. Record the purchase and reissuance of treasury stock under the cost method.

3. Identify the differences between the cost and par methods.

4. Describe the accounting for share retirement.

Exam Tip

CPA Exams in the past have listed a firm's treasury stock in the investment section of the balance sheet in questions calling for the candidate to identify errors. This requires the candidate to recognize that treasury stock is not an asset of the firm. It is reported as a contra-owner's equity account. These questions are solved by reducing the investment account by the amount recorded as treasury stock and reinstating the treasury stock account as a reduction from total OE.

I. **Accounting Generalizations About Treasury Stock**—The following statements hold regardless of the method used to account for treasury stock, which are shares of a firm's common stock purchased (bought back) by that firm.

   A. No one owns treasury stock—there is no shareholder for this stock. A firm cannot own itself.

   B. Treasury stock is not an asset.

   C. A firm cannot record any income account in a treasury stock transaction.

   D. A firm cannot profit from treasury stock transactions.

   E. The treasury stock account is debited upon purchase of treasury stock. The account is a contra OE account. The common stock account is not affected by treasury stock transactions because treasury stock is considered issued stock.

   F. Treasury stock reduces the number of shares outstanding but not the number of shares issued, because treasury stock is issued stock.

   G. When treasury stock is purchased, earnings per share increases because the denominator of EPS is reduced with no effect on the numerator.

   H. The net assets and owners' equity of the firm decrease by the cost of treasury shares purchased.

   I. Retained earnings can be decreased in some cases, but never increased by treasury stock transactions.

II. **Accounting for Treasury Stock**

   A. There are two methods to account for treasury stock:

   1. **Cost Method**—Records the treasury stock account at the cost of shares reacquired;

   2. **Par Value Method**—Records the treasury stock account at the par value of shares reacquired.

   B. Owners' equity is reduced by the same amount, regardless of which method is used, but the balances of certain OE accounts are different under the two methods.

III. Cost Method

A. Description of the Cost Method—
At purchase, treasury stock is debited for the cost of the shares purchased. The contributed capital in excess of par account that was credited when the stock was issued is not affected. Reissuances credit the treasury stock account at cost, and the difference between the purchase price and reissue price is recorded in contributed capital from treasury stock.

B. Journal Entry Example:
(The par of common stock is $5, original issuance price was $20, a total of 700 shares have been issued, and retained earnings is $4,000.)

Purchase 200 shares of treasury stock for $25 a share:

Treasury stock (cost) 200 × $25	5,000	
Cash		5,000

Reissue 50 shares of treasury stock for $30 a share (greater than cost):

Cash 50 × $30	1,500	
Contributed capital from treasury stock ($30 − $25)50		250*
Treasury stock 50 × $25		1,250**

*Excess of reissue price over cost of treasury stock
**FIFO, average or specific identification can be used to measure the cost of treasury stock sold when there is more than one cost represented in the treasury stock account.

Reissue 50 shares of treasury stock for $18 a share (less than cost):

Cash 50 × $18	900	
Contributed capital from treasury stock	250*	
Retained earnings	100**	
Treasury stock 50 × $25		1,250

*Reduces the balance to zero.
**The total excess of cost over reissue price is 50($25 − $18) = $350. The contributed capital from treasury stock account accounts for $250 of that amount. The remainder is taken from retained earnings.

Analysis

Treasury stock purchases reduce the firm's total assets, net assets, and total OE. Erroneously recording treasury stock as an asset (e.g., an investment) would have no effect on these amounts and thus would serve to overstate the firm's assets and OE.

When a firm purchases its own stock, it literally contracts in size. Firms buy back their own stock for a variety of reasons, such as to increase EPS, return cash to the shareholders, and to thwart hostile takeovers.

IV. Balance Sheet Presentation—Treasury stock is subtracted at the very bottom of the OE section of the balance sheet. The balance is $2,500 (100 treasury shares remaining × $25 cost). The common stock and original contributed capital in excess of par accounts are unaffected.

OE section:	
Common stock 700($5)	$ 3,500
Contributed capital in excess of par 700($20 − $5)	10,500
Contributed capital from treasury stock	0
Retained earnings $4,000 − $100	3,900
Less treasury stock at cost	($2,500)
Total OE	$15,400

V. Par Value Method

A. This is the second of two methods allowed for treasury stock accounting. The first is the cost method, covered in the previous lesson.

B. Description of the Par Value Method—At purchase, the treasury stock account is debited for par value, and the contributed capital in excess of par account that was credited when the stock was issued is debited for the original amount recorded. Reissuances are treated as a regular issuance of stock except that treasury stock is credited, rather than common stock.

C. Journal Entry Example—The initial data for the cost method (previous example) is used (par of common stock is $5, original issuance price was $20, a total of 700 shares have been issued, and retained earnings is $4,000) but, the transactions in this example are not the same as for the cost method so that the main aspects of the par method can be shown.

Purchase 100 shares of treasury stock for $15 a share (less than original price):

Treasury stock (par) 100 × $5	500	
Contributed capital in excess of par, common ($20 − $5)100	1,500	
Contributed capital from treasury stock ($20 − $15)100		500
Cash		1,500

This entry reduces the original contributed capital in excess of par as if the stock were going to be retired.

Purchase 100 shares of treasury stock for $22 a share (greater than original price):

Treasury stock 100 × $5	500	
Contributed capital in excess of par, common ($20 − $5)100	1,500	
Contributed capital from treasury stock ($22 − $20)100	200	
Cash 100 × $22		2,200

It is important to remember that the contributed capital in excess of par account is always reduced by the original amount received when the stock was issued ($1,500).

The excess of the cost ($22) over original issue price ($20) is first taken from any previous contributed capital from treasury stock transactions. In this case, $500 is available from the previous treasury stock purchase.

If this amount were insufficient to complete the debit side of the entry, retained earnings would be reduced by the remaining amount. (If the purchase price had been $28, then retained earnings would be reduced by $300.)

Reissue 150 shares of treasury stock for $18 a share:

Cash 150 × $18	2,700	
Contributed capital in excess of par ($18 − $5)150		1,950
Treasury stock 150 × $5		750

This entry is essentially the same as for the issuance of unissued stock. The only difference is that treasury stock, rather than common stock, is credited.

    D. Balance Sheet Presentation—Treasury stock is reported as a subtraction from the common stock account in the balance sheet. The balance is (50 treasury shares remaining × $5 par) = $250. Assume that 700 shares of common stock have been issued. The balance sheet would show:

OE section:

Common stock 700 ($5)	$ 3,500
Less treasury stock at cost (50 × $5)	(250)
Common stock outstanding	3,250
Contributed capital in excess of par	
700($20 − $5) − $1,500 − $1,500 + $1,950	9,450
Contributed capital from treasury stock	
$500 − $200	300
Retained earnings	4,000
Total OE	$17,000

(The total OE for the cost and par value method examples are not equal because the transactions were different. If the transactions were the same, the total OE would be the same although the component balances other than the common stock account could be different.)

VI. Comparison of Cost and Par Value Methods

    A. When treasury shares are purchased at a cost greater than par but less than original issue price, what is the relative impact of the cost and the par value methods on additional paid-in capital and retained earnings?

        1. Cost Method—Under the cost method, when treasury stock is purchased for an amount less than original price, the treasury stock account is debited. This is a contra OE account. Additional paid-in capital and retained earnings are unaffected.

        2. Par Value Method—Under the par value method, the treasury stock account is debited for par value, and additional paid-in capital is debited for the amount in proportion to the original issue price. Because less was paid for the treasury stock than was received on original issuance, retained earnings is unaffected. Rather, additional paid-in capital from treasury stock is credited for the difference, but not by as much as the debit to the original issuance additional paid-in capital account.

        3. Therefore, additional paid-in capital decreases under the par value method relative to the cost method, but there is no difference in the effect on retained earnings under the conditions imposed.

B. Use of the contributed capital from treasury stock account when treasury shares are reissued or purchased:

	Cost Method	Par Value Method
Increase in Contributed Capital from Treasury Stock	Reissue at a price exceeding cost	Purchase at a price less than original issue price
Decrease in Contributed Capital from Treasury Stock	Reissue at a price less than cost	Purchase at a price exceeding original issue price

VII. Share Retirement

A. Sometimes firms retire their shares after purchasing them on the market, rather than treating them as treasury shares. Retired shares are placed back into the authorized but unissued category. Accounting for the purchase and retirement of shares is the same as the purchase of treasury shares under the par value method, except that common stock account is used instead of the treasury stock account.

1. If the purchase price is less than the original issue price, then contributed capital from stock retirement is credited.

2. If the purchase price is greater than the original issue price, then contributed capital from stock retirement is debited until exhausted, and retained earnings is debited for the remainder, if any.

B. Subsequent issuance of the retired shares is recorded as a normal stock issuance, because the retired shares were treated as unissued.

Dividends

This lesson considers cash and other property dividends, which are distributions of the firm's earnings (reduction in retained earnings).

After studying this lesson, you should be able to:

1. Identify the important dates for recording dividends.

2. State the accounting treatment of dividends in arrears.

3. Record a property dividend using the correct amount.

4. Prepare the journal entries for declaration and payment of a scrip dividend.

5. Note the main difference between liquidating dividends and other cash and property dividends.

I. Cash and Other Property Dividends

A. Cash, and other property dividends reduce the distributing firm's assets and retained earnings. A liability is recognized for these liabilities on the date of declaration. Stock dividends also reduce retained earnings but do not involve a distribution of assets. No liability is recognized for stock dividends.

1. **Relevant dates**—In relation to dividends, there are three important dates (listed in chronological order).

a. The **declarative date** is the date the board of directors formally declares the dividend. This is the most important date in terms of the effect on the firm's resources and therefore its balance sheet. At this date, the firm recognizes a liability and a reduction in retained earnings. The firm's net assets are reduced.

b. The **date of record** is simply a cut-off date. The shareholders of record on this date will be the recipients of the dividend payments. This date is used because it requires a certain amount of time to compile the list of shareholders as of a particular date.

c. The **payment date** is the date the dividends are actually distributed to the shareholders. Firms typically pay dividends quarterly. The time lag between declaration and payment can be a few weeks. The fourth-quarter dividend is declared near the end of the fiscal year, but payment often occurs early the next year. Therefore, the amount of dividends declared in a year often is not the same as the amount of dividends paid in that year. Payment does not reduce the firm's retained earnings and net assets; rather, it is the *declaration* that reduces retained earnings and net assets.

B. **Cash Dividends**

1. The distribution of earnings will take the form of a cash distribution. The related liability will be recognized on the date of declaration. The typical entries related to a cash dividend are shown below. Dividends are not recognized as an expense for the firm paying the dividends.

Date of Declaration: Retained Earnings*   xx

         Dividends Payable   xx

*Some firms debit the temporary account Dividends Declared rather than debit retained earnings directly. At year-end, the Dividends Declared account is closed to retained earnings.

---

2. Date of Record:	No Entry	
3. Date of Payment:	Dividends Payable	xx
	Cash	xx

C. Dividends in Arrears—Unpaid dividends for a particular year on cumulative preferred stock. Dividends are not required to be paid but are said to accumulate if unpaid. However, no liability is recognized for dividends in arrears until there has been a dividend declaration. The cumulative feature of preferred stock simply means in the event of a dividend declaration, preferred shareholders are entitled to be paid the dividends in arrears before any distribution related to the current period occurs. Dividends in arrears are disclosed in the footnotes.

D. Other Property Dividends

1. In this type of dividend, the distribution of earnings will take the form of a noncash distribution. The related liability and the gain or loss on disposal of the asset is recognized on the date of declaration. The dividend is recorded at the asset's fair value *at declaration date*. The typical entries related to a property dividend are shown below.

Date of Declaration:	Retained Earnings	xx
	Dividends Payable	xx

2. The above entry is recorded at the fair value of the asset to be distributed. Retained earnings are reduced by the true economic sacrifice of declaring the dividend at the time of making the commitment to distribute the asset. The liability is also measured at fair value. In addition to the above entry, one of the following two entries is made to adjust the asset to fair value at declaration date. The amount recorded is the difference between book value and fair value.

Asset	xx	
Gain on Disposal		xx

or

Loss on Disposal	xx	
Asset		xx

3. Remaining entries:

Date of Record:	No Entry	
Date of Payment:	Dividends Payable	xx
	Asset	xx

The credit to the asset is for the adjusted book value, which equals the fair value on the declaration date. Ignoring income tax effects, the net reduction in retained earnings resulting from a property dividend is the book value of the asset to be distributed. Retained earnings is reduced by the fair value of the asset distributed, but the gain or loss decreases or increases that effect to a net amount equaling the book value of the asset distributed.

Example

A firm declares and pays a property dividend. The book value of the asset distributed is $4,000, and the fair value is $6,000.

Retained Earnings	6,000	
Dividends Payable		6,000
Asset	2,000	
Gain on Asset Distribution		2,000
Dividends Payable	6,000	
Asset		6,000

Retained earnings is decreased a net of $4,000 ($6,000 from recording the dividend – $2,000 gain on asset), an amount equaling the book value of the asset.

II. **Scrip Dividends**—A scrip dividend is first distributed in note payable (scrip) form because the firm does not have the cash at the date of declaration to pay the dividend but wants to assure the shareholders that the dividend is forthcoming.

　A. **Interest Paid**—Interest is paid on the note until cash is paid.

　B. **General Entries**

At declaration:

Retained Earnings	Amount of dividend declared
Scrip Dividend Payable	A liability account

At payment:

Scrip Dividend Payable		Amount of dividend declared
Interest Expense	xx	
Cash		Dividend plus interest

　C. **Interest expense** is computed from the date of declaration to the date of payment using the interest rate in the note. The principal amount is the amount of dividend declared.

　D. **Partial Payment**—If a partial payment is made after declaration (to shareholders of record), then the interest expense is computed from the date of that partial payment to the date the final payment is made. The principal amount on which interest is computed is the amount of the final payment.

　E. **Returns on Capital**—Cash, property, and scrip dividends are returns on capital. They are distributions of earnings, not contributed capital.

III. **Liquidating Dividends**—A liquidating dividend is a return of capital, rather than a return on capital. It is a return of contributed capital—an amount invested by the shareholder.

　A. **Reduces Contributed Capital Account**—The liquidating portion of a dividend reduces a contributed capital account, rather than retained earnings, and must be disclosed as a liquidating dividend.

　B. **Capital Account Debited**—Rather than debiting retained earnings for the liquidating portion, a contributed capital account is debited.

　C. **Liquidating Dividend Occurrence**—One situation in which a liquidating dividend occurs is the payment of a dividend in excess of earnings by a firm in the extractive industries.

1. In this case, because the depletable resource will not be replaced (as would be the case for depreciable assets), a dividend equal to net income plus depletion can be distributed without harming the ability of the firm to maintain capital.

Examples

1. A firm has net income of $10,000 which reflects $2,000 of depletion. A dividend of $12,000 can be paid because the depletable resource will not be replaced. If $12,000 of dividends is declared, the entry is:

Retained Earnings	10,000	
Contributed Capital	2,000	
Dividends Payable		12,000

The liquidating portion is $2,000.

2. A firm in the extractive industries declared a cash dividend of $40,000. The dividend is legal in this state. The following data pertain to the firm just prior to the dividend:

Accumulated Depletion	$10,000
Capital Stock	50,000
Additional Paid-In Capital	15,000
Retained Earnings	30,000

Retained earnings is used first as a source of capital for the dividend ($30,000 of the $40,000 total dividend).

The remaining $10,000 reduces additional paid-in capital and is a liquidating dividend.

The accumulated depletion justifies the liquidating portion because it is a recognized reduction in net income that represents the allocated cost of an investment that will not be replaced. Dividends in excess of income are allowed to the extent of accumulated depletion less any prior liquidating dividends.

Stock Dividends and Splits

Stock dividends reduce retained earnings but cause no reduction in the firm's assets.

After studying this lesson, you should be able to:

1. Identify the differences between cash dividends, stock dividends, and stock splits.
2. List the effects of stock dividends on shares outstanding and on the accounts.
3. Record large and small stock dividends.
4. Note the effects of stock splits on the accounts.

I. **Stock Dividends**—A stock dividend is a distribution by a firm of its stock to its shareholders in proportion to their existing holdings. The shareholder does not pay for these shares. Stock dividends do not involve a future transfer of assets or a future provision of services. Therefore, in relation to stock dividends, no liability is recorded. Each investor simply holds more shares, but each share is worth proportionately less than before the dividend. Each investor maintains the previous ownership percentage.

Example
If a firm has 10,000 shares of common stock outstanding and issues a 5% stock dividend, then 500 shares are distributed to the current shareholders at no cost to them.

If a specific shareholder owned 2,000 shares before the dividend (20% ownership), he or she would receive 100 shares (2,000 × .05). After the dividend, the shareholder owns 2,100/10,500 or 20% of the firm (no change in percentage ownership).

A. **Effect of Dividend**—The effect of a stock dividend is to increase the number of shares issued and outstanding.

B. **EPS Decreased**—Earnings per share is decreased by a stock dividend.

C. **Stock Dividend Purpose**—Stock dividends are distributed to reduce the market price of the firm's stock (often because the stock price has become too high for potential investors) and also to reduce demand by shareholders for cash dividends.

D. **Permanent Capitalization**—A stock dividend is a permanent capitalization (reduction) of retained earnings (or possibly paid-in capital for large stock dividends) into contributed capital. The firm's net assets are unaffected. Only OE accounts are affected.

E. **Accounting for Dividends**—Accounting for stock dividends depends on the size of the stock dividend (small or large).

1. **Small stock dividend**—(% of dividend is less than 20–25%) Capitalize at market price.

Example
Assume a firm has 20,000 shares of $5 par common stock outstanding and declares a 5% stock dividend when the market price (fair value) is $20 per share.

This is a small stock dividend because 5% is less than 20%–25%.

Entry:

Retained earnings 20,000(.05)($20)	20,000	
Common stock 20,000(.05)($5)		5,000
Contributed capital in excess of par, common		15,000

If there is a significant period of time between declaration and distribution of shares, or if the two events occur in different fiscal periods, the account Stock Dividend Distributable is credited instead of Common Stock in the above entry. At distribution, Stock Dividend Distributable is debited and Common Stock is credited.

2. **Market price measure**—The market price of the stock at the **declaration date** is used to measure the stock dividend because that is the date on which the commitment to distribute the dividend is made.

   a. **Market to pay dividend**—Market price is used on the assumption that the market price of the stock will not change given the small size of the dividend, and the shareholder then can sell the shares received while maintaining the predividend market value of the investment. In effect, the firm is using the market to pay the dividend.

   b. **Debit to retained earnings**—Under the above assumption, the debit to retained earnings is the value of the stock distributed and therefore represents the amount of retained earnings to be permanently capitalized to contributed capital. This amount of retained earnings will never be available for cash dividends.

3. **Large stock dividend**—(% of dividend is greater than 20%–25%). Capitalize at par value.

Example

Assume a firm has 20,000 shares of $5 par common stock outstanding and declares a 40% stock dividend when the market price (fair value) is $20 per share.

This is a large stock dividend because 40% is greater than 20%–25%.

Entry:

Retained earnings 20,000(.40)($5)	40,000	
Common stock		40,000

In this case, the assumption cannot be made that the market price of the stock will remain unchanged because of the large dilution in the number of shares outstanding.

Thus, only the par value of shares issued is permanently capitalized. Subsequent changes in market price do not affect the accounting.

   a. Large stock dividends also can be accounted for as a stock split effected in the form of a stock dividend. The debit would be to contributed capital in excess of par, rather than retained earnings in the above example. As such, retained earnings is not capitalized to permanent capital if this alternative is chosen.

   b. We have distinguished small and large stock dividends by referring to "less than 20%–25%," which is sufficient in most cases. However, for SEC registrants, less than 25% is considered small. For other firms, if the dividend percentage is between 20% and 25%, the firm may choose to record the dividend at fair value or at par value of the shares. If less than 20%, fair value is used; if more than 25%, par value is used. The expectation is that the CPA Exam would not use a percentage of 20–25% in order to avoid this confusion.

4. **Change in total OE**—Neither type of stock dividend causes a change in total OE, but retained earnings is reduced and contributed capital is increased (except for a large stock dividend accounted for as a stock split).

   a. **No liability recorded**—It is important to remember that no liability is recorded for a stock dividend because it does not involve the distribution of goods or services, and therefore, does not meet the definition of a liability.

II. Stock Splits—A stock split is not a dividend. Rather it is an adjustment to par value and number of issued shares.

    A. A 2-for-1 split halves the par value and doubles the number of shares. The reason firms split their shares is to reduce the market price and make the shares available to a larger number of shareholders.

    B. No accounting entry is needed although firms may make a memo entry to record the split.

        1. No change in OE—There is no change in any account balance within owner's equity.

    C. Dividend/Split Similarity—Although both a 100% stock dividend and 2-for-1 stock split double the number of shares outstanding, there are few other similarities.

        1. Comparison of dividend/split—Comparison of a 100% stock dividend and 2-for-1 stock split.

	100% stock dividend	2-for-1 stock split
Effect on total OE	None	None
Effect on retained earnings	Decrease	None
Effect on par value	None	Cut in half
Effect on shares outstanding	Double	Double
Effect on contributed capital	Increase	None
Effect on common stock account	Increase	None

III. Additional Aspects

    A. Treasury shares usually do not receive stock dividends. However, if the treasury shares were intended to be used to meet a commitment under a stock option plan for example, then the treasury shares would be adjusted for the stock dividend.

    B. Real estate trusts and other firms may declare dividends that may be paid in cash or shares at the election of the shareholders with a potential limitation on the total amount of cash that all shareholders can elect to receive in the aggregate. For this type of distribution, the stock portion of the distribution is treated as a stock issuance, not a stock dividend.

Dividend Allocation

The final lesson about dividends considers the order and allocation of dividends between preferred and common stock.

After studying this lesson, you should be able to:

1. Allocate dividends when there are dividends in arrears.

2. Determine the dividends to common when the firm has partially participating preferred stock.

3. Calculate the dividends to both classes of stock when the firm has fully participating preferred stock.

I. Introduction

A. Nonparticipating preferred stock is entitled only to the annual dividend percentage noted in the stock certificate—the annual dividend requirement.

B. When the full amount of preferred stock dividend is not paid on cumulative preferred stock for any given year, the unpaid dividends are in arrears and must be paid before any other dividend, including the current-year dividends on preferred stock.

C. If the preferred stock is noncumulative and any part of the current-year dividends are not paid, then they are never paid.

D. When preferred stock does not participate beyond its annual percentage or amount, the order of dividend payments is:

1. Preferred: Any dividends in arrears (only if preferred stock is cumulative)

2. Preferred: Current-period dividend

3. Common: Remainder

Example

a. A firm has 200 shares of 5%, $100 par cumulative nonparticipating preferred stock.

b. The annual dividend requirement on the stock is $1,000 (.05 × 200 × $100).

c. This preferred stock might also be referred to as $5 preferred stock (rather than 5%) indicating the annual dividend per share.

d. The firm also has 4,000 shares of $10 par common stock outstanding.

e. Two years of dividends are in arrears as of the beginning of the current year and $7,000 of dividends are declared for the current year.

f. The dividend allocation is (P = preferred; C = common):

		P	C
i. Preferred:	arrears	$2,000	
ii. Preferred:	current	1,000	
iii. Common:	remainder		$4,000
Total		$3,000	$4,000

II. Preferred Stock Is Participating—When preferred stock is participating, the stock may receive dividends in addition to the annual current dividend requirement. When preferred participates, common receives a matching amount. Preferred stock may be fully or partially participating.

458

A. Fully Participating

1. After any dividends in arrears are allocated, the remaining dividends are allocated based on the total par value of the preferred and common stock outstanding.

2. If total dividends are not sufficient to provide common with a matching amount equal to the preferred percentage times total par value of common, then there is no participation and common receives all the dividends after the current year preferred dividend requirement and any dividends in arrears are allocated.

B. Partially Participating

1. The preferred stock receives dividends up to an additional percentage.

    a. Common stock receives a matching amount equal to the preferred percentage times total par of common stock outstanding before the preferred stock receives its additional allocation.

    b. Common stock receives any dividends in excess of the additional amount allocated to preferred.

2. If the total dividends declared are not sufficient to provide the maximum additional participating percentage to both preferred and common (after common receives its share based on the preferred percentage), then each class of stock receives a share of the remainder in proportion to total par.

3. The steps in the allocation are:

    a. Preferred: Any dividends in arrears

    b. Preferred: Current-period dividend

    c. Common: Matching amount: preferred percentage x total par of common outstanding

    d. Preferred: Additional percentage

    e. Common: Remainder

III. Examples—Common information: A firm has 200 shares of 5%, $100 par cumulative participating preferred stock. The annual dividend requirement on the stock is $1,000 (.05 × 200 × $100). The firm also has 4,000 shares of $10 par common stock outstanding.

		Percentage
Total par value of preferred stock outstanding:	$20,000	1/3
Total par value of common stock outstanding:	40,000	2/3
Total par value	$60,000	

Example
1. *Fully participating*

The preferred stock is fully participating. Two years of dividends are in arrears and total dividends declared are $11,000.

	P	C
a. Preferred: Arrears	$2,000	
b. Preferred: Current	1,000	
c. Common: Matching amount .05($40,000)		$2,000
Dividend remaining =		
$6,000 ($11,000 − $5,000 allocated above)		
d. Preferred: Participation (1/3)($6,000)	2,000	
e. Common: Participation (2/3)($6,000)		4,000
Total	$5,000	$6,000

If total dividends were less than $5,000 but more than $3,000, then common would receive the entire amount above $3,000. There would be no dividends available for participation to either class of stock because common did not receive its matching amount.

2. *Partially participating*

The preferred stock is participating to a maximum additional percentage of 4% (for a total of 9%). Two years of dividends are in arrears, and total dividends declared are $14,000.

	P	C
a. Preferred: Arrears	$2,000	
b. Preferred: Current	1,000	
c. Common: Matching amount .05($40,000)		$2,000
Dividend remaining =		
$9,000 ($14,000 − $5,000 allocated above)		
This amount exceeds 4% of total par of both classes of stock: ($2,400 = .04 × $60,000)		
d. Preferred: Participation (.04)($20,000)	800	
e. Common: Remainder ($9,000 − $800)		8,200
Total	$3,800	$10,200

If the remaining dividends after Step 3 were less than $2,400, then the remaining dividends are allocated in proportion to total par value. Using the same information except that total dividends declared are $6,800:

	P	C
a. Preferred: Arrears	$2,000	
b. Preferred: Current	1,000	
c. Common: Matching amount .05($40,000)		$2,000
Dividend remaining		
$1,800 ($6,800 − $5,000 allocated above)		
This amount is less than 4% of total par of both of stock: ($2,400 = .04 × $60,000)		
Therefore the remaining dividend is allocated in proportion to total par value.		
d. Preferred: (1/3)($1,800)	600	
e. Common: (2/3)($1,800)		1,200
Total	$3,600	$3,200

Stock Rights, Retained Earnings

Accounting for stock rights, and the retained earnings statement is the focus of this lesson.

After studying this lesson, you should be able to:

1. Account for stock rights issued to existing shareholders and for rights issued to outside parties.

2. Articulate the reasons for retained earnings appropriations and restrictions.

3. Record retained earnings appropriations.

4. Prepare a Statement of Retained Earnings.

5. Describe each item found in the Statement of Retained Earnings.

I. Stock Rights—This section covers the issuance of stock rights to existing shareholders and to outside parties for services. A later lesson covers stock option plans for employees. The main question is whether the issuance of the rights is an event to be recognized in the accounts.

Definition

Stock Right: Gives the holder the option to purchase a certain number of shares of the issuing firm at a specified price during a specified time period.

    A. Stock rights are often used to convey preemptive rights.

    B. The existing shareholders are given rights (via a stock warrant) to purchase their pro rata number of shares to keep their current percentage in the firm.

    C. The rights have an expiration date and must be exercised by this date.

Entries for rights to existing shareholders

At issuance of rights:	No journal entry is made. No resources have been transferred.
At exercise of rights:	The usual entry to record the issuance of stock is made. The issue price is the exercise price as specified in the stock warrant, not the market price on the date of exercise.
If rights lapse:	No entry is made if the shareholder does not exercise the rights.

    D. Stock Rights Issued to Outside Parties for Services

At issuance of rights:	Record an expense and owners' equity account equal to the difference between the market price and exercise price, times the number of shares under option.
At exercise of rights:	Record the stock issuance at the exercise price and remove the OE account credited at issuance of the rights.

Example
A firm issues 300 rights to an attorney for services rendered to the firm. Three rights entitle the holder to purchase one share of the firm's $5 common stock for $20. The market value of the stock on the day the rights were issued was $30.

Entries:

At issuance:

Legal expenses ($30 – $20)(300/3)	1,000	
Stock rights outstanding (OE)		1,000

The $1,000 recorded amount represents the opportunity cost to the firm of committing to an issuance of 100 shares of stock for $20 when the market price is currently $30. Subsequent changes in market price do not enter into the accounting.

At exercise:

Cash (300/3)($20)	2,000	
Stock rights outstanding	1,000	
Common stock (300/3)($5)		500
Contributed capital in excess of par, common		2,500

II. Valuation of Bundled Securities

A. Two securities may be bundled (sold) together for one price when initially issued. A common example is when stock warrants are issued with a debt security (the host security). The stock warrants are sometimes referred to as an "equity kicker." Since the stock warrants are detachable from the bonds, the two securities should be reported and valued separately for accounting purposes.

B. When the total fair value of the combined security is equal to the fair value of each security individually, the measurement for reporting purposes is straightforward: report each component at its fair value. However, often the fair value of the combined security is not equal to the sum of the fair value of the individual securities or the valuation of one of the securities is unknown.

C. There are two methods used to determine the value of each security. The proportional or the incremental method. Use the proportional method when the fair value of both securities is known and use the incremental method when only one of the fair values is known.

1. The proportional method allocates the total fair value of the combined security to the individual components based on the proportion of the fair value of each individual security.

Fair value allocated to the bond	(900,000 ÷ 1,200,000) × 1,000,000 =	$750,000
Fair value allocated to the warrant	(300,000 ÷ 1,200,000) × 1,000,000 =	250,000
Total fair value		$1,000,000

i. Assume the total fair value of a bond with a detachable stock warrant has a fair value of $1 million. The fair value of the bond is $900,000 and the fair value of the warrant is $300,000 of a sum of $1.2 million. The proportional method would value the bond and warrant as follows:

ii. The difference between the face value of the bond and the value assigned upon issuance is the discount or premium on the bond. In this example, the issuer will record Discount on Bonds Payable of $250,000 ($1,000,000 face value - $750,000 issue price).

2. The incremental method is used when the fair value of one of the securities is unknown.

    i. Assume the total fair value of bond with a detachable stock warrant has a fair value of $1 million. The fair value of the bond is $900,000 and the fair value of the warrant is unknown. The incremental method would value the bond and warrant as follows:

Total fair value of the bond and warrant	$1,000,000
Fair value of the bond alone	900,000
The fair value allocated to the warrant	$ 100,000

    ii. The difference between the face value of the bond and the value assigned upon issuance is the discount or premium on the bond. In this example, the issuer will record Discount on Bonds Payable of $100,000 ($1,000,000 face value - $900,000 issue price).

    iii. Bonds Payable is a liability account with a natural credit balance. Premium on Bonds Payable is an adjunct account with a natural credit balance. Discount on Bonds Payable is a contra-Bonds Payable (contra-liability account) with a natural debit balance. Paid-in-Capital – Stock Warrants is an equity account with a natural credit balance.

III. Appropriations of Retained Earnings

A. Unappropriated Retained Earnings

1. Available for declaration—This portion of retained earnings is available for dividend declaration. In other words, the future use of this amount of retained earnings has not been determined.

2. No specific purpose—Unappropriated retained earnings have not been earmarked for a specific purpose.

3. Not all are paid—Not all unappropriated retained earnings must be paid in dividends, however.

B. Appropriated Retained Earnings

1. Declared off-limits—This amount of retained earnings has been declared off-limits for dividends so that funds may be conserved for a specific purpose or objective.

    a. Financial planning—The purpose might be related to financial planning, such as debt retirement or plant expansion.

    b. Legal requirement—The purpose or objective might be related to some legal requirement, such as the appropriation of retained earnings related to treasury stock transactions.

    c. Contractual obligation—Finally, the purpose of the appropriation might be related to a contractual obligation, such as a clause in a loan agreement requiring the appropriation.

2. End result—When retained earnings are appropriated, the amount of unappropriated retained earnings declines, and the amount of possible dividend declarations declines as well.

C. Formal communication—A retained earnings appropriation is management's formal communication that a portion of retained earnings has been declared off-limits for dividends.

D. Appropriation Entry—The entry for an appropriation is:

Retained earnings	amount appropriated
Retained earnings, appropriated for X purpose	amount appropriated

1. **No reduction**—This entry does not reduce total retained earnings nor does it necessarily reduce dividends.

2. **When purpose fulfilled**—When the purpose for which an appropriation is made has been fulfilled, the above entry is reversed, reinstating the amount to unappropriated retained earnings.

    a. **No effect**—The entry to reverse the appropriation also has no effect on total retained earnings.

  E. **Partition retained earnings**—Retained earnings appropriations have no effect on assets. They do not "reserve" assets. They simply partition retained earnings into two parts.

IV. **Restrictions on Retained Earnings**

The Tiger Company
Statement of Retained Earnings
For the Year Ended December 31, 20X7

Retained Earnings, January 1, 20X7	XX
Prior Period Adjustment	(±) XX
Change in Accounting Principle (Catch-Up Adjustment)	(±) XX
Restated Balance, January 1, 20X7	XX
(±)Net Income	(±) XX
(−)Cash and Property Dividends Declared	(−) XX
(−)Stock dividends	(−) XX
(=)Retained Earnings, December 31, 20X7	XX

Footnote: The retained earnings balance on December 31, 20X7, is $XX. Of that amount, $YY has been appropriated for …

  A. **Effect Like Appropriation**—It has the same effect as an appropriation and may be accompanied by an appropriation.

Examples
States Restrict—States may restrict retained earnings in the amount of the cost of treasury stock held by the firm. This is a protection for the creditors. It forces the firm to maintain its legal capital.

Bondholders Restrict—Bondholders may restrict retained earnings through the debt agreement or bond covenant. This is also a protection for the creditors but this time is protection for a specific group of creditors—the bondholders themselves who want the firm to conserve cash so that their claims can be met.

  B. **Disclosure**—Both restrictions and appropriations are disclosed in the notes to the financial statements.

Note
Both restrictions and appropriations may cause the amount of dividends to be reduced. However, a firm need not appropriate retained earnings or be subject to a constraint on retained earnings in order to lower the amount of dividends paid. The firm simply needs to reduce the amount of dividends declared. However, an appropriation supports this decision and may make such a decision more acceptable to shareholders.

Example
If total retained earnings is $400,000, and a $100,000 appropriation is recorded, and the firm was planning to declare only $150,000 in dividends, the appropriation does not reduce dividends although it may still accomplish its communication objective.

V. Statement of Retained Earnings

A. **Purpose**—The purpose of the **Statement of Retained Earnings** is to provide the reader of the financial report with a detailed account of increases and decreases in retained earnings that were recorded in a given accounting period. The retained earnings statement may be shown separately, or more frequently, as part of the statement of changes in equity. If part of the Statement of Changes in Equity, the Statement of Retained Earnings occupies one column.

1. A typical Statement of Retained Earnings is shown below.

The Tiger Company
Statement of Retained Earnings
For the Year Ended December 31, 20X7

Retained Earnings, January 1, 20X7	XX
Prior Period Adjustment	(±) XX
Change in Accounting Principle (Catch-Up Adjustment)	(±) XX
Restated Balance, January 1, 20X7	XX
(±)Net Income	(±) XX
(−)Cash and Property Dividends Declared	(−) XX
(−)Stock dividends	(−) XX
(=)Retained Earnings, December 31, 20X7	XX

Footnote: The retained earnings balance on December 31, 20X7, is $XX. Of that amount, $YY has been appropriated for ...

Note
All amounts in the statement can be negative, but cash, property, and stock dividends are always negative amounts. Also, where relevant, amounts are always after-tax amounts.

B. **Adjusted for Prior Adjustments**

1. As you can see, the beginning retained earnings balance is adjusted initially for any prior period adjustment (corrections of errors in prior year net income) recorded during the year and for the catch-up adjustment related to changes in accounting principle.

2. **Restated balance**—The restated balance is increased by reported income and decreased by any dividend declarations that occurred during the year.

Book Value per Share

This lesson includes miscellaneous OE items such as the book value per share ratio, and accounting for quasi-reorganizations.

After studying this lesson, you should be able to:

1. Compute book value per share.

2. Analyze the effect of transactions on book value per share.

3. Identify the reasons and effects of a quasi-reorganization.

4. Record the journal entries for a quasi-reorganization.

5. Prepare the post-reorganization Balance Sheet.

I. **Book Value per Share (of Common Stock)**—Among the ratios tested on the CPA Exam, book value per share is among the ratios tested. Its calculation tests a number of details concerning owners' equity.

   A. **Definition**

   Definition
   Book Value per Share Ratio Equals: Common stockholders' equity per share of outstanding common stock, at the end of the period.

   1. **Common Stockholders' Equity**—Common stockholders' equity is total OE after preferred dividend claims are removed.

   2. **Statistic Represents**—The statistic represents the historical value of the firm per common share and may be used as a benchmark for comparisons with market value per share.

      a. However, it is very unlikely that book value per share would ever equal market value per share for most firms.

   B. **Equations**

   Book Value per Share Outstanding =
   Common Stockholders' Equity/Ending Common Shares of Common Stock Outstanding

   Common Stockholder's Equity =
   Total OE – Liquidation Preference of Preferred Stock–Preferred Stock Dividends in Arrears

   C. **Amount Payable**—The liquidation preference of preferred stock is the amount payable on liquidation of the company. It must be paid before the common stock receives any assets.

Examples

1. *Book Value per Share*

The stockholders' equity section for a firm's balance sheet shows:

6% noncumulative preferred stock, $100 par (liquidation value $105 per share)	$10,000
Common stock	33,000
Retained earnings	12,500
Treasury stock	(6,000)
Total OE	$49,500

At the end of the period, the firm has 100 shares of preferred stock outstanding, 3,300 shares of common stock issued, and 300 common treasury shares.

Book value per share is $13.00 = ($49,500 − 100($105)) / 3,000. Only 3,000 shares of common are outstanding.

If the preferred stock was cumulative and there were dividends in arrears, they also would be subtracted from total owners' equity in the numerator.

The par value of preferred stock is not used in the calculation if it is different from the liquidation preference, as is the case here.

2. *Book Value per Share—Effect of Treasury Stock Purchase*

A firm purchased treasury shares at a cost exceeding the original issuance but less than book value per share. This transaction reduces total stockholders' equity but increases book value.

Explanation:

The purchase of treasury stock at any price decreases total owners' equity.

When the purchase price per share is less than book value per share, then the denominator of book value per share decreases by a greater percentage than does the numerator, and book value per share increases.

Assume that the total owners' equity and number of shares before the treasury stock purchase is $4,000 and 400 respectively. Book value per share is $10. The firm purchases 20 shares of treasury stock for $8 (less than book value). The new book value per share is: ($4,000 − $160)/(380) = $10.11. Book value per share has increased.

Exam Tip
The CPA Exam often asks candidates to analyze the effect of prospective transactions on book value per share.

II. **Quasi-Reorganization**—An alternative to bankruptcy in some cases, quasi-reorganization allows a firm a fresh start and new, more conservative asset values.

   A. **Conditions**—Operating losses have created a deficit in retained earnings (negative balance) and certain asset values are overstated.

      1. **Positive prospects**—However, the firm has positive prospects for the future but will be unable to pay dividends until the deficit is absorbed by future income.

      2. **Updated balance sheet**—Rather than continue with unrealistic asset values and negative retained earnings (the inability to pay dividends will hurt the firm's ability to raise capital), a quasi-reorganization will provide an updated balance sheet with no retained earnings deficit.

B. Requirements for a Quasi-Reorganization

1. **Approval**—Shareholder and creditor approval.

2. **Balance becomes zero**—The retained earnings balance must be zero immediately after the quasi-reorganization.

3. **No negative balance after**—No contributed capital account can have a negative balance after the quasi-reorganization.

4. **Assets down to market**—Assets must be written down to market value (asset write-ups are possible but would be rare).

5. **Dated years after**—Retained earnings must be dated for a period of 3 to 10 years after the quasi-reorganization to indicate that the balance reflects income earned after the quasi-reorganization.

C. Accounting Steps

1. **Write assets down to market value**, further reducing retained earnings (increasing the deficit).

2. **Reduce contributed capital** to absorb the retained earnings deficit.

3. **Change value/number of shares**—If needed, change par value or the number of shares of common stock to absorb the remaining deficit.

Example

A firm has the following balance sheet (abbreviated):

Assets	$10,000	Liabilities	$4,000
		Common stock ($1 par)	3,000
		Contributed capital in excess of par	5,000
		Retained earnings	(2,000)

Certain plant assets with a book value of $5,000 are worth only $1,000. The firm elects to reduce par value to accomplish the quasi-reorganization.

Entries:

Retained earnings	4,000	
Plant assets		4,000

The retained earnings deficit is now $6,000.

Contributed capital in excess of par	5,000	
Retained earnings		5,000

The retained earnings deficit is now $1,000.

The common stock is reduced to $2,000 to absorb the remaining deficit.

This means that par value must be reduced to $.67

$2,000 = (3,000 shares)(new par value)

$2,000/3,000 = $.67 = new par value

Common stock	1,000	
Retained earnings		1,000

The balance sheet immediately following the quasi-reorganization is:

Assets	6,000	Liabilities	4,000
		Common stock ($.67 par)	2,000
		Contributed capital in excess of par	0
		Retained earnings	0

Select Transactions

Revenue Recognition

Five Steps of Revenue Recognition

This lesson on revenue recognition reviews the definition of revenue and the five steps of revenue recognition.

After studying this lesson, you should be able to:

1. Define revenue.

2. Explain the five steps of revenue recognition.

3. Identify separate performance obligations.

4. Recognize the contract terms that impact the transaction price.

5. Evaluate whether a performance obligation is satisfied at a point in time or over time.

6. Identify the methods of measuring revenue when a performance obligation is satisfied over time.

7. Record Contract Liabilities and Contract Assets.

Five Steps of Revenue Recognition

Step 1—Identify the contract with a customer.

Step 2—Identify the performance obligation(s) in the contract.

Step 3—Determine the transaction price.

Step 4—Allocate the transaction price to the performance obligation(s) in the contract.

Step 5—Recognize revenue when the entity satisfies the performance obligation(s).

Definition

Revenue: "Inflows or other enhancements of assets of an entity or settlements of its liabilities (or a combination of the two) from delivering or producing goods, rendering services, or other activities that constitute the entity's ongoing major or central operations."

I. Identify the Contract with a Customer.

  A. "A contract is an agreement between two or more parties that creates enforceable rights and obligations."

  B. Contract Criteria—A contract should be accounted for when it meets the following criteria:

   1. The parties have approved the contract verbally, in writing, or by implication consistent with customary business practices.

   2. Each party's rights to goods or services can be identified.

   3. Payment terms can be identified.

   4. The contract has commercial substance.

   5. Collectibility of substantially all of the consideration is probable (i.e., the entity will probably collect substantially all of the agreed-upon amount from the customer).

  C. Criteria Not Met—A contract does not exist if each of the parties may cancel the contract before any goods or services are transferred to the customer and before any consideration (typically payment) has been made to the provider (seller) without compensating the other party.

The cancellation occurs when the contract is wholly unperformed (i.e., no goods or services have been provided and no consideration has been paid yet).

II. Identify the Performance Obligations in the Contract. A performance obligation is a promise to transfer a distinct good or service, or a series of distinct goods or services that are basically the same, to a customer.

    A. Single Performance Obligation

        1. A contract with a single performance obligation is one in which only one distinct good or service is being provided to the customer.

        2. A good or service is **distinct if a customer can benefit from the good or service on its own** or together with other resources that the customer has readily available and the seller's promise to transfer the good or provide the service can be identified separately from other promises in the contract.

    B. Multiple Performance Obligations

        1. When a contract has more than one performance obligation, **each performance obligation should be allocated a portion of the transaction price and accounted for separately.**

        2. A contract that includes equipment, an installation service, and a training service may have three performance obligations if the promises in the contract are distinct from each other.

III. Determine the Transaction Price. The transaction price in most contracts can be easily identified as the amount the buyer agrees to pay the seller.

    A. Contracts with **terms that impact the transaction price** require further analysis to determine the transaction price.

    B. Contracts may include **variable consideration, significant financing components, noncash consideration, and consideration payable to the customer.**

IV. Allocate the Transaction Price to the Performance Obligation(s) in the Contract. After determining the transaction price, the price should be allocated to the performance obligations in the contract.

    A. If there is only one performance obligation in the contract, then the entire transaction price is assigned to the single performance obligation.

    B. If there are multiple performance obligations, then the transaction price is allocated proportionately to the performance obligations based on their standalone prices. If the standalone prices are not observable, then the entity should estimate the standalone selling price.

V. Recognize Revenue when the Entity Satisfies the Performance Obligation(s). An entity should recognize revenue when it has satisfied the performance obligation.

    A. Satisfaction of the Performance Obligation—A performance obligation is satisfied when the good is transferred to the customer or the customer obtains control of the asset/good.

    B. Control of the asset (and therefore transfer of the good) may be indicated by the buyer's ability to use the asset to produce goods, enhance the value of other assets, pay expenses or settle liabilities, hold on to or sell the asset or good, or pledge the asset as collateral.

    C. A seller may satisfy a performance obligation at a point in time or over a period of time.

        1. Satisfaction of performance obligations at a point in time. When an entity satisfies a performance obligation at a single point in time, it may recognize revenue and record the receipt or cash or promise of payment (i.e., accounts receivable) or, although seen less frequently, the forgiveness of a liability. To determine that control has passed to the customer and the entity has satisfied the performance obligation, the entity considers the following indicators:

a. The entity has a present right to payment for the asset or service.

b. Customer has legal title to the asset.

c. Physical possession has transferred to the customer.

d. Significant risks and rewards of ownership have transferred to the customer.

e. The customer has accepted the asset.

Example
Point in Time
O'Hara Corp. sold goods for $5,000 that had a cost of $3,000. The customer immediately accepted and took possession of the goods and paid for the goods using cash. O'Hara will record the following journal entries to record the sale.

Cash	$5,000	
Sales Revenue		$5,000
Cost of Goods Sold	$3,000	
Inventory		$3,000

---

2. **Satisfaction of performance obligations over time.** Indicators that a performance obligation is being satisfied over time include any one of the following:

   a. The customer receives and consumes the benefits provided by the entity simultaneously as the entity performs its obligation.

   b. The customer controls the asset that is being enhanced or created by the entity as the entity works on it.

   c. The entity creates an asset that does not have an alternative use to the entity and the entity has the right to payment for work completed to date.

3. Entities should consistently apply a revenue recognition approach that measures the progress toward completion of the performance obligation. To recognize revenue over time, an entity may use an output or input method to measure progress toward satisfying the performance obligation as long as progress may be reasonably measured using reliable information.

   a. **Output methods.** An entity recognizes revenue based on the value of the goods or services transferred to the customer to date relative to the remaining goods or services promised under the contract. Output methods may not be practical if measures of progress are not directly observable. In such case, the input method is used.

   b. **Input methods.** An entity measures revenue based on the proportion of input compared to the total expected inputs. For example, a company that expects to incur $100,000 in total project costs would measure revenue relative to the amount of the total project costs incurred. If the company has incurred $25,000 of the $100,000 total costs, then the company would recognize 25% of the revenue associated with the performance obligation.

4. Companies may receive payment up front, in which case, a liability will be recorded (such as unearned revenue) and the deferred revenue will be recognized as the performance obligation is satisfied.

VI. Presentation of a Contract Liability or a Contract Asset When either party to the contract has performed, the entity should present a Contract Liability or Contract Asset in its statement of financial position (i.e., Balance Sheet), depending on which party to the contract has performed.

    A. Contract Liability. If the customer pays consideration before goods or services have been transferred to the customer, then the entity will record a contract liability to represent its obligation to satisfy the performance obligation for which the customer has paid. For example, if a customer pays cash for a year's rent of office space in advance, the entity will record the cash received (debit) and the Unearned Revenue (credit; contract liability) to represent its obligation to provide office space for the next year. The contract liability will be decreased as the performance obligation is satisfied over the next year. As the contract liability is decreased (debit to Unearned Revenue), revenue is recognized (credit to Rent Revenue).

Example
Contract Liability

Gator Company entered into a contract with Croc Company to transfer product to Croc Company for a sales price of $50,000. The product has a cost of $35,000. Croc Company paid Gator Company the full $50,000 sales price in advance. Gator Company will make the following journal entries:

On the date the cash is received:

Cash	50,000	
Unearned Sales Revenue		50,000

On the date the performance obligation is satisfied (e.g. the product is delivered to Croc and control has passed):

Unearned Sales Revenue	50,000	
Sales Revenue		50,000
Cost of Goods Sold	35,000	
Inventory		35,000

Unearned Sales Revenue (natural credit balance) represents the Contract Liability.

    B. Contract Asset. If the entity performs by transferring goods or services to the customer, before the customer pays consideration, then the entity may recognize a contract asset. A contract asset represents the entity's right to consideration. The right may be unconditional or conditional.

        1. Unconditional Right to Contract Asset. An unconditional right to a contract asset occurs when an entity has earned the right to payment and is only waiting for the time to pass to receive payment. Accounts Receivable represents an unconditional right to a contract asset. The entity has satisfied the performance obligation and is waiting to be paid (i.e. receive consideration).

        2. Conditional Right to Contract Asset. A conditional right to a contract asset occurs when a company completes one performance obligation in the contract, but must complete another performance obligation before it is entitled to consideration from the customer. Conditional rights to receive consideration should be reported as a Contract Asset (as opposed to a receivable as shown above when an unconditional right exists).

Example
Contract Asset

Hamilton Company entered into a contract with Burr Company to transfer two products to Burr Company for a sales price of $950,000. The contract requires the delivery of Product 2 before payment on Product 1 will be remitted. Delivery of Product 1 will occur first and delivery of Product 2 will occur second. Product 1 has a sales price of $600,000 and Product 2 has a sales price of $350,000. Hamilton delivers Product 1 to Burr on April 2, 20X9 and delivers Product 2 to Burr on June 30, 20X9.

On April 2, 20X9, after Hamilton delivers Product 1, Hamilton records the following journal entry:

Contract Asset	600,000	
Sales Revenue		600,000

On June 30, 20X9, after Hamilton delivers Product 2, Hamilton records the following journal entry:

Accounts Receivable	950,000	
Contract Asset		600,000
Sales Revenue		350,000

Hamilton records the conditional right to payment for Product 1 by recording a Contract Asset upon delivery of Product 1. By delivering Product 2 to Burr, Hamilton has an unconditional right to payment for both Product 1 and Product 2. The Contract Asset (representing conditional rights) is credited and the amount is debited to Accounts Receivable (representing unconditional rights) in addition to the amount due for Product 2.

Determining Transaction Price

Recall the five steps of revenue recognition. This lesson focuses on Step 3—determining the transaction price when the contract includes terms that impact the amount of revenue to be recognized. These terms include variable consideration, significant financing components, noncash consideration, and consideration payable to the customer.

After studying this lesson, you should be able to:

1. Determine the transaction price when there is variable consideration.

2. Determine the transaction price using the expected value method.

3. Determine the transaction price using the most likely amount method.

4. Identify the impact of a significant financing component and quantify the interest revenue.

5. Account for revenue when noncash consideration is received.

6. Analyze the impact on revenue of consideration payable to the customer.

Five Steps of Revenue Recognition

Step 1—Identify the contract with a customer.

Step 2—Identify the performance obligation(s) in the contract.

Step 3—Determine the transaction price.

Step 4—Allocate the transaction price to the performance obligation(s) in the contract.

Step 5—Recognize revenue when the entity satisfies the performance obligation(s).

I. **Introduction to Determining Transaction Price**—Most contracts cover a single performance obligation and explicitly state the transaction price. Typically, an entity sells goods to the buyer for a fixed price. For example, Conover Company sold and delivered 50 units of product to Rochelle Inc. for $2,000. When the performance obligation is satisfied (i.e., control of the 50 units of product transfers to Rochelle), then Conover recognizes revenue of $2,000.

Contracts may include terms that impact the transaction price. The transaction price in a contract may be impacted by variable consideration, a significant financing component, noncash consideration, or consideration paid to the customer.

II. **Variable Consideration.** When a contract includes pricing terms that will be impacted or determined by a future event, then the contract's transaction price is impacted by consideration that will vary based on the outcome (e.g., discounts, rebates, refunds, credits, incentives, and performance bonuses). There are two methods for determining the amount of revenue to recognize when the contract includes variable consideration: the **expected value method** and the **most likely amount method.**

A. **Expected Value Method**—Uses the sum of probability-weighted outcomes to determine the transaction price. Use the expected value method when an entity has many contracts with similar characteristics.

Example
Expected Value

Wesley Co. builds custom manufacturing equipment. Craig Co. engages Wesley to build a large piece of manufacturing equipment. The price of the equipment is $75,000. Craig agrees to pay an additional amount to Wesley if the equipment is delivered early; otherwise, the equipment is expected to be delivered by July 15. If Wesley delivers the equipment by June 30, then Craig will pay Wesley a bonus of $10,000. If the equipment is delivered by July 5, Craig will pay a bonus of $7,000; if it is delivered by July 10, Craig will pay a bonus of $5,000. Wesley frequently enters into contracts with terms similar to this one. Wesley's management estimates that there is a 60% probability that the equipment will be delivered by June 30, a 20% probability the equipment will be delivered by July 5, a 10% probability the equipment will be delivered by July 10, and a 10% probability the equipment will be delivered on July 15. Determine the transaction price.

Solution

Because Wesley commonly enters into contracts such as this one with similar terms, Wesley should use the expected value method to estimate the transaction price. The expected value method uses a probability-weighted approach to estimate the total transaction price. In this case:

June 30th delivery:	60% ($75,000 + $10,000) =	$51,000
July 5th delivery:	20% ($75,000 + $7,000) =	$16,400
July 10th delivery:	10% ($75,000 + $5,000) =	$8,000
July 15th delivery:	10% ($75,000 + $0) =	$7,500
Estimated total transaction price		**$82,900**

OR

Estimated variable compensation

June 30th delivery:	60% ($10,000) =	$6,000
July 5th delivery:	20% ($7,000) =	$1,400
July 10th delivery:	10% ($5,000) =	$500
July 15th delivery:	10% ($0) =	$0
Estimated variable consideration		**$7,900**

After the impact of the estimated variable consideration is calculated, the estimated variable consideration is added to the sales price for the equipment to determine the total transaction price.

Set sales price for the equipment	$75,000
Estimated variable consideration	$7,900
Estimated total transaction price	**$82,900**

B. **Most Likely Amount Method**—Uses the most likely outcome to determine the amount of revenue to recognize. Use the most likely amount when an entity has two possible outcomes (e.g., they earn the performance bonus or they do not).

Example

Most Likely Amount

Wesley Co. builds custom manufacturing equipment. Craig Co. engages Wesley to build a large piece of manufacturing equipment. The price of the equipment is $75,000. Craig agrees to pay an additional amount to Wesley if the equipment is delivered by June 30; otherwise, the equipment is expected to be delivered by July 15. If Wesley delivers the equipment by June 30, then Craig will pay Wesley a bonus of $10,000; otherwise, no bonus will be paid. Based on prior experience, Wesley's management estimates that there is a 70% likelihood that the equipment will be delivered by June 30. Determine the transaction price.

Solution

Because there are two discrete outcomes, the most likely amount method should be used to determine the transaction price. The transaction price is **$85,000** ($75,000 for the equipment + $10,000 for the bonus because the most likely outcome is that Wesley will deliver the equipment by June 30).

    C. **Constraining Estimates of Variable Consideration**—If there is significant uncertainty about the receipt of the variable consideration, then the company does not record revenue associated with the variable consideration. The company must consider whether it is probable that a significant reversal of revenue would occur if the revenue from the variable consideration is recognized. For example, if the receipt of variable consideration is dependent on a factor outside of the company's control such as weather, then estimating variable consideration is constrained.

III. **Significant Financing Component.** Contracts that allow the buyer to pay at a much later date (more than one year) typically include a significant financing component. The transaction includes both sales revenue and interest revenue.

    A. Interest revenue is accrued over time and measured using an imputed interest rate.

        1. The imputed interest rate is either the rate that would be offered on a similar instrument to an entity with a similar credit rating or the rate that discounts the note to a value reflective of the current sales price of the goods or services.

2. The interest rate may be explicitly stated, as in the example below.

> ### Example
> ### *Significant Financing Explicitly Provided and Reflective of a Rate Associated with a Separate Financing Transaction*
> On October 1, 20X9, Jordan Company sold (and transferred control of the) equipment to Curry Company for $1,000,000 and accepted a 5-year note with an interest rate of 5% and monthly installments of $18,871. The equipment costs Jordan $750,000.
>
> How much revenue should Jordan recognize on October 1, 20X9, assuming control of the goods has passed to Curry? **$1,000,000**
>
> Jordan should recognize revenue for the amount that reflects the price that Curry would have paid for the equipment had Curry paid cash when the equipment was transferred.
>
> Jordan records the following journal entries on October 1, 20X9:
>
> | | | |
> |---|---|---|
> | Notes Receivable | 1,000,000 | |
> | Sales Revenue | | 1,000,000 |
> | Cost of Goods Sold | 750,000 | |
> | Inventory | | 750,000 |
>
> Assuming this is the only interest revenue Jordan earns, how much interest revenue should Jordan report on its December 31, 20X9, income statement?
>
> | Month | Monthly Installment | Interest Revenue per Month | Principal Reduction per Month | Note Receivable (NR) Balance |
> |---|---|---|---|---|
> | October 1, 20X9 | (Given) | (NR balance × Interest rate / 12 months) | (Monthly installment – Interest amount) | $1,000,000 |
> | October 31, 20X9 | $18,871 | 4,167 | 14,704 | 985,296 |
> | November 30, 20X9 | $18,871 | 4,105 | 14,766 | 970,530 |
> | December 31, 20X9 | $18,871 | 4,044 | 14,827 | 955,703 |
> | **Total Interest Revenue for 20X9** | | **$12,316** | | |
>
> The journal entry to record the monthly payment received on October 31, 20X9, follows:
>
> | | | |
> |---|---|---|
> | Cash | 18,871 | |
> | Interest Revenue | | 4,167 |
> | Notes Receivable | | 14,704 |

IV. Noncash Consideration. When consideration received from a customer is in a form other than cash such as goods, services, or even shares of stock, the seller recognizes revenue at an amount that reflects the fair value of the noncash consideration received.

> **Example**
> *Noncash Consideration*
>
> Wolf Company sold goods to Frank Company for the rights to a patent. The fair value of the patent is $75,000. The inventory costs Wolf $40,000.
>
> Wolf Company records the following journal entries associated with the sale:
>
> | | | |
> |---|---|---|
> | Patent | 75,000 | |
> | Sales Revenue | | 75,000 |
> | Cost of Goods Sold | 40,000 | |
> | Inventory | | 40,000 |

V. Consideration Payable to Customer. Sellers may offer terms to incentivize buyers to pay quickly or to purchase a certain volume of goods. Contract terms may include discounts or rebates. A seller may offer a discount to customers who pay within a certain period of time to induce quick payment or the seller may offer a discount to customers who buy a certain volume of goods. Commonly the seller reduces the revenue recognized by the discount offered. If the buyer does not pay within the discount period or purchase the required volume of goods to qualify for the discount, then the seller recognizes Sales Discounts Forfeited and reports it as Other Revenue.

> **Example**
> *Sales Volume Discount*
>
> Fritz Company offers a 2.5% discount to customers who purchase more than $1,000,000 of goods during the year. Mike Company is a customer of Fritz Company and has regularly exceeded the $1,000,000 volume threshold of purchases in the preceding five years. In March, Mike Company purchases $450,000 of goods. The inventory costs Fritz Company $370,000.
>
> Fritz Company records the following journal entries associated with the March sale:
>
> | | | |
> |---|---|---|
> | Accounts Receivable | 438,750 | |
> | Sales Revenue | | 438,750 |
> | Cost of Goods Sold | 370,000 | |
> | Inventory | | 370,000 |
>
> Assuming Mike Company **meets the volume discount** threshold, the following journal entry will be recorded to reflect the collection of the accounts receivable:
>
> | | | |
> |---|---|---|
> | Cash | 438,750 | |
> | Accounts Receivable | | 438,750 |
>
> If Mike Company **does not meet the volume discount** threshold, then the sales discount is forfeited and the journal entry to record the cash collection of the accounts receivable is as follows:
>
> | | | |
> |---|---|---|
> | Cash | 450,000 | |
> | Accounts Receivable | | 438,750 |
> | Sales Discounts Forfeited | | 11,250 |
>
> Sales Discounts Forfeited (natural credit balance) is a revenue account reported as Other Revenue.

Allocating Transaction Price

Recall the five steps of revenue recognition. This lesson applies Step 2 by identifying separate performance obligations and focuses on Step 4 by demonstrating the allocation of a transaction price to separate performance obligations.

After studying this lesson, you should be able to:

1. Allocate the transaction price to a single performance obligation.

2. Identify multiple performance obligations in a contract.

3. Calculate the relative proportion of the standalone price represented by each performance obligation.

4. Allocate the transaction price to multiple performance obligations.

5. Prepare the journal entry to reflect revenue recognition when multiple performance obligations exist.

6. Prepare the journal entry when revenue from a performance obligation is recognized over time.

Five Steps of Revenue Recognition

Step 1—Identify the contract with a customer.

Step 2—Identify the performance obligation(s) in the contract.

Step 3—Determine the transaction price.

Step 4—Allocate the transaction price to the performance obligation(s) in the contract.

Step 5—Recognize revenue when the entity satisfies the performance obligation(s).

I. **Single Performance Obligation.** Most contracts cover a single performance obligation to which the entire transaction price is assigned. The performance obligation is satisfied and the entity records revenue for the stated transaction price.

Example
Single Performance Obligation
Walken Company sold and delivered 80 units of product to Timberlake Inc. for $5,000. The units had a cost of $3,000. The 80 units of product represent a single performance obligation to which the entire $5,000 transaction price is allocated. When the performance obligation is satisfied (i.e., control of the 80 units of product transfers to Timberlake), then Walken recognizes revenue of $5,000 and records the following journal entries:

Cash or Accounts Receivable	5,000	
Sales Revenue		5,000
Cost of Goods Sold	3,000	
Inventory		3,000

II. **Multiple Performance Obligations.** Contracts may include more than one performance obligation but list only one transaction price.

A. When multiple performance obligations exist in a contract with one total transaction price, the transaction price should be allocated to the performance obligations based on the relative proportion of the total standalone price represented by each performance obligation. There are **two major steps** to this process:

1. **Identify the separate performance obligations.**

   a. A performance obligation is considered separate if the good or service is distinct from the other goods or services in the contract.

   b. To be distinct, the good or service must meet both of the following criteria:

      i. The customer can benefit from the good or service on its own or with other resources that are readily available.

      ii. The good or service can be separately identified from other promises in the contract.

2. **Allocate the transaction price to each performance obligation.**

B. If the standalone selling price is not directly observable, then the entity should estimate the standalone selling price.

Example
Multiple Performance Obligations

Smith Company produces equipment and offers installation and training services to its customers. Westbrook Company enters into a contract with Smith Company to purchase a piece of equipment, have the equipment installed, and receive training on the equipment. Westbrook Company has the expertise to install the equipment and train its employees on the equipment but has chosen to contract Smith to complete those tasks. Smith and Westbrook agree to a total contract price of $1,200,000. In other sales transactions, Smith sells the equipment alone for $1,100,000 and offers installation services for $70,000 and training for $130,000 each. Installation and training services are performed when the equipment is delivered. The equipment has a cost to Smith of $900,000.

Solution

Step 1. Identify the separate performance obligations. There are three performance obligations in this contract: (1) equipment, (2) installation, and (3) training. Because Westbrook could install and train its employees on the equipment, the performance obligations are distinct from each other. Any one of the performance obligations could be purchased separately. Westbrook is choosing to purchase each one in this contract.

Step 2. Allocate the transaction price to each performance obligation. The transaction price is allocated using the relative proportion of the total standalone pricing represented by each performance obligation. The standalone prices are provided as:

	Standalone Price
Equipment	$1,100,000
Installation	70,000
Training	130,000
Total Standalone Price	$1,300,000

Westbrook calculates the proportion of the standalone price represented by each performance obligation.

Equipment	$1,100,000/1,300,000 =	84.62%
Installation	70,000/1,300,000 =	5.38%
Training	130,000/1,300,000 =	10.00%
		100%

Hint: Total the proportions for the performance obligations to double check that they add up to 100%. Because the proportions are based on the total standalone price, added together they should total 100%.

Westbrook allocated the total contract transaction price based on the proportions calculated above.

	Total Contract Price	×	Contract Price Proportion	=	Allocated
Equipment	$1,200,000		84.62%		$1,015,440
Installation	$1,200,000		5.38%		64,560
Training	$1,200,000		10.00%		120,000
					$1,200,000

Hint: Total the allocated portions of the transaction price for each performance obligation. Double check that the total transaction price allocated equals the total contract price.

After calculating the amount of the transaction price to allocate to each performance obligation and satisfying the performance obligations, Smith will make the following journal entries to recognize revenue and record costs of goods sold from this transaction:

Cash	1,200,000	
Sales Revenue		1,015,440
Service Revenue (Installation)		64,560
Service Revenue (Training)		120,000
Cost of Goods Sold	900,000	
Inventory		900,000

- In this example, installation and training are completed at the same time as delivery of the equipment.

- In the journal entry presented above, service revenue is shown in two parts to correspond to the separate performance obligations. It could also be recorded as one total credit to Service Revenue for both the installation and the training.

- The cost to provide the installation and training would be reflected in the journal entry to record salaries expense for the period so it is not shown as a separate journal entry here.

Example
Recognizing the Service Revenue from Training over a Period of Time
Using the example above, assume that the training will take place over the course of six months as opposed to occurring at the time of delivery. In this case, the calculation to allocate the transaction price among the equipment, installation, and training does not change. However, the journal entry on the date of delivery and installation does change and appears as follows:

Cash	1,200,000	
Sales Revenue		1,015,440
Service Revenue (Installation)		64,560
Unearned Service Revenue (Training)		120,000

"Unearned service revenue" is a liability account that represents a promise to perform over the next six months. As the training is completed (assume a monthly adjusting journal entry), the unearned service revenue is recognized as revenue in a journal entry that appears as follows:

Unearned Service Revenue	20,000	
Service Revenue		20,000
(120,000/6 months)		

Special Issues in Revenue Recognition

This lesson illustrates special accounting issues under revenue recognition such as warranties, sales with a right of return, goods on consignment, nonrefundable upfront fees, bill-and-hold arrangements, and principal-agent considerations.

After studying this lesson, you should be able to:

1. Calculate the appropriate amount and timing of revenue for service-type warranties.

2. Determine when revenue is to be recognized under a right of return.

3. Account for revenue from goods on consignment.

4. Determine the timing and amount of revenue to be recognized from nonrefundable upfront fees.

5. Describe the circumstances surrounding bill-and-hold arrangements.

6. Calculate the revenue recognized by agents in a principal-agent consideration.

I. **Introduction**—Contracts may include additional terms that impact revenue recognition. Sellers may offer service-type warranties as separate performance obligations, or they may offer the customer the right to return the product for any number of reasons. A seller may consign goods to a consignor for sale in the consignor's store. A customer may request that the seller hold onto the product until the customer is able to accept delivery. These terms present **special issues when determining the timing and amount of revenue** to recognize.

II. **Warranties**

    A. Regular warranties are offered by many companies at no charge to the customer. Some warranties offer the customer assurance that the product will function to agreed-upon specifications (assurance warranties). Other warranties provide service in addition to assurance (service-type warranties).

        a. Assurance-type warranties are not considered a separate performance obligation.

        b. Service-type warranties that go beyond the assurance-type warranty are considered separate performance obligations.

    B. A warranty is accounted for as a separate performance obligation when the customer has the option to purchase the warranty as a distinct service separate from the product and the warranty provides a service in addition to the promises made under the assurance-type warranty.

        1. When the warranty represents a separate performance obligation, the seller should allocate a portion of the transaction price to the warranty.

        2. When the customer pays for the extended (service-type) warranty, an unearned revenue account (liability) is recorded. The reporting issue involves the timing of revenue recognition.

    C. **Accounting for Extended (Service-Type) Warranties**

        1. The unearned revenue is recognized as revenue over the life of the contract.

        2. Warranty expense (cost to service claims) is recognized as incurred.

Example
Warranty

A firm's sales totaled $3,000,000 for the year. This figure includes $150,000 for two-year extended service-type warranty contracts covering the goods sold. The firm expects to incur a total of $120,000 in costs to service warranty claims on these contracts. During Year 1, $20,000 of warranty costs were incurred.

Journal entries for the sale and warranty in Year 1:

Cash or Accounts Receivable	3,000,000	
Sales		2,850,000
Unearned Warranty Revenue		150,000
Warranty Expense	20,000	
Cash, Inventory, Other		20,000
Unearned Warranty Revenue	25,000	
Warranty Revenue		25,000*

*Alternatively, firms may recognize warranty revenue using the straight-line approach. In this case, the company would recognize $75,000 of warranty revenue in Year 1.

$25,000 = ($20,000 / $120,000)$150,000. One-sixth of expected total claims service has been performed. Therefore, one-sixth of $150,000 is recognized as revenue.

The remaining $125,000 of warranty revenue ($150,000 − $25,000) is recognized in the second year of the contract, regardless of the actual cost incurred in the second year, because the benefits cease at the end of the second year. At that point all the revenue is earned.

III. Sales with a Right of Return

A. Sellers often provide a right of return. A right of return is not accounted for as a performance obligation. The seller may offer a full or partial refund of any consideration paid, a credit to be applied against any amounts owed, or an exchange of the product for another product.

B. When a right of return exists, the seller should account for the transfer of products by recognizing revenue in an amount reflective of the amount to which the seller expects to be entitled. Revenue should not be recognized for products expected to be returned, however; most companies record the full revenue amount on the date of the sale and then use adjusting entries at the end of the period to adjust revenue to the amount the seller expects to be entitled.

Example
Right of Return

Dave Inc. sells 200 phones for $50 each to a buyer on credit. Each phone costs Dave $30. Dave allows the buyer to return the phones for any reason and expects the buyer to return 10 phones.

On the date of the sale, Dave records the following journal entries:

Accounts Receivable	10,000	
Sales Revenue (200 × $50)		10,000
Cost of Goods Sold	6,000	
Inventory (200 × $30)		6,000

Two weeks later the buyer returns four of the phones and Dave records the following journal entries:

Sales Returns and Allowances	200	
Accounts Receivable (4 × $50)		200
Returned Inventory	120	
Cost of Goods Sold (4 × $30)		120

At the end of the reporting period, Dave makes the following **adjusting journal entries** to record the additional phones expected to be returned:

Sales Returns and Allowances	300	
Allowance for Sales Returns and Allowances		300
(6 × $50)		
Estimated Inventory Returns	180	
Cost of Goods Sold (6 × $30)		180

- Sales Returns and Allowances (natural debit balance) is a contra-revenue account.
- Allowance for Sales Returns and Allowances (natural credit balance) is shown as a contra-asset account to Accounts Receivable.
- Returned Inventory and Estimated Inventory Returns are asset accounts related to Inventory.

Assume the same facts as above, but the sale was a cash sale instead of credit.

On the date of the sale, Dave records the following journal entries:

Cash	10,000	
Sales Revenue (200 × $50)		10,000
Returned Inventory	6,000	
Inventory (200 × $30)		6,000

Two weeks later the buyer returns four of the phones, and Dave records the following journal entries:

Sales Returns and Allowances	200	
Accounts Payable (4 × $50)		200
Returned Inventory	120	
Cost of Goods Sold (4 × $30)		120

At the end of the reporting period, Dave makes the following **adjusting journal entries** to record the additional phones expected to be returned:

Sales Returns and Allowances	300	
Accounts Payable (6 × $50)		300
Estimated Inventory Returns	180	
Cost of Goods Sold (6 × $30)		180

- Accounts Payable reflects the refund liability that Dave expects to pay to the customer in the future.
- Estimated Inventory Returns reflects the asset that Dave has the rights to recover products from the customer when the refund liability (e.g., Accounts Payable) is settled.

IV. Goods on Consignment

A. In a consignment arrangement, the consignor (owner of goods) uses the consignee's premises to sell its goods. For example, the magazines in a supermarket (consignee) often are owned by the publisher (consignor). The focus here is on the recognition of revenue for the consignor.

B. No revenue is recognized by the consignor when it ships goods to the consignee, because no sale has yet taken place. The consignor includes unsold goods in its inventory even though they are on the consignee's premises, typically "moving" the goods from the Finished Inventory account to the Inventory (Consignments) account.

C. When a retail customer purchases consigned goods on the consignee's premises, only then does the consignor recognize a sale. The consignee typically retains a percentage of each sale (its fee, a revenue) and remits the remainder to the consignor. The amount of revenue recognized by the consignor is the total sales amount. The consignee's fee is treated as an expense by the consignor (Commission expense).

D. The amount of any reimbursable expenses (e.g., handling and advertising) incurred by the consignee also is withheld and recognized as an expense by the consignor.

Example
Consignment

Ron Inc. is the consignor, and Ed Co. is consignee. Note that the example focuses on revenue and does not show the cost of goods sold.

Ron incurs $30 of freight cost to ship goods to Ed (recorded on Ron's books):

Inventory	30	
Cash or Accounts Payable		30

Ed incurs $70 of reimbursable expenses related to the goods on consignment (recorded on Ed's books):

Receivable from Ron	70	
Cash or Accounts Payable		70

Ed sells $500 of merchandise of Ron's goods it holds on consignment and retains a 5% commission (recorded on Ed's books):

Cash or Accounts Receivable	500	
Payable to Ron		475
Commission Revenue		25

Ron is notified of above sale (recorded on Ron's books):

Accounts Receivable	475	
Commission Expense	25	
Sales Revenue		500

Ed remits payment to Ron (recorded on Ed's books):

Payable to Ron	475	
Receivable from Ron		70
Cash		405

Ron receives payment (recorded on Ron's books):

Cash	405	
Expenses	70	
Accounts Receivable		475

V. Nonrefundable Upfront Fees. Some sellers include a nonrefundable upfront fee at or near the inception of the contract.

    A. Most nonrefundable upfront fees represent an advance payment for goods or services that will be provided in the future.

    B. Revenue should be recognized as the goods or services are provided.

> **Example**
> *Nonrefundable Upfront Fee*
> A health club collects a nonrefundable upfront fee of $120 and charges $60 per month for membership to the health club. The average customer belongs to the health club for 12 months. The health club will recognize $10 ($120 / 12 months) per month over the course of 12 months in revenue associated with the upfront fee and $60 per month from the monthly membership dues. The revenue associated with the nonrefundable upfront fee is recognized over the expected time period during which services are delivered.

VI. Bill-and-Hold Arrangements

    A. A contract with a bill-and-hold arrangement allows the seller to retain physical possession of the goods (i.e., hold the goods) until the buyer is ready to receive the goods at a future point in time.

    B. The seller may recognize revenue from the contract before transferring the goods to the buyer if the buyer has control of the goods and the following criteria are met:

        1. There is a substantive reason for the bill-and-hold arrangement (e.g., the customer requested the arrangement because its facility does not have available space to receive the goods).

        2. The seller separates the product from the other inventory and identifies it as belonging to the customer.

        3. The product is currently ready for transfer to the customer.

        4. The product cannot be used by or directed to another customer.

VII. Principal-Agent Relationships or Considerations. The term "principal-agent relationship" is also used in auditing. Note that the meaning is different in a financial reporting context.

    A. In a principal-agent arrangement, the agent provides access to the goods or services to the customer while the principal provides the actual goods or services.

    B. The principal controls the goods or services until they are transferred to the customer, and the principal is primarily responsible for fulfilling the promise of goods or services.

    C. An entity is an agent if its performance obligation is to arrange for the customer to be provided with the goods or services from another party (i.e., the principal).

    D. The agent recognizes revenue based on a commission or fee to which it expects to be entitled in exchange for arranging the transaction.

> ### Example
> #### *Principal-Agent Fee*
> Traveler's Treats is a website that sells vacations to customers on behalf of airlines and hotels. When a vacation is booked, both the airline and the hotel pay fixed rate commissions to Traveler's Treats. The airline and the hotel provide the services directly to the customer. The airline and hotel are the principals, and Traveler's Treats is the agent.
>
> Although the customer pays Traveler's Treats for the entire amount of the airline and hotel fees, only the commission portion is revenue to Traveler's Treats. By recording the commission only as revenue (as opposed to the entire amount paid by the customer for the hotel and the airline ticket), Traveler's Treats is using the net approach to recognize revenue as opposed to the gross method.
>
> Assuming Traveler's Treats charges a fixed rate commission of 3% for all services booked through its website, when a customer books a $10,000 vacation, Traveler's Treats recognizes $300 in commission revenue.

Contract Modifications and Other Considerations

This lesson on revenue recognition addresses contract modifications that result in a new separate contract and contract modifications that modify an existing contract resulting in a blended price for the products. Other contract considerations, such as the cost to fulfill a contract and the recognition of franchise or gift card revenue, are covered.

After studying this lesson, you should be able to:

1. Identify contract modifications that result in a new separate contract.

2. Identify contract modifications that modify an existing contract.

3. Calculate a blended price for products in the case of a modification to an existing contract.

4. Recognize when to expense a cost to fulfill a project.

5. Recognize when to amortize a cost to fulfill a project.

6. Account for revenue from initial franchise fees.

7. Account for gift card revenue.

8. Account for container deposits.

9. Determine the amount of revenue to be recognized from given data about deferred revenues.

I. Contract Modifications

A. "A contract is an agreement between two or more parties that creates enforceable rights and obligations."

B. The parties to the contract may modify a contract to include additional goods or services. When a contract is modified, **one of two results** will determine the accounting for the contract:

    1. A **new separate contract** results from the modification **if:**

        a. The modification is for new or additional promised goods or services that are distinct **AND**

        b. The consideration for the new or additional goods or services reflects standalone prices.

            i. **Then:** A contract modification that results in a new separate contract will be accounted for separate from the existing contract. This does not impact the accounting for the original contract.

    2. An existing contract is modified and accounted for using a prospective approach **if:**

        a. The products or services covered by the modification are not distinct from the existing contract's products or services **OR**

        b. The products or services are not priced at a standalone selling price.

            i. **Then:** The contract is modified and accounted for using a prospective approach. For example, recognize revenue for the remaining products going forward using a blended price based on the original price and the price for the goods in the modified contract.

Examples

Contract Modification

Additional Goods for Consideration Reflective of a Standalone Selling Price

Herring Company promises to sell 80 products to a customer for a contract price of $12,000 ($150 per product). After transferring control of 40 products to the customer and recognizing the revenue associated with those products, the contract is modified to include the delivery of an additional 25 products. The additional 25 products are priced at $140 each resulting in an additional $3,500. The pricing for the additional 25 products reflects an appropriate standalone price and the products are distinct.

Solution. Because the consideration for the additional products is reflective of an appropriate standalone selling price and the products are distinct, **a new separate contract** results from this modification. Revenue will be recognized for the remaining products as control is transferred to the customer. Revenue from the remaining 40 products in the original contract will be recorded at $150 each, and the revenue from the additional 25 products will be recorded at $140 each.

Additional Goods for Consideration that Is Not Reflective of a Standalone Selling Price

Using the example from above, imagine that Herring Company agrees to sell the additional 25 products to their customer but that either the products are not distinct from the original 80 products or that the consideration for the additional 25 products does not reflect an appropriate standalone selling price. In this case, the modification is to the existing contract, and a blended price for the remaining products may be used to recognize revenue.

Herring agrees to sell the additional products to the customer for $80, a price that does not reflect typical standalone pricing.

Solution. Because the modification does not reflect standalone pricing, the existing contract is modified. Revenue of $150 per product for the original 40 products that have already been transferred to the customer would have already been recognized. A prospective approach for the 40 products remaining from the original contract (40 × $150 = $6,000) and the additional 25 (25 × $80 = $2,000) products will result in a blended price of $123.08 ($8,000 / 65). As the products are transferred to the customer, $123.08 of revenue is recognized per product.

Decision Guide to Contract Modifications

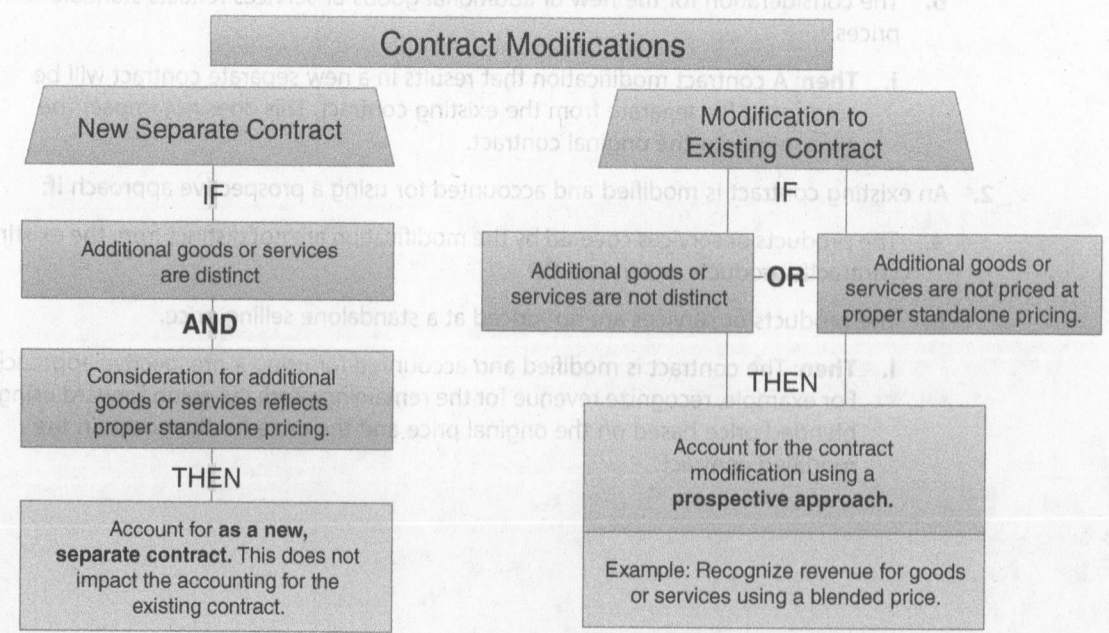

II. **Costs to Fulfill a Contract**—Costs to fulfill a contract are either expensed as incurred or give rise to an asset.

   A. **Costs Expensed as Incurred**

      1. Costs that are expensed as incurred include general and administrative costs or costs that result in an asset with an amortization period of less than one year. The company will expense those costs in the period incurred.

      2. For example, a manager spends time reviewing a contract. The manager's time will likely be recognized as part of salaries expense and expensed in the period incurred.

   B. **Costs that Give Rise to an Asset**

      1. Costs that give rise to an asset to be amortized include incremental costs that the companies would not have incurred if not for the contract. These costs are considered **direct and incremental**.

      2. For example, a company providing technology support to its customer under a five-year contract must create a platform to support the technology. The cost of the platform will be capitalized as an asset and amortized over the five-year contract, assuming the platform is useful only for that particular customer's five-year contract.

      3. **Additional example**—A company pays a real estate agent commission of $15,000 to secure a tenant for a five-year building lease. The commission would be capitalized and amortized over five years at a rate of $3,000 per year.

III. **Collectibility**—An entity must assess whether it is probable that it will collect substantially all of the consideration to which fulfillment of the contract entitles it. The customer's ability and intention to pay are considered as part of the process to identify that a valid contract exists. If the customer lacks the ability or intention to pay substantially all of the consideration, then the contract is considered not to exist because the criteria for a contract have not been met.

IV. **Initial Franchise Fee**

   A. **Recognized as Revenue**—When the franchisor (e.g., McDonald's Corporation) sells a franchise to a franchisee, the latter can sell the franchisor's products under the franchise agreement. The franchisor charges an initial fee and continuing fees. The initial franchise fee is recognized by the franchisor as revenue when all material services or conditions have been substantially performed or satisfied by the franchiser. These services include training of the franchisee and constructing the facilities, for example. The fee is recorded as unearned revenue until it is recognized as revenue.

   B. **Commencement of Operations**—The commencement of operations by the franchisee is generally presumed to be the earliest point at which performance has been completed.

   C. **Questions About Collectibility**—If there are questions about the collectibility of the initial franchise fee or if the amount will be collected over an extended time period and no estimate of uncollectibility can be made, it is appropriate to employ a cost recovery basis to recognize the revenues related to the initial franchise fee.

   D. **Extended Time Period**—If the goods and services related to the initial franchise fee are to be provided over an extended time period, it is appropriate to employ an input or output method of measurement recognize the revenues related to the initial franchise fee.

   E. **Accrual Basis**—The revenues and expenses related to continuing franchise fees should be accounted for under the accrual basis of accounting. The franchisor typically recognizes the revenue as it provides goods and services (including advertising) to the franchisee. The related costs are matched against this revenue in the same period the revenue is earned.

V. **Gift Certificates/Cards**

   A. When a retailer sells a gift certificate or gift card, it records an unearned revenue account (a liability). The transaction is a cash receipt for a possible future sale. When the customer uses the card for a purchase, the liability is reduced, and sales (and cost of goods sold) are recognized.

B. In the case of forfeiture by a customer, the retailer still recognizes revenue, subject to certain legal constraints, if present. Some cards have definite expiration dates that allow for accurate determinations of forfeited cards. Other cards have no expiration dates. For these arrangements, after a certain amount of time and based on past experience, the retailer can assume that a certain percentage of cards will not be redeemed. To the extent that state law requires the firm to remit any or all of the forfeited gift revenue to the state, that portion of the gift card liability is not recognized as revenue.

Example

Gift Card

The beginning balance of a retailer's gift card liability (unearned revenue) for the current year is $4,600,000. During the year, $32,000,000 of gift cards were sold and $28,000,000 of cards were used by customers to purchase goods at a 60% average gross margin percentage. From past experience, the firm estimates that 20% of the beginning gift card liability balance has been forfeited by customers.

Journal entries for the year:

Receipt of cash:	Cash	32,000,000	
	Gift Card Liability		32,000,000
Customer redemption:	Gift Card Liability	28,000,000	
	Sales		28,000,000
	Cost of Goods Sold	11,200,000	
	Inventory		11,200,000
	$11,200,000 = $28,000,000(.40)$		
Forfeiture:	Gift Card Liability	920,000	
	Forfeited Card Revenue		920,000

*This account is typically merged with sales in practice; no cost of goods sold is recognized.

$920,000 = $4,600,000(.20)$

The ending liability balance of $7,680,000 represents the remaining sales that could be recognized in the future on card redemptions. If forfeiture experience changes, the rate applied in the adjusting journal entry at year-end uses the new rate (change in estimate). Eventually, all cash received from customers for gift cards is recognized as revenue, unless state law requires that the firm remit all or a portion of forfeited card receipts to the state.

VI. Container Deposits

A. In some industries, and for certain retail products, the seller requires a container deposit, which is paid by the customer and reimbursed when the container is returned. Accounting for container deposits is similar to that for gift cards. The amount received from the customer is a liability until the container is returned. However, this liability is much less an unearned revenue account because containers are not meant to be sold. However, some containers are never returned and the deposit is forfeited; a nonsales revenue is recognized at this point. An expense is recognized for the cost of containers not returned by customers.

B. Sample Journal Entries

Receipt of deposit:		
Cash	##	
Container deposit liability		##
Return of container:		
Container deposit liability	##	
Cash		##
Forfeiture:		
Container deposit liability	##	
Miscellaneous revenue		##
Miscellaneous expense	##	
Inventory of containers		##

C. If there is a specified return period (e.g., one year), then the forfeiture entries are recorded after that period has elapsed. If not, and the firm honors returns indefinitely, an estimate of forfeitures is used for the forfeiture entries.

D. Are gift card and container deposit liabilities definite liabilities?

    1. The answer is yes. The firm has a liability at the point of receiving cash from the customer. The liability is not contingent on a future event. The firm has an obligation for the amount received. The liability will be extinguished regardless of action or inaction by the customer. These liabilities are not contingent on a future event.

VII. Deferred Revenues

Definition
Deferred Revenue: A liability recognized when cash is received before the service is provided or before the goods are shipped to customers.

A. Deferred revenues are liabilities representing cash received for goods not yet delivered or services to be performed. Recognition of revenue occurs when the firm provides the good or service, at which point the deferred revenue (liability) is reduced. These liabilities often are reduced in adjusting entries. For example, a company may prepare an adjusting entry to recognize rent revenue and reduce unearned rent revenue.

B. Cash representing revenue that will be earned in the future is credited to one of the following accounts, which are simply different names for the same account:

    1. Deferred revenue

    2. Unearned revenue

    3. Revenue received in advance

C. Each of the above accounts is a liability. CPA Exam questions in this area ask the candidate to determine the ending balances of two accounts:

    1. Revenue to be recognized in income for the period *and*

    2. The amount of unearned revenue to be reported in the balance sheet.

D. In the case of deferred revenue, the cash collection occurs before the earnings process is complete. Such revenue is common for firms that require partial or full payment before providing service. Examples include real estate management companies (unearned rent), publishing companies (magazine subscriptions), and airline companies (flight liability).

E. A liability is recognized upon receipt of cash. As the service or good is provided, the liability is extinguished because the revenue is earned. In many cases, the contract need not be fully executed before some revenue is recognized. In these cases, the revenue is recognized based on the percentage of the total contract that has been provided.

Examples

Several examples are provided to illustrate the variations in problems that may be encountered on the CPA Exam.

Subscription Revenue

Duration Magazine Inc. collects subscriptions in advance from customers and records deferred revenue (a liability account). As magazines are distributed over the subscription period, revenue is recognized. The beginning balance of deferred subscription revenue is $24,000. During the year, $87,000 of cash is collected. At the end of the year, the firm calculates from subscription data that the subscription value of magazines yet to be distributed is $37,000.

Solution

The adjusting entry to record revenue for the period is:

Deferred Subscription Revenue	74,000*	
Subscription Revenue		74,000

*$24,000 + $87,000 − $37,000 = $74,000

Rent Revenue Example with Journal Entries

A tenant pays a building management firm $24,000 for two years' rent on August 1, 20X3 ($1,000 per month). The rental period begins on that date and the building management firm has a calendar fiscal year. Provide the journal entries for 20X3.

Solution

Aug 1, 20X3

Cash	24,000	
Unearned Rent		24,000

Dec 31, 20X3 (adjusting journal entry)

Unearned Rent	5,000	
Rent Revenue		5,000

$5,000 = $1,000 per month × 5 months August–December

The 20X3 income statement will reflect $5,000 of rent revenue. The ending balance in unearned rent for 12/31/X3 is $19,000 ($24,000 − $5,000) of which $12,000 is a current liability (the portion relating to 20X4) and $7,000 is a noncurrent liability (the portion relating to 20X5).

Airline Revenue Example with Account Balances

The beginning and ending balances of unearned revenue for an airline company appear below. These amounts represent cash collected from customers for flights to be provided in the future.

	Beginning	Ending
Unearned Revenue	$300,000	$410,000

During the year, the firm collected $760,000 from customers for flights.

How much revenue was recognized during the year?

Solution

Any operating account such as unearned revenue can be analyzed using a T account or an equation. The equation approach is illustrated below:

Beginning Balance of Unearned Revenue + Increase − Decrease = Ending Balance of Unearned Revenue

The increase for this account is the amount of cash received during the period; the decrease is the amount of revenue recognized.

Beginning Balance + Cash Received − Revenue Earned = Ending Balance
$300,000   + $760,000   − ?   = $410,000

Solving for revenue earned yields $650,000. This amount is reported in the income statement.

Summary journal entries can be reconstructed:

Cash	760,000	
Unearned Revenue		760,000
Unearned Revenue	650,000	
Revenue		650,000

Reporting Cash as Revenue on Receipt

In some cases, firms record all cash received as revenue and then make an adjusting entry (1) to recognize the amount of unrecognized revenue to report in the balance sheet and (2) to adjust revenue.

At the beginning of the year, the balance in rent collected in advance (liability) was $56,000. During the year, the firm collected $520,000 in rent from tenants representing rentals of $2,000 per month. At year-end, 10 tenants had an average of eight months' rent (at $2,000 per month) remaining on their contracts. The summary journal entries assuming that cash collected is recognized immediately as rent revenue are as follows:

Cash	520,000	
Rent Revenue		520,000
Rent Revenue	104,000	
Rent Collected in Advance		104,000

The ending liability balance (rent collected in advance) = 10 tenants × 8 months remaining on average × $2,000 per month = $160,000

Beginning Balance + Cash Received − Rent Revenue Earned = Ending Balance
$56,000   + $520,000   − ?   = $160,000

Solving for rent revenue earned for the year yields $416,000. Because the firm has already recorded $520,000 in revenue upon cash collection, the adjustment is $104,000: $520,000 rent recognized previously less the actual revenue earned of $416,000. In this case, the liability balance is directly computed; the amount of revenue recognized is computed as one of the components of the change in the liability account.

F. **Total Revenue to Be Recognized**—You may encounter situations in which firms require cash to be paid in advance for some services, while for other services the firm bills the customer after the service is provided. In this case, both unearned revenue and accounts receivable must be analyzed to uncover the total revenue to be recognized for the period.

Example
Using Accounts Receivable and Unearned Revenue to Calculate Total Revenue
The following amounts were taken from the comparative financial statements of a large local firm:

	12/31/X4	12/31/X3
Accounts receivable	$20,000	$12,000
Unearned revenue	34,000	28,000

The accounts receivable represents billings after service was provided to customers. Unearned revenue represents cash collected before service was provided. Total cash received from customers during 20X4: $126,000.

What amount of service revenue was recognized during the period?

Solution

Accounts receivable is recognized when revenue is earned. The customer is billed after the service is provided. Unearned revenue is recognized when customers pay in advance, before service is provided. Cash received increases the unearned revenue account while reducing accounts receivable. Recognizing earned revenue has the opposite effect: It reduces unearned revenue while increasing the accounts receivable account.

Again, a T account or equation analysis helps. Although the amount of cash received on accounts receivable and the amount of cash received in advance from customers cannot be determined from the information provided, the total cash received from both sources is provided. The solution strategy is to set up the analysis of the two balance sheet accounts and place the revenue amounts on the same side of the respective equations:

Accounts receivable:

Beg. Bal + Revenue Earned − Cash Received = End. Bal
Revenue Earned = End. Bal + Cash Received − Beg. Bal

Unearned revenue:

Beg. Bal + Cash Received − Revenue Earned = End. Bal
Revenue Earned = Beg. Bal + Cash Received − End. Bal

Repeat the last equation for each account, insert the known amounts, recall that total cash received amounted to $126,000, and add the equations together.

AR:	Revenue Earned = End. Bal + Cash Received	− Beg. Bal
	= $20,000	$12,000
Unearned Rev:	Revenue Earned = Beg. Bal + Cash Received	−End. Bal
	= $28,000	$34,000
Sum:	Revenue Earned = $48,000 + $126,000	−$46,000
	= **$128,000**	

Therefore, total revenue to be recognized for 20X4 equals $128,000. However, from the information provided, the revenue cannot be broken down by source (customers paying in advance versus customers paying after service is provided).

Accounting for Construction Contracts

This lesson about contract accounting covers the rationale for the applicable methods and the journal entries for the typical case. It also addresses the accounting for losses on a contract.

After studying this lesson, you should be able to:

1. Determine when to use the percentage of completion method and the completed contract method.

2. Record the three summary journals each year for a contract under both methods.

3. Record annual gross profit under the percentage of completion method.

4. Close the contract accounts under both methods.

5. Prepare the financial statement presentation of the accounts.

6. Distinguish the two types of losses on contract.

7. Account for a single period loss on a profitable contract.

8. Record the loss when a contract turns unprofitable under both methods of accounting.

Note
Multiple terms may be used in accounting for long-term construction contracts. The two key approaches used in accounting for long-term construction contracts are the percentage-of-completion method and the completed contract method. Candidates may see the term "cost-to-cost basis" associated with percentage-of-completion contracts. For example, percentage-of-completion contracts using a cost-to-cost basis are using an input measure approach to recognizing revenue. Accounting for construction contracts follows the overall five-step process for revenue recognition; accounting for construction contracts uses either the percentage-of-completion or the completed contract method to determine when the revenue should be recognized. Therefore, long-term construction contracts will use the percentage-of-completion method (which may also be referred to as cost-to-cost basis) or the completed contract method (which may also be referred to as completion-of-production method). Contract accounting may impact other areas of the CPA Exam, such as accounting for changes in accounting principles and deferred taxes. As an exam tip, it is possible to see questions in those areas that reference a company changing from a completed-contract approach to a percentage-of-completion approach.

I. **Methods of Revenue Recognition for Long-Term Contracts**—Long-term contracts pose a unique revenue recognition problem. The seller/contractor performs its obligation over a long period of time. Cash collection generally is not an issue because projects generally are financed by third parties. Should the contractor recognize revenue as work progresses, or wait until the entire project is complete? Because of the long-term nature of construction contracts, the answer to this question has a significant impact on the contractor's income during the contract period. Two methods are used for revenue recognition in this context:

   A. **Completed Contract Method**—No gross profit or revenue is recognized until the contract is complete. This method is required if estimates of the degree of completion at interim points cannot be made.

B. **Percentage of Completion**—Recognize gross profit in proportion to the degree of completion. This method is required if estimates of the degree of completion at interim points can be made **and** reasonable estimates of total project cost (and therefore profitability) can be made, **and** when the buyer and seller can be expected to perform under the contract. The percentage of completion equals cost incurred to date divided by the total estimated project cost.

II. **Basic Illustration**—The following example provides an illustration of both methods.

A contractor begins construction of a building for a client. The contract price is $10,000. Data for two years follows. The estimated remaining cost is updated at the end of each year. The project is incomplete at the end of Year 2 because costs remain for completion after Year 2. Each year for each contract, three summary journal entries are recorded under each method. A fourth journal entry under the percentage of completion method recognizes revenue and gross profit.

	Year 1	Year 2
Cost incurred in year	$2,000	$4,000
Estimated remaining cost to complete at end of year	6,000	1,500
Progress billings in year	1,000	3,500
Collections on billings in year	800	3,000

III. **Year 1**

A. The first three summary journal entries for Year 1 are the same for both methods:

Construction in progress (inventory)	2,000	
Materials, cash etc.		2,000
Accounts receivable	1,000	
Billings		1,000
Cash	800	
Accounts receivable		800

B. Construction in progress is an inventory account and a current asset. Although the contract may run for several years, the operating cycle of a construction firm is the length of its contracts. Thus, the inventory account is classified as a current asset. Construction in progress is debited only when costs are incorporated into the project. Purchases of materials for the project are recorded in the materials account.

C. Billings is contra to construction in progress. In the balance sheet, if the balance in construction in progress exceeds cumulative billings to date, the net difference is a current asset: Excess of construction in progress over billings on contracts. If cumulative billings exceed the construction in progress balance, the difference is disclosed in the current liability section. By subtracting billings from construction in progress, the seller is transferring its equity in the project from the physical asset to the financial asset (to accounts receivable and then ultimately to cash).

D. The completed contract method recognizes no gross profit in Year 1 (or even in Year 2). The percentage of completion recognizes gross profit each year. Completed contract records no further entries for the first two years.

E. The fourth entry (below) is recorded for percentage of completion only, and is an adjusting entry. This entry records the gross profit on the project for the year based on the percentage of completion, which is 25% at the end of Year 1. 25% = ($2,000/($2,000 + $6,000)). The expected total cost of the project is $8,000 at the end of Year 1 and $2,000 of cost has been incurred.

F. Adjusting entry for percentage of completion only (the fourth journal entry):

Construction in progress	500	
Construction expenses	2,000	
Construction revenue		2,500

G. $2,500 revenue = 25%($10,000). The project is 25% complete allowing 25% of the total revenue to be recognized. The $2,000 of construction expense is the cost incurred in the period. The $500 gross profit can be directly computed as the percentage of completion times the total estimated gross profit: .25($10,000 − $8,000) = $500. The $500 gross profit is recorded in the inventory account because it represents the increase in the value of the inventory. When $500 of gross profit is recognized, the net assets of the seller must also increase.

H. **Caution**—The total estimated cost of the project at the end of any year equals cost incurred to date + estimated remaining costs to complete at year-end. This amount generally must be computed by the candidate. This amount is the denominator of the percentage of completion and also is used to compute gross profit to date. For example, the $8,000 figure would not be provided for the candidate. This amount changes each year of the project.

I. The balance sheet and income effects for both methods at the end of Year 1:

	Completed contract	Percentage of completion
Income statement		
Recognized gross profit	$0	$500*
*The $2,500 revenue less $2,000 expense also can be reported.		
Balance sheet (current assets)		
Accounts receivable	200	200
Construction in progress	$2,000	$2,500
Less billings	(1,000)	(1,000)
Excess of construction in progress over billings	1,000	1,500

If no losses are expected, the balance in construction in progress at any balance sheet date is:

Completed contract:	Total cost to date
Percentage of completion:	Total cost to date + Total recognized gross profit to date

The construction in progress and billings accounts are separate accounts. Billings is subtracted from construction in progress only for reporting in the balance sheet.

Analysis

What is the impact of the four journal entries (under percentage of completion) on the Year 1 financial statements for the contractor?

Although the effects may appear involved, their entire effect is summarized in the fourth entry: an increase in net assets and pretax net income of $500. The first three journal entries cause various account balance changes but net to a zero effect on net assets and net income.

IV. **Year 2**

    A. The first three journal entries are the same as the first year's except for the amounts. Both methods record these entries. These entries are not shown; the amounts are: $4,000, $3,500, and $3,000.

    B. The fourth entry (for percentage of completion below) shows how the gross profit for the second year is computed as the total gross profit to date less the gross profit recognized in earlier years. After the first year, there is no direct way to compute gross profit for the year because total gross profit through the end of each year uses the estimated remaining cost amount and percentage of completion through the end of the year, both of which change each year.

    C. The percentage of completion at the end of Year 2 = Cost to date/Total estimated cost = ($2,000 + $4,000)/($2,000 + $4,000 + $1,500) = $6,000/$7,500 = 80%.

    D. Note that the estimated remaining cost to complete ($1,500) is the only difference between the numerator and denominator. When working a problem in this area, simply repeat the numerator amounts in the denominator and then add the estimated remaining cost to complete to the denominator.

Gross profit recognized in Year 2	=	Total estimated gross profit through Year 2
	−	Gross profit recognized in previous periods
	=	.80($10,000 −$7,500) − $500
	=	$1,500

Adjusting entry for percentage of completion only:

Construction in progress	1,500	
Construction expenses	4,000	
Construction revenue		5,500

$5,500 = .80($10,000) −$2,500 revenue in Year 1

V. **End of Contract—Year 3**

    A. Assume that total cost incurred by the contractor for the project was $7,500 with completion occurring in Year 3. Under percentage of completion, the final adjusting entry (fourth entry in year) would record gross profit for that year and update the construction-in-progress account. That entry is:

Construction in progress		500
Construction expenses	$7,500 – $6,000	1,500
Construction revenue	$10,000 – $8,000	2,000

B. The entries to complete the contract and close the accounts are:

Completed contract:			Percentage of completion:		
Billings	10,000		Billings	10,000	
Construction expenses	7,500		Construction in progress		10,000
Construction in progress		7,500			
Construction revenue		10,000			

C. Only in the final year of the contract is gross profit recognized under the completed contract method. At completion, $2,500 of gross profit is recognized (revenue less expenses). Under the percentage of completion method, the construction in progress account balance is total cost plus total gross profit, or $7,500 + $2,500 = total contract price of $10,000. The billings account reflects the full contract price under both methods.

VI. Contract Accounting, Losses

A. Losses on Contracts

1. For accounting purposes, there are two kinds of losses on long-term contracts: (1) single-period losses and (2) overall losses.

2. They require very different accounting. In particular, a single-period loss is treated exactly the same way as gross profit during the year, for both percentage of completion and completed contract methods. Overall losses require very different reporting.

B. Single-Period Loss—When the total gross profit through the end of a given year is less than the gross profit recognized in previous years, a loss has occurred in the given year although the contract still may be profitable.

In the current example under percentage of completion, the firm has recognized $2,000 of gross profit through the first two years. If the normal computation of gross profit resulted in total gross profit through Year 3 of $1,700, then a single-period loss of $300 has occurred. The entries are the same as before. The adjusting entry for gross profit is computed as usual. The only difference is that construction in progress is credited (reduced) for $300 rather than debited.

1. The completed contract method is unaffected by single-period losses.

C. Overall Losses—GAAP requires, for both methods (percentage of completion and completed contract), that when an overall loss on a contract is anticipated, the loss must be recognized in full. An overall loss occurs when the total estimated costs of the project exceed the contract price.

Example

Year 3 is added to the data for the basic illustration in the previous example. The information for Years 1 and 2 are the same as before. Through Year 2, a total of $2,000 gross profit was recognized.

	Year 1	Year 2	Year 3
Cost incurred in year	$2,000	$4,000	$2,400
Estimated remaining cost to complete at end of year	6,000	1,500	1,800

At the end of Year 3 the overall anticipated loss is $200:

= total estimated project cost − contract price

= $2,000 + $4,000 + $2,400 + $1,800 − $10,000 = $200

The loss is recognized in full for both methods. Any previous gross profit under percentage of completion also is removed from the construction in process account. In the first two years under percentage of completion, recognized revenue was $8,000 and recognized gross profit was $2,000 from the previous example. The adjusting entries to record the loss are:

Adjusting entry for percentage of completion:

Construction expenses	2,435[#]	
Construction in progress		2,200*
Construction revenue		235^

The loss recorded by this entry is $2,200, the difference between the revenue and expense.

[#]A plug figure. When an overall loss is anticipated, the amount recorded as construction expense is no longer the year's incurred cost

*$2,000 profit in Years 1 and 2 plus the overall loss of $200

^The percentage of completion is now ($2,000 + $4,000 + $2,400)/($2,000 + $4,000 + $2,400 + $1,800)= .8235. .8235($10,000) − $8,000 previous revenue = $235

The construction in progress account balance is now total cost to date less the overall loss. The same holds for completed contract. No previous profit must be removed however, and the entry under the completed contract method is:

Loss on construction contract	200	
Construction in progress		200

Share-Based Payments

Stock Options

This lesson begins several concerning stock-based compensation. Stock options are one type of compensation plan.

After studying this lesson, you should be able to:

1. Account for stock option plans available to most or all employees of the firm.

2. Understand how the variables used as inputs to the calculation of the fair value of an option affect the value of the stock option.

3. Compute and record compensation expense for a stock option plan.

4. Prepare the entry for the exercise and expiration of options.

5. Understand and account for the impact of forfeitures.

I. **Stock Purchase Plans Open to All Employees**

A. Before discussing stock option plans, plans for the rank and file are presented as a background to this significant reporting area. In this type of plan, employees purchase stock directly from firms, they may receive a small discount, and the employer may match a portion of the purchase.

1. **Criteria for recognizing compensation expense**

a. Such plans are considered **noncompensatory** (no significant compensation is provided) if all apply:

i. Essentially all employees can participate.

ii. Employee must decide within one month of the firm setting the price for the stock whether to enroll in the plan.

iii. Discount does not exceed the employer cost savings inherent in issuing directly to employees ($\leq$ 5% market price meets this criterion).

iv. Purchase price must be based solely on the market price of the stock.

v. Employees can cancel their enrollment before purchase date and obtain a full refund.

2. **Noncompensatory plan**—If noncompensatory, the shares are recorded as any other stock issuance. The only expense is the portion "paid for" by the firm (the matching portion), if any. The employer does not actually pay any cash; rather, it bears the matching portion as its cost.

Example

The par value of common stock is $1 and market price is $100. Employees of the firm can purchase their firm's stock for $98 (2% discount)—and the other criteria are met.

This plan is noncompensatory (2% < 5%).

The firm pays 50% of the employee's cost, and an employee buys 20 shares.

Compensation expense	980		employer cost .50($98)(20)
Cash	980		
Common stock		20	employee payment 20($1 par)
Paid-in capital in excess of par, common		1,940	20($98 − $1)

If the firm did not match any of the cost, the employee would pay $1,960 (= 20 × $98), and no compensation expense would be recognized. The $100 market price is not used because the discount is considered small.

3. **Compensatory plan**—If not all five criteria are met, then the plan is compensatory. For example, if the discount is substantial, then that total discount amount is recorded as expense.

Example

Assume the same facts as for the above noncompensatory example except that the employee can purchase the stock for $90 (10% discount). This is a compensatory plan because the discount exceeds 5% of the market price.

Compensation expense	1,100*		
Cash	900		.50($90)20 employee payment
Common stock		20	20($1 par)
Paid-in capital in excess of par, common		1,980	20($100 − $1)

*.50($90)(20) matching portion + ($100 − $90)20 the discount portion (the total discount)

In the first example (noncompensatory), total contributed capital is based on the discounted price (< 5%). Compensation expense reflects only the portion not paid by the employee.

In the second example (compensatory), total contributed capital is based on the current share price, and compensation expense reflects the larger discount and the portion paid by the employer.

B. The remaining parts of this lesson pertain to incentive plans for selected employees—typically upper management. The terms of these plans provide an incentive for the employee to provide significant value and be well-compensated.

II. Stock Option Plans

Definition

Stock Option Plan: Provides an employee with the option to purchase shares of employer firm stock at a fixed price in the future, after a reasonable service period. The options expire beyond a certain point.

A. The value of such a grant stems from the potential for the stock price to increase. The ability of employees to influence the stock price provides the incentive.

B. Basic Example—On 1/1/Y1, selected executives of Flowers Inc. are granted the option to purchase 10,000 shares of the firm's $1 par common stock for $5 per share during the two-year period beginning 1/1/Y5 and ending 12/31/Y6 (exercise period). The market price of the stock on the grant date also is $5. To maintain their eligibility for the option plan, the employees must continue to be employed by the firm for the four years after the grant date.

1. **Features of the plan**

   a. The $5 fixed price of the stock is called the option price or exercise price.

   b. The four-year period before the option can be exercised is called the service period, vesting period and amortization period.

   c. During the service period, compensation expense is recognized.

   d. To fully exercise the option, the employees must pay $50,000 for the 10,000 shares.

   e. The options vest at the end of the service period. (The ability to exercise the option is no longer contingent on continued employment with the firm at this point.)

   f. This type of plan is called a *fixed* plan because the relevant terms are set at the grant date.

   g. This plan illustrates *cliff* vesting because all options vest at the same time.

C. Measuring Compensation Expense

1. GAAP requires that the fair value of the options granted be estimated using an option-pricing model as of the grant date. Various option-pricing models are available that use the following six variables at grant date to determine the value of the option (including Black-Scholes, lattice, and others):

   a. Exercise price (option price)—*Higher fair value with lower option price (less must be paid to obtain the shares)*

   b. Expected average life of the option (service period + exercise period)—*Higher fair value with longer option period (there is a greater chance the stock price will increase and the time value of money is greater)*

   c. Current stock price—*Higher fair value with higher price (the fair value of the option is in part a function of current stock price)*

   d. Expected volatility of the stock—*Higher fair value with greater volatility (there is a greater chance of price increase – decreases don't hurt the holder)*

   e. Risk-free rate of interest—*Higher fair value with higher interest rate (the option holder can invest the exercise price and earn interest during service period)*

   f. Dividend yield at the grant date—*Higher fair value with lower dividend yield (higher stock price with lower dividends)*

2. **Fair Value Method**—Assume that Flowers's choice of option-pricing model at grant date establishes the fair value of one option to be $2.20. Note that the market price of the stock at grant date is not used for measuring the cost of the option plan to the firm.

   a. Total compensation expense for the four-year service period is $22,000 (10,000 × $2.20). This amount is allocated on a straight-line basis. The following journal entries illustrate the accounting.

12/31/Y1, Y2, Y3, Y4,		
Compensation expense	5,500	$22,000/4
PIC-stock options		5,500

b. If stock options vest immediately at grant, then the entire compensation expense as measured by the option's fair value is recognized immediately.

c. When the firm issues a stock dividend or splits its stock, unexercised options are adjusted. The number of shares under option, fair value and exercise price are proportionately adjusted. For example, a two-for-one split doubles the number of shares under option, and halves the fair value and exercise price. The total fair value and compensation expense to be recognized remain unchanged.

d. Compensation expense is reported as a component of income from continuing operations. For manufacturing firms, a portion may be allocated first to an inventory account and then to cost of goods sold. PIC-stock options (paid-in capital from stock options) is an owners' equity account which will be closed to another contributed capital account upon exercise.

D. At Exercise

At exercise			
Cash	50,000		10,000($5)
PIC-stock options	22,000		5,500 (4)
Common stock		10,000	10,000($1)
PIC-CS		62,000	

1. Analysis—What is the net effect of the accounting through exercise?

  a. Earnings is reduced $5,500 for each year in the service period.

  b. Retained earnings is reduced $22,000 from compensation expense.

  c. Contributed capital increases $72,000 = the fair value of the options at grant date ($22,000) + cash paid in by employee ($50,000).

  d. Net effect on total OE = $72,000 – $22,000 = $50,000 = cash increase.

2. Essentially, retained earnings is converted into permanent capital for the amount of the fair value of the option, but its placement on the income statement is the key idea. The firm increases its permanent value by the value of the manager's services. The stock price at exercise date is not used in the accounting.

E. Expiration of Options—When the market price fails to increase above the option price (here $5), the options expire. There is no retroactive adjustment and the compensation expense remains (because there was value at grant date), and the PIC-stock options account is simply renamed.

1. Assume all 10,000 options expire—entry at end of exercise period:

PIC-stock options	22,000	
PIC-stock options		22,000

2. Net effect of all the journal entries is to reduce retained earnings by $22,000 (through compensation expense), and increase permanent capital by the value of the grant ($22,000).

F. Forfeitures—Employees may leave the firm before completing the service requirement under the grant. This results in a forfeiture of their shares, requiring an adjustment to total compensation expense. Firms must make an entity-wide accounting policy election concerning accounting for forfeitures. This election affects all share-based payment plans where forfeitures relate to employee turnover; the policy must be disclosed. This election does not affect performance plans. Firms must choose one of the following:

1. **Recognize forfeitures as they occur (when employees leave).** If this alternative is chosen, the initial total compensation expense amount is based on all covered employees until some employees forfeit their grants.

2. **Estimate forfeitures and adjust the estimate as new information is forthcoming.** Forfeitures are estimated when it is no longer probable that an employee will continue with the firm and therefore the employee will not meet the service requirement of the grant.

Example
Assume Flowers chooses to estimate forfeitures:

If, as of the grant date, 10% of the 10,000 options were expected to be forfeited, then only 90% of the $22,000 total fair value is used for the accounting (.9 × $22,000 = $19,800). The entries would be the same except use $19,800 in place of $22,000, and 9,000 options in place of 10,000.

If there is a change in estimated forfeitures, the amount of compensation expense in the year the change is determined is increased or decreased by the effect of the change on all previous years and current year (but no retroactive application). The year of the change receives the entire "catch up" adjustment.

The result is that the amount of compensation expense recognized through the end of that year reflects the amount of expense that would have been recognized using the new estimate all along. In effect, the new estimate is applied to periods before it was known. This procedure is contrary to the usual approach to estimate changes that would allocate the remaining expense over the remaining service period.

Example
Assume in the Flowers example that initially there were no forfeitures expected, but in Y3 new information implies that a total of 10% of the options will be forfeited. The entries for the first two years are as above. Relevant amounts at the end of Y2:

PIC-stock options balance, $11,000 (5,500 × 2)

Compensation expense recognized to date, $11,000

New estimate of total compensation expense, $19,800 (.9 × $22,000)

12/31/Y3

Compensation expense	3,850		$19,800(3/4) − $11,000
PIC-stock options		3,850	

By the end of Y3, three-quarters of the total compensation expense is recognized. The entire impact of the estimate change on three years is recognized in the year of the change (Y3) rather than spread over the remaining years in the service period.

12/31/Y4

Compensation expense	4,950		$19,800(1/4) (SL)
PIC-stock options		4,950	

Total compensation expense recognized over the 4 years = $11,000 + $3,850 + $4,950 = $19,800.

Constant percentage of estimated forfeiture: A quick calculation of total compensation cost is possible if the firm anticipates a constant percentage of estimated forfeitures each year during the service period. For example, a plan grants 100,000 options on 1/1/Y1. The fair value of each option is $2.45, service period is four years, and the anticipated forfeiture rate is 4% per year during the service period.

Total compensation expense = $100,000(\$2.45)(1 - .04)^4 = \$208,090$

G. **Use of Actual Forfeitures Rather than Estimated Forfeitures**—If the firm instead chose to recognize forfeitures as they occur rather than estimate, the same procedure illustrated above is used except actual forfeitures are used rather than estimated forfeitures. Total compensation expense is adjusted when actual forfeitures occur, and a catch-up adjustment to compensation expense is made in that year.

Example

Assume the Flowers data with no forfeitures the first year (Y1). Then in year 2, employees holding 2,000 options leave the firm. As of 1/1/Y2, PIC-stock options balance, $5,500, compensation expense recognized to date, $5,500.

New total compensation expense, $17,600 (8,000 options × $2.20).

12/31/Y2

Compensation expense	3,300*	
PIC-stock options		3,300

*$3,300 = $17,600(2/4) − $5,500

Compensation expense recognized in each of the last two years is $17,600/4 or $4,400.

III. **Nonemployee Share-Based Payments**

1. Many entities enter into agreements in which the third-party vendor is paid with share-based awards (options, rights, etc.) rather than in cash. In general, a share-based payment with a nonemployee is accounted for the same as a share-based payment transaction with an employee.

2. The timing of the recognition of the expense for a nonemployee share-based payment is recognized in the same period as if the issuing entity had paid cash for the goods or services.

3. The share-based payment and the resulting good or service is recognized at fair value as of the grant date.

   a. The grant date is the date that the entity is obligated to issue the share-based payment (typically when the good or service is delivered).

   b. If there is a future performance condition associated with the share-based payment, recognize the cost of the goods or services when the performance condition is probable, not when the performance condition is achieved.

4. The nonemployee share-based payment is always recognized at the fair value of the equity instrument that was issued (not the fair value of the good or service received).

   a. If the issuing entity is nonpublic, the estimated fair value of the share-based payment is determined using a practical expedient. The practical expedient requires the entity to calculate a value using the industry sector index to aid valuation.

IV. Deferred Tax Asset (DTA)

1. The lessons on accounting for income tax provide in-depth coverage of deferred income tax assets. In order to explain the effect of share-based compensation plans on the DTA, a quick review is in order.

   Whenever a current temporary difference between books and tax yields a future deductible difference causing future taxable income to be less than future pretax account income, a DTA is recorded for the tax effect of that difference.

   In the case of compensation expense recognized for share-based plans, pretax accounting income is reduced currently for the amount of compensation expense recognized. The tax deduction typically will not be received by the firm until the shares vest or are exercised (in the future). Therefore, in the future, the firm will reduce its taxable income due to a transaction that has already occurred. As a result, a DTA is created during the years compensation expense is recorded and is eliminated in the future years when the deduction is received.

   The increase in the DTA each year during the service period equals the future tax rate multiplied by compensation expense for that year.

   In some cases—for example, when the market price of the stock equals the option (exercise) price at grant date (there are other tax requirements as well)—there is no tax deduction, in which case there are no tax consequences and no effect on the deferred tax asset (DTA).

2. For plans providing a tax deduction to the firm, the recognized compensation expense per GAAP may be different from the tax deduction ultimately received by the firm. The difference between the actual tax benefit and the recognized DTA through vesting is recognized in income tax expense.

   Example

   a. The total compensation expense for a stock option plan computed at grant date is $3,000,000. The plan has a three-year service period. Assume a 30% tax rate.

   b. Each year during the service period, $1,000,000 of compensation expense is recognized and the required ending DTA is increased $300,000 ($1,000,000 × .30). Income tax expense is reduced $300,000 each year without a tax deduction; therefore, the DTA is increased. By the end of the three-year service period, the DTA has an ending balance of $900,000.

   c. The actual amount of the future tax deduction is not known until exercise. Until then, total compensation expense is used as the estimate of the future deduction.

   d. When the options are exercised, the firm's tax deduction becomes known. Any difference between the tax benefit already recognized (the DTA) and the tax benefit of the actual deduction is recognized as an increase or decrease in income tax expense in the year of exercise.

   Assume the allowed deduction is $3,300,000, which is the number of shares exercised multiplied by the difference between the market price at exercise and the option price. This amount exceeds total compensation expense of $3,000,000 recognized over the three years.

   The tax benefit of the $3,300,000 deduction is $990,000 (.30 × $3,300,000) which exceeds the DTA by $90,000 ($990,000 − $900,000). The $90,000 difference is recognized as a decrease in current income tax expense. If the deduction were less than $3,000,000, the tax effect of the difference is recognized as an increase in income tax expense.

V. Graded Vesting Options

A. Graded vesting refers to groups of options within one award that vest at different dates. For example, one-third of the options in an award may vest one year from grant date, with the rest vesting two years after the grant date.

B. Under U.S. standards, the entire award may be accounted for as a single award using the fair value of the "average" option in the award.

C. Alternatively, each group may be accounted for separately (with separate fair values). In addition, if this approach is chosen, firms may choose a simplified straight-line method whereby the total compensation expense for all groups is allocated over the longest vesting period. Either way, the minimum annual expense is the amount applicable to vested options.

Stock Awards

This lesson discusses another type of stock-based compensation plan. The calculation of total compensation expense is more direct under stock awards, relative to stock options.

After studying this lesson, you should be able to:

1. Compute total compensation expense for stock awards.

2. Record periodic compensation expense using the gross or net methods.

3. Prepare the journal entry for vesting.

4. Modify the recording of compensation expense for forfeitures.

5. Understand how RSUs are similar to stock award plans.

6. Understand the basics for ESOPs.

I. **Stock Award Plans (Restricted Stock)**

   A. Under stock award plans, stock is awarded for continuing employment but the employee cannot sell the stock (the main restriction) until the award is vested—and the employee may not receive the shares until vested. Employees acquire the normal rights of shareholders at grant.

   B. For such plans, total compensation expense is the number of shares awarded multiplied by the market price of the stock at grant date (the fair value at that date). This amount is recognized as expense over the period the employee provides the service for which the grant was awarded. When the award vests, there is no additional incentive and expensing is complete. Changes in stock price after the grant have no effect on the accounting. If the award vests immediately at grant, then the entire compensation expense is recognized immediately.

Example

January 1, 20x1, 500 shares of restricted stock are granted to each of two employees (1,000 shares in total). The stock is $1 par common stock and the market price is $6 on the grant date. The employees must work 3 years at which time the award is vested. This example shows the *gross* method whereas the previous illustrations of accounting for stock options used the *net* method. Both are acceptable and yield the same financial reporting.

Total compensation expense = $6,000 (1,000 × $6)

1/1/x1 (Grant date)

Deferred comp expense	6,000	
Common stock		1,000
PIC-CS		5,000

Deferred compensation expense is a contra OE account. The effect of the above entry on total OE is zero.

12/31/x1, x2, x3

Compensation expense	2,000	
Deferred comp expense		2,000

Under the "net" method, the firm makes no entry on 1/1/x1. At each 12/31, compensation expense is debited for $2,000 and a PIC account is credited. (PIC-stock award)

12/31/x3 (Vesting)

No entry is needed under the "gross" method because the full amount of compensation expense is recorded, deferred compensation expense is closed, and the stock was recorded at grant date. Under the "net" method, the vesting entry replaces the PIC account created during the service period and the permanent OE accounts are credited:

PIC-stock award	6,000	
Common stock		1,000
PIC-CS		5,000

The net effect of the accounting:

- An expense equal to the value of the stock at grant date is recognized.

- Contributed capital increases by that amount.

- Retained earnings is reduced by the same amount permanently.

- There is no net effect on OE. (The firm did not pay or receive anything that can be objectively measured.)

C. **Forfeitures:** As with stock options, firms must decide whether to estimate forfeitures or to wait and recognize them as they occur. If employees do not continue employment through the vesting date then the expense recognized on those awards is reversed. The effect is to reduce compensation expense in the current year by the amount of compensation expense recognized in previous years' on the forfeited stock. Reversal is recorded because the stock is taken back— ultimately the firm did not give anything to the employee in this case. The forfeiture is treated as an estimate change; retrospective application is not permitted.

Example

Assume the firm recognizes forfeitures when they occur. One of the two employees in the example above leaves the firm at the end of 20x2. The deferred compensation expense balance under the gross method is $4,000 ($2,000 for the employee leaving) before recognizing compensation expense.

12/31/x2

Common stock	500
PICCS	2,500
Deferred comp expense	2,000
Compensation expense	1,000

The above gross method entry "takes back" the $1,000 of compensation expense recognized on this employee in 20X1, and removes the contributed capital accounts for the employee. The entries continue for the remaining employee. Under the net method, PIC-stock award is debited $1,000 and compensation expense credited $1,000.

12/31/x2, x3 (gross method)

Compensation expense	1,000
Deferred comp expense	1,000

Under the net method, the 12/31/x2, x3 entries are:

Compensation expense	1,000
PICstock award	1,000

Either way, the $1,000 compensation expense for remaining two years before removing the prior expense recognized on forfeited shares = (500 remaining shares)($6)/(3 year service period) = $1,000. Another way to calculate this amount is: ($6,000 original total compensation expense – $2,000 expense for x1 – $2,000 expense for x2 and x3 on forfeited shares)/2.

For 20x2, there is no net compensation expense ($1,000 decrease and $1,000 increase), and in 20x3, $1,000 of compensation expense is recognized. With the $2,000 recognized in 20x1, a total of $3,000 of compensation expense is recognized for one employee for which the award vested. At this point, the deferred compensation expense balance is zero and there are no further entries.

If the firm chooses to estimate forfeitures, the procedure followed for stock options is applied to stock awards as well. The initial total compensation expense amount is reduced by estimated forfeitures before allocating to the service periods. There is no need to reverse previous compensation expense amounts in this case unless actual and estimated forfeitures are different.

II. Restricted Stock Units (RSUs)

An RSU is the right to receive a specified number of shares. When vested, the shares are issued. Such awards are very similar to stock awards. The benefits are the same. The difference is that the shares are not issued until vested and thus the holders typically do not receive the normal rights of shareholders until the RSU vests.

The accounting is the same as for restricted stock awards. Total compensation expense is determined at grant date using the share price on that date. That total expense is allocated over the vesting period. The same JEs are recorded (gross or net method). Forfeitures are treated the same way as under stock awards.

III. Employee Stock Ownership Plans (ESOPs)

A. An employee stock ownership plan (ESOP) is a qualified stock bonus plan whereby the firm invests primarily in qualifying employer securities, including stock and other marketable obligations for the benefit of the employees. The shares are distributed to the employees as part of their compensation, and often are held by the firm until the employee retires. This discussion focuses on accounting by the employer.

B. Income Statement Effects

1. The employer recognizes compensation expense for the amount the employer contributed, or committed to contributing to an ESOP in the year. This includes cash, and its stock measured at fair value.

C. Balance Sheet Effects

1. In some instances, the ESOP will borrow funds from a bank or other lender in order to acquire shares of the employer's stock. If such an obligation of the ESOP is guaranteed by the employer (assumption by the employer of the ESOP's debt), it should be recorded as a liability in the employer's financial statements. The offsetting debit to the liability should be accounted for as a reduction of shareholders' equity.

2. Shareholders' equity will increase symmetrically with the reduction of the liability as the ESOP makes payments on the debt.

3. Assets held by an ESOP are not to be included in the employer's financial statements, because such assets are owned by the employees, not the employer.

Example

On January 1, Year 1, Fay Corporation established an employee stock ownership plan (ESOP). Selected transactions relating to the ESOP during year 1 were as follows:

- On April 1, Year 1, Fay contributed $30,000 cash and 3,000 shares of its $10 par common stock to the ESOP. On this date, the market price of the stock was $18 a share.

- On October 1, Year 1, the ESOP borrowed $100,000 from Union National Bank and acquired 5,000 shares of Fay's common stock in the open market at $17 a share. The note is for one year, bears interest at 10%, and is guaranteed by Fay.

- On December 15, Year 1, the ESOP distributed 6,000 shares of Fay common stock to employees of Fay in accordance with the plan formula.

In its Year 1 income statement, Fay reports $84,000 of compensation expense relating to the ESOP. This is the amount contributed or committed to be contributed to the ESOP in Year 1: the contribution of $30,000 cash plus the common stock with a fair value of $54,000 (3,000 × $18).

In its December 31, Year 1 balance sheet, Fay will report $100,000 in liabilities for its ESOP obligation because the obligation is covered by either a guarantee by Fay or a commitment by Fay to make future contributions to the ESOP sufficient to meet the debt service requirements.

The offsetting $100,000 debit is reported as a reduction of Fay's stockholders' equity.

Stock Appreciation Rights

The final lesson on stock-based compensation addresses the accounting for a plan that bases total compensation on the increase in the firm's stock price over a period of years. A liability is recorded under certain circumstances.

After studying this lesson, you should be able to:

1. Explain when a liability is recorded for an SAR.

2. Compute and record periodic compensation expense.

3. Modify the calculation of periodic compensation expense for forfeitures.

4. Identify the period over which compensation expense is computed.

I.   Stock Appreciation Rights (SARs)

   A. These plans are different from stock option plans: (1) employee receives the difference between the stock price at grant date, and the stock price at exercise date, (2) pays nothing, (3) the SAR specifies payment of the benefit in either cash or stock (employee may have a choice). The accounting issue is whether the arrangement involves debt or equity.

   B. If the SAR plan allows the employer to issue stock, then the SAR is accounted for as a stock option plan. The fair value of the SAR is estimated at grant date and the total fair value is allocated to compensation expense over the service period.

   C. If the SAR plan specifies that payment is in cash or allows the employee to choose cash payment:

   1. The firm records a liability rather than paid-in-capital when compensation expense is recognized.

   2. For each year in the service period, the fair value of each right is reestimated in light of new information using an option pricing model.

   3. Compensation expense is recorded each year based on the fair value at the end of the period (fair value is reestimated each year through exercise), for the portion of the service period elapsed using the catch up procedure for stock options. Expense recognition continues through the exercise date.

   4. Estimated forfeitures are built into the calculation of total compensation expense as illustrated previously for stock options; or the firm may choose to recognize forfeitures as they occur.

   5. At exercise date, the fair value of the SAR equals the difference between price at grant date and the price paid for the stock.

Example

On 1/1/x1, several executives are granted SARS on a total of 10,000 shares, which, at exercise, pay cash equal to the difference between the $5 per share market price at grant date and the market price at exercise. The market price of the stock on the grant date is $5. To continue owning the SARs, the employees must work for four years at which time the SARs are exercisable, for the two years following that date.

Fair value per SAR:

12/31/x1 $3

12/31/x2 4.50

12/31/x3 2.80

12/31/x4 3.50

12/31/x5 3.90

1/1/x1

no entry

12/31/x1

Compensation expense 10,000($3)/4	7,500	
Liability under SAR plan		7,500

12/31/x2

Compensation expense 10,000($4.50)(2/4) − $7,500	15,000	
Liability under SAR plan		15,000

12/31/x3

Liability under SAR plan	1,500	
Compensation expense		1,500

(Through this date, $21,000 of compensation expense is to be recognized: $21,000 = 10,000($2.80) (3/4). Through this date, $22,500 has been recognized = $7,500 + $15,000. Note that both the liability and compensation expense are reduced this year for the difference.

12/31/x4

Compensation expense 10,000($3.50)(4/4) − $21,000	14,000	
Liability under SAR plan		14,000

The SARs have vested, but the liability and expense continue to be adjusted until exercise or lapsing because the firm must report the liability at the amount of probable payment.

12/31/x5

Compensation expense 10,000($3.90) − $35,000	4,000	
Liability under SAR plan		4,000

During 20x6, the SARs are exercised. The market price at exercise date is $8.40 (fair value of SAR is $3.40, the difference between $8.40 and $5 price at grant).

Liability under SAR plan 10,000(3.40) − $39,000	5,000	
Compensation expense		5,000
Liability under SAR plan	34,000	
Cash 10,000($8.40 − $5)		34,000

Total compensation expense recognized over the entire period is $34,000. If the SAR had no value at the end of exercise period (because the market price was not greater than $5), the entire liability is extinguished and compensation expense is reduced by the same amount as the liability balance at that time.

Income Taxes

Income Tax Basics

The first lesson of several about accounting for income tax provides the big picture of the area and the major issues. Terminology is emphasized so that later lessons can be understood within the context of the larger issues.

After studying this lesson, you should be able to:

1. Note that the emphasis of interperiod tax allocation measurement is on the appropriate recognition of assets and liabilities.

2. Explain how income tax expense is computed in general.

3. Identify the major categories of differences between tax accounting and financial reporting.

4. Define taxable income, income tax liability, current and deferred income tax provision, and other terms.

I. Overview

    A. The reporting principles for GAAP and for tax law are not the same. The amount of taxes due for a period is set by tax law, not by GAAP. The question then is: how to measure income tax expense? In determining the income tax cost and the related ending balances of tax assets and liabilities for the period, GAAP applies the accrual basis of accounting. Income tax expense as reported for the books is generally not the same as the amount of tax due for the period.

    B. Income tax expense is recognized when it is incurred, regardless of when the payment is actually made to the Internal Revenue Service. The process of recognizing income tax expense and associated deferred tax accounts is called "interperiod tax allocation." Interperiod tax allocation is the application of accrual accounting to the measurement of income tax effects on the financial statements.

    C. GAAP adopted the asset/liability approach for measurement of income tax effects.

        1. The emphasis is on the correct measurement of the income tax assets and liabilities.

        2. Deferred tax assets and liabilities are measured directly, along with the income tax liability.

        3. Income tax expense is a derived amount—a derived figure.

    D. **Summary**—The main effects of applying the asset/liability approach for interperiod tax allocation are:

        1. Income tax expense for the period reflects the amount that will ultimately be payable on the year's transactions, even though the timing of payment and expense recognition will not coincide.

        2. The income tax payable account, deferred tax asset account, and deferred tax liability account report the tax receivables and obligations from transactions that have already occurred as of the balance sheet date but that have not yet been received or paid.

II. Terminology and Definitions—Several terms and definitions are provided early in the discussion to help you with the concepts and procedure.

    A. **Taxable Items**—Amounts that cause income tax to increase. This is an Internal Revenue Code term and typically refers to revenues that cause taxable income to increase.

    B. **Deductible Items**—Amounts that cause income tax to decrease. This is an Internal Revenue Code term and typically refers to expenses that cause taxable income to decrease.

C. Pretax Accounting Income—Income before income tax for financial accounting purposes as determined by GAAP.

D. Taxable Income—Income before income tax for tax purposes. This is the analog of pretax accounting income. Taxable income is the amount to which the tax rates are applied in determining the income tax liability for the year.

E. Income Tax Liability—The amount of income tax the firm must pay on taxable income for a year. Firms pay this liability in estimated quarterly installments with the last installment due early in the year following the tax year.

F. Income Tax Expense—The account reported in the income statement that measures the income tax cost for the year's transactions. Income tax expense equals the income tax liability plus or minus the net change in the deferred tax accounts for the period.

G. Current Income Tax Provision—Also called current portion of income tax expense and current provision for income tax. This term is used in the income statement to refer to the amount of income taxes due for the year. This amount is the same as the income tax liability for the year.

H. Deferred Income Tax Provision—The amount of income tax expense for the year that is not currently due. This amount equals the net sum of the changes in the deferred tax accounts.

Example

Assume the following year-end income tax accrual entry. For simplicity, we assume that the entire year's tax liability is paid early the following year. The $40,000 income tax expense amount is derived from the other amounts. It is not directly computed.

Income Tax Expense	40,000	
Deferred Tax Asset	6,000	
Deferred Tax Liability		9,000
Income Tax Payable		37,000

Current income tax provision:	$37,000	(income tax liability)
Plus deferred income tax provision	3,000[1]	
Equals total income tax expense	$40,000	

[1]$9,000 increase in deferred tax liability less $6,000 increase in deferred tax asset

---

I. Permanent Difference—An amount that appears in the tax return or income statement but never both. These include items of revenue or expense that are never taxable or deductible; also taxable and deductible items that never appear in the income statement. This type of difference is also called a nontemporary difference.

Example

A fine or penalty that is never deductible but is treated as an expense or loss for income statement purposes is a permanent difference. These types of differences do not enter into the process of interperiod tax allocation. They have no deferred tax consequences.

J. Temporary Difference—An item of revenue or expense that, over the total life of the item, will affect pretax accounting income and taxable income in the same total amount, but will be recognized in different amounts in any given year for financial reporting and tax purposes.

Example
Depreciation can be different in any given year for income reporting and tax purposes, but total depreciation is the same over the life of the asset under the two reporting systems.

K. Net Operating Loss—Negative taxable income (strictly a tax term). A net operating loss can be carried forward indefinitely to reduce up to 80% of taxable income in a year and therefore an NOL reduces the tax liability in future tax years. A net operating loss gives rise to a deferred tax asset. Note that the deferred tax asset does NOT equal the net operating loss. The deferred tax asset is a function of the net operating loss multiplied by the enacted tax rate.

L. Deferred Tax Asset—The recognized tax effect of future deductible temporary differences. These differences, caused by transactions that have occurred as of the balance sheet date, will cause future taxable income to **decrease** relative to pretax accounting income.

M. Deferred Tax Liability—The recognized tax effect of future taxable temporary differences. These differences, caused by transactions that have occurred as of the balance sheet date, will cause future taxable income to **increase** relative to pretax accounting income.

N. Interperiod Tax Allocation—The process of measuring and recognizing the total income tax consequences of transactions in the year. Only temporary differences and net operating loss carryforwards enter into this process. Interperiod tax allocation gives rise to deferred tax accounts because the total tax consequence of the period's transactions is not equal to the current income tax liability. The current tax liability (measured at the current tax rate) measures a part of that total, but there will be additional tax consequences in the future because of transactions that have occurred as of the balance sheet date. Hence the need for the deferred tax accounts. Deferred tax accounts are measured at the **future enacted** tax rate.

III. Three Types of Differences—Between GAAP and Income Tax Law

A. The three types of differences between the two reporting systems in terms of their effect on accounting for income taxes are:

1. Permanent differences

2. Temporary differences

3. Net operating losses

B. For interperiod tax allocation, temporary differences are the most important. Most firms have both temporary and permanent differences, but net operating losses are less common. Thus, the two main differences to be aware of in accounting for income taxes are temporary and permanent differences.

Permanent Differences

One of the two major types of differences between tax accounting and financial reporting is discussed here. This type of difference does not cause a deferral of tax and is treated in a more straightforward way relative to temporary differences.

After studying this lesson, you should be able to:

1. Describe the general effect of permanent differences on the measurement of income tax expense.

2. List important specific permanent differences.

3. Note how each specific difference affects the tax accrual entry.

I. **Nature of Permanent Differences**

   A. The permanent differences are those, due to the existing tax laws, that will not reverse themselves over an extended period of time. The treatment of permanent differences under the two reporting systems is **permanently** different. Some of the more common permanent differences follow. Permanent (nontemporary) differences are not used in computing the change in deferred tax accounts.

   B. For purposes of the CPA Exam, our recommendation is to be familiar with the most common specific permanent differences. There are far fewer of these relative to temporary differences. Also, be able to identify a new difference as permanent, if given sufficient information about how the item is treated for financial reporting and for tax.

II. **Specific Permanent Differences**

   A. **Tax-Free Interest Income**—An example of this difference is the interest income earned on an investment in state or municipal bonds. The interest income is included in pretax accounting income, but not in taxable income.

   B. **Life Insurance Expense**—The insurance premiums on a life insurance policy for a key employee where the firm is the beneficiary are not deductible from taxable income, but are an expense for financial reporting.

   C. **Proceeds on Life Insurance**—In the event of the death of the key employee, the proceeds from the insurance policy are not taxable but are included as a gain for financial reporting purposes.

   D. **Dividends Received Deduction**—The dividends received deduction is a deduction for tax purposes equal to 80% (amount subject to change) of qualified dividends received. It is an amount of dividends received that is not subject to tax. However, the entire amount of dividends received is included in pretax accounting income. There is no similar deduction for financial reporting purposes. The difference between the total dividend (included in book income) and the amount taxable (e.g., 20%) is the permanent difference (80% of the dividend).

   E. **Fines and Penalties**—Many fines, penalties, and expenses resulting from a violation of law are not deductible for tax purposes, but are recognized as an expense or loss for financial reporting purposes.

   F. **Depletion**—GAAP depletion (cost depletion) is based on the cost of a natural resource used up. Tax depletion is based on revenues of resource sold. The difference in any year is a permanent difference.

III. **General Rule for Accounting for Permanent Differences**—For each of the differences listed above, an amount is recognized in one system of reporting but not in the other. The difference never reverses as it does with temporary differences. But the income tax law is what ultimately determines whether an item is considered for tax purposes. Hence the rule for permanent differences: **The effect of a permanent difference on income tax expense is the same as its effect on the income tax liability for the period.**

Example

Pretax accounting income is $20,000 and taxable income is $22,000. The only difference is a $2,000 fine that is recognized for accounting purposes but is not deductible for tax purposes. If the tax rate is 30%, the income tax accrual entry is:

Income Tax Expense*	6,600	
Income Tax Payable		6,600

*($22,000 × .30)

The fine will never be deductible for tax purposes. Therefore, financial reporting treats the item giving rise to the permanent difference (through income tax expense) in the same way the tax code treats the item—it is not deductible. Permanent differences are not considered when computing the balances of deferred tax accounts. Permanent differences are not allocated; they do not affect the process of interperiod tax allocation.

Note that income tax payable is directly computed as taxable income multiplied by the current tax rate. Because there are no changes in deferred tax accounts, income tax expense equals income tax payable because income tax expense is a derived amount. It is the amount that completes the entry in terms of equality of debits and credits. Income tax expense is not directly computed.

Temporary Differences

This lesson discusses the basics of accounting for the more involved type of difference between tax accounting and financial reporting.

After studying this lesson, you should be able to:

1. Explain the basic nature of an item causing a temporary difference.

2. Identify specific temporary differences.

3. Note that both revenues and expenses can be recognized for financial reporting before or after they are recognized for tax reporting.

4. Define originating and reversing temporary differences.

5. Categorize temporary differences into taxable and deductible differences.

6. Calculate taxable income from pretax accounting income and additional information.

I. Nature of Temporary Differences

A. In contrast with permanent differences, which never reverse over time, temporary differences do reverse. These are the differences involved with the process of interperiod tax allocation—the recognition of deferred tax accounts.

Example

A firm provides services for a client for a fee of $4,000. The service is provided near the end of the year. The client is expected to remit the fee early the following year. For financial accounting purposes, the $4,000 of revenue is recognized in the year the service is provided but for tax purposes is taxable in the year the fee is received. Over the two years, both systems recognize the same amount of revenue. The temporary difference of $4,000 originated in the first year, and reversed in the second. At the end of the first year, the firm has a future difference of $4,000. That is the basis for the recorded deferred tax account at the end of the first year.

1. The only difference between the two reporting systems (GAAP and tax) is one of timing of recognition.

2. The concept of future temporary differences is one way to refer to the underlying differences leading to the deferred tax accounts. Another is in reference to an item's tax basis compared with its amount for financial reporting purposes. For example, the cost of a plant asset is $100,000 and for financial reporting the asset has been depreciated $15,000 through the current balance sheet date (book value $85,000). The asset has been depreciated $25,000 for tax purposes through the balance sheet date. For tax purposes, this asset is said to have a tax basis of $75,000. The difference between the book value and tax basis is $10,000, which also is the future taxable difference. The $10,000 future difference is the amount that enters into the computation of the deferred tax liability at the end of the current year.

II. Some Temporary Differences

Some of the more frequently observed temporary differences are listed and described below. In many cases, a balance sheet account reflects the amount of the difference to reverse in the future.

A. **Taxable After Recognized for the Books**—Revenues or gains that are taxable after they are recognized in financial income.

Examples

1. An example of this type of difference involves the use of the installment sales basis of accounting for income tax purposes. The accrual basis of accounting is used by the entity for financial reporting purposes, while a version of the cash basis, the installment sales basis, is used for income tax purposes. The net installment accounts receivable at year-end reflects the future temporary difference. Only the amount of cash received in a year is taxable in that year; but the entire sale is recognized as revenue for the books in the year of sale.

2. The use of the equity method to recognize income from investments in equity securities is another example. The equity method is used for financial reporting purposes, and the amount of income reported on the income statement corresponds to the percentage of stock owned in the investee multiplied by the reported earnings of the investee. Investment income recognized for tax purposes will be equal to the dividends received in a given year (after the dividends received deduction, if applicable).

B. Deductible After Recognized for the Books—Expenses or losses that are deductible after they are recognized in financial income

Example

An example of this type of difference involves the recognition of warranty expense. For financial reporting purposes, warranty expense is usually estimated and recognized in the year the related merchandise is sold. For tax purposes, warranty expense is recognized in the year customers request warranty service, often after the year of sale. The warranty liability reflects the future temporary difference.

C. Taxable Before Recognized for the Books—Revenues or gains that are taxable before they are recognized in financial income

Examples

1. An example of this type of difference involves the recognition of rent revenue or subscription revenue. For financial reporting purposes, the rent revenue or subscription revenue is recognized in the year that it is earned. For tax purposes, the rent revenue or subscription revenue is recognized in the year that the related cash payment is received. The unearned subscription revenue account reflects the future temporary difference.

2. On September 1, 20X7, the Dolphin Company rented a vacant warehouse to the Raider Company. The lease term was one year, from September 1, 20X7 through August 31, 20X8. The warehouse annual rental fee was $24,000, which was paid in full on September 1, 20X7. For financial reporting purposes, $8,000 rental revenue will be reported in 20X7, and $16,000 rental revenue will be reported in 20X8. For tax purposes, the entire $24,000 will be reported on the 20X7 tax return. The total rent revenue is the same under the two systems of reporting but the timing of recognition is different in each year affected. At the end of 20X7, the $16,000 balance in unearned rent (a liability) equals the future temporary difference to reverse in 20X8.

D. Deductible Before Recognized for the Books—Expenses or losses that are deductible before they are recognized in financial income

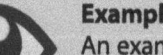

Example

An example of this type of difference is depreciation recorded for income tax purposes. For financial reporting purposes, depreciation is recorded over the estimated useful life of an asset. For tax purposes, depreciation is recorded over shorter time frames called recovery periods. In addition, for tax purposes, an accelerated depreciation method is typically employed.

III. Categorizing Temporary Differences

A. Originating/Reversing

1. When an item causing a temporary difference first occurs, the difference is called an originating difference.

2. In later years, the difference attributable to the item is called the reversing difference.

B. Future Differences
The classification of temporary differences is based on the future reversal rather than the originating amount because deferred tax asset and liability balances reflect the future tax consequences of transactions that have already occurred.

C. Two Categories
For purposes of interperiod tax allocation and recording the annual income tax accrual entry, temporary differences are classified into two categories.

1. The first category, called **Taxable Temporary Differences**, involves differences that initially cause a postponement in the payment of taxes.

   a. In the year of origination, the item causes taxable income to decline relative to pretax accounting income.

   b. When the item reverses, the item causes future taxable income to exceed pretax accounting income. This is why these differences are called taxable differences. They increase taxable income relative to pretax accounting income in the *future*.

   c. Future taxable differences give rise to deferred tax liabilities.

2. The second category, called **Deductible Temporary Differences**, involves differences that initially cause a prepayment of taxes.

   a. In the year of origination, the item causes taxable income to increase relative to pretax accounting income.

   b. When the item reverses, the item causes future taxable income to be less than pretax accounting income. This is why these differences are called deductible differences. They reduce taxable income relative to pretax accounting income in the *future*.

   c. Future deductible differences give rise to deferred tax assets.

D. Examples of Taxable Temporary Differences
Future taxable income > future pretax accounting income:

1. **Depreciation**

Example
For financial reporting and tax purposes, depreciation on a plant asset purchased Year 1 will be:

Year	Book Depreciation	Tax Depreciation
1	$10,000	$16,000
2	10,000	9,000
3	10,000	5,000
Totals	$30,000	$30,000

At the end of Year 1, the future taxable difference is $6,000, because in the future, after Year 1, $20,000 of depreciation expense will be recognized for book purposes ($10,000 + $10,000), but only $14,000 of depreciation will be deducted for tax purposes ($9,000 + $5,000). After Year 1, the future difference of $6,000 will cause taxable income to exceed pretax book income by $6,000 because less depreciation will be deducted than expensed for book purposes. At the end of Year 1, if the future tax rate is 30%, this difference contributes $1,800 to the firm's ending deferred tax liability balance ($6,000 × .30).

At the end of Year 2, the difference in Year 2 has reversed, reducing the future taxable difference to $5,000 ($10,000 book depreciation – $5,000 tax depreciation) which contributes $1,500 to the firm's ending deferred tax liability balance ($5,000 × .30). If there were no other differences, the deferred tax liability would be reduced $300 at the end of Year 2 ($1,800 – $1,500)

At the end of Year 3, there are no future differences, and the deferred tax liability is closed (assuming no other differences).

2. Installment Sales

Example
During Year 1, a firm sells $6,000 worth of goods on the installment basis. For financial reporting purposes, the firm uses the point-of-sales method to record revenue and recognizes the entire $6,000 in Year 1. For tax purposes, the firm uses the installment method, which postpones revenue recognition until cash is received. No cash is received in Year 1 on the sale and the firm has no tax liability for this amount.

At the end of Year 1, the firm has a future taxable difference of $6,000. In a later year, when cash is received, the firm's taxable income will exceed pretax accounting income by $6,000 because of transactions that have occurred through the end of Year 1.

The future temporary difference is found on the balance sheet in the Installment Receivable account, which has a balance of $6,000, the amount not yet collected.

E. Examples of Deductible Temporary Differences—(future taxable income < future pretax accounting income)

1. Warranty expense

Example
Warranty expense
On sales for Year 1, the firm recognizes $8,000 of estimated warranty expense. For the books, the entire estimated expense is recognized in the year of sale. Also during Year 1, $1,000 was spent servicing warranty claims. The firm can deduct only the $1,000 on its Year 1 tax return because tax law limits the deduction to the actual cost of claims service. At the end of Year 1, the firm has a $7,000 future deductible difference because the firm expects to spend $7,000 in the future servicing warranty claims at which time that amount will be deductible. Next year, when the remaining claims are serviced, the firm's taxable income will fall by $7,000 relative to pretax accounting income.

The future temporary difference is found in the warranty liability, which has a balance of $7,000, the amount of future claims expected.

2. Revenue received in advance

Example
Revenue Received in Advance
During Year 1, the firm collected $22,000 in advance of providing its services to customers. By the end of the year, the firm had performed $10,000 worth of service. The full $22,000 is taxable in Year 1 but only $10,000 of revenue is recognized in the income statement. At the end of Year 1, the firm has a $12,000 deductible difference. Next year, when the remaining service is provided, the firm's pretax accounting income will increase $12,000 with no effect on taxable income. Future taxable income will be less than pretax accounting income.

The future temporary difference is found in the unearned revenue account, which has a balance of $12,000, the amount of paid services yet to be provided.

IV. Relationship Between Pretax Accounting Income and Taxable Income

A. Frequently, examination problems provide only one of the two before-tax income measures: (pretax accounting income or taxable income). If taxable income is not provided, it must be computed from pretax accounting income and the differences between the two reporting systems. To prepare the year-end tax accrual entry, which involves the deferred tax account changes, and income tax expense, the candidate must be able to determine taxable income. The income tax liability equals the tax rate multiplied by taxable income and is recorded in the journal entry.

Only current-year differences (both temporary and permanent) are involved in determining taxable income from pretax accounting income. This is in contrast with deferred tax account balances, which use only future temporary differences.

B. When taxable income is not provided, start with pretax accounting income and adjust for differences between pretax accounting income and taxable income. Both temporary and permanent differences are involved. Ask yourself how each difference affects both pretax accounting income and taxable income. The difference in these effects leads to the amount of the adjustment and also the decision about whether to add or subtract from pretax accounting income.

Examples
1. *Short Examples*

Pretax accounting income is given and is $40,000. But you need to determine taxable income. Prepaid rent of $5,000 from the beginning of the year was expensed during the year (a reversing temporary difference). $7,000 of insurance was prepaid at year-end (an originating temporary difference). $3,000 of tax-free interest was received from municipal bonds (a permanent difference). To prepare the tax accrual entry, you need taxable income.

Pretax accounting income	$40,000
Rent expense	5,000
Prepaid insurance	(7,000)
Tax-free interest	(3,000)
Taxable income	$35,000

The logic: Pretax accounting income was reduced by $5,000 of rent expense not paid for this year. This amount was deducted in a previous year when paid. There is no deduction this year so taxable income is not reduced this year; add back to pretax accounting income.

Pretax accounting income was not reduced by the insurance expenditure because no expense was recognized. But it is deductible in the year paid (this year); subtract from pretax accounting income.

Pretax accounting income includes the tax-free interest because it is a revenue, but taxable income excludes it due to its nontaxable nature; subtract from pretax accounting income.

2. *Longer Example*

The four temporary differences from previous examples are repeated below, along with additional information for Year 1. Pretax income is given; you must determine taxable income.

Year 1 Information

Pretax accounting income	$100,000
Fines and penalties	9,000
Municipal bond interest received	14,000
Depreciation deduction	16,000
Depreciation expense recognized for books	10,000
Taxable installment sales	0
Installment sales revenue recognized for books	6,000
Warranty deduction	1,000
Warranty expense recognized for books	8,000
Taxable service revenue	22,000
Service revenue recognized for books	10,000

Computation of taxable income:

		Balance sheet account:
Pretax accounting income	$100,000	
Plus nondeductible fines and penalties	9,000	
Less nontaxable municipal bond interest received	(14,000)	
Excess of tax over book depreciation	(6,000)	Equipment book value
Excess of book over tax sales revenue	(6,000)	Installment receivable
Excess of book over tax warranty expense	7,000	Warranty liability
Excess of tax over book service revenue	12,000	Unearned revenue
Taxable income	$102,000	

The first two adjustments—fines and penalties, and municipal bond interest—are permanent differences. Pretax accounting income was reduced by fines and penalties but they are not deductible for tax purposes and therefore must be added back in computing taxable income. The opposite is true for municipal bond interest. It is included in pretax accounting income but is not taxable and therefore is subtracted in computing taxable income.

The remaining adjustments are temporary differences. $16,000 of depreciation is deducted for tax purposes, but pretax accounting income reflects only $10,000 of depreciation. Thus, an additional $6,000 must be subtracted in computing taxable income.

Pretax accounting income reflects $8,000 of warranty expense, but only $1,000 of deduction was allowed (cost to service claims). To adjust pretax accounting income that was reduced $8,000 to taxable income that is reduced only $1,000, the difference of $7,000 must be added to pretax accounting income.

Pretax accounting income reflects $10,000 of service revenue, but taxable income includes all $22,000 received from customers. Therefore, add $12,000 to pretax accounting income. Taxable income then reflects all $22,000 collected in the year.

Tax Accrual Entry

This lesson integrates previous lessons on accounting for income tax by illustrating the tax accrual entry. This entry recognizes the firm's tax liability, changes in deferred tax accounts, and income tax expense.

After studying this lesson, you should be able to:

1. Identify the types of differences causing deferred tax assets and liabilities.

2. Record the tax accrual entry when there are no beginning balances in deferred tax accounts.

3. Compute income tax expense as a derived amount.

4. Note that it is the future temporary differences which are involved in computing deferred tax account balances.

I. General Tax Accrual Entry

A. The previous definitions and categorization of future differences as permanent and temporary are used in this lesson to develop the year-end tax accrual entry.

B. The following entry is a generalization of the year-end tax accrual entry assuming that the year's full tax liability is paid early the following year. Both the deferred tax asset and liability show an increase, but both can be decreases as well, depending on the situation.

Income Tax Expense	a ``plug'' figure
Deferred Tax Asset	see below*
Deferred Tax Liability	see below**
Income Tax Payable	Taxable Income × Current Tax Rate

*The amount to increase the deferred tax asset to its required ending balance, which is the total future deductible temporary difference multiplied by the future enacted tax rate. Estimated tax rates are not used, only enacted tax rates. If the required change were a decrease, the asset would be credited.

**The amount to increase the deferred tax liability to its required ending balance which is the total future taxable temporary difference multiplied by the future enacted tax rate. If the required change were a decrease, the liability would be debited. Future tax rates are used to measure the deferred tax accounts because the future tax consequences will be settled or recovered at the future tax rate.

> **Note**
> The future and current tax rates are the same if Congress has not enacted a new rate for future years by the end of the current year.

II. Illustrative Example (No Beginning Deferred Tax Balances)

A. A firm in its first year has $100,000 of operating income composed of items that are recognized in the same amounts for both financial reporting and tax purposes. **In addition**, the firm has:

1. $10,000 of municipal bond interest

2. Rent expense of $20,000 for book purposes

3. Rent expense of $25,000 for tax purposes

B. The $5,000 difference in rent expense is the ending prepaid rent. This amount is deductible in Year 1 but is not recognized as rent expense until Year 2. The tax rate for year 1 is 30% but the Year 2 rate, enacted at the close of Year 1, was increased to 35%.

C. Tax accrual entry for Year 1:

Income Tax Expense	24,250	
Deferred Tax Liability ($5,000 × .35)		1,750
Income Tax Payable ($75,000 × .30)		22,500*

*Taxable income = $100,000 − $25,000 = $75,000. The municipal bond interest is not taxable. It is not included in the $100,000 amount common to the two reporting systems. Taxable income applies the current (Year 1) tax rate, while the computation of the deferred tax liability uses the future enacted tax rate.

D. The future temporary difference of $5,000 is a taxable temporary difference because taxable income in Year 2 will increase relative to pretax accounting income by this amount when the prepaid rent is recognized as expense for book purposes only. The resulting deferred tax liability is measured using the future enacted tax rate at which the tax will be paid.

E. Income tax expense is the sum of the increase in the deferred tax liability and income taxes payable. This is the only way to compute income tax expense. It is not the product of the current tax rate and pretax accounting income. The $24,250 income tax expense is the total amount of tax expected to be paid on transactions occurring in Year 1. This total amount is allocated via interperiod tax allocation to the current provision of $22,500 (the income tax liability for Year 1) and $1,750 (the amount deferred to Year 2). The $1,750 is the amount of tax payable in the future based on transactions that occurred by the end of Year 1.

Abbreviated income statement for Year 1

Operating Income Before Rent Expense	$100,000
Rent Expense	(20,000)
Municipal Bond Interest	10,000
Pretax Accounting Income	90,000
Income Tax Expense (from tax accrual entry)	(24,250)
Net income	$ 65,750

F. The **total income tax expense** is classified into two parts, which must be reported either on the face of the income statement or in the footnotes:

Current Provision of Income Tax	$22,500
Plus Deferred Provision of Income Tax	1,750
Total Income Tax Expense	$24,250

G. **Notice** that the income tax expense recognized is not equal to the current tax rate times pretax accounting income (.30 × $90,000 = $27,000). In other words, the current tax rate of 30% is not the effective tax rate for this firm. The effective tax rate is the ratio of income tax expense to pretax accounting income. For this firm, that rate is 26.95% ($24,250/$90,000).

H. Two factors explain the difference: (1) the municipal bond interest is included in pretax accounting income but is not taxed (this lowers the effective tax rate), and (2) the higher rate of 35% is applied to the future temporary difference and is reflected in income tax expense (this raises the effective rate). Because of these types of differences, a tax reconciliation footnote is a required disclosure. That footnote would show:

Statutory Tax Rate:	.3000
Effect of Nontaxable Municipal Bond Interest	(.0333) $10,000(.3)/$90,000
Effect of Future Rate Increase on Future Temporary Differences	.0028 $5,000(.35 − 30)/$90,000
Effective Tax Rate	.2695 $24,250/$90,000

III. Analysis: Practice Example (Permanent and Temporary Difference)—Gem has no beginning deferred tax balances and uses the equity method to account for its 25% investment in Gold. During 20X2, Gem received dividends of $30,000 from Gold and recorded $180,000 as its equity in the earnings of Gold. Additional information follows:

   A. All the undistributed earnings of Gold will be distributed as dividends in future periods.

   B. The dividends received from Gold are eligible for the 80% dividends received deduction.

   C. There are no other temporary differences.

   D. Enacted income tax rates are 30% for 20X2 and thereafter.

   E. Required: In its December 31, 20X2 balance sheet, what amount should Gem report for deferred income tax liability?

   F. Solution: With no beginning deferred tax balances, the ending balance in the deferred tax liability equals the change in the deferred tax liability for the period. The change in the deferred tax liability is the future tax effect of the amount of income from the investment that is expected to be taxable in the future, using enacted tax rates. That amount is $9,000 = .30(.20)($180,000 − $30,000). The ($180,000 − $30,000) factor is the total future earnings difference between tax and book accounting. The .20 is the amount taxable after considering the dividends received deduction. The tax rate is 30%. The final result, $9,000, is the anticipated future tax liability, based on current transactions.

   G. This problem has both permanent and temporary differences. The permanent difference is the 80% dividends received deduction. Of the $180,000 earnings, 80% or $144,000 will never be taxed. Therefore, 20% or $36,000 will be taxed. By 20X2 year's end, .20($30,000 dividends received) or $6,000 has been taxed, leaving $30,000 as the future temporary difference. The $30,000 is the amount recognized in 20X2 earnings but will not be taxed until later years. The tax effect of this difference, $9,000 (.30 × $30,000) is the ending deferred tax liability.

IV. Differences Originating and Reversing Over More than One Period

   A. Depreciable plant assets often require more than one year for the full temporary difference to originate. In early years, future temporary differences appear to be deductible but should not be treated as such. The entire net future temporary difference for a depreciable asset is treated as a taxable temporary difference.

Example

A plant asset is purchased at the beginning of Year 1 and will be depreciated as indicated:

Year	Tax Depreciation	Book Depreciation
1	$400	$200
2	300	200
3	200	200
4	100	200
5	0	200
Totals	$1,000	$1,000

At the end of Year 1, the total future temporary difference is $200, the difference between Years 2–5 depreciation for the two systems ($200 + $200 + $200 + $200) – ($300 + $200 + $100). More depreciation ($200 more) in the future (after Year 1) will be recognized for book purposes than for tax purposes. Thus, future taxable income will exceed pretax accounting in the future in total causing the difference to be classified as taxable at the end of Year 1.

Although the difference for Year 2 (only) appears to be a deductible difference (because Year 2 taxable income will be less than pretax accounting income by $100), that difference is an originating difference, not a reversing difference. Thus, the correct approach is to treat the entire future difference at the end of Year 1 as a taxable difference.

    B. Other examples include prepaids and warranties covering more than one year. In each case, the full future difference at the end of each year is treated the same—either as a future taxable difference (prepaid) or deductible difference (warranty).

Interperiod Tax Allocation Process

This lesson provides a summary of the interperiod tax allocation process by including beginning balances of deferred tax accounts, temporary differences reversing in the current period, and new temporary differences originating in the current period.

After studying this lesson, you should be able to:

1. List the steps leading to the tax accrual entry in the most general case.

2. Compute the ending balance in the deferred tax asset and liability accounts.

3. Determine the change in the deferred tax asset and liability accounts.

4. Complete the tax accrual entry.

5. Identify the treatment of temporary differences that do not originate in only one period.

6. Modify the tax accrual entry for changes in the tax rate and tax law.

I. **General Steps for Interperiod Tax Allocation: Adjusting the Deferred Tax Accounts**

   A. In the previous examples, only one temporary difference was used, and there were no beginning deferred tax account balances. This section completes the discussion by including more than one temporary difference and beginning deferred tax account balances. A general process leading to the tax accrual entry is used.

   B. **Steps Leading to the Tax Accrual Entry:**

1. Compute taxable income and multiply by current tax rate.	
Result = income tax payable ———— to tax accrual entry ————>	XX
2. Analyze all future individual temporary differences, separating them into taxable and deductible categories.	
3. Apply the future enacted rate(s) to the taxable differences and aggregate.	
Result = required ending deferred tax liability balance =	XX
Subtract beginning deferred tax liability balance	(XX)
Equals required increase or decrease in deferred tax liability ————>	XX
4. Apply the future enacted rate(s) to the deductible differences and aggregate.	
Result = required ending deferred tax asset balance =	XX
Subtract beginning deferred tax asset balance	(XX)
Equals required increase or decrease in deferred tax asset ————>	XX
5. Net sum equals income tax expense	XX

   C. **Caution**—Occasionally the CPA exam has asked questions requiring the candidate to determine the income tax payable ending balance after the payment of estimated tax payments. Assume the current tax liability is $50,000 (taxable income × current tax rate). If the firm has made a total of $35,000 of estimated tax payments, then the income tax liability to be reported in the balance sheet is $15,000 ($50,000 − $35,000). This aspect has little effect on the main issue at hand: completing the tax accrual entry.

II. Example—Beginning Deferred Tax Account Balances, Multiple Differences

Example

Year 1 Pretax accounting income:	$60,000
Ending prepaid insurance balance (coverage for Year 2)	10,000
Recognized lawsuit contingent liability (recognized loss) (to be resolved in Year 2)	15,000
Tax rates: current (30%), enacted for Year 2 and later (35%)	

Steps:

			To tax accrual entry
1.	Taxable income = $60,000 − $10,000 + $15,000 = $65,000	=	$19,500
	The prepaid insurance is subtracted because it is an amount paid in Year 1, but not recognized as expense for the books. The contingent loss is added because it is a recognized loss for the books but is not deductible for taxes until paid. Income tax payable = $65,000(.30)		
2.	Future taxable difference: $10,000 prepaid insurance. (Future pretax accounting income will decrease relative to taxable income when the insurance expense is recognized for the books.) Future deductible difference: $15,000 contingent liability. (Future taxable income will recognize the loss as a deduction when paid reducing taxable income relative to pretax accounting income.)		
3.	Required ending deferred tax liability = $10,000(.35) = $3,500		
	Beginning deferred tax liability	(0)	
	Increase in deferred tax liability		3,500
4.	Required ending deferred tax asset = $15,000(.35) = $5,250		
	Beginning deferred tax asset	(0)	
	Increase in deferred tax asset		(5,250)
5.	Income Tax Expense		$17,750

Year 1 Tax Accrual Entry:

Income Tax Expense	17,750	
Deferred Tax Asset	5,250	
Deferred Tax Liability		3,500
Income Tax Payable		19,500

Current Provision of Income Tax Expense	$ 19,500
Less Deferred Provision ($5,250 − $3,500)	(1,750)
Equals Total Income Tax Expense	$17,750

Example
Year 2 Pretax Accounting Income $80,000
Depreciation for financial reporting and tax purposes on a plant asset purchased Year 2 will be:

Year	Book Depreciation	Tax Depreciation
2	$10,000	$16,000
3	10,000	9,000
4	10,000	5,000
Totals	$30,000	$30,000

$5,000 of municipal bond interest was received.

$8,000 worth of goods were sold on the installment basis. The entire amount is recognized in revenue for book purposes. No cash is collected in Year 2.

$11,000 of estimated warranty expense is recognized; $4,000 was spent to service claims.

Tax rates have not changed. Current and future years are taxed at 35%.

Steps:

To tax accrual entry

1. Taxable Income:

	To tax accrual entry
Pretax Accounting Income	$80,000
Municipal Bond Interest	(5,000)
Expiration of Prepaid Insurance from Year 1	10,000
Lawsuit Loss from Year 1, Paid in Year 2	(15,000)
Excess of Tax Depreciation over Book Depreciation	(6,000)
Installment Sales Revenue Recognized for Books	(8,000)
Excess of Warranty Expense over Warranty Deduction	7,000
Taxable Income	$63,000
Income Tax Payable = $63,000 × (.35) =	22,050

The expiration of the prepaid insurance from Year 1 reduced pretax accounting income but does not reduce taxable income in Year 2 because the entire prepayment was deducted in Year 1. The lawsuit loss was not recognized in pretax accounting income because it was recognized in Year 1. It is paid in Year 2 and therefore deducted in Year 2.

2. Future taxable differences:

	To tax accrual entry
Excess of book depreciation over tax depreciation	$ 6,000
Installment sales revenue to be recognized for tax	8,000
Total future taxable differences	$14,000
Future deductible difference:	
Excess of warranty expense over warranty deduction	$7,000

(Note that the temporary differences from Year 1 have reversed and no longer are "future" differences with respect to the end of Year 2.)

		To tax accrual entry
3. Required Ending Deferred Tax Liability = $14,000(.35) =	$4,900	
Beginning Deferred Tax Liability	(3,500)	
Increase in Deferred Tax Liability		1,400
4. Required ending deferred tax asset = $7,000(.35) =	$2,450	
Beginning deferred tax asset	(5,250)	
Decrease in deferred tax asset		2,800
5. Income Tax Expense		$26,250

Year 2 Tax Accrual Entry

Income Tax Expense	26,250	
Deferred Tax Asset		2,800
Deferred Tax Liability		1,400
Income Tax Payable		22,050

Current provision of income tax expense	$22,050
Plus deferred provision ($1,400 + $2,800)	4,200
Equals total income tax expense	$26,250

III. Tax Rate Considerations

A. As already discussed, the future enacted tax rate is used to measure the change in the deferred tax accounts for the year-end tax accrual entry.

B. When the tax rate is changed **during** the year, the new rate is applied as of the beginning of the year (estimate change) to recompute the deferred tax balances. This results in an immediate change to income tax expense. For annual reporting, the normal year-end tax accrual entry automatically accomplishes this effect.

C. Since 1/1/2018, corporations are taxed at a flat rate of 21%.

D. When a future temporary difference is expected to reverse at a different rate than the regular tax rate (for example, a capital gains rate), then the specific rate applying to the difference is used when measuring that portion of the change in the deferred tax account.

Valuation Allowance for Deferred Tax Assets

The reported amount of net deferred tax assets is the subject matter of this lesson.

After studying this lesson, you should be able to:

1. Determine when a valuation allowance is required for a deferred tax asset.

2. Describe the evidence used to determine whether a valuation allowance is required.

3. Explain the sources of support for the realization of a deferred tax asset.

4. Record the appropriate amount of a valuation allowance from given information.

I. Limitation on Deferred Tax Assets

A. A deferred tax asset, like any other asset, is an asset only if it has future benefit. A deferred tax asset will reduce income tax payments in the future, if there is taxable income in the future to reduce. (A few other sources of benefit exist as well but future taxable income is the main one).

B. When there is not a sufficient probability of realizing the deferred tax asset, a valuation allowance (contra account) is recorded to reduce the deferred tax asset to the amount expected to be realized.

II. Net Amount of Deferred Tax Asset Reported

A. **Definition—Realization** of a deferred tax asset means that the asset will provide its expected benefits.

B. When there is **at least a 50% chance of realizing** the deferred tax asset, it is reported free of any valuation account.

C. When there is less than a 50% chance of the deferred tax asset being fully realized, it is reported but also is reduced by a valuation allowance (contra to deferred tax asset) to the amount that has at least a 50% chance of being realized.

D. Another way to say this is: If, based on available evidence, it is more likely than not that some portion of the deferred tax asset will not be realized, the deferred tax asset is reduced by a valuation allowance to the amount more likely than not to be realized.

E. The valuation allowance account, if needed, is treated as a negative deferred tax asset account. The ending balance is the amount required at the end of a period, and the change in the valuation account is the increase or decrease from the previous period. Thus, the same process for updating deferred tax accounts applies to the valuation allowance account.

III. Assessing Whether a Valuation Allowance Valuation Account Is Needed

A. A valuation account is suggested if any of the following are present:

1. A history of unused net operating losses;

2. A history of operating losses;

3. Losses expected in future years; *or*

4. Very unfavorable contingencies.

B. Evidence suggesting that a valuation account is not needed must also be considered, as exemplified by the following:

1. Existing contracts or sales backlog will produce more than enough taxable income to realize the deferred tax asset.

2. An excess of appreciated asset value over the tax basis of the entity's net assets will produce more than enough taxable income to realize the deferred tax asset.

3. A strong earnings history suggests that taxable income in the future will be enough to realize the deferred tax asset.

C. Both positive and negative evidence is used when making the decision about whether to recognize a valuation allowance.

IV. Sources for Realizing the Deferred Tax Asset

A. If any one of the following sources is present in sufficient amount (to achieve the 50% threshold), then no valuation allowance is required. More than one source can be used to support a deferred tax asset.

1. Expectation of future taxable income;

2. Future taxable differences; *or*

3. Tax planning strategies.

B. First Source—The *first* source is the one most frequently used. If sufficient future taxable income is expected, then the deferred tax asset most likely will be realized. The deferred tax asset is credited upon realization, rather than crediting income taxes payable. No valuation account is necessary.

C. Second Source—The *second* source to realize a deferred tax asset involves offsetting future taxable differences (that would give rise to a deferred tax liability) with future deductible differences (that would give rise to a deferred tax asset). Assume a firm has a future $4,000 deductible temporary difference (giving rise to a $1,200 deferred tax asset assuming a 30% tax rate), and it also has a $6,000 future taxable difference. The deductible difference will cancel or offset $4,000 of the taxable difference. Both the deferred tax asset and deferred tax liability will be recorded, but the effect uses the deferred tax asset and no valuation allowance is needed.

D. Third Source—The *third* source, tax planning strategies, are actions that (1) must result in the realization of deferred tax assets, (2) might not be taken otherwise, and (3) are prudent and feasible.

V. Reporting the Deferred Tax Asset and Valuation Allowance

A. The full-deferred tax asset and valuation allowance are reported in the balance sheet. Alternatively, the deferred tax asset is reported net in the balance sheet with the footnotes reporting the full asset and the valuation allowance.

B. The valuation allowance is classified as is the deferred tax asset—noncurrent.

C. The tax rate used to measure the deferred tax asset is based on the source of realization. In other words use the enacted future years' tax rates, if available, to measure the deferred tax asset by multiplying the amount of the temporary difference expected to reverse in a given year by the enacted tax rate for that year. For example, a temporary difference of $1,000 is expected to revise next year when the enacted tax rate is 25%. The current year's tax rate is 30%. The deferred tax asset is $250 ($1,000 multiplied by 25%) because the company will use the enacted tax rate for the year in which the difference is expected to reverse to measure the deferred tax asset arising from that specific difference.

Uncertain Tax Positions

This lesson considers the accounting for beneficial tax positions that are uncertain.

After studying this lesson, you should be able to:

1. Determine the appropriate reporting when the chance of the position being *sustained is less than or equal to 50%*.

2. Record the resolution of the uncertainty for a tax position with less than or *equal to a 50% chance of being sustained.*

3. Prepare the journal entry when it is more likely than not that the position will be *sustained*.

4. Record the resolution of the uncertainty for a tax position with more than a *50% chance of being sustained*.

I. Uncertainty in Income Tax—The Issue

A. The preparation of a firm's tax return is affected by many estimates and uncertainties. Uncertain tax positions are those that may not be sustainable on audit by the IRS. Examples include uncertain deductions, tax credits, and revenue exemptions. The firm includes the uncertain position in its tax return thus reducing its income tax liability, but there remains uncertainty about the actual benefit of that deduction. If there is at least a one-third probability that the tax position will be sustained, there is no legal or professional censure for taking that position.

B. This lesson explains how the financial benefit of such uncertain tax positions is reported. Income tax expense is reduced (benefit recognized) for an uncertain tax position only if it is "more likely than not" (> 50%) that the position will be sustained upon audit by the IRS.

C. A two-step approach is applied: (1) Is the uncertain position more likely than not to be sustained?; (2) If yes, then a probabilistic approach is applied to determine the amount of benefit recognized in the current year.

II. Probability Less than or Equal to 50%

A. If it is **not** "more likely than not" that the position will be sustained upon audit by the IRS, then income tax expense is not reduced and an additional tax liability is recognized. No benefit is recognized in the current year.

Example
Taxable income is $20,000 and the tax rate is 30%. Taxable income reflects an uncertain deduction of $2,000. The firm believes there is less than a 50% chance of the $2,000 deduction being allowed.

Income tax expense	6,600	
Income tax payable ($20,000 × .30)		6,000
Liability for unrecognized tax benefit ($2,000 × .30)		600

Income tax expense is not reduced by the uncertain deduction—the deduction is not recognized in the financial statements. Upon resolution however, future income tax expense is reduced if the deduction is upheld.

The liability for unrecognized tax benefits should not be netted against deferred tax accounts. The reason for this second liability is that the firm is proceeding with the uncertain benefit on its tax return; thus the income tax payable reflects the uncertain deduction. The firm will pay only the smaller amount in the current year with resolution of the unrecognized benefit later. The above entry reflects the expectation that the firm will have to pay the additional $600 at a later date.

B. Resolution of the Uncertainty

1. If the deduction is disallowed, the journal entry in the year of resolution is:

Liability for unrecognized tax benefit	600	
Cash		600

Additional amounts may be due for interest and penalties. These amounts are recognized as an expense in the year of payment.

2. If all or a portion of the deduction is allowed, income tax expense is reduced in the year of payment (change in estimate) for the tax benefit received. Assume that $667 of the deduction was allowed (one-third of the $2,000 deduction taken) yielding a $200 reduction in the amount of tax due, and income tax expense ($667 × .30 = $200).

Liability for unrecognized tax benefit	600	
Cash		400
Income tax expense		200

III. Probability > 50%

A. If it **is** "more likely than not" that the position will be sustained upon audit by the IRS, then the firm must estimate specific outcomes of the audit and probabilities associated with each. The amount of benefit recognized is the largest amount for which the cumulative probability of realization exceeds 50%.

Example
Taxable income is $20,000 and the tax rate is 30%. Taxable income reflects an uncertain deduction of $2,000. The firm believes there is more than a 50% chance of a deduction in some amount being allowed. Estimated amounts of allowable deductions along with their probabilities appear below:

Amount Allowed	Probability	Cumulative Probability
$2,000	.15	.15
1,600	.20	.35
1,400	.30	.65
400	.20	.85
200	.15	1.00

The tax benefit recognized is based on the $1,400 amount, which is the largest amount for which the cumulative probability exceeds 50%. No reduction in income tax expense is recognized for the remaining portion of the deduction ($600).

Income tax expense	6,180	
Income tax payable ($20,000 × .30)		6,000
Liability for unrecognized tax benefit ($600 × .30)		180

Income tax expense is reduced by $420 as a result of the recognition of the current tax benefit associated with the $1,400 amount ($1,400 × .30 = $420).

B. The process of identifying outcomes and estimating probabilities must assume that the taxing authority will have full knowledge of the tax situation.

C. The classification of the liability for unrecognized tax benefit is based on the period of expected settlement. Tax cases often require more than one year for resolution. Therefore, the liability is classified as noncurrent unless there is reason to believe resolution will occur within one year of the balance sheet, in which case the liability is classified as current.

IV. Resolution of the Uncertainty

A. In a later year, if the expected $1,400 deduction is allowed:

Liability for unrecognized tax benefit	180	
Cash ($2,000 − $1,400).30		180

B. When the benefit recognized in income tax expense in a prior year is not the same amount as the final actual benefit determined upon resolution, the difference is recognized in income tax expense in the year of resolution (change in estimate).

1. If no deduction is allowed:

Income tax expense	420	
Liability for unrecognized tax benefit	180	
Cash ($2,000 × .30)		600

2. If a $1,600 deduction is allowed:

Liability for unrecognized tax benefit	180	
Income tax expense ($1,600 − $1,400) × .30		60
Cash ($2,000 − $1,600).30		120

3. If the entire $2,000 deduction is allowed:

Liability for unrecognized tax benefit	180	
Income tax expense ($2,000 − $1,400).30		180

V. The Same Approach Is Applied to Future Temporary Differences—For example, if there is uncertainty about the deductibility of a future deductible difference giving rise to a deferred tax asset, the same two-step approach is applied. The result is a reduced deferred tax asset, increased deferred tax liability, or both.

Net Operating Losses

The relevant provisions of the tax law and general accounting treatment are discussed in this lesson. It also illustrates the journal entries when a firm has a net operating loss. Other aspects including disclosures for taxes are discussed.

After studying this lesson, you should be able to:

1. Note the important footnote disclosures for income tax.

2. Record the journal entry for the carryforward of a net operating loss.

I. **Net Operating Losses**

    A. A net operating loss (NOL) is negative taxable income for a year—a loss for income tax purposes. An NOL occurs when taxable deductions exceed taxable revenues. This provision is solely within the tax code.

    B. The tax law allows an NOL to be carried forward indefinitely to reduce taxes in those years. A company may offset 80% of its taxable income each year as it applies the NOL carryforward. Therefore, even if a company has enough NOL to offset its entire taxable income in a given year, it is limited to offsetting 80% of the taxable income. Sometimes this is referred to as the 80% limitation.

    C. Recognition of the carryforward produces a deferred tax asset (DTA). Now there are two sources of DTAs: future deductible differences and tax loss carryforwards.

II. **Carryforward**—When a firm has an NOL, the firm will carryforward the NOL indefinitely to absorb future taxable income.

III. **Tax Credits**

    A. Some tax credits also have the carryback/carryforward feature and may expire more quickly than the NOL. Tax credits reduce income tax by the amount of the credit and are thus more valuable dollar for dollar. Thus, it may be advantageous to use prior year taxable income for these credits.

IV. **Cautions in Applying the NOL**

    A. An NOL absorbs taxable income through the carryforward feature, NOT income tax. A $10,000 NOL is worth only $3,000 to the firm if the tax rate is 30%.

    B. The taxable income of the earliest future year is absorbed first, in a carryforward. (FIFO)

    C. NOLs themselves are used on a FIFO basis. An NOL must be completely utilized before a later NOL can be carried forward.

    D. The positive taxable income of any year can be absorbed only once in the realization of the tax benefit of an NOL carryforward.

V. Example: NOL Carryforward

This example illustrates how an NOL carryforward operates. A firm's history of taxable income follows:

Year	Taxable Income	Tax Rate
A	$1,000	20%
B	2,000	25%
C	3,500	30%
D	4,000	35%
E	(11,000)	38%
F	1,500	40%
G	6,000	40%

A. Accounting for the Carryforward

1. The NOL is carried forward to years F and G absorbing the 80% of the taxable income in each of those years. In other words, the NOL offers 80% of the taxable income for Years F and G. The combined taxable income for the two years is $7,500. The NOL offsets $1,200 ($1,500 × 80%) in Year F and $4,800 ($6,000 × 80%) in Year G. Thus, $5,000 ($11,000 NOL − $6,000 NOL used in Years F and G) of the NOL remains to be carried forward to future years. The value to the firm of the remaining NOL at the end of year G is $2,000 ($5,000 × .40) assuming a future tax rate of 40%.

VI. Accounting for NOLs

A. Carryforward

1. A *carryforward* generates a deferred tax asset. This is the same account that is produced by future deductible differences. Both a carryforward of an NOL and a future deductible difference reduce future taxable income relative to pretax accounting income. The tax benefit of a carryforward is recognized in income in the period of the loss. The carryforward is recorded as follows (in the NOL year):

Deferred Tax Asset	(future enacted rate)(remaining NOL)
Income Tax Benefit	(future enacted rate)(remaining NOL)

2. The required amount of deferred tax asset from a carryforward contributes to the total required ending deferred tax asset balance, along with the future deductible differences. The deferred tax asset stemming from an NOL is subject to the valuation allowance requirements.

VII. Example—Accounting for NOL Carryforwards—The data from the previous example is repeated below. Assume no temporary or permanent differences (pretax income equals taxable income). The tax rates are enacted in the year before they are effective. For example, the tax rate listed for year F (40%) applies to year F but was enacted in year E. Assume sufficient estimated future taxable income to support a deferred tax asset. (No valuation allowance is required.)

Year	Taxable Income	Tax Rate
A	$1,000	20%
B	2,000	25%
C	3,500	30%
D	4,000	35%
E	(11,000)	38%
F	1,500	40%
G	6,000	40%

A. Carryforward

Year E Accounting:

Deferred tax asset	4,400	
Income Tax Benefit		4,400

The NOL carryforward results in a DTA of $4,400 = $11,000(.40).

Reported net income in year E is negative $6,600 (– $11,000 taxable income + $4,400 income tax benefit).

Year F Accounting:

$1,200 ($1,500 net income × 80% limitation) of the $11,000 NOL is used to absorb taxable income in year F, leaving

$9,800 to carry forward.

Required ending DTA balance:	$3,920	$9,800 remaining NOL × .40
Beginning DTA balance	4,400	
Decrease in DTA	$ 480	

Journal Entry:

Income tax expense	480	
Deferred tax asset		480

The firm pays $120 ($300 × .4) tax in year F.

Year G Accounting:

$4,800 ($6,000 × .8) of the remaining $9,800 NOL is used to absorb taxable income in year G leaving $5,000 to carry forward.

Required ending DTA balance:	$2,000	$5,000 remaining NOL × .40
Beginning DTA balance	3,920	
Decrease in DTA	$1,920	

Journal entry:

Income tax expense	1,920	
Deferred tax asset		1,920

The firm pays $480 (80% limitation applied to $6,000 in income leaves $1,200 in taxable income multiplied by 40% tax rate results in $480 in tax) tax in year G.

Caution: One of the most important aspects of NOL accounting illustrated by this example is to remember to first compute the ending DTA from the remaining NOL. Computing the amount of NOL "used up" by the current year's taxable income using the current year rate will not always yield the correct answer because the tax rate may have changed, as illustrated in this example.

VIII. NOLs and Temporary Differences

A. Temporary Differences and Carryforwards

Both (1) future deductible temporary differences and (2) NOL carryforwards give rise to the required ending deferred tax asset balance. Treat the remaining NOL carryforward amount just like you would a future deductible difference. Always compute the required ending deferred tax asset balance first. Then compare that amount to the beginning balance to determine the change—the amount to enter into the journal entry. The required ending deferred tax asset will reflect the remaining NOL.

> **Note**
> The NOL carryforward and the future deductible difference are treated the same way for purposes of computing the deferred tax asset balance.

 **Example**

A firm has the following beginning deferred tax account balances for the current year (year 3):

Deferred tax liability	$4,000
Deferred tax asset	6,000

The tax rate for year 3 is 40%, and the enacted tax rate for future years is 30%. At the end of year 3, the firm anticipates the following future temporary differences:

Taxable	$5,600
Deductible	3,000

The firm's tax return shows an NOL of $30,000 in year 3 (negative taxable income). Note that the computation of the ending deferred tax liability and asset balances are independent. They do not interact.

Required ending deferred tax liability: $5,600(.30) =	$1,680
Beginning deferred tax liability	4,000
Decrease in deferred tax liability	$2,320
Required ending deferred tax asset = ($3,000 + $30,000)(.30) =	$9,900
Beginning deferred asset	6,000
Increase in deferred tax asset	3,900

Entry for year 3:

Deferred tax asset	3,900	
Deferred tax liability	2,320	
Income tax benefit		6,220

B. Disclosures for Income Taxes

1. Current and deferred portions of income tax expense

2. Any investment tax credits and other credits taken

3. Benefits of operating tax loss carryforwards and, remaining amounts

4. Government grants to the extent they are used to reduce income tax

5. Adjustments to deferred tax accounts (and valuation allowance) as a result of a change in enacted tax rates or tax status of the firm

6. Total of all deferred tax liabilities

7. Total of all deferred tax assets

8. Total valuation allowance recognized for deferred tax assets

9. Net change in the valuation allowance

10. Approximate tax effect of each type of temporary difference (and carryforward)

11. Reconciliation of reported income tax expense on income from continuing operations, with the tax that would have resulted from applying the statutory tax rate to income from continuing operations

12. Any change in the tax status of the firm

Accounting Changes and Error Corrections

Types of Changes and Accounting Approaches

This is the first of several lessons addressing accounting changes. This lesson provides a description of the types of changes and of the accounting approaches that apply to them.

After studying this lesson, you should be able to:

1. Identify the types of accounting changes allowed by GAAP.

2. Note the available accounting approaches.

3. Choose the appropriate accounting approach for a given accounting change.

4. List items that do not qualify as accounting principle changes.

5. Contrast the basic aspects of the two available accounting approaches.

6. Distinguish direct and indirect effects of accounting principle changes.

I. **Background and Summary**

   A. **Accounting Changes and Error Corrections**—GAAP specifies how to account for changes in accounting. The four items addressed:

      1. Accounting principle changes (example: change from FIFO to weighted-average method)

      2. Accounting estimate changes (example: change the useful life of a plant asset)

      3. Changes in reporting entity (example: change in the composition of the subsidiary group in a consolidated enterprise)

      4. Corrections of errors in prior financial statements (example: discover that an item expensed in a prior year should have been capitalized and amortized)

   B. Error corrections are not considered an accounting change but the procedures for recording are the same as for accounting principle changes and thus are covered in this set of lessons.

II. **Accounting Approaches are Specified for Accounting Changes and Errors**

   A. **Retrospective**—Application of a principle to prior periods as if that principle had always been used. The procedure records the effect of the change on prior years as an adjustment to the beginning balance in retained earnings for the year of change rather than in income; prior year financial statements reported comparatively with the current year statements are adjusted to reflect the new method. The result is that the financial statements of all periods presented reflect the same (new) accounting principle. Retrospective application enhances comparability (a quality from the conceptual framework) across the financial statements of different years reported comparatively. Therefore the term *retrospective application* implies that the company applied the new standard it adopted to all periods shown unless it was impracticable to determine the cumulative effect or the period-specific change. When there is retrospective application the entity must disclose the effects on income and income taxes.

   B. **Prospective**—Apply the change to current and future periods only; prior year statements are unaffected.

   C. **Restatement** is the term reserved specifically for error changes. Restatement requires correcting the comparative financial information presented along with correcting the opening retained earnings balance. The entity must disclose the nature of the error and the effect on current and prior periods.

III. **Summary of Accounting**—The following summarizes the types of items found in the accounting changes area, and the associated accounting approach.

Accounting Change or Item	Accounting Approach
Accounting principle change	Retrospective
Accounting principle change—determining prior year effects impracticable	Prospective
Accounting estimate change*	Prospective
Change in reporting entity	Retrospective
Correction of accounting error	Restatement**

*Includes changes in depreciation, amortization and depletion methods, which are treated as a change in estimate effected by a change in accounting principle.

**This is the same accounting procedure as retrospective but the difference in terminology highlights the distinction between a voluntary accounting principle change and the correction of an error, called a prior period adjustment.

IV. **Accounting for Principle Changes—Retrospective Application**

Definition

Change in Accounting Principle: A change from one generally accepted accounting principle to another when there are at least two acceptable principles, or when the current principle used is no longer generally accepted. A change in the method of **applying** a principle is also considered a change in accounting principle.

Example
Changing inventory cost flow assumption (LIFO to FIFO); changing the accounting for long-term construction contracts (completed contract to percentage of completion), change in method of applying LC-M / LC-NRV to inventory (individual, group, aggregate).

A. Changes in depreciation method, amortization method, and depletion method are treated as **estimate changes**.

B. The following are **not accounting principle changes:**

1. Initial adoption of a new principle to new events for the first time or for events that were immaterial in their effect in the past

Example
Capitalizing interest for the first time because in the past the firm was not involved in construction activities to a significant extent. This is not an accounting principle change.

2. Adoption or modification of a principle for transactions that are clearly different in substance from those in the past

3. A change in method that is a planned procedure as part of the normal application of a method (example: the change to the straight-line method late in the life of an asset depreciated on the double-declining balance method)

4. The change from a principle that is not generally accepted to one that is accepted (treat as an error correction)

C. Retrospective Application—The following steps are performed to implement retrospective application of an accounting principle change.

1. The cumulative effect of the change on periods before those presented is reflected in the carrying amounts of affected assets and liabilities as of the beginning of the earliest period presented, along with an offsetting adjustment to the opening balance of retained earnings for that period.

2. The financial statements for prior periods presented comparatively are recast to reflect the period-specific effects of applying the new principle. Each account affected by the change is adjusted as if the new method had been used in those periods.

3. Through a journal entry, the beginning balance of retained earnings in the year of the change is adjusted to reflect the use of the new principle through that date. The amount of this cumulative effect is generally not the same amount as that for Step 1 above because different periods are covered in each.

Example

In 20X5, a firm changes from the weighted-average (WA) method of accounting for inventory to FIFO. The 20X3 and 20X4 reports reissued comparatively with 20X5 will now reflect the FIFO method even though in those prior years the WA had been used. The journal entry to record the change will adjust beginning 20X5 inventory and retained earnings to the amounts that would have been in those accounts at that date had FIFO always been used (this is the cumulative effect recorded in the entry, through 1/1/X5). In the retained earnings statement, the beginning balance in retained earnings for 20X3 will be adjusted for the effects of the change on income for all years before 20X3 (this is the cumulative effect reported in the retained earnings statement, through 1/1/X3). The two cumulative effect amounts cover different numbers of years.

D. Justification for Principle Change—An accounting principle change can be made only if the change is required by a new pronouncement, or if the entity can justify the use of an allowable new principle on the basis that it is preferable in terms of financial reporting. The allowable new principle must improve financial reporting given the environment of the firm. Common justifications include changing business conditions, and better matching of revenues and expenses.

1. Caution: When new accounting standards are adopted, retrospective application may not be required, even though the standard may require that a new accounting principle or method be applied. In such cases, the transitional guidance of the new standard is to be followed.

E. Direct and Indirect Effects—Retrospective application of a change in accounting principle is limited to the direct effects of the change and related tax effects. *Direct effects* are those recognized changes in assets or liabilities necessary to effect the change (e.g., the change to inventory due to change in cost flow assumption). Related effects on deferred tax accounts, or an impairment adjustment resulting from applying LC-M valuation to the new inventory balance are also examples of direct effects.

1. *Indirect effects* are changes in current or future cash flows resulting from making a change in accounting principle applied retrospectively. Such changes are recognized in the period of change. Prior period financial statements are not adjusted although a description of the effects, amounts and per share amounts are disclosed in the footnotes.

Example
A change in nondiscretionary profit-sharing plan resulting from a principle change affecting earnings causes the firm to increase profit-sharing payments in the current period as a result of restating prior period income. The payments are recognized in the current year, not retrospectively.

2. Litigation settlements from lawsuits initiated in previous years but paid or received in the current year are also not treated retrospectively. They are considered an event of the period of settlement and included in that period's earnings.

F. **Disclosures for Principle Changes**—Disclosures in the year of change and also the interim period of change include the following. Subsequent financial statements need not repeat these disclosures.

1. Nature and reason for the change including why the new change is preferable (a change caused by the adoption of a new standard is sufficient justification)

2. Method of applying the change

3. For current and prior periods retrospectively adjusted, the effect of the change on income from continuing operations and net income, and all other affected line items (for income statement, balance sheet, and statement of cash flows), and any affected per-share amounts. A firm may provide only the line item information, or may disclose the entire statements as adjusted, in the notes

4. The cumulative effect on retained earnings (or other relevant equity accounts) as of the beginning of the earliest period presented

5. If it was not practicable to apply the retrospective method to all periods, the reasons why and a description of the alternative method used to report the change

6. Summaries of financial results (such as major financial statement subtotals for the previous ten years) as reported in the notes are also retrospectively adjusted for the change

Retrospective Application

After studying this lesson, you should be able to:

1. Record the journal entry for an accounting principle change.

2. Discuss how prior year financial statements are recast for reporting in the year of change.

3. Prepare the comparative retained earnings statements for an accounting principle change.

4. Explain the modifications to the procedures when it is impracticable to determine prior year effects.

I. Accounting Principle Change—Retrospective Application

A. A firm changed its method of inventory valuation from WA (weighted-average) to FIFO in 20X8 and reports the previous two years' financial statements comparatively with 20X8. The change was made for financial reporting purposes only. Management believes that the FIFO method more accurately portrays the movement of goods and provides a better matching of revenues and expenses. The income tax rate is 40%. Net income for 20X8 as computed under WA would have been $12,000. The retained earnings balance at the beginning of 20X6 was $42,000. The firm has not declared dividends during the last four years.

	Ending inventory balances		Income recomputed under
	WA	**FIFO**	**FIFO**
20X8	$56,000	$68,000	$14,400
20X7	42,000	50,000	12,800
20X6	30,000	34,000	10,200
20X5	25,000	27,000	

B. Journal Entry to Record the Principle Change:

1/1X8		
Inventory ($50,000 − $42,000)	8,000	
Cumulative effect of accounting change (.60 × $8,000)		4,800
Deferred income tax liability		3,200

C. **The Cumulative Effect**—Is closed to retained earnings. It does not appear in the income statement. The $8,000 amount is the difference in total pretax income for the firm from its beginning to 12/31/x7 between WA and FIFO. If the firm had been on FIFO for those years, then cost of goods sold for those years would have been $8,000 less because FIFO ends that period with $8,000 more inventory.

   1. The accounting change increases income for financial reporting in years before 20X8. Therefore, income tax expense has increased for those years causing the deferred tax liability to increase as well through the beginning of 20X8.

D. The 20X8 journal involving inventory and cost of goods sold will reflect the FIFO method.

E. Comparative Statements

1. The income statements and balance sheets for 20X7 and 20X6 will now report cost of sales, income, inventory, and any other related account based on the FIFO method.

2. 20X8 statements reflect the application of the FIFO method.

3. The retained earnings statement reports the effect of the change on income for all years before 20X6. The income amounts reported in the statement reflect the FIFO method.

F. Retained Earnings Statements

	20X8	20X7	20X6
Retained earnings, January 1			$42,000
			1,200*
	$66,200	$53,400	$43,200
Net income	14,400	12,800	10,200
Retained earnings, December 31	$80,600	$66,200	$53,400

*Post-tax difference in beginning 20X6 inventory amounts ($27,000 − $25,000) x .6 = $1,200. Note that the $1,200 amount is the reported cumulative effect and is different from the $4,800 amount recorded. The income amounts shown for 20X6 and 20X7 are the updated amounts reflecting FIFO and thus update the retained earnings balances subsequent to the 1/1/X6 retained earnings balance. Ultimately, by 1/1/X8, a $4,800 increase is reflected in the retained earnings balances reported.

II. Inability to Determine Prior Year Effects—It is not always possible to apply a method retrospectively because required information is not available. In such cases, the usual procedures are not applied.

Example
The change to LIFO requires the firm to apply LIFO all the way back to the beginning of the firm (or a point at which there was no inventory). The procedure requires the identification of cost layers for any prior year for which inventory increased in physical amount. This information may be difficult or impossible to obtain. Purchase price information may no longer be available. Even more challenging would be to apply LIFO retrospectively in a manufacturing context where possibly hundreds of different items are integrated into many different products.

A. Impracticability Exception—The retrospective approach is not to be applied if any of the following applies:

1. After making a reasonable effort to apply the principle to prior periods, the entity is unable to do so.

2. Assumptions about management's intent in prior periods are required and such assumptions cannot be independently substantiated.

3. Retrospective application requires estimates of amounts based on information that was unavailable in the prior periods or on circumstances that did not exist in the prior periods.

B. **Two Impracticability Cases**

1. When it is impracticable to determine the period-specific effects of the change for one or more prior periods presented, the change is applied as of the beginning of the earliest period for which retrospective application is practicable (which may be the current period).

2. When the cumulative effect as of the beginning of the current period cannot be determined, then the change is made prospectively as of the earliest date possible.

Example

A firm changes from FIFO to LIFO in 20X4, but the cumulative effect for prior years cannot be determined. However, records enable the firm to apply LIFO beginning in 20X1. The FIFO ending inventory balance for 20X0 is used as the beginning LIFO balance for 20X1. LIFO is applied from that point. No cumulative effect is recorded.

III. Change in Reporting Entity—Retrospective Application

A. **Change in Reporting Entity**—A change in reporting entity results in financial statements of a different reporting entity. A change in reporting entity is limited mainly to:

1. Presenting consolidated or combined financial statements in place of financial statements of individual entities

2. Changing the set of subsidiaries that make up a consolidated group

3. Changing the entities included in combined financial statements

B. A business combination accounted for by the purchase method, or the consolidation of a variable interest entity is not a change in reporting entity.

C. **Retrospective Method**—The retrospective method is applied (not considered a restatement of prior financial statements). Prior financial statements are recast as if the new entity existed in those prior periods.

D. **Disclosures Required for Current Period**—(Subsidiary subsequent financial statements need not repeat these disclosures).

1. Nature of the change and reason for it

2. Effect of the change on income from continuing operations, net income, other comprehensive income, and related per-share amounts

Prospective Application

This lesson provides detailed guidance on how to account for accounting principle changes.

After studying this lesson, you should be able to:

1. Identify accounting estimate changes.

2. Prepare the appropriate reporting for estimate changes.

3. Account for changes in depreciation, amortization and depletion methods.

I. Accounting for Estimate Changes—Prospective Application

Definition

Change in Accounting Estimate: Is derived from new information and is a change that causes the carrying amount of an asset or liability to change, or that changes the subsequent accounting for an asset or liability. Estimate changes are the most frequent type of accounting change.

Example
Most areas within financial accounting are subject to estimation. Bad debts, warranties, depreciation, pension accounting, lower of cost or market, asset impairment, and many others are examples.

A. Recall that this category of accounting change—**estimate changes**—now also includes changing a method of depreciation, amortization, or depletion. Such a principle change cannot be distinguished from a change in estimate, because the method change reflects a change in the expected pattern of benefits to be received from the asset in the future. Therefore, a change in depreciation method is considered to be a change in estimate affected by a change in accounting principle.

   1. In general, when a change in principle cannot be distinguished from a change in estimate, the change is treated as a change in estimate (prospectively). For example, a cost that has been capitalized and amortized in the past is now expensed immediately because future benefits are no longer probable. The change to immediate expensing is treated as a change in estimate (no future periods are expected to benefit).

B. **Prospective Application**—Changes in accounting estimate are accounted for in the current and future periods (if affected). Prior period statements are not affected in anyway nor are there disclosures with respect to prior statements. The new information prompting the change was not known until the current year and is not relevant to prior periods.

   1. There is no *cumulative effect* account for estimate changes.

   2. For estimate changes affecting only the current period, the new estimate is used and the usual accounting procedure applies.

   3. For changes affecting current and future periods, the book value of the relevant account at the beginning of the current year is used as the basis for applying the new estimate.

   4. For changes in method of depreciation, amortization, or depletion, the book value at the beginning of the current period is used as the basis for expense recognition over the asset's remaining useful life, along with new estimates of salvage value and useful life if necessary. The new method is applied as of the beginning of the period of change.

C. **Disclosures for Estimate Changes**—For the current period, the following are required:

1. Effect of the change on income from continuing operations, net income, and related per-share amounts for the period of change for estimate changes affecting current and future periods

2. For estimate changes affecting only the period of change, the above disclosures are required only if material.

D. **Numerical Example—Change in Estimate of Useful Life**—In 20X8, a firm using the sum-of-years-digits (SYD) method of depreciation changed the total useful life of a plant asset (cost $19,000; residual value $4,000) from ten years to five years. The revised estimate of residual value is $1,000. The asset was purchased 1/1/X5.

Example

Original SYD = 1 + 2 + ... + 9 + 10 = 55

Revised SYD = 1 + 2 = 3 (only two years remain in revised useful life at 1/1/X8)

Book value at 1/1/X8 = $19,000 − ($19,000 − $4,000)[(10+9+8)/55] = $11,636

Depreciation for 20X8 = ($11,636 − $1,000)*[(2/3)] = $7,091

Journal entry for depreciation, 12/31/X8

Depreciation expense	7,091	
Accumulated depreciation		7,091

If the estimates were not changed, depreciation in 20X8 would have been: ($19,000 − $4,000)(7/55) = $1,909. The increase in depreciation is $7,091 − $1,909 = $5,182. Assume a 30% tax rate. The decrease in income for the current year due to the estimate change is .70($5,182) = $3,627.

Footnote: During the current year, the useful life and salvage values of equipment were reduced resulting in a decrease in current year income of $3,627.

E. **Numerical Example—Change in Depreciation Method**—In 20X6, management changes from the double-declining balance method (DDB) to the straight-line method (SL) to reflect new information suggesting that the asset will provide more uniform benefits and for a longer period of time than originally expected. The affected asset was purchased at the beginning of 20X5 for $22,000. Original estimates were: 5-year total useful life; $2,000 residual value. As of the beginning of 20X6, the revised estimates are: 9-year total useful life; $200 residual value.

Example

Book value at 1/1/X6 = $22,000 − $22,000(2/5) = $13,200

Depreciation for 20X6 = ($13,200 − $200)/(9 − 1) = $1,625

(at the beginning of 20X6, eight years remain in the asset's useful life)

Journal entry for depreciation, 12/31/X6

Depreciation expense	1,625	
Accumulated depreciation		1,625

The same entry would be recorded for the remaining seven years of the asset's life after 20X6 unless additional estimate or method changes were made.

Accounting Errors—Restatement

The final lesson on accounting changes considers errors affecting income of prior periods.

After studying this lesson, you should be able to:

1. Identify when an error has occurred, and if it affects income of prior periods.

2. Record a prior period adjustment from given information.

3. Describe how statements of prior periods are restated for an error correction.

4. Determine when a prior period adjustment is recorded in a journal entry, and when it is reported in the retained earnings statement.

I. **Correction of Error in Prior Financial Statements—Restatement**

A. **Error in Prior-Period Financial Statements**—An error in a prior-period financial statement is caused when information existed at the time the statements were prepared enabling correct reporting, but a misstatement was made causing erroneous recognition, measurement, or disclosure. The presumption is that the correct reporting could have been accomplished in the past. Errors made in the current year but discovered before the closing process are corrected without special procedures.

1. Recall that the change from an inappropriate accounting principle to one that is generally accepted is considered an error correction.

2. Changes in estimates that reflect negligence or those that were made in bad faith are also considered error corrections.

B. **Restatement of Prior Financial Statements**—Although not an accounting change, an error correction uses the same accounting procedures as accounting principle changes and is addressed by the same accounting standard. However, the term *restatement* is used rather than *retrospective application* to distinguish voluntary principle changes from restatements due to errors and to reduce potential confusion between the two.

C. The procedure for **error corrections** is the same as for retrospective application except for the use of the term *restatement*.

1. The effect of the error correction on periods before those presented is reflected in the affected real accounts as of the beginning of the earliest period presented, including an adjustment to the opening balance of retained earnings (prior period adjustment) for that period, for the effect of the change on all periods before that date.

2. The financial statements for prior periods presented comparatively are recast to reflect the effect of the error correction.

3. Through a journal entry, the beginning balance of retained earnings in the year of the correction is adjusted to reflect the correct accounting through that date (prior period adjustment).

D. **Numerical Example**—In 20X8, a firm discovered that in 20X5, a cash advance of $600,000 received from a client as a prepayment for advertising services was credited to revenue. The contract called for the firm to provide services evenly over thefive years ending 12/31/X9. Net income for 20X7 was $300,000 and for 20X8 was $400,000 before the error correction. The retained earnings (RE) balance 1/1/X7 was $800,000. 20X8 and 20X7 are shown comparatively in 20X8 annual report. No dividends were paid in either year. Ignore income tax effects.

Examples
1. **Journal entry to record the error correction:**

1/1/X8:

Prior period adjustment	240,000	
Unearned revenue		240,000

The prior period adjustment is closed to retained earnings.

2. **Analysis of error:**

(annual revenue = $120,000 = ($600,00/5))

Amount of revenue recorded through 1/1/X8:	$600,000
Correct amount of revenue earned through 1/1/X8:	
$120,000(3 years)	360,000
Overstatement of RE at 1/1/X8	$240,000
(this is the prior period adjustment through 1/1/X8)	
Amount of revenue recorded through 1/1/X7:	$600,000
Correct amount of revenue earned through 1/1/X7:	
$120,000(2 years)	240,000
Overstatement of RE at 1/1/X7	$360,000
(this is the prior period adjustment through 1/1/X7)	

3. **Corrected net income amounts:**

20X8: $400,000 + $120,000 = $520,000 (correct)
20X7: $300,000 + $120,000 = $420,000 (correct)

4. **Journal entry 12/31/X8:**

Unearned revenue	120,000	
Revenue		120,000

5. **Comparative statements:** The 20X7 statements will be recast to show the corrected amounts of unearned revenue, revenue, and other affected accounts.

6. **Retained Earnings Statements**

	20X8	20X7
Retained earnings, January 1		$800,000
Prior period adjustment, error correction		(360,000)
Retained earnings, January 1, as corrected	$ 860,000	440,000
Net income	520,000	420,000
E 12/31	$1,380,000	$860,000

Footnote: The firm discovered an error in recognizing revenue recorded in 20X5 and has restated the financials for 20X7 and 20X8. The error understated income for 20X7 previously reported by $120,000.

7. The amount of the prior period adjustment to the beginning balance of retained earnings for each year shown is to be reported. For consistency with accounting principle changes, this example reports the adjustment only for the earliest year reported in the retained earnings statement. Firms may report the other amounts in the footnotes.

   E. Disclosures for Error Corrections—Disclosures in the period of correction include the following. Subsequent financial statements need not repeat these disclosures.

      1. A statement that previous financial statements were restated, and the nature of the error

      2. Effect of the correction on each financial statement line item and related per share amounts for each prior period presented

      3. The total cumulative effect of the change on retained earnings as of the beginning of the first period presented

      4. Pre- and post-tax effects of the correction on net income for each prior period presented

II. Counter-Balancing Errors—Many accounting errors counterbalance or *self-correct* after a certain period of time if they are not corrected. These errors require no entry to correct retained earnings or other current account balance after the error counterbalances. However, prior year financial statements remain in error.

Example

1. In counting its ending inventory for the 20X3 accounting year, one row of merchandise in the warehouse was counted twice. The result of this error is that ending inventory for 20X3 was overstated by $5,000. The error was detected on December 28, 20X7. Ignore income tax considerations.

20X3 effects:

*ending inventory is overstated $5,000

*cost of goods sold is understated $5,000

*net income is overstated $5,000

*ending retained earnings is overstated $5,000

20X4 effects:

*beginning inventory is overstated $5,000

*cost of goods sold is overstated $5,000

*net income is understated $5,000

*ending retained earnings is now correct because the income effects for 20X3 and 20X4 cancel each other

The error was detected on December 28, 20X7. At that time, the balance in retained earnings was correct, and no correcting entry is needed. Most likely, neither the 20X3 nor 20X4 statements will be reissued comparatively with those of 20X7—no prior year financial statements require restatement.

2. However, now assume the same error was discovered in 20X4 instead. Beginning retained earnings is overstated $5,000, and beginning inventory for 20X4 is overstated. The following entry is required and illustrates a prior period adjustment:

As of 1/1/X4:

Prior period adjustment	5,000	
Inventory		5,000

Although this is a counterbalancing error, if it is discovered before it has a chance to counterbalance, an error-correcting entry is needed.

Business Combinations

Introduction to Business Combinations

This lesson addresses accounting requirements when control is acquired and, therefore, a business combination has occurred. This lesson also discusses that one of the elements in determining the correct accounting to use for a business combination is the legal form that the combination takes. When a business combination occurs, the operating results of two or more entities are combined. This lesson considers the determination of combined operating results of entities included in a business combination as of the date of the business combination and at the end of subsequent periods.

After studying this lesson, you should be able to:

1. Define *business combination* and identify the elements in that definition.

2. Distinguish the type of accounting required for each of the legal forms of a business combination.

3. Identify when a business combination is effected via a transaction or event.

4. Understand what constitutes the consolidated income of affiliated entities: (a) as of the date of the business combination, (b) as of the end of the period of the combination, and (c) for periods subsequent to the period of the combination.

I. **Definition**—*A business combination* is a **transaction or an event** in which an acquirer obtains **control** of a **business**. First we break down each of the significant components of this definition.

   A. A **transaction** is when there is an exchange of consideration between two parties. A transaction where consideration is paid to the acquiree is the typical way a business combination occurs. However, a business combination can be completed when an **event** occurs where one party gains control over another party without an exchange of consideration.

      1. For example, in the diagram below, Co A is a 40% owner with veto rights and Co B is a 60% owner of Co C. The veto rights require that Co A be in agreement with any major decisions made by Co B. Since Co A has veto rights, Co B does not control Co C. However, if Co A's veto rights expire, then Co B would obtain control of Co C.

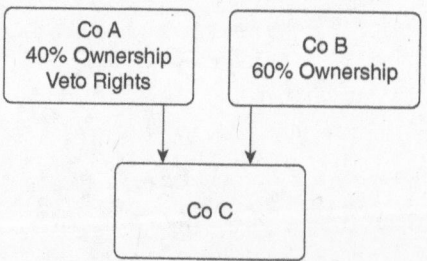

   B. **Control** is defined as voting control and is essentially greater than 50% voting interest.

   C. A **business** is defined as "an integrated set of activities and assets that is capable of being conducted and managed for the purpose of providing a return..." This definition means that the set of activities and assets does not need to be profitable to be considered a business. A start-up company that has yet to generate profits would be considered a business.

1. Because this definition is quite broad, the FASB issued ASU 2017-01 that provides a screen to determine if the group of assets is not a business (eligible for testing on the CPA exam on or after January 1, 2018). The screen states that if "substantially all of the fair value of the gross assets acquired is concentrated in a single identifiable asset or group of similar assets, the set is not a business." This screening means that if the acquisition value is concentrated in only one type of asset, then the acquisition is an asset acquisition, not a business combination.

2. If the screen is not met (all the value is not concentrated) and there are no outputs, the acquisition would be a business if there is an input and substantive process that together contribute to the ability to create an output. Outputs are not required for the set of assets to be a business. But the set must be evaluated to determine if there are both an input and substantive process (e.g., an assembled work force).

3. Why is it important to distinguish between the acquisition of a business versus a group of assets? Because the accounting is quite different. As discussed in these lessons, the accounting for a business combination is quite specific and may result in the recognition of goodwill. There is no goodwill recognized in an asset acquisition.

II. Business Combination Overview

A. The diagram below summarizes the alternative issues and treatments in accounting for business combinations. Specifically, this diagram, is used to show (1) the relationships between the legal forms of business combinations, (2) the use of the acquisition method of accounting to record those combinations, (3) whether consolidated financial statements will be required, and (4) the accounting methods the parent may use to carry its investment in the subsidiary on its (parent's) books prior to preparing consolidated financial statements.

B. The lessons in this section ("Business Combinations") describe and illustrate the accounting treatments for the alternatives depicted in this model. One of the fundamental differences in treatments derives from differences in the legal form of a business combination, as shown in the second column (from the left) in the model.

C. This overview should be used as a frame of reference as you study the lessons in this section.

III. Introduction to Legal Forms of Business Combinations—The legal form of a business combination is concerned with the legal (or statutory) means by which businesses are combined or come under common control. Although the legal form of a combination is distinct from the accounting treatment of the combination, the legal form will determine certain aspects of accounting for a combination.

    A. Legal Forms of Business Combinations—The three legal forms of business combinations are merger, consolidation, and acquisition.

        1. Merger—One preexisting entity acquires either a group of assets that constitute a business or controlling equity interest of another preexisting entity and "collapses" the acquired assets or entity into the acquiring entity.

           a. Graphic illustration

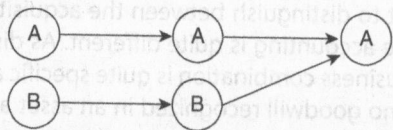

           b. Note: Only one entity (A) survives. (B) (a group of assets or another entity) ceases to exist separate from (A).

        2. Consolidation—A new entity consolidates the net assets or the equity interests of two (or more) preexisting entities.

           a. Graphic illustration

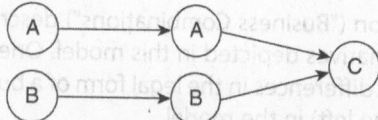

           b. Note: Only one entity (new C) exists; it consolidated the net assets or equity interests of (A) and (B) into it. (A) and (B) cease to exist as legal entities.

        3. Acquisition—One preexisting entity acquires controlling equity interest of another preexisting entity, but both continue to exist and operate as separate legal entities.

           a. Graphic illustration

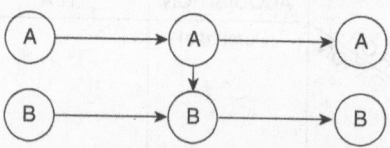

           b. Note: Both entities survive, with (A) owning controlling interest in (B). Both (A) and (B) continue to exist and operate as separate legal entities.

    B. Legal Merger/Consolidation—In a legal merger or consolidation, all of the assets and liabilities of the acquiree are recorded on the acquirer's general ledger.

        1. The acquirer records the group of assets or the assets and liabilities of the acquiree(s) onto its books. (The acquiree will no longer exist.)

Example Entry:

DR: Assets received $_____ (per Acquisition Method)

    CR: Liabilities assumed $_____ (per Acquisition Method)

    CR: Consideration given $_____ (at date of acquisition)

2. The legal form—merger or combination—determines the kinds of accounts (i.e., various assets and liabilities) used to record the combination.

3. The acquisition method of accounting determines the values to be used in the combination entry. (Determination of those values is covered in detail in later lessons.)

4. After this type of combination, only one entity exists, therefore there is no need to prepare Consolidated Financial Statements.

C. **Legal Acquisition**—In a legal acquisition, one entity (the acquirer) buys controlling interest (> 50%) of the voting stock of a target entity (the acquiree) and both entities (acquiring and acquired entities) continue as separate legal and accounting entities.

   1. The acquirer records its ownership of the stock of the acquiree as a long-term investment.

      a. The acquirer does **not** record (pick up) on its books the assets and liabilities of the acquiree.

      b. The assets and liabilities of the acquiree stay on that entity's (separate) books.

Example Entry:

DR: Investment in subsidiary $_____(Per Acquisition Method)

    CR: Consideration given $_____(at date of Acquisition)

---

      c. The legal form—acquisition—determines the kind of asset (an investment!) used to record the combination.

      d. The acquisition method of accounting determines the values to be used in the combination entry. (Determination of those values is covered in detail in later lessons.)

      e. Since, after an acquisition, two entities exist, one controlled by the other, an acquisition usually **does** require preparation of Consolidated Financial Statements, those of the acquirer together with those of the acquiree(s).

D. **Income Determination at Date of Combination**

   1. Only the acquirer's (acquiring firm's) operating results (income/loss) up to the date of combination enter into determination of consolidated net income **as of the date of the combination**.

   2. The acquiree's (acquired firm's) operating results (income/loss) up to the date of combination are part of what the acquirer purchases when it acquires the acquiree (i.e., makes its investment in the acquiree), and are not part of consolidated net income as of the date of combination.

      a. The acquiree's operating results up to the date of the combination will be closed (or treated as closed) to its retained earnings.

      b. The acquiree's retained earnings as of the date of the combination is part of the equity "paid for" by the acquirer when it makes its investment.

      c. The acquiree's retained earnings as of the date of the combination will be part of the acquiree's equity eliminated against the acquirer's investment account in the consolidating process. (The consolidating process is covered as the next major topic.)

IV. Income Determination at the End of the Year of Combination and Subsequent Years

    A. Income at the end of the period (e.g., year) of combination: The acquirer's operating results (income/loss) for the entire year **plus** the acquiree's operating results (income/loss) **after the date of the combination** enter into the determination of consolidated income for the year of combination.

    B. Income for periods (e.g., years) subsequent to combination: In periods subsequent to the period in which the combination occurs, both the acquirer's and the acquiree's operating results (income/loss) for the entire reporting period enter into the determination of consolidated net income or loss.

V. Summary of Determining Income/Loss Associated with a Business Combination—The following timeline graphic summarizes what operating results are included or excluded in determining consolidated income or loss following a business combination. The timeline should be read from left to right.

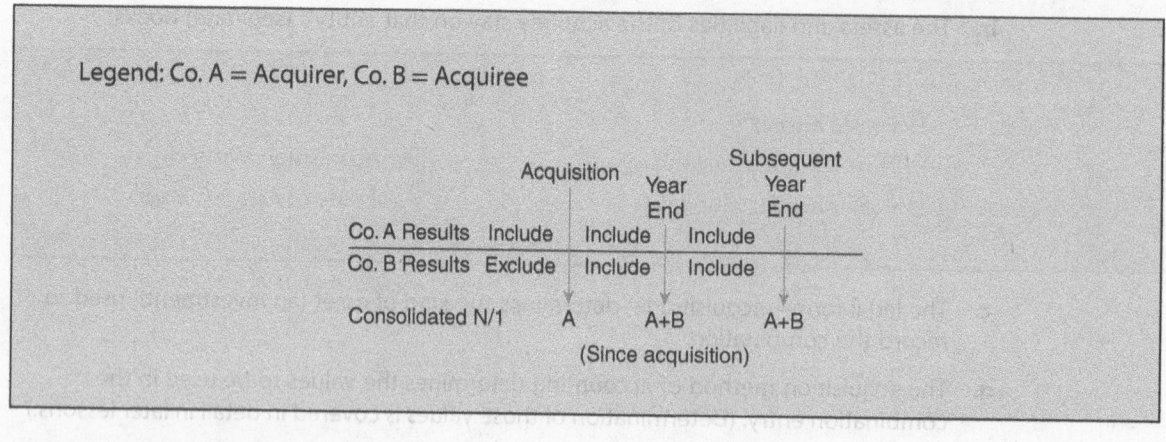

Acquisition Method of Accounting

Introduction to the Acquisition Method of Accounting

Application of the acquisition method of accounting to a business combination involves several requirements: (1) Identifying the acquirer, (2) Determining the acquisition date and measurement period, (3) Determining the cost of the acquisition, (4) Recognizing and measuring the assets acquired, liabilities assumed, and noncontrolling interest in the acquiree, and (5) Recognizing and measuring any goodwill or bargain purchase amount. This lesson covers the first and second of those requirements.

Subsequent lessons cover the remaining acquisition requirements and related issues.

After studying this lesson, you should be able to:

1. List the steps for applying the acquisition method of accounting to a business combination.

2. Identify the nature of the acquirer.

3. Describe the criteria for determining the acquiring entity (acquirer) in a business combination.

4. Define and determine the acquisition date and the measurement period.

5. Describe the effects of changes made to accounts and amounts during the measurement period.

I. Acquisition Method

A. The topic of business combinations is part of ASC 805 in the codification of accounting standards. ASC 805 requires the use of the acquisition method of accounting for business combinations, which is a variation of the purchase method of accounting, and applies to all transactions or events in which an entity obtains control of one or more businesses (including a group of assets that constitute a business). The following transactions are exempt from applying the acquisition method of accounting:

   1. The formation of a joint venture

   2. The acquisition of an asset or group of assets that does not constitute a business

   3. A combination between entities under common control

   4. A combination between not-for-profit organizations

   5. The acquisition of a for-profit entity by a not-for-profit organization

B. ASC 805 specifies how the acquiring entity (acquirer) in a business combination should:

   1. Recognize and measure the identifiable assets acquired, the liabilities assumed, and any noncontrolling interest in the acquired business

   2. Recognize and measure goodwill or a bargain purchase amount

   3. Disclose information about a business combination to enable financial statement users to evaluate the business combination

II. Applying the Acquisition Method

A. Recording a business combination using the acquisition method of accounting involves the following steps:

   1. Identifying the acquiring entity (the acquirer)

   2. Determining the acquisition date and measurement period

   3. Determining the cost of the acquisition

4. Recognizing and measuring the identifiable assets acquired, the liabilities assumed and any noncontrolling interest in the acquired business (the acquiree)

5. Recognizing and measuring goodwill or a gain from a bargain purchase, if any

III. The First Step in Applying the Acquisition Method—Identifying the Acquiring Entity.

A. The acquisition method requires identifying the acquiring entity (i.e., the acquirer).

1. The acquirer is the entity that obtains control of a business.

2. A business (as defined by the FASB) is an integrated set of activities and assets that is capable of being conducted and managed through the use of inputs and processes for the purpose of providing economic benefits to owners, members, or participants.

3. A business may be a group of assets/net assets or a separate legal entity.

B. The acquirer should be determined based on the facts and the circumstances of the combination.

1. A business combination effected primarily through the distribution of cash or other assets or by incurring liabilities (or a combination thereof) to obtain control of a group of assets or a separate entity. The acquiring entity is the one that distributes assets or incurs liabilities.

2. As a general rule, ownership, directly or indirectly, of more than 50% of the outstanding voting shares of another entity (acquiree or investee) establishes the investor as the acquiring entity.

3. In a combination effected through an exchange of equity interest (e.g., common stock for common stock), the entity that issues (new) equity interest is generally the acquiring entity; however, all pertinent facts and circumstances should be considered, including:

   a. The relative voting rights in the combined entity after the combination—If all else is equal, the acquiring entity is the combining entity whose owners as a group have the larger portion of the voting rights in the combined entity.

   b. The existence of a large minority voting interest when no other owner(s) have a significant voting interest: If all else is equal, the acquiring entity is the combining entity whose owner(s) hold the largest minority voting interest in the combined entity.

   c. The composition of the governing body of the combined entity: If all else is equal, the acquiring entity is the combining entity whose owner(s) have the ability to select or remove a voting majority of the governing body of the combined entity.

   d. The composition of the senior management of the combined entity: If all else is equal, the acquiring entity is the combining entity whose former management dominates that of the combined entity.

   e. The terms of the equity exchange: If all else is equal, the acquiring entity is the combining entity that pays a premium over the precombination fair value of the equity interest of the other combining entity(ies).

4. The acquirer usually is the combining entity whose relative size (e.g., measured in assets, revenues or earnings) is significantly larger than that of the other combining entity (ies).

5. A new entity formed to effect a business combination is not necessarily the acquirer.

   a. If the new entity transfers cash or other assets or incurs liabilities to effect a business combination, the new entity is likely the acquirer.

   b. If a new entity is formed to issue equity interest to effect a business combination, one of the preexisting combining entities must be determined to be the acquiring entity based on available evidence, including taking into account the guidance, above.

6. If more than two entities are in the combination, in addition to the guidance, above, consideration should be given to which combining entity initiated the combination and the relative assets, revenues and earnings of the combining entities.

7. The acquirer of a variable interest entity is the primary beneficiary of the variable interest entity.

   a. Simply put, a variable interest entity is one in which contractual, ownership or other pecuniary interests in the entity change with changes in the fair value of the entity's net assets, excluding the variable interest.

   b. An entity will consolidate a variable interest entity when it has an investment or other interest that will absorb a majority of the investee entity's expected losses, receive a majority of the entity's expected residual returns, or both.

   c. The entity that consolidates a variable interest entity is the primary beneficiary of that entity.

IV. **The Second Step in Applying the Acquisition Method—Determining the Acquisition Date and Measurement Period.**

   A. The acquisition date is the date on which the acquirer obtains control of the acquiree (i.e., the business).

      1. It is normally the date on which the acquirer legally transfers consideration for, acquires the assets of, and assumes the liabilities of the acquiree.

      2. The acquisition date could be the *closing date* for the combination.

      3. However, the acquisition date can be before or after the closing date, if by agreement or otherwise the acquirer gains control of the acquiree at an earlier or later date.

      4. An acquirer should consider all pertinent facts and circumstances in determining the acquisition date.

   B. The measurement period is after the acquisition date. If the initial accounting for a business combination is not complete by the end of the reporting period in which the combination occurs, the acquirer will report provisional amounts in its financial statements for items for which the accounting is incomplete and adjust those amounts during the measurement period.

      1. The **measurement period** is the period after the acquisition date during which the acquirer may adjust any provisional amounts.

      2. The measurement period provides the acquirer reasonable time (not to exceed one year) to obtain information needed to identify and measure, **as of the acquisition date**, the following:

         a. Identifiable assets, liabilities, and noncontrolling interest in the acquiree

         b. Consideration transferred to obtain the acquiree

         c. Any precombination interest held in the acquiree

         d. Any goodwill or bargain purchase gain

      3. During the measurement period, new information about facts **that existed at the acquisition date** that would have affected the recognition of assets or liabilities, or that would have affected the measurement of amounts recognized, will be used to adjust the provisional amounts in the reporting period in which the adjustment amounts are determined.

         a. The recognition of additional identifiable assets or asset amounts will result in a decrease in the amount of (provisional) goodwill, if any.

         b. The recognition of additional identifiable liabilities or liability amounts will result in an increase in the amount of (provisional) goodwill, if any.

        c. Adjustments to provisional accounts and/or amounts must be reflected in current period earnings for changes in depreciation, amortization, or other income effects. Effective with ASU 2015–16, retroactive application to prior period financial statements is **not** required.

        d. The effect of the changes in provisional amounts must also be disclosed in the footnotes of the financial statements.

   4. The measurement period ends when the acquirer obtains information it was seeking about facts **that existed at the acquisition date** or learn that no additional information is available.

        a. In no case should the measurement period exceed one year from the acquisition date.

Determining the Cost of the Business Acquired

Application of the acquisition method of accounting to a business combination involves the following requirements: (1) Identifying the acquirer, (2) Determining the acquisition date and measurement period, (3) Determining the cost of the acquired business, (4) Recognizing and measuring the assets acquired, liabilities assumed, and noncontrolling interest in the acquiree, and (5) Recognizing and measuring any goodwill or bargain purchase amount. This lesson covers the third of these requirements, determining the cost of the acquired business.

Subsequent lessons cover the remaining requirements and related issues.

After studying this lesson, you should be able to:

1. Describe the ways that an acquirer may gain control of a business.

2. Identify the elements of consideration that may be transferred to complete a business combination.

3. Demonstrate the accounting for contingent consideration as part of the cost of the business acquired.

4. Demonstrate how to account for acquisition costs related to a business combination.

I. The third step in applying the acquisition method is to determine the cost of the business acquired.

II. **An Acquirer May Obtain Control of a Business in Two Ways**

    A. By transferring consideration to either another entity or its owner(s):

        1. To obtain a group of assets that constitute a business, *or*

        2. To gain control of another entity.

    B. Without transferring consideration. For example, by contract or through the lapse of the minority veto rights of others.

III. **Obtaining Control by Transferring Consideration**

    A. The consideration used by the acquirer may take a number of forms, including:

        1. Transferring cash, cash equivalents, or other assets,

        2. Incurring liabilities,

        3. Issuing equity interests, including common and preferred stock, options and warrants, or

        4. A combination of transferring assets, incurring liabilities or issuing equity

    B. The consideration used to effect a business combination generally must be measured at fair value (see exception in D, below).

    C. If any assets or liabilities transferred by the acquirer (except as noted in D, below) have a carrying value before transfer that is different than fair value at acquisition, the assets or liabilities must be adjusted (remeasured) to fair value at the date of the combination and the related gains or losses recognized in current income by the acquirer.

Example

P, Inc. acquires a group of assets that constitute a business from the shareholders of S, Inc. As payment for the group of assets, P transfers cash and land to the shareholders. The land was acquired by P 12 years ago for $126,000. It had a fair value of $150,000 at the time of the business acquisition. Prior to transferring the land to S, P should make an entry to revalue the land to fair value and recognize a gain.

DR: Land	$24,000
CR: Gain on Land Revaluation	$24,000

(Fair value $150,000 – Carrying value $126,000 = $24,000 gain.)

The land, with a new carrying value of $150,000, would then be transferred to the shareholders of S as part of the consideration for the acquired business.

D. An exception to the requirement that assets and liabilities to be transferred as consideration in a business combination be remeasured to fair value applies when the transferred assets or liabilities remain under the control of the acquirer.

    1. In that case, the assets or liabilities are not adjusted to fair value, but are transferred at carrying value and no gain or loss is recognized.

Example

P, Inc. gained control of S, Inc. by acquiring more than 50% of S's voting common stock. As a part of its acquisition of S's stock, P transferred land with a carrying value of $126,000 and a fair value of $150,000 to S for 10,000 shares of S's common stock. The land will remain on the books of S. Because P has controlling interest in S, P also retains control of the land transferred to S. Therefore, the land should be transferred at the carrying value, $126,000, not fair value, and no gain (or loss) will be recognized.

E. Contingent Consideration as Part of the Cost of the Acquired Entity

    1. The consideration transferred by the acquirer to the acquiree may include a contingent element.

    2. Contingent consideration is either:

        a. An obligation of the acquirer to transfer additional assets or equity interest to the former owner(s) of the acquired business as part of the consideration if future events occur or conditions are met, or

        b. A right of the acquirer to a return of previously transferred consideration if specific conditions are met.

    3. Contingent consideration should be recognized on the acquisition date at fair value as part of the consideration transferred in exchange for the acquired business.

        a. An obligation to pay contingent consideration should be recognized as either a liability or as equity (according to the provisions of ASC 480, *Distinguishing Liabilities from Equity*).

        b. A right to the return of previously transferred consideration should be recognized as an asset.

    4. Changes in the fair value of contingent consideration after the acquisition date that result from new information about facts and circumstances **that existed at the acquisition date** should be accounted for as measurement period adjustments (and, therefore, as adjustments to the cost of the acquired business).

5. Changes in the fair value of contingent consideration **resulting from occurrences after the acquisition date**—including meeting earning targets, reaching a specified share market price, or reaching research and development milestones—are not measurement period adjustments and do not enter into the cost of the business combination.

   a. Changes resulting from occurrences after the acquisition date related to contingent consideration classified as equity are not remeasured; subsequent settlement should be accounted for as an equity adjustment.

   b. Changes resulting from occurrences after the acquisition date related to contingent consideration classified as assets or liabilities are remeasured to fair value at each balance sheet date until the contingency is resolved, with changes recognized in current income.

6. **Acquirer's Share-Based Payment Awards as Cost Elements**

   1. An acquirer may exchange its share-based payment awards for awards held by the acquiree's employees as part of a business combination.

      a. For example, in a merger the acquirer may exchange its stock options (options to acquire its stock) for the stock options in the acquiree held by the acquiree's employees at the date of the merger.

      b. Such an exchange would be a modification of share-based payment awards under ASC 718, *Stock Compensation*, and would be treated as the exchange of the original award for a new award.

   2. The treatment of the exchange of share-based awards in a business combination depends on whether the acquirer is obligated to make the exchange or does so at its own discretion.

   3. An acquirer may be obligated to exchange share-based awards because of:

      a. The terms of the acquisition agreement

      b. The terms of the acquiree's awards

      c. Applicable laws or regulations

   4. If the acquirer is obligated to exchange awards:

      a. The portion (all or part) of the replacement awards (measured in accordance with the provisions of ASC 718) that relates to precombination services based on conditions of the acquiree's awards will be part of the consideration transferred in the business combination.

      b. The portion (all or part) of the replacement awards (measured in accordance with the provisions of ASC 718) that relates to postcombination services (the amount not allocated to precombination services) will be treated as compensation expense in post-combination financial statements.

   5. If the acquirer elects to replace acquiree share-based awards, even though it is not obligated to do so, all the value of the awards (measured in accordance with the provisions of ASC 718) will be treated as compensation expense in postcombination financial statements.

IV. **Obtaining Control Without Transferring Consideration**

   A. An entity (acquirer) may acquire control of another entity (acquiree) without transferring any consideration. Examples include:

   1. An entity reacquires a sufficient number of its own outstanding shares from select investors so that another investor's ownership results in control over the entity.

   2. Minority veto rights lapse that previously kept a majority owner (acquirer) from controlling the investee (acquiree).

3. Two entities agree to combine by contract alone; neither entity owns controlling equity interest in the other entity.

B. When a business combination occurs as a result of a contract between entities:

1. One of the combining entities must be identified as the acquirer and, therefore, the other entity is the acquiree.

2. The equity interests in the acquiree held by parties other than the acquirer are noncontrolling interest in the postcombination financial statements of the acquirer, even if all (100%) of the equity interest in the acquiree is attributable to the noncontrolling interest (i.e., the entity designated as the acquirer has no equity interest in the acquiree).

V. Treatment of Acquisition-Related Costs

A. Acquisition-related costs are costs the acquirer incurs to carry out the acquisition (of a group of assets that constitute a business or an entity).

B. Acquisition costs include:

1. Finder's fees

2. Advising, legal, accounting, valuation (appraisal) and other professional and consulting fees

3. General administrative costs, including the cost of an internal acquisitions department

4. Cost of registering and issuing debt and equity securities in connection with an acquisition

C. Acquisition-related costs (except as noted in D, below) should be expensed in the period in which the costs are incurred and the services are received; these costs are not included as part of the cost of an acquired business.

D. The cost of issuing debt and equity securities for the purposes of a business combination are not treated as cost of the acquired business, but should be accounted for as provided for by other applicable GAAP. Although current GAAP is not uniform with respect to treatment of issuance costs, generally, the following would apply:

1. Debt issuance costs (legal, printing, etc.) may be either recognized as a deferred asset and amortized over the life of the debt, or expensed when incurred.

2. Equity issuance costs (legal, printing, registering, etc.) reduce the proceeds from the securities issued and, in effect, reduce Additional Paid-in Capital.

VI. Summary—In summary, the cost of an acquired business is the sum of:

A. Fair value of assets transferred by the acquirer

B. Fair value of liabilities incurred by the acquirer

C. Fair value of equity interest issued by the acquirer

D. Fair value of contingent consideration (net) obligations of the acquirer

E. Fair value of share-based payment awards for precombination services that the acquirer is obligated to provide

Recognizing/Measuring Assets, Liabilities, and Noncontrolling Interest

Application of the acquisition method of accounting to a business combination involves the following steps: (1) Identify the acquirer; (2) Determine the acquisition date and measurement period; (3) Determine the cost of the acquisition; (4) Recognize and measure the assets acquired, liabilities assumed, and noncontrolling interest in the acquiree; and (5) Recognize and measure any goodwill or bargain purchase amount. This lesson covers the fourth of these requirements, recognizing and measuring the assets acquired, liabilities assumed, and noncontrolling interest in the acquiree.

Subsequent lessons cover the remaining steps and related issues.

After studying this lesson, you should be able to:

1. Identify and record the items that should be recognized as assets or liabilities in a business combination.

2. Identify items that are exceptions to the general recognition and measurement guidelines.

3. Calculate the values associated with business combinations achieved in stages.

4. Demonstrate how noncontrolling interest in an acquiree is recognized and measured.

I. **The Fourth Step in Applying the Acquisition Method**—In the fourth step, you would recognize and measure the assets acquired, liabilities assumed, and any noncontrolling interest in an acquiree.

II. **Recognition**—At the acquisition date, the acquirer must recognize (distinct from goodwill, if any) the identifiable assets acquired, liabilities assumed and any noncontrolling interest in the acquiree.

   A. Identifiable assets and liabilities must meet the definition of assets and liabilities in the **FASB Conceptual Framework,** *Elements of Financial Statements*.

      1. Rights or obligations that do not exist at the date of acquisition, even if expected to exist in the future, are not recognized as assets or liabilities acquired.

      2. Benefits received or obligations that occur but do not exist at the date of acquisition are recognized as post-combination items, as called for by the provisions of other appropriate GAAP. They are not part of the business acquisition. For example:

         a. Costs expected to be incurred to exit an acquired activity

         b. Costs expected to be incurred in terminating or relocating employees of the acquiree

   B. To qualify for recognition as part of the business combination, the assets and liabilities must be part of what the acquirer and acquiree exchanged in the business combination, not the subject matter of any separate transaction.

      1. A pre-combination transaction or arrangement that primarily benefits the acquirer or the subsequent combined entity, rather than the acquiree or the former owner(s), is likely to be a separate transaction.

      2. The following would be separate transactions, not a part of the combination transaction:

         a. A transaction that settles a preexisting relationship between the acquirer and the acquiree

         b. A transaction that compensates employees or former owner(s) of the acquiree for future services

         c. A transaction that reimburses the acquiree or its former owner(s) for paying the acquirer's acquisition-related costs

C. The acquirer can recognize assets and/or liabilities not previously recognized by the acquiree. For example, an internally developed brand name, patent or other asset for which costs were expensed by the acquiree would be recognized as identifiable assets by the acquirer.

   1. This would include in-process research and development (IPRD) costs incurred by the acquiree. That is, the acquirer can capitalize IPRD purchased from the acquiree as part of a business combination. This will result in the acquirer recording an intangible asset for this IPRD.

D. An intangible asset (separate from goodwill) is identifiable and would be recognized by the acquirer if it either:

   1. Is capable of being separated from the acquiree and sold, transferred, leased, rented, or exchanged (e.g., customer lists); *or*

   2. Arises from contractual or other legal rights.

E. Goodwill on the books of the acquired entity prior to a business combination would not be recognized by the acquirer in recording the combination. Any goodwill attributable to the acquiree would be separately determined by the acquirer. (See the "Recognizing/Measuring Goodwill or Bargain Purchase Amount" lesson.)

III. Classification and Designation— At the acquisition date, the acquirer must classify or designate the identifiable assets acquired and liabilities assumed so as to subsequently apply GAAP requirements.

A. Classification or designation will be made on the basis of related contractual terms, economic conditions, operating and accounting policies, and other relevant conditions that exist at the acquisition date.

B. Example of items that need classification or designation include:

   1. Investments in debt and equity securities as being held to maturity, trading, or available for sale

   2. Derivatives to determine whether they are hedging instruments, and if so, the particulars

   3. Embedded derivatives to determine whether they will be treated as separate from the host instrument

   4. Long-term assets to determine whether they will be used or held for sale

C. Leases (lease contracts) and insurance/reinsurance contracts should continue to be classified as established at inception of the contract (unless subsequent modifications of the contract have warranted reclassification).

IV. Measuring (Recording) at Fair Value—At the acquisition date, identifiable assets, liabilities and any noncontrolling interest in the acquiree should be measured (recorded) at fair value at that date.

A. Fair value for identifiable assets and liabilities acquired should be determined using the guidelines and techniques established in ASC No. 820, *Fair Value Measurement*.

B. Fair value for each identifiable asset and liability, or group of related assets or related liabilities, should be determined based on its specific attributes, including condition, location, highest and best use, and so on.

C. Subject to the requirements of ASC 820, the following may be a basis for determining fair value of certain assets acquired and liabilities assumed:

   1. Marketable securities—Quoted prices in active markets

   2. Receivables—Present value of amounts to be received

   3. Inventories (finished goods and merchandise)—Estimated selling price less the cost of disposal and a reasonable profit

   4. Inventories (work-in-process)—Estimated selling price less costs to complete, cost of disposal, and a reasonable profit

5. **Inventories** (raw materials)—Current replacement cost

6. **Plant and equipment held for use**—Current replacement cost

7. **Plant and equipment held for disposal**—Fair value (based on market or cost valuation) less cost of disposal

8. **Intangible assets**—Estimated fair value (based on market, income, or cost valuation)

9. **Land and natural resources**—Fair value (based on market, income or cost valuation)

10. **Accounts and notes payable, long-term debt, and other liabilities**—Present values of amounts to be paid determined using appropriate current interest rates

V. **Exceptions**— Certain exceptions to the general recognition and/or measurement principles apply to specific identifiable assets and liabilities; those exceptions include:

A. **Contingencies**—Recognition principle exception to ASC 450:

1. A contingency is an existing condition involving uncertainty as to possible gain or loss that will be resolved when one or more future events occur or fail to occur. If the contingency meets the criteria of probable and estimable (ASC 450) then the liability would be accrued.

2. Contingencies related to existing contracts (*contractual contingencies*—e.g., warranty obligations) should be recognized and measured at fair value.

3. Contingencies not related to existing contracts (*noncontractual contingencies*—e.g., lawsuits) should be recognized and measured at fair value only if it is more likely than not as of the acquisition date that the contingency will give rise to an asset or a liability, and the fair value is readily determinable. Note that this is a lower threshold than the criteria for ASC 450 (probable and estimable).

B. **Income Tax Issues**—Recognition and measurement principles exceptions:

1. The acquirer will recognize and measure a deferred tax asset or liability related to assets acquired and liabilities assumed in a business combination as provided by the provisions of ASC 740.

2. The acquirer will account for the potential tax effects of temporary differences, carry forwards and income tax uncertainties of an acquiree at the acquisition date, or that will result from the acquisition, as provided for by the provisions of ASC 740, *Tax Provisions*.

C. **Employee Benefits**—Recognition and measurement principles exceptions. The acquirer will recognize and measure a liability (or asset, if any) related to the acquiree's employee benefit arrangements in accordance with applicable GAAP.

D. **Indemnification Asset**—Recognition and measurement principles exceptions:

1. An indemnification represents the promise by the seller to reimburse (indemnify) the acquirer if there are any adverse outcomes from a contingent liability. Typically in a business combination the indemnification would establish a seller's guarantee, which limits the acquirer's liability for the outcome of an uncertainty related to an identifiable asset or liability.

2. The acquirer normally would recognize the indemnification benefit as an asset (indemnification asset) at the time and using the same measurement basis as the indemnified asset or liability.

E. **Reacquired Rights**—Measurement principle exception:

1. Prior to a business combination, the acquirer may have granted the acquiree the right to use an asset of the acquirer; for example, the right to use the acquirer's trade name as part of a franchise agreement.

2. If, as part of the business combination, the acquirer reacquires that right, it should be recognized by the acquirer as an intangible asset and measured on the basis of the remaining contractual term of the contract that granted the right.

3. Subsequent to the business combination, the intangible asset "reacquired right" should be amortized over the remaining period of the contract that granted the right.

F. **Share-Based Payment Awards**—Measurement principle exception:

1. An acquirer may grant its share-based payment awards (e.g., employee stock options) for awards held by the acquiree's employees.

2. The liability or equity recognized as a result of such awards should be measured in accordance with the provisions of ASC 718.

G. **Assets Held for Sale**—Measurement principle exception:

1. Long-term assets acquired by the acquirer, which it classifies as held for sale at the acquisition date should be measured in accordance with the provisions of ASC 360.

2. Basically, ASC 360 requires that assets held for sale must be measured at fair value less cost to dispose.

VI. **Fair Value of Previously Held Equity**—Fair value of acquirer's previously held equity interest in acquiree, if any.

A. At the acquisition date, the acquirer must measure (determine) the fair value of its previously held equity interest in the acquiree, if any.

1. An acquirer would have an equity interest in the acquiree prior to the acquisition date if the business combination were achieved in stages (also called a step acquisition).

Example

On January 2, **2007,** Investco, Inc. acquired 35% of the voting stock of Lowco, Inc. That level of equity ownership likely gives Investco significant influence over Lowco, but does not give it control. Therefore, Investco would account for its investment in Lowco using the equity method of accounting. On January 2, **2009,** Investco acquires in the market an additional 40% of Lowco's voting equity. Thus, as of January 2, **2009,** Investco owns 75% of Lowco's voting equity, which gives it control of Lowco, and a business combination has occurred as of January 2, **2009.**

In this example, Investco would need to determine the fair value of its 35% ownership of Lowco as of January 2, **2009,** the date of the business combination.

B. Any difference between the fair value of the acquirer's precombination equity interest in the acquiree and the carrying value of that interest on the acquirer's books would be recognized by the acquirer as a gain or loss in income of the period of the combination.

1. If the acquirer had accounted for its precombination equity ownership using the equity method of accounting (as in the preceding example), the carrying amount of the investment using that method would be used in determining any gain or loss related to the previously held equity interest.

Example

On January 2, **2007,** Investco, Inc. acquired 35% of the voting stock of Lowco, Inc. for $150,000. Because its investment gave Investco significant influence over Lowco, it used the equity method to account for its investment. On January 2, **2009,** Investco acquired in the market an additional 40% of Lowco's voting stock, which resulted in a business combination. At that time, Investco's investment in the 35% of Lowco acquired in January, **2007,** had a carrying value of $185,000 and a market value of $200,000. As a part of its acquisition accounting for the business combination, Investco must revalue its 35% precombination investment in Lowco to fair value at the date of the business combination and recognize a gain.

Entry

DR: Investment in Lowco, Inc. $15,000

    CR: Gain on Investment Revaluation $15,000

(Fair value = $200,000 – Carrying value $185,000 = $15,000 gain)

The fair value of Investco's precombination investment in Lowco ($200,000) would be included as a part of the cost of Investco's acquisition of Lowco.

    C. The fair value of the equity owned prior to the acquisition date (i.e., the business combination) would become part of the "cost" of the investment in the acquiree.

VII. Fair Value of Noncontrolling Interest

    A. At the acquisition date, the acquirer must measure (determine) the fair value of the noncontrolling interest in the acquiree.

        1. A noncontrolling interest in an acquiree occurs when the acquirer obtains less than 100% of the equity interest of the acquiree.

        2. The percentage of equity interest not owned either directly or indirectly by the acquirer is the noncontrolling interest and must be measured at fair value at the acquisition date.

    B. The value assigned to the noncontrolling interest should not be based simply on the noncontrolling interest's proportional interest in the identifiable assets acquired, liabilities assumed and share of goodwill, but rather on the separately determined fair value of the noncontrolling interest in the acquiree.

        1. If an active market price for the equity shares of the acquiree is available, the acquisition date fair value of the noncontrolling interest would be based on the market value of the equity shares not held by the acquirer.

        2. If an active market price for the equity shares of the acquiree is not available, the acquirer would use some other valuation technique to value the equity shares not held by the acquirer.

    C. The fair value of the acquirer's interest on a per-share basis may be different than the fair value of the noncontrolling interest on a per-share basis, due mainly to a *control premium* associated with the acquirer's ownership.

Recognizing/Measuring Goodwill or Bargain Purchase

Application of the acquisition method of accounting to a business combination involves the following steps: (1) Identify the acquirer; (2) Determine the acquisition date and measurement period; (3) Determine the cost of the acquisition; (4) Recognize and measure the assets acquired, liabilities assumed, and noncontrolling interest in the acquiree; and (5) Recognize and measure any goodwill or bargain purchase amount. This lesson covers the last of these requirements, recognizing and measuring goodwill or a bargain purchase amount in a business combination.

After studying this lesson, you should be able to:

1. Describe how to determine whether or not goodwill or a bargain purchase amount exists.

2. Calculate the goodwill arising from a business combination.

3. Calculate the bargain purchase arising from a business combination.

I. **The Fifth and Final Step in Applying the Acquisition Method**—Recognizing and measuring goodwill or a gain from a bargain purchase, if any.

II. **At the Acquisition Date**—The acquirer must recognize and measure any goodwill or gain from a bargain purchase that resulted from the business combination.

III. **Amount of Gain**—The amount of that goodwill or bargain purchase gain, if any is determined using

   A. The *investment value* of the acquired business, *and*

   B. The fair value of the net identifiable assets acquired and liabilities assumed in the business combination.

IV. **Investment Value**—The *investment value* is the sum of the following elements (The term *investment value* is not used in the FASB, but has been adopted here to include the sum of A. and B., as follows):

   A. The consideration transferred (cost) to effect the business combination (as detailed in the earlier lesson "Determining the Cost of the Business Acquired"), including the fair value of the following:

   1. Assets transferred

   2. Liabilities incurred

   3. Equity interest issued

   4. Contingent consideration (at acquisition date)

   5. Required share-based payment awards to employees for precombination services

   6. Precombination equity of the acquiree held by the acquirer (if the combination was achieved in stages or steps)

   B. The fair value of the noncontrolling interest in the acquiree, if any (as detailed in the prior lesson "Recognizing/Measuring Assets, Liabilities, and Noncontrolling Interest.")

   Investment Value = Costs (in A, above) + FV of NCI

V. **Measured at Fair Value**—The identifiable assets acquired, the liabilities assumed and any noncontrolling interest in the acquiree as of the acquisition date generally would be measured at fair value (with certain exceptions as noted in the prior lesson "Recognizing/Measuring Assets, Liabilities and Noncontrolling Interest").

VI. **Goodwill**—Goodwill results when the investment value (see IV., above) is **greater** than the net fair value of assets assumed and liabilities incurred at the date of the business combination (see IV., above).

A. Simply put, goodwill (if it exists) is the excess of the fair value of the investment in the acquiree (including the fair value of the claim of the noncontrolling interest) over the fair value (or other required measure) of the identifiable net assets of the acquired business.

Example

1. On January 2, 2009, Investco, Inc. acquired all of the outstanding common stock of Lowco, Inc. in the market for $1,000,000 cash and merged the assets acquired and liabilities assumed into Investco. At that date the fair values of Lowco's identifiable assets and liabilities were:

Accounts Receivable	$ 200,000
Inventories	400,000
Property, Plant and Equipment	800,000
Other Identifiable Assets	200,000
TOTAL ASSETS	$1,600,000
Accounts Payable	300,000
Other Current Liabilities	200,000
Long-term Liabilities	200,000
TOTAL LIABILITIES	$ 700,000
FAIR VALUE OF NET ASSETS	$ 900,000

2. Goodwill calculation:

Investment value = $1,000,000 − Fair value of net assets = $900,000 = $100,000 Goodwill.

B. Postcombination treatment of goodwill provides that:

1. Goodwill is not amortized.

2. Goodwill is assessed at least annually for impairment, as provided by ASC 350.

VII. **Bargain Purchase**—A bargain purchase results when the investment value (see IV., above) is **less** than the net fair value of assets assumed and liabilities incurred as of the date of the business combination (see V., above).

A. Simply put, a bargain purchase (if it exists) is the excess of the fair value (or other required measure) of the net assets of the acquired business over the fair value of the investment in the acquiree (including the fair value of the claim of noncontrolling interest).

B. A bargain purchase may result from the following reasons, among others:

1. The business combination occurs when the owner(s) of the acquired entity are under compulsion to carry out the sale (i.e., a "forced" sale), resulting in a bargain purchase by the acquirer.

2. The valuation of assets acquired and/or liabilities assumed is constrained by the exceptions to the use of fair value, as detailed in the prior lesson "Recognizing/Measuring Assets, Liabilities and Noncontrolling Interest."

C. If the acquirer determines that the fair value (or other required measure) of the net assets of the acquiree is greater than the investment in the acquiree (an apparent bargain purchase), before recognizing a gain from a bargain purchase the acquirer must fully reassess whether all assets acquired and liabilities assumed have been identified and properly measured according to the provisions of ASC 805, including the measurement of:

1. Identifiable assets acquired and liabilities assumed
2. Acquirer's precombination equity interest in the acquiree
3. Noncontrolling interest in the acquiree
4. Consideration transferred

D. If, after reassessment, the acquirer still concludes that a bargain purchase exists, the amount of that bargain purchase shall be recognized as a gain in earnings as of the date of the business combination.

Example

1. On January 2, 20X9, Investco, Inc. acquired all the outstanding common stock of Lowco, Inc. in the market for $850,000 cash and merged the assets acquired and liabilities assumed into Investco. At that date, the fair values of Lowco's identifiable assets and liabilities were:

Accounts Receivable	$ 200,000
Inventories	400,000
Property, Plant and Equipment	800,000
Other Identifiable Assets	200,000
TOTAL ASSETS	$1,600,000
Accounts Payable	300,000
Other Current Liabilities	200,000
Long-term Liabilities	200,000
TOTAL LIABILITIES	$ 700,000
FAIR VALUE OF NET ASSETS	$ 900,000

2. Bargain purchase calculation:

Fair value of net assets = $900,000 - Investment value = $850,000 = $50,000 Bargain purchase amount. This amount would be recognized as a gain in the period of the business combination.

(Note: See the entry for this example in the subsequent lesson, "Recording Business Combinations.")

3. The gain is attributable only to the acquirer.

VIII. Special Circumstances—Special circumstances may affect the determination and measurement of goodwill or a bargain purchase amount. These include the following:

A. If the business combination is carried out solely through the exchange of equity (e.g., acquirer's common stock for acquiree's common stock), the fair value of the acquiree's equity interest at the acquisition date may be a more reliable measure of fair value than the acquirer's equity interest and, if so, the amount of goodwill or bargain purchase should be based on the acquiree's equity interest instead of the equity interest transferred by the acquirer.

B. If no consideration is transferred in carrying out the business combination, goodwill or a bargain purchase amount should be determined using a valuation technique, instead of the value of the consideration transferred.

Post-Acquisition Issues

Prior lessons presented the steps required in the application of the acquisition method of accounting to a business combination. Following the combination, most items recognized in a combination will be measured and accounted for following the requirements of GAAP for those specific items. However, some items recognized in a combination have specific post-combination requirements. This lesson presents the accounting for those items.

After studying this lesson, you should be able to:

1. Identify which items recognized in a business combination require specific postcombination treatment.

2. Illustrate how to measure and account for items that require specific postcombination treatment.

3. Demonstrate how to recognize postacquisition measurement period adjustments for assets acquired.

4. Illustrate pushdown accounting and explain how it impacts the financial statements of the acquiree.

I. **Conventional Treatment**—Once the business combination has been recorded using the acquisition method of accounting, the acquirer generally will measure and account for assets acquired, liabilities assumed or incurred, and equity issued in the combination in accordance with the provisions of established GAAP for those items.

II. **Specific Treatment**—However, certain items acquired or issued in carrying out a combination require specific treatment as provided by ASC 805; those items are:

   A. **Assets and Liabilities Arising from Contingencies**

   1. An asset or liability arising from a contingency recognized at the time of a business combination should be accounted for based on subsequent information about the contingency.

   2. Until new information about the possible outcome of a contingency is received, the acquirer will continue to report the contingency at its fair value at the date of the combination.

   3. When new information about the possible outcome of a contingency is received, the acquirer will measure and report the item according to the following rule:

      a. If the contingency is a liability, it will be measured and reported at the *higher* of:

         i. Its acquisition-date fair value, *or*

         ii. The amount that would be recognized if the requirements of ASC 450 were followed.

      b. If the contingency is an asset, it will be measured and reported at the *lower* of:

         i. Its acquisition-date fair value, *or*

         ii. The best estimate of its future settlement amount.

   4. A contingency recognized in a business combination will be derecognized only when the contingency is settled or expires.

   B. **Indemnification Assets**

   1. An indemnification asset recognized in a business combination should be measured and reported on the same basis as the liability or asset that is indemnified, subject to any contractual limitations.

   2. An indemnification asset recognized in a business combination will be derecognized only when it is settled or expires.

C. Contingent Consideration

1. Contingent consideration recognized in a business combination should be measured and reported at fair value.

2. Changes in information about the fair value of contingent consideration as it existed at the date of the business combination are measurement period adjustments and change the cost of the investment.

3. Changes in the fair value of contingent consideration that results from events after the business combination (including reaching a specific share price, meeting an earnings target, etc.) are not measurement period adjustments and do not change the cost of the investment; these changes should be accounted for as follows:

   a. Contingent consideration classified as equity is not remeasured and its subsequent settlement is accounted for within (by adjusting) equity;

   b. Contingent consideration classified as an asset or liability is remeasured at each reporting date and recognized in earnings (unless the contingent consideration is a hedging arrangement, in which case the changes in value are recognized in other comprehensive income).

III. Post-Acquisition Measurement Period Adjustment

There is much complexity associated with determining acquisition-date fair value of the assets acquired and liabilities assumed. Added to this complexity is the timing of the acquisition in relation to the issuance of the financial statements, where the acquisition could occur on December 15 and the financial statements are issued on December 31. Therefore, it is likely that the initial values of the assets acquired and liabilities assumed are measured at a provisional value based on best estimates available as of the reporting date.

A. The measurement period for the provisional values is one year post-acquisition for information that existed as of the acquisition date and, if known, would have impacted the valuation of the assets and liabilities as of that date.

B. During the measurement period, the acquirer recognizes increases (or decreases) in the value of the provisional amounts with the respective adjustments to depreciation, amortization, and goodwill. The impact on the income statement is reported in the period in which the adjustments to the provisional amounts are determined.

Example
The Appendix to ASU 2015-16 provides the following example of how the measurement period adjustment would be reflected in the current financial statements.

Assume the Acquirer purchases the Target on September 20, 20X7, and obtained a tentative fair value estimate for plant equipment of $30,000 and estimated the remaining life to be 5 years. In the December 31, 20X7, financial statements, the Acquirer reported the plant equipment at $30,000 and accumulated depreciation and depreciation of $1,500 ($30,000/5 years × 3/12).

At the end of March, the appraisal of the equipment is completed and the acquisition-date fair value is determined to be $40,000. In the March 31, 20X8, interim financial statements, the acquirer would report the effect of the measurement period adjustment as follows:

1. The carrying amount of the plant equipment would be increased by $9,000. The $10,000 increase in fair value less the $1,000 difference in additional depreciation that would have been taken [$40,000 / 5 years × 6/12) – ($30,000 / 5 years × 6/12) = $1,000].

2. The carrying value of goodwill would be decreased by $10,000.

3. Depreciation expense for the period ended March 31, 20X8, would be increased by $1,000 to reflect the impact on earnings for the change in the provisional amount of the plant equipment.

IV. Pushdown Accounting

A. The acquiree has the option to apply pushdown accounting anytime there is a change in control as defined in ASC 805 and 810. If the acquiree elects to apply pushdown accounting, it would revalue all of the assets and liabilities to acquisition date fair value as determined by the acquirer in its application of ASC 805. The acquiree may elect to apply pushdown accounting each time there is a change in control. If the acquiree elects to apply pushdown accounting in a reporting period subsequent to the change in control, then the election is a change in accounting principle and should be accounted for in accordance with ASC 250.

> **Note**
> *Acquisition accounting at the parent level is the same, regardless of whether it is pushed down to the acquired subsidiary.*

B. Pushdown accounting allows the acquiree to recognize a new basis for all assets and liabilities and any goodwill that results from the application of acquisition method accounting. If there was a bargain purchase the acquiree would recognize an adjustment to additional paid-in capital, not a gain on the income statement. All subsequent accounting for the new basis of the assets and liabilities of the acquired company would be in accordance with the applicable U.S. GAAP. If the acquirer was not required to apply ASC 805 (e.g., the acquirer was an investment company), the acquiree can still elect pushdown accounting and would recognize the new basis for assets and liabilities had ASC 805 been applied by the acquirer.

Example

Assume that Passing Corporation (P) acquired Score Company (S) for $400,000 on July 1, 2015, and on that date S had the following summarized balance sheet with the book values and fair values shown:

	Book Value	Fair Value
Accounts Receivable (net)	$40,000	$40,000
Inventories	80,000	80,000
Plant and Equipment (net)	160,000	200,000
Land	120,000	160,000
TOTAL ASSETS	$400,000	$480,000
Accounts Payable	$20,000	$20,000
Short-term Note	30,000	30,000
Bonds Payable	70,000	90,000
TOTAL LIABILITIES	$120,000	$140,000

If S elects to use pushdown accounting, the incremental fair values of the assets and liabilities would be recorded by S. In addition, S would record the goodwill that results from the business combination. Below is the entry that would be recorded by S on July 1, **2015:**

Plant and Equipment (200,000 − 160,000)	40,000	
Land (160,000 − 120,000)	40,000	
Goodwill (400,000 − (480,000 − 140,000))	60,000	
Bonds Payable (90,000 − 70,000)		20,000
Revaluation Capital		120,000

C. If the acquiree applies pushdown accounting, it should disclose the effects of the pushdown accounting on its separate financial statements so that the financial statement user can evaluate the effects of pushdown accounting. If the acquiree does not elect to apply pushdown accounting, the entity should disclose that it has undergone a change in control event and that it elects to prepare its separate financial statements using its historical basis.

Disclosure Requirements—Acquisition Method

A business combination is a significant event and impacts the reporting of the acquiring entity. Therefore, disclosures are required not only for the period in which the combination occurs, but also in subsequent periods. This lesson describes the most significant of the required disclosures associated with business combinations.

After studying this lesson, you should be able to:

1. Identify the required disclosures associated with business combinations.

I. **Business Combination Disclosure Requirements**—The acquirer in a business combination is required to disclose considerable information related to the combination and effects of postcombination event. The following summarizes those disclosure requirements.

A. There are disclosures that enable users of the acquirer's financial statements to evaluate the nature and financial effects of a business combination that occurs either: (1) during the current reporting period, or (2) after the reporting period, but before the financial statements for that period are released, including the following:

1. The name and a description of the acquiree, the acquisition date, and the percentage voting equity interest acquired (if any)

2. The primary reasons for the business combination and a description of how the acquirer obtained control of the acquiree

3. A quantitative description of the factors that make up the goodwill recognized (if any), such as expected synergies from combining operations, intangible assets that do not qualify for separate recognition (e.g., an assembled workforce), and other factors

4. The acquisition-date fair value of the total consideration transferred and the acquisition-date fair value of **each major class** of consideration transferred

5. For contingent consideration:
   a. The amount recognized as of the acquisition date
   b. A description of the arrangement and the basis for determining the amount of payment
   c. An estimate of the (undiscounted) range of outcomes or, if a range cannot be estimated, that fact and the reasons why a range cannot be estimated
   d. If the maximum amount of payment is unlimited, disclosure of that fact

6. For most receivables, disclosure for **each major class** of receivable the fair value, the gross contractual amounts receivable, and the best estimate as of the acquisition date of the contractual cash flows not expected to be collected

7. The amount recognized at the **acquisition date** for **each major class** of assets acquired and liabilities assumed

8. For assets and liabilities arising from contingencies, the amount recognized or why no amount was recognized, the nature of recognized and unrecognized contingencies, and an estimate of the (undiscounted) range of outcomes or, if a range cannot be estimated, that fact and the reasons why a range cannot be estimated

9. The total amount of goodwill that is expected to be deductible for tax purposes

10. The amount of goodwill assigned to each reportable segment (if segment information is required)

11. For any transactions between the acquirer and acquiree (or its former owners) that are recognized separately from the acquisition of assets and assumption of liabilities in the business combination the following:

   a. A description of each transaction

   b. How the acquirer accounted for each transaction

   c. The amounts recognized for each transaction and the line item(s) in the financial statements where each amount is recognized, including those amounts recognized as expenses and, separately, issuance costs not recognized as expenses

12. For a bargain purchase, the amount of gain recognized, the line item in the income statement where the gain is recognized, and a description of why the transaction resulted in a gain

13. For business combinations in which the acquirer owns less than 100% of the equity interest of the acquiree at the acquisition date, the fair value of the noncontrolling interest at the acquisition date and the valuation techniques and inputs used to measure that fair value

14. For a business combination achieved in stages, the fair value of the equity interest held by the acquirer immediately prior to the combination, the amount of any gain or loss resulting from remeasuring the interest to fair value at the date of the combination, and the line item in the income statement where the gain or loss is recognized

15. For public business enterprises (publicly traded entities), the following:

   a. The amount of revenue and earnings of the acquiree occurring since the acquisition date that is included in consolidated statements for the period

   b. The revenue and earnings of the combined entity for the current reporting period as though the acquisition date for all business combinations that occurred during the period had been at the beginning of the annual reporting period (this would be *supplemental pro forma information*)

   c. For comparative statements, the revenue and earnings of the combined entity for the comparable prior reporting period(s) as though the acquisition date for all business combinations that occurred during the current year had occurred as of the beginning of the comparable prior annual reporting period(s) (this would be *supplemental pro forma information*)

   d. For any of the above information that is impracticable to provide, disclosure of that fact and the reasons why the disclosure is impracticable

B. There are disclosures that enable users of the acquirer's financial statements to evaluate the financial effects of adjustments recognized in the current reporting period that relate to business combinations that occurred in the current or prior reporting periods, including the following:

1. If the initial accounting for a business combination is incomplete for particular assets, liabilities, noncontrolling interests, or items of consideration, and only provisional amounts have been recognized, the following information:

   a. The reasons that the initial accounting is incomplete

   b. The assets, liabilities, equity interests, or items of consideration for which the initial accounting is incomplete

   c. The nature and amount of any measurement period adjustments recognized during the reporting period

2. For contingent assets or liabilities that remain unsettled, the following should be provided in each reporting period:

      a. Any changes in the recognized amounts, including any differences arising as a result of settlement

      b. Any changes in the (undiscounted) range of outcomes and the reasons for those changes

      c. The disclosures required by ASC 820, *Fair Value Measurement*, which deal with how fair value was determined

   3. Reconciliation of the carrying amount of goodwill at the beginning and end of the reporting period.

C. Any additional information necessary to meet the objectives set forth in A and B, above.

Recording Business Combinations

Prior lessons have described and illustrated the legal forms of an acquisition: legal merger, legal consolidation, and legal acquisition. These lessons, have also described the requirements of the acquisition method of accounting for a business combination. This lesson presents the entries to record a business combination under the alternative legal forms.

After studying this lesson, you should be able to:

Complete the entry to record a merger/consolidation under the following circumstances:

1. When there is goodwill and the acquirer has no precombination ownership of the acquiree.

2. When there is goodwill and the acquirer has precombination ownership of the acquiree.

3. When there is a bargain purchase and the acquirer has no precombination ownership of the acquiree.

4. When there is a bargain purchase and the acquirer has precombination ownership of the acquiree.

I. **Legal Form and Acquisition Accounting**—The legal form of a business combination determines the accounts that the acquirer will use in recording a business combination; the acquisition method of accounting determines the amounts at which those accounts will be recorded and is required, regardless of the legal form.

II. **Recording a Legal Merger or Legal Consolidation**

   A. Recall the characteristics of a legal merger and legal consolidation:

      1. **Legal merger**—One preexisting entity (acquirer) acquires either a group of assets that constitutes a business or controlling interest in the stock of another preexisting entity (acquiree) and merges the acquired assets or other entity (assets and liabilities) into the acquirer entity.

      2. **Legal consolidation**—A new entity is created to consolidate two or more preexisting entities.

         a. The preexisting entities cease to exist as legal entities.

         b. Under the acquisition method of accounting, if only equity interest is issued by the new entity, one of the preexisting entities must be determined to be the acquirer, not the new legal entity.

      3. **In either legal form**—Only one entity remains after the business combination.

   B. The basic entry by the acquirer to record a legal merger (or group of assets that constitute a business) or a legal consolidation using the acquisition method of accounting is:

      1. Entry:

$$\left. \begin{array}{l} \text{DR: Assets acquired (at FV)} \\ \quad \text{CR: Liabilities assumed (at FV)} \\ \quad \text{CR: Consideration Paid (at FV)} \end{array} \right\} = A - L = \text{Net Assets}$$

2. Assets acquired and recognized may be:

   a. Tangible (e.g., equipment) or intangible (e.g., patent)

   b. Severable—separately "sellable" (e.g., investments) or nonseverable (e.g., trademark)

3. Assets recognized would *not* include preexisting goodwill of the acquiree.

4. Assets acquired and liabilities assumed by the acquirer would be measured at fair value, with the following exceptions:

   a. Acquired income tax-related items, including deferred tax asset or deferred tax liability related to assets acquired or liabilities assumed, and tax effects of temporary differences, carry forwards, and tax uncertainties, would be measured under the provisions of ASC 740

   b. Employee benefit liabilities (or assets), using the provisions of applicable GAAP

   c. Indemnification asset, using the same measurement basis as the indemnified liability

   d. Reacquisition rights, using the remaining contractual term of the contract that granted the right

   e. Share-based employee payment awards, using the provisions of ASC 718

   f. Assets held for sale, using the provisions of ASC 360

5. Consideration paid by the acquirer could include the following and would be measured at fair value (except when transferred assets (or liabilities) remain under the control of the acquirer; then, they would be measured at carrying value to the acquirer):

   a. Cash and cash equivalents transferred

   b. Other assets transferred

   c. Liabilities incurred

   d. Equity interest issued, including common and preferred stock, options, and warrants

   e. Any combination of the above forms of consideration

C. **Goodwill** would be recognized if the investment value in the acquiree is greater than the fair value of the net assets of the acquiree at the acquisition date.

   1. Investment value in the acquiree is the sum of the fair value of consideration transferred to effect the combination + the fair value of any precombination equity owned by the acquirer + the fair value of the noncontrolling interest in the acquiree, if any.

   2. The fair value of the acquiree's net assets is the difference between the acquiree's total assets at fair value and total liabilities at fair value:

Total Assets (@ FV) – Total Liabilities (@ FV) = FV of Net Assets

3. If investment value > fair value of net assets, goodwill is recognized.

Example

No Precombination Ownership of the Acquiree by the Acquirer

a. Facts: On January 2, 20X9, Investco, Inc. acquired all of the outstanding common stock of Lowco, Inc. in the market for $1,000,000 cash and merged the assets acquired and liabilities assumed into Investco. At that date the fair values of Lowco's identifiable assets and liabilities were:

Accounts receivable	$200,000
Inventories	400,000
Property, plant, and equipment	800,000
Other identifiable assets	200,000
TOTAL ASSETS	$1,600,000
Accounts payable	300,000
Other current liabilities	200,000
Long-term liabilities	200,000
TOTAL LIABILITIES	$700,000
FAIR VALUE OF NET ASSETS	$900,000

b. Goodwill calculation:

Investment value = $1,000,000 – Fair value of net assets = $900,000 = $100,000 Goodwill.

c. Entry:

DR: Accounts receivable	$ 200,000	
Inventories	400,000	
Property, plant, and equipment	800,000	
Other identifiable assets	200,000	
Goodwill	100,000	
CR: Accounts payable		$300,000
Other current liabilities		200,000
Long-term liabilities		200,000
Cash		1,000,000

Example
With Precombination Ownership of the Acquiree by the Acquirer

a. Facts: (The following accounts and amounts are taken from a disclosure illustration in ASC 805; the other facts are assumed.)

On January 2, 20X8, Topco, Inc. acquired 15% of the voting equity of Noco, Inc. for $1,200 and subsequently accounted for the investment at fair value. On June 30, 20X9, Topco, Inc. acquired the remaining 85% of Noco, using the following consideration:

Cash	$8,300
Common stock (1,000 shares × $4)	4,000
Contingent consideration obligation	1,000
Total consideration at combination	$13,300

At that date, the fair value of Topco's original 15% was $2,000. Topco incurred $1,250 of acquisition-related costs. Topco's common stock is $1.00 par, with a market value of $4.00 per share at the acquisition date

The fair values and other appropriate values assigned to Noco's identifiable assets and liabilities were:

Financial assets	$3,500
Inventory	1,000
Property, plant, and equipment	10,000
Identifiable intangible assets	3,300
Total Assets	$17,800
Financial liabilities	$4,000
Liability arising from a contingency	1,000
Total Liabilities	$5,000

b. Goodwill calculation:

Investment value:

Acquirer's consideration at combination	$13,300
Acquirer's precombination equity @ FV	2,000
Total Investment Value	$15,300
Fair Value of Net Assets ($17,800 − $5,000)	$12,800
Goodwill = Investment Value > FV of NA	$2,500

c. Entry:

DR: Financial assets*	$3,500	
Inventory*	1,000	
Property, plant, and equipment*	10,000	
Identifiable intangible assets*	3,300	
Goodwill****	2,500	
CR: Financial liabilities*		4,000
Liability arising from contingency*		1,000
Contingent consideration obligation**		1,000
Cash**		8,300
Investment***		2,000
Common stock ($1 par)**		1,000
Additional paid-in capital**		3,000

*Identifiable assets and liabilities acquired.

**Consideration transferred at combination.

***Precombination Investment in Noco at fair value—now part of the cost of the assets and liabilities acquired.

****Computed goodwill

d. Comments on Entry:

[1]The acquirer would have to classify or designate the assets acquired and liabilities assumed to subsequently apply the appropriate GAAP. For example, if any financial assets are investments, the acquirer would need to identify how any equity or debt investment would be classified.

[2]Since the precombination investment in Noco was classified carried at fair value, there is no gain or loss on the previous held 15% interest.

[3]Goodwill recognized by Topco will not be amortized, but will be assessed at least annually for impairment.

[4]The $1,250 cost incurred to carry out the combination is not part of the consideration used to acquire Noco, but would be expensed by Topco when incurred.

D. A bargain purchase would be recognized if the fair value of the net assets of the acquiree at the acquisition date is greater than the investment value in the acquiree.

1. Investment value in the acquiree is the sum of the fair value of consideration transferred to effect the combination + the fair value of any precombination equity owned by the acquirer + the fair value of the noncontrolling interest in the acquiree, if any.

2. The fair value of the acquiree's net assets is the difference between the acquiree's total assets at fair value and total liabilities at fair value:

Total Assets (@ FV) – Total Liabilities (@ FV) = FV of Net Assets

3. If fair value of net assets > investment value, a bargain purchase gain is recognized.

Example
No Precombination Ownership of the Acquiree by the Acquirer

a. Facts: On January 2, 20X9, Investco, Inc. acquired all of the outstanding common stock of Lowco, Inc. in the market for $850,000 cash and merged the assets acquired and liabilities assumed into Investco. At that date the fair values of Lowco's identifiable assets and liabilities were:

Accounts receivable	$200,000
Inventories	400,000
Property, plant, and equipment	800,000
Other identifiable assets	200,000
TOTAL ASSETS	$1,600,000
Accounts payable	300,000
Other current liabilities	200,000
Long-term liabilities	200,000
TOTAL LIABILITIES	$700,000
FAIR VALUE OF NET ASSETS	$900,000

b. Bargain purchase calculation: Fair value of net assets = $900,000 − investment value = $850,000 = $50,000 bargain purchase amount. This amount would be recognized as a gain in the period of the business combination.

c. Entry:

DR: Accounts receivable	$ 200,000	
Inventories	400,000	
Property, plant, and equipment	800,000	
Other identifiable assets	200,000	
CR: Accounts payable		$300,000
Other current liabilities		200,000
Long-term liabilities		200,000
Cash		850,000
Bargain Purchase Gain		50,000

Example
With Precombination Ownership of the Acquiree by the Acquirer
a. Facts: (The following accounts and amounts are taken from a disclosure illustration in ASC 805; the other facts are assumed.)

On January 2, 20X8, Topco, Inc. acquired 15% of the voting equity of Noco, Inc. for $1,200 and subsequently accounted for the investment at fair value. On June 30, 20X9, Topco, Inc. acquired the remaining 85% of Noco, using the following consideration:

Cash	$5,000
Common stock (1,000 shares × $4)	4,000
Contingent consideration obligation	1,000
Total consideration at combination	$10,000

At that date, the fair value of Topco's original 15% was $2,000. Topco incurred $1,250 of acquisition-related costs. Topco's common stock is $1.00 par, with a market value of $4.00 per share at the acquisition date.

The fair values and other appropriate values assigned to Noco's identifiable assets and liabilities were:

Financial assets	$3,500
Inventory	1,000
Property, plant, and equipment	10,000
Identifiable intangible assets	3,300
Total Assets	$ 17,800
Financial liabilities	$4,000
Liability arising from a contingency	1,000
Total Liabilities	$5,000

b. Bargain purchase calculation:

Investment value:	
Acquirer's consideration at combination	$10,000
Acquirer's precombination equity @ FV	2,000
Total Investment Value	$12,000
Fair Value of Net Assets ($17,800 − $5,000)	$12,800
Bargain Purchase Gain:	
FV of NA > Investment Value	$ 800

596

c. Entry:

DR: Financial assets*	$ 3,500	
Inventory*	1,000	
Property, plant, and equipment*	10,000	
Identifiable intangible assets*	3,300	
CR: Financial liabilities*		4,000
Liability arising from contingency*		1,000
Contingent consideration obligation**		1,000
Cash**		5,000
Investment***		2,000
Common stock ($1 par)**		1,000
Additional paid-in capital**		3,000
Bargain purchase gain****		800

*Identifiable assets and liabilities acquired.

**Consideration transferred at combination.

***Precombination investment in Noco at fair value—now part of the cost of the assets and liabilities acquired.

****Computed bargain purchase gain

d. Comments on Entry:

[1]The acquirer would have to classify or designate the assets acquired and liabilities assumed to subsequently apply the appropriate GAAP. For example, if any financial assets are investments, the acquirer would need to identify how any equity or debt investment would be classified.

[2]Since the precombination investment in Noco was carried at fair value, no gain or loss would be recognized.

[3]The bargain purchase gain will be recognized by Topco in its earnings for the period of the business combination.

[4]The $1,250 cost incurred to carry out the combination is not part of the consideration used to acquire Noco, but would be expensed by Topco when incurred.

III. Recording a Legal Acquisition

A. Recall the characteristics of a legal acquisition:

1. One preexisting entity (acquirer) acquires controlling interest in the voting stock of another preexisting entity (acquiree) and both entities continue to exist and operate as separate legal entities.

2. Example: Company P acquires more than 50% of the voting stock of Company S and Company P does not merge Company S into Company P; rather, Company S continues to exist as a separate corporation with Company P holding the majority of its voting stock.

3. In this legal form, both entities continue to exist, operate, and maintain separate accounting records, but one entity has controlling interest in the other entity.

4. Since the controlling entity may not have 100% ownership of the acquired entity's voting stock, there can be other shareholders with an interest in the acquired entity; those shareholders are the noncontrolling interest.

B. The basic entry by the acquirer to record a legal acquisition using the acquisition method of accounting is:

1. Entry:

> DR: Investment in Subsidiary X (at FV of Consideration Paid)
> CR: Consideration Paid (at FV)

2. Consideration used by the acquirer could include the following and would be measured at fair value (except when transferred assets (or liabilities) remain under the control of the acquirer—then, they would be measured at carrying value to the acquirer):

a. Cash and cash equivalents transferred

b. Other assets transferred

c. Liabilities incurred

d. Equity interest issued, including common and preferred stock, options and warrants

e. Any combination of the above forms of consideration

3. As a result of the acquisition and related entry:

a. A parent-subsidiary relationship is established.

b. The firms operate and maintain accounting books and records as separate entities.

c. The parent carries Investment in Subsidiary on its books using the cost, equity, or other method.

4. The subsidiary will be reported in the consolidated statements of the parent, unless the parent lacks effective control of the subsidiary. (The consolidating process, including when a parent lacks effective control over a subsidiary, is covered in later lessons.)

Example
No Precombination Ownership of the Acquiree by the Acquirer and No Noncontrolling Ownership

1. Facts: On January 2, 20X9, Investco, Inc. acquired all of the outstanding common stock of Lowco, Inc. in the market for $1,000,000 cash in a legal acquisition.

2. Entry:

> DR: Investment in Lowco, Inc. (Subsidiary) $1,000,000
> CR: Cash $1,000,000

3. At that date, Investco also would have to determine the following information:

a. The book values of Lowco's assets and liabilities

b. The fair value of Lowco's assets and liabilities

c. Any goodwill or bargain purchase amount implicit in the relationship between its investment and the fair value of Lowco's net assets

4. The information determined and "captured" in 3, above, will be the basis for the preparation of consolidated financial statements; the preparation of those statements will include, among other things:

   a. Revaluing Lowco's assets and liabilities to fair value as of the date of the business combination

   b. Recognizing any goodwill or bargain purchase amount implicit in the business combination

Example
With Precombination Ownership of the Acquiree by the Acquirer and a Noncontrolling Interest

1. Facts: (The following accounts and amounts are taken from a disclosure illustration in ASC 805; the other facts are assumed.)

On January 2, 20X8, Topco, Inc. acquired 15% of the voting equity of Noco, Inc. for $1,200 and subsequently accounted for the investment at fair value. On June 30, 20X9, Topco, Inc. acquired an additional 65% of Noco, using the following consideration:

Cash	$5,000
Common stock (1,000 shares × $4)	4,000
Contingent consideration obligation	1,000
Total consideration at combination	$10,000

At that date, the fair value of Topco's original 15% was $2,000. Topco incurred $1,250 cost of acquisition-related costs. The remaining 20% ownership in Noco is the noncontrolling interest. Topco's common stock is $1.00 par, with a market value of $4.00 per share at the acquisition date.

2. Entry:

DR: Investment in Noco, Inc. (Subsidiary)	$12,000	
CR: Contingent consideration obligation		1,000
Cash		5,000
Investment		2,000
Common stock ($1 par)		1,000
Additional paid-in capital		3,000

3. Comments on Entry:

   a. Since the precombination investment in Noco was carried at fair value, no gain or loss would be recognized on the acquisition date.

   b. The $1,250 cost incurred to carry out the combination is not part of the consideration used to acquire Noco, but would be expensed by Topco when incurred.

4. At that date, Topco would also have to determine the following information:

   a. The book values of Noco's assets and liabilities.

   b. The fair value of Noco's assets and liabilities.

   c. The fair value of the 20% noncontrolling interest.

   d. Any goodwill or bargain purchase amount implicit in the relationship between the investment value in Noco (Topco's consideration transferred—$10,000, plus its precombination investment at fair value—$2,000, plus the fair value of the noncontrolling interest) and the fair value of Noco's net assets.

5. The information determined and "captured" in 4, above, will be the basis for the preparation of consolidated financial statements; the preparation of those statements will include, among other things:

   a. Revaluing Noco's assets and liabilities to fair value as of the date of the business combination

   b. Recognizing the fair value of the noncontrolling interest in Noco as an equity item

   c. Recognizing any goodwill or bargain purchase amount implicit in the business combination

6. On Topco's books, it will carry its investment in its subsidiary Noco as an asset using the cost method, the equity method, or the fair value method; that investment will be eliminated in the consolidating process and consolidated financial statements will be issued for Topco and Noco.

Financial Instruments

Financial Instruments Introduction

This lesson begins a set of lessons (a new study unit) that covers financial instruments, including derivatives and the use of financial instruments and other contracts for speculation and hedging purposes. Specifically, this lesson introduces the material by defining financial instruments, giving common examples of financial instruments that are (financial) assets and (financial) liabilities, and providing an overview of the other lessons covering financial instruments and related matters.

After studying this lesson, you should be able to:

1. Define financial instruments.

2. Identify asset and liability accounts that are financial instruments.

I. **Introduction**—The term **financial instruments** includes a diverse variety of items found in business activity. Financial instruments include cash, accounts/notes receivable, accounts/notes payable, bonds, common stock, preferred stock, stock options, foreign currency forward contracts, futures contracts, various financial swaps, and so on. Some of these items are common, well understood, and have long-established accounting treatments. Other financial instruments are not so common nor are they well understood, and often they challenge accounting principles. Those challenges are further complicated by the ongoing development of even more exotic financial instruments.

II. **Financial Instruments**

    A. **Defined**—Other contracts that are also considered financial instruments meet the following criteria as presented in ASC 825:

        1. **Cash**—Including foreign currency and demand deposits

        2. **Evidence of an ownership interest in an entity**—(Including investments in common and preferred stock, warrants and options to purchase stock, and partnership and limited liability company interest)

        3. **Contracts that result in an exchange of cash or ownership interest in an entity and that both**

            a. **Impose on one entity a contractual obligation or duty (liability)**

                i. To deliver cash (e.g., trade accounts payable, loan obligations, bonds payable, etc.) or another financial instrument (e.g., a note payable in US Treasury bonds) to a **second entity**, *or*

                ii. To exchange financial instruments on potentially unfavorable terms with a **second entity**.

            b. **Conveys to a second entity a contractual right (asset)**

                i. To receive cash (e.g., accounts receivable, investment in bonds, etc.) or another financial instrument from the **first entity**, *or*

                ii. To exchange financial instruments on potentially favorable terms with the **first entity**.

        4. Derivatives are a special form of financial instrument, which will be defined and described in a subsequent lesson.

    B. Common Examples—Many of the items covered in prior lessons were financial instruments, either financial assets or financial liabilities. Those items (accounts), as well as other financial assets and financial liabilities, include:

        1. Financial assets

            a. Cash and cash equivalents

            b. Accounts receivable

            c. Investments in debt (notes, bonds, etc.) and equity securities (common and preferred stock, etc.)

            d. Interest in partnerships, limited liability entities, and joint ventures

            e. Option contracts (w/favorable terms)

            f. Futures and forward contracts (w/favorable terms)

            g. Swap contracts (w/favorable terms)

        2. Financial liabilities

            a. Accounts payable

            b. Notes and bonds payable

            c. Option contracts (w/unfavorable terms)

            d. Futures and forward contracts (w/unfavorable terms)

            e. Swap contracts (w/unfavorable terms)

III. Transaction Costs—The treatment of cost associated with acquiring a financial asset or incurring a financial liability depends on the nature and treatment of the particular financial instrument:

    A. For all financial instruments (assets or liabilities) to be measured at fair value, the transaction costs associated with acquiring or incurring the item are excluded from the cost of the financial instrument.

    B. Except for certain costs associated with the purchase of (investment in) debt and lending activities, transaction costs directly attributable to the financial item are expensed when incurred.

    C. Costs associated with debt issuance (incurring financial liabilities) are treated as deferred charges.

IV. Impairment Assessment—Financial assets must be assessed for impairment and, if it is determined that fair value is less than carrying value and the decline is other than temporary, the asset must be written down and (generally) a loss recognized in current income.

    A. If the financial asset is classified as available for sale, it must be assessed for impairment because, even though it is carried at fair value, changes in fair value are not reported through income; an impairment loss must be reported through income.

    B. If the financial asset is a debt security, then the treatment of the loss depends on whether or not the entity expects to dispose of the security before its carrying amount is recovered.

        1. If the entity does not expect to hold the debt security until recovery of its carrying amount, the loss is recognized in current income.

        2. If the entity expects to hold the debt security until recovery of its carrying amount, the loss must be separated into two components:

            a. Any portion of loss in fair value attributable to credit standing of the issuer is recognized in income; *and*

            b. Any other loss in fair value is recognized in other comprehensive income, net of tax.

V. Preview—The following lessons dealing with financial instruments cover:

   A. The required and recommended disclosures that apply to all financial instruments, including derivatives.

   B. The definition of derivatives, as a special form of financial instrument, and the measurement requirements, which apply to all derivatives.

   C. The different accounting requirements, which apply depending on the specific purpose for which a derivative instrument is held. Four possible purposes are identified for accounting:

   1. To speculate;

   2. As a fair value hedge;

   3. As a cash flow hedge; *or*

   4. As a foreign currency hedge.

Financial Instruments Disclosures

This lesson identifies and describes the financial statement disclosures required and recommended for all financial instruments, including derivatives. Requirements include fair value disclosures and concentration of credit risk disclosures; market risk-related disclosures are recommended, but not required.

After studying this lesson, you should be able to:

1. Describe the disclosure requirements recommended (but not required) for all financial instruments.

2. Describe the disclosures that are required.

I. **Fair Value and Related Disclosure Requirements That Apply to All Financial Instruments**

   A. **The following must be disclosed for all financial instruments, whether recognized or not recognized in the balance sheet (except as noted in D, below), for which it is practicable to estimate fair value.**

      1. Fair value

      2. Related carrying amount

      3. Whether the instrument/amount is an asset or liability

   B. **Practicable to Estimate**—Means that fair value estimates can be made without incurring excessive costs; it is a cost/benefit assessment. If it is not practicable to estimate fair value, the following must be disclosed:

      1. The reasons that it is not practicable to estimate fair value, *and*

      2. Information pertinent to estimating fair value, such as carrying amount, effective interest rate, and maturity.

   C. **Fair Value Measurement**—Should be determined in accordance with the definition and requirements of ASC 820, *Fair-Value Measurement*.

      1. *Fair value* is the price that would be received to sell an asset or paid to transfer a liability in an orderly transaction between market participants at the measurement date.

      2. Quoted market prices in an active market provide the most reliable evidence of fair value.

   D. Disclosures about fair value **are not required** for the following financial items:

      1. Employer's and plan's obligations for pension benefits, postretirement benefits, postemployment benefits, employee stock option and stock purchase plans, and other forms of deferred compensation arrangements

      2. Substantially extinguished debt

      3. Insurance contracts (other than financial guarantee insurance contracts) and certain investments made by insurance entities

      4. Lease contracts

      5. Warranty obligations and rights

      6. Unconditional purchase contracts

      7. Investments accounted for under the equity method

      8. Noncontrolling interest in a consolidated subsidiary

      9. Equity instruments issued and classified in shareholders' equity

E. No fair value disclosure is required for trade accounts receivable or trade accounts payable when their carrying amounts approximate fair value.

F. **Netting**—Fair values of different financial instruments may not be netted, even if they are of the same class or otherwise related.

G. **Required Disclosures**—May be in either the body of the financial statements or in the footnotes. If in the footnotes, one note must show fair values and carrying amounts for all financial instruments.

II. **Concentration of Credit Risk Disclosure Requirement That Apply to All Financial Instruments**

A. **Disclosures Required**—Entities must disclose all significant concentrations of credit risks arising from all financial instruments (with limited exceptions) whether from a single party or a group of parties engaged in similar activities and that have similar economic characteristics.

B. **Credit Risk Defined**—Credit risk is the possibility of loss from the failure of another party (or parties) to perform according to the terms of a contract.

C. **Concentrations of Credit Risk Defined**—Concentration of credit risk occurs when an entity has contracts of material value with one or more parties in the same industry or region or having similar economic characteristics (e.g., receivables from a group of highly leveraged entities).

D. **The Following Must be Disclosed**—About each significant concentration of credit risk:

1. **Information about the common activity, region, or economic characteristic that identifies the concentration;**

2. **The maximum amount of loss due to the credit risk** (measured as the gross fair value of the financial instruments) that would occur if the other parties failed completely to perform according to the terms of the contract and assuming any collateral was of no value;

3. **The entity's policy of requiring collateral or other security to support financial instruments subject to credit risk**, a brief description of any collateral, and information about the entity's access to the collateral; *and*

4. **The entity's policy of entering into master netting arrangements to reduce the credit risk associated with financial instruments**, a brief description of any such arrangements, and the extent to which such arrangements would reduce the entity's maximum risk of loss.

III. **Market Risk Disclosures Are Recommended**

A. **Market risk disclosures for financial instruments are NOT required** but are encouraged.

B. **Market risk** is the possibility of loss from changes in market value due to changes in economic circumstances, not necessarily due to the failure of another party.

C. **Entities are encouraged to disclose quantitative information about the market risk of financial instruments**, including the following possible disclosures:

1. More details about current position and related period activity

2. Hypothetical effects on income of different changes in market prices

3. An analysis of interest rate repricing or maturity dates

4. Duration of financial instruments

5. The entity's value at risk from derivatives

IV. **Other Disclosures**

A. **Qualitative Disclosures**

1. Except for disclosures related to concentrations of credit risk, U.S. GAAP does not require substantive qualitative disclosures about financial instruments.

2. Under SEC requirements, SEC registrants are required to provide qualitative disclosures about:

      a. Market risk

      b. Interest rate risk

      c. Foreign currency risk

      d. Commodity price risk

      e. Similar risks

3. The SEC qualitative disclosures are provided in management's discussion and analysis and not in the financial statements or notes thereto.

B. Quantitative Disclosures

1. Except for disclosures related to concentrations of credit risk, required quantitative disclosures about financial instruments under GAAP are nominal.

2. Under SEC requirements, SEC registrants are required to provide quantitative disclosures only about financial instrument market risk, and those disclosures are in management's discussion and analysis, not in the financial statements or notes thereto.

C. Class Disclosures—Under SEC requirements, SEC registrants are required to provide separate presentation in the balance sheet of financial instruments by class; however, there is no comparable requirement under GAAP for entities that are not SEC registrants.

Derivatives and Hedging

Derivatives Introduction

This lesson defines derivatives and provides guidance on recognition and measurement. Specifically, it identifies the elements necessary for a financial instrument to be a derivative, gives examples of common derivatives and items that are not derivatives, and explains the concept of embedded derivatives. The general recognition requirement applicable to all derivatives is also presented.

After studying this lesson, you should be able to:

1. Define and describe a derivative financial instrument.

2. Identify common derivatives and contracts that are not derivatives for accounting purposes.

3. Identify the criteria for determining when a contract includes an embedded derivative.

4. Describe the general recognition and measurement requirement applicable to all derivatives.

I. **Definitions**

  A. A **derivative** is a financial instrument (or other contract) with all three of the following elements:

    1. **It has one or more** *underlyings* **and one or more** *notional amounts* or payment provisions (if this happens, then that will happen).

      a. An **underlying** is any financial or physical variable that has either observable changes or objectively verifiable changes. Therefore, underlyings include traditional financial measures such as commodity prices, interest rates, exchange rates, or indexes related to any of these items. More broadly, measures such as an entity's credit rating, rainfall, or temperature changes also meet the definition of an underlying.

      b. **Notional** amounts are the "number of currency or other units" specified in the financial instrument or other contract. In the case of options, this could include bushels of wheat, shares of stock, and so on.

      c. The **settlement amount** of a financial instrument or other contract is calculated using the underlying(s) and notional amount(s) in some combination.

        i. Computation of the settlement amount may be as simple as multiplying the fair value of a stock times a specified number of shares.

        ii. However, calculation of the settlement amount may require a very complex calculation, involving ratios, stepwise variables, and other leveraging techniques.

    2. **Derivatives require little or no initial net investment.** Derivatives can be purchased for an amount that is smaller than would be required for other types of similar contracts.

      a. Many derivative instruments require no net investment or simply a premium as compensation for the time value of money.

        i. Futures contracts may require the establishment of a margin account with a balance equal to a small percentage (2–3%) of the value of the contract.

        ii. A call option on a foreign currency contract would cost only a small fraction of the value of the contract.

        iii. These are typical contracts that would meet this definition and would be included in the definition of derivative instruments.

3. **Its terms require or permit a net settlement**—The instrument can be settled for cash or an asset readily convertible to cash in lieu of physical delivery of the subject matter of the contract.

   a. Require or permit net settlement, either within the contract or by a means outside the contract.

      i. Net settlement means that a contract can be settled through the payment of cash rather than the exchange of the specific assets referenced in the contract.

      ii. This type of settlement typically occurs with a currency swap or an interest rate swap.

   b. Provide for the delivery of an asset that puts the recipient in a position not substantially different from net settlement.

      i. This might include a futures contract where one party to the contract delivers an asset but a "market mechanism" exists (such as an exchange) so that the asset can be readily converted to cash. Convertibility to cash requires an active market and is a determining factor in whether a financial instrument or other contract will be treated as a derivative instrument.

Note

The term *notional amount* is sometimes used interchangeably with *settlement amount*.

Read carefully to determine if the context in which the term is used calls for a number of units (notional amount) or a dollar value (settlement amount).

II. **Derivative Examples**—The following contracts are examples of common derivatives.

   A. **Option Contracts**—For example, a stock option that requires the maker to deliver shares of stock at a later time in exchange for a fixed—option—price. The value of the option contract is a function of market price of the stock (compared to the option or strike price) and the number of shares.

   B. **Futures Contracts**—Made through a clearinghouse (e.g., to deliver or receive a commodity or foreign currency in the future at a price set at the present).

   C. **Forward Contracts**—Not made through a clearinghouse (e.g., like a futures contract, but made directly between contracting parties).

   D. **Swap Contracts**—For example, an agreement to exchange currencies, debt securities, or interest rates (e.g., swap fixed rate debt for variable rate debt).

   E. **Other Contracts**—Some contracts have characteristics comparable with those in the above list and should be accounted for as derivative contracts.

III. **Items Not Derivatives**—The following contracts are not derivatives for accounting purposes:

   A. Normal purchases and sales contracts (for something other than a financial instrument)

   B. Regular security trades

   C. Traditional life insurance and property and casualty insurance contracts

   D. Investments in life insurance

   E. Contracts indexed to a company's own stock

   F. Contracts issued in connection with stock-based compensation arrangements

   G. Contracts to enter into a business combination at a future date

   H. Other contracts as listed in ASC 815

IV. Recognition and Measurement—All derivative instruments must be recognized as either an asset (contractual right) or a liability (contractual obligation) and measured at fair value.

    A. The measurement of derivatives at fair value will result in gains and losses.

    B. The accounting treatment of the resulting gains and losses depends on whether the derivative has been designated (and qualifies) as a hedge and, if so, the purpose of the hedge.

V. Embedded Derivative Instruments

    A. A host contract (debt instrument, lease, or equity instrument) may have a feature that results in a derivative *embedded* into the contract.

        1. An embedded derivative exists when the host contract contains a term or component that behaves like a derivative. That is, if the feature stood alone, it would meet the definition of a derivative.

        2. The instrument containing both the host contract and the embedded derivative is called a hybrid instrument.

    B. **Bifurcation** is the process of separating an embedded derivative from its host contract. The process is necessary so that hybrid instruments can be separated into their component parts, each being accounted for by using the appropriate valuation techniques. Bifurcation occurs if the embedded feature meets all of the following requirements:

        1. The economic characteristics and risks of the embedded derivative are not clearly and closely related to the characteristics and risks of the host contract (Example: Debt instrument that is convertible into a fixed number of the debtor's common stock is contingent on an event that has nothing to do with the debt element or the potential equity interest. The contingent event could be a hostile take-over that is not clearly and closely related to the host);

        2. The hybrid instrument (host contact with derivative instrument) is not itself remeasured to fair value with changes reported in current income as they occur; *and*

        3. As a separate instrument, the embedded instrument would meet the requirements of a derivative instrument.

    C. If a single host contract contains more than one embedded derivative that meets the requirements to be accounted for as a separate derivative instrument, those embedded derivatives must be bundled together and treated as a single, compound embedded derivative, which is accounted for separately.

    D. When an embedded derivative is separated from its host contract, the carrying value of the host contract (before bifurcation) is allocated between the embedded derivative and the host contract as follows:

        1. The derivative is initially recorded at its fair value.

        2. The difference between the carrying value of the hybrid contract and the fair value of the derivative element is the initial value of the remaining host contract.

    E. The host contract, without the embedded derivative, will be accounted for based on GAAP applicable to that type of instrument.

    F. A number of hybrid instruments that would normally require bifurcation are listed next.

        1. A bond payable with an interest rate based on the S&P 500 index

        2. An equity instrument (stock) with a call option, allowing the issuing company to buy back the stock

        3. An equity instrument with a put option, requiring the issuing company to buy back the stock at the request of the holder

        4. A loan agreement that permits the debtor to pay off the loan prior to its maturity with the loan payoff penalty based on the short-term T-bill rates

VI. Accounting for Derivatives Not Designated for Hedge Accounting

A. In this case, the derivative (contract) is not intended to hedge (offset) a separate risk or does not meet the accounting requirements to qualify as a hedge. For example, the derivative (e.g., a stock option contract) may have been entered into for speculative purposes (i.e., to make a profit).

B. Initial Recognition

1. An acquired contract that is a derivative instrument is initially measured and recorded at the then-current fair value.

2. Sample entry, assuming the acquisition of a derivative asset with value at the date of acquisition:

DR: Investment in Derivative

    CR: Cash (or other compensation)

C. Subsequent Measurement and Recognition—Changes in the fair value of these derivatives result in:

1. Adjusting the carrying value of the derivative instrument to current fair value (i.e., increase or decrease an asset or a liability); *and*

2. Recognizing the related gain or loss in current income.

D. Below is a brief description of the value components of options. Options have both intrinsic value (strike price less market price) and time value (option value less intrinsic value). Options can also be *in-the-money* or *out-of-the-money*.

1. Options

a. Call (right to buy)—A call is in-the-money when the strike price is less than the spot price.

b. Put (right to sell)—A put is in-the-money when the strike price is greater than the spot.

c. Assume—Stock with a $30 market value has an at-the-money option with a strike price of $30 (market = strike so the entire option value at the time of purchase is time value—this is an *at-the-money* option), and this option sells for $2 and is good for 60 days.

	Market price $35	Market price $25
Call (right to buy)	In the money	Out of the money
Put (right to sell)	Out of the money	In the money

d. Option value = intrinsic value + time value. In the next table, assume that the option price is quoted to be $8 per option.

e. **Intrinsic value = in-the-money (ITM) value**

	Option value = (quoted value)	Intrinsic Value + (ITM value)	Time value (quoted value—ITM)
Call (right to buy)	8	5 (35 Market—30 Strike)	3
	8	0 (25 Market—30 Strike)	8
Put (right to sell)	8	0 (35 Market—30 Strike)	8
	8	5 (25 Market—30 Strike)	3

f. The accounting for the intrinsic value and time value can be different depending on how the derivative is used. Time value is associated with the time value of money or the anticipated passage of time—where intrinsic value is value associated with the amount of benefit that is associated with the derivative terms relative to the market price.

2. **Futures and forwards**

   a. Time value for futures and forwards is most commonly calculated as the time value of money.

E. The following simplified example illustrates the accounting for a derivative held for speculative purposes (i.e., to make a profit).

Example

On December 1, year 1, Echo, Inc. purchased options to buy (a call option) 1,000 shares of Levy, Inc. in 60 days at a strike price of $45 per share when Levy's stock was selling for $43 per share in the market. Echo's purchase of the options was based on its intent to earn a profit on expected short-term increases in the market price of Levy's stock. On December 31, year 1, Levy stock was selling in the market for $46 per share.

Because the options have a strike price of $45 per share, Echo can purchase 1,000 shares of Levy from the option counterparty for $45 per share, even though the stock is selling in the market for $46 per share. Thus, on December 31 the options have a fair value of $1,000 (1,000 options × ($46 – $45) = $1,000).

1. Echo would make the following entry as of December 31, year 1:

   DR: Stock Options (market price > strike price) $1,000
       CR: Gain on Stock Options $1,000

2. The gain would be recognized in current income.

VII. Hedging

A. Hedging Is a Risk Management Strategy—Hedging involves using offsetting (or counter) transactions or positions so that a loss on one transaction or position would be offset (at least in part) by a gain on another transaction or position (and vice versa).

1. You would "hedge a bet" by offsetting a possible loss (from betting on one team to win) by also betting on the other team to win.

2. You would hedge against a possible loss in inventory value by entering into a contract to sell comparable inventory at a fixed price (set now) for future delivery.

B. For accounting purposes, derivative financial instruments that meet certain criteria may be used as hedges of the risks associated with certain economic undertakings and account balances.

C. For accounting purposes, nonderivative financial instruments may not be used to hedge an asset, liability, unrecognized firm commitment, or forecasted transaction, except that a nonderivative instrument denominated in a foreign currency may be used to hedge the foreign currency exposure of an unrecognized firm commitment to be settled in a foreign currency or a net investment in a foreign operation. (Certain concepts used in this **item** are developed in the immediately following lessons dealing with hedging.)

Hedging Introduction

This lesson makes the distinction between hedging and hedge accounting. There are three broad categories of hedge accounting. This lesson identifies those categories and the documentation required in order to get hedge accounting. In addition, this lesson describes the elements in a hedging relationship, the general kinds of risk that may be hedged, the specific risk components that may be hedged for accounting purposes, and the items and instruments that cannot be used for accounting hedges.

After studying this lesson, you should be able to:

1. Identify the possible uses of derivatives for accounting purposes.

2. Identify and describe the basic elements of a hedge relationship.

3. Identify the basic kinds of hedges for accounting purposes.

4. Identify the specific kinds of risks that can be hedged for accounting purposes.

5. Identify items and instruments that cannot be used for accounting hedges.

I. Hedging

A. Hedging means that the entity utilizes a derivative financial instrument to offset the risk related to a transaction, item, or event:

1. **Natural or economic hedges**—A derivative can be used as a natural hedge with no special hedge accounting treatment. In a natural hedge, both the underlying risk and the derivative instrument are marked-to-market value through earnings. The changes in the value of the hedged risk and derivative offset—to the extent these match, there is no impact on net income.

2. **Hedge accounting**—If certain conditions are met, a derivative may be specifically designated as a hedging instrument and special hedge accounting can be used. The gain (loss) on the derivative (the hedging instrument) is used to match the loss (gain) on the hedged item.

II. Criteria to Use Hedge Accounting

A. Criterion #1—Formal designation and documentation at inception of the hedge including the hedging relationship, the entity's strategy and objective for undertaking the hedge, the nature of the risk being hedged, and the methods used to assess effectiveness.

B. Criterion #2—Eligibility of hedged items and transactions

C. Criterion #3—Eligibility of hedging instruments

D. Criterion #4—Hedge effectiveness; the hedge should be expected to be highly effective throughout its life

1. Effectiveness is measured by analyzing the hedging instrument's ability to generate changes in fair value or cash flows that offset the changes in value or cash flows of the hedged risk item both retrospectively and prospectively.

2. At a minimum, effectiveness will be measured quarterly and whenever earnings or financial statements are reported. The entity will determine whether the hedging relationship has been highly effective in achieving offsetting changes in fair value or cash flows through the date of assessment. An entity can base the measurement on regression or other statistical analysis.

3. The method used to assess effectiveness must be used throughout the hedge period and must be consistent with the approach used for managing risk.

III. Hedge Elements—Hedging involves two basic elements; those elements are:

  A. Hedged Item—The recognized asset, recognized liability, commitment, or planned transaction that is at risk of loss; it is the possible loss on the hedged item that is hedged.

  B. Hedging Instrument—The contract or derivative instrument that is entered into to mitigate or eliminate the risk of loss associated with the hedged item.

IV. Types of Hedge Accounting—Hedge accounting generally provides for matching the recognition of gains and losses of the hedging instrument and the hedged asset or liability. Instruments that qualify as hedging instruments will be accounted for using hedge accounting in one of the following three ways:

  A. Fair Value Hedge:

   1. A hedge of the exposure to changes in the fair value in one of the following:

      a. A recognized asset or liability *or*

      b. An unrecognized firm commitment

  B. Cash Flow Hedge:

   1. A hedge of the exposure to variability in the cash flows in the following:

      a. A recognized asset or liability *or*

      b. A forecasted transaction

  C. Foreign Currency Hedge:

   1. A hedge of the foreign currency exposure in one of the following:

      a. An unrecognized firm commitment

      b. An available-for-sale security

      c. A forecasted transaction

      d. A net investment in a foreign operation *or*

      e. Foreign currency–denominated assets and liabilities

V. Items Eligible for Hedge Accounting—For accounting purposes, there are risks that can be designated as the hedged item.

  A. For financial assets and financial liabilities, the following risks can be hedged:

   1. Commodity price risk

   2. Interest rate risk

   3. Foreign exchange risk

   4. Credit risk (except not for investments in available-for-sale securities)

VI. Items Not Eligible for Hedge Accounting—For accounting purposes, a number of items are specifically excluded from being designated as a hedged item. Those include, among others, the following:

  A. An investment accounted for using the equity method of accounting

  B. A firm commitment to carry out a business combination

  C. A noncontrolling interest in a subsidiary

  D. Transactions between entities included in consolidated statements, except for foreign currency–denominated forecasted intra-entity transactions

  E. Transactions with shareholders as shareholders (e.g., projected purchase of treasury stock or payment of dividends)

VII. Summary of Hedged Item and Fair Value Versus Cash Flow Hedge Accounting

Item	Fair Value Hedge	Cash Flow Hedge
Recognized asset or liability	Hedges the risk of changes in the fair value of the hedged item	Hedges the risk related to the cash flows of the hedged item
Firm commitment	Hedges the risk related to the fair value changes of the commitment. The firm commitment is recognized as an asset or liability if hedged.	Not applicable
Forecasted transaction	Not applicable	Hedges the cash flows related to a forecasted transaction. The forecasted transaction must be specifically identifiable, probable, and with a party external to the reporting entity.
Gain or loss on hedged item	Recognized in income statement line item associated with hedged risk[1]	Recognized in other comprehensive income[2]
Gain or loss on hedging instrument	Recognized in income statement line item associated with hedged risk (offsetting above)[1]	Recognized in other comprehensive income[2]

[1]Gains and losses on hedged item and the hedging instrument shall be recognized in current earnings. To the extent that the hedge is effective, the gains and losses will offset in the same line item on the income statement. To the extent that the hedge is ineffective, the effect will show in current earnings as a gain or loss with no offset.

[2]The gains or losses deferred in OCI are reclassified to net income in the period that the hedged item impacts earnings. The reclassification is to the line item associated with the hedged risk.

VIII. Two Common Transactions to Which Hedge Accounting Is Applied

A. Forecasted Transaction

1. A transaction that is expected to occur for which there is no firm commitment. Because no transaction or event has yet occurred, when the transaction or event does occur, it will be at the prevailing market price (ASC 815).

2. The forecasted transaction must be:

   a. Specifically identifiable, probable to occur (ASC 450), with an external party, and does not involve future assets/liabilities that will be remeasured through earnings

3. Accounting for a forecasted transaction—unhedged:

   a. A forecasted item is recorded at the market value on the day the forecasted transaction occurs.

Example

Assume that on May 1, the company anticipates the purchase of 1,000 barrels (bbls) of fuel oil in six months (November 1). The quantity of the fuel oil is what is normally used in the course of business. The company has not selected a specific vendor or set a price. The spot price of fuel oil on May 1 is $70 bbl and the spot price on November 1 is $85 bbl. No entry would be made at the forecast date or at any time during the forecast period. An entry is made on November 1 when the fuel oil is actually purchased. The entries would be:

Date	May 1		November 1	
Price	($70 bbl)		($85 bbl)	
Entry	No entry	DR: Fuel Oil	$85,000	
		CR: Cash		$85,000

4. **Risk—cash flows**—The cash flows on November 1 are uncertain and have variability and are dependent on the price on November 1.

5. **Benefits of a forecasted transaction:**

   a. Flexibility with respect to vendor, price, quantity, quality, delivery specifics

   b. Allows the company to complete due diligence on potential vendors

   c. Allows the company to "shop around" on the days prior to the purchase

   d. Increased possibility for price concessions in the days prior to the purchase (i.e., discounts and incentives)

   e. Prices may decrease and the purchase price will be lower

6. Limitations of a forecasted transaction:

   a. Prices may increase.

   b. Shortage of supply and cannot obtain the fuel oil (or must obtain substandard quality)

   c. No opportunity to build a relationship with a single vendor

B. Firm Commitment

1. An agreement with an unrelated party that is binding on both parties and usually legally enforceable. The agreement usually specifies all significant terms (including quantity to be exchanged, fixed price, timing of the transaction) and includes a disincentive for nonperformance that is sufficiently large enough to make performance probable (ASC 815).

2. Accounting for a firm commitment—unhedged:

   a. A firm commitment is also known as a purchase (or sales) commitment and is recorded at the commitment price on the date specified in the firm commitment.

Example

Assume that on May 1, the company enters into a firm commitment with a specific vendor to purchase 1,000 barrels (bbls) of fuel oil in six months. The firm commitment specifies the quantity, quality, price and delivery terms. The firm commitment price agreed to on May 1 is $70 bbl with delivery on November 1. The spot price of fuel oil on May 1 is $70 bbl and the spot price on November 1 is $85 bbl. No entry would be made on the date of the firm commitment (May 1) or at any time during the firm commitment period. An entry is made on November 1 when the fuel oil is actually purchased and the fuel oil would be recorded at the firm commitment price. The entries are as follows:

Date	May 1		November 1	
Price	($70 bbl)		($85 bbl)	
Entry	No entry	DR: Fuel Oil	$70,000	
		CR: Cash		$70,000

---

3. **Risk—fair value**—The fair value of the $70,000 contract goes up if the price goes up to $85 (because you can get the oil cheaper than the market price). The fair value of the contract goes down if the price goes down to $65 (because you have to pay a price higher than the market price).

4. Benefits of a firm commitment:

   a. Certainty with respect to vendor, price, quantity, quality, delivery specifics

   b. Permits better budgeting

   c. Allows the company to develop a relationship with a specific vendor

   d. Increases the likelihood of obtaining the product if there is a shortage

   e. Mitigates the risk of prices increasing

5. Limitations of a firm commitment:

   a. Prices may decrease

   b. Vendor may go bankrupt

   c. Less opportunity to build relationships with other vendors

   d. Cannot take advantage of last minute discounts

IX. **Exclusions**—For accounting purposes, a number of instruments are specifically excluded from being used as a hedging instrument. Those include, among others, the following:

   A. A nonderivative instrument (e.g., U.S. Treasury note), except as permitted in certain intracompany cases for:

      1. Hedging changes in the fair value of an unrecognized firm commitment attributable to foreign currency exchange rates, *or*

      2. Hedging the foreign currency exposure of a net investment in a foreign operation.

         a. The net investment in foreign operations is a very common risk that is hedged and is permitted under ASC 805 (listed above). In fact, the hedge of net investments in foreign operations is so common that the rules that restrict the hedging instrument are relaxed so that the net investment of foreign operations can be hedged with nonderivative instruments.

   B. Components of a compound derivative instrument used for different risks.

   C. A hybrid financial instrument if:

      1. It is irrevocably elected to be measured in its entirety at fair value under the fair value option, *or*

      2. It has an embedded derivative that cannot be reliably identified and measured.

Fair Value Hedges

This lesson covers the accounting for fair value hedges. As the name implies, the purpose of this hedge is to offset changes in the fair value of the hedged item. This lesson will define fair value hedges, the requirements that must be met in order for a derivative to be treated as a fair value hedge, and the accounting treatment of derivatives and related hedged items in a fair value hedge.

After studying this lesson, you should be able to:

1. Define a fair value hedge.

2. Describe the criteria that must be met for a derivative to qualify as a fair value hedge.

3. Describe the accounting for derivatives used as fair value hedges and for the related hedged item.

4. Describe the accounting when the requirements for a fair value hedge are no longer satisfied.

I. **Accounting for Fair Value Hedges**

A. A fair value hedge is the hedge of an exposure to changes in fair value of a (recognized) asset, liability, or an unrecognized firm commitment due to a particular risk. A fair value hedge converts a fixed price to a floating price.

1. For example, the use of a futures contract to hedge the fair value of a recognized asset or liability such as inventory.

2. A derivative can also be used to hedge the fair value of an **unrecognized firm commitment.** A firm commitment exists when an entity enters into a contract to buy or sell (i.e., a purchase commitment).

a. Unhedged firm commitments are not recognized because the purchase has not yet occurred. Once the firm commitment is designated as the hedged item, the changes in the fair value of the firm commitment are recognized.

b. A firm commitment to purchase an item is at a fixed price. The changes in the market price relative to the firm commitment price will increase or decrease the fair value of the firm commitment contract.

i. For example: Assume a company has a firm commitment to purchase fuel oil at $60 a barrel. If the market price of the fuel oil rises to $65 a barrel, the fair value of the firm commitment contract has increased because the company can buy the fuel oil at a price less than the market price. If the price of the fuel oil declines to $50 a barrel, then the fair value of the firm commitment contract will decrease because the company is locked into a price that is higher than the market price.

B. A derivative may be used to create a fair value hedge only if both the hedging instrument (the derivative) and the hedged item (asset, liability, or firm commitment) meet **certain criteria**, including:

1. There must be **formal documentation** of (1) the hedging relationship, (2) the objective and strategy for undertaking the hedge, (3) identification of the hedging instrument and the hedged item, (4) the nature of the risk being hedged, (5) how effectiveness of the hedge will be assessed, and (6) when a firm commitment is the hedged item, how the related asset or liability will be recognized.

2. Both at inception of the hedge and on an ongoing basis, the hedge must be expected to be **highly effective** in offsetting changes in fair value of the hedged item, **with an assessment** of effectiveness required **when financial statements are prepared and at least every three months.**

3. The hedged item (1) is specifically identified as a recognized asset, liability, or firm commitment (or portion thereof), (2) presents exposure to changes in fair value that could affect reported income, (3) is not accounted for at fair value with changes reported in income, (4) not an investment accounted for using the equity method, (5) not a noncontrolling interest or an equity interest in a consolidated subsidiary and (6) if a debt security classified as held-to-maturity, the risk being hedged is the creditworthiness of the obligor (not the interest rate because the investor intends to hold to maturity).

C. **Additional Qualifications**

1. The following interest rates may be hedged:

   a. Direct U.S. Treasury obligations

   b. London Interbank Offer Rate (LIBOR)

   c. The securities industry swap rate (Securities Industry and Financial Markets Association [SIFMA] Municipal Swap Rate)

2. If the hedged item is a nonfinancial asset or liability, the risk being hedged is the risk of change in the fair value of the entire hedged asset or liability, not a portion of the asset or liability.

D. **Changes**—Changes in fair value of both the derivative qualifying as a fair value hedge (hedging instrument) and the asset, liability, or firm commitment being hedged (hedged item) are accounted for by:

1. **Adjusting the carrying amount of both the derivative and the hedged item to fair value**.

   a. If the hedged item is a firm commitment, an asset or liability is recognized on the balance sheet when the initial adjustment occurs.

   b. The amount of the adjustment to the hedged item becomes a part of the carrying amount of the item and is accounted for as such.

2. **Recognizing gains and losses from revaluing both the derivative and the hedged item in current income**.

   a. If the hedged item is normally adjusted through "other comprehensive income" (i.e., an available-for-sale debt investment), the change in fair value, if hedged, must be recognized in current income.

   b. The gains or losses on the hedged item and hedging instrument are reported on the same line item in the income statement (typically the line item associated with the risked that is being hedged). To the extent the gain or loss on the hedging instrument offsets the loss or gain on the hedged item, the hedge is "effective." To the extent the gain or loss on the hedging instrument is more or less than that on the hedged item, the hedge is "ineffective" and will result in a net effect (gain or loss) on current income.

E. If the criteria for fair value hedges are no longer met, the derivative may no longer be accounted for as a hedge.

    1. If the hedged item was an unrecognized firm commitment, the asset or liability created to account for its change in value must be written off and a corresponding gain or loss recognized in current income.

F. Hedged assets and liabilities should continue to be assessed for impairment.

Cash-Flow Hedges

This lesson covers the accounting for a cash flow hedge. As the name of the use implies, the purpose of this hedge is to reduce the variability related to uncertain future cash flows. This lesson defines cash flow hedges, the requirements that must be met in order for cash flow hedge accounting, and an overview of the accounting for the derivative and related hedged item.

After studying this lesson, you should be able to:

1. Define a cash flow hedge.

2. Describe the criteria that must be met for a derivative to qualify as a cash flow hedge.

3. Describe the accounting for derivatives used in cash flow hedges and for the related hedged item.

4. Describe the accounting when the requirements for a cash flow hedge are no longer satisfied.

I. Accounting for Cash Flow Hedges

A. A cash flow hedge is the hedge of an exposure to variability (changes) in the cash flow associated with a (recognized) asset, liability, or a forecasted transaction due to a particular risk. A cash flow hedge converts a floating price to a fixed price.

   1. For example, the use of an interest-rate swap to hedge the cash outflow from variable-rate debt, or the use of a futures contract to hedge the cash inflow from a forecasted sale.

   2. A **forecasted transaction** is a planned or expected transaction with a third party, but for which there is not yet a firm commitment and there are not yet any established rights or obligations associated with the planned transaction.

B. A derivative may be accounted for as a cash flow hedge only if both the hedging instrument (the derivative) and the hedged item (asset, liability, or forecasted transaction) meet **certain criteria**, including:

   1. There must be **formal documentation** of (1) the hedging relationship, (2) the objective and strategy for undertaking the hedge, (3) identification of the hedging instrument and the hedged item, (4) the nature of the risk being hedged, and (5) how effectiveness of the hedge will be assessed.

   2. Both at inception of the hedge and on an ongoing basis, the hedge must be expected to **be highly effective** in offsetting change in cash flow of the hedged item, with an assessment of effectiveness required when financial statements are prepared and at least every 3 months.

   3. A forecasted transaction can be hedged only if it is (1) specifically identified as a single transaction or group of individual transactions with the same risk exposure, (2) probable of occurring, (3) with an external party (except for certain intercompany hedges), (4) capable of affecting cash flows that would affect earnings, and (5) not for the acquisition of an asset or the incurrence of a liability, which is accounted for at fair value with the change reported in current income.

C. Additional Qualifications

   1. If the hedged item is the cash flow from a forecasted transaction related to an investment classified as held to maturity, the risk being hedged is the risk of changes in cash flow attributable to credit risk, foreign exchange risk, or both.

   2. If the hedged item is the cash flow from a forecasted transaction, it cannot involve:

      a. A business combination;

      b. A parent's equity interest in a subsidiary; or

      c. An entity's own equity instruments.

D. Changes in Fair Value of Derivatives Qualifying as Cash Flow Hedges (Hedging Instrument) are Accounted for by

1. Determining for each period the change in (1) the fair value of the derivative (hedging instrument) and (2) the present value of the cash flows associated with the asset, liability, or forecasted transaction being hedged (hedged item)

2. Determining for each period (1) the cumulative change in the fair value of the derivative and (2) the cumulative change in the present value of the cash flows associated with the hedged item

3. Recognizing in other comprehensive income the change in the fair value of the derivative for the period (write up or write down the derivative)

4. Recognizing in other comprehensive income the amount equal to the (cumulative) change in the present value of cash flows associated with the hedged item

E. In a cash flow hedge, deferred gains/losses are reported as a component of **Other Comprehensive Income** in the Statement of Comprehensive Income for the period and in **Accumulated Other Comprehensive Income** in the Balance Sheet **until the period(s) in which the hedged item affects income**. For example:

1. The hedge of a forecasted sale would be reclassified to (and recognized in) income in the period of the sale.

2. The hedge of a forecasted purchase of a depreciable asset would be reclassified to (and recognized in) income over the periods depreciation expense is taken on the asset.

F. If the criteria for cash flow hedges are no longer met, the derivative may no longer be accounted for as a hedge.

1. The deferred gain or loss remaining in accumulated other comprehensive income should be reclassified to (and recognized in) income in the period(s) in which the hedged items affect income.

2. If a hedged forecasted transaction is no longer expected to occur, the deferred gain or loss in accumulated other comprehensive income should be reclassified to (and recognized in) income immediately.

G. Assets and liabilities for which related cash flows have been hedged should continue to be assessed for impairment.

1. If an impairment loss is recognized, any deferred gain in accumulated other comprehensive income should be reclassified (recognized) to offset the loss.

Foreign Currency Hedges

This lesson covers the hedge of amounts denominated (to be settled) in a foreign currency. As the name of the use implies, the purpose of these derivatives is to offset changes in the dollar value of expected transactions, commitments, transactions and balances measured in a foreign currency. This lesson identifies and describes the alternative foreign currency hedges; lessons included in the "Foreign Currency Denominated Transactions" section cover these hedges in detail.

After studying this lesson, you should be able to:

1. Define a foreign currency hedge.

2. Identify and describe the specific kinds of foreign currency items that may be hedged.

I. **Accounting for Derivatives That Qualify as Foreign Currency Hedges and Other Eligible Contracts Used as Foreign Currency Hedges**—(This is a summary introduction; the full details of such hedges are covered in subsequent lessons.)

> **Definition**
> *Foreign Currency Hedge*: The hedge of an exposure to changes in the dollar value of assets or liabilities (including certain investments) and planned transactions that are denominated (to be settled) in a currency other than an entity's functional currency (i.e., a foreign currency).

A. An entity may **hedge foreign currency exposure of** the following kinds:

1. **Forecasted foreign-currency-denominated transactions**—(including inter-company transactions). The risk being hedged is the risk that exchange rate changes will have on the **cash flow** from nonfirm but planned transactions to be settled in a foreign currency. For example, the dollar value of royalty revenue **forecasted to be received** in a foreign currency from a foreign entity, including a related entity.

2. **Unrecognized foreign-currency-denominated firm commitments**—The risk being hedged is the risk that exchange rate changes will have on the **fair value** or **cash flow** of firm commitments for a future sale or purchase to be settled in a foreign currency. For example, a commitment (contract) to purchase custom-built equipment from a foreign manufacturer with payment to be made in a foreign currency.

3. **Foreign-currency-denominated recognized assets**—(e.g., receivables) **or liabilities** (e.g., payables). The risk being hedged is the **fair value** or **cash flow**, measured in dollars of:

   a. An already booked asset or liability to be settled in a foreign currency (fair value or cash flow hedge), *or*

   b. A forecasted functional-currency-equivalent cash flow associated with a recognized asset or liability (cash-flow hedge), *or*

   c. An investment denominated in a foreign currency.

   > **Note**
   > *The dollar value of or cash flows from such assets and liabilities may change as a result of changes in the foreign exchange rate between recognition and settlement of the asset or liability.*

4. **Investments in available-for-sale securities**—The risk being hedged is the risk that exchange rate changes will have on the **fair value** of investments in available-for-sale securities (debt or equity) denominated in a foreign currency.

5. **Net investments in foreign operations**—The risk being hedged is the risk that exchange rate changes will have on the **fair (economic) value** of financial statements converted from a foreign currency to the functional currency. In this case, the accounting for the hedging instrument (derivative) must be treated like the accounting for the translation adjustment for the associated foreign investment.

B. The accounting treatments for these foreign currency-hedging purposes generally are consistent with the fair value and cash-flow hedge treatments described in earlier lessons and are discussed in detail in subsequent material.

Effectiveness and Disclosure

In order to qualify for hedge accounting, the company must document how it will assess hedge effectiveness. In addition, this lesson presents the disclosure requirements associated with hedging.

After studying this lesson, you should be able to:

1. Identify and describe how effectiveness is assessed when hedging is used.

2. Describe the most significant disclosures required when hedging is used.

I. **Effectiveness**

   A. To qualify for hedge accounting, the hedging instrument must be highly effective, both at inception of the hedge and on an ongoing basis, in offsetting changes in the fair value or the cash flows of the hedged item. This correlation must be between 80 and 125% in order for the hedge to qualify for hedge accounting.

   B. If the hedge is determined to be effective, then hedge accounting is permitted.

II. **Assessing Hedge Effectiveness**—Hedge effectiveness is assessed in two stages.

   A. **Prospective Consideration**—A forward-looking assessment of the entity's expectations that a planned hedging relationship will be highly effective over future periods in achieving offsetting changes in fair value or cash flows.

      1. The prospective assessment should consider all reasonable possible changes in fair value and/or cash flows of both the hedged item and the hedging instrument.

      2. The prospective assessment can be based on:

         a. Regression analysis or other statistical analysis of past changes in fair value or cash flows

         b. Qualitative assessment of the extent to which the critical terms (e.g., nominal amounts, expiration date, etc.) of the hedging instrument and the hedged item match

      3. Generally, the prospective assessment involves a probability-weighted analysis of the possible changes in fair value and/or cash flows.

   B. **Retrospective Evaluation**—When a relationship between an instrument and an item qualifies as a hedge for accounting purposes, the relationship must continue to be assessed for effectiveness whenever financial statements are reported, and at least every three months.

      1. A single method of evaluating effectiveness is not specified by GAAP.

      2. The retrospective evaluation can be accomplished using a number of approaches, including:

         a. **A dollar-offset approach**—an assessment based on how well the dollar change in the hedging instrument actually has offset the dollar change in the hedged item, with the assessment performed either on a period-by-period basis or on a cumulative basis.

         b. **Regression analysis or other statistical analysis.**

c. Qualitative assessment

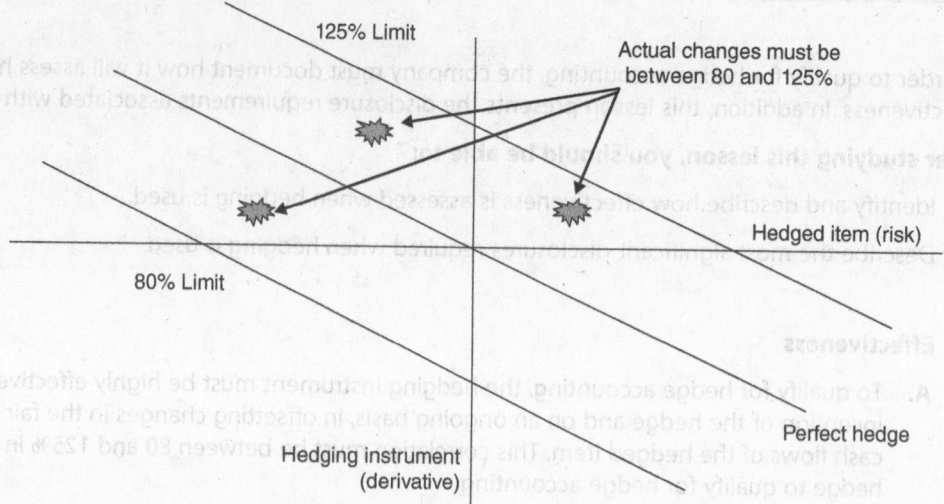

III. Effectiveness Testing

A. In the graph above, the boundaries of 80–125% indicate that the plotted changes in the value of the hedged item and the hedging instrument need to fall within these boundaries. As long as the change in the hedged item and hedging instrument is between the boundaries of 80% and 125%, hedge accounting is permitted. If the change is outside of this range hedge accounting is no longer permitted.

B. Effectiveness is the change in the fair value of the derivative divided by the change in the value of the hedged item.

$$\frac{\Delta FV\ derivative}{\Delta FV\ hedged\ risk} = 80 - 125\%$$

C. Effectiveness of the hedge must be assessed throughout its life with a review at least every three months (i.e., that hedging instrument gain or loss covers hedged item's loss or gain).

D. The straight line through the axis of the above graph represents a "perfect hedge" where changes in the value of the hedged item and hedging instrument offset each other perfectly.

1. A qualitative assessment of effectiveness is allowed when the critical terms of the hedged item and hedging instrument are perfectly matched. When these conditions occur, the entity can perform qualitative assessment of hedge effectiveness subsequent to the hedge inception.

    a. The shortcut method is a simplified way to assess hedge effectiveness. The shortcut method applies to certain hedging relationships of interest rate risk that involve a recognized interest-bearing financial asset or liability (hedged item) and an interest rate swap (hedging instrument).

    b. The shortcut method assumes that (and is possible because) the change in value of the interest-rate swap is a perfect proxy for the change in the value of the interest-bearing financial instrument.

    c. The shortcut method can be used by an entity only if all aspects of the hedging relationship exactly match (e.g., nominal amount, expiration date, etc.) and other criteria are met.

    d. If all of the criteria are met, an entity may assume no ineffectiveness in the hedging relationship, and the entity can use qualitative assessment of effectiveness testing.

IV. Disclosure Requirements

A. An entity that issues or holds derivatives (or other contracts used for hedging) must disclose (mostly in the footnotes) a considerable amount of information in both annual and interim financial statements, including:

1. General disclosure requirements

a. Its objectives for issuing or holding the derivatives (or other contracts), the context needed to understand those objectives, and its strategies for achieving those objectives.

b. Information must distinguish between instruments used for risk management (hedging) and those used for other purposes (e.g., profit).

c. Information must be disclosed in the context of each instrument's underlying risk exposure, including, for example: interest rate risk, credit risk, foreign currency exchange risk, overall price risk, etc.

d. Information must distinguish between instruments designated as fair value hedges, cash flow hedges, hedges of foreign currency exposure of net investments in foreign operations, and any other derivatives.

e. Information that would enable users to understand the volume of its derivative activities

f. Quantitative disclosures must be presented in tabular format.

g. If information on derivatives is disclosed in multiple footnotes, the derivative-related footnotes must be cross-referenced.

B. Balance Sheet–Related Disclosures—The following specific balance-sheet-related disclosures are required:

1. The location (line item) and fair value amounts of derivative instruments

2. Fair value must be presented as a gross (not net) amount.

3. Fair value amounts must be shown separately as assets and liabilities, and segregated between those derivatives that are hedges and those that are not.

4. For derivatives used as hedges, the fair value amounts must be presented separately for each type of hedge contract (e.g., interest rate contract, foreign currency contract, commodity contract, etc.).

5. The amounts reclassified from Accumulated Other Comprehensive Income to Current Income

C. Income Statement–Related Disclosures—The following specific income-statement-related disclosures are required:

1. The location (line item) and amounts of gains/losses on derivative instruments.

2. Gains/losses must be presented separately for:

a. Derivatives designated as fair value hedges and for the related hedged item

b. Derivatives designated as cash-flow hedges and net-investment hedges, separating the effective and ineffective portions

c. Derivatives not functioning as hedges

d. Amounts reclassified from Accumulated Other Comprehensive Income to Current Income

e. Amounts recognized from hedged firm commitments that no longer qualify for hedge treatment

D. Cash Flow–Specific Disclosures—For derivatives designated as cash flow hedges and for the related hedged item the following specific disclosures are required:

1. A description of transactions or other events that will result in the reclassification (recognition) of accumulated other comprehensive income into income and an estimate of the amount to be reclassified during the next 12 months

2. The maximum length of time over which the entity is hedging cash flows for forecasted transactions

3. The gain/loss recognized in earnings from hedged forecasted transactions that no longer qualify for hedge treatment

E. Credit-Risk-Related Contingent Features—Specific Disclosures

1. Credit-risk-related contingent features are provisions in a derivative (or other instrument) that trigger immediate settlement (or other consequences) if a specific event or condition occurs or fails to occur. For example, an interest rate swap may provide for immediate settlement if an entity's credit rating is downgraded.

2. For derivatives that contain credit-risk-related contingent features the following specific disclosures are required:

   a. The existence and nature of credit-risk-related contingent features and the circumstances in which the features could be triggered for derivatives that are liabilities

   b. The aggregate fair value amounts of derivatives that contain credit-risk-related contingent features that are liabilities

   c. The aggregate fair value of assets (1) that are already posted as collateral, (2) additional assets that would be required as collateral and/or (3) needed to settle the instrument immediately if the contingent feature is triggered

V. Note on Derivatives and Hedging Disclosures—The required disclosures related to the issuing and/or holding of derivatives and the use of derivatives (and other instruments) for hedging purposes are extensive, detailed, and continuously changing (usually resulting in more disclosures). The disclosures identified and described above are those that are most significant.

Foreign Currency Denominated Transactions

Introduction and Definitions

This lesson begins a series of lessons covering foreign currency denominated transactions. The first set of lessons discusses the accounting for foreign currency denominated transactions; the second set of lessons deal with foreign currency conversion. This lesson distinguishes between foreign currency transactions and foreign currency translation and gives examples of each. In addition, currency exchange rates and the alternative ways those rates may be expressed are presented.

After studying this lesson, you should be able to:

1. Define and describe foreign currency conversion.

2. Display your understanding of changes in exchange rates.

3. Define direct quote, indirect quote, spot rates and forward rates.

Describe how to account for changes in currency exchange rates at the following dates:

*   When transaction is initiated; and

*   On the balance sheet date; and

*   On the settlement date.

4. Define and describe foreign currency denominated transactions.

I. Foreign Currency Denominated Transactions

Definition
Foreign Currency Transactions: Transactions of a domestic entity denominated in (to be settled in) a foreign currency, but to be recorded on the domestic entity's books in the domestic currency.

Example
A U.S company buys goods from a Japanese company and agrees to pay for the goods with yen, rather than dollars. In this case, the transaction is denominated in yen, but the amount recorded on the books of the U.S. entity is measured in U.S. dollars; therefore, the transaction amount must be converted from yen to dollars.

II. Foreign Currency Translation

Definition
Foreign Currency Translation: Financial statements denominated in (expressed in terms of) a foreign currency, but to be reported in the financial statements expressed in the domestic currency.

Example
A U.S. company has a French subsidiary that maintains its books and prepares its financial statements in euros. In this case, the financial statements are denominated in euros, but must be converted to dollars in order to be consolidated by the U.S. parent.

III. Terms and Definitions

A. **Direct Quote**—This is a direct exchange rate and it measures how much domestic currency must be exchanged to receive one unit of a foreign currency. $1.25 = 1 €.

B. **Indirect Quote**—This is an indirect exchange rate and it measures how many units of foreign currency may be purchased with one unit of domestic currency. $1.00 = .80 €. The indirect quote is the reciprocal of the direct quote (1 € / $1.25 = .80 €).

C. **Spot Rate**—The number of units of a currency that would be exchanged for one unit of another currency on a given date.

D. **Forward Rate**—The number of units of one currency that would be exchanged for units of another currency at a specified future point in time.

KEY CONCEPTS

1. A foreign currency transaction is when a transaction is denominated in a currency other than the domestic currency.

2. An unsettled foreign currency transaction creates a payable or receivable in a foreign currency.

3. This payable or receivable presents a risk because of the changes in the exchange rates before settlement.

IV. Strengthening or Weakening of Currencies

A. A strengthening or weakening dollar means that the dollar buys more or less of the foreign currency. It also means we receive less or more of the foreign currency owed to us.

B. If we have a payable denominated in the € and the dollar strengthens, since we have to pay a fixed amount of €s, and they are now worth fewer dollars, we have experienced a gain on the liability. The gains or losses arising from transactions denominated in a foreign currency are foreign currency transaction gains or losses.

C. The following chart illustrates the relationship between fluctuations in exchange rates and exchange gains and losses.

	Accounts Receivable Denominated in Foreign Currency	Accounts Payable Denominated in Foreign Currency
Domestic Currency **Weakens**	Exchange Gain	Exchange Loss
Domestic Currency **Strengthens**	Exchange Loss	Exchange Gain

Example
If the dollar weakens:

	from	to
indirect	$1.00 = 0.80 €	$1.00 = 0.625 €
direct	$1.25 = 1 €	$1.60 = 1 €

It will take more U.S. dollars to acquire one unit of foreign currency (€ = foreign currency unit).

Imports become more expensive to the U.S.

U.S. exports become less expensive to the foreign country.

If the dollar strengthens:

	from	to
indirect	$1.00 = 0.80 €	$1.00 = 0.909 €
direct	$1.25 = 1 €	$1.10 = 1 €

It will take fewer U.S. dollars to acquire one unit of foreign currency.

Imports become less expensive to the U.S.

U.S. exports become more expensive to the foreign country.

V. General Principles/Rules

A. Transaction terms provide that the transaction will be settled (by a domestic entity) in a foreign currency.

B. The domestic entity will ultimately pay or receive a foreign currency.

VI. General Rules

A. Measure and record transaction on books in terms of the functional currency.

Example
For a U.S. entity, the transaction must be measured and recorded in dollars.

B. Convert foreign currency units (FC units) to functional currency units ($) using spot exchange rate at date of transaction.

C. Recognize the effects of exchange rate changes:

1. On accounts denominated in a foreign currency (e.g., Receivables/Payables)

2. In the period in which the exchange rate changes

3. As adjustment to account balance, and as exchange loss or gain

VII. Application at Date of Transaction

    A. Determine FC units to settle transaction.

    B. Translate (convert) FC units to reporting currency (U.S. dollars) by:

> # FC Units × Spot Exchange Rate = Dollar Amount to Settle

    C. Record transaction at dollar amount to settle.

VIII. Application at Balance Sheet Date

    A. Determine (New) Dollar Amount to Settle Currently by

> #FC Units × Balance Sheet Date Spot Exchange Rate = Dollar Amount at Balance Sheet Date

    B. Determine difference between recorded dollar amount to settle and new (current) dollar amount at balance sheet date.

    C. Record Difference as

        1. Adjustment to recorded receivable/payable

        2. Exchange loss or gain

    D. Report exchange loss or gain in current-period income statement as component of income from continuing operations.

IX. Application at Settlement Date

    A. Determine (New) Dollar Amount to Settle Currently by

> #FC Units × Settlement Date Spot Exchange Rate = Dollar Amount to Settle.

    B. Determine difference between recorded dollar amount to settle and new (current) dollar amount to settle at settlement date.

    C. Record Difference as

        1. Adjustment to recorded receivable/payable

        2. Exchange loss or gain

    D. Report exchange loss or gain in current-period income statement as component of income from continuing operations.

    E. Record settlement of adjusted receivable/payable account balance.

X. Summary

A. Below is a summary of the accounting for foreign currency denominated transactions (described above) in table form:

At Date Transaction Initiated	At Balance Sheet Date, If Before Settlement Date	At Date Transaction Is Settled
Translate transaction into dollars using current spot exchange rate:	Determine dollar amount to settle transaction at balance sheet date (settlement amount):	Determine dollar amount to settle transaction (settlement amount):
(#FC units × ER/spot = $ value)	(#FC units × ER/spot = $ value)	(#FC units × ER/spot = $ value)
Record asset, liability, revenue, expense, loss and/or gain on transaction at dollar amount.	Determine difference between recorded amount and settlement amount.	Determine difference between recorded amount and settlement amount.
	Record difference as:	Record difference as:
	—Adjustment to recorded account balance (receivable/payable), and	—Adjustment to recorded account balance (receivable/payable), and
	—Loss or gain for the period.	—Loss or gain for the period.
	Report loss or gain in current-period income statement as component of income from continuing operations.	Record settlement of adjusted account balance.
		Report loss or gain in current-period income statement as component of income from continuing operations.

Import Transactions

When a domestic entity (assume U.S. entity) imports (purchases) an item from a foreign entity and the settlement of the transaction is in the foreign currency, the transaction is denominated in the foreign currency, but reported in the U.S. dollar equivalent of that foreign currency. This lesson illustrates a foreign currency denominated import transaction at initiation of the transaction, adjustment for changes in exchange rates at the balance sheet date, and settlement of the transaction.

After studying this lesson, you should be able to:

1. Record the entries for foreign currency denominated import transactions:

   • Calculate the effect of the changes in the exchange rates and related gains and losses, and

   • Record the entries for the initial transaction, interim balance sheet date, and the settlement date.

I. Simple Illustration—Purchase (Import) Transaction Denominated in Foreign Currency

Assume: On October 1, 20X2 we entered into a transaction to purchase goods payable in a Foreign Currency (FC) on January 31, 20X3. The purchase was for 1 FC worth of merchandise.

The exchange rates are as follows:

Transaction date:	October 1	$2.00 = 1 FC (direct quotation)
Balance sheet date:	December 31	$1.00 = 1 FC
Settlement date:	January 31	$1.50 = 1 FC

October 1: The entry to record the purchase.

Inventory	$2	
Accounts Payable (FC)		$2

December 31: The FC is worth $1. The change in the exchange rate is recorded.

Accounts Payable (FC)	$1	
Foreign currency transaction G/L (IS)		$1

Note: Foreign currency transaction gain/loss (G/L) could be a debit (loss) or credit (gain) depending on the changes in the exchange rates. Also, this account is recognized in earnings on the Income Statement (IS).

January 31: The FC is worth $1.5. Below are the following entries to: 1) record the change in the exchange rate, 2) the purchase of the FC, and 3) settle the transaction.

1. Foreign currency transaction G/L (IS)	$.50	
Accounts Payable (FC)		$.50
2. Investment in FC	$1.50	
Cash		$1.50
3. Accounts Payable (FC)	$1.50	
Investment in FC		$1.50

II. Illustration: Purchase (Import) Transaction Denominated in Foreign Currency

Assume: On November 15 a U.S. Co. purchases equipment from Foreign Co. for 500,000 units of Foreign currency (500,000 FC) with the full amount payable on January 31.

The exchange rates are as follows:

November 15	1 FC = $.75 (direct quotation)
December 31	1 FC = $.74
January 31	1 FC = $.76

November 15: The entry to record the purchase (500,000 × .75 = 375,000).

Equipment	$375,000	
Accounts Payable (FC)		$375,000

December 31: The change in the exchange rate is recorded. It will now take fewer dollars to settle the obligation in FC. (500,000 × (.75 − .74)) = 5,000

Accounts Payable (FC)	$5,000	
Foreign currency transaction G/L (IS)		$5,000

January 31: It will now take more dollars to settle the obligation in FC. Below are the following entries to: 1) record the change in the exchange rate from December 31 to January 31 (500,000 × (.74 − .76) = 10,000), 2) the purchase of the FC (500,000 × .76 = 380,000), and 3) settle the Accounts Payable in FC.

1. Foreign currency transaction G/L (IS)	$10,000	
Accounts Payable (FC)		$10,000
2. Investment in FC	$380,000	
Cash		$380,000
3. Accounts Payable (FC)	$380,000	
Investment in FC		$380,000

Complete a T-account for the Account Payable in Foreign Currency (FC) as a double check to make sure you have recorded everything properly:

Accounts Payable FC

		375,000 (500,000 × .75)	Nov 1
Dec 31 MTM	5,000		
		370,000 (500,000 × .74)	Dec 31
		10,000 MTM	Jan 31
Jan 31 Payment	380,000		
		0 Ending Balance	

Now try to work through the above problem using indirect exchange rates. With indirect exchange rates you divide the foreign currency amount by the exchange rate. Using the rates below, you will get the exact same journal entries and T-accounts shown above.

The exchange rates are as follows:

November 15	1.333333 FC = $1 (indirect quotation)
December 31	1.351351 FC = $1
January 31	1.315789 FC = $1

Export Transactions

When a domestic entity (assume U.S. entity) exports (sells) an item to a foreign entity and the settlement of the transaction is in the foreign currency, the transaction is denominated in the foreign currency but reported in the U.S. dollar equivalent of that foreign currency. This lesson illustrates a foreign currency denominated export transaction At initiation of the transaction, adjustment for changes in exchange rates at the balance sheet date, and settlement of the transaction.

After studying this lesson, you should be able to:

Record the entries for foreign currency denominated export transactions:

- Calculate the effect of the changes in the exchange rates and related gains and losses, and

- Record the entries for the initial transaction, interim balance sheet date, and the settlement date.

I. Simple Illustration—Sale (Export) Transaction Denominated in Foreign Currency

Assume: On October 1, 20X2 we agreed to sell goods with the receivable to be paid in euros on February 1, 20X3, for 1 FC worth of merchandise.

The exchange rates are as follows:

Transaction date:	October 1	$2 = 1 FC
Balance sheet date:	December 31	$1 = 1 FC
Settlement date:	February 1	$3 = 1 FC

October 1: The entry to record the sale at the current exchange rate.

Accounts Receivable (FC)	$2	
Sales		$2

December 31: The entry to record the change in the exchange rate. (We will now receive only $1 worth of FC instead of $2).

Foreign currency transaction G/L (IS)	$1	
Accounts Receivable (FC)		$1

Note: Foreign currency transaction gain/loss (G/L) could be a debit (loss) or credit (gain) depending on the changes in the exchange rates. Also, this account is recognized in earnings on the Income Statement (IS).

February 1: The FC is now worth $3. Below are the following entries to: 1) record the change in the exchange rate, 2) the receipt of FCs, and 3) convert the FCs to dollars.

1. Accounts Receivable (FC)	$2	
Foreign currency transaction G/L (IS)		$2
2. Investment in FC	$3	
Accounts Receivable (FC)		$3
3. Cash	$3	
Investment in FC		$3

II. Illustration: Sale (Export) Transaction Denominated in Foreign Currency

Assume: On December 15 a U.S. Co. sells goods to a Foreign Co. for 500,000 units of Foreign Currency (500,000 FC) with the full amount payable on January 15.

The exchange rates are as follows:

December 15	1 FC = $.75 (direct quotation)
December 31	1 FC = $.72
January 15	1 FC = $.74

December 15: The entry to record the sale (500,000 × .75 = 375,000).

Accounts Receivable (FC)	$375,000	
Sales		$375,000

December 31: The change in the exchange rate is recorded. When 1 FC is received, it is worth fewer dollars. (500,000 × (.75 − .72)) = 15,000

Foreign currency transaction G/L (IS)	$15,000	
Accounts Receivable (FC)		$15,000

January 31: When 1 FC is received, it is worth more dollars. Below are the following entries to: 1) record the change in the exchange rate (500,000 × (.72 − .74) = 10,000), 2) the receipt of the FC to settle the account receivable (500,000 × .74 = 370,000), and 3) convert the FC to dollars.

1. Accounts Receivable (FC)	$10,000	
Foreign currency transaction G/L (IS)		$10,000
2. Investment in FC	$370,000	
Accounts Receivable (FC)		$370,000
3. Cash	$370,000	
Investment in FC		$370,000

Complete a T-account for the Account Receivable in Foreign Currency (FC) as a double check to make sure you have recorded everything properly:

Accounts Receivable FC					
Dec 15	(500,000 × .75)	375,000			
			15,000	MTM	Dec 31
Dec 31	(500,000 × .72)	360,000			
Jan 31	MTM	10,000			
Jan 31	(500,000 × .74)	370,000			
			370,000	Collection	Jan 31
		0			

Now try to work through the above problem using indirect exchange rates. With indirect exchange rates you divide the foreign currency amount by the exchange rate. Using the rates below, you will get the exact same journal entries and T-accounts shown above.

The exchange rates are as follows:

December 15	1.333333 FC = $1 (indirect quotation)
December 31	1.388888 FC = $1
January 15	1.351351 FC = $1

Foreign Currency Hedges

Introduction to Forward and Option Contracts

The objective of this lesson is to provide an overview of the accounting for forward and option contracts to buy or sell a foreign currency. This lesson defines forward and option and gives examples of each.

After studying this lesson, you should be able to:

1. Define terms related to forward and option contracts, including:

    *   Forward contracts,

    *   Foreign currency forward exchange contracts, and

    *   Foreign currency option contracts.

2. Describe and compute the value of a forward and option contract, including:

    *   At inception of the contract,

    *   At subsequent Balance Sheet dates, and

    *   At settlement of the contract.

3. Record the entries to account for both forward exchange contracts and forward option contracts.

I. Definitions

A. Forward Contracts

Definition
Forward Contracts: Agreements (contracts) to buy or sell (or which give the right to buy or sell) a specified commodity in the future at a price (rate) determined at the time the forward contract is executed.

B. For Accounting Purposes—The most important types of forward contracts are:

1. Foreign Currency Forward Exchange Contracts (FXFC)

Definition
Foreign Currency Forward Exchange Contracts (FXFC): An agreement to buy or sell a specified amount of a foreign currency at a specified future date at a specified (forward) rate.

    a. Under an FXFC contract, the obligation to buy or sell is firm; the exchange must occur.

    b. This contract is an *exchange* because the contract provides for trading (exchanging) one currency for another currency.

Example
A U.S. entity enters into an FXFC to pay a predetermined price in U.S. dollars for a predetermined quantity of euros.

2. Foreign currency option contracts (FCO)

> **Definition**
> *Foreign Currency Option Contracts (FCO)*: An agreement that gives the right (option) to buy (call option) or sell (put option) a specified amount of a foreign currency at a specified (forward) rate during or at the end of a specified time period.

    a. Under an FCO contract, the party holding the option has the right (option) to buy or sell, but does not have to exercise that option. The exchange will occur at the option of the option holder.

 **Example**
A U.S. entity acquires an option (right) to buy euros but does not have to buy the euros.

    b. If the option is exercised, there is an exchange of currencies.

    c. FCO contracts are significantly more costly to execute than FXFC contracts because the option must be purchased by paying an option premium to the counterparty for the right to buy or sell the currency.

    d. The benefit of an FCO (over an FXFC) is that if changes in the exchange rate do not warrant it, the contract does not have to be exercised; therefore, only the option premium (cost) is incurred.

II. The Accounting Treatment

    A. Derivative Instruments—Both foreign currency forward exchange contracts and foreign currency option contracts are derivative instruments.

        1. All derivative instruments are adjusted to and reported at fair value.

        2. Changing fair value of derivatives result in gains and losses.

        3. When derivatives are used for hedging purposes, gains and losses on those derivatives serve to offset losses or gains on the hedged item.

    B. Determining Fair Value of Forward Exchange Contracts

        1. A forward exchange contract requires the parties to the contract to exchange currencies at the maturity of the contract (or to otherwise settle the contract).

        2. The fair value of a forward exchange contract is determined by **changes** in the forward (exchange) rate during the life of the contract, discounted to its present value.

        3. Changes in the forward rate can result in an increase in fair value (a gain) or a decrease in fair value (a loss).

        4. At the inception of a forward contract, it typically has no value (there has been no **change** in the forward rate); changes in value (and gains or losses) occur as the forward rate changes.

5. Illustration

a. Facts: On November 2, year 1, Usco, Inc. enters into a forward exchange contract to sell 10,000 euros (€) in 90 days. The relevant direct exchange rates are:

	Spot Rates	Forward Rates (to January 31, year 2)
November 2, year 1	$1.20	$1.25
December 31, year 1	1.22	1.23
January 31, year 2	1.24	1.24

b. November 2—Contract Initiated:

   i. The contract amount is 10,000€ × $1.25 = $12,500, and since that is based on the quoted rate at that date, it has no intrinsic value; anyone could obtain a 90-day forward contract at $1.25.

   ii. Entry: No entry required; no payment was made and the contract has no value.

c. December 31—Balance Sheet Date:

   i. The forward rate at December 31 is $1.23, a decrease of .02 per euro. Thus, the contract amount is now 10,000€ × $1.23 = $12,300, a change (decrease) of $200. Since Usco has a contract that enables it to sell 10,000€ for $1.25 each and 10,000€ could be sold now (December 31) for only $1.23 each, the $200 change is the nominal value of the contract—the value of Usco's right to sell 10,000€ at $1.25 each. The fair value (and amount of gain) is the present value of the $200. That would be determined by discounting the $200 for one month (31 days in January) at the appropriate discount rate (e.g., the firm's incremental borrowing rate).

   ii. If the appropriate discount rate is 12%, or 1% per month, the present value of $200 due in one month (January 1–31) would be $200 × .99 = $198, the fair value of the contract asset on December 31. The entry would be:

DR: Forward Contract	$198	
CR: Gain on Forward Contract		$198

   1. If the contract was entered into for speculative purposes (i.e., to make a profit), the gain would be recognized in current (year 1) income.

   2. If the contract was entered into as a qualifying hedge, the treatment of the gain would depend on the nature of the hedge (see subsequent lessons).

d. January 31—Settlement Date:

e. The forward rate is the spot rate, $1.24 (the forward and spot rate converge upon the maturity of the forward contract), an increase of .01 per euro since December 31. Thus, an increase of .01 per euro since December 31. The current amount to satisfy the contract is 10,000€ × $1.24 = $12,400, the amount that would be paid to acquire 10,000€ to satisfy the contract (and the amount that would be received if the euros were sold on the current spot market). As provided by its forward contract, however, Usco will receive 10,000€ × $1.25 = $12,500, not $12,400. Thus, its entry would be:

DR:	Cash (sell 10,000€ × $1.25)	$12,500	
	Loss on Forward contract	98	
	CR: Cash (buy 10,000€ × $1.24)		$12,400
	Forward Contract (booked 12/31)		198

f. The net effect over the life of the contract is a $198 gain in year 1 and a $98 loss in year 2, for a net gain of $100, which is the difference between the dollar cost of buying 10,000€ at $1.24 = $12,400 and the dollar amount received from reselling the euros under the forward contract, 10,000€ at $1.25 = $12,500.

C. Determining Fair Value of Forward Exchange Option Contracts

1. A forward exchange option contract gives the holder of the contract the right to buy (call option) or sell (put option) a foreign currency, but does not require the holder to do so.

2. The determination of the fair value of a forward exchange option contract depends on the market in which the option is traded, if any.

3. Alternatives for determining forward exchange option fair value:

a. Exchange-traded options: Market price quoted on exchange = fair value

b. Over-the-counter options: Price quoted from option dealer = fair value

c. Not traded in active market: Option pricing model (e.g., modified Black-Scholes option price model) = fair value

4. At the inception of a forward option contract, the buyer will pay a premium (option premium) to the counter party for the right to buy from or sell to the counterparty according to the terms of the contract; the amount of the premium would be a function of the intrinsic value of the option and the "time value" factor.

a. **Intrinsic value**: The difference between the current spot rate for the currency and the strike price—that is, the price at which exercise of the option would result in a gain

b. **Time value**: The "value" assigned to the probability that the relationship between the changing spot price and the strike price will increase the value of the option during its life

5. Illustration

a. **Facts:** On November 2, year 1, Usco, Inc. enters into a call option contract to buy 10,000 euros (€) in 90 days with a strike price of $1.21. The exchange rates and option premiums for the option period are:

	Spot Rate	Forward Rates (to January 31, year 2)	Option Premium
November 2, year 1	$1.20	$1.25	$200
December 31, year 1	1.22	1.23	350
January 31, year 2	1.24	1.24	300

b. November 2—Contract Initiated:

    i. Usco paid a premium of $200 for the contract; that is its fair value at that date.

> Entry:
>
>   DR: Foreign Currency Option $200
>   CR: Cash $200

c. December 31—Balance Sheet Date:

    i. The option premium, as quoted by option sellers for a contract with comparable terms, has increased from $200 to $350, an increase (gain) of $150.

> Entry:
>
>   DR: Foreign Currency Option $150
>   CR: Foreign Currency Option Gain $150
>
> If the contract was entered into for speculative purposes (i.e., to make a profit), the gain would be recognized in current (year 1) income.
>
> If the contract was entered into as a qualified hedge, the treatment of the gain would depend on the nature of the hedge (see subsequent lessons).

d. January 31—Settlement Date:

    i. The option premium is $300, the intrinsic value of the option at that date, computed as 10,000€ × ($1.24 – $1.21) = 10,000€ × .03 = $300. At the settlement date, there is no time value associated with the contract; it has only intrinsic value.

> Entry:
>
>   DR: Foreign Currency (Euros) $12,400
>   Loss on Foreign Currency Option   50
>   CR: Cash (10,000€ × $1.21) $12,100
>   Foreign Currency Option   350

e. The net effect over the life of the contract is a $150 gain in year 1 and a $50 loss in year 2, or a net gain of $100. Thus, the difference between the cost of euros if purchased January 31 of $12,400 (10,000€ × $1.24) and the cost of the euros purchased under the option contract of $12,100 (10,000€ × $1.21) of $300 is reflected in the $200 cost of the option and a net gain of $100.

D. Both foreign currency forward exchange contracts and foreign currency option contracts are referred to as *forward contracts* in these lessons.

Natural (Economic) Hedge

This lesson illustrates a natural or economic hedge that is not accounted for using hedge accounting. This lesson illustrates the hedge of a purchase and sale denominated in a foreign currency.

After studying this lesson, you should be able to:

1. Define *hedging*.

2. Describe how a forward exchange contract can be used to hedge a receivable denominated in a foreign currency.

3. Record entries associated with a foreign currency receivable, the hedging of that receivable, and the settlement of both the receivable and the hedging instrument.

I. Hedging Definition

Definition
Hedging: A risk management strategy, which generally involves offsetting or counter transactions so that a loss on one transaction would be offset (at least in part) by a gain on the other transaction.

A. You would "hedge a bet" by offsetting a possible loss from betting on one team (to win) by betting on the other team to win.

B. You would hedge against a possible loss in the dollar value of a foreign currency to be received in the future by selling that foreign currency now at a specified rate for delivery when you receive it in the future (a forward contract).

II. Purchase Denominated in Foreign Currency with Natural Hedge

A. Purchase Denominated in Foreign Currency with Natural Hedge

1. Pumped Up Company purchased equipment from Switzerland for 140,000 francs on December 16, 20X7, with payment due on February 14, 20X8. On December 16, 20X7, Pumped Up also acquired a 60-day forward contract to purchase francs at a forward rate of SFr 1 = $.67. On December 31, 20X7, the forward rate for an exchange on February 14, 20X8, is SFr 1 = $.695. The spot rates were:

December 16, 20X7	1 SFr = $.68
December 31, 20X7	1 SFr = .70
February 14, 20X8	1 SFr = .69

	December 16	December 31	February 14
Spot rate	$.68	$.70	$.69
Forward rate	$.67	$.695	$.69

Entries with Company
 	
Hedged item
 	
Changes in the spot
	Equip 95,200
	  AP (SFr) 95,200
	(140,000 SFr × .68)
		Fx G/L (IS) 2,800
		  AP (SFr) 2,800
		(140,000 × (.68 − .70))
			AP (SFr) 1,400
			  Fx G/L (IS) 1,400
			(140,000 × (.70 − .69))
			
			AP (SFr) 96,600
			  Invest in (SFr) 96,600
			  (Pay Swiss Co.)
			  (.69 × 140,000)

Entries with Broker
 	
Hedging instrument
 	
Changes in the forward
	AR (SFr) 93,800
	  AP ($) 93,800
	(140,000 SFr ×
	.67)
		AP (SFr) 3,500
		  Fx G/L (IS) 3,500
		(140,000 × (.67 − .695))
			Fx G/L (IS) 700
			  AP (SFr) 700
			(140,000 × (.695 − .69))
			
			AP ($) 93,800
			  Cash 93,800
			  (Pay Broker)
			  (.67 × 140,000)
			
			Invest in (SFr) 96,600
			  AR (SFr) 96,600
			  Receive SFr (.69 ×
			  140,000)

Accounts Receivable Sfr		Accounts Payable Sfr	
(140,000 × .67) 93,800			95,200 (140,000 × .68)
3,500			2,800
(140,000 × .695) 97,300	700	1,400	98,000 (140,000 × .70)
(140,000 × .69) 96,600			96,600 (140,000 × .69)

III. Sale Denominated in Foreign Currency with Natural Hedge

A. Alman Company sold pharmaceuticals to a Swedish company for 200,000 kronor (SKr) on April 20, with settlement to be in 60 days. On the same date, Alman entered into a 60-day forward contract to sell 200,000 SKr at a forward rate of 1 SKr = $.167 in order to manage its exposed foreign currency receivable. The forward rate on May 31 was 1 SKr = $.168. The forward contract is not designated as a hedge. The spot rates were:

April 20	SKr 1 = $.170
May 31	SKr 1 = .172
June 19	SKr 1 = .165

	April 20	May 31	June 19
Spot rate SKr	.170	.172	.165
Forward Rate	.167	.168	–

Entries with Company	AR (SKr) 34,000
	  Sales 34,000
		AR (SKr) 400
		  FX G/L (IS) 400
			Fx G/L(IS) 1,400
			  AR (SKr) 1,400

Hedged item	(200,000 × .17)	((.170 − .172) × 200,000)	((.172 − .165) × 200,000)
Changes in the spot			Invest in SKr 33,000 AR (SKr) 33,000 (Receive SKr) (.165 × 200,000)

Entries with Broker	AR $ 33,400
	  AP (SKr) 33,400
		Fx (G/L) (IS) 200
		  AP (SKr) 200
			AP(SKr) 600
			  Fx G/L (IS) 600

Hedging instrument	(200,000 × .167)	((.167 − .168) × 200,000)	((.168 − .165) × 200,000)

Changes in the forward			AP (SKr) 33,000
			  Invest in SKr 33,000
			(Pay Broker)
			
			Cash 33,400
			  AR 33,400
			(Receive $)

Accounts Receivable SKr		Accounts Payable SKr	
(200,000 × .17) 34,000			33,400 (200,000 × .167)
400			200
(200,000 × .172) 34,400	1400	600	33,600 (200,000 × .168)
(200,000 × .165) 33,000			33,000 (200,000 × .165)

IV. Hedging Costs

A. Hedging Minimizes or Prevents Losses—From exchange rate changes (per se), but usually involves some costs of doing so, including:

1. Fees or other charges imposed by the other party to the forward contract

2. Differences between spot rates and forward rates at the date the forward contract is initiated

Hedging Forecasted Transactions and Firm Commitment

When forward currency forward exchange contracts are used for hedging, GAAP defines the kinds of risks that may be hedged for accounting purposes. This lesson identifies those types of risks and provides discussion of the hedge of a foreign currency–denominated forecasted transaction and firm commitment.

After studying this lesson, you should be able to:

1. Describe the criteria and accounting treatment for the hedge of a foreign currency–denominated transaction.

2. Identify and describe the items that can be hedged for accounting purposes.

I. **Purpose of Hedging**—GAAP identifies the following types/purposes of using forward contracts for hedging purposes when the item hedged is denominated in a foreign currency:

   A. **Forecasted Transaction**—Hedge a forecasted transaction denominated in a foreign currency; to offset the risk of exchange rate changes on nonfirm but budgeted (planned) transactions to be denominated in a foreign currency

   B. **Unrecognized, Firm Commitment**—Hedge an unrecognized, but firm commitment denominated in a foreign currency; to offset the risk of exchange rate changes on firm commitments for a future purchase or sale to be denominated in a foreign currency

   C. **Recognized Assets or Liabilities**—Hedge recognized (exposed) assets (e.g., receivables) or liabilities (e.g., payables); to offset the risk of exchange rate changes on already booked assets and liabilities denominated in a foreign currency

   D. **Available-for-Sale Investment**—Hedge an investment in available-for-sale securities; to offset the risk of exchange rate changes on this class of investments denominated in a foreign currency

   E. **Net Investment in Foreign Operation**—Hedge a net investment in a foreign operation (e.g., subsidiary); to offset the risk of exchange rate changes on an investment in a foreign operation (e.g., translated value of financial statements expressed in a foreign currency)

II. **Relationships**

   A. The first three types of hedges listed above can occur as a sequence of events (hedges). In sequence of occurrences, these hedges are of:

      1. A forecasted transaction, which may become

      2. An identifiable foreign-currency commitment, which results in a recorded transaction that creates

      3. A recognized asset (receivable) or liability (payable).

 **Example**
A U.S. entity may include in its annual budget the purchase of a major piece of equipment from a foreign entity to be paid in the foreign currency (a forecasted transaction).

During the budget period, the U.S. entity enters into a contract with a foreign entity to construct the equipment (an identifiable firm commitment).

Upon receiving the equipment, the U.S. entity records the asset and the payable to the foreign entity (a recognized liability).

III. Hedging Forecasted Transactions

A. Purpose—To offset the risk of exchange rate changes on non-firm, but budgeted (planned) foreign currency transactions (e.g., purchase or sale) between the time the transaction is planned and when it becomes firm or is executed.

Examples

1. Hedge import or export transactions (denominated in a foreign currency), which are included in a firm's annual budget (i.e., planned).

2. Hedge dividends from a foreign subsidiary that are budgeted for the coming year.

B. Designation

1. **Criteria for designation**—Use of a forward contract, either an exchange contract or an option contract, to hedge a forecasted transaction requires that (these requirements generally apply to all hedges):

    a. The forecasted transaction must be identified, probable of occurring, and present an exposure to foreign-currency price changes.

    b. Use of a forward contract to hedge must be consistent with company risk management policy, designated and documented in advance as intended as a hedge, and be highly effective as a hedge.

2. A firm commitment denominated in a foreign currency has two risks. There is fair value risk associated with the value change of the firm commitment contract and there is cash flow risk associated with the change in the currency exchange rates.

    a. Assume an entity enters into a firm commitment to purchase kiwi from New Zealand for 100 NZD (New Zealand dollar) per bushel. There is fair value risk in the firm commitment if the price of kiwi changes (i.e., the price goes from 100 NZD to 150 NZD per bushel). The firm commitment contract would increase or decrease in value depending on the market price of kiwi (since the firm commitment price is fixed, there is no cash flow risk). Hedging the firm commitment contract for kiwi would be a fair value hedge.

    b. The entity must clearly document whether it is hedging fair value or cash flows when it holds a firm commitment denominated in a foreign currency because hedging the firm commitment itself is a fair value hedge and hedging the exchange rate is a cash flow hedge.

    c. However, there is also cash flow risk associated with the USD/NZD exchange rates. If the exchange rates change from $.60 to $.65 per 1 NZD then it will cost more U.S. dollars to buy one NZD because the cash flows needed to purchase a NZD are not fixed. Hedging the USD / NZD exchange rate is a cash flow hedge.

C. Accounting Treatment

    a. The **change in the fair value** of the forward exchange contract, measured as the change in the forward exchange rate, should be recognized as an increase or decrease in the contract carrying value with a corresponding loss or gain recognized.

    b. The change in the value of the forward contract should be deferred and reported as a component of *other comprehensive income*.

    c. Amounts (losses and gains) deferred in *other comprehensive income* should be recognized in net income in the period(s) in which the related forecasted transaction(s) affect net income.

IV. Hedging Firm Commitments

A. Purpose—To offset the risk of changes in a firm commitment for a future purchase or sale denominated in a foreign currency. In a firm commitment, a contract has been entered into and changes in the market price relative to the firm commitment price will change the value of the firm commitment contract (fair value risk).

> **Example**
>
> A purchase order is placed with a foreign entity to manufacture and deliver equipment with payment to be made in a specified amount of foreign currency. The buying party has a contractual obligation to "take and pay" on delivery of the equipment, but under GAAP will not record the obligation until the equipment is delivered.

B. Designation

1. **Criteria for designation**—The use of a forward contract, either an exchange contract or an option contract, to hedge a firm commitment requires that:

   a. The commitment being hedged **must be firm**, be identified, and present exposure to foreign currency price changes.

   b. The forward contract must be designated and effective as a hedge of a commitment and be in an amount that does not exceed the amount of the commitment. (To the extent the amount of the forward contract exceeds the amount of the commitment, the forward contract is treated as speculation, not a hedge.)

2. **Nature of designation**—A hedge of the firm commitment is a fair value hedge (the hedge is to offset changes in the fair value of the firm commitment).

Hedging Asset/Liability, Available-for-Sale, and Foreign Operations

This lesson covers the hedge accounting for a foreign currency denominated asset or liability, an available-for-sale security, and an investment in foreign operations.

After studying this lesson, you should be able to:

1. Describe the hedge accounting of a hedge of a foreign currency denominated asset or liability.

2. Describe the hedge accounting of a hedge of a foreign currency denominated available-for-sale security.

3. Describe the hedge accounting of a hedge of an investment in foreign operations.

I. **Hedging Foreign Currency Denominated Asset or Liability**—To offset the risk of exchange rate changes on an existing (already booked) asset or liability.

Example
Hedge the risk of exchange rate changes reducing the dollar value of a receivable denominated (to be received) in a foreign currency, or the risk of exchange rate changes increasing the dollars required to settle a payable denominated (to be paid) in a foreign currency. For example, a receivable denominated in a foreign currency will result in collection of a fixed number of foreign currency units, but the dollar value of those units will vary with changes in the exchange rate between that foreign currency and the dollar. A U.S. company could enter into a forward contract now to sell those foreign currency units when received in the future and thus hedge the receivable.

A. **Criteria for Designation**—Use of a forward contract, either an exchange contract or an option contract, to hedge a recognized asset or liability requires that:

1. The asset or liability is denominated in a foreign currency and has already been booked (recognized).

2. The gain or loss on the hedged asset or liability must be recognized in earnings.

B. **Nature of Designation**—A hedge of a recognized asset or liability can be either a cash-flow hedge or a fair value hedge.

1. To qualify as a cash-flow hedge, the hedging instrument must completely offset the variability in (dollar) cash flows associated with the receivable or payable.

2. If the instrument does not qualify as a cash-flow hedge or if management so designates, the hedging instrument will be a fair value hedge.

C. **Accounting Treatment**—The accounting for the hedge of a recognized asset or liability would depend on the designated purpose of the hedge—whether to hedge cash flow or to hedge fair value.

1. If to hedge cash flow, the treatment would include:

a. Adjusting the hedged item (receivable or payable) to fair value each balance sheet date using the spot exchange rate and recognizing the change in fair value as a gain or loss in other comprehensive income.

b. Adjusting the hedging instrument to fair value each balance sheet date using the forward exchange rate and recognizing the change in fair value as follows:

         i. An amount up to the amount equal to the gain or loss recognized on the hedged item is recognized as a loss or gain in other comprehensive income to offset the gain or loss on the hedged item.

    2. If to hedge fair value, the treatment would include:

        a. Adjusting the hedged item (receivable or payable) to fair value each balance sheet date using the spot exchange rate and recognizing the change in fair value as a gain or loss in current income

        b. Adjusting the hedging instrument to fair value each balance sheet date using the forward exchange rate and recognizing the change in fair value as a gain or loss in current income

        c. To the extent the change in fair value of the hedging instrument and the change in the fair value of the hedged item are different there will be a net effect in current income.

D. Alternate Accounting Treatment—A firm can mitigate the risk of exchange rate changes on recognized accounts receivable and accounts payable denominated in a foreign currency without using hedge accounting. See the lesson "Natural (Economic) Hedge" for an illustration of this type of hedge.

II. Hedging Foreign Currency Denominated Available-for-Sale Security—To offset the risk of exchange rate changes on an investment in debt securities that are held available for sale.

Example

Hedge the risk of exchange rate changes on the (dollar) fair value of an investment in debt securities held available for sale that will be settled in (sold for) a foreign currency.

A. Criteria for Designation—Use of a forward contract, either an exchange contract or an option contract, to hedge an available-for-sale investment requires that:

    1. The securities being hedged must be identified and must not be traded in the investor's currency.

    2. The forward contract must be designated and highly effective as a hedge of the investment, and in an amount that does not exceed the amount of the investment being hedged. (To the extent the amount of the forward contract exceeds the investment, the forward contract is treated as speculation, not a hedge.)

B. Nature of Designation—A hedge of an investment available for sale is a fair value hedge; the hedge is to offset changes in (dollar) fair value of an investment.

    1. Accounting treatment

        a. The change in fair value of the forward contract (the hedge), measured as the change in the forward exchange rate, should be recognized as an increase or decrease in the carrying value of the forward contract with a corresponding gain or loss in net income.

        b. The change in fair value of the investment (the hedged item), measured as the change in market value, should be recognized as an increase or decrease in the carrying value of the investment with a corresponding gain or loss in net income.

        c. To the extent the gain or loss on the forward contract does not exactly offset the loss or gain on the investment, there will be a net gain or loss reported in current net income.

> **Note**
> *This treatment requires recognizing changes in the fair value of available-for-sale investments in net income, not in other comprehensive income as otherwise would be required under GAAP.*

III. Hedging Foreign Investment in Foreign Operations—To offset the risk of exchange rate changes on the translation (conversion) of the financial statements of a foreign operation, (branch, investee or subsidiary) from the foreign currency to dollars.

> **Example**
> There is risk that the dollar value of an investment in a foreign subsidiary will fluctuate as a result of exchange rate changes. Translation (conversion from foreign currency units to dollars) of accounts on the financial statements of the foreign subsidiary requires use of varying exchange rates, which subject the investment carried by the parent to fluctuate solely as a result of exchange rate changes.
>
> The U.S. parent could (1) borrow in the foreign currency of the subsidiary (a liability) to offset (hedge) the effects of changes in the exchange rate on conversion of the financial statements (a net asset) or (2) acquire a foreign currency call option to offset (hedge) the effects of changes in exchange rate on the conversion of the financial statements (a net asset).

A. Criteria for Designation—Use of a hedge instrument (e.g., borrowing or derivative contract) to hedge a net investment in a foreign operation requires that the contract be designated as a hedge of the net investment and be highly effective. The FASB classified this type of hedge as a **fair value hedge.** It is not classified as a cash flow hedge because it is highly unlikely that the investor will be liquidating its foreign investment to create a cash-flow risk. That is, if the investor holds significant ownership (>20% for equity method) or control (>50%), the investor is not likely to frequently sell that foreign investment; therefore, the **risk is the changes in value,** not the cash flows from liquidating the investment. However, what is unique is that the unrealized gains and losses are classified in OCI to offset the translation adjustment associated with the conversion of the foreign investment.

B. Accounting Treatment

1. The change in fair value (in dollars) of both the hedging instrument (e.g., a borrowing) and the change in the translated value of the balance sheet of the foreign entity (hedged item) should be determined.

2. The change in fair value (in dollars) of the hedging instrument and the change in the translated balance sheet (from 1. above) are both recorded in the cumulative translation adjustment (an item of other comprehensive income) as offsets to each other.

Speculation and Summary

Forward contracts can be used for speculative purposes. In this case, there is no existing obligation (to pay or receive a foreign currency) being hedged, rather the forward contract is entered into to make money. This lesson also presents a summary of the use of forward contracts and the accounting treatment for such contracts.

After studying this lesson, you should be able to:

1. Describe the accounting treatment of a forward contract used for speculation.

I. Purpose

A. The purpose of speculation is to make a profit as a result of exchange rate changes either by buying foreign currency for future delivery at a price lower than its value when delivered or by selling foreign currency for future delivery at a price higher than it can be bought at the delivery date. In this case, there is no existing obligation or other conversion being hedged; rather, the forward contract is entered into to make a profit (i.e., for speculative purposes).

Example

A U.S. entity enters into a forward contract to purchase euros in 180 days at a rate (forward rate) existing now in the belief that the existing forward rate is less than the spot rate will be in 180 days. To the extent the forward contract rate is less than the spot rate on the date the contract expires, the entity would make a gain. (Of course, if the spot rate at expiration is less than the forward contract rate, the entity would incur a loss.)

B. Any derivative that does not meet the requirements to qualify as a hedging instrument would be treated as held for speculative purposes.

II. Criteria for, and Nature of, Designation—When a forward contract is used for speculation, there is no separate risk being hedged. The forward contract and the resulting loss or gain stand alone. They are not intended to offset any existing exposure.

III. Accounting Treatment

A. The forward exchange contract is measured (valued) and recorded at the forward exchange rate (quoted now) for exchanges that will occur at the maturity date of the contract.

B. If a balance sheet date occurs between initiation of the contract and maturity (settlement) of the contract, the contract must be revalued (at the balance sheet date) by using the forward exchange rate quoted at that time for the maturity date of the contract. Any change between the balance sheet date value of the contract and the already recorded value of the contract, will be recognized as a gain or loss in net income for the period.

C. At the settlement date (maturity date of the contract), the contract must be revalued by using the spot (current) exchange rate for the maturity date of the contract. Any change between the settlement date value of the contract and the already recorded value of the contract, will be recognized as a gain or loss in net income for the current period.

D. In summary, all gains and losses on derivative instruments held for speculative purposes or treated as for speculative purposes are recognized in current income.

IV. Summary of Foreign Currency Hedges

A. Summary of Accounting for Forward Exchange Contracts by Purpose of Contracts

HEDGE OF:	Type of Hedge	Basic Approach	Treatment of Gain/Loss	Comments
Forecasted Transaction: to offset risk of changes on forecasted transaction	Cash flow	Adjust derivative to fair value	Defer to other comprehensive income (OCI)	Gain/loss reclassified out of AOCI to net income when forecasted transaction effects income
Firm Commitment: to offset risk of rate changes on a firm commitment	Fair value	Adjust derivative and firm commitment to fair value	Recognize in current income	The firm commitment is recognized when designated as the hedged item
Recognized Asset or Liability: to offset risk of changes in assets or liabilities	Cash flow OR fair value	Adjust derivative and recognized asset or liability to fair value	Cash flow: defer to OCI Fair value: Recognize in current income	Must document the risk being hedged as cash flow or fair value
Investment in Available-For-Sale (AFS) Securities: to offset risk of exchange rate changes on investment	Fair Value	Adjust AFS investment and derivative to fair value	Recognize in current income	Only debt securities are classified as AFS
Net Investment in Foreign Operation: to offset risk of exchange rate changes on conversion of financial statements	Foreign currency hedge	Adjust derivative to fair value	Offset translation adjustment; any gain more than the translation adjustment is reported in net income	None
SPECULATION: Entered for profit not hedging a risk	None	Adjust carrying value of derivative to fair value	Recognize in current net income	Risk enhancing

Conversion of Foreign Financial Statements

Introduction to Conversion of Foreign Financial Statements

This lesson begins a series of lessons covering foreign currency conversion. Conversion is the process of expressing financial statements expressed in one (foreign) currency to a (domestic) currency. There are two methods of conversion: translation and remeasurement. The key criteria for determining the method of conversion is to determine the entity's functional currency. This lesson describes the nature of foreign currency conversion and how to determine the functional currency.

After studying this lesson, you should be able to:

1. Identify and define currency concepts relevant to foreign currency conversion, including: a) recording currency; b) reporting currency; and c) functional currency.

2. Determine which currency is the functional currency of an entity.

I. **Conversion—The Conversion of Financial Statements from One Currency to Another Currency Involves Two Major Steps:**

   A. Determining the functional currency of the entity that prepared the original financial statements, and

   B. Applying the correct conversion process based on the functional currency of the entity that prepared the original financial statements.

   C. Foreign-currency conversion occurs when a domestic (U.S.) entity must convert financial statements denominated (expressed) in a foreign currency into their domestic (dollar) equivalents.

II. **Sources of Financial Statements**—The financial statements denominated in the foreign currency could be those of a branch, joint venture, partnership, equity investee or subsidiary of the domestic entity.

III. **Conversion Needed**—The conversion could be needed in order to:

   A. Apply equity method by U.S. investor

   B. Combine with other entities

   C. Consolidate with U.S. parent (and other subsidiaries)

IV. **Conversion Objectives**—The objectives of foreign-currency conversion are:

   A. To provide information that is generally compatible with the expected economic effects of rate changes on an enterprise's cash flows and equity, *and*

   B. To reflect in consolidated statements the financial results and relationships of the individual consolidated entities as measured in their functional primary currencies in conformity with U.S. GAAP.

V. **Currency Concepts**—The following currency concepts are relevant to foreign currency translation:

   A. **Recording Currency**—The currency in which the foreign entity's books of account are maintained

   B. **Reporting Currency**—The currency in which the final (e.g., consolidated) financial statements are expressed

    C. **Functional Currency**—The currency of the primary economic environment in which an entity operates and generates net cash flows

VI. **Conversion Methodology**—The specific translation methodology to use to convert financial statements expressed in a foreign currency into domestic (dollar) equivalents depends on the functional currency of the foreign entity. The functional currency of the foreign entity can be:

    A. **The Recording Currency**—The foreign entity's local foreign currency

    B. **The Reporting Currency**—The currency of the final reporting entity (the dollar for a U.S. entity)

    C. **Another Foreign Currency**—A foreign currency other than the recording currency

VII. **Determining Functional Currency**—Generally, the functional currency of the foreign entity will be determined according to the following guidelines:

    A. **Functional Currency= (Local, Foreign) Recording Currency**—If operations of the foreign entity are relatively self-contained and integrated within the country in which it is located.

        1. **EXCEPTION**—If the local economy is highly inflationary (i.e., cumulative inflation of 100% or more over a three-year period) the functional currency = reporting currency (the $ if a U.S. subsidiary).

    B. **Functional Currency= U.S. Reporting Currency**

        1. If operations are a direct and integral component or extension of a U.S. entity's (e.g., Parent's) operations, or

        2. When the foreign entity is located in a country with a highly inflationary economy, defined as cumulative inflation of 100% or more over a three-year period.

    C. **Functional Currency= Another Foreign Currency**—(Other than local foreign recording currency or the reporting currency) If the foreign entity generates most of its cash flows in the currency of another foreign country or if required by law or contract.

VIII. **Role of Functional Currency**—The functional currency of the entity issuing financial statements to be converted to another currency will determine the method to be used to convert the financial statements. Two methods are possible:

    A. **Translation**

    B. **Remeasurement**

Conversion Using Translation

This lesson identifies the exchange rates to use when the translation method of conversion is used and how to treat the resulting translation adjustment.

After studying this lesson, you should be able to:

1. Describe the sequence of requirements when financial statements are converted using translation.

2. Identify the exchange rates to use for converting different financial statement accounts using translation.

3. Describe how the translation adjustment amount is treated when financial statements are converted using translation.

4. Apply the translation method in converting financial statements from one currency to another currency.

5. Describe and apply the reporting of the translation adjustment in a set of converted financial statements.

I. **Translation Process—Local Recording Currency= Functional Currency**—Use translation to convert from foreign currency to reporting currency (the $):

   A. Convert accounts from foreign-currency units (FCU) to dollars using a current exchange rate (CR) —also called spot rate.

      1. **Example**—Conversion: FCU × CR = $

   B. **Current Exchange Rates (CR) to use**

      1. **Revenues, expenses, gains, and losses**—Use the weighted average rate for the period can be used.

      2. **Assets and liabilities**—Use spot rate at Balance Sheet date (except paid-in-capital and retained earnings, see below).

      3. **Paid-in capital**—Use historic rate in existence when paid-in capital arose (but not earlier than investment in foreign entity).

      4. **Retained earnings**—Calculated as beginning R/E (end of prior period) + translated N/I – dividends declared converted at spot rate at date of declaration = ending R/E ($).

II. **Translation Adjustment**—The amount needed to make the Balance Sheet (expressed in dollars) balance is the amount of the translation adjustment.

   A. Under **Translation** (method of converting) the Translation Adjustment does NOT enter into determination of Net Income, but is treated as Other Comprehensive Income for reporting purposes.

   B. Accumulated Other Comprehensive Income (including the accumulated translation adjustment) is reported as an item in Shareholders' Equity in the translated ($) Balance Sheet.

III. Illustration (simple) of translation (local foreign currency is the functional currency):

Example

Assume a U.S. entity has a Mexican subsidiary, which maintains its accounting records and prepares its financial statements in the local currency, the Mexican peso (MP).

Relevant exchange rates are:

Historic rate when subsidiary was established:

1MP = $.0950

Average rate for the current-period 20X8:

1 MP = $.1000

Spot rate at date of dividend declaration:

1 MP = $.1010

Spot rate at end of current-period 12/31/X8:

1 MP = $.1020

IV. Translation—Of the (simple) financial statements from MP to U.S. dollars would occur as follows:

Foreign Subsidiary Statements

For the Year Ended 12/31/X8		Translation Process	
Statement of Net Income and Comprehensive Income (20X8)	MP	Rate for Translation	US$
Sales	100,000	$.1000	$10,000
COGS	(50,000)	.1000	(5,000)
Depreciation	(10,000)	.1000	(1,000)
Other Expenses	(5,000)	.1000	(500)
Net Income	35,000		$ 3,500
Net Income			
Other (Items of) Comprehensive Income: (from B/S below) Translation Adjustment			680
Comprehensive Income			4,180
Retained Earnings (20X8)			
Beginning R/E	60,000	(End 20X7)	$ 5,700
Add: N/I (20X8)	35,000	(Above)	3,500
Deduct: Dividends 20X8	(20,000)	.1010	(2,020)
Ending R/E	75,000		$ 7,180

Balance Sheet (12/31/X8)

Cash and Accounts Receivable	20,000	.1020	$ 2,040
Inventory	80,000	.1020	8,160
Fixed Assets	25,000	.1020	2,250
Total Assets	125,000		12,750
Liabilities	20,000	.1020	2,040
Common Stock	30,000	.0950	2,850
Retained Earnings	75,000	(Above)	7,180
Subsidary Totals	125,000		12,070
Accumulated Other Comprehensive Income		(To Balance)	680
Total Liability + Equity	125,000		$12,750

A. Items to note in above illustration:

1. All revenue (sales) and expense items were assumed to have occurred evenly throughout the year.

2. Beginning Retained Earnings is the dollar value at the end of the prior year.

3. Dividends are translated at the exchange rate in effect on the date of declaration.

4. Common stock is translated at the exchange rate in effect the day the stock was issued (since parent created the sub).

5. The translated Balance Sheet does not balance (Assets= $12,750; Liabilities+ Equity= $12,070) until the translation adjustment is included. The amount of the translation adjustment is the amount needed to make the Balance Sheet balance ($680). The $680 is "plugged."

6. The Translation Adjustment is reported in the Shareholders' Equity Section of the Balance Sheet and as an item of Other Comprehensive Income in reporting Comprehensive Income.

Conversion Using Remeasurement

If the final reporting currency is the functional currency, rather than the local foreign currency, the foreign financial statements will be converted using remeasurement, instead of translation. Similarly, if another foreign currency (other than the recording currency) is the functional currency, the foreign financial statements will have to be remeasured to the functional currency, and then translated to the reporting currency. This lesson identifies the exchange rates to be used when the remeasurement method of conversion is used and how to treat any resulting remeasurement adjustment.

After studying this lesson, you should be able to:

1. Describe the sequence of requirements when converting financial statements using remeasurement.

2. Identify the exchange rates to use for converting different financial statement accounts using remeasurement.

3. Describe how the translation adjustment amount is treated when financial statements are converted using remeasurement.

4. Apply the remeasurement method in converting financial statements from one currency to another currency.

5. Describe and apply the reporting of the remeasurement translation adjustment in a set of converted financial statements.

I. **Remeasurement Process—U.S. Dollar= Functional Currency**—Use remeasurement to convert from foreign currency to reporting currency (the $):

    A. Convert accounts from foreign currency units (FCU) to dollars using temporal method:

        1. For monetary items—current exchange rate (CR).

        2. For nonmonetary items—historical exchange rate (HR), that is, exchange rate in existence when account item arose. Monetary items are those where value is fixed by contract (examples: cash, accounts receivable, accounts payable, bonds and notes, etc.)

        3. Examples

> FCU of Monetary $\times$ CR = $
>
> FCU of Non-Monetary $\times$ HR = $

    B. Historic Exchange Rate—Basically, use historic exchange rate for nonmonetary items:

        1. Past price valuation—Assets and liabilities valued at past prices (not for assets and liabilities measured at amounts promised).

            a. Examples

                i. Securities carried at cost, if any

                ii. Inventories carried at cost

                iii. Prepaid costs

                iv. Fixed assets/accumulated depreciation

                v. Intangibles (goodwill, etc.)

                vi. Deferred revenue

                vii. Paid-in capital

2. **Historic rate conversion**—Revenue and expenses related to assets and liabilities converted at Historic Rate (only).

    a. **Examples**

        i. COGS (when Inventory at cost)

        ii. Depreciation

        iii. Amortization of Intangibles (not GW!)

II. Use Current Exchange Rates for

  A. All other (monetary) Assets and Liabilities

  B. All other Revenue, Expense, Gain, and Loss Items

III. Remeasurement Adjustment—Amount needed to make the trial balance debits and credits (expressed in dollars) balance is amount of remeasurement adjustment:

  A. The remeasurement adjustment is reported as a gain or loss in the income from continuing operations section of the income statement (expressed in dollars).

  B. The remeasurement adjustment "flows through" the Income Statement to Retained Earnings.

IV. Illustration (Simple) of Remeasurement (Reporting Currency Is the Functional Currency)

Example

'Assume a U.S. entity has a Mexican subsidiary, which maintains its accounting records and prepares its financial statements in the local currency, the Mexican peso (MP). Because the Mexican subsidiary is a sales unit that purchases its inventory for its U.S. parent, it is basically an extension of its parent, not independent of it. Therefore, its functional currency is the U.S. dollar.

Relevant exchange rates are:

Historic rate when subsidiary was established:

1 MP = $.0950

Historic rate when subsidiary Fixed Assets were acquired:

1 MP = $.0975

Average rate for the current-period 20X8:

1 MP = $.1000

Spot rate at date dividend declared:

1 MP = $.1010

Spot rate at end of current-period 12/31/X8:

1 MP = $.1020

V. Remeasurement Illustration

Remeasurement Illustration

For the Year Ended 12/31/X8 Income Statement (20X8)	MP	Translation Process Rate for Translation	US$
Sales	$100,000	.1000	$10,000
COGS	(50,000)	.1000	(5,000)
Depreciation Expense	(10,000)	.0975	(975)
Other Expenses	(5,000)	.1000	(500)
Preliminary Net Income	35,000		$ 3,525
Translation Adjustment			
Gain			383
Net Income			3,908
			======
Retained Earnings (20X8)			
Beginning R/E	$60,000	(End 20X7)	$ 5,700
Add: Preliminary N/I (20X8)	35,000	(Above)	3,525
Deduct: Dividends 20X8	(20,000)	.1010	(2,020)
Preliminary End R/E	75,000		$ 7,205
	======		
Add: Adjustment to NI			
(Translation Gain)			383
Ending R/E (Final)			$ 7,588
			======
Balance Sheet (12/31/X8)			
Cash and Accounts Receivable	$20,000	.1020	$ 2,040
Inventory (at cost)	80,000	.1000	8,000
Fixed Assets	25,000	.0975	2,438
Total Assets	125,000		12,478
	======		======
Liabilities	$20,000	.1020	$2,040
Common Stock	30,000	.0950	2,850
Preliminary R/E	75,000	(Above)	7,205
Preliminary subsidiary totals	$125,000		$12,095
	======		======
Deduct: Preliminary R/E			$7,205
Add: Final R/E			7,588
Total Liability + Equity			$12,478

Calculation of Cumulative Translation Adjustment (to be carried to Preliminary Net Income)

Total Assets	$12,478	
subsidiary (L + E)	12,095	
Adjustment to NI	$ 383	("Flows through" to Retained Earnings)

A. Items to note in previous illustration:

1. Revenues (sales) are assumed to have occurred evenly throughout the year.

2. All inventory sold during the year and remaining on hand at year-end is assumed to have been acquired from the parent evenly throughout the year.

3. Fixed assets and depreciation expense are translated at the exchange rate in effect when the fixed assets were acquired.

4. Dividends are translated at the exchange rate in effect on the date of declaration.

5. Common stock is translated at the exchange rate in effect the day the stock was issued (since the parent created the subsidiary).

6. The preliminary translated Balance Sheet does not balance (assets = $12,478; Preliminary Liabilities + Equity = $12,095). The difference ($383) is not reported as a Translation Adjustment in Shareholders' Equity.

7. The amount needed to balance the Balance Sheet ($383) is recognized as a Translation Adjustment Gain in the Income from Continuing Operations section of the Income Statement, which increases Net Income, which, in turn, increases Ending Retained Earnings resulting in balancing the Balance Sheet.

8. Since the translation adjustment is recognized in net income, it is not shown as an item of Other Comprehensive Income.

Remeasurement and Translation

Under special circumstances, both the remeasurement and the translation methods of converting foreign currency financial statements will be required. This lesson identifies when that would be necessary and the accounting treatment, including the handling of the remeasurement and translation adjustments.

After studying this lesson, you should be able to:

1. Describe when both the remeasurement and translation forms of conversion of financial statements will be required.

2. Demonstrate the application of the remeasurement and translation processes in combination when both are required.

I. **Remeasurement, then Translation**—A foreign currency other than the recording currency = functional currency.

   A. In this case, both remeasurement and translation will be required:

      1. **Remeasure**—(As previously described) from recording currency to functional currency (which is another foreign currency), then

      2. **Translate**—(As previously described) from functional currency to U.S. $ reporting currency.

II. **The Translation Adjustments**—Resulting from each of the conversion processes will be reported as follows:

   A. **Remeasurement** (Translation) **Adjustment**—In Income Statement.

   B. **Translation** (Translation) **Adjustment**—In Other Comprehensive Income for reporting purposes and, subsequently, in Accumulated Other Comprehensive Income in the Shareholders' Equity section of the Balance Sheet.

Example
A subsidiary of a company in the United States is in England. The subsidiary functions in the euro. The local currency is the British pound, the functional currency is the euro, and the reporting currency is the U.S. dollar.

The financial statements would be *remeasured* from British pound to euro and then *translated* from euro to the U.S. dollar.

Leases

Background, Short-Term Leases, and Operating Leases

> This is the first of several lessons addressing the accounting for leases. This lesson provides the accounting for short-term and operating leases by the lessee and the lessor.
>
> **After studying this lesson, you should be able to:**
>
> **1.** Distinguish between short-term, operating, and finance leases.
>
> **2.** Account for a short-term lease for the lessee and the lessor.
>
> **3.** Account for an operating lease for the lessee and the lessor.
>
> **4.** Compute the annual lease expense for a lessee with an operating lease.

I. Background

We will cover different types of leases in the lease lessons. Be aware of the role that you are studying (lessee or lessor) and the type of lease being accounted for. We will use the diagram below as a concept map to note the role and type of lease we are covering in most of our examples. In addition to the lease types shown, we will also cover sale-leasebacks.

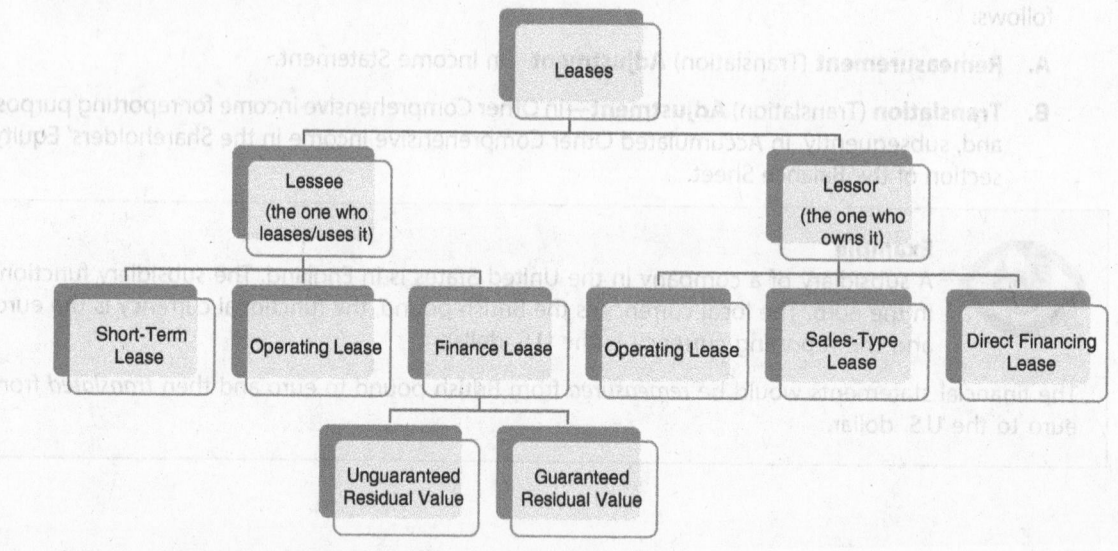

II. Definitions and Short-Term Leases

A. Definitions

1. Lease: A lease is a contractual agreement between a lessor and lessee conveying the right to use property, plant, or equipment for a specified period of time in exchange for consideration ("consideration" is usually cash payments).

2. Operating Lease: A lease that does not transfer control (or ownership) of the leased asset to the lessee. This is a lease that is not classified as a finance lease by the lessee, is not classified as a sales-type lease or direct-financing lease by the lessor, and has a lease term greater than 12 months. The lessee does capitalize a lease liability and records a right-of-use asset.

3. Finance Lease: A lease that transfers control (or ownership) of the leased asset to the lessee. The lessee recognizes a right-of-use asset and a lease liability on its books and recognizes interest expense and amortization over the lease term. The lessee "capitalizes" the leased asset. The lessor removes the asset from its books, replaces it with a financial asset (lease receivable), and recognizes interest revenue over the lease term.

B. When a lease is recorded as **a finance lease** by the lessee, the present value of the future lease payments is debited to the leased asset (right-of-use asset) and credited to the lease liability accounts. For the lessor, the present value of lease payments is debited to the financial asset (a receivable) created at inception (beginning of the lease). Finance leases are discussed in a later lesson.

C. For the lessee, a lease is recorded as a finance lease when it meets the lease capitalization criteria (discussed later).

D. A lease that is less than 12 months is considered **a short-term lease.**

    1. The lessee records lease or rent expense as time passes, typically on a monthly basis.

        a. Lessee monthly journal entries:

            i. Lease Expense (debit)

            ii. Cash or Accounts Payable (credit)

    2. The lessor records lease or rent revenue as earned, also typically on a monthly basis.

        a. Lessor monthly journal entries:

            i. Cash or Accounts Receivable (debit)

            ii. Lease Revenue (credit)

E. A lease that does not meet the finance lease criteria for the lessee (not a finance lease) and the lessor (not a sales-type lease or a direct financing lease) and is longer than 12 months is an **operating lease**.

III. Operating Lease Example. The next example covers accounting for an operating lease by the lessee and the lessor. See the bold positions in the diagram below.

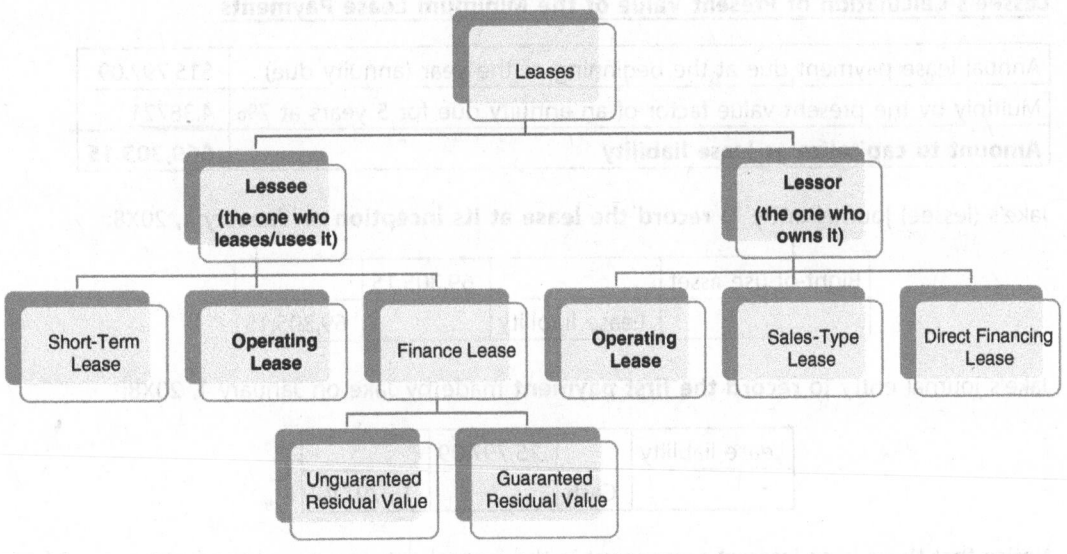

> **Example**
> On January 1, 20X8, Jake Co. (lessee) leased equipment from Paul Co. (lessor) for a 5-year lease term. The equipment has a cost and fair value of $80,000 and a useful life of 7 years with no salvage value. The contract does not contain a renewal option or a purchase option, and the equipment will revert back to Paul. Co. at the end of the lease term. The equipment has alternative uses. The equipment has an unguaranteed residual value of $15,000, and the implicit rate, of which Jake is aware, is 7%. Paul uses the straight-line method of depreciation.

Payments are due at the beginning of the year (annuity due). See below for Paul's (lessor's) calculation of the lease/rental payments to charge Jake.

Lessor's Calculation of Lease Payments

Fair value of the equipment		$80,000
Less: Present value of the unguaranteed residual value	(15,000 × .71299*)	10,694.85
Amount to be recovered through lease payments		69,305.15
Divide by the present value factor of an annuity due for 5 years at 7%		4.38721**
Annual lease payment to charge the lessee		**$15,797.09**

*Present value factor of a single sum for 5 years at 7% = .71299
**Present value factor of an annuity due for 5 years at 7% = 4.38721

Jake Co. evaluates the terms of the lease and determines that it does not meet the finance lease criteria (no transfer of ownership, no purchase option, lease term does not exceed 75% of the economic life of the asset, the present value of the lease is less than 90% of the fair value of the asset, and the asset does have alternative uses).

The lease term is 5 years for an asset with a 7 year useful life; therefore, the lease term covers 71.4% of the asset's useful life.

The present value of the lease (see calculation below), $69,305.15, is less than 90% of the asset's fair value (69,305.15 / 80,000 = 86.6%).

The lease is longer than one year but does not meet any of the lease criteria to be categorized as a finance lease for either the lessee or the lessor. The lease is classified by the lessee and the lessor as an operating lease.

Lessee's Calculation of Present Value of the Minimum Lease Payments

Annual lease payment due at the beginning of the year (annuity due)	$15,797.09
Multiply by the present value factor of an annuity due for 5 years at 7%	4.38721
Amount to capitalize as lease liability	**$69,305.15**

Jake's (lessee) journal entry to **record the lease at its inception** on January 1, 20X8:

Right-of-use asset		69,305.15	
	Lease liability		69,305.15

Jake's journal entry to **record the first payment** made by Jake on January 1, 20X8:

Lease liability		15,797.09	
	Cash		15,797.09

Notice that there is no interest component in the journal entry to record the first payment because in the case of an annuity due, the first payment is likely to happen on the same day as the inception of the lease. No time has passed, so no interest has accrued.

The lessee must complete two calculations to determine how to record subsequent lease payments.

1. Calculate the interest to be included in the lease expense by using the effective interest method.

2. Calculate the amortization of the right-of-use asset based on the portion of lease payment assigned to the lease liability and to the amortization of the right-of-use asset.

The first calculation is to measure the interest to be included in lease expense by applying the effective interest method and setting up an amortization table. This calculation/table is used to figure out how much interest to assign to each payment.

A second calculation is done to allocate the lease expense between the interest portion and the amortization of the right-of-use asset.

The first calculation to figure out how much interest to assign to each lease payment follows.

Lessee's (Jake's) Lease Amortization Schedule to Calculate Interest				
Date	Lease payment	Interest (7%) on lease liability	Reduction in lease liability	Lease liability
1/1/X8				69,305.15
1/1/X8	15,797.09		15,797.08	53,508.07
1/1/X9	15,797.09	3,745.56	12,051.53	41,456.54
1/1/X0	15,797.09	2,901.96	12,895.13	28,561.41
1/1/X1	15,797.09	1,999.30	13,797.79	14,763.62
1/1/X2	15,797.09	1,033.47*	14,763.62	0.00
12/31/X2	End of Lease			

*Rounded 1,033.44 three cents to 1,033.47.

The second calculation to figure out how much of each lease payment is assigned to interest and how much is assigned to amortization of the right-of-use asset follows.

Lessee's (Jake's) Lease Expense Schedule				
Date	Lease expense	Interest (7%) on lease liability	Amortization of right-of-use asset	Carrying value of right-of-use asset
1/1/X8				69,305.15
12/31/X8	15,797.09	3,745.56	12,051.53	57,253.62
12/31/X9	15,797.09	2,901.96	12,895.13	44,358.49
12/31/X0	15,797.09	1,999.30	13,797.79	30,560.70
12/31/X1	15,797.09	1,033.48*	14,763.61	15,797.09
12/31/X2	15,797.09		15,797.09	0.00

*Rounded 1,033.47 one cent to 1,033.48.

We use information from the two calculations to determine our journal entries.

Lessee's (Jake's) Journal Entries over the Life of the Operating Lease and after the Date of Inception.

12/31/X8	Lease expense		15,797.09	
		Right-of-use asset*		12,051.53
		Lease liability**		3,745.56
	*Amortization of the right-of-use asset			
	**Recording the interest into the lease liability			
1/1/X9	Lease liability		15,797.09	
		Cash		15,797.09

12/31/X9	Lease expense			15,797.09	
		Right-of-use asset			12,895.13
		Lease liability			2,901.96
1/1/X0	Lease liability			15,797.09	
		Cash			15,797.09
12/31/X0	Lease expense			15,797.09	
		Right-of-use asset			13,797.79
		Lease liability			1,999.30
1/1/X1	Lease liability			15,797.09	
		Cash			15,797.09
12/31/X1	Lease expense			15,797.09	
		Right-of-use asset			14,763.61
		Lease liability			1,033.48
1/1/X2	Lease liability			15,797.09	
		Cash			15,797.09
12/31/X2	Lease expense			15,797.09	
		Right-of-use asset			15,797.09

Lessor's (Paul) Accounting for the Operating Lease

The lessor receives payment in advance of each lease year (the payment by the lessee is made on January 1 for the following year) and records the receipt of cash and unearned lease revenue at the beginning of each year. As time passes, the lessor recognizes the unearned revenue (shown here on an annual basis) as lease revenue.

Because the lease is an operating lease, the lessor retains the asset on its books and records depreciation on the asset each year over its useful life. Paul Co. uses the straight-line method of depreciation. The asset has a cost basis of $80,000 and a 7-year useful life.

Lessor's (Paul's) Journal Entries over the Life of the Operating Lease

1/1/X8	Cash			15,797.09	
		Unearned lease revenue			15,797.09
12/31/X8	Unearned lease revenue			15,797.09	
		Lease revenue			15,797.09
	Depreciation expense			11,428.57	
		Accumulated depreciation			11,428.57
	($80,000/7 years = $11,428.57)				
1/1/X9	Cash			15,797.09	
		Unearned lease revenue			15,797.09
12/31/X9	Unearned lease revenue			15,797.09	
		Lease revenue			15,797.09
	Depreciation expense			11,428.57	
		Accumulated depreciation			11,428.57
	($80,000/7 years = $11,428.57)				
1/1/X0	Cash			15,797.09	
		Unearned lease revenue			15,797.09

12/31/X0	Unearned lease revenue		15,797.09	
		Lease revenue		15,797.09
	Depreciation expense		11,428.57	
		Accumulated depreciation		11,428.57
	($80,000/7 years = $11,428.57)			
1/1/X1	Cash		15,797.09	
		Unearned lease revenue		15,797.09
12/31/X1	Unearned lease revenue		15,797.09	
		Lease revenue		15,797.09
	Depreciation expense		11,428.57	
		Accumulated depreciation		11,428.57
	($80,000/7 years = $11,428.57)			
1/1/X2	Cash		15,797.09	
		Unearned lease revenue		15,797.09
12/31/X2	Unearned lease revenue		15,797.09	
		Lease revenue		15,797.09
	Depreciation expense		11,428.57	
		Accumulated depreciation		11,428.57
	($80,000/7 years = $11,428.57)			

Finance Lease Basics

The second lesson on lease accounting establishes the terminology and conceptual underpinnings for the remaining lessons on leases.

After studying this lesson, you should be able to:

1. Determine the applicable interest rates for both parties (implicit or incremental).

2. List the items included in minimum lease payments for both parties to the lease.

3. Define the important terms relevant to finance lease accounting, including lease term, bargain purchase option, unguaranteed residual value, minimum lease payments, and others.

4. List and understand the five criteria for a finance lease.

5. Identify the different types of leases for lessees and lessors.

I. Finance Lease Terminology

A. Lease Term and Renewal Option—The **lease term** is the period during which the lessee can reasonably be expected to continue leasing the asset. It is the fixed noncancelable term of the lease plus periods covered by bargain renewal options plus all periods covered by renewal options during which there is a loan outstanding from the lessor to the lessee. The lease term will not extend beyond the exercise date of a bargain purchase option, even if the lease specifies payments after the date of the bargain purchase option. (Those later payments would not be paid because the asset will be purchased before those payments.)

B. Bargain Purchase Option—The bargain purchase option (BPO) is an option whereby the lessee will have an opportunity in the future to purchase the asset at an amount that is significantly less than the asset's fair market value on that future date. The price is sufficiently low to reasonably assure exercise of the option by the lessee. If the lessee accepts the terms of the lease contract, the accounting for both parties assumes the purchase option will be exercised, in which case title transfers to the lessee. The exercise ends the lease term.

   1. The option is not really a bargain, however. The lessor expects the option to be taken and structures all of the payments, including the BPO, to provide the required rate of return. The BPO amount is really just another lease payment.

C. Residual Value, Guaranteed or Unguaranteed—The guaranteed residual value clause is typically found in lease agreements in which there is no bargain purchase option or transfer of title. It is related to the condition of the property at the time that it reverts back to the lessor. If the lessee guarantees the residual value, the lessee is responsible for the condition of the asset at the conclusion of the lease term. If there is no guaranteed residual value in the lease agreement, the lessee is not responsible for the condition of the asset at the conclusion of the lease agreement. Third parties may also guarantee residual values.

   1. If the lessee guarantees a residual value, the expectation is that the title does not transfer to the lessee at the end of the lease term. The lessee will pay the lessor any shortfall between the amount guaranteed and the actual market value of the asset at the end of the lease term.

   2. An unguaranteed residual value is the expected salvage value of the leased asset at the end of the term that has not been guaranteed. The guarantee of residual value, or lack thereof, does not change the amount of the residual. The residual value is a best, good-faith estimate of what the asset will be worth at the end of the lease.

Examples
Residual Value
The estimated value of a leased asset at the end of the lease term is $3,000. With or without a guarantee, the value is expected to be $3,000. This is the same residual or salvage value discussed in the lessons on depreciation of plant assets, except that it is measured at the end of the lease term, which may be well before the end of the asset's economic life.

D. Executory Costs—Executory costs include casualty insurance, maintenance, and property taxes. These costs are usually not capitalized by either party; rather they represent annual expenses associated with owning and maintaining the asset. Executory costs are discussed in more detail in a later lesson.

E. Lessee Minimum Lease Payments—The minimum lease payments for the lessee are all the payments the lessee is expected to make under the lease. These payments include all the rental payments that the lessee is obligated to make in connection with the leased property, with some typical exclusions, such as executory costs.

The components of the lessee's minimum lease payments are listed next.

1. The annual lease payments

2. Bargain purchase option

3. If no bargain purchase option exists, any residual value guaranteed and expected to be paid (the difference between guaranteed residual value minus the expected value at the end of the lease) by the lessee at the expiration of the lease term

4. Any penalty payments the lessee is required to make for not renewing the lease term

5. Excluded are payments required by the lessee for damage, extraordinary wear and tear, or excessive usage because they cannot be estimated. Rather, they are treated as expenses or losses in the period incurred.

F. Lessor Minimum Lease Payments to Be Received

The lessor measures the lease receivable using the minimum lease payments. From the lessor's perspective, the minimum lease payments are the same as those identified for the lessee with one additional element. The minimum lease payments also include any residual value guaranteed by a third party unrelated to either the lessee or the lessor. An unguaranteed residual is not included in the minimum lease payments of the lessor or lessee because it represents value outside the lease arrangement; however, it may be included in the lessor's recording of the lease receivable.

G. Interest Rate

1. **Lessor**—The implicit interest rate is sometimes described as the lessor's required rate of interest or rate of return. Mathematically, the implicit interest rate is the rate that equates the market value of the leased asset with the sum of the present value (PV) of the minimum lease payments (lessor's perspective) plus the PV of any unguaranteed residual value. This is the rate used by the lessor for all PV calculations in a finance lease and for computing interest revenue.

   This rate is the annual compounded rate of return to the lessor over the lease term. The unguaranteed residual value is included in the calculation because it is part of the value of the asset (as is the case with the salvage value for any plant asset).

2. **Lessee**—Whenever readily determinable, a lessee should use the interest rate implicit in the lease. If the rate of interest implicit in the lease is not readily determinable, a lessee may use its incremental borrowing rate. The lessee's incremental borrowing rate is the rate, at lease inception date, the lessee would have incurred to borrow the funds necessary to purchase the leased asset rather than lease it.

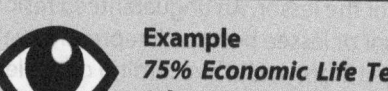

Example
Lessor's Perspective

A lease requires 10 equal annual lease payments of $4,000 to be paid each January 1. The inception of the lease is January 1, Year 1. The market value of the asset leased is $27,807. The unguaranteed residual value at the end of the lease term is $2,000. The lessor's implicit rate in the lease is 10%. The discounted cash flows, including the unguaranteed residual value, are related to the market value as shown in the equation:

$27,807 = Market value of asset = PV of the lease payments + PV of unguaranteed residual value

$27,807 = $4,000(PV ann.due,I = 10%, N = 10) + $2,000(PV$1, I = 10%, N = 10)

$= $4,000(6.75902) + $2,000(.38554)

If the cash flows are received as expected, the lessor will earn 10% on a compounded basis annually from its investment in the leased asset. From the lessor's perspective, all residual values at the end of the lease term are treated the same way in the above equation. It makes no difference in terms of the lessor's equation if the residual is guaranteed or not. The residual value is the best estimate of the value of the asset that the lessor will receive back at the end of the lease term.

II. Finance Lease Criteria

A. The **five criteria** used to determine whether a lease is a finance lease follow. Both parties use these criteria.

B. In all cases, the lease must be noncancelable for it to be a finance lease. This is generally assumed, if not mentioned, in a problem.

> **Tip**
> **Caution:** To facilitate the discussion, the lease capitalization (finance) criteria are referred to by number, but for the CPA Exam, candidates should know the criteria by their descriptions, as provided.

Criterion 1—The lease agreement **transfers ownership** of the leased asset to the lessee at the conclusion of the lease term (title transfer).

Criterion 2—The lease contains a bargain purchase option (BPO).

Criterion 3—The lease term is for the major part of the asset's remaining economic life, effectively measured as at least 75% of the remaining estimated economic life of the leased asset at inception (term is 75% or more of useful life).

Example
75% Economic Life Test

A **lessor** leases an asset with an original useful life when new of 20 years. After two years, the asset is leased for 12 years. The third criterion is not met because 12/18 = .67, which is less than .75. The remaining useful life at inception is 18 years. The lease term is less than 75% of the 18-year remaining useful life. If none of the other four criteria is met, the lease is an operating lease.

Criterion 4—The **present value** of minimum lease payments at the inception of the lease equals or exceeds substantially all of the fair value of the leased asset, effectively measured as at least 90% of the market value of the leased asset at that time (PV is 90% or more of market value). Review the definition of minimum lease payments. Criterion 4 is the reason that minimum lease payments were defined.

a. For criterion 4, the lessor uses the rate implicit in the lease to measure the present value.

b. If the lessee knows or can determine the lessor's implicit interest rate, then the lessee uses the lower of the lessor's implicit interest rate and the lessee's incremental borrowing rate.

c. The parties use these interest rates not only in measuring the present value for criterion 4 but also for capitalizing the minimum lease payments for recording the lease liability or lease receivable and for computing interest.

Example
90% Present Value Test

A lessor leases an asset with a market value of $100,000 for 10 years. Annual end-of-year lease payments are $15,000 (note—the payments are due at end of year so this is an ordinary annuity). The lessor's implicit rate and lessee's borrowing rate are 10%. The lease calls for no other payments by the lessee, and the asset reverts to the lessor at the end of the lease term.

$$\text{PV of minimum lease payments} = \$15,000(\text{PV ord.ann.},I = 10\%, N = 10)$$

$$= \$15,000 \times 6.14457$$

$$= \$92,169 > 90\% \times \$100,000$$

The fourth criterion is met for both parties because the present value of minimum lease payments for both lessor and lessee ($92,169) exceeds 90% of the market value of the asset. Thus, the lease is a finance lease.

Note
Caution 1: The present value of minimum lease payments may be different for the lessor and lessee because:

A. Different cash flows may be included in their minimum lease payments; and

B. Their interest rates may be different. The **lessor** will always use the implicit interest rate. However, when the **lessee** does not know the implicit rate of interest or when the implicit rate of interest is higher than the incremental borrowing rate, then the lessee will use its incremental borrowing rate. The incremental borrowing rate may differ from the implicit interest rate.

Note
Caution 2: When the lease term begins at or near the end of the asset's useful life (typically considered to be within the last 25% of the total useful life of the asset), criteria 3 and 4 no longer can be used to determine whether a lease is a finance lease. In this case, title must transfer or a bargain purchase option must be present for a lease to be capitalized.

Example
25% Useful Life Remaining

An asset's original useful life is 20 years. After 15 years of using the asset, a firm leases it to another firm for 4 years. Normally, this lease would qualify as a finance lease because the lease term is 80% of the remaining useful life at inception (4/5). But at inception, only 25% of the total useful life of the asset remains (5/20). Therefore, criteria 3 and 4 can no longer be used for lease capitalization. Most of the asset's useful life is over. If this lease does not transfer title or include a bargain purchase option, then it is an operating lease.

Criterion 5—Alternative use—If the asset is specialized in nature and does not have an alternative use to the lessor at the end of the lease term, then the alternative use test is met and the lease is a finance lease. In other words, answering "no" to alternative use, meaning the asset does not have an alternative use, meets criterion 5, and the lease is a finance lease.

C. Criteria are met or not met—If none of the five criteria is met, the lease is an operating lease for the lessee and an operating or direct financing lease for the lessor.

    1. Lessee

        a. If one or more of the criteria is met, the lease is a finance lease for the lessee.

        b. If none is met and the lease is greater than 12 months, then the lessee has an operating lease.

    2. Lessor

        a. If one of the five criteria is met, then the lease is a sales-type lease for the lessor.

        b. If none of the five criteria is met, then the lessor has either an operating lease or a direct-financing lease. To determine if the lessor has an operating lease or a direct-financing lease, two additional criteria are considered.

            i. Additional Criteria 1—The present value of the sum of the lease payments and guaranteed residual value is greater than or equal to the fair value of the asset.

            ii. Additional Criteria 2—Collectibility of the lease payments and guaranteed residual value is probable.

            iii. If the two criteria are both met, then the lessor has a direct-financing lease. If they are not met, then the lessor has an operating lease.

III. Classification of Leases

The following is the breakdown of leases for both parties.

    A. Lessee

        1. Short term

        2. Operating

        3. Finance

    B. Lessor

        1. Operating

        2. Sales-type (defined later)

        3. Direct financing (defined later)

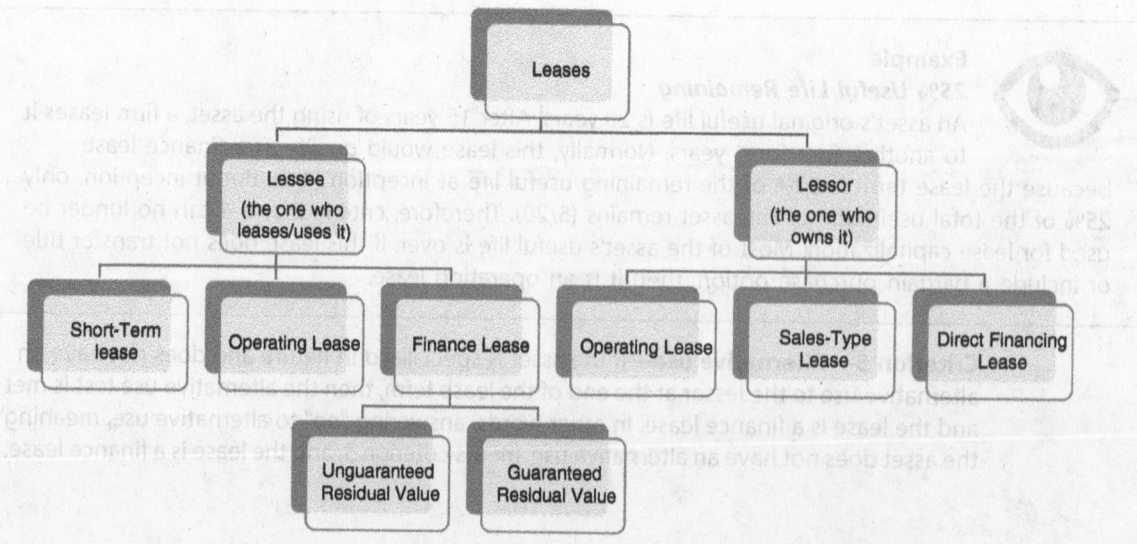

Finance Leases—Lessee

This lease accounting lesson covers the specifics for recording a finance lease for the lessee.

After studying this lesson, you should be able to:

1. Identify a finance lease from given information for the lessee.

2. Record the inception journal entry for the lessee.

3. Prepare the journal entries for interest and amortization expense recognition over the life of the lease.

4. Use the effective interest method to amortize the lease liability for the lessee.

5. Prepare the journal entries for a lessee's finance lease with guaranteed residual value and with unguaranteed residual value.

I.   **Background**—Here we cover accounting for finance leases for the lessee. We start with a finance lease with no residual value and then cover finance leases with guaranteed and unguaranteed residual values.

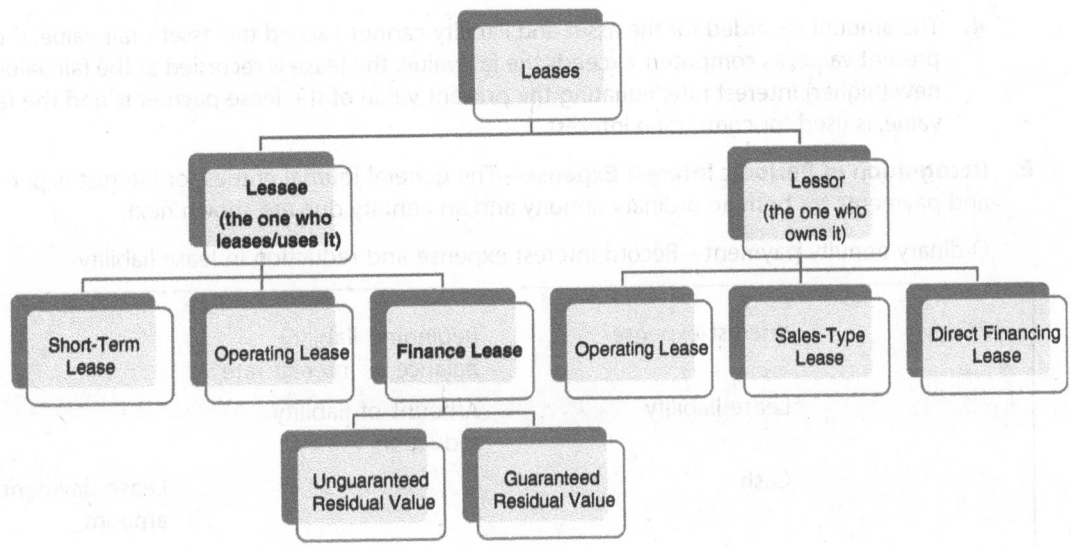

II. **Finance Lease Basics**

A.   A lessee accounts for a lease as a finance lease when the lease is noncancelable (most problems do not state explicitly that the lease is noncancelable, so account for it as if it is unless otherwise stated) and one of the five finance lease criteria are met. Recall that the five finance lease criteria are:

1.   Transfer of ownership.

2.   Bargain purchase option.

3.   Lease term is greater than the major part of the asset's economic life (75% test).

4.   Present value of the lease payments equals or exceeds the substantially all of the asset's fair value (90% test).

5.   Alternative use test—The asset is specialized in nature and does not have an alternative use to the lessor.

B.   The general entries for a finance lease for a lessee appear below. The numerical examples illustrate the procedures. The entries are affected by whether the lease payment stream is an annuity due or an ordinary annuity.

C. Lessee

	At inception of the lease		
1/1/yr1	Right-of-use asset	Present value of minimum lease payments	
	Lease liability		Present value of minimum lease payments

D. The lessee is capitalizing the right-of-use asset that it does not own and is recording a lease liability based on the lease contract.

1. The leased asset is typically included in plant assets or property, plant, and equipment.

2. The lessee typically uses the net method, which records the liability at its present value. The lease liability has both current (amount due within the next fiscal period, typically one year) and noncurrent components.

3. The present value of the minimum lease payments is computed using the lower of the implicit interest rate (the rate of return set by the lessor), if the lessee knows the rate or can determine it, and the lessee's incremental borrowing rate. This is the same rate used by the lessee and lessor for criterion 4.

4. The amount recorded for the asset and liability cannot exceed the asset's fair value. If the present value, as computed, exceeds the fair value, the lease is recorded at the fair value. A new (higher) interest rate, equating the present value of the lease payments and the fair value, is used for computing interest.

E. Recognition of Periodic Interest Expense—The general journal entries for interest expense and payments for both an ordinary annuity and an annuity due are shown next.

Ordinary annuity payment—Record interest expense and reduction in lease liability

12/31/yr1	Interest expense	Beginning liability balance × Interest rate	
	Lease liability	Amount of liability reduction	
	Cash		Lease payment amount

Annuity due payment—Accrue interest, record payment

12/31/yr1	Interest expense	Beginning liability balance × Interest rate	
	Lease liability	Beginning liability balance × Interest rate	
1/1/yr2	Lease liability	Lease payment	
	Cash		Lease payment

F. At the end of the year, the lessee records amortization expense and decreases the right-of-use asset. Computation of amortization expense is discussed in a later lesson.

12/31/yrX	Amortization expense	Calculation shown later
	Right-of-use asset	

G. Residual Value—As discussed in the "Finance Lease Basics" lesson, residual value is a best estimate of what the asset will be worth at the end of the lease

1. Assets may have no residual value expected at the end of the lease.

2. Assets may have a residual value amount expected at the end of the lease and a guaranteed residual value (GRV) amount. A lease contract may include a GRV by the lessee. The lessee is essentially promising to return an asset worth a certain amount. If the leased asset is worth less than the GRV, then the lessee will need to make up the difference in the form of consideration (typically a cash payment for the difference between the GRV and the actual residual value of the lease asset).

III. Finance Lease—Lessee Example

Example
Finance Lease with No Residual Value
This example covers accounting for a finance lease by the lessee. First, we walk through a finance lease with no residual value, then a finance lease with GRV, followed by a discussion of a finance lease with unguaranteed residual value.

On January 1, Year 1, lessor leases equipment to lessee. Data on the lease:

● Equipment fair value and lessor's book value, $25,771 (asset is new)

● Lessor's implicit rate and lessee's implicit borrowing rate, 8%

● Lease payments due each December 31 through Year 3 (three-year lease term)

● Useful life of equipment, three years (**no residual value**)

Payments are due at the end of the year (ordinary annuity). See below for lessor's calculation of the lease/rental payments to charge lessee.

Though our focus is the lessee in this example, the lessor calculates how much to charge the lessee in lease payments.

Lessor's Calculation of Lease Payments with No Residual Value

Fair value of equipment		$25,771
Less: Present value of residual value	0	0
Amount to be recovered through lease payments		$25,771
Divide by present value factor of **ordinary annuity** for 3 years at 8%		2.57710**
Annual lease payment to charge lessee		**$ 10,000**

This is a finance lease for the lessee because criterion 3 is met (lease term of three years = 100% of useful life at inception). Criterion 4 is also met (present value of minimum lease payments of $25,771 = 100% of fair value at inception). There is no information about criterion 1, 2, or 5, and we cannot assume those are met.

Lessee's Calculation of Present Value of Minimum Lease Payments

Annual lease payment due at the end of the year (ordinary annuity)	$10,000
Multiply by present value factor of ordinary annuity for 3 years at 8%	2.5771
Amount to capitalize as lease liability	**$25,771**

The **lessee's journal entries** for the finance lease are shown next.

Lessee Inception and Year 1 Interest and Amortization

1/1/yr1	Right-of-use asset			25,771	
	Lease liability				25,771
12/31/yr1	Interest expense	($25,771 × .08)		2,062	
	Lease liability	($10,000 – 2,062)		7,938	
	Cash				10,000
12/31/yr1	Amortization expense		($25,771/3)	8,590	
	Right-of-use asset				8,590

The lessee records the leased asset as a right-of-use asset and the lease liability at the present value (net method). One year later (12/31/yr1), interest expense is based on the lease liability balance ($25,771). The lessee uses the straight-line method to amortize the right-of-use asset. $8,590 of amortization expense is recognized in each of the three years. The net book value of the asset and the net lease liability are the same only at inception.

At 12/31/yr1, Book value of leased asset = $25,771 – 8,590 = 17,181. Net lease liability = $25,771 – 7,938 = 17,833. $17,833 is the amount on which interest expense for Year 2 is based.

See the next Lessee Amortization Schedule of the Lease Liability.

Lessee Amortization Schedule of the Lease Liability Ordinary Annuity Basis				
Date	Annual lease payment	Interest (8%) on liability	Reduction of lease liability	Lease liability
1/1/yr1				$25,771
12/31/yr1	$10,000	$2,062	$7,938	$17,833
12/31/yr2	$10,000	$1,426	$8,574	$9,259
12/31/yr3	$10,000	$741	$9,259	$0

Lessee Years 2 and 3 Interest and Amortization.

Once the Year 2 and Year 3 entries have been recorded, both the lease liability and the right-of-use asset have book values of zero.

Study hint: Create the t-accounts to follow the journal entries for both the lease liability and the right-of-use asset.

12/31/yr2	Interest expense	($25,771 – 7,938) × .08	1,426	
	Lease liability	($10,000 – 1,426)	8,574	
	Cash			10,000
12/31/yr2	Amortization expense	($25,771/3)	8,590	
	Right-of-use asset			8,590
12/31/yr3	Interest expense	($25,771 – 7,938 – 8,574 × .08)	741	
	Lease liability	($10,000 – 741)	9,259	
	Cash			10,000
12/31/yr3	Amortization expense	($25,771/3)	8,590	
	Right-of-use asset			8,590

Next, we cover a lessee's accounting for a finance lease with GRV and with unguaranteed residual value.

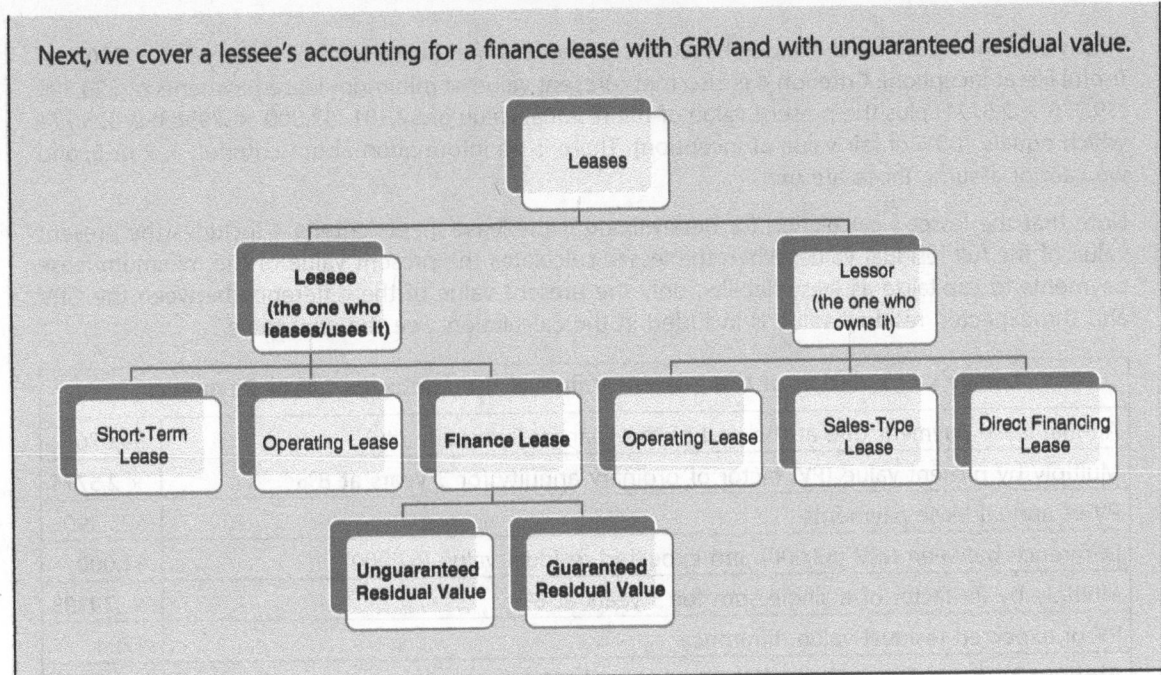

Example
Finance Lease with GRV
A lessee may guarantee the residual value of the lease asset.

If the expected residual value at the end of the lease is less than the GRV, then the lessee should include the present value of the difference in the lease liability.

Using the same fact pattern as the lease above with a slight change regarding residual value, here we cover the lessee's accounting for a finance lease with GRV.

Recall that, on January 1, Year 1, lessor leases equipment to lessee. Data on the lease:

- Equipment fair value and lessor's book value, $25,771 (asset is new)

- Lessor's implicit rate and Lessee's implicit borrowing rate, 8%

- Lease payments due each December 31 through Year 3 (three-year lease term)

- Useful life of equipment, three years

- The lessee **guarantees a residual value of $3,000** associated with the asset at the end of the lease term. The leased asset is expected to have a residual value of $2,000.

Payments are due at the end of the year (ordinary annuity). See below for the lessor's calculation of the lease/rental payments to charge the lessee.

Because the lease contains a residual value, the lessor may charge a bit less in annual lease payments. The table shows the lessor's calculation of lease payments to charge.

Lessor's Calculation of Lease Payments with Residual Value	
Fair value of equipment	$25,771
Less: Present value of residual value ($3,000 × .79383*)	2,381
Amount to be recovered through lease payments	$23,390
Divide by present value factor of an **ordinary annuity** for 3 years at 8%	2.57710
Annual lease payment to charge the lessee	**$ 9,076**

*Present value of single sum (3 years, 8%) = .79383

This is a finance lease for the lessee because criterion 3 is met (lease term of three years = 100% of useful life at inception). Criterion 4 is also met (present value of minimum lease payments of $23,390 ($9,076 × 2.5771) plus the present value of the residual value of $2,381 ($3,000 × .79383) is $25,771 which equals 100% of fair value at inception). There is no information about criterion 1, 2 or 5, and we cannot assume those are met.

Note that the lessee's calculation for determining if the lease meets criteria 4 includes the present value of the full residual value. When the lessee calculates the present value of the minimum lease payments to capitalize as lease liability, only the present value of the difference between the GRV and the expected residual value is included in the calculation. See the next table.

Lessee's Calculation of the Present Value of the Minimum Lease Payments	
Annual lease payment due at the end of the year (ordinary annuity)	$9,076
Multiply by present value (PV) factor of ordinary annuity for 3 years at 8%	× 2.5771
PV of annual lease payments	$23,390
Difference between GRV ($3,000) and expected residual value ($2,000)	$1,000
Multiply by PV factor of a single sum for 3 years at 8%	× .79383
PV of expected residual value difference	$794
Amount to capitalize as lease liability (sum of PVs)	**$24,184**

The **lessee's journal entries for the first year** for the finance lease with a guaranteed residual value are shown next. The journal entries for subsequent years would follow the approach when there is no residual value, and the lessee would use the effective interest method to amortize the lease liability.

Lessee Inception, and Year 1 Interest and Amortization

1/1/yr1	Right-of-use asset		24,184	
	Lease liability			24,184
12/31/yr1	Interest expense	($24,184 × .08)	1,935	
	Lease liability	($9,076 − 1,935)	7,141	
	Cash			9,076
12/31/yr1	Amortization expense	($24,184/3)	8,061	
	Right-of-use asset			8,061

See the Lessee Amortization Schedule of Lease Liability with GRV. Note that at the end of the third year after the lease payment, the remaining lease liability that is not reduced by the lease payments is $1,000, the difference between GRV and expected residual value (RV)

Lessee Amortization Schedule of the Lease Liability with GRV Ordinary Annuity Basis				
Date	Annual lease payment	Interest (8%) on liability	Reduction of lease liability	Lease liability
1/1/yr1				$24,184
12/31/yr1	$9,076	$1,935	$7,141	$17,043
12/31/yr2	$9,076	$1,363	$7,713	$9,330
12/31/yr3	$9,076	$746	$8,330	$1,000

If the **residual value is unguaranteed**, then the lessee would not include the present value of the expected difference between the GRV and the expected residual value in its lease liability computation.

Using the example and assuming unguaranteed residual value, the lessee would capitalize $23,390 as the beginning lease liability. The lessee would use the effective interest method to amortize the lease liability and would amortize the right-of-use asset on the basis of $23,390.

Sales-Type Leases–Lessor

This lesson addresses the specifics for sales-type leases.

After studying this lesson, you should be able to:

1. Identify and define a sales-type lease from given information.

2. Prepare the journal entries for the sales-type lease for the lessor and the finance lease for the lessee.

I. Background

In this lesson, we focus on a sales-type lease for the lessor and also cover the lease as a finance lease with no residual value for the lessee.

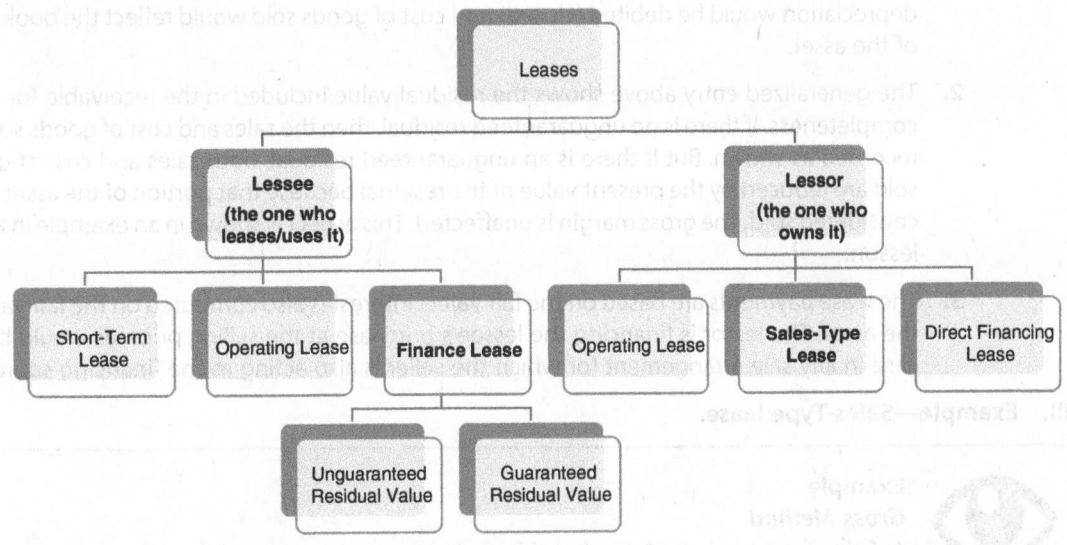

II. Sales-Type Lease (STL) Basics

A. A STL is one of three types of leases for the lessor (the others being operating and direct financing leases). This distinction does not affect the lessee. The lessor derives two types of income from a sales-type lease: interest revenue recognized over the lease term, and gross profit recognized at the inception of the lease agreement.

B. In a STL, the book value or the cost of the lessor's asset is not equal to (usually less than) its fair value. There is gross profit (or loss) on the lease that is recorded at inception. The lessor need not be a manufacturer or dealer for a lease to be a STL for the lessor.

C. The general inception entries for a STL for the lessor appear below. The numerical examples add additional aspects to the entries.

D. Lessor—At inception (although two entries are shown, they can be combined into one):

At inception (lessor assumes a new asset, i.e. Lease Receivable)	
Lease Receivable	sum of minimum lease payments + residual value (if any)
Unearned Interest Receivable	total interest over term
Sales	fair value = selling price
Cost of Goods Sold	cost of asset
Asset	cost of asset

1. The above entry recognizes gross profit immediately. In comparison, a DFL does not. A sale is recorded, as is the cost of goods sold. The gross profit equals sales (recorded at selling price) less cost of goods sold. The net lease receivable (lease receivable less the contra-receivable account called unearned interest revenue) equals the fair value of the asset, which also equals sales. The above entry assumes a new asset. If the asset were used, accumulated depreciation would be debited (closed) and cost of goods sold would reflect the book value of the asset.

2. The generalized entry above shows the residual value included in the receivable for completeness. If there is no unguaranteed residual, then the sales and cost of goods sold are recorded as shown. But if there is an unguaranteed residual, both sales and cost of goods sold are reduced by the present value of the residual because that portion of the asset is not considered sold. The gross margin is unaffected. This aspect is shown in an example in a later lesson.

3. The lease payments are based on the fair value. Interest is also computed on the fair value of the asset. The lessor is financing the lessee's purchase at the selling price, as would be the case in any sale arrangement for which the seller is also acting as the financing source.

III. Example—Sales-Type lease.

Example
Gross Method
A. Sales-Type Lease (note cost and fair value are not equal and the payments occur on the first of the year—annuity due). On January 1, Year 1, Lessor leases equipment to Lessee. Data on the lease:

1. Equipment fair value, $25,771 (asset is new)

2. Lessor's book value (same as cost because asset is new), $20,000

3. Lessor's implicit rate and Lessee's incremental borrowing rate, 8%

4. Lease payments due each January 1 through Year 3 (three-year lease term)

5. Useful life of equipment, three years (**no residual value**)

Lessor's calculation of the annual lease payment (L) is computed as:

$25,771 = Lease payment × (PV ann. due, I = 8%, N = 3)

$25,771 = Lease payment × (2.78326)

Lease payment = $9,259

This is a sales-type lease for the lessor and a finance lease for the lessee because criterion 3 is met (lease term of 3 years = 100% of useful life at inception). Criterion 4 is also met (present value of minimum lease payments of $25,771 = 100% of fair value at inception).

Lessor's journal entries at the inception of the lease.

1/1/yr1	Lease Receivable	(3 payments × $9,259)	27,777	
	Unearned Interest	($27,777–25,771)		2,006
	Sales Revenue			25,771
	Cost of Goods Sold		20,000	
	Equipment			20,000
	Cash		9,259	
	Lease Receivable			9,259

Analysis: Gross profit of $5,771 ($25,771 Sales – $20,000 COGS) is recognized at inception. There is no interest component to the first payment because it takes place at inception before any time has passed. The **net lease receivable** (lease receivable – unearned interest) **before** the first payment is $25,771 ($27,777 – $2,006). The net lease receivable right **after** the first payment is $16,512 ($27,777 – $2,006 – $9,259).

Lessor—Interest Recognition, Year 1

12/31/yr1	Unearned Interest	($16,512 × .08)	1,321	
	Interest Revenue			1,321

A year has passed (note the 12/31/yr1 date) and although no payment is due until the next day, the interest revenue for Year 1 must be accrued as recorded as above. Under accrual accounting, the interest is recognized because it has been earned. It will be received the next day when the lessee makes the second payment to the lessor.

The net lease receivable, after accruing the earned interest revenue on 12/31/yr1, is $17,833 ($27,777 – 2,006 – 9,259 + 1,321). Exam questions are likely to ask about the net lease receivable at the end of the year or immediately following the receipt of a lease payment. The reduction (debit) in unearned interest in the above entry causes the net lease receivable to increase by the amount of recognized interest that has not yet been received.

If the lessor used the net method, the lease receivable would be debited for the unpaid interest (we would not use the contra-receivable account called unearned interest if we used the net method).

When the lessor receives the second lease payment the next day, the lessor records the following journal entry:

1/1/yr2	Cash	9,259	
	Lease Receivable		9,259

The net lease receivable is now $8,574 ($17,833 – 9,259). This is the amount on which interest is computed at the end of year 2. See below.

Lessor—Interest Recognition, Year 2

12/31/yr2	Unearned Interest	($8,574 × .08)	686	
	Interest Revenue			686

The **lessor** records the following journal entry for the last payment on the three-year sales-type lease.

1/1/yr3	Cash	9,259	
	Lease Receivable		9,259

After the last payment, the net lease receivable equals 0 (see the lease amortization schedule below for lessor accounting). Using the preceding journal entries, write out t-accounts for both the Lease Receivable (asset account) and the Unearned Interest (contra-asset or contra-receivable account) to track the net lease receivable (Lease Receivable − Unearned Interest) throughout its life.

Lessor Amortization Schedule
Sales-Type Lease
Annuity Due Basis

Date	Annual Lease Payment	Interest (8%) on Receivable	Recovery of Lease Receivable	Net Lease Receivable
1/1/yr1				$25,771
1/1/yr1	$9,259	$0	$9,259	$16,512
1/1/yr2	$9,259	$1,321	$7,938	$8,574
1/1/yr3	$9,259	$686	$8,574	$0

Lessee Accounting—The lessee accounts for the above lease as a finance lease because criterion 3 and 4 were met. Note that this example is an annuity due (first payment due at inception).

Lessee's journal entries at the inception of the finance lease and the first payment.

1/1/yr1	Right-of-Use Asset	(PV factor of 2.78326 × $9,259)	25,771	
	Lease Liability			25,771

1/1/yr1	Lease Liability		9,259	
	Cash			9,259

The lessee's lease liability immediately following the first payment is $16,512 ($25,771 − $9,259).

Note that the lessee uses the net method to record the lease, i.e. the lease liability is recorded at its present value.

Lessee—Journal entries for payments, interest and amortization recognition over the lease term.

1/1/yr1	Right-of-Use Asset	(PV factor of 2.78326 × $9,259)	25,771	
	Lease Liability			25,771

1/1/yr1	Lease Liability		9,259	
	Cash			9,259

12/31/yr1	Interest Expense	($16,512 × .08)	1,321	
	Lease Liability			1,321

This entry records accrued but unpaid interest and is easy to forget when taking the CPA Exam because no payment is due on this date. Note that the lease liability is increased rather than interest payable, because interest is not separately paid; it is a component of the lease payment.

12/31/yr1	Amortization Expense	($25,771/3)	8,590	
	Right-of-Use Asset			8,590
1/1/yr2	Lease Liability		9,259	
	Cash			9,259
12/31/yr2	Interest Expense	($8,574 × .08)	686	
	Lease Liability			686
12/31/yr2	Amortization Expense	($25,771/3)	8,590	
	Right-of-Use Asset			8,590
1/1/yr3	Lease Liability		9,259	
	Cash			9,259
12/31/yr3	Amortization Expense	($25,771/3)	8,590	
	Right-of-Use Asset			8,590

Lessee Amortization Schedule
Finance Lease
Annuity Due Basis

Date	Annual Lease Payment	Interest (8%) on Liability	Reduction of Lease Liability	Lease Liability
1/1/yr1				$25,771
1/1/yr1	$9,259	$0	$9,259	$16,512
1/1/yr2	$9,259	$1,321	$7,938	$8,574
1/1/yr3	$9,259	$686	$8,574	$0

Direct Financing Leases—Lessor

This lease accounting lesson covers the specifics for recording a direct financing lease for the lessor.

After studying this lesson, you should be able to:

1. Identify a direct financing lease from given information.

2. Record the inception journal entry for the lessor.

3. Prepare the journal entries for lease revenue and deferred gross profit.

4. Use the effective interest method to amortize the lease receivable for the lessor.

I. **Background**—Notice that a lessee may have a finance lease and a lessor may have a direct financing lease. These are different classifications based on the role of the company as the lessee or the lessor so the accounting treatment is very different between the two. In this lesson, **keep in mind that you are the lessor (the one who owns it) and you are accounting for a direct financing lease**.

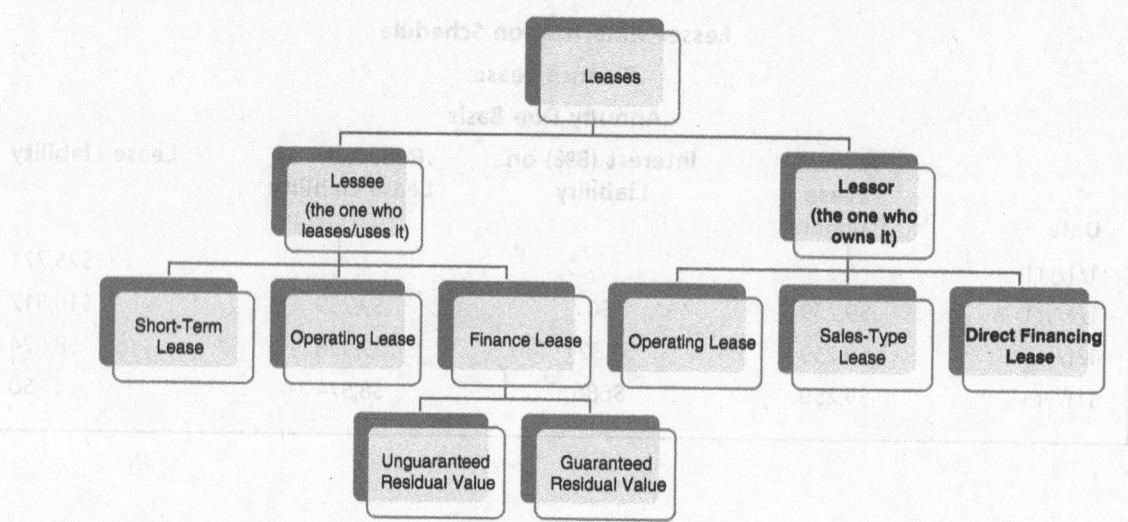

II. **Direct Financing Lease (DFL) Basics—Lessor**

A. A lessor accounts for a lease as a direct financing lease when the lease does *not* meet any of the five lease criteria for a sales-type lease *and* essentially there is a guarantee of residual value by a third party. This is not a very common situation so direct financing leases do not occur often. Recall the sales-type lease criteria:

1. Transfer of ownership

2. Bargain purchase option

3. Lease term is greater than the major part of the asset's economic life (75% test).

4. Present value of the lease payments equals or exceeds the substantially all of the asset's fair value (90% test).

5. Alternative use test: The asset is specialized in nature and does not have an alternative use to the lessor.

B. Usually if the lease does not qualify as a sales-type lease for the lessor (lease does not meet any one of the five criteria just listed), then the lease is an operating lease. The exception to this is when a third party guarantees the residual value and the present value of the lease payments plus the present value of the third-party guarantee of the residual value together exceed the present value test (criterion 4—90% test). If this occurs, then essentially the risks and rewards of ownership have passed to the lessee and the third party (primarily the lessee).

690

C. The general entries for a direct financing lease for a lessor appear below. The numerical examples illustrate the procedures. The entries are affected by whether the lease payment stream is an annuity due or an ordinary annuity.

D. Lessor—Journal entry at the inception of the direct financing lease.

1/1/yr1	Lease receivable	Fair value of the leased asset
	Deferred gross profit	Difference between fair value and cost of asset
	Inventory	Cost of the asset

E. The lessor records a lease receivable for the fair value of the asset, which is also usually the present value of the lease payments and residual value.

F. **Recognition of Periodic Lease Revenue**—The general journal entry for lease revenue for an ordinary annuity follows.

Ordinary Annuity

12/31/yr1	Cash	Lease payment from lessee
	Deferred gross profit	Difference between interest on receivable and lease revenue
	Lease revenue	Lease revenue based on direct financing rate
	Lease receivable	Difference between annual lease payment and interest on receivable

G. Depending on the value of the asset at the end of the lease, the lessor may record the return of the asset as follows.

12/31/yrX	Inventory	Residual value of the asset
	Lease receivable	Remaining lease receivable

H. **Residual Value**—As discussed in the "Finance Lease Basics" lesson, residual value is a best estimate of what the asset will be worth at the end of the lease

1. Assets may have no residual value expected at the end of the lease.

2. Assets may have a residual value amount expected at the end of the lease and a guaranteed residual value amount. A lease contract may include a guaranteed residual value by the lessee or by a third party. A direct financing lease is most likely to occur when a third party guarantees the residual value of the leased asset. If the leased asset is worth less than the guaranteed residual value, then the third-party guarantor will need to make up the difference in the form of consideration (typically a cash payment for the difference between the guaranteed residual value and the actual residual value of the lease asset).

III. Direct Financing Lease Example—Lessor

The next example covers accounting for a **direct financing lease by the lessor**. To account for a direct financing lease, we need to calculate the interest on the receivable as if it were a sales-type lease and then calculate the interest on the receivable as a direct financing lease. The difference between the two interest calculations tells us what the deferred gross profit is for the direct financing lease.

A. On January 1, Year 1, lessor leases equipment to lessee. Data on the lease:

1. Equipment fair value is $40,000, and lessor's carrying value is $37,500 (asset is new).

2. Lessor's implicit rate is 5%.

3. Lease payments due each December 31 through Year 3 (three-year lease term).

4. Useful life of equipment is five years.

5. The equipment has a residual value of $7,000 that is guaranteed by a third party.

Payments are due at the end of the year (ordinary annuity). There will be minor differences in amounts based on rounding; these amounts are noted throughout the example. See below for lessor's calculation of the lease/rental payments to charge lessee.

B. Lessor's Calculation of Lease Payments

Fair value of equipment	$40,000
Less: Present value of residual value ($7,000 × .86384)*	6,047
Amount to be recovered through lease payments	33,953
Divide by present value factor of **ordinary annuity** for 3 years at 5%	2.72325
Annual lease payment to charge lessee	**$12,468**

*Present value factor of single sum (N = 3, 5%) = .86384

C. This is a direct financing lease for the lessor because:

1. There is no transfer of title.

2. There is no bargain purchase option.

3. The lease term is less than 75% of the useful life of the asset (3 years / 5 years = 60%).

4. The present value of the lease payments directly from the lessee is 85% of the fair value of the asset ($33,963 / $40,000).

5. There is no mention that the asset is specialized in nature and that there is no alternative use.

6. However, the present value of the lease payments from the lessee ($33,953) and the present value of the guaranteed residual value that is guaranteed by a third party ($6,047) total substantially all (in this case, 100%) of the fair value of the asset (greater than 90%). The lessor will account for this lease as a direct financing lease.

7. Note that, for the lessee, this is classified as an operating lease because none of the five lease criteria are met. (The residual value is guaranteed by a third party, not the lessee.)

D. The lessor records the **journal entry at the inception** of the lease that effectively recognizes a net lease receivable and removes the asset from the lessor's books. Net lease receivable = Lease receivable – Deferred gross profit. The deferred gross profit in this example is $2,500 (the difference between the fair value of the asset and its carrying value on the lessor's books).

1/1/yr1	Lease receivable	40,000	
	Deferred gross profit		2,500
	Equipment or inventory		37,500

E. The net lease receivable is amortized at a rate that will take it down to zero at the end of the lease term. This rate will be different from (higher than) the implicit interest rate. The rate based on the net lease receivable, and the lease payment that results in a zero ending balance for the net lease receivable is 8.25%. (Note that a rounding error of $7 will exist in the example.)

1. The 8.25% is found by completing an amortization of the net lease receivable that results in an ending balance of zero. The rate will be higher than the implicit rate, so begin by trying a rate a percentage point or two higher and adjusting the rate to fine-tune the outcome.

F. Because the payment calculation done by the lessor is completed using the implicit rate and the gross lease receivable, the difference in interest between the 5% of gross lease receivable calculation and 8.25% of net lease receivable calculation results in the amount of deferred gross profit to be recognized.

G. The lessor must complete two amortization schedules (calculations) to figure out the amounts associated with the annual journal entries for the direct financing lease.

1. The first schedule is the interest calculation based on the implicit interest rate (given in the problem) and the gross lease receivable (this is identical to the amortization calculation completed for a sales-type lease). See below.

Amortization and Interest Calculation for Implicit Rate on Gross Lease Receivable (Sales-Type Lease)

Date	Annual lease payment	Interest (5%)	Reduction in lease receivable	Lease receivable
				40,000
12/31/yr1	12,468	2,000	10,468	29,532
12/31/yr2	12,468	1,477	10,991	18,541
12/31/yr3	12,468	927	11,541	7,000
12/31/yr3	7,000		7,000	0
	44,404	4,404	40,000	

2. The second schedule is the interest calculation based on the effective interest rate (found by tweaking the interest rate until the amortization of the net lease receivable based on the lease payment equals zero) and the net lease receivable.

Amortization and Interest Calculation for Calculated Effective Rate on Net Lease Receivable (Direct Financing Lease)

Date	Annual lease payment	Interest (8.25%)	Reduction in lease receivable	Net lease receivable
				37,500
12/31/yr1	12,468	3,094	9,374	28,126
12/31/yr2	12,468	2,320	10,148	17,978
12/31/yr3	12,468	1,483	10,985	6,993
12/31/yr3	7,000		7,000	-7
	44,404	6,897	37,507	

*$7 rounding error. Effectively, the balance is zero.

H. The difference in the interest between the two calculations ($6,897 – 4,404) is approximately $2,500. (Note that there is a $6 impact from the rounding error of about $7; this small rounding amount is not a concern.) $2,500 is the amount of deferred gross profit that will be amortized by recognizing the difference between the interest per the implicit rate on the gross lease receivable and the interest per the effective rate on the net lease receivable.

I. The **lessor's journal entries** for the direct financing lease are shown next.

12/31/yr1	Cash			12,468
	Deferred gross profit	($3,094 – 2,000)		1,094
	Lease revenue	(Interest at 8.25%)		3,094
	Lease receivable	(Reduction based on 5%)		10,468

12/31/yr2	Cash		12,468	
	Deferred gross profit ($2,320 – 1,477)		844	
	Lease revenue	(Interest at 8.25%)		2,320
	Lease receivable	(Reduction based on 5%, $1 rounding)		10,992

12/31/yr3	Cash		12,468	
	Deferred gross profit ($1,483 – 927)		556	
	Lease revenue	(Interest at 8.25%)		1,483
	Lease receivable	(Reduction based on 5%)		11,541

Reconciliation between Interest Revenue and Lease Revenue for Deferred Gross Profit in Direct Financing Lease for Lessor

Date	Interest on lease receivable (5%)	Lease revenue (8.25%)	Difference (reduction in deferred gross profit)	Deferred gross profit balance
1/1/yr1				$2,500
12/31/yr1	$2,000	$3,094	$1,094	$1,406
12/31/yr2	$1,477	$2,320	$844	$562
12/31/yr3	$927	$1,483	$556	$6 (rounding error)

J. At the end of the lease, the lessor has a lease receivable balance of $7,000 ($40,000 – 10,468 – 10,992 – 11,541) with a $1 rounding error. The $7,000 is the expected residual value of the asset and is guaranteed by the third party. If the asset has a residual value of $7,000 at the end of the lease, then the lessor records the following journal entry.

12/31/yr3	Equipment/Inventory	7,000	
	Lease receivable		7,000

K. If the residual value at the end of the lease is less than $7,000, then the lessor will likely record a journal entry that includes additional consideration from the third-party guarantor. Assume the asset has a residual value of $4,000 at the end of the lease. The lessor will record the following journal entry.

12/31/yr3	Equipment/Inventory	4,000	
	Cash	3,000	
	Lease receivable		7,000

Study Tip

Create t-accounts for both the lease receivable (natural debit balance) and the deferred gross profit (natural credit balance) and trace the journal entries through the life of the lease by updating the t-accounts.

Sale-Leasebacks and Disclosures

This lesson addresses the specifics for sale-leasebacks and the general disclosures required regarding lease accounting.

After studying this lesson, you should be able to:

1. Explain why a firm would enter into a sale-leaseback transaction.

2. Identify when the transaction is a sale or a failed sale.

3. Compute the related gain or loss.

4. Note the general footnote disclosures for leases for both parties.

I. **Nature of the Transaction and Accounting Issues**

   A. A sale-leaseback transaction is actually two related transactions. The owner of the property sells its asset and immediately leases it back. The asset is not physically moved. The transaction is entirely financial.

   B. To qualify as a sale-leaseback, the transaction does need to meet the sales (revenue recognition) criteria. In other words, the control of the asset should transfer to the buyer-lessor from the seller-lessee.

      1. If the transaction meets the criteria for a sale, then the transaction is a sale-leaseback. (An example is shown below.)

      2. If the transaction does not meet the criteria for a sale, then the transaction is a failed sale. (An example is shown below.)

   C. The seller-lessee is the one who owns the asset to begin with and sells it to the buyer-lessor. The seller-lessee intends to immediately lease back the asset it just sold.

      1. Why would the seller-lessee do this?

         a. The seller-lessee may have a lot of money tied up in the asset. Selling the asset and receiving cash up front could be a better financial decision than owning the asset outright for the seller-lessee. The seller-lessee still wants to use the asset but does not want to own it anymore.

   D. The buyer-lessor is the one who buys the asset from the seller-lessee but does not want to use the asset for anything right now. The buyer-lessor is willing to immediately lease the asset back to the seller-lessee.

      1. Why would the buyer-lessor do this?

         a. The buyer-lessor may have money or cash available to invest in something. The buyer-lessor can purchase the asset and then immediately lease it back to the seller-lessee in order to make money through lease revenue.

   E. **Most likely scenario** following a sale-leaseback:

      1. Buyer-lessor purchases the asset, records the purchase, and then leases it back as a lease that qualifies as an operating lease. (In other words, the lease criteria for a sales-type lease are not met.)

      2. Seller-lessee sells the asset and control transfers to the buyer-lessor. Seller-lessee records the sale of the assets (i.e. recognizes a gain or loss), then leases it back under a short-term or operating lease. (Again, none of the lease criteria for a finance lease is met.)

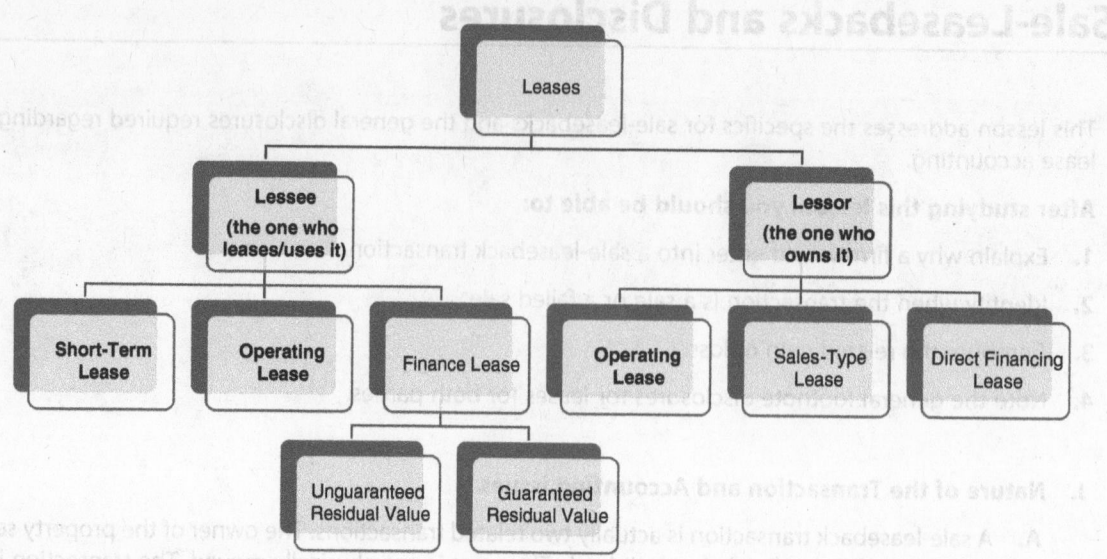

II. Sale-Leaseback Example

Example

On 1/1/X1, QWEL Inc. sells an asset (assume a piece of equipment) for its fair value of $25,771 (cost $40,000; accumulated depreciation $20,000) and leases it back under a three-year lease.

- The lease does not transfer title and does not contain a bargain purchase option, and the asset does have alternative uses.

- The asset has a remaining economic life of 5 years and an estimated unguaranteed residual value of $12,500 at the end of the lease term.

- The annual lease payments provide the lessor an 8% return, and payments are due each December 31 beginning 20X1.

- The buyer-lessor uses straight-line depreciation, and the asset has no salvage value.

- Both the buyer-lessor and the seller-lessee classify the lease as an operating lease because none of the finance lease criteria is met and the lease term exceeds one year.

- No transfer of title back to the seller-lessee.

- No bargain purchase option.

- The lease term is less than the major remaining part of the asset's economic life (3 years / 5 years = 60%; 60% < 75%).

- The present value of the lease payments is less than 90% of the fair value of the asset. $6,150 × PV factor of n = 3, i = 8% (2.5771) = $15,848.

- ($15,848 / $25,771 = 61.5%; 61.5% is less than 90%). See further calculations below.

- The asset has alternative uses to the buyer-lessor.

Buyer-Lessor's Calculation of Lease Payments

Fair value of the equipment		$25,771
Less: Present value of the residual value ($12,500 × .79383)	(PV N = 3, I = 8%) .79383	9,923
Amount to be recovered through lease payments		15,848
Divide by the present value factor of an **ordinary annuity** for 3 years at 8%		2.57710
Annual lease payment to charge the seller-lessee		**$ 6,150**

Control does pass to the buyer-lessor so the transaction is recorded as a sale-leaseback. There are two parts to the transaction to account for and record:

1. Record the sale.

2. Account for the operating lease.

Buyer-Lessor journal entry **to record the purchase** of the asset (equipment) on 1/1/X1.

Equipment	25,771	
Cash		25,771

Seller-Lessee journal entry **to record the sale** of the asset (equipment) on 1/1/X1.

Cash	25,771	
Accumulated Depreciation	20,000	
Equipment		40,000
Gain on Sale of Equipment		5,771

After recording the sale, the **buyer-lessor** will account for the lease as an **operating lease** and will record the following **journal entries** over the three-year lease term. Notice the equipment remains on the buyer-lessor's books so the buyer-lessor records annual depreciation expense.

Buyer-Lessor Journal Entries over the Lease Term—Operating Lease Following the Sale

12/31/X1	Cash	6,150	
	Lease Revenue		6,150
12/31/X1	Depreciation Expense	5,154	
	Accumulated Depreciation		5,154
	($25,771/5 years = $5,154 annual depreciation)		
12/31/X2	Cash	6,150	
	Lease Revenue		6,150
12/31/X2	Depreciation Expense	5,154	
	Accumulated Depreciation		5,154
12/31/X3	Cash	6,150	
	Lease Revenue		6,150
12/31/X3	Depreciation Expense	5,154	
	Accumulated Depreciation		5,154

Seller-Lessee Calculations and Journal Entries over the Lease Term—Operating Lease Following the Sale

Lessee's Calculation of the Present Value of the Minimum Lease Payments

Annual lease payment due at the end of the year (ordinary annuity)	$6,150
Multiply by the present value factor of an ordinary annuity for 3 years at 8%	2.5771
Amount to capitalize as the lease liability	**$15,849***

*$1 rounding error between lessor and lessee, so record as $15,848

Seller-Lessee's Journal Entry at the Inception of the Operating Lease

1/1/X1	Right-of-Use Asset	15,848	
	Lease Liability		15,848

Seller-Lessee's Lease Amortization Schedule to Calculate Interest

Date	Lease Payment	Interest (8%)	Reduction in Lease Liability	Lease Liability
1/1/X1				15,848
12/31/X1	6,150	1,268	4,882	10,966
12/31/X2	6,150	877	5,273	5,693
12/31/X3	6,150	455	5,693	0
12/31/X3	End of lease—note $2 rounding in reduction in lease liability			

Seller-Lessee's Lease Expense Schedule

Date	Lease Expense	Interest (8%)	Amortization of Right-of-Use Asset	Carrying Value of Right-of-Use Asset
1/1/X1				15,848
12/31/X1	6,150	1,268	4,882	10,966
12/31/X2	6,150	877	5,273	5,693
12/31/X3	6,150	455	5,693	0
12/31/X3	End of lease—note $2 rounding in reduction in lease liability			

Notice that the lease amortization schedule for an ordinary annuity operating lease closely follows the seller-lessee's lease expense schedule. This is driven by the timing of the payments and the accrual of interest both occurring at year-end.

Seller-Lessee's Journal Entries over the Lease Term—Operating Lease

Note that the lease payments are due at the end of the year (12/31) for this lease. The example shown in the "Background, Short-Term Leases, and Operating Leases" lesson illustrated the accounting for a lease with lease payments due at the beginning of the year. The journal entries for an operating lease with a payment date at the end of the year are a bit more straightforward.

12/31/X1	Lease Expense	6,150		
	Lease Liability	4,882		
	Right-of-Use Asset*		4,882	
	Cash		6,150	
12/31/X2	Lease Expense	6,150		
	Lease Liability	5,273		
	Right-of-Use Asset		5,273	
	Cash		6,150	
12/31/X3	Lease Expense	6,150		
	Lease Liability	5,693		
	Right-of-Use Asset		5,693	
	Cash		6,150	

*Amortization of the right-of-use asset

III. Failed Sale

A. If the sale-leaseback transaction does not meet the revenue recognition criteria, specifically that control of the asset does not pass from the seller-lessee to the buyer-lessor, then the revenue recognition criteria are not met and the transaction is considered a failed sale.

B. A failed sale is most likely to occur when the terms of the lease that follows qualify the lease as a finance lease. In other words, if the lease criteria for a finance lease are met, then the transaction will be accounted for as a failed sale and will reflect a financing transaction.

C. The failed sale/financing transaction would be recorded as follows:

Cash	XX	
Note Payable		XX

D. Note that the asset does not come off of the seller-lessee's books. The seller-lessee does not record a sale and does continue to depreciate the asset.

IV. Lease Disclosures

A. Lessees are required to disclose:

1. Assets obtained through finance and operating leases.

2. General description of the leases, including important terms and features such as residual values and discount (interest) rates.

3. Breakout of the cost associated with finance leases between the amortization of the right-of-use asset and the interest on the lease liabilities.

4. The cost of operating and short-term leases.

5. Future minimum lease payments in the aggregate and for each of the five succeeding years for both finance and operating leases.

B. Lessors are required to disclose:

1. General description of the leases, including terms such as purchase or renewal options.

2. Allocation of lease payments between lease and nonlease components.

3. A breakout of lease income—from sales-type leases, direct financing leases and interest income.

4. A breakout of the net lease receivable—amount of gross lease receivable, deferred gross profit, and any residual value assumptions.

> **Study Tip**
> When answering an exam question about disclosures, recall the full disclosure principle. To paraphrase, information that would impact the judgment of a reasonable user or would be important to a decision maker should be disclosed.

Additional Aspects of Leases

This lease accounting lesson covers additional terms or payments that impact leases.

After studying this lesson, you should be able to:

1. Calculate amortization recorded by a lessee.

2. Calculate the lease liability for a lease with a bargain purchase option.

3. Calculate the amount to capitalize as a right-of-use asset when initial direct costs are present.

4. Remember and understand the accounting treatment for executory costs and variable lease payments.

5. Prepare the journal entries at lease inception for a lessor's sales-type lease with guaranteed residual value and unguaranteed residual value.

I. Lessee—Finance Leases—Amortization of Right-of-Use Asset

When a lessee accounts for a leased asset under a finance lease, the lessee records amortization of the right-of-use asset over the shorter of the lease term or the useful life of the asset.

A. On the exam, you can expect to see questions in which the lease term is used to amortize the right-of-use asset on a straight-line basis and the lessee records amortization expense at the end of the year.

B. For example, a lessee records a leased right-of-use asset of $30,000 at the inception of a five-year finance lease. The asset has a remaining useful life of six years. The lessee will record amortization expense at the end of the year of $6,000 ($30,000 / 5 years). This scenario is the most likely case.

C. Using the example above, if we change the lease term to five years and the remaining useful life of the asset to four years, then the lessee will amortize the right-of-use asset over the shorter of the two periods (four years). Amortization expense of $7,500 ($30,000 / 4 years) will be recorded. This scenario is not likely.

II. Lessor—Depreciation Expense

A. If a lessor records an operating lease in which the leased asset remains on its books, then it will continue to depreciate the asset using an acceptable depreciation method (such as straight-line or double-declining balance, etc.).

III. Lessee—Bargain Purchase Option

A. A lease containing a bargain purchase option (BPO) that the lessee is reasonably certain to exercise should include the present value of the BPO in the calculation of the present value of the minimum lease payments.

1. The BPO is accounted for just as the difference in the guaranteed residual value and expected residual value amount is.

2. Recall the example in the "Financing Lease—Lessee" lesson, which we adapt here.

3. On January 1, Year 1, lessor leases equipment to lessee. Data on the lease:

   a. Equipment fair value and lessor's book value, $25,771 (asset is new)

   b. Lessor's implicit rate and lessee's implicit borrowing rate, 8%

   c. Lease payments due each December 31 through Year 3 (three-year lease term)

   d. Useful life of equipment, three years

e. The expected value of the asset at the end of the lease is $3,000. The lease contains a BPO of $1,000 at the end of the lease term. It is reasonably assured that the lessee will exercise the option.

f. The lessor charges the lessee an annual lease payment of $9,076.

Lessee's Calculation of the Present Value of the Minimum Lease Payments with a Bargain Purchase Option	
Annual lease payment due at the beginning of the year (annuity due)	$9,076
Multiply by the present value (PV) factor of an ordinary annuity for 3 years at 8%	× 2.5771
PV of the annual lease payments	**$23,390**
BPO	$1,000
Multiply by the PV factor of a single sum for 3 years at 8%	× .79383
PV of the BPO	**$794**
Amount to capitalize as the lease liability (sum of the PVs)	**$24,184**

IV. Initial Direct Costs—Lessee

A. Whether a cost is an initial direct cost depends on timing and execution of the lease and what the cost is.

B. Example of Timing of the Cost

1. A legal fee that is incurred before the execution of the lease may not be considered an initial direct cost; this cost is expensed in the period incurred.

2. A legal fee that is incurred because the lease was executed is considered an initial direct cost; this cost is included in the initial measurement of the right-of-use asset.

C. Other initial direct costs include: document fees associated with preparing the lease documents, commissions paid to agents to secure the lease, and fees paid for third-party guaranteed residual values.

D. An initial direct cost is included in the right-of-use asset and is amortized as part of the right-of-use asset over the life of the lease. Adapting the example from above, assume legal fee of $1,500 was incurred because of the execution of the lease. We see that the initial direct cost is included in the right-of-use asset measurement..

Lessee's Calculation of the Initial Measurement of the Right-of-Use Asset with a Bargain Purchase Option and Initial Direct Costs	
Annual lease payment due at the beginning of the year (annuity due)	$9,076
Multiply by the PV factor of an ordinary annuity for 3 years at 8%	× 2.5771
PV of the annual lease payments	**$23,390**
BPO	$1,000
Multiply by the PV factor of a single sum for 3 years at 8%	× .79383
PV of the BPO	**$794**
Initial direct cost—legal fee from execution of the lease	**$1,500**
Amount to capitalize as right-of-use asset	**$25,684**

V. Lessee—Executory Costs

A. Executory costs tend to be property taxes, insurance, and maintenance costs.

B. When the lessee makes payments directly to the third party, then the lessee should expense the payments as incurred (most likely scenario to see on the exam).

C. When the payments are required fixed amounts and are made to the lessor (similar to how lease payments are made), then the costs should be included in the measurement of the lease liability.

VI. Lessee—Variable Lease Payments

A. Variable lease payments are payments that may change over the course of the lease. The change in the payment may be linked to an external market rate, such as a consumer price index, a performance measure, such as a percentage of sales, or a usage measure, such as mileage.

B. On the exam, you will be expected to remember and understand the accounting treatment for variable lease payments. The question will likely focus on how to account for a variable lease payment arrangement or what to include in the lease liability.

C. If the lease specifies the amount that the payment will increase each year (effectively, the variable lease payments are known throughout the lease and are, in substance, fixed payments), then include the present value of the payment increases in the lease liability.

   1. For example, the lease payment will increase by $3,000 each year over the life of the lease. The lessee will include the PV of each payment increase in the lease liability.

D. If the variable lease payment amount is unknown, either because of unknown index changes or unknown performance or usage factors, then the variable lease payment is not included in the lease liability and is expensed in the period incurred.

VII. Lessor—Sales-Type Lease—Guaranteed versus Unguaranteed Residual Value

(Notice in the graphic the additional lease variations for a lessor's sales-type lease).

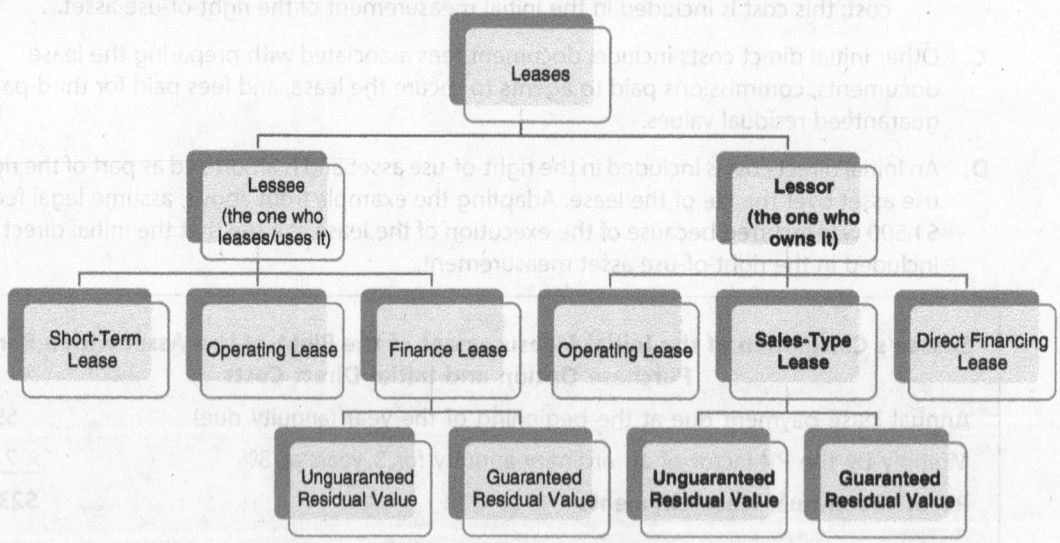

A. A sales-type lease may include guaranteed or unguaranteed residual value.

   1. The calculation of the lease payment to be charged by the lessor is not impacted by whether the residual value is guaranteed or unguaranteed. The lessor will deduct the PV of the guaranteed or unguaranteed residual value from the fair value to calculate the amount to be recovered through lease payments.

   2. **Key conceptual point:** The gross profit will be the same for the lessor regardless of whether the residual value is guaranteed or not.

   3. Consider the journal entry to record the inception of the lease.

a. The **sales revenue and cost of goods sold will be impacted** by whether the residual value is guaranteed or unguaranteed. Because sales revenue and cost of goods sold are both impacted equally, the gross profit remains the same whether the residual value is guaranteed or unguaranteed. Present value of unguaranteed residual value (UGRV) will be subtracted from sales revenue and cost of goods sold; guaranteed residual value (GRV) will not be subtracted.

b. The **lease receivable and the cost of the asset will not be impacted**.

VIII. Example—Sales-Type Lease

Example
Guaranteed versus Unguaranteed Residual Value
Sales-Type Lease

(Note that cost and fair value are not equal and the payments occur on the first of the year—annuity due.) On January 1, Year 1, lessor leases equipment to lessee. Data on the lease:

1. Equipment fair value: $32,000 (asset is new)

2. The cost of the equipment: $29,000.

3. Lessor's book value (same as cost because asset is new): $29,000

4. Lessor's implicit rate and Lessee's implicit borrowing rate: 8%

5. Lease payments due each January 1 through Year 3 (three-year lease term)

6. Useful life of equipment: 3 years

7. Residual value: $4,000

Lessor's Calculation of Lease Payments

(Whether GRV or UGRV, use the same calculation.)

Fair value of equipment		$32,000
Less: PV of residual value (PV factor n = 3, i = 8%)	($4,000 × .79383)	3,175
Amount to be recovered through lease payments		28,825
Divide by the PV factor of an **annuity due** for 3 years at 8%		2.78326
Annual lease payment to charge the lessee		**$ 10,357**

The journal entry to record the inception of the sales-type lease is impacted by whether the residual value is guaranteed or is not guaranteed.

Lessor's Sales-Type Lease Journal Entry at Inception for Lease with GRV

1/1/yr1	Lease Receivable	(3 payments × $10,357, plus residual value $4,000)	35,071	
	Cost of Goods Sold		29,000	
	Unearned Interest	($35,071 gross payments – 32,000 PV of payments and residual value)		3,071
	Sales Revenue			32,000
	Equipment/Inventory			29,000

The lessor's journal entry at the inception of a lease with UGRV is different from a lease with GRV. If the lease has UGRV, then both sales revenue and cost of goods sold are adjusted for the present value of the residual value. In other words, subtract the present value of the residual value from both the sales revenue and costs of goods sold.

Lessor's Sales-Type Lease Journal Entry at Inception of Lease with UGRV

1/1/yr1	Lease Receivable	(3 payments × $10,357, plus residual value $4,000)	35,071	
	Cost of Goods Sold (COGS)	(COGS – PV of UGRV; $29,000 – 3,175)	25,825	
	Unearned Interest	($35,071 gross payments – 32,000 present value of payments and residual value)		3,071
	Sales Revenue	(Sales – PV of UGRV; $32,000 – 3,175)		28,825
	Equipment/Inventory			29,000

The lessor will account for the lease as a sales-type lease by recognizing interest revenue over time and amortizing the unearned interest and lease receivable.

1. Because the net lease receivable (Lease receivable – Unearned interest) is the same regardless of GRV or URGV, the interest revenue will be the same regardless of GRV or URGV.

2. Gross profit remains the same regardless of whether the residual value is guaranteed or not.

   a. Gross profit with GRV = $32,000 – $29,000 = $3,000

   b. Gross profit with UGRV = $28,825 – $25,825 = $3,000

Given the fact pattern above, the lessee will account for this lease as a finance lease. Criterion 3 is met because the lease term is 3 years and the useful life of the asset is 3 years. The lessee's lease liability will depend on the GRV or UGRV and the expected value of the asset at the end of the lease.

Not-for-Profit Organizations

Introduction to Types of Not-for-Profit Entities and Standard Setting

This lesson presents a brief overview of the types of not-for-profit entities and the organizations that set accounting standards for these entities.

After studying this lesson, you should be able to:

1. Recall the purpose and characteristics in the conceptual framework for nonbusiness entities.

2. List the four main categories of not-for-profit organizations.

I. **Background**—Not-for-profit (NFP) organizations comprise a wide variety of institutions, including some governmentally affiliated entities such as state universities and city and county hospitals. For many years, these organizations received little attention and guidance regarding their recording and reporting rules. As a result, standards were developed piecemeal by national industry associations (e.g., National Association of College & University Business Officers) and "industry" audit guides produced by the AICPA. When FASB was created in 1973, NFP organizations were included under its purview, but it was not until the release of Statements #116 (FASB Codification ASC 958-605) and #117 (ASC 958-205 though ASC 958-230) nearly 20 years later that accounting and reporting issues for NFP organizations were addressed in a meaningful, comprehensive manner. Accounting Standards Update 2016-14, issued by FASB in August 2016, is the first major change in NFP financial reporting since Statements 116 and 117. ASU 2016-14 is eligible for testing on the CPA Exam starting the first quarter of 2018. The critical aspects of this ASU are covered in the remaining lessons on NFP entities.

II. **Categories of Not-for-Profit Organizations**

A. Historically, NFPOs have been grouped into the following four categories. Although accounting and reporting differences among the categories have been dramatically reduced, each category retains a few unique characteristics. The four categories of NFP organizations that follow FASB accounting and financial reporting are:

1. **Hospitals and other healthcare entities**—Includes private hospitals (which includes both *for-profit* and *not-for-profit*) as well as nursing homes, home health agencies, continuing care retirement communities, health maintenance organizations, and others:

    a. **Exception:** Public (i.e., government-run) healthcare entities follow accounting and financial reporting standards established by GASB.

2. **Colleges, universities and other educational organizations**—Includes private (e.g., NFP) four-year colleges and universities and other types of schools.

    a. **Exception**—Two-year institutions with taxing authority (i.e., most community colleges) are excluded from this category, as are public (i.e., government-run) educational institutions, such as state-run universities. These types of educational organizations follow the financial reporting model established by GASB.

3. **Voluntary health and welfare organizations (VHWOs)**—These organizations promote research and education in a wide variety of social and health-related areas; they frequently offer free or low-cost services to the general public or to special groups; they receive the majority of their funding from voluntary contributions from the general public and from grants; many of these organizations have local branches that are associated with national organizations with the same objectives.

Example
Arthritis Foundation, United Way, American Cancer Society, Boy Scouts, Girl Scouts, and so on. Almost all these organizations are classified as *private* not-for-profit organizations.

4. **Other nonprofit organizations (ONPOs)**—These encompass a diverse group of organizations including social clubs, political parties, museums, fraternities, unions, athletic clubs, environmental action organizations, etc.; while the vast majority of these organizations are classified as private, governmentally affiliated organizations are occasionally found within this category (public museums, historical sites, etc.).

III. Jurisdiction over Not-for-Profit Organizations

A. **FASB**—Regulates the accounting and reporting practices for all private not-for-profit-organizations; GASB governs governmentally affiliated organizations.

B. **Private NFPs**—Most not-for-profit organizations fall under this category; FAS 116 (ASC 958-605) prescribes the rules for recognition of contributions, and FAS 117 (ASC 958-205 through 230) prescribes the external reporting requirements for all private NFP organizations.

1. Traditional reporting practices (fund model) are still expected to be used for internal reporting and still may appear on the CPA Exam; however, funds are not used for external reporting.

C. **Public (Governmentally Affiliated) NFPs**—These organizations are predominantly publicly funded hospitals and universities, although museums, parks, and landmarks can fall into this category as well.

1. They use fund reporting in their independent statements and for reporting purposes are usually combined with the primary government entity and accounting and financial reporting is determined by the GASB.

D. **Basis of Accounting for Private NFP**—Generally accepted accounting principles established by FASB requires NFP organizations to use full accrual basis accounting. The main objective of financial reporting is to disclose the sources of an NFP's resources and how they were expended rather than the determination of net income.

> **Note**
> Colleges and universities and healthcare organizations can be organized as not-for-profit, governmental, or for-profit commercial entities. If organized as a governmental entity, GASB standards apply. When organized as a not-for-profit or for-profit entity, FASB standards apply.

Financial Reporting

This lesson presents a summary of the primary financial statements for not-for-profit entities.

After studying this lesson, you should be able to:

1. Describe the form and content of the Statement of Financial Position.

2. Describe the form and content of the Statement of Activities.

3. Describe the form and content of the Statement of Cash Flows.

4. Describe the form and content of the Statement of Functional Expenses and know which types of not-for-profits should prepare this statement.

5. Describe the two categories of net assets.

I. **ASU 2016-14 Amended Statement #117 (ASC 958-205 through 958-230)—Financial Statement Presentation**—This statement identifies a single set of statements that is to be prepared for all private not-for-profit (NFP) organizations. In these statements, **fund information is no longer presented**; assets and liabilities from all funds are combined; and the Fund Balances are **translated to one of two classifications of net assets: net assets with donor restrictions or net assets without donor restrictions (958-205-05-6).**

    A. Three statements are required for all organizations (ASC 958-205-05-5):

        1. **Statement of Financial Position**

        2. **Statement of Activity**

        3. **Statement of Cash Flows**

    B. In addition, all NFP organizations must report expenses by nature (e.g., salaries, rent, supplies, etc.) and function (i.e., major program services and supporting activities) in one location, either on the face of the Statement of Activities, as a schedule in the notes to the financial statements, or as a separate financial statement (ASC 958-205-45-6).

II. **Statement of Financial Position**

    A. The Statement of Financial Position is **required** for all NFP organizations.

        1. It does not include any fund information but instead is presented **"for the organization as a whole"** (ASC 958-205-05-7).

        2. Net assets (the residual of assets over liabilities) are broken down into two categories based on whether or not there are any **donor-imposed restrictions**:

            a. **Net assets without donor restrictions**

                i. These net assets represent net assets that are free of donor restrictions on usage and the NFP can use these net assets for any purpose.

            b. **Net assets with donor restrictions**

                i. A donor may place permanent or temporary restrictions on a donation. When the temporary restriction is met, the amount of the restriction met is reclassified from net assets with donor restrictions to net assets without donor restrictions. The two types of temporary restrictions are:

                    1. **Purpose-type restriction**—occurs when the donor stipulates that the resources from the donation must be spent on something specific (e.g., drug-free youth education programs at the YMCA).

2. **Time restriction**—occurs when the donor stipulates that the resources must be spent in a certain time period (e.g., a $50,000 donation to be spent $10,000 yearly for five years).

ii. **Permanent restriction.** A donor may make a contribution with restrictions that it never be spent, such as an endowment fund that is to remain intact but the income from the endowment can be used by the NFP in accordance with the donor's stipulations, if any.

B. **Statement of Financial Position**

Not-for-Profit Organization
Statements of Financial Position
June 30, 20X1 and 20X0
(in thousands)

	20X1	20X0
Assets:		
Cash and Cash Equivalents	$ 75	$ 460
Accounts and Interest Receivable	2,250	1,670
Inventories and Prepaid Expenses	610	1,000
Contributions Receivable	3,025	2,700
Short-term Investments	1,400	1,000
Assets Restricted to Investment in Land, Buildings, and Equipment	5,210	4,560
Land, Buildings, and Equipment (Note A)	61,700	63,590
Long-Term Investments	217,950	203,500
Total Assets	$292,220	$278,480
Liabilities and Net Assets:		
Accounts Payable	$ 2,570	$ 1,050
Refundable Advance		650
Grants Payable	875	1,300
Notes Payable		1,140
Annuity Obligations	1,685	1,700
Long-Term Debt	5,500	6,500
Total Liabilities	$ 10,630	$ 12,340
Net Assets:		
Without Donor Restrictions (Note E)	$ 90,838	$ 78,940
With Donor Restrictions (Note B)	190,752	187,200
Total Net Assets	281,590	266,140
Total Liabilities and Net Assets	$292,220	$278,480

III. **Statement of Activity**

A. The Statement of Activity is required for all organizations. The principal requirement of the statement is to provide the change in net assets for each of the two classifications of net assets (without donor restrictions and with donor restrictions) and for the organization as a whole. This means that all revenue amounts must be reported as belonging to one of these two classifications. Expense amounts are reported only in the **net assets without donor restrictions** category.

> **Exam Tip**
> FASB guidance includes a couple of alternative presentation formats for the Statement of Activity; the format shown in this lesson is the one you will usually see on the CPA Exam.

    B. The Statement of Activity reporting on the changes in net assets without donor restrictions has four principal sections:

        1. Revenues and Gains

        2. Net Assets Released from Restrictions

        3. Expenses and Losses

        4. Change in Net Assets (including reconciliation of beginning and ending Net Assets)

> **Note**
> The reporting of revenues and expenses on the Statement of Activities is heavily tested on the CPA Exam. Be sure to memorize the format of this statement and understand how it is used. The areas of emphasis are classification of revenues, classification of expenses, timing of release of assets from restrictions, and evaluation of the effect on net assets with donor restrictions and net assets without donor-restrictions when donor-restricted monies are spent for their intended purpose.

    C. Statement of Activity Format A

Format A
Not-for-Profit Organization
Statement of Activities
Year Ended June 30, 20X1
(in thousands)

Changes in net assets without donor restrictions:

Revenues and gains:

Contributions	$ 8,500
Fees	5,400
Investment Income on Endowment	3,600
Other Investment Income	2,850
Net Unrealized and Realized Gains on Endowment	4,428
Net Unrealized and Realized Gains on other Investments	3,800
Other	150
Total Revenues and Gains without Donor Restrictions	28,728
Net Assets Released from Restrictions (Note D)	15,220
Total Unrestricted Revenues, Gains, and Other Support	43,948

Expenses and losses:	
Program A	13,100
Program B	8,540
Program C	5,760
Management and General	2,420
Fund Raising	2,150
Total Expenses (Note G)	31,970
Fire Loss	80
Total Expenses and Losses	32,050
Increase in Net Assets without Donor Restriction	11,898
Changes in Net Assets with Donor Restrictions	
Contributions	8,530
Investment Income on Annuity Agreements	180
Investment Income on Endowment	2,520
Net Unrealized and Realized Gains on Endowment	7,572
Actuarial Loss on Annuity Obligations	(30)
Net Assets Released from Restrictions (Note D)	(15,220)
Increase in Net Assets with Donor Restrictions	3,552
Changes in permanently Restricted Net Assets:	
Increase in Total Net Assets	15,450
Net Assets at beginning of year	266,140
Net Assets at end of year	$281,590

IV. Revenues and Gains Section

A. Note the following items in this section:

1. Contribution revenue can be reported in both classifications of net assets; this is also true for investment income and net unrealized and realized gains. Following FASB ASU 2020-07, contributed nonfinancial assets are presented as a separate item in the statement of activities, apart from contributions of cash and other financial assets.

2. Exchange revenues (fees, dues, charges for services, etc.) can only be reported under net assets without donor restrictions.

V. Expenses and Losses Section

A. Note the following items in this section:

1. *All expenses are incurred from net assets without donor restrictions.*

2. Expenses can be reported by nature (e.g., salaries, rent, etc.), by function, or both. If expenses are not reported by nature and function in the face of the Statement of Activities, this information should be reported in the notes to the financial statements or in a separate financial statement. There are two primary functions to classifying the expenses.

3. **Programming services**—Expenditures made to further the main mission of the organization. The line items listed under this category vary substantially from organization to organization but frequently include items such as education, outreach, research, clinical care, etc.

4. **Supporting services**—Expenditures made to provide the organizational infrastructure and to raise resources. Supporting services are always reported on two line items:

   a. **Management and general**—Administrative and support expenses such as the director's salary, office supplies, computer services;

   b. **Fund raising**—Monies used to encourage contributions to the organization including advertisements, promotional literature and mailings, and "special events" such as galas, telethons, auctions, and other fund drives.

Note

The separation of expenses into Program Services and Supporting Services classifications is extremely important as the percentage of revenues spent on Supporting Services is frequently used to measure the efficiency of a NFP organization. The examiners often include questions in which an expenditure is partially for a program service and partially for a supporting service (management and general or fund raising). In these instances, it is important to split the expenditure into the correct functional classifications.

Losses are shown as line items after expenses and can occur in any classification of Net Assets.

VI. **Net Assets Released from the Restrictions Section**

A. Although contributions, which have restrictions on their use, are reported under net assets with a donor restriction, when the monies are expended for the intended purpose, the expense is reported under net assets without donor restrictions, we need a mechanism to **reduce the amount of Net Assets with Donor Restrictions** and to **increase the amount of Net Assets without a Donor Restriction** to cover the expenditure. This is the function of the section titled **net assets released from restrictions.** Whenever the temporary restrictions placed on resources have been "satisfied," we transfer assets from Net Assets with a Donor Restriction into Net Assets without a Donor Restriction.

B. We can move these resources in three instances, which correspond with the three types of restrictions placed on the resources:

   1. **Satisfaction of program restrictions**—The resources have been spent for the intended operating purpose, which always results in the recognition of an expense.

   2. **Satisfaction of asset acquisition restrictions**—The resources have been spent for the intended capital purpose, which always results in the increase of an asset account.

   3. **Satisfaction of time restrictions**—The time or event specified in the restriction on the resources has occurred; note that it is not necessary that the resources be spent.

C. **Note the Following on the Statement of Activities:**

   1. There is always an increase in net assets without a donor restriction.

   2. There is always a decrease in net assets with a donor restriction

VII. **Change in Net Assets**

A. The "bottom line" of the Statement of Activity is entitled **Change in Net Assets,** not Net Income. The Change in Net Assets line item is always followed by the reconciliation of the ending balance in each of the two categories of Net Assets. That is:

Exam Tip

Most questions in this area will ask for the "effect on net assets when monies restricted to a certain type of expenditure are actually expended for that purpose." Two separate transactions must be considered: the expense itself, which will reduce net assets without a donor restriction, and the transfer of resources in the net assets released from restrictions section, which increases net assets without a donor restriction and decreases net assets with a donor restriction.

> + Change in Net Assets
> ± <u>Beginning Net Assets</u>
> = Ending Net Assets

B. Ending net assets totals on the Statement of Activity should reconcile to the Net Asset totals on the Statement of Financial Position.

VIII. Statement of Cash Flows

A. The Statement of Cash Flows is required for all organizations. Its format is identical to the Statement of Cash Flows required by for-profit organizations and consequently it is not heavily tested. The principal difference lies in the treatment of contributions that are restricted for long-term purposes—that is, resources that are subject to capital restrictions—which are reported in the Financing Activities section. Unrestricted contributions and contributions subject to Program or Time Restrictions are reported in the Operating Activities section.

B. The three classifications of cash flows and some examples of the items found in each section are shown below:

1. **Cash flows from operating activities**—Includes **unrestricted contributions, unrestricted investment earnings, revenue restricted for operating purposes (program restrictions)**, revenue from exchange transactions, and **operating expenditures** (salaries, supplies, interest expense), including grants to other organizations;

2. **Cash flows from investing activities**—Includes inflows from the sale of capital assets, marketable securities, etc., and outflows for the purchase of capital assets, etc.;

3. **Cash flows from financing activities**—Has two subsections (i) include contributions and investment revenues restricted for long-term purposes (e.g., restrictions for acquisition of capital assets, endowments) and (ii) other financing activities for debt proceeds, debt repayment, lease payments, etc.

C. Statement of Cash Flows

Indirect Method

Not-for-Profit Organizations

Statement of Cash Flows

Year Ended June 30, 20X1

(in thousands)

Cash Flows from Operating Activities:

Change in Net Assets	$ 15,450

Adjustments to Reconcile Change in Net Assets to Net Cash Used by Operating Activities:

Depreciation	3,200
Fire Loss	80
Actuarial Loss on Annuity Obligations	30
Increase in Accounts and Interest Receivable	(460)
Decrease in Inventories and Prepaid Expenses	390
Increase in Contributions Receivable	(325)
Increase in Accounts Payable	1,520
Decrease in Refundable Advance	(650)
Decrease in Grants Payable	(425)
Contributions Restricted for Long-Term Investment	(2,740)
Interest and Dividends Restricted for Long-Term Investment	(300)
Net Unrealized and Realized Gains on Long-Term Investments	(15,800)
Net Cash Used by Operating Activities	(30)

Cash Flows from Investing Activities:	
Insurance Proceeds from Fire Loss on Building	250
Purchase of Equipment	(1,500)
Proceeds from Sale of Investments	76,100
Purchase of Investments	(74,900)
Net Cash Used by Investing Activities	(50)
Cash Flows from Financing Activities	
Proceeds from Contributions Restricted for:	
Investment in Endowment	200
Investment in Term Endowment	70
Investment in Plant	1,200
Investment Subject to Annuity Agreements	200
	1,680
Other Financing Activities:	
Interest and Dividends Restricted for Reinvestment	300
Payments of Annuity Obligations	(145)
Payments on Notes Payable	(1,140)
Payments on Long-Term Debt	(1,000)
	(1,985)
Net Cash used by Financing Activities	(305)
Net Decrease in Cash and Cash Equivalents	(385)
Cash and Cash Equivalents at Beginning of Year	460
Cash and Cash Equivalents at End of Year	$ 75

IX. Reporting Expenses by Nature and Function

A. All NFPs are required to report expenses according to their natural classification and function. The purpose of this report is to take the functional expense categories (Program Services and Supporting Services) and break them down into "natural expense" categories (i.e., rent, utilities, salaries, depreciation, etc.).

Exam Tip

Prior to ASU 2016-14, only voluntary health and welfare organizations were required to report expense by nature and function. ASU 2016-14 expanded the requirement to not-for-profit organizations. It is highly likely that you will get an exam question on this.

B. **ASC 958-205-45-6** states three options for the report of expenses by nature and function: (1) within the face of the Statement of Activities in the net assets without donor restrictions, (2) as a schedule in the notes to the financial statements, or (3) as a separate financial statement. The following example is in the form of a separate financial statement.

Not-for-Profit Organizations

Statement of Functional Expenses
For the Year Ended December 31, 20X1

	Program Services			Supporting Services			
	Research	Education	Total	Management and General	Fund Raising	Total	Total Expenses
Salaries	$16,000	$ 27,000	$ 43,000	$ 30,000	$15,000	$ 45,000	$ 88,000
Employee Health and Retirement Benefits	1,289	3,340	4,629	4,648	1,284	5,932	10,561
Payroll Taxes, etc.	644	1,670	2,314	2,324	642	2,966	5,280
Total Salaries and Related Expenses	17,933	32,010	49,943	36,972	16,926	53,898	103,841
Professional Fees and Contract Service Payments	34,996	90,710	125,706	13,428	2,283	15,711	141,417
Supplies	4,852		4,852	9,296	6,000	15,296	20,148
Telephone and Telegraph	1,245	1,670	2,915	7,747	5,965	13,712	16,627
Postage and Shipping	1,192	1,670	2,862	6,714	8,015	14,729	17,391
Occupancy	10,000		10,000	15,494	7,707	23,201	33,201
Rental of Equipment	322	835	1,157	1,549	4,567	6,116	7,273
Local Transportation	966	2,305	3,471	11,879	8,563	20,442	23,913
Conferences, Conventions, Meetings	2,577	6,680	9,257	19,626	3,711	23,337	32,594
Printing and Publications	1,289	3,340	4,629	7,231	18,268	25,499	30,128
Awards and Grants	16,106	41,747	57,853				57,853
Interest				20,000		20,000	20,000
Meals					20,000	20,000	20,000
Gratuities					5,000	5,000	5,000
Miscellaneous	322	833	1,155	8,264	5,995	14,259	15,414
Total Expenses before Depreciation	91,800	182,000	273,800	113,000	271,200	246,200	545,000
Depreciation of Buildings, Improvements, and Equipment	12,000	2,000	14,000	13,000	3,000	16,000	30,000
Total Expenses	103,800	184,000	287,800	171,200	116,000	287,200	575,000
Less: Expenses Deducted Directly from Revenues					(25,000)	(25,000)	(25,000)
Total Expenses Reported by Function	$103,800	$184,000	$287,800	$171,200	$91,000	$262,200	$550,000

Donations, Pledges, Contributions, and Net Assets

After studying this lesson, you should be able to:

1. Describe the criteria for recognizing a promise to give ("pledge") as contribution revenue.

2. Describe the criteria for recognizing the value of donated services, donated fixed assets, and donated collections as contribution revenue.

3. Describe *variance power* and how it pertains to the recognition of contribution revenue by not-for-profit organizations that act as an intermediary (agent).

I. **Nonexchange Transactions**—*Contributions* are unconditional, nonreciprocal receipts of assets or services. They are not *exchange* transactions, in which each party in the transaction gives up something of value. FASB ASU 2018-06 clarifies that an exchange transaction occurs when the resource provider receives commensurate value in return for the resources transferred to the not-for-profit. They are asymmetrical transactions in which one party relinquishes something of value to another party, but the other party provides nothing in return. Consequently, since a contribution is both voluntary and nonreciprocal, it is scoped out of FASB ASU 2014-09, *Revenue from Contracts and Customers* (Topic 606). The item of value may be cash, marketable securities, inventory, property, or even services (subject to limitations noted later). Statement #116, *Accounting for Contributions Received and Contributions Made*, provides guidance on revenue recognition for non-exchange transactions.

Study Tip

Many not-for-profit organizations rely on contributions from donors to fulfill their mission. This is particularly true for voluntary health and welfare organizations. Therefore, revenue recognition rules for contributions are a major issue for these not-for-profits, and the topic is consistently tested on the CPA Exam.

II. **Contribution Recognition**

A. *All unconditional contributions are recognized as contribution revenue in the period in which the contribution is made, regardless of whether it is received in cash.* Donations other than cash are recorded at **fair value as of the date of the gift**.

B. **Conditional** contributions depend on the occurrence of some future, uncertain event. In this case, revenue recognition occurs when the condition is met or the chance of not meeting the condition becomes remote. The not-for-profit should account for conditional contributions received (e.g., cash is deposited) as a refundable advance (liability) until the condition is met.

C. **Revenue Classifications**

A. All revenue must be reported in one of two categories based on whether the donor stipulates any restrictions as the use on the revenue. The restrictions can take two forms: (1) restricted as to the purpose of the expenditure (e.g., purchase of new equipment) or (2) the time period in which the revenue can be used (e.g., over the next five years) restrictions are the use of the revenue either in expenditure purpose or time period. The two categories are:

1. **Contributions without donor restrictions** provide resources that are available for expenditure **in the current period for any purpose**.

2. **Contributions with donor restrictions** fall into four main types: (1) resources restricted for specified operating purposes known as "program" or "purpose" restrictions; (2) resources available after a specified time has elapsed known as "time restrictions; (3) resources restricted for acquisition or construction of capital assets known as "capital restrictions; and (4) resources not available for expenditure at any

time, although the earnings on the resources may be expended these permanently restricted recourses are known as "endowments."

3. **Separate presentation of contributions of financial and nonfinancial assets.** Within each category of contributions, with donor restrictions and without donor restrictions, present contributions of nonfinancial assets (e.g., contributed services, buildings, equipment, collections) apart from contributions of cash and other financial assets.

Note

Only revenue from nonexchange transactions (e.g., contributions) can be classified as **contributions with donor restrictions** because the restriction must be made by an external party (the donor); **revenue subject to internal restrictions**, such as might be made by the Board of Directors, **and revenue from exchange transactions** (i.e., dues, sales of goods, charges for services, etc.) are **always classified as contributions without donor restrictions**.

Example

Animal Action recently received $100,000 in contributions. $30,000 of this amount was restricted by donors to covering the costs of a spay/neuter clinic. The director set aside an additional $50,000 of this amount to be used to build an addition to the animal shelter.

Animal Action reports $30,000 of the Contribution of cash and other financial assets as with a donor restriction and reports $70,000 Contribution of cash and other financial assets as without a donor restriction. The $50,000 set aside by the director should be reported as designated resources within the net assets without donor restriction category; because the restriction was internally created, it does not qualify for inclusion in the net assets with donor restrictions category.

D. **Promises to give ("pledges") (ASC 958-605-25-7-15)** —Although FASB prefers the term "promises to give" over "pledges," the CPA Exam may use either term. Do not get tripped up over the semantics, for the exam the two mean the same thing.

A. Promises to give (pledges) may be recognized as contributions as long as they are unconditional. Conditional promises to give are promises that depend on a specific event occurring in the future. They cannot be recognized as contributions until the uncertain future event has occurred. Conditional promises to give are recognized when the conditions are substantially met or when the likelihood that the conditions will **not** be met is remote. An allowance for uncollectible pledges should be recorded in a manner similar to a for-profit organization's accounting for accounts receivable.

Study Tip

The timing of the receipt of cash related to promises to give is a frequent distracter in CPA Exam questions. The examiners will give information about the promise to give and about when the promise to give was paid. The cash payment information should almost always be ignored. **Revenue recognition is not tied to the receipt of cash;** a promise to give in the current period is recognized as revenue when the promise is made, **not** when the cash is received (but see special rules for multiyear promises to give below).

Examples

1. Simmons promises to give $1,000,000 to World Crisis Services to purchase food supplies for a drought-ridden country. Simmons also promises to give an additional $500,000 if the drought is not broken in six months. The $1,000,000 should be

recognized as a Contribution of cash and other financial assets—Donor Restricted Support (a specific purpose) since it is an unconditional promise. The $500,000 cannot be recognized as a Contribution since it is conditioned upon an uncertain future event.

2. Jesse Morgan pledges $10,000 to the McMillan School, a private not-for-profit elementary school that maintains a culturally diverse student body, as long as the average standardized test scores for the student body are above 75% of the national average. The average standardized tests scores for the McMillan School student body have always been above 85% in its 25-year history. Since the likelihood that the test average would fall below 75% for this year is remote, McMillan would recognize the promise to give immediately as a contribution of cash and other financial assets without a donor restriction (no purpose or time restriction exists).

3. QuickCure Hospital receives pledges of $80,000 in November of the current year. It receives $50,000 cash related to the pledges in December and the remaining $30,000 in January. QuickCure's fiscal year runs from January 1 to December 31. QuickCure recognizes revenue of $80,000 in the current year. Remember that the timing of cash receipts does not determine when contribution revenue is recognized.

B. Fundraiser Drives—Are recognized as contribution revenue *net* of the estimated uncollectible pledges (allowance for uncollectible pledges).

Example
Little City Public Television recently held a fund drive and received $300,000 in promises to give. Historically, the station has been unable to collect 30% of its promises to give. Little City Public Television should recognize the contribution revenue of $210,000 ($300,000 − ($300,000 × 30%)).

The accounting entry for promises to give is sometimes tested on the exam:

DR: Pledges Receivable	$300,000	
CR: Estimated Uncollectible Pledges		$90,000
CR: Contribution Revenue without Donor Restrictions		$210,000

E. Promises to Give Made Over Multiple Fiscal Periods—When revenue is to be received over multiple fiscal periods, as happens when contributions are promised over several years (e.g., a promise to give $10,000 per year for four years), special recognition rules apply:

A. Recognize revenue at the *net present value* of the contribution.

B. The portion of the promise that is to be received in subsequent fiscal periods is considered **Contribution of cash and other financial assets - Donor Restricted Support** (time restricted—see below); the portion that is to be received in the current period is recognized as **Contribution of cash and other financial assets - Without Donor Restrictions**, assuming that no other restrictions, such as a purpose restriction, are specified.

C. The net present value of the pledge is recalculated at the end of the period (or whenever the financial statements are prepared) and increases in net present value are booked as *contribution revenue*, **not interest**.

D. When the future payments are received, the assets are reclassified to net assets without a donor restriction, assuming that there are no other restrictions on how the money may be spent, but **revenue is not recognized**. (It was recognized when the promise to give was made and as the interest element was realized.)

Example

On January 1, Fly Free, a raptor preservation organization, received a promise to give without a donor restriction of $10,000 per year for three years (the current year and the next two years).

Assuming an interest rate of 10% and that the first payment is made immediately, the present value of the promise to give is $27,355. Fly Free recognizes $10,000 Contribution of cash and other financial assets without a Donor Restriction (the current year's payment) and $17,355 Contribution of cash and other financial assets - Donor-Restricted Support (the present value of the two remaining payments).

Cash	10,000	
Contributions Receivable	20,000	
Contributions—Revenue—without a Donor Restriction		10,000
Contributions—Revenue—Donor—Restricted Support		17,355
Discount on Contributions Receivable		2,645

At year-end, Fly Free recalculates the present value of the remaining pledge as $19,091. The difference of $1,736 ($19,091 – $17,355) is recognized as Contribution of cash and other financial assets Donor—Restricted Support. Note: Interest revenue is not recognized.

Discount on Contributions Receivable	1,736	
Contribution—Revenue—Donor Restricted Support		1,736

When the second year's payment of $10,000 is received, no additional revenue is recognized (cash increases and pledges decrease). The $10,000 will, however, be reclassified from net assets with donor restrictions to net assets without donor restrictions because the *time restriction* has now been met. (See ASC 958-605-30-4 through 7 for an explanation of how assets are *released from restriction*.)

Cash	10,000	
Contributions Receivable		10,000
Net Assets Released—with a Donor Restriction	10,000	
Net Assets Released—without a Donor Restriction		10,000

At the end of the second year, Fly Free recalculates the present value of the remaining pledge as $10,000. The difference of $909 ($10,000 – $9,091) is recognized as Contribution Revenue with Donor Restrictions category.

Discount on Contributions Receivable	909	
Contribution—Revenue—Donor-Restricted Support		909

When the final payment of $10,000 is received, it will again be reclassified from Net Assets with a Donor Restriction to Net Assets without a Donor Restriction. The total amount of Contribution Revenue recognized over the life of the pledge is $30,000 ($27,355 + $1,736 + $909).

Cash	10,000	
Contributions Receivable		10,000
Net Assets Released—with a Donor Restriction	10,000	
Net Assets Released—without a Donor Restriction		10,000

F. Donated Services (ASC 958-605-25-16-17)

   A. FASB allows NFP organizations to recognize the value of services that are donated to the organization, but only if certain conditions are met. Donated services are recognized if *either*:

   B. Nonfinancial assets are enhanced **or**

   C. Services requiring *a)special skills* are provided *b)by persons possessing those skills* and the services would *c)normally have been purchased* by the organization (e.g., CPA who donates audit services).

G. The entry to record the donated service recognizes the fair value of the service as a *credit to Contribution of nonfinancial assets* and as a *debit to either an asset* (if nonfinancial assets are enhanced) *or as an expense* (if services are provided) account.

Examples

1. ***Nonfinancial Assets Are Enhanced***—Prairie View Prep School is building an auditorium for their fine arts department. The parent of an eighth - grade student is an architect and donates his services to design the auditorium. He normally charges $150,000 for this work, though the going market rate in the area for similar work is $100,000.

   Since architectural fees are normally capitalized as part of the building cost, a nonfinancial asset has been enhanced. Prairie View can recognize the donated services at the fair value of $100,000 with the following entry:

DR: Building	100,000	
CR: Contribution Revenue		100,000

2. ***Service Requiring Special Skills***—Jennifer Rhodes, a professional deep-sea diver, has been hired by Sea Mammals R Us, an international sea mammal conservation group, to help record the activities of migrating whales. The original contract is for five days at $600 per day. However, the process requires an additional two days to complete, and the contract is extended.

   Rather than bill for the additional time, Jennifer contributes her time to the organization. Because Sea Mammals R Us would normally have had to purchase these services and because they are skilled services, they can recognize the value of the services with the following entry:

DR: Research Expenses (Diving Expense)	1,200	
CR: Contribution Revenue		1,200

3. ***Donated Services Not Recognized***—Students at Central University have recently been accosted and robbed and/or threatened when crossing campus late at night. To combat this problem, student groups have banded together to offer escort services to students free of charge. The students estimate that a fair charge for such a service is approximately $10 per trip or $4,500 per month. The university has increased its campus police force in response to the problem and has decided against providing escort services to students.

   Central is *not* able to recognize the value of these services because, even though this might arguably be classified as a "skilled" service, there is no indication that the students possess these skills and this is not a service that the university would normally provide.

Exam Tip

This is a consistently tested area on the exam. Most of the time the value of the services is recognized. Frequently, there are differences between rates charged and *standard* or *fair value* rates: Always record at fair value.

III. **Donated Fixed Assets and Donated Collections**

    A. Donated fixed assets are **recorded at FMV** at date of donation. These assets are generally subject to depreciation.

    B. **Classification of revenue from the donation**—Donated fixed assets are normally considered to be contribution revenue without a donor restriction. If, however, there are restrictions on how the asset must be used or on how proceeds from the sale of the asset may be expended, it should be classified as Contributions of nonfinancial asset revenue - Donor-Restricted Support.

    C. Not-for-profit organizations have the option of not recognizing donated works or art, historical artifacts, rare books, and other similar donated collections as revenues or gains and assets if all of the following conditions are met (ASC 958-360-20):

        1. Held for public exhibition, education, or research in furtherance of public sector rather than financial gain

        2. Protected, kept unencumbered, care for, and preserved

        3. Subject to an organizational policy that requires the proceeds from sales of collection items to be used to acquire other items for collections, the direct care of the remaining collection, or both.

Examples

1. *Fixed Asset Donated without a Donor Restriction*—Newberry Cars donated a demonstration car to the McGrary Foundation, a not-for-profit organization. The car cost Newberry $15,000 and had a retail sales value of $22,000 when new. The car's current market value is $16,000. McGrary records the donation and reports Contributions of nonfinancial asset revenue of $16,000 under Net Assets without a Donor Restriction.

2. *Fixed Asset Donated with a Donor Restriction*—Mary Cochoran donates land to the Newport Home, a not-for-profit organization that provides temporary living accommodations for foster children, with the stipulation that the land be maintained by Newport Home in perpetuity and is used to provide recreational opportunities to the foster children. The land has a basis of $50,000 to Ms. Cochoran and a fair value of $80,000. Newport Home records the donation and reports Contributions of nonfinancial asset revenue of $80,000 under Net Assets with a Donor Restriction.

3. *Donated Work of Art Not Recognized*—Pedro Picasso donates a work of art having a fair value of $50,000 to become part of the permanent collection at the Modern Art Museum. The museum has a policy of not recognizing donations to its collection as revenue or assets. The museum does not recognize the contribution as revenue or record an asset—it should report the donation in the notes to the financial statements.

4. *Donated Work of Art Recognized*—Pedro Picasso donates a work of art having a fair value $5,000 with the understanding that the Modern Art Museum will sell it at an auction and use the funds for its general operating activities. The museum will report $5,000 Contributions of nonfinancial asset revenue under Net Assets Without a Donor Restriction.

IV. **Contributions Raised or Held for Others**

    A. NFP organizations sometimes receive resources that are restricted by the donor to specific recipients. Depending on the degree of the restriction, these monies may represent Contribution Revenue to the NFP organization or they may actually be liabilities of the NFP organization. FASB ASC 958-605 (Statement 136), *Transfers of Assets to a Not-For-Profit Organization That Raises or Holds Contributions for Others,* **addresses these recognition issues.**

    B. **What transactions are covered**—ASC 958-605 applies to transactions in which three entities are identified:

1. A **donor** who has sent resources to a NFP;

2. A **recipient** who is responsible for disbursing the money to a NFP;

3. A **specified beneficiary**, who will ultimately be able to use the funds.

C. FASB requires that when an NFP organization is an intermediary or an agent for the transfer of assets to another NFP organization (beneficiary), that intermediary or agent would not recognize contribution revenue, unless it is granted *variance power* to redirect the resources (i.e., change the beneficiary) or it is financially interrelated to the beneficiary.

1. **Variance power**—The unilateral power to redirect the transferred assets to another beneficiary. Unilateral power means that the recipient entity can override the donor's instructions without seeking approval.

2. **Donor**—The contributor of cash or other assets. The donor decides who the intended beneficiary is. However, if the donor decides to grant variance power, the agent is ultimately responsible for who eventually receives the donation.

3. **Intermediary, agent, or trustee**—The conduit or go-between that holds the contribution. If variance power is granted, the agent acts more as a donee or recipient organization until the contribution is redistributed.

4. **Specified beneficiary**—The ultimate intended recipient of the contribution.

Example

Consider the NFP organization United Way and its work collecting contributions and redirecting the funds to feeder organizations. To the extent that United Way is able to control which feeder organization receives the contribution, it would have variance power.

If a donation is made to a disaster relief NFP organization (e.g., the Red Cross) specifically for the Katrina hurricane relief victims, the NFP is not able to redirect the funds to build a new administrative facility in the state of New York because variance power is not granted.

D. Recognition

1. *Without variance power*, the intermediary will record the receipt of resources (debit) at fair value with an offsetting recognition of a liability (credit) to the ultimate recipient (i.e., specified beneficiary). Likewise, the specified beneficiary is required to recognize a receivable (debit) and contribution revenue (credit).

2. *If variance power is granted*, the NFP recipient organization (i.e., intermediary) would recognize the receipt of resources (debit) and corresponding contribution revenue (credit) instead of a liability because the NFP now has control over the ultimate distribution of the contribution. When the asset is transferred to the beneficiary, an expense is recognized by the NFP (intermediary). A beneficiary would make no entry until contribution is actually received.

3. When the intermediary or agent and the beneficiary are financially interrelated, the intermediary or agent would recognize the receipt of the asset and the associated contribution revenue; the beneficiary would recognize its interest in the net assets of the intermediary or agent. The intermediary would adjust its net assets for the beneficiary's share of the change.

Special Issues—Recent Developments

This lesson describes some special issues pertaining to financial reporting for not-for-profit entities.

After studying this lesson, you should be able to:

1. Describe the accounting and reporting of inexhaustible fixed assets (e.g., collections).
2. List three types of endowments that do not meet the requirements of a regular, "pure" endowment.
3. Describe the reporting for earnings on endowments.
4. Describe the financial reporting for investments.
5. Describe the funds that are used for internal reporting purposes.

I. Inexhaustible Fixed Assets (ASC 958-605-25-19)

A. **Inexhaustible fixed assets** include works of art, cultural treasures, historical documents and property, and so on, and are subject to special rules. In particular:

   1. Inexhaustible fixed assets donated to the organization need *not be capitalized*. This means that, when such an asset is donated to the organization, we do not need to make an accounting entry to record the transaction and the value of the contribution and asset will not appear on the face of the financial statements. Further, if such an item is sold and the proceeds are used to purchase another inexhaustible fixed asset, those transactions also need not be recorded or reported on the face of the financial statements. Note that, although these transactions do not appear on the face of the financial statements, *they are disclosed in the notes*.

   2. Depreciation on these inexhaustible fixed assets *need not* be recorded.

B. In order to use these procedures, the assets must fit the requirements of assets known as *collectibles* or *collections*: Three conditions of the assets must be met. The assets must be:

   1. Held for public exhibition, education, or research rather than financial gain;
   2. Protected, kept unencumbered, cared for, and preserved; *and*
   3. Subject to a policy that requires proceeds from sales of collection items to be used to acquire other items for collections, the direct care of existing collections, or both.

 **Example**

A local collector donates a Picasso painting to the Henderson Museum of Modern Art. Since Henderson already has several Picassos, it sells the painting and uses the proceeds to purchase a Calder mobile. The mobile will be displayed in Henderson's public galleries and will be well protected. Because the art works meet the definition of a *collectible*, Henderson need not record the donation of the Picasso or the subsequent sale and purchase of the Calder. Instead, these transactions are disclosed in the notes.

II. Investments

A. NFP organizations frequently hold significant amounts of investments. ASC 954-320-35 (Statement #124), *Accounting for Certain Investments Held by Not-for-Profit Organizations*, addresses the accounting issues associated with these investments by NFP organizations. For the most part, accounting for these investments is handled in the same manner as it is for-profit organizations. That is, NFP organizations must report (all) their marketable securities at fair value. Changes in market value are recognized on the Statement of Activities as unrealized gains and losses during the period of the change.

B. However, unlike for-profit organizations, NFP organizations do not break debt securities out into Trading, Available-for-Sale, and Held-to-Maturity categories. Because the Held-to-Maturity category is the only one that allows for valuation at other than market value, for NFP organizations, *debt securities* are *always* **valued at fair value**.

III. Endowments

A. **Permanent endowments** are contributions to the organization from third parties for which the principal (corpus) must *remain intact in perpetuity*. Earnings on the endowment may be **expendable-restricted** (expendable but only for specified purposes), **expendable-unrestricted** (expendable at any time, for any purpose), or **nonexpendable**, depending on the stipulations of the donor. Endowments that have these characteristics are called *regular* endowments or *pure* endowments and are recorded as Net Assets with a Donor Restriction. Fund accounting is typically used for endowments for internal purposes but is not used for external reporting for private not-for-profit organizations.

B. **Split-interest agreements** are arrangements whereby both a donor (or beneficiary) and a not-for-profit organization receive benefits, often at different times in a multiyear arrangement. A typical split-interest agreement has two components: a lead interest and a remainder interest. A lead interest provides disbursements throughout the term of the agreement. A final disbursement at the termination of the agreement is a remainder interest.

Example

Roger Smith established a charitable lead trust for a donation to the Salvation Army. Roger put $1,000,000 in the trust to be invested for 10 years. The Salvation Army receives the trust income for the 10-year period (a lead interest). At the end of the 10-year period, the principal of the trust goes to Roger's children (the remainder interest).

C. Other types of contributions are similar to regular endowments but fail to meet one of the regular endowment criteria.

1. **Quasi-endowments**—Amounts set aside by the governing board of the organization, rather than outside sources, of which the principal must be retained and invested. Although these resources act like an endowment, they cannot be considered regular endowments as the restrictions on endowment resources must come from an external party. This type of endowment is known as a **quasi-endowment**. Quasi-endowments are included in **Net Assets without a Donor Restriction**.

    > **Exam Tip**
    > The examiners frequently try to confuse board-designated funds with quasi-endowments. Candidates should pay particular attention to indications of how the principal is to be treated:
    >
    > *If the principal can be spent, it is a board-designated fund.*
    >
    > *If only the earnings can be spent, it is a quasi-endowment.*

2. **Term endowments**—Gifts and bequests from third parties that are to be retained and invested for a period of time or until a specific event occurs. However, after the criterion has been met, the full amount can be spent. The earnings on the invested amount are paid to a separate beneficiary (usually a spouse or a child) until the criterion is met. These contributions are known as **term endowments.** Because they can ultimately be spent, they are **classified as Net Assets with a Donor Restriction** until the criterion is met (e.g., the spouse dies) after which the amount remaining in the endowment is reclassified as **Net Assets without a Donor Restriction.**

3. **Board-designated funds**—Amounts set aside by the governing board of the organization to be spent for specific purposes; these funds are not endowments because the principal can be spent. Board-designated funds frequently are set apart from other unrestricted assets by establishing an account similar to a reservation of Retained Earnings by for profit entities. The account is normally titled Net Assets without a Donor Restriction Designated for _____ and is shown as a line item in the Net Assets without a Donor Restriction category.

Example
Mantega Hospital received a $50,000 gift of securities that are to be retained and invested. The earnings may be used as Mantega wishes. Mantega's governing board designated, for special uses, $30,000 that had originated from gifts without donor restrictions. It set aside $80,000, the earnings from which are to be used to help fund charity care.

Mantega reports $50,000 as a regular endowment (Net Assets with a Donor Restriction); $30,000 is classified as a board designated fund (included in Net Assets without a Donor Restriction); the remaining $80,000 is classified as a quasi-endowment (included in Net Assets without a Donor Restriction).

IV. Earnings on Pure (or "Regular") Endowments

A. Earnings on pure endowments are reported as Endowment Income or Investment Income on the accrual basis. The income may be reported in either of the two classes of net assets depending on whether an external donor has placed restrictions on the use of the income:

1. If there are no restrictions on use, then report income under Net Assets without a Donor Restriction.

2. If the income must be spent for specified purposes, or may not be spent until a specified time or event, report under Net Assets with a Donor Restriction.

3. If the income may not be spent but must be used to increase or maintain the corpus, report under Net Assets with a Donor Restriction.

Example
Erica Gardner gives $100,000 to Borgans Children's Hospital to be used as a loan fund for families traveling to be with their children at the hospital. Interest charged on the loans (endowment earnings) is put back into the fund to increase the amount available to lend. The interest is reported under Net Assets with a Donor Restriction.

V. Underwater Endowment Funds.
ASU 2016-14 changed the financial reporting for "underwater" endowment funds. An endowment is underwater when its fair value is less than original gift amount or a level stipulated by the external donor or by law. When that occurs the NFP will disclose the following information in the Net Assets with a Donor Restriction section of the Statement of Financial Position (ASC 958-205-50-2):

A. The fair value of the endowment

B. The original endowment amount or the level required by the donor or by law

C. The amount of deficiency in the underwater endowment fund

Previously the amount that was "underwater" was reported in unrestricted net assets (the predecessor to net assets without a donor restriction). Since the change is fairly significant, you should anticipate a question on this in the CPA Exam.

VI. Cash flow reporting for the sale of donated financial assets.
Normally, cash received from the sale of donated financial assets, such as debt or equity instruments, are classified as cash inflows from investing activities. Two exceptions to this rule exist. Donated financial assets without a donor restriction that are converted nearly immediately into cash after receipt of the donation will be classified as cash inflows from operating activities. If, however, the donor restricts the use of the sales proceeds for a long-term purpose, such as the construction of a building or creation of an endowment, the cash proceeds should be reported as a cash inflow for financing activities (e.g., contributions restricted to construct building) and simultaneously as a cash outflow for investing activities (e.g., assets restricted for investment in building). In a subsequent period, both the proceeds from the sale of assets restricted to investment in the building and the cost to construct the building shall be reported as cash flows from investing activities.

VII.   Time restrictions on long-term assets. Normally, long-term assets are classified as Net Assets without a Donor Restriction when the assets are placed-in-service. However, if a donor places a time restriction on the long-term asset (e.g., use the donated building for 7 years) then the asset is classified as a Net Asset with a Donor Restriction and Net Assets will be reclassified from With a Donor Restriction to Without a Donor Restriction over the time period stipulated by the donor (e.g., over 7 years). Prior to ASU 2016-14 a NFP could adopt a policy to "imply" a time restriction. ACU 2016-14 eliminated this option.

VIII.   Reporting financial liquidity and flexibility. ASU 2016-14 requires the following information shall be displayed either on the face of the Statement of Financial Position or in the notes to financial statements, unless otherwise required on the face of the Statement of Financial Position:

- Relevant information about the nature and amount of limitations on the use of cash and cash equivalents (such as cash held on deposit as a compensating balance).

- Contractual limitations on the use of particular assets. These include, for example, restricted cash or other assets set aside under debt agreements, assets set aside under self-insurance funding arrangements, assets set aside under collateral arrangements, or assets set aside to satisfy reserve requirements that states may impose under charitable gift annuity agreements.

- Quantitative information, and additional qualitative information in the notes as necessary, about the availability of an NFP's financial assets at the Balance Sheet date to meet cash needs for general expenditures within **one year** of the Balance Sheet date

IX.   Types of Funds Used by Not-for-Profit Organizations—The following seven types of funds are used by not-for-profit organizations:

A.   Unrestricted Current Funds—Account for resources over which the governing board has discretionary control and fund balance is **Net Assets without a Donor Restriction.**

B.   Restricted Current Funds—Account for resources whose use is restricted by external parties for a specific purpose, in which case fund balance is **Net Assets with a Donor Restriction**

C.   Plant Funds—Account for investments in plant and resources available for capital asset acquisition and net assets are typically separated into Net Assets without a Donor Restriction and Net Assets with a Donor Restriction. Plant funds frequently take on other names such as Land, Building, and Equipment Funds, or Plant Expansion Fund; colleges and universities frequently use four subfunds: (1) Unexpended Plant Funds, (2) Funds for Renewal and Replacement, (3) Funds for Retirement of Indebtedness, and (4) Net Investment in Plant.

> **Exam Tip**
> You may see names of funds used by NFP organizations for internal purposes. Since NFP financial reporting is entity wide rather than fund level, you should not be too concerned about NFP fund types. Nonetheless, in case you do see them mentioned in the exam, it is worth covering.

D.   Loan Funds—Commonly used by colleges and universities to account for loans made to students

E.   Endowment Funds—Permanent, term, or quasi (board designated)

F.   Annuity (Life Income) Funds—Account for *split-interest funds* in which the not-for-profit organization shares a beneficial interest with another external party

G.   Agency Funds—Account for resources held by the not-for-profit organization as an agent for a third party

X.   ASU 2019–06 extended accounting for goodwill and intangibles by business entities to not-for-profit entities. Please see the lesson entitled "Conceptual Framework, Standard-Setting and Financial Reporting>Special Purpose Frameworks>Private Company Council" for the accounting alternatives for goodwill and certain intangibles.

Special Industries: Healthcare and Colleges

Healthcare Organizations

This lesson describes basic accounting and financial reporting for healthcare organizations.

After studying this lesson, you should be able to:

1. Recall the financial statements of a not-for-profit healthcare entity and a governmental healthcare entity.

2. Describe differences in format of a not-for-profit healthcare entity's statement of operations and a government healthcare entity's statement of revenues, expenses, and changes in net position.

3. Calculate Net Patient Service Revenue.

I. Reporting Features for Not-for-Profit Healthcare Organizations

A. Revenue recognition. ASU 2014-09 (Topic 606), *Revenue from Contracts to Customers*, eliminated industry-specific revenue guidance for exchange transactions. FASB ASU 2014-09 outlines five steps to be followed in recognizing revenue:

1. Identify the contract(s) with the customer.

2. Identify the separate performance obligations in the contract(s).

3. Determine the transaction price.

4. Allocate the transaction price to the performance obligations in the contract(s).

5. Recognize revenue when, or as, the entity satisfies the performance obligation.

The net effect is that the entity recognizes revenue in the amount that it expects to receive as payment.

For voluntary health and welfare organizations that rely primarily on contributions from donors (i.e., nonexchange transactions), ASU 2014-09 has minimal importance. For healthcare organizations, however, ASU 2014-09 is very important since a significant number of revenue streams are derived from contracts with customers (e.g., patients).

Generally, a patient who has some form of insurance and is admitted to or served by a healthcare provider is viewed as contractually bound. Since insurance usually has a deductible to be paid by the patient, the revenue expected from the patient for the deductible and the amount paid by the third-party insurance should be considered separately. Anyone who has seen insurance claim information associated with hospital bills knows that there is usually a big difference between the gross charges for services and the amount the insurance company will pay. Transaction price is based on the amount the insurance company will pay rather than gross charges. ASU 2014-09 refers to these adjustments to revenue as "variable consideration." In the healthcare industry, variable considerations include: contractual adjustments, discounts, refunds, rebates, price concessions (i.e., uncollectible write-offs), and so on. ASU 2014-09 requires variable consideration to be estimated based on a weighted average probability outcome or by recording the most likely outcome based on past experience. The amount that the healthcare provider does not expect to collect due to a patient's inability to pay is viewed as a "price concession." A price concession is a deduction from gross charges in deriving net patient revenue and is bad debt expense. However, if, in the future, a healthcare provider does not collect some of the amount it expected to collect, this amount would be considered a bad debt and reported as an operating expense.

> **Note**
>
> An interesting situation occurs with patients admitted through the emergency department. Depending on the condition of the patient, the hospital might not be able to conclude that the patient has entered into a contract. It may also be difficult to establish transaction price. There is no valid contact when this occurs, and revenue recognition should be deferred until a valid contract occurs and a transaction price can be estimated.

B. Basic Financial Statements. According to FASB ASC 954-205-45-1, the basic financial statements of not-for-profit healthcare entities consist of a balance sheet, a statement of operations, a statement of changes in net assets, a statement of cash flows, and notes to the financial statements. Not-for-profit healthcare entities present operating information in two separate statements: a statement of operations, which reports changes in net assets without donor restrictions, and a statement of changes in net assets. Alternatively, the two statements can be combined into a single statement of operations and changes in net assets. The following example is in the combined format:

Excel Hospital Statement of Operations and Changes in Net Assets		
	20X2	**20X1**
Revenues, gains, and other support without donor restrictions:		
Net patient service revenue	$390,000	$350,000
Other revenue	20,000	15,000
Contributions	5,000	5,000
Net assets released from donors' restrictions used for operations	15,000	-
Total revenues, gains, and other support	$440,000	$370,000
Patient care and other operating expenses	406,000	340,000
Excess of revenues over expenses	34,000	30,000
Investment return, net, excluding unrealized gains (losses) on other than		
trading debt securities	5,000	10,000
Performance earnings	39,000	40,000
Unrealized gains (losses) on other than trading debt securities	1,000	2,000
Change in net assets without donor restrictions	$40,000	$42,000
Net assets with a donor restriction:		
Gifts and donations	7,000	2,000
Increase in net assets with a donor restriction	7,000	2,000
CHANGE in NET ASSETS	47,000	44,000
NET ASSETS—Beginning of year	100,000	56,000
NET ASSETS—End of year	$147,000	$100,000

Not-for-profit healthcare organizations are required to report a performance indicator in the results of operations. This performance indicator provides a measure comparable to income from continuing operations of a for-profit healthcare organization. In accordance with FASB ASC 954-225, net investment income, excluding unrealized gains (losses) on other-than-trading securities, is included in the performance indicator. FASB ASC 954-225-45-4 also states that because of the importance of the performance indicator, it should be clearly labeled with a descriptive term, such as revenues over expenses, revenues and gains over expenses and losses, earned income, or performance earnings. Not-for-profit business-oriented healthcare entities should report the performance indicator in a statement that also presents the total changes in net assets without donor restrictions. The following items should be reported separately from the performance indicator:

- Transactions with owners
- Equity transfers among related entities
- Donor-restricted contributions
- Contributions of long-lived assets
- Unrealized gains and losses on investments on other than trading securities
- Investment returns restricted by donors or law
- An inherent contribution (a voluntary transfer of assets or service performance in exchange for either no assets or assets of substantially lower value) that increases net assets with donor restrictions

II. Patient Service Revenues

A. Patient Service Revenues—These are gross charges for direct patient care. They include such things as room charges, doctors' fees, medicines, bandages, and so on; *ancillary revenues*—which are revenues for patient-related services such as radiology, pathology, laboratory work, and so on—are also part of patient services revenues.

B. Charity Care—When patients enter the hospital, the *charity cases* are immediately identified and eliminated from the patient service revenue calculations. The amount of revenue as "donated" to charity cases is separately tracked and disclosed in the notes.

C. As paying patients begin to receive services, the charges for those services are *recorded in gross* (e.g., for the full amount). *Patient services revenues* are reduced by *contractual allowances* (price reductions allowed to third party payers such as insurance companies, Medicare, Medicaid, etc.), policy discounts, estimated uncollectible amounts, and administrative adjustments to determine **Net Patient Service Revenues**. Net Patient Service Revenue is the first line in the Statement of Activity. Gross Patient Service Revenues and Contractual Adjustments are displayed in the notes.

+ Gross Patient Service Revenues (*including Ancillary Revenues*)
– <u>Charitable Services</u>
= Patient Service Revenue
– <u>Less Contractual Adjustments and Estimated Uncollectible Amounts</u>
= Net Patient Service Revenue (first line in Statement Activities)

Example
Daily charges for a semiprivate room are $110. However, the hospital has an agreement with an HMO to accept $70 as full payment for the room. The hospital records Patient Service Revenue of $110, records a Contractual Allowance of $40, and reports Net Patient Service Revenues of $70 on the financial statements.

D. Note that ASU 2014-09 (Topic 606), *Revenue from Contracts with Customers*, requires an entity to determine the transaction price, which is the amount of consideration a hospital expects to be entitled to receive in exchange for services and goods to be delivered. Since the delivery of these goods and services often involves significant amounts of variable consideration (e.g., contractual allowances, discounts, concessions for the ability to pay), the entity is required to estimate the variable consideration by either the "expected value" (probability weighted) or "most likely amount." Consequently, estimated bad debt expense is taken into consideration in determining transaction price for net patient service revenue. Any other bad debt expense will be classified as a bad operating expense for all entities.

III. Other Revenue and Support

    A. Other operating revenues and support include revenues from items related to the main operations of the hospital, but not directly related to patient care. Other operating revenues and support include:

        1. Gift shop sales

        2. Parking garage receipts

        3. Cafeteria sales

        4. Tuition from classes offered by the hospital

        5. FMV of donated materials and supplies

        6. Research grants

Example

Bay City Hospital recorded the following revenues:

Delivery room charges (only $15,000 is expected to be collected due to agreements with third-party providers and uncollectible amounts)	$20,000
Cafeteria sales	$3,000
Research grants	$10,000
Radiology charges	$2,000
Nursing fees	$12,000
Gift of medicines used for direct patient care	$1,000

Bay City reports: Net Patient Service Revenues of $29,000 (15,000 + 2,000 + 12,000) and Other Operating Revenues of $14,000 (3,000 + 10,000 + 1,000).

Exam Tip

Categorization of hospital revenue as Patient Service Revenue, Other Operating Revenue, or Nonoperating Gains has been a consistent area of emphasis on the CPA Exam. It is important to know how individual contributions and revenues fit into these categories. Less emphasis has been placed on the expense categories.

IV. Premium Revenues (Capitation Fee Revenues)

    A. Capitation fees are payments made to healthcare providers for comprehensive client coverage provided for a fixed fee (e.g., HMOs). Capitation fee revenues should be recognized during the period covered and estimated obligations related to patient care for this period should be accrued. Capitation fees are shown as a separate line item in the operating section of the statement and may be disclosed as Premium Revenues.

V. Expenses

    A. Expenses include virtually all costs associated with running a hospital, including depreciation, bad debt expense (**except for bad debt related to patient service revenue, which is deducted in determining net patient service revenues**) and losses on disposal of fixed assets. Expenses may be reported by natural categories (salary, supplies, rent, etc.) or by functional categories (inpatient services, ancillary services, administrative, etc.). However, if the NFP healthcare entity chooses to report expenses using natural expense categories (salary, supplies, rent, etc.) it must also report expenses using functional categories either in the Statement of Activities, in the notes to the financial statements, or in a separate financial statement. Functional expenses are based on full cost allocation. Unlike most not-for-profit organizations, nongovernmental not-for-profit healthcare organizations may report depreciation, interest, and bad debt expense, along with functional categories. Following not-for-profit financial reporting guidelines, the NFP healthcare entity must separately disclose program services from supporting activities as the example that follows shows:

1. **Program services**—Inpatient services, outpatient procedures, home health services, research, teaching

2. **Supporting activities**—Management, administrative, fiscal

VI. **Reporting by Governmental Healthcare Entities** Governmental hospitals are subject to the accounting and reporting requirementsfor governmental proprietary funds that are discussed in the lessons devoted to Governmental Organizations. The financial statements of a governmental healthcare entity include:

A. **Statement of Net Position**

B. **Statement of Revenues, Expenses, and Changes in Net Position**

C. **Statement of Cash Flows** (Cash flow statements for governmental entities have four sections of cash flow: operations, investing, capital-related financing, and non-capital related financing).

D. The statement of revenues, expenses, and changes in net position for a governmental healthcare are required to distinguish between operating and nonoperating activities and provide an intermediate subtotal for operating income or loss. This is different from not-for-profit entities that are permitted but not required to display operating and nonoperating information. Moreover, unlike not-for-profit organizations, governmental entities do not have to report transactions by the type of restriction (with and without donor restriction). The governmental statement of revenues, expenses, and changes in net position takes the following format:

Operating revenues (detailed)

Total operating revenues

Operating expenses (detailed)

Total operating expenses

Operating income (loss)

Nonoperating revenues and expenses (detailed)

Income before other revenues, expenses, gains, losses, and transfers

Capital contributions (grant, developer, and other); additions to permanent and term endowments; special and extraordinary items (detailed); and transfers

Increase (decrease) in net position

Net position-beginning of period

Net position-end of period

E. **Bad Debt Expense** Governmental entities never report bad debt expense in financial statements. All revenues are reported net of uncollectible amounts.

F. **Nonoperating Revenue and Gains/Losses**

1. This category includes most **unrestricted** bequests and cash donations, most **donated services**, and **unrestricted** earnings on investments, including endowment income.

Example

Belpark Hospital received the following contributions:

Contributions restricted for cancer research	$50,000
Unrestricted bequest	$25,000
Record-keeping services donated by current employees (these services would have been purchased)	$10,000
Bandages and ointments contributed by a supplier	$5,000
Government grant to fund research on birth defects	$20,000

Belpark reports Other Operating Revenue of $75,000 (50,000 + 5,000 + 20,000) and Nonoperating Gains of $35,000 (25,000 + 10,000).

G. **Contributions Other than Cash**—To properly report these donations, you must carefully evaluate the type and purpose of the contributions:

1. **Materials**—When goods and supplies normally purchased by the organization are donated, the items are **recorded as inventory or as an expense**, as appropriate, and the contribution is reported as Other Operating Revenue.

2. **Services**—Donated services may only be recorded if: (1) a nonfinancial asset is enhanced or (2) special skills are required and the service is provided by someone possessing those skills and the services would have otherwise have been purchased by the organization. If the service can be recognized, then it is necessary to look at the purpose of the service in order to report it:

   a. If the service relates to the main operating mission of the hospital (e.g., a doctor donates a surgical procedure), record it as an operating expense and as Other Operating Revenue

   b. If the service is of a support or administrative nature (e.g., a bookkeeper volunteers to enter transactions), record it as an Operating Expense and a Nonoperating Gain.

   c. NFP healthcare entities are required to include a performance indicator in its income statement. The purpose of reporting the performance indicator to be comparable to income from continuing operations of a for-profit healthcare entity. In this example, Income from Operations is a performance indicator.

Colleges and Universities

This lesson describes basic accounting and financial reporting for colleges and universities.

After studying this lesson, you should be able to:

1. Recall the financial statements for a public (i.e., governmental) college and university.

2. Recall the financial statements for a not-for-profit college and university.

3. Describe the difference between scholarship allowances and scholarships and how each is reported in the Statement of Activities.

I. **Colleges and Universities**—In general, the impact of ASU 2014-09 (Topic 606), *Revenue from Contracts with Customers,* on institutions of higher education is not significant since many of the contracts these institutions entered into are relatively short term in nature (e.g., tuitions and fees paid by students).

   A. **Introduction**—Colleges and universities use their own unique functional classifications for revenues and expenses.

   1. The following summary highlights the major sections of the statement. The following table shows a formal Statement of Activity for a private college. Boldface titles indicate areas often used for CPA Exam questions.

Revenues, gains, and other support:	Net Assets without Donor Restriction	Net Assets with Donor Restrictions	Total
Tuition and Fees, Net	XXX		XXX
Government Grants and Contracts	XXX		XXX
Contributions and Private Gifts	XXX	XXX	XXX
Investment Income	XXX	XXX	XXX
Auxiliary Enterprises	<u>XXX</u>		XXX
Other Revenues	XXX		XXX
Net Assets Released from Restrictions	XXX	(XXX)	
Total Revenues:	XXX	XXX	XXX
Expenditures			
Educational and General			
Instruction	(XXX)		XXX
Research	(XXX)		XXX
Scholarships and Fellowships	(XXX)		XXX
Academic Support	(XXX)		XXX
Student Services	(XXX)		XXX
Institutional Support	(XXX)		XXX
Plant Operation	<u>(XXX)</u>		<u>XXX</u>
Total Educational and General Expenditures	(XXX)		XXX

Auxiliary Enterprises	(XXX)		<u>XXX</u>
Total Expenditures	<u>XXX</u>		<u>XXX</u>
Change in Net Asset	XXX	XXX	XXX
Net Assets at Beginning of Year	XXX	XXX	XXX

II. Tuition Revenues

A. Tuition revenues are shown at net of scholarship allowances and uncollectible amounts. Scholarships, assistantships, fellowships, and tuition waivers that are given in return for services provided to the institutions are reported as expenses for the department and function where the services are provided.

Study Tip

Scholarship allowances and scholarships are not the same thing. Scholarship allowances are the difference between the stated tuition rate and the amount that is actually paid by the student and/or third parties making payments on behalf of the student. Scholarships are actual amounts paid to students by the college rather than a reduction of charges. Tuition waivers given as a result of employment by the university—such as those given to graduate assistants—are reported as expenses. Tuition refunds (i.e., money returned to students because they *did not take* classes) **are** deducted from assessed student tuition and fees to derive gross tuition revenues.

Examples

1. Students at Maplewood College register for classes for which the gross tuition is $1,000,000.

   The college grants student assistantships totaling $250,000 to 50 students in return for a service requirement, scholarships without a work requirement totaling $100,000 to 10 students, and waives tuition of $30,000 for college employees who are also taking classes.

   Refunds of $50,000 are given to students who drop classes before classes start.

   Maplewood reports Gross Tuition Revenue of $950,000 (1,000,000 – 50,000), Tuition and Fees (net) of $850,000 (950,000 – 100,000) and reports $280,000 (250,000 + 30,000) as Scholarship and Fellowship Expense.

2. Assume a university provides a student a $2,000 scholarship based on grades, entering ACT or SAT, and so on. Total tuition and fees for the student is $10,000. The scholarship would be recorded as follows:

Cash	8,000	
Revenue Deduction—Student Scholarships	2,000	
Revenue—Student Tuition and Fees		10,000

3. Assume that a student receives a $2,000 assistantship for services provided to the Biology Department. The assistantship would be recorded as follows:

Cash	8,000	
Expense—Instruction (Biology Department)	2,000	
Revenue—Student Tuition and Fees		10,000

B. Tuition for **academic periods encompassing two fiscal periods** (common in summer semesters) should be recognized proportionately in the two fiscal years affected.

Example
Blondell College's 10-week summer session runs from June 1 until August 15. By the beginning of classes, Blondell had received $500,000 for tuition charges. Another $200,000 was receivable on July 15.

Blondell's fiscal year ends on June 30. The first four weeks of the summer semester occur in June.

The college should recognize $280,000 in tuition revenue (4/10ths) and $220,000 as deferred revenue in the fiscal year ended June 30. $420,000 ($220,000 deferred revenue from the first fiscal year and $200,000 collected in the second fiscal year) is subsequently recognized as Tuition Revenue for the second fiscal year.

Expenditures are handled in a similar fashion.

C. Revenues for **auxiliary enterprises** are aggregated and reported as a single line item in the Revenues section. Expenditures for auxiliary enterprises are aggregated and reported as a single line item in the Expenditures section.

Definition
Auxiliary Enterprises: Activities carried on by the educational institution but not related to the delivery of instruction. Examples include housing services, dining services, athletic programs, college stores, student unions, etc.

D. **Revenue Recognition for Sponsored Research Activities**—Depending on the circumstances, grants received by a higher education institution can be either contributions or revenue from contracts with customers. In most cases, grants from governments, foundations, and other sponsors provide funds to the institution for the performance of research and not the creation of an output for commercial value. In those cases, the grant is a contribution and is subject to the revenue recognition criteria for contributions received by not for profit organizations (Topic 958-605). However, a grantor contracted with the institution to obtain a good or service output with commercial value then the research agreement is subject to ASU 2014-09 (Topic 606).

E. **Functional Classifications**

Revenues:
Tuition and Fees
Federal Appropriations
State Appropriations
Local Appropriations
Federal Grants and Contracts
State Grants and Contracts
Private Gifts
Investment Income
Auxiliary Services

Expenses:

Instruction

Research

Public Service

Academic Support

Student Services

Instructional Support

Student Aid

Auxiliary Services

Note: Program and support expenses should be disclosed in the notes to the financial statements if not shown in the financial statement.

III. **Financial Statements for Not-for-Profit Colleges and Universities**—Not-for-profit colleges and universities, like other not-for-profit organizations, are required to prepare a Statement of Financial Position, a Statement of Activities, and a Statement of Cash Flows following **FASB standards**. Consequently, the college of universities will also report two classifications of net assets:

   A. Net Assets without a donor restriction

   B. Net Assets with a donor restriction

IV. **Financial Statements for Governmental Colleges and Universities**

   A. Governmental colleges and universities, such as the University of North Carolina, are usually reported as a component unit of the primary government that is financially accountable for the college or university (e.g., the State of North Carolina). Separately issued financial statements for the governmental college and university will follow **GASB guidelines** for proprietary funds and, therefore, will include the following:

   1. Statement of Net Position

   2. Statement of Revenues, Expenses, and Changes in Net Position

   3. Statement of Cash Flows

   B. Three components of Net Position are reported:

   1. Net investment in Capital Assets

   2. Restricted

   3. Unrestricted

V. Because private colleges and universities follow FASB reporting guidelines and governmental colleges and universities follow GASB reporting guidelines, differences exist in the format and classification of some items within the financial statements. Please refer to the lesson on healthcare organizations for a description of these differences.

State and Local Governments

State and Local Government Concepts

Introduction to Governmental Organizations

This lesson provides an introduction to governmental organizations.

After studying this lesson, you should be able to:

1. Describe the characteristics that governments operate in that influence their accounting and financial reporting.

2. Describe the how fund accounting is used by governmental entities.

3. Describe the hierarchy of GAAP for state and local governments as established by GASB Statement No. 76.

I. **Exam Coverage**—The AICPA content specifications for accounting for governmental and not-for-profit organizations, including the approximate weighting of the questions, is shown below.

II. **Accounting and Reporting for Governmental Entities (5–15%)**

   A. **Governmental AccountingConcepts**

      1. Measurement focus and basis of accounting

      2. Fund accounting concepts and application

      3. Budgetary process

   B. **Format and Content of Governmental Financial Statements**

      1. Government-wide financial statements

      2. Governmental funds financial statements

      3. Conversion from fund to government-wide financial statements

      4. Proprietary fund financial statements

      5. Fiduciary fund financial statements

      6. Notes to financial statements

      7. Required supplementary information, including management's discussion and analysis

      8. Comprehensive annual financial report (CAFR)

   C. **Financial Reporting Entity Including Blended and Discrete Component Units**

   D. **Typical Items and Specific Types of Transactions and Events**—Recognition, measurement, valuation and presentation in governmental entity financial statements in conformity with GAAP

      1. Net position and its three categories:

         a. Net investment in capital assets

         b. Restricted

         c. Unrestricted

      2. Capital assets and infrastructure

      3. Transfers

      4. Other financing sources and uses

      5. Fund balance and its five types:

       a. Nonspendable

       b. Restricted

       c. Committed

       d. Assigned

       e. Unassigned

    6. Nonexchange revenues

    7. Expenditures

    8. Special items

    9. Encumbrances

    10. Deferred outflows of resources and deferred inflows of resources

  E. Accounting and Financial Reporting for Governmental Not-for-Profit Organizations

III. Characteristics and Types of Governmental Organizations—Accounting and financial reporting for government organizations is greatly influenced by the following unique characteristics of these organizations:

  A. Lack of a clear profit motive

  B. Ownership is collective and nontransferable (i.e., cannot be sold or traded).

  C. Nonexchange transaction—financial resources contributed to the organization are often not in exchange for a direct or proportionate share of services. (e.g., property taxes are paid to finance public schools regardless of the number of children the taxpayer has in school).

  D. Policy decisions are made by a vote of elected or appointed governing bodies.

  E. Policymaking is often open to the public and news media.

  F. The budget is an expression of the policies of the organization and success is frequently determined by the ability or inability to meet the budget.

  G. All the foregoing characteristics lead to an elaborate accounting and financial reporting structure.

IV. Types of State and Local Governments (SLGs)—*General-purpose governments* (cities, states, and counties), *limited or special-purpose governments* (school districts, transit authorities, and municipal utility districts) and various *agencies and commissions* (e.g., employment commission, economic development commission, etc.).

V. Who Makes the Rules?

  A. The governmental GAAP hierarchy is established by GASB Statement No. 76 for fiscal years beginning after June 15, 2015. Statement No. 76 superseded GASB Statement No. 55.

> **Note**
> *Although the federal government is a form of government, it is not included in the state and local government category and, in general, it is not tested on the CPA Exam. The Financial Accounting Standards Advisory Board (FASAB) considers and recommends accounting principles for the federal government.*

    1. State and local governments—The Governmental Accounting Standards Board (GASB) is the primary authority. **GASB Statement No.**76 lists the sources of accounting principles in two categories in descending order of authority as follows:

      a. Category A: Officially established accounting principles; that is, GASB Statements and Interpretations.

      b. Category B: GASB Technical Bulletins, GASB Implementation Guides, and literature of the AICPA cleared by the GASB.

      [Statement No. 55, which was superseded by Statement No. 76, contained four (4) categories:

        i. GASB Statements and Interpretations

    ii. GASB Technical Bulletins and AICPA Industry Guides and Statements of Position cleared by GASB

    iii. AICPA Practice Bulletins cleared by GASB and consensus opinions of a group of accountants organized by GASB

    iv. Implementation guides published by GASB staff and widely recognized practices prevalent in the state and local government.]

    v. If the accounting treatment for a transaction or event is not specified by a pronouncement in Category A, then the governmental entity should consider whether the accounting treatment is specified by a source in Category B.

  c. If the accounting treatment for a transaction or event is not specified by sources in Categories A and B, then the government entity should first consider accounting principles for similar transactions or events within a source in Category A and B and then may consider nonauthoritative accounting literature from other sources—provided it does not contradict authoritative GAAP—such as GASB Concepts Statements, pronouncements and other literature of the FASB, Federal Accounting Standards Advisory Board (FASAB), International Public Sector Accounting Standards Board, and the International Accounting Standards Board, AICPA literature not cleared by GASB, practices that are widely recognized and prevalent in state and local governments, literature of other professional associations and regulatory agencies, and accounting textbooks, handbooks, and articles. Nonauthoritative accounting literature should be evaluated for consistency with GASB Concepts Statements.

2. Hybrid organizations (governmentally affiliated hospitals, universities, and museums)—GASB is the ultimate authority for governmentally affiliated hospitals, universities, and other not-for-profits (e.g., museums). Remember that nongovernmental, not-for-profit hospitals, universities, and other types of not-for-profit organizations follow FASB standards.

GASB Concepts Statements

This lesson describes GASB's conceptual framework by covering GASB Concepts Statements released to date.

After studying this lesson, you should be able to:

1. Understand the unique characteristics of the governmental environment and the two main purposes of financial reporting by governments.

2. List the seven elements of financial statements and describe some examples of deferred items.

3. List the hierarchy of communication methods to convey information to users of the general-purpose external financial reports.

4. Understand the types of measures that can be used to report on service efforts and accomplishments.

5. List the six characteristics of information in financial reporting by governments.

I. **GASB Concepts Statements**—GASB Concepts Statements do not provide authoritative guidance on accounting and reporting; rather, these statements provide the conceptual framework the GASB uses in developing new standards and revising existing standards. Consequently, it is important to understand the main concepts found in the GASB Concepts Statements.

II. **Concepts Statement No. 1,** *Objectives of Financial Reporting* (issued May 1987)

   A. **Scope**

   1. It establishes the objectives of general-purpose external financial reporting by state and local governmental entities.

   2. It applies to both governmental-type and business-type activities.

   3. The concepts statement **does not establish financial reporting standards—it establishes the conceptual framework to be used by GASB in evaluating existing standards and establishing future standards.**

   4. General-purpose external financial reporting includes general-purpose financial statements, notes to the financial statements, required supplemental information, and other supplementary information.

   5. This statement may not meet the needs of users of specific purpose financial reporting:

   a. **Characteristics**

   i. Used to meet the needs of specific users

   ii. Presents financial information on a basis of accounting that differs from GAAP

   iii. Presents financial information in a prescribed format

   iv. Reports on specified elements, accounts, or items taken from the general-purpose financial statements

   b. **Examples**

   i. Offering statements

   ii. Budgets

   iii. Reports to grantor agencies

B. Governmental Environment

1. Primary characteristics

   a. Representative form of government and separation of powers.

   b. Federal system of government and the prevalence of intergovernmental revenues—intergovernmental revenues require state and local governments to be accountable to the governmental entity that provided the resources and to citizenry.

   c. The relationship of taxpayers to services received—governments impose taxes and provide services that may not have a direct relationship between the fees paid the services received:

      i. Taxpayers are involuntary resource providers—They cannot choose whether or not to pay taxes.

      ii. The amount of taxes paid by an individual seldom bears a proportional relationship to the cost or value of services received by the individual.

      iii. There is no "exchange" relationship between resources provided and services received.

      iv. Governments often have a monopoly on the services they provide.

d. Control aspects

   a. The budget is an expression of public policy and financial intent and as a method of providing control—The budget is:

      i. An expression of public policy

      ii. A financial plan

      iii. A form of control having the force of law

      iv. It provides a basis for evaluating performance

   b. The use of fund accounting for control purposes

e. Other characteristics

   a. The dissimilarities between similarly designated governments

   b. Significant investment in nonrevenue producing capital assets

   c. The nature of the political process—Balance the conflicting demands of different groups within the citizenry with the resources made available by the citizenry

f. Users of financial reports

   1. The citizenry—Those to whom government is primarily accountable (e.g., taxpayers, voters, service recipients, the media, advocate groups, public finance researchers)

   2. Legislative and oversight bodies—Those who directly represent the citizens (e.g., state legislatures, county commissions, city councils, board of trustees, school boards)

   3. Investors and creditors—Those who lend or participate in the lending process (e.g., institutional investors, underwriters, bond rating agencies, bond insurers, financial institutions)

g. **Uses of financial reports**

1. Comparing actual financial reports with the legally adopted budget

2. Assessing financial condition and results of operations

3. Assisting in determining compliance with finance-related laws, rules, and regulators

4. Assisting in evaluating efficiency and effectiveness

h. **Purpose of financial reporting**

1. **Accountability**—This is based on the belief that the taxpayer has a "right to know" and is accomplished by providing information to assist users in determining whether the government was operated within the legal constraints imposed by the citizenry.

2. **Interperiod equity**—This is a significant part of accountability by showing whether current-year revenues are sufficient to pay for current-year services or whether future taxpayers will be required to assume burdens for services previously provided.

> **Exam Tip**
> The concepts of *accountability* and *interperiod equity* are extremely important in establishing authoritative guidance by GASB and are consistently asked on the CPA Exam.

i. **Characteristics of information in financial reporting** (TRUCCR ["TRUCKER"])

1. Timeliness

2. Relevance

3. Understandability

4. Comparability

5. Consistency

6. Reliability

III. **Concepts Statement No. 2,** *Service Efforts and Accomplishments (SEA) Reporting* (issued April 1994), and **Concepts Statement No. 5,** *Service Efforts and Accomplishments Reporting—An amendment of GASB Concepts Statement No. 2* (issued November 2008)

A. GASB believes that service effort and accomplishment (SEA) information assists users in assessing accountability and making better informed decisions. However, SEA is voluntary. In June 2010, GASB issue suggested guidelines for voluntary reporting of SEA performance information.

B. **Elements of SEA Performance**

1. Measures of **service efforts** (inputs)—the amount of financial (e.g., cost of road maintenance) and nonfinancial resources (e.g., number of employee hours used in road maintenance) that are applied to a service.

2. Measures of **service accomplishments** (outputs and outcomes)—report what was provided or achieved with the resources used. There are two types of measures of accomplishments:

   a. **Output measures**—Quantity of service provided (e.g., miles of road repaired) or that meets a certain quality requirement (e.g., percentage of buses that meet a prescribed on-time standard).

   b. **Outcome measures**—Indicate the results that occur because of services provided including accomplishments as a result of the services provided (e.g., the clearance rate of serious crimes) and measures of public perception (e.g., residents' rating of their neighborhood's safety).

3. Measures that relate service efforts to service accomplishments (efficiency) measure the resources used to achieve the level of output (e.g., the cost per lane-mile to resurface roads) or measure the resources used to achieve a particular outcome (e.g., cost per lane-mile of road maintained in good condition).

4. GASB states that SEA performance information should focus on measures of service accomplishments (outputs and outcomes) and measures that relate service efforts and service accomplishments (efficiency).

C. **Characteristics of SEA Performance Information**—Should meet the same six characteristics for general-purpose external financial reporting (i.e., GASB Concepts Statement No. 1)—timeliness, relevance, understandability, comparability, consistency, reliability (TRUCCR).

D. **Providing Context for SEA Performance Information**

1. **Comparisons**

   a. With previous years

   b. Entity established targets

   c. Progress toward achievement of goals or objectives

   d. With accepted norms and standards

   e. With other parts of the entity

   f. With other comparable jurisdictions

2. **Unintended effects**—Significant positive or negative indirect consequences

3. **Demand for services**—Competing demand for resources

4. **Factors that influence results**—External (e.g., extreme weather conditions) and internal (e.g., staff shortages)

5. Narrative information

IV. **Concepts Statement No. 3,** *Communication Methods in General Purpose External Financial Reports that Contain Basic Financial Statements* (issued April 2005).

A. **Hierarchy of Communication Methods**

1. Recognition in basic financial statements

2. Disclosure in notes to basic financial statements

3. Presentation as required supplementary information (RSI) is *essential* for placing basic financial statements and notes to basic financial statements in an appropriate context. **RSI is required**

4. Presentation as other supplementary information (SI) is *useful* for placing basic financial statements and notes to basic financial statements in an appropriate context. **SI isnotrequired**, but applicable GASB guidance should be followed when SI is presented.

V. **Concepts Statement No. 4,** *Elements of Financial Statements* (issued June 2007)

A. **Five Elements of the Statement of Financial Position**

1. **Assets**—Resource with present service capacity that the government presently controls

2. **Liabilities**—Present obligations to sacrifice resources that the government has little or no discretion to avoid

3. **Deferred outflow of resources**—A consumption of net assets by the government that is applicable to a future reporting period

4. **Deferred inflow of resources**—An acquisition of net assets by the government that is applicable to a future reporting period

5. **Net position**—The residual of all other elements presented in the statement of financial position

> **Note**
> GASB issued Statement No. 63, *Financial Reporting of Deferred Outflows of Resources, Deferred Inflows of Resources, and Net Position*, to provide financial reporting guidance for deferred outflows of resources, deferred inflows of resources, and the renaming of net assets as net position. Only items identified by GASB as deferred outflows or deferred inflows can be reported as such. For example, GASB Statement No. 53, on derivatives, and GASB Statement No. 60, on service concessions, identify certain items as deferred outflows of resources or deferred inflows of resources.

B. Two Elements of Resource Flow Statements

1. **Outflow of resources**—Consumption of net assets by the government that is applicable to the reporting period; for example, a decrease in fair value of a hedging derivative is a deferred outflow

2. **Inflow of resources**—Acquisition of net assets by the government that is applicable to the reporting period; for example, an increase in fair value of a hedging derivative is a deferred inflow

> **Definition**
> *Resource*: An item that can be drawn on to provide services to the citizenry.

C. Recognition of deferred inflows or resources and deferred outflows of resources is limited to those instances identified and required by GASB in authoritative pronouncements.

>
> **Example**
> GASB Statement No. 53, *Accounting and Financial Reporting for Derivative Instruments*, requires that changes in fair values of hedging derivative instruments be reported as either deferred inflows or deferred outflows of resources.
>
> GASB Statement No. 60, *Accounting and Financial Reporting for Service Concession Arrangements*, requires that certain up-front payments that a government receives from an entity it has contracted with to operate a major capital asset, such as a toll road, be recognized as a deferred inflow of resources. Revenue should be recognized as the deferred inflow of resources is reduced.
>
> GASB Statement No. 65, *Items Previously Reported as Assets and Liabilities*, revises a number of items previously reported as either assets or liabilities.
>
> - **Refunding of debt:** The difference between the reacquisition price and the net carrying amount of the old debt should be reported as a deferred outflow of resources, if a loss occurred, or as a deferred inflow of resources, if a gain occurred.
>
> - **Imposed nonexchange revenue transactions:** Deferred inflows of resources should be reported when resources are received or reported as a receivable before the period in which the levy occurs (e.g., before the property tax levy).
>
> - **Government-mandated nonexchange transactions and voluntary exchange transactions:** In multiyear transactions, such as a grant, time restrictions may exist. The provider should report all resources received before the time requirements are met but all other eligibility requirements are met as a deferred outflow of resources, and the recipient should report them as deferred inflow of resources. The provider should report all resources transmitted before the eligibility requirements are met and without a time requirement as assets, and the recipient should report them as liabilities.
>
> - **Sales of future revenues and intra-entity transfers of future revenues:** The sale or interentity transfer of future revenues should report the amount received as deferred inflows of resources.

- **Leases:** The gain or loss on the sale of property that is accompanied by a leaseback provision should be recorded as a deferred inflow of resources or as a deferred outflow of resources.

- **Loan origination fees and costs:** Points received by a lender in relation to loan origination should be reported as a deferred inflow of resources when received.

- **Rate regulators:** The portion of current rates intended to recover costs that are expected to be incurred in the future (e.g., for utility expansion) should be reported as a deferred inflow of resources when there is an understanding that unused amounts will be returned to the users by a reduction in rate or refund.

- **Revenue recognition in governmental funds:** When an asset is recorded in governmental fund financial statements before the revenue should be recognized, the government should report a deferred inflow of resources until such time as the revenue can be recognized.

GASB Statement No. 68, *Accounting and Financial Reporting for Pensions*, requires that the effects on the total pension liability of (a) changes in assumptions and (b) differences in assumptions and actual experience are to be recognized initially as deferred outflows of resources or deferred inflows of resources and then systematically allocated to expense over the average remaining years of employment of employees. Similarly, the differences between the expected earnings on plan investments and actual experience are to be recognized as deferred outflows of resources or deferred inflows of resources and allocated to expense over a five-year period.

VI. **Concepts Statement No. 6, *Measurement of Elements of Financial Statements***

    A. **Two Approaches to Measuring Assets and Liabilities**

        1. **Initial amount**—Determined at the time the assets is acquired or a liability is incurred.

        2. **Remeasured amounts**—Determined as of the date of the financial statements.

    B. **Four measurement attributes**

        1. **Historical cost**—Price paid to acquire an asset or the amount received as a result of incurring a liability in an actual exchange transaction. This is an **entry value**.

        2. **Fair value**—Price paid that would be received to sell an asset or paid to transfer a liability in an orderly transaction between market participants at the measurement date. This is an **exit value**.

        3. **Replacement cost**—Price that would be paid to acquire an asset with equivalent service potential in an orderly market transaction at the measurement date. This is an **entry value**. A measurement of an asset at the initial transaction date using the replacement cost measurement attribute is referred to as **acquisition value**; such as assets acquired as part of a group of items and donated assets.

        4. **Settlement amount**—The amount at which an asset could be realized or a liability could be liquidated with the counterparty, other than in an active market. A measurement of a liability at the initial transaction date using the settlement amount measurement attribute is referred to as **acquisition value**.

Fund Accounting

This lesson describes fund accounting.

After studying this lesson, you should be able to:

1. List the 11 types of funds used by governmental entities.

2. Describe the measurement focus basis of accounting for each type of fund.

3. Describe the primary purpose of each type of fund.

I. Governmental Accounting Concepts

    A. Governmental entities use several unique accounting methods to provide organizational control

        1. Funds—Segregate resources according to restrictions on use. In the absence of a profit motive, **budgetary accounts** provide control over expenditures. Modification of revenue and expenditure recognition rules changes the flow of transactions through the accounting records to reflect better the nature of the nonexchange transactions that provide most of the resources for governmental expenditures.

    B. Fund Accounting—Many resources received by government entities are restricted to use for specified purposes. Further, they are often required by law to be "separately accounted for." Governmental entities **use funds to segregate resources** by type of restriction.

> **Definition**
> *Fund*: A separate **fiscal** and **accounting** entity with a self-balancing set of accounts (i.e., assets, liabilities, and residual balances).

        1. The accounting equation for a fund is:

> Assets + Deferred Outflows of Resources = Liabilities + Deferred Inflows of Resources + Fund Balance (for governmental fund types or net position for proprietary fund types and government-wide financial statements)

        2. Purpose of a fund—Funds exist:

            a. To improve management accountability and control; *and*

            b. To meet legal requirements.

        3. Types of funds—Governmental entities engage in nonexchange, exchange, and fiduciary transactions. These transactions are segregated into three fund categories:

            a. Governmental funds—Nonexchange revenues such as taxes, intergovernmental revenues, and grants provide resources for the majority of general government expenditures (i.e., expenditures for public health and safety, government infrastructure assets such as roads and bridges, government administration, etc.) These transactions are recorded in a group of funds collectively referred to as governmental funds.

            b. Proprietary funds—Governmental entities sometimes engage in activities in which they operate much like for-profit organizations. Public utilities, convention centers, motor pools, and airports are common examples of these activities. These activities result in exchange transactions, that is, charges to users for the goods and services that they receive. Most exchange transactions are recorded in a group of funds called proprietary funds.

    c. Fiduciary funds—Governmental entities frequently manage and/or process resources on behalf of other entities or individuals. Since these resources do not truly belong to the governmental entity, they are recorded separately in a group of funds called fiduciary funds.

C. Budgetary Accounting

  1. Because governmental entities do not try to earn a profit, they cannot rely on the profit motive—that is, the need to have a positive net income—to control their spending. Instead, **several types of budgetary accounts are incorporated into the accounting records** to control revenues and expenditures and they are **subject to legal spending limits**. In budgetary accounting:

    a. Formal DR/CR accounting entries—Are made at the beginning of the period to record estimated revenues and authorized expenditures (appropriations).

    b. These entries serve as a basis of comparison for actual revenues and expenditures.

    c. Unless there are changes in the budget, the budgetary accounts remain unaltered during the fiscal year.

    d. Since appropriations are usually valid for only one fiscal period, budgetary accounts are closed at the end of the period.

  2. Purpose of budgetary accounting—Budgetary accounting permits organizations to **demonstrate compliance with legislatively prescribed spending limits and purposes**.

D. Encumbrance Accounting—To ensure that the entity does not order more goods than it has the authority to purchase, an estimate of expenditures is recorded at the time an order is placed rather than waiting until the goods are received. This is known as encumbrance accounting.

E. Financial Reporting—Governmental entities produce two distinct sets of financial statements: the **fund statements** and the **government-wide** (or entity-wide) **statements**.

  1. Fund statements—The fund statements include three separate sets of financial statements—one for each of the three fund categories (Governmental, Proprietary, and Fiduciary). Each of these sets of statements is prepared using the "native" basis of accounting for the fund:

    a. Governmental funds—Modified accrual basis

    b. Proprietary funds—Full accrual basis

    c. Fiduciary funds—Full accrual basis

  2. Government-wide statements—The government-wide (or entity-wide) statements are presented for the *organization as a whole* and, therefore, include information from both the governmental and proprietary funds. (Note that fiduciary funds are not included as these resources are managed only on behalf of others and do not actually belong to the governmental entity.) In order to combine information from these two fund categories, they must both use the same basis of accounting. For these statements, the governmental fund transactions are converted from modified accrual basis to full accrual basis so that the **government-wide statements can be presented on a full accrual basis.**

F. Objective of Governmental Accounting

  1. The objective of a governmental entity is the provision of services to its constituents. The objectives of governmental accounting are to:

    a. Assess the availability of current-period resources to finance current-period expenditures (interperiod equity);

    b. Assess the service efforts and accomplishments of the governmental entity; *and*

    c. Demonstrate compliance with the legal authorization to expend.

2. Interperiod equity measures the extent to which current resources are sufficient to finance current expenditures (i.e., we have a balanced budget). Interperiod equity is fundamental to public administration and is a component of accountability.

II. Fund Structure

A. Fund Categories

> **Tip**
> Remember the acronym C-PIPP DRIP the CEG—**DRIP: D**ebt service funds, special **R**evenue funds, **I**nternal service funds, **P**ermanent funds; **CEG: C**apital projects funds, **E**nterprise funds, **G**eneral fund; **C-PIPP: C**ustodial funds, **P**ension trust funds, **I**nvestment trust funds, **P**rivate **P**urpose trust funds—a mnemonic for remembering the 11 types of funds. Governmental funds are the consonants; D, R, P, C, and G, in DRIP-CEG, Proprietary funds are the vowels; I and E, in DRIP-CEG.

1. Governmental entities are organized into **three fund categories**. The fund category determines the basis of accounting that is used for funds within that category, whether budgetary transactions are recorded in the funds, and whether the funds can report capital assets and/or long-term debt and the financial statements that will be prepared for the funds. A fund category may use either modified accrual basis accounting or full accrual basis accounting depending on the fund's activities.

   a. Governmental fund category (modified accrual basis)

   b. Proprietary fund category (full accrual basis)

   c. Fiduciary fund category (full accrual basis)

2. **Fund types**—Within the **three fund categories** are 11 **fund types**.

   a. **Governmental funds (consonants in DRIP CEG)**

      i. **G**eneral fund

      ii. Special **R**evenue funds

      iii. **D**ebt service funds

      iv. **C**apital project funds

      v. **P**ermanent funds

   b. **Proprietary funds (vowels in DRIP CEG)**

      i. **E**nterprise funds

      ii. **I**nternal service funds

   c. **Fiduciary funds (C-PIPP)**

      i. **C**ustodial funds

      ii. **P**ension trust funds

      iii. **I**nvestment trust funds

      iv. **P**rivate **P**urpose trust funds

   d. There is only one general fund. All other fund types may be comprised of many individual funds.

   e. **Number of funds principle**—The number of funds principle states that an organization should **use the minimum number of funds possible, consistent with:**

      a. **Laws and contracts,** *and*

      b. **Sound financial management.**

3. Governmental fund category

a. The five fund types in this category finance most *general government* activities (law enforcement, public safety, schools, capital projects, etc.) All governmental funds are current funds (i.e., they have only current asset and current liability accounts—no long-term items).

   i. They are **expendable funds**—they are not concerned with preserving capital. All resources that are recognized in these funds should be expended, not retained.

   ii. All governmental funds use **modified accrual basis accounting**.

   iii. All governmental funds can use **budgetary accounting** and **encumbrance accounting** (However, at least on the CPA Exam, not all governmental funds use both.)

   iv. **Capital assets** and **long-term debt** related to these funds are **recorded separately in off-books records**. They are not reported in the fund statements, although they **are** included in the government-wide statements.

Accounting Equation

Current Assets + Deferred Outflows of Resources – *Current* Liabilities – Deferred Inflows of Resources = *Fund Balance*

---

b. **Governmental fund types (consonants in DRIP CEG)**

   i. **General fund**—The general fund accounts for ordinary operations of the government.

   a. Revenues typically come from taxes, licenses, fines, fees, etc.

   b. Most **unrestricted resources** are accounted for in this fund.

   c. Expenditures can be made for **any general government services** not specifically accounted for in another fund.

   d. This is the **only required fund** of a governmental unit.

   e. There is **only one general fund**.

   ii. **Special revenue funds**—Account for the proceeds of specific revenues from taxes, grants, entitlements, or other earmarked sources that are restricted or committed to expenditures for specified purposes other than debt service or major capital projects (e.g., a gasoline tax that must be spent on road maintenance, private foundation grants that must be used to provide training opportunities for disadvantaged workers).

   iii. **Capital projects funds**—Account for **monies designated for acquisition or construction of significant capital items** (land, buildings, and equipment). Capital project funds are **short-lived**, existing only long enough to accumulate resources to acquire or construct an asset and to account for the expenditures related to the asset. After acquisition or construction, the fund is closed. Any **monies remaining** in the fund are usually **transferred to a debt service fund** or, if no debt was issued to finance the project, to the general fund.

   iv. **Debt service funds**—Account for **monies set aside to pay interest and principal** on the governmental unit's **long-term general obligation debt**. Note that the debt service fund **does not account for the liability** itself, only for the monies that are set aside to pay the principal and interest. Its function resembles that of a bond sinking fund in financial accounting.

> **Exam Tip**
> Special revenue funds never account for capital asset acquisition, capital asset construction, or debt service transactions on the CPA Exam. CPA Exam questions always assume that these transactions are recorded in the capital projects or debt service funds, respectively.

v. Permanent funds—Account for resources received by the governmental entity with the stipulation that the principal amount remain "intact" but that earnings must be spent, for purposes that benefit the governmental entity (i.e., purchase of library books, park improvements, and cemetery maintenance). These types of funds are more generally known as **endowments**.

    a. Although the permanent fund receives the endowment earnings, any **expendable earnings are transferred to an appropriate governmental fund** (usually a special revenue fund) to make the actual expenditure.

c. Proprietary fund category

    i. The two fund types in this category account for governmental unit activities that charge fees in exchange for goods or services. The activities accounted for in these funds are similar to those of for-profit businesses.

        a. Activities that are *self-supporting*—that is, in which **50% or more of costs are covered by fees**—*must*be accounted for as proprietary funds. Additionally, activities where there is *intent* to cover 50% or more of costs through fees *or* activities that would **benefit from the additional control measures provided by full accrual basis accounting**may be accounted for as proprietary funds. These activities:

            1. Record and report their own capital assets and long-term debt

            2. Use full accrual basis accounting

Accounting Equation
(Current Assets + Capital Assets + Deferred Outflows of Resources) − (Current Liabilities + Long-Term Liabilities + Deferred Inflows of Resources) = Net Position

---

    ii. Proprietary fund types (vowels in DRIP CEG)

        a. Enterprise funds—Account for activities that provide goods and services to the**general public** as well as to the governmental entity itself (i.e., utilities, transit services, golf courses, etc.). A**service fee commensurate with the benefits received** is generally charged.

        b. Internal service funds—Account for activities that provide goods and services **only to other government agencies and departments** (i.e. motor pools, printing services, data processing services, central supplies, etc.). Fees for these services are generally paid through inter-departmental charges.

d. Fiduciary fund category (C-PIPP)—These funds account for monies and other resources held by the governmental unit in a trustee or agent capacity. In general, fiduciary funds use full accrual accounting to record transactions.

    i. Pension trust funds—Pension trust funds account for **contributions made by or on behalf of government employees to provide them with retirement income and postretirement benefits** and for the **actual expenditures made to retirees** and terminated employees. Related transactions such as pension investment earnings and investment management expenses are recorded here as well.

    ii. Custodial funds—Account for monies for which the governmental unit serves as merely an agent in the process of distributing/delivering the monies to their rightful recipient; that is, when the governmental unit acts as a clearing house, collecting monies for other units and then remitting them as appropriate, usually for a small fee. Many of these funds have only current assets and current liabilities— they do not recognize additions or deductions. Custodial funds are also used for investment pools that are not subject to a legal trust or similar arrangement. In that situation, additions and deductions and fiduciary net position are recognized in the custodial fund.

iii. Private purpose trust funds—Account for trust arrangements for which **other entities** (i.e., external organizations or individuals and other governmental entities) **are the beneficiaries rather than the governmental unit itself**. Private purpose trust funds differ from custodial funds in that they **often hold assets for long periods of time**(These funds are often in the form of endowments.), whereas custodial funds hold monies only briefly before they are distributed to the proper recipient.

iv. Investment trust funds—Account for **monies received into an investment pool created through a formal legal trust or similar arrangement from other governmental agencies to be included in the governmental entity's investment pool** (Note: larger, general-purpose governments frequently provide this service to smaller agencies that lie within their jurisdiction). Earnings on the monies invested are also recorded in the investment trust fund. Note that **resources belonging to the governmental entity itself** that are included in the Investment Pool are not reported in the investment trust fund: **only resources from external entities are reported here**. Resources belonging to the governmental entity itself are reported in the funds that made the Investment Pool contributions.

e. Treatment of fixed assets and long-term liabilities—Prior to GASB Statement No. 34, account groups were used to track long-term items (fixed assets and long-term debt) associated with governmental funds. These amounts were also included in the financial statements on the Combined Balance Sheet. The account groups are not part of the GASB Statement No. 34 model and are not included in the fund statements. They are, however, reported in government-wide statements.

Study tip

Even though the Account Groups are not part of the GASB Statement No. 34 reporting model, it is possible that the terms may still appear as possible answers to questions and even that the examiners might ask how transactions that used to be reported in the Account Groups are now reported. Because of this, it is probably a good idea to become familiar with how these account groups were used.

i. In practice, many organizations may still use the two account groups to track long-term items associated with the Government funds. These systems are well established and the information they provide is still needed, so there is little reason to abandon them.

ii. With this in mind, the following information is of interest:

a. General fixed asset account group (GFAAG)—Used to record fixed (long-term) assets purchased by any of the governmental funds (principally the general fund, special revenue fund, and the capital projects fund), as well as items donated to the governmental unit. Assets were recorded at historical cost or at FMV at the date of donation.

b. General long-term debt account group (GLTDAG)—Used to record general obligation long-term debt of the governmental unit, including bonds, notes, and capital leases. As the debt matures (becomes current) the liability is removed from the GLTDAG and placed in a debt service fund for repayment.

Note

GASB Statement No. 10, *Risk Financing Activities,* required that if a single fund is used to accounting for an entity's risk financing activities, that fund should be either the general fund or an internal service fund. GASB Statement No. 66 modifies GASB Statement No. 10 when monies are set aside for risk management by statute. GASB Statement No. 66 states that dedicated revenue restricted by statute for risk financing (e.g., tax levy for tort liabilities) should be accounted for in a special revenue fund.

Measurement Focus Basis of Accounting

After studying this lesson, you should be able to:

1. Describe how the 60-day rule is used.

2. Identify revenues that are subject-to-accrual under the modified accrual basis of accounting.

3. Describe the two criteria that determine revenue recognition under the modified accrual basis of accounting.

4. Describe how capital expenditures are classified under the modified accrual basis of accounting.

I. **Basis of Accounting**—The basis of accounting defines the way in which inflows and outflows of resources are measured and recognized. In governmental accounting, the basis of accounting that is used varies depending on (1) the fund that is used to record the transaction and (2) the report that displays the transaction results. Two bases of accounting are used: **modified accrual basis and full accrual basis.**

A. **Governmental Fund Transactions**—The governmental funds depend on nonexchange revenues to provide the bulk of their resources. Full accrual accounting, which relies on the matching principal to determine the timing of revenue and expense recognition, is not appropriate for these types of transactions. Governmental entities modify the full accrual basis revenue and expenditure recognition rules so that their governmental funds better match the characteristics of these transactions. The resulting basis is known as the modified accrual basis, which is used to record transactions in governmental funds.

1. A major concern for governmental entities is that they have received sufficient *financial resources* to cover their *financial expenses* (*financial resources* can be roughly translated to mean cash and near-cash equivalents). Therefore, the measurement focus for changes in resources during the period (i.e. revenues and expenditures) under modified accrual basis accounting is on *the flow of financial resources*: that is, on *cash* inflows and outflows.

2. Governmental entities also need to know where they stand financially. That is, they need to know the total amount of assets available and liabilities payable at any given point in time. Thus, at the end of the period (e.g., for the balance sheet), the focus of modified accrual basis accounting is on the *financial position* of the organization.

B. **Proprietary Fund Transactions**—Proprietary funds, like for-profit businesses, incur expenses in order to generate revenues sufficient to cover the expenses and maintain the capital invested in the organization. Moreover, like for-profit businesses, most transactions of proprietary funds are exchange transactions. **Full accrual accounting** is, therefore, an appropriate basis of accounting for proprietary funds.

1. A major concern of proprietary entities is that, over the long run, they earn a sufficient return to cover the full cost of providing goods and/or services (i.e., direct expense items such as salaries and cost of goods, as well as the cost of the capital assets used by the entity). The measurement focus of full-accrual basis accounting for changes during the period (revenues and expenses) is, therefore, on *the flow of economic resources, income determination,* or *capital maintenance. Economic resources* are broader in scope than *financial resources* as they encompass financial resources that are not immediately available (e.g., long-term investments, property, plant and equipment).

2. Proprietary entities also need to know where they stand financially. That is, they need to know the total amount of assets available and liabilities payable at any given point in time. Thus, at the end of the period (e.g., for the balance sheet), the focus of **full accrual basis accounting** is on the *financial position* of the organization.

Exam Tip

Questions asking you to relate the basis of accounting to its "measurement focus" appear on almost every CPA Exam. You should memorize the following relationships:

Measurement Focus

Basis of Accounting	During the Period	At the End of the Period
Modified accrual	*flow of **financial** resources*	*net current financial position*
Full accrual	*flow of **economic** resources*	*financial position*

II. Modified Accrual Basis Accounting

A. **A primary objective of for-profit organizations** is to generate a positive **net income**, which ensures that the capital invested in the organization is maintained and that there is a return to the investors. Full accrual basis accounting is designed to measure a for-profit organization's success in achieving this objective. It focuses on the matching of revenues with related expenses to determine net income.

1. Since governments neither have investors who provide capital to fund the organization nor do they raise revenues through the expending of resources (i.e., exchange transactions), the matching of revenues and expenses is not relevant or even possible, for governmental entities. Instead, the emphasis in **governmental entities** is on the **provision of services** and the **availability of resources** to provide those services.

2. Because of the differences in the objectives, full accrual basis accounting is not appropriate for governmental entities. A modification of the full accrual basis revenue and expenditure recognition rules is necessary to create a basis of accounting that is more closely aligned with their objectives. This basis of accounting is called modified accrual basis.

B. **Characteristics of Modified Accrual Basis Accounting**

1. **Measurement focus**—The measurement focus of modified accrual basis accounting is on the *flow of financial resources,* that is, the inflows and outflows of *expendable resources* (i.e., cash and near cash assets such as marketable securities, receivables, etc.), not on the *flow of economic resources, income determination,* and *capital maintenance* as would be the case in the full accrual basis.

2. **Revenue recognition**—Revenues are recognized in the period in which they become measurable and available (not when they are *earned*).

   a. The terms *measurable* and *available* have very specific meanings:

   i. **Measurable**—The amount is known or can be reasonably estimated.

   ii. **Available**—The amount is both:

   1. Legally due

   2. Received in cash either:

      1. By the end of the fiscal period or

      2. *In time to pay for obligations of the current fiscal period* (known as the 60-day rule).

   b. **60-day rule**—A governmental entity may recognize monies received during the first 60 days of a new fiscal period as revenue of the old fiscal period.

   i. **Rationale**—Because many expenditures for the old fiscal period are not known and/ or not due until the new fiscal period (e.g., utility bills), monies received within the first 60 days of the new fiscal period are usually considered received *in time to pay for obligations of the current fiscal period.*

> **Study Tip**
> Full accrual basis revenues are recognized when measurable and earned. The examiners frequently try to confuse candidates by including earned revenue as a factor in modified accrual basis revenue recognition. *Earned* revenue always denotes full accrual basis accounting.

Example
In Fiscal Year X, Bishop County levied property taxes totaling $5,000,000. The County received payments of $4,000,000 by the end of Fiscal Year X, received $300,000 during the first 60 days of the Fiscal Year Y, received an additional $500,000 by the end of Fiscal Year Y, and received the remaining $200,000 during the first 60 days of Fiscal Year Z.

Bishop County recognizes $4,300,000 (4,000,000 + 300,000) of property tax revenue in Fiscal Year X and $700,000 (500,000 + 200,000) of property tax revenue in Fiscal Year Y.

Note
This means that most governmental revenues are recognized when received in cash, as long as they are legally due. Income taxes, sales taxes, licenses, fines, etc. are usually recognized in this manner.

Study Tip
Although governmental entities frequently recognize revenue only when cash is received, this is **not** cash basis accounting. **Cash basis accounting is *never* GAAP** for governmental entities.

    c. **Revenues subject to accrual**—Revenues that are measurable and legally due prior to the receipt of cash are **normally recognized on the accrual basis**. These revenues typically result from charges that are billed to the customer/constituent by the governmental entity. Revenues that are subject to accrual include:

        i. **Property taxes**

        ii. **Interest and penalties on delinquent taxes**

        iii. **Investment revenue**

        iv. **Regularly billed charges for services**

        v. **Taxes collected by other government units but not yet remitted**

Note
Even though revenue is recognized "up front" for these items (e.g., when the receivable is recognized), an adjusting entry is made at the end of the period to defer revenue recognition for any amounts that have not been received in cash within 60 days after the end of the fiscal period.

    d. Therefore, even though we credit revenue when the bill is sent out, the amount of revenue actually reported on the financial statements is consistent with the modified accrual basis revenue recognition rules.

Example
Fayette County Sheriff's Department billed residents $1,200,000 for special security services provided during the year. Of these receivables, $800,000 was paid within the fiscal period and an additional $200,000 was paid during the first 60 days of the next period.

How much revenue should Fayette County recognize when the bills for these services are sent out?

When the bills are sent out, Fayette County recognizes revenue in the full amount of the billing:

DR: Receivables	$1,200,000	
CR: Revenue		$1,200,000

How much revenue is reported for these services on the financial statements?

The revenue reported on the financial statements equals the amount received in cash during the fiscal period or within the first 60 days of the next fiscal period: $1,000,000 ($800,0000 + $200,000)

How should any amounts not recognized as revenue be reported?

The remaining amount should be reported as Deferred Inflows of Resources. The following adjusting entry is made to recognize the deferral:

DR: Revenue $200,000

    CR: Deferred Inflows of Resources $200,000

---

3. **Expenditure recognition**—Expenditures, in general, are recognized on the **accrual basis**, that is, when the liability is measurable and has been incurred, **except for the following four items:**

    a. **Interest on general long-term debt** is not recorded until it is actually due. *Due* in this instance means **on the due date.**

        i. **General long-term debt**—Refers to long-term debt incurred by governmental funds, which are the funds that provide general government services.

        ii. **Specific long-term debt**—Refers to long-term debt incurred by the proprietary funds. Specific debt is reported in the proprietary funds. Interest on specific long-term debt *is accrued.*

Note

Only interest on general long-term debt is treated in this manner. Interest on short-term debt (e.g., accounts payable) and interest on specific long-term debt **are** accrued. The examiners will frequently try to trick you into treating these items as if they were general long-term debt.

Example
The City of Middleton uses a calendar fiscal year. On January 8, $3,000,000 of interest on its general obligation bonds will be due and payable to the bondholders. How much accrued interest on these bonds should be reported on its financial statements dated December 31?

No interest ($0.00) on this debt should be reported on the December 31 financial statements as interest on general, long-term debt is not reported until it is due.

---

    b. **No distinction is made between capital expenditures** (land, buildings, and equipment) **and period expenditures** (wages, rent, utilities, etc.). **All are simply reported as expenditures**.

Example
The City of Bighorn uses general fund resources to purchase a new copier costing $3,000 for the mayor's office as well as $400 of paper, toner, and other supplies to support the copier. Bighorn's Duplicating Service, an internal service fund, purchases a copier costing $10,000 and $600 of supplies, all of which were consumed during the period.

The general fund uses modified accrual basis accounting and the Internal Service Fund uses full accrual basis accounting. Bighorn reports general fund expenditures of $3,400.

The Internal Service Fund reports $600 of expenses and reports an additional asset of $10,000.

---

    c. **Inventoriable materials and supplies**—These may be recognized as **expenditures either when purchased** (purchases method) *or* **when used** (consumption method).

Example
Marriot County purchases $80,000 of inventoriable supplies during the year. Marriot had $40,000 of supplies on hand at the beginning of the year and $30,000 of supplies on hand at the end of the year. If Marriot uses the purchases method, it reports supplies expenditures of $80,000. If Marriot uses the consumption method, it reports supplies expenditures of $90,000 (40,000 + 80,000 − 30,000).

    d. **Prepaid items**—These may be recognized as **expenditures either when purchased** (purchases method) *or* **when used** (consumption method). Unlike inventoriable materials, however, prepaid items are almost always expenditures in full when paid (purchases method).

Example
At the beginning of the year, the City of Whittenville leased space in a strip mall to use for a neighborhood outreach center. Whittenville used general fund resources to pay $36,000 in advance for the three-year lease. If Whittenville uses the purchases method, it reports lease expenditures of $36,000. If Whittenville uses the consumption method, it reports lease expenditures of $12,000 (36,000/3), the value of the lease benefits that expired during the year.

4. **Increases and decreases in fund balance other than revenues and expenditures**—Funds using the modified accrual basis of accounting have a number of transactions that create increases or decreases in fund balance that cannot be classified as revenues or expenditures.

    a. **Other financing sources (OFS)**—Increases in the fund balance of a fund that do not result in an increase in the net position of the organization as a whole.

Example
Receipt of the **proceeds of long-term debt** and **transfers of assets from another fund** are the most common examples of OFS. Other financing sources are either reported with Revenues or netted against other financing uses. In either event, they are **part of the net change in fund balance during the period.**

    b. **Other financing uses (OFU)**—Decreases in the fund balance of a fund that do not result in a decrease in the net position of the organization as a whole.

Example
The transfer of assets to another fund is the most common example of an OFU. Other financing uses are either reported with expenditures or netted against other financing sources. In either event, they are **part of the net change in fund balance during the period.**

Exam Tip
The ability to distinguish OFS and OFU from revenues and expenditures is a consistent area of emphasis on the CPA Exam.

Budgetary Accounting

This lesson describes typical accounting entries related to the government's budget.

After studying this lesson, you should be able to:

1. List the accounts used to record the budget.
2. Prepare journal entries to record the budget.

I. Budgetary Accounting Requirements

A. Budgetary accounting requires the creation of special budgetary accounts, recording of budgetary entries, and preparation of reports that compare budget amounts to actual amounts.

B. In general, only funds that use modified accrual basis of accounting use budgetary accounting. Even then, not all modified accrual basis funds use budgetary accounts. The general fund and special revenue funds are usually budgeted, debt service funds are sometimes are budgeted, but capital projects funds are not usually budgeted.

II. Budgetary Accounts—Budgetary accounts are used to record budget entries. The budgetary accounts parallel the *actual* nominal accounts found in governmental funds. The actual accounts and their normal balances are shown below:

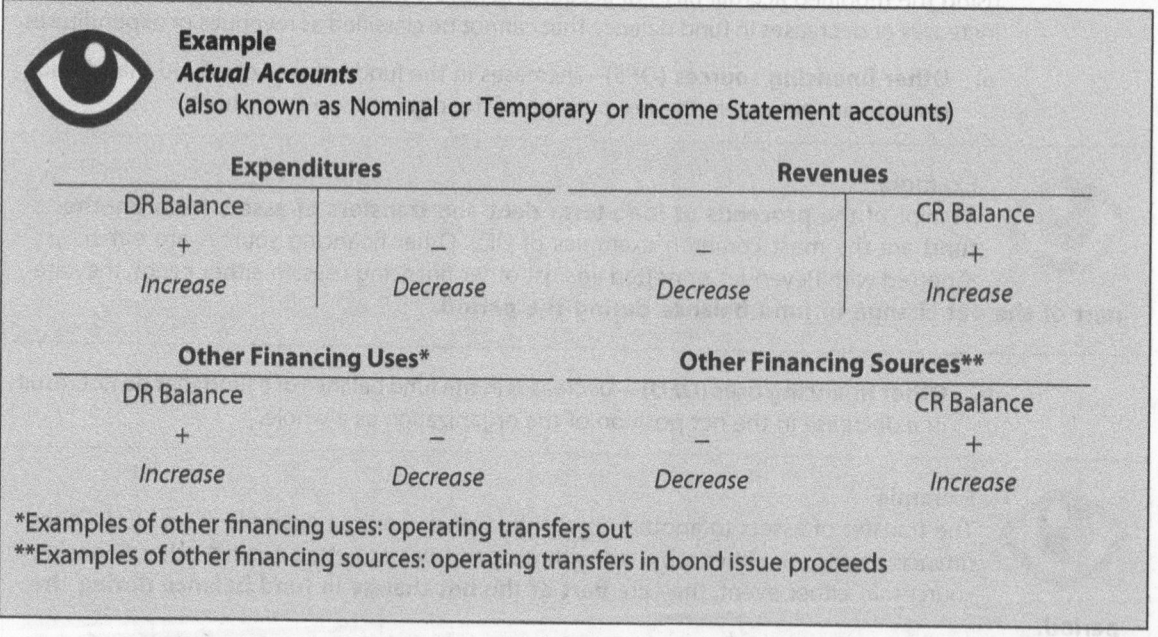

Example
Actual Accounts
(also known as Nominal or Temporary or Income Statement accounts)

Expenditures		Revenues	
DR Balance			CR Balance
+	−	−	+
Increase	*Decrease*	*Decrease*	*Increase*

Other Financing Uses*		Other Financing Sources**	
DR Balance			CR Balance
+	−	−	+
Increase	*Decrease*	*Decrease*	*Increase*

*Examples of other financing uses: operating transfers out
**Examples of other financing sources: operating transfers in bond issue proceeds

A. A parallel budgetary account is established for each of the actual revenue, expenditure, other financing source, and other financing-use accounts. The budgetary accounts and their normal balances are shown below.

Example
Budgetary Accounts
(Note: The normal balances of these accounts are opposite the normal balance of the related actual account.)

Appropriations		Estimated Revenues	
	CR Balance	DR Balance	
−	+	+	−
Close	*Open; Set up*	*Open; Set up*	*Close*

Estimated Other Financing Uses		Estimated Other Financing Sources	
	CR Balance	DR Balance	
−	+	+	−
Close	*Open; Set up*	*Open; Set up*	*Close*

Budgetary Fund Balance	
DR or CR to	*Balance Entry*

B. First, and most important, note that budgetary accounts have **normal balances** *opposite* those of their actual account counterparts. This is the most commonly tested characteristic of the budgetary accounts. You must know whether a DR or a CR is used to "set up" (increase) the budget at the beginning of the year or "close" (decrease) the budget at the end of the year for each of the four budgetary accounts.

1. **Estimated revenues**—Normal balance is a **DR**; the budget office established estimates for this account.

2. **Appropriations**—Normal balance is a **CR**; the legislative body sets these **legally authorized spending limits.**

Note
There is not an account titled Estimated Expenditures. The correct title is Appropriations.

3. **Estimated other financing sources**—Normal balance is a **DR**; this account estimates the inflow of funds that are not properly categorized as revenues (operating transfers from other funds, proceeds of bond issues, etc.)

4. **Estimated other financing uses**—Normal balance is a **CR**; this account estimates the outflow of funds that are not properly categorized as expenditures (operating transfers to other funds, etc.).

5. **Budgetary fund balance**— This is an **offset account** used to balance the budgetary entry; as such, it **does not have a normal balance** but is **debited or credited as necessary** to make debits equal credits within the budgetary entry.

Note
The budgetary fund balance is the technically correct title for this account and is consistently used on the CPA Exam. Some textbooks, however, use **fund balance** as the offset account but this is not what you will see on the CPA Exam. Moreover, for financial reporting GASB Statement No. 54 prohibits reporting reserved and unreserved categories within fund balance and provides five new categories within fund balance to be reported in fund-level financial statements. The five categories are as follows: Nonspendable, Restricted, Committed, Assigned, and Unassigned. Please refer to the "Net Position and Fund Balance" lesson for a more detailed explanation of this change.

> **Study Tip**
> Budgetary accounting is always tested on the CPA Exam. The questions are usually quite simple as long as the candidate remembers:
>
> - The names of the budgetary accounts
> - Budgetary account balances are opposite their actual account counterparts.
> - When budgetary entries are made
> - All of these concepts are tested on nearly every exam.

III. Entry to Record the Budget—The entry to record the budget is **made at the beginning of the year** when the budget is adopted:

Estimated Revenues	XXX	
Appropriations		XXX

DR or CR Budgetary Fund Balance to balance the entry.

    A. There are usually only **two entries** into the budgetary accounts:
        1. The entry to **set up the budget** at the beginning of the year
        2. The entry to **close the budget** at the end of the year
        3. Midyear entries occur only when the legislative body convenes and authorizes additional appropriations or when actual revenues are significantly different from predictions. Note that the offset account used to balance the entry is Budgetary Fund Balance.

Example
In midyear, the Lawrence City Council authorized $150,000 in additional expenditures to repair damages from spring flooding. The entry to record the additional appropriation is:

Budgetary Fund Balance	XXX	
Appropriations		XXX

    B. Entry to Close the Budget—If there have been no changes to the budget during the year, the entry to close the budgetary accounts at the end of the fiscal period simply reverses the original entry.

Appropriations	XXX	
Estimated Revenues		XXX

DR or CR Budgetary Fund Balance to balance the entry.

    A. If there have been changes to the original budget, remember that the purpose of the entry is to close (zero out) the balances in the budgetary accounts, whatever those balances may be. Always DR or CR the Budgetary Fund Balance account to balance the entry.

IV. Budgetary Reporting—For funds that are budgeted, a government produces a budget-to-actual schedule (or financial statement). That report is required to include the original and final budget and the actual amounts. A variance of the final budget to the actual amounts is optional.

Encumbrance Accounting

After studying this lesson, you should be able to:

1. Describe the difference between an encumbrance and an expenditure.

2. Calculate the available balance of an appropriation.

3. Describe how outstanding encumbrances at fiscal year-end are classified in the financial statements.

4. Prepare journal entries related to encumbrances.

I. **Encumbrances Represent the Estimated Dollar Value of Purchase Orders Outstanding**

A. **Using Encumbrances to Control Expenditures**—Appropriations represent legal spending limits prescribed by the entity's governing body. Appropriations are usually established for departmental units and/or for various types of expenditures (salaries, equipment, supplies, etc.). The *unexpended, unencumbered appropriation* is the remaining authorization to spend after taking into account goods still on order (encumbrances) and goods received to date (expenditures). Synonymous terms include: uncommitted appropriations, available balance, unencumbered balance, and free balance. It is calculated as:

> + Appropriations
> − Encumbrances
> − Expenditures
> = Unencumbered, Unexpended Appropriation

Example
Niles County has an appropriation of $10,000 for computer supplies. So far this year, Niles has received and paid for $4,500 of computer supplies. An additional $2,000 of computer supplies have just been ordered. What is Niles' unencumbered, unexpended balance?

	P/O Let
+ Appropriation	+10,000
− Encumbrances	−2,000
− Expenditures	−4,500
= Unencumbered, Unexpended Appropriation	**3,500**

The unexpended, unencumbered balance is immediately reduced by the $2,000 order to $3,500.

When the goods arrive, the encumbrance entry is liquidated (reversed) and the actual cost is recognized as an expenditure, as shown below.

> + Appropriations
> − Encumbrances
> − Expenditures
> = Unencumbered, Unexpended Appropriation

Example
Niles County has an appropriation of $10,000 for computer supplies. So far this year, Niles has received and paid for $4,500 of computer supplies. An additional $2,000 of computer supplies have just been ordered. What is Niles' unencumbered, unexpended balance?

	P/O Let	Goods Received
+ Appropriation	+10,000	10,000
− Encumbrances	−2,000	0
− Expenditures	−4,500	6,500
= Unencumbered, Unexpended Appropriation	**3,500**	**3,500**

1. Note that when the goods are actually received, there is no change in the unencumbered, unexpended appropriation amount: The effect of the transaction has been moved forward to the point of order rather than waiting until the goods arrive.

B. **Encumbrance Accounts**—Two additional budgetary accounts are created to record encumbrances:

Encumbrances		Budgetary Fund Balance Assigned (or Committed) for Encumbrances	
DR Balance + PO Issued	Goods Rec'd	Goods Rec'd	CR Balance + PO Issued

C. **Encumbrances**, like expenditures, is **a debit balance account**. It is increased (debited) when a purchase order is issued. The **fund balance assigned (or committed) for encumbrances** is simply an **offset account** for encumbrances. The balances in the encumbrances and the budgetary fund balance accounts **are always equal, but are opposite each other**. Whether *assigned* or *committed* is used depends on the level of authority required to make the expenditure (i.e., to encumber the amount). If the expenditure is authorized by a formal act of the government's highest decision-maker (i.e., the city council) then *committed* should be used. On the other hand, if the expenditure is authorized by a group (i.e., finance committee) or an official (i.e., business manager) then *assigned* should be used.

II. **Encumbrance Entries**(Note: In this example we assume the expenditures are authorized by a group or an official of the government and, therefore, *Fund Balance—Assigned* is the appropriate category.)

A. **When a Purchase Order is Prepared (or Let)**—The estimated amount of the purchase is recorded as an encumbrance. The entry to record the processing of a purchase order is:

Encumbrances	XXX	
Budgetary Fund Balance—Assigned		XXX

B. **When Goods/Services are Received**—A two-part entry is required.

1. The **encumbrance amount is reversed** (liquidated)

2. The **actual expenditure is recognized:**

Budgetary Fund Balance—Assigned	XXX	
Encumbrances		XXX
Expenditures	XXX	
Vouchers Payable/Cash		XXX

III. **Differences Between Estimated and Actual Expenditures**—When encumbered goods are received at an actual, invoiced price that differs from the estimated (encumbered) amount, the encumbrance is liquidated at the original, estimated amount and the expenditure is recorded at the actual, invoiced amount. As a result of this entry, a corresponding change in the unencumbered, unexpended appropriation balance occurs.

Example
Previously encumbered goods are received at an invoiced cost of $5,500. The estimated cost of the goods was $6,000. The entry to record the receipt of goods is as follows:

Budgetary Fund Balance	$6,000	
Encumbrances		$6,000
Expenditures	$5,500	
Vouchers Payable		$5,500

As a result of this transaction, the balance of the unencumbered, unexpended appropriation increases by $500.

A. **At Year-End**—Encumbered orders not received at fiscal year-end are generally closed out, sometimes as part of the budgetary closing entry. In addition, a portion of the fund balance is set aside to cover the estimated amount of orders outstanding at year-end. Depending on the level of authority by which the encumbrances were established, either Fund Balance—Committed or Fund Balance—Assigned (both are actual Balance Sheet accounts), is used to account for these monies.

Budgetary Fund Balance	XXX	
Encumbrances		XXX
Unassigned Fund Balance	XXX	
Fund Balance—Assigned (or Committed)		XXX

Exam Tip
In the past, the CPA Exam often used these account titles interchangeably: Fund Balance; Unreserved Fund Balance; Unreserved, Undesignated Fund Balance. GASB Statement No. 54 replaced these categories of fund balance with the following five categories: Nonspendable, Restricted, Committed, Assigned, or Unassigned.

Example
After closing all nominal accounts except encumbrances, Morgan City had the following account balances at the end of the year:

Assets	$10,000,000
Liabilities	$7,000,000

There were $2,000,000 of purchase orders outstanding at the end of the year. There were no nonspendable, restricted, committed, or assigned amounts in the fund balance.

Currently, Morgan City's general fund has an unassigned, undesignated fund balance of $3,000,000 ($10,000,000 assets less $7,000,000 liabilities). Since there are no nonspendable, restrictions, commitments, or assigned amounts within the fund balance, this entire amount is available for appropriation (e.g., the legislative body can decide to spend the money).

However, is that money truly available? Consider the outstanding purchase orders. They are not included in liabilities, but they are legal obligations to purchase goods. Should the amount available for appropriation really be $1,000,000 ($3,000,000 less $2,000,000 outstanding purchase orders)?

The closing entry for the encumbrances takes note of this legal obligation:

Budgetary Fund Balance	$2,000,000	
Encumbrances		$2,000,000
Unassigned Fund Balance	$2,000,000	
Fund Balance—Assigned for Encumbrances		$2,000,000

As a result of these entries, the unassigned fund balance is now $1,000,000 ($10,000,000 assets less $7,000,000 liabilities less $2,000,000 outstanding purchase orders/encumbrances). The obligation for the outstanding purchase orders is seen in the Fund Balance—Assigned account balance of $2,000,000.

1. Note that after all closing entries have been made, the balance in the fund balance—assigned (or committed) account includes the amount outstanding encumbrances at year-end. According to GASB Statement No. 54, the fund-level financial statements are not separately displayed in the financial statements, but they should be disclosed in the notes to the financial statements.

IV. **Reversing Entries**—At the beginning of the next fiscal year: The closing entry for encumbrances is usually at least partially reversed. Because of this entry, the prior year encumbrances are then treated like any other encumbrance when the order is received.

Encumbrances—Prior Year	2,000,000	
Budgetary Fund Balance		2,000,000
Fund Balance—Assigned for Encumbrances	2,000,000	
Unassigned Fund Balance		2,000,000

A. Since the fund balance and reservations of fund balance accounts are used only for financial reporting and, therefore, do not affect transaction processing during the year, the reversing entries may not occur. Instead, the balance in the assigned account stays in place throughout the year, and it is simply adjusted to equal the total outstanding encumbrances at the end of the year.

Example

At the beginning of the fiscal year, Bremerton County reported $15,000,000 in its unassigned fund balance and $4,000,000 in its fund balance assigned (for outstanding encumbrances). The outstanding purchase orders were recognized as encumbrances of prior year at the beginning of the year but the fund balance assigned for encumbrances account was not adjusted.

At the end of the fiscal year, all the orders from the prior year had been received but there were $5,000,000 of purchase orders outstanding from the current year. What entry is necessary to close the encumbrance accounts and recognize the outstanding purchase orders on the financial statements?

Budgetary Fund Balance	$5,000,000	
Encumbrances		$5,000,000
Unassigned Fund Balance	$1,000,000*	
Fund Balance—Assigned for encumbrances		$1,000,000*

$5,000,000 CR desired ending balance

$4,000,000 CR beginning balance

$1,000,000 CR is required to achieve the ending balance

Deferred Outflows and Deferred Inflows of Resources

I. **Overview**—GASB Statement No. 63 provides guidance on deferred outflows and deferred inflows of resources. Unlike revenues and expenses, which are inflows and outflows of resources related to the period in which they occur, deferred outflows and deferred inflows of resources are related to future periods. Recognition of deferred inflows or revenues and expenses is deferred until the future period to which the inflows and outflows are related. Consequently, segregating deferred outflows from expenses and deferred inflows from revenues in any given period provides users with information to assess a government's interperiod equity.

II. **Financial Statement Presentation**

   A. **Governmental-Wide Statement of Net Position**

   (Assets + Deferred Outflows of Resources) – (Liabilities + Deferred Inflows of Resources) = Net Position

   B. **Fund-Level Financial Statements**

   1. **Governmental Fund Balance Sheet**

   (Current Assets + Deferred Outflows of Resources) – (Current Liabilities + Deferred Inflows of Resources) = Fund Balance

   2. **Proprietary Fund Statement of Net Position**

   (Assets + Deferred Outflows of Resources) – (Liabilities + Deferred Inflows of Resources) = Net Position

   3. **Fiduciary Fund Statement of Net Position**

   (Assets + Deferred Outflows of Resources) – (Liabilities + Deferred Inflows of Resources) = Net Position

   4. **Types of Deferred Outflows and Deferred Inflows of Resources**—GASB Concepts Statement No. 4 (para. 38) stipulates that recognition of deferred outflows and deferred inflows are limited to those items identified by GASB. The following items have been identified by GASB:

      1. **Derivatives (GASB Statements No. 53 and 64)**—Derivative instruments are reported at fair value. Changes in the fair value of derivatives used for hedging activities are reported as either a deferred outflow (loss in fair value) or a deferred inflow (gain in fair value). On the other hand, changes in the fair value of derivative instruments used for investment purposes are reported as part of current-period earnings. The table below describes how changes in the fair value of derivative instruments are reported:

	Purpose of Derivative Instrument	
	Investment	**Hedging**
Reporting of change in the fair value of the derivative instrument	Investment Revenue—Loss	Deferred Outflow or Deferred Inflow of Resources
Reported in:	Statement of Activities	Statement of Net Position—Balance Sheet

GASBS Statement No. 53 limits the use of the deferred recognition approach to those it describes as effective hedges. In essence, a hedge is considered effective when a change in the fair value of the hedging derivative is offset by the change in the fair value of the underlying hedged item. The standard provides three methods to evaluate the effectiveness of a hedge:

a. **Consistent critical terms method**—If the critical terms of the hedgeable item and the derivative instrument are the same, or very similar, the changes in cash flows or fair values of the derivative instrument will substantially offset the changes in the cash flows or fair values of the hedgeable item.

b. **Quantitative methods**

   i. **Dollar-offset method**—This method evaluates effectiveness by comparing the expected cash flows or fair values of the derivative instrument with the changes in the expected cash flows or fair values of the hedgeable item. If the changes of either the hedgeable item or the derivative instrument divided by the other falls in the range of 80% to 125%, these changes substantially offset and the derivative instrument is considered to be an effective hedge. For example, if the actual results are such that the change in fair value of the derivative instrument is a decrease of $100 and the fair value of the hedgeable item increased by 110, the dollar-offset percentage is 110/100, which is 110%, or 100/110, which is 91%. In either case, the hedging derivative instrument is determined to be effective.

   ii. **Regression analysis method**—This method evaluates effectiveness by considering the statistical relationship between the cash flows or fair values of the derivative instrument and the hedgeable item. The changes in cash flows or fair values of the derivative instrument substantially offset the changes in the cash flows or fair value of the hedgeable item, if all of the following criteria are met:

      a. The R-squared of the regression analysis is at least 0.80.

      b. The F-statistic calculated for the regression model demonstrates that the model is significant using a 95% confidence level.

      c. The regression coefficient for the slope is between –1.25 and –0.80.

c. **Synthetic instrument method**—Sometimes a government will combine an interest-bearing hedgeable item with a derivative instrument to create a third synthetic instrument. This method is limited to cash flow hedges in which the hedgeable items are interest bearing and carry a variable rate. Under this method, the derivative instrument is effective if the actual synthetic rate is substantially fixed. The hedge is considered substantially fixed if the actual synthetic rate is within 90% to 111% of the fixed rate. For example, if an interest-rate swap's fixed payment rate is 7.00%, an actual synthetic instrument rate that falls within a range between 6.30% (90% of 7.00%) and 7.77% (111% of 7.00%) is considered to be substantially fixed and, therefore, the derivative instrument is considered effective.

d. Changes in the fair value of derivative instruments, that do not qualify as effective using one of the methods described above, are reported in the Statement of Activities.

2. **Service concession arrangements (GASB Statement No. 94)**—Service concession arrangements are usually public-private partnerships in which a government receives payments from an operator in return for the right to build, operate, and/or collect user fees on public infrastructure and other public assets during the term of the agreement. Examples include construction and operation of toll roads, operation of convention centers, construction and operation of rest areas, operation of correctional facilities, operation of public golf courses, and so on. A more detailed explanation on service concession arrangements and other forms of public-private partnerships can be found in the lesson on long-term liabilities other than bonded debt.

Example
Suppose Blake City contracts with Kameron Golf for a five-year period to operate its municipal golf course in Year 1. In return for an up-front fee of $250,000 Blake City will allow Kameron Golf to retain 50% of profits. Blake City records the up-front fee in Year 1:

Cash	250,000	
Deferred Inflow of Resources		250,000

Blake City systematically recognizes the revenues in each of the five years:

Deferred Inflow of Resources	50,000	
Revenues		50,000

3. **Items previously reported as assets and liabilities (GASB Statement No. 65)**—Prior to GASB Statement No. 63, deferred outflows of resources had been reported among assets and deferred inflows of resources were reported among liabilities. For example, **imposed nonexhange revenue transaction**, such as property taxes, received in the year before they were due were reported as deferred revenue even though the government has no liability. GASB Statement No. 65 was issued to correct this problem.

Example
Blake City receives $1,000 of Year 2 property taxes in Year 1.

Year 1:

Assets	+ Deferred Outflows	– Liabilities	– Deferred Inflows	= Net Position
$1,000			$1,000	No change

Year 2:

Assets	+ Deferred Outflows	– Liabilities	– Deferred Inflows	= Net Position
			$(1,000)	$1,000

a. Refunding of debt—The difference between the reacquisition price and the net carrying amount of the old debt is reported as a deferred outflow of resources (loss) or deferred inflow of resources (gain) and recognized as a component of interest expense in a systematic manner over the shorter of the remaining life of the old or new debt.

b. Nonexchange transactions

    i. Imposed nonexchange revenue transactions—Deferred inflows of resources should be reported for resources associated with imposed nonexchange revenue transactions that are received or reported as receivable before the taxes are levied or before the period that the resources are required to be used according to enabling legislation that includes time requirements.

    ii. Government-mandated and voluntary nonexchange transactions—Amounts provided by a grant or a government mandated program (e.g., environmental clean-up) in which all eligibility requirements are met other than a time requirement should be reported as a deferred outflow of resources by the provider and as a deferred inflow of resources by the recipient.

Example

Blake City receives a $50,000 cash grant and has not yet met all eligibility requirements including a time requirement:

Eligibility requirements not met, including time requirement

Assets	+ Deferred Outflows	− Liabilities	− Deferred Inflows	= Net Position
$50,000		$50,000		No change

Blake City recognized a liability because it will have to return the monies if it never meets the eligibility requirements.

Example

Kameron City requires a $40,000 cash grant and all eligibility requirements have been met except for a time requirement:

Assets	+ Deferred Outflows	− Liabilities	− Deferred Inflows	= Net Position
$40,000			$40,000	No change

Kameron City recognizes the grant as a deferred inflow of resources because it will have to wait for the time requirement to be met, the inflow is related to a future period and therefore recognition is deferred until the future period.

    c. Sales and intra-entity transfers of future revenues—Sales of future revenues or intra-entity transfers of future revenues (e.g., sale of future tobacco settlement revenues by a county government to its county tobacco settlement authority are recognized as deferred inflows of resources by the county.

    d. Debt issuance costs—These costs are expensed when incurred; that is, they are not deferred outflows.

    e. Leases—Gain or loss on a sale and leaseback transaction are recorded as a deferred outflow (loss) or deferred inflow (gain). Points received by the lender in relation to loan origination are reported as deferred inflow of resources. Loan origination fees, other than points, are reported as revenue.

    f. Regulatory operations—A regulator may set a rate that includes a component to cover expected future costs with the understanding that the rate will be reduced by a corresponding amount if those costs are not incurred. Those amounts should be reported as a deferred inflow of resources and recognized as revenue when associated costs are incurred.

g. Pension (GASB Statement No. 68)—Employer accounting and reporting for pensions was dramatically changed by GASB Statement No. 68. GASB Statement No. 68 changed pension accounting from a funding-based approach to an accounting-based approach, which changed from focus from an actuarially required contribution to a net pension liability. The impacts of benefit changes are immediately recognized. Differences between projected earnings and actual earnings on plan investments are recognized as deferred outflows or deferred inflows and amortized into pension expense over a five-year period. Changes in actuarial assumptions are recognized as deferred outflows or deferred inflows and amortized into pension expense over the average remaining service period of all employees. In general, beginning balances of deferred outflows of resources and deferred inflows of resources related to pensions should be reported at transition only when it is practical to determine all such amounts (**GASB Statement No. 68, para. 137**). However, at transition a government should recognize a beginning deferred outflow of resources for its pension contributions, if any, made subsequent to the measurement date of the beginning net pension liability and the end of the government's reporting period (**GASB Statement No. 71, para. 3**).

h. Government acquisitions—A government may pay and/or assume liabilities of former owner to acquire another entity (e.g., acquire a hospital, private school, or golf course). The acquiring government measures the acquired financial elements at their acquisition value as of the acquisition date. If the payment made by the government exceeds the net position acquired, the difference is reported as a deferred outflow of resources. For example, Blake City acquired King's Crossing Golf Course for $2 million but the net position was $1.7 million. Blake City will report a deferred outflow of resources of $300,000. If Blake City had paid $1.5 million, $200,000 less than the net position acquired, noncurrent asset values will usually be decreased by a corresponding amount.

4. GASB Statement No. 81, *Irrevocable Split-Interest Agreements*

a. Definition of an Irrevocable Split-Interest Agreement—An irrevocable split-interest agreement is created through a trust, or other legally enforceable agreement, in which the donor irrevocably transfers resources to an intermediary (which may be the government or a third party). The intermediary administers the resources for the unconditional benefit of a government and at least one other beneficiary.

b. Types of Interests

i. Lead interest—Receives resources from the trust throughout the term of the split-interest agreement.

ii. Remainder interest—Receives resources as a final disbursement at the termination of the split-interest agreement.

c. Term of the Agreement

i. Period-certain term—A specified time period (e.g., 10 years)

ii. Life-contingent term—Upon the occurrence of a specified event, commonly the death of the donor or a lead interest beneficiary.

d. Recognition when the Government Is the Intermediary

i. Government has a remainder interest—The government should recognize the following:

a. Assets for the resources received or receivable

b. A liability for the lead interest assigned to other beneficiaries

c. A deferred inflow of resource for the government's unconditional remainder interest

      d. At the termination of the agreement, the amount reported as a deferred inflow of resources should be recognized as revenue.

   ii. **Government has a lead interest**—The government should recognize the following:

      a. Assets for the resources received or receivable

      b. A liability for the remainder interest that is assigned to other parties

      c. A deferred inflow of resources for the government's unconditional lead interest

      d. The amount of benefits the government receives in a period should be recognized as revenue and a decrease in the deferred inflow of resources.

  e. **Recognition when a Third Party Is the Intermediary**—The government should recognize an asset and a deferred inflow of resources when the government becomes aware of the agreement and has sufficient information to measure the beneficial interest.

  f. **Asset Recognition Criteria**—Assets should be recognized when *all* of the following criteria are met:

   i. The government is specified by name as a beneficiary in the legal document underlying the donation;

   ii. The donation agreement is irrevocable;

   iii. The donor has not granted variance power to the intermediary with respect to the donated resources;

   iv. The donor does not control the intermediary, such that the actions of the intermediary are not influenced by the donor beyond the specified stipulations of the agreement; and

   v. The irrevocable split-interest agreement establishes a legally enforceable right for the government's benefit (an unconditional beneficial interest).

  g. **Measurement**—The beneficial interest asset initially should be measured at fair value and remeasured at fair value at each financial reporting date. Changes in the fair value of the beneficial interest asset also should be recognized as an increase or decrease in the related deferred inflow of resources.

5. **Use of the term "deferred."** This term is limited to items reported as deferred outflows of resources and deferred inflows of resources (**GASB Statement No. 65, para. 31**).

6. **Major fund criteria**—Combine: (1) assets and deferred outflows of resources and (2) liabilities and deferred inflows of resources in applying the 10% and 5% threshold criteria to determine major funds (**GASB Statement No. 65, para. 33**).

Net Position and Fund Balance

This lesson describes the equity section of each fund type.

After studying this lesson, you should be able to:

1. List the three categories of net position.

2. List the five categories of fund balance.

3. Describe when each category of fund balance should be used.

I. GASB Statement No. 54, *Fund Balance Reporting and Governmental Fund Type Definitions*

   A. Fund Balance and Governmental Fund Types—In February 2009, GASB issued Statement No. 54, entitled *Fund Balance Reporting and Governmental Fund Type Definitions.* The Statement replaces the former *reserved* and *unreserved* fund balance classifications with new classifications and it provides guidance for the types of activities that are accounted for in special revenue, capital projects, and debt service funds. The Statement year-end pertains to fund balance amounts reported in fund-level financial statements for governmental fund types. You should expect questions on the fund balance categories established by GASB Statement No. 54 on the CPA Exam.

      1. GASB Statement No. 54, *Fund Balance Classifications*

         a. Nonspendable—This classification is for amounts that cannot be spent because they are either not in spendable form (e.g., inventory, long-term receivables, or property held for resale) or the government is legally or contractually bound to maintain the amount (e.g., endowments in a permanent fund). However, if the proceeds from the collection of long-term receivables or from the sale of properties are restricted, committed, or assigned, then these amounts should be included in the appropriate spendable fund balance category (i.e., restricted, committed, or assigned). Note also that for government-wide financial statements, amounts held in perpetuity are classified as nonexpendable in the restricted net position category. For fund-level financial statements, however, those amounts should be classified as nonspendable.

         b. Spendable—There are four classifications for amounts that are in spendable form (e.g., fund balance amounts associated with cash, investments, receivables).

            i. Restricted fund balance—Amounts that are restricted to a specific purpose when constraints are placed on the use of resources that are either (1) externally imposed by creditors, grantors, contributors, or laws or regulations of other governments or (2) imposed by law through constitutional provisions or enabling legislation. Enabling legislation refers to legislation that authorizes the government to assess, levy, charge, or mandate the payment of resources and includes a legally enforceable requirement that those resources be used only for the specific purposes stipulated in the legislation. Moreover, the government can be compelled by external parties (e.g., citizens, public interest groups, or the judiciary) to use the resources created by the enabling legislation only for the purposes specified by it.

            ii. Committed fund balance—Amounts that are committed for a specific purpose by formal action of the government's highest level of decision-making (e.g., by city council resolution). In contrast to fund balance restricted by enabling legislation, amounts in the committed fund balance category may be redeployed for other purposes by taking the same kind of formal action (e.g., resolution, ordinance, or legislation) it employed to previously commit the amounts. Moreover, constraints imposed by the governing body are not considered legally enforceable.

            iii. Assigned fund balance—Amounts that are intended by the government to be used for specific purposes that are not classified as restricted or committed. Intent is usually expressed by the governing body, a committee or group (e.g., finance committee), or an official to which the governing body has delegated the authority to assign amounts for specific purposes. In contrast to committed fund balance classification, the authority for making an assignment is not required to be the government's highest decision-making authority. Moreover, constraints imposed on the use of assigned amounts are more easily removed or modified than amounts that are committed. (Note: This is the residual catchall classification for spendable amounts not restricted or committed in a special revenue, capital projects, or debt service fund.) Governments should not report an assignment in the general fund for a specific purpose if the assignment would result in a deficit in unassigned fund balance in the general fund.

    iv. **Unassigned fund balance**—The residual classification for the general fund for amounts not classified as restricted, committed, or assigned. (Note: Typically, this classification is only used by the general fund with one exception: negative fund balance amounts in other governmental fund types are reported as unassigned.)

2. Comparing Old and New Rules on Fund Balance

Pre-GASB 54 Fund Balance Classifications	GASB 54 Fund Balance Classifications
Reserved	Nonspendable
	Restricted
	Committed
Unreserved (Designated)	Assigned
Unreserved	Unassigned

    a. **Stabilization "rainy day" funds**—Many state and local governments formally and systematically set aside amounts for use in emergency situations. Stabilization amounts should be reported as a restricted or committed fund balance if they meet the criteria for being either restricted or committed. Otherwise, the amount should be reported as unassigned fund balance in the general fund.

    b. **Encumbrances**—Prior to GASB Statement No. 54, encumbrances outstanding at the end of the year were shown as a reserve in the fund balance section ("Fund balance reserved for encumbrances"). Since GASB Statement No. 54 removes the *reserved* classification, encumbrances should not be shown in the financial statements. If the encumbered amount has not previously been restricted, committed, or assigned, it should be included within the committed or assigned fund balance depending on the level of authority used to encumber the amount. GASB states that amounts related to encumbrances should be disclosed in the notes to the financial statements.

    c. **Government-wide financial statements**—The term "fund balance" is not used in government-wide financial statements. A summary reconciliation of conversion of total governmental fund balances to net position of governmental activities in the government-wide statement of net position must be prepared.

3. The Statement provides guidance on the types of activities accounted for in the following governmental fund types:

    a. **Special revenue funds**—Used to account for and report the proceeds of specific revenue sources that are restricted or committed to expenditure for specified purposes other than debt service or major capital projects. The "specific revenue sources" should be the foundation of the special revenue fund. Special revenue funds should not be used to account for resources held in trust for individuals, private organizations, or other governments. Restricted or committed fund balance amounts should comprise a significant portion of total fund balance. Effect: This is a *revenues-based* approach. Governments that use an *activity-based* approach (e.g., street maintenance expenditures) will need to examine whether the resources in the fund are restricted or committed amounts.

    b. Capital projects funds—Used to account for and report financial resources that are restricted, committed, or assigned to expenditure for the acquisition or construction of major capital facilities of the general government. Effect: These must be capital, rather than operating expenditures, in addition to nonroutine such as buildings, major building improvements, and infrastructure assets. Nonproject, routine expenditures such as buses, fire trucks, and computers should not be accounted for in a capital project fund.

    c. Debt service funds—Used to account for and report financial resources that are restricted, committed, or assigned to expenditure for principal and interest payments.

II. Net Position (GASB Statement No. 63)

A. Net position represents the difference between assets and liabilities in government-wide financial statements (GASB Statement No. 34) and in fund-level financial statements for proprietary fund types and fiduciary fund types. Basically, there are three categories of net position:

    1. **Net investment in capital assets**—This category indicates the fund's net investment in capital assets and is calculated as the fund's gross capital assets less accumulated depreciation and less the outstanding balance of any capital asset related debt (e.g., mortgages, bonds, and other borrowings). However, the unexpended portion of capital-asset-related debt is not included in this net asset category.

    2. **Restricted net position**—At the fund level, this category indicates the amount of restrictions in excess of noncapital related debt and liabilities directly associated with those restricted assets. To be considered a restriction at the fund level, the constraint on the asset use must be narrower than the general limits of the activity. For example, a Water Utility enterprise fund does not report revenues restricted to use by the water utility as restricted net position. According to GASB Statement No. 46, restrictions may be imposed:

        a. Externally by creditors (e.g., debt covenants), grantors, contributors, or laws and regulations of other governments;

        b. By constitutional provisions; *or*

        c. By enabling legislation of the government that authorizes it to assess, levy, charge, or otherwise mandate payment of resources externally and places a legally enforceable purpose restriction on those net resources.

    3. **Unrestricted**—This category represents the remainder of the fund's net position that does not meet the definition of the other two categories.

    4. **At the government-wide level**—Restricted net position for proprietary fund types (i.e., business-type activities) in the government-wide financial statements may be larger than (and unrestricted net position corresponding less than) the sum of the restricted net position used in the individual proprietary funds because the restriction on asset use is more limited in scope at the fund level than at the government-wide level. For example, assets that are restricted for water utility purposes but can be used for any legitimate purpose by the Water Utility Enterprise Fund increase unrestricted net position in the fund level financial statements. However, the same amount is an increase in restricted net position in the government-wide financial statements because the amounts can only be used by the water utility; they cannot be used by the parks department, street and repair maintenance, and so on.

5. Other points

1. Restricted net position can never be a negative amount.

2. Although it is rare, if some assets are required to be retained in perpetuity (e.g., a permanent endowment), then two subcomponents are used—expendable and nonexpendable restricted net position.

3. The net position of a fiduciary fund is held in trust or in an agent capacity for specific individuals (e.g., employees and retirees), private organizations, or other governments rather than for other funds or component units of the government itself. Therefore, the net position in a fiduciary fund is a restricted net position that is typically labeled as "Net Position Held in Trust."

Note
Designations of unrestricted net position by management indicate that the government does not intend to use those resources for the general operations of the fund. GASB **prohibits** reporting designations of net position on the face of fund or government-wide financial statements.

Note

GASB Statement No. 63, *Financial Reporting of Deferred Outflows of Resources, Deferred Inflows of Resources, and Net Position*, replaces *Net Assets* with *Net Position*. GASB Statement No. 63 was issued because GASB Concepts Statement No. 4 includes net position as one of five elements that make up the government-wide Statement of Financial Position. The need for the change was necessary because GASB Statement No. 53, on derivatives, and GASB Statement No. 60, on service concession agreements, provide for the possible reporting of deferred outflows of resources and deferred inflows of resources, which triggers the use of the term "net position" rather than net assets. Under GASB Statement No. 63, the statement of net position can take the following form:

Assets

+ Deferred Outflows of Resources

− Liabilities

− Deferred Inflows of Resources

= Net Position

Net position has three categories: (1) net investment in capital assets, (2) restricted, and (3) unrestricted.

Governmental Funds

This lesson provides examples of typical accounting entries made in each type of governmental fund.

After studying this lesson, you should be able to:

1. List the five types of government funds and describe the purpose of each.

2. Prepare typical entries for each type of fund.

3. Describe how the modified accrual basis of accounting affects the accounting and reporting for major revenue sources such as property taxes and the acquisition of fixed assets within the fund-level financial statements.

Study Tip

Remember the acronym **C-PIPP DRIP** the **CEG** where **C-PIPP** are the fiduciary funds: **C**ustodial funds, **P**ension trust funds (aka Post-employment trust funds), **I**nvestment trust funds, and **P**rivate-**P**urpose trust funds; **DRIP** refers to **D**ebt service funds, special **R**evenue funds, **I**nternal service funds, and **P**ermanent funds; **CEG** refers to **C**apital project funds, **E**nterprise funds, and the **G**eneral fund. Note that governmental fund types are the consonants in **DRIP CEG** and proprietary funds are the vowels in DRIP and CEG. —**DRIP**: **D**ebt service funds, special **R**evenue funds, **I**nternal service funds, **P**ermanent funds; **CEG**: **C**apital projects funds, **E**nterprise funds, **G**eneral fund; **C-PIPP**: **C**ustodial funds, **P**ension trust funds, **I**nvestment trust funds, **P**rivate **P**urpose trust funds—a mnemonic for remembering the 11 types of funds. Governmental funds are the consonants; D, R, P, C, and G, in **DRIP-CEG**.

I. General Fund

A. **General Fund**—The principal operating fund for all governmental entities. Most "general" revenues (property taxes, fines, penalties, licenses, etc.) and "general" expenditures (police, fire, city administration, etc.) are accounted for in the general fund.

B. **General Fund Characteristics**—The general fund is the only fund that is absolutely required in governmental accounting. There is only one general fund. Like all government funds, the general fund:

   1. Uses modified accrual basis accounting

   2. Uses budgetary and encumbrance accounting

   3. Accounts for current items only

      a. Purchases of fixed assets are recorded in the general fund as expenditures.

      b. Proceeds from the issuance of long-term debt are recorded in the general fund as Other Financial Sources.

Note

Although the fixed assets and the long-term debt are not recorded in the general fund, they *are* recorded "off-books" and are included in the government-wide financial statements. These statements are discussed later in the "Deriving Government-Wide Financial Statements and Reconciliation Requirements" lesson.

C. **General Fund Functions**—In addition to funding most of the current operating costs of the governmental entity, the general fund frequently finances many other funds, such as debt service, capital projects, enterprise, and internal service funds, just to name a few—by transferring monies to these funds. These transfers can take one of several forms:

1. **Loans**—Monies that are transferred to another fund and are expected to be repaid are recorded either as **short-term inter-fund receivables** (*Due from xxxxx fund*) or **long-term inter-fund receivables** (*Advances to xxxxx fund*).

Example

The general fund transferred $80,000 to a newly created capital projects fund to pay for project start-up expenses. The general fund expects the capital projects fund to repay the money in six months when its revenues arrive.

General Fund

DR: Due from Capital Projects Fund $80,000

     CR: Cash $80,000

Capital Projects Fund

DR: Cash $80,000

     CR: Due to General Fund $80,000

If the debt were not to be repaid for several years, the entry would be:

General Fund

DR: Advances to Capital Projects Fund $80,000

     CR: Cash $80,000

Capital Projects Fund

DR: Cash $80,000

     CR: Advances from General Fund $80,000

2. **Transfers**—Monies that are transferred to another fund and are **not** expected to be repaid are recorded as Transfers. Although the general fund occasionally receives monies transferred in from other funds, transfers out from the general fund to another fund are much more common. Transfers are usually made to finance another fund's ongoing operations, to provide investment capital to a fund (purchase fixed assets, increase working capital, etc.) or to remove a deficit position. These transfers are recorded by the fund providing the resources as Other Financing Uses—Transfers Out and by the fund receiving the resources as Other Financing Sources—Transfers In.

D. Common General Fund Entries

1. **Property taxes**—Property taxes are one of the few governmental revenues that are *susceptible to accrual*. This means that the revenues are recorded when the property taxes are levied (i.e., when bills are sent out), rather than waiting until payment is received. The standard entry to record property taxes is:

DR: Property Taxes Receivable—Current	XXX	
CR: Est. Uncollectible Taxes—Current		XXX
CR: Revenues (or Property Tax Revenue)		XXX

    a. Notice that property tax revenue is recognized net of the estimated uncollectible taxes. That is, there is **no** *Bad Debt Expense.* Note also that both the property tax levy and the related uncollectible are designated *Current.*

Exam Tip

Examiners sometimes test candidates' algebraic skills along with their accounting knowledge by asking them how to calculate the amount of the property tax levy based on a specified dollar amount of revenues and given percentage of estimated uncollectible taxes.

Examples

1. Property taxes are levied in December, Year X. The taxes are not due until Year Y and are intended to finance activities in Year Y. The entry to record the tax levy is:

DR: Property Taxes Receivable—Current	XXXX	
CR: Est. Uncollectible Taxes—Current		XXXX
CR: Deferred Inflow of Resources		XXXX

2. Hillborough County levies property taxes sufficient to produce revenue of $475,000. If Hillborough anticipates uncollectible taxes to equal 5% of the total levy, what is the amount of the levy?

$$\text{Levy} - (.05 \times \text{Levy}) = \text{Revenue}$$
$$.95 \times \text{Levy} = \text{Revenue}$$
$$.95 \times \text{Levy} = 475,000$$
$$\text{Levy} = 475,000/.95$$
$$\text{Levy} = 500,000$$

    E. Accounting for Delinquent Taxes—When taxes are not received within a specified period of time, both the receivables and the related uncollectible taxes are reclassified as delinquent.

Property Taxes Receivable—Delinquent	XXX	
Est. Uncollectible Taxes—Current	XXX	
Property Taxes Receivable—Current		XXX
Est. Uncollectible Taxes—Delinquent		XXX

    1. Changes in estimate of uncollectible taxes—At the end of the period, the Estimated Uncollectible Taxes are reevaluated and the allowance account is adjusted appropriately. Note that the offsetting entry is to Revenue. Since property tax revenues are reported net of the allowance for uncollectible taxes, a change in the estimated uncollectible dictates that the revenue recognized from those transactions is also changed.

2. **Original revenue estimate was too high**—Lower the revenue amount.

> DR: Revenues (or Property Tax Revenue)   XXX
>   CR: Est. Uncollectible Taxes   XXX

3. **Original revenue estimate was too low**—Increase the revenue amount.

> DR: Est. Uncollectible Taxes   XXX
>   CR: Revenues (or Property Tax Revenue)   XXX

4. **End-of-period revenue deferral**—Although property tax revenue is recognized when the property tax bills are sent out (e.g., the property taxes are levied), if the taxes are not paid during the fiscal year or in the first 60 days of the subsequent fiscal year, then revenue cannot be recognized. At the end of the period, any revenues not received within the allowable period must be backed out and revenue recognition deferred.

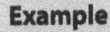

Example
Belmont City levies property taxes totaling $5,000,000 during the current fiscal year. Uncollectible taxes are estimated to be $50,000. When the bills are sent out, Belmont recognizes $4,950,000 in property tax revenue. During the year and in the first 60 days of the subsequent year, Belmont collects property taxes from this levy totaling $4,500,000. Belmont may only recognize the $4,500,000 as revenue during the current fiscal year. Recognition of the remaining $450,000 is deferred by the following entry until the monies are actually collected:

> Revenues (or Property Tax Revenues)   450,000
>   Deferred Inflow of Resources   450,000

F. **Fines and Penalties on Delinquent Taxes**—Fines and penalties assessed by the governmental unit on unpaid taxes are handled exactly as the taxes themselves. That is, they are considered to be "susceptible to accrual" and thus revenue net of estimated uncollectible taxes and penalties is recorded when the fines are levied.

> Fines and Penalties Receivable—Current   XXX
>   Est. Uncollectible Fines and Penalties—Current   XXX
>   Revenues   XXX

G. **Revenues that are not Susceptible to Accrual**—Unlike property taxes, most general fund revenues (i.e., fees for licenses and permits, charges for services, parking fines, etc.) are *notsusceptible to accrual*. These revenues are recorded when they are received in cash, as long as they are legally due.

> Cash   XXX
>   Revenues Control   XXX

1. If they are not yet legally due yet are received by the government, Deferred Inflows of Resources are recognized.

 **Example—The Use of Deferred Inflow of Resources as Required by GASB Statement No. 65**

Note: This is a likely exam question.

Rintner County received an $8,000 property tax payment that was not due until the subsequent fiscal year. Rintner recognizes the receipt as Deferred Inflow of Resources, which is neither revenue nor a liability account, until the taxes are due. (The account title is usually Taxes Received in Advance.)

Cash	8,000	
Deferred Inflow of Resources		8,000
In the subsequent year:		
Deferred Inflow of Resources	8,000	
Property Tax Revenues		8,000

Note

GASB Statement No. 65 limits the use of the term "deferred" to deferred outflows of resources and deferred inflows of resources

H. Long-Term Debt Proceeds—Proceeds received from bonds or other long-term debt issues are not classified as revenues but as Other Financing Sources.

Cash	XXX	
Other Financing Sources—Bond Proceeds		XXX

I. Direct Expenditures—Not all expenditures are encumbered. Bills for services rendered, monthly billings in irregular amounts (e.g., utilities), and items purchased in a retail environment are not usually encumbered. These types of payments are often called **direct expenditures.** They are recorded as expenditures immediately without going through the encumbrance process.

Expenditures	XXX	
Cash/Vouchers Payable		XXX

J. Capital Expenditures— There is no difference in the entry to record payment for a fixed asset such as a computer and a period expenditure such as rent. Both represent *outflows of financial resources* and both are recorded as expenditures. The entry to record purchase of a new fixed asset is:

Expenditures	XXX	
Cash/Vouchers Payable		XXX

II. Special Revenue Funds

Definition

Special Revenue Funds: Funds used to account for monies restricted or "earmarked" for specific types of general government expenditures

A. **Examples of Resources Usually Accounted For**—Special revenue funds include entitlement monies, which must be used to improve public safety, grants to provide housing assistance to low-income constituents, and taxes, which must be used for specified purposes.

   1. All restricted resources can be accounted for in special revenue funds except:

      a. Monies restricted to debt service (these are accounted for in a debt service fund)

      b. Monies restricted for capital projects (these are accounted for in a capital projects fund)

      c. Monies that are permanently restricted (e.g., endowments—these are accounted for in a permanent fund)

B. **Special Revenue Fund Characteristics**—The special revenue fund functions like the general fund except that it accounts only for *restricted resources*. That is, it:

   1. Uses modified accrual basis accounting

   2. Uses budgetary and encumbrance accounting

   3. Accounts for current items only

C. **Special Revenue Fund Entries**—Special revenue funds receive most of their resources from:

   1. Monies transferred to them from the general fund

   2. Intergovernmental transfers

   3. Voluntary grants

D. **Transfers from the General Fund**—These receipts are *always* recorded as Other Financing Sources, *never* as Revenues.

DR: Cash	50,000	
CR: Other Financing Sources—Transfers In		50,000

E. **Intergovernmental Transfers**—Intergovernmental transfers include items such as **grants, entitlements and shared revenues**, which are usually distributed from larger government entities (i.e., the federal government) to smaller government entities (i.e., states, counties, cities).

   1. **Grants, entitlements, and shared revenues**— These are always subject to a **purpose restriction** and may also be subject to **eligibility requirements** and/or **time restrictions**. Recognition of these resources is governed by GASB Statement No. 33. (However, see the note below the examples.)

      a. **Eligibility requirements**—Revenue can be recognized only when all eligibility requirements have been met. *Most* eligibility requirements for entitlements and shared revenues are generic (e.g., they "must provide for the safety of its citizens") and can *usually* be assumed to be met. When there are specific requirements that are **not** met (e.g., they "must have provided training in CPR to all public safety officers"), a liability is recognized until the eligibility requirements are met.

Example

A $50,000 state grant for assistance to single parents of children under the age of three is received. The monies cannot be expended until matching local monies have been appropriated and transferred to the fund (an eligibility requirement).

When the monies are received:

DR: Cash	50,000	
CR: Grant Received in Advance		50,000

After matching monies are transferred to the fund:

DR: Grant Received in Advance	50,000	
CR: Revenues		50,000

b. Time requirements—When resources cannot be used before a specified time or event has taken place, revenue recognition must be deferred.

Example

On February 1, the McClain School District received $500,000 in federal education entitlement monies. $200,000 of the money can be spent in the current period; the remaining $300,000 cannot be spent until September 1 of the following year.

When the monies are received:

DR: Cash	50,000	
CR: Revenues		200,000
CR: Deferred Inflow of Resources		300,000

On September 1 of the subsequent year:

DR: Deferred Inflow of Resources	300,000	
CR: Revenues		300,000

c. Purpose restrictions—The existence of a purpose restriction alone does not delay revenue recognition. This is particularly true when the specified type of expenditure is of an ongoing nature, such as public safety, road maintenance and repair, emergency services, and the like. As long as all other eligibility requirements are met, revenue is recognized immediately.

Example

Lakeland County receives 30% of the tax collected on gasoline sales made inside the county limits. On April 10, Lakeland received $1.5M as its share of taxes collected during the first quarter. By law, these monies must be used to maintain existing roads and bridges.

The requirement to use the money to maintain existing roads and bridges is a purpose restriction, **not** an eligibility requirement. Therefore, revenue related to the transaction can be recognized immediately.

DR: Cash	1.5 M	
CR: Revenue		1.5 M

F. **Voluntary Grants**—While intergovernmental revenues are usually transferred directly to the recipient government for expenditure, most voluntary grants and contracts require that, after a grant is awarded, the recipient government makes the expenditure first and then bills the granting entity for reimbursement. These types of grants are known as expenditure-driven or reimbursement grants.

1. From a revenue recognition viewpoint, the requirement that the governmental entity must first expend resources for the purpose specified in the grant contract can be viewed as an eligibility requirement. Thus, no revenue is recognized when the grant is awarded. When an expenditure is made for the specified purpose, the government entity prepares a reimbursement request. Assuming all other eligibility requirements have been met, the government entity can recognize a receivable and revenue when the reimbursement request is submitted.

Note

Recall that GASB Statement No. 33, which governs revenue recognition for nonexchange transactions such as grants, entitlements, and shared revenues, is a full accrual basis standard. It defines how these revenues will be reported in the government-wide statements (which are prepared on a full accrual basis). However, since special revenue funds use modified accrual basis accounting, GASB Statement No. 33 is not sufficient to determine whether revenue will be recorded in the special revenue funds and reported in the fund statements. The rules governing revenue recognition under the modified accrual basis must be considered on top of the GASB Statement No. 33 rules to make this determination.

Examples

1. A school board makes $20,000 of expenditures in accordance with the specifications of a federal education assistance grant. Documentation of the expenditure and a request for reimbursement is sent to the granting agency.

Expenditure is made:

DR: Expenditures	20,000	
CR: Cash		20,000

Reimbursement is requested:

DR: Grants Receivable	20,000	
CR: Revenue		20,000

2. On November 15, the Town of Live Oak was awarded an expenditure-driven grant of $50,000 by the State Parks Board. This award is appropriately accounted for in a Special Revenue Fund. In December, The town spent $30,000 in accordance with the grant guidelines and properly billed the State Parks Board for the expenditure. Since the State Parks Board normally requires 90 days to process a reimbursement billing request, the Town does not expect to receive the $30,000 reimbursement until late in March. The Town of Live Oak uses a calendar fiscal year.

    According to GASB Statement No. 33, the Town should recognize revenue of $30,000 when the billing is sent to the State Parks Board. However, since the Town will not receive the reimbursement within the current fiscal period or the first 60 days of the subsequent period, modified accrual basis accounting does not permit the revenue to be recognized. Instead, revenue recognition is postponed until the subsequent period. Therefore, the $30,000 is not available under revenue recognition in the modified accrual basis of accounting used by the special revenue fund. GASB Statement No. 65 (para. 30) required use of a Deferred Inflow of Resources in this situation. The entry to record the billing to the State Parks Board then becomes:

DR: Grants Receivable	30,000	
CR: Deferred Inflow of Resources		30,000

    However, the government-wide statements will report revenue of $30,000 during the current year since full accrual basis accounting does not require cash to be received in order to recognize revenue.

III. Debt Service Funds

Definition
Debt Service Funds: Funds used to make interest and principal payments on general long-term debt.

A. **General Debt**—Debt that has been incurred by the governmental fund types. Bonds are the most common form of general obligation long-term debt but other types of long-term debt (i.e., capital leases, long-term notes payable and long-term claims and judgments against the governmental entity, etc.) are also included in this category.

B. **Debt Service Funds**—Do not make payments on *short-term* liabilities or *specific debt* (revenue bonds and other long-term debt attributable to proprietary funds).

Note

Debt service funds do not record or report the long-term debt. They only *service* the debt by making the required interest payments and principal re-payments. The long-term debt is recorded in off-books schedules until it matures (e.g., becomes due). Once the debt has matured, the debt service funds record the currently due portions of the debt. When used in reference to general long-term debt, the terms "current", "due," and "currently due" mean *matured* debt, that is, debt that is on or past the *due date*.

Example

The City of Mayfield uses a calendar fiscal year. On December 31, it has $100,000,000 of general obligation bonds outstanding. Of this amount, $15,000,000 will mature during the next 12 months; $5,000,000 of this amount matures on January 4.

On its fund financial statements dated December 31, Mayfield's debt service funds will not report any of this general obligation debt because none of it is currently due (i.e., *matured*).

On January 4, the due date of the debt, the debt service fund will record the $5,000,000 of debt that matures on that day. The entry to recognize the liability is:

DR: Expenditures—Principal	$5,000,000	
CR: Bonds Payable		$5,000,000

Typically, this liability will remain on the books for less than 24 hours, because the repayment checks to the bondholders are usually written on the maturity date.

DR: Bonds Payable	$5,000,000	
CR: Cash		$5 000 000

C. **Debt Service Fund Characteristics**—Debt service funds use **modified accrual basis accounting** and may use budgetary accounting. Because they use modified accrual basis accounting, **interest expense** on the outstanding debt is **not** accrued, but recorded only when it is actually **due** (i.e., *on the due date*).

1. **Debt service fund entries**

   a. Debt service funds include entries that:

      i. Record receipt of resources to be used to pay interest and repay principal on general obligation long-term debt

      ii. Record investment of those resources and recognition of investment earnings

      iii. Record liabilities related to matured interest and principal on general obligation long-term debt

      iv. Record payment of matured interest and principal

D. **Receipt of Resources**—The majority of resources received by the debt service funds are transferred from the general fund. These transfers are never recorded as revenue; they are always recorded as Other Financing Sources.

Cash	XXX	
Other Financing Sources—Transfers In		XXX

1. **Investment related entries**—are resources accumulated to repay the principal of bonds are usually **invested until they are needed.**

Investments	XXX	
Cash		XXX

   a. Investment earnings—Earnings recognized as **revenues.**

Cash/Interest receivable	XXX	
Interest revenue		XXX

Note
Interest revenue on the debt service fund investments, *unlike interest expense on the long-term liabilities,* **is accrued** as long as the earnings will be received in time to meet modified accrual revenue recognition criteria (e.g., within 60 days of year-end, which is *usually the case.*

   b. Investment management fees—Recognized as **expenditures** in the debt service fund.

Expenditures—Management fees	XXX	
Cash		XXX

2. **Recognition of matured liabilities**—**Interest payable** on general long-term debt is recognized on the day that it becomes due. It is *not* accrued.

Expenditures—Interest	XXX	
Interest Payable		XXX

3. The liability for repayment of matured portions of general long-term debt is recognized on the day that the debt matures.

Expenditures—Principal	XXX	
Bonds Payable		XXX

Note
Under modified accrual basis accounting, both the repayment of principal and payment of interest are recognized as **expenditures** (both require an outflow of financial resources). GASB requires separate reporting of each type of expenditure: **Expenditures—Interest** and **Expenditures—Principal**

E. Payments to Bondholders—If the payable has been accrued, the following entry is used to record payment to the bondholders:

Interest Payable	XXX	
Bonds Payable	XXX	
Cash		XXX

1. Often, however, the expenditure is *not* accrued but is recognized when the payment is made:

Expenditures—Interest	XXX	
Expenditures—Principal		XXX
Cash		XXX

IV. Capital Projects Funds

Definition
Capital Projects Funds: Funds that are used to facilitate resource accumulation and manage expenditures for major capital projects.

A. Capital Projects Funds—Do not have to be used for all capital asset acquisition or construction. The general fund frequently finances purchases of smaller capital assets, such as computers, furniture, and vehicles. Capital projects funds are most useful for large purchases or projects in which funding from multiple sources is involved.

B. Capital Projects Fund Characteristics—Capital projects funds use modified accrual basis accounting and recognized encumbrances. They may also use budgetary accounting (although they almost never do on the CPA Exam).

1. Capital projects funds are *limited life funds*: They exist for the life of the project and are then closed.

2. Surplus monies in the fund at closing are transferred either to a debt service fund or to the general fund. Assets acquired or constructed through capital projects funds are reported in the Government-wide financial statements.

Note
Although the **expenditures** made to construct or acquire capital assets are recognized in the capital projects funds, the **capital asset** itself is **not** recognized in the capital projects fund. Like all governmental funds, capital asset funds cannot recognize fixed assets. This includes *construction in progress*, which represents the cost of an incomplete fixed asset. Assets constructed and construction in progress are reported on the government-wide statements at the actual amount expended to acquire them.

C. Capital Projects Fund Entries—Entries in capital projects funds record:

1. **Receipt of the resources** used to finance the project;

2. **Expenditures** to construct or acquire the capital asset;

3. **Transfers of excess resources** are made when the project is complete (something that rarely happens in practice but is frequently tested on the CPA Exam).

D. Receipt of Resources—Capital projects are usually funded through a combination of bond proceeds, grants, and contributions from the general fund.

1. Debt funding—If **bonds** provide funding, recognize Other Financing Source:

Cash	XXX	
Other Financing Sources—Bond Proceeds		XXX

Note

If bonds are sold at a **premium**, the premium amount is not available for expenditure in to the capital projects fund but is transferred to a debt service fund where it can be used to repay bondholders.

Example

Daley City issued $4 M par value bonds to finance construction of a new police headquarters. The bonds were sold for $4.1 M and the proceeds were accounted for in a capital projects fund. The premium amount is in excess of the amount authorized by voters for expenditure on the project and cannot be expended in the capital projects fund. The bond covenant usually specifies that proceeds received in excess of par value must be used to repay the bond liability. Consequently, premiums are usually transferred to a **debt service fund**.

Record the full amount of the proceeds as an Other Financing Source in the capital projects fund.

Cash	4,100,000	
Other Financing Sources-Bond Proceeds		4,100,000

Record the transfer of the premium to the debt service fund as an Other Financing Use in the capital projects fund and as an Other Financing Source in the debt service fund.

Capital Projects Fund

Other Financing Use—Operating Transfer Out	100,000	
Cash		100,000

Debt Service Fund

Cash	100,000	
Other Financing Source—Operating Transfer In		100,000

E. **Alternative Treatment**—Capital projects funds sometimes separate the premium from the bonds upon receipt of the proceeds, showing only the par value of the bonds as an Other Financing Source and showing the premium as a **liability**(Due to Debt Service Fund). In these instances, the debt service fund may recognize the receipt of the premium as revenue rather than an Other Financing Source. However, most CPA Exam questions do **not** follow this approach.

F. **Grant Funding**

1. If grants provide funding, *Revenue* is usually recognized when the grant is received. However, depending on the terms of the grant contract, revenue recognition may be deferred until eligibility requirements are met or until the monies are actually expended. The general rules prescribed by GASB Statement No. 33 govern recognition of grant proceeds.

Cash	XXX	
Grant Revenues or Grant Received in Advance (a liability)		XXX

2. **Transfers from other funds**—If transfers from the general fund or other fund provide funding, recognize the receipt as an Other Financing Source:

Cash	XXX	
Other Financing Sources—Transfer In		XXX

G. **Expenditures**—All amounts paid for the acquisition or construction of a capital asset, whether for materials, labor, or equipment, are recorded as Expenditures. Somewhat specialized entries occur, however, when construction of the asset is contracted to a private company.

1. When the contract is signed, an encumbrance is created for the entire amount of the contract. As the contractor submits progress billings, the encumbrance is partially liquidated.

Examples

1. Amestown signed a $2 M contract with Bowie Construction to build a new auditorium. Bowie submitted a progress billing for $200,000 when the building was 10% complete.

Entry to Recognize the Contract

Encumbrances	2,000,000	
Budgetary Fund Balance		2,000,000

Entry to Record the Progress Billing

Budgetary Fund Balance	200,000	
Encumbrances		200,000
Expenditures	200,000	
Contracts Payable		200,000

When the progress billing is paid, a portion of the payment is usually withheld. This amount is known as a *retained percentage*. The retained percentage is withheld until the project is satisfactorily completed. If corrections need to be made and the original contractor is unable or unwilling to make the corrections, these monies are available to fund the work. Once the project has been approved any remaining money is remitted to the original contractor.

2. Amestown's contract with Bowie Construction specified that 10% of all billings would be retained.

Entry to Record Payment of the $200,000 Progress Billing Already Recorded

Contracts Payable	200,000	
Retained Percentage		20,000
Cash		180,000

If corrections are required in order for the project to be approved and the original contractor does not elect to complete the work, the work is paid from the Retained Percentage account.

2. **Payments**— Payments for additional work made from the Retained Percentage account do **not** create any additional expenditures

Example
Upon completion of the auditorium, inspection revealed that an additional $80,000 work was needed to correct deficiencies in construction. Bowie elects to forfeit that amount from its retained percentage and let another contractor complete the job.

Entry to Pay the Other Contractor

Retained Percentage	80,000	
Cash		80,000

H. Transfer of Excess Resources—After construction is completed, the capital projects fund is eliminated.

1. Any remaining monies are transferred to other funds. If bonds have been used to finance the project, the transfer is usually to the debt service fund.

Example
Patterson County recently completed a new park headquarters building. The building was financed through bond issues and the construction was accounted for in a Capital Projects Fund. After all bills were paid, $30,000 cash remained in the fund.

Entry to Record the Transfer of the Cash to the Debt Service Fund

Capital Projects Fund:

Other Financing Use—Transfer Out	30,000	
Cash		30,000

Debt Service Fund:

Cash	30,000	
Other Financing Source—Transfer In		30,000

Entry to Close the Capital Projects Fund (assuming all other accounts had been closed prior to transfer of the cash to the debt service fund)

Capital Projects Fund:

Fund Balance	30,000	
Other Financing Use—Operating Transfer Out		30,000

V. Permanent Funds

Definition
Permanent Funds: Funds that account for the principal and earnings of endowments that must be used for the benefit of governmental programs

A. The Endowment Principal—This is typically received as a contribution or a bequest from a private individual or organization. By accepting the endowment, the governmental entity agrees to invest and maintain the principal intact, usually in perpetuity, and to expend the net earnings on the investment for the purposes stated in the endowment agreement. In order to be accounted for in a permanent fund, the purposes must be in support of government programs or for the benefit of the constituents in general.

> **Note**
> Most CPA Exam questions about permanent funds focus on whether it is appropriate to account for a contribution or bequest in a permanent fund. If the resources contributed need **not** be held in perpetuity but may be expended for the governmental purpose, they should be not accounted for in a permanent fund but would most likely be accounted for in a **special revenue fund**. If the purpose of the expenditures is for a nongovernmental purpose or the benefit of specific individuals (e.g., to provide an annual award to recognize an outstanding business), the resources should be accounted for in a **private purpose trust fund**.

B. **Characteristics of Permanent Funds**—Permanent funds use modified accrual basis accounting, but they are not usually budgeted nor do they typically use encumbrances. Although they account for the nonexpendable endowment principal and the expendable earnings on the endowment, they do **not** account for the related expenditures (i.e., expenditures for the purpose(s) specified in the endowment agreement). Instead, the net expendable earnings are transferred to the fund responsible for the specified type of expenditure, which is usually a special revenue fund.

C. **Permanent Fund Entries**—Entries in permanent funds are usually limited to recognition of:

   1. Receipt of the endowment principal

   2. Receipt of investment earnings

   3. Transfer of net expendable earnings

D. **Receipt of Endowment Principal**—GASB Statement No. 33 specifically requires that the receipt of endowment principal (a nonexchange transaction) be recognized as Revenue when received.

E. **Investment Earnings**—Investment earnings have two components: **periodic income** (i.e. interest and dividends) and **capital gains** (gains and losses on the sale of investments). Depending on the endowment agreement, these two components can receive very different accounting treatments.

   1. **Interest and dividends**—Interest and dividends, net of any related expenses, are usually considered fully expendable. The gross revenue is recognized in the permanent fund.

   2. Investment management fees and other expenditures required to maintain the endowment principal are also recognized in the permanent fund. These fees are deducted from investment earnings to determine net expendable earnings.

   3. **Capital gains (and losses)**—In the absence of specific instructions to the contrary, gains (and losses) on the sale of investments are usually considered to be adjustments to the principal. That is, they are **not** expendable.

F. **Transfer of Net Expendable Earnings**—The permanent fund does not make Expenditures for the purpose(s) identified in the endowment agreement. Instead, the earnings are transferred to the fund responsible for the type of expenditure specified in the agreement.

G. **Net Expendable Earnings**—Determined by deducting management fees and other charges necessary to maintain the principal from periodic investment income (interest and dividends).

H. **GASB Statement No. 52, *Land and Other Real Estate Held as Investments by Endowments*—** Prior to this standard, permanent and term endowments, including permanent funds, reported land and other real estate held as investments at their historical cost. This statement requires that endowments report their land and other real estate investments at fair value. Changes in fair value should be reported as investment income.

Example

The City of Towson recently received an endowment consisting of $1,000,000 of cash and securities. The endowment agreement specified that the net earnings on the endowment were to be used to support after-school recreational activities in the city parks. During the year, the endowment received $45,000 of interest revenue and paid $2,000 in investment management fees. Expenditures totaling $20,000 were made for the purposes designated in the endowment agreement.

Entry to Record Receipt of Endowment Principal

Note: The permanent fund is the appropriate fund in which to record the endowment as a provision of recreational activities is a governmental function that benefits the citizenry in general.

Permanent Fund:

Cash/Securities	1,0000,000	
Revenue		1,0000,000

Entry to Record Receipt of Interest Revenue

Permanent Fund:

Cash	45,000	
Revenue—Interest		45,000

Entry to Record Payment of Investment Management Fees

Permanent funds can make expenditures necessary to maintain and manage the endowment principal.

Permanent Fund:

Expenditures—Investment Management	2,000	
Cash		2,000

Entry to Record Transfer of Net Expendable Earnings to an Expendable Fund

In this case, we assume a special revenue fund.

Permanent Fund:

Other Financing Uses—Transfer Out	43,000	
Cash		43,000

Special Revenue Fund:

Cash	43,000	
Other Financing Sources		43,000

Entry to Record Expenditure for the Purpose of the Endowment

Special Revenue Fund:

Expenditures	20,000	
Cash		20,000

Proprietary Funds

This lesson describes the financial reporting for proprietary funds.

After studying this lesson, you should be able to:

1. List the two types of proprietary funds and describe the purpose of each.

2. List the three types of financial statements for proprietary funds.

3. Explain the difference in the primary service user and fee pricing policies for internal service funds and enterprise funds.

4. List the four sections of the Statement of Cash Flows for proprietary funds.

Tip

Remember the acronym **C-PIPP DRIP** the **CEG** where **C-PIPP** are the fiduciary funds: **C**ustodial funds, **P**ension trust funds (aka Post-employment trust funds), **I**nvestment trust funds, and **P**rivate-Purpose trust funds; **DRIP** refers to **D**ebt service funds, special **R**evenue funds, **I**nternal service funds, and **P**ermanent funds; **CEG** refers to **C**apital project funds, **E**nterprise funds, and the **G**eneral fund. Note that governmental fund types are the consonants in **DRIP CEG** and proprietary funds are the vowels in DRIP and CEG.

I. **Internal Service Funds**

    A. **Characteristics**—These funds use full accrual accounting since they are concerned with measuring profit and maintaining capital. Therefore, they:

        1. Carry their own fixed assets and long-term debt

        2. Record depreciation expense

        3. Use standard accounting terminology (i.e., expenses, not expenditures, and net position, not fund balance)

    B. **Reporting in Government-Wide Financial Statements**—Internal service funds are not reported as part of business activities in the government-wide financial statements. Since internal service funds provide services primarily to the reporting government itself, the internal service fund accounts are primarily adjusted into the governmental activities of the government-wide financial statements. Moreover, an internal service fund can never be classified as a major fund for funds-level financial reporting and internal service fund account balances (e.g., total assets) are not used in determining major funds when applying the 10% and 5% rules.

    C. **Look to the Customer**—GASB states that internal service funds should be only if the reporting government is the predominant customer in the activity, otherwise an enterprise fund should be used.

    D. **Financed**—Internal service funds are financed through charges to user departments (which are usually intended to recover at least 50% of operating costs) and contributions from the general fund. Although there are exceptions, the general **pricing policy** in establishing user fees for services and goods provided by internal service funds is to achieve break-even of user fees compared to operating expenses.

    E. **Receive Transfers**—Internal service funds most often receive transfers from the General Fund to provide capital for the initial start-up of the fund or for later expansion. These transfers are reported as Transfers (In) by the internal service fund and as Other Financing Uses—Transfers (Out) by the General Fund. At year-end, the internal service fund will close this amount to its Net Position account.

Note

Under GASB Statement No. 33, no distinctions are made between Residual Equity Transfers (start-up funds or funds transferred out when closing a fund) and Operating Transfers.

F. **Subsidized**—Transfers from the general fund may also subsidize the day-to-day operations of the internal service fund. These transfers are reported as Transfers (In) by the internal service fund and as Other Financing Uses—Transfers (Out) by the general fund. At year-end, the internal service fund will close this amount to its Net Position account.

Example

ABC County maintains a motor pool to provide transportation for county administrators on official business. ABC follows a practice of subsidizing 30% of the operating costs of the motor pool from General Fund resources. During the current period, ABC transferred $36,000 to subsidize current operations and transferred another $80,000 to expand the motor pool by four vehicles. How should these transfers be reported?

General Fund

Other Financing Uses—Operating Transfer-Out	116,000	
Cash		116,000

Internal Service Fund

Cash	116,000	
Operating Transfer-In		116,000

G. **Transactions**—When the internal service fund charges fees to other departments for goods and services, the transactions are recorded just as they would be if the transaction was with an external business. That is, the internal service fund recognizes operating revenue and the recipient fund recognizes an expenditure (or expense, as appropriate for the fund). These transactions are called Quasi-External Transactions.

1. All charges for services (i.e., revenue) that would normally result in a debit to the Accounts Receivable account, are shown as amounts "Due from (fund name)."

Due from General Fund	XXX	
Billings to Departments (an Operating Revenue)		XXX

2. Statement of Revenues, Expenses, and Changes in Fund Net Position distinguishes *operating revenues* (charges for goods and services) from *nonoperating revenues* (interest) from *operating transfers* (regular, recurring transfers from the general fund intended to subsidize operations and grants).

   a. Earnings retained in an internal service fund and contributions to equity made by another fund (e.g., general fund) that are not to be repaid are closed to the equity account Net Position—Unrestricted. Excess of Net Billings to Departments over Costs, if a gain, (or Excess of Costs over Net Billings to Departments, if a loss) is the account title typically used in closing temporary accounts at year's end (i.e., the income summary account name);

   b. Monies from another fund (e.g., general fund) that are used for temporary financing needs and are expected to be repaid are accounted for by crediting "Advances from (fund name)," which is a liability account.

3. The equity section of the Balance Sheet has three principal accounts:

    a. **Net Investment in Capital Assets** (Note: If interfund loans and other debt exceed the internal service fund amount of capital assets net of accumulated depreciation, then there is no net investment in capital assets to report; i.e., only a positive net investment in capital assets is reported),

    b. **Restricted Net Position**—(Typically, internal service funds do not have assets restricted for use by external resource providers or legislative action; when that is the case restricted net position will not appear in the internal service fund Statement of Net Position),

    c. **Unrestricted Net Position**

    d. The general format for the Statement of Revenues, Expenses, and Changes in Fund Net Position is:

> Operating Revenues (detailed)
>
> Total Operating Revenues
>
> Operating Expenses (detailed)
>
> Total Operating Expenses
>
> Operating Income (Loss)
>
> Nonoperating Revenues, Expenses, Gains, Losses, and Transfers (detailed)
>
> Change in Net Position
>
> Net Position—Beginning of Period
>
> Net Position—End of Period

    e. Generally, the Statement of Net Position follows the following format. (Note: Deferred outflows and deferred inflow of resources are not shown since they are unlikely for internal service funds):

> Assets:
>
> Current Assets (detailed)
>
> Capital Assets (detailed)
>
> Total Assets
>
> Liabilities:
>
> Current Liabilities (detailed)
>
> Long-Term Liabilities
>
> Total Liabilities
>
> Net Position:
>
> Net Investment in Capital Assets (a positive amount only)
>
> Restricted (by external resource providers or legislative action)
>
> Unrestricted
>
> Total Net Position

4. The Statement of Cash Flows has four categories (as opposed to the three categories found in for-profit statements):

    a. Operations—From the production of goods and services only (i.e., operating income, not net income) using the **direct method**; this excludes items such as interest and operating transfers, Note: GASB requires a reconciliation of operating income to net cash provided by operating activities is required,

    b. Noncapital financing—from debtor activities not clearly related to capital transactions (e.g., operating grants),

    c. Capital financing—from the acquisition or disposal of capital assets or borrowing and repayment clearly related to capital activities, which can include advances from other funds for the purpose of financing capital acquisitions,

    d. Investing—from gains and losses on investments and creditor activities and interest (less likely for internal services funds than for enterprise funds).

5. **Enterprise Funds**

    1. These funds account for entities that provide goods and services to the general public, such as urban transportation departments, swimming pools, electric and water utilities, airports, ports, government run hospitals, toll roads and bridges, parking lots, parking garages, public housing projects, state-run lotteries, and the like.

    2. GASB requires activities to be reported as enterprise funds if any one of the following criteria in the context of the activity's principal revenues sources is met:

        a. The activity is financed with debt that is secured solely by a pledge of the net revenues from fees and charges of the activity (e.g., revenue bonds);

        b. Laws or regulations require that the activity's costs of providing services including capital costs be recovered with fees and changes, rather than with taxes or similar revenues; *or*

        c. The pricing policies of the activity establish fees and charges designed to recover the costs, including capital costs (such as depreciation or debt service).

    3. **Restricted assets**—Enterprise funds, especially utilities, frequently have assets whose use is restricted by contractual or legal requirements. For example, refundable customer deposits held by a utility are classified as Cash under the Restricted Assets category in the utility's Statement of Net Position. Similarly, assets held for the retirement of revenue bonds as required by bond covenants are also classified under the Restricted Asset category. Another common restricted asset is assets set aside to fund capital acquisitions, replacements, and improvements **Liabilities payable from Restricted Assets**: liabilities Payable from Restricted Assets, such as Refundable Customer Deposits, are reported separately from Current Liabilities. The difference between Restricted Net Assets and Liabilities Payable from Restricted Net Assets is reported as **Restricted Net Position**.

        a. Liabilities Payable from Restricted Assets—Such as refundable customer deposits, are reported separately from Current Liabilities. The difference between Restricted Net Assets and Liabilities Payable from Restricted Net Assets is reported as **Restricted Net Position**.

    4. **Utility plant and construction work in process**—It is common for utility enterprise funds to report utility plant assets and construction work in process in the Statement of Net Position. Net utility plant less related debt is reported in **Net Position as Net Investment in Capital Assets**.

    5. **Customer Advances for Construction**—It is common practice for utilities to require its customers to advance a portion of the estimated cost of construction projects that occur at the request of the customers. These advances are reported as a separate item under liabilities. The amount of the advance refunded to the customer, either wholly or partially, is usually applied against billings for service (i.e., a reduction in account

receivable). The balance of customer advances not refunded (retained by the utility) is reported as **Contributions from Customers** in the statement of revenues, expenses, and changes in fund net position.

6. **Long-term liabilities**—Bonds secured by an enterprise fund's revenues are a common form of long-term debt. However, some bonds also are secured either in part of wholly by the government's full faith and credit. If the intent is to service the bonds from enterprise fund's revenues GASB standards require the bonds to be reported as a liability of the enterprise fund.

7. The general format of a utility enterprise fund statement of net position is:

Assets:
Current Assets
Restricted Assets
Utility Plant
Other Noncurrent Assets
Total Assets
Liabilities:
Current Liabilities
Liabilities Payable from Restricted Assets
Long-Term Liabilities
Total Liabilities
Net Position:
Net Investment in Capital Assets
Restricted
Unrestricted
Total Net Position

Note
GASB Statement No. 62, *Codification of Accounting and Financial Reporting Guidance Contained in Pre-November 30, 1989 FASB and AICPA Pronouncements*, incorporates into the GASB codification guidance that was found in FASB and AICPA pronouncements. The change was necessary because the FASB Accounting Standards Codification, which supersedes the previous FASB pronouncements, would no longer be readily available to some GASB constituents. Through the issuance of GASB Statement No. 62, that guidance is now readily available within the GASB codification. In addition, GASB Statement No. 62 eliminated an election for enterprise funds and business-type activities to apply post-November 30, 1989 FASB Statements and Interpretations that do not conflict with or contradict GASB pronouncements. (November 30, 1989 was the date that the Financial Accounting Foundation reaffirmed GASB as the standard-setting body for governmental entities.)

Fiduciary Funds

This lesson describes the financial reporting for fiduciary funds.

After studying this lesson, you should be able to:

1. List the four types of fiduciary funds and describe the purpose of each.

2. Describe the fund-level financial statements required for each type of fiduciary fund.

3. Understand the difference between single employer and multiple-employer pension plans.

Tip

Remember the acronym **C-PIPP DRIP** the **CEG**—**(DRIP): D**ebt service funds, special **R**evenue funds, **I**nternal service funds, **P**ermanent funds; **(CEG): C**apital projects funds, **E**nterprise funds, **G**eneral fund; **(C-PIPP): C**ustodial funds, **P**ension trust funds, **I**nvestment trust funds, **P**rivate **P**urpose trust funds—a mnemonic for remembering the eleven types of funds. Fiduciary funds are **C-PIPP**.

I. Custodial Funds

A. **Overview of Custodial Fund Transactions**—Governmental entities frequently act as intermediaries in the process of disbursing monies from one governmental entity to another. For example, in a federal program designed to distribute monies to cities across the country, it is common for the federal program to disburse money to the states, which are required to disburse the money to the counties within the state, which are in turn required to disburse the monies to the cities within the counties. When the intermediate entities make these disbursements according to predetermined instructions or a formula, with little or no judgment required, they are acting as custodians and appropriately account for the transactions in a custodial fund.

1. Since the governmental entity has no claim on these resources, but merely acts as a cash conduit, it does not recognize revenues when it receives the monies or recognize expenses when it disburses the monies.

   a. Instead, it recognizes a liability when the monies are received and a reduction in liabilities when the monies are disbursed.

   b. Because the assets (usually cash) recorded in a custodial fund are usually fully offset by a related liability, most custodial funds do not have a net position: In such cases, assets minus liabilities equals zero.

   c. An exception to item (b) above occurs when an investment pool is not subject to a formal trust arrangement. In that case, GASB 84 requires a custodial fund to account for the investment pool and restricted net position is used to account for the amounts related to external entities in the pool.

Example

On July 13, Markson County received $800,000 from the state that is to be distributed to the school districts within the county in proportion to the number of students in each district. On July 22, Markson distributed $250,000 to the Peabody School District, $150,000 to Jim Pierce School District, and $400,000 to Central School District. Prepare the entries to record the receipt of the monies from the state and the disbursement of the monies to school districts:

Custodial Fund

DR: Cash　　　　　　　　　　　800,000
　　CR: Due to School Districts　　　　　800,000

To record receipt of monies payable to the school districts

DR: Due to School Districts　　　800,000
　　CR: Cash　　　　　　　　　　　　　800,000

To record distribution of monies to the school districts

2. **Financial reporting for custodial funds**—Custodial funds, like all fiduciary funds, use full accrual basis accounting. Technically, also like all fiduciary funds, custodial funds prepare a Statement of Net Position and a Statement of Changes in Net Position. An investment pool accounted for in a custodial fund will be reported in a separate column from the other custodial funds.

B. **Tax Collection Custodial Funds**—When several governmental entities have taxing authority over a single piece of property, the governmental entities typically work together to send out a single bill to the taxpayer. The taxpayer returns a single payment to one of the taxing entities (the *collecting entity*, which is typically a county or parish), which in turn disburses the appropriate amount to each of the other taxing entities. These transactions are recorded in a tax collection custodial fund.

1. **Five entries are commonly made in the tax collection custodial fund**

a. **Recognizing the tax levy**—Each taxing entity records its portion of the tax levy in its general fund (or other governmental fund, as appropriate). The gross amount of the total levy across all taxing entities is recorded in the tax collection custodial fund by debiting a receivable account and crediting a generic liability account (e.g., Due to Other Governments).

Example

The Brower County tax collection custodial fund has been established to account for the collection and distribution of the county's and the City of Thurman's property taxes. The tax levies for the year were $600,000 for the County and $400,000 for the City. It is expected that the uncollectible taxes will be $15,000 for the County and $10,000 for the City.

Tax Collection Custodial Fund:

DR: Taxes Receivable for Other Governments　1,000,000
　　CR: Due to Other Governments　　　　　　　1,000,000

To record levy of taxes (note that the full amount of the levy is recognized: *the estimated uncollectible is ignored*).

b. **Recording payments**—When tax payments are received, the collecting entity recognizes the receipt of cash in the tax collection custodial fund and reduces the outstanding Taxes Receivable.

Example

The previous example is continued. The county received $540,000 of tax payments.

Tax Collection Custodial Fund

DR:	Cash	540,000	
	CR: Taxes Receivable for Other Governments		540 000

To record receipt of $540,000 of tax payments

c. **Recognizing amounts payable to specific taxing entities**—When tax payments are received, the collecting entity determines the amounts due to each of the taxing entities according to tax rate schedules. The amount payable to each entity is recognized by creating a specific liability account for each entity and reduces the generic liability account.

Example

The previous example is again continued. After reviewing the relevant tax rate documents, the county determined that $300,000 of the total $540,000 of tax payments belonged to the county and the remaining $240,000 belonged to the city.

Tax Collection Custodial Fund

DR:	Due to Other Governments	540,000	
	CR: Due to Brower County General Fund		300,000
	CR: Due to City of Thurman		240,000

To recognize amounts due to specific taxing entities

d. **Recognizing processing fees**—It is usual for the collecting entity to charge a small fee, usually a percentage of the amount collected, to the other taxing entities. The fee is recognized in the custodial fund by reducing the amounts owed to the other taxing entities and increasing the amount owed to the collecting entity. Note that revenue and expenses related to this transaction are not recognized in the custodial fund: The individual taxing entities will recognize revenue or expense when the monies are distributed.

Example

Suppose that, in the previous example, the county charged a 1% fee to the city to cover the administrative costs associated with collecting and disbursing the property taxes. The processing fee associated with the $240,000 of taxes due to the City of Thurman is $2,400 and is recognized by reducing the amount due to the City of Thurman and increasing the amount due to Brower County.

Tax Collection Custodial Fund

DR:	Due to City of Thurman	2,400	
	CR: Due to Brower County General Fund		2,400

e. **Disbursing the cash payments**—Periodically (once a week, once a month), the collecting entity disburses the collections to the taxing entities. This is recorded in the custodial fund by simply crediting cash and debiting the appropriate liability accounts.

Example

The previous example is completed. At the end of the week, the county disburses the tax payments to its general fund and to the City of Thurmond General Fund in accordance with the individual entity liability accounts.

Tax Collection Custodial Fund

DR: Due to City of Thurman ($240,000—$2,400)	237,600
DR: Due to Brower County General Fund ($300,000+$2,400)	302,400
CR: Cash	540,000

To disburse tax collections to taxing entities.

2. When the taxing entity receives payment for the taxes collected on its behalf, it reduces its Property Tax Receivable account and increases its Cash account. To the extent that there is a difference between the amount of taxes actually collected and the amount disbursed to the taxing entity, the taxing entity recognizes revenues or expenditures for the difference.

Example

In the previous example, Brower County received $302,400, which represented the tax payments collected on its behalf plus a processing fee paid by the City of Thurman. The City of Thurman received $237,600, which consisted of the tax payments collected on its behalf less the processing fee paid to Brower County. Each entity records the receipt of the payment in its general fund as shown next.

Brower County General Fund

DR: Cash	302,400
CR: Property Taxes Receivable—Current	300,000
CR: Revenue—Processing Fees	2,400

To record receipt of tax payments and processing fee

City of Thurman General Fund

DR: Cash	237,600
DR: Expenditures—Processing Fees	2,400
CR: Propery Taxes Receivable—Current	240,000

To record receipt of tax payments and payment of processing fee

C. Special Assessment Custodial Funds—Special assessment projects are often financed with debt issues. Though the debt is to be repaid from special assessments levied on the property owners, the governmental entity usually assumes secondary liability for the debt in the event that the property owners default on their payments. Under these circumstances, the levy of the special assessment and the payments to the bondholders are accounted for in a debt service fund and the special assessment debt is included with other general long-term debt.

1. Sometimes, however, the governmental entity does not assume secondary liability for the debt and merely acts as an agent for the bondholders by collecting the special assessment levy from the property owners and remitting payments for interest and principal to the bondholders. In these cases, the levy of the special assessment and the payments to the bondholders are accounted for in a custodial fund and the special assessment debt is not reported with other general long-term debt.

    a. **Five entries are commonly made in the special assessment custodial fund**

        i. **Levy of the special assessment**—After the project is completed, the special assessment is levied. The full amount of the special assessment is recorded at this time, although it is split into a current and a deferred portion. The debit for the special assessments receivable is recorded just as it would be in a debt service fund. However, instead of crediting revenues, the offsetting credit is to a liability account (usually titled Due to Bondholders).

Example

Mill City recently completed a street improvement project that was to be paid for in part by a special assessment of $800,000 levied on the property owners who benefited from the improvements. The special assessment is payable over 10 years, with $80,000 of the assessment becoming current each year. $800,000 of special assessment bonds, which were not secondarily backed by the city, were issued to cover the construction costs. Interest expense and principal repayments on the bonds are to be paid from the special assessment collections. The entry to record the levy of the special assessment is as follows: (Note that the actual liability for the bonds is not recorded as the city does not assume any liability for the bonds but merely acts as an agent in remitting payments to the bondholders.)

Special Assessment Custodial Fund

DR:	Special Assessments Receivable—Current	80,000	
DR:	Special Assessments Receivable—Deferred	720,000	
	CR: Due to Bondholders		800,000

To record levy of the special assessment

---

        ii. **Receipt of payments from the property owners**—In general, the entry to record payment of the currently due portion of the special assessment is straightforward: Debit Cash and credit Special Assessments Receivable for the amount of the payment. Sometimes, however, the payment may also include interest and penalties for late payment. If the additional amounts have not been accrued (as is usually the case), these amounts are simply shown as being "due to the bondholders."

Example
Mill City received $78,000 in special assessment collections. This amount represented payment of $77,000 of currently due special assessment receivables and $1,000 in interest and penalties associated with assessments that were not paid on a timely basis. (The interest and penalties have not been recorded as receivables.)

Special Assessment Custodial Fund

DR:	Cash	78,000	
	CR: Special Assessments Receivable—Current		77,000
	CR: Due to Bondholders		1,000

To payment of special assessments

      iii. Payment of interest and principal to bondholders—The payment of interest and any currently due portions of principal to the bondholders is recorded by decreasing cash and decreasing the liability account Due to Bondholders by a corresponding amount. No expense is recognized.

Example
At the end of the year, interest of $32,000 was due to the bondholders. In addition, $40,000 of the bond principal matured at the end of the year. The entry to record this payment to the bondholders is shown next.

Special Assessment Custodial Fund

DR:	Due to Bondholders	72,000	
	CR: Cash		72,000

To payment of interest and principal to bondholders

II. Investment Trust Funds

  A. Overview of Investment Trust Fund Transactions—In order to maximize earnings on their investments, governmental entities frequently *pool* or commingle idle cash from many funds into a single Pooled Investment account. Some governments also permit external governmental entities to contribute monies to the investment pool, especially if the external entities lack sufficient size and/or the expertise to manage efficiently their investments themselves. When an investment pool includes external participants, GASB requires the use of an investment trust fund to record and report the interests of the external participants when the pool is established by a formal trust arrangement. (GASB 84 requires a custodial fund when the investment pools are not subject to a formal trust arrangement.).

    1. Valuation of the investment pool assets—Securities held by the investment pool are reported at fair value. The pool is revalued whenever investment income is distributed to the participants and whenever a participating entity adds to or withdraws resources from the pool.

      a. Because of this, investment income is typically distributed to participants on a monthly or quarterly basis and participants can change their investment in the pool only at these points in time.

    2. Distribution of investment income—Interest, dividends, and realized and unrealized gains and losses on investments are distributed to participants in the pool based on their proportionate share of the investment.

a. Income-sharing ratios are established whenever participants add to or withdraw resources from the pool. However, distribution of income does not change the income-sharing ratio since the income is distributed to all participants proportionately.

3. **Reporting participation of external entities**—The net interest of external entities participating in the investment pool is reported as Net Position of Investment Trust Fund.

   a. Each external entity has a separate Net Position account, which is typically listed as Net Position Held in Trust for XXXXX.

   b. Investment pool resources related to internal participants are shown as a liability in the Investment Trust Fund. See the following illustration.

Statement of Net Position Investment Trust Fund

Assets		Liabilities	
Cash	$ 1,000,000	Due to General Fund	$ 10,000,000
Investments	19,000,000	Due to Capital Projects Fund	5,000,000
Total Assets	$20,000,000	*Total Liabilities*	$15,000,000
		Net Position	
		Held in Trust for City X	$ 3,000,000
		Held in Trust for School District	2,000,000
		Total Net Position	$5,000,000
		Total Liabilities and Net Position	$20,000,000

---

4. **Reporting changes in investment**—Changes in a participant's investment in the investment pool arise from three principal sources:

   a. Contribution of resources to the investment pool—This may be the initial contribution of a new participant or an additional contribution from a current participant.

   b. Withdrawal of resources from the investment pool—The withdrawal may be a partial or complete withdrawal.

   c. Net investment earnings (here used in the broadest sense to include realized and unrealized gains and losses on the investment assets, interest revenue, and dividends) Net of any management fees and transaction costs.

   d. Although the investment trust fund, like the other fiduciary funds, uses full accrual basis accounting rules to recognize revenues and expenses, because these resources do not belong to the governmental entity, they are reported on the financial statements as Additions and Deductions, respectively.

      i. Common items listed under Additions include Contributions and Investment Earnings.

      ii. Common items listed under Deductions include Withdrawals and Management Fees.

   e. Only increases and decreases in the investment assets of external pool participants are reported in the investment trust fund's statements. The internal pool participants report increases and decreases in their respective funds.

Statement of Changes in Net Position Investment Trust Fund

Additions:	
Investment Earnings	$ 300,000
Contributions	50,000
Total additions:	350,000
Deductions:	
Withdrawals	100,000
Total withdrawals:	100,000
Change in Net Position	$ 250,000
Beginning Net Position	4,750,000
Ending Net Position	$5,000,000

Note

The following entries are provided to add depth to your understanding of the purpose and use of investment trust funds. However, the entries themselves are rarely tested on the CPA Exam.

B. **Recognition and Distribution of Investment Income**—Although most investment pools distribute income to participants periodically, investment income, such as interest revenue, dividends, and the like, accrues on a continuous basis. Therefore, as income accrues, it is first recorded in a holding account and then later distributed to the pool participants. Changes in the fair value of the pool investments are handled in a similar manner.

1. **Common entries in investment trust funds**—There are four principal entries in investment trust funds.

    a. **Entry to record investment income**—When investment income is received or accrues, the appropriate asset account is debited and a holding account titled Undistributed Earnings on Pooled Investments is credited.

Example

During the quarter, the Investment Pool for Grimes County received dividends totaling $50,000 and interest totaling $120,000. At the end of the quarter, an additional $30,000 in interest had accrued. The income is placed in the holding account to await distribution as shown next.

Investment Trust Fund

DR:	Cash	170,000
DR:	Interest Receivable	30,000
	CR: Undistributed Earnings on Pooled Investments	200,000

To record investment income for the quarter

    b. **Entry to record sale of securities**—When securities are sold, the gain or loss on the sale is placed in a holding account until the end of the period. See the following example.

Example
During the quarter, the securities costing $500,000 were sold for $450,000, resulting in a realized loss of $50,000. The entry to record the sale is shown next.

Investment Trust Fund

DR:	Cash	450,000	
DR:	Undistributed Change in Fair Value of Pooled Investments	50,000	
	CR: Investments		500,000

To record sale of securities at a loss

   c. **Entry to record revaluation of the portfolio**—Whenever income is scheduled to be distributed to the pool participants or when participants add or withdraw resources from the investment pool, the fair value of the investment pool is determined and the change in fair value is calculated. This unrealized gain or loss is combined in the holding account with the realized gains and losses on the sale of securities for distribution to the pool participants.

Example
At the end of the quarter, the fair value of the securities held in the investment pool was $19,350,000. The book value of the investments at the end of the quarter was $18,500,000, resulting in an unrealized gain of $850,000. This gain is recorded as shown next.

Investment Trust Fund

DR:	Investments	850,000	
	CR: Undistributed Change in Fair Value of Pooled Investments		850,000

To record change in fair value of the investment portfolio

   d. **Entry to record distribution of investment earnings to pool participants**—Both the Undistributed Earnings on Pooled Investments and the Undistributed Change in Fair Value of Pooled Investments are periodically distributed to the pool participants in accordance with their proportionate interest in the investment pool. Since distributions to external participants increase the net position of the investment trust fund, they are recorded as revenues (additions) to the investment trust fund. Distributions to internal participants, however, simply increase the liability to the internal participants recorded in the investment trust fund: The internal participants will report the revenue in their fund statements.

Example

At the end of the quarter, the investment earnings and change in the fair value of the investment portfolio are distributed to the participants in proportion to their interest in the pooled investment. The internal and external participants interests are:

Internal Participants		Proportionate Interest
General Fund	$ 10,000,000	50%
Capital Projects Fund	5,000,000	25%
External Participants		
City X	$ 3,000,000	15%
School District	2,000,000	10%
Total Interest in Investment Pool	$20,000,000	100%

The balance in the Undistributed Earnings on Pooled Investments account of $200,000 and the balance in the Undistributed Change in Fair Value of Pooled Investments account of $800,000 are distributed as shown next.

Investment Trust Fund

DR:	Undistributed Earnings on Pooled Investments	200,000	
	CR: Due to General Fund (50% × $200,000)		100,000
	CR: Due to Capital Projects Fund (25% × $200,000)		50,000
	CR: Additions—Investment Income (10% + 15%) × $200,000)		50,000

To distribute investment earnings to investment pool participants

Investment Trust Fund

DR:	Undistributed Change in Fair Value of Pooled Investments	800,000	
	CR: Due to General Fund (50% × $800,000)		400,000
	CR: Due to Capital Projects Fund (25% × $800,000)		200,000
	CR: Additions—Investment Income (10% + 15%) × $800,000)		200,000

To distribute realized and unrealized gains and losses on investments to participants

2. **Recognition of investment earnings of internal participants**—Internal participants are notified when investment earnings are distributed to investment pool participants. Each internal participant makes an entry to recognize revenue in the appropriate fund and increases their Pooled Investment account to reflect the increase in the investment trust fund.

Example

The investment trust fund notifies the internal participants of their earnings. Each fund makes an appropriate entry in their fund accounts, as shown.

General Fund

DR:	Pooled Investments ($100,000 + $400,000)	500,000
	CR: Investment Revenue	500,000

To record quarterly earnings on pooled investments

Capital Projects Fund

DR:	Pooled Investments ($50,000 + $200,000)	250,000
	CR: Investment Revenue	250,000

To record quarterly earnings on pooled investments

III. **Pension Trust Funds and Other Postemployment Benefit Plan (OPEB) Trust Funds**

   A. **Overview of Pension Plans**—Pension plans are categorized in several different ways.

   1. **Defined contribution versus defined benefit plans**—There are two broad types of pension plans: **defined contribution** plans and **defined benefit** plans. In defined contribution plans, the employer and the employee make contributions to the plan, which are invested and earn a return. Upon retirement, the employee is entitled to the total contributions made on his or her behalf plus the accumulated earnings on those contributions, whatever they may be. Thus, while the *contributions* to these funds are defined, the *benefits* are determined by the performance of the invested assets. Because plan benefits are based on existing resources, *no actuarial calculations are necessary* to determine the plan liability or the required contribution to the plan. In **defined benefit plans**, the employer promises the retiree a defined future benefit over a future time period and the employer bears the risk associated with unknown future economic factors.

      a. Defined benefit plans specify, in relative terms, the future benefits that the plan will pay out (e.g., two-thirds of the average annual salary during the last three years of employment). Actuarial calculations are necessary to establish the present dollar value of these benefits and to determine the annual contribution necessary in order to have sufficient resources available to pay retirement benefits.

   2. **Single employer plans versus multiple employer plans**—*Single-employer* plans are exactly what they say. They are individual plans set up by an individual governmental employer to cover a specified class or classes of employees. A single-employer plan, however, does not necessarily mean single-*plan*. Many governmental entities offer several different pension plans to different classes of employees (e.g., one plan for public safety personnel and another plan for administrative personnel). A governmental entity may offer several different single-employer plans.

      a. Sometimes, in an effort to provide better-quality, lower-cost plans to their employees, smaller employers band together and jointly create a retirement plan that covers all of their employees. These plans are known as *multiple-employer plans*. States frequently provide a plan that is available to all the employees of any governmental entity within its jurisdiction. These plans are known as Public Employee Retirement Systems (PERS). There are two types of multiple-employer plans.

         i. Agent multiple-employer plans pool the administrative and investment functions for multiple employers to reduce overhead but each individual employer plan assets maintained in separate accounts to pay benefits to only its plan members.

    ii. Cost-sharing multiple-employer plans pool the assets and obligations of all participating employers and use plan assets to pay benefits to any participating plan members.

  3. IRC Section 457 Deferred Compensation Plans—GASB Statement No. 97 requires reporting defined benefit Section 457 plans as either a pension plan or an other employee benefit plan (OPEB). In some cases, Section 457 plans do not have a governing board. If the primary government performs the duties that a governing board typically would perform, the absence of a governing board should be treated the same as a government that appoints of a voting majority of a governing board for purposes of determining financial accountability. Defined contribution Section 457 plans are exempt from the provisions of GASB No. 97.

B. Reporting for Pension Trust Funds—GASB Statement No. 67 establishes reporting requirements for defined benefit pension trust funds. Two financial statements are required: (1) Statement of Fiduciary Net Position and (2) Statement of Changes in Fiduciary Net Position. All of the amounts presented in the pension trust fund statements are in nominal (actual) dollar amount: *No actuarial amounts are presented.*

  1. Statement of fiduciary net position—This statement is required for all types of pension plans. The most distinctive feature of the statement is the title of the net position section: Net Position Held in Trust for Pension Benefits.

Statement of Fiduciary Net Position
Pension Trust Fund

Assets	
Cash	$ 15,000,000
Interest Receivable	500,000
Investments	54,500,000
Total Assets	*70,000,000*
Deferred Outflows of Resources	
Liabilities	
Accounts Payable	$500,000
Annuities Payable	1,500,000
Total Liabilities	*$2,000,000*
Deferred Inflows of Resources	
Net Position Held in Trust for Pension Benefits	$68,000,000

---

  2. Statement of changes in fiduciary net position—This statement is also prepared for both defined contribution and defined benefit plans. Note that the statement presents *Additions* and *Deductions* rather than Revenues and Expenses. This terminology reflects the fact that these resources do not belong to the governmental entity and so cannot generate revenues and expenses for the governmental entity.

    a. Additions (revenues) and Deductions (expenses) are recognized on the full accrual basis.

    b. The principal Additions (revenues) recognized in the pension trust fund consist of:

      i. Contributions to the plan from the employee

      ii. Contributions to the plan from the employer

      iii. Investment earnings

Exam Tip
Some CPA Exam questions still ask about the amount of Revenue or Expense recognized in Fiduciary Funds. Although GASB now requires Fiduciary Funds to *report* Additions and Deductions in their financial statements, it is permissible to *record* Revenues and Expenses in the fund and simply convert them to Additions and Deductions for reporting purposes. Consequently, questions that ask about Revenue or Expense recognition in the funds can be answered without undue concern about the terminology used in the question.

Statement of Changes in Fiduciary Net Position
Pension Trust Fund

Additions:

Contributions:

Employer	$ 1,200,000
Employee	800,000
Total Contributions:	2,000,000

Investment Income:

Interest and dividends	1,800,000
Net increase in fair value of investments	400,000
Total Investment Income:	2,200,000
Total additions	4,200,000

Deductions:

Retirement annuities	1,400,000
Disability benefits	400,000
Refunds to terminated employees	200,000
Administrative expenses	300,000
Total deductions	2,300,000

Net Increase — 1,900,000

Net Position Held in Trust for Pension Benefits:

Beginning of year	66,100,000
End of year	$68,000,000

c. The principal Deductions (expenses) recognized in the pension trust fund consist of payments to retirees, refunds to terminated employees, and investment management fees.

    i. Required supplementary information (RSI)

      a. All plans:

        i. Plan description

        ii. Investment policies

        iii. Receivables

        iv. Allocated insurance contracts

        v. Reserves

        vi. Deferred Retirement Option Program (DROP)

        vii. 10-year schedule of Actuarially Determined Contributions

      b. Single-employer and cost-sharing multiple employer plans:

        i. Components of net pension liability

        ii. Significant assumptions

        iii. Actuarial valuation date

        iv. 10-year schedule of changes in net pension liability

        v. 10-year schedule of Net Pension Liability

        vi. 10-year schedule of Money-Weighted Rates of Return

C. Accounting for Pension Trust Funds—The transactions accounted for in pension trust funds are straightforward. The funds follow full accrual basis accounting rules when recognizing Revenues (Additions) and Expenses (Deductions) and adjust their investments to reflect market value at the end of the period. Questions on the CPA Exam usually ask only whether a particular item can be recognized as a Revenue (Addition) or an Expense (Deduction) in the fund.

Note

GASB Statement No. 68 provides new standards for accounting and financial reporting for pensions that apply to most governments that provide their employees with pension benefits. Together with GASB Statement No. 67, GASB Statement No. 68 represents a significant shift from the *fund-based* approach used in the past to an *accounting-based* approach. GASB 68 is effective for fiscal years beginning after June 15, 2014.

D. Annual Pension Expense—Annual pension expense includes the following items:

Benefits earned during the year

+ Interest on the total pension liability

+/– Changes in benefit terms

– Projected earnings on plan investments

+/– Changes in plan net position from other than investments

Changes in plan net position from other than investments: Differences between projected and actual earnings on plan investments are initially recognized as deferred outflows or resources or deferred inflows of resources and will be amortized to pension expense over a five-year period. Differences in some assumptions used to develop the projected total future pension benefit are initially recognized as deferred outflows or resources or deferred inflows of resources and will be amortized over the average remaining service period of all employees in the plan (active and inactive). (Prior to GASB Statement No. 68 this difference was amortized in a period up to 30 years. Be on guard for a question that includes a 30-year amortization answer—this is a trick answer!) The unamortized amounts are reported in the balance sheet as either a deferred outflow of resources, if the difference is unfavorable, or as a deferred inflow of resources, if the difference is favorable.

1. **Pension liability**—For **single-employers** and **agent employers** is the net pension liability calculated as the difference between the employer's total pension liability less the amount of plan assets as indicated by the net position of the plan. For cost-sharing employers the net pension liability is its proportionate share of the cumulate net pension liability in the cost-sharing plan. Measuring total pension liability is a three-step process:

    a. **Projection of the future benefit payments**—For current and inactive employees including projected salary increases, service credits, automatic cost-of-living adjustments (COLA), and other automatic benefit changes.

    b. **Discount rate**—This is used to determine the present value of the projected future benefit payments. The rate is based on the long-term expected rate of return on plan investments to the extent that plan assets are available to meet the pension liability; thereafter, a tax-exempt, high-quality (an average rating of AA/As or higher) 20-year municipal bond index rate would be incorporated into the measurement of a blended **discount rate** (in effect the premise is that the government would issue bonds to meet the pension obligation remaining after plan assets are exhausted).

    c. **Attributing the present value to specific time periods**—After the projected benefit payments have been discounted they are allocated to past, current, and future time periods. Total pension liability represents the portion that is attributed to each employee's past and current periods of service. GASB Statement No. 68 requires employers to use the entry age actuarial cost method applied as a level percentage of payroll.

    d. **Actuarial valuations**—Should be performed at least biennially. If a valuation is not prepared as of the measurement date, the total pension liability will be based on a roll forward of information from an earlier actuarial valuation to the measurement date (the earlier valuation should be no more than 24 months earlier than the pension plan's fiscal year-end).

Example

Planerville City maintains a single-employer, defined benefit pension plan for city employees and, as required by GASB, records transactions related to the plan assets in a Pension Trust Fund. The current balances in the Pension Trust Fund are as follows:

Account	DR	CR
Cash	35,000	
Interest Receivable	5,000	
Investments	530,000	
Pension Annuities Payable		10,000
Net Position Held in Trust—Pension Benefits		560,000

During the year, the following transactions occurred:

*   Planerville contributed $30,000 to the pension plan on behalf of city employees. Contributions from the employees totaled $20,000.

*   Interest of $18,000 and dividends of $4,000 were received in cash during the year ($5,000 of the interest had been previously accrued). Accrued interest at year's end totaled $7,000.

*   Annuity payments to retirees during the year totaled $35,000, including the $10,000 that had been previously accrued. Accrued pensions payable at the end of the year totaled $15,000.

*   Terminated employees requested and received refunds of their contributions totaling $5,000.

*   Investment management fees of $8,000 were paid.

Pension Trust Fund

DR: Cash   50,000
     CR: Contributions—Employers   30,000
     CR: Contributions—Employees   20,000
To record receipt of employer and employee contributions.

DR: Cash   22,000
     CR: Interest Receivable   5,000
     CR: Additions (Revenue): Investment Income   17,000
To record receipt of investment income.

DR: Interest Receivable   7,000
     CR: Additions (Revenue): Investment Income   7,000

DR: Deductions (Expenses): Retirement Annuities   25,000
DR: Pension Annuities Payable   10,000
     CR: Cash   35,000
To record payment of retirement annuities.

DR: Deductions (Expenses): Retirement Annuities   15,000
     CR: Pension Annuities Payable   15,000
To record accrual of retirement annuities.

DR: Deductions (Expenses): Refunds   5,000
     CR: Cash   5,000
To record payment of refunds to terminated employees.

DR: Deductions (Expenses): Management Fees   8,000
     CR: Cash   8,000
To record payment of refunds to terminated employees.

E. **Supplemental Disclosures**—Although the Pension Trust Fund accounts for pension assets only in nominal dollars, actuarial information must be disclosed in two required schedules by GASB Statement Nos. 67 and 68: the Schedule of Changes in Net Pension Liability (which replaced the Schedule of Funding Progress) and the Schedule of Employer Contributions (similar to what was required before GASB Statement Nos. 67 and 68). Both schedules are included in the Required Supplementary Information (RSI) section of the Comprehensive Annual Financial Report (CAFR).

1. **Schedule of Changes in Net Pension Liability**

   a. This is a 10-year schedule of changes in the net pension liability, presenting for each year; the beginning and ending balances of total pension liability, the pension plan's fiduciary net position, and net pension liability; service cost, interest on the total pension liability, changes in benefits terms, differences between expected and actual experience in measurement of the total pension liability, changes of assumptions or other inputs, contributions from the employer, contributions from nonemployer contributing entities, contributions from employees, pension plan net investment income, benefit payments, pension plan administration expense, and other changes.

   b. Two key ratios are also presented:

      i. The **funded ratio**, which is the ratio of the plan fiduciary net position divided by total pension liability

      ii. Net pension liability (asset) as a percentage of covered payroll.

         a. As required supplemental information (RSI) contributions to the actuarially determined contribution as a percentage of covered payroll is presented.

2. **Schedule of Employer Contributions**—This schedule presents the actuarially determined contribution, the amount actually contributed by the government, the difference between the two, and the percentage of the amount that was actually contributed to the actuarially determined contribution amount. A ratio of the amount of contribution recognized by the pension plan as a percentage of covered payroll is also presented. This schedule also presents information for a 10-year period.

3. **GASB Statement No. 78 Exclusion**—Excludes GASB Statement No. 68 requirements for pensions provided to employees of state or local governments through a cost-sharing multiple-employer defined benefit plan that (a) is not a state or local governmental pension plan, (b) is used to provided defined benefit pensions both to employees of state and local government employers and to employees of employers that are not state or local governments, and (c) has no predominant state or local governmental employer. In these situations, a government employer may not be able to obtain the measurements and other information needed to comply with the requirements of GASB Statement No. 68. Therefore, GASB Statement No. 78 excludes those government employers from the requirements of Statement No. 68 and prescribes recognition and measurement of pension expense, expenditures, liabilities, disclosures, and RSI for these pension plans.

   > **Note**
   > *Prior to GASB 67 and 68, the actuarially determined contribution was termed as the "annual required contribution." With GASB Statement Nos. 67 and 68, GASB shifted the focus from a funding-based approach to an accounting-based approach. GASB stated that funding was a policy decision by the government. Hence, the change from annual required contribution to actuarially determined contribution reflects GASB's shift in philosophy regarding pensions.*

   a. **Recognition and measurement in financial statements prepared using the economic resources measurement focus**—Pension expense equal to the employer's required contributions to the pension plan for the reporting period and a payable for unpaid required contributions at the end of the reporting period.

   b. **Recognition and measurement in financial statements prepared using the current financial resources measurement focus**—Pension expenditures equal to the employer's required contributions to the pension plan for pay periods within the reporting period and a payable to the extent it is normally expected to be liquidated with expendable available resources.

c. **Disclosures**

    i. Description of the plan

    ii. Whether the pension plan issues a publicly available report

    iii. Description of benefits

    iv. Description of contribution requirements

    v. Information about employer's payables

d. **Required supplemental information (RSI)**—A 10-year schedule of the employer's required contributions.

F. **Recognition of Pension Costs in the Employing Funds**—The amount of pension costs actually recognized in the employing fund varies according to the basis of accounting used by the fund.

    1. **Governmental funds**—Governmental funds recognize pension cost on the modified accrual basis: Employers report the portion of the annual pension cost that has been or will be *funded with current resources of the governmental funds* as expenditures. This amount may be more or less than the current period's annual pension cost.

        a. Liability for any unfunded amount is not recorded in the fund but is maintained off-books by adding it to the Schedule of General Long-Term Debt.

Example

Largo County's offers a defined benefit pension plan to its employees. The annual pension cost for the fund for the current year is $100,000. However, the county was only able to contribute $50,000 to the pension plan. The county does not currently have plans to pay the additional $50,000 due to the pension plan.

DR:	Expenditures—Pension Cost	50,000	
	CR: Cash		50,000

To record pension cost. (Note that no fund liability is accrued for the additional $50,000 that the county should have paid into the pension plan for the current year because the county has not yet committed resources to pay these costs.)

    2. **Proprietary funds**—When employees are paid using proprietary fund resources, the employer's pension contributions are recognized on the full accrual basis (i.e., whenever a fund liability is incurred. A fund liability is incurred whenever an enforceable claim is made against fund resources.

Example

The previous example is continued with the exception that the employees are paid using proprietary fund resources.

DR:	Expenses—Pension Cost	100,000	
	CR: Pension Liability		50,000
	CR: Cash		50,000

To record pension cost (Note that the full actuarially calculated pension cost is recognized even though the county has not yet committed resources to pay these costs; this is because full accrual basis accounting requires recognition of the full actuarially calculated liability in the period that the employee services were rendered.)

G. Other Postemployment Benefit Plan (OPEB) Trust Funds—Fortunately with GASB Statement No. 74, on financial reporting by plans that administer OPEB benefits, and GASB Statement No. 75, on a government's accounting and financial reporting of OPEB benefits that it provides to its employees, GASB adopted approaches that are similar to those used for pensions under GASB Statement Nos. 67 and 68. The next table provides a summary.

	Pensions (GASB Statement Nos. 67 and 68)	OPEB (GASB Statement Nos. 74 and 75)
Total liability	Total pension liability	Total OPEB liability
Difference between total liability and plan fiduciary net position	Net pension liability	Net OPEB liability
Discount rate	Long-term expected rate of return on plan assets, if any, are expected to be available to make projected benefit payments and be invested using a strategy to achieve a return and a 20-year tax-exempt high quality general obligation municipal bond yield or index rate to the extent the plan assets are projected to be insufficient to cover projected benefits and administrative expenses	
Actuarial cost method	Entry age actuarial cost method with each period's service cost determined as a level percentage of pay	
Required supplementary information	Schedule of Changes in Net Pension Liability (ten years)	Schedule of Changes in Net OPEB Liability (10 years)
	Schedule of Employer Contributions (10 years)	Schedule of Employer Contributions (10 years)

Note

Governments that fund OPEB on a "pay-as-you-go" approach will not have an OPEB Trust Fund and will report the Total OPEB Liability in their financial statements.

IV. Private Purpose Trust Funds

A. Resources Managed in Trust

Definition

Private Purpose Trust Funds: Funds used to account for any resources managed in trust by the governmental entity, where the beneficiaries are outside of the governmental entity itself. The beneficiaries may be individuals, private organizations or businesses, or other governmental entities.

1. Individual private purpose trusts may be either expendable or nonexpendable (e.g., endowments, where the principal must be retained and only the earnings may be expended).

2. Earnings from nonexpendable trust funds are often transferred to another fund for the actual disbursements to be made.

3. As with permanent Funds, capital gains and losses related to nonexpendable trusts are attributed to the principal unless specifically directed to attribute elsewhere.

4. Under GASB Statement No. 52, land and other real estate held as investments are reported at fair value with the change in fair value for the period reported as investment income/loss.

Format and Content of Annual Comprehensive Financial Report (ACFR)

The Annual Comprehensive Financial Report

This lesson describes the Annual Comprehensive Financial Report (ACFR) and the types of financial statements presented in it.

After studying this lesson, you should be able to:

1. List two government-wide financial statements and describe which fund types are included in the statements.

2. List the three main sections of the CAFR and the three items that make up the *basic financial statements*.

3. Describe items that require supplemental information (RSI).

I. **Annual Comprehensive Financial Report (ACFR)**

A. **Reporting Requirements**—GASB specifies two levels of reporting for governmental entities: the General Purpose Financial Statements and the The Annual Comprehensive Financial Report (ACFR)

1. **General Purpose Financial Statements (GPFS)**—The General Purpose Financial Statements represent the minimum requirements for external reporting. The GPFS contain three principal components (all three components are discussed in more detail both below and in the GASB Statement No. 34, *Basic Financial Statements—and Management's Discussion and Analysis—for State and Local Governments*, Reporting lesson):

   a. Management's discussion and analysis (MD&A)

   b. Basic financial statements

   c. Required supplementary information (RSI)

2. Though the GPFS represent the minimum reporting requirements (sometimes phrased on the exam as the "minimum that can be separately released"), most medium to large governmental entities find it necessary to provide significantly more information in order to meet the needs of the users of the financial statements.

3. **Annual Comprehensive Financial Report (ACFR)**—In order to meet the information needs of external users of the financial statements, most governmental entities produce an Annual Comprehensive Financial Report (ACFR), which is the equivalent of the annual report of a for-profit organization. GASB specifies the structure of the ACFR, which is broken up into three main sections. Each section contains several required elements:

   a. Introductory section

   b. Financial section

   c. Statistical section

Study Tip
The items included in each of the sections of the ACFR are frequently tested on the CPA Exam.

ACFR Structure

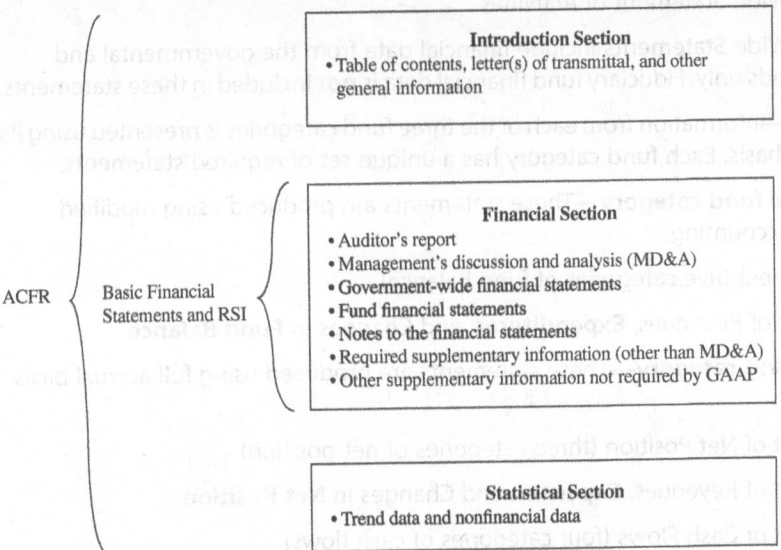

ACFR {
  Basic Financial Statements and RSI {

    ┌───┐
    │ **Introduction Section** │
    │ • Table of contents, letter(s) of transmittal, and other │
    │   general information │
    └───┘

    ┌───┐
    │ **Financial Section** │
    │ • Auditor's report │
    │ • Management's discussion and analysis (MD&A) │
    │ • Government-wide financial statements │
    │ • Fund financial statements │
    │ • Notes to the financial statements │
    │ • Required supplementary information (other than MD&A) │
    │ • Other supplementary information not required by GAAP │
    └───┘

    ┌───┐
    │ **Statistical Section** │
    │ • Trend data and nonfinancial data │
    └───┘
}

B. ACFR—Financial Section—In addition to the required financial statements, the Financial section includes explanatory text and a number of supporting schedules. The following items are included in the Financial section:

1. **Auditor's report**—This is the first item presented in the section and, in addition to providing the auditor's opinion on the fairness of the statements, specifies the scope of the audit.

   a. The Basic Financial Statements are always covered by the auditor's opinion but the accompanying information in the management's discussion and analysis (MD&A), the required supplementary information, the combining statements, and other schedules, is **not** usually audited.

2. **Management's discussion and analysis (MD&A)**—The purpose of the MD&A is to help the user assess the overall financial condition of the governmental entity and determine whether the government's position has improved or deteriorated during the period. MD&A should compare current year results to prior year results with an emphasis on the current year.

   a. The analysis of the MD&A is based on currently known facts and conditions. In its evaluations, forecasts or subjective information are not permitted.

   b. The information presented typically includes an analysis of balances and transactions in individual funds, descriptions of capital asset and long-term debt activity during the year, and an analysis of significant variations between original and final budget amounts and final budget amounts and actual budget results.

3. **Basic financial statements**—Basic financial statements consist of three separate items:

   a. Government-Wide Statements

   b. Fund Statements

   c. Notes to the Financial Statements

4. **Government-wide statements**—These statements present information for the government as a whole and are presented on a full accrual basis. Two statements are required:

Note
GASB Statement No. 63 replaced *net assets* with the term *net position* for Government-Wide Financial Statements, Proprietary Fund Financial Statements, and Fiduciary Fund Financial Statements. Governmental Fund Financial Statements report fund balances rather than Net Position.

    a. Government-Wide Statement of Net Position

    b. Government-Wide Statement of Activities

    c. Government-Wide Statements include financial data from the governmental and proprietary funds only. Fiduciary fund financial data is **not** included in these statements.

5. **Fund statements**—Information from each of the three fund categories is presented using its native accounting basis. Each fund category has a unique set of required statements.

    a. **Governmental fund category**—These statements are produced using modified accrual basis accounting.

        i. Balance Sheet (five categories of fund balance)

        ii. Statement of Revenues, **Expenditures**, and Changes in **Fund Balance**

    b. **Proprietary fund category**—These statements are produced using full accrual basis accounting.

        i. Statement of Net Position (three categories of net position)

        ii. Statement of Revenues, **Expenses**, and Changes in **Net Position**

        iii. Statement of Cash Flows (four categories of cash flows)

    c. **Fiduciary fund category**—These statements are produced using full accrual basis accounting.

        i. Statement of Fiduciary Net Position

        ii. Statement of Changes in Fiduciary Net Position

> **Exam Tip**
> The examiners frequently ask candidates to identify which statements are required for a fund type or category or, conversely, what funds are included in a specified statement.

6. **Notes to the financial statements**—The GASB requires numerous disclosures in the Notes. The Notes are considered an integral part of the Financial Statements. Common disclosures include:

    a. **Summary of significant accounting policies**, including policies for:

        i. Budgetary basis of accounting

        ii. Reporting capital assets, including estimating useful lives and depreciation expense

        iii. Description of pension plans and other postemployment benefits, annual pension cost, and net pension obligation

        iv. Schedule of debt service costs to maturity

        v. Schedule of capital assets (beginning balances, additions, deductions, ending balances)

        vi. Schedule of long-term liabilities (beginning balances, additions, deductions, ending balances)

    b. **Other required supplementary information (RSI)**—The RSI is presented after the Basic Financial Statements and is used to display additional information other than that included in the MD&A or the Notes. The information presented in the section varies depending on the activities of the governmental entity:

C. **Budgetary Comparison Statement**—This statement is required for **all funds subject to an annual budget.** The statement must present:

    a. Original budget (**required**)

    b. Final budget (*as amended*) (**required**)

    c. Actual revenues and expenditures (**required**)

    d. Variance (final budgeted amounts less actual amounts) (**encouraged but not required**)

e. The Budgetary Comparison Statement is **presented on the budgetary basis that is used by the legislative body, which may be cash basis or near cash basis (required when applicable)**.

f. A reconciliation between the revenues and expenditures using the GAAP basis (usually modified accrual basis) and the budgetary basis is required when the budget basis is non-GAAP.

D. **Pension Plan and Other Postemployment Benefit (OPEB) Plan Disclosures**—Actuarial information about pension plan liabilities and funding is presented in two required schedules (the specific requirements of these schedules are discussed in the Fiduciary Fund study text):

   a. For pensions: Schedule of Changes in Net Pension Liability and Related Ratios; For OPEB: Schedule of Changes in Net OPEB Liability and Related Ratios

   b. For pensions: Schedule of Employer Contributions; For OPEB: Schedule of Employer Contributions;

   c. The schedules show historical trends by presenting information for a 10-year period.

E. **Information Related to Infrastructure Assets Accounted for Using the Modified Approach**—Governmental entities using the modified approach to calculation and reporting of depreciation expense related to infrastructure assets (streets, bridges, sidewalks, drainage systems, etc.) are required to disclose and justify their methods for determining depreciation in this section. The following information is usually presented:

   a. Description of the method used to assess condition of the assets

   b. Results of the most recent condition assessments

   c. Estimate of costs necessary to maintain the assets at the prescribed level of condition

   d. Comparison of actual maintenance costs to estimated costs

F. **Combining Financial Statements and Individual Fund Financial Statements**—Although they are not specifically required by GASB, most governmental entities provide combining statements for all aggregate columns. Individual fund statements may be presented whenever the governmental entity deems it appropriate.

   a. Combining statements are used to show the individual entities included in the aggregated columns of the Financial Statements, for example, the "Non-Major Funds" columns found in the Fund Statements and the Component Units column in the Government-Wide Statements.

II. **ACFR—Statistical Section**—The purpose of the Statistical section is to assist the user in evaluating the current and future performance of the governmental entity in the broader context of its social and economic environment. GASB 44 defines five categories of information that should be presented in the Statistical section and recommends that data be provided for a **10-year** period in order to facilitate trend evaluation.

   1. **Financial trends information**—Schedules in this category help the user understand how the governmental entity's financial position has changed over the past 10 years. It typically displays key fund balances and key net position category balances for this period.

   2. **Revenue capacity information**—This information helps the user understand the ability of the governmental entity to generate its own revenues. Information included in this section typically includes:

      a. Significant sources of revenue

      b. Principal taxpayers

      c. Property tax levy and collection

3. **Debt capacity information**—This section assists the user in understanding the governmental entity's obligation to service existing debt as well as its ability to finance future operations through debt. It includes information such as:

   a. Ratios of outstanding debt to personal income

   b. Schedules of direct and overlapping debt

   c. Legal debt limitations and debt margins

   d. Revenues pledged to service debt

4. **Demographics and economic information**—The economic and social environment in which the governmental organization operates is presented in this section. Trend information that is frequently provided includes:

   a. Per capita income

   b. Level of education achieved and distribution of current students across educational level

   c. Major employers and industries

   d. Employment and unemployment rates

5. **Operating information**—The purpose of this section is to provide the user with a better understanding of the government's operations and resources. At a minimum, the following schedules of operating information should be provided:

   a. Number of government employees

   b. Operating indicators—Indicators are indicators of the demand or level of service provided, such as the number of building permits issued, number of park visits, average daily school attendance, etc.

6. **Narrative explanations**—The statement requires explanatory information regarding the sources, methodologies, and assumptions used to produce each schedule and to provide narrative explanations of:

   a. The objectives of statistical section information

   b. Unfamiliar concepts

   c. Relationships between information in the statistical section and elsewhere in the financial report

   d. Atypical trends and anomalous data that users would not otherwise understand

7. **GASB Statement No. 34,** *Financial Reporting*

   A. **GASB Statement No. 34 reporting model**—This reporting model modifies the traditional "fund-based" statements somewhat and then adds to them two highly aggregated, entity-wide statements. This set of nine statements constitutes the *Basic Financial Statements*. The Basic Financial Statements represent the minimum amount of financial information that can be taken out of the ACFR and released separately.

State and Local Governments

MD&A	Basic Financial Statements	RSI

Government-Wide Financial Statements	Fund-Level Financial Statements	Notes to the Financial Statements
• Statement of Net Position • Statement of Activities	**Governmental Funds** • Balance Sheet • Statement of Revenues, Expenditures, and Changes in Fund Balance **Proprietary Funds** • Statement of Net Position • Statement of Revenues, Expenses, and Changes in Fund Net Position • Statement of Cash Flows **Fiduciary Funds** • Statement of Net Position • Statement of Changes in Net Position	

8. **Government-wide financial statements**—The traditional fund-based statements are complemented by two highly aggregated/government-wide statements.

   1. **Characteristics of government-wide statements**

      a. Distinguish *governmental activities* from *business-type activities* but do **not** identify funds.

      b. The measurement focus is on *economic resources* (i.e., revenues and expenses) and thus uses full accrual based accounting.

   2. **Classification of funds**

Governmental Activities	Business-Type Activities	Not Reported in Government-Wide Statements
General Fund	Enterprise Fund	Pension Trust Fund
Special Revenue Fund		Investment Trust Fund
Debt Service Fund		Private Purpose Trust Fund
Capital Projects Fund		Custodial Funds
Permanent Fund		

Internal service funds are not reported in the government-wide financial statements; rather, the amounts in the ISF are blended into governmental activities and business activities according to the use by each of ISF services.

   3. The account groups are not reported in the GASB Statement No. 34 model, but the net position and long-term debt from the account groups are included under Governmental Activities.

9. **Statement of net position**

   1. Government-Wide Financial Statements

| | Primary Government | | | |
	Governmental Activities	Business-Type Activities	Total	Component Units
Assets				
(listed by liquidity)	xxxxx	xxxxx	xxxxx	xxxxx
Deferred Outflows of Resources	xxxxx	xxxxx	xxxxx	
Total Assets	xxxxx	xxxxx	xxxxx	xxxxx
Liabilities				
(listed by maturity)	xxxxx	xxxxx	xxxxx	xxxxx
Deferred Inflows of Resources	xxxxx	xxxxx	xxxxx	
Total Liabilities	xxxxx	xxxxx	xxxxx	xxxxx
Net Position				
Net Investment in Capital Assets	xxxxx	xxxxx	xxxxx	xxxxx
Restricted for:				
Capital Projects	xxxxx	xxxxx	xxxxx	xxxxx
Debt Service	xxxxx	xxxxx	xxxxx	xxxxx
Community Development	xxxxx	xxxxx	xxxxx	xxxxx
Other Purposes	xxxxx	xxxxx	xxxxx	xxxxx
Unrestricted	xxxxx	xxxxx	xxxxx	xxxxx
Total Net Position	xxxxx	xxxxx	xxxxx	xxxxx

10. **Assets**— These include both current and fixed assets.

    a. **Interfund payables and receivables**—Among governmental activities funds and among business-type activities funds have been eliminated.

    b. **Internal balances**—Any remaining interfund payables and receivables between government-type and business-type funds are identified as **Internal Balances** under each activity type and are eliminated in the Total column.

    c. **Capital assets**—include fixed assets previously reported in the General Fixed Assets account group but they must be reported net of accumulated depreciation and includes intangible assets, as provided by GASB Statement No. 51, net of amortization.

    d. **GASB Statement No. 51,** *Accounting and Financial Reporting for Intangible Assets.* (This content is from the lesson "Special Items—Recent Developments.") GASB Statement No. 51 was issued to resolve inconsistencies that had developed in accounting and financial reporting for intangible assets. The types of intangible assets held by governments include the following: water rights, timber rights, patents, trademarks, computer software, and easements. Easements are mentioned in GASB Statement No. 34 para. 19, as a type of capital asset, and it is this reference that is considered the source of the inconsistencies in accounting for intangible assets observed in practice.

        i. **Characteristics of intangible assets**—An intangible asset is an asset that possesses all of the following characteristics:

            a. **Lack of physical substance**—The asset may be contained in, or on an item of, physical substance (e.g., software on a computer disc) or closely associated with another item that has physical substance (e.g., the underlying land in the case of a right-of-way). These modes of containment and associated items are not considered when determining whether an asset lacks physical substance.

- **b. Nonfinancial nature**—The asset is not in monetary form nor does it represent a claim or rights to assets in monetary form.
- **c. Initial useful life** extending beyond a single reporting period

ii. **Exceptions**—The provisions of GASBS Statement No. 51 do not apply to the following intangible assets:

- **a.** Those acquired or created for the purpose of obtaining income or profit, which should follow guidance for investments
- **b.** Assets resulted from capital lease transactions reported by lessees
- **c.** Goodwill created through combination

iii. **Recognition**—An intangible asset should be recognized in the statement of net position, if it is identifiable. One of the following two conditions must be met for intangible assets to be considered identifiable:

- **a.** The asset is separable. It is capable of being separated or divided from the government and sold, transferred, licensed, rented, or exchanged
- **b.** The asset arises from contractual or other legal rights

iv. **Internally generated intangible assets**—Internally generated intangible assets are capitalized only when all three of the following conditions are met. Outlays prior to meeting the three conditions should be expensed as incurred.

- **a.** The project is expected to provide an intangible asset upon completion of the project.
- **b.** Technical or technological feasibility for completion of the project is demonstrated so that the intangible asset will provide its expected service capability.
- **c.** The intention, ability, and presence of effort to complete or continue development of the intangible asset is demonstrated.

v. **Internally generated computer software**—Activities involved in developing and installing internally generated computer software can be grouped into three stages:

- **a. Preliminary project stage**—Activities include the conceptual formulation and evaluation of alternatives, the determination of the needed technology, and the final selection of alternatives. Treatment: Expense.
- **b. Application development stage**—Activities include design, software configuration and interfaces, coding, hardware installation, and testing. Treatment: Capitalize.
- **c. Postimplementation/operation stage**—Activities include application training and software maintenance. Treatment: Expense.
- **d.** Activities in the preliminary project stage and the postimplementation/ operation stage should be expensed. Outlays in the application development stage should be capitalized; however, the following two criteria must be met in order to capitalize application development stage activities:

  - **i.** The activities in the preliminary project stage are completed; *and*
  - **ii.** There is an ongoing authorization and commitment to funding.

vi. **Modification of computer software**—Additional criteria must be met to capitalize outlays associated with an internally generated modification of computer software that is already in operation. One of the following criteria must be met:

- **a.** An increase in the functionality of the computer software;
- **b.** An increase in the efficiency of the computer software; *or*
- **c.** An extension of the estimated useful life of the software.

vii. Amortization—The amortization period should not exceed the period of service capacity provided in contractual or legal rights. Renewal periods related to such rights may be considered if there is evidence that the government will seek to achieve the renewal and that the outlays associated with the renewal are nominal in relation to the level of service capacity expected to be obtained by the renewal. An intangible with an indefinite useful life should not be amortized (e.g., a permanent right-of-way easement).

viii. Estimated historical cost—If the actual historical cost of an intangible asset is not known, the government should report the estimated historical cost for intangible assets acquired after June 30, 1980.

e. Infrastructure assets—Roads, sidewalks, street lights, signs, and bridges must be included as part of capital assets net of depreciation.

    i. Modified approach—The depreciation requirement for infrastructure assets can be waived under the following conditions:

        a. The inventory of infrastructure assets is up-to-date, information on asset condition is available, and the amount necessary to maintain and preserve the infrastructure assets is estimated.

        b. Complete condition assessments of infrastructure assets are made every three years.

f. Artwork and historical treasures—Capitalize at historical cost or fair value at date of donation. However, these items do not have to be depreciated.

g. Collections—Special rules are available, however, for collections. Items are considered part of a collection if they are:

    i. Held for public exhibition, education, or research;

    ii. Protected and preserved; *or*

    iii. Subject to a policy that requires proceeds from sales of collection items to be used to acquire other items for collections. FASB has a proposed accounting standards update that would also allow the proceeds to be used to maintain the rest of the collection.

h. Impairments—GASBS No. 42, *Accounting and Financial Reporting for Impairment of Capital Assets and for Insurance Recoveries*. This Statement requires governmental entities to recognize impairments of capital assets using criteria that mirror the requirements in financial accounting.

    i. Recognition—A capital asset should be considered impaired if its service utility has declined significantly and unexpectedly.

        a. The decline must be large in magnitude and the event or change in circumstance that caused the decline must be outside the normal life cycle of the capital asset. Exclusions:

            i. Events or changes that might be expected to occur during the life of the asset

            ii. Capital assets accounted for under the modified approach (GASB Statement No. 34)

            iii. Impairments caused by deferred maintenance

    ii. Procedures

        a. Indicators of impairment

            i. Evidence of physical damage

            ii. Change in legal or environmental factors

            iii. Technological development or evidence of obsolescence

            iv. Change in the manner or expected duration of usage of a capital asset

            v. Construction stoppage

  b. Tests of impairment—factors to consider:

   i. Magnitude of the decline in service utility

   ii. Unexpected nature of the decline

  c. Measurement depends on whether the capital asset will continue to be used by the government.

   i. Assets continue to be used. The amount of the impairment is a portion of the historical cost. Use one of the following methods that best reflects the value-in-use or remaining service utility of the impaired capital asset:

    a. The restoration cost approach is typically used for impairments resulting from physical damage (e.g., fire damage to a city building). The amount of the impairment is derived from the estimated costs to restore the utility of the capital asset.

    b. The service units approach is generally used for impairments resulting from changes in legal or environmental factors or from technological development or obsolescence (e.g., new water quality standards that a water treatment plant does not meet). The amount of impairments is determined by evaluating the maximum service units or total estimated service units throughout the life of the asset before and after the event or change in circumstances.

    c. The deflated depreciated replacement cost approach is generally used for impairments resulting from a change in the manner or duration of use. The current cost for a capital asset to replace the current level of service is identified. This cost is depreciated to reflect the fact that the existing capital asset is not new and then is deflated to convert to historical cost dollars.

    d. Assets are no longer used. Impaired capital assets that will not continue to be used by the government and those impaired from construction stoppage should be reported at the lower of carrying value or fair value.

 iii. **Reporting**—Impaired capital assets should be reported at the lower of carrying value or fair value.

  a. Depending on the circumstances, the impairment loss, if significant, may be reported either as a special item or as an extraordinary item:

   i. Special items are within the control of management but are either unusual in nature or infrequent in occurrence. Special items are reported separately in the statement of activities and before extraordinary items.

   ii. Extraordinary items are unusual in nature, infrequent in occurrence, and outside the control of management.

  b. **Insurance recoveries.** GASB Statement No. 42 also provides guidance on all insurance recoveries. Impairment losses are reported net of insurance recoveries. Only realized or realizable insurance recoveries should be recognized. If an insurer has admitted or acknowledged coverage, an insurance recovery is considered realizable.

 iv. **Liabilities**—Include both short-term and long-term liabilities and are valued using the effective *interest rate method*. This results in long-term liabilities being shown at their *present value*, rather than at their face value, which was the case when they were reported in the General Long-Term Debt account group.

 v. **Net position**—Contains three component parts:

  a. **Net investment in capital assets**—These assets are all fixed, including infrastructure assets, and net of accumulated depreciation less the total of all general obligation long-term debt.

b. **Restricted net position**—These assets are subject to third-party restrictions governing how they may be spent (primarily the fund balances from the restricted funds—special revenue fund, debt service fund, capital projects fund, and permanent fund).

c. **Unrestricted net position**—These assets may be used at any time and for any purpose. They are primarily the fund balance from the general fund.

11. **The statement of activities**—This statement is developed in a functional format that highlights Program revenues and costs. The top half of the statement measures revenues and expenses by Program and categorizes the net result as either a governmental activity or a business-type activity. Net results at the program level are typically negative as much of the cost of providing these programs is financed from other sources. These other sources—general revenues, transfers, and special items—are shown in the bottom half of the statement. The overall net effect is usually to bring overall cash flows to a positive number. All reporting is on the full-accrual basis.

Government-Wide Financial Statements
Statement of Activities

Functions	Expenses	Charges for Services	Operating Grants	Governmental Activities	Business Activities	Total	Comp. Units
		Program Revenues		Net Revenue (Expense) and Changes Primary Government			
Primary Government							
Governmental Activities							
Function #1	xxx	xxx	xxx	xxx		xxx	
Function #2	xxx	xxx	xxx	xxx		xxx	
Total Governmental Activities	xxx	xxx	xxx	xxx		xxx	
Business Type Activities:							
BTA #1	xxx	xxx	xxx		xxx	xxx	
BTA #2	xxx	xxx	xxx		xxx	xxx	
Total Business Type Activities	xxx	xxx	xxx		xxx	xxx	
Total Primary Government	xxx	xxx	xxx	xxx	xxx	xxx	xxx
Component Units	xxx	xxx		xxx			xxx
General Revenues—detailed				xxx	xxx	xxx	xxx
Contributions to Permanent Funds				xxx		xxx	
Special Items				xxx		xxx	
Total General Revenues, etc.				xxx	xxx	xxx	xxx
Change in Net Position				xxx	xxx	xxx	xxx
Net Position—beginning				xxx	xxx	xxx	xxx
Net Position—ending				xxx	xxx	xxx	xxx

1. The **functional format** is divided into governmental activities, business-type activities, and Component Units.

2. A function's **Net Revenue (Expense)** is calculated as: the function's program revenues less the function's expenses.

   a. **Exchange revenue** is recognized on the full-accrual basis.

   b. **Nonexchange revenue** is recognized when all conditions surrounding the receipt of the monies have been met (purpose, time, reimbursement, and other contingencies).

   c. **Derived revenue** (sales taxes, income taxes, gasoline taxes, etc.) should be recognized in the same period as the underlying transaction.

   d. **Imposed nonexchange transactions** (property taxes, fines, penalties, etc.) are recognized as soon as a legally enforceable claim exists.

3. **General revenues, special items, and transfers** are reported below the function section.

12. **Required supplementary information (RSI)**—This information presents schedules and statistical data that supplement the basic financial statements. Note that the RSI is not part of the Basic Financial Statements.

   1. **Budgetary comparison schedules**—include the budget as originally adopted, the final budget, and the actual results.

      a. The basis of accounting used for this schedule **matches the basis used to develop the budget.** Note that **many** governmental entities use the **cash basis** to develop budgets.

13. **Balance sheet conversion adjustments**—Following is a summary of the adjustments required to convert from the GASB Statement No. 34–mandated fund-based balance sheets to the government-wide statement of net position. Note that, with the exception of interfund payables and receivables to enterprise funds and the wholesale inclusion of internal service funds as part of governmental activities, all modifications are made to governmental funds.

   1. Add all internal service fund assets and liabilities to the governmental activities balance sheet. The internal service fund Net Position are added to the Fund Balance of the governmental fund.

   2. Eliminate all interfund payables/receivables except those to/from Enterprise funds.

      a. The Net payable/receivable balance to/from enterprise funds is labeled *internal balances.*

   3. Add *net* general government fixed assets.

      a. Accumulated depreciation *must* be deducted from the assets.

   4. Add *net* general government long-term debt.

      a. Report using the effective interest rate method, instead of par value.

   5. Bring accruals and deferrals up-to-date according to the economic resources measurement focus (full accrual basis).

   6. Report Net Position instead of fund balances.

See the following illustration.

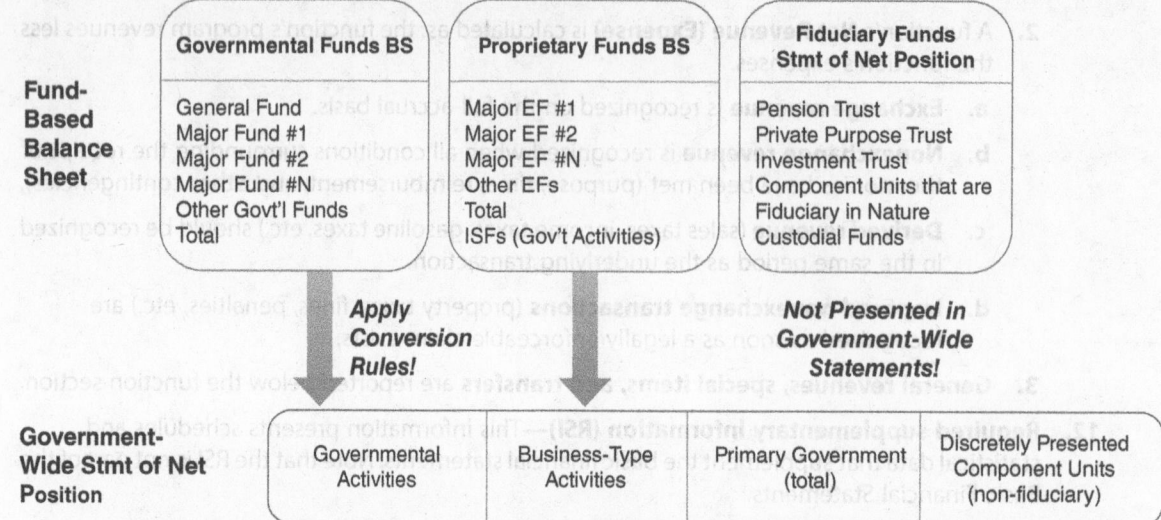

	Governmental Funds BS	Proprietary Funds BS	Fiduciary Funds Stmt of Net Position
Fund-Based Balance Sheet	General Fund Major Fund #1 Major Fund #2 Major Fund #N Other Govt'l Funds Total	Major EF #1 Major EF #2 Major EF #N Other EFs Total ISFs (Gov't Activities)	Pension Trust Private Purpose Trust Investment Trust Component Units that are Fiduciary in Nature Custodial Funds

Apply Conversion Rules!   *Not Presented in Government-Wide Statements!*

Government-Wide Stmt of Net Position	Governmental Activities	Business-Type Activities	Primary Government (total)	Discretely Presented Component Units (non-fiduciary)

14. **Operating statement conversion adjustments**—Following is a summary of the adjustments required to convert from the GASB Statement No. 34 mandated fund-based operating statements to the government-wide statement of activities. Note that, with the exception of interfund payables and receivables to Enterprise funds and the wholesale inclusion of Internal Service funds as part of governmental activities, all modifications are made to governmental funds.

1. Add all net revenue (expense) related to internal service funds:

    a. Add internal service funds' Net Position to governmental funds' total Fund Balance.

2. Eliminate capital outlay expenditures and debt principal expenditures.

    a. Increase the governmental funds' total Fund Balance for these items.

3. Eliminate proceeds from issuance of GLTD and proceeds from fixed asset sales.

    a. Decrease the governmental funds' total Fund Balance for these items.

4. Adjust governmental fund interest expenditures to interest expense under the effective interest method.

    a. Includes amortization of premiums, discounts, and bond issue costs.

    b. Depending on where you are in the amortization process, this could cause the governmental funds' total Fund Balance to increase OR decrease.

5. Record gains/losses on the sale of fixed assets.

    a. Increase or decrease the total Fund Balance of governmental funds for these items, as appropriate.

6. Record depreciation expense on GFA.

    a. Decrease the governmental funds' total Fund Balance for this item.

7. Adjust revenues from modified accrual to accrual amounts.

    a. Increase or decrease the governmental funds' total Fund Balance for these items, as appropriate.

8. Convert expenditures to expenses and adjust for differences between the modified accrual and accrual bases.

    a. Increase or decrease the governmental funds' total Fund Balance for these items, as appropriate.

15. **Changes in the Fiduciary Fund Category**—GASB Statement No. 34 made dramatic changes in the accounting and reporting of the Fiduciary Fund Category. All fiduciary funds now use the full accrual basis of accounting to record revenues and expenses. However, **none** of the fiduciary funds report revenues and expenses, since these monies do not belong to the government entity. Instead, the fiduciary funds **report changes in net position:** additions to net position and deduction from net position.

1. **Additional fiduciary fund**—One completely new fund type has been added to the Fiduciary Fund category:

   a. **Investment trust funds**—These funds are administered through a formal trust or equivalent arrangement and are used to account for monies received from other governmental entities that are pooled with reporting entity's investments. These funds account for the **external portion of the poolonly.**

      i. Portions of the pool belonging to the reporting government should be reported in the funds that hold the equity positions in the pool.

2. **Accounting for some fund types remains the same**

   a. **Pension trust funds**—Report the contributions to and distributions from the governmental entity's pension funds.

   b. **Custodial funds**—These may include only those assets that are ultimately payable to entities outside the reporting government.

      i. For example, a property tax custodial fund could only include those amounts due to other government entities.

      ii. Monies payable to the reporting government must be reported in the appropriate fund.

      iii. Investment pools that are not administered through a trust are accounted for in a custodial fund and will be reported as a separate column from other forms of custodial funds in the financial statements.

16. **GASBS Statement No. 56,** Codification of Accounting and Financial Reporting Guidance Contained in the AICPA Statements on Auditing Standards

   A. This Statement adds accounting guidance in the AICPA auditing literature to the GASB codification in three areas:

   1. **Related party transactions**—State and local governments are required to disclose related-party transactions and should recognize the substance of the transaction rather than its legal form.

   2. **Subsequent events**—Two types of subsequent events are described in the Statement. Recognized events consist of events that provide additional evidence with respect to conditions that existed at the date of the statement of net position and require adjustments to the financial statements. **Nonrecognized events** consist of those events that provide evidence with respect to conditions that did not exist at the date of the statement of net position. These events should not result in adjustment of the financial statements, but they may be disclosed in the notes of the financial statements.

   3. **Going concern considerations**—The Statement requires financial statement preparers to evaluate whether there is a substantial doubt about a government's ability to continue as a going concern for 12 months beyond the financial statement date (or shortly thereafter, which GASB describes as "an additional three months"). Indicators of substantial doubt include:

      a. Negative trends (e.g., recurring budget deficits)

      b. Other indicators of financial difficulties (e.g., loan default)

      c. Internal matters (e.g., work stoppages)

      d. External matters (e.g., legal proceedings)

4. If the evaluation determines that there is substantial doubt about a governmental entity's ability to continue as a going concern, then the notes to the financial statements should include the following disclosures:

    a. Pertinent conditions and events giving rise to the assessment that a substantial doubt exists about the ability of the entity to continue as a going concern

    b. The possible effects of such conditions and events

    c. Government officials' evaluation of the significance of those conditions and events

    d. Possible discontinuance of operations

    e. Government officials' plans

    f. Information about the recoverability or classification of recorded assets amounts or the amounts or classification of liabilities

Determining the Financial Reporting Entity

This lesson describes how the financial reporting entity is determined.

After studying this lesson, you should be able to:

1. Describe a primary government and a component unit.

2. Describe the difference between the blended presentation and discrete presentation of component unit information.

3. Describe the criteria for *fiscal independence* and *financially accountable*.

I. **Other Entities**—Because many governmental entities either authorize or are otherwise associated with a variety of other commissions, agencies, boards, and special districts, a question arises about which, if any, of these *other entities* should be included in the financial statements of the primary governmental unit. If the other entities are included, a further question concerns how their financial information should be presented. Most of these entities are legally separate organizations and enjoy some degree of financial and/or management independence.

II. **Terminology**

Definitions

Primary Government: A state government, a general-purpose local government (cities, counties) or a special purpose government that (1) has a separately elected governing body, (2) is legally separate, and (3) is fiscally independent of other state and local governments. The primary government is also known as the oversight unit. To be *fiscally independent*, the organization must be authorized to take all three of these specific actions without the approval of another government:

1. determine its budget

2. levy taxes or set user fees, and

3. issue bonded debt.

Component Units: Legally separate organizations for which the primary government officials are financially accountable or for which the relationship with the primary government is such that it would be misleading or incomplete to exclude it from the primary government's financial statements.

Financial Reporting Entity: A primary government and its component units.

III. **Deciding Whether an Entity Is a Component Unit**

A. The following circumstances set forth a primary government's financial accountability for a legally separate organization:

1. The primary government is financially accountable if it appoints a voting majority of the organization's governing body *and* either:

a. It is able to impose its will on that organization if primary government has the ability to do any one of the following:

i. Remove appointed members of the organization's governing board at will

ii. Modify or approve the budget of the organization

iii. Modify or approve rate or fee changes affecting revenues, such as utility rate increases

iv. Veto, overrule, or modify decision of the organization's governing body

v. Appoint, hire, reassign, or dismiss those persons responsible for the day-to-day operations of the organization

    b. **OR** there is potential for the organization to provide specific financial benefits to or impose specific financial burdens on the primary government as evidenced by any one of the following conditions where the primary government is:

       i. Legally entitled to or can otherwise access the organization's resources

       ii. Legally obligated or has otherwise assumed the obligation to finance the deficits of, or provide financial support to, the organization

       iii. Obligated in some manner for the debt of the organization

  2. Exception for IRC Section 457 Deferred Compensation Plans. According to GASB Statement No. 97, Section 457 plans that do not have a governing body will be considered financially accountable to the primary government if the primary government performs the duties that a governing body typically would perform.

B. The primary government is financially accountable if an organization is **fiscally dependent** on the primary government and there is a potential for the organization to provide specific benefits to, or impose specific financial burdens on, the primary government regardless of how the organization's governing body is determined.

Recap of combinations of criteria of a potential component unit should be included in the primary government's reporting entity:

Appointment Authority	Financial Accountability Appointment Authority	Fiscal Dependence
+	+	+
Financial Benefit or Burden	**Ability to Impose Will**	**Financial Benefit or Burden**

IV. Include the organization as a component unit in the primary government's financial statements when it would be misleading without the inclusion of the other entity. (Component units can be other organizations for which the nature and significance of their relationship with a primary government are such that exclusion would cause the reporting entity's financial statements to be misleading.)

Example

What are the criteria for recognizing an independent agency as a component unit of a general-purpose governmental unit (i.e., city, county, or state)?

The component unit must be fiscally dependent on the primary government or, if not fiscally dependent, then its board must be appointed by the primary government and either the primary government can impose its will on the component unit or significant financial burdens or benefits can be shifted from one to the other.

V. **GASB Satement No. 39,** *Determining Whether Certain Organizations Are Component Units*—This statement broadens the definition of a component unit. It requires legally separate organizations that are not fiscally dependent on the primary government, and for which the primary government is not financially accountable, to be included in the primary government's financial statements as component units if the organization raises and holds economic resources for the direct benefit of a governmental unit.

A. **Criteria**—Legally separate entities that meet all of the following criteria, should be discretely presented as component units if:

  1. The separate organization holds economic resources entirely, or almost entirely, for the direct benefit of the primary government, its component units, or its constituents

  2. The primary government is entitled to, or has the ability to otherwise access, a majority of the economic resources received or held by the separate organization

3. The economic resources received or held by the separate organization are significant to the primary government

4. GASB Statement No. 80, issued January 2016, provides the blending method should be used for a component unit organized as a not-for-profit corporation in which the primary government is the sole corporate member, as identified in the component unit's articles of incorporation or bylaws.

B. GASB Statement No. 39 requires discrete presentation of component units included in the reporting entity due to the requirements of Statement No. 39.

Example
The Business School alumni of Big X University establish a legally separate, not-for-profit foundation to provide scholarships to students and to establish chaired faculty positions. Although neither the Business School nor the University appoint members of the governing board of the foundation or exert any control over the foundation, all of the money raised by the foundation is channeled to the Business School, which constitutes a significant resource to the Business School and the University. Because all three requirements are met, the foundation is included as a component unit of Big X University.

C. **Presenting the Financial Information**

1. **Blending**

   a. If the component unit is, in substance, a part of the primary government (i.e., a building authority established to construct facilities for the primary government) then the balances for its funds should be included with similar funds in the primary government.

Example
The component unit's capital projects fund should be added to the primary government's capital projects funds; the component unit's debt service fund should be added to the primary government's debt service funds; and so on.

   b. **Exception**—An exception is made for the component unit's general fund, which is considered a special revenue fund for the primary unit.

   c. **A component unit is deemed to be part of the primary government** *in substance* **when any one of the following characteristics occur:**

      i. It has substantively the same governing body as the primary government (i.e., a voting majority of the component unit's governing body is the same as the primary government's governing body; e.g., 4 out of 7) and (1) there is a financial burden/benefit relationship or (2) the primary government's management has day-to-day operational responsibility for the component unit.

      ii. The component unit provides services only or provides benefits only to the primary government.

      iii. The component unit's total debt outstanding is expected to be repaid entirely, or almost entirely by the primary government.

2. **Discrete presentation**

   a. **For all other component units, a special column is added to the right of the primary government's data.** If there are multiple component units, their data may be aggregated into a single column and a combining statement that details the individual units prepared.

Example

How and when is a component unit's financial information presented discreetly with the primary government?

All other component units (i.e., those that provide services to other than the primary government) use discrete presentation. The component unit(s) data is displayed in a separate column to the right of the primary government's information.

D. Reporting Entity Component Unit Disclosures

1. The component units included in the reporting entity

2. The rationale for including each component unit

3. Information about how each component unit was included in the financial statements—blended or discretely presented in the government-wide financial statements or included in the fiduciary fund financial statements (recall that fiduciary funds are not included in the government-wide financial statements)

4. The availability of separate financial statements of each component unit

Major Funds and Fund-Level Reporting

This lesson discusses major funds and fund-level reporting.

After studying this lesson, you should be able to:

1. Describe how major funds are determined.

2. List the types of financial statements required at the fund-level for fiduciary funds.

3. List the types of financial statements required at the fund-level for proprietary funds.

4. List the types of financial statements required at the fund-level for governmental funds.

5. Describe financial reporting for internal service funds.

I. Major Funds and Fund-Based Statements

A. **Reporting**—Based on *major funds*.

1. A major fund is one that comprises 10% of the total assets plus deferred outflows, or liabilities plus deferred inflows, revenues, or expenditures/expenses (excluding extraordinary items) for its fund category (governmental or enterprise funds) **and** one that comprises at least 5% of the corresponding total for all governmental and enterprise funds combined.

Note

Fiduciary funds are never major funds because the assets in fiduciary funds are not government assets and, therefore, are not used to calculate the 5% and 10% tests. The government acts as a trustee, custodian, or agent of assets held by the government for the benefit of others. Fiduciary funds are not included in the government-wide financial statements. In the Annual Comprehensive Financial Report (ACFR) fiduciary funds are reported at the fund level to provide accountability to those for whom the government is acting in a fiduciary capacity.

---

2. The general fund is always considered a major fund.

3. Other funds may be considered major funds because of their significance to the governmental unit and/or the users of the financial statements (based on *professional judgment*).

4. Nonmajor funds are segregated by type (governmental or *business-like*), then presented in total by type in separate columns.

B. A **reconciliation** of amounts listed on the fund-based statements to amounts listed on the government-wide statements must be presented a) on the face of the fund-based financial statements or b) on a separate schedule.

C. **Financial Statements**

1. Proprietary funds and fiduciary funds present a Statement of Net Position, rather than a Balance Sheet (governmental funds still call their statement a Balance Sheet).

2. Since fiduciary funds do not recognize revenue or expense, they produce a Statement of Changes in Net Position, rather than a Statement of Revenues and Expenses.

3. The Statement of Revenues and Expenditures Budget to Actual—essentially the budget comparison statement—appears with Other Required Supplementary Information.

II. Treatment of Fiduciary Funds—The only statements required for fiduciary funds are a Statement of Fiduciary Net Position and a Statement of Changes in Fiduciary Net Position.

    A. Although we **record** additions and deductions for in the trust funds (pension trust, investment trust, and private purpose trust), we **do not report** these funds in the government-wide financial statements.

        1. Because these monies do not belong to us, we cannot recognize either revenue or expense related to them.

    B. Instead, we report Additions to Net Position and Deductions from Net Position.

    C. Except in the case of an investment pool that is not subject to a formal trust arrangement, a custodial fund does not even RECORD additions and deductions, because these funds act simply as a cash conduit;

        1. Monies in these funds belong to someone else and simply flow through the custodial fund.

        2. Hence, the custodial fund records and reports only assets and liabilities.

III. Treatment of Internal Service Funds—Internal service funds are not aggregated with enterprise funds but are, instead, combined with the governmental funds in the government-wide financial statements.

IV. Infrastructure Capital Assets

    A. Capital assets include infrastructure (sidewalks, street lights, roads, etc.) and easements.

Deriving Government-Wide Financial Statements and Reconciliation Requirements

After studying this lesson, you should be able to:

1. Describe which fund types make up governmental activities and which fund types make up business-type activities.

2. Describe how internal service fund financial information is integrated into the government-wide financial statement.

3. Prepare standard entries to adjust fund-level information in deriving governmental activities in the Statement of Net Position.

4. Describe what creates "internal balances" in the Statement of Net Position.

I. **Governmental Activities**—Recall that governmental funds (DRIP CEG) use the modified accrual basis of accounting, which has the flow of financial resources measurement focus. Consequently, a number of conversion steps are required in converting fund-level information to government-wide information. Capital assets and long-term liabilities are not included in the fund-level financial statements of governmental funds; revenues and expenditures are not measured in accordance with accrual accounting; and the five types of fund balances need to be restated in one of the three categories of net position. The conversion process can be summarized as follows (GF: General Fund; ISF: Internal Service Fund; MF: Major Fund; NMF: Nonmajor Funds):

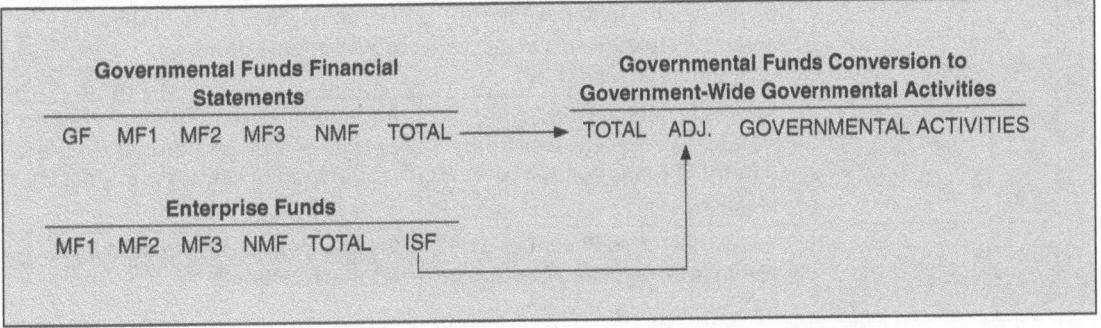

The adjustments need to convert fund level governmental fund balance sheet information into the government-wide balance sheet can be summarized by examining the accounting equation for governmental funds, the government-wide statement, and the adjustments necessary to make the conversion:

Governmental Funds Accounting Equation	Adjustments to Make the Conversion to Government Wide	Governmental Activities Accounting Equation
Current Assets		Current Assets
	General Capital Assets	**+ Capital Assets**
+ Deferred Outflows		+ Deferred Outflows
− Current Liabilities		− Current Liabilities
	General Long-term Liabilities	**− Long-term Liabilities**
− Deferred Inflows		− Deferred Inflows
	Deferred Revenues	**− Deferred Revenues**
= Fund balance	**+/− Net Effect of Changes**	**= Net Position**

Adjustments:

	Government-Wide Financial Statements	
Adjustments	**Balance Sheet**	**Statement of Activities**
General Capital Assets	Add capital assets and accumulated depreciation	Eliminate capital outlay expenditures, add depreciation expense, deduct carrying value of capital asset disposals
General Long-Term Liabilities	Add bonds payable and add (deduct) bond premium (discount), add accrued interest payable	Eliminate other financing sources for bonds and bond premium (or other financing use for bond discount), eliminate expenditures or other financing use for bond retirements, convert interest expenditure to interest expense
	Add other long-term liabilities such as pensions, other post-employment benefits (OPEB), claims, judgments, compensated absences, etc.	Convert expenditures to expenses
Other Adjustments	Add Internal Service Fund (ISF) assets and liabilities	Allocate ISF profit (loss) from interfund sales/services to decrease (increase) expenses
	Eliminate interfund payables to and receivables from governmental funds	Eliminate transfers to and from governmental funds
	Reclassify net interfund payables and receivables from enterprise funds as internal balances	Reclassify net amount of transfers to or from Enterprise Funds as transfers to and from business-type activities
	Reduce Deferred Revenues to eliminate amounts deferred due to resources not available	Convert revenues from modified accrual to accrual

II. Business-Type Activities—Enterprise funds (EFs) are reported as business-type activities in the government-wide financial statements. Since EFs are reported using the flow of economic resources measurement focus and the accrual basis of accounting, the conversion process is rather simple. The main adjustments are to eliminate various interfund transactions and balances. When an Internal Service Fund provides sales and services to EF departments, the profit (loss) experienced by the ISF overstates (understates) the amount recorded by the EF, and an adjustment is required to derive business-type activity expenses in the statement of activities. The net amount of interfund receivables and payables between EFs and governmental funds are reclassified as **internal balances** in the balance sheet (Statement of Net Position). The conversion process can be summarized as follows (GF: general fund; ISF: internal service fund; MF: major fund; NMF: nonmajor funds):

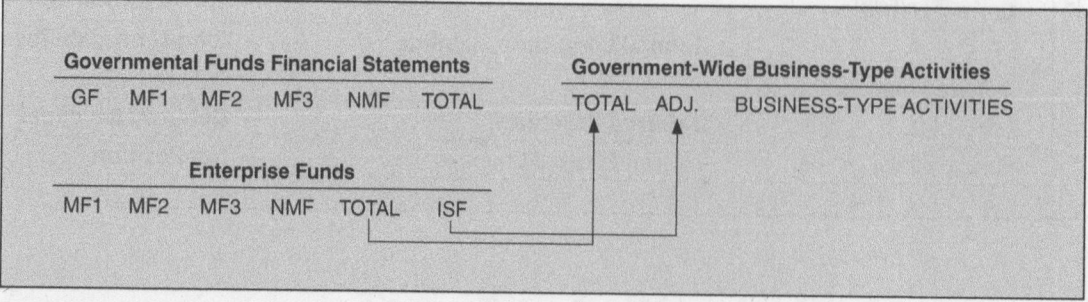

III. Internal Service Funds—Internal service fund (ISF) activities that primarily serve governmental activities are reported as governmental activities. Similarly, ISF activities that primarily serve enterprise funds are reported as business-type activities. If the ISF makes a profit or a loss then the funds the recorded expenditures or expenses from ISF services require an adjustment for the amount of overcharge or undercharge by the ISF.

IV. Fiduciary Funds—Fiduciary fund activities **(PIPPA)** are **not** included in the government-wide financial statements because the government primarily holds and manages resources in fiduciary funds for the benefit of others.

V. Conversion Worksheet—The standard worksheet used to convert governmental funds to government activities takes the following form:

| | Adjustments | | | |
| Governmental Funds | General Capital Asset Balances and Changes | General Long-Term Liabilities Balances and Changes | Other Balances, Changes, and Interfund Items | Governmental Activities |

Example

The City of Carrolton, Texas had the following balances in its balance sheet for governmental funds as of September 30, 20X4:

Assets	
Cash and cash equivalents	$122,925,945
Receivables	
Ad valorem taxes	149,350
Sales taxes	2,385,722
Franchise taxes	3,006,119
Accrued interest	191,398
Other	1,182,311
Due from other funds	1,153,976
Due from other governments	1,067,617
Prepaid items	51,584
Land held for resale	3,032,558
Total Assets	$135,146,580
Liabilities and Fund Balance	
Liabilities	
Accounts payable	$11,543,454
Unearned revenue	723,293
Total Liabilities	12,266,747
Total Fund Balance*	122,879,833
Total Liabilities and Fund Balance	$135,146,850

*For simplicity, only total fund balance is used in this example. Carrolton's balance sheet reports all five categories of fund balance. Government-wide financial statements report three categories of net position rather than fund balance.

Other information related to governmental activities:

1. Capital assets:

Land	$102,700,673
Construction in progress	4,865,419
Buildings	65,622,079
Equipment	30,822,739
Intangibles	6,156,150
Improvements	43,784,292
Infrastructure	259,110,959
Accumulated Depreciation:	
Buildings	(36,944,523)
Equipment	(17,777,803)
Intangibles	(5,637,553)
Improvements	(15,442,257)
Infrastructure	(67,926,595)

2. Long-term liabilities:

Bonds payable	$168,728,244
Compensated absences	13,675,654
Health claims liability	1,105,000
Other post-employment benefits	411,049
Long-term risk liability	2,028,558

3. Internal service fund:

Cash and cash equivalents	$16,854,237
Receivables:	
Accrued interest	22,597
Other	65,477
Inventories	71,275
Prepaid items	176,367
Accounts payable	1,043,264
Net amount allocated to business-type activities	194,753

Other items:

4. Equity interest in North Texas Emergency Communications Center joint venture with two other cities: $583,200

5. Net pension asset: $1,352,103

6. Deferred charges on debt refunding: $2,122,111

7. Interest payable not reported under modified accrual basis of accounting: $971,993

8. Cash and investments restricted by legal and contractual obligations: $30,442,879

9. Adjustment for internal balances

Assets	Governmental Funds	(1) Capital Assets	(2) Long-Term Liabilities	(3) ISF	#	Other Items	Government-Wide
Cash and cash equivalents	$122,925,945			16,854,237	8	(30,442,879)	$109,337,303
Receivables							
Ad valorem taxes	149,350						149,350
Sales taxes	2,385,722						2,385,722
Franchise taxes	3,006,119						3,006,119
Accrued interest	191,398			22,597			213,995
Other	1,182,311			65,477			1,247,788
Due from other funds	1,153,976				9	(1,153,976)	—
Due from other governments	1,067,617						1,067,617
Internal balances				194,753	9	1,153,976	1,348,729
Inventories				71,275			71,275
Prepaid items	51,584			176,367			227,951
Equity interest in joint venture					4	583,200	583,200
Land held for resale	3,032,558						3,032,558
Restricted assets, cash					8	30,442,879	30,442,879
Net pension assets					5	1,352,103	1,352,103
Capital assets (Net)		369,333,580					369,333,580
Total Assets	$135,146,580	369,333,580		17,384,706		1,935,303	523,800,169
Deferred outflow or resources—Debt Refunding Charges				2,122,111	6	2,122,111	2,122,111
Liabilities and Fund Balance							
Liabilities							
Accounts payable	$11,543,454			1,043,264			12,586,718
Accrued interest payable					7	971,993	971,993
Unearned revenue	723,293						723,293
Long-Term Liabilities (Total)			185,978,505				185,978,505
Total Liabilities	12,266,747		185,978,505	1,043,264		971,993	200,260,509
Total Fund Balance*/Net Position	122,879,833	369,333,580	(185,978,505)	16,341,442		963,310	325,661,771

Conversion worksheet: To simplify the example, capital assets are added in the worksheet as a single amount net of accumulated depreciation in adjustment (1) and long-term liabilities are added in total in adjustment (3). It highlight the adjustment for internal service funds adjustment (3) is shown in a separate column. All other adjustments appear in the "Other Items" column with the appropriate reference in the "#" column.

VI. Reconciliation of the Changes in Fund Balance to Changes in Net Position—A reconciliation for the changes in fund balance in the government fund balance sheet to changes in net position in the government-wide statement of net position accompanies the government fund balance sheet.

City of Carrollton, TX

Reconciliation of Governmental Funds Fund Balances to Governmental Activities Net Position
30-Sep-X4

Reconciliation of Fund Balances to Net Assets

	in 000s
Fund Balances—Total Governmental Funds	$122,880
Capital Assets, net of accumulated depreciation, are not reported on the Balance Sheet but are reported on the Statement of Net Position	369,334
Long-term liabilities are not due and payable in the current period and therefore are not reported in the funds.	(185,979)
Unamortized balance of debt refunding costs reported when refunding occurred by the governmental refunding occurred.	2,112
Internal service fund current assets and accounts payable	16,147
Internal balances between governmental activities and business activities	195
Interest is not accrued on long-term debt on the Balance Sheet but is reported on the Statement of Net Position	(972)
Deferred Revenue reported in the funds are not on the Statement of Net Position because of differences in revenue recognition.	1,352
Equity investment in joint venture is not reported in governmental funds balance sheet	583
Net Position of Governmental Activities	$325,662

Note

The $195 amount of internal service fund net position allocated to business-type entities is the only reconciling item between total net position for enterprise funds and net position for business-type activities in the government-wide statement of net position.

Typical Items and Specific Types of Transactions and Events

Interfund Transactions, Construction Projects, and Infrastructure

This lesson describes the types of interfund transactions and special rules related to infrastructure.

After studying this lesson, you should be able to:

1. List the four types of interfund transactions.

2. Understand typical entries related to construction projects.

3. Describe when the *modified approach* for infrastructure can be used.

I. Interfund Transactions

   A. Loans

   1. One fund transfers cash (usually) to another fund with the expectation that this amount will be repaid. The general fund frequently loans or advances monies to an enterprise fund.

   a. General fund

Advances to Enterprise Fund*	XXX	
Cash		XXX

*This account title assumes that the debt is a long-term item; if it is a short-term item, the account titles are changed to Due from the Enterprise Fund (Receivable) and Due to the General Fund (Payable)

   b. Enterprise fund

Cash	XXX	
Advances from General Fund*		XXX

*This account title assumes that the debt is a long-term item; if it is a short-term item, the account titles are changed to Due from the Enterprise Fund (Receivable) and Due to the General Fund (Payable)

   2. When the monies are repaid, the entries are simply reversed.

   B. Quasi-External (Interfund Sales and Purchase) Transactions—These transactions occur when one fund (usually an enterprise or internal service fund) supplies goods/services to another fund. The transaction gives rise to a revenue entry in the fund supplying the services and an expenditure in the fund using the services.

   1. For instance, if the general fund receives copying services from the printing and duplication department (an internal service fund), the following entry is recorded:

   a. General fund

Expenditures	XXX	
Due to Internal Service Fund		XXX

b. Internal service fund

Due from General Fund	XXX	
Revenues		XXX

c. When the amounts are paid in cash, the liability/receivable is eliminated in each of the funds.

C. Expenditure Reimbursements—When one fund pays an expenditure on behalf of another fund and subsequently receives repayment, the expenditure is reduced in the fund that receives the repayment and increased in the fund making the repayment.

1. For example, if the general fund previously paid for an expenditure on behalf of a capital projects fund and the capital projects fund is now reimbursing the general fund, the entry to record the reimbursement is:

2. General fund

Cash	XXX	
Expenditures		XXX

3. Capital projects fund

Expenditures	XXX	
Cash		XXX

D. Residual Equity Transfers—These are nonrecurring, relatively infrequent, transfers of monies between funds, typically to establish or expand the activities of a Proprietary fund (i.e., for capital purposes), remove a deficit equity position in a Proprietary fund, or transfer a remaining balance out of a fund that is being closed.

1. Reporting for Residual Equity Transfers

> **Note**
> *Transfers from the general or special revenue fund to capital projects or debt service funds are classified as operating transfers, not residual equity transfers!*

a. In the GASB Statement No. 33 model, they are titled simply Transfers and are reported in the other financing sources/(uses) section of the government fund fund-based statements and as Transfers by the proprietary fund in a separate line item after the operating income line of the proprietary fund statement of revenues, expenses, and changes in net position.

b. The transfers of proprietary funds are closed to net position.

2. To record the transfer of remaining funds from a terminated debt service fund to the general fund:

E. Debt Service Fund

DR: OFU—Residual Equity Transfer to General Fund	XXX	
CR: Cash		XXX

F. General Fund

DR: Cash	XXX	
CR: OFS—Residual Equity Transfer from Debt Service Fund		XXX

II. **Operating Transfers**—These are regular, routine, or recurring transfers of resources between funds to subsidize current activities. They are classified as Operating Transfers. Examples are when the general fund transfers money to the stores fund (and ISF) to subsidize salary costs or when the general fund transfers monies to a debt service fund to be used for the repayment of a long term liability.

A. Since these transfers do not represent revenues or expenditures for the governmental unit, they are reported as other financing sources/uses in governmental funds and as Transfers In or Out in proprietary funds (in a line(s) after Operating Income).

B. The entry to record a routine transfer from the general fund to the debt service fund is shown below.

C. **General Fund**

DR: OFU—Operating Transfer to Debt Service Fund	XXX	
CR: Cash		XXX

D. **Debt Service Fund**

DR: Cash	XXX	
CR: OFS—Operating Transfer from General Fund		XXX

III. **Entries Relating to Major Construction Projects**

A. **Major Construction Projects**—When a major building project is begun, a series of entries occur that affect the debt service fund and the general fund. These entries are illustrated below.

B. **Introduction**

1. Bonds are issued to pay for the constructions (no entry required for authorization of bond issue).

a. **Capital projects fund**

Cash	10,000,000	
Other Financing Sources—Bond Proceeds		10,000,000

b. **Governmental activities (government-wide financial statements)**

Cash	10,000,000	
Bonds Payable		10,000,000

2. Bonds payable are shown at present value calculated using the effective interest rate method on the government-wide financial statements but are not shown in the fund-level financial statements of the capital projects fund.

3. Progress proceeds on the building.

a. **Capital projects fund**

Expenditures	5,000,000	
Cash (or Vouchers Payable)		5,000,000

b. Governmental activities (government-wide financial statements)

Construction-in-Progress	5,000,000	
Cash (or Vouchers Payable)		5,000,000

4. The general fund transfers monies to the debt service fund to cover interest that is now due on the debt and to provide for retirement of the bonds; the debt service fund pays the interest.

a. General fund

Operating Transfer to Debt Service Fund	2,000,000	
Cash		2,000,000

b. Debt service fund

Cash	2,000,000	
Operating Transfer from General Fund		2,000,000
Expenditures—Interest	1,000,000	
Interest Payable		1,000,000

c. Governmental activities (government-wide financial statements)

Interest Expense	1,000,000	
Interest Payable		1,000,000

5. The project is completed at an additional cost of $4,500,000.

a. Capital projects fund

Expenditures	4,500,000	
Cash (or Vouchers Payable)		4,500,000

b. Governmental activities (government-wide financial statements)

Note
The asset is reported with Net Investment in Capital Assets in the Government-Wide Financial Statements.

Capital Asset	9,500,000	
Cash (or Vouchers Payable)		4,500,000
Construction-in-Process		5,000,000

c. The capital projects fund is closed and the remaining balance is transferred to the debt service fund to be used to repay the bond liability.

a. Capital projects fund

Other Financing Sources	10,000,000	
Expenditures		9,500,000
Fund Balance		500,000
Residual Equity Transfer to Debt Service Fund*	500,000	
Cash		500,000
Fund Balance	500,000	
Residual Equity Transfer to Debt Service Fund*		500,000
Debt Service Fund:		
Cash	500,000	
Residual Equity Transfer from Capital Projects Fund*		500,000

*Per GASB Statement No. 33, these would be reported as transfers.

IV. Infrastructure

A. Infrastructure is capital assets such as highways, bridges, streets, sidewalks, water and sewerage systems, storm drainage, seawalls, and lighting systems that are stationary in nature and can be preserved much longer than most other capital assets (e.g., buildings and equipment).

B. The financial reporting treatment of public infrastructure follows that of other capital assets.

C. In **government-wide financial statements** infrastructure is reported as assets in the Statement of Net Position and, unless the modified approach is adopted, depreciation expense for infrastructure is reported in the government-wide Statement of Activities. Depreciation is also recognized in proprietary and fiduciary fund-level financial statements.

D. In **governmental fund financial statements** additions to infrastructure assets are reported as expenditures.

E. Under the **modified approach** a government can elect not to depreciate certain eligible infrastructure, provided that the following two requirements are met:

1. The government manages the eligible infrastructure assets using an asset management system that includes (a) an up-to-date inventory of eligible assets, (b) condition assessments of the assets and summary of results using a measurement scale, and (c) estimates each year of the annual amount needed to maintain and preserve the eligible assets at a condition level established and disclosed by the government, and

2. The government documents that the eligible infrastructure assets are being preserved approximately at (or above) the condition level established and disclosed in 1(c).

3. Using the modified approach, the government will expense maintenance costs in lieu of depreciation expense. Additions and improvements to infrastructure assets are still capitalized in the government-wide statement of net position and in the proprietary and fiduciary fund-level statements of net position.

Long-Term Liabilities Other Than Bonded Debt

This lesson describes the common types of long-term liabilities other than bonded debt.

After studying this lesson, you should be able to:

1. List four common types of long-term liabilities other than bonded debt.

2. Describe the *general rule* at the fund level, for recognition of expenditures and liabilities.

3. Describe the *general rule* at the government-wide level, for recognition of expenses and liabilities.

I. **Recognition and Reporting of Long-Term Liabilities Other Than Debt in Governmental Funds**

   A. **Recognize a Liability**—In the fund-based statements only when the use of current resources is required. Governmental funds are used to account for sources, uses, and balances of expendable general government financial assets. As a result, in governmental funds:

      1. Long-term assets purchased are reported as fund expenditures rather than as fixed assets.

      2. Proceeds of long-term debt are recorded as other financing sources rather than as long-term debt.

      3. Long-term portions of the liability are kept off the fund-based statements.

         a. Only those portions of the potential liability that are likely to be paid in cash are included. For example, if sick leave does not vest to the employee, then only those portions of sick leave that are reasonably expected to be paid to the employee are reported.

      4. General long-term liabilities are reported in the government-wide financial statements.

         a. All unmatured long-term debt, except for that of proprietary funds or trust funds, is reported in the government-wide Statement of Net Position. Matured general obligation debt, that has been recorded in or will be paid from a debt service fund, is excluded from general long-term liabilities.

         b. General long-term liabilities include unmatured principal of bonds, warrants, notes, capital leases, claims and judgments, certificates of participation, compensated absences, landfill closure and postclosure care, underfunded pension plan and underfunded OPEB contributions, and other forms of general government debt. Unmatured long-term special assessment debt is also included if the government is obligated in any manner on the debt and the debt is not being serviced through an enterprise fund.

   B. **Liabilities in the Government-Wide Statements**—may be reported either at face value or at discounted value, depending on the circumstances.

      1. If there is a *structured settlement plan* (contractual obligations to pay money on fixed or determinable dates as a means of settling a liability), then the discounted value of the plan to discharge the liability is used;

      2. In the absence of a structured settlement plan, the liability is simply reported at face value.

Example

The City of Tima Springs was assessed damages of $1,000,000 pursuant to a liability claim from a citizen who fell into an uncovered manhole. Payment of the claim is scheduled to take place over a 10-year period, with the first payment of $115,000 due in six weeks; the PV of the remaining cash flow is $465,000.

Tima would recognize the currently due portion of the settlement as an Expenditure in its fund-based statements. The government-wide statements would report expenses of $580,000 ($465K + $115K) and report the liability at its $465,000 PV.

II. Common Types of Long-Term Debt Other Than Bonded Debt

A. Claims and Judgments

—These primarily related to construction activities of a government. Litigated and adjudicated claims adverse to the government should be recorded. For claims that not yet been litigated or judgments have not been made, liabilities may be estimated on a case-by-case basis. Accounting and reporting for claims and judgments varies as follows:

1. The amount of claims and judgments recognized as expenditures and liabilities of governmental funds is limited to amount that is payable with current expendable resources available in the fund.

2. The full known or estimated liability and expense is reported in the government activities column of the government-wide statement of net position and statement of activities.

B. Compensated Absences

—Such absences represent paid time off that employees earn in vacation and sick leave. The accounting and reporting for compensated absences is similar to that for claims and judgments, and varies as follows:

1. The amount of expenditure and liability recognized in the financial statements of governmental funds is only that portion of the compensated absences that employees will use in the upcoming fiscal period. That is, the amount that will be paid from current financial resources.

2. The full amount of the liability and expense is recognized in the government-wide financial statements.

Example

General Fund recognizes $50,000 in the amount that it estimates employees will use in the next year:

Expenditures—Compensated Absences	$50,000	
Liability—Compensated Absences		$50,000

The full expense and liability of $200,000 is recognized in the government-wide financial statements:

Expense—Compensated Absences	$250,000	
Liability—Compensated Absences		$250,000

C. Right-to-Use Assets (Leases, PPP, SBITA)

—Three GASB Statements apply a common approach to accounting for contracts that involve the right to use another party's asset (the "underlying asset"). The three GASB Statements are: GASB 87 on leases, GASB 94 on public-private and public-public partnership (PPP) and availability payment arrangements (APA), and GASB 96 on subscription-based information technology arrangements (SBITAs).

In each statement, common features include the definition of the arrangement, determination of the contract's time period (term), accounting for short-term arrangements of 12 months or less, and accounting for long-term arrangements exceeding 12 months.

Definitions

1. **Definition:** The lease, public-private and public-public partnership (PPP), or subscription-based information technology arrangements (SBITA) is a contract that conveys control of the right to use or operate a nonfinancial asset for a period of time in an exchange or exchange-like transactions. "Control" occurs when the party has the right to both the *present service capacity* of the underlying asset and can *dictate the nature and manner of use* of the underlying asset.

2. **Term:** The term is the period of time during which the party has a noncancelable right to use or operate the underlying asset (referred to as the noncancelable period) plus the following additional periods, if applicable:

   a. Include option periods to *extend* the arrangement if it is reasonably certain that the option will be exercised.

    b. Include periods for which there is an option to *terminate* the arrangement if it is reasonably certain that the option *will not* be exercised.

3. **Short-term arrangements:** Contracts of 12 months, or less, should be expensed by the lessee and income for the lessor and revenue for the two parties based on the payment provisions of the contract.

4. **Long-term arrangements:** Contracts exceeding one year will be accounted for in one of two ways: (1) as financed purchase/sale if the contract transfers ownership or (2) as a lease-type arrangement with the right to use or operate an underlying asset.

5. **Leases:** GASB 87 (effective beginning June 15, 2021) established new accounting guidance for leases. The biggest change was replacing the operating and capital lease dichotomy with a single model for lease accounting based on the principle that leases are financings of a right to use an underlying asset. Under GASB 87, there are three types of leases:

    1. Short-term leases of one year or less (including any renewal or extension options)

    2. Contracts that transfer ownership

    3. All other leases

Government-wide accounting for leases:

Type of lease	Lessee Accounting[1]	Lessor Accounting
Short-term leases	Lease payments are expense	Lease payments are revenue
Contracts that transfer ownership	Reported as a financed purchase	Reported as the sale of an asset
All other leases—initial recognition	Debit: Intangible right-to-sue asset Credit: Lease liability	Debit: Lease receivable Credit: Deferred inflow of resources (continue to report leased asset)
All other leases—subsequent to initial recognition	Debit: Lease liability Debit: Interest expense Credit: Cash Debit: Amortization expense Credit: Accumulated amortization	Debit: Cash Credit: Lease receivable Credit: Interest revenue Debit: Deferred inflow of resources Credit: Lease revenue Debit: Depreciation expense Credit: Accumulated depreciation

[1]Expect questions related to the ***lessee*** on the exam.

1. **Public-Private and Public-Public Partnership (PPP, or P3).** GASB 94 (effective beginning June 15, 2022) supersedes GASB 60 on service concession arrangements (SCA). A PPP is an arrangement in which the government (transferor) contracts with an operator (either another government or a nongovernmental entity) to provide public services by conveying control of the right to operate or use a nonfinancial asset for a period of time in an exchange or exchange-like transaction. Essentially, a PPP is contractual relationship in which the transferor and the operator agree to share the risks and rewards associated with the public asset. The partnership can involve some or all of the following aspects of the public asset: design, build, finance, operate, maintain, own.

    Form of PPP: A PPP has three basic forms.

a. Some PPPs meet the definition of a lease and apply GASB 87 guidelines if the operator is not required to improve the existing assets and it is not a service concession arrangement. GASB 94 provides guidance for all other PPPs.

b. Some PPPs are service concession arrangements (SCA) in which all of the following criteria are met:

1. The transferor conveys to the operator the right to provide public services through the use and operation of the underlying PPP asset in exchange for significant consideration.

2. The operator collects and is compensated by fees from third parties (such as tolls).

3. The transferor determines and can modify the services to be provided, to whom the operator is required to provide services, and the prices or rates that can be charged.

4. The transferor retains a significant residual interest in the service utility of the underlying PPP asset at the end of the arrangement.

c. Some P3s are availability payment arrangements (APAs), in which a government procures a capital asset or service for which the operator is compensated by the government instead of being compensated by third parties.

Examples

1. Excel County enters into a public-private partnership arrangement with Swamp Bridge Operators (SBO), under which SBO will operate, maintain, and retain toll fees from the Swamp Movable Toll Bridge. SBO paid Excel County $50 million for the right to operate the toll collection and to receive and retain toll revenues for a period of 25 years. Excel County sets the toll rates and retains ownership of the bridge at the end of the arrangement.

   Based on the facts in this example, this PPP meets the criteria of a SCA. Criterion (b1) is met because there is a significant up-front payment. Criterion (b2) is met since SBO is collecting fees from third parties. Criterion (b3) is met because Excel County established the toll rates and SBO provides the toll collection function in place of the county. Criterion (b4) is met as the PPP asset will remain with the county at the end of the arrangement.

2. Excel County enters into a public-private partnership arrangement with Road Warriors Inc. (RWI) to design, build, and finance construction of a toll road. In exchange, the county pays RWI $15 million at the start of the project, $10 million on the date the toll road is placed into service, and $1 million annually for the design, building, and financing of the toll road. As part of the arrangement, RWI collects all tolls for the toll road for 25 years and remits the collections to the county. RWI will receive $100,000 per month for collecting the tolls.

   Based on the facts of the example, this PPP does not meet the criteria of a SCA because RWI is not charging third parties and retaining the toll fees; hence, criterion (b) is not met. The county is compensating RWI for operating the toll function by paying $100,000 per month. This is an availability payment arrangement (APA).

3. Excel County enters into a public-private partnership arrangement with Road Warriors Inc. (RWI) to design, build, and finance construction of a toll road in exchange for ownership of the toll road at the end of the arrangement. RWI collects and keep all tolls for the toll road for 25 years. This is a PPP arrangement since the county is not paying a fee to the operator.

Initial measurement of a PPP right-to-use asset:

Initial up-front payment received from operator

+ Present value of future installment payments

+ Cost of purchased or constructed underlying PPP asset

+ Cost of improvements to existing underlying PPP asset

+ Initial direct cost necessary to place right-to-use asset into service

Recognition and Measurement for PPP:

	Transferor[1]	Operator
Underlying PPP asset is existing asset owned by transferor. No improvements are required, and PPP is not a SCA.	This is a lease under GASB 87.	This is a lease under GASB 87.
Underlying PPP asset is existing asset owned by transferor. It will be improved by operator and is not a SCA.	At commencement recognize: • Receivable for present value of installment payments • Deferred inflow of resources • Continue recognizing the underlying asset at carrying value	At commencement recognize: • Intangible right-to-use asset • Liability for present value of installment payments
Underlying asset is new asset purchased or constructed by operator. PPP meets definition of a SCA.	At commencement recognize: • Receivable for present value of installment payments • Deferred inflow of resources Recognize asset at acquisition value when placed in service	At commencement recognize: • Intangible right-to-use asset • Liability for present value of installment payments
Underlying asset is new asset purchased or constructed by operator. PPP does not meet definition of a SCA.	At commencement recognize: • Receivable for present value of installment payments • Receivable for the underlying asset • Deferred inflow of resources Recognize asset at acquisition value when placed in service	At commencement recognize: • Deferred outflow of resources • Liability for present value of installment payments • Liability for underlying asset to be transferred Recognize underlying asset until ownership is transferred.

[1]**Exam Tip:** Focus on questions related to the government as the transferor in the PPP arrangement. Questions about service concession arrangements (SCAs) have been asked in the past. Remember that the guidelines for leases are closely followed in PPP arrangements.

2. **Subscription-Based Information Technology Arrangements (SBITAs).** GASB 96 (effective beginning June 15, 2022) basically covers cloud-based computer technology. Borrowing from GASB 87 on leases, a SBITA is defined as a contract that conveys control of the right to use another party's IT software, alone or in combination with tangible capital assets, for a period of time in an exchange or exchange-like transaction. If the contract includes a combination of IT software and tangible capital assets, the software component must be a significant component. If the software is insignificant compared to the underlying tangible asset, as in the case of a smart copier, then lease accounting (GASB 87) should be used.

Definitions

Short-term SBITA: For a SBITA with a term of one year or less, expense outflows when incurred.

Long-term SBITA: The government recognizes a subscription asset and a subscription liability at the commencement of the subscription term. The subscription liability is measured as the present value of total future subscription payments expected to be made to the vendor during the subscription term. The subscription asset is measured as the initial value of the subscription liability plus payments made at the commencement of the SBITA term and minus vendor incentives received at the commencement of the term.

Accounting for outlays related to stages of SBITA implementation:

Preliminary project stage: Expense outlays for activities such as the evaluation of alternatives and final selection of alternatives for the SBITA.

Initial implementation stage: Capitalize outlays for activities to place it in service related to configuration, coding, testing, and installation of the underlying IT assets.

Operation and additional implementation stage: Expense outlays related to maintenance, troubleshooting, technical support, and other measures to maintain ongoing access to the underlying IT assets.

Training costs: Expense training costs as incurred regardless of the stage in which they are incurred.

Example
Excel County enters into a subscription to use Loud Cloud Computing's IT services. Excel: pays $50,000 up front; signs a five-year agreement with 60 monthly installment fees of $20,000 due at the beginning of each month at a 5.9869% discount rate (having a present value of $1,040,000); incurred $20,000 consulting charges to develop the bid criteria and evaluate vendor proposals; incurred $35,000 in implementation costs associated with installing, coding, and testing; and incurred $25,000 to train its staff.

	Debit	Credit
Right-to-use intangible subscription asset	$1,125,000	
IT expense	$45,000	
Discount on subscription-based IT liability	$160,000	
Subscription-based IT liability		$1,200,000
Cash/Payables		$130,000

The subscription asset is the up-front fee ($50,000) plus implementation costs ($35,000) and the present value of the subscription-based liability ($1,040,000). The consulting fees for preliminary project evaluation ($20,000) and the staff training costs ($25,000) are expensed.

D. Municipal Solid Waste Landfills—Landfills incur a variety of costs during the period of operation and after closure. The EPA requires postclosure maintenance and monitoring over a landfill for thirty years. GASB requires measuring and reported estimated total closure and postclosure costs. A portion of the total cost is recognized yearly using the units-of-production method. For example, a landfill in its first year of operation has an estimated capacity of 5,000,000 cubic yards and $10,000,000 in currently estimated closure and postclosure costs. A total of 500,000 cubic yards were used in the first year of operation. Since 10% of the landfills capacity was used, 10% ($1,000,000) of the total closure and postclosure cost will be recognized. The journal entry is as follows:

Expense for Landfill Closure and Postclosure	$1,000,000	
Accrued Landfill Closure and Postclosure Liability		$1,000,000

1. Obviously, the liability amount will increase yearly. Actual costs for closure and postclosure are reported as a reduction of the accrued liability, not as capital assets or expenses.

2. Usually landfills are operated as a proprietary fund. IF the landfill is operated as a governmental fund; e.g., by the general fund, then only amounts actually spent on closure or postclosure activities will be recognized as an expenditure of the fund. The government-wide activities, however, will report the expense and liability in the same manner that a proprietary fund would report.

E. Pension Plans—These plans represent significant costs and liabilities for many governments. Accounting and reporting for pension plans are discussed in the lesson on "Fiduciary Funds." Accounting for pensions in funds that employ government workers is similar to accounting for claims and judgments and compensated absences. Governmental fund types will recognized pension expenditures and liabilities to the extent that the amounts are payable with current available financial resources. Proprietary funds will recognize the full expense and liability.

F. Other Postemployment Plans (OPEB)—Such plans provide retirement benefits other than pensions such as medical, dental, and vision plans. Generally, accounting and reporting for OPEB is similar to that for pension plans and is discussed in the lesson on "Fiduciary Funds."

III. Accounting and Reporting for Pollution Remediation Obligations—Many state and local governments are faced with high costs in their attempts to remediate existing pollution problems. Note, that the statement does not address costs associated with control or prevention of future pollution problems.

A. Liability Recognition Triggers—The government must recognize a liability for pollution remediation if the cost can be reasonably estimated and one of the following five events occurs:

1. **Pollution poses an imminent danger** to the public or environment and a government has little or no discretion to avoid fixing the problem.

2. The government has **violated a pollution prevention-related permit or license.**

3. **The government has been identified by a regulator** (i.e., the Environmental Protection Agency (EPA) as being responsible (or potentially responsible) for cleaning up pollution, or for paying all or some of the cost of the clean-up.

4. **An outcome (or likely outcome) of a lawsuit** will compel the governmental entity to address a pollution problem.

5. **The government begins to clean up pollution** or conducts related remediation activities (or the government legally obligates itself to do so).

B. Expense or Expenditure Recognition—Recognition of the expense varies with the fund responsible for the clean-up costs.

1. **Government-wide financial statements and proprietary fund statements**—Report expenses as the liability related to the pollution remediation is accrued. As the work is preformed and payments are made, the liability is reduced.

2. **Governmental fund statements**—Report expenditures when the payment for the clean-up is made.

C. **Capitalization of Pollution Remediation Costs**—Not every pollution remediation is recognized as an expense. Pollution remediation costs can instead be capitalized when they are used for the following:

1. Prepare property for sale in **anticipation of a sale**;

2. Prepare property for use when the **property was acquired with known or suspected pollution that was expected to be remediated**;

3. Perform pollution remediation that **restores a pollution-caused decline in service utility, which was previously recognized as an asset impairment**;

4. Acquire property, plant, and equipment that have **future alternative use other than remediation efforts**.

IV. **GASB Statement No. 70,** *Accounting and Financial Reporting of Nonexchange Financial Guarantees*

A. **Nonexchange Financial Guarantees**—A government may extend or receive a financial guarantee without receiving or providing equal or approximately equal value in return. For example, a school district may receive a financial guarantee from the state government for its bonds used to construct a new school without providing consideration to the state government. (Note: GASB 70 does not apply to guarantees related to special assessment debt, which is covered by GASB 6).

B. **Recognition**—A government that has extended a nonexchange financial guarantee should consider qualitative factors in assessing the likelihood that the government will **more-likely-than not** be required to make a payment in relation to the guarantee. Example qualitative factors include:

1. Initiation of a process of entering bankruptcy or financial reorganization;

2. Breach of debt contract, debt covenants, default on interest or principal payments;

3. Other indicators of significant financial difficulty.

C. **Measurement**

1. **Proprietary funds** (economic resource measurement focus). Recognize the liability and an expense at the discounted present value of the best estimate of future outflows expected to be incurred as a result of the guarantee. If a best estimate is not available then recognize the minimum value within the range of estimates.

2. **Governmental funds** (current financial resources measurement focus). Recognize a fund liability and expenditure to the extent of the liability expected to be liquidated with expendable and available resources when payments are due and payable on the guaranteed obligation.

Terminology and Nonexchange Transactions

After studying this lesson, you should be able to:

This lesson describes unique terminology and classification schemes used in governmental accounting.

1. List six expenditure classification schemes.

2. Distinguish between an expense and an expenditure.

3. List four types of nonexchange transactions.

4. List seven revenue classifications.

I. Account Terminology and Classifications

A. Revenue Classifications—Revenues of governmental funds are classified by source. The main revenue source classes are:

1. **Taxes**—Property, sales, income, and other taxes; penalties and interest on delinquent taxes

2. **Licenses and permits**—Motor vehicle permits, fishing permits, building permits, alcoholic beverage licenses

3. **Intergovernmental**—Grants, shared revenues, and payments to other governments in lieu of taxes

4. **Charges for services**—Building inspection fees, copying fees, recording fees

5. **Fines and forfeits**—Parking fines, traffic fines

6. **Investment earnings**—Usually on short-term investments

7. **Miscellaneous**—Rents and royalties, escheats. (The net assets of deceased persons who die without a will and with no known relatives revert back to the state.)

B. Expenditure Classifications—Most expenditures of governmental funds are authorized through appropriations. During the budgeting process, appropriations are identified not just by the type of expenditure (i.e., salaries, supplies, utilities) but also by the purpose(s) of the expenditure and its funding source. In order to show compliance with the appropriations, expenditures must also be coded to identify these characteristics.

1. **Fund**—The fund supplying the financial resources

2. **Program or function**—The broad purpose of the expenditure (i.e., public safety, education, health, etc.)

3. **Activity**—A specific goal or objective under a program (i.e., child vaccination, low-income healthcare, AIDS awareness, etc.)

4. **Organizational unit**—The department or agency within the governmental entity that is responsible for managing the expenditure (i.e., community clinic, emergency services, health department, etc.)

5. **Character**—Identifies the period of time benefited by the expenditure:

   a. **Current expenditures**—Benefit the current period only

   b. **Capital outlay**—Benefits current and future periods

   c. **Debt service**—Benefits past periods (and, potentially, current and future periods)

   d. **Intergovernmental transfers**—Nonexchange (and frequently mandatory) transfers of resources from one governmental entity to another

6. **Object**—The "natural" expense category, the specific purpose of the expenditures (e.g., salaries, supplies, and rent).

> **Study Tip**
>
> Of the six classifications listed, four are most frequently seen in CPA Exam questions: *Fund, Program/ Function, Character,* and *Object*.

> **Study Tip**
>
> Expenditures in the fund statements for the governmental funds are reported by character. Expenditures in the government-wide statements for the governmental funds are reported by program/function.

C. **Special Terminology**—Used in modified accrual basis accounting.

1. **Modified accrual basis**—Uses alternate titles for some common accounting terms:

   a. **Expenditures, not expenses**—Under modified accrual basis accounting, decreases in net assets are called **expenditures**, not expenses.

   b. **Fund balance, not retained earnings or owner's equity**—Under modified accrual basis accounting residual equity is called Fund Balance, not Retained Earnings or Owner's Equity.

> **Study Tip**
>
> The examiners frequently use these two terms to indicate which type of fund is being discussed.
>
> If the question uses the terms "expenditures" or "fund balance," then the fund or report in question must be one of the governmental funds, as these are the only funds that use modified accrual basis accounting.
>
> If the question uses the terms "expenses" or "net position," then the fund or report in question must be one of the proprietary funds or fiduciary funds, as these are the only funds that use full accrual basis accounting.

   c. **Vouchers payable, not accounts payable**—The term "Accounts Payable" may be replaced by the term "Vouchers Payable" in any of a governmental entity's funds. No differences in treatment are signified by the alternate terminology.

   d. **Warrants, not checks**—The term *check* may be replaced by the term *warrant* in any of a governmental entity's funds. No differences in treatment are signified by the alternate terminology.

D. **Use of Control Accounts in Governmental Accounting**

1. Accounts such as revenues, estimated revenues, expenditures, appropriations, and encumbrances frequently have the word *control* appended to the account title. The account titles revenues and revenues control refer to precisely the same account (as do expenditures and expenditures control, etc.).

2. The concept of a *control* account here is the same as in financial accounting when it is used with accounts receivable control.

3. The **control account** is a general ledger summary account that reflects the grand total balance of the subsidiary ledger accounts.

4. For example, A/R control represents the total dollar amount of the individual customer accounts:

Cust 1		Cust 2		Cust 3		A/R Control	
	500		100		300		900

5. In government accounting, this concept is applied to the budgetary and actual revenue and expenditure accounts: the account **revenue control** represents the total of the individual revenue accounts:

Rev-Taxes	–	Rev-Fines	–	Rev-Licenses	–	Revenue Control	–
600		200		300		1100	

Note

The form of the account name does not influence the answer to the question. A question about a revenue transaction may refer to the revenue account as revenue control, revenue or zoning fee revenue; in all instances, the answer to the question would be the same.

II. GASB Statement No. 33, *Accounting and Financial Reporting for Nonexchange Transactions*

A. GASB Statement No. 33 provides a comprehensive basis for recognizing nonexchange revenues such as property taxes, sales taxes, shared revenues, entitlements, and grants. It divides the revenues into four classes of transactions and defines separate recognition criteria for each class.

1. Because GASB Statement No. 33 is a full accrual basis standard and most nonexchange revenues are recorded in governmental funds, application of the revenue recognition rules when recording the transactions and when reporting them in the fund statements is a two-step process:

a. Determine whether revenue can be recognized under GASB Statement No. 33 recognition rules. If revenue cannot be recognized, there is no need to go on to the second step: the transaction is recognized as deferred inflow of resources; *and*

b. If revenue can be recognized under GASB Statement No. 33, then we must apply the modified accrual basis recognition standards to determine whether revenue can be recorded in the (governmental) funds. If revenue cannot be recognized under modified accrual basis as well as under GASB Statement No. 33, then the transaction is recognized as deferred inflow of resources.

2. Again, this two-step process is necessary because we use a full accrual basis standard to record and report transactions in funds that use the modified accrual basis of accounting. For reporting in the government-wide statements, which are presented on the full accrual basis, this two-step process is not necessary: Transactions are evaluated using only GASB Statement No. 33 rules.

Note
These timing differences create an ongoing set of adjustments between revenue recognized in the funds and reported in the fund statements and revenue reported in the government-wide statements.

Study Tip

The examiners sometimes ask questions about nonexchange revenue recognition in the government-wide statements and sometimes ask questions about nonexchange revenue recognition in the fund statements and about when the transactions are recorded. Timing differences from revenue recognized/not recognized in prior periods may complicate these questions. It is extremely important to read the question carefully to determine which basis of accounting is being used before attempting to answer the question.

B. **Nonexchange Revenue Classifications**—The following four transaction classifications are used to define and apply revenue recognition rules:

1. **Imposed nonexchange revenues**—Government-assessed amounts, such as property taxes, fines, and interest on delinquent property taxes, are billed and charged to individuals and businesses.

   a. Recognize revenue in the period for which the taxes are levied; *and*

   b. Recognize an asset (property taxes receivable) when there is an enforceable claim or when payment is received (cash).

Example

Property Tax Example

The City of Wellston uses a calendar fiscal year. In November, Year X, the City levied property taxes totaling $25 M to be used to finance the next fiscal year, Year Y. The taxes were due by January 31, Year Y. The City posted collections as follows:

Through December 31, Year X:	$1,5 M
Through December 31, Year Y:	$20.0 M
January 1-February 28, Year Z	$2.5 M
March 1-December 31, Year Z	$1.0 M

According to GASB Statement No. 33, *all* revenue would be recognized in Year Y because the taxes were levied for use in Year Y. Note that when the taxes are levied in Year X, deferred inflow of resources is credited because the revenue cannot be recognized until the following year. Therefore, the Government-wide statements would report:

Year X	Deferred Inflow of Resources	$25 M
Year Y	Property Tax Revenue ($1.5M + $20.0M +$2.5M)	$24 M
Year Z	Property Tax Revenue (amount rec'd after 60 days)	$1 M

In order to record the taxes in the general fund, the requirements of modified accrual basis accounting must be considered in addition to the GASB Statement No. 33 rules (i.e., revenues must be received in cash within 60 days after the end of the fiscal year). This changes the timing of the revenue recognition. Revenue is recorded in the general fund and reported in the fund statements as follows:

Year X	Deferred Inflow of Resources	$25 M
Year Y	Property Tax Revenue	$25 M
Year Z	No revenue—all previously recognized	$0 M

2. **Derived tax revenues**—Taxes resulting from the taxable exchange transactions of individuals and businesses. Principal examples are sales taxes and income taxes. These revenues differ from imposed revenues as the government does not know what the amount will be until it receives the tax.

   a. Recognize both assets and revenue at the time the underlying exchange transaction takes place.

Example
Sales Tax Example

In December, Year X, merchants collected $58M in sales taxes. The merchants filed tax forms on January 31, Year Y and remitted $50M to the state. Because of a downturn in the economy, it was expected that only $5M of the remaining $8M would be collected and that $5M would not be collected until April, Year Y.

The government-wide statements report the net revenue in the period in which the underlying exchange transaction (e.g., the purchase of goods from the merchants) took place:

Year X: Sales Tax Revenue ($50M received within first 60 days of Year Y) $50 M
Year Y: Sales Tax Revenue ($5 M received after first 60 days of Year Y) $5 M

To record the taxes in the general fund, we must consider the timing of the cash receipts in addition to the GASB Statement No. 33 requirements. Thus, the sales taxes would be recorded in the general fund and reported in the Fund statements as follows:

Year X: Sales Tax Revenue ($50M received within first 60 days of Year Y) $50 M
Year Y: Sales Tax Revenue ($5 M received after first 60 days of Year Y) $5 M

Notice that the total amount of revenue recognized over the two-year period is the same in the government-wide statements as in the fund statements. Only the timing of the recognition differs.

C. **Government-Mandated Nonexchange Transactions**—These are intergovernmental transfers of resources including entitlements, shared revenues, and payments in lieu of taxes. Most of these resources: 1) have restrictions on how they may be used; and 2) are only available to the recipient entity if they meet specific conditions known as **eligibility requirements.**

   1. Recognize both assets and revenue when **all** eligibility requirements have been met:

      a. Eligibility requirements include achievement of specified objectives and time requirements.

      b. *Generic* eligibility requirements may be assumed to be met (i.e., in order to receive highway funds, a state must have interstate highways in need of repair; even though no specific repairs may be scheduled when the monies are received, eligibility is assumed to be met because it would be unusual not to have interstate highways in need of repair).

   2. **"On-behalf of" payments**—These are, by definition, recognized as revenue and as a corresponding expenditure. (For example, state governments may make the employer portion payments for elementary and secondary schools on behalf of the school districts in order to provide equal pension benefits to teachers across the state.)

Example
Shared Revenue Example
A state is entitled to 40% of the federal gasoline tax collected on gas sales within its borders. The state receives these monies directly from the retailers and periodically remits 60% of the tax to the federal government. In order to be eligible to receive these monies, the drinking age in the state must be no less than 21 and the state must maintain all interstate highways within its borders at or above a specified level of condition for the entire year.

If the drinking age in this state is below 21, the state may not recognize revenue, even though it has the cash in its possession, because this specific eligibility requirement has not been met. This is the case both for reporting on the government-wide statements and on the fund statements and for recording in the general fund.

If the drinking age is 21, the state may recognize revenue immediately in the Government-wide statements even though it has not maintained all of the interstate highways at the specified condition level for the entire year because this is a generic eligibility requirement and the presumption is that it will be met. Revenue reporting in the fund statements and recording in the general fund is dependent upon the timing of the receipt of cash.

D. **Voluntary Nonexchange Transactions Contracts**—Entered into voluntarily by the participants, who may include individuals and/or other governmental entities; this classification includes competitively awarded grants, cash and/or property contributions or bequests, and endowments; frequently subject to use/purpose restrictions and/or eligibility requirements

   1. Recognize both assets and revenue when **all eligibility requirements have been met**:

      a. The existence of purpose restrictions does **not** affect revenue recognition.

      b. For reimbursement/expenditure-driven grants, reimbursement requirements are considered to be eligibility requirements, so revenue is **not** recognized until the expenditure is made.

      c. Endowments, which could be considered to have an indefinite time restriction, are explicitly required to be recognized as revenue upon receipt.

Example
Bexar City received a $100,000 grant from the Alliance for Education to be used to provide reading programs at neighborhood recreation centers. In order to receive these monies, the city must operate programs in at least three recreation centers, each with an enrollment of at least 30 children between the ages of 5 and 7. Bexar currently operates two centers with substantially more than 30 children within the required age range enrolled in programs. It plans to open a third center in two months and anticipates an enrollment of 5–7 year olds sufficient to meet the grant requirement.

When the grant monies are received, they cannot be recognized as revenue in either the government-wide or fund statements because the specific eligibility requirements have not been met. As soon as the third center is completed and enrollments have reached the specified level (i.e., the eligibility requirements have been met), revenue can be recognized in both the government-wide and the fund statements.

E. **Other Considerations Affecting Revenue Recognition**—Resources from nonexchange transactions often have timing restrictions (restrictions on *when* the resources are to be used) and purpose restrictions (restrictions on how the resources are to be used).

   1. **Time restrictions**—Resources may not be used until a specific date or event has taken place, and revenue must **not** be recognized until the time requirement has been met and a deferred inflow of resources is recognized;

2. **Purpose restrictions**—When resources must be used for specific purposes, revenue is recognized *immediately;* limitations to the availability of the resources are shown by reporting a fund balance—restricted, committed, or assigned depending on the level of authority (fund-based statements) or a restricted net asset (government-wide statements).

III. GASB Statement No. 72, *Fair Value Measurement and Application*

A. **Definition of Fair Value**—Fair value is the price that would be received to sell an asset or paid to transfer a liability in an orderly transaction between market participants at the measurement date. (Note this definition is the same as that in GASB Concepts Statement No. 6, para. 38.)

B. **Valuation Approaches**

1. **Market approach**—Utilizes information resulting from market transactions for identical or similar assets or liabilities (an exit price).

2. **Cost approach**—Based on the amount necessary to replace an asset's present capacity for providing service (an entry price often referred to as current replacement cost).

3. **Income approach**—Calculated by converting future amounts to a single current discounted amount.

C. **Fair Value Hierarchy**—Three levels of inputs into the measurement of fair value pertain to the reliability of the measurement of an asset or liability's fair value.

1. Level 1 inputs are quoted prices from markets with many transactions for *identical* assets and liabilities. Level 1 inputs are derived directly from the market and need not be adjusted in any way.

2. Level 2 inputs are inputs that are observable for *similar* assets or liabilities. Level 2 inputs should not be used unless Level 1 inputs are unavailable.

3. Level 3 inputs are unobservable and based on assumptions a government develops based on information available to it. Level 3 inputs should not be used unless Level 1 and Level 2 inputs are unavailable.

D. **Application of Fair Value**

1. **Investments**—Securities and other assets that a government holds primarily for the purpose of income or profit and with a present capacity that is based solely on its ability to generate cash or to be sold to generate case should be measured a fair value.

2. **Securitized Loans**—Loans acquired or originated by a government that have been securitized should be measured at fair value.

3. **Exceptions:**

a. **Alternative investments**—Some government entities, particularly pension funds and endowments, hold investments for which fair value is not readily determinable. In such circumstances the investment can be valued using a *net asset value per share* (or its equivalent) amount; e.g., the government's proportionate share of the net assets

b. **Acquisition value**—The price paid to acquire an asset with equivalent service potential in an orderly market transaction at the acquisition date or the amount at which a liability could be liquidated with the counterparty at the acquisition date (an entry price). The following assets should be measured at acquisition value:

i. Donated capital assets

ii. Donated works of art, historical treasures, and similar assets

iii. Capital assets that a government received in a service concession arrangement

c. **Equity interests in common stock**—Should be accounted for using the equity method. However, the following investments in common stock are excluded from using the equity method and will use the cost method instead:

i. External investment pools—GASB Statement No. 79, *Certain External Investment Pools and Pool Participants*, describes the criteria for qualifying external investment pools to elect to report investments at amortized cost. Statement No. 79 was issued December 2015, is effective for financial statements beginning after December 15, 2015, and is eligible for testing starting July 1, 2016.

ii. Pension or other postemployment benefit plans

iii. IRS Section 457 deferred compensation plans

iv. Endowments or permanent funds

v. Investments in entities that calculate a net asset value per share (or equivalent)

vi. Equity interest ownership in joint ventures or component units

vii. Investments with a maturity of one year or less at the time of purchase such as money market investments.

viii. Investments in life insurance other than investments in life settlement contracts.

d. Synthetic guaranteed investment contracts that are fully benefit-responsive (GASB Statement No. 53).

E. Disclosures

1. The nature, characteristics, and risks of the assets and liabilities.

2. The level of inputs used to measure the fair value of assets or liabilities.

3. Whether standards specifically require separate disclosure of an asset or liability (such as derivatives per GASB Statement No. 53).

4. The relative significance of assets and liabilities measured at fair value compared to total assets and liabilities.

5. For each type of asset or liability measured at fair value:

   a. The fair value measurement at the end of the reporting period

   b. The value hierarchy (Level 1, Level 2, or Level 3)

   c. A description of the valuation approach used (market, cost, or income)

   d. Any changes in valuation approach and inputs that had a significant impact on the measurement of fair value and the reasons for the changes

IV. GASB Statement No. 77, *Tax Abatement Disclosures*

A. Effective Date—GASB Statement No. 77 was issued August 2015 and is effective for financial statement periods beginning after December 15, 2015. Therefore, it is eligible for testing in July 2016.

B. Definition of Tax Abatement—A reduction in tax revenues that results from an agreement between one or more governments and an individual or entity in which (a) one or more governments promises to forgo tax revenues to which it is entitled and (b) the individual or entity promises to take a specific action after the agreement has been entered into that contributes to economic development or otherwise benefits the entity or the citizens of those entities.

C. General Disclosure Principles

1. Disclosures should distinguish between tax abatements resulting from agreements entered into by (a) the reporting government and (b) other governments that reduce the reporting government's tax revenues.

2. Disclosure information may be provided individually or in aggregate. (Note: A government that chooses to disclose information about individual tax abatements agreements should present only those that meet or surpass a quantitative threshold selected by the government.)

3. Disclosure information should be organized by each major tax abatement program, such as economic development program or film production incentive program.

4. Disclosure information resulting from agreements entered into by other governments should be organized by the government that entered into the abatement agreement and the specific tax being abated.

5. Disclosure should commence in the period in which a tax abatement agreement is entered into and continue until the tax abatement agreement expires. (Note: If the government made commitments other than to reduce taxes as part of a tax abatement agreement, information about those commitments should be disclosed until the government has fulfilled the commitments.)

D. Disclosure Requirements

| | Tax Abatement Agreement Entered into by: | |
Required Disclosures:	1. Reporting Government:	2. Other Governments
(a) Brief description information:		
(1) Names and purpose of the tax abatement program	✓	✓
(2) Specific taxes being abated	✓	✓
(3) Authority under which agreements are entered into	✓	
(4) Criteria that make a recipient eligible to receive abatement	✓	
(5) The mechanism by which taxes are abated including:	✓	
(i) how the taxes are reduced		
(ii) How the amount of the abatement is determined		
(b) Gross dollar amount, on an accrual basis, by which the government's taxes were reduced during the reporting period	✓	✓
(c) If amounts are received or receivable from other governments:		
(1) Names of the governments		
(2) Authority under which the amounts were or will be paid.	✓	✓
(3) Dollar amount received or receivable		
(d) If commitments other than to reduce taxes are made, disclose the types of commitments and the most significant individual commitments made.	✓	
(e) For individually disclosed tax abatements, describe the quantitative threshold the government used to determine which agreements to disclose.	✓	✓
(f) Describe the specific source of any legal prohibition that prohibits a government from disclosing specific required disclosures.	✓	✓

Note

Tax abatement agreements entered into by a government's discretely represented component units should report disclosures according to the requirements for agreements entered into by the reporting government. For blended component units, disclosures should be in accordance with the requirements for agreements entered into by other governments.

Special Items—Recent Developments

This lesson describes recent accounting standards affecting governmental entities.

After studying this lesson, you should be able to:

1. List the three types of leases and create journal entries for each type of lease.
2. Describe the reporting requirements for direct borrowings and direct placement debt.
3. Describe the accounting for interest cost related to construction projects.
4. Explain when a majority equity interest is an investment and when it is a component unit.

I. **Statements**—The following statements have been recently issued and/or implemented by GASB. Though some of these topics have been addressed in other parts of the study text, they are included in this section because, historically, the Board of Examiners tends to include questions on new statements more often than they might otherwise warrant.

II. **GASB Statement No. 87,** *Leases* **(eligible for testing Q3 2021)**

A. **Single Model for Leases**—replaces previous guidance in which leases were classified as either operating or capital. Unless the lease is a short-term lease or transfers ownership at the end of the lease, lessees will recognize a lease liability measured as the present value of payments expected to be made over the lease term and lease asset ("right to use asset") at the commencement of the lease. Similarly, the lessor will recognize a lease receivable and a deferred inflow of resources at the commencement of the lease term. The lessor continues to report the leased asset. GASB 87 lease accounting guidelines have been applied to public-private and public-public partnership arrangements (GASB 94) and to subscription-based technology arrangements (SBITA), such as cloud computing. These topics are covered in the lesson on Long-Term Liabilities other than Bonded Debt.

At commencement of the lease			
	Asset	Liability	Deferred Inflow
Lessee	Right to use asset	Present value of future lease payments	n/a
Lessor	Lease receivable Continue to report leased asset	n/a	Equal to lease receivable plus any up-front cash received

Subsequent period reporting of the lease			
	Asset	Liability	Deferred Inflow
Lessee	Amortize asset	Reduce by lease payments less amount for interest expense	n/a
Lessor	Reduce lease receivable by lease payments less amount related to accrued interest Depreciate leased asset	n/a	Reduce deferred inflow and recognize revenue

B. **Lease Term**—the period during which the lessee has a no cancellable right to use an underlying asset plus (i) periods to extend the lease if it is reasonable that the lessee/lessor will exercise that option, (ii) periods the lessee/lessor can opt to terminate the lease if it is reasonable to assume that the lessee will not exercise that option.

C. **Short-Term Leases**—leases with a lease term of 12 months or less will be recognized as an expense by lessee and revenue by the lessor.

D. **Contracts that Transfer Ownership**—a contract that transfers ownership of the underlying asset to the lessee at the end of the contract is reported as a financed purchase by the lessee and as a sale of the asset by the lessor.

E. **Effective Date**—financial reporting periods beginning after June 15, 2021.

F. GASB Statement No. 96, Subscription-Based Information Technology Arrangements (SBITA), applies rules for leases established in GASB Statement No. 87 to SBITA. Governments with SBITA should recognize a right-to-use intangible asset and a corresponding subscription liability. There is an exception for short-term SBITA of 12 months or less similar to short-term lease arrangements.

III. **GASB Statement No. 88, *Certain Disclosures Related to Debt, including Direct Borrowings and Direct Placements* (eligible for testing Q3 2019)**

A. **Direct Borrowings and Direct Placements**—Requires separate disclosures on direct borrowings and direct placements from other forms of debt. Direct borrowings and direct placements have terms negotiated directly with the investor or lender and are not offered for public sale.

B. **Required Disclosures**—the following items must be reported separately for (i) direct borrowings and direct placements and (ii) other debt:

1. Principal and interest requirement to maturity for each of the next 5 years and in five-year increments thereafter

2. Terms by which interest rates change for variable-rate debt

3. The amount of unused lines of credit

4. Assets pledged as collateral

5. Terms in debt agreements related to (i) events of default, (ii) termination events, and (iii) acceleration clauses.

C. **Effective Date**—financial reporting periods beginning after June 15, 2019.

IV. **GASB Statement No. 89, *Accounting for Interest Cost Incurred before the End of a Construction Period* (eligible for testing Q1 2021)**

A. **Eliminates Capitalization of Interest**—previous guidance provided for the capitalization of interest on constructed assets in government-wide financial statements and enterprise fund-level financial statements. GASB No. 89 eliminates capitalization of interest cost because the cost itself if not a resource that affects the service capacity of the asset.

B. **Classification of Interest Cost:**

1. **Government-wide and Proprietary Financial Statements**—recognize interest cost as expense in the period in which the cost is incurred.

2. **Governmental Fund Financial Statements**—interest cost incurred should be recognized as an expenditure in accordance with governmental fund accounting principles.

C. **Effective Date**—financial reporting periods beginning after December 15, 2020.

V. **GASB Statement No. 90, *Majority Equity Interest* (eligible for testing Q1 2020)**

A. Clarifies that a government that holds a majority equity interest in a legally separate organization will report that interest as an investment if it meets GASB's investment definition (per GASB No. 72):

a. The interest is held primarily for the purpose of income or profit *and*

b. Has a present service capacity based solely on its ability to generate cash or to be sold to generate cash.

      i. Investment measured using the equity method unless (ii) applies.

      ii. Investment measured at fair value if a special-purpose government engaged only in fiduciary activities (a fiduciary fund, an endowment, or permanent fund) holds a majority equity interest in a legally separate organization.

B. If the majority equity interest does not meet the definition of an investment, the interest is reported as a **component unit.**

    a. Measure the interest at **acquisition cost when 100% equity interest is held.**

    b. Measure the interest using the **equity method when less than 100% equity interest is held.**

870

Index

F